Jim Windeal
FIN. AID OFFICE
SCCC

Kleppner's Advertising Procedure

ELEVENTH EDITION

Kleppner's Advertising Procedure

J. Thomas Russell
University of Georgia

W. Ronald Lane
University of Georgia

Annotations by

Jackie Nicholson
Eckerd College

Lecture Outlines by

Rachel Nelson

PRENTICE HALL, Englewood Cliffs, New Jersey 07632

Editorial/production supervision: Nancy Farrell
Production Management: York Production Services
Interior design: Maureen Eide
Manufacturing buyer: Peter Havens
Cover design: Ray Lundgren Graphics
Cover art: Maureen Eide
Photo research: Teri Stratford
Photo editor: Lorinda Morris-Nantz

Part opening photos: Part One: The Granger Collection Part Two: Mel Digiacomo/The Image Bank Part Three: Lou Jones/The Image Bank Part Four: Gregory Heisler/The Image Bank Part Five: Brett Froomer/The Image Bank Part Six: Jules Zalon/The Image Bank

Printed in the United States of America
10 9 8 7 6 5 4 3 2 1

ISBN 0-13-516378-1

Prentice-Hall International (UK) Limited, *London*
Prentice-Hall of Australia Pty. Limited, *Sydney*
Prentice-Hall Canada, *Toronto*
Prentice-Hall Hispanoamericana, S.A., *Mexico*
Prentice-Hall of India Private Limited, *New Delhi*
Prentice-Hall of Japan, Inc., *Tokyo*
Simon & Schuster Asia Pte. Ltd., *Singapore*
Editora Prentice-Hall do Brasil, Ltda., *Rio de Janeiro*

Contents

ABOUT THE ANNOTATED INSTRUCTOR'S EDITION

The Annotated Instructor's Edition has been designed for your convenience. The front matter preceding the text includes:

Lecture Outlines
End of Chapter Questions
Answers to End of Chapter Questions

The page numbering of the Annotated Instructor's Edition is identical to the students' version of the text. We have included annotations in the margins of the instructor's version of the text that are shaded blue to make them easier to find. The annotations were written by Jackie Nicholson at Eckerd College in St. Petersburg, Florida.

RATIONALE FOR ANNOTATIONS

Students in an introductory course in advertising—as in other courses—are confronted with comprehensive, complete material, with an emphasis on theory rather than application. What has proved helpful to assist students in sorting out the *key concepts* have been *descriptive margin notations,* highlighting topics of specific interest and recall.

The Annotated Instructor's Edition of Russell's *Kleppner's Advertising Procedure,* eleventh edition, takes traditional margin notations a step further—by combining theory with application. Each annotation contains *a selected key concept* from the text material, followed by *a contemporary example of its application* in the marketing environment. Emerging areas of advertising, sales promotion, public relations, publicity, outdoor, and direct marketing are featured. References include excerpts from trade journals, business publications, and professional association newsletters, along with personal quotations of "promoters."

A comprehensive list of supplements appears on page AIExi.

ABOUT THE SUPPLEMENTS FOR KLEPPNER'S ADVERTISING PROCEDURE, ELEVENTH EDITION

*ANNOTATED INSTRUCTOR'S EDITION—The student text plus lecture outlines and numerous marginal annotations from recent issues of sources such as *AdWeek* and *Advertising Age* provide applications of key concepts. Also the AIE contains answers to end-of-chapter questions.

- The AIE is also available in a 3-ring binder upon adoption
- Lecture outlines are also available on disk (IBM and MAC)

*TEST ITEM FILE—Contains 25–30 true/false questions, 25–30 multiple choice questions, and 25–30 completion questions per chapter. This comprehensive TIF was written by text authors Thomas Russell and Ronald Lane.

*COLOR TRANSPARENCIES—A set of 50 four-color transparencies, taken from the book, various ads, and other sources, is available to adopters of the text.

*STUDY GUIDE—Helps students to learn basic concepts by providing Learning Objectives and Chapter Outlines; Definitions and Exercises for key terms; Chapter Summaries; hands-on exercises including Multiple Choice, True/False, and Matching questions; and, illustrative articles to supplement key concepts.

*PRENTICE HALL VIDEO SERIES FOR ADVERTISING—Includes more than 20 segments that are 15–20 minutes in length. The series is accompanied by a video guide.

*PRENTICE HALL SLIDE SERIES FOR ADVERTISING II—Includes 150 four-color slides of various selling situations, demonstrations, presentations, and other real-life situations.

*ADWEEK'S BEST SPOTS VIDEOTAPE OF COMMERCIALS—This one-hour video consists of commercials from 1989 and 1990.

*PRENTICE HALL DATA MANAGER—This integrated software package provides a complete classroom management system that allows teachers to design tests, maintain student records, and provide both practice and actual testing at a computer terminal.

PART ONE

The Place of Advertising

CHAPTER ONE

Background of Today's Advertising

Modern advertising can be understood only within the context of the cultural and economic system that inspired it. Advertising, more than any other business function, is linked to the development of the U.S. free enterprise system. Advertising had a mutually influential relationship with the forces that determined our modern system of exchange.

The eleventh edition of *Kleppner's Advertising Procedure* is designed not only to demonstrate advertising techniques, but to show how advertising is an integral part of the U.S. economic, cultural, and social fabric. Consequently, students must understand the concurrent social changes that were initiated as advertising developed into its current form. The chapter must be studied from the broad historical perspective of economic development, rather than as a narrow history of advertising.

LECTURE OUTLINE

I. The process of selling is as old as the exchange of goods.
- **A.** Advertising history can be divided into three broad periods:
  - **1.** Premarketing era
  - **2.** Mass communications era
  - **3.** Research era
- **B.** Advertising is now an integral part of the marketing mix.
- **C.** Advertisers realize that marketing expertise must be accompanied by public trust.

QUESTION: What are some of the primary differences in the mass communications and research eras of advertising?

II. Beginnings.
- **A.** Earliest known evidence of advertising, around 3000 B.C.
- **B.** Babylonia, Egypt, Greece, England, France, and Rome had various forms of advertising.
- **C.** Outdoor signs have been the most enduring medium (the decorative art of inns in the seventeenth and eighteenth centuries).

QUESTION: What were some of the means early people devised to promote their wares?

III. The origin of the newspaper.
- **A.** Offspring of Gutenberg's invention, printing from movable type.
- **B.** First advertisement (in any language), a sheet in a German news pamphlet, about 1525 (an ad featuring the virtues of a mysterious drug).
- **C.** First printed English newspaper came out in 1622, the *Weekly Newes of London*.
- **D.** First ad in English newspaper, 1625.

IV. "Siquis," the tack-up advertisement.
- **A.** Forerunner to present want ads.
- **B.** Handwritten announcement for public posting.

QUESTION: How did the invention of movable type change advertising compared to periods before this invention?

V. Advertising comes to America.
  A. First American newspaper to carry advertisement, the *Boston Newsletter*, 1704 (an ad offering a reward for the capture of a thief).
  B. When the United States was formed, the colonies had 30 newspapers.

VI. Three momentous decades, 1870 to 1900 (The Age of the Industrial Revolution).
  A. America began the nineteenth century as an agricultural society. The Industrial Revolution took hold slowly before the Civil War. By the end of the nineteenth century, the United States was a great industrial nation in which advertising played a role.
  B. Biggest changes took place in the "three momentous decades," 1870 to 1900.
    1. The United States boomed.
    2. Population increased.
    3. Railroads helped open the West.
    4. Inventions and production grew.
    5. Newspapers became widespread.
    6. Magazines made nationwide selling and national advertising possible.
  C. Advertising grew with the country and helped establish its marketing system.

QUESTION: Were some of the specific ways in which the expansion of the railroads affected the growth of advertising?

VII. Media.
  A. Newspapers.
    1. By 1900, about 10,000 papers, with combined circulations of 10 million (90 percent were weeklies, 10 percent were dailies).
    2. In 1900, newspapers were the largest class of media.
    3. Religious publications were the most influential medium for a few decades after Civil War.
  B. Magazines.
    1. Favorable factors included increased literacy, railroads began carrying mail (including magazines), establishment of low second-class postal rate, printing innovations.
    2. Magazine publishers first held advertising in low esteem.
    3. 1890s: magazines of entertainment, fiction, and advice, including *Cosmopolitan* and *Ladies' Home Journal*.
    4. Magazine advertising more than doubled between 1880 and 1890.
    5. An important point to stress: Magazines made possible the nationwide sale of products and they brought national advertising into being.

QUESTION: Compare and contrast the growth of magazines in the latter part of the nineteenth century with other the development of newspapers.

VIII. Patent-medicine advertising.
  A. By 1870s, the largest category of advertisers.
  B. Many fraudulent claims, which tarnished all advertising.

IX. National advertising emerges.
  A. Legitimate manufacturers saw opportunities in country's growth.
  B. Consumer product markets spread.
  C. Railroads carried merchandise coast to coast.
  D. Packaging; trademarks.
  E. Magazines in full swing.

QUESTION: Why was the emergence of nationally branded goods important to the growth of advertising?

X. Mass production appears.
  A. Henry Ford, 1913.
  B. Mass production is dependent upon mass selling, that is, advertising.

XI. The advertising agency.
  A. Agency story deeply rooted in growth of U.S. industry and selling.
  B. Originated to sell space for out-of-town newspapers on a percentage basis.
  C. Later they planned, prepared, and placed the ads, as well as rendered further services.

XII. As America enters the new century.
  A. Moral atmosphere of business after Civil War consisted of corruption, swindling, and fraudulence in the extreme. Advertising contributed to this with its patent-medicine advertising. The need for regulation clear.
  B. Pure Food and Drug Act (1906).
    1. First federal law to protect public's health and the first to control advertising.
  C. Federal Trade Commission Act (1914).
    1. Unfair methods of doing business are hereby declared illegal (protected one businessman from another).
    2. Eventually extended rule to protect public versus misleading and deceptive advertising.
    3. For the first time, America was taking stock of the morality of everyday life.

QUESTION: Why are patent medicines so often cited in discussions of the worst of advertising?

XIII. Advertising comes of age.
  A. Public confidence badly needed; people organized advertising clubs to earn this confidence and trust.
  B. Associated Advertising Clubs of the World (1905).
    1. Now the American Advertising Federation (AAF).
    2. Promoted "truth in advertising."
    3. Vigilante committees ultimately became Better Business Bureau (now autonomous). The BBB, in 1971, became a part of the Advertising Review Council, an all-industry effort aimed at curbing misleading advertising.

QUESTION: Why is the founding of the vigilance committees regarded as a major turning point in the history of modern advertising?

C. Association of National Advertising Managers (1910).
   1. Now called the Association of National Advertisers (ANA).
   2. Purpose is to improve the effectiveness of advertising from the viewpoint of the advertiser.

D. American Association of Advertising Agencies (AAAA, 4A's) formed in 1911.
   1. Objective is to improve the effectiveness of advertising and of the advertising-agency operation.
   2. Over 75 percent of all national advertising is placed by AAAA members.

E. Printers' Ink.
   1. In 1911, this trade paper published a Model Statute for the state regulation of advertising, designed to "punish untrue, deceptive, or misleading advertising."

F. Audit Board of Circulation.
   1. Formed in 1914 by a group of advertisers, agencies, and publishers.
   2. An independent auditing organization that conducts its own audits and issues its own reports of circulation.
   3. Grew out of loose claims about circulation made by many publishers prior to 1914.

QUESTION: Why was the ABC a necessary condition for the growth of mass advertising?

XIV. Advertising in World War I.

A. Advertising agencies and media people offered services to the government's Council of National Defense and became the propaganda arm as the Division of Advertising of the Committee of Public Information.

B. Advertised Liberty Bonds, the Red Cross, conservation of fuel, and observance of meatless and wheatless days.

XV. The 1920s.

A. Many new products, much growth.

B. Radio station KDKA, Pittsburgh, began broadcasting.

C. NBC, CBS, and FCC (originally the Federal Radio Commission) were founded.

D. Manufacture of radio sets boomed. Business boomed. So did advertising.

E. *Saturday Evening Post,* on December 7, 1929, carried 154 pages of advertising—still an all-time record.

F. Decade ended with the Big Crash.

XVI. The 1930 Depression.

A. Complete turmoil.

B. Major resulting developments affected advertising.
   1. Emergence of radio as a major advertising medium. FDR's inaugural address in 1933 had largest audience ever to hear one voice. Radio showed the power to move a nation.
   2. Robinson-Patman Act (1936) protected small merchants from unfair competition of big dealers with high buying power.
   3. Wheeler-Lea Act (1938) gave FTC more direct and sweeping powers over advertising.
   4. Federal Food, Drug and Cosmetic Act (1938) gave FDA authority over labeling and packaging of food, drug, and cosmetic products.

QUESTION: Why was so much legislation affecting business passed during this relatively short period of time?

XVII. Advertising during World War II.

A. Industry turned to war-goods production. Rationing prevalent.

B. Advertising reduced.

C. War Advertising Council (today called The Advertising Council).
   1. Comprised media (space), agencies (creative talent), and advertising (management) who bound together, combined various areas of expertise, and prepared a series of massive public service campaigns.

XVIII. 1950 to 1975: The word was "growth."

A. End of WWII brought fantastic release of pent-up demand for virtually every type of product.

B. Innovations galore. New products, new everything.

C. A period of growth unparalleled in U.S. history.

XIX. Advertising in the period 1950 to 1975.

A. Advertising was swept up in the post-World War II economic growth and experienced a 500 percent increase.

B. The period was also a time of dramatic changes in the character of advertising.
   1. The Justice Department (outlawing the 15 percent commission), Congress (cigarette ban and outdoor restrictions), and the FTC (corrective and comparative advertising) changed the rules of advertising.
   2. The consumer movement had its early beginnings.
   3. Major magazines went out of business, and newspapers saw their readers move to the suburbs.
   4. Radio had to deal with TV and all media had to share the advertising dollar with direct mail.

XX. Advertising in an age of mega-mergers.

A. The development of multinational corporations led to the formation of huge, mega-agencies.

B. Client conflicts have become a major problem of agency mergers.

C. Agencies must convince clients that large agencies can provide personal services.

QUESTION: If you were the president of a medium-size ad agency how would you try to compete against a mega-agency for an account?

D. Four issues facing modern advertising:
   1. Dealing with the legal, ethical, and self-regulatory atmosphere
   2. Adapting to changing lifestyles of consumers
   3. Changing technology and diversification of media and audiences
   4. Gaining international expertise as clients expand into foreign markets

ANSWERS TO QUESTIONS

1. Briefly discuss the three broad periods of advertising history.

(a) The premarketing era was marked by simple product exchange. There were far fewer goods than demand for them, so the problems of promotion never entered the picture. Furthermore, since each person made only a few goods to be sold in the immediate area, the ideas of distribution and mass product were not an issue. (b) The mass communication era was the first period in which people learned of the availability of goods through a primitive mass media. Even in this era, goods were in such short supply that one had only to let people know that goods existed to be assured of sales. (c) The modern era is one of research. Today, the methods of mass production can produce goods far faster than the public demands them. Consequently, sellers must be sure there is a demand for their goods before they make and distribute them.

2. Identify the following:

a. A hoarding was the first printed outdoor sign introduced in England in 1740.

b. A siquis was a handwritten poster introduced in sixteenth century England. The forerunner of the modern want ad.

c. The *Weekly Newes of London* was the first printed English newspaper; it was published in 1622.

d. Williams Claxton is credited with producing the first ad in English.

e. The *Printer's Ink* model statutes were introduced in 1911 as a guide for legislation controlling local advertising by states.

f. Corrective advertising requires that an advertiser found to have run deceptive advertising run other advertising that corrects the earlier deception.

3. Why was the period from 1870 to 1900 so important in the development of modern advertising?

This period introduced the industrial revolution to America. With mass production, an employed and literate public, and dependable national transportation, the stage was set for a national economic boon.

4. What was the role of religious publications in the development of magazines in the nineteenth century?

In the mid-1800s religious publications were extremely influential with large circulations and substantial revenues from advertisers, especially patent medicines. They offered the proof that magazines of more general content could be supported by advertisers and attain huge readership.

5. Discuss the changes in advertising brought about by the introduction of radio in the 1920s.

Radio brought the nation together as a single mass audience. Advertisers took advantage of this new medium to advertise products on a truly national basis. For the first time, new products could be introduced simultaneously throughout the country.

6. Discuss the role of the War Advertising Council. What is its role today?

The War Advertising Council was an organized plan by the advertising industry to aid in the war effort during World War II. It promoted defense-related campaigns such as buying war bonds. After the war, the public service effort was continued by the Advertising Council.

7. What is meant by the term *mega-agency?*

In the last decade, a number of mergers of large agencies have created agencies of unprecedented size. These agencies are intended to provide any possible service for clients. They are especially important to multinational clients.

CHAPTER TWO

Roles of Advertising

Advertising is an extremely diverse marketing tool. It is equally useful promoting products for an international package goods manufacturer as it is selling the services of your neighborhood service station. This chapter introduces students to the many facets of modern advertising and demonstrates the circumstances in which advertising is most useful as well as how it functions cooperatively with the other components of the marketing mix.

The chapter also points out that the advertising process cannot be reduced to a set of checklists. Every advertising campaign is unique to a specific advertiser. The creative execution and media plan so successful for one company might be a complete failure for its nearest competitor. Advertising is indeed an art—not a science! The intent of this chapter is to introduce the student to the wide-ranging arsenal of tools available to the advertiser. It is this flexibility that allows advertising to effectively address the many prospects available in the marketplace.

LECTURE OUTLINE

I. Advertising is the communication component of the marketing mix.
- **A.** Advertising most often fails when it is asked to carry out inappropriate functions that go beyond communication.
- **B.** Advertising should:
  1. Take the consumer's point of view.
  2. Deliver a sales message.
  3. Concentrate on consumer benefits, not product attributes.

II. Advertising and the marketing mix.
- **A.** Advertising has two major components: a marketing foundation and persuasive communication.
- **B.** Advertising functions within a marketing framework that consists of four elements:
  1. Product
  2. Price
  3. Distribution
  4. Communication
- **C.** Advertising must coordinate its efforts with the other factors involved in marketing communication.
  1. Personal selling
  2. Sales promotion
  3. Public relations
  4. Advertising

QUESTION: Why is advertising usually unsuccessful if it attempts to carry out noncommunication goals?

III. Advertising as an institution:
- **A.** To evaluate and understand advertising, you must have an overview of its cultural, social, and economic functions—both intended and unintended.
- **B.** Advertising serves consumers by letting them influence their economic lives and make informed choices.
- **C.** Advertising allows businesses to introduce new products and create new markets to sustain a mass market economy.
- **D.** Advertising supports a diverse media structure and stimulates economic growth.

QUESTION: Briefly discuss what is meant by unintended functions of advertising.

IV. Conditions conducive to the use of advertising.
- **A.** The failure rate of new product introductions is ample evidence that advertising cannot sell products for which there is no consumer interest.
- **B.** New product success depends on three elements.
  1. Consumer needs.
  2. Marketing and production expertise of the firm.
  3. The "fit" of a new product in a niche in the marketplace.

V. Advertising can only be successful promoting a good product with a perceived need.
- **A.** The most advertising can do for a poor product is gain initial trials.
- **B.** Advertising usually cannot sell a product simply by listing product attributes; it must turn these attributes into consumer benefits.
- **C.** A successful product is one that can produce sales and profits for its manufacturer.
  1. As market share increases, the ratio of advertising to sales normally decreases.
  2. Sales and revenues cannot substitute for profits.
- **D.** Product timing is an important aspect of successful selling; advertising may contribute to the acceptability and

adoption of a product but can rarely move a product far ahead of public taste.

E. Advertising can only exist with brand names that ensure consistent quality, an inherent attribute of brand development.

QUESTION: What are some of the reasons for and against brand-name line extensions versus developing new brand names?

F. A key to successful marketing and advertising is a product that is clearly differentiated from its competition. Differentiation has gone through three major periods:
  1. The product era
  2. The image era
  3. Positioning era

QUESTION: How does positioning a product differ from the product era of differentiation?

G. Price is a major factor of product differentiation and must fit in with other aspects of the marketing mix. Remember that price is among the easiest types of differentiation for competitors to meet.

VI. Variations in the importance of advertising.

A. Advertisers demonstrate a wide variance in the amount they spend on advertising.

B. Some of the major reasons why advertising plays a larger or smaller role for advertisers include:
  1. Volume of sales
  2. Advertising's role in the marketing mix
  3. Competitive environment and profit margin of individual brands
  4. Overall management philosophy
  5. Number of new product introductions

QUESTION: How would the type of distribution and sales method for a product affect its level of advertising support?

VII. The place of advertising in the marketing process is often a function of the directness of intended effect and the time over which advertising is supposed to operate.

A. For example, retail advertising is direct, short-term advertising; institutional advertising is indirect, long-term, and so on. The strategy and execution of advertising will change as we move from one level of the marketing process to another.

QUESTION: How does the execution of advertising differ by the extent that advertising contributes to final sales?

B. National advertising.
  1. National advertising is advertising conducted for trademarked products or services sold through different distributors or stores. It does not mean the product is necessarily sold nationwide.
  2. National advertising is the most general type. Its purpose is to announce availability of products. It usually does not include price or specific dealer location.

QUESTION: In what major ways does national advertising differ from retail advertising?

C. Retail advertising.
  1. The largest category of advertising in terms of dollars invested and number of ads.
  2. Retail advertising usually emphasizes dealer services and price over specific brands.
  3. Retail advertising is immediate. It seeks short-term sales: Buy today.

D. End-product advertising.
  1. End-product advertising leapfrogs over the manufacturer to build demand among ultimate consumers of finished products.
  2. End-product advertising presents one of the greatest challenges to the manufacturer.

E. Direct-response advertising.
  1. As lifestyles change and consumers demand greater convenience of purchase, direct-response advertising takes on more importance.
  2. The media use for direct-response advertising has expanded to include virtually all forms.
  3. The telephone and the credit card have opened many new opportunities for direct marketing.
  4. The primary strategy of direct-response advertising is to make a sale quickly.

QUESTION: To what do you attribute the significant increase in direct-response selling in the last decade?

F. Industrial advertising.
  1. Industrial advertising is the most detailed and sophisticated form of advertising. It is directed to manufacturers for the sale of machinery, equipment, or raw materials.
  2. Industrial buying decisions usually involve several people.
  3. Industrial advertising usually sets the stage for personal selling.

QUESTION: How does the market for industrial advertising differ from that of consumer advertising?

G. Professional advertising.
  1. Advertising directed to a professional adviser (e.g., a physician or architect) upon whose advice the buyer depends.
  2. Its aim is to have the professional recommend or specify the advertised product or service.
  3. It seeks to create an indirect demand to ultimate consumers.

H. Institutional advertising.
  1. Institutional advertising takes many forms, but it always seeks to create a favorable image for the total firm as distinct from the short-term sale of a specific product.
  2. It is usually directed to business executives and has a wider audience than trade or industrial advertising.

QUESTION: How does institutional advertising differ from most other advertising in terms of timing and execution?

ANSWERS TO QUESTIONS

1. Advertising is the communications element of the marketing process. Explain and give examples of how advertising's role differs from other marketing techniques.

Advertising is most effective when it is assigned goals that can be accomplished through communication. It is not one-to-one communication such as personal selling but is directed to the masses. It is intended to build long-term brand loyalty, unlike sales promotion. It is a controlled and identified communication, unlike public relations.

2. Briefly discuss the marketing concept's view of consumers.

The marketing concept starts with the needs and demands of the consumer and develops products and advertising appeals that channel these desires. It can be contrasted to a production-oriented concept that tries to get consumers to accept those products that a company can most easily make.

3. What are the four primary elements of the marketing process?

They are product, price, distribution, and communication.

4. Compare and contrast advertising and public relations.

Advertising is identified to its audience. The advertisers pay for the space and control the messages without being edited by the media. Public relations is normally run as news; the media decides whether to accept public relations information and in what form to run it. Both advertising and public relations are intended to persuade specific publics to some point of view or buying behavior.

5. What are two of the primary roles that advertising serves for society?

Advertising supports a diverse and strong media system and is a major stimulant to economic growth by enabling new products and companies to enter the marketplace.

6. Discuss the importance of a product in filling a niche in the marketplace.

Customers usually cannot be convinced to change brands unless they see some additional benefit in doing so. Products that only duplicate the features and benefits of those already on the market will find it very difficult to enter the marketplace with significant success.

7. What are the three eras of product differentiation used by advertisers in this century?

(1) The product era tried to differentiate products on the basis on product features (some of little importance to consumers). (2) The image era of the 1960s attempted to create an atmosphere for products. (3) The positioning era attempts to have a product fill a unique position in the consumer's mind.

8. Identify the following types of advertising:

a. National advertising is used by the owner of branded goods that are sold in a number of locales (not necessarily nationally) and by a number of different retailers.

b. End-product advertising is designed to have manufacturers use certain ingredients in producing final consumer goods.

c. Trade advertising is largely directed to retailers to get them to stock and promote a manufacturer's goods.

d. Industrial advertising is directed to purchasing agents who are buying equipment and goods used in the manufacture of other products.

9. What are some of the reasons for the growing popularity of direct-response advertising?

There are several reasons, but the primary one is convenience. A busy lifestyle, working women, and a growing elderly population all contribute to the popularity of direct-response advertising.

PART TWO

Planning the Advertising

CHAPTER THREE

The Advertising Spiral and Brand Planning

There is a tremendous amount of diversity on advertising functions. This chapter examines the strategic plan: the development of product and marketing objectives before the ads are created. A clear understanding of the product and its users is critical.

The product life cycle is the series of stages a product passes through. The degree of consumer acceptance determines which advertising stage the product is in. The life cycle model consists of three stages: pioneering, competitive, and retentive.

LECTURE OUTLINE

I. The pioneering stage.
- **A.** The stage a product is in until people appreciate the fact that they need the product.
- **B.** Ideas are introduced that make previous ones seem antiquated.
- **C.** Advertising implants a new custom, changes habits, develops new usage, or cultivates new standards of living.
  - **1.** Produce a long-desired product
  - **2.** Reference to the progress of time
  - **3.** Anticipate and answer consumers' questions
- **D.** A product's utility rather than its advantages over competitors is emphasized.

QUESTION: What is the first stage in the product life cycle? What does it tell the consumer?

- **E.** Pioneering can secure customers before competitors get started.

II. The competitive stage.
- **A.** This occurs once consumers are faced with questions of which brand to buy.
- **B.** In the short term, the pioneer has the advantage of leadership.
- **C.** It communicates the product difference to the consumer.

QUESTION: What are the three stages of the life cycle of a product?

III. The retentive stage.
- **A.** Remind the consumer the brand exists.
- **B.** Occurs once a consumer already accepts and uses a product.
- **C.** Visual or name advertising with little or no copy.
- **D.** The goal is to maintain market share and ward off consumer trial of other products.

QUESTION: When does the retentive stage occur? What is its goal?

IV. The advertising spiral is an expanded version of the advertising stages of products.
- **A.** Comparison of stages:
  - **1.** Fewer products in pioneering stage than competitive stage
  - **2.** The advertising depends on the attitude of a group of consumers toward the product.
  - **3.** Retentive stage gets the least amount of advertising.
  - **4.** Change is a continuum.
- **B.** After the retentive stage:
  - **1.** A product can coast for a short period of time before declining.
  - **2.** Retentive stage is most profitable.

3. Two strategies near the end of the stage:
   a) Decide to let the product die
   b) Seek to expand the market into a new pioneering stage

QUESTION: What is the most profitable stage? What choices must be made near its demise?

4. The newer pioneering stage attempts to get more people to use the product.
   a) Product identification
   b) Complete overhaul
   c) Show new ways of using the product
   d) Give reasons for using the product more often

C. New pioneering stage and beyond.
   1. Product is in different stages in different markets.
   2. ''Newest pioneering stage'':
      a) Get more people to use a type of a product.
      b) Creative marketing and a flexible product
      c) Product innovations
   3. Get the consumers to understand what the product is about.
   4. Get more people to buy the brand.
   5. Develop product innovations or advertising-positioning strategies.
   6. Must reach smaller groups of prospects

QUESTION: What kinds of strategies and goals are implemented in the new pioneering stage and those that follow?

D. The advertising spiral as a management decision tool.
   1. Products don't move through each stage at the same speed.
   2. The advertiser must know about the product before creating new advertising ideas:
      a) In which stage is the product?
      b) Use pioneering advertising to attract new users?
      c) Work at competitive advertising to get a larger share of the market?
      d) What proportion should be pioneering? Competitive?
      e) Are we coasting in the retentive stage? Is more aggression needed?

QUESTION: What considerations must be taken into account before creating new advertising strategies?

V. Building strong brands.
   A. Branding was born out of profit squeeze in the 1880s.
   B. Brands exist only in and through communication.
   C. Must be distinct from its competition
   D. Made up of two types of elements:
      1. Rational elements
         a) Embody the content of the brand's proposition
         b) Speak more to the rational side of the brain
         c) Most visible part of the brand
      2. Emotional elements
         a) Set the style, tone, character, mode, mood of execution
         b) Speak more to the intuitive side of the brain
         c) Less visible and more difficult to express and measure

QUESTION: What two elements constitute a brand?

QUESTION: How did brands originate?

VI. Lintas: Link Strategic Planning Process is a planning process to help synergize communications to build strong brand equity.
   A. Brand equity audit
      1. Market context examines the market and consumers
      2. Brand equity indicators
         a) Brand awareness
         b) Market share, price elasticity, shore of voice
         c) Brand sensitivity (price, pack size, model)
         d) Assumed leadership
         e) Consistency of the brand's communication over time
         f) Ranking attributes
         g) Distribution, pricing, product quality, and product innovation
         h) Brand loyalty
      3. Brand equity description identifies and describes consumers' thoughts and feelings that result in brand biases
      4. Competitive strategies and tactics
         a) Analysis of current advertising and other communications
         b) Assessment of problems/opportunities

QUESTION: Discuss four brand equity indicators.

   B. Strategic options and recommended plan
      1. Communication objectives
      2. Audience
      3. Source of business
      4. Brand positioning and benefits
      5. Marketing mix
      6. Rationale
   C. Brand equity probe
      1. Qualitative research step
      2. What are the boundaries?
   D. Creative brief.
      1. Strategy
         a) Key observation
         b) Communication objective
         c) Consumer insight
         d) Promise
         e) Support
         f) Audience
      2. Desired brand equity
      3. Creative guidelines

QUESTION: Briefly describe the components that make up the Lintas: Link Strategic Planning Process. What is the ultimate goal?

ANSWERS TO QUESTIONS

1. What is the pioneering stage?

The advertising stage of a product in which the need for such a product is not recognized by the consumer. The pioneering advertising must demonstrate to consumers that their needs can be met in a new and efficient way. Advertising emphasizes the newness and benefits of products in this stage. It explains what the product is for to many consumers and starts an education process.

2. What determines the stage of a product?

The stage of a product depends on the consumers' perceptions of the product, not age of the product, or budget. Factors other than advertising can influence consumers' perceptions of the product, moving it from one stage to another.

3. How can a product be in more than one stage at a time?

A product can be in different stages of different markets at one time (segmentation). For example, fax machines are in the competitive stage among business users, where their use has been accepted, but they are largely in the pioneering stage in terms of home use. A product may hold ground in one competitive area while it seeks new markets with pioneering advertising aimed at other segments.

4. What is the essence of the advertising message in each stage of the spiral?

Pioneering advertising: The ad tries to answer the consumer's question, "What is the product for?" The result is usually a message selling the generic aspect of the product instead of brand differentiation. It is generally part of an education process. Competitive advertising: The consumer knows about the product and/or product category and asks, "Which brand shall I buy?" The ad message concentrates on brand differences. Retentive advertising: The message is geared to remind the consumer about the product. Generally, the retentive ad is highly visual with only short reminder copy.

5. Why is the retentive stage both good and bad news for some products?

Products in the retentive stage are well known by consumers and may be at their height of popularity. The retentive stage is also likely to be the most profitable stage. The bad news is that the product may simply coast in the retentive stage for long periods and risk decline. If it is totally in the retentive stage, the product category may be in decline.

6. What is brand equity?

The value of the brand. The cumulative value of years or decades of advertising and marketing investment in a brand and the way consumers, distributors, and salespersons perceive that brand in relation to other brands.

7. What are the elements of the Lintas Creative Brief?

There are three elements in the Lintas Creative Brief: (1) The one-page statement of strategy that clearly identifies the target consisting of key observation, advertising objective, consumer insight, promise, support, and audience. (2) Desired brand equity: a list of the rational and emotional components that describe how we want consumers to feel and think about the brand. The desired brand equity is compared to the current brand equity. (3) Creative guidelines: a simple list of dos and don'ts giving the creative team clear direction about the attitude, approach, and tonality of the advertising.

8. Name the four steps in the Lintas: Link strategic planning system.

(1) Brand equity audit, (2) strategic options and recommended plan, (3) brand equity probe (research), and (4) creative brief.

9. Identify:

a. Communication objective: The primary goal the message is to achieve.

b. Left brain: The rationale hemisphere of the brain that reads images, is logical, deals with math, verbal, and memory functions.

c. Advertising Objective: The communication goals designed to accomplish certain tasks within the total marketing program.

d. New Pioneering: The focus of new pioneering advertising is to get more people to use that type of product. This may mean the product must expand to include new markets and/or develop product extensions to attract other consumers. Arm & Hammer expanded its product by creating new uses—refrigerator deodorant for its baking soda.

CHAPTER FOUR

Target Marketing

A strategic plan for targeting your advertising to those consumers most likely to be interested in your product is a wise and necessary move.

This chapter examines those questions that must be answered in order to create such a successful strategic plan. Once initial general questions have been answered, the information must be sorted and further defined so that time and money is not wasted advertising your product to people who are unlikely to buy it.

LECTURE OUTLINE

I. Target marketing is the process designed to pinpoint the best prospects among all consumers.
- **A.** Marketing executives evaluate demographic and product-preference shifts.
- **B.** Identify the predictable changes and opportunities effecting the market in the next century.
- **C.** Income data:
  1. Disposable-after-tax income
  2. Discretionary: amount of money consumers have after paying taxes and buying necessities
  3. Income change
  4. Importance may vary according to product category.

QUESTION: What is target marketing and what is it designed for?

- **D.** Population changes
- **E.** Lifestyle studies:
  1. Activities
  2. Interests
  3. Opinions

QUESTION: What are three typical lifestyle measures?

II. Segmenting innovators for new products.
- **A.** Mediamark Research, Inc. (MRI) published a Consumer Innovators Report
  1. Five categories of consumer/usage, attitudes, and lifestyles
  2. Identifies products, services, and activities representative of innovation
  3. Specific variables cluster consumer segments.
- **B.** Examination of demographic variables yields a profile of the typical U.S. adult.

QUESTION: What valuable information does Mediamark Research, Inc. supply?

III. Target marketing and the marketing concept.
- **A.** Products must be created to fill an existing need rather than forcing a product on the marketplace.
- **B.** Market products meet the needs of a specific consumer group.
- **C.** Market segments are not static.

QUESTION: What is the main concept behind target marketing?

IV. What is a product?
- **A.** A product is designed with satisfactions to match the interest of a particular group of consumers.
- **B.** Target marketing focuses on groups of people seeking similar satisfactions.
- **C.** New-product advertisers must find a place in the market against established competition.
- **D.** Six segments of package-goods brand loyalty:
  1. National brand loyalty
  2. National brand deal
     - *a)* Choose least expensive national brand
     - *b)* Considerable store switching
  3. Private-label loyal
  4. Private-label deal
  5. National-brand switcher
  6. Private-label switcher

QUESTION: What are the six segments of package-goods brand loyalty?

V. What is a market?
- **A.** A market is a group of people identified by a common characteristic, interest, or problem who:
  1. Use the product to advantage
  2. Afford it
  3. Are reached through some medium
- **B.** Majority fallacy assumed every product should be aimed at and acceptable to a majority of all consumers.
- **C.** A group of potential purchasers of a product

QUESTION: What is the majority fallacy?

VI. What is the competition?
- **A.** A brand will gain value in a particular consumer segment by more exactly meeting its needs.
- **B.** May be products outside your product's class as well as in the same sector
- **C.** Widens as the price of the product increases
- **D.** The immediate competition is the other products in the same class.

VII. Planning the advertising.
- **A.** Market segmentation
  - **1.** Geographical segmentation
  - **2.** Product user segmentation
  - **3.** Lifestyle segmentation

QUESTION: What are the three types of market segmentation?

QUESTION: Give an example of product-user segmentation.

- **B.** Niche marketing
  - **1.** A flanking strategy to engage competitors in product markets where they are weak or have little or no presence
  - **2.** Pit your strength against the competitors' weakness.
  - **3.** Once upper limits are reached, sales growth is limited unless company expands beyond its niche.
  - **4.** Gain a product entry into a larger market by attacking a small part of it not served by competitors.
  - **5.** Caters to latent needs existing products don't satisfy

QUESTION: What is the one drawback of niche marketing? What are its two main purposes?

VIII. Positioning.
- **A.** Create a product to meet the needs of a specialized group.
- **B.** Identify and advertise a feature of an existing product that meets the needs of a specialized group.
- **C.** A product can hold different positions at the same time.
- **D.** View the product through the consumer's eyes.

QUESTION: Whose point of view does positioning take? Can one product hold different positions simultaneously? Give an example.

- **E.** Creating a product for selected markets
  - **1.** Variations on a conventional product
  - **2.** Aimed at groups with needs not fully met by existing products
- **F.** Positioning the product by appeal
  - **1.** Easy approach to opening other markets
  - **2.** Risk of competitors' matching the change easily
- **G.** Positioning to expand brand share
  - **1.** Used when a company already has a very high percentage of the market for a type of product
  - **2.** No physical product changes, only different appeals

QUESTION: What is the risk involved in positioning a product by appeal? What is its advantage?

- **H.** In approaching a positioning problem, ask these questions:
  - **1.** What position do we already own in the prospect's mind?
  - **2.** What position do we want to own?
  - **3.** What companies must be outgunned?
  - **4.** Do we have enough marketing money?
  - **5.** Do we have the guts to stick with one consistent positioning concept?
  - **6.** Does our creative approach match our positioning strategy?

QUESTION: What questions must be asked in approaching a positioning problem?

IX. Profile of the market.
- **A.** Determine the overall usage of the type of product.
  - **1.** Dollar sales
  - **2.** Number of units sold
  - **3.** Percentage of using households
- **B.** Category is:
  - **1.** Growing
  - **2.** Stagnating
  - **3.** Declining
- **C.** Compare share of the market to competition.
- **D.** Ask what share trends have been over past several years.
- **E.** Know the chief product advantage featured by each brand.

X. Profile of the buyer.
- **A.** Demographic reports refer to those facts relevant to a person's use of a product.
- **B.** Advertisers seek a profile of the kind of person they want to reach and then select the media that best reaches them.

QUESTION: How do demographics play a role in media selection?

- **C.** Determine who the heavy users are and identify their similarities.

XI. Beyond demographics: Psychographics
- **A.** Differences exist in the nature and extent of purchases between groups of buyers with the same demographic characteristics.
- **B.** Studies lifestyles
- **C.** Psychographic research
- **D.** The need for market testing; measures advertising and promotional variables

XII. Targeting special markets: Hispanics
- **A.** One of the fastest-growing markets
- **B.** Addressed in terms of their own lifestyles, identities, and motivations
- **C.** Buying preferences influenced by peers
- **D.** Brand loyal
- **E.** Difficult in translation of slogans/themes

QUESTION: Why is it important for advertisers to specially address the Hispanic audience? What makes this difficult?

ANSWERS TO QUESTIONS

1. What is target marketing?

It is the accurate identification of current and prospective users of a product. Target marketing means focusing on groups of people who seek similar satisfactions from life and from a product.

2. What is a market?

It is defined as a group of people who can be identified by some common characteristic, interest, or problem and have the ability to purchase the product.

3. Name the key demographic characteristics used by advertisers.

These are age, income, sex, education, marital status, occupation, geographical location, race, size and type of household, and so on.

4. What is the 80/20 rule as it relates to target marketing?

Basically, the 80/20 rule is the concept that a high percentage of sales are generated by a relatively small group of consumers (80 percent of the sales are bought by 20 percent of the consumers).

5. What two purposes can *niche marketing* serve?

(1) It can gain a product entry to a larger market by attacking a small portion of it not being served by competitors. (2) It can also cater to latent needs that existing products do not adequately satisfy.

6. What is positioning?

It is segmenting a market by creating a product (or positioning a product) to meet the needs of a select group or by using a distinctive advertising appeal to meet the needs of a specialized group, without making changes in the physical product.

7. How does a consumer's lifestyle relate to segmentation strategy?

If you are trying to sell golf balls, you must understand golfers (how and where they buy, how often they buy, how often they play, and so on). People with similar interests and lifestyles group themselves. Advertisers can evaluate the importance of such clusters as potential customers. These individuals may cross many demographic categories. The more you think about a person's lifestyle, the easier it is to segment that person.

PART THREE

Managing the Advertising

CHAPTER FIVE

The Advertising Agency, Media Services, and Other Services

The world of the ad agency is one of dramatic change. This chapter explores the traditional agency and many of the changes in progress as well as other advertising services organizations.

Agencies adapt to their environments and the clients they serve. Therefore, the changes in the advertising business reflect those taking place in the corporate world in general. The American Association of Advertising Agencies defines an ad agency as an independent business, composed of creative business people who develop, prepare, and place advertising in advertising media for sellers seeking to find customers for their goods and services.

LECTURE OUTLINE

I. How agencies developed.

- **A.** The Early Age (Colonial times to 1917)
  - **1.** Colonial postmasters first acted as advertising agents.
  - **2.** Space salesmen (1840s)
  - **3.** Space wholesalers (1850s)
  - **4.** The first rate directory (1869)
  - **5.** The agency becomes a creative center (1870s).
  - **6.** Agency-client relationship is established (1875).
  - **7.** The Curtis-no-rebating rule (1891)
  - **8.** Standard commission for recognized agencies established (1917)
  - **9.** The American Association of Advertising Agencies (1917)

QUESTION: Who were the first advertising agents?

QUESTION: What important development in advertising occurred in 1875?

- **B.** The No-Rebate age (1918 to 1956)
  - **1.** Radio
    - *a)* Scopes trial
    - *b)* Prime news vehicle
  - **2.** Television
    - *a)* Nationwide network broadcasts
    - *b)* Major medium for many agencies
  - **3.** Electronic data processing
    - *a)* Computer research

QUESTION: What is the Curtis-no-rebating rule?

- **C.** The Age of Negotiation (1956 to now)
  - **1.** Consent decrees to stop no-rebating provisions.
  - **2.** Review the total compensation an agency should receive for services.

II. The full-service advertising agency today.

- **A.** Offers clients all services necessary to handle the total advertising function
- **B.** Expanded agency departments or subsidiary companies

C. Functions
 1. What is the marketing problem?
 2. The strategy
 3. The creative response
 4. The media plan
 5. The total plan
 6. Notify trade of forthcoming campaign
 7. Billing and payments

QUESTION: What are the six functions of the full-service ad agency?

D. Organization of the Full-Service Agency
 1. Creative department
  a) Responsible for the success of the agency
  b) Traffic department
  c) Creative director is responsible for the finished product.
 2. Account services
  a) Responsible for relationship between agency and client
  b) Keep agency ahead of clients' needs
 3. Marketing services
  a) Media planning and buying
  b) Research
  c) Sales promotion
 4. Management and finance
  a) Financial and accounting control
  b) Office management
  c) Personnel

QUESTION: Name one responsibility of each of the following: creative department, marketing services and management, and finance

E. International agency operations
 1. Large U.S. agencies have offices or affiliates in countries where clients are selling their goods.
 2. U.S. agencies purchase a majority or minority interest in successful foreign agencies.
 3. Two ways of constructing international marketing and advertising:
  a) Universal theme in all countries using the same slogan and visual treatments
  b) Individual themes are tailored in each country, but the same basic advertising strategy is retained.

III. Competing accounts.
 A. Client-agency relationship is professional and confidential.
 B. Agency shouldn't handle competing companies or products.

IV. The agency of record handles the advertising of a large advertiser's various divisions and products.

V. Agency Networks.
 A. Small- and medium-sized agency
 B. Help with information gathering and sharing

QUESTION: What is an agency network? How does it differ from the agency of record?

VI. New developments in the agency world.
 A. The mega-agency
  1. Greater reservoir of talent
  2. Ability to shift portions of accounts from one agency to another
  3. Clout in negotiating with the media
  4. Conflicts with competing accounts
  5. Impersonal and not as creative

QUESTION: What are the advantages and disadvantages of the mega-agency?

 B. Independent creative services
 C. A la carte agency
 D. In-house agency
 E. Rolodex agency
 F. Media-buying services
  1. In-house services
  2. Agencies merging services

VII. Forms of agency compensation
 A. Media commission (15 percent)
 B. Production commissions or markups (17.65%)
 C. Fee arrangements

QUESTION: What is the standard percentage of media commission?

VIII. Other services.
 A. Barter
 B. Research services

IX. Agency of the future.
 A. Fewer levels in every department
 B. Agency branches will disappear.
 C. Become less powerful account services
 D. Creative talent will lead in strategy development.
 E. Greater importance of account planners
 F. Narrowing research responsibilities
 G. Media planning will have considerable clout.
 H. Performance-based incentives
 I. Emerging financial/administrative manager
 J. Top agency talent will work directly on the business.

QUESTION: What are some of the predictions for the agency of the future?

ANSWERS TO QUESTIONS

1. What services do advertising agencies usually perform for clients?

Obviously, an agency develops, prepares, researches, and places advertising. In many cases, the agency assists in the marketing strategy and product development. Today the full-service agency offers sales promotion, public relations, direct marketing, television programming, package designing, and so on—all services necessary to handle the total advertising function.

2. What is the A.A.A.A. (4A's)?

American Association of Advertising Agencies is a national association accounting for the majority of national advertising dollars. Its members must meet strict criteria for membership; they compete against each other.

3. What is an ''agency of record''?

The agency of record is used when a large advertiser employs a number of agencies. The job of the agency of record is to coordinate media buys to ensure that the total media buy for the company is organized and all corporate media discounts are credited properly.

4. What is the role of the independent media-buying service?

They are specialized media-buying businesses that negotiate and buy advertising space and time. They perform any part of the planning or buying function a client desires. Their forte is spot television. They work on a commission basis; in some instances, the rate is lower than a full-service agency.

5. Identify the function of each of the four agency organizational elements.

(1) Creative department: develops, creates, and produces the ads. (2) Account services: manages the day-to-day relationship between the agency personnel and the client. (3) Marketing services: includes media, research, sales promotion, and so on functions. (4) Management and finance: responsible for accounting, billing, personnel, and office management.

6. What changes are predicted for the agency of the future?

The agency of the future will be streamlined with a layer of ''thinkers'' and a layer of ''doers.'' Agency branches will disappear, and account services will be less powerful. Creative persons will be more involved in strategy development. Account planners will become more important as the research function narrows. Media planning will grow in importance. Top agency talent will work directly on the account team.

CHAPTER SIX

The Advertiser's Marketing/ Advertising Operation

The ad agency business responds to the changes that take place in the global business environment. This chapter discusses the marketing-advertising function—the key to the existence of the ad agency.

In these uncertain business times, traditional marketing organizational structure and procedures are being questioned.

LECTURE OUTLINE

I. Marketing-services system developed by Procter & Gamble
- **A.** Marketing activity begins with the product managers assigned to different brands.
- **B.** Marketing services represent the technical talent involved in implementing a marketing plan.
- **C.** Product manager brings together the agency professional and the marketing-services division.

QUESTION: What is the role of the product manager?

II. Evolution: The category manager.
- **A.** All disciplines report to the category manager.
- **B.** Follows the product line and decides how to coordinate each brand
- **C.** Product manager's responsibilities:
  - **1.** Plan strategy and objectives
  - **2.** Gather relevant brand information
  - **3.** Coordinate budget developments and control
  - **4.** Get recommendations from agencies and others for final decision and approval
- **D.** Group product manager approves product manager's plans.
- **E.** Vice-president for advertising:
  - **1.** Reviews and evaluates brand media plans
  - **2.** Attends creative presentations
  - **3.** Acts as adviser and consultant
- **F.** Each brand gets the full marketing attention of its own group, while all brands benefit from the company's special marketing services.

QUESTION: What is the hierarchy of the marketing-services system? What is its great advantage?

III. Setting the budget: Four approaches.
- **A.** Percentage of sales
  - **1.** Ad budget increases only when sales increase.
  - **2.** Competitive pressures
- **B.** Payout plan
  - **1.** Spend at a level that will be acceptable at some future date.
  - **2.** Used for new products requiring high advertising expenditures
  - **3.** Risk of accumulating major debt
- **C.** Competitive budgeting
- **D.** The task method
  - **1.** Specific sales target for a given time to attain a given goal
  - **2.** Spend whatever is necessary to meet that quota.
  - **3.** Brand loyalty factors
  - **4.** Geographical factors
  - **5.** Product penetration
  - **6.** Requires accurate, reliable research, experience, and models

QUESTION: What are the four approaches to setting the budget?

QUESTION: What is the risk involved in the payout plan?

IV. Selecting an agency.
- **A.** Determine what types of service are needed and list them in order of importance.
- **B.** Establish a five-point scale to rate each agency's attributes.
- **C.** Check published sources and select agencies that fit your requirements.
- **D.** Make sure there are no conflicts with accounts at the agency.
- **E.** Start preliminary discussions with interesting agencies.
- **F.** Reduce original list of potential agencies.
- **G.** Prepare a more specific evaluation list on the same scale.
- **H.** Discuss final arrangements.
- **I.** Make sure the arrangements are comfortable.
- **J.** If you're an international company, make sure the agency can handle your nondomestic business.

QUESTION: Discuss the steps involved in selecting an ad agency for your company.

V. Appraising national advertising.
  A. Advertising goals versus marketing goals
    1. Define specifically what the company expects to accomplish through advertising.
    2. Marketing goal is to increase marketing share.
    3. Advertising goal is a specific communication task.
    4. Colley Report appraises advertising by its effectiveness in the communication spectrum, leading to sales.

QUESTION: How does the Colley Report appraise advertising?

  B. Appraising the campaign before it is run
    1. Test idea options in different markets
    2. Tips off competition to what you're planning

QUESTION: What is the drawback of appraising a campaign before it is run?

  C. The company/agency research conflict
    1. The PACT study states advertising's contribution to marketing objectives is the focus of any copy test.
      a) Reinforce current perceptions.
      b) Encourage trial of a product/service.
      c) Encourage new uses of a product or service.
      d) Provide greater saliency for a brand or company name.
      e) Change perceptions and imagery.
      f) Announce new features and benefits.
    2. PACT report sees advertising performing on three levels:
      a) Reception
      b) Comprehension
      c) Response

QUESTION: What does the PACT study hold is the focus of any copy test?

VI. The changing marketing environment.
  A. Supermarkets now demand slotting allowances for shelf space.
  B. SAGE Group, Ltd. indicates new rules:
    1. Marketplace leverage is at the local level.
    2. Building brand equity among retailers should become as important as building brands among consumers.
    3. Marketing decisions must shift to the sales level.
    4. Information is the most important asset.
  C. Research bolsters the value of advertising.

VII. Changes in corporate strategy.
  A. Jim Trout's ideas on bottom-up marketing for the 1990s:
    1. Go down to the front.
    2. Narrow your focus.
    3. Find your tactic.
    4. Build your strategy.
    5. Make the changes.
    6. Launch a big program.
  B. John Naisbitt's future trends:
    1. Transition to a service economy
    2. High-technology explosion is creating a need for a counterbalancing humanism.
    3. Desire for a higher quality of life outside of cities
    4. Socialism is on the wane.
    5. English is emerging as the universal language.
    6. Individual is more important and powerful.
    7. Complex multioption society has evolved.
    8. Global free trade
    9. United States is primed to be a major player in the global economy.

QUESTION: What is Jim Trout's theory on marketing for the 1990s?

QUESTION: Name five of John Naisbitt's future trends.

ANSWERS TO QUESTIONS

1. What are the two traditional ways companies organize their advertising departments?

The oldest advertising structure is the advertising department in which all activities are funneled through the ad manager. More recently, the marketing services system has been developed. In this structure a product manager manages the advertising of a brand somewhat like an independent company. The advertising department is available to provide support for all products within the company. There is the evolution of this system where a category manager is over several competing company brands in the same product category and each product's advertising manager reports to the category manager.

2. What is a category manager?

The category manager is responsible for all aspects of the brand in his/her category. One category manager follows each line of business and decides how to coordinate each brand. One purpose of this structure is to allow the category manager to target brands at different markets reducing the competition between the company's brands.

3. What is a payout plan?

A payout plan is a budget strategy showing the cost of doing business. It is not uncommon for a payout plan to spend more dollars than present sales of a product would warrant. However, as the plan moves into year two or year three, sales should increase and ad spending should stabilize or decrease. It is a system that allows you to evaluate costs and predict when (what year) the product should become profitable.

4. What are the forms of agency compensation?

Standard 15 percent commission, a fee basis, or a combination of commission and fee.

5. Discuss the slotting fee's role in introducing a new product.

Slotting allowances or fees are the admission fee demanded by supermarkets for shelf space for new products. The money primarily comes out of the marketer's trade promotion funds and insures space for about 3 to 6 months. The fee covers the administrative overhead for the supermarket.

6. Differentiate between the traditional "top-down" and Ries and Trout's "bottom-up" marketing approaches.

In "top-down" marketing you decide what you want to do (strategy). Then you figure how to do it (tactics). In "bottom-up" marketing, you start by finding out what you can do and then set up a program to do it. You find your tactic in the mind of the prospect.

PART FOUR

Media

CHAPTER SEVEN

Basic Media Strategy

In recent years, the cost of advertising time and space have increased at a faster rate than most other business expenditures. In fact, media costs make up by far the largest category of advertising expenditures. In light of these increases, it is not surprising that the media function has taken on growing importance to advertisers in recent years. The media planning process is an area where advertisers can achieve great cost efficiency through careful planning. The intent of this chapter is to introduce students to the planning process and attributes of individual media vehicles. From a marketing and advertising perspective, Chapter 7 is a key to understanding this entire section of the text.

LECTURE OUTLINE

I. Advertising media is often overlooked, but it makes up by far the largest category of advertising expenditures.
- **A.** Increased costs have led to a more careful appraisal of the media function and more professionally trained media planners.
- **B.** Media are most generally classified as either mass or nonmass and the term *advertising media* is used to cover a host of promotional devices.

II. Media characteristics are extremely diverse with different vehicles reaching selected target markets with greater or lesser cost and communication efficiency.
- **A.** Advertising media are dominated by three categories: newspapers, TV, and direct-response.
- **B.** No single medium is right for every advertiser, and decisions must be made on a product-by-product basis taking into account intended creative executions and intended prospects.
- **C.** Newspapers are the primary recipient of ad dollars. They reach a broad audience at a low cost but suffer from relatively low reading time and difficulty in reaching young adults.
- **D.** Television is a graphic media combining all the senses. Offers a perishable message and an increasingly fragmented audience. It is becoming more selective, but at a higher cost per viewer.
- **E.** Direct response is the most expensive and selective medium. In recent years it has gained in popularity with many major advertisers due to its ability to reach a mobile and active population.
- **F.** Magazines offer opportunities for reaching specialized audiences in a quality environment. Difficult to reach a sizable proportion of a market with one or a few magazines.
- **G.** Outdoor is a visual medium with high impact. It is excellent for reminder messages and as a complement to other medium in an introductory campaign. Rarely suitable for a complete sales message.

III. The media process must be part of a plan that outlines the way in which the various media are integrated into the total advertising campaign.
- **A.** There is no standard format for a media plan, but most include the basic information outlined in this chapter.
- **B.** A good media plan will follow logically from the marketing and advertising objectives developed for the product.

IV. The basic strategy of media planning must begin with the prospects to be reached by the advertising.
- **A.** The media planner must decide which vehicles will reach the greatest number of prospects at the lowest cost.
- **B.** Proliferation of media choices makes the job of the planner extremely complex.

C. The planner must judge potential media buys on the basis of weighted audiences using the demographic CPM:

$$\text{Weighted CPM} = \frac{\text{ad cost} \times 1000}{\text{demographic audience segment}}$$

D. Prospects are increasingly measured according to a number of variables through the use of clusters such as the PRIZM system.

QUESTION: Why is the target marketing aspects of media planning so crucial to successful advertising?

V. Media planning does not exist outside the constraints of the communication message it delivers.
- **A.** In recent years, there has been a much closer relationship between creative and media personnel.
- **B.** The media planner must choose those media that best communicate the positive attributes of a product, not those that are simply delivered to prospects.
- **C.** The media planner is looking for media vehicles that systematically exclude nonprospects and create the most conducive environment for prime prospects.

QUESTION: How does advertising awareness relate to propensity to purchase in evaluating the success of advertising?

VI. Media planning must take into consideration the distribution of both the product and the media.
- **A.** The more concentrated the prospects, the easier the job of the planner.
- **B.** Media planners are interested in budgeting according to available dollars, current sales, and sales potential. Often they use the Brand Development Index:

$$\text{Brand Development Index} = \frac{\text{percent of sales}}{\text{percent of population}}$$

QUESTION: How will an emphasis on regional advertising strategy by national manufacturers affect media planning?

VII. The media planner must make compromises among reach, frequency, and continuity.
- **A.** The media planner is usually operating with a fixed budget and rarely makes major decisions on continuity.
- **B.** The planner must make sure ad messages fall within an effective range of reach and frequency. That is, the message must reach enough prospects enough times to make impact, but not so many times that wearout occurs.
- **C.** Reach and frequency must be considered with a context of marketing, message, and media environments.

QUESTION: Discuss the concept of empty reach.

VIII. The media schedule outlines the specific media vehicles and timing of the media plan.
- **A.** Media plans usually demonstrate some form of flighting that allows a reduction of advertising dollars without losing impact and awareness.
- **B.** Media plans may also use either seasonal or steady buys.
- **C.** Flighting must consider a number of variables in developing a plan:
  1. Competitive spending
  2. Timing
  3. Advertising decay
  4. Secondary media between flights

QUESTION: Under what circumstances would an advertiser consider a steady media buy?

IX. Media planning is not conducted in a competitive vacuum.
- **A.** The budget, share of market, product quality, and even broadcast media availability are all competitive considerations.
- **B.** A firm must be careful to determine the specific companies and brands with which it competes.
- **C.** Finally, a competitive awareness should not become a defensive, follow-the-leader strategy.

X. As previously noted, the media planner rarely determines the budget.
- **A.** The media planner has major responsibility for fiscal oversight since so much of the total ad budget is allocated to media.
- **B.** In the future, we will see even stricter controls of media costs and more narrowly defined prospect groups.

XI. The role of the media department is becoming more important in the total advertising decision making process.
- **A.** Clients are demanding cost efficiencies that most often start with media.
- **B.** The media planner is being asked to evaluate the qualitative factors that contribute to successful advertising.
- **C.** With the introduction of computer technology, the media department is becoming a major source of marketing information used by all departments.

QUESTION: What are some of the attributes that you would look for in hiring for the media department?

XII. In the future, the media function will become even more complex and the risk to advertisers greater.
- **A.** Greater fragmentation will increase the cost/1000 of media but should result in more narrowly defined audiences.
- **B.** Advertisers will increasing consider regional and local strategies, making the job of the media planner even more difficult.
- **C.** The management of the media function, especially budgeting, will undergo dramatic changes during the 1990s.

The media plan should be reviewed for an overall perspective of media planning. It might be helpful to have students discuss it again at the conclusion of Chapters 8 to 13.

ANSWERS TO QUESTIONS

1. Discuss the concept of mass and less-than mass advertising media.

As media and their audiences become more fragmented, we must take note of those vehicles that deliver very small, targeted audiences. For convenience, advertisers have said that those media vehicles that deliver less than 1 (one) percent of some group are considered less-than mass media.

2. Discuss the major advantages and disadvantages of the following advertising media:

(a) Newspapers reach a broad audience and are extremely flexible for the advertiser. However, they exhibit low reading time and reach a small percentage of teens and young adults on a regular basis. (b) Television encompasses all the senses and offers advertisers prestige. Its message is perishable and is extremely costly, especially in newer fragmented vehicles such as cable where CPM figures can be very high. (c) Direct mail can target virtually any audience with a personal message, but it is expensive on a CPM basis and has a "junk mail" image among many people. (d) Radio can reach a huge aggregate population and can segment many groups, especially teens. Its lack of a visual element means that attention levels are very low. Even though the cost per spot is low, it demands high frequency for most products. (e) Magazines have long life and a colorful, prestige image that can reach virtually any target market. Magazines are expensive and their long closing dates work against many advertisers who depend on timing to react to changing market situations. (f) Out-of-home is a visual medium that is excellent for reminder ads. It generates high reach and frequency levels, but cannot deliver a full sales message and is a low-prestige medium among most buyers.

3. Successful advertising usually begins with the narrow identification of a target market. Explain.

Essentially, the best message delivered to the wrong audience is worse than a mediocre message delivered to the right audience.

4. Compare and contrast the notion of marketing and advertising goals.

Basically, both are attempting to enhance the sale of a product. However, advertising goals are much more narrowly defined in a communication context. For example, a marketing goal is to increase market share two percent; an advertising goal is to increase brand awareness two percent.

5. Discuss the relationship between creative elements and advertising media planning.

Basically, the media planner has to know what the focus of the advertising message is going to be. Radio is normally not suitable for direct-response offers, but television would be excellent for demonstrating a product.

6. Briefly discuss the Advertising Research Foundation model for evaluating media.

The idea of the model is to move from the simplest evaluation of media (vehicle distribution) to the most complex (sales) and show the way prospects become a higher proportion of the total audience at each level.

7. Describe the media concepts of reach, frequency, and continuity. Which of these is usually not controlled by the media planner?

Reach is the number or percentage of a audience that is exposured with no duplication. Frequency is the average number of times this audience is exposed, and continuity is the period of time over which this exposure takes place. Normally, the length of a campaign (continuity) is determined by the client, not the media buyer.

8. Discuss the idea of effective reach and effective frequency. How do they relate to the notion of "quality of exposure"?

The media planner wants to reach an audience enough times to have impact, but not so many that it is clear a purchase decision will not be made or has already been made. As you provide overexposure in a media plan, it probably means that other prospects are not being reached or are being reached inadequately.

9. How does the media planner use flighting to extend the advertising budget?

The premise behind flighting is that there is a continuity of impression in the absence of actual advertising. If a person remembers your product without constant advertising, exposures can be withdrawn for a time at a significant cost savings.

10. How will audience fragmentation affect the media buying process in the future?

Media planners will have to accept a higher level of CPM and make up the difference with less waste circulation through more target media.

CHAPTER EIGHT

Using Television

The difficulty of organizing a discussion of television advertising is that it is no longer a single medium. From an advertising and marketing perspective network, spot, syndicated, and cable programming are designed to reach different audiences with diverse messages and at significant cost differentials. In addition, television must be considered as a social and cultural force as well as a medium of entertainment, news, and advertising.

This chapter divides this complex medium into its component parts. At the same time, every effort has been made to demonstrate the flexibility and synergism that is such an advantage of television. This edition also has expanded coverage of VCR audiences, video cassette advertising, and the difficulties of program ratings in the current fragmented environment.

LECTURE OUTLINE

I. Television is a medium that permeates every facet of our lives.
- **A.** It is a social and cultural medium from which we not only gain information, but validate our environment.
- **B.** In a recent poll watching TV ranked above sleeping and eating as favorite passtimes!
- **C.** Television is fast moving from a broadly based mass medium to one that addresses its programs to the individual. In this sense, TV may become more and more like radio during the next decade.

II. Television is an increasingly fragmented medium.
- **A.** TV fragmentation will result in higher costs/1000, but much greater choice for both viewers and advertisers.
- **B.** Part of viewing fragmentation will result in an increase in noncommercial alternatives, especially among prime prospects for many advertisers.
- **C.** Network dominance will be reduced, but the majority will still view the three major networks.

QUESTION: If you were a network executive, how would you compete in this era of fragmented audiences?

III. Television is second only to newspapers as an advertising medium and the largest medium by far among national advertisers.
- **A.** Among the major advantages of TV are:
  1. TV is indispensable in the lives of many people.
  2. TV provides maximum creative opportunities.
  3. TV is an excellent medium for introducing new products to a mass audience.
- **B.** TV is not ideal for every advertiser or every advertising situation.
  1. TV is costly, especially for small advertisers.
  2. Clutter is a continuing problem as more advertisers seek access to the medium.
  3. Clutter will become even more of a problem with more advertisers using 15-second commercials.

IV. Marketing TV to advertisers has become more realistic in recent years.
- **A.** TV rarely presents itself as the only medium, but rather shows how the medium can work effectively with other vehicles.
- **B.** This complementary approach is called "media synergism."
- **C.** This tactic works very well with local advertisers who will rarely consider a TV-only media plan.

QUESTION: Why has TV been more inclined to adopt a multimedia approach in recent years?

V. The rating-point system.
- **A.** Rating point: the unit of measurement for the size of an audience.
- **B.** A rating point is one percent of the total number of households with television sets in a specified area (whether these sets are turned on or not). A rating of 12 for a program means 12 percent of the television households in a given area watched that show.
- **C.** Gross rating points (GRPs).
  1. The GRP is a measure of advertising weight, or impact against a market.
  2. The GRP is a duplicated audience figure taking into account the ratings of all commercials bought in a particular schedule.
  3. Mathematically, the GRP is expressed:

$$R \times F = GRP$$

$$\frac{GRP}{R} = F$$

$$\frac{GRP}{F} = R$$

Where R = reach expressed as a *percentage* of target audience and F = frequency of exposures against that market.

D. While the GRP system shows the relative weight from market-to-market, audiences generated by a GRP level in one market cannot be compared to another.

E. GRP levels are usually based on rating points against a target population (for example, women 18 to 35), rather than the total viewing audience.

F. The GRP system is an important means of determining what weight can be used within a given budget or the budget needed to achieve a certain impact as measured by GRPs.

VI. The share of audience.

A. While the rating measures the percent of television households watching a show, the share of audience (referred to as the "share") measures the households using television (HUT) who are watching a show.

B. The share is a measure that determines how well a show is doing against its immediate competition; the rating measures how well it compares to all other shows.

QUESTION: Under what circumstances would an advertiser be more interested in the share figure rather than the rating for a show?

C. Discuss some of the ways in which a media planner would use the GRP.

VII. The media planner must approach TV from the perspective that it is in fact a number of media.

A. In the future, we will see even more diversification and a trend toward the viewers taking greater control of their viewing through VCRs, and so on.

B. The advent of information services and interactive TV is going to dramatically change the TV landscape in the future.

VIII. Despite the erosion of network TV audiences, it should be emphasized that the networks still set the agenda for the majority of TV.

A. The networks represent a loosely structured organization of largely independent stations that come together as brokers between program producers and stations with time to sell.

B. The networks depend on station clearances for entry to the marketplace and pay stations compensation for their time.

C. Network time is bought in two phases: up-front for large advertisers and scatter plans for the remainder of the schedule.

D. Time prices are the result of negotiation rather than fixed rates.

E. Part of the negotiation process involved the payment of make-goods if programs miss anticipated ratings levels.

IX. Spot and local TV is used by advertisers who don't have national distribution, have too small a budget to afford network advertising, or want to give added weight to high potential markets.

A. Defining the television territory.

1. Transmission boundaries of broadcast signals do not coincide with sales territories.
2. The Arbitron and Nielsen Rating Companies define broadcast territories. The most familiar designation is the Area of Dominant Influence (ADI) developed by Arbitron. The ADI is an area that consists of all counties in which the home market stations receive a preponderance of viewing. Nielsen has a similar system called the Designated Marketing Area (DMA).
3. The ADI is commonly used to define market areas in other media, demonstrating the dominance of television as a national advertising medium.

B. Spot and local advertising are growing much faster than network.

QUESTION: Why has the ADI designation become popular as a general device to define marketing territories?

D. Four A's has suggested the following procedures for buying spot television.

1. Summary includes general information about the client, budget, target audience, and advertising strategy.
2. Goals by market addresses the advertising weight to be delivered in each market.
3. Buying guidelines are the specific specifications of the buy including make-goods, daypart weights, and reach and frequency goals.

E. The station representative system.

1. Persons with offices in the main advertising centers who act as sales and service agents for stations around the country.
2. They provide the time buyer with market data, the station's programming, and the station's audience. They find out what spots are available for the time buyer, and they help set a firm schedule.

QUESTION: Why has the growth of local and spot TV buys to some extent undermined the traditional rep/station relationship?

F. Local station sales are largely conducted by the station sales force.

1. Local TV is the fastest-growing segment of the TV industry in terms of increase in dollars.
2. This increase is caused by availability of co-op dollars, aggressive selling by local stations, and the increase in independent stations that depend on local advertisers.

X. Specifics of buying television time.

A. The television day.

1. A great deal of spot and local television advertising is bought on a daypart basis.
2. Each daypart has its distinctive characteristics.

B. Pre-emption rate.

1. Spot television advertising is often sold on a preemptible (low-rate) basis, where an advertiser can

claim time if he or she is willing to pay a higher rate than the current advertiser.

2. Types of pre-emptible rate.
   a) Immediately pre-emptible
   b) Pre-emptible with some notice, for instance, two weeks
   c) Nonpre-emptible or fixed rate

QUESTION: What type of advertiser would be most likely to use each of the categories of pre-emptible rates?

C. Run of schedule (ROS).
   1. Advertiser gets a lower rate by allowing station to run his commercials at its (station's) convenience versus specifying a particular position.

D. Package rates.
   1. An assortment of time slots at different periods of the day, sold as a package, at less cost than if the advertiser bought those spots individually.

E. Product protection.
   1. Every advertiser wants to keep competitors' advertising as far away as possible from his.
   2. Some stations say they will keep competitive product commercials 5 to 10 minutes apart.
   3. Most stations will guarantee only that they will not run them back to back.

F. Rotation: Horizontal and vertical (also applies to radio).
   1. Rotation refers to the placement of commercials within a schedule to get the greatest possible showing.
   2. Horizontal rotation. Placement of commercials according to days of the week.
   3. Vertical rotation. Placement of commercials according to time of day.
   4. Two spots a week for four weeks shown only on Monday and Tuesday does not hit people who watch television on the other days; it is poor horizontal rotation.
   5. Three spots on the "Tonight Show," all shown at 12:45 A.M. would miss those who went to sleep earlier; it is poor.

QUESTION: Why would a rotation schedule be more important to a medium or small TV advertiser rather than a very large advertiser?

XI. TV syndication is the sale and distribution of programming on a station-by-station basis.

A. At one time, it was a minor factor for off-network reruns to get a little revenue in fringe periods on local stations.

B. Syndication has become an important factor due to:
   1. The primetime access rule eliminating some network programming.
   2. Competition for lead-ins to local news.
   3. Increase in the number of stations and additional time to fill.
   4. Advertisers are looking for alternatives to increases in network costs.

C. There are several forms of syndication.
   1. Off-network (excluded from network affiliates during access period).
   2. First-run syndication.
   3. Barter, in which syndicated shows are provided to stations who wish some spots to be presold. Many shows are offered on a cash-barter basis.
   4. Fourth network was formally a single "special" syndicated show. Now Fox Broadcasting has established a continuously syndicated network similar to major networks, but with only a few shows.

D. Most syndicated shows are run on a strip basis (either five or seven days a week).

QUESTION: Would you anticipate that syndication would become a larger factor in the future? Why?

XII. Cable has come into its own as an advertising medium, mainly through the establishment of a number of large cable-only networks.

A. Cable now reaches over half of all households, and ad revenues have passed the $1 billion mark.

B. The cable industry is made up of three components:
   1. System operators
   2. Basic cable networks
   3. Pay (or premium) cable networks

C. Cable viewership is concentrated in less than ten services.

D. Advertisers are concerned that viewers of premium channels are prime prospects for many of their products but cannot be reached with their advertising messages.

QUESTION: How has cable contributed to the fragmentation of the TV audience?

XIII. The VCR has offered the first practical means of the audience to take complete control of its viewing.

A. Advertisers have tried to adapt to the VCR by:
   1. Inserting ads in prerecorded material such as movies
   2. Placing ads on boxes in which rental movies are taken out of the store

B. The flexibility of VCR use (fast-forwarding, time-shift viewing, and so on) has made advertisers concerned about traditional rating methods and tracking VCR users.

XIV. Other broadcast services include:

A. Subscription television (STV)

B. Direct Broadcast Satellite System (DBSS)

C. Multipoint Distribution System (MDS)

D. Low Power Television (LPTV)

E. Information services
   1. Teletext is a broadcast service that allows a viewer to receive several hundred "pages" (screens) of information using a converter.
   2. Videotex is a more flexible system that interconnects with a central computer to provide unlimited two-way service for banking, shopping, or making reservations.

QUESTION: Why have the information services not grown as anticipated?

XV. Advertisers don't buy programs; they buy the people who are watching these programs. Consequently, the rating services that verify these audiences are critical to the industry.

A. A. C. Nielsen and the Arbitron Ratings Company are the two major providers of TV ratings.

B. There are several methods of gathering TV ratings:

1. In medium and small markets the diary is the most popular method.
2. In large markets the household meter is largely replacing the diary for basic rating information; diaries are still used for demographics.
3. The newest advance in ratings is the people meter that provides each individual in the household with access to the meter.
4. In the future, we will see widespread use of a combined audience rating device with a means of determining purchase behavior.

QUESTION: What are the necessary technological ingredients to put together a system such as ScanAmerica?

C. The final type of ratings are the so-called qualitative ratings made popular by Marketing Evaluations' Q Reports.

1. The key to Q Ratings are popularity, not size of audience.
2. The ratings are extremely controversial among some performers and TV executives.

ANSWERS TO QUESTIONS

1. Discuss the role of the three major networks in contemporary television. How has this role changed in the last decade?

There has been a great deal of discussion over the erosion of network audiences during the last decade. In fact, network share have gone from approximately 90 percent to around 70 percent (slightly lower in households with pay cable services). While this is of major concern to the networks, it should not mask the fact that the networks still set the agenda for most TV and provide the benchmark against which other services are judged. Even the most pessimistic predictions say that the networks will maintain collective shares of over 50 percent into the next century.

2. Discuss the concept of the fragmented audience and the major implications of this concept on advertisers.

Basically the fragmentation of TV has led to opportunities for market segmentation formerly unavailable in the medium. Unfortunately, it also has resulted in higher CPM figures for advertisers.

3. Identify:

a. Most advertising on TV (particularly network) is bought on the basis of spots distributed (scattered) throughout a number of network shows.

b. Clutter is any nonprogram material, usually commercials.

c. Gross rating points are the accumulated ratings over several TV or radio spots.

d. Cost per point is the cost per rating point generated by a broadcast media schedule.

e. Program syndication are programs distributed and sold on a station-by-station basis in contrast to network programming.

f. Clearance is when a station clears a time period to allow a network program to appear.

g. Spot advertising is bought by national advertisers on a station-by-station basis rather than through networks.

h. Up-front buys are commercials bought at a premium by large advertisers at the opening of the buying season in the spring for the next fall season.

i. Area of Dominant Influence is a term coined by the Arbitron Rating Company; it refers to the area in which a station has its majority audience. Each county in the United States is in an exclusive ADI.

4. What is the difference between a rating and a share?

A rating is the percentage of households tuned to a station; a share is the percentage of sets-in-use or households-using-television tuned to a program.

5. Compare and contrast the three primary methods of gathering audience ratings (that is, diary, household meter, and people meter).

The diary is the least expensive method, but it suffers from people not filling it out on a regular basis. The household meter accurately measures the number of households watching a particular show but cannot give demographic breakouts of the audience. The people meter provides a device for each member of the household to record viewership and combine the best features of the diary and meter.

6. How does a syndicated network differ from a traditional network in television?

A traditional network has a list of station affiliates which, in most cases, will automatically clear a high percentage of their time for their home network. A syndicated network is like any syndicated show, in that, it must sell each station individually. The only difference is that the syndicated network generally asks that each station broadcast the program at the same time.

7. Discuss the role of television reps in selling television time.

Basically the rep sells for local stations on a percentage basis. He or she calls on major advertisers and their agencies and, in effect, becomes a local station's sales representative in various markets where the station could not afford to have a full-time salesperson.

8. Discuss the role of barter syndication as an outlet for national advertising.

The normal approach to barter syndication is that a producer provides a station with a program where a certain number of spots already have been sold to national advertisers. The station is provided with time to sell a few spots to local advertisers. The program is given free to the station or at a reduced price.

9. What are the advantages and disadvantages of checkerboarding and stripping?

Checkerboarding will accumulate more reach since different people like different shows. However, the problem is finding enough shows to fill a week's worth of programming. Stripping will gain high levels of frequency, but unless there are many episodes of a show the available audience wearout occurs due to reruns.

10. Discuss the potential of videotext as an advertising medium.

Videotext has great potential in that it can reach a known, selective audience that is upscale and already interested in the services provided and the advertising for these services. Whether the potential will be realized is a matter of enough people buying the computers and softwear that run the systems.

11. How do the "Q" ratings differ from more traditional audience rating services?

Basically, the Q rating is a measure of popularity, whereas traditional services are measures of audience size.

CHAPTER NINE

Using Radio

Most students are extremely heavy radio listeners and, hence, very interested in the medium. The discussion of radio is also an excellent place to emphasize the target marketing of the 1980s and 1990s and the role that radio plays in niche marketing using several media in a single campaign. Finally, radio is an excellent example of the way a medium often must adapt to changing public tastes and an evolutionary marketplace. As we point out in this chapter, radio successfully made the transition from a mass medium to an individual medium when TV came on the scene. Will AM radio be successful in stemming the tide of FM?

LECTURE OUTLINE

I. Radio set the example for the target marketing media of recent years.
- **A.** Radio is so pervasive that set ownership statistics are meaningless.
- **B.** Radio is a necessary habit for every demographic group, both at home and in the car.
- **C.** Today, radio is a successful competitor with newspapers and other media for local advertising dollars.

II. Radio has many features that make it a prime medium for a diversified list of advertisers.
- **A.** Radio is a personal medium, speaking to each person on a one-to-one basis.
- **B.** Radio is broadly selective, reaching a large number of listeners in all age categories.
- **C.** Radio can deliver light users of other media.
- **D.** With its large out-of-home audience, radio delivers a group of listeners who are already in the marketplace.

QUESTION: As an advertiser, what do you see as the two major advantages of radio?

III. As the case with most media, radio is not suitable for all advertising situations.
- **A.** The major problem with radio is the lack of a visual element.
- **B.** Radio also has a small per station audience that requires high frequency to reach most target markets.
- **C.** Radio has little potential as a major player in the direct-response field so popular with other media.

QUESTION: What are some of the ways radio advertisers can overcome the lack of a visual element?

IV. A few useful technical points on radio:
- **A.** Radio signals are transmitted by radio waves that differ in terms of frequency. Each station is assigned its own frequency by the Federal Communications Commission.
- **B.** Differences between AM and FM radio:
  1. There are approximately 4,750 AM and 3,550 FM stations.
  2. AM (amplitude modulation) radio waves vary the amplitude of the sound wave while the frequency remains constant.
  3. FM (frequency modulation) radio waves vary their frequency while the amplitude remains constant.

V. Selling radio time is complex because of the number of station options and formats.
- **A.** Local sales account for about 75 percent of radio revenues so the sales department of a local station is crucial.
- **B.** In recent years local radio has been dramatically upgraded, offering good career opportunities for college graduates.
- **C.** Network radio has become much more popular in recent years, but still accounts for less than 10 percent of total revenue.
  1. Satellite downlinks provide easy access to stations for national programming.
  2. Radio stations may belong to a number of these national program services.
  3. There is a danger that radio will lose its local flavor if too much programming is provided by satellite services.
  4. Major users of network radio are stations in medium and small markets.
- **D.** Spot radio is very soft with advertisers either buying straight local advertising or using national networks.
- **E.** The future of the rep-initiated nonwired networks is in doubt as spot continues to fall.

QUESTION: If you were a radio rep, how would you compete with national satellite networks in selling advertising?

VI. In recent years FM has come to totally dominant the radio audiences with the exception of the over-55 age group.
  A. FM now has 75 percent of the total radio audience large due to:
    1. The 1972 nonsimulcast rule of the FCC
    2. Better sound quality of FM
    3. The decline of the cost of FM sets
    4. FM appeals to those audience segments of most importance to advertisers

QUESTION: If you were general manager of an AM station, how would you market your station against FM competition?

VII. Most radio advertising is bought by time classifications called dayparts.
  A. Dayparts are used since most stations have few program segments.
  B. East daypart is dominated by a specific target audience.
  C. Cost of radio is largely determined by the daypart in which an ad runs.

VIII. Types of programming.
  A. Ratings for most radio stations are in the one to five range.
  B. Radio programming provides distinct audiences for the advertiser.
  C. Radio is especially adept at enhancing a media schedule by:
    1. Giving added weight to a prime prospect segment.
    2. Reaching nonusers of other media (for example, teens)
    3. Offering local market flexibility for national advertiser

IX. Radio ratings are dominated by Arbitron and Birch at the local level.
  A. Arbitron, the largest radio rating service, uses the diary method with follow-up telephone calls to encourage participation.
  B. Birch uses a telephone-interview technique covering the last 24-hour listening pattern.
  C. Both services make special efforts to provide ratings on Hispanic listeners, a large portion of the radio audience in many markets.
  D. RADAR (Radio All Dimension Audience Research) is the major service for network ratings. It uses the telephone interview method.

QUESTION: Would you expect radio ratings to be more difficult to obtain than those in TV? Why?

X. Radio differs from TV in that you are buying stations and dayparts rather than programs.
  A. Drive time is the most desired and highly rated period for most stations.
  B. Advertisers usually buy time in terms of packages. The most popular is the total audience plan (TAP) which rotates spots throughout the broadcast day to reach various segments of the listening audience.

XI. Negotiation is the basis for buying radio time.
  A. Negotiation should follow certain rules.
    1. Do your homework.
    2. Be fair; look for a long-term relationship.
    3. Know your counterpart.
    4. Don't be greedy.
  B. Most radio negotiation is the result of on-the-job training.

QUESTION: As an agency time buyer, what information would you gather before going into a negotiation session with a radio salesperson?

XII. Buying radio is based on two primary characteristics of the medium.
  A. It is done on the basis of narrow audience segments.
  B. The time is perishable.

XIII. In using radio ratings, we need to remember that buying radio stations is similar to buying television programs.
  A. Listeners tend to concentrate their radio in only a few stations based on format and personalities rather than individual programs, which are largely nonexistent.
  B. Radio media planners must understand several definitions of radio ratings.
  C. Geographical patterns of radio ratings.
    1. Metro survey area (MSA) the central city from which most of a stations' audience originates
    2. Total survey area (TSA) the area that encompasses the MSA and selected counties in the listening area
  D. The basic pattern for audience ratings in radio are accumulated audiences over a period of time. These ratings are usually expressed as Average Quarter-Hour Estimates in terms of:
  E. Radio ratings are expressed as average quarter-hour estimates in terms of:
    1. Average persons
    2. Average ratings
    3. Metro share
    OR
  F. Cume Estimates:
    1. Cume persons
    2. Cume ratings

QUESTION: Why does radio depend so much on accumulated audience estimates?

XIV. Planning reach and frequency schedules in a market.
  A. The first step is to rank stations by target market rating.
  B. Next, we must see how multistations' schedules accumulate reach and frequency.
  C. Finally, we must evaluate how our radio schedule complements other media that we are considering.

ANSWERS TO QUESTIONS

1. Discuss some of the marketing techniques that allowed radio to compete with the introduction of television as an advertising medium.

Basically, radio began to sell itself as a local, rather than a national medium. It also positioned itself as a supplemental medium, selling to advertisers as a necessary means of reaching light users of other media.

2. Discuss the primary advantages and disadvantages of radio as a medium.

Radio is low cost, reaches audiences such as teens who are light users of other media, and generates high aggregate audience figures. However, radio lacks the visual element that is so important to many advertisers. Also, the fragmented audience of the medium means that advertisers must pay for high levels of frequency.

3. Briefly discuss the differences between AM and FM radio as an advertising medium.

Basically, FM dominates radio with its better tonal quality. AM is dominant only among older (55+) listeners and in the talk and news formats.

4. Discuss the status of network radio and its development during the last few years.

Network radio still provides less than 10 percent of radio advertising revenues. However, many small stations are using network services delivered through satellite for a majority of their programming.

5. Discuss the three primary radio ratings services for local and network radio audiences.

(a) Arbitron is the largest service and uses the diary method to obtain local market ratings. (b) Birch, using telephone interviews, is the other major service for local ratings. (c) Radio All-Dimension Audience Research (RADAR) provides network radio ratings through telephone interviews.

6. Identify:

a. Drive time is the early morning and late afternoon periods when most stations have their peak audiences and highest rates.

b. Package plans are designed to place radio spots throughout the broadcast day in order to reach all segments of the listening audience.

c. The Metropolitan Survey Area (MSA) is the area of concentrated audience for most stations. It is a designation used to define the central geographical area for rating services.

d. Cume is short for accumulated audience or the total audience listening to a station over several quarter hours or dayparts.

e. Average quarter hour rating is the base unit for most radio ratings. It refers to the percentage of a population that is listening in an average 15-minute period.

7. Discuss some of the primary reasons for the emergence of FM radio.

(a) The better tonal quality, which is important since most radio programming is musical. (b) The FCC dictated in the early 1970s that FM and AM jointly owned stations could not simulcast and therefore FM was positioned as a separate medium. (c) The cost of FM sets has dropped dramatically, making it practical for people to buy them; this is especially important for cars.

8. How is radio used by most advertisers in their media planning?

Radio is used as a supplemental medium to reach audience segments who are not regular users of other media. It is also used as a means of providing additional weight against prime prospects at a reasonable cost.

CHAPTER TEN

Using Newspapers

Newspapers are the largest medium in terms of total advertising revenue and number of different advertisers. Newspapers carry advertising ranging from a full-page for General Motors to a classified notice for free kittens. Daily newspaper readership is over 60 million and is increasing each year.

Despite these impressive numbers and the continuing popularity of newspapers as an advertising medium, there are some dark clouds on the horizon. Newspaper readership is not keeping up with population growth, and household formation and readership is especially soft among young adults. Also, despite various attempts at changing the situation, national advertisers have not embraced the medium. Newspapers also face aggressive competition from local TV and radio stations, suburban weeklies and shoppers, and direct mail pieces prepared by large chain outlets. The future of newspaper advertising remains bright, but marketing will be the key to continued success.

LECTURE OUTLINE

I. Newspapers remain the leader in advertising revenues, but they face a changing competitive situation at the local level.
- **A.** Both broadcast media and a host of local print alternatives are vying for the retail dollar.
- **B.** At the same time, newspapers face higher operating costs that threaten to cut into profits.
- **C.** Newspapers are fortunate in that they experience little internal competition and therefore can offer a united front against inroads from other media.
- **D.** It remains to be seen if national newspapers such as *USA Today* can generate the ad dollars needed to be profitable.

II. Despite the popularity of newspapers as an advertising medium, marketing has become necessary to defend themselves against aggressive competition.
- **A.** Marketing takes two avenues:
  - **1.** Gaining new and retaining old readers, especially among young adults
  - **2.** Increasing ad dollars, especially among national advertisers and large retail chains
- **B.** There are several trends that bode well for future gains in newspaper advertising:
  - **1.** Increasing regional strategies by national advertisers
  - **2.** Newspapers can compete against the 15-second TV commercial.
  - **3.** Newspapers offer a flexibility of format to reach customers.
  - **4.** Newspapers offer immediate results.

III. Newspapers must serve both small retailers and large retail chains. To do so, most major dailies offer zoned editions and total market coverage (TMC).
- **A.** Zoned editions offer coverage of only a portion of the market for small retailers or those who want additional weight given to a certain segment of the total market.
- **B.** Total market coverage gives a retailer total penetration of all households by supplementing newspaper circulation with direct mail or a once-a-week free edition.

QUESTION: Discuss some of the local retailers in your community who would be likely to use zoned editions or TMC programs.

IV. There are three primary categories of newspaper advertising.
- **A.** Classified advertising is often overlooked, but is one of the most profitable segments of newspaper advertising. It accounts for approximately 37 percent of total revenue.
- **B.** Three categories—employment, real estate, and automotive—account for 75 percent of classified advertising revenue.
- **C.** Local newspaper advertising is the workhorse of the industry.
- **D.** In recent years, much of the decision-making for local stores has been consolidated in corporate headquarters, changing the relationship between the retailer and the local newspaper salesperson.
- **E.** National newspaper advertising continues to lag behind other categories.
- **D.** There are three issues that must be addressed if newspapers are to gain significant national advertising:
  - **1.** Standardization of format from one newspaper to another as well as group billing procedures
  - **2.** Better positioning opportunities and reproductive quality

3. A decrease in the local versus national rate differentiation

QUESTION: Why is the classified category of newspaper advertising so profitable?

QUESTION: As a newspaper publisher, how would you defend the national newspaper rate for most dailies?

V. Newspapers as an advertising medium.
   A. Newspapers have high audience penetration and readership on a daily basis.
   B. Newspaper advertising is most used by the public.
   C. Newspapers accumulate audiences on both a reach and frequency basis.

QUESTION: Will newspapers successfully stave off competitors and remain the number one advertising medium through the 1990s?

VI. The rate structure.
   A. The SAU system has simplified the national advertising buying process. However, a number of decisions must be made by both local and national newspaper advertisers.
   B. Discounts.
      1. Flat rate papers offer no discounts.
      2. Open rate papers may offer a number of discounts. The most popular are frequency or bulk discounts.
   C. Run-of-paper (ROP) and preferred-position rates.
      1. ROP rates are the basic rates quoted by a newspaper where the ads are placed at the discretion of the publisher.
      2. Preferred positions may assure placement in a certain section of the paper or place on the page. Preferred positions are not as common as in past years, but advertisers may still request certain positions.
   D. Combination rates.
      1. The most common combination rate is for advertising in both the morning and evening editions of jointly owned newspapers.
      2. Group owners also may offer combination rates for advertising in two or more markets.
      3. Finally, independently owned newspapers may offer combination buys through a central source.

QUESTION: Why is the SAU system generally more important to national rather than local advertisers?

VII. The rate card.
   A. Includes rates, copy requirements, mechanical requirements—all the information an advertiser needs to place an order
   B. Standard Rate and Data Service (SRDS) publishes all rate-card information.
   C. SRDS information applies only to national newspaper rates.

VIII. As newspapers have attempted to increase national advertising revenue, they have moved toward the CPM as the major means of comparing costs.
   A. The CPM comparison reflects the fractional-page buys through the SAU.
   B. It also allows inter-media comparison on a basis that is used currently by national advertisers.

QUESTION: What are some of the limitations on using inter-media comparisons for media costs?

IX. Newspapers must develop a means of adjusting the space bought by advertisers during a contract period.
   A. You enter into the space contact if the paper gives a scale of discounts depending on the amount of lineage run over 12 months. (If a paper has a flat rate, there is no need for a space contract.)
   B. A space contract is an agreement of the rate you will pay for any space that has been run during the year in question.
   C. Requires two steps.
      1. Estimate of space needed, with an agreement to make any needed adjustments at year's end. (You are then billed during the year at the selected rate.)
      2. Total lineage is added at end of the year. If the estimate equals the actual, no adjustment is necessary. If you failed to run enough space to earn that rate, you will have to pay at the higher rate charged for that lineage bracket (called the short rate).
   D. To make sure the students understand this concept, it is advisable to go over the text example in complete detail.
   E. If space run actually exceeds the estimate and qualifies for a better line rate, the advertiser gets a rebate.

X. Newspapers must provide advertisers with various reports concerning their circulation and readership.
   A. The most widely used service is the Audit Bureau of Circulations (ABC) reports that consist of a Publisher's Statement and ABC Audit.
   B. The *Circulation and Penetration Analysis of Print Media* provides county-by-county penetration of various print media as well as by ADI.
   C. Finally, Simmons and Scarborough provide standardized information for a number of major dailies.
      1. Syndicated services are of major importance to national advertisers who buy hundreds of papers in their media schedules.
      2. These services provide demographic information, buying data, and media usage.

QUESTION: As a newspaper ad salesperson, how would you use each of the three types of research services to sell advertising?

XI. Newspaper Marketing and Merchandising Services.
   A. Newspapers have reacted to their new competitive environment by developing a number of strategies to promote the medium to advertisers.
   B. The emphasis on marketing has taken several forms.
      1. Promoting the newspaper as the best source of information, entertainment, and advertising.
      2. Promoting the newspaper to local retailers to keep or increase their business.

3. Promoting newspapers to national advertisers as part of their total media schedules.
4. Providing more and better research—especially to national advertisers.

QUESTION: Why have newspapers put so much emphasis on marketing and merchandising in recent years?

XII. The newspaper magazine supplement has long been a popular vehicle for national and regional advertisers as well as local advertisers in a few cities.

A. The largest Sunday supplements are *Parade* and *USA Weekend,* which are circulated in, respectively, 315 newspapers (31 million circulation) and 286 newspapers (14.5 million circulation).

B. In addition, a few large newspapers have large independently produced Sunday magazines. Among these are the *Los Angeles Times, New York Times,* and *The Washington Post.*

C. Generally, the trend is away from locally edited Sunday supplements, with fewer than 40 still being published.

D. There are also a few opportunities for weekday supplement advertising. These supplements tend to be oriented toward some topic such as sports, food, and so on.

XIII. The black-oriented and ethnic press are demonstrating diverse trends in adding and retaining readers.

A. As blacks become more integrated into society, the black press has lost significant circulation. As metropolitan dailies become more sensitive to total coverage of the community, the black press may have continuing problems.

B. In contrast, the Hispanic press is growing rapidly. As the Hispanic population of many major cities continues to increase, we will probably see even more growth in this sector of the press.

QUESTION: How can the black-oriented press stem the tide of decreasing circulation?

XIV. The weekly press is in a period of transition from a rural, small-town medium to one serving an upscale, suburban audience.

A. Approximately two-thirds of weeklies are published in urban areas.

B. Weeklies range from well-edited full-service newspapers to shoppers with very little editorial content.

XV. One of the sections of the newspaper (especially Sunday) that has the highest readership are the comics.

A. Some advertisers are increasing their use of syndicated comics such as Puck to take advantage of estimated Sunday comic readership of 60 million.

B. In addition to ads placed in the comics, the spadea wrap gives advertisers what amounts to a ''cover'' on the outside of the comic section.

ANSWERS TO QUESTIONS

1. Discuss some of the primary reasons for newspaper leadership in advertising revenue.

Newspapers appeal to a wide range of advertisers and readers. They can be used by someone placing a one-time want ad, a major retail store, or a national advertiser. In addition, newspapers reach over 60 million readers each day. Readers generally are better educated and have higher incomes than the total population.

2. Marketing has become a key factor in the success of many newspapers. Discuss.

The days when newspapers held a monopoly position among local advertisers are over. Today, newspapers must compete with media ranging from TV to suburban weeklies for advertising dollars. In addition, newspapers must market themselves to readers who have a number of media outlets vying for their time and money.

3. Discuss zoning and total marketing coverage. How do these functions present both problems and opportunities to newspapers?

On the one hand, the fact that newspapers must provide both total coverage and spot coverage of a market is an indicator of the breath of advertiser support they have. On the other hand, the two types of coverage present severe technical and distribution problems for local papers.

4. Why have newspapers shown a growing aggressiveness in competing for national advertising in recent years? What are some of the steps they have taken to accommodate national advertisers?

Newspapers realize that national advertising is a largely untapped potential market for future growth—especially with their local clients coming under pressure from other media to shift dollars away from newspapers. Papers have tried to bring in national dollars through creative selling, offering standardized formats, and, in some cases, network-type buying systems. The one area where little has been done is narrowing the national/local rate differentiation.

5. Why has the CPM calculation replaced the milline rate in comparing newspaper rates?

As newspapers have moved to fractional page sizes rather than line rates, the CPM is more easily adaptable. Second, national advertisers, which newspapers are trying to sell, are more comfortable with the CPM, which allows them to make intermedia cost comparisons.

6. Why has syndicated audience research only recently become an important part of newspaper advertising?

When newspapers were selling largely to local advertisers or there was little local media competition, there was little incentive to provide nationally standardized research. However, national advertisers demand this type of intermarket research in making media-buying decisions.

7. What is the role of the Advertising Checking Service?

The service provides proof that ads were run and run in the proper space with good quality reproduction.

8. From an advertising and marketing perspective, what is the role of the syndicated newspaper distributed magazine?

It offers national advertisers the ability to reach a national audience with one insertion order and one bill. It also provides a newspaper audience with the buying convenience of a magazine.

9. Briefly discuss the process of audience verification used by the Audit Bureaus of Circulations.

Twice a year, publishers provide a statement of their circulation according to guidelines set forth by the ABC. Then once a year, the ABC audits each publication to verify that the information in the publisher's statements was correct.

10. Under what circumstances would the short rate be used by a newspaper?

When an advertiser fails to buy the contracted amount of space and, therefore, does not qualify for a particular discount, the newspaper will recalculate the proper space cost using the short rate.

11. Discuss newspaper readership trends in recent years and some of the approaches newspapers have taken to increase newspaper penetration.

Basically, newspaper circulation has failed to keep up with household formation and population increases. This shortfall has been particularly acute among young adults. Newspapers have attempted many approaches to gaining readers. Promotions and aggressive selling, special sections of interest to young readers, and more colorful redesign of the paper are among some of the techniques tried by different publications.

CHAPTER ELEVEN

Using Magazines

Magazines have many qualities that make them an excellent medium for several categories of advertisers. Magazines, with few exceptions, represent a credible vehicle for advertisers with a prestige image that carries over to the products they promote. Magazines also provide quality color reproduction and opportunities for regional (even local) advertising. Advertisers must plan ahead to use magazines since ad deadlines are often far ahead of actual publication. Finally, magazines are second only to direct mail in terms of CPM. Consequently, advertisers must choose carefully to make sure the magazines they use provide minimal waste circulation.

The discussion of magazines offers an interesting contrast to newspapers. Whereas newspapers have little internal competition, magazines often compete directly with dozens of other titles for reader time and advertiser dollars. It is also helpful to contrast the marketing goals of consumer versus business and farm publications. The contrast offers a view of the flexibility of magazines and the different problems faced by the various categories.

LECTURE OUTLINE

I. Magazines were the first national medium; their growth can be traced to the growth of U.S. business in general.
- **A.** Magazines were the prime national medium from the mid-1800s until the introduction of radio in 1920.
- **B.** It wasn't until the coming of TV in the late 1940s that magazines began to make significant changes in the way they approached advertising.

II. Magazines as a selective medium.
- **A.** Beginning in the early 1960s, magazines sold the quality, rather than the quantity, of their audiences.
- **B.** The major magazine success stories of the 1970s and 1980s were among selective circulation publications.
- **C.** Today there are many more magazines with lower average circulation than 20 years ago.

III. Magazines are extremely diversified but share several characteristics.
- **A.** Advantages.
  - **1.** Audience selectivity.
  - **2.** Ability to achieve reach among selective targets.
  - **3.** Long life.
  - **4.** Availability of demographic and geographic editions.
  - **5.** Credibility and believability.
- **B.** Disadvantages.
  - **1.** High cost per thousand among selective publications.
  - **2.** Long closing dates.
  - **3.** Ad banking (clustering ads together) among some publications.

IV. Since magazines are relatively expensive, there must be good reasons for advertisers to pay this premium.
- **A.** Magazines tend to deliver a quality audience of generally upscale readers.
- **B.** By its very nature, a magazine requires a level of audience involvement lacking in most other media.
- **C.** Because of the selective editorial content of most magazines, it stands to reason that readers will be more interested in the advertising that is associated with these publications.
- **D.** In a study by *Folio* magazine advertisers were asked to outline the factors most important in making magazine advertising decision. They were:
  - **1.** Advertising reproduction quality
  - **2.** Audited circulation
  - **3.** Ads that are included throughout the editorial content of a magazine
  - **4.** Syndicated audience research available
  - **5.** Recommendation of ad agency
  - **6.** Prefer an established publication
  - **7.** The magazine should be unique in some way from competing titles
  - **8.** Lack of audience duplication with competing titles
  - **9.** Make sure publication will make its rate base or guaranteed circulation
  - **10.** Opportunity for far forward advertising

QUESTION: Can you think of other factors that an advertiser should consider in choosing a magazine?

V. On occasion, advertisers need to purchase magazine ad space on very short notice.
- **A.** Some magazines offer advertisers the opportunity to buy space on a fast-close basis.

   B. Many times advertisers will reserve magazine space but not make a final decision on the specific ad until right before publication.

VI. Magazines with their ability to reach a segmented market are becoming popular vehicles for coupon and direct-response advertising.

   A. Magazines have long life and can generate returns for a much longer period of time than most media.

   B. Magazines also have large enough space to accommodate coupons.

VII. In order to compete for advertisers using regional strategies and those with less than national distribution, magazines have developed a sophisticated system of partial run advertising opportunities.

   A. Geographic and demographic editions:

      1. Geographic and demographic editions (called partial run editions) allow large circulation magazines to compete with more specialized publications.

      2. Magazines are currently offering editions keyed to upscale zip codes to give advertisers even more flexibility.

      3. Partial run advertising currently accounts for 13 percent of magazine revenues.

   D. Advantages of partial run editions:

      1. Advertiser only buys in his/her sales territories.

      2. Supports promotions run in only some regions.

      3. Can be used for testing prior to national product introduction.

      4. Reaches scattered markets with one order.

      5. Can encourage retail support by listing retailers in various regions.

      6. Allows prestige of national medium for local and regional advertisers.

   E. Disadvantages of partial run editions:

      1. Cost per thousand is much higher than national editions.

      2. Closing dates are usually earlier.

      3. Every partial run may not be available in each edition of a publication.

      4. Partial run ads may be more likely to be banked in a special section.

   F. In the future, we will see more use of editorial editions as well as partial run advertising.

QUESTION: What are some of the categories of advertising that might be most likely to use partial run advertising?

VIII. Because of the specialized nature of many magazines, advertisers are interested in the style of publications as well as their audience numbers.

   A. Magazines have an image for readers and advertisers much more than other media.

   B. Systems such as PRIZM (discussed in Chapter 7) are very important to magazine advertisers in evaluating various publications.

IX. Magazine elements.

   A. Magazine sizes.

      1. Page size is the type area, not the size of the actual page.

      2. Two sizes mainly.

         a) Standard size: about 8" x 10," like *Time*.

         b) Small size: about 4⅜ x 6½," like *Reader's Digest*.

      3. Sizes do change.

   B. Magazine space-buying designations.

      1. First cover page: front cover (not sold in American consumer magazines, but is sometimes in business or industrial magazines).

      2. Second cover page: inside of front cover.

      3. Third cover page: inside of the back cover.

      4. Fourth cover page: the back cover.

      5. A premium charge is made for the second, third, and fourth cover position, and there is usually a waiting list for these positions.

      6. Space is usually sold in terms of full, half, or quarter pages; also in units of 3, 2, or 1 column.

   C. Gatefolds.

      1. An extra page that folds out, giving the ad a big spread

      2. High premium cost

      3. Used on special occasions (new product, and so on)

   D. Bleed ads.

      1. An ad with no margins; ad seems to run over the page.

      2. Usually an extra charge

      3. Done to get attention

   E. Inserts and multiple page units:

      1. Gain greater impact, but are not particularly cost efficient

      2. Good for launching new products

      3. Can develop new marketing strategies

      4. Useful in enhancing consumers' perception of a product

      5. Helpful in promoting a range of products under a single brand name

QUESTION: What products are usually associated with multipage ads?

X. How space is sold.

   A. For national advertisers, buying magazine space is a straightforward process.

   B. The one-time, no-discount space buy is the basic or open rate. All discounts are figured from the open rate.

   C. Magazines are compared on the basis of CPM and weighted CPM calculations.

   D. Discounts.

      1. All discounts are computed from the one-time full-page rate of a publication—referred to as its basic or open rate.

      2. Frequency discount—the more often the advertiser runs within the contract year, the lower the cost per unit.

      3. Volume (dollar) discount—the more total space the advertiser uses within a contract year, measured in dollars, the lower the rate.

QUESTION: Why would a large multi-brand company be more likely to use volume as opposed to frequency discounts?

4. Special discounts.
   a) Mail-order discount.
   b) Travel discount.
   c) Trade-book discount.
   d) Multiple-page discount.
   e) Seasonal-adjustment discount.
   f) Consecutive-page discount.
5. In addition to all these discounts is a corporate or total dollar discount based on the total dollars spent by all of a corporation's divisions in a year.

E. Remnant space.
1. Unsold space when the magazine is ready to go to press.
2. Rather than run empty space, it is sold as remnant space at a big discount.
3. Great for direct response advertiser, each of whose ads stands on its own and is not part of a continuing campaign (material for such space must be ready immediately).

F. Rate negotiation.
1. Formerly, magazine rates were not negotiated as is the case of broadcast time.
2. With greater competition, some magazines are negotiating rates with large advertisers.

G. The magazine short rate.
1. If an advertiser signs a space contract at the beginning of the year (cannot be signed retroactively), he agrees to make any adjustment necessary at the end of the year if he does not run all of the space anticipated. Also, the publisher agrees to give a better rate if the advertiser exceeds the estimate.
2. You should go over the text example of the short rate computation in full detail.

QUESTION: Why is it impractical for most advertisers to depend on remnant space for their magazine advertising?

QUESTION: In what significant ways does the magazine short rate differ from the short rate in newspapers?

XI. Gaining entry for magazine advertising involves several relatively simple steps.

A. Involves two major steps: the space contract and the insertion order.
1. Space contract.
   a) An agreement to pay the current rate schedule for such space as is used.
   b) *Not* an order for a specific amount of space.
   c) If advertiser plans to use a certain magazine for the coming 12 months, he will sign a space contract to get the best rate.
   d) Advertiser estimates his space and is billed for the discount rate to which that amount of space entitles him.
   e) Advantage to advertiser: He is protected during that time from a rate increase.
2. Insertion order.
   a) When advertiser is ready to run an ad, he sends the insertion order to the publisher, specifying date of issue, size of ad, and contract rate.

B. Magazine dates.
1. Cover date: date appearing on cover.
2. On-sale date: date when it is issued.
3. Closing date: When the print or plates needed to print, the ad must be in the publisher's hands in order to make a given issue.

XII. Magazine networks make it easier for an advertiser to buy several publications at once.

A. There are two basic types of magazine networks.
1. Single publisher networks that sell several publications of one company
2. Independent networks that contract with several publishers to sell related magazines

QUESTION: From the standpoint of the advertisers that use them, how do the two types of magazine networks differ?

XIII. Split-run advertising.

A. Magazines divide a geographic edition for testing purposes.

B. Simplest example: Advertiser supplies two different ads, same size and shape, each to be run in half an edition, in the same position, and each calling for a coupon response.

C. Both are distributed equally in the same territory or in adjacent territories having similar demographic characteristics (which is the key to comparability).

D. Advertiser then compares results.

XIV. As is the case with all media, advertisers buy audiences, not magazines.

A. Magazines guarantee a certain level of circulation; if they fail to meet this guarantee, they must pay a rebate to advertisers.

B. Failing to meet a circulation guarantee can be damaging to a magazine since there are usually many competitors ready to take advantage of the situation.

C. The ABC audits magazines, as it does newspapers.
1. The magazine's books
2. Number of copies printed
3. Number sold at newsstands
4. Number returned
5. Number sold by subscription
6. How subscriptions were obtained
7. Rate of renewal

D. The audited circulation is the figure that determines what audience the magazine will guarantee, and the rate base determines ad costs.

E. Primary circulation versus pass-along circulation.
1. Readership usually refers to paid and pass-along circulation.
2. Most syndicated readership services base their estimates on a sample of total readers, not audited primary circulation.

3. SMRB surveys 110 magazines using the through-the-book method of personal interviews.
4. MRI measures 280 magazines with the recent-reading technique.

QUESTION: What are the primary strengths of the MRI and SMRB methods of measuring magazine readership?

XV. As competition for magazine advertising increases, the merchandising of this advertising takes on greater importance.
- **A.** Merchandising is a method of differentiating one title from another.
- **B.** There are several common forms of merchandising a magazine's advertising.
  1. "As advertised in" point-of-purchase displays
  2. Direct mail campaigns to retailers
  3. Shopping guides listing advertisers in each issue
  4. Shows and in-store promotions

XVI. Ask students to take each of the magazine media plans and see if there are suitable substitutes to reach the audience goals and objectives of the products.

XVII. The business press differs in several ways from the consumer publications discussed to this point.
- **A.** The competition for ad dollars comes from direct response, trade shows, and even personal selling.
- **B.** The audience of business publications is generally better educated and expert in particular fields.
- **C.** Advertising is profit-, rather than benefit-oriented.
- **D.** Business publications are most often used to:
  1. Establish contact
  2. Create awareness
  3. Arouse interest
  4. Build product preference
  5. Keep customers sold
- **E.** Pass-along readership is more valuable in the business press.

XVIII. General categories of business publications.
- **A.** The business press is divided into several categories.
  1. Trade publications, which are directed to those who buy products for resell.
     - *a)* Emphasis on profitability to retailer for stocking certain types of goods.
     - *b)* Greatest number and diversity of business publications are in this category.
  2. Industrial publications, which are directed to people who buy goods to make other products.
     - *a)* Relatively small circulation magazines.
     - *b)* Tend to carry very specific and technical advertising.
  3. Professional journals, which are directed to people such as doctors, who recommend products to others.

XIX. Business publications; general practices.
- **A.** Controlled circulation: Many business publications are sent free to a select group of readers involved in some occupation.
- **B.** Audits.
  1. Business Publications Audit of Circulation, Inc. (BPA), an organization for the business press.
  2. ABC and the Verified Audit Circulation Company (VAC) also audit business publications.
- **C.** Vertical and horizontal publications.

XX. Farm publications.
- **A.** Farm magazines are facing increased competition from other media for the agribusiness ad dollar.
- **B.** Farm magazines must compete with the consumer media for their general circulation and trade media (such as direct mail) for their business advertising.
- **C.** In terms of both geographic and demographic offerings, farm publications are among the most diversified media.
- **D.** Farm publications fall into three general categories:
  1. General farm publications
  2. Regional farm publications
  3. Vocational farm publications
  4. Selective binding has given great flexibility to farm publications.

ANSWERS TO QUESTIONS

1. Discuss how magazines, beginning in the 1950s, began to change their marketing strategy to compete with television.

Magazines moved away from a mass marketing strategy to one of audience segmentation and selectivity. Rather than reach everyone, each magazine attempted to define a portion of the total audience that they could most effectively reach.

2. How has reader support of magazines changed during recent years? What opinion do advertisers have of this change?

During the last two decades, advertising support of magazines has gone from over 60 percent of total revenues to approximately 50 percent. Advertisers support this change since it means readers have more of a stake in the publication and, presumably, will spend more time with the magazines they buy.

3. Discuss the primary advantages and disadvantages of magazines as a consumer advertising medium.

Magazines reach a narrowly defined, generally upscale audience with quality reproduction. They also have a longer life than any other major medium. On the negative side, most magazines have high CPMs and long closing dates, making them difficult to react to short-term changes in the marketplace.

4. Discuss the qualitative elements of magazines as an advertising medium.

Magazines demonstrate high levels of involvement with their readers. Because of the specialized nature of most magazines, readers identify with the editorial and associate with the advertising in a way that most other media do not.

5. Discuss the procedure of the Audit Bureau of Circulations (ABC) in verifying consumer magazine audiences.

The ABC is interested only in paid readership. It basically verifies the twice-a-year publisher's statements that are issued by each ABC member publication.

6. Identify:

a. Fast close provides advertisers with a method of getting their ads into a publication much faster than the regular closing date.

b. Partial-run circulation is primarily either demographic or geographic editions that are not sent to the total circulation of a magazine.

c. Bleed ads are run to the edge of the page without a margin.

d. Volume discounts are based on the total amount of money spent by an advertiser in a magazine.

e. Remnant space is the cheapest space in a magazine. It usually comes from unbought partial-run advertising in other editions.

f. The closing date is the date when all ad materials must be at the publisher.

g. Controlled circulation is made up of those people who qualify to have a free issue of a magazine sent to them. Most often used in business-to-business publications.

h. Industrial publications are those that are sent to purchasing agents in various industries.

7. Why is psychographic research so important to magazines?

Since magazines try to set a tone for their readers to gain involvement, it is important to understand the reasons behind their readers' behavior.

8. What are the primary advantages and disadvantages of multiple units and magazine foldouts?

They gain high impact and readership, which is excellent to introduce a new product or model or to describe a complex product. On the other hand, they are usually more expensive than regular ads on a CPM basis.

9. What is the role of magazine networks in selling advertising?

Primarily magazines networks allow an advertiser to buy a number of publications with one insertion order and at a higher discount than buying them individually.

10. What is the primary competition for business magazines in gaining advertising dollars?

Traditionally, personal selling has been the major competitor, but in recent years direct-response, both mail and telephone, have become important competitors.

11. How is pass-along readership viewed by consumer and business publications?

Consumer publications know that advertisers give much less importance to readers who don't have the interest or income to be primary buyers of the publication. However, advertisers generally regard pass-along readers of business publications as equal to primary readers. They know that people usually don't browse through a technical publication unless they have some interest in it.

12. What is the difference between a vertical and a horizontal industrial publication?

Horizontal publications cover one job category within a number of industries. Vertical publications cover all aspects of a single industry.

13. Discuss the changing competitive environment for agribusiness publications.

Agribusiness publications are facing many of the same problems as business magazines. However, the competition for agribusiness is coming from segmented programming directed to the farm community on traditional media outlets. We are seeing agribusiness companies using broadcast, newspapers, and even outdoor advertising to reach their audiences.

CHAPTER TWELVE

Out of Home Advertising

The term *out of home advertising* has replaced ''outdoor advertising,'' reflecting the creativity and flexibility that have come to stand for this area of advertising.

This chapter discusses this oldest form of advertising and mass communication. Dating as far back as the ancient Egyptian wall paintings on tombs and clay tablets to the tavern signs of fifteenth-century England providing landmarks and lodging information, out of home advertising has passed through many stages. The modern era of advertising began with World War I and the propaganda devices used to spur the war effort. The common marketing objective is to reach consumers in the market place with a colorful, spectacular message.

LECTURE OUTLINE

I. Outdoor advertising.
- **A.** Highway poster/billboard is the most common.
- **B.** An overview of the outdoor industry:
  - **1.** Smallest in revenues
  - **2.** Mostly in or near metropolitan areas
  - **3.** Standardized posters and painted signs
  - **4.** Supplemental medium
  - **5.** Most successful when used by companies that:
    - *a)* Introduce a new product and want immediate brand-name recognition
    - *b)* Want to provide reminder advertising for established, well-known brands

QUESTION: What is the most common form of outdoor advertising?

QUESTION: Which companies implement outdoor advertising most successfully?

- **C.** Several factors have benefitted outdoor advertising recently:
  - **1.** Increasingly mobile population and dispersed shopping and commuting patterns
  - **2.** Modern interstate highway system
  - **3.** Legislative restrictions banning liquor and cigarettes from broadcast media
- **D.** Primary advantages:
  - **1.** Media-mix reinforcement
  - **2.** Frequency of exposure
  - **3.** Strengthened market presence
  - **4.** Target audience capability
  - **5.** Dominant visual impact

QUESTION: What factors benefited from outdoor advertising in recent times?

- **E.** Primary disadvantages
  - **1.** Creative limitations
  - **2.** Little audience selectivity
  - **3.** Problem of availability

QUESTION: Discuss the primary advantages and disadvantages of outdoor advertising.

- **F.** The image of outdoor:
  - **1.** Has suffered due to association with liquor, beer, and tobacco advertisers
    - *a)* Declining categories with retail advertising replacing alcohol as second largest category
    - *b)* More diversification
  - **2.** Means of selectively targeting high potential markets
  - **3.** Gets a message across with minimal clutter
  - **4.** Regarded as a scenic pollutant
    - *a)* Highway Beautification Act of 1965 (''Lady Bird Bill'') restricted placement of signs along interstate highways within 660 feet of interstate roads
    - *b)* Banning and decrease of number of signs
    - *c)* Public interest groups limit construction of new billboards making existing sites more valuable and profitable
  - **5.** Economic expansion and population mobility with result in future growth

QUESTION: What is the prime argument against outdoor advertising, and what type of legislation has been passed to ensure against it?

II. The Traffic Audit Bureau's Outdoor Advertising Plan.
- **A.** Set clear objectives.
  - **1.** Gain broad awareness.
  - **2.** Add seasonal weight.

3. Target segments not easily reached by other media.

B. Choose strategic paths.

C. Define target markets already reached by other media.

D. Develop creative executions.

E. Arrange production and inspect results.

QUESTION: What five-part plan has the Traffic Audit Bureau come up with for outdoor advertising?

QUESTION: What kinds of objectives may be set.

III. Form of outdoor advertising.

- **A.** Poster panels
  - **1.** Typical 30-sheet and bleed posters, 12 x 25 feet
  - **2.** Illuminated and nonilluminated panels
    - ***a)*** High traffic volume locations use illuminated panels.
    - ***b)*** Illuminated panels have 24-hour exposure.
  - **3.** Thirty-day contract period with rotation on different thoroughfares
- **B.** The eight-sheet poster
  - **1.** Five feet high, 11 feet wide
  - **2.** Affordable to the small business person
  - **3.** Meets regulations, offering geographical flexibility
  - **4.** Reaches preselected demographic groups
  - **5.** Eight-Sheet Outdoor Advertising Association (ESOAA)

QUESTION: What are the two typical forms of outdoor advertising? Which type would the small business person prefer?

- **C.** Buying poster advertising
  - **1.** Gross rating points (GRPs or showings)
    - ***a)*** Purchases in units of 100, 75, 50, or 25
    - ***b)*** Measure percentage of duplicated audience exposed daily
- **D.** Outdoor networks
- **E.** Sources of outdoor audience data
  - **1.** Traffic Audit Bureau
    - ***a)*** Audits each market and provides circulation figures and basic information
    - ***b)*** Counts the number of pedestrians and/or automobiles passing any advertising structure during a period of time
  - **2.** Out-of-home Measurement Bureau
    - ***a)*** Promotes development of credible information about out of home media
    - ***b)*** Encourages standards of practice
  - **3.** Simmons Market Research Bureau and Audience Measurement by Market of Outdoor
    - ***a)*** Product and media usage data from a sample of the population
    - ***b)*** Conduct surveys

QUESTION: What are three sources of outdoor audience data?

- **F.** Painted bulletins
  - **1.** Permanent
  - **2.** Rotary
  - **3.** More expensive than posters
    - ***a)*** Higher production costs
    - ***b)*** Placed at high-traffic locations
  - **4.** Special embellishments
- **G.** Spectaculars
  - **1.** Made by specialists in steel construction
  - **2.** Prime locations to attract many passerbys

QUESTION: What accounts for the great expense of painted bulletins?

IV. Criteria for selecting outdoor locations.

- **A.** Length of unobstructed approach
- **B.** Type of traffic
- **C.** Characteristics of placement
- **D.** Immediate surroundings
- **E.** Size and physical attractiveness
- **F.** Price

V. Creativity in outdoor advertising.

- **A.** Product name should register quickly.
- **B.** Use brisk, compact, provocative copy.
- **C.** Legible type
- **D.** Eliminate nonessential elements.
- **E.** Big illustrations
- **F.** Simple background
- **G.** Bold colors

QUESTION: What creative principles are used in designing an outdoor poster?

VI. Cooperative advertising in outdoor.

- **A.** Manufacturers and retailers share cost of space for production
- **B.** Increases dollars available to the medium

VII. Trends in outdoor advertising.

- **A.** New fabric and plastic materials offering great illumination and lower maintenance costs
- **B.** Consolidation of ownership
- **C.** Diversify the product categories using the medium
- **D.** Awareness of environmental and public policies

QUESTION: What are four predominant trends in outdoor advertising?

VIII. Transit advertising.

- **A.** Broad reach of a mobile population
- **B.** New transit systems
- **C.** Low cost
- **D.** Excellent supplemental and reminder medium

QUESTION: What factors account for the popularity of transit advertising?

IX. Station and shelter advertising.

- **A.** Attract attention and generate involvement
- **B.** Generate attention in daylight hours
- **C.** Aids in registering a brand name with the public and communicating sales messages
- **D.** Enhances effectiveness of the shelter
- **E.** Evokes favorable comments such as convenient, safe, clean, and easy to see

ANSWERS TO QUESTIONS

1. Discuss the two primary types of outdoor advertising.

Posters and the much more expensive (about five times more) painted bulletins.

2. Why has the term *out-of-home* begun to replace "outdoor" in describing the general use of these media?

Out-of-home is more descriptive of the tremendous range of signs and posters that make up all aspects of what was formerly confined to a few outdoor media vehicles.

3. Briefly discuss the major advantages and disadvantages of outdoor advertising.

Outdoor can reach a broad spectrum of the population many times and a cost much lower than other media. However, it cannot provide a complete sales message and must be primarily reminder-type advertising. It also suffers from an image problem among a sizable portion of the population.

4. Discuss the image problems of outdoor advertising and some ways in which the industry has moved to correct them.

The two major problems facing outdoor are the controversy over whether outdoor is a visual pollutant and the concentration of alcohol and tobacco products in outdoor. The outdoor industry has tried to bring other product categories into the industry to demonstrate a more diversified image. It also has tried to convince critics that the standardized industry is mostly in industrially zoned areas and actually has decreased the number of posters in recent years. The problem is that most critics make no distinction between standardized signs and on-premise or retailer originated signs.

5. Discuss the roles of the Traffic Audit Bureau and the Out-of-Home Measurement Bureau.

The TAB's activities are confined to audience analysis of 30-sheet posters and painted bulletins. The OMB audits circulation for eight-sheet posters and shelter advertising.

6. Discuss some of the reasons for the growing popularity of the eight-sheet poster.

The eight-sheet poster meets zoning regulations that traditional posters sometimes do not. Also, it is less expensive than 30-sheet posters and research shows it has about the same audience impact.

7. If an advertiser purchases a 50-GRP showing in a market, what audience level is being bought?

The advertiser will be buying an exposure level equal to one-half of the market's population on a daily basis.

8. Discuss some of the major factors in the recent growth of transit advertising.

Transit systems have entered or greatly improved in a number of markets. This trend has resulted in a more upscale ridership for advertising. In addition, transit is the least expensive of all recognized media. It delivers a colorful message with maximum impact and, in the case of inside signs, reaches a captive audience already in the marketplace.

CHAPTER THIRTEEN

Direct-Response and Direct-Mail Advertising

Today, the direct-mail industry has grown and changed tremendously from the minor, insignificant medium it was 20 years ago. This chapter looks closer at this fastest-growing marketing activity and the different distributive methods it employs: media, trade practices, and traditions.

Direct-response advertising enables advertisers to identify and reach prospective consumers. It encompasses a number of media vehicles and is used by nearly every major advertiser for all sorts of products.

LECTURE OUTLINE

I. Definitions.
- **A.** Direct marketing
  - **1.** Encompasses direct-response and direct-mail advertising and the research and support activities
  - **2.** Allows advertisers greater control over the communication process
- **B.** Direct-response advertising
  - **1.** Any advertising used in selling goods directly to consumers
  - **2.** Doesn't have to come through the mails

QUESTION: What two kinds of advertising does the term *direct marketing* encompass? What is its advantage for the advertiser?

II. Growth of direct-response advertising.
- **A.** Societal factors
  - **1.** Fast-paced lives of executives and working women
  - **2.** Senior citizens
- **B.** The image problem of direct response
  - **1.** Had a reputation as a haven for the disreputable
  - **2.** Proposed legislation to restrict the industry's operations
- **C.** The search for alternative media by advertisers
  - **1.** Clutter has become a problem.
  - **2.** Greater emphasis on creative values means higher production costs.

QUESTION: Where does the image problem of direct response stem from?

- **D.** Target marketing and direct response
  - **1.** ZIP codes allow for audience segmentation.
  - **2.** Combine with demographic information
  - **3.** Psychographic information
  - **4.** Synchographics studies the timing of lifestyle changes.
- **E.** Research in direct response
- **F.** Use of computers and credit cards in direct response
  - **1.** Eliminates waste circulation
  - **2.** Determines duplication
  - **3.** Allows for personalized direct-response messages

QUESTION: What is synchographics, and how is it advantageous to target marketing?

- **G.** Telemarketing
  - **1.** Outbound: seller calls prospects
    - *a)* Immediate
    - *b)* Flexible
    - *c)* Can be tested quickly and inexpensively
  - **2.** Inbound: order-taking operation used with some other medium
  - **3.** Steps to success:
    - *a)* A targeted list
    - *b)* Scripts
    - *c)* Testing
    - *d)* Trained personnel
    - *e)* Record keeping

QUESTION: What are the five basic steps to telemarketing success?

  - **4.** States limit telemarketing by:
    - *a)* Requiring registration
    - *b)* Prohibiting calls to people who have notified a commission they don't want such calls
    - *c)* Limiting calls to specified hours
    - *d)* Permitting people to place an asterisk by their number to indicate no calls
  - **5.** 900 numbers
    - *a)* Listen to prerecorded message
    - *b)* Respond to opinion polls

QUESTION: What are some of the ways by which states can limit telemarketing?

III. Television and direct response.
- **A.** The traditional straight sale
  - **1.** 30-second to two-minute television commercial offering low-cost merchandise offered through an 800 number
  - **2.** Now offer greater products in more upscale tones
  - **3.** Combining television, telephone, and credit card selling, advertisers gain:
    - *a)* Immediate response
    - *b)* Ability to offer consumers maximum convenience
  - **4.** Off-hours spots at low rates
  - **5.** PI (per inquiry): station runs the ad as often as desired and gets a percentage of money received or so much for each inquiry
  - **6.** Bonus-to-payout: fixed schedule of spots with agreed-upon return

QUESTION: When are television direct-response ads usually run? Discuss two methods of placement.

- **B.** Long-form television direct response
  - **1.** Program-length shows
  - **2.** Aired on UHF independent stations or cable networks
- **C.** Television shopping networks
- **D.** Videocassettes
  - **1.** Used primarily by business-to-business advertisers, incorporated with total marketing plan
  - **2.** Supplement to print and broadcast advertising

IV. Radio and direct response.
- **A.** Supplements other forms of direct response
- **B.** Relatively low cost

V. Magazines and direct response.
- **A.** Advantages
  - **1.** Audience selectivity
  - **2.** Distinctive audience
  - **3.** Long life
  - **4.** Size and color
  - **5.** Prestige

QUESTION: What are five advantages of magazines in direct-response advertising?

- **B.** Discounts: special mail-order rate or mail-order section

VI. Newspapers and direct response.
- **A.** Freestanding inserts (FSI)
- **B.** Sunday supplements

VII. What makes a good direct-response product?
- **A.** Don't sell a product available at a neighborhood store, unless a special price is offered
- **B.** Distinguishing quality or useful service
- **C.** Small, for mailing
- **D.** Opens door to repeat business
- **E.** A good value

QUESTION: What elements make a product suitable for direct-response advertising?

VIII. Types of direct-response offers.
- **A.** Category one: direct sales. Intent is to close a sale.
  - **1.** One-step purchase of a specific product
  - **2.** Catalogs
  - **3.** Fulfillment: total customer-service departments
  - **4.** Negative options: book and record clubs

QUESTION: What type of direct-response offer is the book-of-the-month club?

- **B.** Category two: lead getting. It paves the way for a sale.
  - **1.** The two-step sales operation
    - *a)* Determine potential consumers
    - *b)* Follow-up to close the sale
  - **2.** Business-to-business direct marketing
    - *a)* Relatively small market
    - *b)* Concentrated buying decisions
    - *c)* High average per-purchase expenditures
    - *d)* Flexibility

IX. Direct-response copy
- **A.** Calls for immediate response
- **B.** Longer, more informative, stronger promise-of-benefit headline
- **C.** More personal
- **D.** Immediate

QUESTION: How does direct-response copy differ from general consumer advertising (four ways)?

X. Direct-mail advertising.
- **A.** Advantages
  - **1.** Selectivity
  - **2.** Ideal for response
  - **3.** Personal impact
  - **4.** Flexibility of format and timing
  - **5.** Measureability
- **B.** Four primary objectives
  - **1.** Building sales
  - **2.** Cultivating customers
  - **3.** Supporting dealers
  - **4.** Providing internal benefits

QUESTION: What are the four primary objectives of direct-mail advertising?

- **C.** The mailing list
  - **1.** Data-based marketing identifies best prospects for a product from a larger pool.
  - **2.** Renting the list from a list broker
    - *a)* Understand the product
    - *b)* Understand the total process
    - *c)* Negotiate for lists
    - *d)* Clean up lists
    - *e)* Follow up
- **D.** List protection against multimailings beyond agreed-upon limit is abuse:
  - **1.** Include decoy/fictitious names
  - **2.** Never allow renters to possess lists

QUESTION: What are two forms of protection against misuse of lists?

E. Types of mailing lists
  1. Compiles lists
  2. Response lists
    a) House lists
    b) Rental lists
F. Merge/purge removes duplicates from lists
G. Other direct-mail techniques
  1. Package inserts
  2. Cooperative (joint) mail advertising
  3. Syndicate mailings
H. The best direct-mail prospects
  1. Customers who have recently ordered or who order frequently
  2. Buyers of similar products
  3. Volume buyers
  4. Those who have shown interest in a related product
  5. People with demographic interest in a product
  6. Those known to reply to direct mail

QUESTION: What types of people make up the best direct-mail prospects?

I. The direct-mail package includes:
  1. Envelope
  2. Letter
  3. Brochure
  4. Order form
  5. "Act now" statement
  6. Reply envelope

XI. Testing direct mail.
  A. The mailing list
  B. The message
  C. Timing

XII. A mail-production program.
  A. Check weight and size with Post Office
  B. Select printing process
  C. Select paper
    1. Writing stocks
    2. Book stocks
      a) News stock
      b) Antique finish
      c) Machine finish
      d) English finish
      e) Coated
    3. Cover stocks
  D. Basic weights and sizes
  E. Select the printer
  F. Select the letter shop (mailing house)

QUESTION: What decisions must be made in working through a direct-mail schedule?

ANSWERS TO QUESTIONS

1. What is meant by the term *direct marketing?*

Direct marketing is the general term that encompasses direct-response and direct mail advertising as well as the research and support activities that make them possible.

2. Discuss some of the major societal factors that have led to the significant increase in direct-response advertising.

The major advantage of direct-response is that it saves time for people on the move. In addition, it has been helped by the growth of working women and the elderly who have money to spend but have an aversion to traditional shopping.

3. What steps have been taken by the direct-response industry to upgrade its image and standing with consumers?

One of the major means of changing the image of direct-response has been the number of major national companies who are using the technique. In addition, the Direct Marketing Association has undertaken educational programs designed to warn consumers about dishonest direct-response sellers as well as enable consumers to be removed from any mailing list.

4. What are the primary advantages and disadvantages of the following direct-response vehicles?

a. Direct mail can pinpoint virtually any consumer with a personalized message delivered at the time the advertiser wishes. On a CPM basis, direct mail is among the most expensive types of advertising, and it has a "junk mail" image with some consumers.

b. Telemarketing has the same advantages of direct mail and can also deliver a flexible message and answer any consumer questions immediately. It is controversial since many people think sellers should not intrude on prospects' privacy.

c. Catalogs can provide full information to a very select audience. The problem is that there are so many catalogs sent that it is hard to distinguish yours from competitors.

d. Television can demonstrate the product and provide immediate opportunities for sales through 800-number telemarketing. It is expensive and gets fairly low returns.

e. Magazines provide selective audiences, higher return rates than most other media, and an upscale image with quality reproduction. A major drawback is that the timing of some publications may not meet the needs of a seller.

5. Briefly discuss the use of inbound telemarketing. Inbound telemarketing is used in connection with other media to provide a personal contact for immediate sales or customer service. It personalizes the largely impersonal process of mass advertising.

6. Discuss the use of direct-response advertising to build leads rather than achieve direct sales.

In the case of complex or high-priced merchandise, direct-response (or most other types of advertising) cannot accomplish the entire sales job. However, direct-response can build leads by having prospects send for more information or ask that a salesperson call.

7. Compare and contrast direct-response advertising with traditional media advertising.

Direct-response is usually more personal than media advertising. To be effective, direct-response should offer merchandise that is not readily available from traditional outlets or at a competitive price. It is also effective when used in connection with traditional media advertising to offer a means of closing the sale.

8. Discuss database marketing and its applications to direct-response advertising.

Databases are dynamic sources of marketing information. Each time a contact is made with a customer, information is added to the database. For instance, what the person bought, changes in product preferences that may signal a change in lifestyle, and so on.

9. Discuss the role of the list broker in building a successful direct-mail advertising program.

The major job of the broker is, of course, to provide the most up-to-date list at the most economical price. However, beyond that, the broker is a consultant to his/her clients recommending when the list should be used, how to test a list, what type of message might be used for different segment of the list, and so forth.

10. Identify:

a. A merge/purge operation is used by list compilers to merge several lists and at the same time eliminate duplicate names.

b. Ride-alongs are ads sent with other merchandise or bills to customers.

c. Joint-mailings consist of ads for several products and companies where the cost of mailing is shared rather than each company having to individually incur the cost.

d. The fulfillment function is simply the sending of ordered merchandise as well as the customer service that accompanies it.

e. 900-telemarketing requires that the user pay a fee for information or telephone entertainment. It differs from 800-telemarketing in which the service is provided free to those who use it.

CHAPTER FOURTEEN

Sales Promotion

Sales promotion is not advertising, but it resembles it closely. Therefore, this chapter will examine sales promotion and the techniques and formats it encompasses. Much larger than advertising in terms of expenditure and diversification, sales advertising requires an understanding of marketing and advertising objectives in order to be executed successfully. Poor planning and a lack of integration with the total marketing mix are the prime causes of sales promotion failures.

LECTURE OUTLINE

I. Promotion and advertising.
- **A.** Sales promotion is a temporary incentive to buy a product in addition to the normal merits.
- **B.** Consumers expect some type of promotion with every sale.
- **C.** Three types of promotion:
  - **1.** Consumer advertising: traditional media advertising
  - **2.** Consumer sales promotion: sales-promotional incentives directed to the consumer
  - **3.** Trade promotion: designed to encourage a company's sales force to push its products more aggressively

QUESTION: What are the three types of sales promotion? Which type would a cents-off coupon fall under?

- **D.** Reasons for promotional growth
  - **1.** Greater competition in product categories
  - **2.** Reduced consumer spending
  - **3.** High retail inventories
  - **4.** Quick payout-free publicity for the sponsor

QUESTION: What are some of the reasons for the recent growth of promotional activities?

II. Forms of sales promotion.
- **A.** Point-of-purchase advertising
- **B.** Premiums
- **C.** Specialty advertising
- **D.** Coupons
- **E.** Sampling
- **F.** Deals
- **G.** Sweepstakes and contests
- **H.** Cooperative advertising
- **I.** Booklets and brochures
- **J.** Trade shows and exhibits
- **K.** Directories and yellow pages
- **L.** Trade incentives

III. Point-of-purchase advertising.
- **A.** Aisles and shelves of stores
- **B.** Provide information to the consumer and persuade him or her to purchase
- **C.** Generate impulse sales
  - **1.** Candy and gum
  - **2.** Cosmetics
  - **3.** Oral hygiene products
- **D.** Problem of clutter

QUESTION: What items are most often bought out of point-of-purchase advertising? What is the problem with this form of advertising?

- **E.** Uses of point-of-purchase advertising
  - **1.** Informing
  - **2.** Reminding
  - **3.** Persuading
  - **4.** Merchandising
- **F.** Forms of display must:
  - **1.** Be eye-catching
  - **2.** Conserve space
  - **3.** Produce greater profitability for retailers
- **G.** Display ideas:
  - **1.** Product as central theme
  - **2.** Tie-ins with other advertising
  - **3.** Demonstrations

QUESTION: What are the four uses of point-of-purchase advertising and in what ways can they be displayed?

- **H.** Audio and interactive point-of-purchase

IV. Premiums are extra incentives to encourage a consumer to make a purchase.
- **A.** An item offered in exchange for customer action
- **B.** Traffic-building premiums are given merely for visiting.
- **C.** The value of a premium is judged by:
  - **1.** Use to customers

2. Uniqueness among competitive promotions
3. Relation to the product
4. Ease of promotion with the product
5. Quality expected by consumers at a price the advertiser can afford
6. Safety

D. Largest users: food-product manufacturers

QUESTION: How is a successful premium judged?

E. Self-liquidating premiums are sold to consumers at a price that covers the cost of the item and handling.

F. Direct premiums are given free to the consumer at time of purchase.
1. On-pack
2. In-pack
3. Near-pack
4. Container

G. Free mail-in premiums require sending a proof-of-purchase for a free gift.

H. Tie-in premiums
1. Promote two products in the same product line
2. Cross-industry promotions

I. Fulfillment firms open, organize and respond to requests for mail-in premiums

QUESTION: What are four types of premiums? Which type are the baseball cards found in Topp's bubble gum?

V. Specialty advertising.

A. Giving gifts to consumers to build goodwill and result in a future purchase

B. Used to build consumer and trade support

C. Supplement to other promotional and marketing plans

D. Organization of the specialty advertising industry
1. Suppliers
2. Distributers
3. Direct houses
4. The advertiser

E. Calendar specialties
1. Used on a daily basis
2. Items consumers need
3. Expensive
4. Clutter

QUESTION: What are the advantages and disadvantages of calendar specialties?

F. Executive gifts
1. Sent to present customers
2. Something for the office

VI. Coupons.

A. Coupon distribution
1. Freestanding inserts
   a) Clutter
   b) Concentration of certain product categories
2. Direct-mail couponing

B. In-store direct mail

C. Coupon redemption fraud

QUESTION: What are two forms of coupon distribution?

VII. Sampling.

A. Distribution of samples
1. Door-to-door delivery
2. Direct-mail
3. Magazines
4. Coupons
5. In-store sampling
6. Cooperative product sampling

B. Advantages
1. Reaches new users
2. Introduces the product by building trial
3. Demonstrates product improvement
4. Opens new markets and forces distribution

C. Disadvantages
1. Lacks precision
2. Waste and expense

QUESTION: What are the major advantages and disadvantages of sampling?

VIII. Deals.

A. Temporary price reduction or "sale"

B. Merchandising deal: three products wrapped together and sold at a reduced price

C. Attach package of a new member of a product family to a package of an older member

D. Save money on an additional purchase of the same product

E. Cash rebates

IX. Sweepstakes and contests.

A. Sweepstakes depend on some form of random drawing.
1. Random drawing sweepstakes
2. Lucky number sweepstakes
3. Games

B. Contest
1. Require some element of skill
2. Requires time of participants

C. Marketing objectives
1. Heighten the involvement of present consumers
2. Differentiate the product from other brands
3. Introduce a new product
4. Increase dealer support

QUESTION: What are the basic differences of sweepstakes and contests?

QUESTION: What are the common marketing objectives of both sweepstakes and contests?

X. Cooperative advertising. National manufacturers reimburse local retailers for placing their advertising in local media.

A. Advantages for the national manufacturers:
1. Gains local identification for its product
2. Creates goodwill among participating retailers
3. Saves money by sharing costs
4. Enables qualification for local rates

B. Advantages for the retailer:
1. Identifies the local establishment with national brands

2. Extends local advertising budget
3. Improves quality of advertising

C. Advantages for the media:

1. Increases spending by present advertisers in a medium
2. Helps attract new advertising

QUESTION: Discuss the different advantages cooperative advertising offers to the manufacturers, retailers, and media.

D. Vendor programs are custom programs designed by retailers.

E. Controlling Co-op dollars

1. Retailers submit documentation or proof of performance for payment.
2. Co-op fraud
   a) Retailers bill manufacturers for ads that never ran.
   b) Double billing; overcharging

QUESTION: What are two methods of co-op fraud?

XI. Trade shows and exhibits.

A. Reaches dealers and customers in environment condusive to current sales and leads to follow up

B. Attract serious prospects with little or no waste circulation

C. Most often incorporated when:

1. Products are early in the life cycle
2. Sales are high
3. Customer concentration is low
4. Exhibitor has aggressive product plans

XII. Directories and Yellow Pages.

A. Advantages of directories

1. Reach only prospects
2. Information is directly associated with product information needed by the customer.
3. Used by decision makers at time of a purchase

QUESTION: What are three advantages of directories in relation to the targeting of consumers?

B. Consumer directories

1. Yellow Pages
2. Future electronic directories

C. Trade directories

XIII. Trade incentives.

A. Dealer incentives are directed to retailers and whosesalers.

B. Sales incentives are directed to the company's own salespeople.

ANSWERS TO QUESTIONS

1. Compare and contrast sales promotion and advertising.

Sales promotion is a short-term, extra incentive offered to consumers to close a sale. Advertising, with the possible exception of retail, tends to be a long-term effort to build consumer loyalty to a brand.

2. Some advertisers fear that an overuse of sales promotion may damage consumer loyalty created by advertising. Discuss.

When sales promotion becomes expected, consumers choose products on the basis of which brand is making the best "deal." When this happens, manufacturers actually lose profits by having to cut prices or provide other inducements to consumers.

3. Point-of-purchase advertising is one of the fastest growing segments of sales promotion. Why?

In a self-service economy where a majority of products are bought on the basis of impulse, it is imperative that consumers be reminded of brands as close to the time of purchase as possible. Point-of-purchase accomplishes this.

4. Compare and contrast premiums and specialities.

Both premiums and specialities provide a reward to consumers. However, premiums are given as a result of a consumer making a purchase. Specialities are a free gift given to build good will and encourage future purchases.

5. What is the primary appeal of self-liquidating premiums to advertisers?

Unlike other premiums, the consumer pays all or a portion of the cost of self-liquidating premiums. In some cases, the self-liquidating premium actually can be very profitable to the manufacturer.

6. What is the function of a fulfillment firm?

Fulfillment firms operate to process orders, ship merchandise, and answer consumer problems in connection with either direct-response or sales-promotion offers.

7. What are the primary advantages and disadvantages of couponing as a sales-promotion technique?

Couponing offers consumers a price reduction without actually lowering the stated price of the product. The problem with coupons are that they tend to be overused and are open to fraud. Because consumers expect them, they can be seen as a type of permanent price reduction.

8. Compare and contrast sweepstakes and contests. Why have sweepstakes become more popular in recent years?

Sweepstakes are based on chance and luck; contests have an element of skill associated with them. Sweepstakes are much more popular because they are easier to administer and have a higher level of consumer participation.

9. Discuss the use of cooperative advertising as a sales-promotion device.

Co-op advertising serves several purposes. Usually the cost of advertising is shared between the manufacturer and retailers, it promotes goodwill at the retail level, and it more closely identifies the national brand with local retailers.

10. Discuss, from a marketing standpoint, the advantages and disadvantages of consumer versus trade promotion.

Basically, trade promotions are trying to push products through the marketing channel by building support among various levels in the marketing channel. Consumer promotion is trying to pull the product through the channel by building consumer demand. In fact, both techniques are often used together in coordinated sales-promotion plans.

PART FIVE

Creating the Advertising

CHAPTER FIFTEEN

Research in Advertising

Predicting consumer behavior in order to develop a solid foundation for building campaigns is complex. This chapter examines the various research techniques available and the ways in which they help marketers understand the consumers. It will also discuss ways to judge whether an ad will communicate effectively to consumers before it is actually run.

LECTURE OUTLINE

I. What kind of research is needed?
- **A.** Market research tells us about the product, the market, the consumer, and the competition.
- **B.** Pretesting ads and campaign evaluation

II. Anthropology and advertising.
- **A.** Emotional connection between products and consumer values
- **B.** Certain needs and activities are common to all people.
- **C.** Each society attaches its own values and traditions.
- **D.** Sharpens understanding of differences in cultural heritage, regional variations, rites of passage, and changing cultural roles

QUESTION: What connection does anthropology make between products and consumer values?

III. Sociology and Advertising.
- **A.** Examines structure and function of organized behavioral systems
- **B.** Studies group influences on the individual
- **C.** Social class and stratification
  - **1.** Using several variables gives a more accurate prediction of consumer behavior
  - **2.** People's aspirations take on flavor of social class just above their own.
- **D.** CUBE Concept: Consumer behavior research determines consumer behavior on the basis of habits developed in childhood.
  - **1.** How people control their circumstances
    - *a)* Take-control
    - *b)* Yield-control
  - **2.** How people act
    - *a)* Act-first
    - *b)* Think-first
  - **3.** How people judge information
    - *a)* Fact-based
    - *b)* Feeling-based

QUESTION: What is the theory behind the CUBE concept? What are its three dimensions of decision making?

  - **4.** Eight distinct consumer segments with individual profiles
    - *a)* Traditionals
    - *b)* New middle Americans
    - *c)* Home-and-community-centereds
    - *d)* Rising stars
    - *e)* Good ol' girls and boys
    - *f)* Young socials
    - *g)* Moralists
    - *h)* Aging hippies

QUESTION: What eight consumer segments does the CUBE concept devise?

IV. Psychology and Advertising.
- **A.** Motivation
- **B.** Cognition
- **C.** Learning

D. Values and Lifestyle 2 (VALS 2) classifies consumers along two key dimensions
  1. Self-orientation—fundamental need to define a social self-image and create a world in which it can thrive
  2. Resources—range of psychological and material resources available to sustain the self-concept
  3. Three general psychological orientations
    a) Principle
    b) Status
    c) Action

QUESTION: Along what two dimensions does VALS 2 classify consumers?

QUESTION: What are the three general psychological orientations?

  4. Actualizers: successful, active, high self-esteem, abundant resources
  5. Fullfilleds and believers: principle-oriented
  6. Achievers and strivers: status-oriented
  7. Experiencers and makers: action-oriented
  8. Strugglers' lives constricted

QUESTION: Are achievers and strivers principle-oriented, status-oriented, or action-oriented? Explain.

V. Research today.
  A. Research and the invisible brand. Consumer research helps advertisers create messages that deliver newer, stronger images.
  B. The changing role of research. Discern not only who buys but why.
  C. Account planners versus researchers
    1. Define client's problem
    2. Identifies target audience
    3. Provides guidance for creative department

QUESTION: What is the account planner's role in the relationship to the client?

  D. Single-source data
    1. Information comes from one supplier
    2. Information is extracted from a single group of consumers

QUESTION: What are the series of research steps in advertising.

  A. Market, product, competitive, and consumer research
    1. Situation analysis defines the market the product competes in.
    2. Prospect research defines who is expected to buy the product.
  B. Creative research and success in advertising
    1. Research should fuel the creative process.
    2. Sometimes a great advertising concept just happens.

QUESTION: What do situation analysis and prospect research each define?

  C. Advertising strategy or message research
    1. Focus group research
      a) Main methods of qualitative research
      b) Costly
      c) Elicit spontaneous reactions
    2. Pretest research
      a) Rough copy research
      b) Finished copy research
    3. Campaign evaluation research

QUESTION: What kinds of research are implemented to test advertising strategy?

VI. Testing creative research; copy testing.
  A. Should provide measurements relevant to the advertising objectives
  B. Specify action standards before results are in
  C. To succeed, an ad must be received, understood, and make an impression.
  D. Results vary according to the degree of finish of the test.
  E. Forms of testing:
    1. Concept testing-target audience evaluation of creative strategy
      a) Card concept test
      b) Poster test
      c) Layout test
    2. Test commercials

QUESTION: What are measures of a good copy test?

VII. Post-test research
  A. Burke Day-After Recall
  B. Starch Reports: Who reads magazine ads?

ANSWERS TO QUESTIONS

1. What is the role of the social sciences in advertising?

The social sciences can tell us a lot about how people live, think, and function in society. Advertising is a technique designed to influence people's behavior. It can be successful only if we fully understand the motivations, culture, and peer pressures that influence the ultimate behavior of the people seeing our messages.

2. How is CUBE (Comprehensive Understanding of Buyer Environments) research used by advertisers?

CUBE is a means of determining consumer behavior on the basis of habits developed in childhood. It segments the population into eight groups according to: how people control their circumstances, act, and judge information. It can be used to measure product usage, media preferences, and identify market segments.

3. VALS 2 classifies consumers along what two key dimensions?

(1) Self-orientation: the fundamental human need to define a social self-image and create a world in which it can thrive.

(2) Resources: the range of psychological and material resources available to sustain that self-concept.

4. What is single-source data?

Information supplied from one research company that integrates retail tracking data from store scanners with household panel data on consumer purchase patterns and ad exposure information. All of this information is gathered from one group of consumers.

5. Differentiate between card concept and layout tests.

Card concept testing is a system for evaluating advertising ideas using written concepts with no ad copy or illustrations. A layout test evaluates consumer reaction to the visual and copy in rough art form.

6. What is the purpose of Burke-Day-After-Recall testing?

Burke is a means of testing television commercials after they have been aired. They use telephone interviews the day after the commercial is run. It gives the advertiser information on how many people saw and heard the commercial, a summary of what they remembered (recall of key advertising messages), and a verbatim transcript of what the consumer said.

CHAPTER SIXTEEN

Creating the Copy

Appeals must be planned carefully and implemented in advertising. Strategies must be created in order to successfully create appeals based on various common elements.

This chapter discusses those elements all advertisements work with in creating an appeal: the headline, the copy style, slogans, and comparative advertising.

LECTURE OUTLINE

I. The Nature and Use of Appeals.
  A. Advertising motivates people by appealing to their problems, desires, and goals and offering solutions
  B. Selecting the appeal
    1. Concept testing determines the best of a number of possible appeals.
    2. Focus groups offer direct responses to products and benefits and problems the prime prospects see.
    3. Motivational research seeks to find the underlying reasons for consumer behavior.
      a) Emotions
      b) Open-ended responses

QUESTION: What are three techniques that help us decide on appeals?

II. Structure of an advertisement.
  A. The promise is the whole ad.
  B. The promise acts as the headline, requires fuller exposition.
    1. Promise of benefit
    2. Spelling out of promise
    3. Amplification
    4. Proof of claim
    5. Action to take
  C. The headline is the most important part.
    1. Use short, simple words.
    2. Include invitation to the prospect, primary product benefits, name of brand, interest-provoking idea.
    3. Selective words
    4. Action verb
    5. Give enough information to say something about product and its benefits.
    6. Four categories:
      a) Present a new benefit
      b) Directly promise an existing benefit
      c) Curiosity-invoking and provocative
      d) Selective

QUESTION: What are the four most common categories of headlines? What characteristics compose a good headline?

  D. The subheadline spells out the promise the headline presents.
    1. Can be longer
    2. Can invite further reading
    3. Can serve as a transition to the opening paragraph of copy
  E. Application presents your case for the product and explains how the headline promise will be fullfilled.
    1. Emphasize product or service features of primary importance
    2. Builds confidence in the company's resourcefulness

QUESTION: What does the subheadline do? Amplification?

  F. Proof of product performance
    1. Emphasize manufacturer's reputation
    2. Trial offers
    3. Seals of approval
    4. Demonstrations
    5. Money-back guarantees
    6. Warranties
    7. Testimonial

QUESTION: What are five ways a product can reassure its consumers of good performance?

III. Copy style.
  A. Factual approach
    1. Product's advantages
    2. Open to different advantages
  B. Imaginative approach
    1. Saying a familiar thing in an unfamiliar way
  C. Emotional approach
    1. Strong illustration supports emotional headline
  D. Copy for special-interest groups

QUESTION: Give examples of the factual, imaginative, and emotional types of copy style.

IV. Comparative advertising.
  A. Never started by the leader in a field

B. The stronger the proof that products are otherwise identical, the better.
C. The different features should be of importance to the customer.

V. Slogans
A. Sum up the theme for a product's benefits to deliver an easily remembered message.
B. May be combined with a catchy tune to make a jingle
C. Institutional slogans
1. Establish a prestigious image for a company
2. Change infrequently
D. Hard-sell slogans
1. Change with campaigns
2. Epitomize the special significant features of product advertised
3. Strongly competitive claims

QUESTION: What are the three basic rules applied to comparative advertising?

E. Elements of a good slogan
1. Short, clear, and easy to remember
2. Bold
3. Parallel
4. Apt
5. Incorporates the product name

QUESTION: What are five elements of a good slogan?

VI. Reviewing the copy.
A. Copy strategy is what you say to whom and why.
B. A Big Idea
C. Strong execution of the Big Idea

ANSWERS TO QUESTIONS

1. How do you tell if you have a strong appeal?

There is no foolproof way to select one advertising appeal over another, but these three research techniques allow us to evaluate advertising appeals at different levels: concept testing, focus groups, and motivational research. This kind of research arms the advertiser with consumer's viewpoints about appeals before deciding on a final ad direction.

2. What does copy style mean?

The style of the copy is its personality as contrasted to its factual content. There are many ways to tell the same story; the creative essence of copywriting is to see a product in a fresh way. There are many writing techniques that allow a writer to present information differently. Advertising tries to present information in a fresh, interesting manner.

3. Name some factors that should be considered in evaluating strong headlines.

There is no formula that guarantees a good headline, but the following factors should be considered. Use short, simple words, usually no more than ten; include an invitation to the prospect, primary benefits, name of the brand, and an interest-provoking idea to gain readership in the heads; use words that are selective, appealing only to prime prospects; use action verbs; give enough information so that the consumer who reads only the headline learns something about the product and its benefits.

4. Most headlines fall into four categories. Discuss one of them.

(1) Heads that present a new benefit: A product with a new benefit generally offers news to the consumer. (2) Heads that directly promise an existing benefit: This approach focuses on one of the product's benefits. (3) Curiosity heads: attracts attention and invites the consumer to read more and deeper into the ad. (4) Selective headlines: aim at a particular prospect directly and may use the same techniques as the other three.

5. What makes a good slogan?

The most important aspect of a slogan is that it be remembered. It should be short and clear and convey some important attribute to consumers.

6. What do we mean by amplification of the body copy?

The body copy is where you present your case for the product and explain how the promise in the headline is to be fulfilled. The body copy builds on the headline and illustration.

CHAPTER SEVENTEEN

The Total Concept: Words and Visuals

The creative team in an ad agency consists of a writer and an art director who work together to come up with the Big Idea—a concept that is expressed clearly and combines words and visuals.

In this chapter, the actual construction of an ad is explored. The creative team works together in a systematic manner that can sometimes become highly unpredictable. The important thing to keep in mind is that there is no rule about how to work to develop the Big Idea. However, the ultimate goal must always be to solve your prime prospect's problems through an idea that must come alive.

LECTURE OUTLINE

I. In advertising, the total concept is:
- **A.** A fresh way of looking at something
- **B.** A novel way of talking about a product or service
- **C.** A dramatic new dimension that gives the observer a new perspective
- **D.** A Big Idea
  - **1.** Expressed clearly
  - **2.** Combining words and visuals

II. Advertising creatives.
- **A.** The Creative Team consists of:
  - **1.** Writer
  - **2.** Art director
- **B.** Creative process is done in a systematic manner in order to solve the prime prospect's problem
- **C.** The end result is the Big Idea

III. Creative ideas do two important things:
- **A.** Make the prime prospect realize that he or she should consider your project first
- **B.** Implants your brand name indelibly into the prime prospect's mind and connects it to the positive attributes of the product

QUESTION: Who comprises the creative team and what are they striving for?

IV. Visualizing the Big Idea.
- **A.** Creative team forms mental pictures of how the basic appeal can be translated into a selling message.
  - **1.** Find the words that work with the visual for the most powerful effect.
  - **2.** Make as many versions of the idea as possible.
- **B.** Ads created for a specific marketing purpose
  - **1.** Ads for a product should conform to the same set of objectives.
  - **2.** Promise or basic theme is the one thing you would say about the product.

V. The Creative Leap.
- **A.** Write many headlines.
- **B.** Consider appropriate visual ideas.
  - **1.** Free association
  - **2.** Brainstorming

VI. The Layout.
- **A.** The ad has a variety of elements, including:
  - **1.** Headline
  - **2.** Illustration
  - **3.** Copy
  - **4.** Logotype
- **B.** Putting all these elements together is the layout of the ad.
  - **1.** The total appearance of the ad
  - **2.** Physical rendering of the design of the ad-blueprint
- **C.** Layout person as editor.
  - **1.** The visualizer translates an idea into visual form.
  - **2.** A layout person uses that illustration and all other elements to make an orderly, attractive arrangement.
  - **3.** Art director and writer review all elements.
    - *a)* Decide what is most important
    - *b)* Should product be shown
    - *c)* Fast story versus long-copy ad

QUESTION: Name four elements of the layout.

VII. Working hard to get noticed.
- **A.** Attracting attention is the primary creative objective of an ad.
- **B.** All the creative elements must be strongly executed.
  - **1.** The illustration is usually the key.

2. Headline completes the communication.
C. Illustrations must have strong relationship to the selling concept.
D. Three basic means of attracting attention are:
1. The visual alone
2. The headline alone
3. The combination of the visual and headline

VIII. Basic Design Principles
A. Unity
B. Harmony
C. Sequence
D. Emphasis
E. Contrast
F. Balance
1. Formal balance
a) Elements of equal weight, sizes, and shapes on the left and right sides
b) Impression of stability and conservatism
2. Informal balance
a) Seemingly random spacing of elements
b) Imaginative and distinctive results

QUESTION: Name and discuss the six basic design principles.

IX. Other composing elements.
A. Color
1. Attention-getting device
2. Certain products can only be presented realistically in color.
3. Highlights specific elements within an ad
4. Psychological language of color sets the mood for the ad.
B. White space
1. Helps unify the ad and emphasize other elements
2. Keep it outside of the ad

QUESTION: What are the purposes of color and white space in ads?

X. Search for distinction.
A. Break away from the layout trend in the same field.
B. Size
1. Full page gets more attention than half page.
2. Cost considerations
C. Extra-large headline
D. Different style of artwork
E. Use long narrative copy and catchy headlines.

XI. Preparing the layout.
A. For the first ad of a new campaign of color magazine ads, a series of layouts are prepared:
1. Thumbnail sketches
2. Rough layouts
3. Comprehensive, mechanical layout

XII. Computer Design.
A. Computer graphics is the ability to draw or display visual information on a video terminal.
B. Raster Scan Graphics is the most common computer display.
C. The pixel is each spot on the screen.
1. Represents the location in the computer's memory
2. Determines the resolution of the image
D. Professional mastery of layout increasingly demands knowledge of photography, computers, printers, and electronic imaging

QUESTION: What are the three steps in preparing the layout for a first ad in a campaign?

QUESTION: What is a pixel and what does it determine?

XIII. Layout for small advertisements.
A. Must gain attention in a busy setting
B. Abstract the one or two most essential elements of a large ad and emphasize them

XIV. The artist's medium is the tool or material used to render an illustration.
A. Photography is the most popular.
B. Pen and ink, pencil, crayon, and wash
C. Choice depends on:
1. Desired effect
2. Paper on which the ad is printed
3. Printing process
4. Availability of an artist who is effective in the desired medium

XV. Trade practice in buying commercial art.
A. Requires written permission of a legal release from anyone whose picture is used
B. Arrange all terms in advance

QUESTION: What factors influence the choice of the artist's medium?

XVI. Other sources of art and photography.
A. Clip art
B. Stock photos
C. Computer clip art

ANSWERS TO QUESTIONS

1. What role does marketing play in visualization?

Advertising, both words and illustrations, are executed to carry out some marketing objectives. Pretty pictures and beautiful prose, in themselves, do not represent effective advertising.

2. What are the basic design principles?

The following design principles will attract the reader and enhance the chances of the message being read. UNITY: every design must have unity; otherwise, the elements (copy, art, head, logo) will compete with each other creating visual problems for the eye. There must be visual integration of elements. HARMONY: all the elements must work together—not against each other—in attracting the eye. SEQUENCE: there needs to be an orderly arrangement so the ad can be read from left to right. Structural or gaze motion layouts can help guide the eye through the ad elements. EMPHASIS: this is focusing on one (or a few elements) to stress that element. Don't give all elements equal emphasis because nothing will stand out. CONTRAST: using different sizes, shapes, and tones make the layout more interesting. BALANCE: makes the ad look secure and natural.

3. What is informal balance?

A layout that does not have equal weights of elements on each side (not symmetrical). Elements may appear to be placed more at random on the page.

4. What is meant by the creative leap?

Basically, this is the bridge between the development of broad appeals and concepts and the actual execution of advertising.

5. What is the creative team?

In print, the creative team is usually a writer and an art director.

CHAPTER EIGHTEEN

Print Production

Once the idea for an ad has been developed, and the copy, layout, and illustrations have been prepared, the advertiser or agency is responsible for print production—that is, the conversion process to a finished product.

Production requirements differ from ad to ad, depending on the size of the agency, ranging from small agencies with only one production expert to large agencies with numerous specialists. In this chapter, the role of quality in traditional graphics preparation and production as well as computer technology's influence are explored. These elements influence the production of ads in all agencies.

LECTURE OUTLINE

I. Print production is the conversion process from a developed idea to the finished product.
- **A.** Requirements differ from ad to ad.
- **B.** Production organization varies according to the size of the agency.

II. Graphics by computer.
- **A.** Enables one person to both create and produce
- **B.** Gives production managers more choices
- **C.** Time required for art and production people to learn the software may be a hindrance.
- **D.** Creating layouts on the computer is much faster.

QUESTION: What are some of the advantages and disadvantages of using computers in production?

III. Production data.
- **A.** Each publication determines the due dates and mechanical specifications for an ad:
  1. Type of edition desired
  2. Printing process
  3. Kinds of proofs needed
  4. Film size
- **B.** SRDS (Standard Rate and Data Service) Print Media Production Data publication carries essential production information for the major national and regional publications

IV. Production planning.
- **A.** Time schedule is planned for the creative and production work.
- **B.** The closing date is the date/time when all material must arrive at the publication.
  1. Black and white ads require two to three days to make printing materials and revisions.
  2. Process color ads require 20 days.

QUESTION: What is SRDS and what service does it perform? Why is this so important?

V. Selecting the printing process usually depends on the medium in which the ad is running.
- **A.** First step is to decide which printing process is most suitable
  1. Letterpress printing: printing from a raised surface
  2. Offset lithography: printing from a flat surface
  3. Rotgravure: printing from an etched surface
- **B.** Sheet-fed versus web-fed presses
  1. Sheet-fed presses feed sheets of paper through the press one at a time.
  2. Web-printing feeds paper continuously and the printing is very rapid.
- **C.** Screen printing
  1. Especially good for short runs
  2. Uses a stencil
  3. Economical and can print on almost any surface

QUESTION: What are the three most common printing processes? Discuss their advantages and disadvantages.

- **D.** Flexography
  1. Presses are simpler to operate, cheaper to run, and cleaner to use because they print with water-based inks.
  2. A direct-relief printing process that uses photopolymer plastic plates on web presses.
- **E.** Di Litho printing combines the use of offset-type planographic plates with direct transfer of the image from the plate to the web.

QUESTION: What is the difference between screen printing and flexography?

VI. Planning the typography.
- **A.** Typography is the art of using type effectively.
  1. Select the style (typeface) and sizes of type.

2. Decide on spacing between letters, words, and lines.
3. Prepare the specifications for the typesetter.

B. Typefaces

C. Type fonts are complete assortments of types of one size and face.
1. All the lowercase and capital characters, numerals, and usual punctuation marks.
2. Roman font is the upright letter form.
3. Italic form is oblique.

D. Type family is two or more series of types that are variants of one design.

QUESTION: What types of decisions are involved in planning the typography?

E. Measurement of type
1. Point system is used to measure the size of type (heights of letters)
   a) 72 points to an inch
   b) Type is set from six to 120 points
   c) Display or headline type are types sizes above fourteen points
   d) Used to measure the height of space between lines, rules and borders as well
2. A pica is a linear unit of measure.
   a) 12 points of space or 6 picas to an inch
   b) Used to indicate width or depth and length of line
3. An em is a square of the type size and is used for indentation of copy blocks and paragraphs.
4. An agate is a measure of the depth of space, with 14 agate lines to a column inch.
5. Line spacing or leading is the vertical space between lines of type and is measured in points.
   a) Added to make type more readable
   b) Should be no more than 20 percent of the type size

QUESTION: What are the five measurements of type?

VII. Typesetting methods.

A. Software packages for the microcomputer are usually rather limited and commercial quality requires expensive output typesetters.

B. Desktop laser printers cost substantially less.

C. None of the major packages provides em, en, or thin spacing.

D. Major problem with desktop publishing is the lack of design/typography background on the part of the operators.

E. Desktop systems offer speed.

QUESTION: What are some of the drawbacks of desktop computers as opposed to traditional commercial typesetting methods?

VIII. Mechanical and artwork.

A. Type is pasted up on the mechanical in the proper place and sent to the photoplatemaker.

B. Photoplatemaking is the preparation of the artwork for printing by producing a printing plate/image carrier for publication printing.

C. For letterpress printing, the advertiser produces photoengravings, combining photography, and chemical engravings.
1. Line plates
   a) Line art is artwork drawn in black ink on white paper using lines and solid black areas.
   b) Line tint gives line art variation in shades by breaking up the solid color with screen tints or benday screens.
   c) Line color plates provide a more inexpensive method of printing in color with effective results.
2. Halftone plates are used for continuous-tone artwork that have a range of tonal values between pure blacks and pure whites.
   a) The art is broken into dots.
   b) The size of the dots vary according to the contrast of tone to the original.
3. The halftone finish is the treatment of the background.
   a) Square halftone
   b) Silhouette
   c) Surprint
   d) Mortise
4. Line conversion transforms a continuous-tone original into a high-contrast image of only black and white tones similar to line art.
5. Two-color halftone plates allow a two-color reproduction to be made from monochrome artwork.
   a) Screen tint in a second color is printed over a black halftone.
   b) Duotone: Artwork is photographed twice, changing the screen angle so the dots fall between those of the first plate.
6. Four-color process printing reproduces a color photo with a set of four-color plates (red, yellow, blue, and black).
   a) Color separation is the process of preparing plates of the various colors and black.

QUESTION: Discuss the differences between line plates and halftone plates.

D. Desktop color separations allow agencies and advertisers to produce their own color separations at huge savings, but the quality of color separations is inferior.

IX. Color proofing.

A. Press proofs provide a virtually exact representation of the final product.
1. Separate proof for each color as well as a proof for each color combination.

B. Off-press proofs are less expensive and faster and don't require plates or printing.
1. Overlay proofs
2. Adhesive or toner transfer proof

X. Making duplicate material.

A. Letterpress duplicates
1. Stereotypes
2. Photopolymer plates
3. Electrotype
4. Cronapress plates

B. Repro proofs
C. 3M scotchprints
D. Satellite transmission systems
E. Color copies

QUESTION: Name four types of letterpress duplicates.

ANSWERS TO QUESTIONS

1. Differentiate between letterpress and offset printing.

Letterpress prints from a raised surface. All elements—copy, art, and photos—must be made into a raised plate. The raised surface is inked and comes in direct contact with the paper. The image transfers from the plate (raised surface) to the paper. Offset lithography prints from a flat surface and is based on the principle that grease and water don't mix. The ink adheres to the exposed image on the flat plate and is transferred to a rubber blanket. The image is then offset from the rubber blanket to the paper. The paper does not come in direct contact with the plate.

2. What is continuous tone copy?

Any copy having a range of tonal value between pure whites and pure blacks. A photograph is an example of continuous tone art. Oil paintings, water-color paintings, and marker art can also be continuous tone copy.

3. When do you need to make a halftone?

If you desire to reproduce the range of tones in continuous tone art, a halftone is needed. Photographs have that range of grays (black and white photos) or range of colors (color photos). Black ink is never gray, so a halftone is made to break up the different tonal areas into a dot pattern. The size of the dots varies according to the contrast of the original photo. What appears to be gray is really different-sized black dots, giving the illusion of gray. The reader's eyes perceive the halftone as a range of tonal value instead of dots.

4. What are points and picas?

A point is 1/72 inch or there are 72 points to an inch. In production, we measure the height of type in terms of points. Therefore, 72-point type is about 1 (one) inch high; 36-point type is about one-half inch high; 18-point type is about one-quarter inch high. Picas are linear units of measure. There are 6 picas to an inch. Production people measure the width of lines, columns, spaces, and so on in terms of picas.

5. What are color separations?

To reproduce color photographs (color pictures, art) color separations are necessary. It is the process of isolating the light (red, yellow, blue plus black) in color artwork. A filter is used on the copy camera that only allows that spectrum of light onto the negative. This process is repeated for each of the process colors using different filters. What results is a halftone negative with yellow light, one with red light, another with blue light, plus your black negative. Each of these negatives is exposed to a separate printing plate. Then each of the printing plates are printed on top of each other with the appropriate process color inks. The final result is a blending of these four colors.

6. What kinds of color proofs do advertisers use?

Achieving quality color reproduction is one of the crucial roles of production managers. There are two major categories of color proofs. (1) Press proofs, which provide virtually exact representation of the final product. The progressive proof (progs) is made on special proofing presses. The progs give the advertiser a separate proof for each of the process colors, as well as a proof of each color combination (red and yellow, red and blue, blue and yellow)—seven printed proofs in all. (2) Off-press proofs, of which there are several kinds. Overlay proofs are made on clear polyester in each color. No plate or printing is involved. The color separation negatives are each exposed to the appropriate color-sensitized polyester sheets. The resulting four overlays are stacked on top of each other to produce the composite. Adhesive or toner transfer proofs uses dry pigments to produce images on photosensitive adhesive polymers. Chromalin is generally considered the superior adhesive process.

7. What is line art?

Line art has no tonal values and is solid color or white. Ink drawings are line art.

8. What colors are used in process color?

Red (magenta), blue (cyan), yellow, and black. Each of these process colors is always the same standard process color (not just any red, process red; not just any blue). They are the exact same colors at any printer or publication.

9. Where do you find publication mechanical requirements?

Each publication's production department can supply an advertiser with its mechanical requirements. Also, SRDS Print Media Production Data provides production requirements for newspapers and most major national and regional magazines.

CHAPTER NINETEEN

The Television Commercial

The danger of commercial clutter and audience boredom in television advertising has led to innovation in the creativity of television commercials. Today's advertisers have refined their innovations and now have an array of new techniques and variations on old ones.

This chapter explores some of these techniques including the serial, the split ad, the documercial, handheld camerawork, and reality advertising, all of which have invigorated the work of those involved in creating and producing television commercials.

LECTURE OUTLINE

I. Creating the television commercial.

A. Visual techniques

1. Spokesperson delivers the copy directly to the viewer.
a) May display/demonstrate the product
b) Should be likable and believable but not overwhelm the product

2. Testimonials by celebrity personalities will grab viewers' attention.
a) Match the person to the product.
b) Fictional figures work well.
c) Noncelebrities may add credibility.

3. Demonstration is popular because television is ideal for demonstrating how the product works.
a) Use close shots.
b) Make the demonstration relevant and involving.
c) Legally, the demonstration must correspond to the actual usage.

4. Close-ups

5. Story line technique is similar to making a miniature movie except the narration is done offscreen.

6. Direct product comparison answers questions about the two products for the viewer.
a) Danger of lawsuit by a competitor
b) Must be credible to avoid inducing sympathy for the competition

QUESTION: Why is it so critical not to try and fool the viewer in a demonstration commercial? (2 reasons)

7. Still photographs and artwork allow you to structure a well-paced commercial.
a) Zoom lenses
b) Panning the camera

8. Slice of life is based on a dramatic formula: predicament + solution = happiness.
a) Viewers must see the problem as real.
b) Reward must fit the problem.

9. Customer interviews involve nonprofessionals.

10. Vignettes and situations are useful in creating excitement and motivation.

11. Humor makes the commercial more interesting.
a) Danger of the viewer remembering the humor and not the product
b) Make the humorous copy relevant to the product

QUESTION: What is the dramatic formula of slice-of-life commercials?

12. Animation
a) Cartoons create a warm, friendly atmosphere.
b) Simplifies technical product demonstrations

13. Stop motion occurs when an object is photographed in a series of different positions, simulating movement.

14. Rotoscope techniques allow animated and live-action sequences to be produced separately and then optically combined.

QUESTION: What are the differences and similarities between animation, stop motion, and rotoscope techniques? Name some examples of each.

15. A combination of techniques is widely used.

16. Mood imagery is expensive and difficult, combining several techniques to set a certain image for the product.

B. The search for new techniques

1. Serials can be highly effective in sustaining viewer interest.
a) Each spot must be able to stand on its own.
b) Risky to expect to sustain interest over a period of weeks or months

2. Split spots: Two related 15-second spots run with an unrelated 30-second spot between them.

3. In bookend commercials, the first sets up the second, but each works separately.

4. Documercials attempt to make an audience feel like they are watching real-life events.

QUESTION: Two commercials for one product that run back to back but are unrelated are called what? How do they differ from split spots?

II. Planning the television commercial involves many considerations.
- **A.** Establish a relationship between sight, sound, and motion.
- **B.** The words should interpret the picture and advance the thought.
- **C.** Television is more effective at showing than telling.
- **D.** The number of scenes should be planned carefully.
- **E.** Conceive the commercial as a flowing progression.
- **F.** Television is a medium of close-ups.

QUESTION: List three considerations in planning a television commercial and discuss their importance in terms of viewer effectiveness.

- **G.** Action of a commercial takes more time than a reading of copy.
- **H.** Consider the use of words on the screen of the basic theme.
- **I.** Show the brand name.
- **J.** Communicate one basic idea.
- **K.** Read the audi aloud to catch tongue twisters.
- **L.** Sentences should be short and uncomplicated.
- **M.** Describe your scene and action completely in writing video description.

III. Sensory visuals involve the audience more.
- **A.** Special effects
- **B.** Slow motion
- **C.** Motion with meaning

IV. Writing the script.
- **A.** Use simple, easy-to-pronounce, easy-to-remember words.
- **B.** Be brief.
- **C.** Think of words and pictures simultaneously.
- **D.** Write copy in a friendly, conversational style.
- **E.** Try to match the audio with the visual.

QUESTION: What type of language is ideally used in television commercials as opposed to print advertising?

V. The storyboard consists of a series of sketches showing key scenes developed in the script.
- **A.** Two frames for each scene
  1. Top frame represents the television screen (video)
  2. Bottom frame describes the video and the audio
- **B.** Gives the agency, client, and production house personnel a common visual starting point

VI. Producing the television commercial.
- **A.** Production is a two-part process: shooting and editing.
  1. Casts
  2. Directs the talent
  3. Directs the cameraperson in composing each picture
  4. Assumes responsibility for the setting
- **C.** The film commercial is shot out of sequence and are put in place by the editor.
- **D.** Scenes are usually shot more than once.

QUESTION: Discuss the responsibilities and functions of the director in shooting a television commercial.

VII. Other elements of the commercial.
- **A.** Opticals are necessary to provide smooth visual continuity.
  1. Cuts are used to indicate simultaneous action, speed up action, and for variety.
  2. Dissolve is an overlapping effect.
  3. Fade-ins allow the scene to fade into vision from total black.
  4. Fade-outs allow the scene to fade into total black.
  5. Matte is when one part of one scene is placed over another.
  6. Super is the superimposition of one scene or object over another.
  7. Wipes occur when a new scene wipes off the previous scene with a geometric pattern.
     - *a)* Flip
     - *b)* Horizontal
     - *c)* Vertical
     - *d)* Diagonal, closing door
     - *e)* Bombshell
     - *f)* Iris
     - *g)* Fan
     - *h)* Circular
  8. Zoom is a smooth move from a long shot to a close-up or vice-versa.

QUESTION: What is a wipe? What is it used for? Discuss some of the various types.

- **B.** Sound track is the audio portion of the commercial.
  1. Music can set the mood, tone, and accent the selling words.
     - *a)* Stock music
     - *b)* Original music
  2. Sound editing manipulates and shapes the sounds to achieve the desired effect.
  3. New technology is improving the quality of sound in commercials.
- **C.** Processing occurs after all the scenes have been shot when all scenes are developed and the film is delivered for viewing as rushes or dailies.

VIII. The film editor's function.
- **A.** Decides how to assemble the shots that will appear
- **B.** Coordinates sound and music with video

IX. Videotape.
- **A.** Videotaping avoids the process of film developing
- **B.** Gives greater definition and clarity
- **C.** Unique advantages
  1. Played back immediately
  2. Fascinating trick effects

QUESTION: Name three advantages of shooting with videotape as opposed to film.

X. Role of the producer.
  A. Prepares the specs so production studios can compute bids
  B. Meets with studios and explains storyboards and specs
  C. Analyzes the bills and recommends the studio to the client
  D. Arranges for equipment
  E. Arranges auditions through a talent agency
  F. Participates in preproduction meeting
  G. Represents both the agency and the client
  H. Arranges for the recording session
  I. Participates in editing
  J. Arranges screenings for agency associates and clients
  K. Handles billings and invoices

QUESTION: Briefly describe the responsibilities of the producer.

XI. Controlling the costs of commercial production.
  A. Labor and equipment are the major cost items.
  B. Inadequate preplanning is the chief waste of money.
  C. Local advertisers pay much less than national.
  D. Union scale is the minimum payment allowed.
  E. Residual fees are re-use fees paid to performers every time the commercial is aired.

QUESTION: What are some of the factors involved in the high cost of television production?

ANSWERS TO QUESTIONS

1. What are the elements of a television script?

On the left, you describe the video action. On the right, you write the audio portion including sound effects and music. Some agencies use a third column, usually down the middle of the script, for rough sketches of the video, or a mini-storyboard.

2. What is the purpose of the television storyboard?

The storyboard is the blueprint of the commercial. It is used to visualize the original idea, to gain client approval, and to guide the execution of the commercial. If you only use a script, each person reading it will visualize the scenes differently. The storyboard illustrates the major frames or scenes in the script.

3. Who creates a television script?

At the agency, usually an art director and a copywriter create the concept and script together. In the major agencies, a television producer is part of the creative team.

4. A commercial that ends with "To be continued" is an example of what technique?

This technique is known as "serial commercials." Each spot should be able to stand on its own in terms of communicating your objectives. This technique is considered somewhat risky, but offers a great creative opportunity.

5. How has the role of the jingle changed?

Today creatives want music that isn't as "up ending" as the traditional jingle. Rock music isn't as popular in commercials and jingles as in the past (this doesn't imply that rock music isn't used anymore). The jingle sets the slogan or the lyrics to music.

6. What is a residual?

This is a fee paid to certain talent on a commercial every time the commercial is run after 13 weeks for the life of the commercial. It is referred to "as the cost that never ends."

7. Trace what happens to a commercial from after it has been shot until after it is delivered to the TV station.

Here are the typical steps in production after the commercial has been shot. After shooting, the editor and agency screen dailies for scene selection. The agency screens rough cut. Sound and music are recorded on tracks. All sound tracks are placed on a single track. An interlock is made for client approval consisting of sound and work print. The editor makes changes on interlock. Original negative of selected scenes sent to lab for an inter-positive (IP). The IPs are sent to the optic lab for the adding of titles, dissolves, and other opticals. The optical negative is sent to the lab for a silent print called an answer print optical. The APO and mixed track are given final approval. The mixed magnetic track is sent to the lab to make optical track negatives. The optical picture negative is combined with the optical picture negative, and color corrections are made. Client and agency view print for final approval. Release prints are ordered. Distribution to stations.

8. What are the differences between shooting on film and shooting on videotape?

The differences are not as great as in the past due to dramatic changes in videotape equipment. The preference by directors for film over videotape is subjective. Film is considered to have a softer, more glamorous image and makes it easier to create some types of special effects. Film editing takes weeks. With videotape, you can see the results immediately. If the commercial is one long take from beginning to end, the commercial may be through after the last frame has been shot. Videotape can give you greater definition and clarity than you can achieve on film.

9. What is the role of the director?

The director is the key person in the shooting of the commercial. The director takes part in the casting and directing of the talent, directs the shots the cameraperson shoots, and is responsible for putting the entire commercial together.

CHAPTER TWENTY

The Radio Commercial

Radio is a medium for the ears alone. It cannot rely on interesting visuals to attract the audience's attention. Sound messages can be powerful, but radio requires a different style of advertising, and it is a highly selective medium due to the tremendous choice of sounds in every market. The ultimate goal in radio advertising is to create a verbal message that instills a positive feeling for the product in the minds of the audience.

LECTURE OUTLINE

I. The nature of the medium.
- **A.** Radio is a highly selective medium for advertisers.
- **B.** Relatively low cost allows positioning of a "sound" to specific audiences.

II. Creating the commercial.
- **A.** Words are the basic building blocks of effective radio commercials.
  - **1.** Describe the product
  - **2.** Grab attention
  - **3.** Create interest
  - **4.** Build desire
  - **5.** Evoke a response from the listener
- **B.** Sound can unlock the listener's imagination and create feelings.
  - **1.** Manual effects are produced live.
  - **2.** Recorded effects are available from records, tapes, or professional sound libraries.
  - **3.** Electronic effects are produced electronically on special studio equipment.
- **C.** Music catches the listener's attention and evokes feelings.
  - **1.** "Universal Language"
  - **2.** Jingles make a slogan memorable.

QUESTION: What are the three major elements the copywriter uses in radio commercials? Discuss their effects on the audience.

III. Structuring the commercial.
- **A.** Introduction serves as attention-grabber.
- **B.** Product benefits
  - **1.** Describe one fundamental aspect.
  - **2.** Emphasize the benefits of owning the product.
  - **3.** Explain the selling points.
  - **4.** Demonstrate ownership enjoyment.
  - **5.** Illustrate disadvantages of not owning the product.
- **C.** Close
  - **1.** Invitation to act
  - **2.** Product theme
  - **3.** Solution to the problem
  - **4.** Punch line

QUESTION: What are the three standard components that make up the structure of a radio commercial?

IV. Writing the commercial.
- **A.** Simplicity
- **B.** Clarity
- **C.** Coherence
- **D.** Rapport
- **E.** Pleasantness
- **F.** Believability
- **G.** Interest
- **H.** Distinctiveness
- **I.** Compulsion

V. Some techniques used to create mental pictures are:
- **A.** Straight announcer. Success depends on the copy and the warmth and believability of the performer.
- **B.** Two-announcer. Allows for a fast pace and generates excitement
- **C.** Announcer-actor. Actor's voice reacts to or supplements the message delivered by the announcer.
- **D.** Slice-of-life. Reenacts a true-to-life scene, involving the listener.

QUESTION: Discuss the differences between straight announcer, two-announcer, and announcer-actor techniques in creating mental pictures over the radio.

- **E.** Jingle-announcer. Jingle is pleasant, easily remembered, and sets the ad apart.
- **F.** Customer interview. Announcer talks with actual consumers.
- **G.** Humor. The test is whether the customer remembers the product, not the commercial.
- **H.** Combination. Radio techniques may be used in countless ways.

VI. Timing of commercials.
- **A.** 10 seconds, 25 words
- **B.** 20 seconds, 45 words

C. 30 seconds, 65 words
D. 60 seconds, 125 words

VII. Musical commercials leave no room for subtlety.
A. Intro: beginning of song establishes the tempo and lyrics
B. Verse: middle of the song where the message is developed
C. Theme or Chorus: may be the conclusion of the song
D. Commercial music is very flexible.

QUESTION: What are the three main elements to writing commercial music?

E. A mass marketer can position a sound to a specific audience.

VIII. Methods of Delivery.
A. The live commercial
1. Delivered in person
2. Script may be revised to complement the announcer's style.
3. Ad-libbing should be discouraged.
4. Some are delivered partly live and partly prerecorded.
5. Popular announcers are accepted.
6. Low cost

B. Station announcer
1. Reads copy written by the agency
2. Allows for frequent changes in copy at no cost

C. Prerecorded commercials
1. Undertaking a regional or national campaign
2. Assures an identical commercial is aired each time

QUESTION: Discuss the three methods of delivery of radio commercials.

IX. Producing the radio commercial.
A. Agency or advertiser appoints a producer.
B. Producer prepares cost estimates.
C. Producer selects a recording studio.
D. Producer (and casting director) casts the commercial.
E. Producer selects a musical director, chooses the music, or selects stock music.
F. Rehearsal is held.
G. Studio tapes music and sound separately.
H. Studio mixes music and sound with voices.
I. Producer sees the master tape is prepared for distribution and shipped to stations.

QUESTION: Compare the role of the producer in television versus radio commercials.

ANSWERS TO QUESTIONS

1. Describe the characteristics of radio advertising.

Radio is designed to be heard; therefore, sound is the tool that makes it tick—that is, playing with sound in the theater of the listener's mind. Of course, you're playing against the clock of usually 30 to 60 seconds. Radio is also a highly segmented medium; different stations carry different sounds appealing to different kinds of people. This segmentation offers great opportunity for specific-appeal advertising.

2. Sound effects can come from what three sources?

MANUAL: effects produced in the studio live using props. RECORDED: sound effects that are available from records, tapes, or professional sound libraries. These include almost every conceivable sound from computer sounds to cars racing. ELECTRONIC: sound effects that are created electronically with special studio equipment using filters, oscillators, and reverbs. Electronic effects usually come from a device that generates an electrical impulse.

3. What kind of sentence structure is used in radio scripts?

Short, simple conversational sentences. There are no hard and fast rules for structuring radio scripts. Usually, the left section of the page is for information relating to voices, announcer, music, and sound, and is keyboarded in ALL CAPS. The right side of the script consists of copy and directions. This section should be keyboarded double-spaced. Use CAPS or underline for emphasis. The typical script will contain an introduction, product benefits, and a close.

4. What do we mean by "theater of the mind?"

The theater of the mind or listener's imagination is the concept where a writer has the opportunity to paint pictures in the mind of the listener through the use of sound. The listener can visualize what is being heard.

5. What is the role of the producer in the process of making a radio commercial?

The producer prepares a cost estimate and gets a budget approved, selects a recording studio and a casting director (if any), makes all the arrangements to get music (if any), directs the rehearsal before the recording session and the recording session, mixes the different sound and music tracks (if necessary), and supervises the preparation of the master tape for distribution (on tape of cassettes).

6. What is the maximum number of words for a 30-second commercial?

The maximum words in a natural sounding 30-second commercial is 65. If you don't mind people rattling off words, you might be able to push 75 to 80 words. Of course, these numbers don't take into account any jingles, sound effects, and so on that may take away from words being spoken.

7. How can music be effective in reaching different audience with the same message?

Using the same lyrics and tune, an advertiser can change the tempo of the music to appeal to a specific station format and listener. The advertiser can create chorus, rock, country and western, rhythm and blues, and so forth versions of the same basic commercial.

CHAPTER TWENTY-ONE

Trademarks and Packaging

A strong, effective image builds brand equity. This chapter focuses on the strategies for creating strong brand names such as Pepsi, Kodak, and Coca-Cola, as well as the methods for integrating packaging into the overall marketing program.

Developing and protecting trademarks, logos, and package designs is an expensive task, but well worth the cost, for they distinguish one firm's products from its competitors'. Trademarks are also valuable to the consumer in that they assure that one tube of toothpaste will be of the same quality as the same brand purchased elsewhere. There is a strong need to protect these valuable trademarks, and a whole body of law has been created to assure these needs are met.

LECTURE OUTLINE

I. Trademarks.
- **A.** A trademark is any symbol, sign, word, name, or device that distinguishes a product from those made or sold by others.
  - **1.** Protects the public from being deceived
  - **2.** Protects the owner from unlawful use of his/her property
- **B.** A logotype (logo) is the combination of a trademark and some pictorial or design element.
  - **1.** Achieves a level of name recognition among consumers
  - **2.** The most successful packages combine intriguing design schemes with provocative logotypes.
- **C.** A trade name is the name under which the company does business.
- **D.** Requirements must be met to qualify for an exclusive trademark.
  - **1.** It must be used in connection with an actual product.
  - **2.** It must not be confusingly similar to trademarks on similar goods.
  - **3.** It must not be deceptive.
  - **4.** It must not be merely descriptive.

QUESTION: What is a trademark, and how does it differ from a logo?

QUESTION: Discuss four requirements necessary for qualifying for a trademark.

II. Protecting a trademark.
- **A.** Factors considered in judging trademark infringement:
  - **1.** The distinctiveness of the complainant's mark
  - **2.** The similarity of the marks
  - **3.** The proximity of the parties' products
  - **4.** The likelihood of the complainant bridging the gap between noncompeting products
  - **5.** The similarity of the parties' trade channels and advertising methods
  - **6.** The quality of the alleged infringer's products
  - **7.** The sophistication of the particular customers
- **B.** The economics value of a trademark is a major consideration in lawsuits.
- **C.** The best evidence in showing confusion is consumer surveys.

QUESTION: What factors effect proving trademark infringement?

III. Forms of trademarks.
- **A.** Dictionary words
  - **1.** Familiar words used in an innovative manner
  - **2.** Common name as an identifier
- **B.** Coined words
  - **1.** Words made up of a new combination of consonants and vowels
  - **2.** New and phonetically pleasing
  - **3.** Created by computer or mathematical calculations
- **C.** Personal names
  - **1.** Real people, fictional characters, historical characters, mythological characters, foreign names
  - **2.** Secondary meaning: through usage, the public recognizes a name as representing the product of one company only
- **D.** Geographical names
  - **1.** A place name that has acquired secondary meaning

QUESTION: What is secondary meaning and why is it important?

- **E.** Initials and numbers
  - **1.** Hardest form to remember
  - **2.** Easiest to confuse and imitate
- **F.** Pictorial
  - **1.** A distinctive artistic device
  - **2.** Lettering, design, insignia, or picture

QUESTION: Name the six forms of trademarks and give examples of each.

IV. The successful trademark.
- **A.** Distinctive
- **B.** Complements the manufacturer's product and image
- **C.** Adaptable to a package
- **D.** Adaptable to many different advertising campaigns over many years

QUESTION: What factors make up a successful trademark?

V. Logos to promote a distinctive product or service.
- **A.** Continuity of design builds product recognition

VI. New trademark law aids United States in global markets.
- **A.** 1870's laws were based on the use of the mark in commerce.
- **B.** 1946 laws required owners to submit proof of prior use when applying to register their marks.
- **C.** New law permits companies to base trademark applications on an intent to use the mark.
  - **1.** Brings the U.S. laws in harmony with worldwide standards
  - **2.** Ten-year registration period; can be renewed indefinitely
  - **3.** Prohibits false statements in advertising about a competitor's product

QUESTION: Trace the changes in U.S. trademark policy from the nineteenth century until now.

VII. Trademark Notice.
- **A.** Indicates a trademark has been registered
- **B.** Exception when a trademark is repeatedly used in an ad

VIII. Putting a lock on trademarks.
- **A.** Make sure the trademark word is capitalized or set off in distinctive print.
- **B.** Follows the trademark with the generic name of the product
- **C.** Don't speak of it in the plural.
- **D.** Don't use it in a possessive form or as a verb.

QUESTION: What are the steps involved in putting a lock on the ownership of a trademark?

IX. House, Service, and Certification Marks.
- **A.** House marks denote the firm that produces several different trademarks.
- **B.** Service marks identify companies that render services.
- **C.** Certification marks certify that a user of a firm's identifying device is doing so properly.

X. Company and product names.
- **A.** Name change craze
- **B.** Steps for creating memorable names
  - **1.** Describe what you are naming.
    - *a)* Key features and characteristics
    - *b)* Competitive advantages
  - **2.** Summarize what you want your name to do.
  - **3.** Describe whom you are targeting with the name.
    - *a)* Identify targets and their demographic characteristics.
    - *b)* List name qualities that would appeal to them.
  - **4.** List names you like and dislike.
  - **5.** Build a list of new name ideas.
    - *a)* Start with a list of names you like.
    - *b)* Add to it from sources.
  - **6.** Combine name parts and words.
  - **7.** Pick your favorites.

QUESTION: What are the steps for creating memorable company and product names?

- **C.** Verify name availability.
- **D.** Test your name before using it.

XI. Packaging
- **A.** Must protect the package contents
- **B.** Must meet reasonable cost standards
- **C.** Marketing issues
  - **1.** Adopt a package conducive to getting shelf space at the retail level.
  - **2.** Easy to handle, store, and stack
  - **3.** Soil resistant packages
  - **4.** Product should come in full range of sizes and packaging.

QUESTION: What are two requirements of package protection?

QUESTION: What marketing issues must be taken into account?

- **D.** Computers and package design
  - **1.** Quicker design
  - **2.** More efficient review process
  - **3.** Faster approval
  - **4.** Lower design costs
- **E.** Changing package design and marketing is responding to a more sophisticated, discerning consumer
- **F.** Packaging and color influence
  - **1.** Each color produces a psychological reaction.
  - **2.** Informs consumers about the type of product
  - **3.** Influences consumers' perceptions of quality, value, and purity

QUESTION: What benefits do computers offer in package design?

XII. Common approaches to the successful use of a package as a marketing tool:
- **A.** The type of product and function of the package
- **B.** The type of marketing channels to be used for the product
- **C.** The prime prospects for the product
- **D.** Promotion and advertising for the product and its package
- **E.** The relationship to other packages in a product line
- **F.** The typical consumer use of the product

XIII. Legal Aspects of Packaging
- **A.** The Fair Packaging and Labeling Act of 1966
  - **1.** Informed consumers are essential to the functioning of a free economy.
  - **2.** Packages and labels should enable consumers to obtain accurate information.

B. Food packages must display the ingredients prominently.

C. Drug products must display instructions for use, precautions, and instructions in case of overdose.

QUESTION: What is the fair Packaging and Labeling Act of 1966 and why is it so crucial?

XIV. Corporate identity: logo and whole package.

A. A marketing program incorporates research, corporate definition, and communication.

ANSWERS TO QUESTIONS

1. Why does a trademark become more valuable every year?

If the brand is being promoted, each year more people should be more familiar with your trademark, thereby increasing brand equity. The trademark is the brand's asset.

2. What is a logotype?

A logotype is simply a trademark that includes some pictorial display.

3. Briefly discuss the major changes in U.S. trademark laws in recent years.

In the past, you could not register a trademark in the United States before you used it on a product. To bring U.S. trademark practices closer to international regulations, several changes have been made: You can apply for a trademark before using it on a product, your trademark rights start when the application is made, you have six months to actually use the trademark (although you can apply for five six-month extensions), registration period has been reduced from 20 years to 10 years (although renewal can be applied for indefinitely).

4. What are the main reasons for so many new corporate names in the last decade?

The majority were associated with mergers and acquisitions; others reflected divestitures, spinoffs, sale of assets, and leveraged buyouts. Foreign acquisitions of U.S. companies resulted in a large number of changes and foreign companies establishing plants in the United States often simplified their foreign names to make them easier for consumers to remember.

5. How has high-quality imagery in packaging changed in recent years?

Design firms are redesigning packages to suit marketing strategies. Packaging is being used to shore up store brands with high-quality imagery. Packaging is being used to create upscale private-label brands. A shift from packaging that suits the manufacturer to packaging that is "consumer-friendly," in terms of opening and use, reclosing, and portions.

CHAPTER TWENTY-TWO

The Complete Campaign

The concept of brand equity goes beyond the development of a single ad, commercial, or promotional piece. This chapter discusses campaigns—that is, series of ads and commercials with established strategies and goals. Campaigns run over longer periods of time and integrate advertising strategies into sales and marketing programs.

Campaigns bring together all the advertising elements discussed so far. In order to achieve this, a plan is needed. The first step in creating this plan is to understand the marketing goals.

LECTURE OUTLINE

I. Situational analysis establishes a starting point in order to create future advertising.
- **A.** The product
  - **1.** Unique consumer benefits the product will deliver
  - **2.** Value of the product relative to the proposed price
  - **3.** Availability of adequate distribution channels
  - **4.** Maintenance of quality control
- **B.** Prime-prospect identification
  - **1.** Who buys the product and what are their demographic characteristics?
  - **2.** Who are the heavy users of the product?
  - **3.** Examine the prime prospect's problems.
- **C.** Competitive atmosphere and marketing climate
  - **1.** How do we compare in market position?
  - **2.** What are the specific product features of competing brands?
  - **3.** What are competitors' marketing strategies?

QUESTION: What three elements are examined in situational analysis? What kinds of factors are explored?

II. Creative objectives and strategy.
- **A.** Determine what specific claim will be used in advertising copy.
- **B.** Consider various advertising executions.
- **C.** Develop the copy and production of advertisement.

III. Creative criteria for campaigns.
- **A.** Visual similarity
  - **1.** Same typeface or layout format
  - **2.** Same spokesman or continuing character
  - **3.** Same demonstration
- **B.** Verbal similarity
  - **1.** Certain words/phrases to sum up the product's benefits
  - **2.** Copy format
  - **3.** Tagline used in each television commercial
- **C.** Sound similarity
  - **1.** Same music or jingle
  - **2.** Same announcer's voice
  - **3.** Same sound effect
- **D.** Attitude similarity

QUESTION: What are the four creative criteria for campaigns? Cite examples of each.

IV. Media objectives.
- **A.** Media strategy
  - **1.** Prospect identification: Match prospects for a product with users of specific media.
  - **2.** Timing
    - *a)* Media closing dates
    - *b)* Production time required
    - *c)* Campaign length
    - *d)* Number of exposures desired
  - **3.** Creative considerations

QUESTION: What is prospect identification, and what does it do?

- **B.** Media tactics
  - **1.** Media vehicles
  - **2.** Advertising weight
  - **3.** Appropriate budget allocations
- **C.** Media scheduling

QUESTION: Discuss the three media objectives: strategy, tactics, and scheduling.

V. The sales-promotion plan
- **A.** Dealer displays
- **B.** Premiums
- **C.** Cooperative advertising
- **D.** Couponing offers
- **E.** Sales promotion material

VI. Getting the campaign approved.
- **A.** Present a statement of the company's marketing goals.

B. Objectives
  1. Launch a new product.
  2. Increase sales.
  3. Raise the firm's share of the market.
  4. Promote a specific service of a firm.
C. Describe the philosophy and strategy of the ad.
D. Present the ads or commercials.
  1. Media proposal
  2. Plans for coordinating the entire effort with the sales department

QUESTION: What are the steps involved in getting the campaign approved?

QUESTION: What kinds of objectives are listed in this process?

VII. Research post-tests.
A. Expected results are defined in specific and measurable terms.
  1. Increase brand awareness by 10%.
  2. Improve advertising recall by 25%.
B. Conduct research to see if goals were met.
  1. Separate results of advertising campaign from consumer behavior that would have occurred in any case
  2. Research design is used as a pretest.

ANSWERS TO QUESTIONS

1. What is the basic purpose of an ad campaign?

To develop a series of ads with established strategy and goals. Any advertising plan (for a campaign) should be integrated into the sales promotion and marketing program.

2. What is included in the situation analysis?

The situation analysis encompasses an examination of the product, competition, and prospects to find opportunities for unique approaches to advertising.

3. How does the 80/20 rule relate to prospect identification?

The 80/20 rule indicates that a small portion of your customers or potential customers buy a large percentage of the product. They are the heavy users and may offer the greatest potential for success (but your competition also may come to this conclusion so the competition is probably great for these users or potential users). The point here is that an advertiser needs to have a clear understanding of the prime prospect before aiming an ad campaign toward anyone.

4. What is the advantage of continuity of layout and copy throughout a campaign?

People begin to recognize your ads. They may or may not read, look, or listen to every ad, but they know you are advertising. The continuity helps drive home the overall campaign strategy because the consumer becomes familiar with your campaign: Each ad reinforces, to varying degrees, all the other ads. Remember, brand advertising takes time, with one message building upon the next message.

5. What is continuity of attitude?

All advertisements have a similarity in attitude. For example, all ads may communicate "fun." Each ad in such a campaign expresses a consistent attitude toward the product and the people using it.

6. Must creative and media strategy be done simultaneously? Discuss briefly.

The creative and media components of the ad campaign originate from the common foundations of marketing strategy and prospect identification. A successful campaign depends on the balance between the two areas. One is not superior to the other; therefore, they must be considered together as a equal part of the campaign. You can't create television ads if media isn't planning or can't afford television. They need to work together simultaneously.

7. How does a campaign relate to the Link process?

The four components of Link are synthesized into an action plan for the development of all communications for the brand, including advertising, promotions, public relations, and direct marketing. The guiding principle is that everything you do should build equity for the brand.

PART SIX

Other Environments of Advertising

CHAPTER TWENTY-THREE

Retail Advertising

Most retailing takes place in retail stores such as those found in retail shopping malls. However, recently, nonstore retailing by mail, phone, door-to-door, and vending machines has grown tremendously.

This chapter focuses on the means by which a retailer advertises. The large retailer will often use a media mix, which requires planning, target identification, and media selection. Retailers number in the millions and use nearly every advertising and promotion method, often on a daily basis.

LECTURE OUTLINE

I. Changing retail environment.
- **A.** Retailing in the 1950s and 1960s
  - **1.** Low prices and cheap goods
  - **2.** Discount department stores adopt self-service.
  - **3.** Centralized checkout and fewer salespeople bring down labor costs.
- **B.** Growth in the 1970s
  - **1.** Discounters expand.
  - **2.** Major retailers enter discount business.
  - **3.** Increase in the number of households fueled general merchandise sales.
- **C.** More for less in the 1980s
  - **1.** Customers demand better service, ambiance, and merchandise.

QUESTION: Trace the changes in retailing from the 1950s through the 1980s. What accounted for these changes?

- **D.** Present and future trends
  - **1.** Hypermarkets: range from 200,000 to 325,000 square feet
  - **2.** Pricing effects advertising
    - *a)* Low everyday prices
    - *b)* Promotional pricing
- **E.** Retailers are looking to successful competitors for guidance.
- **F.** Reasons consumers patronize a store
  - **1.** Price
  - **2.** Selection
  - **3.** Quality
  - **4.** Service functions as a tie-breaker.

QUESTION: What are the two pricing strategies that affect advertising?

QUESTION: What are the prime reasons customers patronize a specific store?

- **G.** A marketing emphasis
  - **1.** Retailers expect local media vehicles to define their audiences.
  - **2.** Universal Product Code (UPC)
    - *a)* Intended to speed up checking out of customers and aid in inventory control
    - *b)* Scanner determines when and where products are bought.
    - *c)* Important retail research device

II. Differences between national and retail advertising.
- **A.** National advertising
  - **1.** Done by a marketer
  - **2.** Get people to buy the marketer's branded goods wherever they are sold

3. Difficult to trace effectiveness quickly

B. Retail advertising
1. Done by local merchants or service organizations
2. Attract customers to buy goods and services they have to offer
3. Easy to trace effectiveness quickly
4. Fast tempo

C. Some firms do both national and retail advertising.

D. In the future, the distinction will be less clear.

QUESTION: What are the differences between national and retail advertising? Are they ever used simultaneously? Give examples.

III. Types of Retail Advertising (as suggested by the Newspaper Advertising Bureau).

A. Promotional
1. Emphasis on high-scale volume at a reduced price
2. Discount stores

B. Semipromotional
1. Sales offerings interspersed with regular-priced items
2. Department stores and supermarkets

C. Nonpromotional
1. No-sale advertising strategy
2. Plays down price and emphasizes quality

D. Assortment ads
1. Show large variety of products
2. Promote store as a place for one-stop shopping

E. Omnibus ads
1. More clearly sales-oriented
2. Feature items for several departments

F. Institutional ads
1. Emphasizes a store's unique characteristics
2. Tells a story of importance to customers

QUESTION: What are the six categories of retail advertising as proposed by the Newspaper Advertising Bureau?

QUESTION: Which type of advertising is best suited for discount stores? Why?

IV. Retail business cycles vary according to the product or service category.

V. Sales and media promotions are recognition periods for a cause, special interest, appreciation or, more often, holiday.

VI. The retail advertising mix.

A. Retail advertising must:
1. Determine goals and objectives of the marketing and advertising programs
2. Identify target markets
3. Develop a copy and media strategy

B. Newspapers in retailing
1. Primary local advertising vehicle
2. ZIP code information used to:
   a) Target best customers
   b) Make more efficient and media buys
   c) Locate sites for new outlets
   d) Analyze sales performance
3. Suburban editions reach select countries or communities.
4. "Special sections" are published throughout the year to promote special interests.

QUESTION: What are the three jobs retail advertising must accomplish?

C. Radio in retailing
1. Local advertising is very important.
2. Flexibility in spot scheduling
3. Strong promotions
4. Good reminder medium
5. Allows for creativity

QUESTION: What is ZIP code information used for and in which medium is it found?

D. Television in retailing
1. Impressive financial gains due to:
   a) Growth of independent television stations
   b) Cable television is the fastest-growing retail media segment.

E. Direct response in retailing
1. Promotes special sales
2. Reaches a specific segment of customers
3. New technology
   a) Video shopping service
4. Cross-over between mail-order and in-store selling
5. Federal Trade Commission's Mail Order Rule
   a) Order must be shipped within promised time
   b) If no time is promised, must ship within 30 days or send option notice.
6. Direct-response television advertising

QUESTION: What are five elements of radio that make it advantageous for retail advertising?

QUESTION: What is the Federal Trade Commission Mail Order Rule and what medium is it found in?

VII. Cooperative advertising.

A. Chief advantages
1. Helps the buyer stretch his/her advertising capability
2. Provides good artwork and copy of the advertised product
3. Store earns a better volume discount for advertising

B. Chief disadvantages
1. Store's 50 percent payment may be disproportionate for the amount of sales and profit.
2. Brand name is emphasized at expense of store's name.

C. Acceptance depends on the product's importance to the store.

D. Association of National Advertisers, the Radio Advertising Bureau, and the Television Bureau of Advertising designed a form to assure the vendor the commercials run as scheduled.

QUESTION: What are the advantages and disadvantages of cooperative advertising?

ANSWERS TO QUESTIONS

1. How does a retailer's pricing policy affect the amount of advertising it does?

Retailers with "low everyday prices" rarely have a sales and do little advertising. The appeal to consumers is that a basket full of products will cost less than the same basket at a promotional discounter. The promotional pricing discounter relies on the proposition that "Americans love a good sale." This kind of retailer depends on advertising to attract consumers to their sale.

2. If price is the main motivator to shop at a store, how does service influence customers?

Depending on the nature of the store and the nature of the store's prospects, all things being equal (prices, quality, selection, and so on) service can function as a "tie-breaker."

3. How does retail advertising differ from national advertising?

The retailer is trying to get people into his or her store to buy a host of items on a daily basis. The advertising reflects this urgency and variety: "Come in today and buy these specials." National advertising is trying to get prospects to buy their specific product at any kind of store.

4. What are the six types of retail advertising?

The Newspaper Advertising Bureau has suggested six categories of retail advertising. (1) Promotional: Here, the emphasis is on sales and high sales volume at reduced prices. (2) Semipromotional: Sales offerings are interspersed with many regular-priced items. (3) Nonpromotional: Here, there is a no-sale advertising strategy, where their advertising plays down price and emphasizes quality of merchandise and expertise. (4) Assortment ads: The intent is to show a large variety of products and ads are institutional in nature. (5) Omnibus ads: These are similar to assortment ads, but are more clearly sales oriented. (6) Institutional ads: This advertising promotes unique character of the store.

5. How are newspapers using ZIP/postal codes?

They are furnishing retailers (and national advertisers) with custom ZIP/postal code circulation reports. Most newspapers offer a number of zones for advertisers to target certain prospects. They may have special sections aimed at certain areas of their coverage area. In short, newspapers are using direct mail's strategic selling tool to offer advertisers more flexibility in targeting customers.

6. What is the fastest-growing medium in retail advertising?

Cable television is the fastest-growing media segment in retail advertising. Even though the CPM figure is generally higher for these cable spots, the actual cost is within the budgets of even small advertisers.

CHAPTER TWENTY-FOUR

International Advertising

In the last decade, the international sector of the advertising industry has undergone tremendous change. Where years ago, international marketing and advertising was concerned primarily with the export of U.S. products and services, today foreign advertising agencies compete effectively with U.S. agencies.

This chapter examines this movement from total U.S. control of international advertising to the competition that has evolved. Now, U.S. companies must have the capability to meet client demands throughout the world.

LECTURE OUTLINE

I. Global marketing and advertising.
- **A.** Developing a unique marketing plan for each country would:
  - **1.** Be tremendously expensive
  - **2.** Deny the advantage of using already successful techniques
- **B.** Global marketing suggests a corporation can develop a master marketing strategy.
  - **1.** Assumes consumers are basically alike all over the world
  - **2.** Allows the development of a single, coordinated marketing strategy
  - **3.** Reduces cost of advertising production
  - **4.** Saves on media-planning costs
  - **5.** Tends to place the corporation's interest above those of the consumer
    - ***a)*** Consumers aren't "global."
    - ***b)*** Consumers don't generally buy global brands or products.
    - ***c)*** Customers place personal/individual values on the brands they buy.
    - ***d)*** Foreign origin isn't an instant value, but a barrier.

QUESTION: What are the major advantages of a global marketing strategy over developing a unique plan for each country?

QUESTION: What consumer characteristics must be kept in mind?

- **C.** 1992: The Economic Unification of Europe
  - **1.** EEC (European Economic Community) barriers will be removed.
  - **2.** Uniform standards for television commercials.
  - **3.** Don't fall prey to a blind allegiance to global marketing.
- **D.** Global marketing is an ideal rather than a practical blueprint.

II. The multinational advertising agency.
- **A.** Building the multinational agency
  - **1.** U.S. agencies generally acquire an in-country agency or a majority interest in one.
  - **2.** Keep a sense of corporate identity.
  - **3.** Corporate compatibility must be present.
  - **4.** Establish a centralized management.
- **B.** Benefits of centrally coordinated campaigns
  - **1.** Cost savings
  - **2.** Sharing of experience
  - **3.** Effective control of the overall advertising budget
  - **4.** Ensures the account will get the benefit of the agency's top resources
  - **5.** Positioning and image for a product can be built over time and across territory.

QUESTION: What are the benefits of centrally coordinated campaigns?

III. The Advertising Function in International Advertising
- **A.** Transcultural assumption can be misleading and risky.
- **B.** Creative considerations
  - **1.** Misuse of language
  - **2.** Balance forces of efficiency and creativity
  - **3.** Simplifying factors:
    - ***a)*** Growing cultural understanding and commonality among nations
    - ***b)*** Greater understanding of graphic and visual advertising approaches in overcoming cultural differences
    - ***c)*** Creative directors better understand how to integrate a central theme with local input

QUESTION: What are some of the factors that make international creative considerations easier?

- **C.** Media considerations
  - **1.** Media buying is difficult outside the United States.

2. Feasibility of large multinational agencies establishing worldwide media operations:
   a) Growth of non-U.S. billings
   b) Coordination of media buys
   c) Buying expertise
   d) Availability of media discounts and buying flexibility

QUESTION: What are the factors that make the establishment of worldwide media operations appealing?

3. Drawbacks of pooled buying
   a) Reluctance for one media-buying organization to represent competing brands
   b) Whether media abroad would long be content to deal with combines as single entities

IV. Media trends.
   A. Television will grow dramatically.
   B. Print media will grow, at a slower pace.
   C. Advertising expenditures will increase around the globe.
   D. Political and economic changes will pave the way for globalization.

QUESTION: What are two drawbacks to pooled buying?

ANSWERS TO QUESTIONS

1. Why have U.S. advertising agencies become so aggressive in expanding into international markets in recent years.

The major push for U.S. agencies to go international came from their clients. It is rare to find a major national company that does not have a large international sales component. Obviously, these companies look to their agencies to support these efforts on both the national and international scene. In addition, we have seen more and more foreign companies enter the U.S. market and domestic agencies want to compete for these accounts.

2. Discuss the concept of global marketing as it relates to advertising.

In its strictest definition, global marketing seeks to develop a single marketing and advertising plan that can be used across international boundaries. In fact, it has come to mean that agencies and their clients seek to find areas of commonality that can save time and money in developing marketing plans from one country to another. There is a realization that true global marketing strategies are very unlikely for most products.

3. What is the significance of the year 1992 to marketing and advertising in Europe?

In 1992, many of the barriers to free trade will be lifted among members of the European Economic Community. The idea is that people, products, and promotion will be able to more easily cross the political boundaries of these countries.

4. What are some of the basic strategies used by advertising agencies to expand into international markets?

At one time, U.S. agencies attempted to build their international presence through the importation of American talent into foreign countries and starting agencies from the ground up. However, in the last decade, most U.S. agencies have expanded by acquiring existing agencies in various countries and keeping the management team in place to give a local presence and expertise to these agencies.

5. What are the advantages and disadvantages of centralized management by multinational agencies?

A centralized approach may hold costs to a minimum, especially if ads can be used in several countries. It allows testing of concepts to be implemented in several countries. Finally, it offers the company a more consistent advertising approach from one country to another. The disadvantage is that, depending on the degree of control, local management may not be able to react to fast-changing market conditions.

6. Discuss the idea of multinational media-buying combines among major advertising agencies.

The advantage of such a system is that it allows agencies to concentrate both their talent and combine international accounts for greater efficiency and cost savings. This is a major factor in countries where agencies (or buying units), as opposed to clients, receive media discounts. The problem in such a system is that some clients see a conflict of interest with a single group buying for competing brands.

7. Discuss the ramifications to advertising agencies of the continuing consolidation of worldwide marketing by major corporations.

First, as corporations get larger and more complex, the agencies serving them must follow suit. In the future, we will see larger and fewer agencies, each with worldwide expertise. We will also see more problems of client conflicts.

CHAPTER TWENTY-FIVE

Legal and Other Restraints on Advertising

Advertising is the most regulated of all business enterprises, ranging from language laws to restrictions on the size and placement of outdoor signs. Consumers of today are more aware than ever of abuses in advertising. Consequently, the legal regulatory environment has become increasingly complex.

In this chapter, three primary constraints on advertising are discussed: those of legally constituted bodies, media control, and self-regulation by advertisers. Laws shielding the public from false and misleading advertising has replaced the old-fashioned notion of caveat emptor: Let the buyer beware.

LECTURE OUTLINE

I. The Federal Trade Commission (FTC).

A. Several factors dictate the FTC's role as an enforcement agency.

1. It cannot satisfy all its constituencies.
2. Tends to concentrate on major national issues and sets the national regulatory agenda for advertising
3. Bad publicity generated by an FTC false advertising charge is worse than any penalty

B. Some basic FTC rules and legal findings

1. Fairness: An ad can be ruled unfair or harmful even if truthful.
2. Total impression: A "tendency to deceive" may be found illegal.
3. Clarity: protect the credulous and gullible.

QUESTION: What factors dictate the FTC's role as an enforcement agency?

4. Fact versus puffery
5. The question of taste does not involve the FTC.
6. Demonstrations must not mislead viewers.
7. Warranties—Magnuson-Moss Warranty Act requires the following information be provided.
   - *a)* Nature and extent of guarantee
   - *b)* Manner in which the guarantor will perform
   - *c)* Identity of the guarantor
8. "Free" terms/conditions must be stated clearly.
9. Lotteries—a person must not have to pay to enter a lottery conducted by an advertiser.
10. Testimonials—an endorser engaging in deceptive promotion is liable along with the agency and advertiser.

QUESTION: What are six basic FTC rules and legal findings?

C. Methods of FTC enforcement

1. Consent decrees: Advertiser signs an agreement saying the deceptive practice/advertising will be stopped.
2. Cease and desist orders: issued if the deception is substantial
   - *a)* Serious, formal action
   - *b)* Hearing before administrative law judge
3. Corrective advertising: required when major advertising themes are the basis for consumers' choices
   - *a)* Counteracts residual effect of deceptive advertising
   - *b)* Advertiser runs ad at own expense to dissipate the deceptive effects

QUESTIONS: What form of FTC enforcement requires a court hearing? What form counteracts residual effects of deceptive advertising?

D. Deception, standards of disclosure, and substantiation

1. Substantiation is the key to advertising regulation.
2. Intent to deceive is not a factor.
3. False advertising isn't illegal, deceptive is.
4. Perception is subjective; proving deception must show:
   - *a)* Misrepresentation or omission that can mislead the consumer
   - *b)* The misrepresentation or omission is likely to mislead the consumer.
   - *c)* The misrepresented/omitted information is important to the consumer.

QUESTION: What must be shown in proving an ad is deceptive and not merely false?

E. Three-law "Package"
   1. 1890 Federal Sherman Antitrust Act
   2. 1914 Clayton Antitrust Act; eliminated preferential price treatment
   3. 1936 Robinson-Patman Act
      a) Prevents manufacturers from providing a "promotional allowance" to one customer unless it is also offered to competitors
      b) Lack of aggressive enforcement due to changing retail climate and broader interpretation of what constitutes legitimate business practices today
      c) Strong deterrent to antitrust practices at the retail level

QUESTION: What kind of unfair practice does the Robinson-Patman Act deter? What makes enforcement less aggressive?

II. The Federal Food, Drug and Cosmetic Act (1938)
   A. Requires ingredients on labels
   B. Labels must be:
      1. Truthful and not misleading
      2. Supported by scientific evidence
      3. Consistent with medical and nutritional principles
      4. Accompanied by the required nutrition information level

QUESTION: What must be included on all health claim labels and how must they be presented?

III. The Federal Control of Advertising.
   A. Alcohol tax unit of the U.S. Treasury Department
      1. Labeling
      2. Standards of bottle sizes
      3. Advertising of alcoholic beverages
      4. Independent state laws
   B. Securities and Exchange Commission
      1. Full disclosure of relevant company facts
      2. Sell stock so the investor can form an opinion
   C. U.S. Postal Service stops delivery of mail to firms guilty of using the mails to defraud.

QUESTION: Which federal department imposes alcohol advertising restrictions?

QUESTION: What two elements foes the Securities and Exchange Commission insist on?

IV. Advertising and the First Amendment
   A. Commercial speech enjoys some protection.
   B. Distinction between degree/kind of protection for commercial speech and other forms.
   C. Commercial speech is viewed as less serious/important.
   D. No concrete doctrine of commercial speech
   E. Virginia State Board of Pharmacy versus Virginia Citizens Consumer Council (1976)
      1. Ruled banning advertising of prescription drug prices as unconstitutional
      2. Society benefits from free flow of commercial information.
   F. Friedman versus Rogers (1979) ruled
      1. First Amendment protection for commercial speech is not absolute.
      2. Regulation of commercial speech can be allowed even when restrictions would be unconstitutional in realm of noncommercial expression.
   G. The Central Hudson Four-Part test to determine when commercial speech is constitutionally protected and when regulation is permissible
      1. Is the commercial expression eligible for first amendment protection?
      2. Is the governmental interest asserted in regulating the expression substantial?
      3. Will the prohibition further the government's goals?
      4. Is the regulation more extensive than necessary to serve the government's interest?

QUESTION: What are the four parts of the Central Hudson test and what is its purpose?

V. Advertising of Professional Services.
   A. Bates versus State Bar of Arizona rules laws forbidding advertising by attorneys are unconstitutional
   B. In 1988, Supreme Court extended attorneys' rights to advertise their professional services.

QUESTION: What triumph for professionals did Bates versus State Bar of Arizona yield?

VI. State and Local Laws Relating to Advertising.
   A. Printers' Ink Model Status (1911) punished untrue, deceptive, or misleading advertisers.
   B. National Association of Attorneys General (NARG) at the forefront of advertising regulation.
   C. Aggressive stance by states in reviewing national advertising

VII. Comparison Advertising.
   A. Types
      1. Head-to-head comparisons
      2. Your brand against the world
      3. Brand X comparisons

QUESTION: What are the three main types of comparative advertising?

   B. Lanham Act enforces strict penalties for deceptive and damaging comparative advertising

VIII. The Advertising Clearance Process
   A. Checks and balances systems of advertisers, agencies, and media
   B. Newspapers form a first line of defense.
   C. Television's broadcast standard department deals with questions of taste.
      1. Standards are mostly consistent across the networks.
      2. May question advertising acceptable in magazines or cable TV
   D. Media may be held liable for advertising they carry.

QUESTION: What types of systems do advertisers, agencies, and media use to protect themselves against liability?

IX. Self-Regulation by Industry-Wide Groups

A. Better Business Bureaus exert a major influence on truth and accuracy in advertising with no legal authority.

B. The National Advertising Review Council strives to sustain high standards of truth and accuracy in national advertising.

1. National Advertising Division (NAD)—investigative
2. National Advertising Review Board (NARB)—refers matters to appropriate government agency
3. NAD/NARB system cannot:
   a) Order the stop of an ad
   b) Impose a fine
   c) Bar anyone from advertising
   d) Boycott advertiser/product
4. Brings to bear judgment of the advertiser's peers

QUESTION: What are the two branches of the NARC and how do they interact? What can these branches not do? What is their key source of power?

C. The Children's Advertising Unit if the NAD studies:

1. Product presentation
2. Adequate disclosure
3. Sales pressure

QUESTION: What areas of children advertising does the CARU examine?

V. Copyrighting Advertising.

A. Nature of copyrights

1. Grants owner exclusive rights to print, publish, reproduce an original work for a specific period of time
2. Protects the expression of but not the concept, idea, or theme
3. Must contain substantial amount of text or picture

B. How to register a copyright

1. Write to Register of Copyrights, the Library of Congress, for forms.
2. The word "copyright" (or abbreviation or symbol) should appear with the name of the advertiser.
3. Send two copies of the ad with the forms and fee to the register of Copyrights.

ANSWERS TO QUESTIONS

1. Discuss the three major types of restraints on advertising.

a. Laws and regulations. Laws at both the local, state, and federal levels as well as the various regulatory bodies such as the Federal Trade Commission play an important role in advertising.

b. Media controls. The various media impose a number of restraints on the type of advertising and the product categories that can be used.

c. Self-regulation. Organizations such as the National Advertising Division of the Council of Better Business Bureaus serve to protect consumers' interests.

2. Why has the notion of caveat emptor been largely rejected by advertising regulators in this century?

The idea of caveat emptor (let the buyer beware) assumes a simple economy where both buyers and sellers have equal information. Since that is obviously not true in a complex society, some protection must be afforded the consumer.

3. Discuss the role of the Federal Trade Commission in regulating advertising.

The FTC, once it has determined that some advertising is false or misleading, issues consent decrees where the advertiser agrees to stop the practice. If a consent decree is not signed then a cease and desist order is issued forcing the company to stop the practice. A consent decree can be appealed to the full Commission or fought through the courts (as a practical matter, this rarely happens). In addition, to the formal role of the FTC, many think the bad publicity a company gains from an FTC citation is of more practical importance than the actual regulation by the Commission.

4. Intent is not a relevant factor in determining deceptive advertising. Explain.

A lack of intent to deceive is not a defense for deceptive advertising. The FTC does not have to prove malice or whether an ad was intented to deceive in order for a company to be cited. Remember, it is the protection of the consumer that is the paramount issue considered by the FTC.

5. Discuss the Robinson-Patman Act as it relates to cooperative advertising.

The intent of Robinson-Patman is to protect retailers from unfair trade practices. The primary use of Robinson-Patman is to make manufacturers provide advertising allowances (such as co-op) on a equal basis to all categories of retailers.

6. Discuss the importance of the so-called Central Hudson four-part test.

The Central Hudson test is the best general guideline provided by the Supreme Court as to what tests must be met before a governmental body can restrict advertising. It offered insight into the areas where advertising speech cannot be abridged by government.

7. What was the significance of the Shapero case as it relates to the advertising of professional services?

The case involving the mail solicitation by an attorney, extended the circumstances under which the advertising of professional services would be protected.

8. What are the ramifications to national advertising of the recent actions of the National Association of Attorneys General?

First, it indicates a dissatisfaction by the NAAG with the enforcement of advertising and other trade practice violations by the FTC. Of more importance, it might signal the coming of a number of contradictory laws from one state to another that would make national advertising very difficult.

9. Why are the television network standards offices of such importance to national advertising?

Primarily because over half of all national advertising dollars are spent in TV. A commercial that would not be allowed on TV could greatly disrupt a campaign.

10. Briefly outline the steps and procedures used by the National Advertising Review Council.

The Council has two operating arms:

a. The National Advertising Division is an investigative body which initiates action as well as receiving complaints from outside. When it determines that a complaint against an advertiser is valid it negotiates with the advertiser to correct the problem.

b. When the NAD and an advertiser cannot reach agreement the National Advertising Review Board is asked to review the matter and reach a final decision. It should be noted that neither the NAD or the NARB have legal authority to implement their decisions.

CHAPTER TWENTY-SIX

Economic and Social Effects of Advertising

Advertising's primary purpose is to encourage the consumption of goods and services, and is a major social force. Some even claim that advertising sets social and cultural agendas.

This chapter examines the responsibility advertisers have to both their clients and the public. There is a dual component: balancing economic efficiency and social responsibility.

LECTURE OUTLINE

I. The Economic Role of Advertising.
- **A.** Efficiency
  - **1.** Cheapest means of reaching large numbers of consumers
  - **2.** Advertising evaluation is directly ties to sales
- **B.** Corporate profits
  - **1.** Advertising must be an investment in future profitability to be justified.
  - **2.** Must see supplementary role of advertising in creating sales
  - **3.** Advertising-generated profitability achieved through product sales
  - **4.** Qualitative value created through product awareness
- **C.** Advertising should contribute to the overall welfare of the economy. There are four categories:
  - **1.** Counterproductive
  - **2.** Unproductive
  - **3.** Somewhat productive
  - **4.** Most productive
- **D.** Difficult to deal in generalities

QUESTION: What are the three components of the economic role of advertising?

QUESTION: What are the four categories of advertising's effects on the economy?

II. The social role of advertising.
- **A.** Concentrates on the advertisement's unintended consequences
- **B.** Mirror of society
- **C.** Shaper of society
- **D.** Three major periods:
  - **1.** The era of exaggerated claims 1865 to 1900
  - **2.** The era of public awareness 1900 to 1965
    - *a)* Pure Food and Drug Act of 1906
    - *b)* Protection against literal fraud
  - **3.** The era of social responsibility 1965 to present
    - *a)* Consumer movements of the 1960s
    - *b)* Environmental safety concerns
    - *c)* Heightened awareness of social issues

QUESTION: Trace the changes in the social role of advertising from the nineteenth century until now. What legislation was passed in 1906?

- **E.** Special-interest groups demand advertising fairly reflect the society.
  - **1.** Include a diverse population
  - **2.** Include minorities without even noticing it
- **F.** Advertising restricts competition and raises prices.
  - **1.** Brand monopolies
  - **2.** Brand switching with no overall economic gain for consumers
  - **3.** Higher prices for the buying public
  - **4.** Consumer choice as a director of production
- **G.** Advertising promotes unwanted purchases.
  - **1.** Presumes degree of human irrationality
  - **2.** Few consumers spend in such a manner.
- **H.** Advertising sells inferior products.
  - **1.** Contradictory to the reality of the marketplace
- **I.** Advertising is an unnecessary expense.
  - **1.** Benefits both sellers and buyers
    - *a)* Consumers gain wide choice of products and lower prices.
    - *b)* Sellers are allowed product entry into the marketplace.

QUESTION: What are some of the negative views associated with the social role of advertising and how can they be argued?

III. Advertising's role in communicating social issues.
- **A.** Direct advocacy of a social-responsibility theme

B. Depiction of certain social groups in a favorable light
C. Favorable illustration of a social-responsibility goal

QUESTION: "Don't litter" is an example of what type of advertising role in communicating social issues?

QUESTION: Give examples of the three roles advertising plays in communicating social issues.

IV. Advertising and ethical considerations.
- **A.** Today, concerns are openly discussed.
- **B.** Formal studies conducted on ethical issues
- **C.** Six most frequently cited ethical problems:
  1. Treating clients fairly
  2. Creating honest, nonmisleading, socially desirable ads
  3. Advertising unethical products
  4. Treating suppliers, vendors, and media fairly
  5. Treating agency employees and managers fairly
  6. Treating other agencies fairly

QUESTION: What are the six most frequently cited ethical problems in advertising?

ANSWERS TO QUESTIONS

1. Compare and contrast advertising's social and economic roles.

The primary purpose of advertising is to engage in supporting the economic system by enhancing the efficiency with which companies sell their goods and services. However, because advertising is such a high profile activity, it also sets the social and economic agenda for a large segment of our culture. Not just the products that are advertised, but where they are advertised and the manner in which they are presented play a role in the way society reacts to products.

2. What are some of the primary economic roles against which advertising success should be judged?

a. Is advertising more efficient than alternative means of selling?

b. Does advertising contribute to corporate profits? Is it an investment or an expense?

c. What contribution does advertising make to the overall economy?

3. What is the proper sales criteria on which to judge advertising?

With the exception of retail and direct mail, advertising rarely can be judged solely on whether sales take place. Instead, advertising is often judged on the basis on consumer attitude changes, awareness, or recall of a brand, increased store traffic, or even inquiries about a product.

4. Is advertising an expense or an investment?

Like any business cost, advertising is an expense to the seller. However, the question is do advertising expenditures result in greater profits than alternative marketing activities or if no advertising had been conducted. The answer must, of course, depend on the individual advertising program.

5. Discuss the circumstances in which advertising is most productive in terms of overall economic welfare.

Advertising is most productive when both buyer and seller profit equally. For example, when advertising is the most efficient means of communicating product benefits that result in sales. And, the product is one that offers the greatest overall benefit to the consumer from among the alternatives at his or her disposal.

6. In your opinion, should advertising for otherwise legal products be banned or restricted in some way?

[Note: students should be judged on the quality of their response since there is no "right" answer.] However, if a student argues that no ban or restrictions should be imposed, the instructor might point out the many cases of such impositions where advertisers do not object. That is, certain types of advertising to children and requirements for disclosure of financial and medical information.

7. In the text, the present period was characterized as one of social responsibility. How does this period compare to the earlier period of "truth in advertising"?

Truth in advertising is recognized as a minimal standard. The fact that a company tells the truth in its advertising is an expectation rather than a reason for applause. Today, advertisers must convey information in an environment that meets the broad requirements of consumers and does so in a manner that is conducive to the best interests of society as a whole.

8. Discuss the concept of brand monopoly.

Unlike traditional monopolies where a producer has control over the supply of a product, a brand monopoly is largely a manner of brand loyalty on the part of consumers. Here, a particular brand has garnered such a large share of the market that satisfied consumers have little reason to look for alternatives. Therefore, it becomes extremely difficult for competitors to find a niche to compete with this "monopoly" brand.

9. Discuss truthful advertising and ethical advertising.

As we discussed in Chapter 25, an ad may be literally truthful and yet convey an overall misleading impression to the consumer. Both the FTC and most advertisers realize that it is not the truth of each statement in an ad that is important but, rather, the overall impression left by the message. That is why advertisers are expected to make full disclosure of pertinent facts. Errors of omission can be just as important as misleading statements.

Kleppner's Advertising Procedure

THE PRENTICE HALL SERIES IN MARKETING
Philip Kotler, Series Editor

Abell/Hammond	STRATEGIC MARKET PLANNING: PROBLEMS AND ANALYTICAL APPROACHES
Corey	INDUSTRIAL MARKETING: CASES AND CONCEPTS, 3rd ed.
Green/Tull/Albaum	RESEARCH FOR MARKETING DECISIONS, 5th ed.
Keegan	GLOBAL MARKETING MANAGEMENT, 4th ed.
Kotler	MARKETING MANAGEMENT: ANALYSIS, PLANNING, IMPLEMENTATION, AND CONTROL, 6th ed.
Kotler	PRINCIPLES OF MARKETING, 4th ed.
Kotler/Andreasen	STRATEGIC MARKETING FOR NONPROFIT ORGANIZATIONS, 3rd ed.
Lovelock	SERVICES MARKETING: TEXT, CASES, AND READINGS
Nagle	THE STRATEGY AND TACTICS OF PRICING: A GUIDE TO PROFITABLE DECISION MAKING
Ray	ADVERTISING AND COMMUNICATION MANAGEMENT
Russell/Lane	KLEPPNER'S ADVERTISING PROCEDURE, 11th ed.
Stern/El-Ansary	MARKETING CHANNELS, 3rd ed.
Stern/Eovald	LEGAL ASPECTS OF MARKETING STRATEGY: ANTITRUST AND CONSUMER PROTECTION ISSUES
Urban/Hauser	DESIGN AND MARKETING OF NEW PRODUCTS

PRENTICE HALL, Englewood Cliffs, New Jersey 07632

ELEVENTH EDITION

Kleppner's Advertising Procedure

J. Thomas Russell
University of Georgia

W. Ronald Lane
University of Georgia

Library of Congress Cataloging-in-Publication Data

Russell, Thomas
Kleppner's advertising procedure.

(The Prentice Hall series in marketing)
Rev. ed. of: Kleppner's advertising procedure/Thomas Russell, Glenn Verrill, W. Ronald Lane. 10th ed. c1988.
Includes bibliographical references.
1. Advertising. I. Lane, W. Ronald. II. Kleppner, Otto. Advertising procedure. III. Title. IV. Title: Advertising procedure. V. Series.
HF5823.K45 1989 6539.1 89-25588
ISBN 0-13-516337-4

Editorial/production supervision: Nancy Farrell
Production Management: York Production Services
Interior design: Maureen Eide
Manufacturing buyer: Peter Havens
Cover design: Ray Lundgren Graphics
Cover art: Maureen Eide
Photo research: Teri Stratford
Photo editor: Lorinda Morris-Nantz

Part opening photos: Part One: The Granger Collection Part Two: Mel Digiacomo/The Image Bank Part Three: Lou Jones/The Image Bank Part Four: Gregory Heisler/The Image Bank Part Five: Brett Froomer/The Image Bank Part Six: Jules Zalon/The Image Bank

Printed in the United States of America
10 9 8 7 6 5 4 3 2 1

ISBN 0-13-516337-4

Prentice-Hall International (UK) Limited, *London*
Prentice-Hall of Australia Pty. Limited, *Sydney*
Prentice-Hall Canada, *Toronto*
Prentice-Hall Hispanoamericana, S.A., *Mexico*
Prentice-Hall of India Private Limited, *New Delhi*
Prentice-Hall of Japan, Inc., *Tokyo*
Simon & Schuster Asia Pte. Ltd., *Singapore*
Editora Prentice-Hall do Brasil, Ltda., *Rio de Janeiro*

Brief Contents

Contents

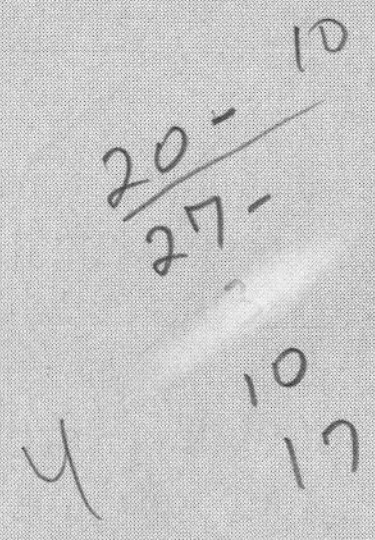

TEN

Using Newspaper 233

ELEVEN

Using Magazines 265

TWELVE

Out-of-Home Advertising 307

THIRTEEN

Direct-Response and Direct-Mail Advertising 335

TWENTY-FIVE

Legal and Other Restraints on Advertising 629

TWENTY-SIX

Economic and Social Effects of Advertising 653

P.S.

Getting Your Job in Advertising and Succeeding in Your Job Career 669

Preface

The eleventh edition of *Kleppner's Advertising Procedure* is designed to reflect the changing world of modern advertising and marketing. In a business environment of mergers, mega-agencies, new product introductions, and increasingly demanding and sophisticated consumers, advertising's job has become more difficult than in any past period. As we near the twenty-first century, the advertising practitioner of tomorrow will be a person well versed in marketing, psychology, consumer behavior, and legal regulation. The authors seek to reduce the complexities of advertising to manageable and organized units throughout the text.

This edition is intended for both students who plan a career in advertising and those to whom advertising is an interesting supplement to other disciplines such as marketing, commercial art, and psychology. In addition, all students, regardless of their major, are consumers of advertising and the text seeks to make advertising understandable as part of the overall economic system.

Kleppner's Advertising Procedure offers the reader a broad overview of the history, purpose, and role of advertising in our multifaceted economy. No one can fully understand advertising without some notion of its roots. Part One offers a review of the background of advertising. In Chapter 1 we examine the cultural and historical events that influenced modern advertising. Chapter 2 demonstrates the great number of uses of advertising as a marketing tool and what advertising can and cannot do as part of the marketing process.

Part Two introduces the planning and research functions so crucial to successful advertising. Successful advertising is built on a foundation of knowledge of both the consumer and the product. Chapter 3 outlines the life cycle of a product and the interaction between products and consumers. A new feature of the chapter includes a discussion of the importance of building brand equity to ensure brand survival in an increasingly competitive marketplace. Chapter 4 provides an overview of the consumer and points out the various means an advertiser has to identify potential consumers.

In Part Three we discuss advertising as a business. Advertising is unusual in that it is a business in itself and also serves a staff function for other businesses. Advertising agencies, as other businesses, have accountants, office managers, and salespersons (called account execs). However, the success of an agency is determined by how well it meets the needs of its clients. It is the personal and working relationships between agency and client that will be discussed in Chapters 5 and 6.

Part Four begins our discussion of the techniques and execution of advertising. In Chapter 7 the media strategy that underlies all advertising campaigns is examined. In recent years, the expenditures for media have grown significantly and now represent well over $100 billion of the total spent on advertising activities. Throughout the rest of this section the various media are discussed individually.

Starting with broadcast media in Chapters 8 and 9, we see the fragmentation of advertising vehicles. The growth of cable, VCR penetration, and increased selectivity of radio stations have resulted in media outlets reaching fewer people at a greater cost per person, but with an ability to more clearly identify prospects. The print media are discussed in Chapters 10 and 11, and we see that many of the same attempts at audience selectivity used by broadcasters are prevalent in newspapers and magazines.

We conclude this media section with a discussion of more specialized advertising media and related options such as sales promotion. In outdoor, direct-response media, and sales promotion we see that advertising is complemented by a number of related sales forces. The elusive consumer cannot be successfully reached by any one technique.

In Part Five we begin our discussion of the message—that combination of words, pictures, and psychological environment that will move a consumer to purchase one brand over another or make a buy today instead of tomorrow. The creation of advertising is both science and art. In Chapter 15 we examine the various research techniques that offer insights into consumer motivations. However, the same research will result in vastly different creative executions depending on the interpretations of the creative team. It is the ability of creative people to take research and view it in unique ways that separates great advertising from the also-rans. In Chapter 22 we present some ways in which the whole creative process is accomplished.

Finally, in Part Six, some of the more specialized advertising topics are presented. From the fast-paced world of retailing in Chapter 23 to the problems of international commerce in Chapter 24, advertising is truly part of the global village. In Chapters 25 and 26 the authors seek to examine the legal and regulatory restraints placed on advertising. Special emphasis is placed on the importance of self-regulation and the gatekeeper function of the media in accepting advertising. We conclude the text with a discussion of the social and economic effects of advertising. In a sense we ask the question, ''What is the value of advertising to society.''

As *Kleppner's Advertising Procedure* enters its seventh decade, the authors have attempted to retain the traditions of earlier editions while reflecting the many changes in the practice of advertising. We continue to base our approach to advertising on its marketing roots. However, the new cases and illustrations demonstrate that competitive pressures-demand that basic marketing fundamentals be presented in increasingly creative ways with cost efficiency an ever-present concern.

As in past editions, we approach the study of advertising with anticipation and excitement. We hope that at the conclusion of the text you share our enthusiasm over what is the most dynamic of business enterprises.

ACKNOWLEDGMENTS

The publication of *Kleppner's Advertising Procedure* is not a result of the efforts of the authors alone. Rather, this eleventh edition is the product of the cooperation of dozens of individuals, agencies, clients, and trade associations who have kindly allowed us to exhibit their creative work and research for more than 60 years in this and past editions. The authors are indebted to these people who have not only given us permission to use their material, but more importantly have also spent a great deal of time discussing their philosophy of advertising as well as the current state of the business. In a real sense, the eleventh edition is as much a compilation of these ideas as those of the authors.

While space does not permit us to name each person or organization that was instrumental in the publication of this text, we have attempted to give credit for each exhibit as it appears in the book. However, this identification can offer only a small token of the gratitude the authors express for the splendid cooperation in this and previous editions. The ultimate benefactors of this cooperation are the countless students who will pursue a career in advertising based on the lesson learned from these contributors.

About the Authors . . .

Otto Kleppner

(1899–1982)

A graduate of New York University, Otto Kleppner started out in advertising as a copywriter. After several such jobs, he became advertising manager at Prentice-Hall, where he began to think that he, too, "could write a book." Some years later, he also thought that he could run his own advertising agency, and both ideas materialized eminently. His highly successful agency handled advertising for leading accounts (Dewar's Scotch Whisky, I. W. Harper Bourbon and other Schenley brands, Saab Cars, Doubleday Book Clubs, and others). His book became a bible for advertising students, and his writings have been published in eight languages.

Active in the American Association of Advertising Agencies, Mr. Kleppner served as a director, a member of the Control Committee, chairman of the Committee of Government, Public and Educator Relations, and a governor of the New York Council. He was awarded the Nichols Cup (now the Crain Cup) for distinguished service to the teaching of advertising.

J. Thomas Russell

Thomas Russell is Professor of Advertising and Dean of the College of Journalism and Mass Communication at the University of Georgia. Russell received his Ph.D. in Communications from the University of Illinois and has taught and conducted research in a number of areas of advertising and marketing. He was formerly editor of the *Journal of Advertising* and is the author of numerous articles and research papers in both academic and trade publications.

In addition to his academic endeavors, Russell has worked as a retail copywriter as well as a principal in his own advertising agency. Russell is a member of a number of academic and professional organizations including the American Academy of Advertising, the American Advertising Federation, and the Association for Education in Journalism and Mass Communication. He has also served as a judge and faculty member for the Institute of Advanced Advertising Studies sponsored by the American Association of Advertising Agencies.

W. Ronald Lane

Ron Lane has worked in most aspects of advertising. He began in advertising and promotion for a drug manufacturer. He then worked as an ad manager for a retail drug chain and later for its small agency. After moving to Atlanta, he worked on such accounts as: Coca-Cola (Tab, Fresca, Sprite, Fanta brands), National Broiler Council, Minute-Maid, and Callaway Country Store. Ron has worked in creative and account services.

He is a Professor of Advertising at the University of Georgia. He is formerly advertising director of the *Journal of Advertising* and its current business manager. Ron has been a coordinator of the Institute of Advanced Advertising Studies sponsored by the American Association of Advertising Agencies. He is also a partner in SLRS Communications, Inc., an advertising-marketing agency.

Lane is a member of the American Advertising Federation Academic Committee and a recipient of AAF District Seven Outstanding Educator Award. He has served as an ADDY Awards judge numerous times and has been on the faculty of the Advertising Age Creative Workshop. He is a member of the American Academy of Advertising and the American Marketing Association.

PART ONE

The Place of Advertising

Advertising is often viewed as a communication tool of fairly recent origin. In fact, advertising is as old as civilization and commerce. It has always been necessary to bring buyers and sellers together. The only thing that has changed over the centuries is the degree of sophistication of the advertising function. In Chapter 1, we trace the development of advertising from its primitive beginnings on clay tablets and tavern signs to the electronic age.

In Chapter 2, we review the many facets of advertising. Advertising is not a single technique, but one that can be adapted to virtually any product or company. The versatility of advertising as a tool to solve marketing problems is one of its predominate characteristics. No aspect of business demands the breadth of knowledge required to create successful advertising.

ONE

Background of Today's Advertising

Advertising is often considered a recent phenomenon. It is true that modern advertising, with its multibillion-dollar budgets and tremendous influence in the marketing process, is in many ways a creation of the post–World War II business revolution. However, the process of communicating a sales message is as old as human history. We can divide advertising history into three broad periods:

1. *The Premarketing Era*. From the start of product exchange in prehistoric times to the middle of the eighteenth century, buyers and sellers communicated in very primitive ways. For most of this period, "media" such as clay tables, town criers, and tavern signs were the best way to advertise a product or a service. Only toward the end of this era was printing used.
2. *The Mass Communication Era*. From the mid-1700s to the early decades of this century, advertisers were increasingly able to reach large segments of the population, first with faster presses and later through broadcast media.
3. *The Research Era*. During the last 50 years, advertisers have methodically improved the techniques of identifying and reaching narrowly targeted audiences with messages prepared specifically for each group or individual (in the case of direct mail). Modern communication technology has aided in this quest for the perfect advertising campaign.

The focus of advertising has narrowed, paralleling the growth of marketing, as a technique to reach specific target markets. Coca-Cola's "other" diet cola, TAB, had been aimed at *hard-core dieters*. New ads in the '90s will feature TAB as the drink for the *upscale market*.

In its evolution as a marketing power, advertising has become a major economic and social force. Advertising practitioners have come under close public scrutiny and now find themselves working within a complex legal and regulatory framework. Perhaps the most important change in twentieth-century advertising is advertisers' sense of social responsibility. Many advertising practices that were almost routine a century ago are universally condemned by the industry today. Contemporary advertisers realize that public trust is the key to successful advertising. Throughout the remainder of this chapter, we will discuss the historic forces that have shaped contemporary advertising.

BEGINNINGS

The urge to advertise seems to be a part of human nature, evidenced since ancient times. Of the 5,000-year recorded history of advertising right up to our present TV satellite age, the part that is most significant begins when the United States emerged as a great manufacturing nation about 100 years ago. The early history of advertising, however, is far too fascinating to pass by without a glance.

It isn't surprising that the people who gave the world the Tower of Babel also left the earliest known evidence of advertising. A Babylonian clay tablet of about 3000 B.C. bears inscriptions for an ointment dealer, a scribe, and a shoemaker. Papyri exhumed from the ruins of Thebes show that the ancient Egyptians had a better medium on which to write their messages. (Alas, the announcements preserved in papyrus offer rewards for the return of runaway slaves.) The Greeks were among those who relied on town criers to chant the arrival of ships with cargoes of wines, spices, and metals. Often a crier was accompanied by a musician who kept him in the right key. Town criers later became the earliest medium for public announcements in many European countries, and they continued to be used for centuries. (At this point, we must digress to tell about a promotion idea used by innkeepers in France around A.D. 1100 to tout their fine wines: They would have the town crier blow a horn, gather a group—and offer samples!)

Roman merchants, too, had a sense of advertising. The ruins of Pompeii contain signs in stone or terra-cotta, advertising what the shops were selling: a row of hams for a butcher shop (Exhibit 1.1), a cow for a dairy, a boot for a shoemaker. The Pompeiians also knew the art of telling their story to the public by means of painted wall signs like this one (tourism was indeed one of advertising's earliest subjects):

- Traveler
- Going from here to the twelfth tower
- There Sarinus keeps a tavern
- This is to request you to enter
- Farewell

Hoarding. *First printed outdoor sign, forerunner of modern outdoor advertising.*

Our modern day *billboards* resemble the outdoor advertising signs of early Rome and seventeenth century England. The newest version of billboards are "movable"—on the sides of trucks! U-Haul's moving trucks feature "splashy slices of Americana" and soon will display local events, such as circuses, rodeos, and jazz festivals.

Outdoor advertising has proved to be one of the most enduring forms of advertising. It survived the decline of the Roman empire to become the decorative art of European inns in the seventeenth and eighteenth centuries. That was still an age of widespread illiteracy, so inns vied with one another in creating attractive signs that all could recognize. This accounts for the charming names of old inns, especially in England—such as the Three Squirrels, the Man in the Moon, the Hole in the Wall (Exhibit 1.2). In 1614, England passed a law, probably the earliest on advertising, that prohibited signs from extending more than 8 feet out from a building. (Longer signs pulled down too many house fronts.) Another law required signs to be high enough to give clearance to an armored man on horseback. In 1740, the first printed outdoor poster (referred to as a "hoarding") appeared in London.

ORIGINS OF NEWSPAPER ADVERTISING

William Claxton. *English printer who is credited with producing the first printed ad in English.*

The next most enduring advertising medium, the newspaper, was the offspring of Johann Gutenberg's invention of printing from movable type (about 1438), which, of course, changed communication methods for the whole world. About 40 years after the invention, William Caxton of London printed the first ad in English—a handbill of the rules for the guidance of the clergy at Easter. This was tacked up on church doors. (It became the first printed outdoor ad in English.) But the printed newspaper was a long

EXHIBIT 1.1

One of the oldest signs known. It identified a butcher shop in Pompeii.

EXHIBIT 1.2
Signs outside seventeenth-century inns.

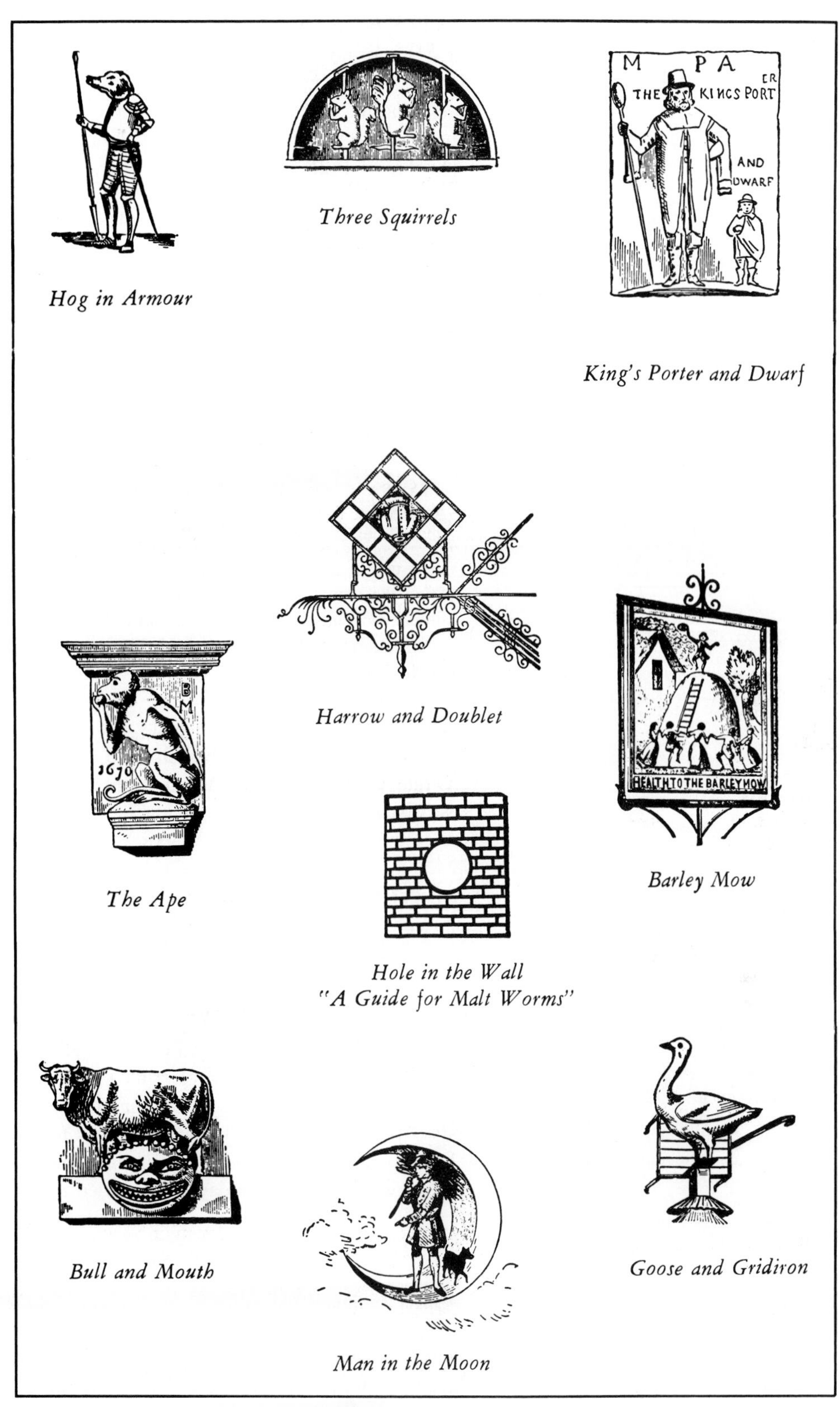

time coming. It really emerged from the newsletters, handwritten by professional writers, for nobles and others who wanted to be kept up-to-date on the news, especially of the court and important events—very much in the spirit of today's Washington newsletters.

The first ad in any language to be printed in a disseminated sheet appeared in a German news pamphlet in about 1525. And what do you think this ad was for? A book extolling the virtues of a mysterious drug. (The Food and Drug Administration did not exist in those days.) But news pamphlets did not come out regularly; one published in 1591 contained news of the previous three years. It was from such beginnings, however, that the printed newspaper emerged. The first printed English newspaper came out in 1622, the *Weekly Newes of London*. The first ad in an English newspaper appeared in 1625.

Siquis—Tack-Up Advertisements

The forerunner of our present want ads bore the strange name of *siquis*. These were tack-up ads that appeared in England at the end of the fifteenth century. Of these Frank Presbrey says:

> These hand-written announcements for public posting were done by scribes who made a business of the work. The word "advertisement" in the sense in which we now use it was then unknown. The advertising bills produced by the scribes were called "Siquis," or "If anybody," because they usually began with the words "If anybody desires" or "If anybody knows of," a phrase that had come from ancient Rome, where public notices of articles lost always began with the words "Si quis."
>
> First use of manuscript siquis was by young ecclesiastics advertising for a vicarage. . . . Soon the siquis poster was employed by those desiring servants and by servants seeking places. Lost articles likewise were posted. Presently also tobacco, perfume, coffee, and some other luxuries were thus advertised. The great percentage of siquis, however, continued to be of the personal, or want-ad type.[1]

Advertising in the English newspapers continued to feature similar personal and local announcements. The British have, in fact, shown so much interest in classified ads that until a few years ago the *London Times* filled its first page with classified advertising.

Advertising Comes to America

***Boston Newsletter.** It was the first American newspaper to carry advertising, first published in 1704.*

Newspaper advertising became the first printed vehicle to publicly announce personal needs, such as servants. The outgrowth of these announcements is *classified advertising*. Classified's growth rate in number of ads has leveled off—but an 8.1% increase in total spending is expected over the 1989–1993 period.

The Pilgrims arrived on American shores before the *Weekly Newes of London* was first published, so they had had little chance to learn about newspapers. But later colonists acquainted them with the idea, and the first American newspaper to carry ads appeared in 1704, the *Boston Newsletter* (note the newsletter identification). It printed an ad offering a reward for the capture of a thief and the return of several sorts of men's apparel—more akin to the ad offering a reward for returned slaves written on Egyptian papyrus thousands of years before than to the advertising printed in the United States today. By the time the United States was formed, the colonies had 30 newspapers. Their advertising, like that of the English newspapers of the time, consisted mostly of ads we would describe today as classified and local.

THREE MOMENTOUS DECADES: 1870 TO 1900

Neither those ads nor all the ads that appeared from ancient Egyptian days until the American industrial revolution explain the development of advertising in the United States. The history of advertising in the United States is unique because advertising took hold just as the country was entering its era of greatest growth: Population was soaring, factories were springing up, railroads were opening the West. Advertising grew with the country and helped establish its marketing system. The United States entered the nineteenth century as an agricultural country, following European market-

[1]Frank Presbrey, *History and Development of Advertising* (Garden City, NY: Doubleday, 1929).

ing traditions, and ended the century as a great industrial nation, creating its own patterns of distribution. A new age of advertising had begun.

We pick up the story in about 1870, when this era of transition was crystallizing. Among the major developments, transportation, population growth, invention, and manufacturing ranked high.

Transportation

Here was a country 3,000 miles wide. It had sweeping stretches of rich farmland. It had minerals and forests. It had factories within reach of the coal mines. It had a growing population. But its long-distance transportation was chiefly by rivers and canals.

Railroads today are fighting for survival, but 100 years ago they changed a sprawling continent into a land of spectacular economic growth. In 1865, there were 35,000 miles of railroad trackage in the United States. By 1900, this trackage was 190,000 miles. Three railroad lines crossed the Mississippi and ran from the Atlantic to the Pacific. Feeder lines and networks spread across the face of the land. Where railroads went, people went. No longer limited to the waterways, they established farms, settlements, and cities across the continent. The goods of the North and the East could be exchanged for the farm and extractive products of the South and the West. Never before had a country revealed such extensive and varied resources. Never since has so vast a market without a trade or language barrier been opened. This was an exciting prospect to manufacturers.

People

In 1870, the population of the United States was 38 million. By 1900, it had doubled. In no other period of American history has the population grown so fast. This growth, which included those recently freed from slavery, meant an expanding labor force in the fields, factories, and mines; it also meant a new consumer market. About 30 percent of the new population were immigrants. But all the settlers before them had been immigrants or descendants of immigrants who had had the courage to pull up stakes and venture to the New World, a land far away and strange to them, in search of a new and better life. The result was a people who were mobile, both in their readiness to move their homes and in their aspirations to move upward in lifestyle.

Inventions and Production

The end of the nineteenth century was marked by many notable inventions and advances in the manufacture of goods. Among these were the development of the electric motor and of alternating-current power transmission, which relieved factories of the need to locate next to waterpower sources, thus opening the hinterland to development and growth. The internal combustion engine was perfected in this period; the automobile age was soon to follow.

It was the age of fast communications; telephone (Exhibit 1.3), telegraph, typewriter, Mergenthaler linotype, high-speed presses—all increased the ability of people to communicate with one another.

In 1860, there were 7,600 patent applications filed in Washington. By 1870, this number had more than doubled to 19,000; by 1900, it had more than doubled again, to 42,000.

Steel production has traditionally served as an index of industrial activity. Twenty *thousand* tons of steel were produced in 1867, but 10 *million* tons were produced in 1900. There is also a direct correlation between the power consumption of a country and its standard of living. By 1870, only 3 million horsepower was available; by 1900, this capacity had risen to 10 million. More current means more goods being manufac-

EXHIBIT 1.3
The first telephone ad (1877).

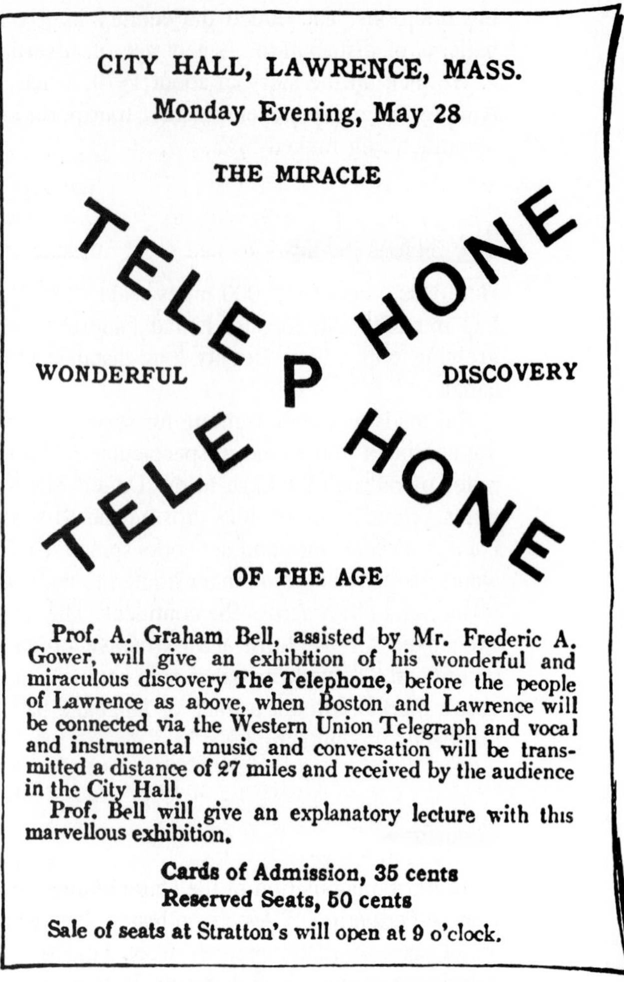

CITY HALL, LAWRENCE, MASS.
Monday Evening, May 28
THE MIRACLE
TELEPHONE
WONDERFUL
DISCOVERY
TELEPHONE
OF THE AGE
Prof. A. Graham Bell, assisted by Mr. Frederic A. Gower, will give an exhibition of his wonderful and miraculous discovery The Telephone, before the people of Lawrence as above, when Boston and Lawrence will be connected via the Western Union Telegraph and vocal and instrumental music and conversation will be transmitted a distance of 27 miles and received by the audience in the City Hall.
Prof. Bell will give an explanatory lecture with this marvellous exhibition.
Cards of Admission, 35 cents
Reserved Seats, 50 cents
Sale of seats at Stratton's will open at 9 o'clock.

tured; it also means that more people are using it for their own household needs. Both types of use form a good economic index.

The phonograph and the motion-picture camera, invented at the turn of the century, enhanced the American lifestyle.

The Columbian Exhibition in Chicago in 1893 was attended by millions, who returned home to tell their friends breathlessly about the new products they had seen.

Media

The growth of newspapers in the United States spawned opportunities for printed advertisements—to help reduce the costs of publishing. Circulation, in recent years, has declined drastically, but is predicted to rebound, due to better demographics, increases in morning and Sunday circulation, and stability of circulation of evening papers.

Newspapers. Since colonial times, newspapers had been popular in the United States. In the 1830s, the penny newspaper came out. In 1846, Richard Hoe patented the first rotary printing press, and in 1871, he invented the Hoe web press, which prints both sides of a continuous roll of paper and delivers folded sheets. By the end of the nineteenth century, about 10,000 papers were being published, with an estimated combined circulation of 10 million. Ninety percent of them were weeklies (most of the rest dailies) published in the county seat, and contained farm and local news. By 1900, 20 of the largest cities had their own papers, some with as many as 16 pages. Newspapers were the largest class of media during this period.

To save on the cost of paper, many editors (who were also the publishers) bought sheets already printed on one side with world news, items of general interest to farmers, and ads. They would then print the other side with local news and any ads they could obtain (forerunners of today's color insert). Or else they would insert such pages in their own four-page papers, offering an eight-page paper to their readers.

Religious Publications. Religious publications today represent a very small part of the total media picture; but for a few decades after the Civil War, religious publications were the most influential medium. They were the forerunners of magazines. The post–Civil War period was a time of great religious revival, marking also the beginning of the temperance movement. Church groups issued their own publications, many with circulations of no more than 1,000; the biggest ran to 400,000. But the combined circulation of the 400 religious publications was estimated at about 5 million.

Religious publications had great influence among their readers, a fact that patent-medicine advertisers recognized to such an extent that 75 percent of all religious-publication advertising was for patent medicines. (Many of the temperance papers carried advertisements for preparations that proved to be 40 percent alcohol. Today we call that 80 proof whiskey.)

Magazines. Most of what were called magazines before the 1870s, including Ben Franklin's effort in 1741, lasted less than six months—and for good reason: They consisted mostly of extracts of books and pamphlets, essays, verse, and communications of dubious value. Magazines as we know them today were really born in the last three decades of the nineteenth century, at a time when many factors were in their favor. The rate of illiteracy in the country had been cut almost in half, from 20 percent in 1870 to a little over 10 percent in1900. In 1875, railroads began carrying mail, including magazines, across the country. In 1879, Congress established the low second-class postal rate for publications, a subject of controversy to this day, but a boon to magazines even then. The Hoe high-speed rotary press began replacing the much slower flatbed press, speeding the printing of magazines. The halftone method of reproducing photographs as well as color artwork was invented in 1876, making magazines more enticing to the public. (*Godey's Lady's Book,* a popular fashion book of the age, had previously employed 150 women to hand-tint all of its illustrations.)

Literary magazines intended for the upper middle classes now appeared—*Harper's Monthly, Atlantic Monthly, Century*—but their publishers did not view advertising kindly at first. Even when, at the turn of the century, Fletcher Harper condescended to "desecrate literature with the announcements of tradespeople," he placed all the advertising in the back of his magazine.

Ladies Home Journal. *The first magazine to achieve one million circulation and usher in mass national advertising.*

Inspired by the success of popular magazines in England, a new breed of publishers came forth in the 1890s to produce magazines of entertainment, fiction, and advice, forerunners of today's women's and general magazines. Magazines brought the works of Rudyard Kipling, H. G. Wells, Mark Twain, and Conan Doyle to families across the face of the land. By 1902, *Munsey's* had a circulation of 600,000; *Cosmopolitan,* 700,000; *Delineator,* 960,000. The *Ladies' Home Journal* hit the million mark—a great feat for the age. The 10-cent magazine had arrived.

The amount of advertising that magazines carried was comparable to modern magazine advertising. *Harper's* published 75 pages of advertising per issue; *Cosmopolitan,* 103 pages; *McClure's,* 120 pages. Today a typical issue of the *Ladies' Home Journal* has 100 pages of advertising; *Reader's Digest,* 75; *Better Homes & Gardens,* 125. Magazines made possible the nationwide sale of products; they brought into being nationwide advertising.

Magazine ads first promoted patent medicines. It all dates back to 1886, when John Styth Pemberton, an Atlanta pharmacist, concocted a syrup to be dispensed in local soda fountains as a smooth-tasting tonic for headaches. It was his bookkeeper, Frank Robinson, who suggested the name *Coca-Cola,* and coined the flowing script.

Patent-Medicine Advertising

Patent-medicine advertisers had been around for a long time, and by the 1870s, they were the largest category of advertisers. After the Civil War, millions of men returned to their homes, North and South, many of them weak from wounds and exposure. The only kind of medical aid available to most of them was a bottle of patent medicine. As a result, patent-medicine advertising dominated the media toward the end of the nineteenth century, its fraudulent claims giving all advertising a bad name (Exhibit 1.4).

EXHIBIT 1.4
One of the more restrained ads in the patent-medicine category. Electricity, the new, magic power of the 1890s, was offered in a curative belt.

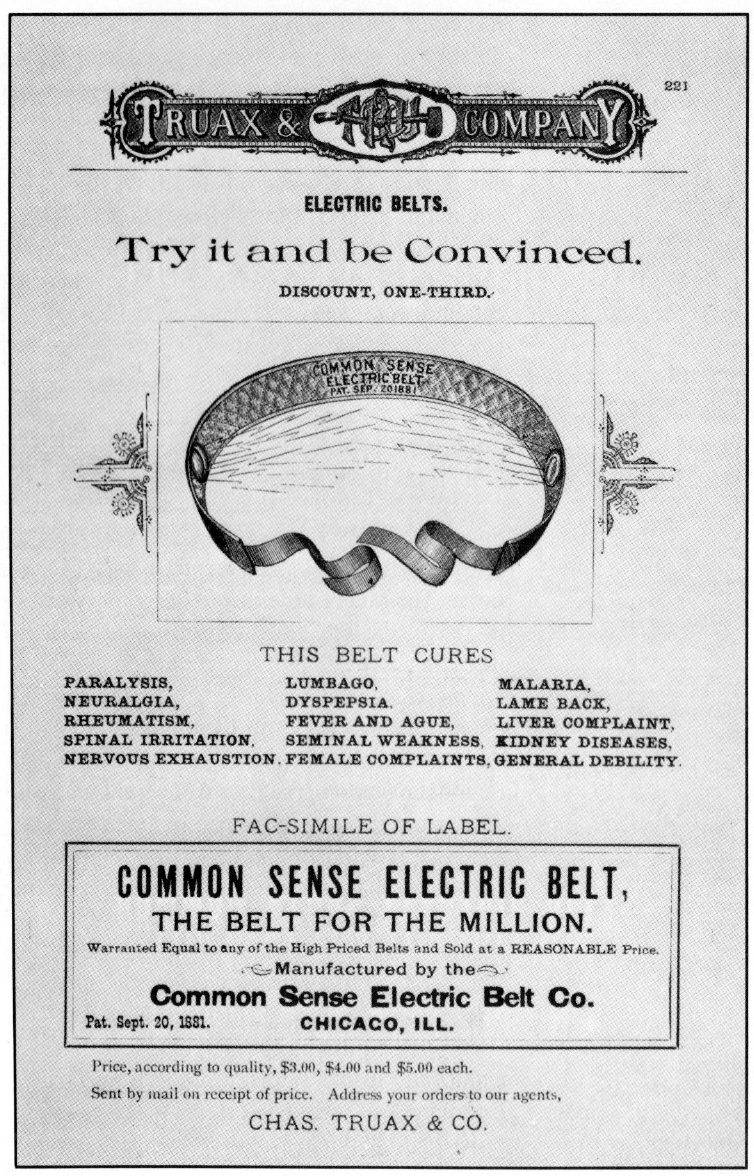

National Advertising Emerges

National distribution of products was helped by magazine ads. Lately, consumer magazine advertising has had large increases in *automotive, toiletry,* and *cosmetics* ads. Growth in readership also has helped circulation revenue, which now exceeds advertising expenditures. Industry spending is projected to grow 7.6% over the next five years.

Meanwhile, legitimate manufacturers saw a new world of opportunity opening before them in the growth of the country. They saw the market for consumer products spreading. Railroads could now transport their merchandise to all cities between the Atlantic and Pacific coasts. The idea of packaging their own products carrying their own trademarks was enticing, particularly to grocery manufacturers; for it allowed them to build their business on their reputation with the consumer instead of being subject to the caprices and pressures of jobbers, who had previously been their sole distributors. Magazines provided the missing link in marketing—magazine advertising easily spread the word about manufacturers' products all over the country. Quaker Oats cereal was among the first to go this marketing route, followed soon by many others (Exhibit 1.5).

This was the development of national advertising, as we call it today, in its broadest sense, meaning the advertising by a producer of his trademarked product, whether or not it has attained national distribution.

EXHIBIT 1.5

Leaders in national advertising in the 1890s. (Reproduced from Presbrey, *History and Development of Advertising*, p. 361.)

LEADERS IN NATIONAL ADVERTISING IN 1890'S

A. P. W. Paper
Adams Tutti Frutti Gum
Æolian Company
American Express Traveler's Cheques
Armour Beef Extract
Autoharp
Baker's Cocoa
Battle Ax Plug Tobacco
Beardsley's Shredded Codfish
Beeman's Pepsin Gum
Bent's Crown Piano
Burlington Railroad
Burnett's Extracts
California Fig Syrup
Caligraph Typewriter
Castoria
A. B. Chase Piano
Chicago Great Western
Chicago, Milwaukee & St. Paul Railroad
Chicago Great Western Railway
Chocolat-Menier
Chickering Piano
Columbia Bicycles
Cleveland Baking Powder
Cottolene Shortening
Cook's Tours
Crown Pianos
Crescent Bicycles
Devoe & Raynolds Artist's Materials
Cuticura Soap
Derby Desks
De Long Hook and Eye
Diamond Dyes
Dixon's Graphite Paint
Dixon's Pencils
W. L. Douglas Shoes
Edison Mimeograph
Earl & Wilson Collars
Elgin Watches
Edison Phonograph
Everett Piano
Epps's Cocoa
Estey Organ
Fall River Line
Felt & Tarrant Comptometer
Ferry's Seeds
Fisher Piano
Fowler Bicycles
Franco American Soup
Garland Stoves
Gold Dust
Gold Dust Washing Powder
Gorham's Silver
Gramophone
Great Northern Railroad
H-O Breakfast Food
Hamburg American Line
Hammond Typewriter
Hartford Bicycle
Hartshorn's Shade Rollers
Heinz's Baked Beans
Peter Henderson & Co.
Hires' Root Beer
Hoffman House Cigars
Huyler's Chocolates
Hunyadi Janos
Ingersoll Watches
Ives & Pond Piano
Ivory Soap
Jaeger Underwear
Kirk's American Family Soap
Kodak
Liebeg's Extract of Beef
Lipton's Teas
Lowney's Chocolates
Lundborg's Perfumes
James McCutcheon Linens
Dr. Lyon's Toothpowder
Mason & Hamlin Piano
Mellin's Food
Mennen's Talcum Powder
Michigan Central Railroad
Monarch Bicycles
J. L. Mott Indoor Plumbing
Munsing Underwear
Murphy Varnish Company
New England Mincemeat
New York Central Railroad
North German Lloyd
Old Dominion Line
Oneita Knitted Goods
Packer's Tar Soap
Pearline Soap Powder
Peartltop Lamp Chimneys
Pears' Soap
Alfred Peats Wall Paper
Pettijohn's Breakfast Food
Pittsburgh Stogies
Pond's Extract
Postum Cereal
Prudential Insurance Co.
Quaker Oats

Mass Production Appears

The words *chauffeur, limousine,* and *sedan* remind us that some of the earliest motorcars were made and publicized in France. In the United States, as in France, they were virtually handmade at first. But in 1913, Henry Ford decided that the way to build cars at low cost was to make them of standardized parts and bring the work to the man on the assembly-line belt. He introduced to the world a mass-production technique and brought the price of a Ford down to $265 by 1925 (when a Hudson automobile cost $1,695 and the average weekly wage was $20). But in a free society, mass production is predicated upon mass selling, another name for advertising. Mass production makes possible countless products at a cost the mass of people can pay and about which they learn through advertising. America was quick to use both.

The Advertising Agency

We have been speaking of the various media and their advertising. The media got much of that advertising through the advertising agency, which started out as men selling advertising space on a percentage basis for out-of-town newspapers. Later they also planned, prepared, and placed the ads and rendered further services. The story of the advertising agency is deeply rooted in the growth of American industry and advertising. Later in the book we devote a whole chapter (Chapter 5) to the American agency, from its beginning to its latest patterns of operation. Until then, we need keep in mind only that the advertising agency has always been an active force in developing the use of advertising.

AMERICA ENTERS THE TWENTIETH CENTURY

The moral atmosphere of business as it developed after the Civil War reflected laissez-faire policy at its extreme. High government officials were corrupted by the railroads, the public was swindled by flagrant stock market manipulations, embalmed beef was shipped to soldiers in the Spanish-American War. Advertising contributed to the immorality of business, with its patent-medicine ads offering to cure all the real and imagined ailments of man. There was a ''pleasing medicine to cure cancer,'' another to cure cholera. No promise of a quick cure was too wild, no falsehood too monstrous.

The Pure Food and Drug Act (1906)

As early as 1865, the *New York Herald-Tribune* had a touch of conscience and eliminated ''certain classes'' of medical advertising, those that used ''repellent'' words. In 1892, the *Ladies' Home Journal* was the first magazine to ban *all* medical advertising. The *Ladies' Home Journal* also came out with a blast by Mark Sullivan, revealing that codeine was being used in cold preparations and a teething syrup had morphine as its base. Public outrage reached Congress, which in 1906 passed the Pure Food and Drug Act, the first federal law to protect the health of the public and the first to control advertising.

The Federal Trade Commission Act (1914)

Federal Trade Commission (FTC). *The agency of the federal government empowered to prevent unfair competition and fraudulent, misleading, or deceptive advertising in interstate commerce.*

In addition to passing laws protecting the public from unscrupulous business, Congress passed the Federal Trade Commission Act, protecting one businessman from the unscrupulous behavior of another. The law said, in effect, ''Unfair methods of doing business are hereby declared illegal.'' John D. Rockefeller, founder of the Standard Oil Company, got together with some other oilmen in the early days of his operation and worked out a deal with the railroads over which they shipped their oil. They arranged not only to get a secret rebate on the oil they shipped, but also to get a rebate on all the oil their *competitors* shipped. Result: They were able to undersell their competitors and drive them out of business. What was considered smart business in those days would be a violation of the antitrust laws today.

In time, the FTC (Federal Trade Commission) extended its province to protecting the public against misleading and deceptive advertising—a matter of which all who are responsible for advertising today are very much aware. Of this period of exposure and reform, the historian James Truslow Adams said, "America for the first time was taking stock of the morality of everyday life."

Yet, despite these praiseworthy efforts at self-regulation and many others in the years that followed, and general acceptance, the advertising industry was and continues to be the target of criticism for its social effects. Chapter 26 answers such criticism, and it has been placed at the end of the book so that in judging the criticisms you will have had the benefit of the advertising background that the intervening chapters provide.

ADVERTISING COMES OF AGE

American Advertising Federation (AAF). *An association of local advertising clubs and representatives of other advertising associations. The largest association of advertising people. Very much interested in advertising legislation.*

Better Business Bureau. *An organization, launched by advertisers and now with wide business support, to protect the public against deceptive advertising and fraudulent business methods. Works widely at local levels. Also identified with the National Advertising Review Board.*

Printers Ink Model Statutes (1911). *The act directed at fraudulent advertising, prepared and sponsored by* Printer's Ink, *which was the pioneer advertising magazine.*

Audit Bureau of Circulations (ABC). *The organization sponsored by publishers, agencies, and advertisers for securing accurate circulation statements.*

In about 1905, there emerged a class of advertising men who recognized that their future lay in advertising legitimate products and in earning the confidence of the public in advertising. They gathered with like-minded men in their communities to form advertising clubs.

These clubs subsequently became Associated Advertising Clubs of the World (now the American Advertising Federation). In 1911, they launched a campaign to promote truth in advertising. In 1916, they formed vigilance committees. These developed into today's Council of Better Business Bureaus, which continues to deal with many problems of unfair and deceptive business practices. In 1971, the bureaus became a part of the National Advertising Review Council, an all-industry effort at curbing misleading advertising. The main constituency of the American Advertising Federation continues to be the local advertising clubs. On its board are also officers of the other advertising associations.

In 1910, the Association of National Advertising Managers was born. It is now known as the Association of National Advertisers (ANA) and has about 500 members, including the foremost advertisers. Its purpose is to improve the effectiveness of advertising from the viewpoint of the advertiser. In 1917, the American Association of Advertising Agencies was formed to improve the effectiveness of advertising and of the advertising agency operation. Over 75 percent of all national advertising today is placed by its members, both large and small.

In 1911, *Printers' Ink,* the leading advertising trade paper for many years, prepared a model statute for state regulation of advertising, designed to "punish untrue, deceptive or misleading advertising." The *Printers' Ink* Model Statute has been adopted in its original or modified form in 44 states, where it is still operative.

Up to 1914, many publishers were carefree in their claims to circulation. Advertisers had no way of verifying what they got for their money. However, in that year, a group of advertisers, agencies, and publishers established an independent auditing organization, the Audit Bureau of Circulations, which conducts its own audits and issues its own reports of circulation. Most major publications belong to the ABC, and an ABC circulation statement is highly regarded in media circles. The ABC reports of circulation are fully accredited in most areas. (Today similar auditing organizations are operating in 25 countries throughout the world.)

In June 1916, President Woodrow Wilson addressed the Associated Advertising Clubs of the World convention in Philadelphia, the first president to give public recognition to the importance of advertising. Advertising had come of age!

Advertising in World War I

When the United States entered World War I in 1917, a number of advertising agency and media men offered their services to the government but were turned down; for "Government officials, particularly Army chiefs, believed in orders and edicts, not persuasion."[2] But when these groups offered their services to the Council of National Defense, they were welcomed and became the Division of Advertising of the Committee of Public Information—the propaganda arm of the government.

The committee's first job, to help persuade all eligible men to register for the draft, resulted in the registration of 13 million men in one day without serious incident. The committee also succeeded in persuading advertisers to use their own paid space to advertise Liberty Bonds and the Red Cross and to carry messages of the Fuel Administration (to use less fuel) and the Food Administration (to observe its meatless and wheatless days).

World War I provided the impetus for advertising to show what it could do to persuade people to be patriotic; public service and non-profit advertising were born. To encourage sales of "healthful" products, the American Heart Association and the American Dental Association have participated in advertising and sales promotion campaigns by endorsing those products that meet their standards.

The 1920s

The 1920s began with a minidepression and ended with a crash. When the war ended, makers of army trucks were able to convert quickly to commercial trucks. Firestone spent $2 million advertising "Ship by Truck." With the industry profiting by the good roads that had been built, truck production jumped from 92,000 in 1916 to 322,000 in 1920. Door-to-door delivery from manufacturer to retailer spurred the growth of chain stores, which led, in turn, to supermarkets and self-service stores.

The passenger car business boomed, too, and new products appeared in profusion: electric refrigerators, washing machines, electric shavers, and, most incredible of all, the radio. Installment selling made hard goods available to all. And all the products needed advertising.

Federal Communications Commission (FCC). *The federal authority empowered to license radio and TV stations and to assign wavelengths to stations "in the public interest."*

Radio Arrives. Station KDKA of Pittsburgh was on the air broadcasting the Harding-Cox election returns in November 1920, some months before its license to operate had cleared. Many other stations soon began broadcasting. There were experimental networks over telephone lines as early as 1922. The first presidential address to be broadcast (by six stations) was the message to Congress by President Coolidge in 1923. The National Broadcasting Company (NBC) started its network broadcasting in 1926 with six stations and had its first coast-to-coast football broadcast in 1927. That was the year, too, that the Columbia Broadcasting System (CBS) was founded and the Federal Radio Commission (now the Federal Communications Commission, FCC) was created.

Making radio sets proved to be a boon to industry (Exhibit 1.6). According to Irving Settel:

> Radio created one of the most extraordinary new product demands in the history of the United States. From all over the country, orders for radio receiving sets poured into the offices of manufactures. Said *Radio Broadcast Magazine* in its first issue. May 1922:
>
> "The rate of increase in the number of people who spend at least a part of their evening listening in is almost incomprehensible . . . It seems quite likely that before the market for receiving apparatus becomes approximately saturated, there will be at least five million receiving sets in this country."[3]

During the '20s and '30s, it was *radio* that proved it alone could reach and influence more people than any other medium. Over the next several decades, radio stations have maintained steady listenership and have become *the primary out-of-the-home medium*. Ad growth of 9.2% is predicted over the next five years.

Business boomed in the mid-1920s—and so did advertising. The December 7, 1929, issue of *The Saturday Evening Post,* is historic. It was the last issue whose advertising had been prepared before the stock market crash of October 1929. The magazine was 268 pages thick. It carried 154 pages of advertising. The price: 5 cents a copy. Never again would *The Saturday Evening Post* attain that record. It was the end of an era.

---

[2] James Playsted Wood, *The History of Advertising* (New York: Ronald, 1958).

[3] Irving Settel, *A Pictorial History of Radio* (New York: Citadel, 1960), p. 41.

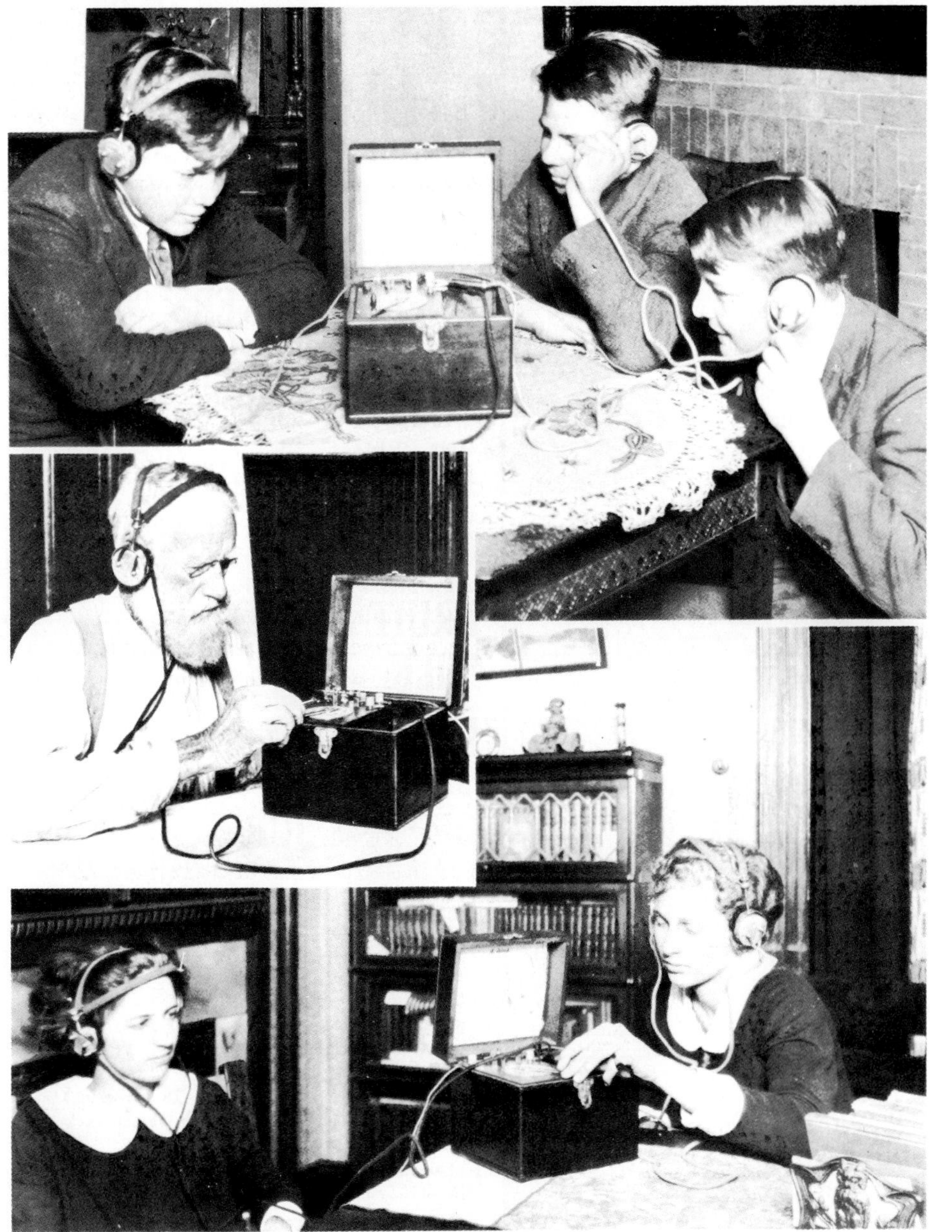

EXHIBIT 1.6

The earliest radio sets. The Aeriola Junior had heavy use in the early 1920s. Rural listeners, particularly, turned to their sets for farm information, weather reports, and even church services. (From Irving Settel, *A Pictorial History of Radio* [New York: Grosset & Dunlap, 1967.] © Irving Settel, 1967.)

The 1930s Depression

The stock market crash had a shattering effect on our entire economy: Millions of people were thrown out of work; business failures were widespread; banks were closing all over the country (there were no insured deposits in those days). There was no social security, no food stamps, no unemployment insurance. Who had ever heard of pensions for blue-collar workers? There were bread lines, long ones; and well-dressed men on street corners were selling apples off the tops of boxes for 5 cents. (See Exhibit 1.7.) The Southwest was having its worst windstorms, carrying off the topsoil and killing livestock and crops. Farmers abandoned their farms, packed their families and

EXHIBIT 1.7
Chain-store ad, 1932.

SPECIAL	PRICES TODAY	PRICES A YEAR AGO	CHANGE IN PRICE
POTATOES MAINES 100 lb. bag / PRINCE EDWARD ISLES 90 lb. bag	$2.35	3.17	—82¢
PEACHES CALIFORNIA	2 lgst. cans 25¢	2 for 46¢	—21¢
UNEEDA BAKERS MACAROON SANDWICH	3 pkgs. 25¢	NEW PRODUCT	....
STRING BEANS STANDARD QUALITY	3 No. 2 cans 28¢	3 for 30¢	— 2¢
TOMATOES STANDARD QUALITY	3 No. 2 cans 20¢	3 for 30¢	—10¢
AUNT JEMIMA PANCAKE FLOUR	2 pkgs. 25¢	2 for 30¢	— 5¢
AUNT JEMIMA BUCKWHEAT FLOUR	2 pkgs. 25¢	2 for 34¢	— 9¢
DEL MONTE FRUIT SALAD	lgst. can 29¢	41¢	—12¢
MILK WHITEHOUSE BRAND	3 tall cans 22¢	3 for 23¢	— 1¢
CATSUP BLUE LABEL	sm. bot. 13¢	15¢	— 2¢
CATSUP BLUE LABEL	lge. bot. 19¢	23¢	— 4¢
ORANGE JUICE	2 ... 15¢	2 for 20¢	— 5¢

		PRICES TODAY	A YEAR AGO	CHANGE IN PRICE
Red Circle Coffee	lb.	29¢	39¢	—10¢
Eight O'Clock Coffee	lb.	25¢	35¢	—10¢
Bokar Coffee	lb. tin	35¢	45¢	—10¢
Grandmother's Bread	20 ounce loaf	7¢	8¢	— 1¢
Jack Frost Sugar	5 lb. cotton sack	25¢	29¢	— 4¢
Pure Lard	lb.	15¢	17¢	— 2¢
Nucoa	lb.	23¢	25¢	— 2¢
Salt	4 lb. sack	8¢	10¢	— 2¢
Pea Beans	lb. package	10¢	17¢	— 7¢
Lima Beans	lb. package	17¢	23¢	— 6¢
Sunnyfield Flour	24½ lb. sack	75¢	89¢	—14¢
Sunsweet Prunes	2 lb. package	15¢	29¢	—14¢
Puffed Wheat	package	12¢	13¢	— 1¢
Puffed Rice	package	14¢	15¢	— 1¢
FRESH MEATS & FOWL AT A&P MARKETS				
PORK LOINS HALF OR WHOLE	lb.	25¢	31¢	— 6¢
Prime Ribs of Beef (CUT FROM FIRST 6 RIBS)	lb.	35¢	41¢	— 6¢
Sirloin Steak	lb.	49¢	55¢	— 6¢
Loin Lamb Chops	lb.	35¢	51¢	—16¢
Roasting Chickens (3½ to 4 lbs.)	lb.	39¢	42¢	— 3¢

furniture into old pickup trucks, and headed west. (Steinbeck wrote his *Grapes of Wrath* around this experience.) The government finally launched the Works Progress Administration (WPA) for putting men to work on public-service projects, but the bread lines continued to be long.

Out of that catastrophe came three developments that affect advertising to this day:

1. Radio emerged as a major advertising medium. In March 1933, President Franklin D. Roosevelt made the first inaugural address ever to be broadcast by radio, giving heart and hope to a frightened people. His line "We have nothing to fear except fear itself," spoken to the largest audience that had ever at one time heard the voice of one man, became historic. In one broadcast, radio showed its power to move a nation. Radio had arrived as a major national advertising medium. It quickly became part of the life of America. The 1930s began with 612 stations and 12 million sets; they ended with 814 stations and 51 million sets.
2. The Robinson-Patman Act (1936) was passed to help protect the little merchant from the unfair competition of the big store with its huge buying power. This law is still operative today.
3. Congress passed the Wheeler-Lea Act (1938), giving the FTC more direct and sweeping powers over advertising, and the Federal Food, Drug and Cosmetic Act (1938), giving the administration authority over the labeling and packaging of these products. These laws, which we discuss in Chapter 25, Legal and Other Restraints on Advertising, are a pervasive consideration in advertising today and a forerunner of the government's increasing interest in advertising.

Robinson-Patman Act. *A federal law, enforced by the FTC. Requires a manufacturer to give proportionate discounts and advertising allowances to all competing dealers in a market. Purpose: to protect smaller merchants from unfair competition of larger buyers.*

Advertising During World War II (1941 to 1945)

With World War II, industry turned to the production of war goods. Since all civilian material was severely rationed, many firms curtailed their advertising. Others felt that though they were out of merchandise, they were not out of business, and they wanted to keep the public's goodwill, so they applied their advertising efforts to rendering public service. The Goodyear Tire & Rubber Company's advice on how to take care of your tires in days of product shortages was akin to ads that were to appear in 1974 and 1975.

The War Advertising Council. When the government turned to the advertising industry for help in enlisting civilian aid in the war effort, the industry organized the War Advertising Council. It was composed of media, which contributed the space; agencies, which contributed the creative talent; and advertisers, who contributed management. Among the council's succession of massive public-service campaigns were those for putting workers on guard against careless talk ("The enemy is listening"), salvaging scrap metals, purchasing war bonds, writing V-mail letters, wartime recruiting (especially of women), preventing forest fires, and planting victory gardens. More than a billion dollars of space, time, and talent went into this effort. So successful was the project that it was continued after the war, to deal with public-service problems. It was renamed The Advertising Council and is very active to this day.

After World War II, industry went into high gear, supplying the pent-up demand for cars, homes, appliances, and all the other postponed purchases. Many new and improved products appeared, made possible by materials and processes originally developed for war use, leading directly to the historic growth period of 1950 to 1975.

Advertising from 1950 to 1975: The Word Was *Growth*

Wrote Richard Manchester, in speaking of this period:

> A surge of abundance was everywhere. Technological change had never held a greater fascination for Americans. . . . The sheer number of innovations was bewildering. . . . One by one they appeared, were assimilated into the general experience. Millions of men and women of the swing generation realized that in countless little ways life had become more tolerable, more convenient, more interesting—in a word, more livable.[4]

[4]Richard Manchester, *The Glory and the Dream* (Boston: Little, Brown, 1973), p. 946.

Also in discussing this era, John Crichton reported:

The great growth period of 1950–75 produced an *abundance of products and* the need to convey information about those products, in order to sell them. Chuck King created *tiki beach huts,* in order to promote his new suntan lotion. For a quarter, the beachcomber can get an all-over spray. King expects to sell 800 of his "sun centers" in 1989, generating an estimated $5 million for his K-Sun, Inc.

> In 1950 many markets were either infantile or virtually nonexistent. Travel and leisure, second homes, food franchises, second, third, and fourth cars, many frozen and instant foods, many of the synthetic fabrics and combinations of them, many of the devices like color television, snowmobiles, the Sunfish and the Hobie Cat, mobile homes, and campers were all in the future. In 1950 the United States, untouched by the ravages of the Second World War, was embarked on a period of growth unparalleled in our history. It was a period of great buoyancy and confidence.[5]

The Figures Also Said Growth. Between 1950 and 1973,[6] the population of the United States increased by 38 percent, while disposable personal income increased by 327 percent. New housing starts went up by 47 percent, energy consumption by 121 percent, college enrollment by 136 percent, automobile registrations by 151 percent, telephones in use by 221 percent, number of outboard motors sold by 242 percent, retail sales by 250 percent, families owning two or more cars by 300 percent, frozen-food production by 655 percent, number of airline passengers by 963 percent, homes with dishwashers by 1,043 percent, and homes with room air conditioners by 3,662 percent.

Advertising not only contributed to the growth but was part of it, rising from an expenditure of $5,780 million in 1950 to $28,320 million in 1975—a growth of 490 percent. There were many developments in advertising during this time:

- In 1956, the Department of Justice ruled that advertising agencies could negotiate fees with clients rather than adhere to the then-required 15 percent commission on all media placed. This encouraged the growth of specialized companies, such as independent media-buying services, creative-only agencies, and in-house agencies owned by advertisers.
- The voice of the consumer became more powerful.
- Congress passed an act limiting outdoor advertising alongside interstate highways. Cigarette advertising was banned from television.
- The FTC introduced corrective advertising by those who had made false or misleading claims. Comparison advertising (mentioning competitors by name) was deemed an acceptable form of advertising.
- The magazine-publishing world saw the disappearance of the old dinosaurs—*The Saturday Evening Post, Collier's,* and *Woman's Home Companion.* There was no vacuum at the newsstand, however, for there was an immediate upsurge in magazines devoted to special interests.
- Newspapers felt the effect of the shift of metropolitan populations to the suburbs. Freestanding inserts became an important part of newspaper billings.
- Radio took a dive when TV came along. The story of how it came out of that drastic decline is a good example of turning disadvantages into advantages.
- Direct-response advertising soared from $900 million in 1950 to $8 billion in 1980, reflecting the growth of direct marketing.
- The two biggest developments to emerge were TV and electronic data processing. TV has changed America's life as well as the world of advertising. Data-processing systems have brought before the eyes of management a wealth of organized information. This, together with the syndicated research services, has revolutionized the entire marketing process and the advertising-media operation.

Corrective advertising. *To counteract the residual effects of previous deceptive advertising, the FTC may require the advertiser to devote future space and time to disclosure of previous deception. Began around the late 1960s.*

As advertising grew, so did concern over its influence. Consumer input, placement bans, and corrective messages began to impact on the "choices" of advertisers. In an effort to curb the vast amounts of *children's television advertising,* bills have been proposed in Congress to limit commercial time and "program-length" commercials, like G. I. Joe.

Advertising in an Age of Mega-Mergers

During the remaining decade of this century, advertising must deal with a changing economic order, both internally and externally. Internally, the mergers of huge agencies have created mammoth organizations with billings ten times those of large agen-

[5]John Crichton, "We're in the Last Quarter," paper presented at the Western Region Convention of the American Association of Advertising Agencies, 1975, p. 3.

[6]We select 1973 as the last full year before the high inflation brought on by the oil embargo of 1974.

cies only a decade ago. While these mergers give the mega-agencies immense resources and financial stability, they are not without their problems. It is difficult to merge agencies of this size without serious client conflicts. In some cases, major companies have withdrawn millions of dollars' worth of business as a result of such merger-created conflicts. Almost as large a problem is the perception among some clients that personal advertising services cannot be maintained in these large agencies, especially for medium-size accounts.

Advertising agencies find that their expansion increasingly comes from international accounts. An agency that hopes to achieve a position among the top 50 agencies must have the capacity to service accounts in an international environment. Modern agencies must deal with uncertainties of international currency and competition from foreign agencies (notably in Europe and the Far East), and still provide traditional services to domestic clients.

Despite the importance of these changes, the agency business still represents only one area of the total advertising landscape. The issues facing the modern advertiser go far beyond agency-client relationships. Among the issues we will address in coming chapters are:

1. There is growing consumer sophistication toward advertising as an information source. The legal, ethical, and self-regulatory atmosphere in which advertising functions has never been more publicly debated. The legal problems facing advertising span the spectrum from bans on the advertising of legal products such as smokeless tobacco to individual state restrictions on billboard size and placement.
2. Advertisers will have to adapt to changing lifestyles and family living arrangements. The working couple, single-person and single-parent households, and other nontraditional living arrangements are altering consumption patterns and reactions to advertising. The traditional modular family of working husband, housewife, and children now makes up less than 15 percent of American households. Advertising strategy must deal with a marketplace that has more Americans over 65, few under 21, more educated and affluent middle-aged people, and more single-person households than ever before. The ramifications of these changes will affect the purchase and promotion of everything from housing to diapers.
3. Changes in technology and diversification of the communication system will have profound effects on advertising. Cable TV, home video recorders, a proliferation of specialized magazines, the success of direct-mail and home-shopping techniques, and the growth of sales promotion are changing the practice of advertising in fundamental ways. The successful advertising practitioner of the next century will be a marketing generalist who is competent at evaluating research and, most of all, who understands the psychology of consumer behavior.
4. Finally, the practice of advertising will operate on an international stage, utilizing huge multinational agencies with international research and media-buying capabilities. Some clients fear a lessening of personal services and even creativity among these so-called mega-agencies. The agencies claim that, to the contrary, consolidation will bring about greater efficiencies and cost savings for clients.

''Non-traditional'' approaches—in voice and media—to reach the ''new'' consumer is advertising's challenge of today. Marketing research, in the field of consumer behavior, will be relied on to help predict trends and changes in the marketplace. One of the *biggest* areas of the United States people are continuously watching for changes is New York City. The ''Big Apple'' is becoming a Latin city; its white population is aging, while the Hispanic population is relatively young and consistently producing large families. Predictably, more ads will appear in Spanish and in the Spanish media.

The period of consolidation and growth of advertising that started in the 1950s will continue throughout the next decade. However, given the new media technologies, the movement to a service economy, and the fragmented audience, the future of advertising is difficult to predict. Still, it is safe to say the remaining years of this century will be marked by dramatic change, with success going to those who can best predict its direction.

SUMMARY

Most of us think of advertising as having recent origins. Certainly the sophisticated marketing and advertising of the 1980s is a post–World War II phenomenon. However, the desire to persuade others through various means of communication dates back to prehistoric times. Mass advertising has its roots in the German and English handbills of the sixteenth century, which were either handed out or, more frequently, posted in central locations.

The history of advertising as we know it dates back to the American industrial revolution of the latter nineteenth century. During this period, a growing middle class, mass production, expanded transportation, and high-speed printing presses combined to pave the way for modern marketing and advertising.

The years 1900 and 1920 saw the introduction of a number of legal and regulatory restrictions on advertising. This period was also marked by a sense of professionalism in advertising and self-regulation from within the industry as people began to understand the immense power of advertising.

The period from 1950 to 1975 was one of consolidation and growth. Advertising budgets grew at unprecedented rates and took on a new importance in the selling of virtually all products. If this period was one of growth, the present era may become known as one of change. The new communication technology, only a dream ten years ago, is today a reality. With it come opportunities and responsibilities that advertisers of earlier periods could not have imagined.

QUESTIONS

1. Briefly discuss the three broad periods of advertising history.
2. Identify the following:
   (a) Hoarding
   (b) Siquis
   (c) *Weekly Newes of London*
   (d) William Claxton
   (e) *Printers' Ink* Model Statute
   (f) Corrective advertising
3. Why was the period from 1870 to 1900 so important in the development of modern advertising?
4. What role did religious publications play in the development of magazines during the nineteenth century?
5. Discuss the changes in advertising brought about by the introduction of radio in the 1920s.
6. Discuss the role of the War Advertising Council. What is its role today?
7. What is meant by the term *mega-agency*.

READINGS

BRUNER, GORDON C. II: "The Marketing Mix: A Retrospective and Evaluation," *Journal of Marketing Education,* Spring 1988, p. 29.

FULLERTON, RONALD A.: "How Modern Is Modern Marketing? Marketing's Evolution and the Myth of the 'Production' Era," *Journal of Marketing,* January 1988, p. 108.

HOTCHKISS, GEORGE BURTON: *Milestones of Marketing Thought* (New York: Macmillian, 1938).

MARCHANT, ROLAND: *Advertising the American Dream* (Berkeley: University of California Press, 1985).

POPE, DANIEL: *The Making of Modern Advertising* (New York: Basic Books, Inc., 1983).

PRESBREY, FRANK: *History and Development of Advertising* (Garden City, NY: Doubleday, 1929).

WOOD, JAMES PLAYSTED: *The Story of Advertising* (New York: Ronald Press, 1958).

TWO

Roles of Advertising

Advertising is the communications arm of the marketing process. Like any communications technique, advertising can tell a number of stories, each with its own goals and objectives. When advertising fails as a promotional tool, it is often because it is being asked to accomplish noncommunication goals—that is, it is being used where a promotional or marketing technique would be more successful.

Advertising is a method of delivering a message from a sponsor, through an impersonal medium, to many people. (The word *advertising* comes from the Latin *ad vertere,* meaning ''to turn the mind toward.'') The roles of advertising are many: It can be designed to dispose people to buy a product, to support a cause, or even to do less consuming (''demarketing''). It may be used to elect a candidate, raise money for charity, or publicize union or management positions during a strike (''advertorials''). Most advertising, however, is for the marketing of goods and services.

Demarketing. *The use of advertising and other promotional techniques to convince consumers to consume less of a product or service.*

Regardless of advertising's role in a particular instance, there are three primary rules for developing effective advertising:

In its role as marketing communicator, advertising informs, persuades, and reminds its publics about products, services, and causes. When Rich Cronin joined MTV Networks' Nickelodeon—Nick at Nite, he knew creating ''breakthroughs'' would be necessary. He's invested in ''scratch 'n' sniff'' ads, irreverent commercials showing giant iguanas swallowing policemen, mock ''teach-ins'' at schools—all to keep the network's audiences aware of its programming.

Rule 1: *All advertising must take the customer's view.* In the last quarter century, it has been recognized that products must meet the needs of consumers, not just the needs of sellers. That is, in developing new products, we start with potential consumer demand rather than with what products can be produced most efficiently. This notion of placing the consumer first is known as the *marketing concept.*

Rule 2: *Advertising is delivering sales messages.* The motive of advertising is not to write great literature, to present the prettiest picture, or to entertain the audience—though some or all of these elements are often present in advertising. Advertising is first and foremost a sales tool, and we must never lose sight of that fact.

Rule 3: *Customers buy benefits, not attributes.* Few advertisements consist of a list of product characteristics. Instead, advertisers show the consumer how the product meets some perceived need or desire. Consumers want to know ''What's in it for me?'' before they purchase a product. One of the basic mistakes novice advertisers make is to assume that consumers will see the benefit in their products. Be direct in pointing out consumer benefits. The distinction between attributes and benefits is a key one for developing effective advertising strategies.[1]

ADVERTISING AND THE MARKETING MIX

Regardless of its specific purpose and execution, successful advertising has two components: a marketing foundation and persuasive communication.

Advertising functions within a marketing framework. The American Marketing Association defines marketing as "the process of planning and executing the conception, pricing, promotion, and distribution of ideas, goods, and services to create exchanges that satisfy individual and organizational objectives."[2]

Marketing consists of four primary elements: product, price, distribution, and communication. While advertising is primarily concerned with communication, it depends on sound management decisions in the other three areas of the marketing mix[3] for its success. An inferior product, an overpriced product, or a product with inadequate distribution will doom even the finest advertising campaign.

In assessing the role of advertising, we must begin with an examination of the total marketing communication of the firm. Increasingly, firms are developing total promotion budgets rather than allocating funds to the various elements of marketing individually. In this way, advertising can complement, reinforce, and be coordinated with the other areas of the marketing mix. To understand the complex relationships among advertising and other marketing communications, we need to briefly review the following four elements:

Sales promotion. *Short-term incentive to create immediate sales of a product.*

1. *Personal selling*. Personal selling is face-to-face communication with one or more persons with the intent of making an immediate sale or developing a long-term relationship that will eventually result in a sale.
2. *Sales promotion*. Sales promotion is an extra incentive for a customer to make an immediate purchase. The incentive may be a reduced sale price, a cents-off coupon, or a chance to win a trip to Hawaii in a sweepstakes. Ideally, advertising builds long-term brand loyalty, while sales promotion acts as a short-term boost to sales.
3. *Public relations*. Public relations is a management tool designed to establish support among a firm's various internal and external publics. It differs from advertising in that while the advertiser directly pays for exposure of the message, controls in what medium and how often it will appear, and dictates exactly what it will say, public relations can influence all these elements, but has no precise control over them.
4. *Advertising*. Advertising is a message paid for by an identified sponsor and delivered through some medium of mass communication. Advertising is persuasive communication. It is not neutral; it is not unbiased; it says "I am going to sell you a product or an idea." In many respects, it is the most honest and frank type of propaganda.

One of the primary jobs of the marketing manager is to assess the role that advertising should play in the marketing-communications mix. This assessment includes an evaluation of marketing goals and strategies, identification of prime prospects, product characteristics, and the budget available for communication.

The emphasis in this chapter is on the diversity of the advertising function and how advertising must complement other areas of marketing objectives.

---

[1]Don E. Schultz and Stanley I. Tannebaum, *Essentials of Advertising Strategy* (Lincolnwood, IL: NTC Business Books, 1988), p. 9.

[2]Committee on Definitions, *Marketing Definitions: A Glossary of Marketing Terms* (Chicago: American Marketing Association, 1985).

[3]*Marketing mix* is a term coined in the early 1930s by Professor Neil H. Borden of the Harvard Business School to denote a marketing process that includes such factors as distribution, advertising, personal selling, and pricing.

ADVERTISING AS AN INSTITUTION

Gaining a broad perspective of advertising's role as an economic and social institution is critical to understanding the day-to-day functions of advertising. Advertising does not function in a vacuum. Rather, it is part of the changing social, cultural, and business environment of which it is a part. For example, "shifts in social values result in changes to consumer behaviors. Thus, it is critical for advertisers and marketers to keep track of shifts in values of their target segments if they hope to deal effectively with the resultant changes in behavior."[4] The ability to both accurately predict and react to a changing society is basic to successful advertising.

Advertising is an extremely complex institution. Not only does it have many segments, but its interactions with other sectors of society are not easily traced. Joseph E. De Deo, president of Young & Rubicam Europe, advocates viewing advertising's roles from the perspective of its contributions to consumers, business, and society.[5]

What Advertising Does for People

By imparting product knowledge, advertising has produced a world of informed consumers. Research has shown the benefits of educating customers in the use of correct film speeds. If consumers can be convinced to use different film speeds for different occasions, that increases satisfaction with 35mm photography, which in turn builds sales, says Fuji's Rod King, Senior Marketing Manager.

The most important thing advertising does is give consumers influence—or more accurately, *more* influence—over their economic lives. It does this by providing them with the knowledge they need to make informed choices about available products and services. It gives them the ability to judge the performance of the products and services they buy. It creates in them expectations that make them more demanding customers. And it produces a dialogue between producer and consumer, which forces the former to understand what the latter wants and how to best satisfy his or her desires.

What Advertising Does for Business

Without advertising, businesses would not be able to bring new products to the attention of enough consumers fast enough to make the enormous cost of creating, developing, manufacturing, and distributing these products a rational business proposition. In a large mass market economy, there is simply no other way to create a viable market for a new product or service. In addition to creating new markets, advertising is instrumental in revitalizing old markets and maintaining and defending markets for established brands.

What Advertising Does for Society

Advertising revenues maintain a highly diverse and innovative media structure at relatively low cost to people. Advertising is also a major stimulant to vigorous economic growth and stability. Finally, advertising promotes a more efficient use of national resources. It is the key link in the marketing process, the aim of which is to produce what the market needs and can absorb.

CONDITIONS CONDUCIVE TO THE USE OF ADVERTISING

Advertising is part of a "promotion mix" of communication variables, which also includes sales promotion, public relations, publicity, and personal selling. Graceland, Elvis Presley's former home in Memphis, spent only $100,000 in ads in 1988, but has poured efforts in more rewarding promotional strategies, such as sales promotions and public relations.

As we said earlier, a manufacturer has an enormous array of communication tools to choose from in selling a product. Generally, a company does not choose one technique over another, but rather determines the proper proportion of investment to make in

---

[4]Lynn R. Kahle, Basil Poulos, and Ajay Sukhdial, "Changes in Social Values in the United States During the Past Decade," *Journal of Advertising Research*, February/March 1988, p. 40.

[5]Joseph E. De Deo, "Why Over $109,800,000,000 Was Spent on Advertising in America Last Year," a presentation to Soviet managers.

advertising, sales promotion, and so on. They key to successful promotion is choosing the combination of techniques that produces the greatest sales volume at the lowest cost.

Exhibit 2.1 shows the wide variation in advertising efficiency among companies and industries in the United States. Whirlpool Corporation is an example of a company that has achieved outstanding efficiency in its advertising program. In fact, the company was recognized as the most efficient advertiser in the country in 1988. Exhibit 2.2 is an example of the type of advertising that has helped Whirlpool achieve such success. It should be noted that the figures in Exhibit 2.1 are *not* measures of management skill, since companies vary greatly in the tasks they assign to advertising. It is also true that sales per advertising dollar tend to decrease as total sales increase—that is, very large companies achieve economies of scale more easily than smaller ones.

Product line extension. *Using the same brand name to market a number of products. The technique is most successful when products are sold to one consumer segment.*

The risk of product failure and the tremendous increase in advertising costs have resulted in a more conservative approach to marketing new products. Many companies are developing extensions and variations on their present product lines to take advantage of already established consumer awareness. For example, in the extremely competitive cereal market, Nabisco introduced Blueberry-Filled Shredded Wheat and Kellogg added Nutri-Grain Biscuits as an extension of its successful Nutri-Grain cereal line. Several years ago the use of established brands in line extensions was less common. For example, Coca-Cola resisted using its brand identity when it introduced its first diet drink, Tab. However, more recently, both Coke and Pepsi marketed a number of diet cola variations under their brand names.

If we accept the fact that advertising is not the solution to every marketing problem, it is imperative that we identify those conditions most conducive to the effective use of

EXHIBIT 2.1

Note the wide variation in sales per advertising dollar among different industries. (Courtesy: *Advertising Age*, May 23, 1988, p. 48.)

Revenues per $1 in advertising expenditures for 100 leading national advertisers

		U.S. ad spending		U.S. 4th qtr. sales		Sales per $1 advertising		%
Primary business	**Advertiser**	**1987**	**1986**	**1987**	**1986**	**1987**	**1986**	**chg.**
AIRLINES	Texas Air Corp.	$6,491	$10,073	$2,078,554	$1,096,023	$320.25	$108.81	194.3%
	AMR Corp.	12,153	13,067	1,694,700	1,349,100	139.45	103.25	35.1%
	Allegis Corp.	19,890	14,834	2,100,000	2,536,000	105.58	170.96	-38.2%
	Delta Air Lines	17,955	15,435	1,614,856	1,137,150	89.94	73.67	22.1%
	Trans World Airlines	8,667	7,787	638,629	570,087	73.68	73.21	0.6%
APPLIANCES	General Electric Co.	29,277	27,262	10,952,760	11,163,880	374.10	409.51	-8.6%
	Xerox Corp.	11,450	10,087	2,940,000	2,590,000	256.77	256.76	0.0%
	International Business Machines	36,622	42,762	8,824,900	8,305,500	240.98	194.23	24.1%
	Hewlett-Packard Co.	6,629	5,458	1,183,680	939,600	178.57	172.15	3.7%
	Whirlpool Corp.	8,022	14,594	972,100	942,900	121.18	64.61	87.6%
	Matsushita Electric Industrial Co.	15,349	26,141	1,401,010	1,302,860	91.28	49.84	83.1%
	Eastman Kodak Co.	30,222	33,100	2,302,800	2,682,800	76.20	81.05	-6.0%
	Philips N.V.	27,267	26,488	1,151,400	1,288,200	42.23	48.63	-13.2%
	Tandy Corp.	29,816	29,906	1,120,580	1,028,560	37.58	34.39	9.3%
	Polaroid Corp.	16,522	11,156	300,133	301,254	18.17	27.00	-32.7%
AUTO	Ford Motor Co.	108,692	112,534	15,040,000	13,040,000	138.37	115.88	19.4%
	General Motors Corp.	225,983	166,480	23,476,420	22,719,030	103.89	136.47	-23.9%
	Chrysler Corp.	118,287	107,726	6,976,060	5,090,540	58.98	47.25	24.8%
CHEMICALS	Mobil Corp.	11,550	11,650	5,794,940	4,625,000	501.74	396.99	26.4%
	E.I. du Pont de Nemours & Co.	25,705	29,999	5,479,290	4,607,130	213.16	153.58	38.8%
	Monsanto Co.	7,460	9,731	1,236,820	1,051,900	165.80	108.09	53.4%
	Goodyear Tire & Rubber Co.	12,963	13,045	1,679,360	1,498,240	129.55	114.86	12.8%
	Dow Chemical Co.	13,873	15,753	1,654,620	1,283,860	119.27	81.50	46.3%
	American Cyanamid Co.	13,596	9,163	676,698	626,736	49.77	68.40	-27.2%
ENTERTAINMENT	Gulf & Western Industries	11,343	9,186	1,365,820	950,340	120.41	103.45	16.4%
	Capital Cities/ABC	14,490	11,291	1,408,139	1,187,324	97.18	105.16	-7.6%
	Warner Communications	10,318	10,568	846,600	682,260	82.05	64.56	27.1%
	CBS Inc.	11,615	12,685	672,510	691,650	57.90	54.52	6.2%
	Time Inc.	35,519	35,186	1,081,100	977,550	30.44	27.78	9.6%
	MCA Inc.	21,887	15,013	532,780	507,485	24.34	33.80	-28.0%
	Walt Disney Co.	32,079	23,570	734,600	660,900	22.90	28.04	-18.3%
FOOD	Borden Inc.	7,282	4,197	1,461,240	1,098,360	200.66	261.70	-23.3%
	Geo. A. Hormel & Co.	6,463	5,071	554,887	440,480	85.85	86.86	-1.2%
	Castle & Cooke	3,348	1,442	286,898	281,348	85.70	195.06	-56.1%
	Kraft Inc.	36,719	58,384	2,065,600	1,619,200	56.25	27.73	102.8%
	IC Industries	18,454	23,407	1,025,280	922,040	55.56	39.39	41.0%
	CPC International	7,474	7,523	362,681	444,666	48.52	59.11	-17.9%
	RJR Nabisco	115,141	118,452	4,419,000	4,217,000	38.38	35.60	7.8%
	Sara Lee Corp.	59,846	53,496	2,247,400	2,028,100	37.55	37.91	-0.9%
	Philip Morris Cos.	164,904	202,006	4,874,160	4,521,570	29.56	22.38	32.1%
	Hershey Foods Corp.	23,545	21,459	665,719	614,971	28.27	28.66	-1.3%
	Ralston Purina Co.	54,989	58,264	1,323,450	1,285,200	24.07	22.06	9.1%
	H.J. Heinz Co.	29,176	22,458	701,680	660,276	24.05	29.40	-18.2%
	Pillsbury Co.	77,516	78,497	1,516,500	1,424,700	19.56	18.15	7.8%
	Campbell Soup Co.	63,260	57,765	1,095,602	1,023,852	17.32	17.72	-2.3%

EXHIBIT 2.2

Whirlpool utilizes effective advertising to produce high sales/advertising ratios. (Courtesy: Whirlpool Corporation.)

advertising. While there are few guarantees of product success, three elements seem to be crucial in introducing new products:

1. *Consumer need*. First and foremost, a product must meet the needs of present and prospective consumers. As we noted earlier in this chapter, marketplace success begins with a determination of consumer desires. The profitable product is one that meets consumer demand in a unique and creative way.
2. *Marketing product expertise*. Product failure often results when a company brings to the marketplace a product with which it has had no previous experience. More and more companies are bringing out product line extensions to take advantage of existing expertise and tap into past successes. For example, Noxell, long a leader in cosmetics and skin care with its Cover Girl and Noxzema brands, achieved great success with Clarion cosmetics for those with sensitive skin.
3. *Filling a niche in the marketplace*. A product may be needed by consumers and fall within the marketing and production expertise of a firm. However, if another brand is already meeting the demand, there may be no opportunity to profitably add the new brand to the category. Is there a need for another cola drink?

A GOOD PRODUCT THAT MEETS A PERCEIVED NEED

The success of new product introduction is not dependent on advertising alone. Advertising creates awareness and encourages consumers to try new products—but it cannot make up for products' deficiencies. Ads touting the benefits of "hypoallergenic" Good Start infant formula got the new product off to a "good start." The same ads were recalled, when investigations revealed that some babies had allergic reactions to the product.

> The fact of the matter is we are successful in selling good products and unsuccessful in selling poor ones. In the end, consumer satisfaction—or lack of it—is more powerful than all our [promotional] tools and ingenuity put together. . . . You know the story. We had the perfect dog food except for one thing—the dog wouldn't eat it.[6]

Advertising can often gain a product initial trials from a number of consumers. However, it cannot achieve long-term repeat sales for an inferior product. A perfect example of a product that failed despite strong advertising support and initial consumer enthusiasm is Premier cigarettes. Introduced as a cleaner, "smokeless" cigarette, it was welcomed by smokers when it rolled out in a test market. However, most of those who tried the cigarette thought it tasted terrible, and sales fell far short of original forecasts.

Advertisers must realize that consumer demand is not created simply by product characteristics and function. Rather, it encompasses a host of product benefits of a qualitative and psychological nature. Consumption is determined by a complex environment in which the consumer lives and works.

> We have seen that in the consumer society the consumer, not the product, is the core of the message system about the sphere of consumption. Not the consumer as isolated individual, however: the act of consumption is always a social process. In selecting, using, and enjoying things people look around to find out what others are doing. We can call this need for individuals to relate their tastes and choices to those of others the "intersubjective" aspect of consumption activity. It is bound up with a more general behavior pattern that appears to be deeply rooted in the human personality—the concern with "relative standing," the continual scanning of the social landscape to ascertain how others are doing and to compare one's own condition with theirs.[7]

Many advertisements for upscale products portray a sense of style rather than specific product benefits (see Exhibit 2.3).

Sales, Revenues, and Profit Potential

Advertising, in its ability to reach large numbers of consumers, is the *least expensive* means of promotion—on a sales versus exposure basis. With the help of Hollywood stuntman, the new frozen novelty, Citrus Snowburst, from Kraft General Foods, climbed out of the clutter of summertime snacks. The "delivery man" headed up the New York Daily News skyscraper on a trapeze to bring the new thirst-quencher to a roofing crew—while hundreds of people gathered below to watch the "feat."

Before considering advertising, a company must examine the potential for sales, revenues, and profits from its products. A study of industrial products found that the higher a company's market share, the more it typically spends on media advertising (see Exhibit 2.4). As we will see later in this chapter, consumer product advertising usually demonstrates the opposite relationship between advertising and sales: As market share for consumer products increases, the ratio of advertising-to-sales decreases. Advertising is generally regarded as the least expensive means of market communication. Companies and brands with high market shares tend to be those that are most established in the marketplace. Consequently, these companies can devote a high proportion of their promotional budget to advertising. Smaller companies may find it necessary to spend more money in relatively expensive promotional categories such as dealer incentives or even personal selling to compete with larger competitors.

Regardless of a company's relative competitive situation, the important factor in advertising is to develop a plan that contributes to profitability. Don't fall into the trap of viewing sales and revenues as a substitute for profits. A quick review of the last decade would show that some of the largest companies in the United States (in terms of sales volume) experienced some of the largest losses.

---

[6]*The Role of Advertising in America,* a publication of the Association of National Advertisers, 1988.

[7]William Leiss, Stephen Klein, and Sut Jhally, *Social Communication in Advertising* (New York: Methuen Publications, 1986), p. 247.

EXHIBIT 2.3

For many products, the emotional environment of an ad is more important than the copy. (Courtesy: Remy Martin.)

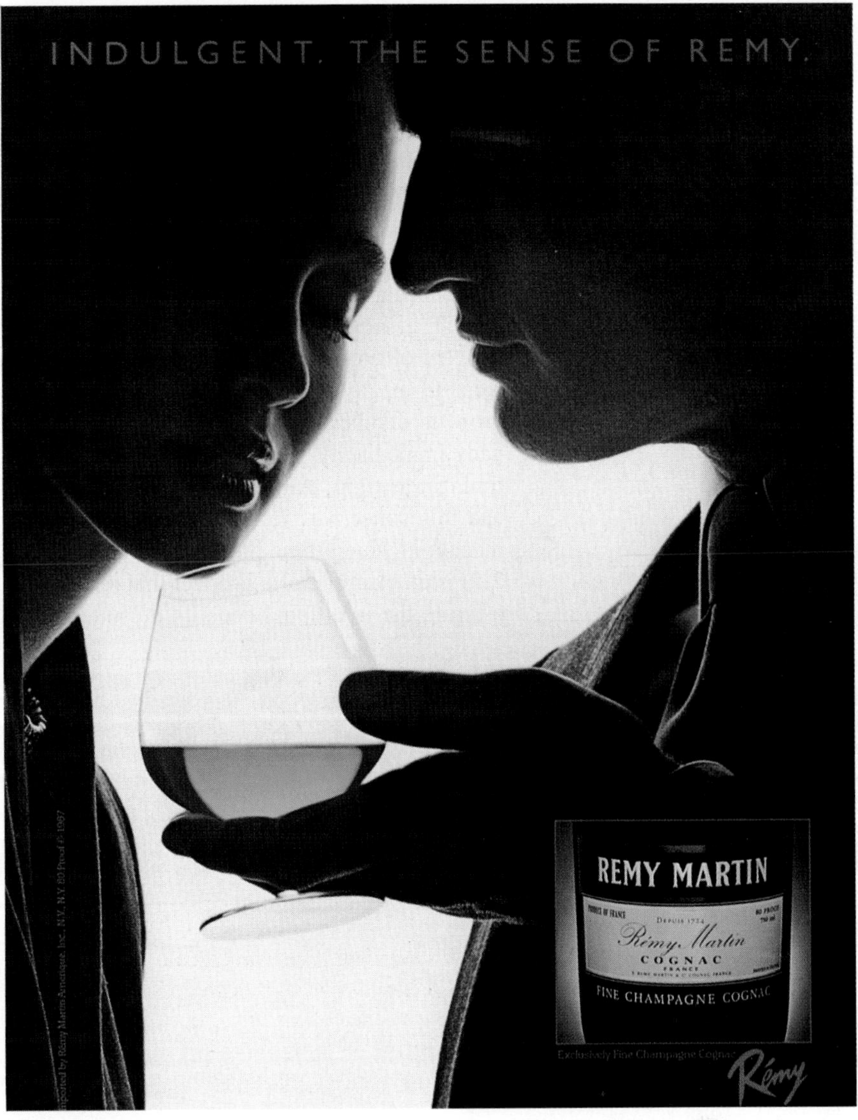

EXHIBIT 2.4

Market share is closely related to the amount of money industrial companies spend on advertising. (Courtesy: Cahners Publishing Company.)

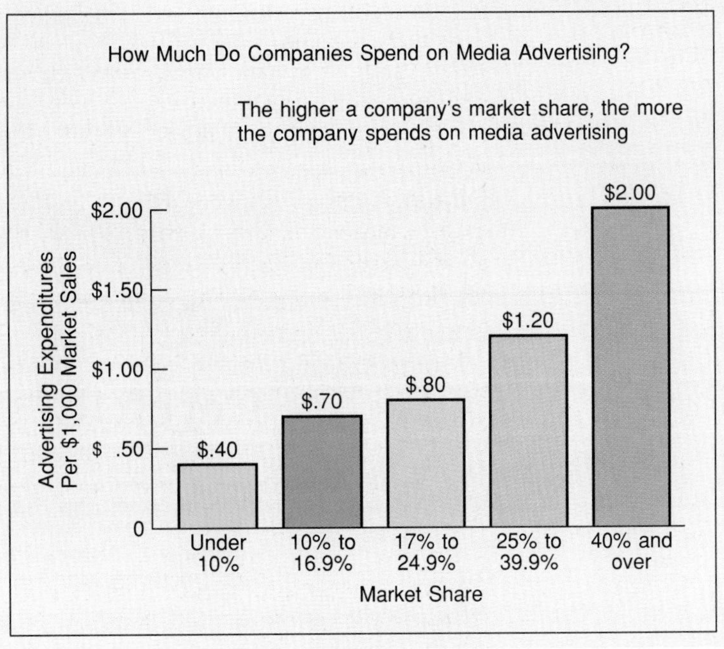

Product Timing

In introducing a product to the market, advertising is the vehicle to use to *inform* the public. New car, Saturn, will not show its car in initial advertising, but will use its first generation ads, instead, to build consumers' anticipation about the vehicle.

Product quality must be combined with proper timing if advertising is to be successful. That is, the best-made product for which there is no demand will be no more successful than the most inferior product. However, advertising may contribute to the acceptability and adoption rate of certain products by showing how a product meets an underlying consumer need unfulfilled by existing products.

The major product success stories tend to be about new products that caught a social trend just before it became a primary consumer demand. In the early 1980s Del Monte introduced a line of salt-free canned vegetables that became a major part of its product line. The same introduction ten years earlier would have been premature since the dangers of consuming excessive sodium were not well publicized. Likewise, Orval Kent Company recognized both the desire for more healthy eating habits and the growing number of singles in the population and marketed Salad Singles. The company immediately gained a 50 percent share of the prepared salad market because its timing was right. A healthy lifestyle is important to a growing number of Americans, and this concern is reflected in both the type of products being introduced and the manner in which these products are being marketed. PAM Cooking Spray (see Exhibit 2.5) is an example of a product that recognizes consumers' changing eating habits by offering the traditional benefits of butter minus the cholesterol.

EXHIBIT 2.5

Appeals to consumers' desire for a healthy lifestyle are an increasingly important component of many food ads. (Courtesy: Boyle-Midway Household Products, Inc.)

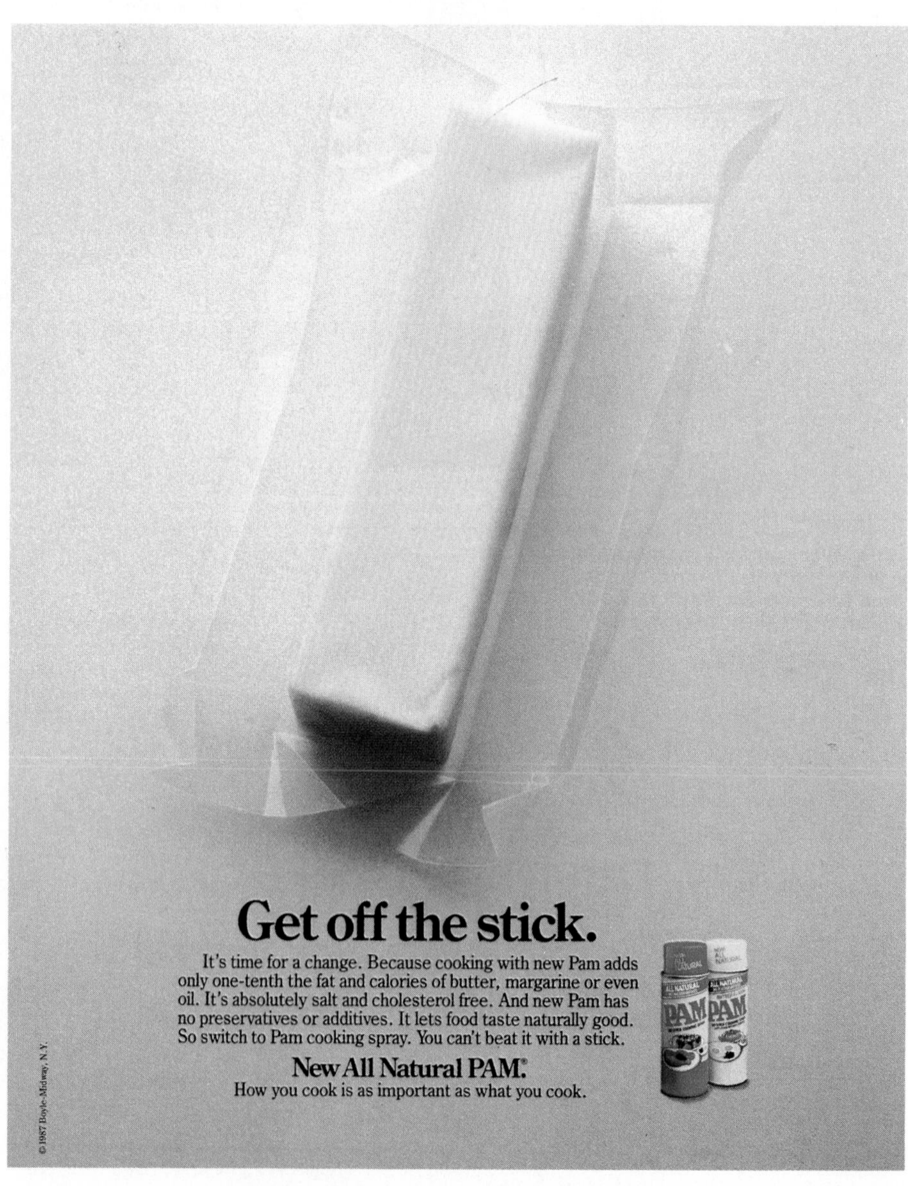

Get off the stick.
It's time for a change. Because cooking with new Pam adds only one-tenth the fat and calories of butter, margarine or even oil. It's absolutely salt and cholesterol free. And new Pam has no preservatives or additives. It lets food taste naturally good. So switch to Pam cooking spray. You can't beat it with a stick.
New All Natural PAM.
How you cook is as important as what you cook.
© 1987 Boyle-Midway, N.Y.
PAM
PAM

On the other hand, poor timing can be fatal to a marketing plan. Poor timing can consist of either entering a market for which insufficient demand has been established, or staying with a product too long after it has passed its sales peak, or introducing a brand into a saturated market whose potential has been largely exhausted. These problems stem from the failure to read changing consumer attitudes properly. For example, Sears, Roebuck & Company, while selling huge amounts of basic clothing, has a problem marketing fashion lines. ''Once driven by price and value, the mass-market clothing business today rides on status and style. But Sears has failed to move with the industry. For fashion apparel—and today, that includes sports clothes as well as one-of-a-kind evening gowns—sends the clearest message to the market about whom a store wants to serve.''[8]

Brand Name

Advertising accentuates the use of *brand names*—whether they are family brands or individual brands. *Roper Report's* the recognition of differences among brands is on the *rise*. Wealthier people are more likely to find differences among brands, and men are far more likely than women to draw distinctions among products, such as automobiles, television sets, gasoline, and beer.

Advertising is only possible because of the use of brand names. Without the guarantee of consistent quality that is inherent in brand development, advertising could serve only a limited function. As we shall show in Chapter 21, its brands and other identifying trademarks are among a company's most valuable assets, and firms go to great lengths to protect them.

Manufacturers often wonder whether they should distribute new products under their own brand names, develop new brands for them, or even sell them through large retail outlets under the stores' private brands. Actually, only a few products can be marketed successfully under store labels, so the choice for most manufacturers is between introducing a new product under the existing brand name and marketing it as a different brand.

Because of the time and expense involved in establishing individual brands, the trend in recent years has been to emphasize corporate identity. Large companies such as General Motors, Del Monte, and Du Pont increasingly promote their corporate identity as well as the individual brands they distribute. Often their advertisements are part of institutional messages that, in effect, sell the total company's commitment to quality (see Exhibit 2.6). The strategy of corporate identification works much better when the brands have some common usage or target market to which they are directed.

Product Differentiation

One of the keys to a successful product is that it have some attribute(s) unavailable in other products. Sometimes this differentiation is as obvious as a lower price; other times it may be a beneficial, but hidden, characteristic or a qualitative feature of style or prestige that the company and its advertising have created for the product.

To show consumers how different products are, advertising is used to help illustrate intrinsic characteristics. Consumers will get to ''mouth feel'' Lite Fantastic ice cream in Iowa supermarkets very soon. It's the only way to impart its creaminess resembling real ice cream, while promoting its unique properties—no sugar, no fat, and no cholesterol.

In every instance, consumers' perception of the product differentiation is crucial. Take a product being sold at a lower price than its competitors. Does this pricing cause the consumer to perceive the product as a bargain? Or does it reflect poorly on the quality of the product, making it seem a cheap brand to be avoided? A bargain-priced TV set is entirely different from a bargain perfume in marketing strategy and perceived differentiation by the consumer.

In searching for the competitive advantage of a product difference, advertisers often make one of two mistakes. The first is to promote a feature that is of little importance to consumers or is taken for granted. For example, a grocery store has wider aisles than other stores, but is this of major importance to shoppers? The second error advertisers make is to overlook consumer benefits that are shared by other brands, but haven't been promoted to consumers. Most beer is drunk at night. Michelob took this simple fact and turned it into a theme: ''The Night Belongs to Michelob.'' By combining that

[8]David Snyder and Peter D. Waldstein, ''Sears' Clothes Woes,'' *Advertising Age*, July 18, 1988, p. 18.

EXHIBIT 2.6

Du Pont sells corporate quality in a dramatic fashion. (Courtesy: Du Pont.)

The difference between a shattered windshield and a shattered life.
On November 17, 1986, the car in which Tara Meyer was riding was in an accident. Unfortunately, she wasn't wearing her seat belt. So like 150,000 other victims each year, her head hit and shattered the windshield.
But unlike many of the others, Tara suffered no facial cuts or lacerations.
The difference?
A new idea developed by a group of Du Pont engineers. They believed that a thin layer of plastic along the inside of the windshield would keep the razor-sharp, shattered glass on the outside—away from the occupants.
Their idea helped make more than just a safer windshield... it made a difference.
And that's something we try to do in everything we do.
At Du Pont, we make the things that make a difference.

Better things for better living.
DU PONT

theme with sophisticated, sometimes mysterious slice-of-life advertising, it was able to successfully differentiate itself from other upscale beers.

Positioning: The New Differentiation

Sellers have always attempted to differentiate their products. Marketing has seen three major techniques of product differentiation in its history.

Positioning. *The creation of a particular attitude toward a product in the mind of consumers.*

1. *The product era.* Advertising during the product era focused on product features. Every product tried to be different, and those that couldn't copied the features of the leaders in each product category. Your "better mousetrap" was quickly followed by two more just like it, both claiming to be better than yours.
2. *The image era.* In the 1960s, companies found that reputation, or image, was more important in selling a product than any specific product feature. David Ogilvy and his "man in the Hathaway shirt" is credited with ushering in this period. However, as every company tried to establish a reputation for itself, the noise level became so high that relatively few companies succeeded.
3. *The positioning era.* Positioning is not what you do to a product, but what you do to the mind of the consumer. To succeed in our overcommunicated society, a company must create a position in the prospect's mind, a position that takes into account not only the company's own strengths and weaknesses, but also those of its competitors. In the positioning era, it's not

enough to invent or discover something new. Rather, you must be first to get into the prospect's mind.[9]

By positioning a product to occupy a unique "space in the mind of a consumer," the marketer can use advertising to convey a distinctive message. Carnival Cruise Lines, the firm behind the repositioning of the cruise business, started the trend when it stopped selling a voyage on an ocean liner and began selling *fun*.

Successful advertising must communicate a message that makes the product stand apart from all others. Modern advertising has been criticized for trying to make obscure and inconsequential product differences important. There is no question that some advertising offers little information to the consumer, but the best and most successful ads are for products that are clearly different from their competitors and convey this difference effectively. The Hormel Bacon Bits advertisement (see Exhibit 2.7) is an example of such an effective differentiation.

Price

The *price-quality ratio* is more easily illustrated, when advertising is employed to *show* consumers the value of the product. Mary Kay Cosmetics is shifting away from its image of an old-fashioned, down-home company. Using full-page ads in upscale women's magazines, it has discontinued its "all-pink" policy and has given way to more sophisticated off-white. And the old logo is set in more modern, block type to appeal to contemporary women.

We often think that the product with the lowest price has a competitive advantage over its competition. But another way of viewing price is that it must be *right*. By right price, we mean one that is considered and promoted within the general marketing strategy of the brand. A premium price and the quality that such a price implies can be important elements in a product's success. A L'Oréal hair color ad that states "It costs a little more, but I'm worth it" is obviously using a different marketing strategy than a Suave shampoo ad that says the only difference between it and other brands is "it costs less."

A product's price will largely determine what advertising strategy can be used in selling it. Will price be emphasized? Will the product be sold primarily through discount stores? Will it be sold as an upscale brand emphasizing quality? The answers to these questions are usually decided by the company's pricing policy relative to its competition. Manufacturers often go to great lengths to protect their price structure. For instance, some major television manufacturers announced that they would not provide advertising allowances to retailers who undercut their minimum prices. The U.S. Supreme Court affirmed the right of companies to stop selling to retailers and wholesalers who engaged in heavy price-cutting of their products.

[9] Al Ries and Jack Trout, *Positioning: The Battle for Your Mind* (New York: McGraw-Hill Book Company, 1986), pp. 23–24.

EXHIBIT 2.7

Product differentiation is the central theme of effective comparative advertising. (Courtesy: Geo. A. Hormel & Company.)

VARIATIONS IN THE IMPORTANCE OF ADVERTISING

Reebok shoes increased their advertising budget 33 percent, to $40 million, for 1989. Nike's $34 million advertising budget represented a jump of 36 percent for the same period. The fierce competition between these two manufacturers of sports shoes required significant increases in advertising expenditures. The 30+ percent increase of Reebok and Nike compares to an 8 percent increase in total U.S. advertising expenditures. The point is that companies vary widely in their advertising expenditures.

Competitive forces in the marketplace may encourage increases in forms' advertising budgets—*beyond* what they would consider reasonable to meet their goals. Tretorn, the tennis footwear maker, has *tripled* its advertising budget and increased its public relations budget *by tenfold*, just to try to keep pace with industry leaders, Nike and Reebok.

There are a number of reasons for the variations. No single reason may explain why advertising plays such a large role for one firm and a relatively insignificant one for another. However, the following guidelines provide insight into the differences:

1. *Volume of sales*. In almost every case, as sales increase, the percentage of dollars spent on advertising decreases. This is largely a matter of economies of scale—that is, regardless of a company's sales figures, there are only so many prospects to be reached with advertising. After sales reach a certain level, the ad budget may continue to rise, but at a slower rate.
2. *Advertising's role in the marketing mix*. As we stated earlier in this chapter, advertising is only one element of the marketing-communications process. Companies often lower the proportion of dollars they devote to advertising as they invest money in sales promotions, dealer incentives, or personal selling.
3. *Competitive environment and profit margin*. As we saw in the Reebok/Nike example, competition usually leads to increases in advertising budgets. How much these budgets go up is often a function of profit margins. For instance, industries such as pharmaceuticals and soaps and cleaners traditionally are able to spend a higher percentage of their sales on advertising since the cost of producing their goods is relatively low.
4. *Overall management philosophy of advertising*. Obviously, the ultimate factor in the use of advertising is management's decision to use advertising versus some other promotional tool. In the end, the money spent on advertising reflects top management's confidence in advertising as a marketing tool and the need to spend promotional dollars. For instance, Ryan's steak houses, a southeastern restaurant chain, does no advertising. This very successful operation depends solely on word-of-mouth.
5. *New-product introductions*. The greater the number of new products it introduces and the higher the percentage of its total revenues from new products, the greater a company's advertising budget will be. Exhibit 2.8 shows the companies that introduced the most new products during 1985–1987. Almost without exception, these companies had greater-than-average advertising-to-sales ratios.

EXHIBIT 2.8
(Courtesy: *Advertising Age*.)

Top product introducers

Number of introductions 1985, 1986, 1987	
1. Campbell Soup Co.	354
2. General Foods	326
3. Lever Bros./Lipton	260
4. Kraft Inc.	243
5. RJR Nabisco	231
6. ConAgra	216
7. Nestlé	213
8. General Mills	197
9. H.J. Heinz	191
10. Sara Lee	184

Source: New Product News

We now move on to the next big step—fitting advertising into the marketing process.

THE PLACE OF ADVERTISING IN THE MARKETING PROCESS

One of the problems in discussing advertising is how to convey a sense of commonality about a business function that is used in such diverse ways. There are a number of approaches to the study of the functions and execution of advertising. But no matter what approach one takes, advertising must be viewed within a general marketing perspective.

A common thread running through all advertising is that it is a special form of marketing communication. Effective advertising must be successful on two levels: (1) communicating and (2) carrying out marketing goals. Unfortunately, success on one level often means failure on the other—for example, people enjoy and remember a certain humorous ad, but can't identify the brand of the product it advertises.

Perhaps the easiest way to evaluate advertising's role in the marketing process is according to the *directness* of the intended communication effect and the anticipated *time* over which that effect is supposed to operate. In other words, how much of the total selling job should be accomplished by advertising and over what time frame should the job be accomplished?

Different kinds of advertising are designed to produce different responses—immediate response or long-term, direct or indirect. Northwest Airline's World Horizons Program, which offers travel packages and discounts to senior citizens, features commercials showing the early days of retirement. They're designed to invoke immediate reaction, if the audience is over 65—or "gifts" for family—or interesting options for the future.

Advertising designed to produce an immediate response in the form of purchase of a product is called *direct-action, short-term advertising*. Most retail advertising falls into this category. An ad that runs in the newspaper this morning should sell some jeans this afternoon. Advertising used as a direct sales tool, but designed to operate over a longer time frame, is called *direct-action, long-term advertising*. This advertising category is used with high-ticket items (washers and automobiles) for which the purchase decision is a result of many factors and the purchase cycle is relatively long.

Another category of advertising is used as an indirect sales tool. Such indirect advertising is intended to affect the sales of a product only over the long term, usually by promoting the general attributes of the manufacturer rather than specific product characteristics. Included in this category are most institutional and public relations advertisements. The exception would be remedial public relations advertising designed to overcome some negative publicity concerning product safety, labor problems, and the like.

Regardless of the category it falls into, advertising should advance a product or service on its journey through the marketing channel. The objectives and execution of advertising will change as we move along this channel, which means there will be different forms of advertising for different levels of distribution.

Advertising to the Consumer:

- National advertising
- Retail (local) advertising
- End-product advertising
- Direct-response advertising

Advertising to Business and Professions:

- Trade advertising
- Industrial advertising
- Professional advertising
- Institutional advertising

National advertising is *general* in its approach, seeking to establish demand for a product. Better known brands have achieved high percentage of consumer loyalty. Kodak, the number one camera and film maker in the United States, uses the "family" approach in its heavy reliance on sales promotion at entertainment and theme parks. Promotions for its *single-use* and *waterproof cameras* are aimed at *vacationers,* who are heavy users of Kodak picture-taking products.

National advertising. *Created to sell a branded product through a number of outlets in different parts of the country. It does not have to be truly national in character.*

ADVERTISING TO THE CONSUMER

National Advertising

The term *national advertising* refers to advertising by the owner of a trademarked product (brand) or service sold through different distributors or stores, wherever they may be. It does not necessarily mean that the product is sold nationwide.

National advertising is usually the most general in terms of product information. Items such as price, retail availability, and even service and installation are often omitted from national advertising. Since each retailer will play a major role in the final sale of the product, national ads for companies such as Campbell Soup cannot be extremely specific (see Exhibit 2.9). National advertising seeks to establish demand for a product, especially one sold through self-service outlets. Ideally, the customer comes into the retail store already presold on a certain brand because of its national advertising. The better known and established the brand, the greater the potential brand loyalty.

EXHIBIT 2.9

National advertisers such as Campbell Soup rarely offer specific price information in their ads or list retailers stocking their products. (Courtesy: Campbell Soup.)

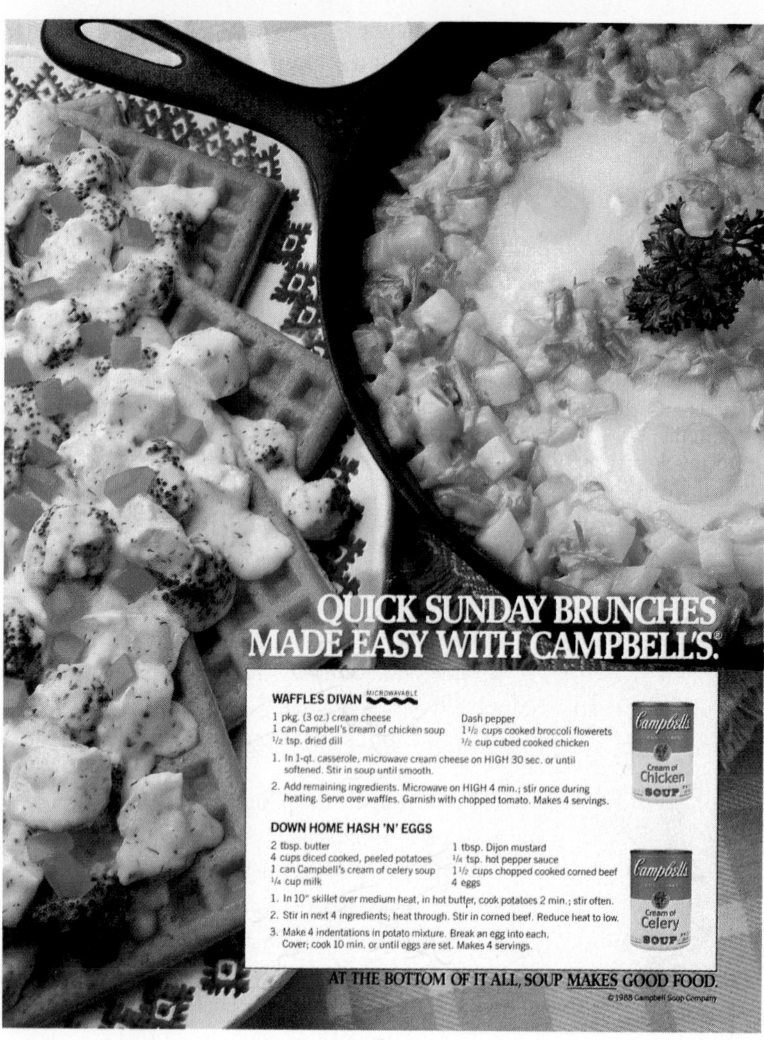

Retail (Local) Advertising

Retail advertising. *Advertising that attempts to bring consumers into a particular store to buy any brand of merchandise that the store carries.*

Retail advertising is usually selling not only individual products, but also the retail establishment as the place to buy a number of brands. Most retail advertising has a distinctive style that is used regardless of the particular product being advertised. It is also very specific about the items being advertised as well as about the store.

Retail advertising often includes price information, service and return policies, location of the store, and hours of operation—information that the national advertiser cannot provide. Often retailers include a number of products in a single advertisement to show the range of merchandise available. Many retail advertisements are designed to feature sale merchandise that will build store traffic, with the hope that customers will buy other full-priced items once they are inside the store.

The *focus* on retail and local advertising is on the *outlet,* where products can be purchased. An innovative way to get women to buy cosmetics in department stores is to feature *custom-blending products* in their ads, says Bloomingdale's. It personalizes the products and turns them into something that can't be found anywhere else.

End-Product Advertising

Although end-product advertising is primarily directed at consumers, it is a hybrid category because it is also intended for the trade and industrial levels. Basically, a company such as Monsanto (see Exhibit 2.10) or Du Pont advertises one of its products that is used in the manufacture of other products. Often these advertisements carry a line indicating that consumers should ask for products that contain a particular component, such as 100 percent wool, Teflon, Scotchgard, or Stainblocker.

As we said, end-product advertising functions at several levels of the marketing channel simultaneously. Successful end-product advertising creates a demand among

EXHIBIT 2.10

Monsanto uses effective end-product advertising to encourage consumers to buy products with Monsanto components. (Courtesy: Monsanto Company.)

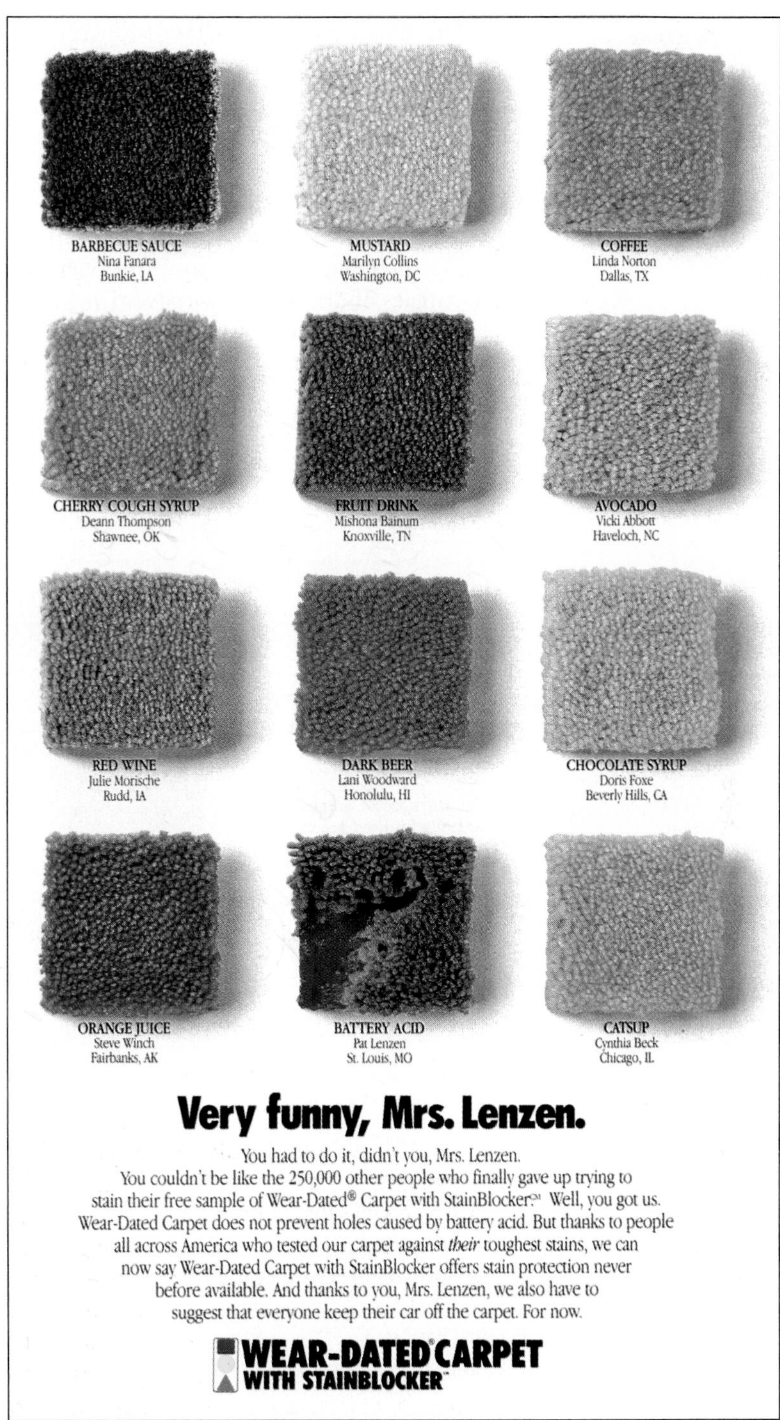

BARBECUE SAUCE
Nina Fanara
Bunkie, LA
MUSTARD
Marilyn Collins
Washington, DC
COFFEE
Linda Norton
Dallas, TX
CHERRY COUGH SYRUP
Deann Thompson
Shawnee, OK
FRUIT DRINK
Mishona Bainum
Knoxville, TN
AVOCADO
Vicki Abbott
Haveloch, NC
RED WINE
Julie Morische
Rudd, IA
DARK BEER
Lani Woodward
Honolulu, HI
CHOCOLATE SYRUP
Doris Foxe
Beverly Hills, CA
ORANGE JUICE
Steve Winch
Fairbanks, AK
BATTERY ACID
Pat Lenzen
St. Louis, MO
CATSUP
Cynthia Beck
Chicago, IL
Very funny, Mrs. Lenzen.
You had to do it, didn't you, Mrs. Lenzen.
You couldn't be like the 250,000 other people who finally gave up trying to stain their free sample of Wear-Dated® Carpet with StainBlocker.SM Well, you got us. Wear-Dated Carpet does not prevent holes caused by battery acid. But thanks to people all across America who tested our carpet against *their* toughest stains, we can now say Wear-Dated Carpet with StainBlocker offers stain protection never before available. And thanks to you, Mrs. Lenzen, we also have to suggest that everyone keep their car off the carpet. For now.
WEAR-DATED CARPET
WITH STAINBLOCKER

End-product advertising uses "pull" strategy to make consumers aware of certain ingredients used in the manufacture of products, hoping they will ask for these ingredients when they make their purchases. Sears and du Pont will jointly advertise a new Lasting Images line of furniture, featuring *du Pont's Future Style support system,* to be sold exclusively by Sears.

consumers that leapfrogs the manufacturer of the finished product. Monsanto and other end-product advertisers hope that if they build consumer demand, manufacturers will be more inclined to use specific end products in their finished products. They also hope that retailers will either put pressure on manufacturers to meet this consumer demand or will buy from manufacturers who do.

Building demand through end-product advertising is not easy. A company must have a product that both manufacturers and consumers recognize and can be convinced will improve other products. These advantages are often not obvious in the finished product, so extensive advertising is required to make consumers aware of them. End-product advertising is a variant of the more traditional national advertising that asks the consumer to buy a product by name.

Direct-response advertising. *Advertising that promotes goods that are sold without going through a retailer. Any medium can carry direct-response advertising.*

Direct-Response Advertising

Consumers' changing lifestyles have prompted an increasing number of manufacturers to use direct marketing: selling a product from marketer to consumer without going through retail channels. The advertising used in direct marketing is referred to as *direct-response advertising* (see Exhibit 2.11). The primary benefit it offers is convenience. The number of women working, the increase in younger adults with more discretionary income, and the trend to a self-service economy have combined to make in-store shopping less convenient for many consumers.

Examples of direct-response advertising can be found in all the media. Products sold this way are most often available by mail, but companies are increasingly supplementing mail order with telemarketing to make direct buying even easier. Today credit cards and 800 toll-free service make immediate sales of a variety of merchandise possible. Cable television shopping channels and videocassettes give some consumers the opportunity to see merchandise "live" before ordering it from their living rooms. The future holds much promise for innovative ways of communicating with prospects.

EXHIBIT 2.11

A fast-paced lifestyle has created a number of opportunities for direct-response and shop-at-home buying. (Courtesy: Lenox Collections.)

Direct-response advertising promotes manufacturers' products directly to consumer, thereby by-passing wholesalers and retailers. The vehicles used include catalogs, bill-stuffers, television, and telemarketing. Before entering a market, Luminsque, a new cosmetic, conducts a massive direct mail campaign to potential users. The letters invite 35–45-year-old affluent women to chosen stores for customized "face-overs" and reduced price products.

A jewel of nature
to enjoy in your home

BLUEBIRD

Intricately crafted of the finest bisque porcelain and meticulously painted by hand

An original work of art available exclusively from Lenox

The vivid blue songbird gracefully alights amid pink roses, his plumage gleaming like a precious jewel in the summer sun. He is as beautiful and welcome as the roses that bloom around him... and as he sings, his cheerful spirit touches every heart.

Now you can enjoy all his vibrant charm and sweetness in *Bluebird,* an original work of art in fine bisque porcelain—exclusively from Lenox.

Bluebird is a sculpture delightfully true to life—from the bird's tiny beak and bright expression to its brilliant plumage. Even the sweetheart roses are perfectly recreated, down to the last petal of each pale pink flower and the tiniest vein of each delicate leaf.

Entirely painted by hand, *Bluebird* will provide a refreshing touch of nature and a striking flourish of color to your home. The burnt orange and rich blue of the feathers, the green leaves and blushing rose petals... all will be captured with convincing realism. And, as a continuing reminder of its superb quality, each imported work of art will also bear the Lenox® trademark in pure 24 karat gold.

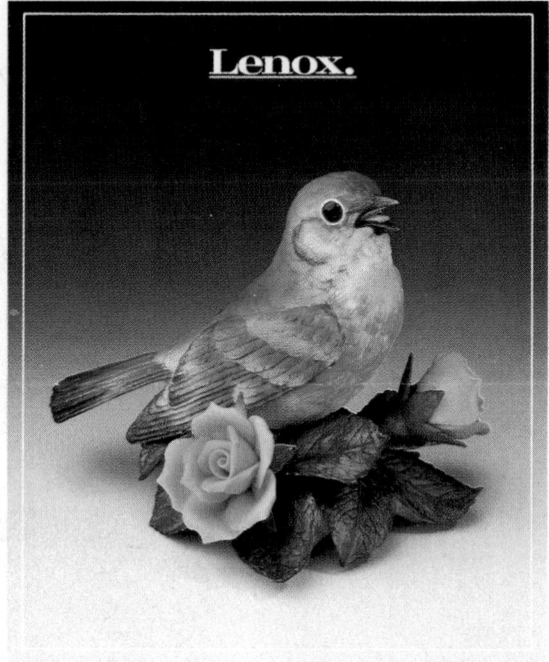

© Lenox, Inc. 1988

Shown actual size

Bluebird is available only direct from Lenox. To acquire this enchanting Lenox garden bird sculpture for your home, simply mail your reservation no later than April 30, 1988. Or, on credit card orders, call **TOLL FREE,** 24 hours a day, 7 days a week, **1-800-537-1600 ext. 988.** 39713

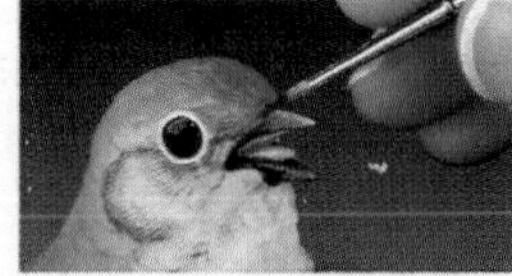

Painted by hand to reveal every detail of the bluebird's rich colors.

RESERVATION APPLICATION

Please enter my reservation for *Bluebird* by Lenox.
I need send no money now and prefer to pay as follows:

☐ DIRECT. I will be billed in 3 monthly installments of $13* each, with the first installment due in advance of shipment.

☐ BY CREDIT CARD. After shipment, please charge the full amount of $39* to the credit card indicated below:
☐ MasterCard ☐ VISA
☐ American Express

Account No. ______

Expires ______

*Plus $3.25 per sculpture for shipping and handling. State sales tax will be billed if applicable. Please allow 4 to 6 weeks for delivery.

Signature ______
All orders are subject to acceptance.

Name ______
PLEASE PRINT

Address ______

City ______

State ______ Zip ______
39713

Your application should be postmarked by April 30, 1988.

Mail to:

Lenox Collections
One Lenox Center • PO Box 3025
Langhorne, Pennsylvania 19093-0026

ADVERTISING TO BUSINESS AND PROFESSIONS

The average person doesn't see a very important portion of advertising because it is aimed at store buyers, doctors, architects, bankers, and others who are in a position to specify the advertiser's product for others to buy. This type of advertising is done in addition to advertising products to consumers for their personal use. Advertising to business takes several different forms.

Trade Advertising

> ***Trade advertising.*** *Advertising directed primarily to retail and wholesale merchants to convince them to carry certain national products in their inventory.*

Before consumers have an opportunity to purchase a product, it must be available in retail stores. Manufacturers use trade advertising to promote their products to wholesalers and retailers. Trade advertising tends to emphasize the product's profitability to retailers and the consumer demand that will create high turnover of the product for the retailer (see Exhibit 2.12).

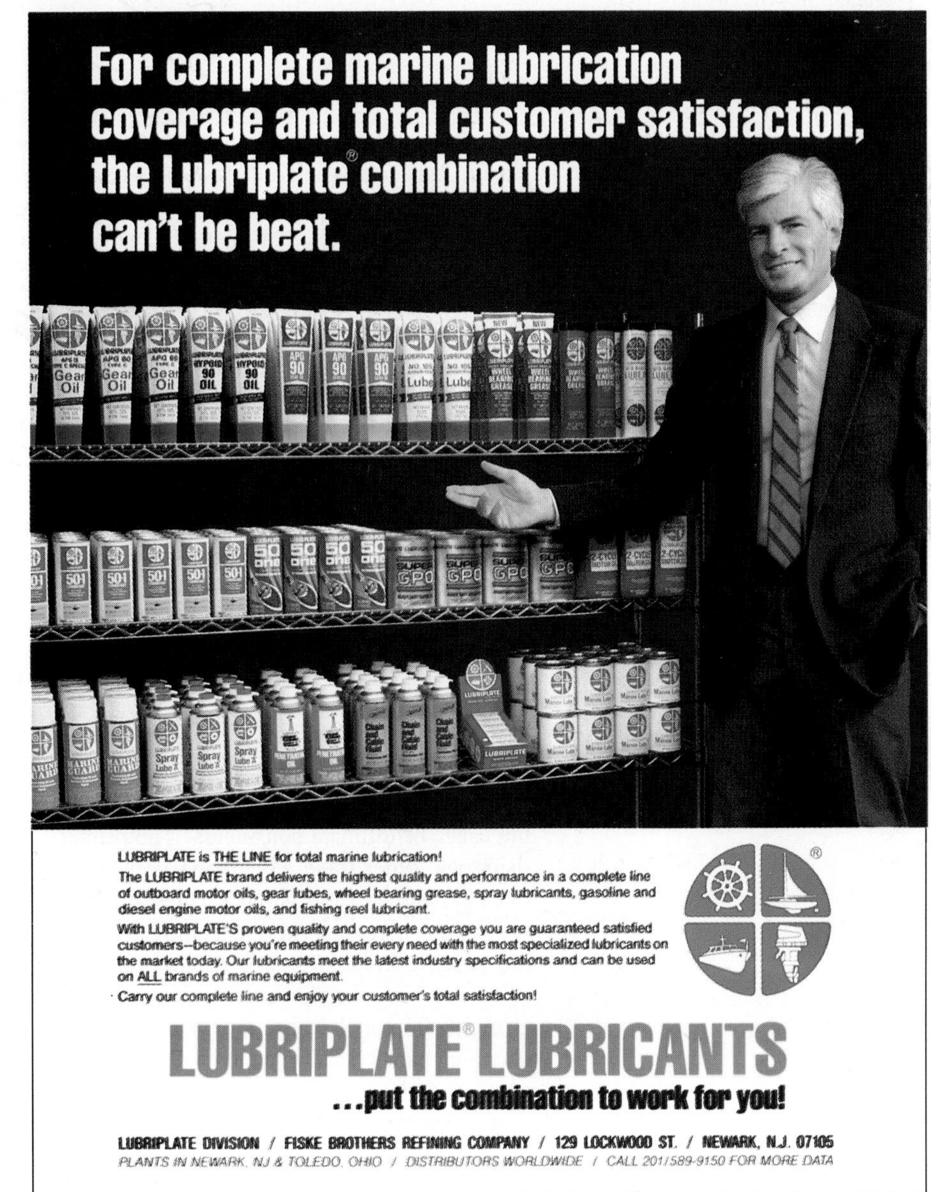

EXHIBIT 2.12

Note the manner in which trade advertising speaks directly to retail customers. (Courtesy: Lubriplate Lubricants.)

Trade advertising can be used to do three things:

1. *Get an initial trial for a product.* Manufacturers are interested in increasing the number of retail outlets that carry their brands. Trade advertising can create brand recognition for follow-up by personal salespersons, or it can offer coupons and 800 numbers for retailers to get more information.
2. *Increase trade support.* Manufacturers compete with countless other brands for shelf space and dealer support. For example, the typical grocery store stocks over 6,000 different items. Trade advertising can encourage retailers to give a prominent position to a company's products, use a manufacturer's point-of-purchase material, or take advantage of dealer incentives offered by a company.
3. *Announce consumer promotions.* Many trade advertisements offer a schedule of future consumer promotions. Manufacturers do this to let dealers know that they are supporting them with their own advertising and to encourage dealers to coordinate local promotions with the manufacturer's national advertising efforts.

Manufacturers often use trade advertising to encourage wholesalers and retailers to carry their products. HMK Advertising of Boston came up with the "Mystery Vacationer Promotion" to encourage travel agents to mention certain clients' vacation packages *first* to clients. The agents' reward is $1,000, not to mention free hotel stays and cruises.

There are approximately 8,000 trade publications—several for virtually every category of retail business. Although the average consumer probably has not heard of most of them, trade journals such as *Progressive Grocer* and *Drug Topics* play an important role in the advertising plans of most national advertisers.

Industrial Advertising

Industrial advertising. *Intended to those purchasing agents who buy industrial goods used in the manufacture of other products. Often used to introduce personal salespeople who actually make the sale.*

A manufacturer is a buyer of machinery, equipment, raw materials, and components used in producing the goods it sells. Those companies that produce machinery, equipment, or material to sell to other producers address their advertising to them in their industry publications. This method is quite unlike consumer advertising and is referred to as *industrial advertising*.

Industrial advertising is directed at a very specialized and relatively small audience. The target audience of most industrial advertising is industrial purchasing agents in a specific industry. Because industrial advertisements are written for experts, they often contain product specifications and details that only those well versed in a particular manufacturing segment would understand (see Exhibit 2.13).

Industrial advertising rarely seeks to sell a product directly because the purchase of industrial equipment is usually a complex process that includes a number of decision makers. Industrial advertising normally occupies a much less important role than consumer advertising. Its job is to establish a quality image and name recognition for a product, to communicate major product benefits, and perhaps most importantly, to open doors for salespersons who actually make the sale.

Advertising by manufacturers to other manufacturers to increase their awareness about the seller and his products is called industrial advertising. It is the most concentrated of all advertising categories, in that it seeks a very small, specialized audience. J. R. Simplot, with the promotional strategy of Director of Marketing Blaine Jacobson, went from a small potato firm to become McDonald's biggest potato supplier. It directed its trade advertising in the biggest uses of staples—fast-food organizations.

Professional Advertising

Professional advertising is similar in intent to other types of trade advertising. That is, it is directed toward people who are not the actual users of a product, but who influence the usage of ultimate consumers. The primary difference between professional advertising and other trade advertising is the degree of control exercised by professionals over the purchase decisions of their clients.

Whereas a grocery store encourages consumer purchases of certain goods by stocking specific brands, people can go to another store that has greater variety, lower prices, or better-quality merchandise. On the other hand, few people would think of changing doctors because a physician doesn't prescribe a certain brand of drugs or of changing banks because a bank orders checks for its customers from one printer versus another. Consequently, professionals often make the final purchase decision for their customers. Most customers are unaware of how professional advisers decide on the various brands of professional products and services they recommend (see Exhibit 2.14).

EXHIBIT 2.13

Industrial advertising is written in technical language for a knowledgeable, sophisticated audience. (Courtesy: Texaco Chemical Company.)

TEXACO'S NEW JEFFAMINE® EDR-148.
THE TOUGH, FLEXIBLE DIAMINE
SEEDED TO CURE FOUR TIMES FASTER.

Texaco Chemical's new JEFFAMINE EDR-148, used as a curing agent for epoxy resins, has the flexibility and toughness of our JEFFAMINE D, T, and ED series. Plus something extra.

EDR-148 cures four times faster at room temperature. Because it's not sterically hindered.

This fast-reacting polyether amine also has good electrical properties, is miscible in a wide range of solvents, and has excellent impact resistance and thermal shock properties. Which makes it a natural for epoxy resin curing in adhesives, coatings, casting, laminating, potting, encapsulating, and composites, as well as for fiber modification.

If you'd like to speed up your cure without sacrificing flexibility or toughness, make JEFFAMINE EDR-148 your top seed. Call or write: Marketing Manager, Specialty Chemicals, Texaco Chemical Company, P.O. Box 430, Bellaire, Texas 77401, (713) 432-3465.

JEFFAMINE EDR-148 structure: $H_2NCH_2CH_2OCH_2CH_2OCH_2CH_2NH_2$

QUALITY AMINES FROM QUALITY MINDED PEOPLE.

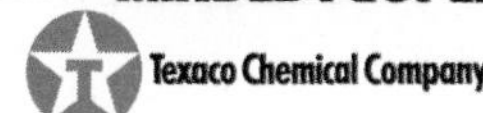

0736R2

EXHIBIT 2.14

Professional advertising often determines the products and services professionals recommend to their clients. (Courtesy: GE Capital.)

More Capital ideas. From the people who grew them.
For over 50 years, GE Capital has been providing American business with the capital it needs to grow on. And all that time, we've also been providing something else: ideas. A constant flow of thoughts, inspirations and innovative suggestions for making maximum use of every last dollar.
Today, our capital ideas are as much a part of our portfolio as the capital itself. In equipment leasing, acquisition funding, real estate and a dozen other areas, our people never tire of putting money to work in new and better ways (a few of which are detailed below).
If any of our capital ideas have started you thinking that we may be able to help your business, call GE Capital at our special toll-free number: 800 243-2222.
Let us put our brains and our resources to work for you.
Capital Ideas Grow at GE Capital.
Sailing The Ocean Blue Without The Green.
You can't keep your head above water in the highly competitive shipping business by sinking your working capital into containers and ships. That's why GE Capital has financed over $1 billion in ships and hundreds of thousands of containers for shipowners worldwide.
POLICY
Cancelling An Insurance Fallacy.
"Considering all the litigation, legislation and assorted red tape, structuring a leveraged buyout within the insurance industry is a near-impossibility." Not quite. In 1987, GE Capital put together two of the first major insurance LBOs–for a total of nearly $500 million.
Wheel Dealing, From Cradle To Grave.
For many auto dealers, GE Capital is a start-to-finish partner. We can finance the dealer's buildings and real estate, floor-plan his vehicle inventory, provide full leasing plans to retail customers–even liquidate trade-ins and end-of-lease vehicles through our network of auto auctions.
GE Capital

Institutional advertising. *Designed to sell the image and expertise of a company rather than the products it makes. It is basically an indirect, long-term sales technique.*

Should a firm decide to promote its *own image* in the marketplace, rather than its products, it will use institutional advertising. Like public relations, it puts the firm in the best possible "light." Since its vehicles have been chosen the official vehicles of the Universal Studios in Hollywood and Florida, Chrysler will be promoting the company's selection in forthcoming ads and commercials.

Institutional Advertising

You need to have a clear understanding of what differentiates institutional, or corporate, advertising from the other types of advertising discussed in this chapter. Institutional advertising is basically a promotional technique intended to portray a corporate image of overall excellence, apart from the benefits of any single product. Institutional advertising may show that the company is a good corporate citizen; that its products are both functional and socially responsible; or that its reputation for quality is beyond compare.

It often differs from other types of business advertising in that it appears in upscale consumer media and is addressed to a wider audience (see Exhibit 2.15).

NONPRODUCT ADVERTISING

Idea Advertising

Not all advertising is designed to sell a product or service. Both companies and nonprofit organizations often use advertising to convey ideas about some topic. Idea advertising may address tax legislation, union relations, or some other area of concern to a company. Other idea advertising addresses issues of more general concern to a group or an organization, such as church attendance or freedom of speech (see Exhibit 2.16).

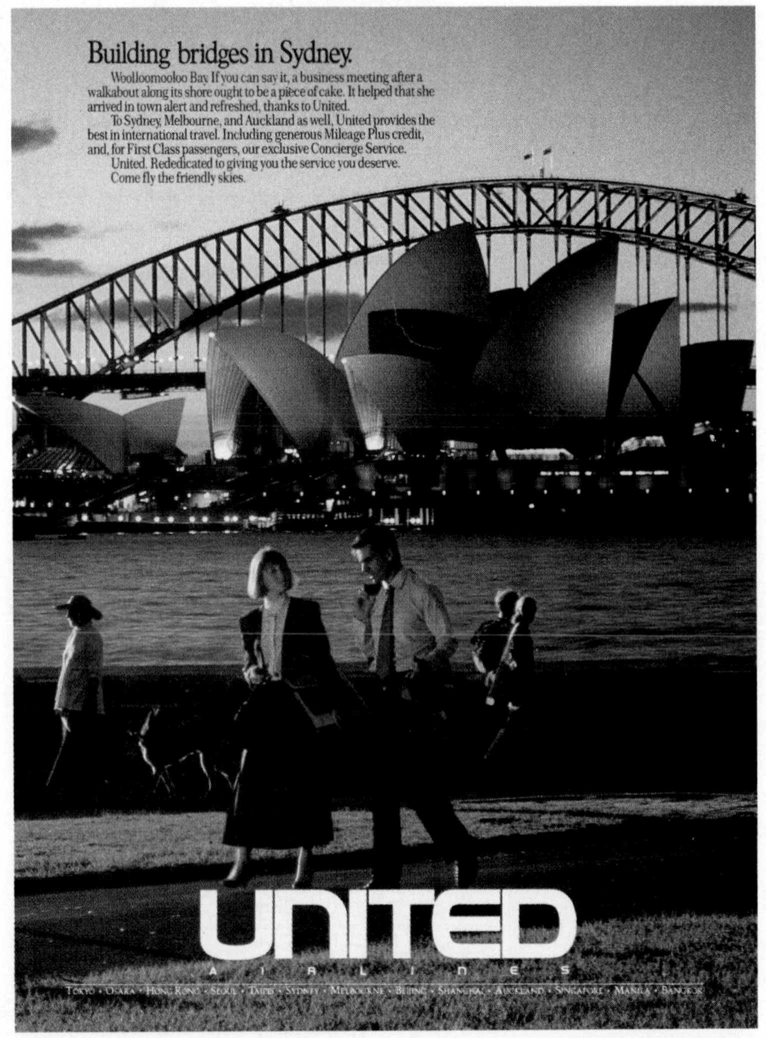

Building bridges in Sydney.
Woolloomooloo Bay. If you can say it, a business meeting after a walkabout along its shore ought to be a piece of cake. It helped that she arrived in town alert and refreshed, thanks to United.
To Sydney, Melbourne, and Auckland as well, United provides the best in international travel. Including generous Mileage Plus credit, and, for First Class passengers, our exclusive Concierge Service.
United. Rededicated to giving you the service you deserve.
Come fly the friendly skies.
UNITED
AIRLINES

EXHIBIT 2.15

Institutional advertising sells a corporate image rather than products. (Courtesy: United Airlines.)

To convey a special interest message to a particular target market, the sponsoring organization may use "idea" advertising as a promotional effort. Anheuser-Busch has created a department of consumer awareness and education to encourage responsible use of their products. Chairman August A. Busch III announced a fourfold increase in the budget supporting the "Know when to say when" television ad campaign.

EXHIBIT 2.16

Advertising effectively promotes ideas as well as products. (Courtesy: The Freespeech Committee.)

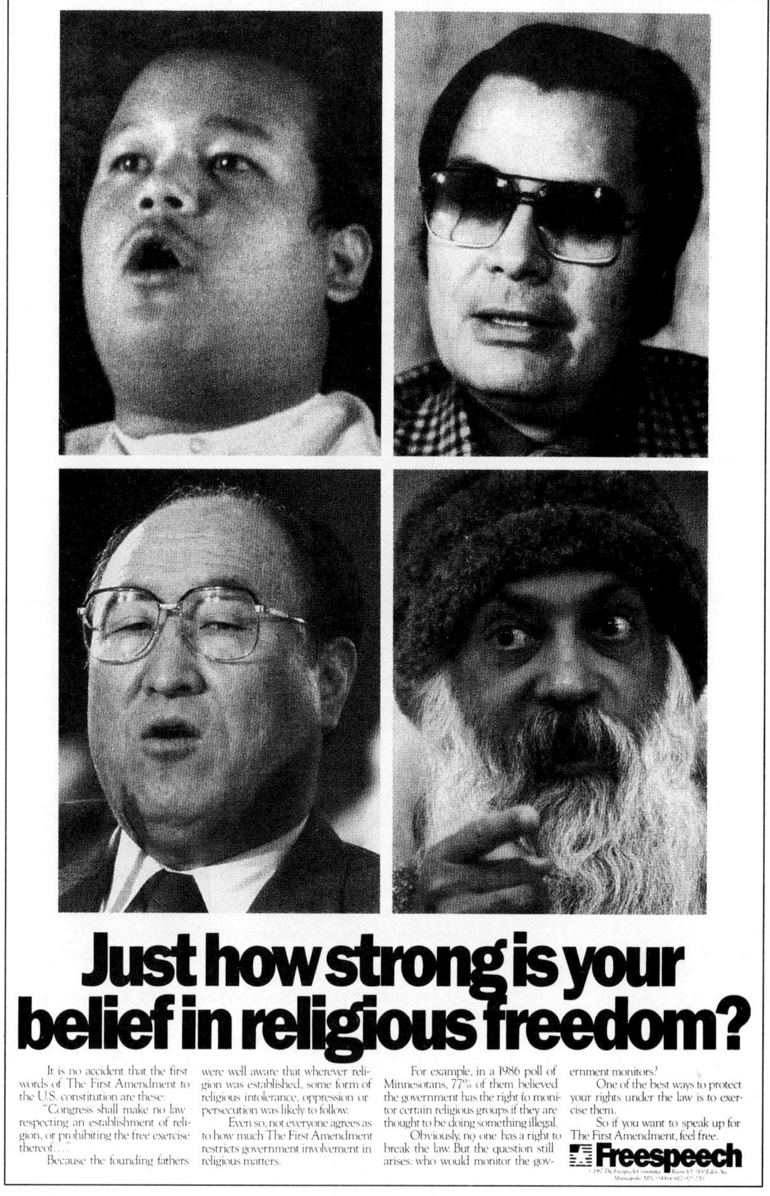

Just how strong is your belief in religious freedom?
It is no accident that the first words of The First Amendment to the U.S. constitution are these:
"Congress shall make no law respecting an establishment of religion, or prohibiting the free exercise thereof. . . ."
Because the founding fathers were well aware that wherever religion was established, some form of religious intolerance, oppression or persecution was likely to follow.
Even so, not everyone agrees as to how much The First Amendment restricts government involvement in religious matters.
For example, in a 1986 poll of Minnesotans, 77% of them believed the government has the right to monitor certain religious groups if they are thought to be doing something illegal.
Obviously, no one has a right to break the law. But the question still arises: who would monitor the government monitors?
One of the best ways to protect your rights under the law is to exercise them.
So if you want to speak up for The First Amendment, feel free.
Freespeech

Depending on the topic and the sponsoring organization, some idea advertising may be fully protected by the First Amendment, rather than having the limited protection of commercial speech.

Services need to be advertised as they are bought and sold like products—but without tangibility, it is difficult to convey their identity. Often, tangible items are used to represent them in their ads. In promoting the *tourist business,* the city of Denver features its location and its beauty in its ads. Recalling the locomotives of a century ago and its new airport of today, it shows tangible elements of progress, against a backdrop of history and nostalgia.

Service Advertising

Service industries have expanded significantly in recent years. National service industries that are major advertisers include airlines, rental cars, motel and hotel chains, tourist attractions, travel agencies, banks, insurance companies, and legal services. Ads for services differ from those for commodities because of the difference in the way the two are marketed.

Since services are basically people enterprises, service advertising almost always has a strong institutional component. Often service companies keep the same slogan, theme, or identifying mark for a long time to increase consumer awareness (see Exhibit 2.17). Since service industries are so similar (and often legally regulated), it is difficult to develop a distinct differentiation among competitors. Banks and insurance companies have a particularly hard time in establishing an effective identity.

EXHIBIT 2.17

Wausau Insurance has developed its trademark into a long-running advertising theme. (Courtesy: Wausau Insurance.)

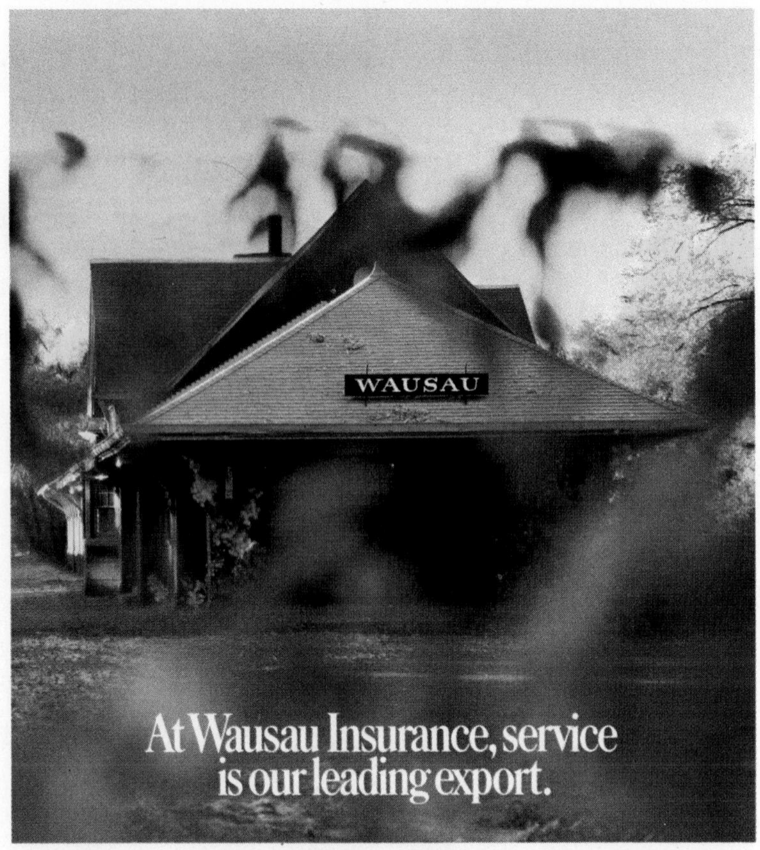

This little depot — the symbol of a hometown spirit of helpfulness — is where Wausau Insurance came of age. From here we've exported, all across America, our reputation for exceptional business insurance service.

When your company considers teaming up with Wausau, you can do it with confidence. Because we realize one of the most valuable assets we protect is our own reputation for service.

With Wausau, expect excellence in claims service. Excellence in loss-control service. Openness in communications. Alertness in response to your needs and problems.

And remember, it's always wise to ask what you'll *get* for your money. *That's* what determines value. Re-discover the simple joy of getting your money's worth.

WAUSAU INSURANCE

Wausau Insurance Companies, 2000 Westwood Drive, Wausau, Wisconsin 54401 Telephone (715) 845-5211 A Member of the Nationwide® Group

SUMMARY

The intent of this chapter was to give you an overview of the many roles of advertising. No communication tool can reach more people so effectively and at such a reasonable cost as advertising. Advertising is equally adept at selling goods at the corner drugstore and for the country's largest corporations. However, just as no two products adhere to the same marketing and advertising strategies, no two advertisements have exactly the same purpose. Since advertising is so flexible, it is important for the advertiser to determine exactly what role advertising is to play in the overall marketing program. To do this, it is necessary to identify those conditions conducive to successful advertising. A limited list of conditions would include a branded product of standardized quality with beneficial differentiation from its competitors that is sold at a reasonable price.

The key to successful advertising is developing an interesting message that will reach potential customers in an appropriate editorial environment at the proper time. Planning is the key to accomplishing these tasks. During the remainder of the text, we will discuss the techniques and executions of successful advertising.

SUGGESTED EXERCISES

- Bring to class two examples of advertisements that clearly note the way a product fulfills a consumer need.
- Note three advertisements that attempt to differentiate their products from the competition. At least one of these ads should name one or more competing brands.
- Collect two advertisements for relatively new products and two for products that have been on the market for some time. Compare and contrast the advertising approaches used by each.

QUESTIONS

1. Advertising is the communications element of the marketing process. Explain and give examples of how advertising's role differs from that of other marketing techniques.
2. Briefly discuss the marketing concept's view of consumers.
3. What are the four primary elements of the marketing process?
4. Compare and contrast advertising and public relations.
5. What are two of the primary roles that advertising serves for society?
6. Discuss the importance of a product in filling a niche in the marketplace.
7. Identify and briefly describe the three eras of product differentiation used by advertisers in this century?
8. Identify the following types of advertising:
   (a) national advertising
   (b) end-product advertising
   (c) trade advertising
   (d) industrial advertising
9. What are some of the reasons for the growing popularity of direct-response advertising?

READINGS

BOGART, LEO: ''Advertising: Art, Science, or Business,'' *Journal of Advertising Research,* December 1988/January 1989, pp. 47–52.

FANNIN, REBECCA: ''Crunching the Competition,'' *Marketing & Media Decisions,* March 1988, p. 70.

FANNIN, REBECCA: ''Seeing Is Believing,'' *Marketing & Media Decisions,* February 1988, p. 51.

FREEMAN, LAURIE: ''Brand Profit Is Focus for 1990s,'' *Advertising Age,* March 13, 1989, p. 32.

MARTIN, STEPHEN H.: ''An Objective for Everyone,'' *Marketing & Media Decisions,* March 1988, p. 124.

''The Power of Advertising,'' *Advertising Age* (special issue), November 9, 1988.

PRIEMER, AUGUST B.: ''Developing Your Theory of How Advertising Works,'' *Journal of Media Planning,* Spring 1988, p. 15.

SETTLE, ROBERT B., AND PAMELA L. ALRECK: ''Positive Moves for Negative Times,'' *Marketing Communications,* January 1988, p. 19.

WILCOX, DENNIS L., PHILLIP H. AULT, AND WARREN K. AGEE: *Public Relations Strategies and Tactics* (New York: Harper & Row Publishers, 1989), Chap. 9.

PART TWO

Planning the Advertising

The key to successful advertising is reaching prime prospects with a meaningful message in the proper media environment. However, these elements don't just happen. Behind virtually every good ad is sophisticated planning and an awareness of the market. Although from time to time great advertising is created through simple intuition, hard work and research are the norm.

Good advertising can rarely sell a bad product. The quality of the product, its competition, and its stage of development will affect advertising's role. Chapter 3 traces the introduction, maturity, and eventual decline of products through the concept of the advertising spiral. In Chapter 4, we consider the specific niche that a product occupies in the marketplace. It is increasingly apparent that successful marketing depends on products that are narrowly targeted to a clearly defined group of consumers. Target marketing is the key to product development and, as we shall see, to the media-buying process.

THREE

The Advertising Spiral and Brand Planning

The stage in a *product's life cycle* determines the advertising message. As Danskin, the predominant company responsible for dancers' apparel and shoes, expands into *running, cycling, and tennis clothing,* it'll use the theme, "Not just for dancing." Coincidentally, it used the same theme to introduce *exercise clothing* in 1967—more than 20 years ago.

This chapter examines the tremendous diversity of advertising's functions. Critical to successful advertising is the development of product and marketing objectives prior to making ads—the *strategic plan.* It is extremely important to have a clear understanding of the product and its users and potential users when making strategic advertising decisions.

Products pass through a number of stages, from introduction to ultimate demise, known as the "product life cycle." The manner in which advertising presents a product or brand to consumers depends largely upon the degree of acceptance the product has earned with consumers. It is this degree of acceptance that determines what "advertising stage" the product is in.

The life-cycle model discussed in this chapter consists of three primary stages (Exhibit 3.1):

- Pioneering stage
- Competitive stage
- Retentive stage

The nature and extent of each stage are discussed in the following sections.

EXHIBIT 3.1
Primary stages of the life-cycle model.

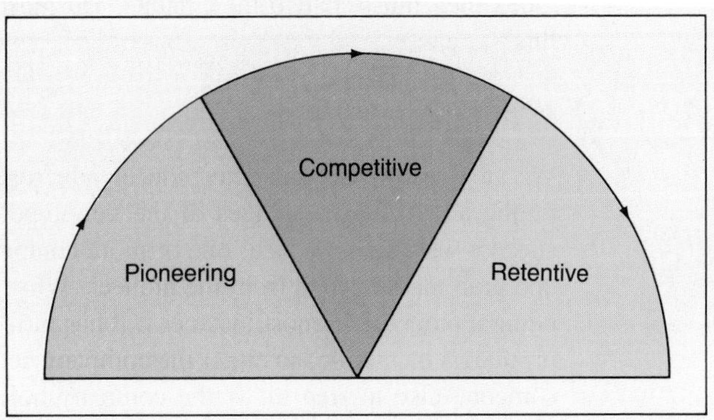

THE PIONEERING STAGE

> ***Pioneering stage.*** *The advertising stage of a product in which the need for such product is not recognized and must be established or in which the need has been established but the success of a commodity in filling those requirements has to be established.* See *Competitive stage, Retentive stage, Spiral.*

Advertising, in the early stages of a product's life cycle, serves to "educate" consumers about a new product or service. Facing declines in its premium-price beers, *Coors* will introduce its first contender in the *popular-price segment.* The company will market Keystone only in *cans, but in cans with a difference.* Coors will advertise Keystone as being available in *specialty lined cans,* that take away the metal taste of canned beers.

At the early stage of a product's introduction to the marketplace, a great deal of *advertising money* is spent to acquaint the targets with the product's "unique" advantage. *Saturn,* a new import by General Motors, will be launched in the fall of 1990, with a *start-up ad budget of* \$80–\$100 million! The first advertising will consist of a dealer film, TV, print, and major auto shows. "The extra push is needed," confessed Thomas Shaver, director of marketing services, "to position Saturn away from GM's other 2 relatively low-price car divisions, Chevrolet and Pontiac."

Just because a manufacturer develops a revolutionary new product, it doesn't necessarily follow that consumers feel compelled to purchase it. Until people appreciate the fact that they need a product, that product is in the pioneering stage.

The advertising used in the pioneering stage introduces an idea that makes previous conceptions appear antiquated. It shows how methods long accepted as the only ones possible have been improved upon. For example, diapers came in only one style for all babies until Scott Paper Company differentiated them by gender in the early 1970s with its Raggedy Ann and Raggedy Andy disposables. They had only limited success. Today, however, Luv Deluxe for Boys and Luv Deluxe for Girls are hot sellers. Advertising, by educating consumers to the new diapers' advantages, created demand for them. The advertising for a product in the pioneering stage must do more than simply present a new product—it must implant a new custom, change habits, develop new usage, or cultivate new standards of living.

Manufacturers may produce a product that does something many people have long desired—a VCR, a fax machine, a car phone, for example (see Exhibit 3.2). Advertising in these cases will not exhort consumers to raise their standards of acceptance, but rather will aim at convincing them that they can now accomplish something not possible before—through the use of the new product.

An interesting feature of pioneering advertising is its reference to the progress of time: Some variant of "Now you can do this" or "At last you can do that" is often found in the copy. The advertising anticipates and answers the consumer's question: What is the product for? It sells the generic aspect of the product category or tries to educate the consumer about what the product does. The Water Grabber ads in Exhibit 3.3 try to change plant care habits by educating the consumer about this new product's technology: ". . . granules act as tiny reservoirs. They hold up to 500 times their weight in water" and "release water as your plants need it, so you can go for weeks without watering your plants."

The pioneering stage of a product is not usually profitable for the manufacturer. The seller must obtain and expand distribution, generate consumer trials, and increase geographical markets. At the same time, most consumer products require heavy promotional and advertising expenditures during the pioneering stage.

Advertisers tend to assume that consumers understand, or are aware of, the product's advantages when they may in fact have little knowledge about the product. When a manufacturer overestimates the consumer's knowledge and/or appreciation of the product, it may engage in premature competitive advertising. Until the target market clearly understands the benefits of the product, the advertising should emphasize the product's utility rather than its advantages over competing products. Trying to gain a competitive advantage over other products when there is no interest in the product category is fruitless.

The Water Pik ad in Exhibit 3.4 tries to convince consumers that brushing and flossing aren't enough for healthy teeth and gums. For many years Water Pik has tried to educate consumers that the key to healthy teeth is healthy gums, and to have healthy gums they must change their habits. Do most consumers understand and agree with this?

Why Be a Pioneer?

We've already seen that the pioneer advertiser incurs the expense of educating the public about the advantages of the new type of product. If the advertiser has some success with the new idea, one or more competitors will quickly jump into the market and grab market share from the pioneer. Why, then, would a company take the risk of being a pioneer? In most instances, it has little choice if it wants to be successful: The product is inevitable, so either the company decides to enter the market first or to allow someone else to step in. If the company holds back, it may cost more to enter the market later because then it will be necessary to go up against competitors' advertising.

BELLSOUTH MOBILITY

SFX: (AMBIENT OUTDOOR SFX, BIRDS, WATER) (CASTING REEL AND KERPLUNK)
MAN A: What are you doing over there?
MAN B: That's where the fish are.
SFX: (CASTING REEL AND KERPLUNK)
MAN A: Oh no, they're right over there.

MAN B: Dollar on the first fish?
MAN A: How about five on the biggest?

MAN B: Okay.

ANNCR: While we can't promise a BellSouth Mobility car phone. . .

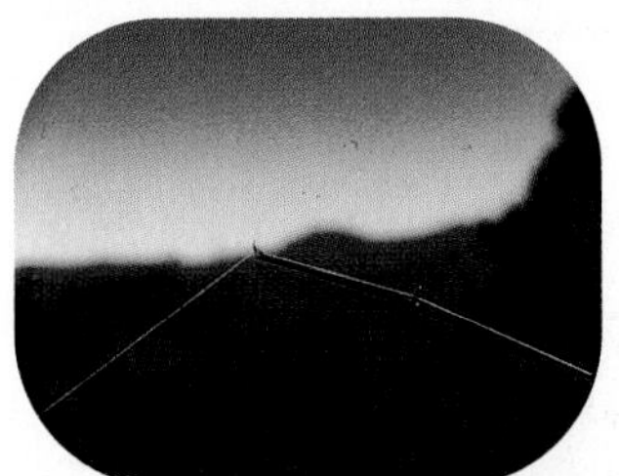

ANNCR: . . .will help you cacth bigger fish. . .

MAN A: Oh, this is big. This is real big.

ANNCR: We can promise it will give you more time to try.
MAN A: Ooo!

SFX: (SPLASH)
ANNCR: BellSouth Mobility. The phone company for your car.
MAN B: Ed? Ed. . . ?

EXHIBIT 3.2

BellSouth Mobility television commercial depicts advantages of the cellular phone. Do people want car phones? Does the cost prohibit this market from rapidly expanding? (Courtesy: BellSouth Mobility.)

Now you can love 'em and leave 'em.

"Thanks to WATER GRABBER,™ I can water my temperamental ferns and go on a cruise with a clear conscience."

The fact is, WATER GRABBER™ granules act as tiny reservoirs. They hold up to 500 times their weight in water. Just add these safe, non-toxic granules to the soil of ANY indoor or outdoor plant. Then you can water (even fertilize), go away for several weeks and let WATER GRABBER™ care for your plants!

WATER GRABBER™ granules swell when you water, which "shakes" or aerates the soil, encouraging root growth. Then they slowly release 95% of the water. It's water on demand for your plants. And those who enjoy watering frequently don't have to worry. With proper drainage, WATER GRABBER™ prevents waterlogging of the roots.

WATER GRABBER™ is just as effective for outside flower beds and vegetable gardens. The granules can even be pre-mixed with water-soluble fertilizer. WATER GRABBER™ gradually releases both water and fertilizer as needed. (It also makes other water-soluble nutrients in the soil more readily available to roots.)

WATER GRABBER,™ a longstanding commercial trade secret, has been tried and proven by major U.S. and European landscapers. Now it's finally available to consumers. So if you love your plants–get WATER GRABBER.™ Then you can safely love 'em and leave 'em and keep 'em healthier and greener.

One small packet can absorb up to a quart of water! Five 4-gram packets for only $2.99 let you care for ten 6″-pot plants. Or try the 69¢ introductory packet. Available at major supermarkets, plant and garden centers, and other retail outlets.

WATER GRABBER

Water Retention Granules for ALL Plants

Now available at: Home Depot, Kroger, Pike Nurseries, Winn-Dixie, K-Mart, Dunaway Family Drugs, Smith Ace Hardware, Williams Bros. and other retail outlets.

EXHIBIT 3.3A

A revolutionary new product trying to find consumers.

Confessions of a Plant Killer.

"I'm a good person. Really I am. But I've got to confess. I used to be a killer. A plant killer.

"I wouldn't water them for weeks and then I'd drown them. I love plants and the guilt was killing *me*.

"Then I discovered new WATER GRABBER.™ I've never seen anything like it. It's so easy to use and inexpensive, too, so I can use it in all my plants–indoors and out. I don't kill plants anymore. I make them thrive. With WATER GRABBER,™ I don't feel guilty anymore."

WATER GRABBER™ granules are like tiny reservoirs. They absorb up to 500 times their weight in water. Just add these safe, non-toxic granules to the soil and then water. WATER GRABBER™ releases the water as your plants need it, so you can go for weeks without watering your plants. You can go on a long trip with a clear conscience.

WATER GRABBER™'s absorbing and releasing action aerates the soil, encouraging root growth. And if you over-water occasionally, don't worry. With proper drainage, WATER GRABBER™ prevents waterlogging of the roots.

WATER GRABBER™ is also ideal for outdoor plants and vegetables. They'll thrive even in too-wet or too-dry weather.

Now available at: Home Depot, Kroger, Pike Nurseries, Winn-Dixie, K-Mart, Dunaway Family Drugs, Smith Ace Hardware, Williams Bros. and other retail outlets.

F-P Products, 263 Kelley Street, Lake City, South Carolina 29560

EXHIBIT 3.3B

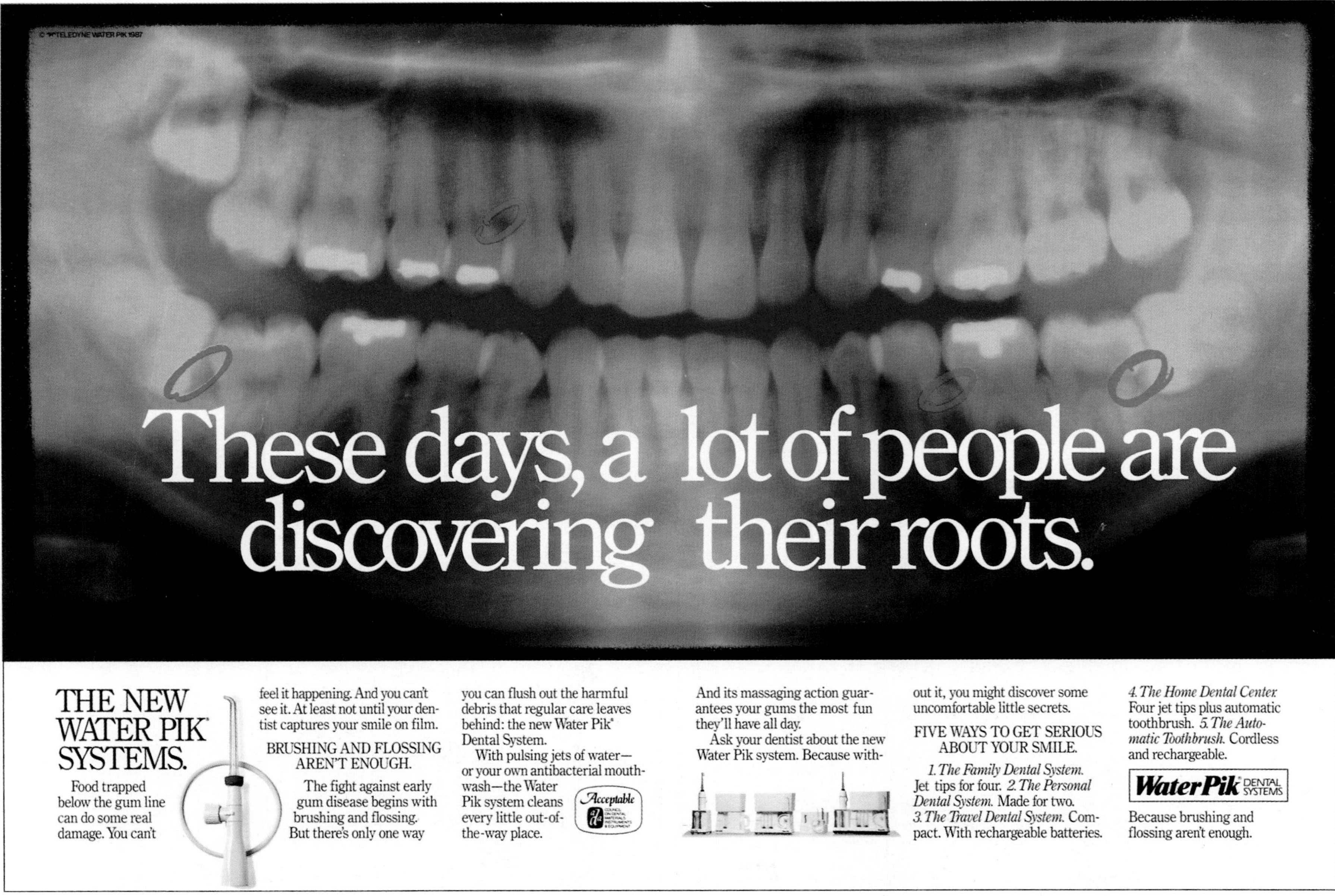

© TELEDYNE WATER PIK 1987
These days, a lot of people are discovering their roots.
THE NEW WATER PIK® SYSTEMS.
Food trapped below the gum line can do some real damage. You can't feel it happening. And you can't see it. At least not until your dentist captures your smile on film.
BRUSHING AND FLOSSING AREN'T ENOUGH.
The fight against early gum disease begins with brushing and flossing. But there's only one way you can flush out the harmful debris that regular care leaves behind: the new Water Pik® Dental System.
With pulsing jets of water—or your own antibacterial mouthwash—the Water Pik system cleans every little out-of-the-way place.
Acceptable
And its massaging action guarantees your gums the most fun they'll have all day.
Ask your dentist about the new Water Pik system. Because without it, you might discover some uncomfortable little secrets.
FIVE WAYS TO GET SERIOUS ABOUT YOUR SMILE.
1. The Family Dental System. Jet tips for four. 2. The Personal Dental System. Made for two. 3. The Travel Dental System. Compact. With rechargeable batteries. 4. The Home Dental Center. Four jet tips plus automatic toothbrush. 5. The Automatic Toothbrush. Cordless and rechargeable.
WaterPik® DENTAL SYSTEMS
Because brushing and flossing aren't enough.

EXHIBIT 3.4

Water Pik shows consumers that brushing and flossing are not enough to assure they will have healthy teeth and gums. They are trying to change consumer habits. (Courtesy: Teledyne Water Pik.)

The one sure advantage a pioneering advertiser has is time—the opportunity to become the leader in the field with a substantial head start over others. Often the pioneer's name is the first to come to people's minds whenever they think of that type of product for year afterward. So a pioneering effort can secure customers before competitors get started.

THE COMPETITIVE STAGE

Once a new product is generally accepted by consumers, there is going to be competition. The consumer now knows what the product is and how it can be used. At this point, the main question the consumer asks is: Which brand shall I buy? When this happens, the product has entered the competitive stage and the advertising for it is referred to as *competitive advertising*. (Note that this is a restrictive meaning of the term, not to be confused with the looser meaning that all ads are competitive with one another.)

Competitive stage. *The advertising stage a product reaches when its general usefulness is recognized but its superiority over similar brands has to be established in order to gain preference.*

In the short term, the pioneer usually has an advantage of leadership that can give it dominance in the market. Generally, in the early competitive stage, the combined impact of many competitors, each spending to gain a substantial market position, creates significant acceleration in the rate of growth. If the pioneer can maintain market share during this initial period of competitors' growth, it can more than make up for the earlier expenditures associated with its pioneering efforts.

In the *second stage* of the PLC, competition has entered the marketplace—if the product is successful. The idea of promotion now is to differentiate the advertiser's product from the competition *by some form of persuasion*. After a year of profitable sales from its *cross-trainers sneaker line*, Nike will attempt to align its product with versatile athlete, Bo Jackson. *Only in Nike's* cross-trainers can *he* compete effectively in baseball, football, basketball, tennis, running, cycling, *and* weights, claims the 60-second TV spot. The viewer (hopefully) is left with the impression that *only Nike's C-Ts* can help the any-sport athlete accomplish "all" by "just doing it. . . ."

Among the many everyday products now in the competitive stage are deodorants, soaps, toothpastes, cars, detergents, headache remedies, shaving creams, razors, shampoos, televisions, VCRs, dog food, computers, and packaged foods. The purpose of competitive-stage advertising is to communicate the product difference to the consumer; the advertising features the differential of the product. For example, the Dunlop tennis ad in Exhibit 3.5 says, "Unlike other wide-bodies, the Plus and Pro are widest and stiffest at the point of impact. This provides a more powerful, more stable hitting surface. The frame tapers into the grip for more forgiving flex and greater control . . ." Competitive advertising shows how unique features, or differentials, of one brand make it better than all others.

Here are some competitive headlines:

Now you can rent a car without standing in any lines, stopping at any counters, filling out any contracts, or even starting the engine.

(*Hertz*)

What's the first thing you take off when you get home at night? If it's your shoes, you're probably wearing the wrong ones.

(*Naturalizer*)

Introducing pantyhose for spring in all the latest flavors.

(*No Nonsense*)

Few things so fulfilling are so unfilling.

(*diet Coke*)

Plastic wrap leave you steamed? We make microwaving easier.

(*Cut-Rite*)

Notice that these ads don't tell you why you should use their "type" of product; it is taken for granted that you know why. Instead, each headline sets out to tell you why you should select that particular brand from all the others in the field.

The *reminder stage* of advertising assumes the target knows about the product and has used it. The idea is to keep the customer *focused* on a particular brand for its ability to *maintain satisfaction*. That's the whole idea behind the new Budget Rent-a-Truck ads. Mike Ditka, the new spokesperson for the company, will declare, in his notoriously stern face, "*Next to me*, Budget's trucks are the toughest thing on wheels. I'm not changing my coaching habits, and they *still* have the most reliable vehicles around."

THE RETENTIVE STAGE

Products that reach maturity and widescale acceptance enter the retentive, or reminder, stage of advertising.

When consumers already accept and use the product, there may be no point to

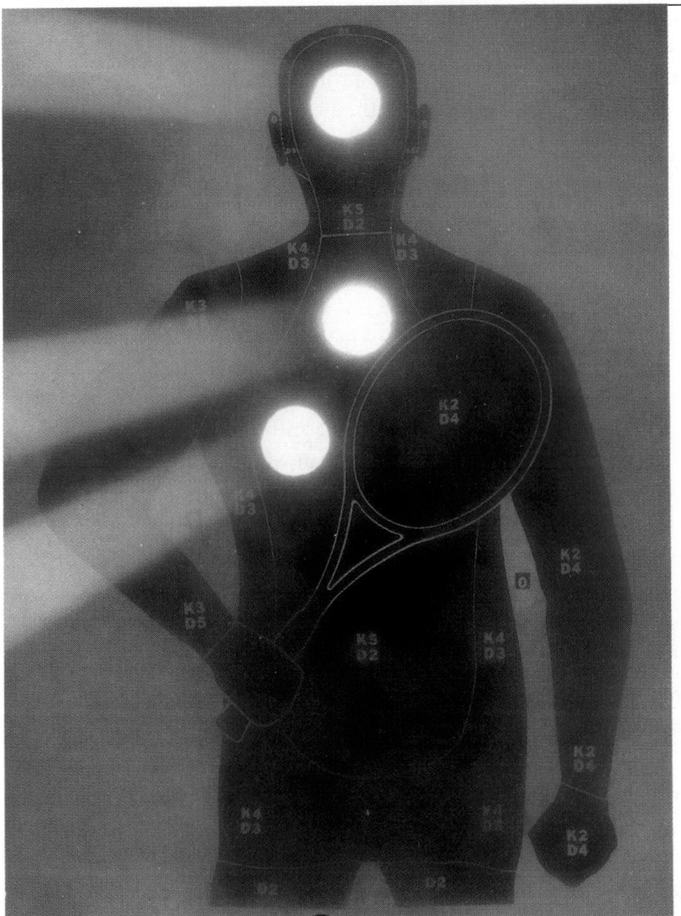

INTRODUCING WIDE-BODIES WITH THE ACCURACY TO HIT A BALL ANYWHERE YOUR CONSCIENCE PERMITS.
You cradle the weapon firmly in your palm. Take careful aim across the net. Then fire a bullet. Right on the mark.
Welcome to tennis with Dunlop's new Max Impact racquets. The Max Impact Plus, Max Impact Pro and Max Impact Mid. Three new graphite wide-bodies like nothing you've ever played. Because they give you the awesome power you expect from a wide-body tennis racquet. Without sacrificing control.
Unlike other wide-bodies, the Plus and Pro are widest and stiffest at the point of impact. This provides a powerful, more stable hitting surface. The frame tapers into the grip for more forgiving flex and greater control. And, because wider racquets create more shock, the Plus and Pro feature "Impact Modulators." A vibration dampening system that utilizes Kevlar® and Sorbothane.® Two materials that have remarkable ability to absorb the vibration caused by shock.
The result is a solid, more comfortable feel. Less wear and tear on your arm. And a racquet that is more responsive. For greater control and accuracy of shots.
Go demo the Max Impact Plus, Max Impact Pro or our powerful mid-size wide-body, the Max Impact Mid. You'll be amazed at the power and control.
Your opponents will be blown away.
DUNLOP TENNIS
© 1989 Dunlop Slazenger Corporation. and Dunlop are registered trademarks of DNA (Housemarks) Limited.
Sorbothane is a registered trademark of BTR PLC. Kevlar is a registered trademark of DuPont, Inc.

EXHIBIT 3.5

Introducing a new product feature. (Courtesy: Dunlop Tennis & Cole Henderson Drake, Ken Lewis, copyrighter.)

competitive advertising. The product has been around for along time and consumers have made their brand choices. The advertiser may think: Everybody knows about my product and likes or dislikes it . . . so why advertise? History, however, tells us that when successful brands stop advertising, consumers are likely to quickly forget about them. Therefore, most astute advertisers try to retain the customers they have by keeping the brand name before them. This is called *reminder advertising—it simply reminds consumers the brand exists*. This kind of advertising is usually visual or name advertising, meaning the ad gives little reason to buy the product. Most reminder ads look like posters—they have a few large words and a dominant illustration of the product. Generally, there is little or no body copy, since there is no need to give consumers much information.

> ***Retentive stage.*** *The third advertising stage of a product, reached when its general usefulness is everywhere known, its individual qualities are thoroughly appreciated, and it is satisfied to retain its patronage merely on the strength of its past reputation.*

Very few advertisers reach the point where they can consider their product entirely in the reminder stage. Usually there are other products in the pioneering and competitive stages challenging their leadership position. In fact, if your product is truly all alone in the retentive stage, that may be cause for alarm. It may mean the product category is in decline and the competition sees little future in challenging you for consumers.

The advertiser's goal in the retentive stage is to maintain market share and ward off consumer trial of other products. Products in the retentive stage don't necessarily cut back on their advertising expenditures, but they do adopt different marketing and promotional strategies than those used in the pioneering and competitive stages. When a brand is used by a large portion of the market, its advertising is intended to keep present customers and increase the total market, on the assumption that the most prominent brand will get the largest share of the increase.

Generally, products in the retentive stage are at their most profitable levels because developmental costs have been amortized, distribution channels established, and sales contacts made. The development of advertising and promotion may often be routine at this stage. Obviously, companies like to maintain their products in the retentive stage as long as possible.

THE ADVERTISING SPIRAL

The advertising spiral (Exhibit 3.6) is an expanded version of the advertising stages of products. It provides a point of reference for determining which stage or stages a product has reached at a given time in a given market and what the thrust of the advertising message should be. This can be important information for deciding on strategy and giving the creative team a clear perspective on what information they need to communicate to prospects. In many respects, the advertising spiral parallels the life cycle of the product (Exhibit 3.1), except that it shows what has to be done at each stage and where the product can go when it reaches a high level of success.

Comparison of Stages

When a product occupies more than 1 stage in the PLC—*because of different targets—separate campaigns* need to be designed to appeal to each one. Porsche, *in one of the most targeted campaigns ever,* mailed 100,000 laser-printed personalized posters, showing a recent model with a vanity license place bearing the recipient's name. It obviously "hit" the *special* upscale climbers it wanted to reach, because the company reported increased showroom traffic and sales.

There are fewer products in the pioneering stage than in the competitive stage. The development of new types of products or categories does not take place very frequently. Most advertising is for products in the competitive stage. As we have pointed out, such advertising often introduces a new product feature that is in the pioneering stage and gets the spotlight for a period of time.

In using the advertising spiral, we deal with one group of consumers at a time. The advertising depends upon the attitude of "that" group toward the product. A product in the competitive stage may have to use pioneering advertising aimed at other groups of consumers to expand its markets. Fax machines are in the competitive stage among businesspeople, where their use is accepted, but they are largely in the pioneering stage for home use. Thus, pioneering and competitive advertising will be going on simultaneously for fax machines. Each series of ads, or each part of one ad, will be aimed at a different audience for this same product.

Products in the retentive stage usually get the least amount of advertising. This stage, however, represents a critical moment in the life cycle of a product, when

EXHIBIT 3.6
The advertising spiral.

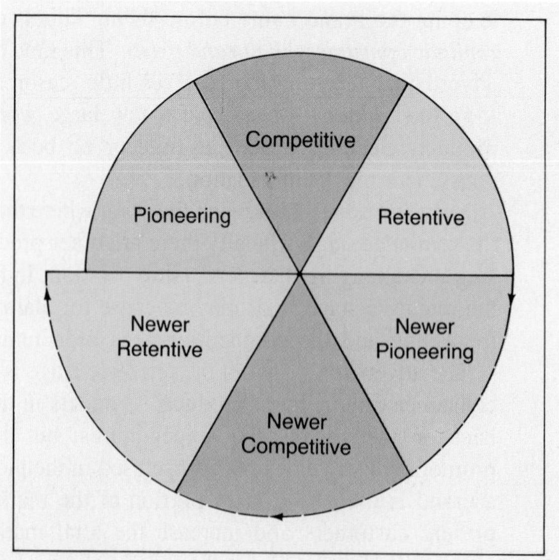

important management decisions must be made. Hence it is important to create effective advertising in this stage.

Significant improvements in a product remove it from the *second or competitive stage* and put it back in *stage 1*—as it once again needs to *inform* its customers about the changes it made. When the City of Miami wanted to "get the word out" about its new *image,* it took advantage of Super Bowl XXIII's presence and provided the committee with an estimated $2 million for festivities and public relations efforts.

When a product loses its popularity—mostly because newer versions or replacements have joined the marketplace or its customer base is declining—an advertiser can continue to *remind* the public about its presence—or cease promotion altogether. *Denny's,* the largest family restaurant chain, elected to promote its "basics." "In an age of fast-food and upscale dining, we still maintain there's room for a 'coffee shop'," quotes Sam Maw, president-CEO. "Our customer base dwindled in the last few years—not because we weren't providing a needed product, but because we lost our identity, and weren't communicating. . . ." To build its broad franchise, Denny's introduced its new Corlick Sisters TV campaign, costing $20 million.

Product in Competitive Stage, Improvement in Pioneering Stage. It is not unusual for a new brand to enter the competitive stage without doing any pioneering advertising. A new product entering an established product category must hit the ground running to differentiate itself from the competition. Every new brand thus enjoys whatever pioneering advertising has already been done in the product category.

Change is a continuum: As long as the operation of a competitive product does not change, the product continues to be in the competitive stage, despite any pioneering improvements. Once the principle of its operation changes, however, the product itself enters the pioneering stage. Think about the change from the needle record player to compact disc technology. When a product begins to move into more than one stage, the changes are not always easy to categorize.

Whenever a brand in the competitive stage is revitalized with a new feature seeking to differentiate it, pioneering advertising may be needed to make consumers appreciate the new feature. Huggies diapers added a soft elastic band. If its advantages had not been advertised, consumers might have ignored the feature.

After the Retentive Stage

The life of a product does not cease when it reaches the retentive stage. In fact it may then be at the height of its popularity, and its manufacturer may feel it can just coast along. But a product can coast for only a short period of time before declining.

As we noted earlier, the retentive stage is the most profitable one for the product. But all good things must come to an end. A manufacturer has a choice between two strategies when the product nears the end of the retentive stage.

In the first strategy, the manufacturer determines that the product has outlived its effective market life and should be allowed to die. In most cases, the product is not immediately pulled from the market. Rather, the manufacturer simply quits advertising it and withdraws other types of support. During this period, the product gradually loses market share but remains profitable because expenses have been sharply curtailed. This strategy is the one typically presented in textbook descriptions of the product life cycle, but not necessarily the one that corresponds to actual product development.

The problem with the model in Exhibit 3.7 is that it portrays an inevitable decline in the product life cycle, whereas most long-term products go through a number of cycles

EXHIBIT 3.7
A typical product life-cycle model.

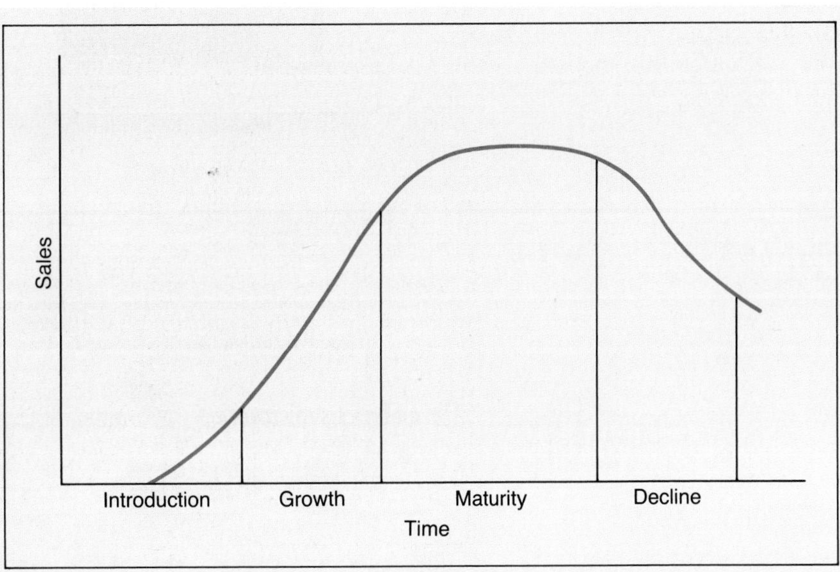

of varying peaks and duration before they are finally taken off the market. The advertising spiral depicted in Exhibit 3.6 shows these cycles. The advertising spiral, the second strategy available to the manufacturer of a product nearing the end of the retentive stage, does not accept the fact that a product must decline. Instead, it seeks to expand the market into a newer pioneering stage.

The three basic stages of the spiral shown in the top half of Exhibit 3.6 (pioneering, competitive, and retentive) are straightforward and easy to understand. However, the stages in the bottom half (newer pioneering, newer competitive, and newer retentive) are trickier. In order to continue to market an established product successfully and profitably, creative marketing is necessary.

Successful products, which have reached their saturation level in one market may have "new life" in other markets (example: business to home). An alternative way to increase market share would be to advertise *additional uses* to the same or expanded markets. *American Express,* attempting to boost credit card purchases of high-ticket items, created in 1986, "Buyer's Assurance," which doubled a manufacturer's product warranty up to 1 year. In 1987, "Purchase Protection" followed—with significant success.

The newer pioneering stage attempts to get more people to use the product. Basically, there are two ways to enter this new stage. This first is by product modification. This can be relatively minor, such as adding a new ingredient to a detergent or a deodorant to a bar of soap, or—in the other direction—taking caffeine out of a soft drink or coffee. Alternatively, it may entail a complete overhaul of a product such as a radical model change for an automobile. In some cases, advertising alone may be enough to get customers to look at the product in a new light.

Advertisers cannot afford to simply rely on old customers because they die off, are lured away by the competition, or change their lifestyles. Smart advertisers will initiate a change in the direction of their advertising when their product is enjoying great success. They will show new ways of using the product and give reasons for using it more often. For instance, if you're a successful soup company and your customers are eating your canned soup with every meal, you have reached a saturation point. How can you increase sales? Simply by encouraging people to use soup in new ways. You create recipe advertising—showing new food dishes, casseroles—requiring several cans of your product. You now have your customers eating your soup as soup, along with casseroles made from your soup. Of course, this means more sales and a new way of thinking about soup. Obviously, Kraft Cheese Whiz processed cheese spread is not a pioneering product, for it has been around for many years. However, Exhibit 3.8 shows an ad geared toward new consumer lifestyles: "*The* marvelous microwave in-a-

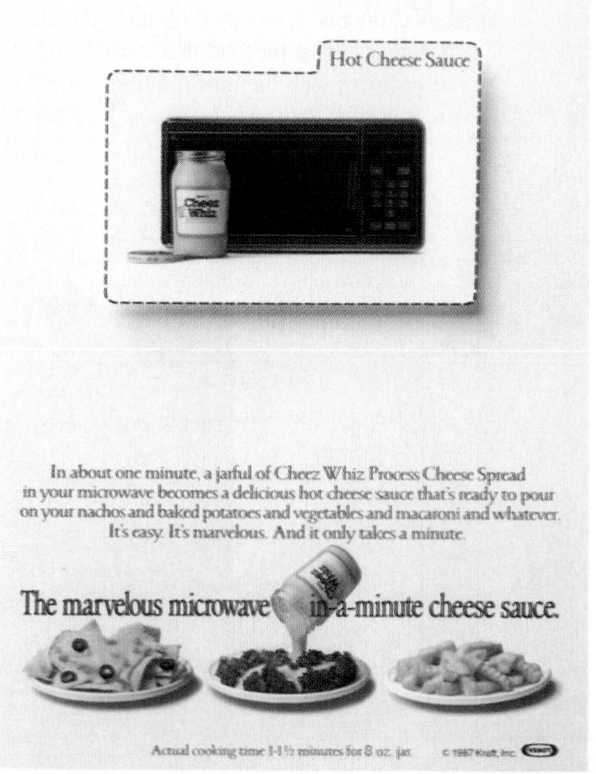

EXHIBIT 3.8
An old product offering new pioneering features. (Courtesy: Kraft, Inc.)

minute Mexican cheese sauce.'' The product is adapting to the environment with features often found in an introductory marketing strategy.

New Pioneering Stage and Beyond

A product entering the new pioneering stage is actually in different stages in different markets. Long-time consumers will perceive the product as in the competitive or retentive stage. New consumers will perceive it as being a pioneer. For instance, the personal computer is in the competitive stage for most large and many medium-sized businesses, but in the pioneering stage for small businesses and home users. Hence the dual nature of computer advertising. Some advertising focuses on the number of users and the sophistication of the computer, assuming that the firm has already bought a competing system. Other computer ads are clearly trying to sell the value of having a computer. We will soon see computers becoming pioneers in other markets. Think about the opportunities for expanding the market for desktop publishing as prices fall on hardware and software becomes easier to use. At this point, the advertising spiral will have entered still another cycle (see Exhibit 3.9), which we call the ''newest pioneering stage,'' where the focus is on getting more people to use this type of product.

The *newer* pioneering or introductory stage—where the advertiser is seeking new targets—can often achieve success with a *product line extension*. The ''original'' product is ''reworked,'' with a newer formula and a newer name, but is ''related'' to the original version. Neutrogena, the ''pure'' facial soap, added eye cream, night cream, and sunblock in 1988. As a result, sales increased 32% to an estimated $179 million. For 1989, Diana Temple, a vice-president with Solomon Brothers, predicted a healthy 27% increase for Neutrogena this year. ''The expanded line is particularly effective in drug stores, where the additional products have helped the company achieve added shelf space,'' she added.

The product in this stage is faced with new problems and opportunities. Can you convince segments of the market not using your product that they should? Obviously, you have to understand why they were not interested in the product earlier. Creative marketing and a flexible product help this process.

Many manufacturers of brands that achieved retentive-stage status—Pepsi-Cola, Jell-O, Budweiser, Crisco Oil, Coca-Cola—began to look for ways to move the product beyond the retentive stage. Pepsi-Cola, Coca-Cola, and Budweiser moved into the new pioneering stage with product innovations: Diet Pepsi, diet Coke, and Bud Light. Today Bud Light is in the newer competitive stage fighting off a host of competitors. Diet Coke and Pepsi are in the early part of the new retentive stage. Anheuser-Busch is introducing Bud Dry in the fledgling dry-beer market in hopes of dominating this new beer segment (it owns Michelob Dry, the first national dry beer). Dry beers have already captured about 40 percent of the Japanese market, so American brewers have hopes that consumers here will also learn to like them. Despite the present lack of consumer acceptance, much competition is expected in the dry-beer category in the future.

The advertising focus in the newer pioneering stage is on getting consumers to understand what the product is about. Michelob's research found that consumers had

EXHIBIT 3.9
The expanded advertising spiral.

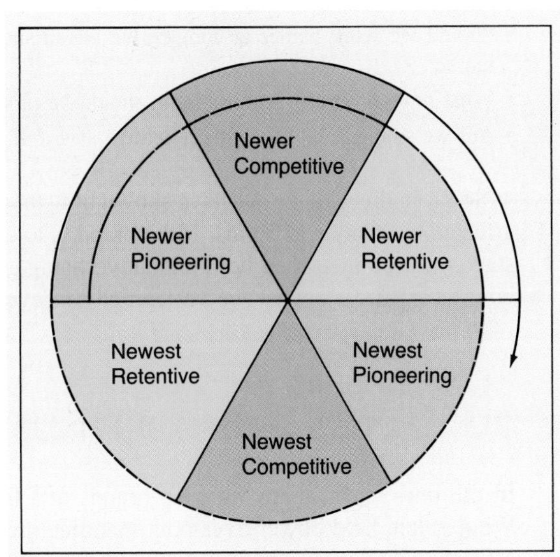

absolutely no idea what *dry* meant when it came to beer. Advertising in the newer competitive stage aims at getting more people to buy the brand. The newer retentive stage relies on existing prestige to keep current customers. Diet Pepsi and diet Coke are looking for ways to enter the newer pioneering stage. If Pepsi discovered that its product would remove warts, they might consider this new market potential and create appropriate advertising. This is an extreme example, of course, but it does illustrate how the spiral can continue (see Exhibit 3.9).

Movement to the new pioneering, competitive, or retentive stage is not easy. First, the manufacturer must develop either product innovations or advertising-positioning strategies that make the product different in the eyes of the consumer. Also, as we move to the newer stages of the spiral (the bottom half of Exhibit 3.6), there are usually fewer prospects for the product. Therefore, a company must become more efficient at reaching smaller groups of prospects.

Brands entering additional cycles do not return to the point at which they started their life. When IBM introduced its midrange computers to businesses, these were not pioneer products in the same sense that a new product introduced by a new company would be, for IBM was then the computer leader. The company's advertising said: "Presenting the affordable IBM midrange computers. Because you're getting too big to think small." The copy went on: "For as little as $15,000, you can store all your data in one place and streamline your entire operation."

The Advertising Spiral as a Management Decision Tool

A product may hold its ground in one competitive area while it seeks new markets with pioneering advertising aimed at other groups (see Exhibit 3.10). Products do not move through each stage at the same speed. A product may go swiftly from one stage in one cycle to a newer stage in another cycle. This change may also be a matter of corporate strategy. A company may believe it can secure more business at less cost by utilizing pioneering advertising that promotes new uses for the product. It is possible that the same result could be obtained by continuing to battle at a small profit margin in a highly competitive market. A retentive advertiser may suddenly find its market slipping and plunge right into a new competitive war, without any new pioneering work. Like a compass, the spiral indicates direction; it does not dictate management decisions.

Before attempting to create new ideas for advertising a product, the advertiser should use the spiral to answer the following important questions:

- In which stage is the product?
- Should we use pioneering advertising to attract new users to this type of product?
- Should we work harder at competitive advertising to obtain a larger share of the existing market?
- What proportion of our advertising should be pioneering, what proportion competitive?
- Are we simply coasting in the retentive stage? If so, should we be more aggressive?

So far in this chapter we have shown how the life cycle of a product or brand may be affected by many conditions. If the brand is to continue to be marketed, its advertising stage must be identified before its advertising goals can be set. Next we will examine how to expand on what we've learned to develop a strategic plan for a brand.

BUILDING STRONG BRANDS

In the mid-1880s, there were no brands and little quality control by manufacturers. Wholesalers held power over both manufacturers and retailers. Manufacturers had to offer the best deal to wholesalers in order to get their product distributed. This created a

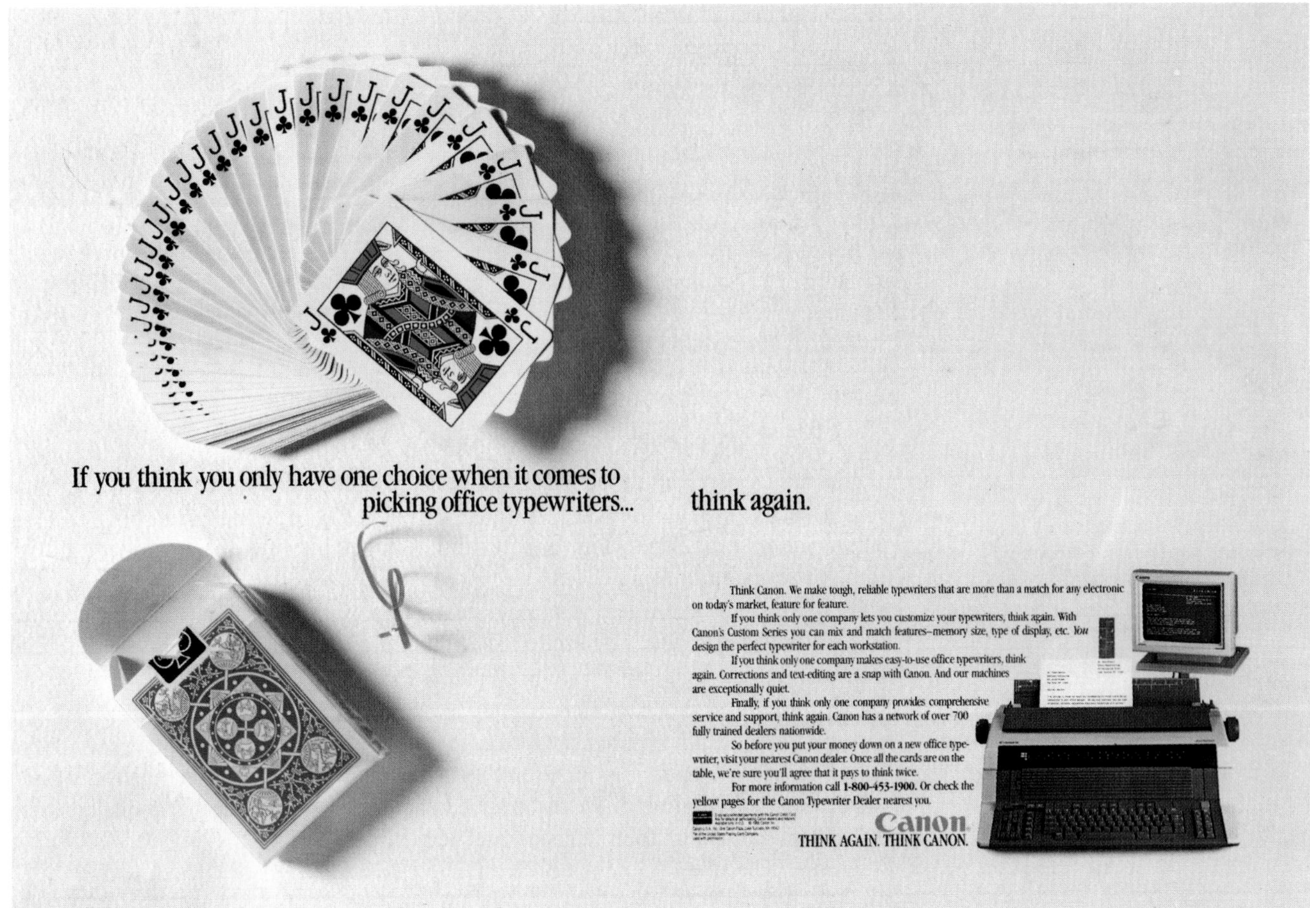

EXHIBIT 3.10
A brand trying to expand its market. (Courtesy: Canon.)

Manufacturers' brands were developed to evade the scrutiny of greedy wholesalers by appealing to their *targets directly with brand names*. Even today, manufacturers, in highly competitive situations, may want to by-pass intermediary distributors. Proctor & Gamble, thinking it could promote *Crush Orange Soda and Hires Root Beer* better and cheaper than its local bottler in San Antonio, threatened to *sell directly to Wal-Mart*. (The impending sale of the two labels prevented the deal from going through.)

squeeze on profits. As a result of this profit squeeze, some manufacturers decided to differentiate their products from the competition. They gave their products names, obtained patents to protect their exclusivity, and used advertising to take the news about them to customers, over the heads of the wholesalers and retailers. Thus was the concept of branding born. Among the early brands still viable today are Levi's (1873), Maxwell House Coffee (1873), Budweiser (1876), Ivory (1879), Coca-Cola (1886), Campbell Soup (1893), and Hershey Chocolate (1900).[1]

Since brands are the most valuable assets a marketer has, we need to thoroughly understand what they are all about. The product is *not* the brand. A product is manufactured; a brand is created. A product may change over time, but the brand remains. A brand exists only in and through communication. The communication of the brand proclaims its singular and durable identity, its territory as a brand. It is therefore not sufficient for a brand to promote a motivating quality of the product, for another product can always equal or copy it. The brand must be distinct from its competition. In fact, it is the competition that helps form the brand's identity. A brand is a memory bank carrying all its history, which constitutes its accumulated capital.

At any point in time a brand is made up of two types of elements (see Exhibit 3.11).

The *rational elements* stem predominately from "what" the brand is doing, telling, showing. They

- Embody the content and theme of the brand's communications, its proposition or promise.

[1]Norman Berry, "Revitalizing Brands," *Viewpoint,* July–August 1987, p. 18.

EXHIBIT 3.11
The basic elements of a brand.

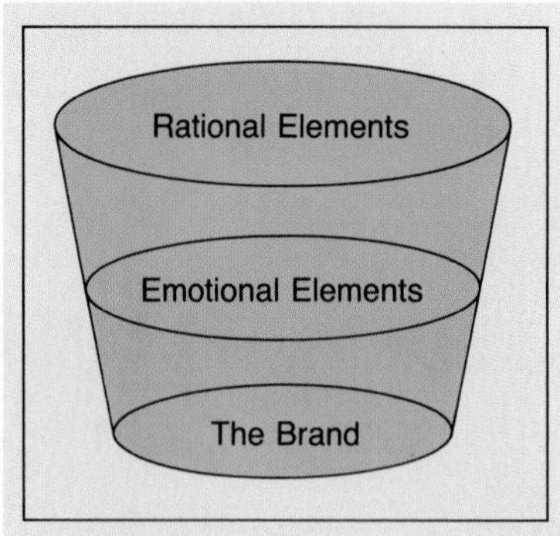

There are *rational* (thinking) and *emotional* (feeling) *elements* involved with brand names. Promotion tries to exploit both. Up to now, Absolut Vodka has used a straightforward message in its ads, stressing the "reasons why smart people drink their product." They've now extended their ad campaign into the *emotional arena* by inviting consumers to create their own Absolut ads, using watercolor paints contained in the contest insert.

- Speak more to the left or rational side of the brain.[2]
- Are the most visible part of the brand, the easiest part to articulate and measure.

The *emotional* elements stem mainly from "how" the brand is expressing itself, telling, showing, promising. They

- Set the brand's style, tone character, mode, mood of execution.
- Speak more to the right or intuitive-nonverbal side of brain.
- Are less visible and therefore more difficult to express directly and measure.

In evaluating a brand, it is important to understand both the rational and the emotional elements that define it. We can decide to act directly on either group of elements, and the implications of each decision are very different.

MANAGING THE BRAND-COMMUNICATION MIX

Brand Equity. *The value of how consumers, distributors, salespersons, etc. think and feel about a brand relative to the competition over a period of time.*

In today's marketing environment, it is essential that every communication reinforce brand personality in the same manner. Advertising, public relations, packaging, display, sales merchandising, and promotion must all be managed to build the brand's equity by communicating the same brand message to consumers.

Lintas: USA, one of the major advertising agencies, uses a planning process called Lintas:Link to help synergize communications to build strong brand equity (see Exhibit 3.12). The most important factor in determining the actual value of a brand is its equity in the market: how consumers (end users and other publics like employees, salespeople, and distributors) think and feel about the brand.

Lintas:Link Strategic Planning Process

The following steps help us understand the brand.

Brand Equity Audit. This step identifies the present equity of the brand and the factors that have a significant impact on it so that the most effective communication

[2]The brain is divided into two hemispheres: the left brain and the right brain. The left brain is the rational side. It reads images, is logical, and deals with math, verbal, and memory functions. It is the conservative side of the brain. The right brain is intuitive. It scans images, controls the creative process, and thinks nonverbally. It is the emotional side of the brain.

People obviously use both sides of their brain, but it is not unusual for one side to be dominant. The following occupations are supposed to attract left-brain individuals: accounting, the law, research, engineering, medicine. Right-brain individuals are more likely to take up art, photography, music, acting, etc. and other occupations that require intuitive thinking.

EXHIBIT 3.12

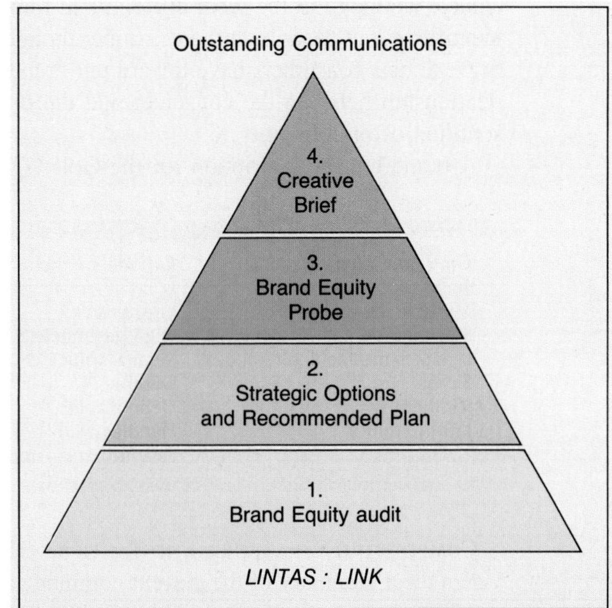

In developing *a brand equity audit,* the advertiser should begin with *the market itself.* The *second step evaluates the brand* and how it's received versus competition. "The name, *Clorox,* is synonymous with 'clean'," admits Hugh Zurkerblen, Solomon Brothers' analyst. Their market, he found, is relatively "quiet," so Clorox has "a pretty wide birth to diversify." *Clorox Clean-Up,* a new general-purpose liquid cleaner that mixes bleach with detergent, is the latest example to "test" its name in the marketplace. "Against its main competitors—Pine-Sol, Mr. Clean, and Lysol—it should do well," predicts another Wall Street analyst.

Consumers' thoughts and feelings about a particular brand are considered to be the most difficult to discern *and* important to record. The audit gathers both *emotional and rational elements* to provide a *complete* brand equity description. "By projecting a 'bad-boy' image for its *Jose Cuervo Tequila,* Steven Goldstein, Heublein director of public relations revealed, "we're reaching the 'traditional' tequila drinker." Research showed the company would be better off maintaining the product's "toughness" through ads placed in off-beat publications, such as *Rolling Stone.*

***Market Share.** Sales of one brand divided by total product category sales.*

strategy can be developed. The specific aim is to find out how consumers think and feel about the brand versus the competition. The brand equity audit is divided into four areas.

MARKET CONTEXT. We examine the existing state of things from two angles: the market and the consumer. What is our market and whom do we compete with? What other brands/product categories? What makes the market tick? Is it segmented? How? What segment are we in? Are products highly differentiated? What kind of person buys products in this category? In the mind of these consumers, what drives the market or holds it back (needs, obstacles, etc.)? Is the product bought on impulse? How interested are consumers in the product? Do they tend to be brand loyal?

The sole purpose here is to set the scene. We look at the market from varying angles and select only the ones relevant to building brand equity.

BRAND EQUITY INDICATORS. Once we understand the market context, we go on to examine current brand equity—how strong or weak consumer bias is toward our brand, relative to other brands. Here we must be selective and shrewd, picking out those indicators that will provide maximum insight. The following is a list of indicators often used:

- Brand awareness—top-of-mind is best
- Market share, price elasticity, share of voice, and the like
- Brand sensitivity—the relative importance of brand to other factors involved in the purchase, such as price, pack size, model
- Assumed leadership—consumers' perception of leadership of the brand
- Consistency of the brand's communication over time
- Image attribute ratings, or ranking attributes
- Distribution, pricing, product quality, and product innovation
- Brand loyalty—the strength of a brand lies in the proportion of its customers who buy it as a brand rather than just as a product

Once the key indicators have been identified, they are used for future tracking purposes.

BRAND EQUITY DESCRIPTION. Now that we understand the market in which our brand operates and have a clear indication of the strength or weakness of our brand

Current promotion strategies are appraised in the *fourth stage* of the audit. These are contrasted with competitors' in an effort to decipher the advertiser's strengths versus weaknesses. *Tom's of Maine,* a regional producer of all-natural deodorants and toothpastes, has begun to use *national print and radio* to promote its products in major cities. However, it's unable to afford *television*—one reason why it may have to settle for a *3% market share, versus 67%* for Proctor & Gamble and Colgate-Palmolive. It also confesses to *prices* ranging from 25%–50% more than the leading brands, which prohibit cost comparisons in ads.

Push Strategy. *Strategy using salesforce and trade promotion to push a product through the channels to consumers.*

Pull Strategy. *Depends on advertising and consumer promotion to build up consumer demand.*

The next step encompasses the *recommendations, with various options.* Should an additional target market input be necessary, "probes" are executed for further insights into the rational and emotional elements. When Polaroid launched its *One Film*—35 mm single-speed film, designed to eliminate consumer confusion over which speed to buy—both *Kodak and Fuji* filmmakers went back to *their* drawing boards. Kodak's research unit recommended that they introduce *new packaging* for its Kodacolor Gold *200* film, that positions it as "multipurpose." Fuji, too, will be rolling out a multipurpose film called Super HG 200. Not to forsake their conventional markets, and in case the "one speed" concept attracts the strictly amateur market, as predicted, both Kodak and Fuji are committed to maintaining substantial inventories of film with various speeds.

equity, we move to the most difficult and important area in the brand equity audit—identifying and describing the consumer thoughts and feelings that result in the strong or weak bias consumers have toward our brand relative to other brands. This personal relationship between the consumer and the brand provides the most meaningful description of brand equity.

A brand equity description for the Golf GTI automobile might look like this:

Emotional Elements	*Rational Elements*
My little sports car	Inexpensive
Sets me free	High gas mileage
It makes me feel/look good	Retains value
Simple	Durable
It's there when I want it	Dependable
I'm in control	Handles well
	Easy to park—small

COMPETITIVE STRATEGIES AND TACTICS. This area of the audit is designed to provide a clear summary of the current communication strategies and tactics of our brand and of key competitors. It should include an analysis of current advertising and other communications in relation to brand equity. Is the strategy designed to reinforce current brand equity or to change it? Who is the target audience? Are there different target audiences? What are the theme and executional approach? How are the marketing funds being spent (consumer pull versus trade push, advertising, promotions, direct marketing, etc.)? An assessment of problems/opportunities is also in order here.

Strategic Options* and *Recommended Plan. This step in the Lintas:Link strategic planning process draws on the conclusions from the brand equity audit to develop a viable recommended plan. The strategic options include:

- *Communication objectives:* What is the primary goal the message aims to achieve?
- *Audience:* Whom are we speaking to?
- *Source of business:* Where are customers to come from—brand(s) or product categories?
- *Brand positioning and benefits:* How are we to position the brand and what are the benefits that will build brand equity?
- *Marketing mix:* What is the recommended mix of advertising, public relations, promotion, direct response, etc.
- *Rationale:* How does the recommended strategy relate to, and what effect is it expected to have on, brand equity?

Alternative plans can be developed by changing the content of any of the major options.

Brand Equity Probe. The probe is the proprietary, qualitative research step in the Lintas:Link process. It is exploratory and task oriented. Here we need to determine which element(s) of brand equity must be created, altered, or reinforced in order to achieve our recommended strategy, and how far we can stretch each of these components without risking the brand's credibility. In other words, what are the boundaries we should not cross?

Example: Our brand is seen as too technical and aloof. How far can we take it to make it more friendly?

If not enough information is available, from previous research to complete this step, we may need to do the brand equity probe right at the start of the Link process. If sufficient information is available, simply summarize the results here.

The probe results in a revised list of rational and emotional elements that describe *how we want consumers to think and feel about our brand in the future.*

Will it be yours?

Of the 50 million dogs in America, a million will now enjoy a dry dog food never before available.

A dog food for the fortunate one dog in fifty.

Will it be yours?

That depends on the price you place on quality.

Because quality is what our new dog food is all about.

We named our dog food Purina O.N.E.® Short for "Optimum Nutritional Effectiveness." "Optimum" because, ounce for ounce, there is no leading dog food that is more nutritious than Purina O.N.E.

We used a number of expensive ingredients not used in most other dry dog foods.

Our main ingredient is chicken—a highly digestible source of protein and other nutrients for dogs.

What you won't find in Purina O.N.E. is important, too. It's free of fillers, and artificial colors and flavors. It only has good things for your dog.

But even the best dog food won't do your dog any good if he won't eat it.

Dogs don't always know what's good for them, but they usually know what they like.

So good taste isn't just a nicety. It's a necessity.

Happily, your dog will love the taste of Purina O.N.E. Taste tests prove it's more palatable

than even the leading dry dog food.

Unhappily, not all dogs will get the chance to eat Purina O.N.E.

For one thing, we can't make enough of it to go around.

But the real determining factor is cost.

Not every dog owner is willing to pay the price for a dog food of this quality.

We suggest you pick up a bag of Purina O.N.E., and compare its ingredients to the dog food you're now serving.

Then compare the price. And decide if your dog is worth the difference.

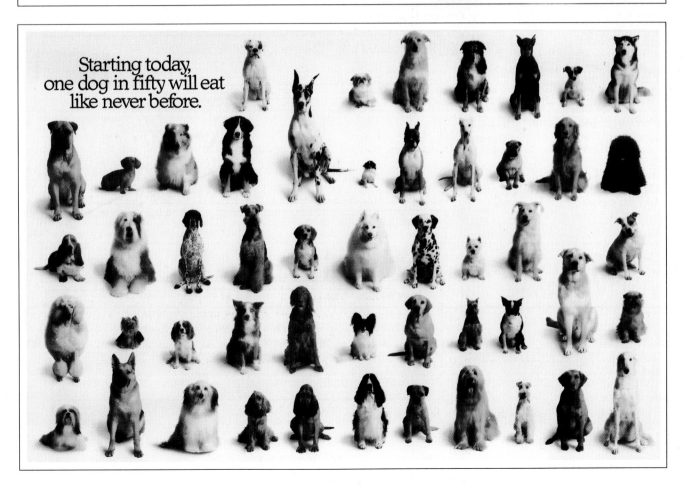

Starting today, one dog in fifty will eat like never before.

EXHIBIT 3.13

A new product tries to build brand equity. This new product would start the Link Process with a brand equity probe. (Courtesy: Purina.)

Creative Brief. In this step, we synthesize the first three Link steps into an action plan for the development of all communications for the brand: advertising, promotion, public relations, direct marketing, and so on. The creative brief consists of three elements.

STRATEGY: This is a one-page statement that clearly defines what audience we are talking to; how they think, feel, and behave; what communication is intended to achieve; and the promise that will create a bond (link) between the consumers and the brand. The strategy consists of:

- *Key observation:* The most important market/consumer factor that dictates the strategy.
- *Communication objective:* The primary goal the advertising aims to achieve.
- *Consumer insight:* The consumer ''hot button'' our communication will trigger.
- *Promise:* The link between the consumer and the brand: what the brand should stand for in the consumer's mind.
- *Support:* The reason the brand gives the consumer permission to believe.
- *Audience:* Whom are we speaking to? How do they think and feel about the brand?

The key to writing the strategy is to have one idea per element (or box in Exhibit 3.14).

EXHIBIT 3.14

You need to fill in one idea in each box in the creative brief.

LINTAS:LINK

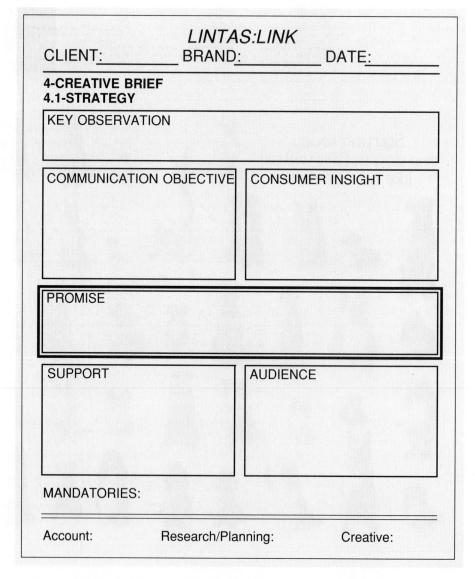

CLIENT:__________ BRAND:__________ DATE:__________

4-CREATIVE BRIEF
4.1-STRATEGY

KEY OBSERVATION

COMMUNICATION OBJECTIVE

CONSUMER INSIGHT

PROMISE

SUPPORT

AUDIENCE

MANDATORIES:

Account: Research/Planning: Creative:

The audit process ends with a ''creative brief'' or *action plan* for all communication variables—the entire ''advertising mix.'' *Strategy* for reaching the target audience; the desired ''equity'' or rational/emotional elements considered ''ideal;'' and, lastly, the ''creative tone'' the campaign should assume are included. This spring Chesebrough-Pond's Prince Matchabelli unit broke a $4.5 million campaign for a new scent called *Night Rhythms*—aimed at *teens and young women*. ''The changing lifestyle of *today's mother* is helping the younger segments,'' revealed an industry spokesperson. *Night Rhythms* is billed as ''The fragrance that dances 'til dawn,'' uses bold colors and graphics, and has more sophisticated positioning. Ads in teen and fashion magazines direct the young consumers' to upscale specialty stores, such as Bloomingdales, Saks Fifth Avenue, and Bullock's.

Desired Brand Equity. This is the list of rational and emotional components that describes how we want consumers to think and feel about the brand in the future. The *desired* brand equity is compared to the *current* brand equity to clearly show, side by side, the changes the communication program is intended to create (see Exhibit 3.15). Changes in brand equity, especially in the emotional elements, come very slowly. We would expect the differences between current and desired brand equity to be subtle—or, if substantial, to take a long time to be achieved.

Creative Guidelines. This part of the creative brief is written in close cooperation with the creative director on the brand and is based on insights gained from the brand equity probe as well as on judgment and experience. The creative guidelines are a simple list of do's and don'ts giving the creative team clear direction about the attitude, approach, and tonality the advertising should take in order to create the desired brand equity.

EXHIBIT 3.15

The desired brand equity is compared to current brand equity, showing changes the communications program is intended to create. This information is part of the creative brief, along with creative guidelines for all communications.

LINTAS:LINK

CLIENT:________ BRAND:__________ DATE:______

CURRENT BRAND EQUITY

EMOTIONAL ELEMENTS	RATIONAL ELEMENTS

DESIRED BRAND EQUITY

EMOTIONAL ELEMENTS	RATIONAL ELEMENTS

ALL COMMUNICATIONS

SHOULD	SHOULD NOT

NIKE
AIR
AIR FREIGHT.
The Force Series from Nike. When it absolutely, positively has to be in someone's face.
Air Force STS
Air Delta Force ST
FORCE.

NIKE
AIR
THIS IS ONE CROSS-TRAINER THAT ISN'T AFRAID TO TAKE A BATH.
Nike-Air® washable cross-training shoes. (Sink. Washing machine. Tub. They don't care.) Don't even need a dryer. Sounds like something to get lathered up about.
Bo Jackson. Baseball player & football hobbyist.

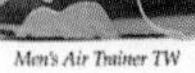

Men's Air Trainer TW

EXHIBIT 3.16

Ads working hard to build strong brand equity. (Courtesy: Nike and Wieden & Kennedy, Inc.)

SUMMARY

Products pass through a number of stages, from introduction to ultimate demise, known as the "product life cycle." Advertising plays a different role in each stage of product development. Until consumers appreciate the fact that they need a product, that product is in the pioneering stage of advertising. The competitive stage tries to differentiate one brand from another. The retentive stage calls for reminder advertising.

A product's age has little to do with the stage it is in at any given time. Rather, consumer attitude or perception determines which stage a product is in. As consumer perception changes, moving it from one stage to another, the advertising message should change. In fact, the advertising may be in more than one stage at any given time. Creative marketing can propel a product through new pioneering, new competitive, and new retentive stages. And it is even possible for a product to continue on into newest pioneering, competitive, and retentive stages. As products age, so do their consumers, which is why no product can survive without constantly attracting new consumers. Long-term success depends on keeping current customers while constantly creating new ones.

In the mid-1880s there were no brands. Manufacturers differentiated their products and gave them names as the concept of branding was born.

Brands are among the most valuable assets a marketer owns. The product is not the brand. A product is manufactured; a brand is created and is made up of both rational and emotional elements. In today's marketing environment it is essential that every communication reinforces brand personality in the same manner: advertising, public relations, packaging, promotion, etc. The most important factor in determining the actual value of a brand is its equity in the market: how consumers think and feel about the brand.

Lintas' Link is an example of a strategic planning system that involves the brand equity audit, strategic options and recommended plan, brand equity probe, and the creative brief.

QUESTIONS

1. What is the pioneering stage?
2. What determines the stage of a product?
3. How can a product be in more than one stage at a time?
4. What is the essence of the advertising message in each stage of the spiral?
5. Why is the retentive stage both good and bad for some products?
6. What is brand equity?
7. What are the elements in the Lintas Creative Brief?
8. Name the four steps in the Lintas' Link strategic planning system.
9. Identify:
   (a) communication objective
   (b) left brain
   (c) advertising objective
   (d) new pioneering

SUGGESTED EXERCISES

1. Find an ad for a product in each of the three basic stages of the advertising spiral from current publications. Briefly explain how each ad's message relates to the specific stage?
2. Find two ads that are in both the pioneering and competitive stages at the same time. Briefly explain.

3. Find two ads for brands you consider to have strong brand equity.
4. Find two ads that are for products that are attempting to build strong brand equity.

READINGS

Berry, Jon: "Brand Preference: The Missing Link?" *Adweek,* August 24, 1987, p. 32.

Dagnoli, Judann: "Columbian Arrival," *Advertising Age,* April 3, 1989, p. 60.

Eliashberg, Jehoshusa, and Thomas S. Robertson: "New Product Preannouncing Behavior: A Market Signal Study," *Journal of Marketing Research,* Vol. 25., August 1988, pp. 282–292.

Freeman, Laurie: "Johnson Takes Raid to the Max," *Advertising Age,* March 6, 1989. p. 41.

Ries, Al, and Jack Trout: Positioning: The Battle for Your Mind (New York: McGraw-Hill, 1986).

Sloan, Pat: "Reebok Responds to Nike," *Advertising Age,* February 20, 1989, p. 2.

Strazewski, Len: "Apple Uses New Marketing Strategy to Take a Slice of Competitor's Pie," *Marketing News,* September 12, 1988, p. 7.

Tellis, Gerard J., and Claes Fornell: "The Relationship Between Advertising and Product Quality Over the Product Life Cycle: A Contingency Theory," *Journal of Marketing Research,* Vol. 25, February 1988, pp. 64–71.

FOUR

Target Marketing

In the brand equity audit discussed in the last chapter, we examined the existing state of the brand in the context of markets and consumers. Now it is time to get specific about the types of information available and how to use them in planning advertising decisions for almost any product or service.

Let's say you have developed a great product and want to sell it and get rich. You give the product a name and decide to advertise. But to whom? Everybody who has any money? That wouldn't be very smart. You would be much wiser to draw up a strategic plan for targeting your advertising to the best prospects—those consumers most likely to be interested in your product.

To make strategic planning work, you need to know the answers to a lot of questions. Who are the best prospects? Where do they live? Are they male or female? Are significant numbers of them Hispanic, black, Asian, or other special groups? What about geographical differences? How important is education or income? What kind of lifestyles do your prospects have? How do they spend their time? How do they think and act? Are there enough of these people for you to make a profit?

Target marketing. *Identifying and communicating with groups of prime prospects.*

You answer these questions, but wonder which of this information is really important to your decision making. At this point, do you know enough to define your target market? Or do you need to know more to reach your prospects? For instance: What do you want people to think of and feel about your brand as a result of being exposed to your advertising? Perhaps you'd better do more homework before spending any money!

You need to identify your prime prospects so you don't waste time and money advertising your product to people who are unlikely to buy it. The process designed to pinpoint your best prospects among all consumers is called *target marketing*. The Hercules ad in Exhibit 4.1A doesn't try to appeal to everybody who can use this kind of wrap. Instead, it targets snack food manufacturers—a very limited but profitable market for Hercules. The *Wall Street Journal* ad in Exhibit 4.1B targets advertisers of products for the affluent businessperson.

The process of finding prime prospects can be complex because there are so many ways of looking at consumers in a constantly changing environment. Marketing executives need to evaluate significant shifts in demographic and product-preference pat-

Too often, snack foods go stale on the shelf. Then they go out with the twice weekly pick-ups.

What a waste.

Especially when you could be using laminations made of Hercules* oriented polypropylene films. Our films provide excellent barriers against oxygen and moisture. For better flavor retention. And longer shelf life.

Of course, there is more than one kind of snack. And Hercules makes a variety of films to suit the specific needs of each. We offer saran-coated, Surlyn*-coated and co-polymer sealable oriented polypropylene films. As well as opaque and metallized films to protect snacks from light.

But the benefits aren't limited to what's inside the package. Hercules has a higher consistency of quality. Your converters can meet delivery requirements quickly and with fewer problems.

Our films provide a wide sealing range. So you don't have to make adjustments as often. We even have slip-modified films that provide superb machinability.

And you're never alone when you work with Hercules. Our Film Applications Lab provides technical support unsurpassed in the industry. Whatever snack packaging needs you have, we can help you meet them. With just the right film.

To get more information on Hercules films for snacks, write Hercules Product Information, Hercules Incorporated, Hercules Plaza, Wilmington, DE 19894. Or call 1-800-247-4372.

Otherwise, you're just throwing your money away.

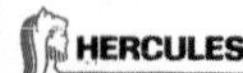

EXHIBIT 4.1A

Hercules aims its polypropylene film at snack food manufacturers. (Courtesy: Cole Henderson Drake, Inc.)

EXHIBIT 4.1B

***The Wall Street Journal* targets advertisers. (Courtesy: *The Wall Street Journal.*)**

You don't want to miss.

Because, in target marketing, aim is everything.

You have to reach the people who can buy what you have to sell.

Which is why, if your target is business or the affluent, there's just one place to aim.

The Wall Street Journal.

Every business day, we reach 6.2 million people with the power to say "Yes." And with the affluence and influence to turn "Yes" into sales.

Our subscribers have an average household income of $107,800. And an average household net worth of nearly $800,000.

Among those in business and the professions, over half hold top management positions. With the authority to initiate and approve major purchases.

That makes The Journal's audience the perfect target for marketers of everything from computers and convention sites to luxury homes and cars.

And if you're targeting one part of the country?

In addition to Journal editions, we now offer Southern California and Southeastern Regions. So you can target your advertising to two of the fastest growing economic areas in the world.

No matter which editions or regions you select, you'll reach those who can say the one word every marketer wants to hear.

"Yes."

The Wall Street Journal.

Where target marketers make a big splash.

THE WALL STREET JOURNAL.

IT WORKS.

To be an *effective* and *successful* marketer, the advertiser needs to identify *prime prospects*—the people most likely to buy the product or service. The process is called *target marketing*. In promoting its maritime heritage in *Forbes, Palm Beach Life, Power and Motor, Yacht, and Yachting,* Brooke Yachts *knows* it's reaching potential customers. The ads for yachts in the $3–30 million range emphasize the company's *expertise* and *longevity*—two important characteristics valued by their upscale targets.

The first step in "targeting" is to identify "*shifts*" in the marketplace. *Disposable and discretionary income levels* are key indicators for marketing projections. *Spiegel, the fashion-conscious cataloger,* combined additional family income with increased numbers of women working and produced a successful market strategy. Its multiple, up-to-date catalogs promote *advantages,* not readily available in the marketplace: *sophisticated clothing and home furnishings, with convenience.* The emphasis on familiar brand names breaks down any consumer resistance—and "personalized service" promotes repeated "*direct*" *shopping.*

terns. The first step in this process is to identify the predictable changes and opportunities that will affect the market into the next century.

What are the marketing implications of delayed marriages on furniture, appliances, and other household basics? Since 1980, the number of married couples under age 25 has dropped by 38 percent as young people continue to postpone marriage (see Exhibit 4.2). Does this trend mean fewer household products will be sold, or does it mean advertising for these products must be aimed at a different type of consumer? Nonfamily households under age 25 outnumber married-couple households in the this age group—44 percent versus 35 percent.[1] What are the implications for advertisers?

Income is another method of segmenting consumers. The Census Bureau is the biggest supplier of income data, which it collects from some 60,000 households each year. To use income data from any source, you need to decide how many income categories you need. If you simply use households making $25,000 plus, you will be unable to differentiate between middle- and upper-income levels. Moreover, income numbers can be misleading. The *mean* (or average) can be skewed by a few extremes. If five people have the following incomes: $5,000, $6,000, $7,000, $8,000, and $100,000, the mean income would be $25,200—which is not reflective of anyone in the group. A better measure is *median* income—the point at which half the individuals have lower incomes and half have higher incomes. The median income for this group is $7,000.

Disposable income and discretionary income are two measures often used by marketers. *Disposable income* is after-tax income. *Discretionary income* is the amount of money consumers have after paying taxes and buying necessities like food and housing. Exhibit 4.3 examines another important variable, *income change*. In 1990, 13.4 percent of all U.S. households earned between $30,000 and $39,999, and these households accounted for 20.1 percent of the country's total consumer income. In 1995, 14.3 percent of all U.S. households will have an income in this bracket, and will account for 18.7 percent of the country's total consumer income. The importance of income may vary significantly according to product category—it means little in selling soft drinks, but is very important in selling different makes and models of cars.

The study of population changes is also helpful in planning marketing and advertising activities. Population growth and decline may affect the weight of advertising in different states or regions of the country. Exhibit 4.4 gives the Census Bureau's projection of population changes up to the year 2010 for selected states. California, Texas,

[1] Judith Waldrop, "Inside America's Households," *American Demographics,* March 1989, pp. 20–27.

EXHIBIT 4.2

Change in number of householders aged 15 to 24, 1980–1988.

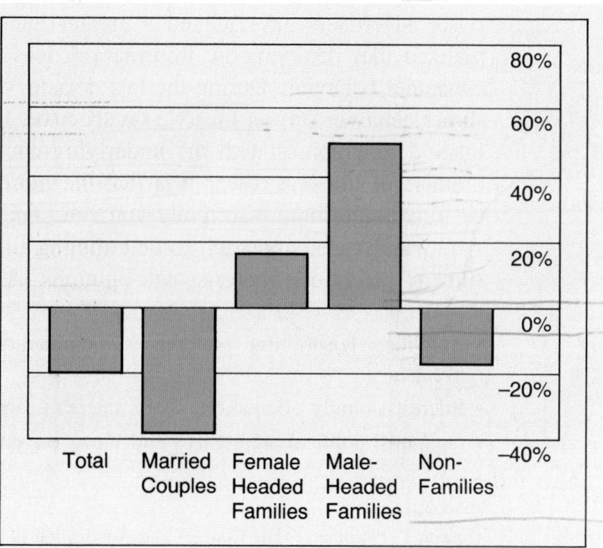

EXHIBIT 4.3

Household income as percentage of income, 1985–1995.

Percent of U.S. Households			*Income Level*	*Percent of Total U.S. Consumer Income*		
1985	*1990*	*1995*		*1985*	*1990*	*1995*
30.0	26.0	22.5	Under $10,000	8.3	6.3	4.9
29.3	26.2	23.3	$10,000–19,999	21.8	16.8	13.0
21.1	21.2	19.9	$20,000–29,999	25.9	22.9	18.6
11.1	13.4	14.3	$30,000–39,999	19.0	20.1	18.7
4.4	6.5	9.0	$40,000–49,999	9.8	12.5	15.0
3.0	4.9	8.0	$50,000–74,999	9.0	12.8	17.8
1.1	1.8	3.0	$75,000 & Over	6.2	8.6	12.0
100%	100%	100%	TOTAL	100%	100%	100%

Source: CARR Reports, Cahners, Publishing Co.

EXHIBIT 4.4

Selected states' population changes, 1990–2010.

				1990–2000		*2000–2010*	
	1990	**2000**	**2010**	**Change**	**Percent**	**Change**	**Percent**
U.S. total	249,891	267,747	282,055	17,856	7.1%	14,308	5.3%
Arizona	3,752	4,618	5,319	866	23.1	701	15.2
California	29,136	33,500	37,347	4,374	15.0	3,847	11.5
Florida	12,818	15,415	17,530	2,597	20.3	2,115	13.7
Georgia	6,663	7,957	9.045	1,294	19.4	1,088	13.7
Illinois	11,612	11,580	11,495	−32	−0.3	−85	−0.7
Iowa	2,758	2,549	2,382	−209	−7.6	−167	−6.6
Kansas	2,492	2,529	2,564	37	1.5	35	1.4
Michigan	9.293	9,250	9,097	−43	−0.5	−153	−1.7
Texas	17,712	20,211	22,281	2,499	14.1	2,070	10.2
Wyoming	502	489	487	−13	−2.6	−2	−0.4

Source: U.S. Bureau of Census.

and Florida will have more than half of the U.S. population growth between 1990 and the year 2000, and Arizona is expected to be the fastest-growing state during the 1990s. Iowa will lose 21,000 people per year during the same period of time. What are the implications for advertisers? Exhibit 4.5 illustrates that the U.S. population is growing, but the birth rate is declining. Again, what does this mean for advertisers?

Population migrations also dictate where increased advertising dollars should be spent. Increasing attention is being focused on *California, Texas and Florida*—and other *Sunbelt* states. Recognizing the spiraling growth of the area, *Luby's of San Antonio,* a mid-priced cafeteria, plans on opening 100 restaurants in Florida in the next 20 years! Their prime target—retirees.

As advertisers have gained a greater understanding of the consumer, they have realized that demographic information does not provide an adequate prediction of consumer behavior. During the last decade, the emphasis has been on studying consumer behavior from a lifestyle prospective. Lifestyle studies attempt to combine primary demographics with the underlying causes of consumer behavior. "The basic premise of lifestyle research is that the more you know and understand about your customers the more effectively you can communicate and market to them."[2]

A widely used approach to determining lifestyle characteristics is to identify consumers' activities, interests, and opinions (AIO). Typical AIO measures are:

AIO (activities, interests, and opinions). *Widely used in identifying consumers for lifestyle studies.*

- Activities: leisure-time preferences, community involvement, and preferences for social events.
- Interests: family orientation, sports interests, and media usage.
- Opinions: political preferences and views on various social issues.

[2]Joseph T. Plummer, "The Concept and Application of Life Style Segmentation," *Journal of Marketing,* January 1974, p. 33.

EXHIBIT 4.5

Projected growth of the U.S. population. (*Source:* Carr Reports, Cahner's Publishing Company.)

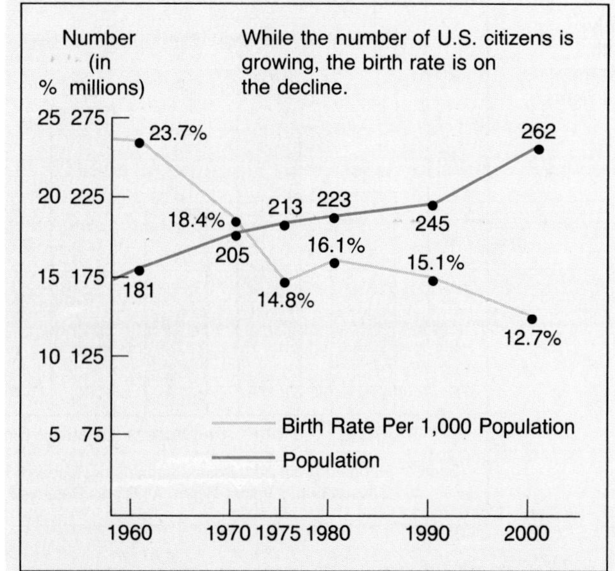

Geographics and demographics—the quantitative factors—don't tell the whole story. Advertisers use consumer behavior studies—*lifestyle analysis*—to identify the *activities, interests, and opinions* (AIO) of various individuals. Such psychographic research has revealed an interest in seeing more information about pharmaceuticals broadcast on television. *Lexis* is proceeding with plans to air TV spots for its N.E.E. 1/35 birth control pills. Although the networks, earlier this year, refused TV advertising for the oral contraceptive, Lexis plans to run the spots on an independent channel. A company spokesperson admitted that, "most informed women refer to *specialized programming* anyway, for meaningful health information."

Innovators are marketers' best targets, as they are the consumers most likely to buy *new products*. *The Limited* began their meteoric rise by appealing to teens and young 20s, who appreciated "saavy" clothes. Once they bought, management knew it wouldn't be long before their peers would be clamoring for the same styles. To continue the cycle, the "innovative" chain keeps the individual assortments coming to stores at "quick clips"—so that there's *always* something "new" to feature. Other outlets, such as department and specialty stores, are still rooted in the "seasonal rut."

Looking at Exhibit 4.6, you can see that consumers A and B are identical demographically, but that an advertiser would detect important differences by examining their lifestyles.

SEGMENTING INNOVATORS FOR NEW PRODUCTS

Billions of dollars are spent on new-product introductions each year despite a failure rate as high as 80 percent. Evidence suggests that poor marketing is one of the problems. Marketers need to know which consumers have a predeliction to purchase new products and how they can be reached most efficiently.

One company that supplies this kind of information is Mediamark Research Inc. MRI publishes a *Consumer Innovators Report*, identifying the consumers most likely to be responsive to new products. There are five categories of consumer/usage, attitudes, and lifestyles (see Exhibit 4.7), and within each category, products, services, and activities that are representative of innovation are identified. Specific variables are used to cluster consumer segments. Overall, 45 percent of U.S. adults have a proclivity to purchase and try new products and services in one or more categories.

A profile of the average or typical U.S. adult emerges from an examination of basic demographic variables. The degree to which the consumer innovator segments diverge

EXHIBIT 4.6

Consumer demographic and lifestyle profiles.

	Demographic Profile	*Lifestyle Profile*
Consumer A	Age: 38; sex: male; race: white; occupation: managerial; income: $40,000; married, two children	Republican, President of Rotary Club, Member Board of Directors Little League Baseball, Member of the Town and Gown Theater, and the Rolling Hills Sports Car Club
Consumer B	Age: 38; sex: male; race: white; occupation: managerial; income: $40,000; married, two children	Politically independent, President of the Carlton Coin and Stamp Club, and Executive Secretary of the Woodland Preservation Society

EXHIBIT 4.7

Percent of U.S. adults in innovative segments. (*Source;* Reprinted with permission. Mediamark Research Inc. *Consumer Innovators Report.* All rights reserved.)

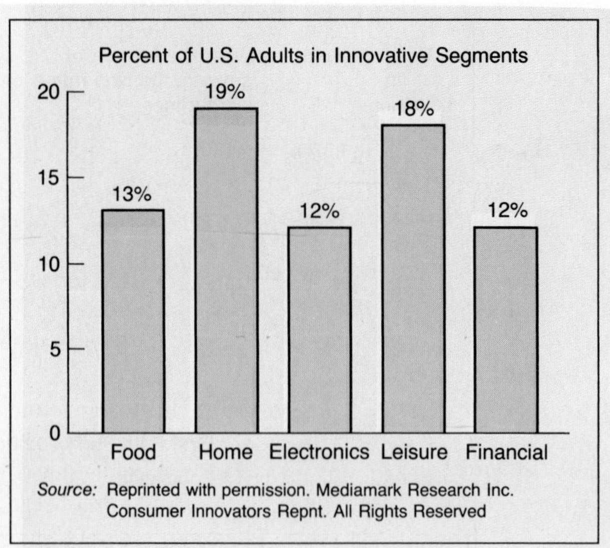

from this profile is critical in determining each segment's socioeconomic status and lifestyles. Exhibit 4.8 shows a distinct difference between the innovators and noninnovators. A general description of innovators is: They are almost equally divided between men and women who are in the 35–54 age group, they are married with children; and they are 54 percent more likely than the average American to have a college education and 50 percent more likely to have a household income exceeding $50,000.

This kind of information arms marketers of new products and line extensions with the knowledge they need to identify consumers most likely to purchase their new products. Reaching these innovators effectively will strengthen an advertiser's chances of successfully launching a new product.

EXHIBIT 4.8

Demographics of innovators versus noninnovators. (*Source:* Reprinted with permission. Mediamark Research Inc. *Consumer Innovators Report.* All rights reserved.)

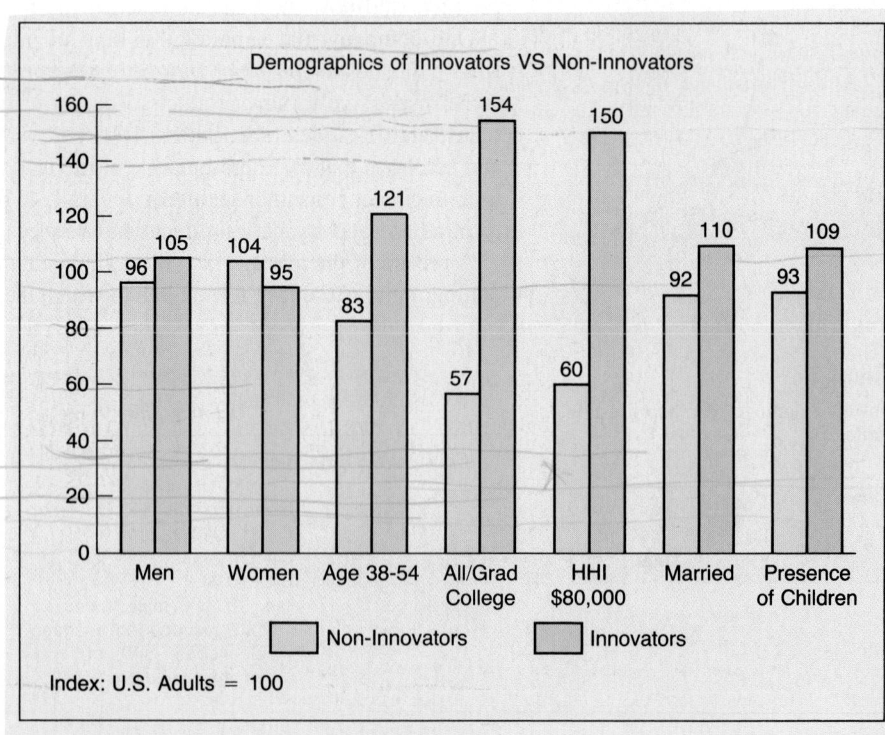

TARGET MARKETING AND THE MARKETING CONCEPT

Marketing concept. *A management orientation that views the needs of consumers as primary to the success of a firm.*

As markets reach the saturation level when basic demands have been satisfied, *new products* emerge to satisfy *specific needs* of smaller groups or "targets." A new chicken feed supplement has been launched by C. R. Eggs of King of Prussia, Pennsylvania, which actually reduces cholesterol in eggs. "It's so exciting," beams Jerry Siano, N. W. Ayer vice-chairman, "that it could actually make *ordinary eggs 'obsolete!'*"

Market segmentation is an extension of the *marketing concept,* defined by Philip Kotler as a management orientation that holds that the key to achieving organizational goals is determining the needs and wants of target markets and adapting the organization to delivering the desired satisfactions more effectively and efficiently than its competitors.[3]

The marketing concept developed from the recognition that an exclusive emphasis on product production could not be continued once modern production exceeded general consumer demand. Successful products would be those developed to solve a consumer problem rather than those that could be manufactured most efficiently; so companies realized that they should be creating products to fill an existing consumer need rather than forcing a product on the marketplace. Furthermore, sellers found that the best strategy was to market products that met the needs of a specific consumer group (or target) rather than to try to satisfy all consumers with a single product.

The research ingenuity and expense that go into finding the unfilled marketing niche can be tremendous, but the rewards for success make the effort extremely worthwhile. However, the advertiser must realize that these market segments are not static. As products change and new competitors enter the marketplace, consumers look for product alternatives. Advertising must adapt to these alternatives in the marketplace. Exhibit 4.9 illustrates how BellSouth Mobility's lifestyle approach goes beyond the mere need for cellular phone service. As the market for cellular phones expands, so does the technology. What happens to the call to your car phone if you step out for lunch? The answer is a cellular phone with a built-in answering machine. And, of course, all good

[3]Philip Kotler, *Principles of Marketing* (Englewood Cliffs, NJ: Prentice Hall, 1980), p. 22.

EXHIBIT 4.9
BellSouth Mobility uses a lifestyle approach to reach their target. (Courtesy: BellSouth Mobility.)

salespeople will want to send and receive orders and information to and from the office over their cellular phone with the built-in fax machine. Obviously, not everybody needs such technology, but these kinds of innovations often create a broader spectrum of tastes, habits, and needs among consumers.

The award-winning advertising in Exhibit 4.10 illustrates how a state has segmented tourists. "The best place to hear old English music is 3,000 miles west of London" targets music lovers and adventurers.

Not only do you have to target your audience, but you must do it with effective communication.

WHAT IS A PRODUCT?

Consumers don't buy "products"—they buy *satisfaction. Combining cigarette smoking with music,* Salem cigarettes will launch its most ambitious promotional marketing program to date. "This is the largest, fully integrated music-marketing program in history," bragged Larry Gershman, director of sales promotion for FCB/Lever Katz Partners' Integrated Communications Group. "Sound Waves" focuses on what introductory ads call "the refreshest new music"—in a play on Salem's current ad theme—that promotes mainly "cutting edge" rock music from up-and-coming performers. . . . with little attention to the actual cigarette or smoking.

Brand loyalty. *Degree to which a consumer purchases a certain brand without considering alternatives.*

Normally, consumers don't go to the store to buy cetylpyridinium chloride, domiphen bromide. (.005 percent), and SD alcohol 38-F (16.6 percent) in a mouthwash base of water, glycerin, polysorbate 80, sodium saccharin, benzoic acid, flavor, and FD&C Blue No. 1. They go to buy Scope. Scope is more than a physical object. It represents a bundle of satisfactions—clean breath, clean taste, relief of dryness, self-esteem—that are considered more or less important by each consumer.

Different people have different ideas about what satisfactions are important. Products are designed with satisfactions to match the interest of a particular group of consumers. We are judged in large measure by our physical possessions—think of yuppies and their BMWs or Jags. The products that we purchase say something about us and group us with people of like tastes and brand preferences. Target marketing means focusing on groups of people who seek similar satisfactions from life and products.

It is difficult for a new product to find a place in the market against established competition. Its manufacturer must be selective in defining the most profitable market segments because the cost of introducing a new product can be very expensive.

How can a new-product advertiser estimate the chances of getting a heavy user of another brand to try the new brand? One technique is to define market segments according to their brand loyalty and preference for national over private brands. Studies of package-goods brand loyalty have found six segments:

1. *National-brand loyal.* Members of this segment buy primarily a single national brand at its regular price.
2. *National-brand deal.* This segment is similar to the national-brand-loyal segment, except that most of their purchases are made on deal (that is, the consumer is loyal only to national brands but chooses the least expensive one). To buy the preferred national brand on deal, the consumer engages in considerable store switching.
3. *Private-label loyal.* Households in this segment primarily buy the private label offered by the store in which they usually shop (e.g., Eckerds, A&P, and other store brands).
4. *Private-label deal.* This segment shops at many stores and buys the private label of each store, usually on deal.
5. *National-brand switcher.* Members of this segment tend not to buy private labels. Instead, they switch regularly among the various national brands on the market.
6. *Private-label switcher.* This segment is similar to the private-label-deal segment, except that the members are not very deal-prone and purchase the private labels at their regular price.[4]

Price, product distribution, and promotion also affect the share of market coming from each competing brand. However, a new national brand would expect to gain most

[4]Robert C. Blattberg, Thomas Buesing, and Subrata K. Sen, "Segmentation Strategies for New National Brands," *Journal of Marketing,* Fall 1980, p. 60. (Courtesy *Journal of Marketing,* a publication of the American Marketing Association.)

Discover what happened to the English pub when it came to North Carolina.

When the English came to the New World, they brought one of their oldest institutions:

Their local pub.

Yet, after a century or two in North Carolina, it evolved into something even better:

Our country store.

Walk in the door, and time slips into another dimension.

You can join in a game of checkers, which some of us still play with bottle caps.

Meet everybody from the blacksmith to the barber.

And take home a maple walking stick, a fly swatter, or a sack of moon pies.

All across North Carolina, you'll find places that continue to dwell happily in the past.

Like Wilmington, the port city where Cornwallis spent a two-week vacation. Here, you can explore 200 blocks of historic district, and a restored Victorian waterfront.

Or, follow the high road to miles of white beaches.

And to the little village of Southport, where the pace is so relaxed, it takes three days to celebrate the fourth of July.

So, come soon. To our shore, our midlands, and blue-misted mountains.

And you'll find that, even though the English discovered us four hundred years ago, we're worth discovering again.

North Carolina

Call toll-free, 1-800-VISIT NC, Operator 846.

The best place to hear old English music is 3,000 miles west of London.

When English settlers came to North Carolina, they brought a priceless treasure:

Ancient melodies, airs and ballads, some as old as the language itself.

Over the years, music like this has almost vanished in England. But it's taken root and flourished here.

We play it on porches in summer. Around hearth fires in winter. At the largest folk gathering in the country. Or, you can hear it in many small festivals all across our state.

And in a tiny mountain church named Morning Star, where the hymn tunes are still sung from old-time shape notes.

It's music so precious, the National Endowment for the Arts helps preserve it.

And it's so contagious, it could inspire you to make a joyful noise all your own.

So, come.

And discover that what the English carried across an ocean in their hearts can be taken home in yours.

North Carolina

Call toll-free, 1-800-VISIT NC, Operator 838.

EXHIBIT 4.10

of its initial sales from segments 2 and 5, while segments 1 and 3 would normally be poor prospects to try a new brand.

WHAT IS A MARKET?

Market. *A group of people who can (1) be identified by some common characteristic, interest, or problem; (2) use a certain product to advantage; (3) afford to buy it; and (4) be reached through some medium.*

Against established competition, a new product advertiser should promote to those consumer segments who are most likely to "switch." While several massmarketers offer clothing to women, size 12 and up, the trend is just taking root among *fashion-conscious merchants and designers,* such as Claiborne. "This is a market segment 'screaming' for additional merchandise," reveals Allen McNeary, senior vice-president. This year it entered the $10 billion-plus large-size market with its Elizabeth line. McNeary reported that 40% of the women in the United States are over size 12. With out-of-home jobs, college educations, and incomes of $30,000 or more, they are looking—desperately—for "an updated silhouette."

The *competition* for a new product may be *narrow*—within its product category (example: King Cola versus Coca-Cola)—or *broad* (example: Sony VCR versus Disney World). By enlarging their product base beyond home improvement items, *Wal-Mart* now competes in multiple markets. As more chains and regional stores join the discounting or low-price sector (example: Sears), their competitors are as near to their customers as *they are.*

For our purposes, a *market* can be defined as a group of people who can be identified by some common characteristic, interest, or problem; could use our product to advantage; can afford to buy it; and can be reached through some medium. Examples of potential markets are computer owners, golfers, mothers with young children, newlymarrieds, physicians, weight watchers, stamp collectors, football fans, indoor-sports fans, do-it-yourselfers, and runners.

Majority fallacy is a term applied to the assumption, once frequently made, that every product should be aimed at, and acceptable to, a majority of all consumers. Alfred Kuehn and Ralph Day have described how successive brands all aimed at a majority of consumers in a given market will tend to have rather similar characteristics and will neglect an opportunity to serve consumer minorities. They use chocolate-cake mixes as an example: Good-sized minorities would prefer a light chocolate cake or a very dark chocolate cake to a medium chocolate cake, which is the majority's choice. So while several initial entrants into the field would do best to market a medium chocolate mix to appear to the broadest group of consumers, later entrants might gain a larger market share by supplying the minorities with their preferences.[5]

We shall pursue the question of how to define a market throughout this book. Here it is enough to say that a market is a group of potential purchasers of our product.

WHAT IS THE COMPETITION?

Who are our competitors? What other brands? What other product categories? Are there many brands or only a few? What impact, if any, do store brands and generics have? Are there any strong, long-established brands or is the market volatile? In this context, how would you define Mountain Dew's (see Exhibit 4.11) competition? Sprite? 7-UP? Mellow Yellow? Colas? Iced tea? It could be any or all of these products. A major purpose of target marketing is to position a brand effectively within a product category (soft drinks) or subcategory (lemon-lime soft drinks).

Marketing strategy for a brand should seek to demonstrate how that product meets the needs of a particular consumer group. Your brand will gain value in a particular consumer segment by more exactly meeting its needs. Your ability to accomplish this will enhance the chances of your brand's success against a more generally positioned brand, which may not fully satisfy any single consumer segment. Products are normally competitive within a segment rather than across several groups. Shampoos, for example, are manufactured to meet a wide range of preferences—for clean hair, for manageable hair, for permed hair, for oily, dry, and regular hair. In Chapter 3, we illustrated how new brands must appeal to different segments of the general market according to their brand preferences and loyalty.

While most advertising emphasizes direct brand competition (7-Up versus Sprite or Colgate versus Crest), we consider competition more broadly, as including all the forces that inhibit the sales of a product. Thus, competition may be products outside your product's class as well as products in the same subclass as your product.

The competitive array can widen even further as the price of the product increases. For example, in terms of the family budget, the real competition for Interplak's tartar-

[5]Alfred A. Kuehn and Ralph A. Day, "Strategy of Product Quality," *Harvard Business Review,* November–December 1962, pp. 100ff.

EXHIBIT 4.11

Mountain Dew uses a lifestyle approach to reach their young target audience. (Courtesy: Pepsi-Cola Company.)

New, precise data on *local and regional markets* have given rise to market segmentation strategies. With increased *interest* and *usage* of *bath-related products in West Germany*, Colgate Palmolive is adding shower gel and foam bath to its line of Cleopatra skin care products. "There has been absolutely no consumer-led demand for a *single* European market," said Martin Sorrell, chief executive of the WPP Group, London, "so we're continuing targeting areas that appear *strong* . . . until the others catch up . . ."

fighting toothbrush (similar to what dentists use and selling for about $79) may not be other brands, but rather tartar-control toothpaste or tartar-control prerinse mouthwash. The competition for a brand of life insurance may be an alternative investment.

Still, the immediate competition for a product already on the market is other products in its class. How does your product compare with others in differentials? In total sales? In market share? In the sale of this particular brand? What do consumers like and dislike about the products being offered, including your?

PLANNING THE ADVERTISING

Market Segmentation

> ***Market Segmentation.*** *Dividing a total market of consumers into groups whose similarity makes them a market for products serving their special needs.*

There are a number of factors to be considered in planning advertising to take advantage of market segmentation. The first step is to determine the variable to use for dividing a market. In addition to demographics, the major means of market segmentation are geographical, product user, and lifestyle segmentation.

Geographical Segmentation. Designating customers by geographical area is the oldest form of segmentation and dates to an earlier period when distribution was the primary concern of manufacturers. Today geomarketing is of particular importance to media planners in deciding on national, regional, and local ad campaigns. It is only recently that geomarketing has been elevated to a marketing discipline the way that demographics was in the 1950s and psychographics in the 1970s. In this instance, consumers haven't changed, but marketers' awareness of regional marketing has. Geodemographic marketing is just another way of segmenting the market for companies in search of growth.

There has been a "data explosion" on local markets. Some of the information comes from such companies as Nielsen, but there is also a growing trend among retailers to collect their own market research data for use in merchandising and buying decisions. Recently, Ogilvy & Mather recognized the shift toward geodemographic marketing by expanding on a concept called "The Nine Nations of North America" (see Exhibit 4.12). For example, San Franciscans drink almost twice as much domestic

EXHIBIT 4.12
Summary of Garreau's Nine Nations of North America.

Nation	Capital City	Location	Values of Differential Importance
New England	Boston	Extends north from central Connecticut, generally following traditional definition	Not sense of accomplishment, self-fulfillment
Québec	Québec City	Province of Québec	Self-respect?
The Foundry	Detroit	Surrounds the Great Lakes (excluding Superior) and extends to the Atlantic	Sense of accomplishment, being well-respected?
Dixie	Atlanta	Traditional South extended north to Indianapolis and St. Louis, cut off in the west at Dallas, and excluding south Florida	Not self-fulfillment, self-respect?
The Islands	Miami	South Florida and the Latin American Rim	Security
Empty Quarter	Denver	Rocky Mountains; excludes eastern Colorado but includes eastern Washington, Oregon, and California	Sense of belonging, sense of accomplishment
Breadbasket	Kansas City	Well north of Winnipeg, west nearly to Denver, as far east as Indianapolis—it excludes Midwestern cities such as Milwaukee, Chicago, and Cincinnati but includes most of the farmland in Illinois, Wisconsin, the Dakotas, Nebraska, and Oklahoma.	Not fun and enjoyment in life, warm relationships with others
MexAmerica	Los Angeles	Extends as far north as San Joaquin Valley of California and Pueblo, Colorado, but not as far north as Las Vegas or Austin	Sense of accomplishment, self-respect
Ecotopia	San Francisco	Follows the Pacific Ocean from south of San Francisco to Alaska	Not sense of accomplishment, self-fulfillment

(Source: Lyne R. Kahle, "The Nine Nations of North America and the Value Basis of Geographic Segmentation," Journal of Marketing, *April 1986, pp. 37–47.)*

table wine as New Yorkers. Some automobile manufacturers even use this kind of information to determine the popularity of car colors for certain markets—for sports cars, it's white on the West Coast and black in the Northeast.

Despite the importance of national distribution, there are still certain industries that have local and regional brands (Budwine and Cheerwine are local and regional soft drinks that taste like cherry cola). In these industries, geographical segmentation is a distribution strategy rather than a promotional one. Exhibit 4.13 shows a typical geographical market segmentation. Note that New England has the highest index for diet colas; however, compare its population number to the Southeast's. Exhibit 4.14 illustrates individual markets for hard candy.

Many national companies are dividing their marketing and advertising efforts into regional units in order to better respond to the competition. McDonald's, for instances

EXHIBIT 4.13
Diet colas' geographical segmentation.

Region	Population (000's)	All Buyers Index
New England	5010	119
Middle Atlantic	13166	99
East Central	10291	98
West Central	12097	102
Southeast	13445	98
Southwest	8138	92
Pacific	13322	103

(*Source:* Reprinted with permission. Copyright Spring 1988. Mediamark Research Inc. All rights reserved.)

EXHIBIT 4.14

Some individual markets for hard roll candy.

Metro Area	All Buyers Index
Oakland MSA	111
San Francisco MSA	84
San Jose MSA	118

(*Source:* Reprinted with permission. Copyright 1986. Mediamarket San Francisco. Mediamark Research Inc. All rights reserved.)

uses a major advertising agency to handle its national advertising and numerous (generally smaller) agencies to handle franchise and regional efforts supplementing the national effort. This gives McDonald's the ability to react to the marketplace by regions, cities, or even individual stores.

Product user segmentation. *Identifying consumers by the amount of product usage.*

Product User Segmentation. User segmentation is a strategy based on the amount and/or consumption patterns of a brand or product category. The advertiser is interested in product usage rather than consumer characteristics. As a practical matter, most user segmentation methods are combined with demographic or lifestyle consumer identification. Here the advertiser is interested in market segments that have the highest sales potential. Typically, a market segment is first divided into all users, and then subdivided into heavy, medium, and light users. Exhibit 4.15 segments a market not only according to geographical areas, but also according to product usage. It shows, for example, that diet cola usage among medium users is strongest in the West. The *heavy user* of diet colas is defined as a person who consumes more than five drinks or glasses within seven days; the *medium user* consumes two to five diet colas per week; and the *light user* consumes fewer than two diet colas per week. As you would expect, the definition of usage varies with the product category. You can compare usage of all soft-drink consumers, of regular soft-drink consumers, or of diet soft-drink consumers; you can compare any of these against caffeine-free soft usage; or you can look at lemon-lime versus orange usage—by category, flavor segment, or individual brands. As you can see, product user segmentation can get quite complex, but this kind of information allows marketers to use a rifle approach instead of a shotgun approach.

Lifestyle segmentation. *Identifying consumers by combining several demographics and lifestyles.*

Lifestyle Segmentation. In lifestyle segmentation, we make the assumption that if you live a certain way, so do your neighbors, and therefore any smart marketer would want to target clusters filled with these clones. Lifestyle clusters are more accurate characterizations of people than any single variable would be.

Each research company has its own terminology for the various clusters it identifies. For example, SRI developed a system called VALs that classifies people according to their values and lifestyles. It has recently been updated to VALs 2, which puts less emphasis on values and more on the psychological underpinings of behavior (see

EXHIBIT 4.15

Market segmentation by geographical area and product usage.

	Adults (000's) Usage of Diet Colas			
Region	**All Users (index)**	**Heavy Users (index)**	**Medium Users (index)**	**Light Users (index)**
Northeast	16896 (105)	6636 (96)	5453 (104)	4807 (119)
North Central	18910 (102)	8606 (108)	5862 (97)	4441 (96)
South	24732 (95)	11445 (103)	7494 (88)	5892 (91)
West	14931 (101)	5487 (87)	5776 (121)	3667 (100)

(*Source:* Reprinted with permission. Copyright Spring 1988. Mediamark Research Inc. All rights reserved.)

EXHIBIT 4.16

Personal investments in common or preferred stock.

Lifestyle Categories	*Index (Upper-Deck) Affluent Population) Average = 100*
Well-feathered nests	106
No strings attached	138
Nanny's in charge	71
Two careers	80
The good life	92

(*Source:* "Upper Deck Report," Mediamark Research Inc. Reprinted by permission. Copyright 1986. All rights reserved.)

Many national companies use *two approaches to promotion—national and regional.* Each approach may be handled by different advertising agencies, using alternative media. *Arby's* planned expansion in Philadelphia, Boston, Memphis, and Toronto "has prompted *a consistent TV campaign* for the first time," stated Mark Stein, vice-president-communications. W. B. Doner & Company is the national agency responsible. "Regional promotions—mostly P-O-P, radio, and FSIs—are handled by franchisee groups," added Stein, "who select *local agencies.*"

"Heavy users" of a particular product—or those with *above average potential*—are prime prospects for advertisers. *Gentlemen's Quarterly* magazine cites its "power" to attract males "who *'work out' 6 days out of 7.*" Their ad to advertisers features the shoes that are worn on each of those 6 days—"an athletic footwear wardrobe that didn't exist 10 years ago." "When *GQ* says so, over 4 million readers jump, run, hurdle, swing, shoot, tackle, and dribble," says the copy. For advertisers looking for heavy users of athletic equipment—*GQ* says "it's the one."

***Niche marketing.** A combination of product and target-market strategy. It is a flanking strategy that focuses on niches or comparatively narrow "windows of opportunity" within a broad product market or industry. Its guiding principle is to pit your strength against their weakness.*

Chapter 15 for a discussion of VALs 2). Another example is the clusters of investors depicted in Exhibit 4.16. These clusters are extracted from Mediamark Research's Upper Deck survey of affluent investors (people whose incomes are in the top 10 percent). Financial companies would be interested in the "well-feathered nests" and the "no strings attached" segments.

Education, income, race, place of residence, and family life cycle (e.g., single, married, widowed, childless) are some of the variables in a typical cluster.

Niche Marketing

"Niche marketing is not another buzzword for marketing segmentation," according to Alvin Achenbaum.[6] It is essentially a flanking strategy, the essence, which is to engage competitors in those product markets where they are weak or, preferably, have little or no presence. The guiding principle of niche marketing is to pit your strength against the competitor's weakness. No-frill motels didn't exist for many years. They were a logical means of competing against the other motel segments.

Porsche has managed to carve a formidable niche in the automobile industry by truly understanding its customers. It has identified what they generally have in common: They love to drive and place great stock in how a car handles; they appreciate styling and thoroughness in design versus flashiness and chrome; and they are achievers who set high standards for themselves and expect the same from the cars they drive. In 1989, Porsche expanded its U.S. market beyond sports car enthusiasts to include upscale consumers. High performance is still Porsche's notable feature, but the company sees opportunities in the luxury market.[7] Porsche's 1989 campaign reflected this shift: advertisements highlighted luxury features and driving pleasure with taglines like "Think of it as a Mercedes with Tabasco sauce" and "Fire the chauffeur."

In another example of studying the market and finding a niche, Noxell, the maker of Cover Girl makeup, discovered through market research in the late 1950s that a number of women would buy makeup they thought was good for the skin. So when Noxell introduced *Cover Girl* cosmetics, it presented them as therapeutic, rather than just enhancing to looks. By using world-class models to endorse its "clean makeup" throughout the 1960s, 1970s, and 1980s, Cover Girl has expanded this segment of the market substantially.

It should be noted that while segmentation is extremely important to successful advertising, it is not without risks. One problem is that once the upper limits of the niche are reached, sales growth will be limited unless the company can expand beyond its niche. Reebok International's niche was the aerobic shoe segment. As that market became saturated, Reebok had to enter other shoe markets to keep growing. By too

[6]Alvin Achenbaum, "Understanding Niche Marketing," *Adweek,* December 1, 1986, p. 62.

[7]Allan J. Magrath, *Market Smarts* (New York: John Wiley & Sons), pp. 8–18.

By catering to areas of a market, which large competitors don't cater to—or by aiming at markets currently "unserved"—*the niche marketer* can successfully carve a "porthole" or "window of opportunity." That's just what *Bain de Soleil* did, when it aimed its ads at upscale targets who were "bored" with drugstore suntan products. By emphasizing its moisture restoring and deep tanning properties, it downplayed its expensive price. That also helped in carving distribution *in specialty stores*—where suntan lotions and creams hadn't penetrated.

By "positioning" a product, we can create *a distinctive personality,* made up of real and perceived elements, which can be recalled by the targeted consumer. Ads for *Lawnboy* feature a "revolutionary" new M-Series walk-behind mower, with an oil system that allows longer engine life *without* premixing the oil. Spot TV commercials, themed "The most important oil change in history," illustrate a distinct, new product break-through—but also position Lawnboy as the maker of the *most efficient and least bothersome lawnmowers.* The company is especially anxious to attract *women* with their new approach.

When *selected markets* show evidence of strong demand, it may be profitable to market a product primarily to those markets. The producer anticipates *expanding* the market base—once success is achieved locally or regionally. Three such success stories of this approach are what Quaker Oats did with *Gatorade,* Proctor & Gamble with *Folgers Coffee,* and General Foods with *Entenmann's.* All three products *now* enjoy national distribution.

narrowly defining your market—that is, by excessive segmenting—you can become very inefficient in buying media, creating different ads, and obtaining alternative distribution channels. Stanback headache powders have been unable to crack the California market despite several attempts because the headache powder appeals to a peculiar southern proclivity to self-medicate.

Niche marketing can serve at least two purposes. It can gain a product entry to a larger market by attacking a small part of it not being served by competitors. It can also cater to latent needs that existing products do not adequately satisfy.

POSITIONING

Without distinctive positioning, your brand is lost. *Positioning* is another term for fitting the product into the lifestyle of the buyer. It refers to segmenting a market by either or both of two ways:

1. Creating a product to meet the needs of a specialized group.
2. Identifying and advertising a feature of an existing product that meets the needs of a specialized group.

Example:

Your birth control pills could be robbing you of essential vitamins and minerals.

Estrovite vitamins recognized a potential problem among women on birth control pills and created a product positioned to fulfill that need.

A product can hold different positions at the same time. Arm & Hammer baking soda has been positioned as a deodorizer for refrigerators, an antacid, a freezer deodorizer, and a bath skin cleaner, without losing its original market as a cooking ingredient.

Positioning is viewing the product through the eyes of the consumer. You position your product by placing it a certain way in the consumer's mind. You might try to get the following reactions from consumers to a new line of frozen-food entrees that are low in calories and have larger servings than the competition's:

Before seeing your advertising, the consumer thinks:

> "I like the convenience and taste of today's frozen foods but I don't usually get enough of the main course to eat. I would like to try a brand that gives me plenty to eat but is still light and healthy—and, most importantly, it's got to taste great."

After seeing your advertising, the consumer thinks:

> "I usually buy Judi's Frozen Food entrees. They taste great and I get plenty to eat, but they are still low enough in calories so that I don't feel I'm overeating. They're better for me because they have less salt and fat than others. And there is enough variety so that I can eat the foods I like without getting bored by the same old thing."

The point is to try to develop a position that has a certain difference.

Creating a Product for Selected Markets

One of the ways that marketers attract a focused interest group is through variations on a conventional product. New variation looks for groups with needs not fully met by existing products. In addition, products in the retentive stage may see variation as a means of rejuvenating a product whose sales have gone flat.

Wine coolers have grown rapidly to a billion-dollar industry since their introduction in 1981 by California Coolers. They were born on the California beaches as a refreshing summer drink. About one-third of their sales come from ordinary wine drinkers and the rest are split between soft-drink and new users. The cooler producers established niches in the ''refresher'' market because they met consumer preferences for cool, sweet, portable beverages and capitalized on the trend toward a more moderate and healthier lifestyle. California Coolers is strongest among the 21–29 age group, but targets 21–34-year-olds. The company has taken advantage of being the original wine cooler by positioning itself as ''The real stuff'' (see Exhibit 4.17).

In the pet health category, Heartgard-30 positioned itself as the once-a-month heartworm medicine for dogs. The product's advantage is absolutely clear in comparison to the daily required dosage of other heartworm medications, but now there are other 30-day medications available. Still, Heartgard-30 is positioned in the pet owner's mind as ''the once-a-month'' heartworm medication.

Positioning the Product by Appeal

Appeal. The motive to which an add is directed and which is designed to stir a person toward a goal the advertiser has set.

Sometimes you can advantageously position a product, or reposition it, just by changing the advertising appeal. Depending on the product, this may be the easiest approach to opening other markets. The risk is that competitors can match this type of change much easier than significant product changes.

Examples of this type of advertising are numerous. DeBeers meets the challenge of fewer marriages by appealing to men to buy a diamond ring ''that says you'd marry her all over again.'' OXY is positioned as the serious acne medicine, ''because zits are no laughing matter.'' Lee's Relaxed Rider Jean are positioned as the jeans that conform to the contours of a woman's body: ''The brand that fits.''

Positioning to Expand Brand Share

Positioning—or, more accurately, repositioning—can be an effective method of increasing brand share when a company already has a very high percentage of the market for a type of product. Let's assume our company, Acme Widgets, has 80 percent of the widget market. Two strategies that the company might adopt are shown in Exhibits 4.18 and 4.19.

EXHIBIT 4.17
California Cooler positions itself as the real stuff. (Courtesy: Chiat/Day Advertising.)

EXHIBIT 4.18

Strategy 1: Traditional brand promotion (no brand repositioning).

1988		1989	1990	
Brand Share, %		**Advertising**	**Brand Share, %**	
A,	10		A,	9.9
B,	5	$10 million spent against brands A, B, and C	B,	5.0
C,	5		C,	5.0
Acme,	80		Acme,	80.1
Total	100			100.0

EXHIBIT 4.19

Strategy II: Acme Widgets' brand repositioning.

1988		1989	1990	
Brand Share, %		**Advertising**	**Brand Share, %**	
			Primary market:	
A,	10	$6 million spent to keep present market share	A,	10
B,	5		B,	5
C,	5		C,	5
Acme,	80		Acme,	80
Total	100			100
			Alternative market:	
		$4 million spent to promote repositioned Acme Widget to new market	Other products and brands already in market,	85
			A,B,C,	5
			Acme	10
Total				100

If the original approach of a promotional strategy has "exhausted" its market appeal, *"repositioning"* can take place by alternating its approach. R. J. Reynolds Tobacco, in an effort to shift its appeal to smokers ages 21 to 24—from a current base of female smokers in their mid-30s, is repositioning core cigarette brands around themed ads and promotions. *Winston* has adopted a *sports focus,* while *Camel* has centered on *humor,* depicting the "Old Joe" cartoon mascot as a "Smooth Character."

In Exhibit 4.18, Acme, by engaging in direct brand competition, has increased its market share very slightly. However, it is extremely doubtful that further sales can be profitably taken from the competition. Increased advertising expenditures to make inroads into brands A, B, and C will probably cost proportionally more than the revenues realized.

The repositioning strategy depicted in Exhibit 4.19 has allowed Acme to keep its overwhelming share. At the same time, by spending 40 percent ($4 million of its $10 million advertising allowance) of its budget to position the company in a new market, acme gained 10 percent of this formerly untapped market segment rather than the 0.1 percent of the primary market it achieved with the first strategy. In this example, no physical changes were made in the product—only different appeals were used. This is the basis for positioning by choice of appeal.

How to Approach a Positioning Problem

Not all products lend themselves to the type of repositioning discussed here. The advertiser must be careful not to damage current product image by changing appeals and prematurely expanding into new markets. Jack Trout and Al Ries say that the advertiser who is thinking about positioning should ask the following questions:

1. What position, if any, do we already own in the prospect's mind?
2. What position do we want to own?
3. What companies must be outgunned if we are to establish that position?
4. Do we have enough marketing money to occupy and hold that position?

5. Do we have the guts to stick with one consistent positioning concept?
6. Does our creative approach match our positioning strategy?[8]

Positioning Examples:

- Peak was positioned as the toothpaste with baking soda. Although Peak had a unique product difference, it managed to obtain only a small market share because that difference was unimportant to consumers. People really interested in brushing their teeth with baking soda used real old-fashioned baking soda instead.
- Check-up toothpaste was introduced as the plaque attacker.
- Edwards baking company is positioned as the ''pie people.''
- Milk-Bone brand dog biscuits clean teeth and freshen breath.
- Affinity shampoo is for women over 40.
- Nature Valley Granola Bars are essentially the same as Carnation's Breakfast Bar, but they are positioned as a ''healthy snack food'' instead of a ''breakfast substitute.''
- Cheer is the detergent for all temperatures.
- Surf detergent is positioned as the ''dirt and odor remover.''
- Liquid Clorox 2 is the color-safe bleach that whitens whites and brightens colors.
- Fresh step is the cat litter that freshens with each step.
- Spray 'n Wash is the tough stain remover for laundry.
- Lever 2000 deodorant soap is better for your skin.

PROFILE OF THE MARKET

Advertisers should be aware of their ''strength''—share—of their markets and of their consumers' profiles. Frito-Lay's $4.1 billion sales in 1988, or 54.6% of the salty-snack market, made it the number 1 producer. Realizing *an expanded and nostalgia-hungry market,* they've brought back the ''Ruffles have ridges'' campaign—with a new twist. With Porky Pig stuttering the r's, they hope to ''awaken'' followers of the brand and attract Warner Brothers loyal cartoon watchers.

So far we have discussed specific market segments. Now we will examine the overall market for a product.

First, we determine the overall usage of the type of product. This is usually defined in terms of dollar sales, number of units sold, or percentage of households that use such a product. Then we determine if the category is growing, stagnant, or declining. We compare our share of the market to the competition (see Exhibit 4.20). Next we ask what the share trends have been over the past several years. Finally, we want to know the chief product advantage featured by each brand.

Windex regular, lemon scent, and vinegar have almost a 50 percent share of the $200 million glass-cleaner category. Glassworks, a newer product, has mustered about a 20 percent share. Other product categories and shares: Airwick holds a 25 percent share of the air-freshener market. Endust has a remarkable 80 percent of the dusting-aid segment, and Vanish holds about 30 percent of the toilet-bowl cleaner market.

EXHIBIT 4.20
Domestic liquor brands.

Brand	*Share (%)*
Bacardi	5.0%
Smirnoff	4.7
7 Crown	2.7
Popov	2.5
Canadian	2.3
Jim Beam	2.2
Jack Daniels	2.1
Seagram's gin	2.0

(Source: Advertising Age, February 27, 1989, p. 74.)

[8]Jack Trout and Al Ries, *The Positioning Era* (New York: Ries Cappiello Colwell, 1973), pp. 38–41.

It is important for the advertiser to know not only the characteristics of the product's market, but also similar information about the media alternatives. Most major newspapers, magazines, and broadcast media provide demographic and product-user data for numerous advertising categories.

PROFILE OF THE BUYER

Many small-business owners know the majority of their customers personally—their age, family status, financial status, and lifestyles. The bigger the business, the tougher this kind of knowledge is to come by for the owner. The best a large advertiser can do is try to form a clear mental picture of the typical consumer of the product in order to discover what kind of person must be appealed to in reaching for more business. The advertiser attempts to prepare a demographic profile of that person.

Demography is the study of vital economic and sociological statistics about people. In advertising, demographic reports refer to those facts relevant to a person's use of a product. Recently, advertisers have recognized the increased importance and differences of consumers over 50 years of age. They are about 64 million strong in 1990, and will probably number more than 76 million by the turn of the century. Right now these consumers control about 42 percent of all consumer income and approximately 50 percent of the country's discretionary income. An Ogilvy & Mather study found that people over 50 say they've "worked hard enough," and that 46 percent of them are determined to do more of what they want and can afford to do. They are mature enough to understand how precious life is, which is why they are concerned about their health and have stopped taking relationships with others for granted. In a focus group, one of them blurted out: "You know, I feel a little sorry for my son and daughter. I know they're not going to have it as good as we did." They are quite satisfied with their lot in life. They think of themselves as individuals, but believe in traditional social values. Still, the new sense of ease they are feeling in maturity has allowed them to relax their conventional attitudes to some extent and become more tolerant about differences and more self-indulgent. Thus, they are willing to spend on premium products for themselves. Now that the kids are gone, for example, they are likely to refurbish their homes. They feel at least 15 years younger than their chronological age; but as they get older, they become more afraid of being isolated from the rest of us.

The "over 50" market looms as one of high potential—with a large number of consumers, who *know* what they want, have the necessary dollars, and *want* to spend money on themselves. Now *another* magazine geared to the over 50 segment has been launched. *Mature Outlook,* published by Allstate Insurance Companies, will hit newsstands in 16 states. Anticipating huge demand by consumers and advertisers alike, circulation will be pegged at nearly *1 million*. Jack Fleish, publisher, forecasted increased growth, due *to the growing number of products and services* wanting to reach the "mature market."

Using an index of 100 for all adults, the over-50 crowd's index for the microwave oven is 133, new porch or patio 146, new carpet 152, new mattress 122, and so on, making them seem a lucrative market. O&M's research shows that explicit targeting may backlash, however, if it is clumsy. For example, a well-meaning commercial for Affinity shampoo had a middle-aged man admiring a middle-aged woman and saying to himself: "Beautiful hair. I wonder how old she is?" She turns to the viewer and says: "Over 40—and proud of it." The company had come up with a product that really helps "older" hair—but no older person wants to be reminded that he or she has "older" hair. Lesson: Never obviously isolate the over-50s from other people.[9]

The aging population does offer numerous opportunities, if marketing is done creatively and tactfully. The following niches have great potential: health care, home, leisure, financial services, educational services, and antiaging products and services.

All advertisers will seek to prepare a profile of the kind of person they want to reach. Lifewise, when a medium tries to sell space or time to an advertiser, it will supply a profile of its readers or viewers. The advertisers will then match the two profiles to see whether that medium reaches the type of people targeted. This is the basis for media selection.

Exhibit 4.21 is targeted at a specific lifestyle. To help make such matching possible,

[9]David Ward, *Over 50s: How to Reach Out to an Ignored Consumer* (Ogilvy & Mather Worldwide, 1988).

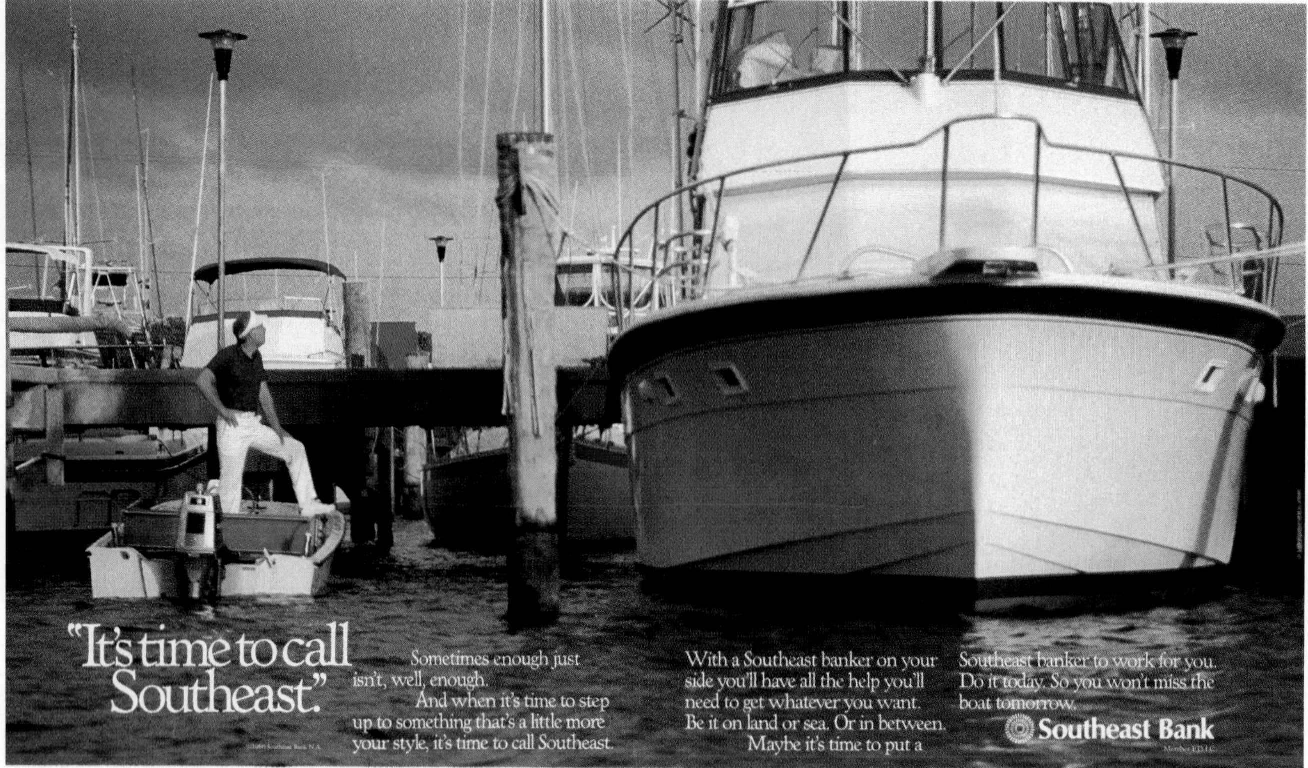

"It's time to call Southeast."
Sometimes enough just isn't, well, enough.
And when it's time to step up to something that's a little more your style, it's time to call Southeast.
With a Southeast banker on your side you'll have all the help you'll need to get whatever you want. Be it on land or sea. Or in between.
Maybe it's time to put a Southeast banker to work for you. Do it today. So you won't miss the boat tomorrow.
Southeast Bank

EXHIBIT 4.21
Southeast Bank understands its prime prospects and their lifestyle. (Courtesy: Southeast Bank.)

the American Association of Advertising Agencies has recommended a standardized breakdown for consumer media data so that the advertiser can prepare a list in terms of the standard classification that the media will be using. Exhibit 4.22 shows several of these categories.

Heavy Users

For any product, a small percentage of users are responsible for a disproportionately large share of sales. The principle of heavy usage is sometimes referred to as the 80/20 rule—that is, 80 percent of the units sold are purchased by only 20 percent of the

EXHIBIT 4.22
AAAA's recommended standard segments for demographic characteristics in surveys of consumer media audiences.

RECOMMENDED AUDIENCE SEGMENTS FOR CONSUMER MEDIA DATA

Explanation of 1986 Revisions

The purpose of these revisions to the AAAA's recommended breakdowns is to provide agency users (and suppliers) of media and marketing data with comparable reporting standards. These revised breakdowns reflect recent demographic, economic, and sociological changes in the population. In addition, consideration has also been given to data refinements which will permit the user to further differentiate between the marketing media characteristics of population segments, such as reporting the number of children under 18. This type of data will help to distinguish differences in the living patterns of families that have children vs. those that do not have any children.

AAAA's RECOMMENDED STANDARD SEGMENTS FOR DEMOGRAPHIC CHARACTERISTICS IN SURVEYS OF CONSUMER MEDIA AUDIENCES

DATA TO BE GATHERED AND REPORTED (IF POSSIBLE, TO BE DIRECTLY ACCESSIBLE)

CHARACTERISTIC	MINIMUM BASIC DATA TO BE REPORTED	ADDITIONAL DATA — HIGHLY VALUED
I. PERSONS CHARACTERISTICS		
A. HOUSEHOLD RELATIONSHIP	PRINCIPLE WAGE EARNER IN HH (DEFINES HH HEAD)	
	PRINCIPLE SHOPPER IN HH (DEFINES HOMEMAKER)	
	SPOUSE	
	CHILD	
	OTHER RELATIVE	
	PARTNER/ROOMMATE	
	OTHER NON-RELATIVE	
B. AGE	UNDER 6	2 - 5
	6 - 11	6 - 8
	12 - 15	35 - 49
	16 - 20	25 - 49
	18 - 20	
	16 OR OLDER	
	18 OR OLDER	
	18 - 24	
	25 - 34	
	35 - 44	
	45 - 49	
	50 - 54	
	55 - 64	
	65 - 74	
	75 OR OLDER	
C. SEX	MALE	
	FEMALE	
D. EDUCATION	LAST GRADE ATTENDED:	
	GRADE SCHOOL OR LESS (GRADE 1-8)	
	SOME HIGH SCHOOL	
	GRADUATED HIGH SCHOOL	
	SOME COLLEGE (AT LEAST 1 YEAR)	
	GRADUATED COLLEGE	ANY POST GRADUATE WORK
	IF CURRENTLY ATTENDING SCHOOL	— (IF PERTINENT TO STUDY) —
		LIVE HOME
		LIVE AWAY
		— LIVE IN STUDENT HOUSING
		— LIVE OFF CAMPUS
	FULL-TIME STUDENT	
	PART-TIME STUDENT	
E. MARITAL STATUS	MARRIED	SPOUSE PRESENT SPOUSE ABSENT
	WIDOWED	
	DIVORCED OR SEPARATED	SPOUSE WORKING
	SINGLE (NEVER MARRIED)	
	PARENT	ENGAGED
	PREGNANT	
	'LIVING TOGETHER'	

EXHIBIT 4.22 (continued)

CHARACTERISTIC	MINIMUM BASIC DATA TO BE REPORTED	ADDITIONAL DATA — HIGHLY VALUED
F. RELIGION — POLITICAL		PROTESTANT / CATHOLIC / JEWISH / OTHER / NONE — ACTIVE (Practicing) / INACTIVE (Non-Practicing) POLITICAL — CONSERVATIVE — LIBERAL — MODERATE
G. RACE	WHITE BLACK OTHER	
H. PRINCIPLE LANGUAGE SPOKEN AT HOME	ENGLISH SPANISH OTHER	
H1. OTHER LANGUAGES SPOKEN AT HOME	ENGLISH SPANISH OTHER	
I. INDIVIDUAL EMPLOYMENT INCOME	UNDER $10,000 $10,00 - 14,999 $15,000 - 19,999 $20,000 - 24,999 $25,000 - 29,999 $30,000 - 39,999 $40,000 - 49,999 $50,000 - 74,999 $75,000 AND OVER	$75,000 - 99,000 $100,000 AND OVER IEI INCOME BY QUINTILE AS DETERMINED BY THE SURVEY ZIPTILES. OTHER INCOME

IEI BY QUINTILE
INCOME INTERVAL

QUINTILE	% ADULTS	LOW -	HIGH	MEDIAN INCOME
1	20	—	10,156	6,391
2	20	10,757	19,999	13,959
3	20	20,000	29,999	24,953
4	20	30,000	43,243	34,967
5	20	43,244	—	60,150

EXHIBIT 4.22 (continued)

CHARACTERISTIC	MINIMUM BASIC DATA TO BE REPORTED	ADDITIONAL DATA — HIGHLY VALUED
J. OCCUPATION AS DEFINED BY BUREAUS OF THE CENSUS	**ARMED FORCES**	
	CIVILIAN LABOR FORCE	HOLD MORE THAN ONE JOB
	EMPLOYED	IN HOME OUT-OF HOME
	— FULL TIME (35 or More Hours Per Week) — PART TIME (Less than 35 Hours Per Week)	
	SELF EMPLOYED	PRIVATE COMPANY GOVERNMENT
	UNEMPLOYED — LOOKING FOR WORK	PREDOMINANTLY — DAY WORK — EVENING/NIGHT WORK
	MAJOR OCCUPATIONAL CATEGORIES — MANAGERIAL, PROFESSIONAL — TECHNICAL	TECHNICAL RELATED SUPPORT OCCUPATIONS
	— ADMIN. SUPPORT (INCL. CLERICAL) — SALES — OPERATIVE, NON-FARM LABORERS, SERVICE WORKERS, PRIVATE HOUSEHOLD WORKERS	
	— FARMERS, FARM MANAGERS, FARM LABORERS	
	— CRAFTSMEN	
	— OTHER	
	INDUSTRY OF EMPLOYMENT	
	JOB TITLE	
	NOT EMPLOYED	
	RETIRED	
	STUDENT (FULL TIME)	
	HOMEMAKER (Not Employed Outside Home)	
	DISABLED	
	TEMPORARILY UNEMPLOYED	
	OTHER	
II. HOUSEHOLDS CHARACTERISTICS		
A. COUNTY SIZE	A COUNTY B COUNTY C COUNTY D COUNTY	
B. GEOGRAPHIC AREA AS DEFINE BY BUREAU OF THE CENSUS	INSIDE METROPOLITAN STATISTICAL AREA ... — MSA CENTRAL CITY — MSA SUBURBAN — MSA OTHER OUTSIDE METROPOLITAN STATISTICAL AREA	METROPOLITAN STATISTICAL AREA POPULATIONS 4,000,000 AND OVER 1,000,000 — 3,999,999 500,000 — 999,999 250,000 — 499,999 100,000 — 249,999 50,000 — 99,999
	URBAN	URBAN: URBANIZED AREA — CENTRAL CITY — URBAN FRINGE — OTHER URBAN — PLACES OF 10,000 — 50,000 POPULATION — PLACES OF 2,500 — 9,999 POPULATION
	RURAL	
C. GEOGRAPHIC REGION	AS DEFINED BY BUREAU OF THE CENSUS .... — NORTHEAST — NORTH CENTRAL — SOUTH — WEST NIELSEN GEOGRAPHIC AREAS — NORTHEAST — EAST CENTRAL — WEST CENTRAL — SOUTH — PACIFIC	CENSUS GEOGRAPHIC DIVISION — NEW ENGLAND — MID ATLANTIC — EAST NORTH CENTRAL — WEST NORTH CENTRAL — SOUTH ATLANTIC — EAST SOUTH CENTRAL — WEST SOUTH CENTRAL — MOUNTAIN — PACIFIC MAJOR MARKET UNDUPLICATED TV COVERAGE AREAS
D. PRESENCE/AGE OF CHILDREN IN HOUSEHOLD	NO CHILDREN UNDER 18 YOUNGEST CHILD 6-17 YOUNGEST CHILD UNDER 6	YOUNGEST CHILD 12-17 YOUNGEST CHILD 6-11 YOUNGEST CHILD 2-5 YOUNGEST CHILD UNDER 2
E. HOUSEHOLD TYPE		FAMILY MEMBERS ONLY NON-FAMILY MEMBERS ONLY BOTH FAMILY AND NON-FAMILY MEMBERS

EXHIBIT 4.22 (continued)

CHARACTERISTIC	MINIMUM BASIC DATA TO BE REPORTED	ADDITIONAL DATA — HIGHLY VALUED
F. HOUSEHOLD SIZE	1 MEMBER 2 MEMBERS 3 MEMBERS 4 MEMBERS	NUMBER OF ADULTS (Persons 18 and Over) MALE/FEMALE HH FEMALE ONLY HH MALE ONLY HH
G. NUMBER OF CHILDREN UNDER 18 IN HOUSEHOLD	NONE ONE MORE THAN ONE	NUMBER OF CHILDREN 6 - 17 NUMBER OF CHILDREN UNDER 6 NUMBER OF CHILDREN BY HOUSEHOLD SIZE
H. HOUSEHOLD INCOME	SEE I., INDIVIDUAL EMPLOYMENT INCOME	$ 75,000 - 99,999 $100,000 AND OVER HOUSEHOLD INCOME BY QUINTILE AS DETERMINED BY SURVEY ZIPTILES
I. OTHER HOUSEHOLD CHARACTERISTICS		NUMBER OF ADULTS EMPLOYED FULL TIME
J. HOME OWNERSHIP	OWN HOME — PRIVATE OWNERSHIP — COOPERATIVE OWNERSHIP — CONDOMINIUM RENT HOME	RESIDENCE FIVE YEARS PRIOR TO SURVEY — LIVED IN SAME HOUSE/HOME — LIVED IN DIFFERENT HOUSE/HOME — IN SAME COUNTY — IN DIFFERENT COUNTY — IN SAME STATE — IN DIFFERENT STATE
K. TYPE HOUSING UNIT	SINGLE FAMILY HOME MULTIPLE FAMILY HOME APARTMENT MOBILE HOME OR TRAILER	

NOTE: THE RECOMMENDED MINIMUM AND ADDITIONAL DATA STANDARDS APPLY TO GENERALIZED SURVEYS. THOSE SURVEYS DONE TO MORE SPECIFIC PURPOSES—E.G. PARTICULAR GEOGRAPHIC SECTIONS OF THE COUNTRY, AFFLUENT MARKETS, PUBLICATIONS DIRECTED TOWARDS A SPECIFIC TARGET, ETC.—MAY CHOOSE TO COLLAPSE OR EXPAND CHARACTERISTIC SEGMENTS AS APPROPRIATE TO THEIR CONTEXT.

EXHIBIT 4.22 (continued)

consumers. Of course, the exact figure varies with each product and product category, but the 80/20 rule is representative of most product sales. Heavy users are identified not only by who they are, but also by when they buy and where they are located. In Exhibit 4.23, for example, we find that the heavy users of brand X are women aged 55 and older. In addition, the most effective selling is done from January through June in the East Central and Pacific regions.

In defining your market, then, you must determine who the heavy users are and identify their similarities, which would define your marketing goals.

EXHIBIT 4.23
Users of brand X.

1. Target Audience: Current Consumers

Women	Pop., %	Consumption, %	Index
18-24	17.5	5.0	29
25-34	21.9	10.1	46
35-54	30.1	24.0	80
55 +	30.5	61.0	200
Total	100.0	100.0	

2. Geography: Current Sales

Area	Pop., %	Consumption, %	Index
Northeast	24	22	92
East Central	15	18	120
West Central	17	16	94
South	27	24	89
Pacific	17	20	118
	100	100	

3. Seasonality

Period	Jan.-Mar.	Apr.-Jun.	Jul.-Sept.	Oct.-Nov.
Consumption, %	30	36	20	14
Index	120	144	80	56

BEYOND DEMOGRAPHICS: PSYCHOGRAPHICS

Driving on a highway past modest-sized backyards of middle-class homes, one is struck first by their similarity. But a harder look is more illuminating; for behind the similarities lie differences that reflect the interests, personalities, and family situations of those who live in such homes. One backyard has been transformed into a carefully manicured garden. Another includes some shrubs and bushes, but most of the yard serves as a relaxation area, with outdoor barbecue equipment and the like. A third yard is almost entirely a playground, with swings, trapezes, and slides. A swimming pool occupies almost all of the space in another yard. Still another has simply been allowed to go to seed and is overgrown and untended by its obviously indoor-oriented owners.

Psychographics. *A description of a market based on factors such as attitudes, opinions, interests, perceptions, and lifestyles of consumers comprising that market.*

If you want to advertise to this community, you would be speaking to people of different interests, different tastes. There may be a big difference in the nature and extent of purchases between any two groups of buyers who have the same demographic characteristics. The attempt to explain the significance of such differences has led to an inquiry beyond demographics into psychographics.

Emanual Demby, president of Demby & Associates and considered one of the founders of psychographics, has described psychographics as:

> The use of psychological, sociological, and anthropological factors, such as benefits desired (from the behavior being studied), self-concept, and lifestyle (or serving style) to determine how the market is segmented by the propensity of groups within the market—and their reasons—to take a particular decision about a product, person, ideology, or otherwise hold an attitude or use a medium. Demographics and socioeconomics are also used as a constant check to see if psychographic marketing segmentation improves on other forms of segmentation, including user/nonuser groupings.[10]

Publications use both demographic and psychographic information about their readers to attract specific kinds of advertisers. Exhibit 4.24 illustrates *Esquire*'s market uniqueness in more than mere income figure: ". . . fewer than 1% of American men spent $1000 or more on a watch in the past year. What should be no surprise to you is that more than four times as many *Esquire* men did."

Psychographics—studying lifestyles—sharpens the search for prospects beyond the demographic data. Using lifestyle information, good creative people can devise copy that appeals to one or more psychographic segments (see Exhibit 4.25). "Quick and nutritious" appeals to career women and men with great time demands of them as well as to mothers concerned about their children's need for wholesome foods. The agency and client media people select media vehicles likely to deliver that special target group or groups.

Psychographic Research

Psychographic information, combined with other segmentation variables, can be purchased from a variety of research sources. One such firm features its "trade-off analysis." This procedure helps determine which characteristics of a product are most important to a prospect and estimates the dollar value of each. "Understanding how prospects prioritize the factors that influence purchase decisions," claims *Walker Research and Analysis,* "takes more than luck."

Different syndicated research companies specialize in different types of information. Each publishes reports for subscribers. The various reports give information on what type of product people buy and which brands; who buys them and their demographic status and psychographic distinctions; how people react to products and to ads; people's styles of buying and what media reach them. In the broadcast field, the services report their estimates of how many TV households are listening to or viewing which programs on which stations. One of the uses of such data is to help the advertiser select the target market.

Advertisers can also order "customized" data from these services and a number of other research companies. Here are a few examples:

- *BrandTab.* Introduced in late 1988, BrandTab contains the entire Mediamark consumer data base, along with more than 30 formats for brand management. The data base includes demo-

[10]Emanual H. Demby, "Psychographics Revisited: The Birth of a Technique," *Marketing News,* January 2, 1989, p. 21.

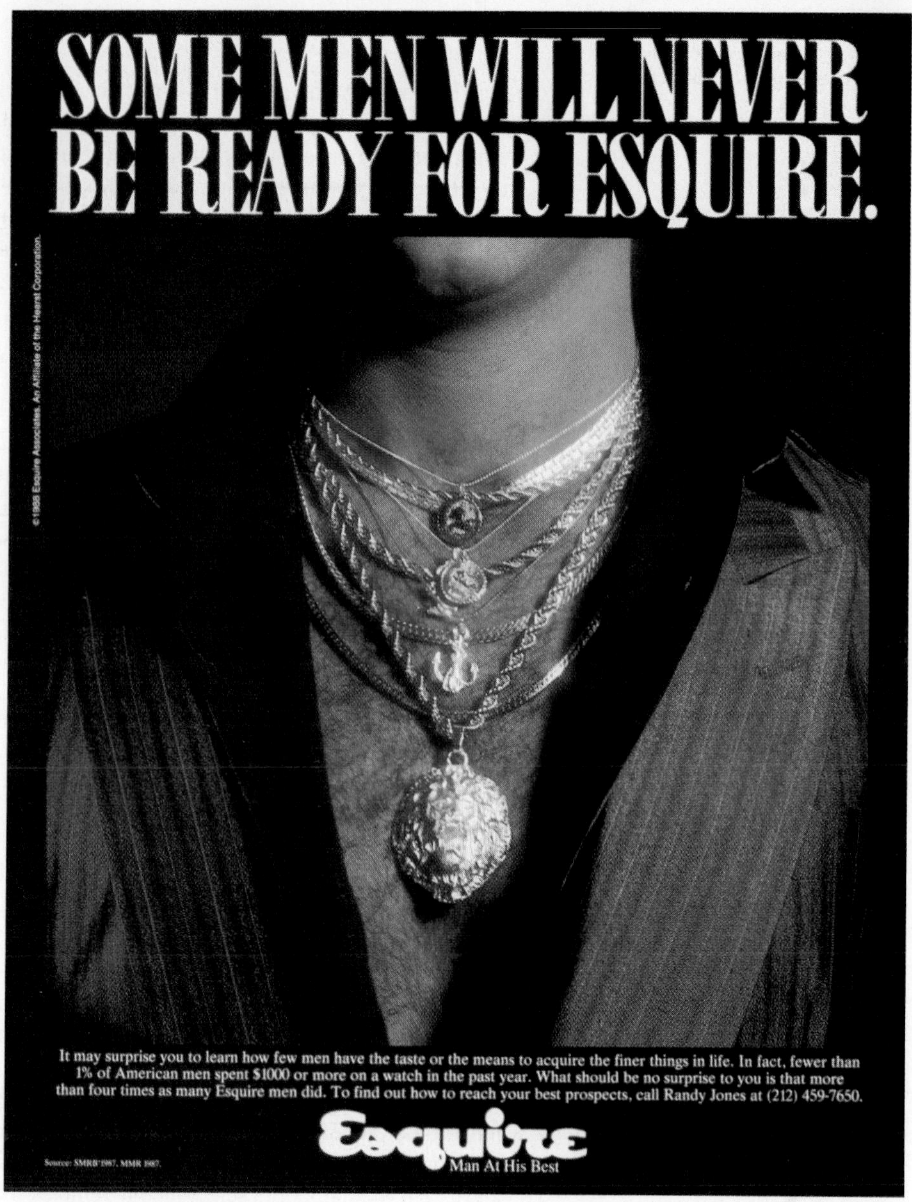

EXHIBIT 4.24

Media often promote the lifestyle of their readers to advertisers. (Courtesy: *Esquire*.)

graphic, lifestyle, and usage data for more than 450 product categories and 5,700 different brands (see Exhibit 4.26)

- *ACORN (A Classification of Residential Neighborhoods)*. The ACORN market segmentation system, developed by CASI, classifies U.S. households according to a set of 49 socioeconomic, demographic, and housing characteristics.
- *ClusterPlus*. A product of Donnelley Marketing Information Services, this is a segmentation system that classifies every neighborhood into one of 47 lifestyle categories. ClusterPlus is linked to the Residential Master file, which includes the names, addresses, and demographic characteristics of 90 percent of U.S. households.
- *Upper Deck Report on the Affluent Market*. This is an annual report on the lifestyles of the top 10 percent of households by income.
- *Consumers Innovators Report*. This MRI study of actual new-product purchasing behavior in five important groupings (food and kitchen environment, the home environment, electronics, leisure activities, money and financial products) describes innovative consumers in more than 300 product categories.
- *Scantrack*. Information from a sample of supermarkets in about 50 metropolitan areas is

EXHIBIT 4.25

"Only the Strong Survive" uses lifestyle to attract its target for Sunbeam Lite.

obtained using UPC (universal product code) scanner categories. Scantrack is part of A. C. Nielsen's single-source research.

- *MRI Mediamarket Reports*. Viewing, listening, and reading habits are cross-tabulated with demographic and product purchasing data covering 10 local markets.
- *Prism*. Claritas LP's system classifies some 540,000 units of neighborhood geography, including census block groups, postal carrier routes, and zip codes, into 40 basic lifestyle clusters.
- *MRI Business-to-Business Report*. This is an annual report identifying the media usage and purchasing patterns of key decision makers.

The Need for Market Testing. Although extremely helpful, psychographic research cannot replace market testing as the ultimate guide to successful advertising and marketing. Manufacturers rarely introduce a new product without doing some prior test marketing. Today there are numerous electronic test markets, which get products into immediate distribution, then track purchases by scanners in supermarkets on a weekly or a monthly basis. Traditional test marketing involves choosing cities for testing that

EXHIBIT 4.26

Mediamark promotes its syndicated service, which includes demographic, lifestyle, and usage data. (Courtesy: Mediamark Research, Inc.)

Finally. A better way to keep tabs on your brands.

BrandTab.™ The revolutionary new brand management tool.

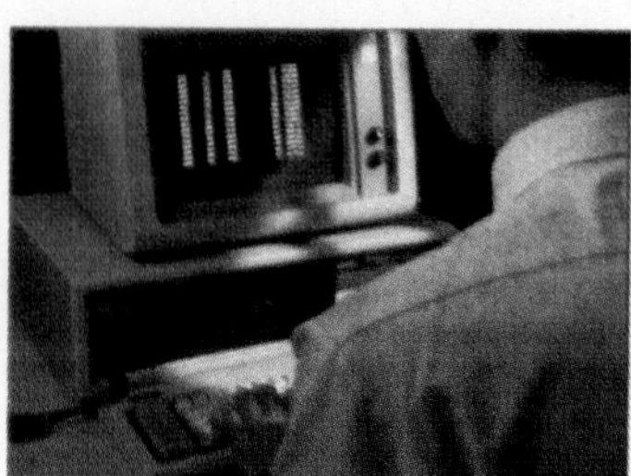

Now, in minutes, you can assess brand loyalty, analyze your strengths and weaknesses versus the competition, discover new growth opportunities, and much more.

Because now there's BrandTab, a brand management tool unlike anything you've ever encountered. It contains the largest consumer database available anywhere. It features nearly 50 pre-programmed analysis formats. And it works on your own office PC.

BrandTab is a product of Mediamark Research Inc., one of the nation's leading consumer research companies. Since 1979, Mediamark has conducted an annual survey of 20,000 adult consumers, covering demographics, lifestyle characteristics, exposure to major media, and usage of more than 5,700 products and services.

The BrandTab system combines data from this survey with software designed specifically for brand management applications, enabling you to perform—with surprising ease—virtually any consumer analyses you want:

- Product category analyses
- Single brand analyses
- Multiple brand user analyses
- Analyses of volume of use by multiple brand users

See for yourself how BrandTab can help you keep tabs on your brands. Call the Mediamark office nearest you to arrange for a free demonstration.

MEDIAMARK RESEARCH INC.
341 MADISON AVENUE, NEW YORK, NY 10017 (212) 599-0444
500 N. MICHIGAN AVE., CHICAGO, IL 60611 (312) 329-0901
414 JACKSON STREET, SAN FRANCISCO, CA 94111 (415) 788-0927

are similar demographically to the general population, that are isolated from larger markets, and that have reasonably priced media. Testing generally measures advertising and promotional variables.

TARGETING SPECIAL MARKETS: HISPANICS

Hispanic-Americans have become one of the fastest-growing markets for advertisers. Strategy Research Corporation estimates that there are 21.2 million Hispanics in the United States—a complex market made up of Mexicans, Cubans, Puerto Ricans, and Central and South Americans.

The Hispanic market is a challenge to advertisers, not least because of its geographical dispersal. Once concentrated in the inner cities, today many Hispanics live in the suburbs, where job opportunities are better and Latinos meet with less discrimination than some other groups. In California, the Hispanic population grew 34.9 percent in Los Angeles County between 1980 and 1988, 61 percent in San Bernardino County, 52 percent in Ventura Country, and 42.6 percent in Orange County. Other fast-growing Spanish-speaking areas are New Jersey's Hudson County, Manhattan, Chicago, New Orleans, Washington, Hartford, and Milwaukee (see Exhibit 4.27).

Most advertising and marketing people agree that Hispanics have to be addressed in terms of their own lifestyles, identities, and motivations.[11] As a result, major advertising agencies have formed their own Hispanic subsidiaries or have affiliated with Hispanic agencies to better reach this segment of the population.

In recognizing specific lucrative segments, advertisers are now directing specific campaigns to the Hispanic markets. Aside from its diversity, its appeal is its *loyalty for national brands.* Proctor & Gamble, a company whose reputation was made *by brand development,* will enhance its participation in the Hispanic market to the tune of *$35 million!* It's sponsoring a new magazine titled, *''La Familia de Hoy,''* an every-other-monthly Spanish language publication. Distribution will be in Hispanic areas through 11,000 doctor and dentist offices and beauty salons.

Up to 50 percent of Hispanics are immigrants, and the majority are under the age of 25. Their buying preferences are often influenced by their peers. Minority consumers typically are very brand loyal and are willing to pay extra for brand names. Hence companies that sell to this special market can count on long-term loyalty to their products. However, Hispanics, like all ethnic groups, want positive media images that hold out the promise of upscale lifestyles. Reaching them can be difficult because of their dual English/Hispanic media habits and because it is sometimes hard to translate into Spanish a sales message that worked well in English.

Saatchi & Saatchi DFS had problems creating ads for Toyota for the Hispanic market. In 1987, Toyota's general market theme, ''Who could ask for anything more?'' didn't translate very well—the idiom in Spanish was so different that the obvious response would be: ''We could ask for a lot of other things.'' When Saatchi subsidiary Conill Advertising took over the account, their first move was to change the question into a declarative statement: *''Toyota siempre le da mas''* or Toyota always gives you more. It is estimated that Toyota spent about $3.5 million on advertising through Conhill to reach the Hispanic market—this time much more successfully.

Coors beer also had problems with translation. Their ''Get loose with Coors'' slogan translated into Spanish as ''Get the runs with Coors.''

Procter & Gamble was the first major company to set aside an amount of money for Hispanic media and promotion that reflected the percentage of business it does in the Hispanic market. It was also one of the first companies to establish a multitiered corporate Hispanic marketing infrastructure. P&G's program is perhaps the most evolved—with Hispanic group brand managers for specific product groups—and illuminates what may become the norm as corporate investment in this market segment grows.

For a number of years, 7-Up created different radio commercials for the different Hispanic communities in this country—California, Miami, Texas, etc.—using basically the same lyrics but different music tempos. Today 7-Up has its Hispanic agency, Cassanova/Pendrill, create entire campaigns aimed specifically at this complex market (see Exhibit 4.28).

Hispanics living in the Northeast and Southeast tend to buy more brands from companies that show a particular interest in Hispanic consumers. They generally like

EXHIBIT 4.27
Selected metro Hispanic populations.

Los Angeles	2,373,000
New York	1,509,000
Miami	648,000
San Antonio	587,000
Chicago	534,000
Houston	481,000
San Diego	342,000
Phoenix	267,000
Dallas	223,000
Denver	190,000
Jersey City	143,000
Tucson	130,000

[11] Edmond M. Rosenthal, ''Advertising in the Big League,'' *Television/Radio Age,* November 1988, p. A13.

EXHIBIT 4.28

Samples frames of 7-Up Hispanic commercial. (Courtesy 7-Up Corp.)

JINGLE: Refrescame. . .7 Up
Una lluvia de frescura
quita la sed como ninguna
Disfruta de su sabor.

Refrescame. . .7-Up
Refrescame. . .7-Up

JINGLE: Refresh me. . .7-Up
A shower of freshness
quenches your thirst
like no other. Enjoy
its taste.

Refresh me. . .7 Up
Refresh me. . .7-Up

Cae la lluvia tan fresca
Cae con ritmo sabroso
por eso me hace bailar.

Refrescame. . .7-Up

The rain falls so fresh
it falls with such good
rhythm, that's why it makes
me wanna dance.

Refresh me. . .7 Up

DONUT: :15 seconds

DONUT: :15 seconds

JINGLE: Cae la lluvia tan fresca
Cae con ritmo sabroso
por eso me hace bailar.

JINGLE: The rain falls so fresh
it falls with such good
rhythm, that's why it makes
me wanna dance.

Refrescame. . .7-Up
Refrescame. . .7-Up

Refresh me. . .7 Up
Refresh me. . .7-Up

American-made products and believe brand-name products are superior to store brands, but there are significant buying differences from region to region. Therefore, to attract Hispanic customers require astute marketing and advertising.

SUMMARY

The accurate identification of current and prospective users of a product will often mean the difference between success and failure. The targeting of advertising to these prospects in an efficient media plan with appropriate creative is critical.

This chapter has concentrated on fundamentals: What is a market? competition? positioning? Numerous methods of examining segmentation and other important considerations in the planning of any advertising program have been discussed. Understanding these basic concerns through research is part of the process. Research is the key to successful target marketing. Market research to define prime market segments, product research to meet the needs of these segments, and advertising research to devise the most appropriate messages are mandatory for the success of a firm in a competitive environment. Also, we need to be familiar with the multitude of research services providing data for aiding our planning—ACORN, MRI Mediamarket Reports, Scantrack, Prism, etc.

Advertisements are increasingly using a rifle instead of the shotgun approach. In the media section, we will learn how it is becoming easier to tailor messages through a variety of special-interest media vehicles.

Advertisers are placing more importance on lifestyle characteristics than on demographic factors. Advertisers recognize that purchase behavior is the result of a number of complex psychological and sociological factors that cannot be explained by a superficial list of age, sex, or occupational characteristics.

Finally, we need to keep abreast of changes in population and better understand such important market segments as Hispanics and blacks. We need to know more than just the numbers and locations. We need to understand their lifestyles, identities, and motivations.

QUESTIONS

1. What is target marketing?
2. What is a market?
3. Name the key demographic characteristics used by advertisers.
4. What is the 80/20 rule as it relates to target marketing?
5. What are the two purposes of niche marketing?
6. What is positioning?
7. How does a consumer's lifestyle relate to segmentation strategy?

SUGGESTED EXERCISES

1. Choose two ads whose headlines clearly identify, and appeal to, heavy users of a product.
2. Find print ads that are obviously developing new markets.
3. Discuss current television commercials using lifestyle themes.

READINGS

CANNON, HUGH M., AND DAVID L. WILLIAMS: "Toward a Hierarchical Taconomy of Magazine Readership," *Journal of Advertising,* Vol. 17, No. 2, 1988, p. 15.

GRECO, ALAN J.: "The Elderly as Communicators: Perceptions of Advertising Practitioners," *Journal of Advertising Research,* June/July, 1988.

KAHLE, LYNN R., BASIL POULOS, AND AJAY SUKHDIAL: "Changes in Social Values in the United States During the Post Decade," *Journal of Advertising Research,* February/March, 1988, p. 35.

KAMINS, MICHAEL A.: "Celebrity and Noncelebrity Advertising in a Two-Sided Context," *Journal of Advertising Research,* June/July, 1989, p. 34.

KOHLI, AJAY: "Determinants of Influence in Organizational Buying: A Contingency Approach," *Journal of Marketing,* July, 1989, p. 50.

LEVINE, STEVEN, AND MARTIN FRIEDMAN: "A New Look at Television Efficiency and Its Impact on Media Strategy Development," *Journal of Media Planning,* Spring, 1989, p. 9.

PART THREE

Managing the Advertising

Advertising is a business. This obvious fact is sometimes lost in the exciting, fast-paced world of clients, creativity, and million-dollar budgets. In many respects, success in advertising depends on the same sound business practices that apply in any other field. In other respects, the advertising business is different from all other enterprises.

Chapter 5 concentrates on advertising agencies. Agency managements realize the importance of people. Unlike other businesses, they are largely labor intensive. Agencies are, in fact, little more than office furniture and the ideas of their employees. They also differ from other companies in that they are largely organized according to the needs of their clients. An advertising agency is like a company with a limited number of customers, each of whom must be serviced individually.

Chapter 6 views the advertising process from the client's perspective. An agency works as a team with a company's advertising department. It is crucial that this teamwork operate efficiently. The choosing of an agency and the long-term working relationship are among the most important decisions a corporation can make.

FIVE

The Advertising Agency, Media Services, and Other Services

Ad agencies *of late* have gone through tremendous changes in recent years. Once thinking that centralization was the ''key'' to a well-coordinated promotional campaign, Burger King has switched to ''regionalization.'' It recently tapped Rosenfeld, Serowitz, Humphrey, & Strauss, New York, *for a regional program in the East.* That puts the chain another step closer to implementing a layer of regional agencies and breaking up its centralized $200 million account, now at N. W. Ayer, New York.

With increasing emphasis on worldwide marketing, advertising agencies are expanding to foreign markets. In order to become familiar with the *British market, Ad Week* magazine offers the *Design and Art Direction Annual and Showreel*—the best 600 ads and 68 commercials of the current year. They're advertised as ''everything you want to know about the current state of British advertising.''

The world of the advertising agency is one of dramatic change. Agencies once known for their personalities and definite ad philosophies have either disappeared or merged at the international, national, regional, or local level. Many of the new agencies haven't existed long enough in their merged state to develop a personality or a clear image of themselves.

There are a lot of opinions about the changes, pro and con. In this chapter, we'll look at the traditional agency and many of the changes in progress there. We'll also look at some other advertising services organizations.

TODAY'S ADVERTISING AGENCY

Many of the changes taking place in the advertising agency business reflect the changes taking place in the corporate world in general—mergers, leveraged buyouts, foreign acquisitions, and an increasing emphasis on global marketing. Agencies are, like all successful institutions, adapting to the environment within which they operate and to the clients they serve. For all the changes, advertising agencies continue to be the most significant companies in the development of advertising and marketing in the world.

The American Association of Advertising Agencies' definition of an advertising agency is: An independent business, composed of creative and business people, who develop, prepare, and place advertising in advertising media for sellers seeking to find customers for their goods and services.

According to the United States Census Bureau, there are over 10,000 agencies operating in this country. More than 4,000 of them are listed in the *Standard Directory of Advertising Agencies* (also known as the *Agency Red Book*). The *AdWeek Agency Directory* lists over 5,000 advertising agencies and some 300 media-buying services. There are at least 2,000 agencies listed in the New York Yellow Pages alone. The majority of these agencies are small one- to ten-person shops (we'll say more about size and services later in the chapter).

HOW AGENCIES DEVELOPED

Before we discuss present-day agencies further, let us take a look at how advertising agencies got started and how they developed into large worldwide organizations that play such a prominent role in the marketing and advertising process.

The Early Age (Colonial Times to 1917)

It is not generally known that the first Americans to act as advertising agents were colonial postmasters:

> In many localities, advertisements for Colonial papers might be left at the post offices. In some instances the local post office would accept advertising copy for publication in papers in other places; it did so with the permission of the postal authorities. . . . William Bradford, publisher of the first Colonial weekly in New York, made an arrangement with Richard Nichols, postmaster in 1727, whereby the latter accepted advertisements for the New York Gazette at regular rates.[1]

Space Salesmen. Volney B. Palmer is the first person known to have worked on a commission basis. In the 1840s, he solicited ads for newspapers that had difficulty getting out-of-town advertising. Palmer contacted publishers and offered to get them business for a 50 percent commission, but often settled for less. There was no such thing as a rate card or a fixed price for space or commission in those days. A first demand for $500 by the papers might be reduced, before the bargain was struck, to $50. (Today we call that negotiation.) Palmer opened offices in Philadelphia, New York, and Boston. Soon there were more agents, offering various deals.

Rates for space were first published by George Rowell. The average cost for *a Super Bowl 30-second spot* has "shot up" from $450,000 in 1984 to approximately $675,000 in 1989. Meanwhile, ratings have decreased from a high of 48 in 1986 to a low of 42 last year. With soaring prices, sponsors remaining are beer, soft drinks, and automobile companies—those products that have *wide* consumer appeal. Dropping out are computers and financial services.

Space Wholesalers. During the 1850s in Philadelphia, George P. Rowell bought large blocks of space for cash (most welcome) from publishers at very low rates, less agent's commissions. He would sell the space in small "squares"—one-column wide—at his own retail rate. Rowell next contracted with 100 newspapers to buy one column of space a month and sold the space in his total list at a fixed rate per line for the whole list: "An inch of space a month in one hundred papers for one hundred dollars." Selling by list became widespread. Each wholesaler's list was his private stock in trade. (This was the original media package deal.)

The First Rate Directory. In 1869, Rowell shocked the advertising world by publishing a directory of newspapers with their card rates and with his own estimates of their circulation. Other agents accused him of giving away their trade secrets; publishers howled too because his estimates of circulation were lower than their claims. Nevertheless, Rowell persisted in offering advertisers an estimate of space costs based on those published rates for whatever markets they wanted. This was the beginning of the media estimate.

Calkins and Holder showed that an advertising agency could do more than just write ads. It became the "creative center for advertising ideas." MCA, the sponsor of teenage singer Tiffany's shopping mall concert in 1987, has decided to integrate the mall-tour concept into its current promotion efforts. Its agency has devised, "MCA Presents . . . The Magic of Hollywood," with music acts, Hollywood memorabilia, and interactive exhibits. All MCA's divisions will be represented—Universal Pictures, Universal Studios Tour, MCA Home Video, and MCA Records.

The Agency Becomes a Creative Center. In the early 1870s, Charles Austin Bates, a writer, began writing ads and selling his services to whoever wanted them, whether advertisers or agents. Among his employees were Earnest Elmo Calkins and Ralph Holden, who in the 1890s founded their own agency, famous for 50 years under the name of Calkins and Holden. These men did more than write ads. They brought together planning, copy, and art, showing the way to combine all three into effective advertising. Not only was their agency one of the most successful for half a century, but the influence of their work helped establish the advertising agency as the creative center for advertising ideas. Many of the names on the list of firms advertising in 1890

[1]James Melvin Lee, *History of American Journalism*, rev. ed. (Boston: Houghton Mifflin, 1933), p. 74.

(see Chapter 1) are still familiar today; their longevity can be attributed to the effectiveness of that generation of agency people who developed the new power of advertising agency services. The business had changed from one of salesmen going out to sell advertising space to one of agencies that created the plan, the ideas, the copy, and the artwork, produced the plates, and then placed the advertising in publications from which they received a commission.

To this day, the unique contribution to business for which agencies are most respected is their ability to create effective ads.

The *agency-client relationship* evolved when advertisers agreed to deal with agencies and have the agencies deal with the media. Eventually, agencies were extracting their fees from the media—not from their clients—who paid the agencies and the media the same rates. That's the approach Lowe Tucker Metcalf uses in their trade paper ads to attract clients. They claim their ads receive *the best starch figures—and the best sales figures—* because of unusual creativity and highly accurate media placement. Above all, they stress a personal interest by President Bill Tucker—who promises to make a client's ad more visible and memorable, than the client could make himself.

Agency-Client Relationship Established. In 1875, Francis Ayer established N. W. Ayer & Son (one of the larger advertising agencies today). Ayer proposed to bill advertisers for what he actually paid the publishers (that is, the rate paid the publisher less the commission), adding a fixed charge in lieu of a commission. In exchange, advertisers would agree to place all their advertising through Ayer's agents. This innovation established the relationship of advertisers as clients of agencies rather than as customers who might give their business to various salespeople, never knowing whether they were paying the best price.

The Curtis No-Rebating Rule. In 1891, the Curtis Publishing Company announced that it would pay commissions to agencies only if they agreed to collect the full price from advertisers, a rule later adopted by the Magazine Publishers of America. This was the forerunner of no-rebating agreements, which were an important part of the agency business for over 50 years. (Agency commissions, however, ranged from 10 to 25 percent in both magazines and newspapers.)

Radio, soon established as a major entertainment source, became a major advertising vehicle as well. In its hotly competitive, specialized marketplace, local stations ofttimes need all the "professional help they can get." *Radio Works* is a professional radio production agency, which supplies "concepts and copy—at affordable prices, plus *fast* turn-around." For openers, it'll send a demo tape, along with statistical data on demographics of likely targets for its material and geographical placements. Local businesses, interested in advertising, would be approached with this "persuasive" information.

Standard Commission for Recognized Agencies Established. In 1917, newspaper publishers, through their associations, set 15 percent as the standard agency commission, a percentage that remains in effect for all media to this day (except local advertising, for which the media deal directly with the stores and pay no commission). The commission would be granted, however, only to agencies that the publishers' associations "recognized." One of the important conditions for recognition was an agency's agreement to charge the client the full rate (no rebating). Other criteria for recognition were that the agency must have business to place, must have shown competence in handling advertising, and must be financially sound. Those three conditions are still in effect. Anyone may claim to be an agency, but only agencies that are recognized are allowed to charge a commission.

Today's agencies still receive commissions from the media for space they buy for clients. However, artwork and the cost of production are generally billed by the agency to the advertiser, plus a service charge—usually 17.65 percent of the net, which is equivalent to 15 percent of the gross. By preagreement, a charge is made for other services.

American Association of Advertising Agencies (AAAA, 4 A's). *The national organization of advertising agencies.*

The American Association of Advertising Agencies. The most important agency association is the American Association of Advertising Agencies (written as A.A.A.A. or 4A's), established in 1917. This organization has continuously acted as a great force in improving the standards of agency business and advertising practice. Its members, large and small, place over 80 percent of all national advertising today.

The No-Rebate Age (1918–1956)

We shall summarize the events of this era that left their mark on today's agency world.

Radio. One of the main events of 1925 was the notorious Scopes trial, and the main advent was radio. They did a lot for each other. Radio dramatized evolution-on-trial in Tennessee; it brought the issue of teaching scientific evolution home to Americans and it brought people closer to their radios. Tuning in to radio soon became a major part of

American life, especially during the Great Depression and World War II. Radio established itself as a prime news vehicle. It also gave advertising a vital new medium and helped pull agencies through those troubled years. A number of agencies handled the entire production of a radio program as well as its commercials. By 1942, agencies were billing more for radio ($188 million) than they were for newspaper ($144 million) advertising. The radio boom lasted until TV came along.

Television took radio's place—as the most popular medium for entertainment and advertising. Anheuser-Busch spent $5 million on Bud Bowl I—only *six* 30-second spots during the Super Bowl! With the largest TV audience in attendance for the year, Bud's spots are during the pre-game show, the kickoff, and one at the end of each quarter. To encourage continued viewing *throughout* the game, "scorecards" will be available in point-of-purchase displays.

Television. TV became popular after 1952, when nationwide network broadcasts began. Between 1950 and 1956, TV was the fastest-growing medium (see Exhibit 5.1). It became the major medium for many agencies. National advertisers spent more on TV than they did on any other medium. Television expenditures grew from $171 million in 1950 to $1,225 million in 1956.

Electronic Data Processing. The computer entered advertising through the accounting department. By 1956, it was already changing the lives of the media department, the marketing department, and the research department—all having grown in competence with the increasing number of syndicated research services. Agencies prided themselves on their research knowledge and were spending hundreds of thousands of dollars for research every year to service their clients better.

Business was good, and American consumers were attaining a better standard of living than they had ever enjoyed before. The period from 1950 to 1956 proved to be the beginning of the biggest boom advertising ever had: Total expenditures jumped from $4.5 billion in 1950 to $9.9 billion. Over 60 percent of this spending was for national advertising placed by advertising agencies. And the agency business was good, too.

The Age of Negotiation (1956 to Now)

Consent Decrees. In 1956, a change occurred in the advertiser-agency relationship. The United States Department of Justice held that the no-rebating provision between media associations and agencies limited the ability to negotiate between buyer and seller and therefore was in restraint of trade and a violation of antitrust laws. If the people involved in such provisions consented in writing to stop the practices now found unlawful, however, the Justice Department promised to drop all charges against them. Consent decrees to stop no-rebating provisions were entered into by all media associations on behalf of their members.

Although the Justice Department's ruling in no way affected the 15 percent commission agencies were accustomed to getting from the media, it opened the way to review the total compensation an agency should receive for its services, with the 15 percent commission a basic part of the negotiations. We shall shortly see the effects this has had on the agency-client relationship.

Full-service agencies offer their clients a large variety of services—from sales promotion, public relations, direct marketing to logo and packaging design, and even television programming. McDonald's recent decision to top last year's $400 million in United States media spending and to increase the number of promotions will be handled by Leo Burnett USA, Chicago for TV and Simon Marketing, Los Angeles promotion. In-store promotions include cups with peel-off stickers revealing prizes. Additional spots will feature new products being tested in regional markets. The agencies are responsible for coordinating themes, designing new, distinctive packages, and arranging for community involvement in the new product launches.

THE FULL-SERVICE ADVERTISING AGENCY TODAY

In the simplest terms, the *full-service agency* offers clients all the services necessary to handle the total advertising function. In recent years, this concept has expanded to include new communications services through expanded agency departments or subsidiary companies. Today's full-service agency may offer sales promotion, public relations, direct marketing, logo and package design, and even television programming.

Lintas:USA is an example of an agency expanding integrated marketing services to its clients. In Chapter 3, we reviewed the Lintas: Link system for strategic development. Lintas describes its multiservice process as "one advertiser, one voice," carrying the message about the product through a variety of disciplines—advertising, sales promotion, public relations, direct marketing, and so forth—with a tight marketing focus so that the brand image is reinforced every time the consumer is contacted. Most

EXHIBIT 5.1

Leslie Advertising, Inc., targeted potential clients with this direct-mail piece telling of great recall scores for their new client's television commercials. (Courtesy: Leslie Advertising, Inc., Greenville, S.C.)

large agencies have subsidiaries or divisions that offer a range of specific services. Ogilvy & Mather calls its diversified services "Ogilvy Orchestration." Young & Rubicam pioneered the concept with its "whole egg" approach in the 1970s.[2] (Exhibit 5.2 is an example of the diversity of specialized services available in one agency.)

Functions of the Full-Service Agency

Initial work by a full-service agency begins with a description of the *target* and the *market*. The *new target* for the Wine Institute of San Francisco, a trade association for California wineries, are those people who have *never* tasted wine. Its "mellow image" campaign will be a combination of advertising, promotions, and educational programs to "break down some of the 'mystique' that *average Americans* associate with wine."

When a new account or a new product is assigned to a full-service agency, work on it will generally proceed along the following lines.

What Is the Marketing Problem? The marketing problem entails gathering and analyzing all the information necessary to market the product or service. Who are the prime prospects? Where are they? What are their demographic and psychographic characteristics? How does the product fit into their lifestyle? How do they regard this type of product? This particular brand? Competitive products? What one benefit do consumers seek from such a product? In what distinctive way can the product solve the prime prospects' problem? What media will best reach your market? Exhibit 5.3 illustrates one agency's savvy in asking the right questions before developing creative.

The Strategy. Using the answers to these questions, you formulate a strategy that positions the product in relation to the prime-prospect customer and emphasizes the attribute that will appeal to the prime prospect.

The Creative Response. Once the overall strategy is determined, you decide on the creative strategy, write copy, and prepare rough layouts and storyboards.

---

[2]Jon Lafayette, "Lintas Tries Integrated Approach," *Advertising Age,* December 19, 1988, p. 4.

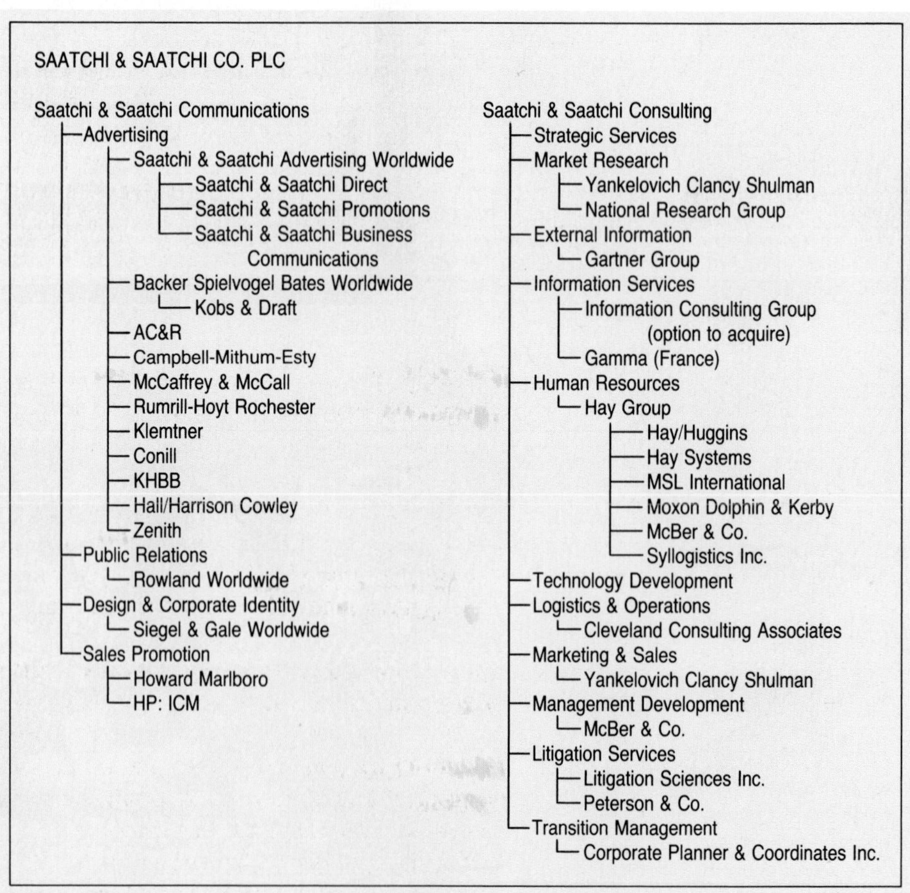

EXHIBIT 5.2

Saatchi & Saatchi integrates a number of independent support companies specializing in public relations, design, sales promotion, market research, information and, other services for clients. (Courtesy: *Advertising Age*.)

EXHIBIT 5.3

An agency is concerned to get the right information before it attempts to create ads. (Courtesy: Longwater, Inc.)

To get the right answers, you first have to ask the right questions.

We all know examples of advertising strategies that skidded straight from the showroom to the junk heap. It's not that they didn't come up with suitable answers—they just didn't ask the right questions.

At Longwater Advertising, we're driven to create work that's fresh and innovative, yet steered by sound marketing and research. We avoid answers that are someone else's retreads, and communicate with our clients to insure the most mileage for their advertising dollar.

Shopping for an agency can be like looking for a new car. Some sport a lot of chrome and glitter outside, but ultimately it is what's under the hood that really counts.

So take a look around, and be sure to kick the tires at Longwater. Because when it comes to your advertising agency, the last thing you need is a lemon. Or an Edsel.

619 Tattnall Street
Savannah, Georgia 31401,
912-233-9200
FAX 912-233-1663

Longwater Inc.

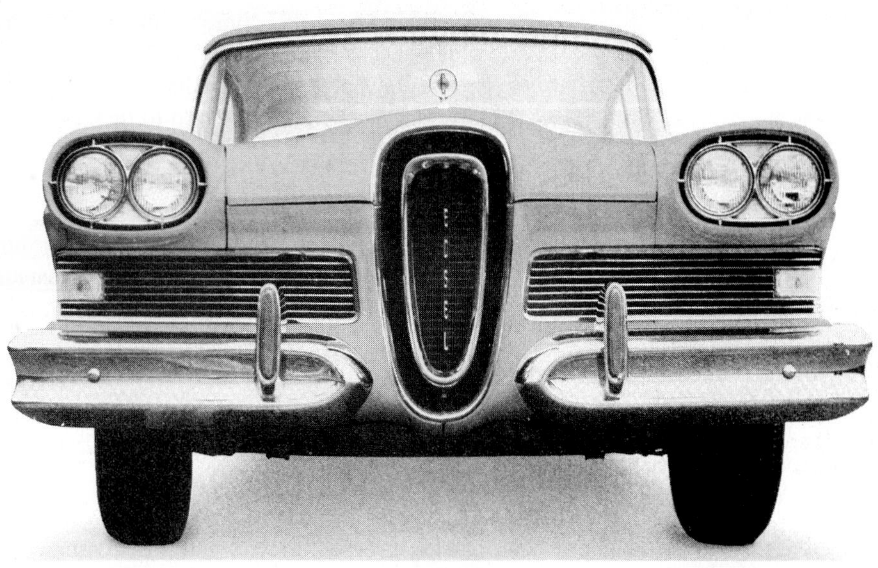

The *advertising plan* is based on the *strategy* that positions a product, appropriately, in the mind of the selected *target*. From that point, the *creative execution* and the *media plan* are developed. Conair chose, as their new celebrity spokesman, *Joe Namath*—specifically for his *lack* of sex appeal! It's positioning its lather warmer, electric shaver, and beard trimmer as "sensible" additions to the male grooming process. Conair is upping its ad budget by 30% in the product lines Namath will hype—which will appear in "clean" gray and red modern "packages" on television and in well-known male magazines, such as *GQ*.

The Media Plan. Next you define media strategy, checking objectives to ensure that they parallel your marketing objectives. Then you select media and prepare schedules with costs.

The Total Plan. You present roughs of the copy, layout, and production costs, along with media schedules and costs—all leading to total cost.

When the total plan is approved, you proceed with the production of ads, issue media orders, and ship plates and prints to media or tapes and films, as required.

Notify Trade of Forthcoming Campaign. You inform dealers of the campaign details early enough so that they can get ready to take advantage of the ad campaign.

Billing and Payments. When ads are run, you take care of billing to client and payment of bills to media and to production vendors. As an example of the billing procedure, let us say that through your agency an advertiser has ordered an ad in *Leisure-Time* magazine for one page, worth $2,000. When the ad appears, the bill your agency gets from the publisher will read something like this:

1 page, October *Leisure-Time* magazine	$2,000
Agency commission @ 15% (cash discount omitted for convenience)	300
Balance due	$1,700

Your agency will then bill the advertiser for $2,000, retain the $300 as its compensation, and pay the publisher $1,700.

The agency commission applies only to the cost of space or time. In addition, as mentioned earlier, your agency will send the advertiser a bill for production costs for such items as:

- Finished artwork
- Typography
- Photography
- Retouching
- Reproduction prints
- Recording studios
- Broadcast production

These items are billed at actual costs plus a service charge, usually 17.65 percent (which is equivalent to 15 percent of the net).

Organization of the Full-Service Agency

Advertising agencies come in all sizes and shapes. The largest employ hundreds of people and bill hundreds of millions of dollars every year. The smallest are one- or two-person operations (usually a creative person and an account manager). As they grow, they generally must add to their organizational structure to handle all the functions of a full-service agency.

All agencies do not structure themselves in exactly the same manner. For discussion purposes, we have chosen a typical organizational structure under the command of major executives: the vice presidents of (1) the creative department, (2) account services, (3) marketing services, and (4) management and finance (see Exhibit 5.5). We shall discuss briefly how each department is organized.

Setting the *tone* and *direction* of a full-service agency is the *creative department*. Backer Spielvogel Bates, New York received special distinction from the advertising press for its print campaign in business and lifestyle magazines for British Airways. It featured the *"free extras"* first-class passengers receive on flights—drinks, food, and headsets—with the tag line, "The Best Things in Flight are Free." The ad's objective was to appeal to the "cheapskate," without appearing "tacky." "It worked," revealed advertising director, George Hadley.

Creative Department. As the head of the creative department, the creative director is responsible for the effectiveness of all advertising produced by the agency. The success of the agency depends on this department. The creative director sets the creative philosophy of the agency and its standards of craftsmanship, and generates a stimulating environment that inspires the best people to seek work there.

At first, all writers and artists will work right under one creative director; but as the business grows, various creative directors will take over the writing and art activities of different brands. A traffic department will be set up to keep the work flowing on schedule.

The print production director and the television manager also report to the creative director, who is ultimately responsible for the finished product—ads and commercials.

Account Services The vice president in charge of account services is responsible for the relationship between the agency and the client, and is indeed a person of two

EXHIBIT 5.4

This is an example of an agen‿, creative self-promotion. This direct-mail piece touting Buntin as a "hot southeastern agency" was sent to prospective clients. (Courtesy: Buntin Advertising, Inc.)

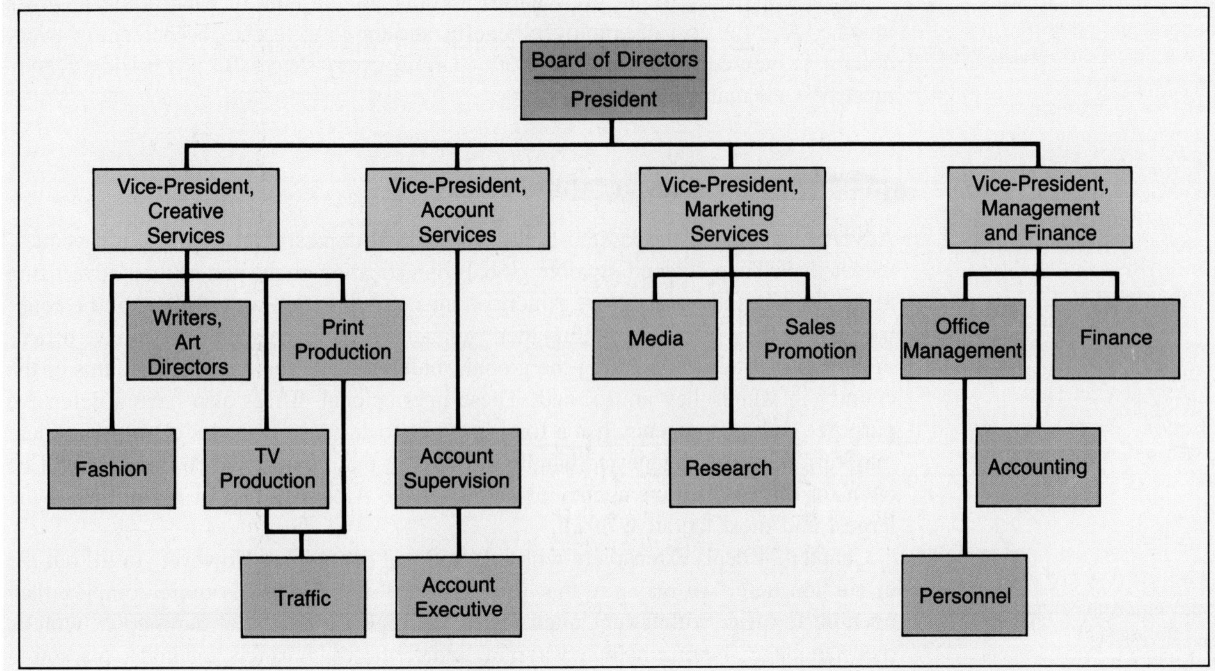

EXHIBIT 5.5
Organization of a typical full-service agency.

worlds: the client's business and advertising. This vice president must be knowledgeable about the client's business, profit goals, marketing problems, and advertising objectives. He or she is responsible for helping to formulate the basic advertising strategy recommended by the agency, for seeing that the proposed advertising prepared by the agency is on target, and for presenting the total proposal—media schedules, budget, and rough ads or storyboards—to the client for approval. Then comes the task of making sure that the agency produces the work to the client's satisfaction.

As the business grows and takes on many clients, an account supervisor will appoint account executives to serve as the individual contacts with the various accounts. Account executives must be skillful at both communications and follow-up. Their biggest contribution is keeping the agency ahead of its clients' needs. But the account supervisor will continue the overall review of account handling, maintaining contacts with a counterpart at the client's office.

The "business" side of an agency is involved in *account services*—the "link" between the agency and the client. *Media selection and buying* is a separate department, as is *management and finance*. Currently, WPP Group Chief Executive Martin Sorrell is involved in research and analysis in *brand name valuation*—both for his own business units and for his clients. "The objective for a company is to 'warn' a possible suitor what the 'real' company is worth," stated John Murphy, chairman of Interbrand Group, a branding consultancy. "*Brand valuation* can also be used as a brand management tool to analyze strengths and weaknesses of brands to arrive at the appropriate levels of advertising and promotional support agencies should recommend."

Marketing Services The vice president in charge of marketing services is responsible for media planning and buying, for research, and for sales promotion. The marketing vice president will appoint a media director, who is responsible for the philosophy and planning of the use of media, for the selection of specific media, and for buying space and time. As the agency grows, there will be a staff of media buyers, grouped according to media (print, TV, or radio), accounts, or territory. The media staff will include an estimating department and an ordering department, as well as a department to handle residual payments due performers. The media head may use independent media services, especially in the purchase of TV and radio time.

The research director will help define marketing and copy goals. Agencies usually use outside research organizations for field work; but in some agencies, research and media planning are coordinated under one person. The division of work among the executives may vary with the agency.

The sales-promotion director takes care of premiums, coupons, and other dealer aids and promotions.

Management and Finance Like all businesses, an advertising agency needs an administrative head to take charge of financial and accounting control, office management, and personnel (including trainees).

There's more demand than ever for international promotional campaigns. Agencies today have their own affiliates abroad—or have agreements with foreign agencies, in order to serve their global clients more effectively. That's precisely why *Pan Am World Airways* selected Della Femina, McHaynee WCRS to handle its $5.5 million account. Della Femina was created by British parent firm WCRS—out of Della Femina Travisano & Partners/New York and HBM Creemer/Boston—because it believed "a single combination of worldwide agencies would have a better chance of winning big accounts."

The same message or a variation of the original message can enable the international advertiser to use the same theme worldwide. The Gilette Company of Boston is using a new $70 million international campaign to re-introduce its Atra Plus blade shaving system. The new TV spots from BBDO/New York feature men working, playing sports, getting married, and becoming fathers. The "image ads" will appear in 14 languages in Europe and North America. All use local-language versions of the tagline: "The best a man can get."

As indicated in Exhibit 5.6, salaries account for the bulk of each dollar of gross income. Add the cost of employee benefits and the total reaches 64 percent of every dollar. As you can see from the profit margin, every successful advertising agency must be well managed.

International Agency Operations

Advertising outside the United States has passed domestic advertising in revenues. Clients have been demanding more global sophistication on the part of their advertising agencies. Virtually every large American agency has offices or affiliates in the countries where their clients are selling their products. American agencies now have offices in over 100 countries handling the global, multinational, and national accounts of the country in which they are located. These international offices also have a defensive purpose: Unless an agency has a foreign office to serve an overseas client, that client may turn to a local agency to handle business in that country. Then the door will be open for the competitive agency to take over the American part of the billings—the largest and most lucrative of all.

Chapter 24 deals extensively with international operations. However, to fill out the discussion here, we may say that setting up a foreign office is more complex than opening an office within the United States. Each country is a different market, with its own language, buying habits, ways of living, mores, business methods, marketing traditions, and laws. So instead of trying to organize new agencies with American personnel, most American agencies now purchase a majority or minority interest in successful foreign agencies. They usually have a top-management person as the head of an overseas office. Key members of the international offices regularly gather at the home office for an intensive seminar on the philosophy and operation of the agency, picking up ideas to carry back and adapt as they see fit.

International marketing and advertising can be conducted in two basic ways:

1. A universal theme is applied to all marketing-advertising problems in all countries, using the same slogan and visual treatment. Thus, Coca-Cola employs the same basic theme in all of its global advertising, with necessary modifications for clarity and understanding. It would be extremely expensive and inefficient for Coca-Cola to run totally different messages in each country where it sells its product. (An excellent example of universal theme advertising is the Apple Computer ad in Exhibit 5.7).

EXHIBIT 5.6

The distribution of gross income for the typical advertising agency. (Courtesy: American Association of Advertising Agencies.)

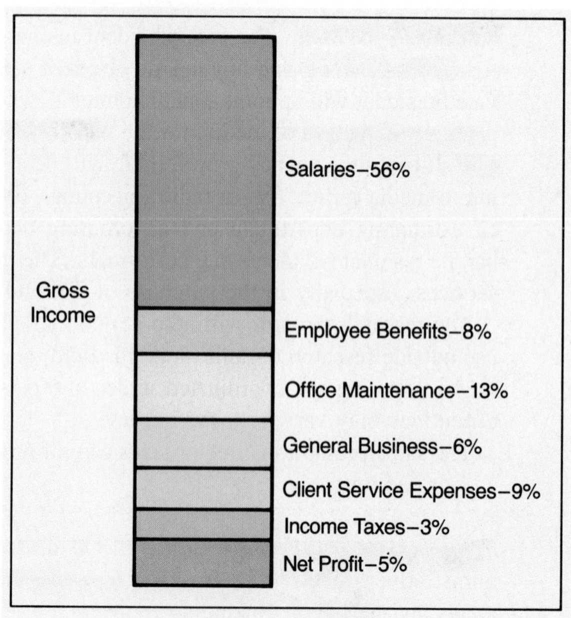

EXHIBIT 5.7

Apple ad uses the same theme in many countries—only the copy is translated. (Courtesy: Apple Computer.)

2. Individual themes are tailored to the marketing climate, competitive situation, and advertising practices in each country, but the same basic advertising strategy created for the product is retained. Here the thought is that national differences are too great to allow the same message to be used everywhere, and simply translating American ads into a foreign language has proved dangerous. Frank Perdue's Spanish translation of "It takes a tough man to make a tender chicken," actually said, "It takes a sexually excited man to make a chick affectionate."[3]

An agency's ability to provide advertising services throughout the world is very often crucial to its success in winning significant new business and retaining old accounts. As clients grow and market their products in more and more countries, they often feel the need for the services of a worldwide agency. Many account switches have been made almost solely because the new agency could provide worldwide service whereas the old one could not. Exhibit 5.8 lists the major global agencies as of this writing.

COMPETING ACCOUNTS

Clients generally don't "permit" agencies to handle accounts, which conflict with their businesses. *Recent mergers*—by clients and agencies alike—have made exclusivity difficult. *Colgate-Palmolive* may delay the national launch of its *Colgate low-price, over-the-counter medicines*—until it resolves an apparent conflict involving a key agency. Sources say Colgate is "uncomfortable" with HDM, a joint venture of Young & Rubican, Dentsu and Eurocom. Y&R currently handles Advil and Anacin, potential competitors.

The client-agency relationship is a professional one. Much of the information exchanged between client and agency is confidential. This may include plans for new products or new marketing strategies. Therefore, the client generally will not approve of an agency handling companies or products in direct competition. Sometimes agencies will handle accounts for the same type of product if they don't compete directly—for example, banks that don't compete in the same markets may be handled by the same agency. Many client-agency conflicts result from mergers in which one merger partner handles an account for a product that competes with one the other merger partner is already handling. When agencies consider merging, the first question is: Will any of our accounts conflict? Currently, a number of the large national agencies run their local offices independently in the hope that clients won't view the same type of account in another office as a conflict (see Exhibit 5.9). Competing accounts also present a problem in dealing with outside creative services and are conceivably an inhibiting factor.

EXHIBIT 5.8
Major global agencies.

1. Dentsu, Inc.
2. Young & Rubicam
3. Saatchi & Saatchi Worldwide
4. Backer Spielvogel Bates Worldwide
5. McCann-Erickson Worldwide
6. FBC-Publics
7. Ogilvy & Mather Worldwide
8. BBDO Worldwide
9. J. Walter Thompson Company
10. Lintas: Worldwide
11. Hakuhodo International
12. Grey Advertising
13. D'Arcy Masius Benton & Bowles
14. Leo Burnett Company

[3]Stephen Baker, *The Advertiser's Manual* (New York: John Wiley & Sons, 1988), p. 219.

EXHIBIT 5.9

BBDO domestic agency network. (This list does not include all BBDO agencies.)

- Baxter, Gurian & Mazzel, Beverly Hills
- BBDO, New York
- BBDO, Atlanta
- BBDO, Los Angeles
- Blair Advertising, Rochester
- Caravetta Allen Kimbrough, Miami
- Frank J. Corbett, Chicago
- Tracy-Locke, Dallas
- Ingalis, Quinn & Johnson, Boston
- Tycer Fultz Bellack, Palo Alto

THE AGENCY OF RECORD

Large advertisers employ a number of agencies to handle the advertising of their various divisions and products. To coordinate the total media buy and the programming of products in a network buy, the advertiser will appoint one agency as the agency of record. This agency will make the corporate media contracts under which the other agencies will issue their orders, keep a record of all the advertising placed, and transmit management's decisions on the allotment of time and space in a schedule. For this service, the other agencies pay a small part of their commissions (usually 15 percent of their 15 percent) to the agency of record.

Agency networks have several agencies located in different areas—for the purpose of being able to share information and provide better regional coverage for clients. Gary Gelpin, the new president of the National Advertising Agency Network, representing smaller advertising agencies, claims. "The NAAN network provides the larger structure that lets the small agency *keep* its entrepreneural enthusiasm, its excitement." Founded in 1932, NAAN provides a confidential exchange of information and assistance. It represents one full-service agency in each of 50 markets in the United States and Canada. "It allows small shops to tap into the resources of the worldwide network."

AGENCY NETWORKS

In general, the agency networks are composed primarily of small- and medium-sized agencies that have a working agreement to help with information gathering or sharing. In the 1920s, Lynn Ellis, an advertising management consultant, saw that middle-sized agencies that had no branch offices had difficulty in dealing with the regional problems of their clients. He organized such agencies (one agency in each main advertising center) into an agency network so that they could help one another cope with problems in their respective areas and could exchange ideas, experiences, and facilities. Today there are a number of agency networks operating throughout the country.

Don't confuse associations like the American Association of Advertising Agencies with agency networks. A.A.A.A. members are in direct competition with one another—there may be dozens of A.A.A.A. agencies in the same city.

The development of the "mega-agency" has provided clients with the advantage of diversified talent and media clout—but, in some cases, with impersonalization and loss of status. *Saatchi & Saatchi* consolidated its United Kingdom media buying in late 1988, thus touching off the next wave of multinational acquisition activity in Europe. At the same time, the agency acquired two Madison Avenue "mainstays," Compton Advertising and Dancer-Fitzgerald-Sample. Pretax profits for fiscal 1989 were $279 million, while their *average growth* has been *59%* during the past ten years.

NEW DEVELOPMENTS IN THE AGENCY WORLD

The Mega-agency

Saatchi & Saatchi PLC, London, began one of the most significant recent changes in the advertising business by systematically expanding from a small agency in 1986 to a $13.5 billion mega-agency network operation by 1988. Saatchi & Saatchi Advertising Worldwide and Backer Spielvogel Bates Worldwide accounted for $10.1 billion of the Saatchi advertising empire in 1988 (see Exhibit 5.2 for a summary of Saatchi & Saatchi PLC holdings). For the moment, Saatchi's holdings make it the world's biggest advertising concern. New York–based Interpublic Group of Companies is the second-largest mega-agency. Martin Sorrell, a former senior executive at Saatchi & Saatchi, heads another London mega-agency, WPP Group PLC, which had grown very rapidly to 289

EXHIBIT 5.10
Worldwide ranking of Mega-Agencies.

Group	Income (millions)	Billings (millions)
Saatchi & Saatchi PLC, London	$1,900	$13,529
Interpublic Group of Companies, New York	1,260	8,402
WPP Group PLC	1,173	7,825
Ominicom Group	986	7,072

(Source: *Advertising Age*, March 29, 1989.)

offices worldwide by the end of 1988. The four largest mega-agencies, by billings and gross income, are listed in Exhibit 5.10.

Mega-agencies offer several advantages to their clients, among which the most important are: a greater reservoir of talent; an ability to shift portions of accounts from one agency to another without going through the time-consuming, and often confusing, agency review (Coca-Cola has switched assignments for their brands between Interpublic's McCann-Erickson and Lintas:Worldwide); and superior clout in negotiating with the media. There are also some disadvantages for clients dealing with a mega-agency, the most important of which is conflicts with competing accounts.

Smaller agencies claim that the mega-agency is quite impersonal and not as creative in advertising clients' products. The fact is that all agencies—large and small—are composed of small units or teams that work on an assigned account or group of accounts. The ability of the team and its dedication to creative and professional excellence are dictated by the talent and innovative abilities of individuals, not the size of the company they work for. Many medium and smaller agencies are in fact traveling the merger road themselves in order to become more competitive.

The size and structure of an agency will attract or repel clients, depending on what level and quality of services they are seeking. Some large corporations have been critical of agency mergers and mega-agencies. Yet, in truth, the advertising business is following business in general in attempting to diversify, economize, and become more efficient and profitable.

"Boutiques" have been organized for those clients preferring a more innovative and personalized approach to *creative*. Such an agency is the *Blue Chip Marketing Group* of Stamford, Connecticut, which specializes in reaching top executives with exceptionally creative upscale gifts and presentations. It recently helped the Phoenix Mutual Life Insurance Company identify and send two mailings to 300 prospects Phoenix salespeople weren't reaching by phone. Each potential client received a box containing his/her nickname carved in wood and a page of copy about Phoenix.

Other Advertising Services

New services are continually springing up in competition with advertising agencies. Each new service is designed to serve clients' needs a little differently. This competition has impacted agency structure and operations.

Independent Creative Services. Some advertisers seek top creative talent on a free-lance, per-job basis. Many creative people do free-lance work in their off-hours. Some make it a full-time job and open their own "creative shop" or "creative boutique."

À La Carte Agency. Many agencies offer for a fee just that part of their total services that the advertiser wants. The à la carte arrangement is used mostly for creative services and for media planning and placement.

In-House Agency. When advertisers found that all the services an agency could offer were purchasable on a piecemeal fee basis, they began setting up their own internal agencies, referred to as *in-house agencies.*

In-house agency. *An arrangement whereby the advertiser handles the total agency function by buying individually, on a fee basis, the needed services (for example, creative, media services, and placement) under the direction of an assigned advertising director.*

Under the in-house agency operation, an advertiser can employ an agency or a creative service to originate advertising for a fee or markup. A media-buying service will buy the time or space, and an agency will place ads for a fraction of the usual 15 percent commission. Whereas the older house agency was equipped with a complete full-service staff, the in-house agency is an administrative center that gathers and directs varying outside services for its operations and has a minimum staff. The term

In-house agencies, today, functions as "administrative centers," directing various independent services to perform specific functions, such as creative, media buying, etc. They don't generally compete with full-service agencies—they simply prefer to *direct* the promotion operations for the firm, rather than the agency. Because of constant changes in promotions, merchandise, and prices, *Zayre Discount Stores* maintained an in-house agency—to coordinate its various promotion functions. Now that Ames Department Stores has acquired the 361-store chain, it's considering an "everyday low price" marketing strategy that would halve the number of promotional circulars and cut the $20–$25 million ad budget. Still, Ames would keep the *in-house* concept, as "the best workable set-up for rapid turnover merchandisers," quoted a management source.

The "art" of media buying has fostered the growth of *separate media-buying services,* especially for spot television. The vast majority of agencies with multinational aspirations are now seeking to build *a network* of media independents in Europe. Knowing how vital media placement is for their clients—especially in diverse markets—*WCRS and Saatchi and Saatchi* have made the boldest moves so far. With the approach of 1992, when the European Community will dismantle trade barriers, agencies anticipate more demand for European promotion, "and they will expect to have *first-rate European media services,*" acknowledged HMS Media Services' Kai Hiemstra.

in-house distinguishes the talent-assembling type of agency operation from the self-contained full-service house agency born in the earliest days, when large advertisers owned agencies (e.g., Procter & Gamble had its own Procter and Collier agency) geared to perform almost all advertising functions. These house agencies generally fell out of favor as advertisers discovered that they could get better advertising from an independent agency. The few such house agencies operating today often use outside services to supplement their own staffs.

Saving money is not the only, or even the chief, reason some firms use an in-house agency. For industrial companies that have highly technical products that constantly undergo technological changes and advances, it may well be more efficient to have in-house technical people prepare the ads. This saves endless briefings that would be necessary if outside industrial writers were used. But the companies place their ads through an agency of their choice, at a negotiated commission.

Rolodex Agency. An agency run by several advertising specialists, usually account and/or creative people, that has no basic staff is called a *rolodex agency.* It hires specialists—in marketing, media planning, creative strategy, writing, whatever—who work on a project basis. The concept is similar to hiring free-lance creative people to execute ads, except that the experts are hired as needed. The rolodex agency claims to be able to give advertisers expertise that small full-service agencies can't match.

Media-Buying Services. Media-buying services developed with the rapid growth of television in the 1960s, when every TV station was constantly concerned about unsold time—a cardinal sin because it meant an irreversible loss of revenue. At the same time, agency media directors came under great pressure to make the most effective use of their budgets by planning, placing, and negotiating the best deal for a schedule. Negotiating became a sophisticated art—so much so that some media directors decided to open their own time-buying services to perform whatever part of the total media operation an advertiser or agency might require.

While media services plan and buy all media, their forte is spot television. It is estimated that media services place 25 to 30 percent of national spot advertising dollars.[4] Most media services work on a commission basis, like the agencies, although sometimes at lower rates. These services are used by advertisers and agencies (usually small to medium in size).

IN-HOUSE SERVICES. A few large advertisers have taken the media-buying function in-house so they will have more control over the buying operation. Thomas J. Lipton and Lever Brothers formed L & L Media, Inc., in late 1988, in an attempt to integrate the media-buying function to make it more efficient. This is not likely to become a trend, however. It is more probable that advertisers will keep a seasoned media consultant on staff to ride herd on their agency or media service's performance.

AGENCIES MERGING SERVICES. The agreement between Omnicom and the Ogilvy Group to jointly buy media in Europe started a trend to strengthen agency media-buying clout by combining media-buying operations. Client conflicts are one of the problems this concept must overcome to be successful. The European trend in consolidation of agencies' media-buying units is unlikely to spread rapidly to the United States.

FORMS OF AGENCY COMPENSATION

As we saw in the section on the history of advertising, agency compensation was fairly standardized for most of this century. Recently, however, it has been all over the map, ranging from the traditional commission to incentive compensation systems tied to the

[4]George Swisshelm, "Media Services Enter New Era," *Television/Radio Age,* February 20, 1989, pp. 32–34.

success of the advertising. However, there are still only two basic forms of advertising agency compensation: commissions and fees.

Agencies are compensated by the standard *15% commission* and/or by *fees for special services*. However, those companies doing business in foreign markets are now being confronted with compensation "variations." When *Sara Lee/ Douwe Egberts division,* based in Utrecht, Netherlands, aligned its business by product category in about a dozen European countries, four global agencies became "the winners." Compensation methods are still being discussed, including a combination of fee and commission payments. Each agency will have its own arrangement.

- *Media commission.* The traditional 15 percent commission is the most common form of agency income. Outdoor advertising companies allow a 16⅔ percent commission.
- *Production commissions or markups.* As indicated earlier, agencies subcontract production work (type, photography, illustrators) and charge the client the cost plus a commission—with 17.65 percent being norm.
- *Fee arrangements.* Sometimes the 15 percent commission isn't enough for agencies to make a fair profit (e.g., it may cost an agency more to serve a small client than a large one). As a result, a fee arrangement (e.g., flat fee, cost plus fee, flat fee plus direct costs, project fee) or a commission plus a fee arrangement may be agreed to by the client and agency. The fee will be based on the type of work being done (e.g., copy writing at hourly or fixed rates, artwork charges based on salary of involved personnel).

The Association of National Advertisers conducts biennial surveys among its members to determine the agency compensation used by advertisers. The 1989 study indicates that the original 15 percent commission system is continuing to decline as companies try to lower costs (see Exhibit 5.11). Labor-based fees—a method of compensation that had recently been on the rise—also declined in the latest survey results, to 24 percent usage among the ANA members surveyed. Reduced commissions seems to be gaining as an agency compensation method among ANA members; it increased from 25 percent in 1986 to 29 percent in 1989.[5]

Procter & Gamble shifted to higher agency compensation for its 1990 fiscal year in hopes of elevating creative quality. The new system keeps the 15 percent commission rate on traditional media, but on top of that P&G is paying a 15 percent commission for creative done for promotional vehicles (such as supermarket shopping carts) and ads for alternative media (such as controlled-circulation magazines). The fee for new product development has also been increased.[6] This action is significant to the agency business because it places promotion on an equal footing for commissions with conventional measured media.[7]

[5]Assocation of National Advertisers, Inc., *Current Advertiser Practices in Compensating Their Agencies: 1989.*

[6]Laurie Freeman, "P&G Seeks New Creative Thrust," *Advertising Age,* February 20, 1989, p. 3.

[7]"P&G Levels the Playing Field," *Advertising Age,* February 27, 1989, p. 16.

EXHIBIT 5.11

Advertising agency compensation arrangements. (Courtesy: *ADWEEK.*)

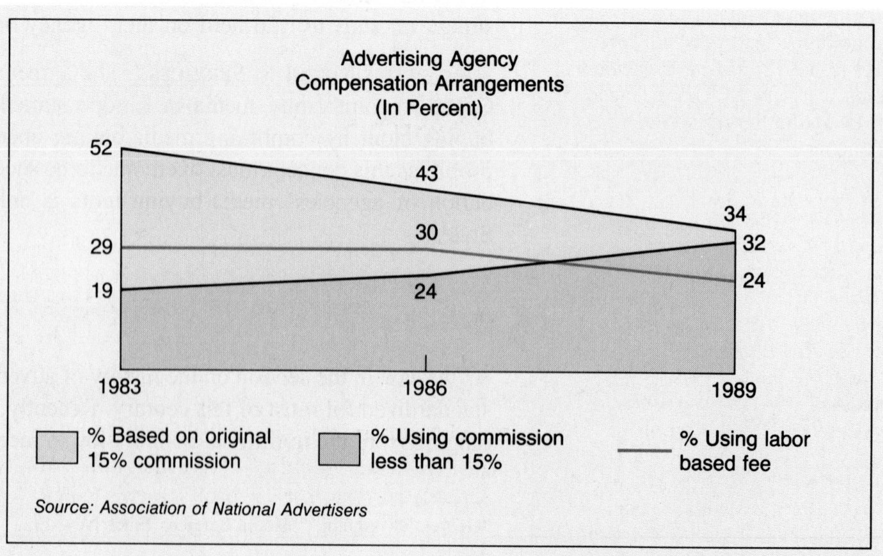

OTHER SERVICES

Barter. *Acquisition of broadcast time by an advertiser or an agency in exchange for operating capital or merchandise. No cash is involved.*

Barter

Barter is another way for an advertiser or agency to buy media below card rates, especially TV and radio time.

When the Advertiser Is the Buyer. Long before radio and TV appeared on the scene, hotels began a practice that they continue to this day: They bartered their rooms for advertising space in newspapers and magazines.

Barter in broadcasting began in the early days of radio. Cash was always tight (it still is), but studios have to spend a lot of money for equipment. Firms that handle barter supply a station with anything it needs in exchange for time. The bartered material may be furniture, equipment, even travel tickets, but it is most often program material in the form of films—a constant need of TV stations, which usually must rent them from independent film syndicators. Generally included are Hollywood films, films of popular old TV programs, and, most important, films of current popular TV series that the barter houses control. There is no cash outflow for the station.

Some barter houses become virtually brokers or wholesalers of time. They build inventories of time accumulated in various barter deals. These inventories, known as *time banks,* are made available to advertisers or agencies seeking to stretch their TV or radio dollars.

Barter has its drawbacks, of course. Often the weaker stations in a market use it the most. Some stations won't accept barter business from advertisers already on the air in the market. Much of the time is poor time (even though it is still good value at the low rate paid). Frequently, the advertiser or agency does not deal directly with the station, so problems of make-goods can be sticky. Nevertheless, barter is used by many well-known advertisers.

The roles are changing, however. Now agencies themselves are using barter on behalf of their clients. This is how it works: The agency goes to a station and offers a syndicated show free. All the station must do is retain three or four minutes in the half hour for the agency's client. The station is then free to sell three or four minutes on its own. The advantage to the advertiser of *trade-out shows,* as they are often called, is not only a possible saving in TV costs, but, more important, control over the quality of the environment in which the commercial appears. Competitive commercials or commercial overcrowding can be fended off.

This arrangement has proved so successful that a number of agencies have gone into the barter business, creating syndicate shows, bartering time for them on various stations, accumulating their own time banks, and then offering the time to their clients at less than rate-card costs.

Research Services

Research of potential advertising effectiveness, in the form of custom-made client studies, is extremely popular. When the California Automobile Dealers Association wanted to know what specific factors attracted customers to their showrooms, they had J. D. Powers and Associates conduct a study among buyers of new cars. New ads were designed to focus on the "greeting of prospects" and "the efficiency of completing the necessary paperwork"—as a result of the direct mail study.

In addition to the syndicated research services previously discussed, which regularly report the latest findings on buyers of a product—who and where they are, how they live and buy, what media they read, watch, and listen to—there is a vast array of advertising and marketing research services. These services offer custom-made research reports to marketers and their agencies, answering their questions about their own products and their advertising. Studies cover such subjects as advertising effectiveness, TV and print pretesting and post-testing, concept testing, market segmentation, positioning of products, media preferences, purchasing patterns, and similar problems directly affecting advertising decisions.

A fascinating variety of techniques are used in gathering such information. They include field surveys, consumer mail banks, focus groups continuous-tracking studies, cable TV testing of commercials, image studies, electronic questionnaires, opinion surveys, shopping center intercepts, and media-mix tests.

EXHIBIT 5.12

The Bottom-Line's self-promotion ad sells its personality. (Courtesy: The Bottom-Line.)

Word Processor

Made of 100% all natural ingredients. Fully portable, rechargeable and works under adverse operating conditions. Comes with unlimited warranty.

This model is guaranteed to generate words that motivate your customers, clients and consumers to action.

To do something.

To buy something.

In a word—to say "yes."

Whoever that guy was who said one picture is worth a thousand words must have flunked fifth grade English.

Pictures are wonderful.

Baby pictures.

Wedding pictures.

Moving pictures. And pictures of your fishing trip to Lake Lotsaluck.

Pictures are pretty.

But they need words.

That's why Hollywood invented talkies.

(Hey, those guys weren't dumb.)

Don't get me wrong. I like visual images—a lot. In fact, I've included one here to show to you that our new market-driven word processor is currently in stock and available.

Words can set us free—all by themselves.

You didn't notice any illustrations in the Declaration of Independence, did you?

Or photographs accompanying the Gettysburg Address?

(Don't feel bad. I couldn't find any either.)

You don't need pictures to appreciate The Wall Street Journal. Or Willie Nelson.

Can you dig it?

Today's consumers (that's thee and me and ol' Bubba makes three) are savvy. We want to know the truth and nothing but. So help us, Lee Iacocca.

We want to read words that leap off the printed page and grab us around the old attention span.

We want words that illuminate the world around us. That extend the boundaries of our vision. Words that scratch us where we itch. Prose written and designed to reach out into the marketplace, press people's buttons and make them glow.

Some of these people are your prospective customers. And when we help you communicate your story to them with impact, clarity and credibility, you bet your P&L they're gonna respond.

After all, when you reduce marketing to its essence, that's . . .

The Bottom Line
Marketing Strategies That Help You Gain The Competitive Edge

The Bottom Line, Inc.
107 Mills Avenue, Greenville, SC 29605-4017 803-233-1930

Regardless of the technique used in gathering information for a research report, its real value lies in the creative interpretation and use made of its findings.

AGENCY OF THE FUTURE

Predicting the future of the advertising agency is difficult and risky, but here is an attempt by the chairman of the Bloom Agency to identify qualitative changes of the future:[8]

- Agencies will function with fewer levels in every department. The streamlined agency of the future will have a layer of "thinkers" and a layer of "doers."

---

[8]Robert Bloom, "The Agency of the Future," *Adweek*, November 7, 1988, p. 32.

Future predictions for the execution of effective advertising visualizes more agency-client cooperative decision-making, more "hands on" involvement by top executives in promotional strategy, and greater use of the computer in financial planning. "For the long-term health of agency/client relations," remarks Philip Morris Chairman, Hamish Maxwell," we believe in promoting *value-added products* and in building *brand loyalty*. Both are effectively done with *advertising*." He added that the most effective advertising will come from *clients,* which are smart enough to ensure that "great work has a chance of getting through the decision-making process."

- Multiple offices will become an anachronism. Agency branches will virtually disappear, because they have always been impractical from the standpoint of quality control and profit.
- Account services will become less powerful. Already, it is no longer the exclusive path to the top. Creatives are many times the highest-paid talent. In many agencies, account services has relinquished its role in strategy development to the account planner and creative directors. This trend will accelerate.
- Creative talent will take the lead in strategy development. No longer content to allow account services to slip a copy of strategy under the door, today's creatives are more assertive, disciplined, and possessed of a strong strategic sense.
- Account planners will become more important. They will not be research "retreads," but will come from media or creative or account services. Agencies will rely more heavily on account planners, who will have to be articulate, persuasive, and compatible with the creative people.
- Research responsibilities will narrow. Clients are seizing this area and agencies are relinquishing it. The agency's research role will be limited to that of a methodology consultant.
- Media planning will have considerable clout. The computer has made media planners the whiz kids of today, and tomorrow they will be even more influential. The plethora of media, with their high cost and complexity, will dictate this.
- Performance-based incentives will become a key component of agency compensation. People do what they are paid to do; that's why management-by-objective, tied to incentives, works. Sophisticated clients and agencies will work together to establish base service compensation on a reward system for high performance.
- The position of financial/administrative manager will emerge because a powerful internal operations executive will be needed to facilitate the return of top agency talent to hands-on client involvement. This person's responsibilities will be internal efficiency.
- Top agency talent will work directly on the business—once again. The agency of the future will be headed by people who enjoy doing the work, rather than administering the bureaucracy.

SUMMARY

Space wholesalers began what is now the full-service advertising agency. Later, agencies charged a standard commission (15 percent) and agreed to the no-rebate rule introduced by Curtis Publishing Company in 1891.

The no-rebate age, when the 15 percent commission system was strictly adhered to, began in 1917 and ended in 1956, when the Department of Justice ruled that the no-rebate provision was in restraint of trade. Consent decrees entered into by all media associations allowed agency and client to review the total compensation that an agency receives for its services.

In 1917, the American Association of Advertising Agencies (A.A.A.A. or 4A's) was formed to improve the standards of advertising business and practice. Today its members place 80 percent of all national advertising.

A full-service agency works on many aspects of the client's marketing problem: strategy, creative response, media planning, and trade campaigns. The agency is usually organized into four divisions: account services, marketing services, creative services, and management and finance. Some agencies have a domestic network of offices or affiliates to service their large accounts better. The growing importance of global marketing to some clients has led agencies to expand internationally. Clients usually pay agencies by commission, fees, or a combination of the two.

There are other types of advertising services besides the traditional advertising agency: in-house agencies, à la carte agencies, creative boutiques, rolodex agencies, and media-buying services. Agencies usually cannot and will not handle two accounts that compete in the same market.

Barter is a method of payment for media that uses goods and services in place of cash. Some agencies barter by producing TV shows and offering them to TV stations in exchange for commercial time.

Research plays a very important part in successful marketing. Studies are done on positioning, concept testing, advertising effectiveness, TV and print pretesting and post-testing, media preferences, and purchasing problems.

Advertising agencies have been changing rapidly in recent years to keep up with their environment. They will continue to change, but perhaps along somewhat different lines. It is predicted that in the streamlined agency of the future, creative talent will take the lead in strategy development, account planners will become more important, research responsibilities will continue to narrow, and media planners will be more influential. The position of financial/administrative manager will emerge to coordinate internal operations and free creative talent to create.

QUESTIONS

1. What services do advertising agencies usually perform for their clients?
2. What is the A.A.A.A. (4A's)?
3. What is an "agency of record"?
4. What is the role of the independent media-buying services?
5. Identify the functions of each of the four agency organizational elements.
6. What changes are predicted for the agency of the future?

SUGGESTED EXERCISE

- Using *Advertising Age, Adweek,* and *Agency Redbook* profile one of the major regional, national, or international agencies. Specifically discuss its size, number of offices, and types of accounts.

READINGS

BARRY, THOMAS E., RON L. PETERSON, AND W. BRADFORD TODD: "The Role of Account Planning in the Future of Advertising Agency Research," *Journal of Advertising Research,* Vol. 27, No. 1 (1987), 15–21.

GARDNER, HERBERT S. JR.: *The Advertising Agency Business* (Lincolnwood, IL: NTC Business Books, 1988).

HORTON, CLEVELAND: "Chiat, Mojo Put on Brakes," *Advertising Age,* April 10, 1989, p. 3.

HILL, JULIE SKUR.: "No. 1 Dentsu Hits Lofty $1.2 Billion in Gross Income," *Advertising Age,* March 29, 1989, p. 1.

MCDONALD, HOWARD E.: "The Uneven Playing Field," *Advertising Age,* April 17, 1989, p. 20.

MEYERS, JANET: "Mars Embraces Fee System," *Advertising Age,* January 23, 1989, p. 3.

"U.S. and Foreign Advertising Agency Income," *Advertising Age,* March 29, 1989.

SIX

The Advertiser's Marketing/Advertising Operation

With increasing structured and organization changes in the business world, the results are being felt in the advertising function. Now that Cadbury Schweppes has acquired *Crush, Hires,* and *Sun-Drop* soft drinks from Proctor & Gamble, "we think these brands will enhance our global opportunities," revealed Brian Walker, CS' manager-corporate communications and public affairs. *Sunkist,* a previous acquisition, is being promoted in England. Agencies in Brussels and Mexico City are already handling *Crush.*

The advertising agency business has responded to the changes taking place in the global business environment as described in Chapter 5. There have been so many articles about mergers at all levels, staffing changes, restructuring of agencies, and so on because the advertising agency is considered the glamorous part of the business. Actually, control of the business lies on the advertiser side, in the marketing-advertising function. Here is the key to the very existence of advertising agencies.

Changes taking place in corporate advertising and marketing departments don't generate the same kind of press coverage, yet they strongly affect the advertising planned and executed by agencies. And there have been changes on top of changes in corporate boardrooms.

These are uncertain times for much of the business world, what with high-risk ventures, leveraged buyouts, mergers, foreign partnership or ownership, Wall Street's incessant demands for high short-term profits, and accountability for every aspect of business, including marketing and advertising. As a result, traditional marketing organizational structure and procedures are being questioned.

Before we examine the various roles of the marketing and advertising personnel in the typical structure, let's look at the structure itself.

MARKETING-SERVICES SYSTEM

The advertising department structure—the traditional system—worked well for most companies (see Exhibit 6.1). However, Procter & Gamble found it less effective as the number of brands it marketed grew. Many of P&G's growing brands developed their own marketing problems, which could not be handled effectively under the traditional organizational structure. As a result, Procter & Gamble developed a new organizational concept: the marketing-services system. This concept has been widely adopted, especially in the package-goods field, for groceries, drugs, and cosmetics. It has also been used by a number of service-oriented companies.

EXHIBIT 6.1
Simple organization chart of an advertising department.

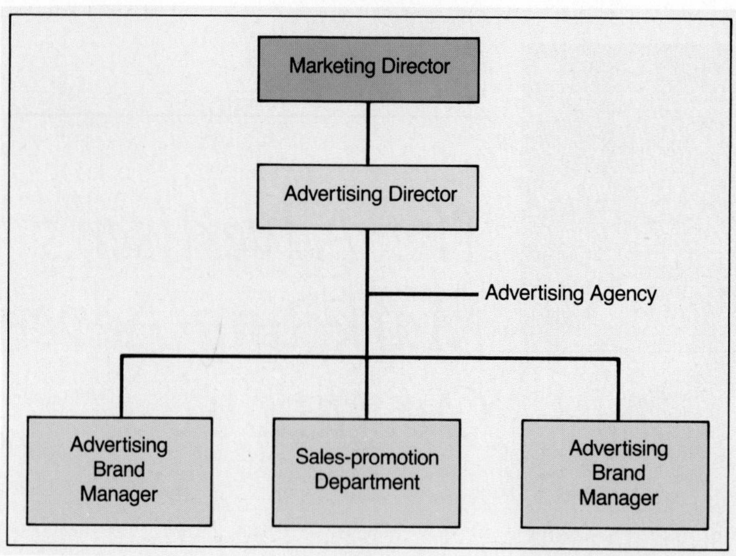

By employing the *marketing-services system,* individual product managers have the availability of *internal* technical talent involved in implementing a marketing plan—plus *external* advertising agency personnel. *Proctor & Gamble's Downy Fabric Softener,* along with Gerber's Products, will sponsor a "Million Dollar Baby" contest on cable TV's adult pop-music channel, VH-1/Video Hits One. The promotion was created in-house; the advertising for the promotion will be handled by Fred/Alan, New York.

The marketing-services system has two parts. One is the *marketing activity,* which begins with the product managers assigned to different brands. The other part is a structure of *marketing services,* which represents all the technical talent involved in implementing a marketing plan, including creative services, promotion services, media services, broadcast programming, advertising controls, and marketing-research services. All of these services are available to the product manager, as is the help of the advertising agency assigned to that manager's brand. The product manager can bring together the agency professional and his or her counterpart in the marketing-services division, giving the company the benefit of the best thinking of both groups—internal and external. The company may assign a different agency to each brand or group of brands. Each group has a group product manager, who supervises the individual product managers (see Exhibit 6.2).

The product manager is responsible for planning strategy and objectives, gathering relevant brand information, coordinating budget developments and control, and getting recommendations from agencies and others up the line for final discussion and approval as quickly as possible. The product manager is also a primary liaison between the marketing department and all other departments, as well as the advertising agency. The product manager's plans must be approved by the group product manager, who then submits them for approval to the vice president for marketing and finally to the executive vice president.

Under this system, the advertising department is a branch of the marketing-services division. The vice president for advertising, responsible for the review and evaluation of brand media plans, attends all creative presentations to act as an adviser and is an adviser and consultant on all aspects of the advertising. The vice president for advertising reports to the senior vice president, director of marketing.

The biggest difference in this operation is that the advertising does not all come through one huge funnel, with one person in charge of all brands. The great advantage, from the corporate viewpoint, is that each brand gets the full marketing attention of its own group, while all brands get the full benefit of all the company's special marketing services and of the accumulated corporate wisdom. The more important the decision, the higher up the ladder it goes for final approval.

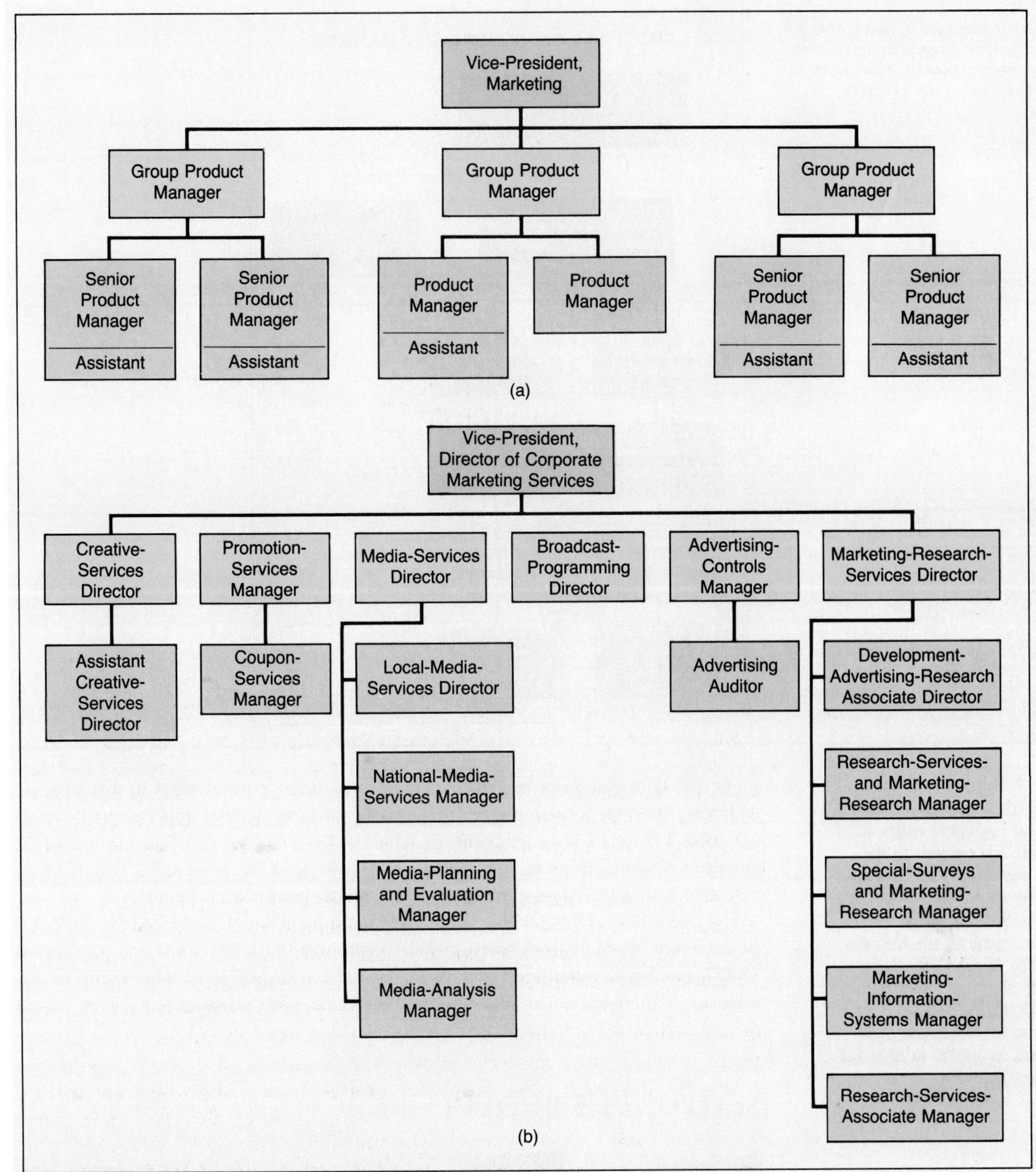

EXHIBIT 6.2

Organization in a large company with a marketing-services division: (a) the marketing department; (b) the marketing-services department, where specialists in creative, media, and research advise product managers and consult with counterparts in agency.

EVOLUTION: THE CATEGORY MANAGER

In late October 1987, Procter & Gamble Company added a layer of management to its brand structure (see Exhibit 6.3). Each of P&G's 39 product categories is run by a category manager, to whom all disciplines—research, manufacturing, engineering, sales, advertising, and so on—report. The category manager follows the product line

EXHIBIT 6.3

The category manager is responsible for all aspects of the brands in his or her category. Each product's advertising manager reports to the category manager.

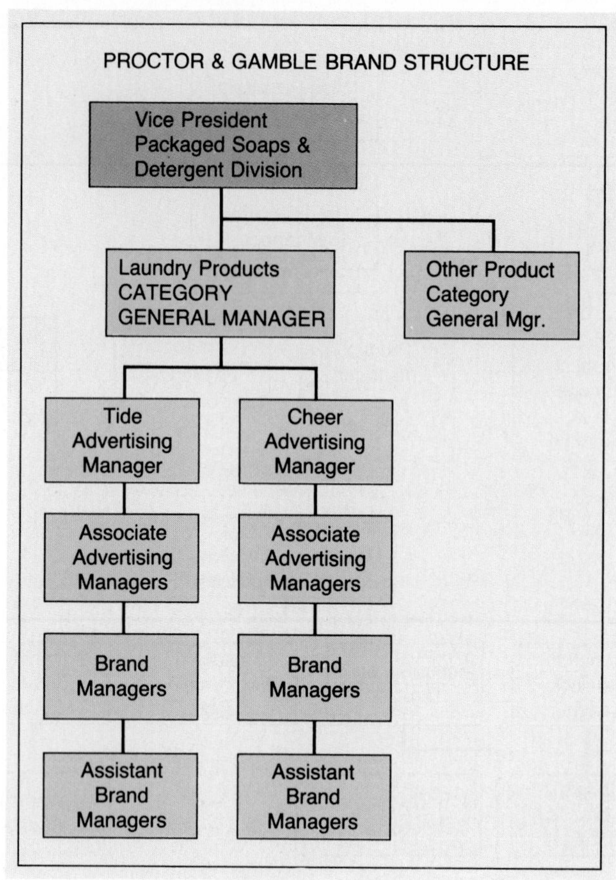

Proctor & Gamble's category manager system combines several brand managers under its "umbrella" according to the product category. The CM decides how to position respective brands in each category. *Revlon,* also, employs the CM system. "The Nines," Revlon's amalgam of brands, which includes Germaine Monteil and Charles of the Ritz, are each positioned to appeal to different age groups and taste levels.

he or she is in charge of and decides how to coordinate each brand in that line. For example, the category manager for laundry products decides how to position and advertise Tide and Cheer detergents to avoid conflicts and overlap. The purpose of this structure is to create marketing strategies that fit all of the company's brands in one category instead of developing competitive strategies for each brand.[1]

Colgate followed P&G with a similar restructuring in which it reduced the number of its detergent products from seven to four. Each brand now has a distinct market position. A number of other large advertisers have also restructured to better compete. The majority of them are not simply copying P&G's category management system, as was the case when the brand manager system was developed in 1931.

SETTING THE BUDGET

The strategic aspect of advertising planning is concerned with accomplishing some objective. This may be the launching of a new product, increasing a brand's awareness level, or neutralizing competitive advertising. How much money will it take to accomplish the objective? If we've been successful with our brand, do we know whether we're spending too much on advertising, or not enough? The largest variable expense in most companies is for consumer-oriented advertising. Despite all the technology available to help us determine how much should be spent, the final decision is a judgment call by corporate management (see Exhibit 6.4 for a list of the decision makers). It will vary across companies and according to objectives. Exhibit 6.5 illustrates when those decisions are made. Two-thirds of advertising budgets are submitted for approval in September or October; almost 80 percent are approved during the

[1] "The Marketing Revolution at Procter & Gamble," *Business Week,* July 25, 1988, pp. 72–76.

EXHIBIT 6.4

Who Prepares Clients' Ad Budgets*

VP/Marketing	63.2%
VP/Advertising	31.6
Ad Manager	22.2
Brand Manager	16.3
Ad Agency	21.7
Sales Promotion	5.6

Who Approves Clients' Ad Budgets*

President or CEO	68.5%
VP/Marketing	37.3
Executive VP	20.9
Division Manager	17.2
VP/Advertising	14.4
Treasurer or Controller	8.6

(* Totals more than 100% due to multiple responses.)
Source: 26th Gallagher Report Consumer Advertising Survey.

EXHIBIT 6.5

When Are Ad Budgets Okayed?

Month	Submitted	Approved
April	5.3%	0.0%
May	10.3	0.0
June	0.0	10.2
July	15.1	0.0
August	5.3	0.0
September	32.5	15.2
October	31.4	32.0
November	0.0	31.9
December	0.0	10.7

Source 26th Gallagher Report Consumer Advertising Survey

period of September through November. As you might expect for such an important decision, most presidents or chief operating officers strongly influence the approval process.

Budgets are usually drawn up using one of four approaches: percentage of sales, the payout plan, competitive budgeting, or the task method.

Percentage of Sales

Advertising budgets may be determined by a *percentage of sales*—either last year's anticipated year's, or some combination of the two. *Zenith* plans on luring more baby boomers in its fold by spending $30 million on TV advertising this year. It's hoped that its new youthful image campaign will help its drive to increase its market share and move closer to the industry's number one TV producer, RCA. The new ad figure represents a 10% increase over previous years' spending or 15% of this year's sales.

Companies using this method base their budget on a percentage of sales. A Gallagher Report indicates that about 9 percent of companies surveyed employ this method of budgeting.[2] Roughly 35 percent use a percentage of anticipated sales, and another 9 percent calculate a medium between last year's actual sales and anticipated sales for the coming year (see Exhibit 6.6). In either method, a change in sales changes the amount of advertising expenditures.

A firm using the percentage-of-sales method of determining a budget won't spend beyond its means because the ad budget will increase only when sales increase. If sales decrease, so will the advertising. However, if competitive pressures are severe, the firm may have to maintain or increase the budget just to retain market share, even though there is no prospect of increased profit.

[2]26th Gallagher Report Consumer Advertising Survey.

EXHIBIT 6.6

How Do Clients Calculate Ad Budgets
34.8% take a percentage of anticipated sales.
30.4% combine needed tasks with percent of anticipated sales.
13.0% outline needed tasks and fund them.
13.0% set arbitrary amounts based on general fiscal outlook.
8.7% take a percentage of the previous year's sales.
8.6% calculate a medium between last year's actual and next year's anticipated sales.
Source: 26th Gallagher Report Consumer Advertising Survey

Carrying the advertising/sales relationship one step further, a firm could use the *payout plan*. The *initial* advertising expenditure is a percentage based on future expectations, which may be *formidable*. The ratio "gets better" as sales "catch up." In introducing *Heartwise*, an oat-bran cereal containing *psyllium*—a widely touted cholesterol-reducing ingredient—Kellogg will be spending $45 million! As one of the first products to directly link food and health claim information, the company anticipates a market "stampede," especially by older targets.

Should a firm find itself in a "hot," competitive environment, it may do what its competition is doing. In that case, advertising approaches and expenditures are dictated by the competition—not by the firm. Eddie Bauer, the "natural clothes" direct merchant, will launch new, frequent catalogs—now that it's part of the Spiegel catalog empire. Its competitors—Land's End, J. Crew, and Tweeds—have been "stepping up the heat" in aiming for the sportswear/outdoor target markets. Bauer will "fire back" with "Eddie Bauer: A Legend for Four Generations"—a 40-page specialty catalog, featuring merchandise that draws on the Bauer heritage.

Payout Plan

This method of budget strategy is more complex. Basically, the advertiser spends at a level that will be acceptable at some future date. The payout plan is normally used for new products that require high advertising expenditures (relative to low initial sales) in order to establish themselves in the marketplace. Whatever the specific payout method used, the underlying principle is that present advertising budgets are based on future sales. Of course, the advertiser who overestimates future sales runs the risk of accumulating major debt.

Exhibits 6.7 and 6.8 are examples of typical payout plans. Let's briefly go through Exhibit 6.7, a payout plan for a fast-food operation. In the first year of operation, the company spent the entire gross profit ($15,274,000) on advertising. In addition, the company invested $10,300,000 in store development, for a first-year operating loss. In the second year, the company again invested gross profits ($48,122,000) in advertising and carried over the $10,300,000 debt from the first year. By the third year, sales had increased to the point where advertising as a percentage of gross sales had dropped to 13 percent, or $46,312,000, leaving a profit of $35,625,000. After covering the first-year debt of $10,300,000, the payout was $25,325,000.

If the company had demanded a 10 percent profit in the first year (0.10 × $84,845,000 = $8,485,400), it would have had to curtail advertising drastically, reduce corporate store investment, or do some combination of both. In that case, the company would have made a profit the first year, but risked future profits and perhaps its own long-term survival.

Competitive Budgeting

Another approach to budgeting is to base it on the competitive spending environment. In competitive budgeting, the level of spending relates to percent of sales and other factors; whether the advertiser is on the offensive or defensive; media strategies chosen

EXHIBIT 6.7

An advertiser can work up a payout plan showing the cost of doing business, figuring in the cost of advertising and profit projections over a specified period of time. This example is for a fast-food operation.

Systemwide Payout (Fiscal Years 1, 2, 3)

		Year 1		Year 2		Year 3
Sales		$84,854,000		$218,737,000		$356,248,000
Food Cost	34%	28,850,000	34%	74,371,000	34%	121,124,000
Paper Cost	5%	4,245,000	5%	10,937,000	5%	17,812,000
Labor	22%	18,668,000	20%	43,747,000	20%	71,250,000
Overhead	21%	17,819,000	19%	41,560,000	18%	64,125,000
Total Op. Exp.	82%	69,580,000	78%	170,615,000	77%	274,511,000
Gross Profit	18%	15,274,000	22%	48,122,000	25%	81,937,000
Advertising/Promo		*$15,274,000*		*$ 48,122,000*	*13%*	*$ 46,312,000*
Store Profit		0		0	10%	35,625,000
Corp. Invest.		10,300,000		0		0
Corp. Profit		(10,300,000)		0		35,625,000
Corp. Profit Cumulative		(10,300,000)		(10,300,000)		25,625,000

Investment Introduction—36 Month Payout	Year 1	Year II	Year III	3-Year Total	Year IV
Size of Market (MM Cases)	8	10	11		12
Share Goal:					
Average	12½%	25%	30%		30%
Year End	20	30	30		30
Consumer Movement (MM Cases)	1.0	2.5	3.3	6.8	3.6
Pipeline (MM Cases)	.3	.2	.1	.6	—
Total Shipments (MM Cases)	1.3	2.7	3.4	7.4	3.6
Factory Income (@ $9)	$11.7	$24.3	$30.6	$66.6	$32.4
Less Costs (@ $5)	6.5	13.5	17.0	37.0	18.0
Available P/A (@ $4)	$ 5.2	$10.8	$13.6	$29.6	$14.4
Spending (Normal $2)	$12.8	$10.0	$ 6.8	$29.6	$ 7.2
Advertising	10.5	8.5	5.4	24.4	5.7
Promotion	2.3	1.5	1.4	5.2	1.5
Profit (Loss):					
Annual	($ 7.6)	$ .8	$ 6.8	—	$ 7.2
Cumulative	($ 7.6)	($ 6.8)	—	—	$ 7.2

EXHIBIT 6.8

This is an example of a package-goods product payout plan. Note the advertising spending levels each year.

(e.g., desire to dominate a medium), or answers to such questions as: Is it a new brand or an existing one? The problem here is that competition dictates the spending allocation (and the competing companies may have different marketing objectives).

Firms operating by "specific objectives" may also want to formulate *advertising objectives*. The budget is then set, based on what they want their promotion strategy to accomplish. Most firms provide quantitative "benchmarks" ahead of time. To coincide with 1990 model-year changes, Chrysler has adopted *a "radical new approach"* to its advertising. Ricardo Montalban and James Earl Jones are "out"—and Tina Turner is "in"—with sassy pitches. . . . "We weren't satisfied with what we've had in the past few years," admitted Arthur "Bud" Liebler, executive director-corporate communications and marketing services. $500 million in promotion expenditures is being set for "breakthrough creative."

The Task Method

Under this method, the company sets a specific sales target for a given time to attain a given goal. Then it decides to spend whatever money is necessary to meet that quota. The task method might be called the "let's spend all we can afford" approach, especially when launching a new product. Many big businesses today started that way. Many businesses that are not here today did too.

This approach can be complex. It involves several important considerations: brand loyalty factors, geographic factors, product penetration. Advertisers who use this method need accurate, reliable research, experience, and models for setting goals and measuring results (see Exhibit 6.9).

The task method is used most widely in a highly competitive environment.

Budgets are under constant scrutiny in relation to sales and usually are formally reviewed every quarter. Moreover, they are subject to cancellation at any time (except for noncancelable commitments) because sales have not met a minimum quota, money is being shifted to a more promising brand, or management wants to hold back money to make a better showing on its next quarterly statement.

No one approach to budgeting is always best for all companies.

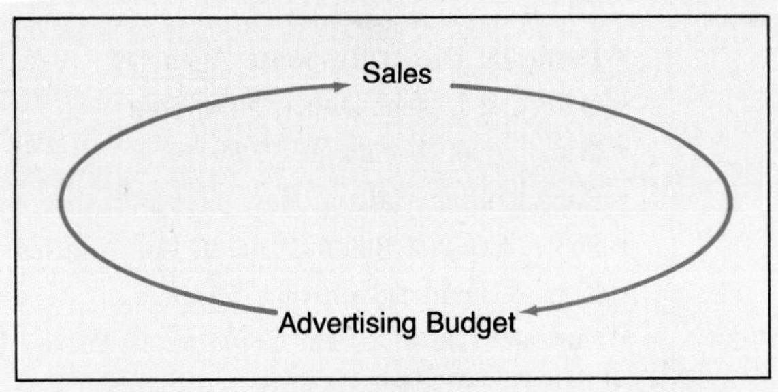

EXHIBIT 6.9

Sales and advertising budgets are interrelated. Generally, budgets are related to sales forecasts and sales generate advertising dollars.

SELECTING AN AGENCY

Agency selection should be based on *need for services,* followed by an objective rating scale of "strengths." In his recent remarks at the *Advertising Age* Creative Workshop, Geoffrey Frost, FCB/Leber Katz Partners Senior Executive VP, called on ad agencies to "reinvent" themselves—that is, evolve into multi-purpose "marketing" agencies. Client service executives, said Frost, should be prepared for clients' needs in *all* areas of marketing communications—advertising, public relations, sales promotion, direct marketing, and other specialties. "And that will help re-establish agencies, not as 'vendors' to clients, but as vital marketing partners," quoted Frost.

Searching out agencies which have run impressive campaigns and/or handled products in the advertiser's field is a recommended next step. *Marden-Kane,* a specialist in sales promotion, advertises to promoters that it's been creating "*results-proven* sweepstakes, contests, games, incentive programs, and premium offers *for over three decades*." They invite inquiries for "free samples" of successful campaigns.

Choosing an agency can be a complicated matter. Do you need a full-service agency, as discussed in the Chapter 5, or would you do better with a specialized agency? There are all sorts of specialized agencies; Exhibit 6.10 shows two representative groups: health care and direct response. Also, many full-service agencies have health-care, direct-response, and other specialized subsidiaries.

After deciding generally whether you want a large or small, specialized or full-service, domestic or global agency, the following points may help you in evaluating specific agencies:

1. Determine what types of service you need from an agency, and then list them in order of their importance to you. For instance: (1) marketing expertise in strategy, planning, and execution; (2) creative performance in TV, print, radio, or outdoor; (3) media knowledge and clout; (4) sales-promotion and/or trade relations help; (5) public relations and corporate- or image-building ability; (6) market research strength; (7) fashion or beauty sense; (8) agency size; (9) location in relation to your office. Your special needs will dictate others.
2. Establish a five-point scale to rate each agency's attributes. A typical five-point scale would be: (1) outstanding, (2) very good, (3) good, (4) satisfactory, (5) unsatisfactory. Of course, you should give different values or weights to the more important agency attributes.
3. Check published sources and select a group of agencies that seem to fit your requirements. Use your own knowledge or the knowledge of your industry peers to find agencies responsible for successful campaigns or products that have most impressed you. Published sources include the annual issue of *Advertising Age* that lists agencies and their accounts by agency size and the "Red Book" *(Standard Advertising Register),* which lists agencies and accounts both alphabetically and geographically. In case of further doubt, write to the American Association of Advertising Agencies, 666 Third Avenue, New York, New York 10017, for a roster of members.
4. Check whether there are any apparent conflicts with accounts already at the agency. When agencies consider a new account, that is the first question they ask (along with the amount of the potential billings).
5. Now start preliminary discussions with the agencies that rate best on your preliminary evaluation. This can be begun with a letter asking if they are interested or a phone call to set up an appointment for them to visit you or for you to visit the agency. Start at the top. Call the president or the operating head of the agency or office in your area, who will appoint someone to follow up on the opportunity you are offering.
6. Reduce your original list of potential agencies after first contact. A manageable number is usually no more than three.

EXHIBIT 6.10
Some examples of specialized agencies.

- **Domestic Health-care Agencies**
- Medicus Intercon International, New York
- Sudler & Hennessey, New York
- Kallir, Philips, Ross, New York
- M.E.D. Communications, Woodridge, N.Y.
- Klemtner Advertising, New York
- Carrafiello-Diehl & Associates, Irvington, N.Y.

- **Domestic Direct-Response Agencies**
- Ogilvy & Mather Direct, New York
- Wunderman Worldwide, New York
- Rapp Collins Marcoa, New York
- Foote, Cone & Belding Direct, Los Angeles
- Kobs & Draft Advertising, Chicago
- Customer Development Corporation, Peoria, Ill.

7. Now again prepare an evaluation list for rating the agencies on the same five-point scale. This list will be a lot more specific. It should cover personnel. Who will supervise your account, and how will the account team be staffed? Who are the creative people who will work on your business? Similarly, who will service your needs in media, production (TV) research, and sales promotion, and how will they do it? What is the agency's track record in getting and holding on to business and in keeping personnel teams together? What is the agency's record with media, with payments? Make sure again to assign a weighted value to each service aspect. If TV is most important to you and public relations aid least, be sure to reflect this in your evaluation.
8. Discuss financial arrangements. Will your account be a straight 15 percent commission account, a fee account, or a combination of both? What services will the commission or fee cover, and what additional charges will the agency demand? How will new-product work be handled from both a financial and an organizational point of view? What peripheral service does the agency offer, and for how much?
9. Do you feel comfortable with them?
10. If your company is an international one, can the agency handle all of your nondomestic business, and if so, how will they do it?

Advertising goals should be *communication goals*—such as awareness of a product—not marketing goals—such as an increase in sales. Warner-Lambert has started a new network TV campaign for Certs mints. It has abandoned the common "medicinal" approach and adopted a more memorable, romantic theme, with the tagline "Two is better than one; two mints in one." The scene features a young, kissing couple, at night, in formal clothes, leaning on a "classic" Porche convertible.

APPRAISING NATIONAL ADVERTISING

The big questions that national advertising and marketing management must answer are: How well is our advertising working? How well is our investment paying off?

How do you measure national advertising, whose results cannot be traced as easily as those of direct-response advertising?

Advertising Goals versus Marketing Goals

Advertising goals. *The communication objectives designed to accomplish certain tasks within the total marketing program.*

The answer is not simple. Much of the discussion on the subject centers around a report Russell H. Colley prepared for the Association of National Advertisers. The thesis of this study is that it is virtually impossible to measure the results of advertising unless and until the specific results sought by advertising have been defined. When asked exactly what their advertising is supposed to do, most companies have a ready answer: Increase their dollar sales or increase their share of the market. However, these are not advertising goals, Colley holds; they are total marketing goals.

National advertising alone cannot accomplish this task. It should be used as part of the total marketing effort. The first step in appraising the results of advertising, therefore, is to define specifically what the company expects to accomplish through advertising. The Colley report defines an advertising goal as "a specific communications task, to be accomplished among a defined audience to a given degree in a given period of time."

Marketing goals. *The overall objectives that a company wishes to accomplish through its marketing program.*

As an example, the report cites the case of a branded detergent. The marketing goal is to increase market share from 10 to 15 percent, and the advertising goal is set as increasing, among the 50 million housewives who own automatic washers, the number who identify brand X as a low-sudsing detergent that gets clothes clean. This represents a specific communications task that can be performed by advertising, independent of other marketing forces.

The Colley report speaks of a marketing-communication spectrum ranging from unawareness of the product to comprehension to conviction to action. According to this view, the way to appraise advertising, is by its effectiveness in the communication spectrum, leading to sales.

Researchers disagree on whether the effectiveness of national advertising—or, for that matter, of any advertising—should be judged by a communication yardstick rather than by sales. As a matter of fact, in Chapter 15 we'll discuss whether an ad's effectiveness should be measured by some research testing score.

A Marketing Science Institute report says:

In general, total sales are not considered a valid measure of advertising effectiveness, because of the presence of other influencing variables. Sales as a criterion may have some validity if advertising is the most prominent variable, or, in the case of mail-order advertising, when it is the only variable.

Exhibits 6.11 and 6.12 illustrate two approaches to service advertising for banks with different geographical locations, competitive situations, and budgets. Each bank has its own goal and approach to measuring the advertising and marketing results.

EXHIBIT 6.11

Our Moment Of Truth Happens

50,000 TIMES A DAY

When was the last time you heard about a banker skipping a coffee break? Or going home late?

Miracles like these happen almost daily at United Carolina Bank. Because we have a different priority than most banks. Our priority is you, the Customer.

We think service should go beyond a teller's smile. To us, our "moment of truth" happens every time our business touches you or your account. Which in our case averages about 50,000 times a day.

It's the kind of Customer-first attitude that's a part of everybody who works for you at UCB. Because in everything we do, we look at it from your point of view. To make ours the kind of bank you've wanted all along.

UNITED
CAROLINA
BANK
"That's What
I Want!"

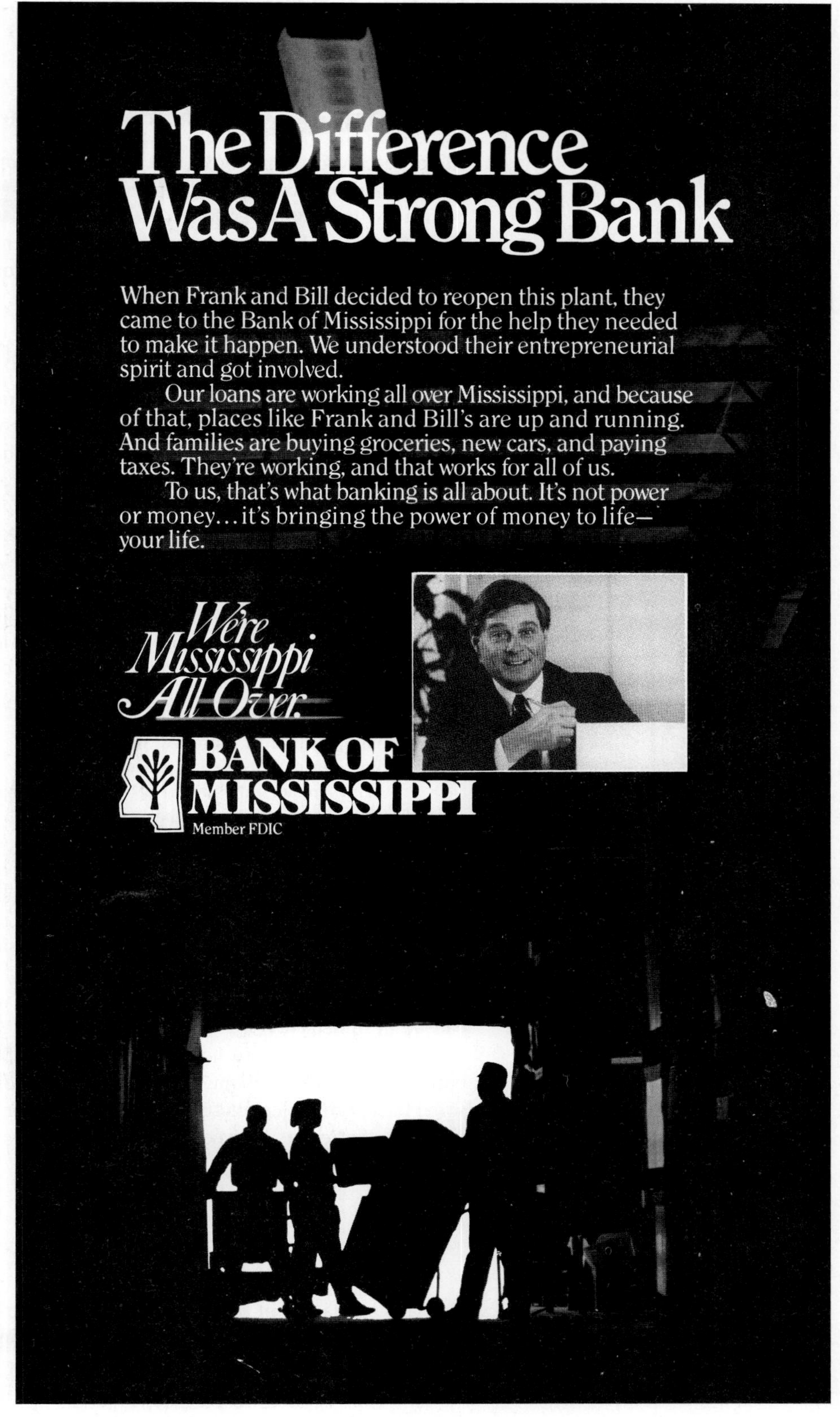

EXHIBIT 6.12
Bank of Mississippi. (Courtesy: Robinson & Associates.)

Local, regional, and national advertisers need to decide which type of measure is most effective in evaluating their advertising.

Appraising the Campaign Before It Is Run

Advertising, like products, can be tested ahead of time—*with different approaches in different markets. Reebok* has confirmed that it's signed superchoreographer Paula Abdul for its new *image-oriented* ads, coming this fall from Chiat/Day/Majo. At the same time, they plan to continue "The physics of physiques" promotion, which concentrates on *performance* of its products. Reebok's management consulting group will make recommendations about which approach should take prominence in the future.

There are those who believe that the time to appraise a campaign is before it is run. They would do this by testing idea options in different markets—a familiar practice, of course, with one big drawback: It tips off the competition to what you are planning to do, and they will try to beat you to it in other markets, especially if the campaign involves a new product or is based on a promotion.

The Company/Agency Research Conflict

Advertising, according to the PACT study, should *contribute* to the overall marketing objectives of a company. Lauren Hutton has been recruited, once again, by Revlon for its *Ciara fragrance ads*. In projecting "the woman of the '90s, who's devastatingly female," the company expects Hutton to attract the successful 40's woman, who began using Ciara 10 years ago, when the brand was first introduced by her. "We think we'll get old users back because Lauren was so strongly associated with the brand," forecasted Sharon Connolly, senior VP-creative marketing at Revlon's Prestige Fragrances group.

Ideally, a company and its agency should have no conflict about the goals of advertising. However, conflicts do arise, often over the different priorities given creative and marketing values by agencies and companies. These different priorities are reflected in the way advertising is evaluated by client and agency.

Twenty-one of the largest advertising agencies jointly examined the question of advertising evaluation and copy testing. The PACT (Position Advertising Copy Testing) Report discusses their findings. Two major aspects of the report should be noted:

1. The PACT study recognized that advertising's contribution to overall marketing objectives should be the focus of any copy test. The copy test for a specific ad should consider the advertisement's potential for achieving its stated objectives. Among these objectives might be:
   - Reinforcing current perceptions
   - Encouraging trial of a product or service
   - Encouraging new uses of a product or service
   - Providing greater saliency for a brand or company name
   - Changing perceptions and imagery
   - Announcing new features and benefits
2. The PACT Report viewed advertising as performing on three levels:
   - Reception (Did the advertising get through?)
   - Comprehension (Was the advertising understood?)
   - Response (Did the consumer accept the proposition?)

The PACT Report offers a starting point from which specific measures of advertising can be designed.

The PACT Report did not solve the copy-testing dilemma nor the inherent conflict between agency and client. However, it did address the general problem and offered some basic principles for further discussion. For us, it also demonstrates the complex marriage that exists between a company and its advertising agency.

THE CHANGING MARKETING ENVIRONMENT

With scarce shelf space, category and/or brand managers must be prepared to pay hefty "strolling" allowances to supermarkets to get products "exposed." Last year, *Campbells* spent *$2 million* in store shelf displays and trade allowances *for its dry soups alone*.

Category managers of the future will have more to worry about than promoting products to consumers. Foremost among their problems will be the fight for, and cost of, shelf space. Today more than five times as many new products are being introduced in grocery and drug stores today than in 1976, while shelf space has remained relatively flat. The result is that supermarkets are now demanding *slotting allowances* for shelf space. This "admission fee" which comes primarily from the marketer's trade promotion funds, ensures space for about three to six months. Supermarkets say the slotting allowance is needed to pay for the administrative overhead for placing a new product in their system, including warehouse space, computer input, communication to individual stores about the product's availability, and the redesign of shelf space. Some supermarkets in the Northeast require a $15,000 to $40,000 slotting allowance in addition to the traditional trade allowances. Many of the giant package-goods manufacturers—e.g., Procter & Gamble and General Mills—have resisted paying the slotting allowance on the grounds that their multimillion-dollar introductory consumer campaigns build enough demand to cancel out the costs of the supermarkets' administrative overhead.

The Federal Trade Commission recently conducted a study of the legal implications of slotting allowances, but hasn't reached a decision as of this writing. Manufacturers say the fees result in higher consumer prices, but supermarkets contend they should be compensated for providing valuable shelf space for unproven products.

SAGE Group, Ltd., a unit of Ogilvy Group, indicates some new rules future product, brand, or category managers must learn:[3]

- Marketplace leverage is at the local level. As consumers' taste, needs, and wants continue to expand and fragment, leverage can only be achieved by delivering relevant products, services, messages, and promotions to consumers as individuals.
- Building brand equity among retailers should become as important as building brands among consumers.
- Marketing decisions must shift to the sales level. Manufacturers' marketing and promotion programs must eventually become store-specific to succeed.
- Information is the most important asset you have. Only the first company to use information wins. As brand building moves from national media to the supermarket shelf, marketing and merchandising executions must be adapted to the needs of each consumer market and store franchise.

Change is frightening; losing can be fatal. But the current turmoil represents an enormous profit opportunity.

Research Bolsters the Value of Advertising

Research indicates that advertising to consumers "pays off" in greater sales dollars than trade promotions. *Frito-Lay,* the nation's number one salty-snack marketer, is spending 50% more on consumer advertising in 1989 than 1988. Last year, the Pepsi Co division spent about $60 million. "We're realizing one of the strongest weapons we have is *brand equity,*" admitted Chris O'Leary, director of marketing for the Chee-Tos, Fritos, and Tostitos brands.

According to a study released in 1989 of more than 360 tests conducted over a decade by Information Resources, Inc., in its BehaviorScan electronic test markets, advertising is more cost-efficient than trade promotions in luring customers to package goods.[4] IRI defines trade promotion as incentives to supermarkets to promote products in their advertising or in special displays, but only over the short term. Results indicate that just 16 percent of short-term promotions justify their expense. Advertising, on the other hand, pays off immediately in 20 percent of the cases, and consumer retention of advertising over a two-year period almost doubles that return.

CHANGES IN CORPORATE STRATEGY

There are many forces at work in today's business environment. The future will bring even more changes in the corporate sector. What will be the competitive effects of the mergers on competition? Will the corporate debt affect the ability to research and develop products, and promote them? What adjustments will have to be made to counter the effects of 1992 in Europe (the reduction of trade barriers among European countries)? Will marketing strategies be affected? Jack Trout, partner in Trout & Ries, thinks so (although most marketers don't necessarily agree). Trout attacks some of management's most cherished concepts, including goals, missions statements and long-term strategic planning. He has developed marketing programs for companies

[3]Spencer Hapoienu, "Supermarketing's New Frontier," *Advertising Age,* April 4, 1988, p. 18.

[4]Ira Teinowitz, "IRI Research Bolsters Value of Advertising," *Advertising Age,* March 6, 1989, p. 71.

such as American Express, Xerox, Merk, and Burger King and believes the competitive environment has made the traditional ''top-down'' approach somewhat obsolete. In top-down marketing you decide what you want to do (the strategy). Then you figure how to do it (the tactics). Below are some of Trout's ideas on how ''bottom-up'' marketing should be practiced in the 1990's:[5]

Trout's ''bottom-up'' approach shifts emphasis from top management to the *firm's prospect*—for the purpose of strategic planning. The *narrower* the focus, the *more precise* the angle, the greater the chances for success. McDonald's, in searching for ways to expand its market after *3pm*, is testing fried chicken in Dallas and Houston. ''Customers said they wanted 'something different' for dinner—after already having breakfast and lunch at McDonald's,'' noted Ron Paul, president of Technamic Consultants, a restaurant consultancy. Point-of-purchase support is being directed in those cities by Moroch & Associates.

- *Go down to the front*. The place to find the answer to your marketing problem is in the mind of the prospect. You start the bottom-up marketing process by finding out what you can do and then setting up a program to do it.
- *Narrow your focus*. Most marketing managers do just the opposite. They try to be all things to all people. Line extensions (Tide, Tide unscented, Tide with Bleach, etc.) run rampant in corporate America. Yet most of the big marketing victories have come from narrowing the focus. Federal Express didn't try to become a full line supplier of air freight services. They focused on small packages overnight. Domino's didn't try to become a pizza restaurant, pizza take-out and pizza delivery service. They focused on home delivery only.
- *Find your tactic*. What single tactic or ''competitive mental angle'' might be exploited to produce a marketing victory? You find your tactic in the mind of the prospect. Do you have a concept or idea to drive your business?
- *Build your strategy*. The next step is to build your strategy or ''coherent marketing direction.'' Most companies start with the strategy and then look for tactics to execute it. An example of the failure of this top-down thinking is Xerox's attempt to get into the computer business. Twenty years and $2 billion dollars later, Xerox still hasn't found a tactic to execute its strategy.
- *Make the changes*. You can't change the marketplace. Xerox means copiers, not computers, and no amount of marketing efforts will overcome this simple fact. To develop an effective strategy, a company has to be willing to make internal changes—in the name, the product, the price. You can't force your way into the consumer's mind.
- *Launch a big program*. You have to launch your program in a big way. There are two basic methods of doing this. The ''big bang'' approach launches the program with as much impact as you can afford to overcome the inertia that always exists in the marketplace. The ''rollout'' approach, which is popular among smaller companies, launches the program in a single city or state/region, then rolls out to other areas as success and resources allow.

Future Trends

John Naisbitt has predicted a number of trends that will affect marketing as we move toward the twenty-first century.[6] Here are a few of his predictions:

Naisbitt sees a gradual transformation *from an industrial to a service economy*. And more and more *services* are airing their ''wares'' in the media. For the first time in their history, the Girl Scouts have launched a print, radio, and TV public service campaign, titled ''Brainstorm.'' It aims at encouraging more girls to become Scouts and to stay in the program as they move into their high school years.

- The gradual transition to a service economy is continuing unabated. Jobs in service sectors now pay more than jobs in industry.
- The high-technology explosion that is transforming our society is creating a need for a counterbalancing humanism. Literature, music, the performing arts, and ''new age'' spiritualism are areas in which participatory interest is on the rise.
- For the first time in 200 years, more people are moving to rural areas than to cities and environs. The main reason is the desire for a higher quality of life. Advancements in electronics and communications have made it possible to be in touch with the world without living in a city or commuting to work in one.
- Socialism is on the wane in all the highly developed nations and many of the less developed ones. Examples are the existence of unregulated markets in China and perestroika, or the restructuring of the economy, that is presently going on in the U.S.S.R.
- English is emerging as the universal language of our times. It is already the standard language of shipping, air travel, science, the youth culture, and information.
- Individuals are becoming more important and powerful in the new global economy. Electron-

[5]Jack Trout, ''Long-term planning a things of the past in new marketing strategy,'' *Television/Radio Age*, October 17, 1988, p. 51.

[6]John Naisbitt, ''John Naisbitt's Ten Latest Trends,'' *Sound Management*, April 1989, p. 30.

ics and information are the prime enablers in this trend. A dichotomy of sorts is becoming apparent: broad global marketing on the one hand and pinpointed niche marketing on the other.

- A complex multioption society has evolved during the twentieth century. Computers, which drive the marketplace, permit more segmentation, which, in turn, is transforming the marketing landscape. More information with more detail is now available far more quickly.
- The world is moving slowly toward global free trade: one marketplace, one economy. The European Common Market countries are scheduled to abolish trade restrictions among themselves in 1992; the United States and Canada recently signed a free trade agreement.
- The United States is primed to be a major player in the global economy of the twenty-first century. The biggest stumbling block is the low quality of American education.

SUMMARY

There are two basic means of handling the advertising operation in a company: an advertising department that supervises the agency and handles all aspects of advertising through the ad manager; and a marketing-services system that uses product managers and specialists in different marketing/advertising services. Procter & Gamble has altered the typical structure of the marketing-services system by adding a category manager. All disciplines—research, manufacturing, engineering, sales, advertising, and so on—report to the category manager.

The selection of an agency involves many factors, the most important of which are how appropriate and experienced the agency is, what kind of work it does for clients, and how well its people can work with the advertiser's people.

Budgets are set in various ways, percentage of sales being the most common.

Evaluation of national advertising begins with a definition of what you want the advertising to accomplish. Advertising goals are not the same as marketing goals; advertising is a specific communication task. The PACT Report addressed the question of what constitutes good advertising and how to measure it.

The marketing environment continues to change. A case in point is the slotting allowances that have become the admission fees to supermarket shelf space for new products. The Sage Group suggests several new rules for new-product/category/brand managers to learn: Marketplace leverage is at the local level; retailers should be concerned about brand equity; marketing decisions must shift to the sales level.

Tests by Information Resources indicate advertising is more cost-efficient than trade promotions.

Ries and Trout say the traditional "top-down" approach to marketing isn't as effective as it used to be and suggest a "bottom-up" approach.

John Naisbitt predicts a number of trends for the future that advertisers should be aware of. The growing individualization in a global economy is one of the most important.

QUESTIONS

1. What are the two traditional ways companies use to organize their advertising departments?
2. What is a category manager?
3. What is a payout plan?
4. What are the forms of agency compensation?
5. Discuss the slotting allowance's role in introducing a new product.
6. Differentiate between the traditional "top-down" and Ries and Trout's "bottom-up" marketing approaches.

SUGGESTED EXERCISE

- Find two articles in current advertising publications that discuss a products budget.

READINGS

BAKER, STEPHEN: *The Advertiser's Manual* (New York: John Wiley & Sons, Inc., 1988).

CAGLEY, JAMES W.: "A Comparison of Advertising Agency Selection Factors: Advertiser and Agency Perceptions," *Journal of Advertising Research,* Vol. 26, No. 3 (1986), pp. 39–44.

DAGNOLI, JUDANN, AND LAURIE FREEMAN: "Campbell, P&G Plan Shift in Agency Compensation," *Advertising Age,* December 26, 1988, p. 1.

KOTLER, PHILIP, AND GARY ARMSTRONG: *Principles of Marketing,* 4th ed. (Englewood Cliffs, NJ: Prentice Hall, 1989).

MAGIERA, MARCY: "Carnation Links Pay, Research," *Advertising Age,* March 6, 1989, p. 1.

PART FOUR

Media

The role of the media planner has taken on added importance in recent years. The costs of time and space have risen to the point that budgetary controls of the media-buying process are essential. The number of media vehicles available to advertisers has also created a need for more experienced media personnel. Whereas a few years ago there were three TV networks, today there are more than 20 distributed by cable, syndication, and over-the-air outlets. Likewise, the number of magazines, radio stations, and out-of-home advertising vehicles has increased dramatically.

The increase in media outlets has resulted in a fragmenting of the viewing and listening audience. This fragmented audience permits media planners to reach narrow target segments, but at a higher cost per person. Media specialization requires media buyers to have a broader knowledge of marketing goals, advertising objectives, audience profiles, and media characteristics.

In this section, we will stress the importance of recognizing the opportunities of reaching specialized market segments. Already we see the term *mass media* being replaced by concepts such as narrowcasting on cable TV and a tremendous growth in specialized print media. Media planners will also need to understand and coordinate their efforts with creative personnel to take full advantage of specialized media. At no time has the need for professionally trained media planners been greater.

SEVEN

Basic Media Strategy

With advertising costs skyrocketing, *accountability* is at an all-time high. Frequently, *celebrities* can induce additional readership. Quaker Oats cereal uses Wilford Brimley, the grandfatherly *Cocoon* movie star, in its ads. It recently ran a sweepstakes promotion, offering $10 toward tickets to the new version, ''a natural and irresistible opportunity,'' said Quaker, ''considering our spokesman.''

***Non-mass media.** A medium which delivers less than one percent of a population.*

The advertising function is generally divided into creative and media elements. These broad classifications, along with their support activities such as account services, traffic, and finance, lead to the finished advertising campaign. Most people regard advertising as the ads and commercials they read and see every day. However, as we shall see in this chapter, it is the buying, selling, and planning of advertising media that account for the major portion of the typical advertising budget. In fact, only the cost of product distribution constitutes a larger portion of the marketing expense of the typical firm.

With total expenditures for advertising about to pass the $140 billion mark, and most of the money going to media advertising insertions, advertisers are paying greater attention to the media-planning function. As one advertising executive pointed out, ''Now more companies are relying on the media people to help them out with their media choices. The demand for accountability is intense, it's increasing.''[1]

We begin our discussion of media with some definitions of the term. In recent years, the proliferation of advertising vehicles has made exactly what should be included in the term *advertising media* problematical. Perhaps the simplest definition of *media* is: ''the means by which advertisements are made public.''

Stephen Phelps, deputy media director at D'Arcy Masius Benton & Bowles, has suggested that there are two dimensions to media:

1. Whether the medium is identified as ''mass'' or ''less-than mass.'' For our purposes, the term *non-mass media* will be applied when the typical vehicle in the category delivers one percent or less of an agreed-upon group, e.g., households.
2. Whether the medium alone, without the advertisement, qualifies as ''communication.'' That is, does it carry a message or information *other* than that contained in the advertisement?[2]

Phelps uses a matrix to demonstrate these dimensions of media (see Exhibit 7.1).

[1]Maureen Goldstein, ''Up the Ladder,'' *Inside Print,* August 1988, p. 31.

[2]Stephen P. Phelps, ''Mediology,'' *Marketing & Media Decisions,* January 1988, p. 47.

EXHIBIT 7.1

Media planners must be aware of the degree of selectivity of the media vehicles they purchase. (Courtesy: *Marketing & Media Decisions*.)

Media Matrix Model		
	Informational	**Non-Informational**
Mass	• Television-Nat'l/Local • Radio—Nat'l • Newspaper—Nat'l/Local • Magazine—Nat'l Consumer	• Billboards • Mass Mailings
Targeted	• Cable • Radio—Local • Newspaper—College/Ethnic • Magazine—Trade; "Buff"	• Direct Mail • Matchbook Covers • "Other" Out-of-Home

He suggests that the next step in the media matrix may be the degree of user interaction with the media. Within two decades, we will probably see much more user control of media, as in consumers "calling up" messages when they need them. At a minimum, we will see a type of electronic Yellow Pages similar to the system already in use in France.

First, the advertiser has to define his promotional strategy—what objectives he wishes the various media to accomplish on behalf of his product. After lopping off the bottom tier of its liquor brands, Seagram has begun to refashion itself as a *marketer of luxury,* rather than liquor. It will be promoting its new image in high-status magazines and specialty stores' catalogs for such brands as Chevas Regal Scotch and V.O. whiskey.

Newspapers are the "best bet" locally, but are not necessarily reaching the youth market. They can, however, be extremely flexible—in size of ad, color, placement, and timing. American Express found that the youth of today prefer their card to other credit cards—"the ultimate symbol of adulthood." Print ads in *college newspapers* proved to be the most successful media strategy in reaching this narrowly-segmented market.

MEDIA CHARACTERISTICS

In the next several chapters, we will be discussing in some detail each of the major advertising media. To set the stage for that examination of basic media strategy, we will briefly outline here the major characteristics of these media. Exhibit 7.2 gives some idea of the tremendous expenditures accounted for by each of the media.

There is no one medium that is right for every advertiser. Each advertiser has special objectives that can be accomplished by some media and not by others. The starting point for any media plan is an analysis of the various media's strengths and weaknesses and how these characteristics fit the particular advertiser's strategy.

Newspapers

Although they are still the primary recipient of advertising dollars, newspapers face increasingly stiff competition in most markets from a host of locally oriented media vehicles.

Pros:

1. Newspapers have wide exposure to a general population.
2. Newspaper advertising is extremely flexible, with opportunities for color, large and small space ads, timely insertion schedules, and some selectivity through special sections and targeted editions.
3. Newspapers reach their audiences at the convenience of the reader.

EXHIBIT 7.2

Estimated Advertising Expenditures in Major Media, 1990

	$ billions	*% of Total*
Newspapers	36	26.1
Television	32	23.2
Direct mail	21	15.2
Radio	9.5	6.9
Consumer magazines	8.1	5.9
Business and farm publications	3.1	2.3
Outdoor	1.3	1.0
Other	27	19.8

Cons:

1. The average person spends less than 30 minutes reading a newspaper. Consequently, most ads go unread.
2. Teenagers and young adults do not demonstrate high newspaper readership.
3. Advertising costs have risen much more sharply than circulation in recent years.

Television

Television, through a combination of sight, sound, motion, and color, is a tremendously dramatic medium. While trailing newspapers in overall advertising dollars, it is the number-one medium for national advertisers.

National advertisers prefer *television*. Its creativity and reach surpass other media by far. But cable and VCRs continue to impact on viewership. NBC hopes to attract more sponsors for the 1992 Summer Olympic Games in Barcelona, Spain, since they've agreed to sell some of the action to a cable outlet.

Pros:

1. Television is an extremely creative and flexible medium. Virtually any product message can be adapted to TV.
2. Network television is the primary vehicle for reaching mass audiences.
3. Television offers advertisers prestige lacking in most other media.

Cons:

1. The television message is perishable and easily forgotten without expensive repetition.
2. The television audience is fragmented, with alternatives such as cable, independent stations, and VCRs vying for audience viewing time.
3. Advertising costs continue to increase. This has led to more and shorter messages, which contribute to commercial clutter.

Radio

Radio is characterized by its many stations, formats, and high reach across virtually every demographic segment. In many respects, radio pioneered the segmented marketing strategy so prevalent in all media today.

No more segmented medium exists than *radio*. It ''travels'' well and reaches ''hard-to-reach'' segments, such as youth and inner-city residents. Royal Crown, in its effort to target *adults,* will be using more radio in its media mix, says President Alfred Burke. In trying to get ''more mileage'' out of their advertising dollars, it's important that they reach their target—without wasted effort. More radio spots will be directed at *commuters* in big cities nationally, the more likely drinkers of RC and Diet Rite colas.

Pros:

1. Radio can more selectively target an audience segment than virtually any other medium, especially teens.
2. Radio goes with listeners into the marketplace, giving advertisers proximity to the sale.
3. Radio, with its relatively low cost for production and immediacy, can react quickly to changing market conditions.

Cons:

1. Without a visual component, listeners often use radio as ''background'' rather than paying full attention.
2. The low average audience of most radio stations requires high frequency to achieve acceptable reach and frequency.
3. Adequate audience research is not always available, especially in medium and smaller radio markets.

Direct Response

Direct response is a medium particularly attuned to the target-marketing philosophy of the 1990s. Efficient use of computers and automation has held down costs despite recent postal increases.

Direct response affords advertisers the opportunity to *reach* narrowly defined segments—but at a relatively *high* cost. Nonetheless, many manufacturers would like to forge relationships *directly* with customers—and *sustain* them, as well. The new Frequent Shopping Advantage Club, says Peter Palmer and Doug Lauder, is the answer. It's a carefully crafted cooperative mail program, where consumers are awarded free merchandise in exchange for UPC codes of products they buy. So far, 12 major marketers, including RJR Nabisco, Lever Brothers, and Frito-Lay have signed on.

Pros:

1. Direct response can target even the most narrowly defined audiences.
2. The timing of the message is at the discretion of the advertiser rather than the media.
3. Direct response offers opportunities for measuring advertising effectiveness unavailable in most other media.
4. Direct response is able to utilize a number of different approaches to deliver a message (e.g., telephone, videocassettes).

Cons:

1. High cost per inquiry is a major problem with many forms of direct response. These include costs for printing, production, and handling and personnel.
2. Provision must be made for keeping prospect lists up-to-date.
3. Direct response, especially direct mail and telemarketing, has an image problem among many consumers.

Magazines

The trend lately has been the growth of *specialized magazines,* which can offer advertisers prestige, demographic and geographic selectivity, and long-life. The new magazine, *Connoisseur,* boasts impressive up-scale readership statistics—median net worth of $866,000; 30.4% with incomes over $150,000; and 74.4% valid passport holders.

Magazines are the oldest of the national advertising media. Intense competition has kept magazine advertising rate increases below those of most other media in recent years.

Pros:

1. The number and range of specialized magazines provide advertisers with an opportunity for narrowly targeting audiences. Both demographic and geographic selectivity can be achieved.
2. Magazines provide a prestige, quality environment for advertisers.
3. Magazine advertising has a long life, especially since issues are often passed along to several readers.

Cons:

1. Magazines are more expensive on an audience-reach basis than any other major medium, with the possible exception of direct mail.
2. Most magazines have relatively long advertising deadlines, which reduce flexibility and the ability of advertisers to react to fast-changing market conditions.
3. A single magazine rarely reaches the majority of a market segment. Therefore, several magazines must be used or alternative media must supplement magazine advertising.

Outdoor

As a supplement to other forms of mass media, *outdoor advertising* can reach a mobile audience at a very low cost. Now that Delta Airlines has become the official airline of Disneyland and Walt Disney World, it's sponsoring an attraction called *Dream Flight*. With the Delta name and logo prominently displayed, visitors will enter the "ride" as though they were boarding a Delta 747 plane.

Outdoor advertising is a visual medium intended for brand-name reinforcement. It has high impact and reaches a mobile audience with extremely high frequency.

Pros:

1. Outdoor can reach most of the population in a market at a very low cost per exposure.
2. It is an excellent means of supplementing other media advertising and building brand-name recall.
3. With the use of color and lighting, outdoor is a medium that can't be ignored.

Cons:

1. Outdoor cannot communicate messages because effective copy is limited to seven to ten words.
2. The effectiveness of outdoor is extremely difficult to measure.
3. Outdoor advertising is controversial in many communities, and its negative image may carry over to the advertiser who uses the medium.

THE COMPONENTS OF THE MEDIA PLAN

Media plan. *The total analysis and execution of the media component of a campaign.*

It goes without saying that a thorough knowledge of the characteristics of the primary advertising media is necessary to develop a media plan. However, a media plan is made up of more than just a descriptive analysis of the various media. While there is no standard format, the following elements are found in most national plans:

- The target audience
- Communication requirements and creative elements
- The efficiency/effectiveness balance—shall we stress reach, frequency, or continuity?
- Geography—where is the product distributed?
- The pressure of competition
- The budget

HOW DO WE DISTINGUISH BETWEEN MARKETING AND ADVERTISING GOALS?

Effective advertising is an extension of the basic marketing plan and is derived from it. However, advertising goals are not the same as marketing goals. The marketing staff sets the marketing goals or objectives. The marketing department decides how to allocate resources to various tasks, including advertising. It also determines how these resources will be distributed to specific target markets and what sales objectives can be expected over time and geography.

Examples of marketing objectives are:

1. Attaining a market share increase from 2 percent of industry sales to 4 percent within 18 months.
2. Increasing distribution by number of retail outlets and/or geographic regions. If a product is currently available to 50 percent of the population or can be found in 50 percent of retail outlets, the marketing goal might be to increase this figure to 60 percent by the end of the year.
3. Increasing total sales. Goals may be set in either number of units sold or dollar volume of sales.

Advertising goals are communication objectives designed to reach the target audience with the appropriate message. Ad goals (media objectives and communication objectives) are based on marketing objectives, but they are not the same as marketing goals.

Advertising objectives might include:

1. Increasing brand awareness from 20 percent to 30 percent among 18-to-34-year-old women within one year.
2. Increasing recall of brand advertising by 10 percent in the next three months.
3. Increasing favorable product attitudes by 10 percent in the next year.

An important point is that both marketing and advertising objectives should be specific, measurable, and attainable. Before any marketing or advertising objective is adopted, the question must be asked: Do I have the ability to measure successful accomplishment of this objective?

The Target Audience

Reaching the *target audience* with the best media vehicles is the primary job of media planners. The newest sales promotion strategy is ''P-O-P Radio,'' an in-store radio network, whose announcements filter through loudspeakers at 7,000 drugstores and will soon be expanded into supermarkets.

Perhaps the most important job of the media planner is deciding which media vehicles will best reach the prime prospects for a product. The entire media-planning function must focus on a clear market profile and remember that it is prospects, not readers or listeners, who are of primary importance to the advertiser.

The job of the media planner is more difficult today because of the proliferation of media vehicles from which to choose. In recent years, media planners have evaluated media on the basis of how they maximize target-audience exposures. While evaluative techniques differ from agency to agency, all agencies tend to use some variation of the *weighted* or *demographic* cost per thousand (CPM). Let's look at an example of the weighted CPM:

The CPM is a means of comparing media costs among vehicles with different circulations. The formula is stated:

$$\text{CPM} = \frac{\text{ad cost} \times 1000}{\text{circulation}}$$

Cost per thousand. *Method of determining the cost of audience delivery for ads in various media.*

McCall's has a circulation of 5,000,000 and a 4/color page rate of \$60,800. Therefore, its

$$\text{CPM} = \$12.16 \frac{(\$60{,}800 \times 1000)}{5{,}000{,}000}$$

Now assume that we are only interested in reaching women with children under 2 years old. We find that 600,000 *McCall's* readers are in this category. Therefore:

$$\text{Demographic CPM} = \$101.33 \frac{(\$60{,}800 \times 1000)}{600{,}000}$$

The demographic CPM simply adjusts the circulation to include only that part of the audience of interest to a particular advertiser. In recent years, advertising research has developed extremely sophisticated techniques for identifying prospects. Most of these new techniques recognize that proper identification of prospects demands the use of several variables.

To return to our *McCall's* example, we realize that all women with children under 2 years of age are not alike. They differ in terms of education, income, housing, geography, and lifestyle. Obviously, these differences must be considered on a number of bases.

PRIZM (Potential Rating Index by ZIP Market). *A method of audience segmentation developed by the Claritas Corporation.*

One attempt to segment markets on a multiple-variable basis is the Potential Rating Index by ZIP Market (PRIZM) system developed by the Claritas Corporation. The system uses eight variables to compute a ranked index or ZIP quality rank. Exhibit 7.3 shows the 40 ZIP-market cluster descriptions assigned to all ZIP codes in the country. For instance, the typical resident of Blue Blood Estates is upper-class affluent (category A), lives in a suburban area with a dominant white population, is married with children, has at least a college degree, is employed in a white-collar job, and lives in a single-family dwelling. The combination of these variables computes to a ZQ score of 83 (based on a scale of 100 and an average for all clusters of 50).

Advertisers rely on a system such as PRIZM, which weights different variables or characteristics of population groups, to determine who their prime prospects will be. If a television program, such as ''Roseanne,'' is known for attracting heavy detergent buyers, Pete Megroz of Arbitron *knows* he can attract makers of laundry products—at a premium price—to purchase viewing time.

The next step, of course, is to match these general categories or clusters with the products and media each is most likely to use. A system such as PRIZM, utilizing a number of weighted variables, is much more useful in identifying prime prospects than any single variable would be.

Before we leave the subject of target marketing, we should mention the problem of uniform target delivery. Uniformity of delivery is especially difficult when dealing with relatively large market segments. For instance, package-goods advertisers often target a group such as ''women 25–54.'' There is a danger of then proceeding to view that target as one uniform mass in all ensuing analyses.

Subsegments within the target market may prove more useful to the advertisers than approaching the market uniformly. Lately, more Los Angeles advertisers are relying on Spanish language media. VHF-TV station KSLD will become Southern California's *third* Spanish language television station this year.

Two approaches are possible to the problem of uneven delivery. One is to more narrowly define the target market (e.g., women 25–54, college educated, living in single-family dwellings, with incomes of $35,000+). The trouble with this approach is that we find it increasingly expensive and difficult to narrow our media plan to such a specific audience. Furthermore, we may exclude prospects who do not meet these narrow criteria. A more reasonable approach is to recognize that total uniform target delivery is an illusion and to plan accordingly.

A target market is the sum of its parts. Those parts are not likely to be equal in value nor to receive their appropriate media weight by chance. That recognition can influence decisions in a number of key strategic and executional areas, including the consideration of alternative media and the weighting of subsegments within the target market for greater sales potential. The net effect is more precision in planning.[3] Exhibit 7.4 shows the market segment for personal computers.

Communication Requirements and Creative Elements

Communications component. *That portion of the media plan that considers the effectiveness of message delivery as contrasted to efficiency of audience delivery.*

The media planner must be constantly aware of the communication component of the media schedule. We sometimes get so caught up in media-audience analysis that we forget advertising must *communicate* to these listeners and readers. In the past, a major criticism of the advertising process was that media and creative functions were not coordinated closely enough. The result, according to the critics, was advertising that did not fully utilize the communicative strengths of the various media vehicles. Fortunately, the separation between the creative and media functions seems to have diminished in recent years. Among major advertising agencies, there seems to be a heightened realization that intra-agency communication is necessary for effective advertising.

If advertisers' main purpose is to communicate information about their products—in order to increase sales—attention needs to be focused on the *criteria* which encourage *focused attention* to ads and commercials. One way to encourage shoppers to read supermarket cart panels is to insert a calculator, says Mike Brennan, a 30-year-old entrepreneur from Tulsa, Oklahoma. Most P-O-P advertising in stores serves no function, but according to Brennan, the "Shoppers Calculator" has utility—adding a whole new *service* for the shopper.

The communication portion of the media plan involves not simply exposure to advertising, but rather *effective* exposure. Intuitively, we know that every ad exposure is not equal. As we will discuss later in the chapter, at some point the rate of advertising awareness diminishes with each additional exposure. In recent year, planners have paid more attention to the quality of exposure from a communication perspective.

Rolf Speetzen, an advertising researcher, identified several criteria that discriminate between readers who pay little attention to a magazine's advertisements and those who read them carefully:

1. How much of an advertisement does the respondent read?
2. Does the respondent read all or most of the articles in the magazine?
3. How far would the respondent go to obtain the magazine?
4. Does the respondent think that advertising is entertaining?
5. Does the respondent think that advertising is helpful?[4]

Advertisers measure *communication effectiveness,* according to whether the ads and commercials achieved their objectives. Merchandising and entertainment tie-ins can enhance the salability of related clothing and toys, while increasing box office receipts. The advertising for Steven Spielberg and George Lucas' *Land Before Time,* was coordinated with instore promotions at more than 1,400 Penney's and 5,800 Pizza Huts to trigger record responses for *all* the sponsors.

Assuming we correctly measure quality of exposure, the question then becomes: Does a difference in exposure quality make any difference in the marketplace? Research data suggest that those respondents who exhibit quality-exposure characteristics not only show higher levels of advertising awareness (Exhibit 7.5a) but also, more importantly, demonstrate a greater propensity to purchase (Exhibit 7.5b).

Effective communication takes place as we systematically exclude nonprospects from the media. No matter what techniques the media planner uses to evaluate the media plan, the goals should be measuring communication effectiveness and, if possi-

[3]Ron Lawrence, "Uniform Target Delivery: An Illusion," *Marketing & Media Decisions,* December 1987, p. 94.

[4]Wally Wood, "Quality, Awareness, and Intent to Buy," *Marketing & Media Decisions,* March 1988, p. 140.

EXHIBIT 7.3

PRIZM: The ZIP-Market cluster system. (Courtesy: Claritas Corporation).

The 10 Cluster Groups		*The 40 Zip-Market Clusters*					
Codes	**Descriptive Titles**	**Numbers**	**Nicknames**				**One-**
S1	Educated, affluent, elite white families in owner-occupied, green-belt suburbs	28	Blue Blood Estates	A	SUBS	DOM	WHITE
		5	Furs & Station Wagons	A	SUBS	DOM	WHITE
		25	Two More Rungs	A	SUBS	MIX	WH/FS
		7	Pools & Patios	A	SUBS	DOM	WHITE
S2	Educated, affluent, semi-urban sophisticates with singles & university enclaves	8	Money & Brains	A	SUBS	MIX	WHITE
		20	Young influentials	A	SUBS	MIX	WHITE
T1	Mobile, upper-middle, child-raising families in new suburbs & ex-urban towns	24	Young Suburbia	A	SUBS	DOM	WHITE
		1	God's Country	B	TOWN	DOM	WHITE
		27	Levittown, U.S.A.	B	SUBS	DOM	WHITE
		17	Young Homesteaders	C	TOWN	DOM	WHITE
U1	Educated singles in hi-rise areas with University, artistic & downscale elements	21	Urban Gold Coast	A	CITY	MIX	WH/FS
		31	Sun-Belt Singles	B	CITY	MIX	WH/MM
		37	Bohemian Mix	B	CITY	MIX	WH/MM
S3	Middle-class, native-white, blue-collar families in industrial urban fringes	30	Blue-Chip Blues	B	SUBS	DOM	WHITE
		16	Middle America	B	SUBS	DOM	WHITE
		40	Blue-Collar Nursery	C	SUBS	DOM	WHITE
U2	Mixed, middle-class, foreign stock & minorities in dense urban row-house areas	23	Bunker's Neighbors	B	CITY	MIX	WH/FS
		3	Old Melting Pot	B	CITY	MIX	FS/BL
		36	Blue-Collar Catholics	B	CITY	MIX	WH/FS
		2	Eastern Europeans	C	CITY	MIX	WH/FS
		4	Heavy Industry	C	CITY	MIX	FS/SP
T2	Lo-mid to downscale mill & factory towns with educated gentry & blue-collar labor	18	Old Brick Factories	C	TOWN	DOM	WHITE
		33	Down-Home Gentry	C	TOWN	DOM	WHITE
		22	Mines & Mills	C	TOWN	DOM	WHITE
		12	Big Fish/Small Pond	C	TOWN	MIX	WH/BL
		13	Norma Rae-Ville	D	TOWN	MIX	WH/BL
R1	Minor cities & rural towns amidst farms & ranches, across agricultural mid-America	29	Coalburg & Corntown	C	TOWN	DOM	WHITE
		19	Shotguns & Pickups	C	TOWN	DOM	WHITE
		34	Agri-Business	C	FARM	DOM	WHITE
		35	Grain Belt	D	FARM	DOM	WHITE
U3	Mixed black, Spanish & foreign stock in aging, center-city, row & hi-rise areas	9	Hispanic Mix	C	CITY	MIX	FS/MM
		26	Ethnic Row Houses	C	CITY	MIX	FS/BL
		14	Emergent Minorities	C	CITY	MIX	BL/MM
		11	Dixie-Style Tenements	D	CITY	MIX	BL/SP
		32	Urban Renewal	D	CITY	DOM	BLACK
R2	Mixed, unskilled whites, blacks, Spanish & Indians in poor rural towns & farms	39	Marlboro Country	D	FARM	DOM	WHITE
		10	Back-Country Folks	D	FARM	DOM	WHITE
		38	Share Croppers	D	FARM	MIX	WH/BL
		15	Tobacco Roads	D	FARM	MIX	WH/BL
		6	Hard Scrabble	D	FARM	MIX	WH/BL

KEY TO ONE-LINERS:
EXAMPLE (Cluster No. 16, Middle America)
Demographic Highlights: 1 2 3 4 5 6 7 8 9
One-Liner Abbreviations: B SUBS DOM WHITE FAM HS BC S-U ZQ17

1. Socio-Economic
   A (Affluent/Upper)
   B (Upper Middle)
   C (Lower Middle)
   D (Downscale/Lower)

2. Type ZIP area
   CITY (Dense, Urban, Row & Hi-Rise Areas)
   SUBS (Suburban Residential Areas)
   TOWN (Ex-Urban, Towns & Minor City Areas)
   FARM Farms, Ranches & Other Rural Areas)

8. Housing Stock
   S-U (Single-Unit Housing)
   2-4 (2-4 Unit Housing)
   M-U (Multi-Unit Housing)

9. ZQ Rank
   ZQ 1-("ZIP-Quality" Rank
   ZQ-40 highest to lowest)

EXHIBIT *(CONTINUED)*

						Estimated 1980 Importance				***Weighted Avg. ZQ* Scores***	
						Percent U.S. Households		**Percent U.S. Population**			
Liners						**Groups**	**Clusters**	**Groups**	**Clusters**	**Groups**	**Clusters**
FAM	CG	WC	S-U	ZQ	1		.67		.71		83
FAM	CG	WC	S-U	ZQ	2		2.85		3.02		75
FAM	CG	WC	M-U	ZQ	4		1.63		1.61		70
FAM	CG	WC	S-U	ZQ	6	9.08	3.93	9.27	3.93	71	67
F/S	CG	WC	M-U	ZQ	3		1.36		1.31		75
F/S	CG	WC	M-U	ZQ	7	4.20	2.84	3.97	2.66	69	65
FAM	CG	WC	S-U	ZQ	8		6.60		6.97		64
FAM	CG	WC	S-U	ZQ	10		2.42		2.49		58
FAM	SC	BW	S-U	ZQ	11		4.59		4.86		57
FAM	SC	BW	S-U	ZQ	19	18.40	4.79	19.11	4.79	57	48
SGL	CG	WC	M-U	ZQ	5		.38		.24		67
F/S	CG	WC	M-U	ZQ	13		3.62		3.12		55
SGL	CG	WC	M-U	ZQ	14	4.79	.79	3.94	.58	56	53
FAM	HS	BW	S-U	ZQ	9		3.90		4.18		58
FAM	HS	BC	S-U	ZQ	17		3.98		4.09		50
FAM	HS	BC	S-U	ZQ	20	9.34	1.46	9.83	1.56	53	47
FAM	SC	WC	M-U	ZQ	12		4.58		4.32		57
FAM	HS	WC	M-U	ZQ	15		1.55		1.43		52
FAM	HS	BW	2-4	ZQ	16		2.42		2.34		51
FAM	HS	BC	2-4	ZQ	18		.13		.13		49
FAM	HS	BC	2-4	ZQ	27	9.59	.91	9.11	.89	53	42
FAM	HS	BC	2-4	ZQ	21		3.11		3.06		46
FAM	EX	BW	S-U	ZQ	22		4.19		4.05		45
FAM	HS	BC	S-U	ZQ	28		2.27		2.28		41
FAM	EX	BW	S-U	ZQ	30		2.97		3.00		40
FAM	GS	BC	S-U	ZQ	33	14.52	1.98	14.40	2.01	42	36
FAM	HS	BC	S-U	ZQ	23		3.79		3.89		45
FAM	HS	BC	S-U	ZQ	29		2.29		2.43		41
FAM	HS	BF	S-U	ZQ	31		2.32		2.31		40
FAM	HS	BF	S-U	ZQ	37	10.31	1.91	10.57	1.94	41	32
FAM	HS	BC	2-4	ZQ	24		.45		.43		43
F/S	HS	BC	2-4	ZQ	25		2.00		1.86		43
FAM	HS	BC	M-U	ZQ	26		1.90		1.87		42
F/S	HS	BC	M-U	ZQ	34		1.86		1.69		36
F/S	GS	BC	M-U	ZQ	36	8.28	2.07	7.85	2.00	39	35
FAM	HS	BC	S-U	ZQ	32		3.37		3.39		38
FAM	CS	BC	S-U	ZQ	35		3.14		3.22		35
FAM	GS	BC	S-U	ZQ	38		2.80		2.89		30
FAM	GS	BC	S-U	ZQ	39		1.21		1.36		30
FAM	GS	BF	S-U	ZQ	40	11.49	.97	11.95	1.09	33	28
					Total U.S.	100.00	100.00	100.00	100.00	50	50

*"ZIP Quality"—a weighted composite of education and affluence variables, which permits Clusters to be ranked and grouped according to recognized socio-economic levels (Avg. US = ZQ 50)

3. Degree of Homogeneity
   DOM (Predominant Pattern),
   MIX (Mixed, or Bi-Modal)

4. Ethnicity
   WH WHITE (Whites)
   BL BLACK (Blacks)
   SP (Spanish Americans)
   FS (Foreign Stock)
   MM (Minority Meld)

5. Life Cycle
   SGL (Singles, Couples Few Children)
   FAM (Families w/ Children)
   F/S (Families w/Singles Elements)

6. Education Level
   CG (College Grad & Above)
   SC (Some College)
   HS (High School)
   GS (Grade School)
   EX Exception, Flat or Bi)

7. Employment Level
   WC (White Collar)
   BC (Blue Collar)
   BW (Blue/White Mix)
   BS (Blue Collar/Farm)

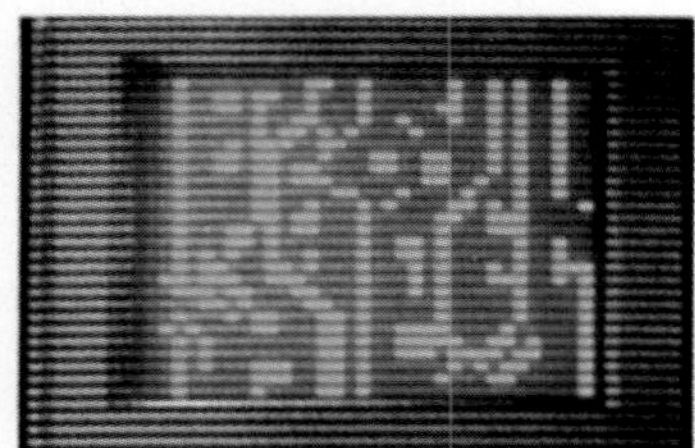

BRAND REPORT INDEX

PERSONAL COMPUTER OWNERSHIP

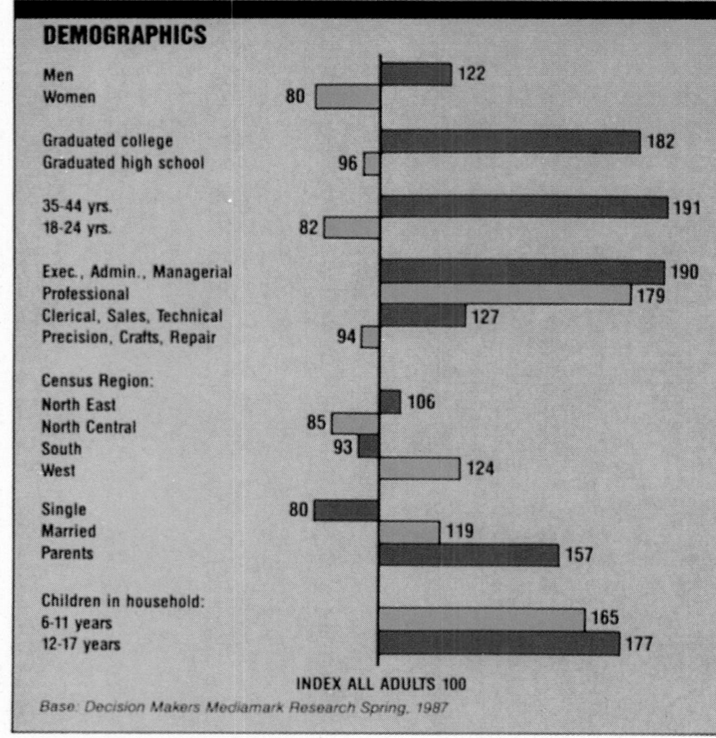

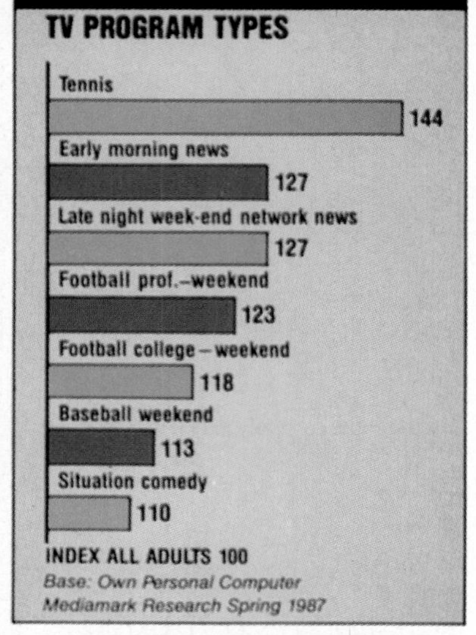

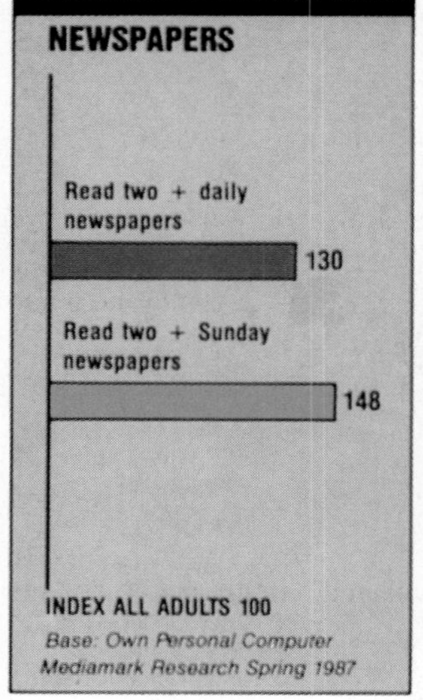

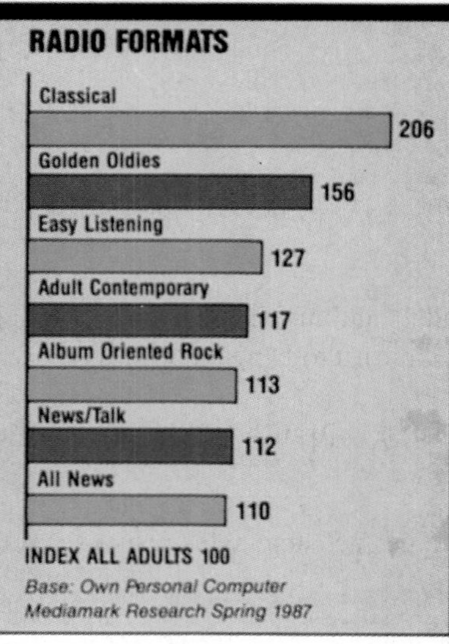

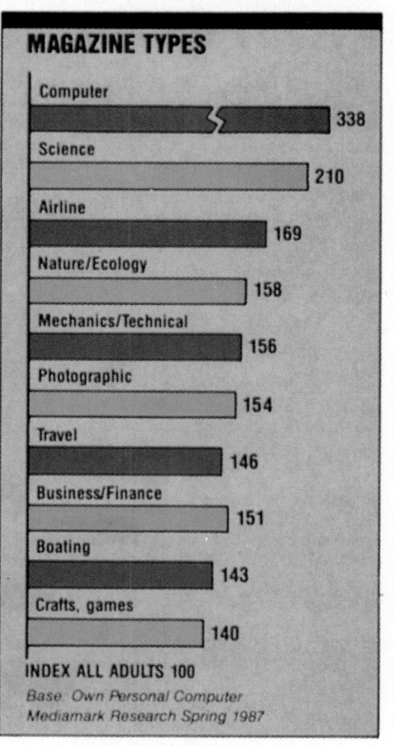

EXHIBIT 7.4

Sophisticated research allows media planners to identify prime prospects for virtually every product category. Courtesy of *Marketing and Media Publications*.

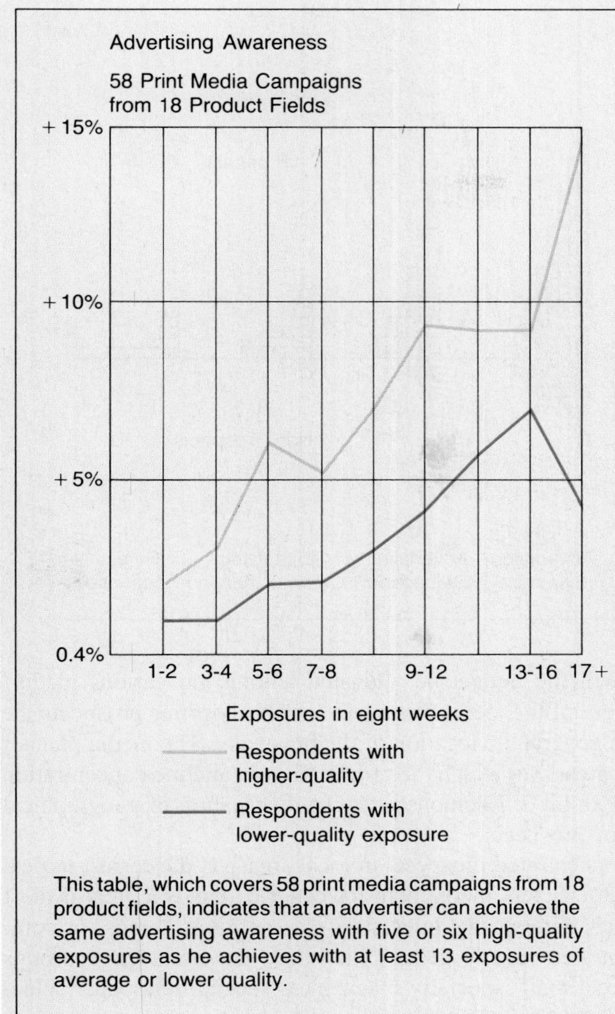

Advertising Awareness
58 Print Media Campaigns from 18 Product Fields
+15%
+10%
+5%
0.4%
1-2 3-4 5-6 7-8 9-12 13-16 17+
Exposures in eight weeks
Respondents with higher-quality
Respondents with lower-quality exposure
This table, which covers 58 print media campaigns from 18 product fields, indicates that an advertiser can achieve the same advertising awareness with five or six high-quality exposures as he achieves with at least 13 exposures of average or lower quality.

EXHIBIT 7.5A

Advertising Awareness: 58 print media campaigns from 18 product fields.

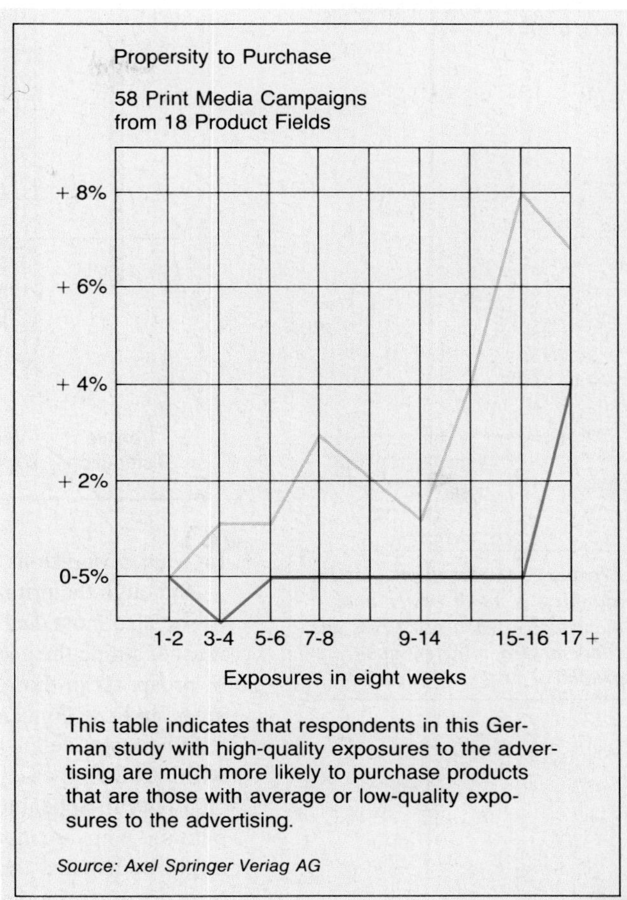

Propersity to Purchase
58 Print Media Campaigns from 18 Product Fields
+8%
+6%
+4%
+2%
0-5%
1-2 3-4 5-6 7-8 9-14 15-16 17+
Exposures in eight weeks
This table indicates that respondents in this German study with high-quality exposures to the advertising are much more likely to purchase products that are those with average or low-quality exposures to the advertising.
Source: Axel Springer Veriag AG

EXHIBIT 7.5B

Propensity to purchase: 58 print media campaigns from 18 product fields.

ble, sales. Exhibit 7.6 shows the various levels of media distribution and communications as they relate to prospects.

The first step in the model is to determine the physical distribution of the medium. For print media, this would be the paid circulation of a newspaper or magazine; for broadcast media, the households who own a TV or radio set. The next step is to add in the pass-along readers and multiple viewers in the average household reached (vehicle exposure). Then we measure the people who actually see the ad or commercial (advertising exposure).

The fourth and fifth steps deal with communication of the ad. Naturally, prospects are much more likely to notice an ad (advertising perception) or to have some deeper involvement with it, such as recalling specific information from the ad (advertising communication). The final step, sales response, is the ultimate goal of all elements in the marketing mix.

Geography—Where Is the Product Distributed?

At this point, the media planner has extensive knowledge about both the target audience and the advertising message. Now the planner must begin the process of putting together the media schedule. Will it concentrate on national, regional, or local media?

EXHIBIT 7.6

Advertising Research Foundation model for evaluating media. (Source courtesy: Audience Concepts Committee, *Toward Better Media Comparisons* [New York: Advertising Research Foundation, 1961], p.15.)

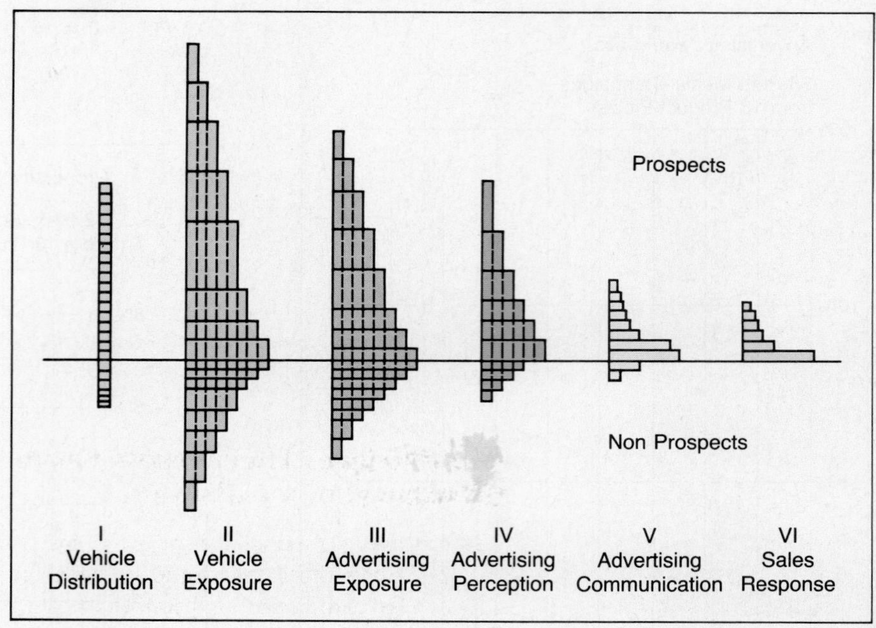

> ***Prospect concentration.*** *Media planning is much easier and inexpensive when prospects are concentrated in a few geographical areas.*

In what proportions? How will the budget be allocated among the various media?

Although the primary concern of the media planner is to identify prime prospects, he or she also must deal with the geographic location of the prospects. The media planner must examine the geographic area(s) in which the product is sold and the concentration of prospects in those areas. Exhibit 7.7 demonstrates the dual nature of geographical areas and the concentration of prospects.

Obviously, cell 1—with concentrated prospects in local area—is the easiest to deal with. At the other extreme, an efficient media plan for cell 9 demands a great deal of creativity to appeal to prospects with special interests—say, antiques, tennis, or computers—who are not concentrated in any geographic area. These selective groups might be reached through direct mail, specialty magazines, special newspaper selections, or even narrowly defined radio or TV programs.

The media planner must also deal with budget allocation by geographic area. One method of geographic budget allocation is to compare sales and population of a market. The resulting brand-development index (BDI) allows the media planner to see the concentration of prime prospects on a market-by-market basis. Exhibit 7.8 demonstrates the use of the BDI.

ACME Appliance has a media budget of $2,000,000 and sells in 20 markets. The media planner wants to allocate the budget in those 20 markets according to the sales potential of each market.

Example: Market 2, based on its population, should have an advertising allocation of $240,000 (0.12 × $2,000,000). however, the sales potential of market 2 is only 67 percent as great as its population would indicate (sales/population or 8/12). Therefore,

EXHIBIT 7.7

Location and concentration of prime prospects.

Prime Prospects	Local	Regional	National
Concentrated	1	2	3
	4	5	6
Dispersed	7	8	9

EXHIBIT 7.8

Computing the brand-development index.

Market	Population %	ACME Sales (%)	Budget by Population (000)	BDI (Sales/ Population)	Budget by BDI
1	8	12	$ 160	150	$ 240,000
2	12	8	240	67	160,800
3	6	6	120	100	120,000
etc.					
20	100%	100%	$2,000		$2,000,000

Reach. *The unduplicated audience delivered by a medium or media schedule.*

Frequency. *(1) The number of waves per second that a transmitter radiates, measured in kilohertz (kHz) and megahertz (MHz). The FCC assigns to each TV and radio station the frequency on which it may operate, to prevent interference with other stations. (2) Of media exposure the number of times an individual or household is exposed to a medium within a given period of time. (3) In statistics the number of times each element appears in each step of a distribution scale.*

Continuity. *A TV or radio script. Also refers to the length of time given media schedule runs.*

the media planner reduces the allocation to market 2 to $160,800 ($240,000 × 0.67) and reallocates funds to markets with greater potential, such as market 1.

The Efficiency/Effectiveness Balance—Shall We Stress Reach, Frequency, or Continuity?

At this stage, the media planner is moving into the specific tactics of the media schedule. The first step is consideration of audience reach, frequency, and continuity. *Reach* refers to the total number of people to whom you deliver a message; *frequency* refers to the number of times it is delivered within a given period (usually figured on a weekly basis for ease in schedule planning); and *continuity* refers to the length of time a schedule runs. Only the biggest advertisers can emphasize all three factors at once, and even they seek to spread their money most efficiently.

Reach, frequency, and continuity must be balanced against the demands of a fixed budget. However, the media planner must also consider the balance between the least expensive media (efficiency) and those most able to communicate the message and reach the best prospects (effectiveness). Exhibit 7.9 shows the relationship among the three elements in some typical media strategies.

In reality, the media planner's primary considerations are reach and frequency. Normally, the budget is predetermined and the planner functions within fairly strict guidelines as to the continuity of the campaign. In other words, the media planner

EXHIBIT 7.9

Reach, frequency, and continuity relationships with a fixed budget.

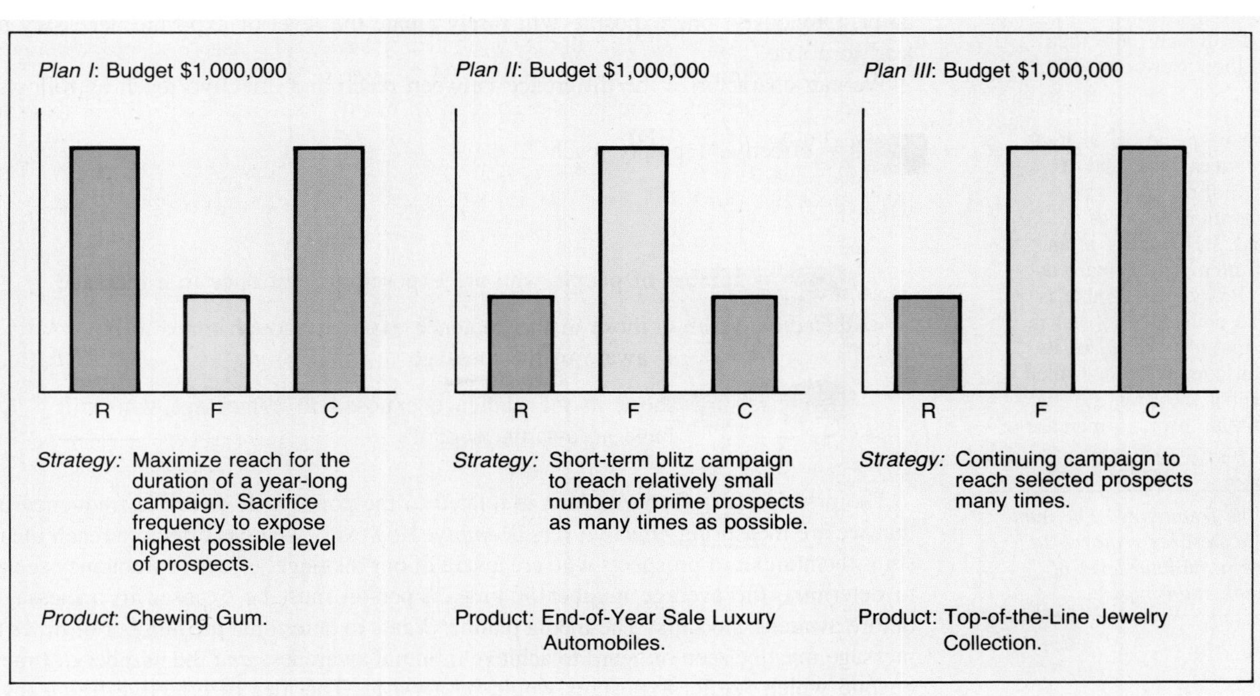

Plan I: Budget $1,000,000
R
F
C
Strategy: Maximize reach for the duration of a year-long campaign. Sacrifice frequency to expose highest possible level of prospects.
Product: Chewing Gum.
Plan II: Budget $1,000,000
R
F
C
Strategy: Short-term blitz campaign to reach relatively small number of prime prospects as many times as possible.
Product: End-of-Year Sale Luxury Automobiles.
Plan III: Budget $1,000,000
R
F
C
Strategy: Continuing campaign to reach selected prospects many times.
Product: Top-of-the-Line Jewelry Collection.

In scheduling ads, the total number of prospects must be balanced with the number of times the ads will run during a specific period, along with the length of time the schedule will run. ConAgra, maker of the newest line of frozen children's meals, Kid Cuisine, anticipates a four-to-six month test in Dallas, Denver, Fort Wayne, Indianapolis, and Salt Lake City. After a four week introductory flight of television spots in family shows, Kid Cuisine advertising will branch off into Saturday morning television and women's magazines to reach the larger audience of child viewers.

rarely has the option of reducing a year-long campaign to six months in order to fulfill reach or frequency goals.

Most media planners start with frequency as the first building block. A determination is made as to the minimum exposures required to make an impact on the prospect during some buying cycle. We might look at the reach/frequency question in terms of total exposures that can be purchased with our ad budget.

Let's say our budget will purchase 2,000,000 exposures. These exposures can be bought in a number of ways as long as they total 2,000,000. However, each time we increase the number of exposures per prospect, we reduce the number of prospects we can reach:

5 exposures × 400,000 prospects = 2,000,000
10 exposures × 200,000 prospects = 2,000,000
2 exposures × 1,000,000 prospects = 2,000,000

As you can see, if we decide to increase the number of exposures per prospect, we risk failing to reach other prospects at all. Yet we must be careful to break the communications barrier or else our ad message will be totally ineffective.

In recent years, planners have been more concerned with the effectiveness of advertising than with simply generating exposure figures. You will recall our earlier discussion of "quality of exposure," that is, the communication component of the media plan. In order to measure communication versus exposure, media planners have adopted the term *effective* reach and *effective* frequency.

Basically, we can measure the effectiveness of reach by determining the number or percentage of those in the audience who have some level of message recall. There are actually two kinds of reach. The kind we usually hear about is the percentage of the target audience exposed to an ad or commercial—exposed at least once, and perhaps only once.

"Quality of exposure" refers to the *effective reach* of the campaign—how many prospects are *aware* of a product. Pepsi-Cola International, in order to reach young video fans, will sponsor the 1989 World Music Video Awards. The two-hour awards will be televised via satellite from London and is expected to reach more than half a billion viewers in 50 countries!

The other type of reach is effective reach, which is different in a number of important ways. The goal of advertising is awareness of a product or service. It's not enough to expose your market once to your advertising, you have to make them *aware* of it. However, awareness is rarely achieved with one exposure, so simply knowing the number of people exposed to at least one message is not a measure of effective advertising. It is estimated that the average consumer sees 1,200 advertising impressions daily. Obviously, one exposure will rarely create the level of exposure necessary to lead to a sale.

We can characterize the difference between reach and effective reach as follows:

Reach = effective + empty reach

where

Reach = number of people who are exposed at least once to a message

Effective reach = those in the audience exposed enough times to be aware of the message

Empty reach = those in the audience exposed to a message who still have no awareness of it

Effective frequency is thought to lie between three and 10 exposures of an ad. Overexposure often produces "wearout." However, in an unusual attempt to capture attention, Procter & Gamble is running a consumer contest in Europe that tests *recall* of its television commercials. Called "Remember the Brands," the contest is an effort to increase viewers of commercials!

Effective frequency. *The number of exposures required to achieve a minimal level of communication impact.*

The principle of effective reach is related to the concept of effective frequency in that we are measuring *effective* versus *empty*. However, whereas effective reach measures the number of prospects who are aware of our message, effective frequency seeks to determine the average number of times a person must be exposed to a message before awareness occurs. The media planner wants to determine the number of times a message must be seen or heard to achieve minimal awareness *and* the number of times beyond which further exposures would be a waste. The idea of effective frequency, then, is to determine a low and high level of exposure. A rough rule of thumb is that three exposures are necessary to pass some minimum threshold of communication, and that, generally, any exposure level over ten is overexposure. Overexposure is defined as continuing to reach a prospect after a purchase decision has been made or to the point of wearout. Obviously, effective exposure varies for each product and campaign.

In order to determine the desirable levels of exposure for a particular campaign, media planners examine three categories of elements that contribute to effective frequency: marketplace, message, and media channels. Exhibit 7.10 offers a review of these primary factors and the subcategories of each.[5] As the exhibit shows, the setting

EXHIBIT 7.10

The marketing, message, and media environments must be coordinated for effective frequency plans.

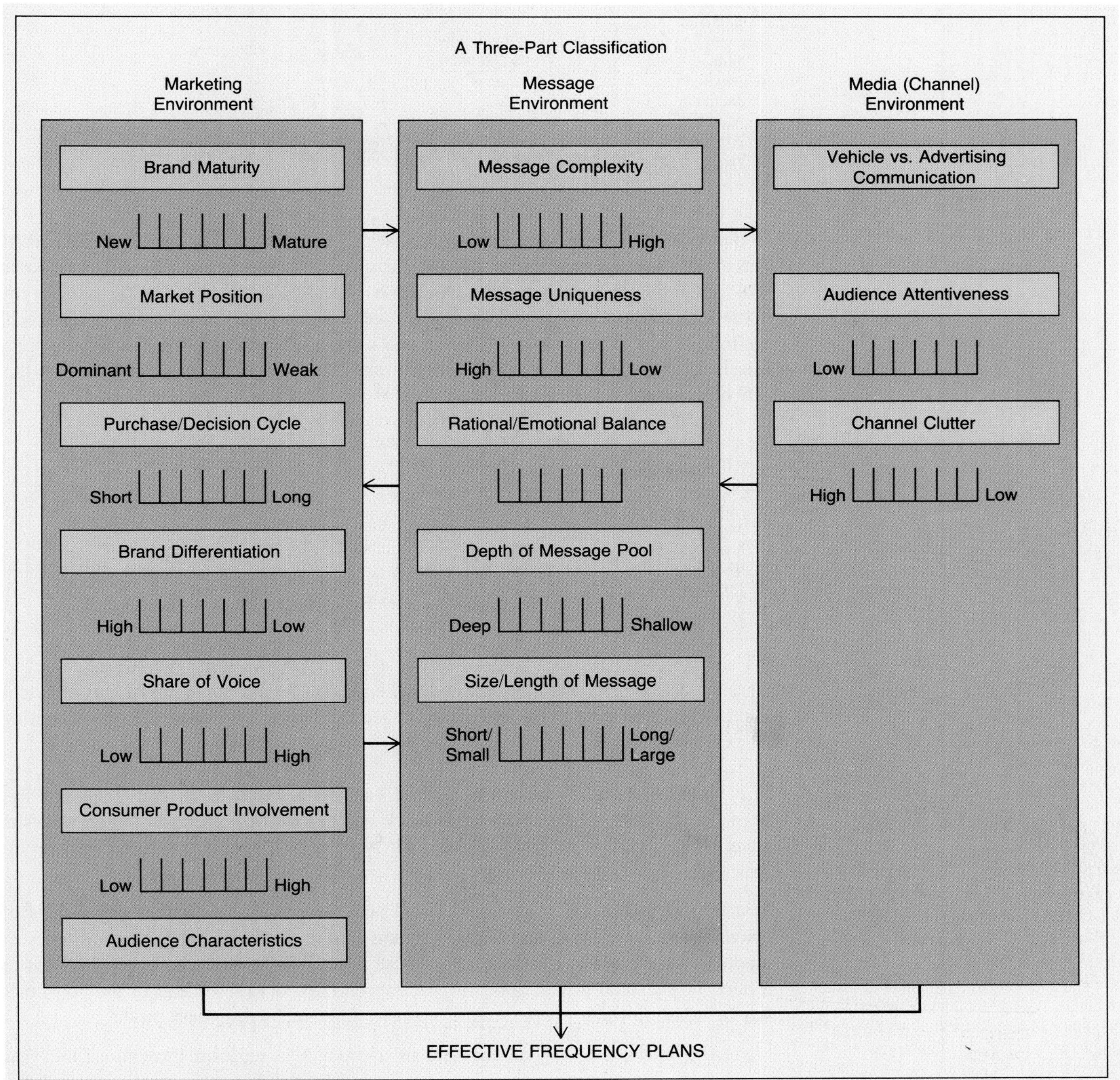

[5]From Peter B. Turk, "Considerations in Setting Effective Frequency Levels," *Journal of Media Planning*, Spring 1987, p. 21.

of any effective frequency level involves many considerations. It also suggests that these variables do not function alone, but display complex interactions and relationships.

To this point we have considered reach and frequency in a very elementary, single-medium perspective. But media schedules are not made up of a single medium. Instead, large national advertisers may use dozens or even hundreds of discrete media vehicles in a single year. Thus, the problem of reach must be dealt with on the basis of audience overlap and duplication.

Let's look at a simple example:

Target Audience:	
Men, 18–34	Reach %
Medium A	25
Medium B	22
Medium C	18
Medium D	16
Duplicated total reach	81

If we simply totaled the reach figures, we would conclude that we had reached 81 percent of our target market of 18–34-year-old males. But in order for this total to be valid, there would have had to have been no overlap in audiences. That is, none of the audience of medium A was exposed to media B, C, or D; none of the audience of medium B was exposed to A, C, or D; and so on. In a national advertising campaign, this lack of duplication would be highly unlikely. A more typical outcome of this schedule would be:

Target Audience:	
Men, 18–34	Reach %
Medium A	25
Medium B	14
Medium C	6
Medium D	2
Unduplicated total reach	57

Here the actual reach, or unduplicated audience, is 57 rather than the 81 earlier calculated. Thus, we find that the original 81 reach figure was obtained by double-counting 24 percentage points.

The Media Schedule. Once the desired balance between reach and frequency has been determined, it is time to begin work on the question of when to schedule the advertising. There is no right answer, but some typical timing patterns might be instructive.

In deciding when to schedule advertising, the *seasonality* or the *steadiness* of a products' sales has to be considered. *Flighting* helps to build audience awareness during periods of advertising inactivity. Recognizing *heavy holiday sales,* Corona Extra will run one of the largest holiday network-television schedules ever developed for an imported beer, estimated to cost $1.7 million for national and regional spots.

SEASONAL PROGRAM. Some products' sales have seasonal fluctuations—sales of cough drops increase in the winter, suntan lotions in the summer, and watches at graduation time and at Christmas. For these products, the advertising is scheduled to reflect the seasonal peaks, appearing in concentrated dosages ahead of the consumer buying season, when people might begin to think of buying such products.

STEADY PROGRAM. When the sale of a product is uniform throughout the year (toothpaste, for example), the advertising could be steadily maintained. Often, however, companies choose to concentrate their advertising. Sometimes a steady schedule spread over 12 months would be too thin, so the preference is for more impressive advertising concentrated during shorter time periods. Sometimes the company needs the money to meet competitive promotional efforts or to finance special local campaigns. During the summer, reading and TV watching decrease and radio listening increases; therefore, many TV network advertisers take a hiatus until fall or switch their advertising to radio.

> ***Flighting.*** *The length of time a broadcaster's campaign runs. Can be days, weeks, or months but does not refer to a year. A flighting schedule alternates periods of activity with periods of inactivity.*

FLIGHTING. One of the most frequently used advertising scheduling techniques is *flighting*. Flighting consists of relatively short bursts of advertising followed by periods of total or relative inactivity. The idea is to build audience awareness for your product so that brand awareness carries over the periods of inactivity. Done correctly, flighting achieves the same brand awareness as a steady advertising schedule, but at a much lower cost.

This concept is obviously appealing to advertisers, who rarely think they have enough funds to reach all their prospects with a consistent advertising program. The problem is that the available research doesn't tell advertisers which levels of awareness will be achieved with any particular flighting strategy. One thing is certain: The advertiser must guard against significant erosion of brand awareness during the hiatus between flights. Exhibit 7.11 demonstrates the ideal outcome of a properly executed flighting strategy compared to a steady schedule, both using the same advertising budget.

Under the steady schedule, audience awareness peaks fairly quickly (after about 20 weeks) and afterward shows little if any increase. The flighting schedule grows much more slowly, but because of budget savings is able to reach more prospects and therefore to achieve higher levels of brand awareness. As we cautioned earlier, an advertiser must be careful to consider the communication component of the media plan. Some media planners think that a flighting plan sacrifices depth of communication even though it achieves minimal awareness.

Regardless of the flighting schedule used, the following factors should be considered:

1. *Competitive spending*. How does your plan coincide with the primary competition's? Are you vulnerable to competition between flights?
2. *Timing of flights*. Does the schedule correspond with any seasonal features found in the product-purchase cycle?
3. *Advertising decay*. Are you spending enough in peak periods to maintain brand awareness between flights?

EXHIBIT 7.11

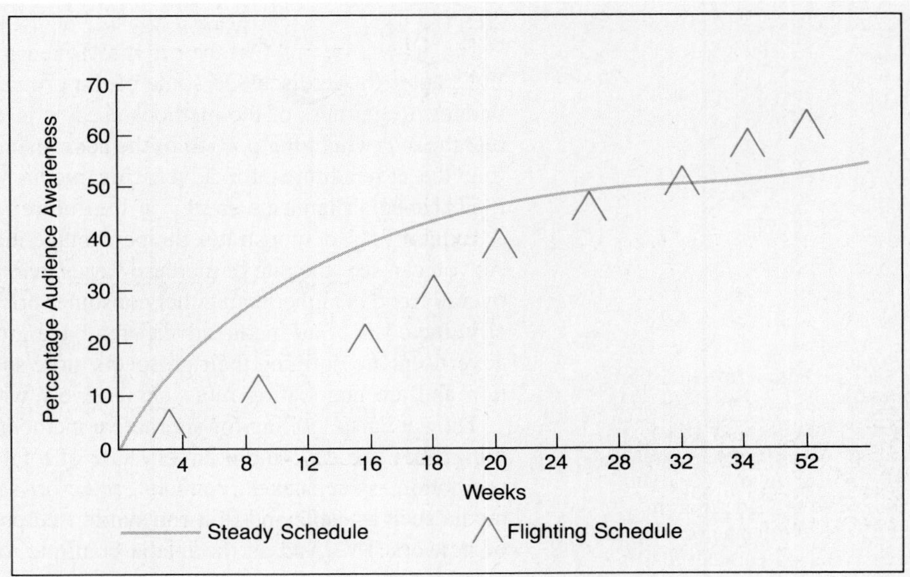

4. *Secondary media*. Should secondary or trade media be used between flights to maintain minimal visibility?

The Pressure of Competition

Competitive ad pressure manifests itself in the *dollars* competitors spend on advertising and in their *comparative product challenges*. Jordache has moved on to imitation Levi's 501 commercials—the street noise, the bluesy music in the background, the bleached footage of groups of teenagers doing self-conscious things. . . . Only, the dialogue is not as sophisticated and comes across as an obvious take-off.

The media planner must deal with the competitive situation. Virtually every aspect of the marketing and advertising function is relative to the competitive environment. Product success is measured in terms of market share. An ad budget is measured against what competitors spend. Comparative advertising challenges the claims of competitors. The advertising professional must know as much about the competition as about his or her own product.

Although the media schedule should be developed with the competition in mind, the planner must not fall into the trap of a defensive, follow-the-leader strategy. Obviously, the advertising plans for the top and bottom firms in an industry will be vastly different and a unique marketing program must be developed to demonstrate these differences.

A firm should examine its competition in several ways. First, what brands have product qualities and prices most competitive with yours? Second, among what consumer groups are you most (and least) successful relative to your competition? You must realize that in a multifirm industry you cannot be equally competitive with all other firms. The more accurately you pinpoint *your* competitive problems, the more successful your promotional activities will be.

It is also important to remember that you are not only competing against other brands of the same generic product, but also against all other products that compete for the consumer's dollars. Advertising has to convince the consumer of the need for tires before the issue of Firestone versus Goodyear can be addressed. In some sense, the competition for tires may be a washing machine or a new suit. Generally, the larger firms in a product category devote at least a portion of their advertising to increasing generic demand, while the smaller firms usually have to concentrate on brand advertising to maintain their market shares.

Several services that report competitive advertising activity are available to advertisers. One of the most prominent companies in the field is Leading National Advertisers (LNA), which provides dollar and space-time insertion figures for over 24,000 brands (see Exhibit 7.12). This information can be extremely valuable for determining the relative weight of alternative media schedules compared to competitive brands.

The Budget

In Chapter 6, we discussed some of the primary means of determining an advertising budget. Regardless of the methods used, it is clear that media will continue to constitute the overwhelming portion of the advertising budget. It is also obvious that controlling the expenditures for advertising media will take an increasing amount of the typical media planner's energy in the future.

Exhibit 7.13 demonstrates the percentage increases in media prices in recent years. As you can see, the rate of increase varies markedly among the different media, but the overall trend is higher than either consumer prices or the gross national product. Generally, the costs of all media advertising have grown faster than audiences. In response, advertisers are defining their prospects more specifically to cut down on waste circulation and are negotiating more aggressively with media salespeople.

As costs continue to climb for all media advertising, advertisers are looking for alternative methods of promotion—such as sales promotion and cable television. For the first time in 100 years, the Tournament of Roses Parade has corporate sponsors—Burger King, Chrysler, and Pepsi-Cola.

They are also looking for alternative methods of promotion and advertising. For one thing, they are devoting a larger share of total promotional dollars to consumer sales promotion (sweepstakes, coupons, price-off sales, etc.). For another, they are using media such as cable and first-run syndicated programming to circumvent the high cost of network TV. And as the media continue to fragment, we will probably see even more experimentation with media vehicles, many of which did not even exist a few years ago.

LNA AD $ SUMMARY–BRAND INDEX

BRAND NAME — CLASS CODE PARENT COMPANY (SUBSIDIARY or DIVISION)		YTD $(000)	MEDIA USED
HARTFORD NATIONAL BANK & TRUST CO	B151	$ 80.6	S
HARTFORD NATIONAL BANK & TRUST CO CONSUMER SERVICES	B151	2.5	O
HARTFORD NATIONAL CORP			
HARTS BREAD	F161	70.2	S
DPF INC (INTERSTATE BRANDS CORP)			
HARTS FAMILY DEPARTMENT STORES	G608	6.3	O
NATIONAL INDUSTRIES INC (BIG BEAR INC)			
HARTS SEEDS	T620	1.2	S
HART CHARLES C SEED CO			
*HARTWICK COLLEGE RESIDENTIAL	B133	1.8	M
HARTZ MOUNTAIN DOG & CAT VITAMINS	G532	877.2	S-R
HARTZ MOUNTAIN DOG CHEWS	G531	143.4	S-R
HARTZ MOUNTAIN FLEA COLLARS	G532	6,103.2	M-N-S-R
HARTZ MOUNTAIN FLEA TAGS	G532	1.8	S
HARTZ MOUNTAIN CORP			
HARTZ MOUNTAIN INDUSTRIES INC REAL ESTATE	G520	16.5	O
HARTZ MOUNTAIN CORP (HARTZ MOUNTN INDUST IN)			
HARTZ MOUNTAIN PET SHAMPOO	G532	297.8	R
HARTZ MOUNTAIN WORMER	G532	639.8	S-R
HARTZ MOUNTAIN CORP			
HARVARD BED FRAMES	H120	22.8	M
RUSCO INDUSTRIES INC (HARVARD MFG CO)			
HARVARD BUSINESS SCHOOL ADVANCED MANAGEMENT PROGRAM	B133	21.1	M
HARVARD BUSINESS SCHOOL RESIDENTIAL	B133	6.3	M
HARVARD EXECUTIVE EDUCATION PROGRAM	B133	24.5	M
HARVARD UNIVERSITY (HARVARD BUSINESS SCHOO)			
HARVARD JR WORLD ENCYCLOPEDIA	B410	5.0	S
EASTERN GUILD INC			
HARVARD MEDICAL SCHOOL HEALTH LETTER	B420	11.3	M-P
HARVARD UNIVERSITY PRESS	B410	4.5	M
HARVARD UNIVERSITY (HARVARD UNIVERSITY PR)			
HARVEST BLEND INSTANT HOT CEREAL	F122	36.2	M-S
RALSTON PURINA CO			
HARVEST MAID FOOD DEHYDRATOR	H220	2.6	M
ALTERNATIVE PIONEERING SYS I			
HARVEST TIME CANNING JARS & LIDS	H235	13.4	M
STONE CONTAINER CORP (NATL PKGING CONSMR GRP)			
HARVESTORE GRAIN SYSTEM	T520	3.6	S-O
SMITH A O CORP (SMITH A O HARV PRO INC)			
HARVEY PROBBER FURNITURE	H120	2.3	P
PROBBER HARVEY INC			
HARVEY RADIO	G605	4.8	M-P
HARVEY GROUP INC (HARVEY RADIO)			
HARVEYS BRISTOL CREAM SHERRY	F320	903.5	M-S
HEUBLEIN INC (HARVEY JOHN & SONS LTD)			
*HARVEYS RESORT HOTEL LAKE TAHOE NEVADA	T431	8.7	M
*HARVEYS SKINDIVING SUITS	G490	18.3	M
HARVEYS WINES	F320	23.6	S
HEUBLEIN INC (HARVEY JOHN & SONS LTD)			
*HARVIE & HUDSON (APPAREL-MEN)	G607	1.8	M
HARWOOD PERFORMANCE RACING COMPONENTS	T154	6.3	M
HARWOOD PERFORM SALES INC			
HARZFELDS (JEWELRY)	G606	.9	M
HARZFELDS (APPAREL-WOMEN)	G607	22.9	M
GARFINCKEL BROOKS BR M & R I (HARZFELDS INC)			
HASBRO DOLLS & ACCESSORIES	G450	1,152.5	N-S
HASBRO TOYS	G450	1,979.1	N-S
HASBRO INDUSTRIES INC			
HASPEL SPORTSUITS MEN	A112	9.4	M
HASPEL SPORTSUITS MEN & WOMEN	A112	31.9	M-P
HASPEL SPORTSWEAR MEN	A115	2.1	M
HASPEL SPORTSWEAR MEN & WOMEN	A115	21.4	M-P
HASPEL SUITS MEN & WOMEN	A112	79.1	M-P
HASPEL SUITS & SPORTSWEAR MEN & WOMEN	A112	3.9	M
HASPEL BROTHERS INC			
HASSELBLAD CAMERA & ACCESSORIES	G230	8.1	M
GILLETTE CO (BRAUN NORTH AMERICA)			
HASSELFORS MARINE HARDWARE	G490	3.0	M
GENERAL SPORTING GOODS CORP (HASSELFORS STLES MAR D)			
*HASTINGS (APPAREL-MEN)	G607	16.7	M
HASTINGS AUTOMOTIVE PRODUCTS	T154	27.0	R
HASTINGS MFG CO			
*HASTINGS MUTUAL INSURANCE	B220	6.4	O
HATHAWAY SHIRTS MEN	A111	11.6	P-S
WARNACO INC (HATHAWAY C F CO)			
HATTERAS YACHTS	G430	48.2	M
AMF INC (HATTERAS YACHT CO)			
*HATTIE (APPAREL-WOMEN)	G607	12.2	M
*HAUMAN HOUSE INC (MISCELLANEOUS)	G608	66.9	M-P
HAV-A-TAMPA CIGARS	G112	15.9	M-S
ELI SECURITIES CO (HAV CORP)			
HAVAHART TRAPS	T550	4.5	M-P
ALLCOCK MFG CO			
*HAVANA FLORIDA CO (MISCELLANEOUS)	G608	.9	M
HAVANA WEED OIL FRAGRANCE FOR WOMEN & MEN	D113	4.7	S
REGENCY COSMETICS INC			
*HAVERFORDS (MISCELLANEOUS)	G608	.9	M
*HAVILAND CHINA	H111	32.8	M-S
*HAWAII HOMES REAL ESTATE	G520	10.2	M
HAWAII RESORT PROMOTION	T432	155.0	M
HAWAII STATE OF (HAWAII VISITORS BUREAU)			
HAWAIIAN CANNED & FROZEN PUNCH	F223	5.0	O
HAWAIIAN CANNED PUNCH	F223	2,243.6	P-N-S-O
REYNOLDS R J INDUSTRIES INC (RJR FOODS INC)			
*HAWAIIAN ISLANDS RESORT PROMOTION	T432	58.1	M
HAWAIIAN PUNCH POWDERED DRINK MIXES	F223	6,088.7	M-P-N-S-O
REYNOLDS R J INDUSTRIES INC (RJR FOODS INC)			
HAWAIIAN TROPIC SUN & SKI PRODUCTS	D111	18.2	M
HAWAIIAN TROPIC SUNTAN PRODUCTS	D111	19.4	S-O
TANNING RESEARCH LABS INC (RON RICE BEACH PRODS)			
*HAWK ENTERPRISES (MISCELLANEOUS)	G608	.6	M
*HAWK REAL ESTATE	G520	34.6	M-P
HAWK TUNE-UP EQUIPMENT	T154	2.3	M
PALPAC			
HAWKER BUSINESS JETS	T300	40.5	M
HAWKER SIDDELEY GROUP LTD (HAWKER SIDDELEY AVIAT)			
*HAWORTH OFFICE FURNITURE	B313	86.3	M
*HAWTHORN BOOKS	B410	$ 25.9	M
HAY-ADAMS HOTEL WASHINGTON	T431	.9	M
SHELDON MAGAZINE ENTERPRISES			
*HAYASHI GRAPHICS (MISCELLANEOUS)	G608	.9	M
*HAYES-LEGER LTD (HOUSEHOLD)	G605	1.9	M
HAYES NATIONAL BANK	B151	.1	O
CHARTER NEW YORK CORP			
HAYMAKER SPORTSWEAR WOMEN	A115	15.5	M-P
GENERAL MILLS INC (HAYMAKER SPORTS INC)			
*HAYNES PUBLICATIONS	B410	10.1	M
HAYOUN SKIN CARE CLINIC	D240	7.4	M
HAYOUN CLINIC			
HAYS IGNITION SYSTEMS	T154	1.0	M
HAYS SALES			
*HAYSTACK MOUNTAIN SKI AREA	T432	.5	O
HEAD-BED BEDDING	H120	8.8	P
BOARDMAN AVERY LTD (HEAD-BED DIV)			
HEAD CAMPS RESIDENTIAL	B133	8.3	M
AMF INC (AMF HEAD DIV)			
*HEAD SHAMPOO	D142	207.2	M-S
HEAD & SHOULDERS LOTION SHAMPOO	D142	315.7	M-P
HEAD & SHOULDERS SHAMPOOS	D142	8,667.3	N-S
PROCTER & GAMBLE CO			
HEAD SKIS	G470	30.8	M
AMF INC (AMF HEAD DIV)			
HEAD SPORTING FOOTWEAR MEN	A132	56.5	M
HEAD SPORTSWEAR MEN & WOMEN	A115	28.2	M
AMF INC (AMF HEAD SPORTSWEAR IN)			
HEAD START KERATIN SHAMPOO	D142	9.6	M
HEAD START VITAMIN & MINERAL COMPOUND	D215	813.2	M-S
BRASWELL INC (COSVETIC LABS CO)			
HEAD STRONG 1 VITAMINS	D215	25.3	M
WEIDER COMMUNICATIONS			
HEAD TENNIS RACKETS	G490	275.1	M-S
AMF INC (AMF HEAD DIV)			
HEADHUGGER HAIR PIECES	D144	6.4	M
AMORA INDUSTRIES INC			
*HEADSTART HAIR FOR MEN HAIRPIECES	D144	9.1	M
HEALD CYCLE KITS	G440	50.9	M
HEALD LAWN & GARDEN MACHINE KITS	T610	47.5	M
HEALD INC			
*HEALTH CLUB FOR WOMEN	D240	2.0	M
*HEALTH MAINTENANCE ORGANIZATION OF PENNSYLVANIA	B210	5.2	O
HEALTH-O-METER SCALES	H150	12.5	M
CONTINENTAL SCALE CORP			
HEALTH-TEX WEARING APPAREL CHILDREN	A115	752.9	M-P-S
CHESEBROUGH-PONDS INC (HEALTH-TEX INC)			
HEALTHKNIT MULTI-PRODUCT ADVERTISING MEN	A121	115.8	M
STANWOOD CORP (STANDARD KNIT MILLS IN)			
HEALTHWAYS DIVING INSTRUMENTS & ACCESSORIES	G222	6.1	M
HEALTHWAYS SCUBA EQUIPMENT	G490	2.0	M
LEISURE DYNAMICS INC (HEALTHWAYS)			
HEALTHY HAIR HAIR VITAMINS	D215	40.9	S
PALM BEACH BEAUTY PRODS CO			
*HEALY INC (JEWELRY)	G606	1.1	M
HEARST CORP NEWSPAPERS	B420	154.1	S
HEARST RADIO STATIONS	B430	357.3	S-O
HEARST TV STATIONS	B440	1.9	O
HEARST CORP			
HEART/AMERICA WOOD STAIN	H541	91.2	S
SCHERING-PLOUGH CORP			
*HEART LAND (MISCELLANEOUS)	G608	1.4	M
*HEART OF ARKANSAS RESORT PROMOTION	T432	6.1	M
HEART OF THE 60S RECORDINGS	H330	138.8	S
MISCELLANEOUS RECORD OFFERS			
HEARTLAND NATURAL CEREALS	F122	293.8	S
HEARTLAND NATURAL CEREALS SWEEPSTAKES	F122	114.8	M
HEARTLAND NATURAL SYRUP	F111	19.9	S
PET INC (PET GROCERY PROD DIV)			
*HEARTS & FLOWERS FLORIST INC WEDDING SERVICES	G602	.7	M
HEAT-CATCHER HEATING SYSTEM HOME	H522	.5	M
LASSY TOOLS INC			
*HEAT KEEPER HEATING SYSTEM HOME	H522	2.7	M
HEAT WAVE PORTABLE HEATERS	H220	16.1	S
INTERMATIC INC			
HEATH CANDY	F211	225.4	S
HEATH L S & SONS INC			
HEATH CO (MISCELLANEOUS)	G608	295.7	M-P-S-O
SCHLUMBERGER LTD (HEATH CO)			
HEATHROW HOTEL LONDON	T431	4.8	M
LEX SERVICE GROUP LTD			
HEATILATOR FIREPLACES HOME	H522	135.2	M-S
HEATILATOR FIREPLACES HOME DEALERS	H522	.3	O
VEGA INDUSTRIES INC (HEATILATOR DIV)			
HEAVEN HILL BOURBON WHISKEY	F330	50.7	O
HEAVEN HILL DISTILLERS INC			
*HEAVENLY VALLEY SKI AREA LAKE TAHOE	T431	39.2	O
HEAVY DUTY DOORS HOME	H525	.4	M
HEAVY DUTY MFG CO INC			
HEAVY METAL MAGAZINE	B420	38.3	M
TWENTY FIRST CENTURY COMM I			
*HEBREW ARTS SCHOOL RESIDENTIAL	B133	.3	M
HEBREW NATIONAL KOSHER FRANKS	F150	1,251.0	S
HEBREW NATIONAL KOSHER MEAT PRODUCTS	F150	1.7	S
COLGATE-PALMOLIVE CO (HEBREW NATL KOSHER F I)			
HECHT CO (APPAREL-WOMEN)	G607	10.4	M
HECHT CO (MISCELLANEOUS)	G608	3.5	M
HECHT CO GENERAL PROMOTION	G608	5.8	M
MAY DEPARTMENT STORES CO (HECHT CO)			
HECKERS FLOUR	F113	18.0	M
STANDARD MILLING CO			
HECKLER & KOCH GUNS	G420	1.4	M
SECURITY ARMS CO INC (HECKLER & KOCH INC)			
*HECKS (MISCELLANEOUS)	G608	73.2	S-O
*HECTORS PLANT COLLARS	T540	25.5	S
HEDDON FISHING EQUIPMENT	G410	49.8	M
KIDDE WALTER & CO INC (HEDDONS JAMES SONS)			
*HEDENKAMP CARDS AGENTS WANTED	G571	46.1	M
HEDMAN HEDDERS	T154	2.3	M
HEDMAN MFG CORP			

MEDIA USED: M–MAGAZINES, P–NEWSPAPER SUPPS., N–NETWORK TV, S–SPOT TV, R–NETWORK RADIO, O–OUTDOOR

*Company and Brand name are the same.

EXHIBIT 7.12

LNA ad dollar summary and brand index. (Courtesy: Leading National Advertisers, Inc.)

EXHIBIT 7.13

Various media categories demonstrate wide variances in cost and CPMS.

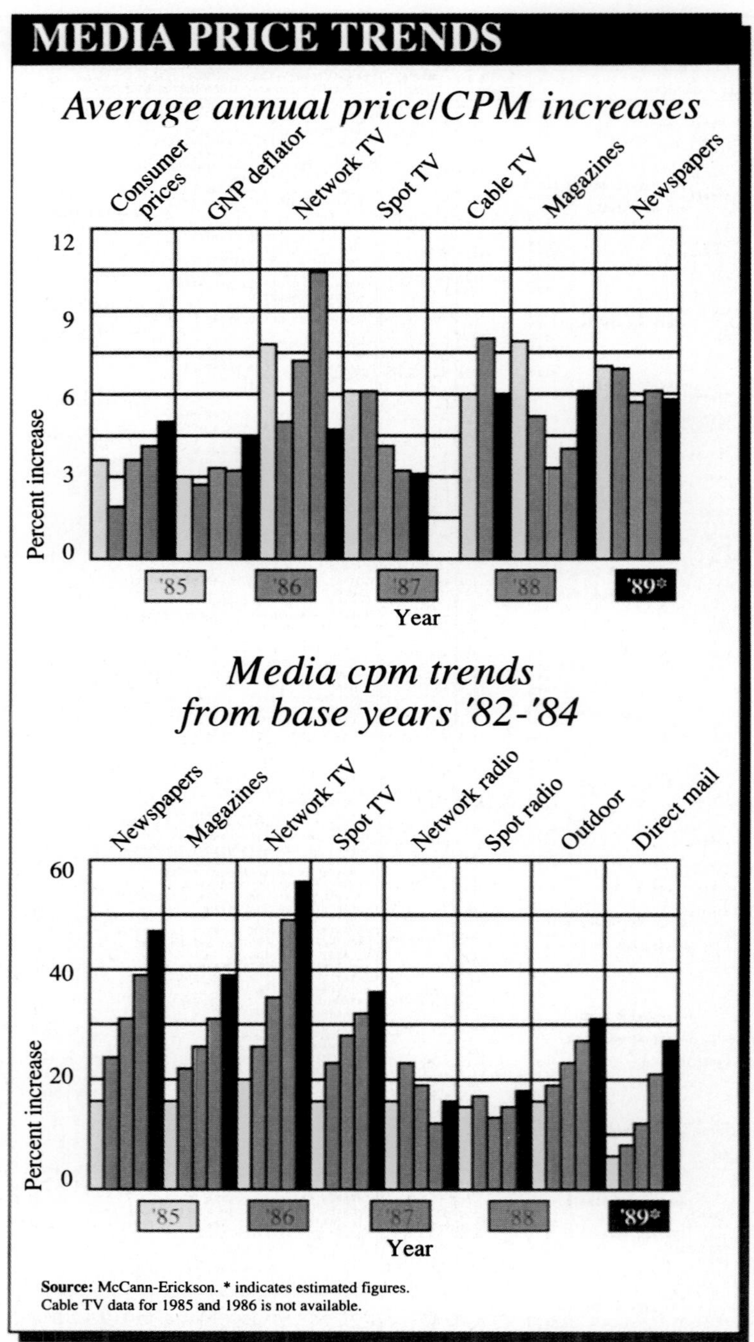

ORGANIZATION OF THE MEDIA FUNCTION

As media costs have escalated, advertisers and agencies have tried to increase efficiency through the organization of the media function. In some sense, the reexamination of media management centers on three factors:

1. *Cost efficiency*. Advertisers are demanding that agencies deliver a narrowly targeted audience at the lowest possible cost. These are often incompatible goals. As we saw earlier in this chapter, CPM delivery rises significantly as we reach more narrowly defined target segments. And as we discussed in Chapter 6, advertisers are turning to independent media-buying

Qualitative factors have given advertisers new information about how to be more cost efficient in reaching heavy-user brand segments. In addition to totaling the *large quantity* of merchandise 12–23-year-olds purchase, life-style research has uncovered the fact that they are *more materialistic* than any age group has ever been. They also pay more attention to the *quality* of the material, than previous generations.

organizations to attain cost efficiency—or at least to provide the threat of competition to their agency media departments.

2. *Qualitative factors*. The renewed attention to the media function has led to an emphasis on marketing factors beyond simple cost efficiency. Issues such as choosing the best media plan to break through communication clutter, knowing how to gain maximum impact in the right markets at the right time, and being able to concentrate on heavy-user brand segments have become as important as the cost of advertising.[6]
3. *Role of the media department*. The media department has become a central part of the advertising process within most agencies. Since the advent of computer technology, the media department is a primary source of marketing information throughout the agency. Many advertisers see the growing importance of the media function as a healthy development that will bring a more balanced approach to the marketing-creative-media triad so crucial to successful advertising.

SUMMARY

The media function will become even more complex in the future. Accompanying this complexity will be a greater financial risk to the advertiser. Agencies will be asked to justify their media planning in more detail than ever before. Basically, the media function will be characterized by three major trends during the decade of the 1990's.[7]

1. *Continued media fragmentation*. Even experienced media buyers are amazed at the extent of the growth in individual media choices. Independent, syndicated, and cable TV all offer major challenges to network television. Daily newspaper circulation has increased some 10 percent in the last decade, but suburban weeklies and shoppers have proliferated even faster, and more are being established every day. The number of consumer magazines has grown by 50 percent in the last 10 to 15 years.
2. *Regionalization and localization*. National advertisers realize that network spots and full-run magazine buys do not deliver uniform advertising weight in each market. Increasingly, they are supplementing national advertising buys with allocations to individual local markets. In the future, we will see a greater proportion of media dollars spent at the local and regional levels. We will also see both network TV and national magazines offering advertisers more less-than-full-run buying opportunities.
3. *Changes in the management of the media function*. The basic media relationship between clients and agencies is changing. The fee and commission structure for paying agencies will be negotiated to a greater extent in the future; the traditional 15 percent commission will soon be the exception rather than the rule. Agencies will face competition from both independent media buyers and in-house media departments established by clients. There has even been talk of a return to brokerage of media buying, whereby agencies buy large blocks of space and time and then resell them to clients. This idea of space brokerage was discussed in Chapter 5 as the beginning of the modern advertising agency.

In the following chapters, we will examine each of the media available to the media planner as well as some promotional techniques associated with advertising. As you will see, the complex nature of the media function requires a media planner who is well versed in quantitative skills, marketing strategy, and, naturally, all aspects of advertising.

SUGGESTED EXERCISES

- Bring in three pieces of direct-mail advertising you have received. Compare these pieces to traditional media advertising in copy and approach.
- Choose a magazine advertisement for a consumer product and rewrite it as a radio and a television commercial, and then as a newspaper advertisement.

[6]Herb Maneloveg, "Media Department and 'Let's Make a Deal,'" *Advertising Age*, May 16, 1988, p. 18.
[7]Herbert Zeltner, "Interesting Times, Yes; Predictable, No," *Advertising Age*, November 30, 1987, p. S-2.

- Invite an executive from a local advertising agency to discuss the organization of the media and creative functions in his or her agency.

QUESTIONS

1. Discuss the concept of mass and less-than-mass advertising media.
2. Discuss the major advantages and disadvantages of the following advertising media:
   (a) newspapers
   (b) television
   (c) direct mail
   (d) radio
   (e) magazines
   (f) out-of-home
3. Successful advertising usually begins with the narrow identification of a target market. Explain.
4. Compare and contrast marketing and advertising goals.
5. Discuss the relationship between creative elements and advertising media planning.
6. Briefly discuss the Advertising Research Foundation model for evaluating media.
7. Describe the media concepts of reach, frequency, and continuity. Which of these is usually not controlled by the media planner?
8. Discuss the idea of effective reach and effective frequency. How do they relate to the notion of ''quality of exposure''?
9. How does the media planner use flighting to extend the advertising budget?
10. How will audience fragmentation affect the media-buying process in the future?

READINGS

BARBAN, ARNOLD M., DONALD JUGENHEIMER, AND PETER TURK: *Advertising Media Sourcebook* (Lincolnwood, IL: NTC Business Books, 1988).

HALL, ROBERT W.: *Media Math* (Lincolnwood, IL: NTC Business Books, 1988).

KAPLAN, RACHEL: ''What Can Media Planners Expect in the 1990s?'' *Inside Print,* January 1989, p. 51.

LANCASTER, KENT, AND HELEN E. KATZ: *Strategic Media Planning* (Lincolnwood, IL: NTC Business Books, 1988).

MANDESE, JOE: ''Planners: The Real Story,'' *Marketing & Media Decisions,* October 1988, p. 36.

MCGANN, ANTHONY F., AND J. THOMAS RUSSELL: *Advertising Media: A Managerial Approach* (Homewood, IL: Richard D. Irwin, Inc., 1988).

MUELLER, GARY: ''Ten Guidelines for Producing Creative Media Plans,'' *Journal of Media Planning,* Fall 1988, p. 40.

SISSORS, JACK, AND LINCOLN BUMBA: *Advertising Media Planning* (Lincolnwood, IL: NTC Business Books, 1988).

SWENSEN, CHESTER A.: ''How to Sell a Segmented Market,'' *Journal of Business,* January/February 1988, p. 18.

CASE HISTORY

Portable Heaters Media Plan

STRATEGIES

Target Audience. Adults 25–54 with HHI of $20M+. This group represents the single largest cluster of homeowners most likely to purchase heat-saving devices. Emphasis should be placed on male purchaser.

Seasonality. Schedule support, to the extent affordable, to provide continuous activity during late August–February. This period accounts for over 95 percent of total unit sales.

Geography. Allocate funds in accordance with market-volume contribution. A national/local spending analysis reveals that markets displaying 100+ BDIs represent 35 percent of total volume. The resulting national/local allocation is:

	BDI 100 +	*BDI 99–*	*Total*
%US	20.5	79.5	100
National $	1,460M	5,850M	7,310M
Local $	1,690M	—	1,690M
Total $	3,150M	5,850M	9,000M
%	35%	65%	100%

Communication Goals. The effective frequency level for both national and high BDI markets will be 2+ exposures over a typical four-week advertising period. This relatively low frequency goal reflects:

- The lack of competitive advertising presence in this category
- The clean and straightforward presentation of product benefits (rather than image) in creative executions

Recognizing the different, "selling environment" between high and low BDI markets, the effective reach goal in spot markets is adjusted upward to reflect the increased household penetration opportunities existing there.

National: 50 High BDI: 66

PLAN DESCRIPTION

National Media. The recommended media plan places 67 percent of total national expenditures into network television, with the remaining 33 percent allocated to national consumer magazines. All media activity has been scheduled during a six-month period, mid-August through late January.

NFL Football TV represents the primary media vehicle, accounting for 41 percent of this total. Activity is scheduled in an alternate week sponsorship of the "Half-Time" on the Monday Night NFL Football TV broadcasts. This sponsorship consists of a 5-second voice-over billboard and two 30-second commercials within each of the "Half-Time"shows on a total of ten different dates.

Twenty percent of the total budget has been identified for primetime scatter announcements scheduled over a 14-week period.

Six percent of the total budget has been allocated for 35 participations in the NBC "Today" show. Two 30-second announcements per week will be scheduled for 18 weeks. Each announcement will appear in the first network TV break position within the weather forecast.

All broadcast activity is scheduled so that continuity is maintained throughout the winter season. Lighter-weight levels, however, are exhibited in December and January because:

- The preoccupation of consumers with the holidays during this period is felt to have a negative effect on generating sales.
- Monthly sales patterns reveal that consumers are more inclined to purchase a heater during the late fall and early winter months in preparation for the colder weather temperatures.

Thirty-three percent of the total national budget has been allocated to consumer magazines. Activity is scheduled to run within eight different publications. Magazines were selected on the basis of their efficiencies and reach of the target group, as well as their appropriate editorial environment. Also taken into consideration in the magazine selection process was the "merchandising potential" these books would have with the distributor force. Minimum insertion frequency for each of the publications is as follows:

Magazine	*Minimum Frequency*	*Schedule*
Weeklies		
Time	5	Once every 6 weeks
Sports Illustrated	5	Once every 6 weeks
Newsweek	5	Once every 6 weeks
Monthlies		
Better Homes & Gardens	3	Once every other month
House Beautiful	3	Once every other month
Money	3	Once every other month
Annuals/Bi-Annuals		
BH&G Home Energy Ideas	1	Once per season
House Beautiful's Home Remodeling	1	Once per season

The print activity begins with the corporate spread, with subsequent ads, spreads and pages featuring specific products. Overall magazine activity is scheduled to ensure continuity throughout the six-month selling season.

Local Media. Recognizing the particular regional sales skew of these products, 18 percent of the total media budget has been allocated to spot TV markets providing BDIs of 100 + (20.5 percent U.S.). Activity has been planned in a news/late fringe mix to take advantage of local market efficiencies/viewing patterns.

Spot TV activity has been planned for 10 continuous weeks and frontloaded in these markets to follow monthly sales trends.

CHANGES VERSUS YEAR AGO

The following changes have been implemented to improve upon last year's plan.

- Homeowners have been added to the demographic definition for magazine selection to better aid in pinpointing potential prospects.
- Though still skewed toward men, less emphasis is being placed on them in order to capitalize on the joint (male and female) purchase decision.
- Increased attempts will be made to further merchandise our involvement in the NBC "Today" show to dealers by buying Fridays only. (Heater sales are concentrated on the weekend.)
- "Today" show commercials will be 25 seconds in length, with the resident weatherman giving a 5-second opening lead-in to the commercials.
- Prime-time network scatter TV has been added to the schedule to capitalize on the reach capabilities of this medium. It is also highly merchandisable to the trade.
- The print schedule provides a more extensive mix of books, extending the presence in the newsweekly and home categories.
- Specific additions to the print recommendation are *Newsweek, House Beautiful, BH&G Home Energy Ideas, House Beautiful's Home Remodeling,* and *Money*. Further, minimum frequency requirements are satisfied with each publication's recommended number of insertions.

PERFORMANCE AGAINST STRATEGIC GOALS

Strategy	*Plan Performance*
Demographic: Adults 25–54/HHI $20M+. (Emphasis on male purchaser.)	The plan delivers a 4-week national target audience reach of 74%, with an average frequency of 2.2. Impression delivery is split 59%/41% between men and women.
Communication Goals	The plan achieves a typical 4-week reach of 45% at the 2+ exposure level. While this represents a 41% increase versus a year ago, it is short of going-in objectives. This is due, for the most part, to the use of spread units during the campaign's introduction; they were judged indispensable during the introductory phase.
Seasonality: Schedule support leading into and during the peak sales period.	TV and print activity is scheduled from August through January. This provides continuity throughout the peak selling season.
Geography: National support/local overlay to reflect regional purchase patterns.	The plan uses network TV, national magazines, and spot TV to align support with U.S. population and volume contribution.
Environment: Select prestigious, highly visible vehicles.	The plan utilizes the leading magazines in each editorial classification. NFL Monday Night Football is one of the highest-rated prime-time shows.

	Typical 4-week (2nd Qtr. Average)			*Total Activity (2nd Qtr. Total)*	
	Reach/Frequency	**GRPs**	**ER*@2+**	**Reach/Frequency**	**GRPs**
NFL Football	14%/2.9x	120		59%/5.1x	300
Today Show	14%/1.3x	18		39%/2.7x	104
Prime scatter	29%/1.4x	48		72%/3.3x	240
Total network	59%/3.1x	186		89%/7.2x	644
Print	47%/1.5x	72		59%/3.5x	208
Total national (79.5% US)	78%/3.3x	258	51%	93%/9.2x	852
Spot TV (20.5% US)	65%/3.7x	240		86%/7.0x	600
Total nat'l/spot	84%/5.9x	498	65%	96%/14.9x	1452

*Effective frequency.

Portable Heaters Media Plan A25–54 GRPs

Month / Media	April May June July Aug Sept Oct Nov Dec Jan Feb March	Total $(000)
Network TV		
NFL Football	30 30 30 30 30 30 30 30 30 30	$2,930.2
Today Show	5 5 5 5 5 5 5 5 5 5 5 5 5 5 5 5 5 4 4 4 2	$ 391.5
Prime Scatter	24 24 12 12 12 12 12 12 12 12 12 12 12 12 12 12 12	$1,445.0
Total National TV		$4,770.3
Spot TV (20.5% US)	60 60 60 60 60 60 60 60 60 60	$1,960.0
Magazines	S P S P S P	$2,280.3
Sports Illustrated	S S S P	
Newsweek	S S S P P	
Money	— S ———— P —— —— P ——	
Better Homes	— S ———— P ——— P —	
House Beautiful	— S ———— P —— —— P ——	
BHG—Home Remodeling	S ————————————————————	
HB—Remodeling	S ————————————————————	
Grand Total		$9,010.6

S = Spread 4-Color Bleed; P = Page 4-Color Bleed

Courtesy: Independent Media Services, Inc.

EIGHT

Using Television

Since television arrived on the scene in the late 1940s, it has become more than just another medium of communication. Once an interesting novelty that brought Milton Berle into our living rooms, television is now part of the fabric of our lives. Television is *the* most important aspect of many people's daily routine; they plan their schedule around their favorite news and entertainment programming (see Exhibit 8.1).

Today children who haven't learned their ABC's can recite commercial jingles by heart. When "Monday Night Football" goes into overtime, employers can predict that tardiness and absenteeism will be high the next morning. What we "know" is important is largely what Peter Jennings, Tom Brokaw, and Dan Rather told us was impor-

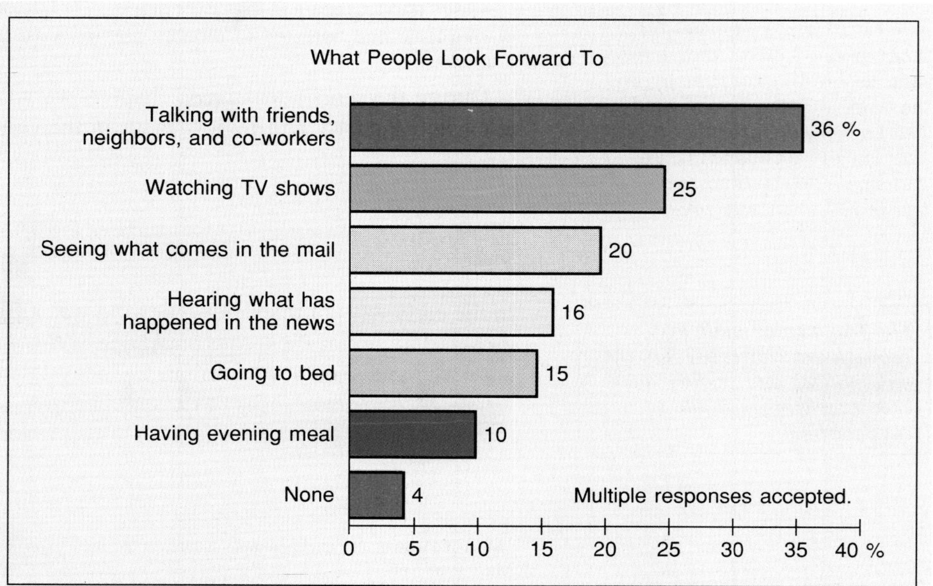

EXHIBIT 8.1

Television has become part of American culture as well as a medium of communication. (Courtesy: Television Information Office.)

tant last evening. Television serves as a validation of reality in America. In 1983, household viewing of television passed the seven-hour mark for the first time.

Although the numbers tell only part of the story, they are impressive. According to the Television Information Office, of total American homes:

- 98 percent have television
- 96 percent have color television
- 60 percent have two or more sets
- 59 percent have a VCR
- 53 percent buy basic cable
- 31 percent receive 30 or more channels
- 28 percent buy one or more pay channels
- 2 percent have satellite dishes

Despite its ubiquity, television is a medium very much in transition. This transition can be traced to the declining role of the big three networks during the last decade.

> At one time, discussions about the TV business would begin and end with the Big Three networks. Now such discussions merely begin with the networks. That is because the networks are crumbling—and the action is moving to competitors.
>
> Not so long ago, any American who wanted to watch TV on Sunday evening could only choose between "Walt Disney," "The Ed Sullivan Show," and "The F.B.I." Pretty tame stuff. Now a viewer can watch bicycle racing on ESPN, rock videos on MTV, congressional hearings on C-SPAN, and young people's programming on Nickelodeon. A viewer can watch movies and first-run syndicated shows on independent TV stations. He can buy zirconia diamonds from Home Shopping Channel, check for hurricanes on The Weather Channel, and ask Dr. Ruth how to have the perfect orgasm![1]

Television networks are facing *heavy competition* from independent TV stations and cable. So, *Capital Cities/ABC* acquired an interest in In-Store Advertising of New York, which will have electronic message boards hanging over supermarket aisles in 7,000 stores by 1991. The deal will enable *the network* to sell time on the boards *as package time* with TV buys of advertisers—another method to increase their revenue base.

The "demographic" revolution is changing lifestyles, necessitating a change in television programming to appeal to the new, less defined audiences. While young professionals who have high incomes might be considered prime targets for extensive lawn equipment for their upscale homes, they have little leisure time to actually do the work. Instead, a new study, *The Lawn and Gardening Market,* actually recommends advertising "luxury timesavers" and professional services.

Thomas F. Leahy, president of the CBS Marketing Division, summed up the networks' view of this new world of television:

> We, as a television industry, will need to develop programming that is tailored to appeal to newly identified, high-value audiences. As we all know, the United States is in the midst of a demographic revolution that will last well into the next century: "baby boomers" are aging; older adults are living longer, wealthier, more active lives; and birth rates, already at historic lows, continue to plunge. Youth markets are losing purchasing power while adult and senior markets are swelling their ranks and gaining in purchasing power. . . . Lifestyles are more varied and less defined than ever before. Traditional demographic views of the market are too simplistic and outdated to reliably predict consumer needs and preferences.[2]

During the remainder of this chapter, we will examine the various elements of the television industry and review them in the context of a radically changing medium.

THE FRAGMENTED TELEVISION AUDIENCE

The fragmented audience. *Technological diversity has created smaller and smaller audience segments available to each medium.*

In the early days of television, viewing was a family activity. Each evening the family gathered around a flickering black-and-white set to watch the limited offerings of the networks and their local affiliates. Today television is much like radio in that each family member has access to his or her own set and individual program choice has replaced family viewing. The growth of program availability has made the appeal of

[1]Merrill Brown, "Can Elephants Learn to Waltz?" *Journalism and Mass Communication Administrator,* May 1988, pp. 7–8.

[2]Robert F. Leahy, remarks to the Rochester Advertising Council, Rochester, NY, June 23, 1988, p. 8.

Individual television viewing has replaced family viewing, which creates opportunities for *selective appeals*. Skippy Peanut Butter, long known for its youth orientation, has launched a new campaign that appeals to the fastest growing segment of peanut butter eaters—*adults*. The commercials will feature *fun* and *versatility* of the product. "Dipping" pretzels and crackers into the jar has replaced smiling kids, with white bread-laden peanut butter. These ads will be aired during the late-night, "snack-viewing time."

Cost per prospect. *Method of calculating relative cost of a media vehicle which considers only prime prospects for a product or brand.*

Offsetting higher costs of television advertising will be less waste circulation and more accurate forecasting of the viewing audience. When Tempo Industries of New York launched the first advertising for Maccabee beer on *Late Night With David Letterman,* it *knew* its 30-second spots would be reaching its prime market—young to middle age ethnic beer drinkers, in large Eastern cities.

Television has tremendous flexibility in presenting messages and is able to *reach all groups*. It's the number one medium among *national* advertisers. Sears is using a *heavy media schedule* to launch its switch to everyday low pricing and other marketing strategies. It used to consider print media, such as Sunday newspaper inserts, the *only* way clothing and descriptive goods, such as tools and appliances, could be adequately promoted. Sears' stores will also feature "videos" of recent commercials.

New products have the *best* opportunity to inform their target markets via television. In introducing a new category of infant nutrition products, Carnation will use television advertising to reach "busy moms and dads, who have 'given up' newspaper reading."

individual viewership even greater. The proliferation of channels has created an increasingly fragmented viewership. There would be little reason for each member of a household to have a television set if there were only three choices of what to watch.

As we noted earlier, almost one-third of U.S. households receive more than 30 television channels. If you add to this number the growing ownership of VCRs, most of which are used to view movies rather than prerecorded TV material, it is obvious that each program alternative will reach a smaller share of audience in future years. This decrease in average program share is exacerbated by the fact that overall television viewership can grow only through population increases or higher levels of viewing; and in recent years, both have been relatively flat. If the viewing pie can't expand significantly, then the slices must become smaller.

The end result of this audience fragmentation will be more expense to advertisers and a new marketing strategy for the medium. As we noted in Chapter 7, Basic Media Strategy, as audience levels decrease, inevitably CPM levels increase. Television CPM levels will certainly continue to increase during the 1990s, but offsetting this higher cost will be greater selectivity of market segments, less waste circulation, and perhaps a lower cost per *prospect* than is the case today. One forecast about television advertising in the year 2000 is that a two-tier system will be in place. The first will be the mass audience delivered by the networks. Even if network share should fall to the 50 percent level, this would still be a tremendously large audience. The second tier will be composed of cable networks, independent stations, advertiser-supported videocassettes, syndicated programming, and other systems. This second tier will provide advertisers with a targeted media alternative to supplement and extend the basic audience exposure achieved by the networks. In this view, the new broadcast services will ultimately provide more competition to narrowly targeted media such as magazines and radio than to mass television-broadcasting outlets.

Frankly, one doesn't have to be much of a prophet to foresee most of these events. Already ESPN and Turner Broadcasting are successfully competing for NFL football and NBA basketball games, which was unheard of only a few years ago. The question is not whether the television audience will be fragmented (it already is), but to what degree and in what direction.

TELEVISION AS AN ADVERTISING MEDIUM

Advantages

Television advertising encompasses several of the senses in a sight, sound, and motion presentation that gives advertisers tremendous creative flexibility. An additional advantage is the degree of audience penetration achieved by the medium. Unlike other media, there are virtually no groups of nonusers of television. From teenagers to the elderly, television is an integral part of most people's day. Exhibit 8.2 shows that the lowest category of television usage is among teenage boys, of whom *only* 68 percent watch every day.

High coverage and maximum creative possibilities have established television as the number-one medium among national advertisers. Almost 55 percent of all national advertising dollars is spent on some form of television. Magazines, which occupy the second position, get only 18 percent of national advertising dollars. Given the expenditures by national advertisers, it is not surprising that the Television Information Office reports that 57 percent of consumers say they are most likely to learn about new products through television.

Disadvantages

Cost. Television is an expensive medium. The typical prime-time spot costs $150,000, and even a commercial on your favorite daytime soap opera can run $25,000 or more. Production of a single network-quality commercial may cost

EXHIBIT 8.2

No audience segment is immune to the power of television. (Courtesy: Television Advertising Bureau.)

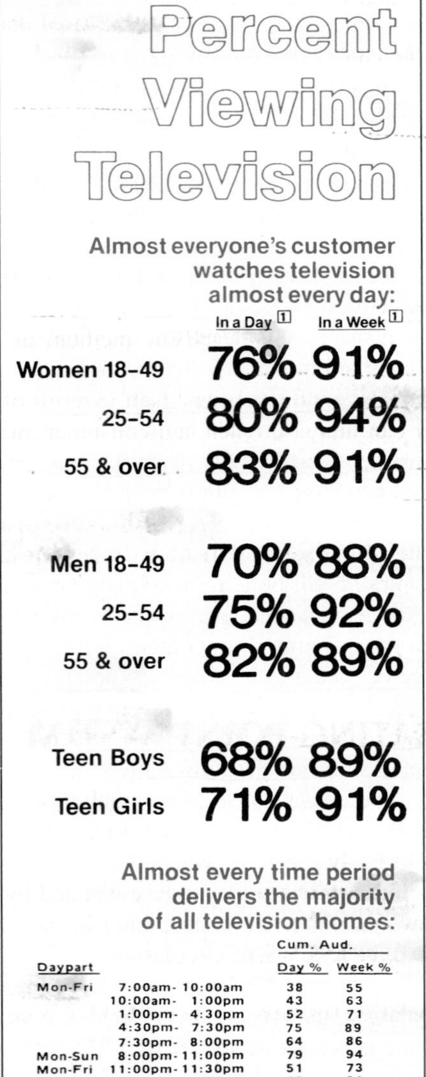

Percent Viewing Television

Almost everyone's customer watches television almost every day:

	In a Day [1]	In a Week [1]
Women 18–49	76%	91%
25–54	80%	94%
55 & over	83%	91%
Men 18–49	70%	88%
25–54	75%	92%
55 & over	82%	89%
Teen Boys	68%	89%
Teen Girls	71%	91%

Almost every time period delivers the majority of all television homes:

Daypart		Cum. Aud. Day %	Cum. Aud. Week %
Mon-Fri	7:00am- 10:00am	38	55
	10:00am- 1:00pm	43	63
	1:00pm- 4:30pm	52	71
	4:30pm- 7:30pm	75	89
	7:30pm- 8:00pm	64	86
Mon-Sun	8:00pm- 11:00pm	79	94
Mon-Fri	11:00pm- 11:30pm	51	73
	11:30pm- 1:00am	40	61

Two disadvantages may impede some advertisers from using television in the future—its progressively increasing *cost* and *clutter*. As audience size decreases for a network, the cost of sponsorship increases. And, with 15-second commercials, viewers may be unable to clearly distinguish individual messages. Jay Kuhnie, national ad manager for Chrysler Corporation's Dodge, said, "15s have added to the clutter and have helped push consumers into zapping past commercials."

> ***Clutter.*** *Refers to proliferation of commercials (in a medium) that reduces the impact of any single message.*

$100,000, with some costing double or triple that. As we have seen, the CPM of these commercials is increasing at a faster rate than actual cost because of audience deflation.

Clutter. Advertisers' criticism of commercial clutter has risen dramatically in recent years. Most advertisers think that the level of television clutter makes achieving consumer awareness of any specific message difficult. The increase in clutter is only partly due to an increase in total time devoted to commercials; it is also a result of shortening their length. For instance, in 1965, approximately 70 percent of all television commercials were one minute long. Beginning in 1970, advertisers moved to the 30-second commercial, and this became the standard length. Then, in 1986, the three major networks agreed to accept 15-second commercials. Today over 20 percent of all network commercials are 15 seconds long, making it even more difficult for consumers to distinguish one advertiser's message from another's.

Advertisers are extremely concerned about clutter. According to one major advertising executive:

> Commercial efficacy is threatened by dramatic increases in clutter, as well as by the greater opportunity (viewing options) and means (remote controls) for viewers to channel-switch

during commercial breaks. The growth of commercial time together with advertisers' propensity to use shorter commercials has increased dramatically the number of commercials to which the typical television viewer is exposed. And even though accurate information on channel-switching is unavailable because of the limitations of existing research services, we believe that viewer tune-out during commercials actually has increased, particularly among cable households with remote-control devices.[3]

Marketing Television Advertising

In selling television today to advertisers, the advantage that's stressed is TV's tie-in with *other media.* DDB Needham New York designed a new television campaign for Amtrak, which combines 60-second spots with newspaper advertising. The television images expose viewers to the beauty of the American countryside, while the print ads supply ''hard'' information about specific trains, such as schedules and accommodations.

One of the major changes in television advertising is the manner in which it is marketed to potential advertisers. At one time, television advertising executives, particularly at the major networks, marketed the medium as *the* best advertising source. With the growing competition from other media, they have recently taken a more realistic stance. Television now markets itself in terms of ''media synergism,'' showing how an advertiser can increase reach and consumer awareness by using television in connection with other media. This approach has proved extremely effective among local advertisers who have had little experience with television. The Television Advertising Bureau (TvB) emphasizes that ''Media synergism is advertising in one medium calling attention to advertising in another . . . and doing what each medium does best for greater results. But a growing number of advertisers say it's television doing what other media can't do alone to improve the advertiser's bottom line.''

THE RATING-POINT SYSTEM

Rating point (TV). *(1) The percentage of TV households in a market a TV station reaches with a program. The percentage varies with the time of day. A station may have a 10 rating between 6:00 and 6:30 P.M., and a 20 rating between 9:00 and 9:30 P.M. (a real hit!) (2) In radio the percentage of people who listen to a station at a certain time. See gross rating points.*

Television advertisers evaluate the medium according to the delivery of certain target audiences. In the case of networks and large affiliates, advertisers tend to look for exposure to fairly broad audience segments such as women 18 to 49. Cable networks and some independent stations are evaluated by their ability to deliver more narrowly defined audiences that are both smaller in size and more expensive to reach on a CPM basis, but have less waste circulation.

The basic measure of television is the rating. The rating, expressed as a percent of some population (usually TV households), gives the advertiser a measure of coverage based on the potential of the market. The rating is usually calculated as follows:

$$\text{Rating} = \text{program audience/total TV households}$$

When ratings are expressed as percents of individuals, the same formula is used, but the population is some target segment rather than households. For example, if we are interested only in 18–34-year-old males, the formula would be:

$$\text{Rating} = \text{18–34 males viewing program/total 18–34 males in population}$$

Prime time network programs usually achieve a rating of between 9 and 25, with the average being around 15. In comparison, Cable News Network/CNN averages 1.3 in primetime and ESPN, the cable sports network, 1.6.

A household rating of 12 for a program means that 12 percent of all households in a particular area tuned their sets in to that station. Prime-time network programs usually achieve a rating of between 9 and 25, with the average being around 15.

Advertisers usually purchase *a package of spots*—rather than an individual program. Georgia Tech, faced with rising costs, is offering sponsors of its football games a total of 100 TV spots over a four-week period on ESPN, CNN, USA Network, and MTV.

As we will discuss later in this chapter, TV advertising is rarely bought on a program-by-program basis. Instead, advertisers schedule a package of spots that are placed in a number of programs and dayparts. The weight of a schedule is measured in terms of the total ratings for all commercial spots bought (the gross rating points, or GRPs).

Let's look at Exhibit 8.3 for a typical TV buy.

[3]Robert H. Bolte, ''Clutter Clatter,'' *Marketing & Media Decisions,* March 1988, p. 144.

EXHIBIT 8.3

Package television buy.

Vehicle	*Rating*	*Cost*	*Spots*	*GRPs*
"All My Children"	8.6	$15,950	25	215.0
"General Hospital"	8.7	15,950	25	217.5
"Guiding Light"	7.4	15,950	19	140.6
"One Life"	7.4	15,950	14	103.6
TOTAL GRPs				676.7

Reach = 99.9
Frequency = 6.77

Gross rating points (GRP). *Each rating point represents 1 percent of the universe being measured for the market. In TV it is 1 percent of the households having TV sets in that area. In radio it is 1 percent of the total population being measured (e.g., adults, male/female, teenagers). In magazines, it is 1 percent of the total population being measured, as 1 percent of the total population being measured, as 1 percent of all women or all men of different ages or teenagers, based on census records. In outdoor it is the number of people passing a sign in one day. The percentage is figured on the population of that market. This includes people who pass the sign more than once a day. Gross rating points represent the total of the schedule in that medium in that market per week or per month.*

GRPs were calculated by multiplying the insertions times the rating. In the case of "All My Children," the rating was 8.6 × 25 (the number of insertions) = 215 GRPs.

Advertisers also use GRPs as the basis for examining the relationship between reach and frequency. These relationships can be expressed mathematically:

$$R \times F = GRP$$

$$\frac{GRP}{R} = F \quad \text{and} \quad \frac{GPR}{F} = R$$

where R = reach and F = frequency

To use these relationships, you must know (or be able to estimate) the unduplicated audience. In the television schedule in Exhibit 8.3, we estimate that we have reached virtually the entire target market (reach = 99.9 percent) and that the average number of times we reached each person in the audience was 6.77. We can check the formulas using the solutions previously calculated:

$$R \times F = GRP \text{ or } 99.9 \times 6.77 = 676$$

$$\frac{GRP}{F} = R \quad \text{or} \quad \frac{676}{6.77} = 99.9$$

$$\frac{GRP}{R} = F \quad \text{or} \quad \frac{676}{99.9} = 6.77$$

One of the principal merits of the GRP system is that it provides a common base that proportionately accommodates markets of all sizes. One GPR in New York has exactly the same relative weight as one GRP in Salt Lake City. GRPs cannot be compared from one market to another unless the markets are of identical size. However, the cost of TV commercial time varies by city size. Exhibit 8.4 gives an idea of the use of GRPs in two markets, Los Angeles and Boston.

After selecting the number of GRP's or weight an advertiser wants to place *in a specific market*, he then must decide the number of channels and the time allocation for each. In testing network spots for the first time in eight years, Pittsburgh Paints decided to concentrate in selected East Coast markets—where its name had the highest recognition. Revenues increased 27%.

The advertiser has to decide how much weight (how many GRPs) to place in his or her markets and for how long a period. This is a matter of experience and of watching what the competition is doing. Suppose the advertiser selects 100 to 150 per week as the GRP figure (considered a good working base). Within this figure, the advertiser has great discretion in each market. How shall the time be allocated: Put it all on one station? Divide it among all the stations? Use what yardstick to decide? The answers depend on whether the goal is reach or frequency.

Look again at the hypothetical pricing structure in Exhibit 8.4.

EXHIBIT 8.4

Use of gross rating points in intermarket comparisons.

	ADI TV HH Population(000)	*Avg. Cost per Spot*	*Avg. Prime Time Rating*
Los Angeles	4,241	$2,800	18
Boston	1,930	2,200	18

If we buy three prime-time spots in these markets, we would expect to receive 54 GRPs (3 spots × 18 average rating). However, it would be a serious mistake to equate a 54 GRP buy in Los Angeles with the same level in Boston. In Los Angeles, 54 GRPs would deliver 2,290,000 household impressions (0.54 × 4,241,000 HH, or households) at a cost of $8,400 (3 spots × $2,800 per spot). On the other hand, a 54 GRP buy in Boston would deliver 1,042,200 households impressions at a cost of $6,600. In order to estimate buys, advertisers often use the cost per rating point (CPP) calculation:

$$CPP = \frac{\text{cost of schedule}}{\text{GRPs}}$$

In this case:

$$\text{Boston:} \quad CPP = \frac{\$6,600}{54} = \$122.22$$

$$\text{Los Angeles:} \quad CPP = \frac{\$8,400}{54} = \$155.55$$

If we make the mistake of comparing GRPs from markets of different sizes, it would appear that a rating point costs 27 percent more in Los Angeles than in Boston. However, a rating point represents 42,000 households (1 percent of 4,241,000) in Los Angeles versus only 19,300 in Boston.The advertiser is actually getting 219 percent more households for 27 percent higher cost in Los Angeles. So Boston is hardly a bargain.

While total number of households or individuals differ from market to market, so do the numbers of *prospects*. When television spots for Mateus Wine are featured, the company is not just aiming at wine drinkers in general, but those who remember the '50s and the '60s—the "Beat Generation." The commercials recall Woodstock, guitar playing, peace symbols—all reminiscences of today's Baby Boomers.

In using a cost-per-point comparison among markets, advertisers can compare target audiences, definition, size, and growth rate. CBS advises advertisers to check with *their 9 national sales offices* "to reach 5 'first class' markets"—such as New York (WCBS-TV Channel 2), Los Angeles (KCBS-TV Channel 2), Chicago (WBBM-TV Channel 2), Philadelphia (WCAU-TV Channel 10), and Miami (WCIX-TV Channel 6).

In addition to the problem of intermarket comparisons, the GRP has other limitations. It does not tell us the number of *prospects* for the product that are being reached by a program. Still, the GRP concept does provide a unified dimension for making scheduling judgments.

It must also be remembered that GRPs alone cannot tell how effectively a broadcast schedule is performing. If an advertiser's target audience is women aged 18 to 49, for example, 5 GRPs will often deliver more women in that group than 10 GRPs will. This, as you would expect, is a function of where the GRPs are scheduled. Five GRPs during a Sunday night movie will almost always deliver many times more women 18–49 than will 10 GRPs scheduled on a Saturday morning.

Because of the shortcomings of GRP measures, the CPP evaluation is becoming more important in media buying.

> Cost-per-point reflects several of the critical decisions built into a media plan. These include: target audiences, definition, the size of this target population, and the growth rate of this population, as well as its CPM. And cost-per-point allows realistic comparison between the cost of this year's plan compared to last year vs. five years ago.
>
> The importance of using cost-per-point is even more apparent if we compare different target audiences; for example, women 18–49 vs. women 25–54. Each of these targets starts with a different cost-per-point, and each is growing at a different rate. Over the past three years the number of women 25–54 has increased 6.9%, while the 18–49 group is up 4.4%. It takes a significantly bigger budget increase to stay even if your target is 25–54.[4]

SHARE OF AUDIENCE

Share of audience. *That portion of the viewing audience tuned to a particular program.*

While the rating is the basic audience-measurement statistic for TV, another measure, the share of audience (or simply, share), is often used to determine the success of a show. The share is defined as the percentage of households using TV that are watching

[4]Robert N. Adler, "The CPP Beats the CPM," *Advertising Age,* September 12, 1988, p.18.

By using the share-of-audience measurement, advertisers can determine how successful a particular show is. *60 Minutes* has been a top-rated show for CBS, with a 22.2 rating and a 34 share. NBC boasts *The Cosby Show;* its rating of 27.9 gives it a 44 share. *Roseanne* is tops for ABC, averaging a 22.4 rating and a 33 share.

a particular show. It is used by advertisers to determine how a show is doing against its direct competition.

Let's assume that the "Today Show" has 5,000 households watching it in a market with 50,000 households. In this case, we know that the rating for the "Today Show" would be 10:

$$\text{Rating} = \frac{\text{“Today” viewers}}{\text{total TV households}} \times 100 = \frac{5{,}000}{50{,}000} \times 100 = 10$$

The share calculates the percentage of households using TV (HUT) that are tuned to the program. Let's assume that of the 50,000 households, 25,000 are watching TV. In this case, the share for the "Today Show" would be 20:

$$\text{Share} = \frac{\text{“Today” viewers}}{\text{HUT}} \times 100 = \frac{5{,}000}{25{,}000} \times 100 = 20$$

It is understood that both the ratings and share of audience are expressed as percentages (hence the factor of 100 in the equations). Therefore, we do not use decimal points or refer to the measures in this example as "10 percent" and "20 percent." Instead, we say that the rating is 10 and the share is 20.

THE MANY FACES OF TELEVISION

Men and women, aged 18–49, the prime market for most national advertisers, don't, as a rule, watch *network programs*. Instead, they often watch cable channels. To reach this upscale, profitable audience, Marketing Communications Networks will roll out *Cable Direct*. The program consists of category-exclusive coupons of national advertisers, mailed to households in markets where *cable systems sell local advertising*. Two 30-second spots will appear on local cable channels to announce the program.

Television is not a unified medium, but rather a multifaceted one with different audiences, technology, buying patterns, and even styles and executions of advertising. The simple days of dealing with three networks and their affiliates and few large-market independent stations are over forever. Exhibit 8.5 shows the viewing preferences of men and women aged 18 to 49, a prime market for most national advertisers. As you can see, less than half of this audience was tuned into network programming.

In the future, not only will television continue to diversify, but, more importantly, viewers will increasingly determine the content of the medium. Already a number of experiments are going on in "interactive television." Basically, interactive television allows viewers to select the program, news, or advertising they wish to see from a menu of available topics. In the case of interactive commercials, viewers are able to get additional information, place an order, and charge their accounts, all without leaving their living room sofa. Although the technology for interactive television is available now, we are some years away from universal availability of such systems. Here we will concentrate on the major elements of television used by advertisers.

Network Television

> In 1985 the seller's market for network TV ended as ad revenues declined for the first time since 1971, when cigarettes were barred from the broadcast media. Network TV became a buyer's market and it has continued on through . . . [the present]. The gradual erosion in network TV ratings, the reduction in daytime TV advertising to non-working women, the increased use of 15-second commercials and the competition from cable and barter syndication all helped keep network rates in check.[5]

Despite the recent decline in network audience shares, we can't overestimate their importance to the television industry. The networks set the agenda for news, entertain-

[5]Robert J. Coen, "TV Forms Hot; Print, Outdoor Waver," *Advertising Age,* November 30, 1987, p. S-2.

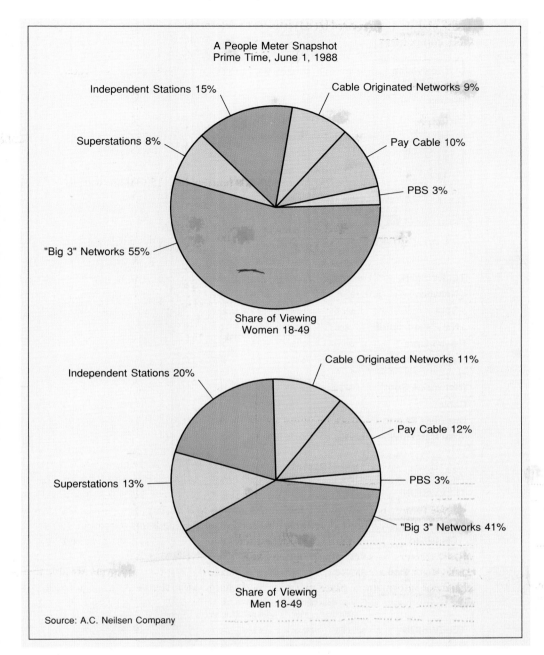

A People Meter Snapshot
Prime Time, June 1, 1988

Independent Stations 15%
Cable Originated Networks 9%
Superstations 8%
Pay Cable 10%
PBS 3%
"Big 3" Networks 55%

Share of Viewing
Women 18-49

Cable Originated Networks 11%
Independent Stations 20%
Pay Cable 12%
Superstations 13%
PBS 3%
"Big 3" Networks 41%

Share of Viewing
Men 18-49

Source: A.C. Neilsen Company

EXHIBIT 8.5

The television audience continues to fragment as new program sources become available. (Courtesy: *Gannett Center Journal.*)

ment, and advertising in all sectors of the medium. Even the decline in network audience share in recent years must be placed in the perspective of the 90 percent share of 15 years ago. Exhibit 8.6 shows the national advertising dollars expended at the network level. In the competitive market for national advertising, network television still accounts for over one-quarter of all national advertising dollars. In the future, the three networks will continue to show increases in advertising revenue, although their share of total advertising dollars will decline.

Organization of the Networks. A *TV network* is defined as two or more stations broadcasting a program originating from a single source. In the case of cable networks, which we will discuss in the cable section, this definition has to be altered slightly, since they do not broadcast in the strictest sense of the word. In addition, there are

EXHIBIT 8.6
(Courtesy: Television Bureau of Advertising, Inc.)

National Ad Volume:

	Millions of Dollars 1986	1987	% Change	% of Total
TELEVISION	$15,512	$16,108	+ 3.8	53.4
Network	8,342	8,500	+ 1.9	28.2
Spot	6,570	6,846	+ 4.2	22.7
Nat'l Syndication	600	762	+27.0	2.5
Newspapers	3,376	3,494	+ 3.5	11.6
Magazines	5,317	5,607	+ 5.5	18.6
Radio (Network & Spot)	1,771	1,743	- 1.6	5.8
Cable	676	760	+12.5	2.5
Business Papers	2,382	2,458	+ 3.2	8.1
Total Major Media	$29,034	$30,170	+ 3.9	100.0

Local Ad Volume:

	Millions of Dollars 1986	1987	% Change	% of Total
TELEVISION	$6,514	$6,833	+ 4.9	17.9
Newspapers	23,614	25,918	+ 9.8	67.8
Retail	14,311	15,227	+ 6.4	39.8
Classified	9,303	10,691	+14.9	28.0
Radio	5,178	5,463	+ 5.5	14.3
Total Major Media	$35,306	38,214	+ 8.2	100.0

Total Ad Volume:

	Millions of Dollars 1986	1987	% Change	% of Total
TELEVISION	$22,026	$22,941	+ 4.2	20.9
Newspapers	26,990	29,412	+ 9.0	26.8
Magazines	5,317	5,607	+ 5.5	5.1
Radio	6,949	7,206	+ 3.7	6.6
Cable	855	963	+12.6	0.9
Business Papers	2,382	2,458	+ 3.2	2.2
All Others	37,621	41,063	+ 9.1	37.5
Total Advertising	$102,140	$109,650	+ 7.4	100.0

Source: McCann-Erickson 5/88

Affiliate. *A station which agrees to broadcast programs originating from a network. Affiliates may be independently owned or owned by a network.*

regional or special-event networks that exist only to broadcast a particular event such as a football or basketball game. The stations that broadcast that game are part of the "network" only so long as the game lasts; afterward their "affiliation" comes to an end.

The Fox Network is an interesting hybrid between the continuing affiliation of the Big Three and the specialty networks for one event. The Fox Network operates on a continuing basis, but on a limited schedule of weekend and late-night programming,

Other than the "Big Three" television networks, the Fox Network operates on a limited schedule of weekend and late-night programming. Recently, it added a third night of original programming, reflecting added viewership and advertising revenues.

Clearance. *The percentage of affiliates that agree to carry a network's shows or the average percentage of a network's shows that are carried by the total affiliate lineup.*

Network compensation. *The network fees paid to affiliates for carrying network programming.*

Affiliates of networks have a choice of accepting local revenue or network compensation. An additional advantage of networks is that it enables stations to fill up their airtime with attractive programming. The public still watches more *network shows* than any others. Network TV ad expenditures rose 13.4% to $6.9 billion for the first 9 months of 1988, as compared with a 9.3% growth for total TV spending.

Network television advertising is bought mainly by a relatively few, very large advertisers—the top 100 national advertisers account for over 75% of all network advertising. The number one advertiser is Procter & Gamble, which spent $172.8 million in 1988 out of a total network tab of $4,735.3 billion! Following P&G closely was General Motors; third and fourth were Philip Morris and Kellogg, respectively. Chrysler was fifth, and Unilever, McDonald's, RJR Nabisco, AT&T, and Anheuser-Busch rounded out the top 10 last year.

featuring such shows as "The Reporters" and "21 Jump Street." The affiliates of Fox are independent stations (they are not affiliated with CBS, NBC, or ABC) that come together as a network on a regular, but limited, basis. It remains to be seen if Fox can develop enough programming to become a true fourth network. Except where otherwise noted, this section is concerned only with the Big Three networks.

The networks are really a loosely structured relationship between CBS, NBC, or ABC, which functions as a broker, and independent local stations. The networks generally contract with producers and studios to supply programs, which they then offer to their local-station affiliates. The networks sell advertising to offset their costs of buying shows and pay a fee (called *compensation*) to local stations to carry their programming.

Each of the networks has approximately 220 affiliates. When a station carries a network program, this is called *clearance* because the local station clears the time for the network show. It is extremely important for a network to have as high a clearance rate as possible so it can offer advertisers total national coverage. Most network programs have 95–100 percent clearance. Shows that fail to achieve clearances in the high 90s are probably so bad that they will soon be canceled anyway.

Clearance is a matter of economics. At one time, network compensation amounted to almost 20 percent of station revenues. However, in recent years, network compensation has fallen far behind other station revenue sources (see Exhibit 8.7). Therefore, an affiliate may realize more revenue by showing an old movie and keeping all the advertising revenue than by clearing a network show and receiving only the network compensation. Network compensation depends on a number of factors, but is usually much lower than a station's normal program charges. Even though total network compensation amounts to almost $500 million, the value of network affiliation is much more important than the money received from the networks.

> Network affiliation allows stations to fill up their airtime. It enables stations to present a variety of popular and special programs, and it generates strong lead-in and adjacent audiences for its local news and syndicated programs. Finally, network affiliation allows stations to "piggyback" on the considerable promotion and publicity value of the networks and their leading stars.[6]

As network audience shares have declined, the relationship between networks and their affiliates has come under closer scrutiny by both groups. Among the topics being discussed are:

- Compensation and preemption (clearance rates)
- Revising the way commercial time is sold and formatted
- A new emphasis on marketing efforts
- Joint financing of major sports and entertainment programs, with affiliates sharing in the risks and also in the ad revenue[7]

Despite the current reexamination of the network-affiliate relationship, its value is indisputable. As Anthony Malara, president of the CBS Marketing Division, said, "I have never met an affiliate who wants to be an independent. . . ."

Buying Network Time. Network television advertising, unlike advertising in other media, is concentrated among a relatively few very large advertisers. *Advertising Age* estimates that the top 100 national advertisers account for over 75 percent of all network advertising. Companies such as Procter & Gamble, Philip Morris, and General

[6]Barry L. Sherman, *Telecommunications Management* (New York: McGraw-Hill Book Company, 1987), p. 111.

[7]James P. Forkan, "TV Web-Affiliate Relationship Seen Changing with Times," *Television/Radio Age*, August 22, 1988, p. 32.

EXHIBIT 8.7

Network compensation has become less important to local stations since the 1970s. During the same period, local television advertising has grown dramatically. (Courtesy: *Television/Radio Age*.)

Sales of U.S. TV stations by advertising category, 1963-1993

Year	Network compensation		National regional spot (In Millions)		Local	
	Amount	% change	Amount	% change	Amount	% change
1963	$203	0.5%	$616	11.2%	$241	5.7%
1964	214	5.4	711	15.4	276	14.5
1965	230	7.5	786	10.5	303	9.8
1966	244	6.1	872	10.9	346	14.2
1967	246	0.8	872	0.0	365	5.5
1968	248	0.8	998	14.4	453	24.1
1969	254	2.4	1,108	11.0	519	14.6
1970	240	−5.5	1,092	−1.4	563	8.5
1971	230	−4.2	1,013	−7.2	637	13.1
1972	224	−2.6	1,167	15.2	778	22.1
1973	233	4.0	1,221	4.5	896	15.2
1974	248	6.4	1,329	8.8	979	9.3
1975	258	4.0	1,441	8.4	1,080	10.3
1976	270	4.7	1,920	4.7	1,390	28.7
1977	288	6.7	1,960	6.7	1,586	14.1
1978	315	9.4	2,326	18.7	1,987	25.3
1979	344	9.2	2,564	10.2	2,245	13.0
1980	369	7.3	2,920	13.9	2,484	10.6
1981	393	6.5	3,302	13.1	2,767	11.4
1982	406	3.3	3,846	16.5	3,088	11.6
1983	416	2.5	4,211	9.5	3,611	16.9
1984	424	1.9	4,715	12.0	4,216	16.8
1985	446	5.2	5,077	7.7	4,665	10.6
1986	454	1.8	5,574	9.8	5,275	13.1
1987	460	1.3	5,795	4.0	5,610	6.4
1988	469	2.0	6,350	9.6	6,325	12.7
1989	476	1.5	6,825	7.5	6,900	9.1
1990	483	1.4	7,275	6.6	7,475	8.3
1991	489	1.3	7,725	6.2	8,025	7.4
1992	497	1.7	8,525	10.4	9,025	12.5
1993	504	1.4	9,150	7.3	9,800	8.6
5-year growth rates:						
(1975–1980)		7.4%		15.2%		18.1%
(1980–1985)		3.9		11.7		13.4
(1985–1990)		1.6		7.5		9.9
10-year growth rates:						
(1975–1985)		5.6%		13.4%		15.8%
(1980–1990)		2.7		9.6		11.6
5-year growth rates:						
(1988–1993)		1.5%		7.6%		9.2%

Sources: FCC television financial data (1963-1980); TELEVISION/RADIO AGE "TV Business Barometer" (1981-1986); Dick Gideon Enterprises (1987—1993)

Motors spend millions of dollars each year on television advertising, over half of which is targeted to network buys. As you can see in Exhibit 8.8, the top ten network advertisers allocate a significant percentage of their total advertising budgets to network television. Network television buys are negotiated by the giants of American corporations and agencies; it is not a game for the fainthearted.

Most network advertising time is bought on the basis of *negotiation* and *scatter plans*. As the term implies, scatter plan means that advertisers don't buy spots on single shows, but rather negotiate for spots on several shows, often in a number of dayparts. These spots, scattered throughout a network's schedule, are purchased according to a two-tier system that considers the size of the advertiser and the timing of scheduling.

EXHIBIT 8.8
The big hitters: TV

Total & Top 10 Media Spenders (January to June, $000,000)

	1988	1987	% chg
NETWORK TV			
Total spending	$4,735.3	$4,066.3	16.5
1. Procter & Gamble Co.	172.8	192.3	−10.1
2. General Motors Corp.	171.4	129.9	31.9
3. Philip Morris Cos.	154.7	181.2	−14.6
4. Kellogg Co.	140.0	109.8	27.5
5. Chrysler Corp.	110.2	66.0	67.0
6. Unilever NV	107.6	124.8	−13.8
7. McDonald's Corp.	107.4	105.4	2.0
8. RJR Nabisco	101.9	93.8	8.6
9. AT&T Co.	97.5	73.1	33.3
10. Anheuser-Busch Cos.	96.1	88.5	8.6
SPOT TV			
Total spending	$4,009.1	$3,548.3	13.0
1. PepsiCo Inc.	130.2	130.9	−0.5
2. Procter & Gamble Co.	102.9	72.8	41.3
3. General Motors Corp.	71.6	36.4	96.5
4. General Mills	66.4	61.2	8.6
5. McDonald's Corp.	58.1	55.1	5.5
6. Anheuser-Busch Cos.	45.7	44.6	2.8
7. Pillsbury Co.	45.7	56.5	−19.2
8. Philip Morris Cos.	45.6	59.9	−23.9
9. Coca-Cola Co.	34.0	35.5	−4.3
10. Nestle SA	31.6	27.5	14.9
TV SYNDICATION			
Total spending	$424.8	$316.9	34.1
1. Procter & Gamble Co.	29.4	20.7	41.7
2. Philip Morris Cos.	27.2	23.7	14.7
3. Kraft Inc.	20.4	10.9	86.6
4. Bristol-Myers Co.	15.7	10.7	47.1
5. Mars Inc.	13.7	6.6	105.5
6. Unilever NV	13.1	16.4	−20.0
7. Kellogg Co.	11.5	10.4	9.7
8. Nestle SA	11.3	11.0	2.9
9. Coca-Cola Co.	10.4	4.8	117.3
10. Eastman Kodak Co.	9.9	7.7	29.2

Source: BAR/LNA Multi-Media Reports. Note: Major spending by auto dealer groups in spot TV (January to June 1988, $000,000)—General Motors Corp. Dealers Association, $85.4; Ford Auto Dealers Association, $48.7; Chrysler Corp. Dealer Association, $45.0; Ford Motor Co. Local Dealers, $42.4; General Motors Corp. Local Dealers, $38.3; Hyundai Group, $37.7.

***Up-front buys.** Purchase of network TV time by national advertisers during the first offering by networks. Most expensive network advertising.*

UP-FRONT BUYS. The process of buying network television advertising begins in April or May, when advertisers and agencies determine the budgets, GRP levels, and daypart buying goals they are seeking for the upcoming fall television season. When the network schedules are announced, agency planners begin the actual negotiations for position and price of the spots they wish to buy. While there are up-front buys in all dayparts (e.g., daytime, early morning, evening news), the major concern of most advertisers is their prime-time schedule.

***Rating guarantees.** Offered when networks promise a certain delivery of rating points to advertisers. If guaranteed GRPs are not met, the network provides advertisers with additional spots to make up for shortfall.*

Before any money is committed, network account executives and agency buyers negotiate a package of programs. While some advertisers might prefer to buy a package of hits such as *The Cosby Show* or *60 Minutes*, the networks rarely sell these shows without throwing a few new or struggling series into the deal.

One of the main reasons advertisers commit to upfront time so far in advance of the television season is because the networks offer rating guarantees for such deals. So-called, short-term "scatter" buys made during the season generally are not similarly covered. However, a buyer who is willing to make a deal without guarantees or cancellation options can win in other ways; namely price concessions.

"Up-front buys" enable advertisers, in advance of the season, to "get in on" the hit shows, especially those in prime time. While they "pay" for that privilege, they are also guaranteed certain ratings, or they may cancel. Anheuser-Busch, Pepsi, and Gillette have already signed on an "official sponsors" for the 1990 Goodwill Games, the international athletic competition scheduled to air on the Turner Broadcasting System. The "packages" for sponsors include television spots and special on-site promotions.

Should ratings fall below the negotiated level, networks "make good" to the advertisers—in the form of additional spots. The first 15 hours of "War and Remembrance" on ABC scored an 18.9 rating and a 29 share, or about 6% below the network's guaranteed ratings estimate of 20.2. It "made good" to sponsors in the next installment.

Once a deal is set, the network puts it on "hold" and allows the agency about a week to go over the buy with their client before making a commitment. No money actually changes hands until the commercial time airs and the networks invoice the order.[8]

MAKE-GOODS. One of the major negotiating points in network television advertising is the guarantee that networks have traditionally given up-front advertisers to "make good" on any ratings shortfall. Generally, these guarantees carry a floor to protect the networks from a complete ratings disaster, but they still provide an important hedge for the advertiser, particularly in buying new shows with no ratings track record. Normally, make-goods are in the form of additional spots given to advertisers to bring their schedule up to some agreed-upon GRP level.

The make-good situation was particularly critical when the switch was made to people-meter ratings. (We will discuss rating methodology later in this chapter.) In some cases, the networks found that people-meter ratings were much lower than anticipated ratings and occasioned significant make-goods to advertisers. For example, the ratings shortfall in children's programming meant that the networks had to make good on over 25 percent ($40 million) of all advertising sold for these programs.

The make-good situation was so severe for the networks in the 1987–1988 season that ABC announced that it would no longer give guarantees for commercial time bought on its Saturday morning schedule.[9] (Earlier, in 1982, CBS had announced that it would no longer guarantee rating levels for certain demographic audience segments, but when many advertisers refused to place advertising without guarantees, the network was forced to rescind its policy.) According to the Associated Press, NBC had to deliver make-goods of approximately $70 million when the 1988 Summer Olympics in Seoul averaged ratings of 17.9, well below the 21.2 guaranteed to advertisers.

Spot and Local Television

***Spot (TV and radio).** Media use; purchase of time from a local station, in contrast to purchase from a network. When purchased by a national advertiser, it is, strictly speaking, national spot but is referred to as just spot. When purchased by a local advertiser, it is, strictly speaking, local spot but is referred to as local TV or local radio. (2) Creative use: the text of a short announcement.*

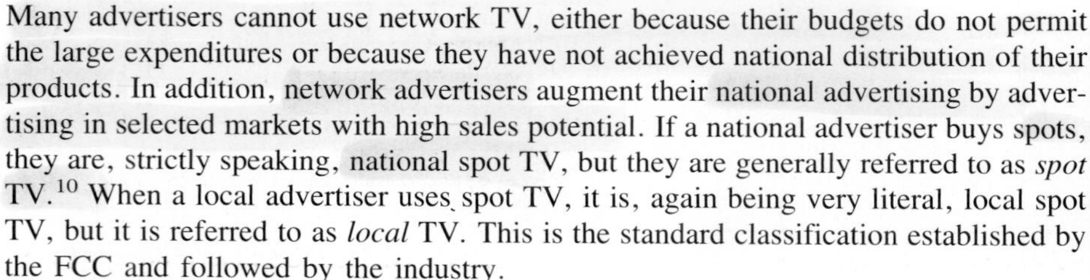

Many advertisers cannot use network TV, either because their budgets do not permit the large expenditures or because they have not achieved national distribution of their products. In addition, network advertisers augment their national advertising by advertising in selected markets with high sales potential. If a national advertiser buys spots, they are, strictly speaking, national spot TV, but they are generally referred to as *spot* TV.[10] When a local advertiser uses spot TV, it is, again being very literal, local spot TV, but it is referred to as *local* TV. This is the standard classification established by the FCC and followed by the industry.

Define the Television Territory. Before the advent of TV, a company traditionally established sales and advertising territories by state boundaries and arbitrary geographical divisions within them. However, a TV transmission wave goes in many directions for varying distances; it is no respecter of man-made maps. How to coordinate sales territories with TV planning for advertising was the problem on which two major research firms worked.

The Arbitron Ratings Company defines a market according to three geographic areas (see Exhibit 8.9) in which spot and local TV audiences are measured:

***Area of Dominant Influence (ADI).** An exclusive geographic area consisting of all counties in which the home-market station receives a preponderance of total viewing hours. Developed by Arbitron Ratings. Widely used for TV, radio, newspaper, magazine, and outdoor advertising in media scheduling.*

1. *Total survey area (TSA).* The TSA is a geographical area composed of those counties in which at least 98 percent of the net weekly circulation of each home-market station occurs.
2. *Area of dominant influence (ADI).* The ADI is an area that consists of all counties in which the home-market stations receive a preponderance of viewing. Each county in the United States (excluding the state of Alaska) is allocated exclusively to one ADI. There is no overlap.

[8] Joe Mandese, "Upfront," *Marketing & Media Decisions,* May 1988, p.37.

[9] Verne Gay, "ABC Pulls Guarantee for Kids' TV Audience," *Advertising Age,* April 4, 1988, p. 2.

[10] The word *spot* is another of those advertising terms that is used in two senses: (1) time-buying use—a way of buying time on a non-network show; and (2) creative use—"We need some 30-second spots."

EXHIBIT 8.9

Map showing Arbitron coverage areas. (Courtesy: The Arbitron Rating Company.)

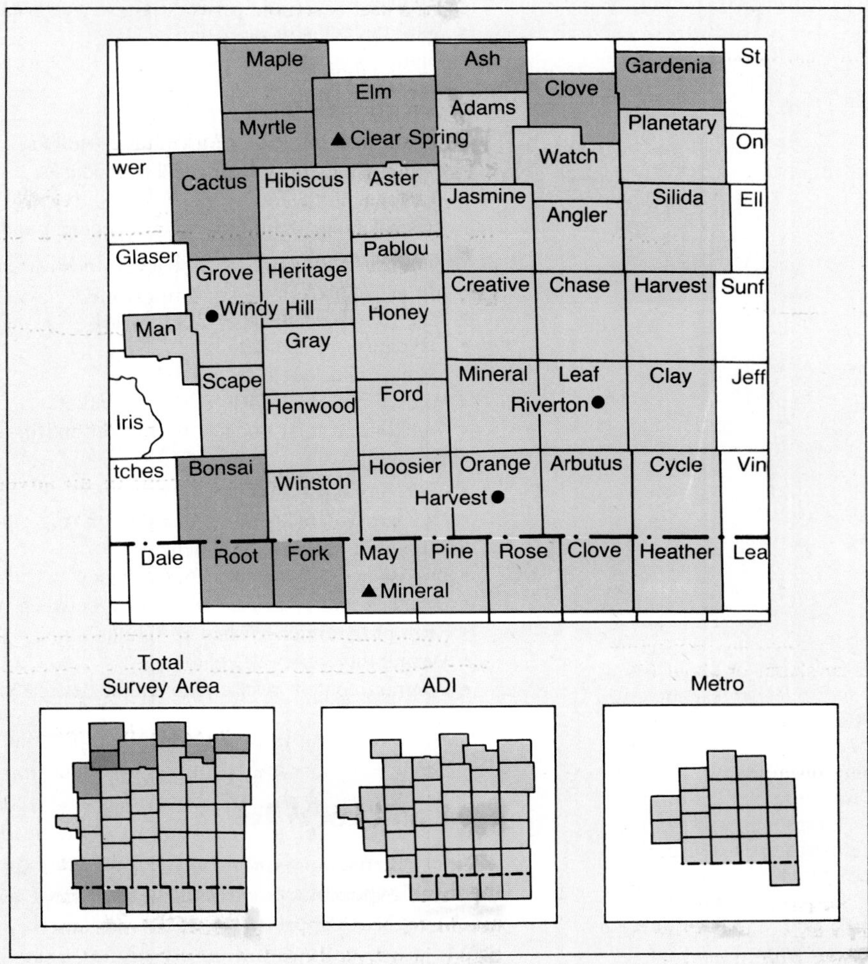

3. *Metro rating area (MRA).* The MRA generally corresponds to the standard metropolitan area.

Designated Market Area (DMA). *A rigidly defined geographical area in which stations located, generally, in the core of the area attract most of the viewing. A concept developed by the A. C. Nielsen Company.*

The A. C. Nielsen Company developed a marketing map based upon important (designated) marketing areas. It selected stations that reached those areas best and referred to these selections as *designated marketing areas,* or *DMA.*

The ADI system is used by most other media to describe which part of the TV ADI their circulation covers. The ADI has thus become a standard of circulation designation in addition to a method of defining broadcast rating areas.

When we speak of TV advertising, we naturally think of network advertisers with their multimillion-dollar budgets and national audience coverage. However, as we have seen, network advertising shares are decreasing at a significant rate. Dollars are increasingly being shifted into spot and local TV. Within the next five years, it is predicted that local TV advertising will become the medium's largest category.

Spot TV. Spot advertising is much more complex than network advertising simply because of the number of stations and markets involved. The American Association of Advertising Agencies (4A's) has suggested a number of procedures for buying spot TV.[11] These buying specifications are divided into three parts:

1. Summary
   - Client

[11] *Spot Television Buying Procedures from Planning Through Post Analysis* (New York: American Association of Advertising Agencies, 1982), pp. 3–4.

- Product
- Total budget
- Flight dates
- Daypart(s)
- Commercial length
- Basis for GRP goals (e.g., ratings; women 18+ ratings)
- Target audience (primary and secondary)
- Test or nontest
- Type of report required (e.g., schedules) and its due date

2. Goals by Market
   - Market name
   - Flight dates (if different by market)
   - Daypart(s) by market
   - Commercial length by market
   - Weekly and total GRP goals by market
   - Weekly and total budgets by market and in total
3. Buying Guidelines
   - Make-good restrictions
   - Daypart weight/spending distribution (e.g., percentage of early versus late fringe)
   - Minimum rating requirement
   - Importance of reach versus frequency
   - Whether money can be transferred between markets
   - Strip programming schedule limitations
   - Desirability of break positions
   - Program content restrictions and/or desired programs

With *spot television,* national advertisers can take a *regional approach* to their advertising—focusing on different sales patterns from one market to another. "Reps" often function as intermediaries between the advertisers and the television stations. Saab, the Swedish automaker, will venture into *regional marketing* next year to try to bolster market share in the Pacific, Southeastern, and South Central states.

Spot advertising is becoming more popular for a number of reasons. Increasingly, national advertisers are taking a regional approach to their advertising. Even the most widely distributed national brands have differential sales patterns from one market to another. Likewise, the viewership of network programs varies from one market to another. In order to even out the sales/ad exposure patterns, advertisers often supplement their network advertising with a spot schedule. A few national advertisers that take a regional approach use spot exclusively. It should be noted that spot television CPMs are usually significantly higher than the same coverage on a network basis. Consequently, spot advertising must serve some specific marketing goal to make it cost efficient. Exhibit 8.10 shows that the leading products using spot advertising are very similar to the major product categories in network.

Rep firm. *An independent company that contracts with stations to sell advertising to national advertisers. The rep receives a commission of the time sold.*

In the past, the process of buying spot time was relatively standardized. Most spot television buys were made through sales representatives, called *reps*. Reps are large national companies with offices in most major markets. They contract with local stations or station groups to sell spot advertising to national advertisers. In effect, the rep provides local stations with a national sales force throughout the country. The rep is paid a commission based on the time sold. This commission is negotiable, but estimates range from approximately 5 percent in the largest markets to slightly more than 10 percent among smaller stations.

While the rep firm is still very important in the spot buying process, the business has become extremely competitive. In 1987 and 1988, many of the larger rep firms bought out smaller firms, were purchased themselves, or merged with competitors. The resulting consolidation caused turmoil in the once-stable relationships between agency media buyers and the reps who handled major stations' spot time. Rep firms usually operate on an exclusive basis with stations in a specific market. The consolidation caused conflicts similar to those caused by agency mergers (discussed in Chapter 5). It has been estimated that as much as $1 billion in billings changed hands among the reps because of these mergers and buyouts.

Some advertising agencies, having lost their old rep, simply began to buy direct from stations. In addition, the regional strategy adopted by many clients resulted in more agency buyers who were comfortable dealing directly with local media: " . . . buyers say the upheaval in station representation is putting a strain on their spot-buying

EXHIBIT 8.10

Automotive and food advertisers spend almost as much as the next ten categories in spot TV. (Courtesy: Television Bureau of Advertising.)

Top 20 Spot Television Categories, 1987

	Millions of Dollars 1987
1. Automotive	$1,152
2. Food & Food Products	987
3. Confectionery & Soft Drinks	373
4. Consumer Services	264
5. Toiletries & Toilet Goods	255
6. Beer & Wine	237
7. Sporting Goods & Toys	221
8. Travel, Hotels & Resorts Outside U.S.	205
9. Proprietary Medicines	194
10. Publishing & Media	169
11. Household Equipment & Supplies	145
12. Soaps, Cleaners & Polishers	136
13. Gasoline, Lubricants & Other Fuels	124
14. Insurance	118
15. Home Electronics Equipment	87
16. Building Materials, Equipment & Fixtures	76
17. Apparel, Footwear & Accessories	61
18. Household Furnishings	51
19. Pet Food & Supplies	51
20. Horticulture	50

Source: BAR

operations and hastening the trend to buy direct.'' As one media buyer pointed out, ''At the very least, it's disruptive to the relationships that buyers have established with the reps who handle their business. Those relationships have to be renewed. In some cases, a buyer will find the new situation uncomfortable, and the station may lose business because of it.''[12]

Despite the altered relationship between reps and agencies, the rep remains an important player in spot television. The good sales rep is both a salesperson and a marketing specialist for advertisers. The rep must be able to show a national advertiser how a schedule on WAWS-TV in Jacksonville or KDKA-TV in Pittsburgh will meet a national company's advertising objectives.

[12] Joe Mandese, ''The Rep Rap,'' *Marketing & Media Decisions,* October 1987, p. 46.

Local Television Advertising

Local *television* appeals to advertisers with *less* than a national market, probably a few regions or counties, who wish to take advantage of television exposure of their products. Makers of Mexican foods, for instance, would want to concentrate their television advertising in El Paso, Albuquerque, and Phoenix, as opposed to Scranton, Albany, and Philadelphia—according to SAMI/Burke researchers.

> Local advertising . . . generally derives from regional [or local] advertisers purchasing time on television stations in their own markets. Increasingly, however, national advertisers are finding advantages in local target marketing; therefore, national advertiser participation in local advertising markets is growing. From the mid-1970s through 1984, spending for local television hovered around 26 percent of all TV ad spending. Between 1984 and 1987, though, local advertising moved up more than three percentage points to 29.2 percent. Conversely, national TV broadcasting's share of TV ad dollars dropped to 70.8 percent. This trend is likely to continue.[13]

Until the early 1970s, local television advertising was a very minor part of the typical station's revenues. Except in the largest markets, stations depended primarily on national spot advertising and, to a lesser degree, network compensation for their revenues. However, in the last decade, local advertising has become a major profit center for stations. Estimates are that by 1992 television advertising expenditures will break down as follows:

	$ millions	*% of Expenditures on TV*
Network	13.3	33.3
National spot	11.85	29.6
Local	13.2	33.0
Barter syndication	1.65	4.1
Total TV advertising	40.0	100.0

Exhibit 8.11 shows the decline in network advertising over a 15-year period among national advertisers. The popularity of local television is the result of several factors.

1. As mentioned earlier, many large advertisers have adopted regional marketing strategies that give increased importance to local and regional advertising compared to national advertising schedules.
2. Co-op advertising plans in which national advertisers and local retailers share advertising expenses have increasingly been made available to television by national companies. (We will discuss the details of co-op later in the text.)
3. Local television stations have become much more aggressive in promoting the medium to advertisers. Categories of local advertising—such as grocery and drug stores, movies, and real estate—that were once the exclusive domain of newspapers now spend millions of dollars on local television. Exhibit 8.12 illustrates the competitive stance taken by the television industry in promoting local advertising.
4. The increase in the number of independent stations and cable outlets has given local advertisers access to television at an affordable price. For example, during the decade 1977–1987, network affiliates increased by 8 (1.2 percent), while independent stations increased by 249 (382 percent).

Once, supermarkets and drugstores *only* advertised in newspapers. Now, they're taking advantage of *local television*. The increase in the number of independent stations and cable outlets have helped make local television advertising *more accessible* and *more affordable*. Cablevision's News 12 Long Island serves 550,000-plus homes in a very desirable portion of New York. Morning and early-evening news 30-second spots range between $300 and $400, versus New York affiliates' spots at $3,500–4,500!

So the decline in network share of advertising dollars does not result from a waning interest in the medium by national advertisers. Rather, more national dollars are being funneled into television through local stations. This change has serious implications for the economic support of the networks, including the future financing of programs.

Buying and Scheduling Spot and Local Television Time. Since advertisers have shifted more of their budgets to local markets, media buyers must be familiar with the specifics of buying spot and local television time.

THE TELEVISION DAY. Spot and local TV advertising are often purchased by daypart rather than by specific program. Each daypart varies by audience size and demographic

[13] *Five Year Communications Industry Forecast* (New York: Veronis, Suhler & Associates, Inc., 1988), pp. 28–29.

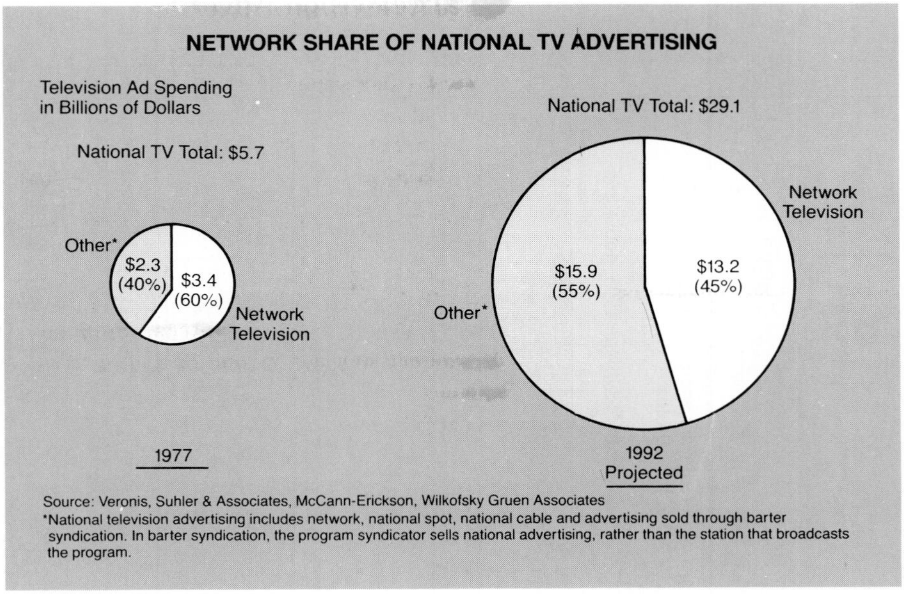

NETWORK SHARE OF NATIONAL TV ADVERTISING

Television Ad Spending in Billions of Dollars

National TV Total: $5.7

Other*: $2.3 (40%) | Network Television: $3.4 (60%)

1977

National TV Total: $29.1

Other*: $15.9 (55%) | Network Television: $13.2 (45%)

1992 Projected

Source: Veronis, Suhler & Associates, McCann-Erickson, Wilkofsky Gruen Associates

*National television advertising includes network, national spot, national cable and advertising sold through barter syndication. In barter syndication, the program syndicator sells national advertising, rather than the station that broadcasts the program.

NETWORKS' SHARE OF NATIONAL TV AD SPENDING, EVERY FIVE YEARS

Year	Network ($ Millions)	National* ($ Millions)	Networks' Share (%)
1977	$ 3,460	$ 5,664	60.1%
1982	6,210	10,889	57.0
1987	8,830	17,255	51.2
1992	13,250	29,100	45.5

Source: Veronis, Suhler & Associates
McCann-Erickson, Wilkofsky Gruen Associates

* National television advertising includes network, national spot, national cable, and advertising sold through barter syndication. In barter syndication, the program syndicator sells national advertising rather than the station that broadcasts the program.

EXHIBIT 8.11

Network dominance of national TV advertising has dropped significantly in the last decade.

Spot and local television advertising are often purchased by *daypart*, which varies in *size and demographic profile*. Advertisers are given the options of preemptability, special features, scheduling, run-of-schedule, package rates, and product protection by separating competing products' commercials. Campbell Soup, in an effort to tie in with the National Football League, went *"regional"* last fall for its *Hungry Man Dinners*. The TV spots are predicted to increase sales and shelf space—but will have different copy, depending on the "nuances" of the particular areas.

Preemption rate. *Lower than normal rate charged to TV advertisers who agree to give up commercial time to other advertisers who are willing to pay a higher time charges.*

profile. Media planners must be familiar with the audience makeup of various dayparts. Some typical daypart designations are:

1. Morning: 7:00–9:00 A.M. Monday through Friday.
2. Daytime: 9:00 A.M.–4:30 P.M. Monday through Friday.
3. Early fringe: 4:30–7:30 P.M. Monday through Friday.
4. Prime-time access: 7:30–8:00 P.M. Monday through Saturday.
5. Prime time: 8:00–11:00 P.M. Monday through Saturday and 7:00–11:00 P.M. Sunday.
6. Late news: 11–11:30 P.M. Monday through Friday.
7. Late fringe: 11:30 P.M.–1:00 A.M. Monday through Friday.

PREEMPTION RATE. A considerable proportion of spot TV advertising time is sold on a preemptible (lower-rate) basis, whereby the advertiser gives the station the right to sell a time slot to another advertiser who may pay a better rate for it or who has a package deal for which that particular spot is needed. Although some stations offer only two choices, nonpreemptible and preemptible advertising, others allow advertisers to choose between two kinds of preemptible rate. When the station has the right to sell a spot to another advertiser any time up until the time of the telecast, the rate is

At one time newspapers were a growth medium. But no longer!

In the 1950's daily newspaper circulation rose 9%. In the 1960's daily newspaper circulation rose a smaller 5%. In the 1970's and 1980's there's been no newspaper growth—0%.

Daily Newspaper Circulation

	(000)	
1950	53,829	
1960	58,882	+9%
1970	62,108	+5%
1980	62,202	+0%
1987*	62,400	+0%

*preliminary TvB estimate

2.

While daily newspaper circulation remains flat, **the number of U.S. households continues to increase.**

A 22% increase in U.S. households in the '50's was followed by 17% in the '60's, 27% in the '70's, and another 14% increase in U.S. households has been added to date in the '80's.

U.S. Households

	(000)	
1950	43,000	
1960	52,500	+22%
1970	61,410	+17%
1980	77,900	+27%
1987	89,130	+14%

3.

Once, the total circulation of daily newspapers out-numbered the total number of U.S. homes. But today that has changed dramatically. **There is only enough circulation for 70% of U.S. households.**

Daily Newspapers Per Household

	Circulation (000)	U.S. Households	Newspapers/ Households
1950	53,829	43,000	1.25
1960	58,882	52,500	1.12
1970	62,108	61,410	1.01
1980	62,202	77,900	.82
1987	62,400	89,130	.70

4.

As daily newspaper circulation failed to match the growing marketplace...a new medium replaced it. **Television is today's growth medium.**

Television was an immediate success with the American public. So much so that TV households increased 1079% in the '50's and continued to grow by 28% in the '60's, 30% in the '70's and 15% to date in the '80's.

Television Households

	(000)	
1950	3,880	
1960	45,740	+1079%
1970	58,500	+ 28%
1980	76,300	+ 30%
1987	87,400	+ 15%

5.

Today, **television households with one or more television sets greatly out-number total daily newspaper circulation.**

1970 was the last year that newspaper circulation was greater than the number of television homes. Today there are 25 million more television homes than there is newspaper circulation.

	Newspaper Circulation (000)	Television Homes (000)
1950	53,829	3,880
1960	58,882	45,750
1970	62,108	58,500
1980	62,202	76,300
1987	62,400	87,400

6.

Television is in virtually every U.S. household. 98.1% of U.S. homes are television homes.

	U.S. Households (000)	Television Households (000)	% TV Homes
1950	43,000	3,880	9.0%
1960	52,500	45,750	87.1%
1970	61,410	58,500	95.3%
1980	77,900	76,300	97.9%
1987	89,130	87,400	98.1%

Sources: Point 1, 3, 5, Editor & Publisher
Point 2, 3, 4, 5, 6, NBC, 1950, 1960;
A.C. Nielsen, 1970, 1980, 1987

(a)

EXHIBIT 8.12

Television stations have become extremely aggressive in their competition with newspapers for local advertising dollars. (Courtesy: Television Bureau of Advertising.)

TvB TELEVISION BUREAU OF ADVERTISING

(Printed from 1" Videotape by Radio TV Reports. Contact Marc David (212) 599-5833)

"FOOD PROCESSOR"

This is a common everyday food processor.

In the newspaper, it looks like this!

On the radio, it sounds like this!

On television, it looks like this! If television can make a common everyday food processor look like this, think what it can do for the products you sell!

Television advertising means business...more business...for you!

"UPS AND DOWNS"

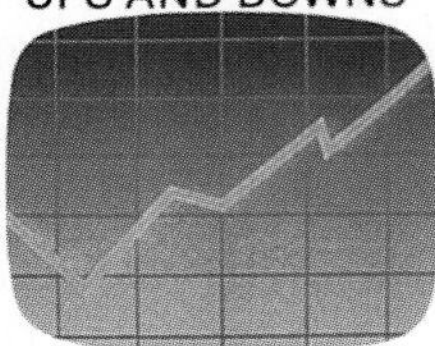

Most businesses have ups...and downs.

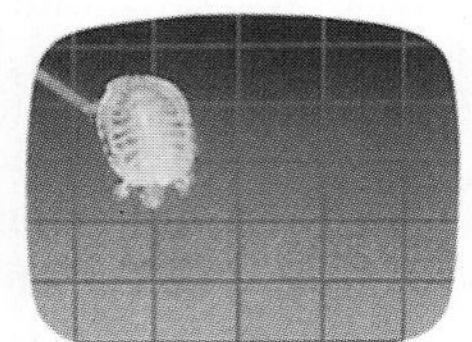

But some have more downs than ups.

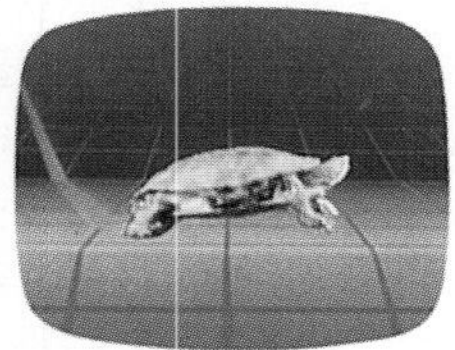

The more they go down... the harder it is to go back up.

One advertising medium can make your business highs higher...and can give you the jump on your competition. Television!

Television advertising means business...more business...for you!

"I WISH"

If you're in business this could happen to you! "I wish I had listened."

"I wish I had stayed away from those four-color print jobs." "I wish I had realized that people don't read all that junk mail."

"I wish I had become a television advertiser."

"Hey, who hired you anyway?"
"Your secretary! She saw us on television!"

Television advertising means business...more business...for you!

"GAME SHOW"

A quiz for newspaper advertisers. Which of these statements is true? Newspaper costs are up!

Newspaper readership is down!

Newspaper coverage isn't even half the homes in my trading area!

Unfortunately, each of those is true. If you're a newspaper advertiser, maybe you'd like an alternative. Try television. I'll bet your competitor has.

Television advertising means business...more business...for you!

"BUSINESS THERAPY"

A sad business story. I told my competitor that television advertising costs too much!

I told him television was only for big business.

Yet, he used television and I did not. His business is now bigger than mine.

For your business the perfect cure could be just a television commercial away.

Television advertising means business...more business...for you!

(b)

called the immediately preemptible (IP) rate (the lowest rate). When the station can preempt only if it gives the original advertiser two weeks' notice, the rate is designated "preemptible with two weeks' notice" and is sold at a higher rate. The highest rate is charged for a nonpreemptible time slot; the two-week preemptible rate is the next highest; and the immediately preemptible rate is the lowest.

Exhibit 8.13 is a quotation from a rate card. The three columns show the preemption rates: column I, the nonpreemptible rate; column II, the rate for preemption on two weeks' notice; and column III, the rate for preemption without notice. Observe how the rate goes down.

SPECIAL FEATURES. News telecasts, weather reports, sports news and commentary, stock market reports, and similar programming are called *special features*. Time in connection with special features is sold at a premium price.

RUN OF SCHEDULE (ROS). An advertiser can earn a lower rate by permitting a station to run commercials at its convenience whenever time is available rather than in a specified position. (This is comparable to ROP in printed advertising; see Chapter 10.)

PACKAGE RATES. Every station sets up its own assortment of time slots at different periods of the day, which it sells as a package. The station creates its own name for such packages and charges less for them than for the same spots sold individually. The package rate is one of the elements in negotiation for time.

Product protection. *When a station agrees not to schedule a commercial for a competing brand within some specified time period.*

PRODUCT PROTECTION. Every advertiser wants to keep the advertising of competitive products as far away from his or her commercials as possible. This brings up the question of what protection against competition an ad will get. Although some stations say that they will try to keep competing commercials 5 to 10 minutes apart, most say that while they will do everything possible to separate competing ads, they guarantee only that they will not run them back to back.

SCHEDULING SPOT AND LOCAL TIME. *Rotation of a schedule* refers to the placement of commercials within a schedule to get the greatest possible showing (see Exhibit 8.14). If you bought two spots a week for four weeks on a Monday-to-Friday basis, but all the spots were aired only on Monday and Tuesday, your rotation would be poor. You would miss all the people who turn to the station only on Wednesday, Thursday, or Friday. Your *horizontal rotation* should be increased.

Vertical rotation assures there will be differences in the time at which a commercial is shown within the time bracket purchased. If you bought three spots on the "Tonight Show," which runs from 11:30 P.M. to 12:30 A.M., but all your spots were shown at 12:15 A.M., you would be missing all the people who go to sleep earlier than that. To avoid this situation, you would schedule one spot in each half hour of the program, vertically rotating your commercial to reach the largest possible audience.

TELEVISION SYNDICATION

Syndication. *The selling and scheduling of TV programs on a station-by-station basis, as contrasted to network programming.*

Television syndication is the sale and distribution of shows on a station-by-station basis, rather than through a network. From an advertising standpoint, syndication encompasses elements of both network and spot buys. Like network, the programs are

EXHIBIT 8.13
Rate and quotation.

Rate-Card Excerpt			
	I	**II**	**II**
Tues., 8–9 A.M.	$135	$125	$115

EXHIBIT 8.14

Schedule demonstrating rotation of television spots. (Courtesy: BDA/BBDO.)

Station KOCO/Ch. 5/ABC			OKLAHOMA CITY (all 30s)					
Day	**Time**	**Program**	**Spots per Week**	**HH Rtg.**	**ADI Men 25–49 Rtg.**	**Homes (000)**	**Men 25–49 (000)**	**Adults 25–54 (000)**
M-S	10-10:30 P.M.	Late News	1	16	14	88	33	75
M-S	10:35-11:10 P.M.	M*A*S*H	2	19/38	16/32	96/192	39/78	83/166
SAT	4-5:30 P.M.	Wide World of Sports	1	7	6	38	12	26
M-F	7-10 P.M.	Prime Orbit*	1	12	11	67	26	59
			5	73	63	385	149	326
*Prime Orbit to Rotate:								
Mon	7:30 CC	Monday Night Baseball	2					
Tue	7-9 P.M.	Happy Days/Laverne & Shirley/Three's Company/ Too Close for Comfort	1					
Fri	8-10 P.M.	ABC Fri. Night Movies	1					

Syndicated shows—those distributed on a station-by-station basis—hold the most opportunity for *local* advertisers. Their popularity, based on previous network affiliation and their versatility in the schedule, have contributed to their demand. The top syndicated shows in 1988 were *Wheel of Fortune*, *Jeopardy*, *Oprah Winfrey Show*, *PM Magazine*, and *Donahue*. "First-run syndications is a major growth area today," stated Mort Marcus, executive vice president of Qintex Entertainment.

produced and provided by an outside source. On the other hand, all or some of the advertising on these shows is sold by the local stations.

At one time, syndication was a very minor part of television advertising revenues. For the most part, it consisted of selling canceled network shows to local stations to fill "dead" time in afternoon or late-night dayparts. The shows were viewed by both stations and producers as having run their course and were deemed to have little value.

Several factors changed the economics of syndication, and today it is the fastest-growing segment of television advertising (see Exhibit 8.15).

1. *The prime-time access rule*. In 1971, the Federal Communications Commission (FCC), in effect, deleted 30 minutes of prime-time programming from the network schedule. Local affiliates scrambled to fill the time formerly programmed by the networks. The ensuing demand for new programming increased the cost of syndicated programming. Since the rule also prohibited affiliates (but not independent stations) from using shows that had formerly been on a network, it also created the need for "first-run" syndication.

EXHIBIT 8.15

National Syndicated ad volume, 1980–1995.
(Source: Television Bureau of Advertising.)

	Millions	$ Chg.	$ TV
1980	50	—	0.4
1981	75	50.0	0.6
1982	150	100.0	1.0
1983	300	100.0	1.8
1984	400	33.3	2.1
1985	530	32.5	2.6
1986	610	15.1	2.8
1987	708	16.1	3.0
1988	827	16.8	3.1
1989	956	15.6	3.3
1990	1,090	14.0	3.4
1991	1,238	13.6	3.5
1992	1,396	12.8	3.5
1993	1,570	12.5	3.6
1994	1,749	11.4	3.7
1995	1,941	11.0	3.7

2. *Growing competition of local evening news.* During the 1970s, local stations ''discovered'' news as a profit center. The competition for ratings (and advertising dollars) in local news involved everything from glamorous personalities, high-tech sets, and helicopters. It also indicated the need for popular ''lead-ins'' to the news hour. Stations learned that the most popular syndicated programs at 5:30 built an audience for the six o'clock news. The competition among affiliates for ''M*A*S*H,'' ''Wheel of Fortune,'' and other popular syndicated shows further escalated their costs.[14]
3. *The increase in the number of outlets.* The affiliates are not the only ones vying for syndicated product; so are the hundreds of independent stations and cable networks. In 1988, the syndicated market saw a major departure from form when the USA Network won the syndication rights to ''Miami Vice'' and ''Murder She Wrote.''
4. *Leverage against network price increases.* Despite falling audience shares, network advertising rates continue to increase. ''The dual effect of higher prices and smaller network audiences was a drastic increase in network TV CPMs, up 10% to 30% in 1987. . . . As a result, advertisers last year began re-evaluating their network TV spending, boosting allocations to alternative media, such as cable and syndication.''[15] Some major advertisers such as Procter & Gamble have shifted significant dollars from the networks into syndicated programming.

There are several types of syndication. As we discuss some of the major ones, remember that a show can fall into more than one category.

Off-Network Syndication

Off-network syndication is the oldest form of syndication. The demand for syndicated shows has fundamentally changed both the economics and the relationship between networks and producers. To be a financial success in syndication, a show has to have been on the network a minimum of four to five years (approximately 100 episodes). Knowing the lucrative syndication market that awaits successful shows, the networks can be very hard-nosed in their negotiations with producers. In some cases, producers claim that network sales do not cover their costs. However, these producers know the residual fees will increase the longer their shows stay on the networks. Nonetheless, as the risks and competition of syndication increase, producers will be less willing to sell to the networks at less than a premium price.

The advantage to advertisers of off-network syndication is that it has quality production, established stars, and a proven track record from its network run. However, with the growth of independent stations and cable networks, many with 24-hour programming schedules, we are seeing shows in syndication that barely had a network run. Off-network shows such as ''Lady Blue,'' which would not even have been considered for syndication a few years ago, are now regularly seen on cable. Filling airtime is a tremendous problem, but the standards of success for networks and syndication are much different. For example, a network rating of 5 would get a show quickly cancelled; the same rating on many cable networks would place the show number one.

First-Run Syndication

First-run syndication. *Syndicated shows that are produced specifically for the syndicated market, as contrasted to off-network reruns.*

Any softness in the off-network syndication market is the result of growth in original programming developed for syndication. At one time, the only first-run syndicated programs were game shows. They were inexpensive to make and were popular with both stations and audiences. However, in recent years, a number of other formats have found their way into syndication. The major breakthrough was ''Donahue,'' which spawned the ''Oprah Winfrey Show,'' ''Geraldo,'' and a host of other imitators.

---

[14]Local affiliates can schedule off-network reruns, such as ''M*A*S*H,'' anytime except during the prime-time access period.

[15]Richard Edel, ''Unwired Nets Snare Marketers' Dollars,'' *Advertising Age*, February 22, 1988, p. S-12.

Besides game and talk shows, syndicators have produced a number of other shows, including "She's the Sheriff," "The New Gidget Show," and "Out of this World." The increased production costs and generally lower ratings achieved by syndicated programming have greatly increased the risk of even the least expensive first-run programming.

Barter Syndication

Barter syndication. *A show that is offered to stations with national commercials already inserted. The station receives the show at no (or lower) cost in return for giving up some commercial time. Additional time is made available for local commercials.*

In barter syndication, a show is offered to a station at a reduced price (even free, in rare cases), with presold national spots. About half the commercial time is sold to national advertisers; the remainder is available for sale by the local station. Consequently, the station gets inexpensive programming and national advertisers get to participate in syndication with the convenience of a network-type buy.

The number of barter syndication shows has increased dramatically in the last five years. However, all is not well in the barter market:

> ". . . although the huge amount of barter syndicated programming being offered will, technically at least, leave buyers in control, the worry is that there is so much product out there that the competition for TV station time slots will be so fierce that few shows will be able to achieve suitable national coverage.
>
> Like network shows, syndicators must guarantee national advertisers that their shows will be carried by enough stations to constitute a "national buy." And since national advertisers rarely accept coverage of less than 70% of the U.S., the current glut of programming in the station marketplace poses a double whammy for barter sales reps.[16]

It is also important to evaluate the quality of the coverage. A clearance at 7 P.M. is much different than a clearance at 2 A.M.

Fourth Network

Another use of the term *fourth network* refers to first-run syndication programming that runs simultaneously in a certain time period, but is sold and distributed on a station-by-station basis. In the past, a fourth network usually existed for one show—a special presentation like the highly rated, but critically slammed "The Mystery of Al Capone's Vault"—and was sold primarily to independent stations.

While syndicators have nibbled at the loyalties of network affiliates in other network programming dayparts, prime time has long been an elusive target. But Paramount has proved that with the right show, affiliates will renounce their network during prime time, if only for one hour a week. The network was third-place ABC, and Paramount pitted a virtually proven property, "Star Trek: The Next Generation," against that network's weakest night. The strategy paid off: No less than a dozen ABC affiliates bumped the network's 8 P.M. Saturday night spot in favor of the one-hour syndicated show. Of course, this doesn't signal a mass defection from the networks by the affiliates—at least not yet.

Stripping and Checkerboarding

Strip programming. *A strip is when the same show is programmed Monday-Friday at the same time.*

A local station's practice of programming the same syndicated show in a time period throughout the week is called *stripping*. That is, the station strips the show across a time period. Virtually all weekday syndication is programmed in this way. Independent stations have long used off-network sitcoms as a counterprogramming technique to compete with local affiliate newscasts and late-night network programming.

---

[16]Joe Mandese, "Testing the Ad Waters," *Marketing & Media Decisions*." February 1988, p. 87.

The opposite of stripping, programming a different syndicated program each night, is known as *checkerboard* programming, or *checkerboarding*. Checkerboarding is used infrequently today because there is a dearth of quality programming. As a television executive noted, "Checkerboarding's problem is more with product than with concept: Hollywood just couldn't keep up the flow of 'first-class' offerings required to keep viewers satisfied. In the old days, viewers had a choice of three shows to watch. Now there are 25 to 30 different things. People don't have to watch anything that is bad or mediocre."[17]

CABLE TELEVISION

There has been a tremendous growth in cable advertising—both in dollars and share of the total revenue. Cable operators predict cable ad spending will grow by about *20%* annually over the next few years. Ad revenues were *$1.45 billion in 1988!*

Cable television achieved two significant benchmarks in 1987. First, the industry passed the 50 percent level of household penetration. And, not coincidentally, advertising allocations to cable hit the $1 billion mark. Exhibit 8.16 shows the tremendous growth of cable advertising. Note that advertising in cable is increasing on both a dollar and a share-of-television-revenue basis. In fact, cable advertising is growing at a much faster rate than household penetration.

Financially, the cable industry has never been healthier. Cable programming attracts an average share of 20 percent of the viewing audience, compared to 11 percent in 1983. Overall, cable operating profits are above $275 million, compared to a $54 million loss in 1983.[18] Exhibit 8.17 shows the dramatic growth in both basic and pay cable channels since the 1970s.

The Organization of Cable Television

Cable television consists of three main components: system operators, basic cable programming networks, and pay cable programming networks. Each component has singular economic characteristics. Cable systems are capital-intensive, largely due to high initial construction and maintenance costs. System operators derive revenues partly from cable subscribers, who pay a monthly fee to receive programming. Like television stations, cable systems distribute programmed entertainment and maintain affiliate relationships with basic and pay cable networks.[19]

Cable television advertising revenues are concentrated in a very few cable networks. There are approximately 50 advertising-supported cable services, but, as Exhibit 8.18 shows, only six services have 40 million or more subscriber households. The number of subscribers begins to fall sharply for the other networks, as does their potential for significant advertising revenues.

EXHIBIT 8.16

Cable advertising is one of the fastest-growing segments of the industry. (Courtesy: Television Advertising Bureau.)

	Cable Ad Volume (millions)	*Cable as a % of Total TV Ad Volume*
1985	$ 751	3.5%
1986	930	4.0%
1987	1,142	4.6%
1990	1,982	5.9%
1995	4,041	7.4%

Source: Paul Kagan Assoc., Inc.; TvB projections.

[17] Alice Z. Cuneo, "Pattern Set for Checkerboard Demise," *Advertising Age*, February 22, 1988, p. S-6.
[18] Richard Zoglin, "Heady Days Again for Cable," *Time*, May 30, 1988, p. 52.
[19] *Five Year Communications Industry Forecast* (New York: Verons, Suhler & Associates, July 1988), p. 56.

EXHIBIT 8.17

Cable penetration is accelerating. It is now 54 percent and is projected to reach 63 percent in the early 1990s. (Courtesy: *Advertising Age*.)

Year	Cable Subscribers (000)	Household Penetration (%)	Pay Subscribers (000)
1988	48,637	53.8	28,114
1987	44,971	50.5	27,600
1986	42,237	48.1	23,709
1985	39,873	46.2	24,165
1980	17,671	22.6	7,599
1975	9,197	13.2	NA
1970	4,498	7.5	NA

- Cable penetration projected to reach 63% by1992.
- The rate of annual cable penetration growth has increased from 200,000 homes per month (Nov. 1986–Nov. 1987) to 300,000 homes per month (Nov. 1987–Nov. 1988).

Source: Nielsen

Despite its overall popularity, cable television is an extremely competitive business. In part, this is the result of the vast amount of programming that is needed to fill a 24-hour day on most of these services. It has been estimated that one week of contemporary television uses more programming than a full year of television did in 1970. Because advertisers are overwhelmed with the sheer number of choices, the successful cable channel must fill one of three niches:

The sheer number of choices offered to cable advertisers forces them to choose one of three niches: (1) general audience; (2) specialized programming, such as sports or news; and (3) distinct demographics, such as Disney Channel for children or Financial News Network. FNN calls itself the business network and "brags" that is reaches the best educated, most affluent audience in television!

1. Be a service that can compete on a broad basis for a general audience. The Turner Broadcasting Service (TBS), with its mix of movies, off-network reruns, and sports, and the USA Network are two prime examples of this type of cable service.
2. Be the leader in a particular programming format. Clearly, ESPN in sports, the Cable News Network (CNN) in news, and MTV in music have achieved this position with both viewers and advertisers.
3. Be a service (sometimes with a relatively small audience) with a distinct demographic or upscale audience. Black Entertainment Television (BET), the Financial News Network (FNN), and the Disney Channel fall into this category.

EXHIBIT 8.18

Cable television audiences are concentrated in a relatively few networks. (Courtesy: *Advertising Age*.)

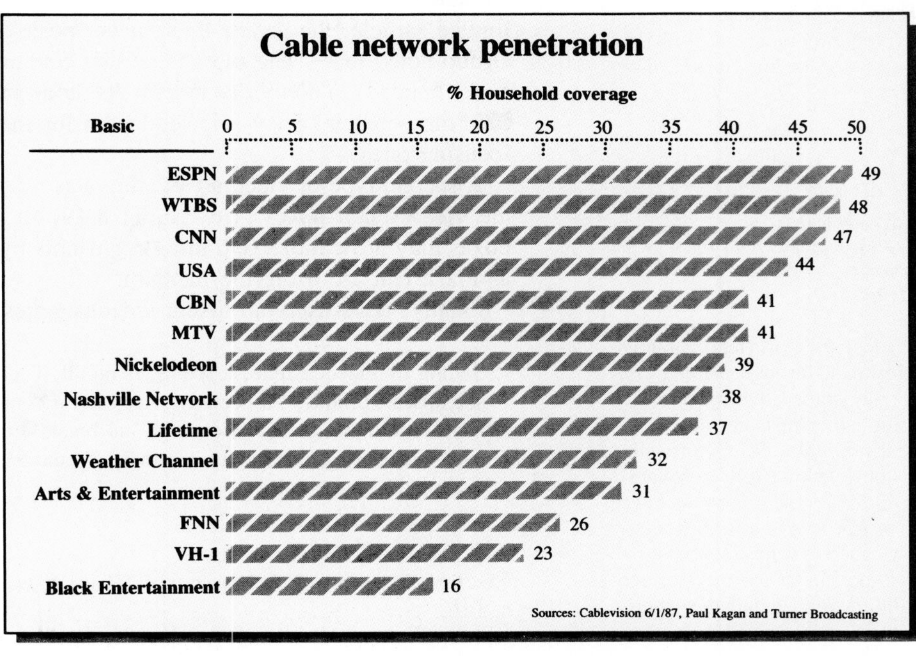

Pay cable. *Networks which are carried exclusively on cable and supported solely by subscribers.*

In addition to advertiser-supported cable networks, there are approximately ten pay (also called *premium*) channels. The oldest, and still the most popular, is Home Box Office, with almost 16 million subscribers. While none of these channels accept advertising, they are an important consideration to both advertisers and commercial cable services since they compete for viewers with commercial outlets. These pay services are all the more troublesome to commercial channels since they attract a younger and more upscale viewing audience, the very people advertisers are trying to reach through commercial outlets.

Local cable system advertising, as a separate advertising medium, has never achieved significant revenues. Only about 10 percent of all cable advertising revenues come from local advertising. Most local commercials are run by cable operators on a "cut-in" basis—that is, operators sell local commercials on time provided by CNN or ESPN in their regular programming. An increasing number of local systems are working with cable networks to sell local advertising spots. The marketing strategy of a music store buying time on MTV, a sporting goods dealer on ESPN, or a pharmacy on the Lifetime network has brought numerous local advertisers to cable in recent years.

The Videocassette Recorder (VCR)

Depending on your point of view, the VCR is either one of the greatest innovations in television technology or one of its most serious competitors. Clearly, it is a phenomenon that must be considered part of the television advertising mix. According to A. C. Nielsen, household VCR ownership will reach 65 percent in 1990, up from just 2 percent in 1980.

There are several indications that advertisers and the television industry are taking the VCR seriously. We will review three areas where the VCR has caused significant changes in the industry.

Since 1987, when Diet Pepsi advertised on the taped release of *Top Gun*, there has been a slow but steady interest in placing commercials on movie tapes. Pepsi has signed, again, to appear in the beginning of movies; this time it's a multi-title deal with Paramount Home Video. The commercials won't be movie-themed, but will, in some way, tie in with the movies.

Advertiser Participation in Videos. Over $5 billion is spent on VCR movie rentals each year. It is estimated that more than 80 percent of VCR owners are regular movie renters. Since most of these people are under 50 years old, a lucrative market is being lost to advertisers who use only traditional broadcast outlets.

Advertising came to the VCR in 1986, when a Diet Pepsi commercial was placed on the taped release of *Top Gun*. Since then, there has been a slow but steady interest on the part of advertisers in placing commercials on movie tapes. *Dirty Dancing, Platoon,* and *Interspace* are among the several tape releases carrying commercials. Based on a limited sample, the results thus far are positive. One research study by the Fairfield Group noted that "The most important finding is that ads placed on videos perform better than ads in non-video media. As far as awareness and recall, they perform about four times better. They [viewers] paid for the video so they are likely going to be focusing on it."[20]

A second type of video advertising was recently introduced. This is advertising on the video rental boxes (see Exhibit 8.19). It is estimated that advertising on rental boxes may grow into a $30 million business by 1990. Already major advertisers such as Pizza Hut are using the medium.

Finally, advertisers are using videocassettes as a direct-response medium.

"Videologs" or video catalogs help break through *printed clutter*, say some advertisers of fashionable, upscale, and technical products. Tyler Software Systems, which sells software to retail stores, prefers to have its prospects view its introductory video—*before* sending sales personnel for indepth consultations and detailed written material.

> Selling by videocassette, it seems, is rapidly becoming one of the most fashionable ways to sell upscale products, especially since most upscale households have a VCR. Direct marketers have started producing "videologs" to break through the clutter of printed catalogs. Now it is the advertisers who are turning their ads and brochures into videos, "bro-videos" or "videochures" if you will.[21]

---

[20]L. Eric Elie, "Ads Make Headway on Home Videos," *The Atlanta Journal,* September 5, 1988, p. 1-D.

[21]Wayne Walley, "Marketers Star in Home Videos," *Advertising Age,* December 7, 1987, p. 58.

EXHIBIT 8.19

The growth of videocassettes has opened a number of advertising opportunities. (Courtesy: ADcorp, Inc.)

How Videotagg Works For You!

Every Rented Video Carries Your Message Home!

Until now rental video cassettes have gone home in plain, protective plastic boxes.

From this day on, those boxes are no longer plain; no longer ordinary!

ADcorp Inc. has transformed these boxes into one of the most effective and dynamic advertising media in the world.

And not just a few boxes.

Millions of video boxes in literally every important market in North America are under contract to carry your color plus Videotagg advertising message.

How It Works

Your Videotagg ad is printed in glossy full color on adhesive-backed material and applied to the covers of video rental boxes in the specific consumer market you wish to reach.

Videotaggs are available in virtually every major market in the United States and Canada. ADcorp has long term contracts with some 8,000 video rental outlets representing more than 20 million video movie boxes available for Videotagg ads.

For further information
call 403-265-3555 or write

ADCORP
ADcorp, Inc.
500, 333 - 11th Avenue S.W.
Calgary, Alberta T2R 1L9

The average rental frequency of video movies and their Videotagg carrying boxes ranges from approximately 12 to 18 times per quarter per movie with some new movie releases renting much more frequently. Exposure of your Videotagg ad is further insured with a minimum of 4 exposures each time a movie enters a home. First when the movie is rented, second when the video box is opened, third when the movie is re-inserted in the box and fourth when the video box is returned to the rental outlet. Even more exposures than these will likely occur during the 24 hour plus rental period.

Market purchases can range from ads reaching an entire market to geographic sub-divisions of markets (blocks). The total video box inventory in any market can also be split market-wide so a Videotagg ad appears only on every second, third or more box. Exclusive market purchases are also available.

Videotagg ads penetrate the entertainment and private areas of VCR owners' homes and deliver multiple exposures for your ad message.

Contact an ADcorp Regional Office for details on our special introductory program. And remember ADcorp offers agency commissions, frequency and volume discounts, and market test programs. ADcorp also specializes in measurable market promotions, couponing and premiums that will verify Videotagg is a powerful and cost effective advertising medium.

National Sales Offices:
New York 201-464-0409,
Chicago 312-416-2353,
Los Angeles 714-660-1220

Take Your Pick!

The 4 inch x 7 inch Videotagg advertising space offers several formats ranging from one ad per Videotagg to alternative layouts offering several smaller space ads sharing the space with other non-competitive (guaranteed) advertisers. Horizontal and vertical formats are available.

Here are only a few examples of how to use Videotaggs.

Videotagg© by ADcorp, Inc.

Rating Services and the VCR. We will discuss the television rating services in detail later in this chapter. Here we note that current considerations given to measuring the VCR audience are another indication of their importance to the industry. Questions are being asked concerning:

> ***Time-shift viewing.*** *Programs which are recorded for viewing at a different time.*

- How much recorded material is played back, and how long after the original telecast is it viewed?
- How does the playback audience differ from the live audience?
- What percentage of commercials are fast-forwarded?
- Are time-shifted viewers (those who view a program at a time different from its original telecast) as valuable to advertisers as viewers of the original telecast?
- How much of VCR play time is devoted to tape rentals?[22]

[22]Steven Sternberg, ''VCRs: Impact and Implications,'' *Marketing & Media Decisions,* December 1987, p. 100.

The VCR and the Average Person's Viewing Pattern. For example, AGB Television Research found:

- Viewing of home-recorded and prerecorded tapes adds 10 percent to the average person's viewing time in VCR homes over a 24-hour day.
- The bulk of viewing is of prerecorded rather than of home-recorded tapes.
- Prerecorded cassettes played in prime time attract a significantly bigger audience within the household than either home-recorded or regular TV programs.
- Taped soap operas are usually played back within 24 hours, prime-time programs within one week.[23]

Regardless of the specific uses, or degree of usage, viewers make of the VCR in the future, it is clear that the technology has forever changed the television landscape. The VCR will increasingly be part of the media considerations of advertisers.

OTHER BROADCAST ALTERNATIVES

We are starting to see alternative delivery systems competing with both cable and traditional TV outlets. Since the advertising potential for these services is so small at the present time, they will only be discussed briefly here.

Subscription Television (STV)

A decoding device takes jumbled broadcast signals and lets the subscriber see first-run movies and other material similar to that offered by pay cable. The advantage of STV is that it doesn't require the capital investments of cable because the signal is broadcast and thus no wiring is needed. On the other hand, the subscriber gets only a single channel rather than the large number of channels delivered by cable.

Direct-Broadcast Satellite Systems (DBS)

Here a signal is transmitted by satellite directly to a subscriber and is picked up by a home receiver dish.

Multipoint Distribution Systems (MDS)

Usually this system is found in hotels or in apartment buildings. It is delivered over a line-of-sight transmission and can provide a multichannel capability over areas of approximately ten miles.

Low-Power TV (LPTV)

As the name implies, these are simply low-powered TV stations with limited coverage. The FCC instituted a freeze on the issuance of licenses for LPTV, and the future of this form of television is very much in doubt.

TELEVISION INFORMATION SERVICES

Not long ago, many people thought that television information services were the growth industry of the future. There were optimistic predictions that by 1990 we would be banking, reserving airline tickets, and conducting routine correspondence over our

[23] "New Data on VCR Playback Viewing: Demos Differ the Second Time Around," *Television/Radio Age*, June 27, 1988, p. 11.

home computers and television sets. The optimists even saw people reading a daily electronic newspaper off their television screens. It has not worked out that way.

There are two basic systems of information delivery: teletext and videotext. While both systems go by a number of names, they have in common the fact that they carry alphanumerics and graphics rather than traditional television pictures.

Teletext

Teletext is a broadcast service that is transmitted to the vertical blanking interval of your television set. The vertical blanking interval is the unused black lines at the top of the picture tube (hidden by the television cabinet). With a converter, the viewer can receive from 100 to several hundred pages or screens of information (see Exhibit 8.20). To date, the major viewer usage for the vertical blanking interval is to carry closed captions for the deaf.

Videotext

Video text. *A service which links a TV set to a central computer to provide a number of informational services such as banking, stock reports, etc.*

While videotext is in some ways similar to teletext, it is a much more flexible system. Basically, videotext links the home television set to a central computer in a two-way communication system. Videotext can be used for information services, but it can also operate as a two-way linkage for shopping and other consumer services (see Exhibit 8.21).

To date, despite significant investments by firms such as Knight-Ridder and Warner Communications, virtually all attempts at home computer/television shopping and information services have failed. The latest, and one of the most ambitious, efforts to launch a successful system is Prodigy Services Company, a joint venture of IBM and Sears Roebuck. Prodigy offers "an at-home electronic service that serves up all kinds of shopping—from clothing to airline tickets—as well as more news and feature-y tidbits than any information junkie might possibly dream of. More than 58 vendors, retailers, brokerage services and advertisers, such as Buick and Levi Strauss, have signed on for what Prodigy promises is a highly personal, compelling and easy-to-use medium that today's harried society will soon realize is a must have."[24]

There are two parts to marketing Prodigy. "First, Prodigy needs to convince exist-

[24] Rebecca Fannin, "The Last Great Hope?" *Marketing & Media Decisions,* February 1988, p. 24.

EXHIBIT 8.20

A broadcast teletext system. (*Source: New Technologies Affecting Radio and Television Broadcasting* [Washington D.C.: National Association of Broadcasters, 1981], p. 23.)

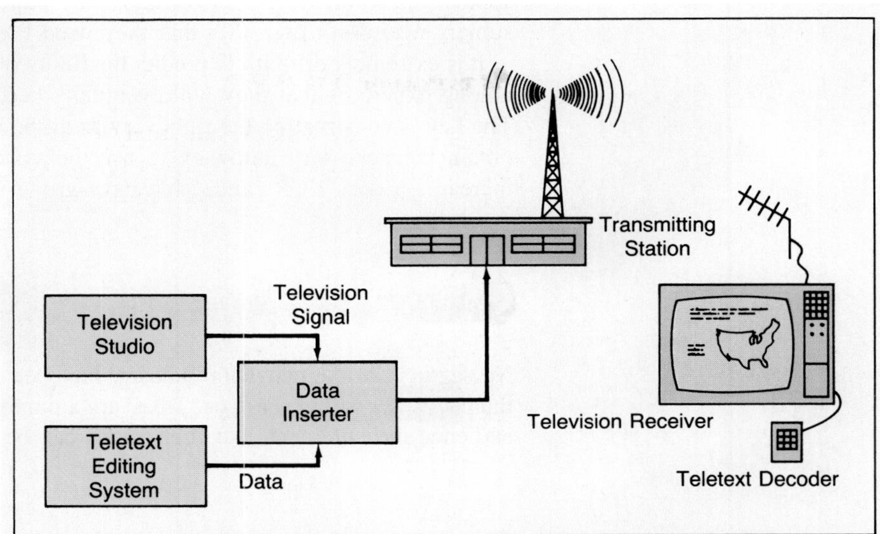

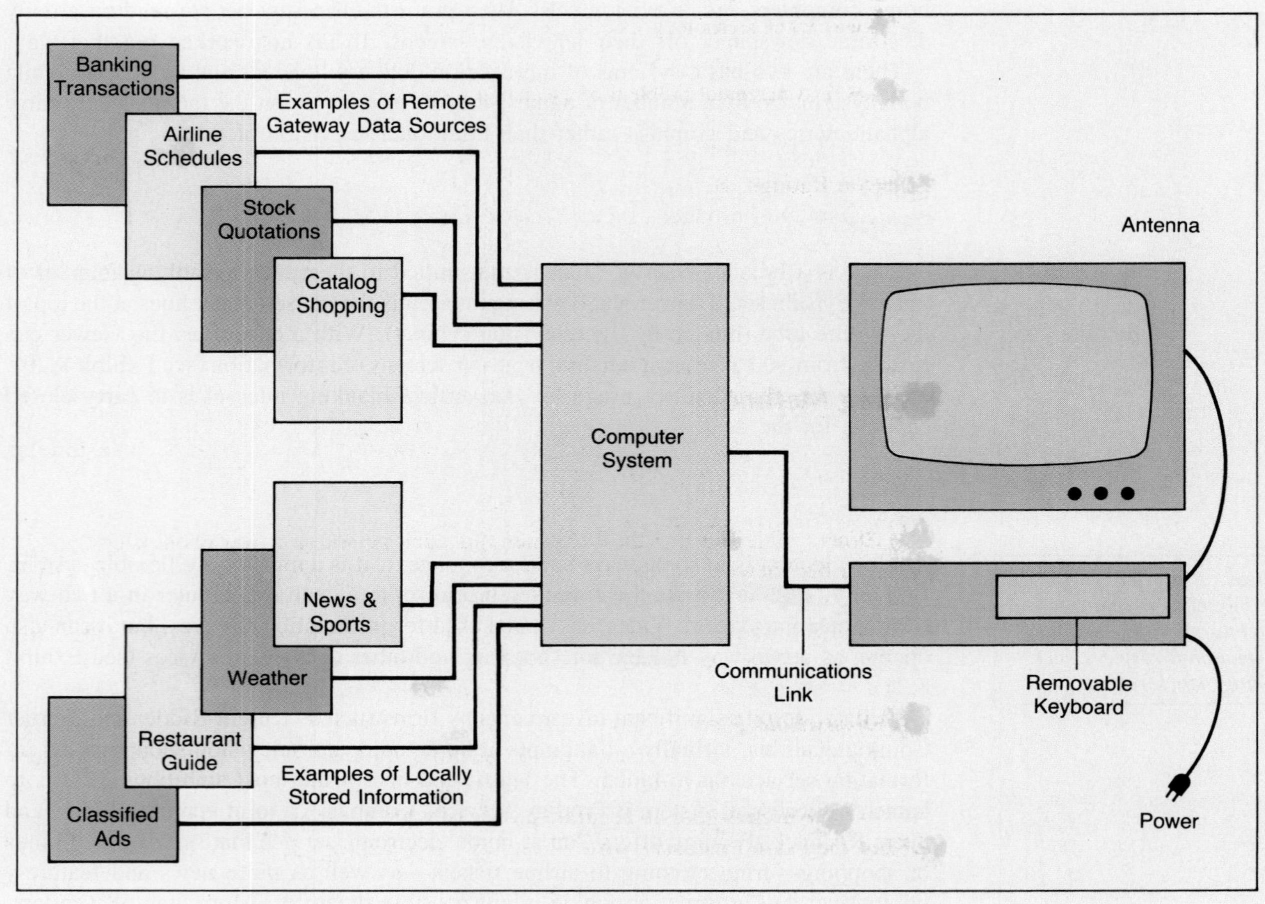

EXHIBIT 8.21
KEYCOM's videotex service. (KEYFAX Teletext is a magazine-format teletext service of Satellite Syndicated Systems and KEYCOM Electronic Publishing.)

ing personal-computer users that they would benefit by signing up with the service. But that market is fairly limited, with an estimated 15 million to 20 million PCs in homes. Of those computers, only about 5 million are powerful enough to operate Prodigy's sophisticated software. Second, and more important, Prodigy needs to convince consumers who don't own PCs that they need Prodigy's services.''[25]

It is extremely difficult to predict the future of these services. However, the thinking among experts is that they will eventually become practical and financially feasible. The key is constructing the right service at the right price to get enough consumers to obtain the necessary hardware to use the system. Once that happens, services will increase, just as VCRs and cable have grown in recent years.

SYNDICATED AUDIENCE RESEARCH

No segment of the television industry has seen more dramatic changes in recent years than audience rating services. There are a number of reasons for this transformation in audience measurement, but four trends can be identified as most significant:

[25]Judith Graham, ''Linkup,'' *Advertising Age,* May 23, 1988, p. 93.

1. Program-viewing alternatives have burgeoned.
2. Measurement technology has become much more sophisticated and refined.
3. The new "Information Society" demands more data and information.
4. There is a perennial problem of escalating media costs.[26]

In the big business of television ratings, two companies dominate: A. C. Nielsen and Arbitron Ratings. Both issue a number of reports dealing with local, national, cable, VCR, and even product usage. Because the industry is so dominated by ratings in terms of programming and revenues, the importance of these rating companies cannot be overestimated.

Rating Methods

The methodology and technology used to gather audience data have gone through several phases over the years.

Ratings' services have placed less reliance on the *diary* alone today and more emphasis on the *Audiometer*—revealing what programs the television set is tuned to—and the *People Meter*—combining set meters *with* diaries. Recent combined figures of the three major networks show their "people meter" scores are slipping. In 1987–88, the first year "people meters" were used, their viewing audiences registered a 71 share. One year later, that figure had slipped to 68. Agency buyers agreed that the decline appeared accurate, with recent growth of cable and independents.

The Diary. The diary method requires that each person in a household keep a record of his or her viewing habits. For many years, the diary was the mainstay of television ratings, and it is still used for smaller market local ratings (see Exhibit 8.22). However, the television of the 1980s cannot be adequately measured by research methods of the 1950s. As a primary source of research data, the diary is on its way out.

The Household Meter. Since 1950, when Nielsen introduced the Nielsen Storage Instantaneous Audimeter (referred to as either the SIA or simply the Audimeter), metered audience measurement has been the principal method of obtaining national ratings. The meters give an accurate profile of what programs the television set is tuned to, but they don't measure who, if anyone, is watching. Also, they are significantly more expensive than diaries.

People Meters. The people meter (see Exhibit 8.23) combines the accuracy of set meters with the diary's ability to gather demographic information, for it records not only what is being watched, but also by whom. Nielsen uses a sample of 4,000 households to gain its people meter ratings. To gauge the reliability of its sample, Nielsen compares its sample households to other households on which data have been obtained from other sources. For example, in a comparison of car registration in the United States versus car registration for Nielsen families, the Nielsen families' car ownership was the same for 6 of 13 models and varied by no more than 3 percentage points on the other 7.

In this way, Nielsen is able to assure advertisers that the audience estimates it provides are accurate "snapshots" of the audience tuned in to television at any particular time. While some people question the size of the sample used by Nielsen and Arbitron, political polling has long shown the accuracy of samples even smaller than these for simple questions. Within the acknowledged margin of error, there is no question that the rating service audience estimates reflect the actual audience. The advantage of the people meter is that it allows the advertiser to gain an accurate demographic profile of the television audience (see Exhibit 8.24).

Combined Television Audience and Purchase Data. It is extremely important for advertisers to know the purchasing behavior of the people who watch television. One system that attempts to combine viewing and purchasing behavior is ScanAmerica, introduced nationally by Arbitron in 1989. The system consists of a people meter that

[26] Alice Sylvester, "Television-Audience Measurement in Transition," *Marketing & Media Decisions,* September 1988, p. 84.

EXHIBIT 8.22

Diaries are still used in smaller markets, but will be largely phased out during the next decade. (Courtesy: Arbitron.)

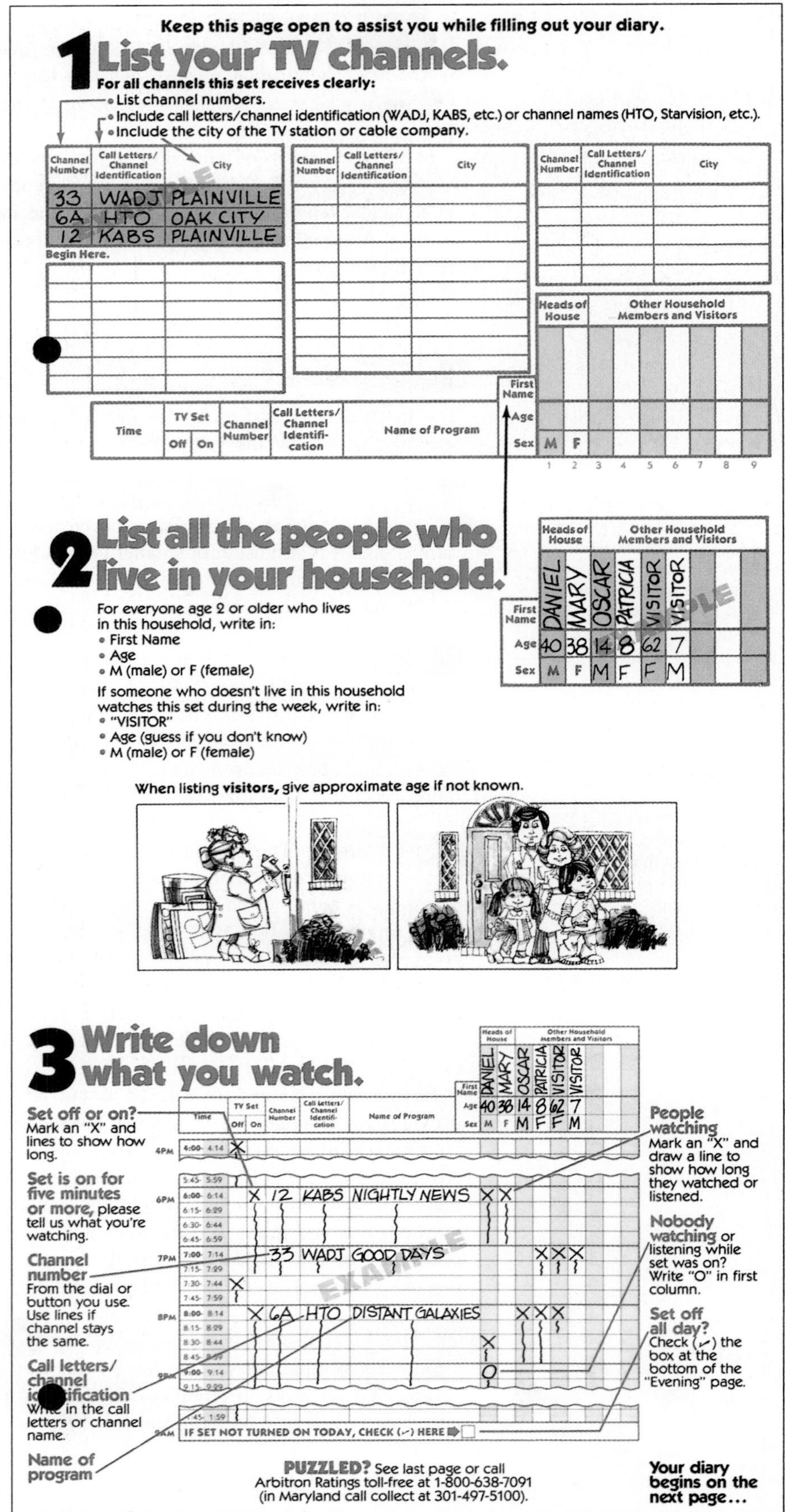

Keep this page open to assist you while filling out your diary.

1 List your TV channels.

For all channels this set receives clearly:

- List channel numbers.
- Include call letters/channel identification (WADJ, KABS, etc.) or channel names (HTO, Starvision, etc.).
- Include the city of the TV station or cable company.

Channel Number	Call Letters/ Channel Identification	City
33	WADJ	PLAINVILLE
6A	HTO	OAK CITY
12	KABS	PLAINVILLE

Begin Here.

Time	TV Set Off	TV Set On	Channel Number	Call Letters/ Channel Identification	Name of Program

	Heads of House		Other Household Members and Visitors						
First Name									
Age									
Sex	M	F							
	1	2	3	4	5	6	7	8	9

2 List all the people who live in your household.

For everyone age 2 or older who lives in this household, write in:

- First Name
- Age
- M (male) or F (female)

If someone who doesn't live in this household watches this set during the week, write in:

- "VISITOR"
- Age (guess if you don't know)
- M (male) or F (female)

	Heads of House		Other Household Members and Visitors						
First Name	DANIEL	MARY	OSCAR	PATRICIA	VISITOR	VISITOR			
Age	40	38	14	8	62	7			
Sex	M	F	M	F	F	M			

When listing **visitors,** give approximate age if not known.

3 Write down what you watch.

Set off or on? Mark an "X" and lines to show how long.

Set is on for five minutes or more, please tell us what you're watching.

Channel number From the dial or button you use. Use lines if channel stays the same.

Call letters/ channel identification Write in the call letters or channel name.

Name of program

	Time	Off	On	Channel Number	Call Letters/ Channel Identification	Name of Program	DANIEL 40 M	MARY 38 F	OSCAR 14 M	PATRICIA 8 F	VISITOR 62 F	VISITOR 7 M
4PM	4:00-4:14	X										
	5:45-5:59											
6PM	6:00-6:14		X	12	KABS	NIGHTLY NEWS	X	X				
	6:15-6:29											
	6:30-6:44											
	6:45-6:59											
7PM	7:00-7:14			33	WADJ	GOOD DAYS				X	X	X
	7:15-7:29											
	7:30-7:44	X										
	7:45-7:59											
8PM	8:00-8:14		X	6A	HTO	DISTANT GALAXIES			X	X	X	
	8:15-8:29											
	8:30-8:44						X					
	8:45-8:59											
9PM	9:00-9:14						O					
	9:15-9:29											
	4:45-4:59											
5AM	IF SET NOT TURNED ON TODAY, CHECK (✓) HERE ☐											

People watching Mark an "X" and draw a line to show how long they watched or listened.

Nobody watching or listening while set was on? Write "O" in first column.

Set off all day? Check (✓) the box at the bottom of the "Evening" page.

PUZZLED? See last page or call Arbitron Ratings toll-free at 1-800-638-7091 (in Maryland call collect at 301-497-5100).

Your diary begins on the next page...

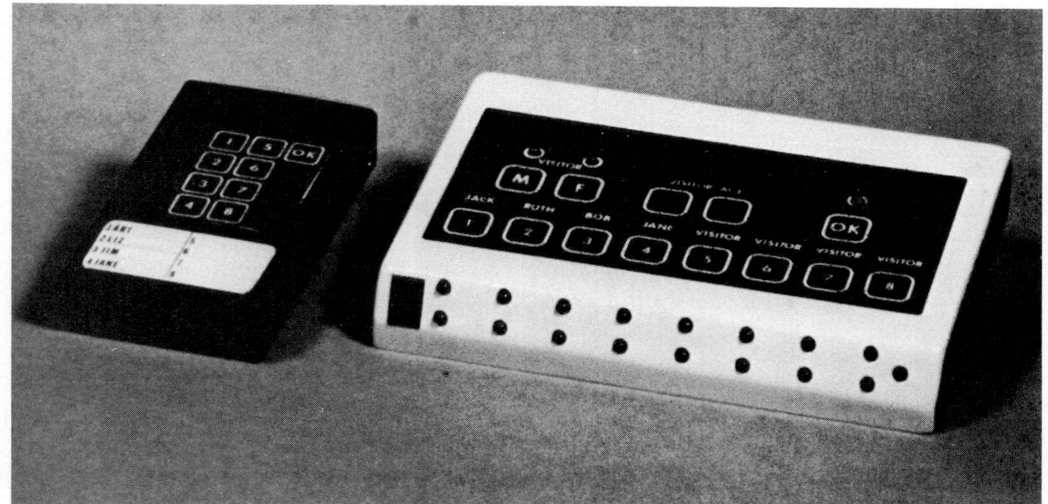

EXHIBIT 8.23

The A-C (Automated Collection of Audience Composition) people meter is a small unit placed on top or beside the TV set. Eight sets of red and green lights on the front are used to indicate if selected people are in the viewing audience (green) or not (red). Each set of lights is assigned to a household family member who can indicate his or her presence as a viewer by pushing an assigned button on the top of the meter, changing its light from red (all red lights are on and flashing when the set is turned on) to green. (Courtesy: A C. Nielsen Company.)

EXHIBIT 8.24

The people meter rating provides valuable information about audience demographics. (Courtesy: A. C. Nielsen.)

22 PROGRAM AUDIENCE ESTIMATES (Alpha) APR. 18–24, 1988

PROGRAM NAME / DAY TIME DUR NET NO. OF / #STNS CVG% TYPE T/C	KEY	HOUSEHOLD AUDIENCES AVG. AUD. %	SH %	AVG. AUD. 0,000	TOTAL PERS (2+)	WORKING WOMEN 18+	WORKING WOMEN 18-49	LOH 18-49 W/CH <3	WOMEN TOTAL	WOMEN 18-34	WOMEN 18-49	WOMEN 25-54	WOMEN 35-64	WOMEN 55+	MEN TOTAL	MEN 18-34	MEN 18-49	MEN 25-54	MEN 35-64	MEN 55+	TEENS TOT. 12-17	TEENS FEM. 12-17	CHILDREN TOT. 2-11	CHILDREN TOT. 6-11
EVENING CONT'D																								
MATLOCK(R)-CONT'D																								
8.00 - 8.30	A	14.3	23	1267	1587	283	208	39^	906	137	359	365	457	483	527	75	185	198	271	299	65	32^	89	55
8.30 - 9.00	A	17.1	26	1515	1608	288	205	35^	911	137	366	380	467	477	557	81	202	222	294	303	63	30^	76	39^
MIAMI VICE(R)	A	9.4	17	833	1638	279	236	105	664	279	503	473	324	114	607	317	466	376	234	114	193	88	174	129
FRI 10.00P 60 NBC 5	B	12.3	23	1090	1660	294	253	102	697	292	507	442	326	152	629	276	450	384	288	139	161	77	173	112
202 98 OP 5	C	12.3	23	1090	1660	294	253	102	697	292	507	442	326	152	629	276	450	384	288	139	161	77	173	112
10.00 - 10.30	A	9.0	16	797	1665	268	228	98	664	277	499	468	321	120	614	317	464	379	236	121	201	93	187	139
10.30 - 11.00	A	9.8	18	868	1613	289	244	112	665	280	507	477	326	109	601	317	467	374	232	107	186	83	161	119
MR. BELVEDERE(R)	A	11.0	20	975	1719	245	185	106	753	247	423	385	335	290	399	151	259	262	188	106	172	99	395	247
FRI 9.00P 30 ABC 5	B	11.2	20	996	1728	276	212	100	755	251	427	395	326	290	424	162	269	244	192	128	197	121	353	232
193 93 CS 8	C	11.4	20	1009	1732	277	219	98	744	255	435	398	328	270	424	160	266	247	195	128	197	121	366	248
MOONLIGHTING(R)	A	11.8	19	1045	1560	307	271	104	663	361	487	376	214	151	450	268	356	286	150	63	257	132	190	122
TUE 9.00P 60 ABC 5	B	14.8	23	1311	1609	347	312	117	728	388	569	470	264	130	459	263	381	319	164	58	218	120	205	134
216 99 PD 23	C	18.0	28	1597	1677	373	333	130	775	415	604	505	283	137	491	278	402	338	182	64	204	116	206	133
9.00 - 9.30	A	12.0	19	1063	1590	309	269	104	661	359	481	377	214	154	435	256	337	272	144	66	273	141	220	137
9.30 - 10.00	A	11.5	18	1019	1543	308	276	104	670	367	497	379	216	149	469	283	379	304	157	61^	243	124	161	107
MURDER, SHE WROTE(R)	A	15.6	26	1382	1620	308	201	36^	892	148	321	347	419	501	601	111	206	239	273	331	47	15^	80	42^
SUN 8.00P 60 CBS 5	B	18.4	30	1634	1611	307	188	36	894	130	320	359	451	501	605	93	217	246	304	333	43	21	70	40
210 99 SM 31	C	20.0	30	1774	1610	313	199	40	899	134	330	365	454	496	592	95	222	246	304	320	52	25	68	41
8.00 - 8.30	A	15.1	26	1338	1616	302	197	37^	879	140	303	329	405	509	615	113	209	241	280	339	42^	12^	79	37^
8.30 - 9.00	A	16.1	26	1426	1624	314	204	36^	904	156	338	364	432	493	588	109	203	238	266	324	51	17^	82	46
NBC MONDAY NIGHT MOVIES(R)	A	18.6	31	1648	1616	329	259	73	835	267	503	490	428	267	503	176	312	299	245	160	147	86	131	78
MON 9.00P 120 NBC 4	B	13.9	22	1234	1590	286	215	67	823	209	446	445	439	315	547	154	298	299	276	207	104	57	116	71
199 97 FF 27	C	16.5	26	1458	1645	325	257	82	846	269	493	456	407	295	507	167	306	289	255	165	143	78	148	92
WHEN THE BOUGH BREAKS																								
9.00 - 9.30	A	17.9	28	1586	1597	316	254	70	791	248	464	454	401	267	463	165	285	280	219	150	156	94	187	110
9.30 - 10.00	A	19.0	30	1683	1632	325	257	74	832	262	503	494	433	262	495	173	301	294	241	158	157	94	147	87
10.00 - 10.30	A	19.1	32	1692	1630	340	264	73	859	279	524	510	443	267	522	182	329	311	258	162	144	82	105	61
10.30 - 11.00	A	18.4	33	1630	1602	335	259	77	854	278	519	501	435	272	530	184	332	312	260	169	131	74	87	54
NBC NEWS SPECIAL(S)	A	13.9	24	1232	1539	310	237	55	846	226	455	446	442	317	525	176	304	278	255	177	86	29^	81	47^
TUE 10.00P 60 NBC																								
197 98 DO																								
WOMEN BEHIND BARS																								
10.00 - 10.30	A	13.7	23	1214	1574	309	237	51^	849	228	456	442	444	322	537	178	308	282	266	187	94	34^	94	58
10.30 - 11.00	A	14.0	25	1240	1515	314	239	58	850	226	457	453	444	314	517	176	303	276	247	169	79	23^	70	37^
NBC SUNDAY NIGHT MOVIE	A	14.0	22	1240	1639	341	256	91	794	308	508	475	345	234	550	241	384	352	244	127	135	76	161	96
SUN 9.00P 120 NBC 5	B	16.2	26	1437	1617	339	256	75	832	250	469	452	409	300	542	191	331	312	258	173	126	75	117	73

measures the television viewing of each person in a household, and a data scan wand that tracks household product purchases. The people meter gathers data on:

ScanAmerica. *A system which allows researchers to track purchase behavior, audience demographics, and viewership.*

- The channel, broadcast or cable, being watched
- Exact time and length of viewing
- The age and sex of each viewer
- Any use of VCRs or other devices with the television set

In order to discover the purchasing behavior of television viewers, ScanAmerican was introduced by Arbitron in 1989. In addition to performing like People Meters, it also registers products brought into the household by UPC symbols. The leading product of 1,100 categories in 50 markets is *microwavable frozen pizza,* according to recent data reports.

The data scan wand (see Exhibit 8.25) registers products brought into the household. All products with a Universal Product Code (UPC) symbol, regardless of place of purchase, can be tracked. ScanAmerica is designed to collect ongoing information about what consumers buy from a projectable sample of 5,000 households. This combination of television viewing information and household purchases, called *single-source research,* is in strong demand within the industry. By gathering both viewing and product-purchasing data, the system can show the interaction of these behaviors—in other words, whether viewers of a program do buy the product advertised on the commercials. Though broadcasters concentrate on the viewing date, and advertisers on the purchasing data, both markets share the ScanAmerica production costs and the results of panel data.[27]

The VCR Audience

One of the major dilemmas faced by the rating services is the use of VCRs by a growing segment of the population. The problem involves research methodology as well as the value of a taped versus an original viewing of a program. The concern with

[27]From *ScanAmerica Information Packet,* published by Arbitron Ratings.

EXHIBIT 8.25

(a)

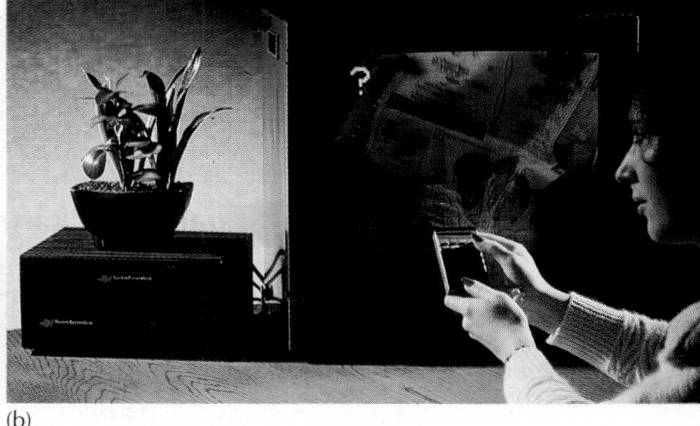
(b)

(c)

including taped viewing (you will recall that this is known as time-shift viewing) in metered ratings is that Nielsen research has found that:

- About 25 percent of these recordings are not played back.
- For about 60 percent of recordings played back, viewers use the fast-forward to skip over commercials.

Advertisers are, of course, exclusively concerned with audience commercial exposure. The ability to zip (fast-forward through commercials) or zap (delete the commercial) with VCRs has made them extremely cautious of counting methods that weight time-shift viewing equally with original viewing. Many in the industry think that taped-playback audiences should be weighted downward—that is, given less value than the original audience watching the show. The problem is how to arrive at a defensible weighting procedure.

Ratings for Commercials

The "ultimate" desire of advertising is a rating system *for commercials. Ad Week Magazine* offers monthly recaps of the "best spots" for $95. They claim they've watched 1,000 hours of commercials to give the viewer 29 minutes of "all the TV commercials that are too good or too important to miss." They also feature a weekly critique of a current commercial.

The ultimate goal for advertisers is a rating system exclusively for commercials. After all, from an advertising standpoint, program ratings are of interest only insofar as they demonstrate *opportunities* for prospects to see a commercial. To date, attempts to develop a commercial rating service have not proved technologically feasible or financially practical.

Still, the search for an affordable and valid system for rating commercials will goes on, and the company that finally develops one will instantaneously become the leader among rating companies. As one advertising executive noted, a commercial rating system "can make us smarter and give us a better understanding of audience dynamics. And it might introduce a new level of precision on our analysis, allowing us to better select the most appropriate programs/slots for ads without the leap of faith we currently make—that the average audience for quarter hours is sufficient to describe the audience we're really communicating with, those who actually are exposed to our communication."[28]

Rating services currently depend on diary reporting of taped playbacks, which has the same shortcomings inherent in all diary procedures. Exhibit 8.26 shows the extent of VCR activity during various dayparts. Since VCR penetration is now over 60 percent, the use of VCRs can only increase and the research problem will become more complex.

Qualitative Ratings

Marketing Evaluations is the best-known *qualitative* research service. Rather than just count viewers, it probes how much or how little various programs are liked. In battling for the "king of late-night talk shows" spot, ME found that Pat Sajak placed only a few points below Johnny Carson, making his show a very attractive alternative for advertisers seeking the same audience.

The foundation of television audience measures is the number of people (or demographic segments) viewing a particular program. However, the traditional rating measures offer no insight into audience involvement or degree of preference for particular television shows or personalities. These measures can be extremely important in determining, for example, what type of person to use in a product testimonial commercial or when once-popular shows are "wearing out."

The best-known qualitative research service is Marketing Evaluations, which compiles a number of "popularity" surveys called "Q" reports. The most familiar of these are the TvQ and Performer Q. "The company's TvQ data indicate how much, or how little, viewers like various television programs and which they regard as their favorites. By dividing the percentage familiar with a particular show into the percentage who like that program, the research arrives at its Q likeability scores. Its Performer Q ranks individual personalities in a similar fashion."[29]

---

[28]Debbie Solomon, "Commercial Ratings: All Things Considered," *Marketing & Media Decisions,* July 1988, p. 135.

[29]The Quality Factor: Did They Like It? TvQ Research Charts the 'Favorites,' " *Television/Radio Age,* June 27, 1988, p. 19.

EXHIBIT 8.26

The VCR has become a fundamental extension of the television set in many households. (Courtesy: A. C. Nielsen.)

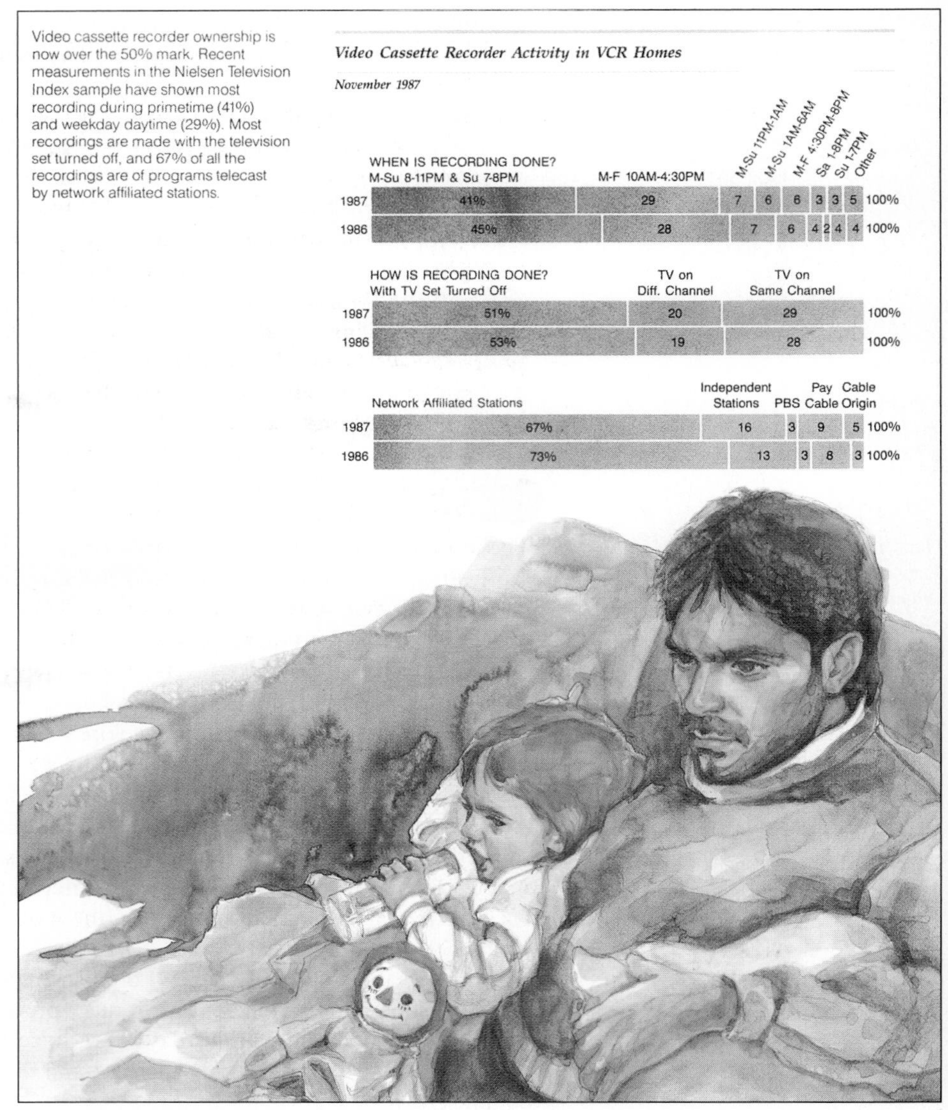

Let's assume that a television show, "Big Bob Monday Night Circus," is familiar to 50 percent of the population and 30 percent of the people rank it as one of their favorite shows. The Q score would be calculated as follows:

$$Q = FAV/FAM \text{ or } 30/50 = 60$$

> ***Q ratings.*** *They measure the popularity of a program or personality rather than the size of the audience as is the case with traditional rating systems.*

The Q ratings have been instrumental in keeping some TV shows on a network's schedule. For instance, it was reported that both "Tour of Duty" and "Wiseguy" were given extra chances because, even though their ratings were low, the viewers who were aware of the shows liked them. On the other hand, critics charge that the Q ratings are extremely artificial measures of both shows and performers. Ed Asner, then president of the Screen Actors Guild, characterized the Q ratings as "McCarthyism—a sort of approval 'whitelist' instead of a blacklist. Casting directors could pit me for a role against Meadowlark Lemon, Miss Piggy, or Victoria Principal—we all have Qs of 32—and that's all we have in common. . . ." According to recent Q scores, the most popular TV "performers" are Bill Cosby, the California Raisins, and Alf.[30]

[30]Dan Hurley, "Those Hush-Hush Q Ratings—Fair or Foul?" *TV Guide,* December 10, 1988, p. 6.

SUMMARY

Television is the primary national advertising medium, and all indications are that it will remain so for the foreseeable future. However, it is very much a medium in transition. Total network dominance is now past history. VCRs and multiple program alternatives have allowed the viewer to increasingly take control of the medium. Today there are opportunities for specialized programming that would have no chance of airing on one of the Big Three networks. The inevitable introduction of two-way television communication will dramatically speed up this process of viewer control.

The proliferation of program choices means television advertisers face some difficult decisions, including: How can we reach the VCR generation? What media planning techniques are needed to develop television buying schedules in this fragmented market? Should cable networks and syndicated programs be considered primary advertising vehicles for national advertisers? The answers to these and many other questions will determine the future use of the medium as an advertising tool.

Finally, marketing will become more of a consideration in the television industry. Television will follow the lead of newspapers and radio in showing advertisers how the medium can function as part of a coordinated media mix. Television marketing will also reach out to local and regional advertisers to compete with local media for additional advertising dollars. Predictions are that television will emerge from the current turmoil as an even stronger force in advertising because it will have a broader base of advertisers and because the fragmented audience offers tremendous opportunities to reach narrowly defined prospects.

QUESTIONS

1. Discuss the role of the three major networks in contemporary television. How has their role changed in the last decade?
2. Discuss the concept of the fragmented audience and the major implications it has for advertisers.
3. Define:
   (a) scatter plans
   (b) clutter
   (c) gross rating points
   (d) cost per point
   (e) program syndication
   (f) clearance
   (g) spot advertising
   (h) up-front buys
   (i) area of dominant influence (ADI)
4. What is the difference between a rating and a share?
5. Compare and contrast the three primary methods of gathering audience ratings: diary, household meter, and people meter.
6. How does a syndicated television network differ from a traditional network?
7. Explain the role of television reps in selling television time.
8. Discuss the role of barter syndication as an outlet for national advertising.
9. What are the advantages and disadvantages of checkerboarding and stripping?
10. Discuss the potential of videotext as an advertising medium.
11. How do the Q ratings differ from more traditional audience rating services?

SUGGESTED EXERCISES

- List your three favorite television shows. How does your list compare with the programs watched by your classmates? With the list of the highest-rated programs in the latest published survey?

- List the television programs available in your community at 8 P.M. on Monday night.
- Count the number of commercials broadcast on one of the network affiliates in your market any evening between 8 and 9 P.M. How many of these commercials were for local businesses?

READINGS

BRAND, STEWART: *The Media Lab: Inventing the Future at MIT* (New York: Viking Penguin, 1987).

EASTMAN, SUSAN TYLER, SYDNEY W. HEAD, AND LEWIS KLEIN: *Broadcast/Cable Programming Strategies and Practices* (Belmont, CA: Wadsworth Publishing Company, 1989).

FULLERTON, HUGH S.: ''Technology Collides with Relative Constancy: The Pattern of Adoption for a New Medium,'' *Journal of Media Economics,* Fall 1988, p. 75.

JAFFE, ALFRED J.: ''Big Market Affiliate Erosion,'' *Television/Radio Age,* February 6, 1989, p. 38.

KATZ, HELEN E., AND KENT M. LANCASTER: ''How Leading Advertisers and Agencies Use Cable Television,'' *Journal of Marketing Research,* February/March, 1989, p. 30.

REESE, CHUCK: ''Don't Bank on Spot,'' *Channels,* February 1989, p. 30.

Special Report: TV Syndication 1989, *ADWEEK,* January 23, 1989.

STERNBERG, STEVE: ''VCRs: A New Medium, a New Message,'' *Marketing & Media Decisions,* January 1989, pp. 81–87.

WALDROP, JUDITH, AND DIANE CRISPELL: ''Daytime Dramas, Demographic Dreams,'' *American Demographics,* October 1988, p. 29.

NINE

Using Radio

Radio is the *most personal* of all mass media, in that it's usually listened to by individuals by themselves. That makes it an excellent vehicle for *target marketing*. "Now the goal is to know the targets and then modify network programming for the markets," said Norm Pattiz, chairman of Westwood One.

Radio is the most personal of all the mass media. It is rarely listened to as a group activity. The exception to this solo listenership is usually car radio, where mobility of audience gives radio another of its primary characteristics. The ownership of radios has become so pervasive that penetration statistics are virtually meaningless. Once every household and car had a radio, the industry began to gather statistics concerning multiset ownership. However, when these figures passed the five-radios-per-household level, they, too, became meaningless. Suffice it to say that everyone has a radio and most listen to some radio program every day. In fact, the sheer numbers of radios, stations, program formats, and listeners is a problem for the media planner. The range of choices available has made determining the proper radio schedule for any particular advertiser a major headache.

What is particularly interesting about this situation is that not many years ago the prevailing opinion was that radio was dying as a major advertising medium. The pessimists predicted that the flight of audiences and advertisers to television, and the resulting reductions in network radio dollars, would soon bring financial ruin. At the same time, radio had to contend with newspapers for local dollars. Clearly the medium had changed drastically from the golden age of network radio, when the family gathered around the radio set to listen to Jack Benny, Fred Allen, and Bob Hope. When the last soap opera moved from radio to television in the 1950s, it marked the end of one era and the beginning of another. Luckily, radio executives were able to develop a strategy that not only saved radio as an advertising medium, but also made it more popular than ever with listeners.

Radio is *diverse*, but specific. It can reach a wide variety of different kinds of consumers, but it *can* tailor a particular message to a narrow group. This is due to the large numbers of stations, formats—and numbers of radios and listeners in the audience. Radio is known to be as fragmented as it can possibly be—yet there's format duplications. That's when the truly innovative stations rise to the top, and the others change their formats.

In many ways, radio is the ideal medium for the target-marketing concept of the 1980s and 1990s because there is virtually no target market that cannot be identified and successfully reached through an existing station and format. In fact, radio can do a better job of reaching some segments with an effective advertising message than any other alternative. Most importantly, it can deliver a narrowly targeted message at a lower cost than any other medium.

This amazing turnaround from the brink of disaster did not just happen. Radio's success in the last 25 years is a tribute to the marketing know-how of radio managers as

Most radio programs originate *locally*, which encourages advertising, also, to relate to the local surroundings. Ads for WQXR, a New York classical radio station, uses notables such as New York's Commissioner of Cultural Affairs, Mary Schmidt Campbell and Doubleday president, Nancy Evans. These people are *true* stars—''our audience identifies with them,'' explained Bob Fearon, chairman at Fearon/Gleckler.

well as to the inherent advantages of the medium. As we will see throughout this chapter, radio is a medium that can adapt to almost any marketing situation. The list of major radio advertisers encompasses virtually every major corporation and product classification. Advertisers as diverse as Listerine mouthwash, True Value Hardware, and American Airlines each spend more than $5 million on radio because it delivers a diverse audience, yet one that can be targeted to the specific needs of almost any advertiser. Exhibit 9.1 demonstrates the persuasiveness of radio in our lives.[1] With all these advantages, it is not surprising that radio not only survived the transition from a national to a local medium, but has prospered to an extent that even its greatest advocates would once have found surprising.

FEATURES AND ADVANTAGES OF RADIO

A Personal Medium

Theater-of-the-mind. *Characteristic of radio that plays to the listener's imagination rather than using the visual cues of other media.*

Radio is not regarded as a mass medium by its audience, but rather as a one-to-one vehicle of entertainment, information, and company. The radio speaks directly to each listener. Since most radio programs originate locally, they can be personal. The very fact that radio utilizes the spoken word makes it conversational and informal. It is a medium of the imagination, a ''theater of the mind,'' and many people would not be without it in their cars, homes, or workplaces.

Broadly Selective

Radio is able to reach *hard-to-reach segments* of the population—working adults, ethnics, and light users of other media. Northwest Airlines, in devoting a third of its $45 million ad budget to promoting Far East travel, wants to single out working adults and those who'd be impressed with their knowledge of Far Eastern culture. Northwest is kicking off its campaign with 5 new radio commercials a week.

There are currently more than 10,000 commercial radio stations, approximately ten times the number of commercial television stations. These radio stations offer advertisers a tremendous array of formats, rate structures, and markets to deliver their messages. Radio also delivers an audience greater than those for competitive media. For instance, radio audiences are larger than television audiences from 5 A.M. until 5 P.M. (see Exhibit 9.2). Radio reaches the great majority of adults, who listen, on average, three hours per day.

Aggregate listenership figures only tell part of the story. As we have said, radio's success is tied to its ability to deliver narrow audience demographics. National advertisers, in particular, view radio as a supplemental medium that reaches audiences missed by their national media schedules. Radio fulfills this role in two ways.

Supplemental medium. *Radio is usually used in conjunction with other media, often to reach radio listeners who are light users of other media vehicles.*

First, it can deliver some market segments better than any other medium. For instance, 99.4 percent of young people 12–17 listen to radio weekly, while approximately 90 percent of both black and Hispanic adults listen to radio at least once a week. Second, radio is particularly adept at reaching light users of other media. As Exhibit 9.3 shows, light users of other media are likely to be heavy users of radio. In fact, very light users of television (those viewing less than one hour per day) listen to radio over three and a half hours a day. Therefore, radio is the idea supplemental

EXHIBIT 9.1
Radio Statistics

Radios in use	527 million
Households with radio	99 percent
Car radios	128 million
Radios per household	5.6
Daily adult listenership	80 percent

[1]Unless otherwise noted, radio statistics in this chapter are courtesy of the Radio Advertising Bureau.

EXHIBIT 9.2

Radio has a very large audience throughout daytime hours. (Courtesy: Radio Advertising Bureau.)

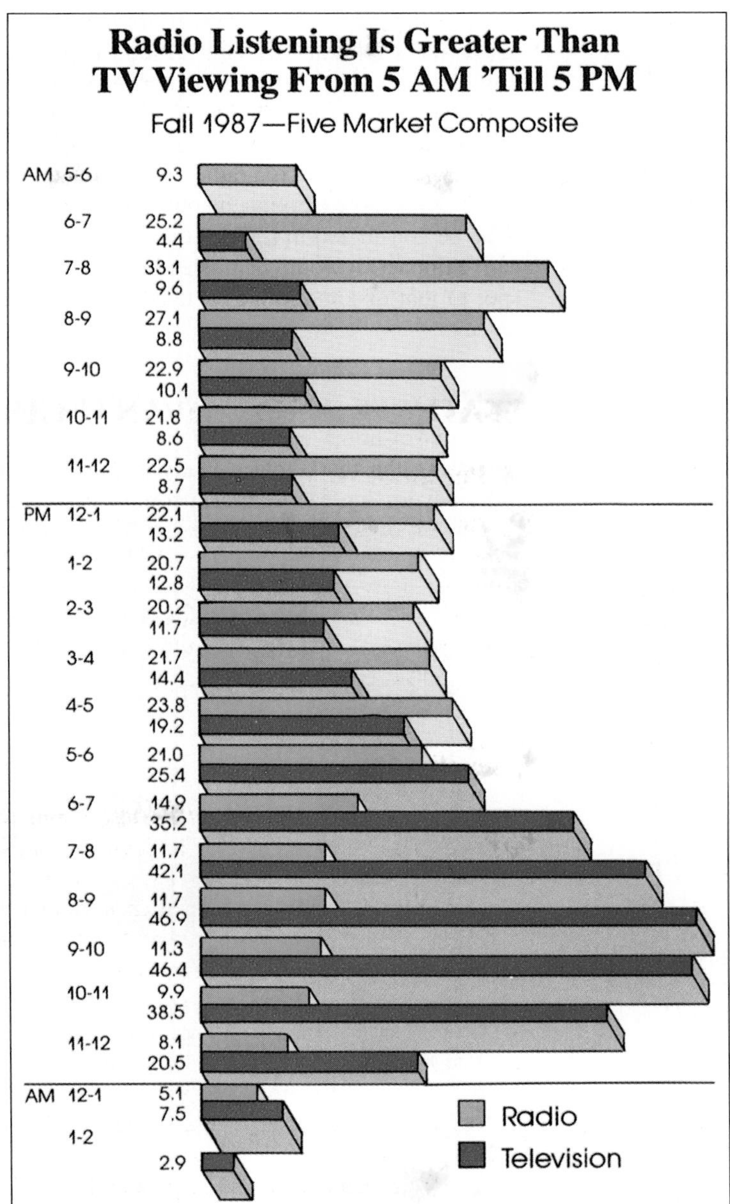

EXHIBIT 9.3

Radio reaches light users of other media. (Courtesy: Radio Advertising Bureau.)

	% of Population	*% of Total Viewing/ Reading*	*Time Spent with Medium*	*Time Spent with Radio*
TV	38%	12%	1:07	3:10
Newspapers	50	13	:11	2:38
Magazines	69	15	:05	2:38

Light Users—Adults 18+

Cost increases have been below those of other media and are forecasted to remain in that position. Audience fragmentation has kept CPM's down on adult-targeted stations. The youth market has been a little stronger because there are fewer outlets.

medium for national advertisers as well as the primary medium for advertisers who need to reach certain market segments.

Low CPM

In Chapter 7, we discussed the growing cost consciousness of advertisers in making media buys. Generally, the cost of advertising media has significantly outpaced the consumer price index (the cost of basic goods and services). Because of the number of

When out-of-the-home, radio can deliver a *complete sales message to consumers*—unlike any other media. This usually occurs during peak shopping hours. Greyhound Lines will break three 30-second radio spots in 9 markets—to promote its new same-day service for its express package business.

stations and the resulting competition for advertising dollars, this upward cost spiral is less evident in radio. In fact, during the period from 1967 to 1988, spot radio CPMs grew less than CPMs for any other medium, and network radio CPMs were ahead of only magazines (see Exhibit 9.4). Predictions are that future increases in radio CPMs will remain in the 3–5 percent range, far less than anticipated increases in other media.

Overall, the CPM for radio (approximately $4.00) is lower than that for all other media with the exception of outdoor ($1.50). Of course, the CPM figures for radio must be considered in light of the frequency needed for effective reach and communicative impact. It would be misleading to compare the CPM of a single, perishable radio spot to that of a magazine ad that can be read and reread at the individual's convenience.

Proximity to purchase. *Radio is one of the most effective media in reaching consumers who are in the marketplace with the intent to purchase goods and services.*

Proximity to Purchase

Only out-of-home advertising matches radio's ability to reach an audience that is already in the marketplace ready to purchase. However, unlike out-of-home media, radio advertising can deliver a complete sales message to these prospects. Currently, 95 percent of all vehicles have a radio and approximately 70 percent of drivers report

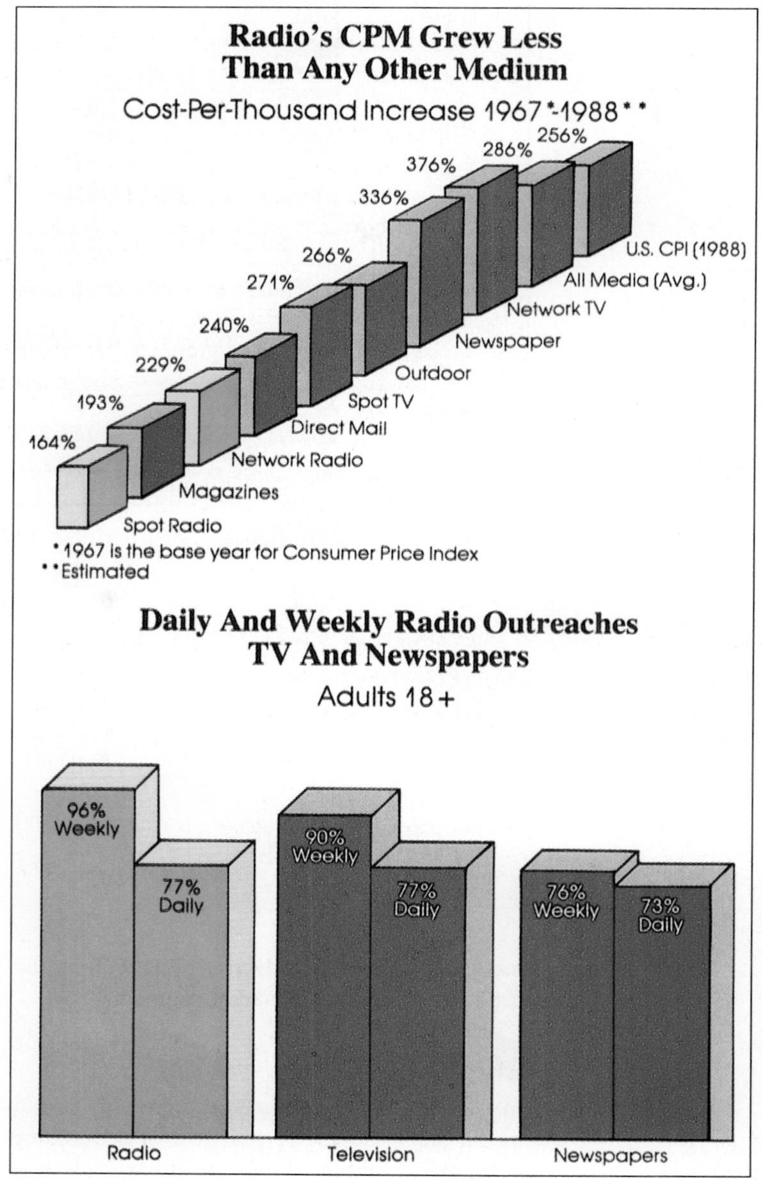

EXHIBIT 9.4

Radio delivers audiences at a relatively inexpensive cost per thousand. (Courtesy: Radio Advertising Bureau.)

that they listen to the radio *every* time they drive. Most of this drive-time listening occurs during peak shopping hours.

Exhibit 9.5 shows the percentage of various audience segments that are reached by the major media within one hour of purchasing a product. Note that radio is particularly successful at reaching the professional/managerial category and households with incomes of $50,000+. These figures are of great interest to retailers whose advertising is extremely perishable and to all those whose advertising must generally create sales quickly or not at all.

By having a fragmented audience—that is, dispersed among a wide variety of stations—advertisers have to be either selective in choosing targets or *repetitive* in duplicating their messages among different stations. That's the kind of dilemma General Foods faced when introducing their new oat bran cereal, Honey Bunches of Oats. They knew a good portion of their market are avid radio listeners, so spot radio is a necessary vehicle—even if it means some "wasteful" or "duplicate" spending.

Radio audiences must be approached *creatively* in order to get advertisers' messages across—due to the lack of a visual element. "White, clean, cold, pure" are the words used to describe Canadian Glacier Natural Mountain Water on the West Coast. Radio spots will try to depict a glacier-fed lake to the listening audience—to compete with top sellers Evian and Vittel from France in the imported, non-carbonated bottled water market.

LIMITATIONS AND CHALLENGES OF RADIO

Some advertisers and agencies are beginning to wonder if radio is becoming a victim of its own success. The great number of stations and formats, which allows advertisers to target specific market segments, also presents a bewildering array of choices. To put the situation in perspective, there are more than twice as many radio stations as television stations, consumer magazines, and daily newspapers combined!

Added to the numbers problem are two other factors that often work to the disadvantage of radio. First, since radio spots are relatively inexpensive, agencies make a much lower per-spot commission than they would by placing the same number of advertising insertions in other media. Second, the audience research available for radio, especially that measuring out-of-home listeners, is often difficult to evaluate and compare to the research done for other media. Consequently, the media planner may have to work harder for less agency profit. Sometimes the path of least resistance is simply to exclude radio as a major part of a client's media plan.

While the logistical problems of buying radio can be countered, a more fundamental problem is radio's lack of a visual element. In this age of self-service retailing and competitive brand promotions, package identification is crucial for many advertisers. The radio industry has developed creative techniques to partially overcome the medium's inability to convey sight images. Sound effects, jingles, pungent copy, and vivid descriptions are used imaginatively to create a mental picture—often at extremely low production costs.

Radio operates at a distinct disadvantage in direct response, a growth area in other media. The medium offers no opportunity for coupon clipping, and taking down a phone number or address while driving down the highway is not practical. The radio

EXHIBIT 9.5
Immediacy to purchase is a major strength of radio advertising. (Courtesy: Radio Advertising Bureau.)

Percent of Shoppers Reached by Four Media Within One Hour of Purchase

	Radio	TV	Newspapers	Magazines	Shopped Past 24 hours	Average Amount Spent ($)
Total Population 12+	50%	21%	15%	12%	63%	62
Teens 12–17	43	25	22	23	51	36
Adults 18–34	63	28	13	15	63	55
Women 18–49	56	22	15	12	73	70
Men 18–49	64	27	16	13	61	59
Adults 50+	35	15	10	7	62	65
Working Women	55	20	14	11	73	67
Full Time Homemakers	48	22	14	10	68	74
Household Income $50,000+	60	19	10	10	73	69
Prof/Mgr Men	63	26	18	11	64	69

Source: R. H. Bruskin & Associates, Spring 1986.

industry has taken steps to encourage more direct-response advertising, such as providing the same phone number for all station-handled orders, but the growth potential for radio direct response is limited.

As we noted earlier, radio has had the lowest CPM and rate increases among the major media in recent years. While an advantage to the advertiser, this does not bode well for the future financial health of the industry. At present, radio revenues are growing at just about the rate of inflation, but national spot sales are almost flat. In addition, the radio advertising dollar and listening audience are continually divided among more and more stations.

TECHNICAL ASPECTS OF RADIO

The Signal

The electrical impulses that are broadcast by radio are called the *signal*. If a certain station has a good signal in a given territory, its programs and commercials come over clearly in that area.

Frequency

Radio waves. *The signals that carry sound are transmitted by electronomagnetic waves.*

Amplitude modulation (AM). *The method of transmitting electro-magnetic signals by varying the amplitude (size) of the electro-magnetic wave, in contrast to varying its frequency (FM). Quality not as good as FM but can be heard farther, especially at night. See Frequency modulation (FM).*

Frequency modulation (FM). *A radio-transmission wave that transmits by variation in frequency of its wave, rather than by size (as in AM modulation). An FM wave is twenty times the width of an AM wave, which is the source of its fine tone. To transmit such a wave, it has to be placed high on the electro-magnetic spectrum, far from AM waves with interference and static. Hence its outstanding tone.*

All signals are transmitted by electromagnetic waves, sometimes called *radio waves*. These waves differ from one another in frequency (the number of waves that pass a given point in a given period of time). Frequencies are measured in terms of thousands of cycles per second (kilohertz, or kHz; formerly called megacycles, or mc). Every station broadcasts on the frequency assigned to it by the FCC, so that it does not interfere with other stations. (The FCC, in fact, acts as the traffic director of the airwaves, assigning frequencies to all users of broadcasting, including television, police radio, citizens' band, navigational aids, and international radio.) A radio station assigned a frequency of 850,000 cycles per second, or 850 kHz, is identified by 85 on the radio dial (the final zero is dropped for convenience).

Differences Between AM and FM Radio

All electromagnetic waves have height, spoken of as *amplitude,* whose range resembles the difference between an ocean wave and a ripple in a pond; and speed, measured by the frequency with which a succession of waves passes a given point per minute, or per second. If, for example, a radio station operates on a frequency of 1,580 kHz, this means that 1,580,000 of its waves pass a given point per second.

On the basis of these two dimensions—amplitude and frequency—two separate systems have been developed for carrying the sound waves. The first system carries the variations in a sound wave by corresponding variations in its amplitude; the frequency remains constant. This is the principle of amplitude modulation (AM) (see Exhibit 9.6a). The second system carries the variation in a sound wave by corresponding variations in its frequency; the amplitude remains constant. This is the principle of frequency modulation (FM) (see Exhibit 9.6b).

There are approximately 5,050 AM and 4,300 FM stations (not including over 1,400 noncommercial stations). Establishment of new AM stations has stabilized at 1 percent annually, while FM stations are increasing at a yearly rate of almost 8 percent.

The technical structure of AM and FM radio has created, in effect, two distinct media, each offering different values to the listener and the advertiser. AM signals carry farther, but are susceptible to interference. FM has a fine tonal reception, but its signal distances are limited. A particular station's quality of reception is determined by atmospheric conditions and station power (broadcast frequency). The hours of operation frequency and signal-coverage areas can be obtained on station rate cards.

EXHIBIT 9.6

In amplitude modulation (a), waves vary in height (amplitude); frequency is constant. Frequency modulation (b) varies the frequency but keeps the height constant. These drawings, however, are not made to scale, which would reveal that width is the significant difference between AM and FM. The FM wave is 20 times wider than the AM wave. This fact helps to explain how FM captures its fine tones.

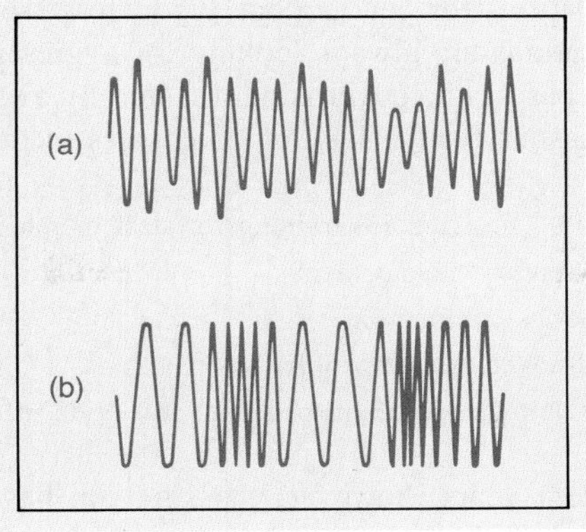

SELLING RADIO COMMERCIAL TIME

Selling advertising is more complex in radio than in any other medium. Whereas a typical market may have one major daily newspaper and a few suburban weeklies, three network affiliates and a couple of independent television stations, and perhaps two out-of-home media companies, there may be 30+ radio stations in a metropolitan area. While radio advertising, like television, is made up of network, local, and spot advertising, the similarity ends there.

Local sales account for 76 percent of radio revenues as contrasted to about 25 percent for television. Obviously, then, the sales department of a local radio station is extremely important to a station's success. In Exhibit 9.7, a typical organization chart for a radio station, we see that the sales manager reports directly to the station manager and is a major member of the executive team of the station.

Before discussing the three categories of radio advertising, it might be useful to examine the sales strategy of radio. Keep in mind that radio selling offers many entry-

EXHIBIT 9.7

Typical radio station organizational chart. (*Source:* Barry L. Sherman, *Telecommunications Management: The Broadcast and Cable Industries* [New York: McGraw-Hill Book Co., 1987], p. 248.)

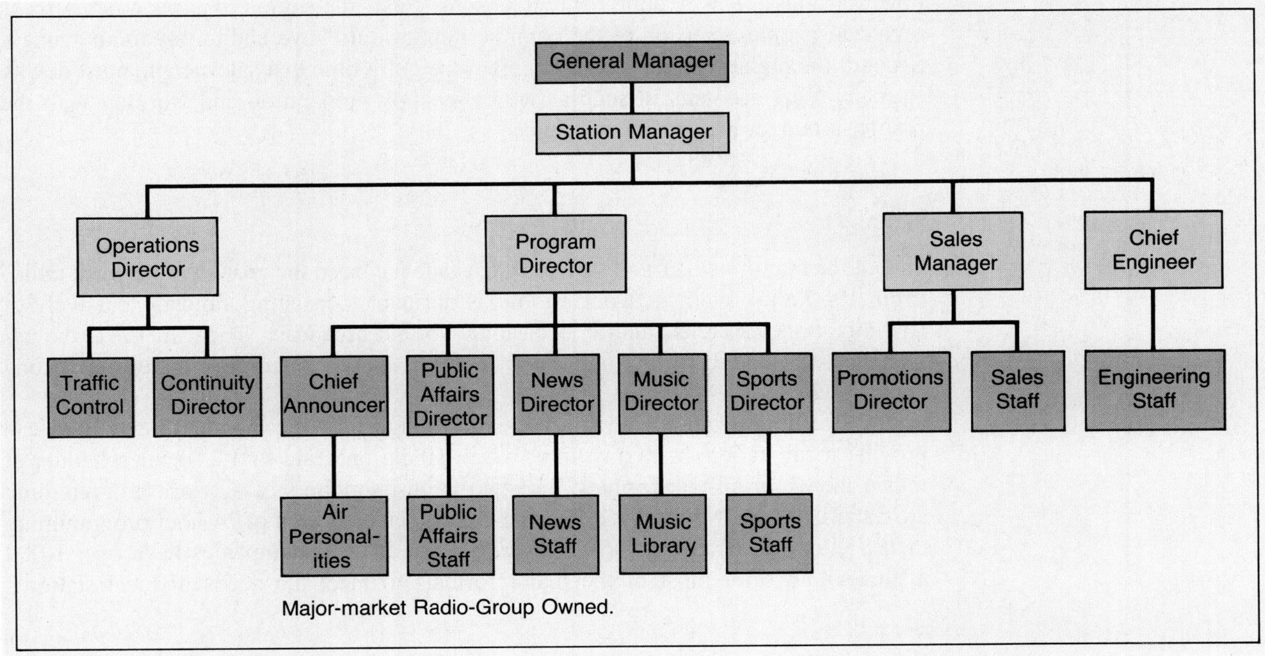

level positions for new college graduates, especially in small and medium markets. Radio stations are always looking for aggressive salespeople.

In the past, radio advertising was hurt by a scarcity of professional salespeople. The major reasons for the lack of good sales techniques were:

- Poor or no formal sales training for staff members
- Poor inventory management
- Tremendous competition
- High turnover of salespeople
- Lack of knowledge of, respect for, and pride in the medium by sales staff[2]

Radio Advertising Bureau (RAB). *National industry-wide organization that promotes the use of radio advertising.*

In recent years, however, the situation has improved dramatically. Two primary factors led to this turnaround in radio sales. First, major stations and industry-wide efforts undertaken through organizations such as the Radio Advertising Bureau (RAB) have been directed at recruiting a better-trained, more professional sales staff. Second, the industry has adopted creative compensation methods designed to reward and retain the best salespeople.

Until recently, most stations paid their sales staff a straight commission or a salary plus commission. Today stations are developing compensation plans that reward their top salespeople with some kind of sliding-scale commission.

One of the simplest sliding-scale techniques is setting a lower commission for the normal sales quota, and then rewarding the salespeople who go over quota. For instance:

Monthly Quota ($10,000)	*Commission*
$20,000	18%
15,000	15
10,000 (meet quota)	10
Under quota	5

Another common sales bonus technique is to pay a higher commission on direct sales than on agency placement. Some stations pay twice as much commission on direct business. This is done for two reasons. First, the station is passing along to its own salespeople a portion of the commission it would have had to pay to an agency. Second, the higher commission recognizes the extra time that salespeople must devote to many local accounts in such activities as copy preparation and working with the retailer's budget and media schedule.

Network Radio

One of the major media trends of the last decade has been the growth of network radio. From 1960 until 1980, network radio was dormant, consisting almost exclusively of five-minute news breaks and an occasional special broadcast. Then, in 1981, the advantages of satellite technology came to radio and the medium entered its second network era.

The satellite downlink, now inexpensive enough for even the smallest station, can provide local stations with anything from a single program to a 24-hour schedule of music, news, or all-talk formats. The two largest suppliers of network programming are Satellite Music Network (SMN), which began the concept of 24-hour programming in 1981, and the Transtar Radio Network. Both of these companies have over 1,000 affiliates and offer most of the major formats to meet the needs of local stations.

[2]James Duncan, Jr., "Trends: American Radio 1977–1987," *Sound Management*, October 1987, p. 34.

Satellite radio networks. *Unlike TV, a single radio network often provides only a portion of a station's total network programming. Relatively inexpensive satellite downlink permits a station to simultaneously be an affiliate of as many as five networks.*

Network radio, due to the growth of satellite technology, has grown tremendously in the past decade. "Networks" supply individual stations with programming on a selective basis, so that one station may have *several* network suppliers. Total network spending on radio amounted to $307.5 million, a 17.6% change over 1987. The top media spenders were Sears ($29.4 million), General Motors ($15.0 million), Bayer Aspirin ($9.7 million), Campbell Soup ($9.6 million), and Proctor & Gamble ($9.0 million).

Radio network affiliation is much different from television network affiliation. There are currently more than 20 radio networks. Radio "networks" are really program suppliers that contract with individual stations. It is not uncommon for a single station to contract with four or five program suppliers, and therefore be part of that many networks.

The advantages to the local stations of the satellite network are:

1. Stations are guaranteed quality programming based on the latest audience research for a particular format.
2. Radio networks give local stations access to celebrities they could not afford otherwise. The revival of network radio has actually created a number of new radio personalities.
3. Even the smallest stations can obtain national advertising dollars when they are part of a network. Stations that would never have been considered by national advertisers for a local spot buy may be included in a network radio schedule.
4. The cost efficiencies of sharing programming with several hundred other affiliates keeps both personnel and programming costs to a minimum.

To date, the primary users of network radio are found in medium and small markets. Stations in the top-ten markets don't want to share their advertising revenue and, furthermore, have the budgets to program their stations themselves. These major stations do, of course, belong to traditional networks for news and special programming, but that is something they have always done.

The most often heard negative comment about the current trend to network radio is that outside formula programming will cause radio to lose its local flavor. Critics point out that radio has worked for the last 25 years to establish itself as a primary local medium for both advertisers and audiences. The key to this success has been local programming and news. In the last two years, we are seeing a movement to get more local input into network programming. however, it is still a major problem for the medium.

Spot Radio

Individual station "buys," of time by advertisers are called "spot radio." As a whole, radio attracted *$7.8 billion* in advertising during *1988*, up 8.2% from the prior year, according to the Radio Advertising Bureau. Of the total, *local spots* accounted for $6 billion, up 9%; national spots totaled $1.4 billion, a 6.6% increase.

When an advertiser buys time on an individual station, it is called *spot radio*. The program originates at the station from which it is broadcast; it is not relayed from a network broadcast. As in television, when a national advertiser uses spot radio, it is, strictly speaking, local spot radio, but it is referred to simply as *spot*.

In recent years, the portion of radio advertising that has been the softest in terms of advertiser demand has been spot. Many industry analysts wonder if there will be any place for spot buys in the future. With the growth of networks, advertisers are finding it much cheaper to buy many stations through a network than to buy the same stations one by one. In addition, a network guarantees consistent quality of programming and advertising across many stations. Finally, the network buy is much easier since the advertiser deals with only a single source and pays one bill.

Nonwired networks. *Groups of radio stations whose advertising is sold simultaneously by station representatives.*

As we discussed in Chapter 8, most spot broadcast purchases are made through reps. Several years ago, radio rep firms started selling combines called *nonwired networks*. These "networks" enabled advertisers to buy many markets with one insertion order and one bill. It was a great simplification for the media planner and helped to increase spot buying, especially among smaller stations. But the problem with the nonwired networks is that they offer neither programming nor context in which to place the advertising. They are really nothing but spot buying made easy. It is questionable whether they can compete with the new programming services that package advertising like traditional television advertising.

The health of spot radio is a major concern to many stations, since spot advertising has long been a major profit center for local stations, particularly those in large markets. However, the advertising mix in radio is yet another example of the volatility of this medium. There is no question that radio will remain an overwhelmingly local medium for the foreseeable future.

AM versus FM as an Advertising Medium

Nowhere is the transition in the radio industry more evident than in the changing roles of AM and FM. The rise of FM can be traced to 1972. In that year, AM radio had 75 percent of the listening audience and an even higher percentage of advertising revenues. Since then, the audience for FM has grown steadily, and now it has the position formerly held by AM (see Exhibit 9.8).

In a period of less than 20 years, a major advertising medium went from a position of preeminence to one of fighting for survival. There are several reasons for the decline of AM and the rise of FM:

In the last 20 years, there has been a significant growth of *FM stations*—due to its better delivery of *music*. Advertisers have switched from AM to FM, since FM is now able to deliver the preferred audience. With Frank Sinatra the new owner of *KFAS-FM* in Casa Grande, 45 miles from Phoenix, the format was changed to ''adult contemporary.'' It, naturally, features his songs and attracts the ''bobby sox'' crowd of the '40s and '50s the station was after.

1. In 1972, the Federal Communication Commission ruled that joint owners of both AM and FM stations in the same market had to program different formats. This ruling opened the way for FM as a separate medium.
2. The sound quality of FM is markedly better than that of AM. Since music is the key to successful radio, FM steadily gained audience share at the expense of AM.
3. The decline in the cost of FM sets coincided with the popularity of the medium. Twenty years ago, radio sets with an FM band were much more expensive than AM-only sets. Also few cars were equipped with FM radio. Currently, 88 percent of car radios are AM/FM, and it is difficult to find a radio without both AM and FM capability.
4. As radio audiences turned to FM for the most popular music formats, AM was left with news, talk, and specialty formats such as religion. With the exception of some popular talk shows, AM formats do not appeal to those market segments most desired by advertisers. Therefore, advertisers quickly followed audiences in switching to FM.

Exhibit 9.9 shows the major radio formats and the share of both AM and FM audiences listening to each. Advertisers, of course, are interested in formats only to the extent that they deliver certain market segments. An examination of Exhibit 9.10 shows the concentration of prime prospects (adults aged 18–49) in the most popular formats. On the other hand, the older age groups listen to the less popular formats such as Nostalgia/Big Band (NO) and News/Talk (NT).

It is clear that AM is a medium in trouble. Technological improvements such as stereo AM, introduced in 1982, have not turned the tide. Nor has AM found a really effective format to bring back listeners. It may well be that AM will become a specialty medium much as FM was 25 years ago.

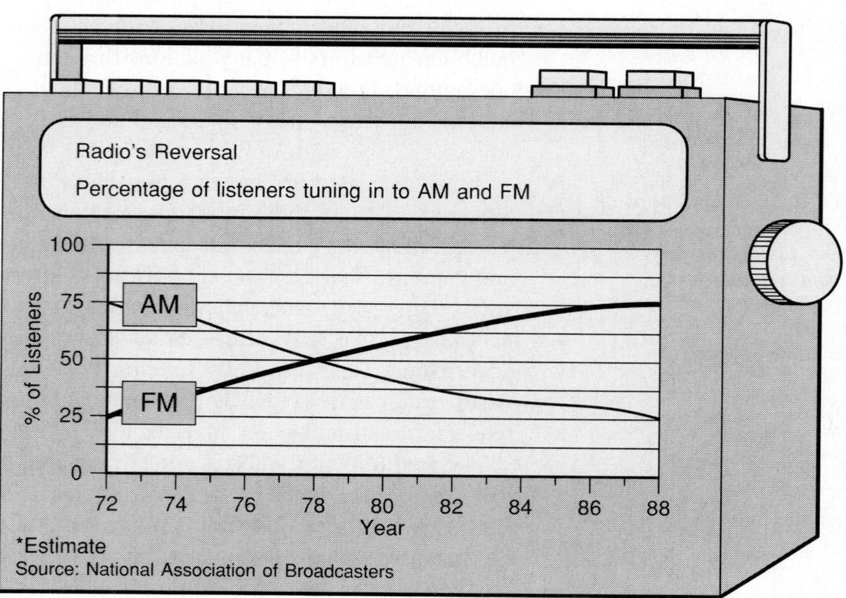

EXHIBIT 9.8

The emergence of FM is the primary story of radio in the 1980s. (Courtesy: *Atlanta Journal and Constitution.*)

EXHIBIT 9.9

How AM/FM Stations Program By Format

There are 4,902 commercial AM stations and 4,041 commercial FM stations licensed by the Federal Communications Commission operating in the United States (as of 12/31/87). 1,301 non-commercial stations can also be found, primarily on the FM dial.

A programming format usually defines the kind of audience attracted to a particular radio station. The following formats are in use:

Percent of AM, FM stations in the top 100 markets programming each format.

Format	AM	FM	Total AM/FM
Adult contemporary	18.3%	21.3%	19.5%
Country	17.8	13.8	16.1
Rock/CHR	2.9	16.7	8.8
Album oriented rock (AOR)	1.3	13.0	6.2
MOR/nostalgia	11.8	1.4	7.4
Easy listening	1.8	8.8	4.8
Religious	14.1	6.1	10.3
News/talk	7.0	0.5	4.2
Black/R&B	4.4	2.3	3.5
Urban contemporary	2.5	3.4	2.9
Golden oldies	6.6	1.8	4.6
Spanish	4.4	0.9	2.9
Classical	0.5	4.0	2.0
All news	2.0	0.0	1.1
Soft contemporary (light)	1.1	4.6	2.3
Variety	0.9	0.5	0.7

EXHIBIT 9.10

Radio formats are designed to appeal to narrowly targeted audiences. (Courtesy: Arbitron.)

Formats	
Contemporary Hit Radio	CHR
News/Talk	NT
Album Oriented Rock	AOR
Easy Listening/ Beautiful Music	BM
AM Adult Contemporary	AM/AC
FM Adult Contemporary	FM/AC
Country	CO
Urban Contemporary/ Black	UR
Classical	CL
Nostalgia/Big Band	NO
Religion	RE
Spanish	SP

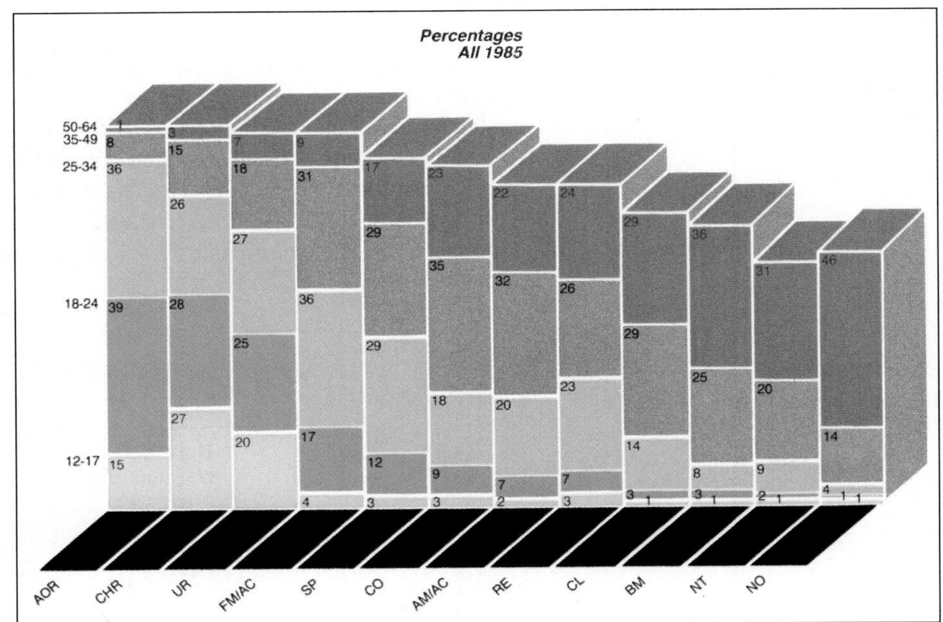

Time Classifications—Dayparts

The *peak* listening time is weekdays between 7 and 10 A.M. That's when a station's *expanded newscasts, all-day weather forecasts,* and *celebrity commentators,* such as Paul Harvey, are likely to be aired. As a result, commercial time is the highest during that period.

In being able to *supplement* other media, radio can deliver additional "weight" to the media schedule, can reach non-users of other media, and can direct programming to *strictly local markets.* Along with Audi's biggest ever TV and print ad campaign, costing $70+ million, dealers are encouraged to buy local radio spots. DDB Needham Worldwide supplies the creative materials. "We're going to take advantage of *all things* coming together. We need to reach *new customers* and build interest in the brand," quoted Anthony Kirton, Audi director of marketing.

Two companies—*Arbitron* and *Birch*—dominate radio ratings. Arbitron uses a written diary, while Birch prefers telephone surveys. A particular subculture, the Hispanics, have been singled out by *both* rating services for special surveys, because of their *numbers* and their *preference of radio* over other media. Ringling Bros. and Barnum & Bailey Circus doesn't treat the Hispanics as part of one homogeneous mass, either. They rely on local radio, using Spanish-speaking performers for direct interviews to "sell" their performances.

The broadcast day is divided into time periods called dayparts (see Exhibit 9.11). Weekends are regarded as a separate time classification. Most radio spot time is sold in 60-second units. The cost varies with the daypart.

The size of radio audiences varies widely from daypart to daypart. The peak listening period is from 7 to 10 A.M., with an average of 31 to 24.5 percent of the audience tuning in during subsequent quarter hours. TV viewing, of course, peaks between 8 and 10 P.M., with average quarter-hour audiences in the 50 percent range. Radio also differs from TV in seasonality of audience levels. Radio listening is remarkedly stable throughout the year, whereas TV audiences fluctuate as much as 25 percent from fall to summer.

Types of Programming

Radio is a quasi-mass medium. Despite its generally high aggregate audiences, the number of people listening to any particular station at a given time is usually quite small. Even the top stations in a major market rarely achieve ratings above 8 or 10, and a rating of 1 to 3 is common. Consequently, radio stations must reach clearly defined target segments that are of prime importance to advertisers (e.g., women 18–34).

As we said earlier, radio is an excellent supplementary medium to the mass-appeal vehicles such as TV or newspapers because of its ability to target audience segments. it can be used in three ways to enhance a media schedule efficiently:

1. Radio can give added weight to a prime-prospect audience segment. Manufacturers of office equipment may reach the business person during morning-drive time; grocery spots may reach the housewife at midmorning; and movie commercials might be played on Friday and Saturday during early-evening time periods.
2. Radio can reach nonusers of other media. Radio is a primary medium for teenagers, many older people, and certain segments of ethnic groups. Without radio advertising, potential customers within these audience segments would be missed.
3. Finally, radio provides a flexible medium to reach local markets that might be given too little advertising weight in the national media schedule. For instance, an advertiser's national TV or magazine campaign may not achieve GRP goals in certain markets. Radio could be added to the media plan on a selective basis to overcome this problem.

As we saw in Exhibit 9.9, advertisers have a number of formats from which to choose in matching audience preferences and stations. Three formats alone—adult contemporary, country, and rock/CHR—account for almost half of all station programming formats. These dominant formats are also the most competitive. Consequently, a station may decide to use another format with less audience appeal, but also with less competition from other stations and therefore a better chance of achieving dominance among a particular audience segment.

EXHIBIT 9.11

The radio broadcast day, Monday to Friday.

Daypart	*Characteristics*
6 A.M.–10 A.M.	Drive time, breakfast audience, interested chiefly in news
10 A.M.–3 P.M.	Daytime, programs characteristic of station, talk, music or all-news
3 P.M.–7 P.M.	Afternoon, drive time; radio prime time and same as morning drive time
7 P.M.–12 A.M.	News, music, talk shows
12 A.M.–6 A.M.	Music, talk shows

RADIO RATINGS SERVICES

> ***Arbitron Ratings Company.*** *Syndicated radio and TV ratings company. Dominant in local radio ratings.*

Local radio station ratings are dominated by two companies: Arbitron and Birch. Arbitron was established in 1964 and was long the only major radio ratings company. Then, in 1977, Birch Radio was founded, and since the early 1980s, it has been a major competitor to Arbitron. However, Arbitron remains the larger of the services in terms of agency and station clients as well as total revenue.

Among any research services there will invariably be differences in reported audience measurements. However, this problem of comparison is made more difficult in the case of Birch and Arbitron since they use completely different methods of surveying radio audiences. Arbitron uses a written diary and Birch employs telephone surveys. The difference in methodologies has caused media planners concern during the last several years.

Arbitron

Arbitron provides each member of a sample household who is at least 12 years old with a diary (see Exhibit 9.12). This diary covers a seven-day period and has places to

EXHIBIT 9.12

A page from the Arbitron diary. (Courtesy: Arbitron.)

Please start recording your listening on the date shown on the front cover.

4 **THURSDAY**

TIME			STATION			PLACE		
			Fill in station "call letters" (If you don't know them, fill in program name or dial setting)	Check One (✓)		Check One (✓)		
							Away From Home	
	From	To		AM	FM	At Home	In a Car	Some Other Place
Early Morning (5AM to 10AM)								
Midday (10AM to 3PM)								
Late Afternoon (3PM to 7PM)								
Night (7PM to 5AM)								

IF YOU DID NOT LISTEN TO RADIO TODAY PLEASE CHECK (✓) HERE ➡ ☐

Each time you listen to the radio, please be sure to use a new line, and write in the station "call letters."

indicate daypart, station call letters, and place of listenership (home, car, other). Arbitron follows up diary placement with phone calls to encourage proper administration of the diary.

Arbitron measures 259 markets with samples varying by population of individual metropolitan areas. Each market is measured at least annually, and the 79 largest markets are measured four times a year. Each survey period lasts 12 weeks. The cost of the Arbitron service is determined by size of market and station share of audience.

The major problem with Arbitron's methodology is human nature. Diaries can be put aside and either not returned or filled in all at once, creating a recall problem. The diary method also demonstrates shortcomings in measuring the increasingly large out-of-home listenership.

As competition between Arbitron and Birch continues and clients demand more segment breakouts, we should see a further proliferation of reports by both services. Exhibit 9.13 shows an example from Arbitron of an audience-composition breakout. To track the frequent shifts in radio listening patterns, Arbitron provides a service called Arbitrends. Arbitrends gives rolling averages of station ratings so media plan-

EXHIBIT 9.13

In this example, station WAAA reaches 13,300 persons 12 and over from 6 A.M. to midnight. Men 35–44 make up 1,400 of this audience, or 11 percent. (Courtesy: Arbitron.)

Audience Composition

Monday - Sunday 6AM - MID

	METRO AQH (00)													
	Persons 12+	Men 18+	Men 18-24	Men 25-34	Men 35-44	Men 45-54	Men 55-64	Women 18+	Women 18-24	Women 25-34	Women 35-44	Women 45-54	Women 55-64	Teens 12-17
WAAA	133	43	9	12	14	5	1	79	21	25	19	5	8	11
%	100	32	7	9	11	4	1	60	16	19	14	4	6	8
WBBB	228	100	13	48	29		5	123	26	49	29	8	7	5
%	100	44	6	21	13		2	54	11	21	13	4	3	2
+ WCCC	488	204	7	14	24	39	46	283	14	11	35	38	72	1
%	100	42	1	3	5	8	9	58	3	2	7	8	15	
WDDD	120	46	9	8	12	4	6	62	8	9	15	6	12	12
%	100	38	8	7	10	3	5	52	7	8	13	5	10	10
WEEE														
%														
WFFF														
%														
WGGG														
%														
WHHH														
%														
WSVB														
%														
WJJJ														
%														
WKKK														
%														
WLLL														
%														
WMMM														
%														
WNNN														
%														
WOOO														
%														
WPPP														
%														
WQQQ														
%														
WRRR														
%														
WSSS														
WTTT														
%														
WUUU														
%														
WVVV														
%														
WSVB														
WXXX														
%														
WYYY														
%														
WZZZ														
%														
KAAA														
%														
KBBB														
%														
KCCC														
%														
KDDD														
%														
KEEE														
%														
KFFF														
%														
TOTALS AQH														
%														

AUDIENCE COMPOSITION

NEW SECTION

DEMOS — P 12+; TEENS (12-17); M&W 18+, 18-24, 25-34, 35-44, 45-54, 55-64 AND EACH DEMO AS A PERCENT OF P 12+

GEOGRAPHY — METRO

ESTIMATES — AQH (00) WITH CUME (00) ON FACING PAGE

DAYPARTS — MON-SUN 6AM-MID

Footnote Symbols: * Audience estimates adjusted for actual broadcast schedule.
\+ Station(s) reported with different call letters in prior surveys - see Page 5B.

Fall 1986 — ARBITRON RATINGS 8 — Anytown, USA

EXHIBIT 9.14

Arbitrends can alert media buyers to fluctuations in a station's ratings. (Courtesy: Arbitron.)

ARBITRENDS Rolling Average Trend Report
ROLLING AVERAGES FOR NOVEMBER-APRIL, 1987-1988

INDIANAPOLIS Metro — DAYPART: Weekend 6a-Mid
DEMOGRAPHIC: Persons 18 PLUS — MARKET POPULATION: 894,600
LISTED BY: Arbitron Sequence

Station	Estimate	No-De-Ja 1988	De-Ja-Fe 1988	Winter 1988	Fe-Ma-Ap 1988
WTLC-FM	AQH Rtg	1.3	1.2	1.4	1.1
	Share	10.1	9.9	10.7	9.2
	Cume Rtg	9.8	9.5	9.9	9.6
WTPI-FM	AQH Rtg	0.4	0.5	0.4	0.4
	Share	3.2	4.0	3.4	3.3
	Cume Rtg	6.1	6.7	5.9	6.1
WTUX-AM	AQH Rtg	0.5	0.6	0.6	0.5
	Share	4.0	4.9	4.6	4.4
	Cume Rtg	4.9	5.5	5.1	5.4
WXIR-FM	AQH Rtg	0.1	0.1	0.1	
	Share	1.1	1.0	0.6	0.3
	Cume Rtg	1.8	1.6	1.2	1.3
WXLW-AM	AQH Rtg	* 0.1	* 0.1	* 0.1	* 0.1
	Share	0.6	0.7	0.5	0.6
	Cume Rtg	1.0	1.3	1.1	0.8
WXTZ-FM	AQH Rtg	1.3	1.3	1.1	1.0
	Share	10.2	10.7	8.7	8.1
	Cume Rtg	11.4	12.3	10.4	10.6
WZPL-FM	AQH Rtg	0.9	0.8	0.9	1.0
	Share	7.1	6.5	7.2	7.7
	Cume Rtg	9.7	9.7	11.1	11.2
WLW -AM	AQH Rtg		**	**	
	Share	0.1	**	**	0.4
	Cume Rtg	0.3	**	**	0.9
MARKET TOTALS	AQH Rtg	13.1	12.5	12.7	12.3
	Cume Rtg	80.3	80.9	81.4	79.7

* Audience estimates adjusted for actual broadcast schedule.
** Station not reported this survey.

ners can track not only current ratings, but also the stability or fluctuations of audiences for a station over time (see Exhibit 9.14).

Birch

Birch Radio. **The primary competition to Arbitron in providing local market radio ratings.**

The Birch radio service uses the telephone interview technique. The respondent is one adult in each sample household, and he or she is questioned about listening patterns in the last 24-hour period. The interview lasts approximately nine minutes and is conducted with the person in the household with the most recent birth date.

As with Arbitron, Birch's methodology is a major concern of advertisers. Obviously, many people will not agree to do a lengthy telephone interview with a stranger. However, Birch has an excellent rate of response, approximately 60 percent, compared to slightly less than 50 percent for Arbitron. Even so, many critics view both services' sample sizes as inadequate. The problem is not with overall sample size, but with whether the size of demographic cells (e.g., males 18–34 listening to station WWCC from 6 A.M.–10 A.M.) is meaningful. Remember, however, that both services claim only to provide audience *estimates*.

Apart from methodology, the services are very similar. Birch samples 250 markets, with the top 108 markets receiving more frequent sampling. Charges are based on market size, but all stations in a market pay the same rate regardless of average ratings.

QUALITATIVE COMPONENTS OF AUDIENCE

	TOTAL WEEKLY AUDIENCE		COMPARATIVE VALUES - READ DOWN						COMPOSITIONAL VALUES - READ ACROSS						
			NONE		CHK/SVGS		M MKT/CD		AQH COMPOSITION %			CUME COMPOSITION %			
	AQH	CUME	% IND	% PEN	% IND	% PEN	% IND	% PEN	NONE	CHK/SVGS	M MKT/CD	NONE	CHK/SVGS	M MKT/CD	
WAAF-FM	132	1602	81	9.8	127	15.4	47	5.6	3.2	91.4	5.4	4.2	81.3	14.4	WAAF-FM
WBCN-FM	319	3068	127	29.4	116	26.9	62	14.3	4.0	76.9	19.1	6.7	74.0	19.3	WBCN-FM
WBET	2	142	*	*	*	*	*	*	*	*	*	*	*	*	WBET
WBOS-FM	97	958	110	8.0	129	9.3	39	2.8	2.9	87.0	10.0	5.8	82.1	12.1	WBOS-FM
WBUR-FM	25	768			91	5.3	135	7.8		59.3	40.7		58.2	41.8	WBUR-FM
WBZ	129	2554	80	15.5	88	16.9	129	24.6	5.2	54.7	40.2	4.2	55.9	39.9	WBZ
WCAP	2	109	*	*	*	*	*	*	*	*	*	*	*	*	WCAP
WCAV-FM	5	143	*	*	*	*	*	*	*	*	*	*	*	*	WCAV-FM
WCGY-FM	61	606	149	6.8	130	5.9	30	1.4	4.3	90.9	4.8	7.8	82.9	9.3	WCGY-FM
WCRB-FM	29	804			115	7.0	85	5.1		60.9	39.1		73.6	26.4	WCRB-FM
WEEI	110	2526	66	12.6	92	17.6	122	23.1	6.6	56.8	36.6	3.5	58.8	37.7	WEEI
WERS-FM	26	272	*	*	*	*	*	*	*	*	*	*	*	*	WERS-FM
WESX*	5	108	*	*	*	*	*	*	*	*	*	*	*	*	WESX*
WEZE	4	135	*	*	*	*	*	*	*	*	*	*	*	*	WEZE
WFNX-FM	36	429			86	2.8	145	4.7		50.0	50.0		55.0	45.0	WFNX-FM
WGBH-FM	62	1144			99	8.5	120	10.3		61.3	38.7		62.9	37.1	WGBH-FM
WHDH	66	1580	254	30.2	62	7.4	153	18.1	11.8	53.0	35.3	13.3	39.5	47.2	WHDH
WILD*	4	246	*	*	*	*	*	*	*	*	*	*	*	*	WILD*
WJIB-FM	84	1129			69	5.9	181	15.3		52.9	47.1		44.0	56.0	WJIB-FM
WLLH	9	311	*	*	*	*	*	*	*	*	*	*	*	*	WLLH
WMEX	4	205	*	*	*	*	*	*	*	*	*	*	*	*	WMEX
WMJX-FM	65	1016			102	7.8	113	8.6		70.3	29.7		65.0	35.0	WMJX-FM
WODS-FM	128	1552	148	17.3	115	13.4	62	7.2	5.1	71.0	23.9	7.8	73.2	19.0	WODS-FM
WPLM		37	*	*	*	*	*	*	*	*	*	*	*	*	WPLM
WPLM-FM	56	514	146	5.7	65	2.5	164	6.3	26.7	40.3	33.0	7.7	41.7	50.7	WPLM-FM
WRKO	141	1820	242	33.2	83	11.4	111	15.2	9.4	51.0	39.6	12.7	52.8	34.5	WRKO
WROL*	17	194	*	*	*	*	*	*	*	*	*	*	*	*	WROL*
WROR-FM	70	1102			98	8.1	121	10.0		54.5	45.5		62.5	37.5	WROR-FM
WSSH-FM	49	824	119	7.4	91	5.7	115	7.1	4.4	50.2	45.4	6.2	58.1	35.7	WSSH-FM
WVBF-FM	44	674			93	4.7	131	6.6		47.0	53.0		59.5	40.5	WVBF-FM
WXKS	13	347	*	*	*	*	*	*	*	*	*	*	*	*	WXKS
WXKS-FM	162	2575	52	10.1	115	22.3	78	15.0	2.3	71.3	26.4	2.7	73.3	24.0	WXKS-FM
WZLX-FM	148	1723	165	21.4	120	15.6	48	6.3	6.2	79.5	14.3	8.7	76.3	15.0	WZLX-FM
WZOU-FM	97	1174	134	11.9	91	8.1	112	9.9	14.6	55.7	29.8	7.1	58.2	34.8	WZOU-FM
WHJY-FM	20	354	317	8.5	113	3.0	36	1.0	24.6	71.6	3.7	16.7	72.2	11.1	WHJY-FM
WOKQ-FM	3	211	*	*	*	*	*	*	*	*	*	*	*	*	WOKQ-FM
PUR	2322	12898	100	97.3	100	97.4	99	96.6	5.3	67.4	27.3	5.3	63.8	30.9	PUR

BIRCH RADIO

CATEGORY DEFINITIONS	ESTIMATED POPULATION (00)
NONE - HAVE NOT USED ANY BANKING SERVICES IN PAST YEAR	696
CHK/SVGS - HAVE USED ONLY CHECKING OR SAVINGS ACCOUNTS IN PAST YEAR	8452
M MKT/CD - HAVE USED SPECIAL SERVICES LIKE MONEY MKT ACCTS/CD'S IN PAST YEAR	4132

EXHIBIT 9.15

Birch Radio provides weekly audience and product data. In this example, 91.4 percent of men 18+ listening to station WAAF used a checking or savings account in the past year. (Courtesy: Birch Radio.)

Birch currently has approximately 1,500 clients versus 3,100 for Arbitron. In recent years, the Birch report has added product-category usage data to the basic radio ratings (see Exhibit 9.15).

Beginning in 1988, Birch began surveys of Hispanic listeners to match similar studies done by Arbitron. Because of language barriers, the Hispanic market is difficult and expensive to survey. However, it is simply too large and affluent a market to ignore, either by advertisers or by rating services. Currently, there are 20 million Hispanics in the United States, and this figure will approach 30 million by the year 2000. Studies show that Hispanics prefer radio to other media, spending an average of 30 hours per week with the medium (see Exhibit 9.16).

Radio All-Dimension Audience Research (RADAR). *Service of Statistical Research, Inc., major source of network radio ratings.*

Network Radio Ratings

Radio All Dimension Audience Research (RADAR). The major source of radio network ratings is RADAR, a service of Statistical Research, Inc. Data used in RADAR reports are collected through telephone recall interviews. RADAR measure-

EXHIBIT 9.16

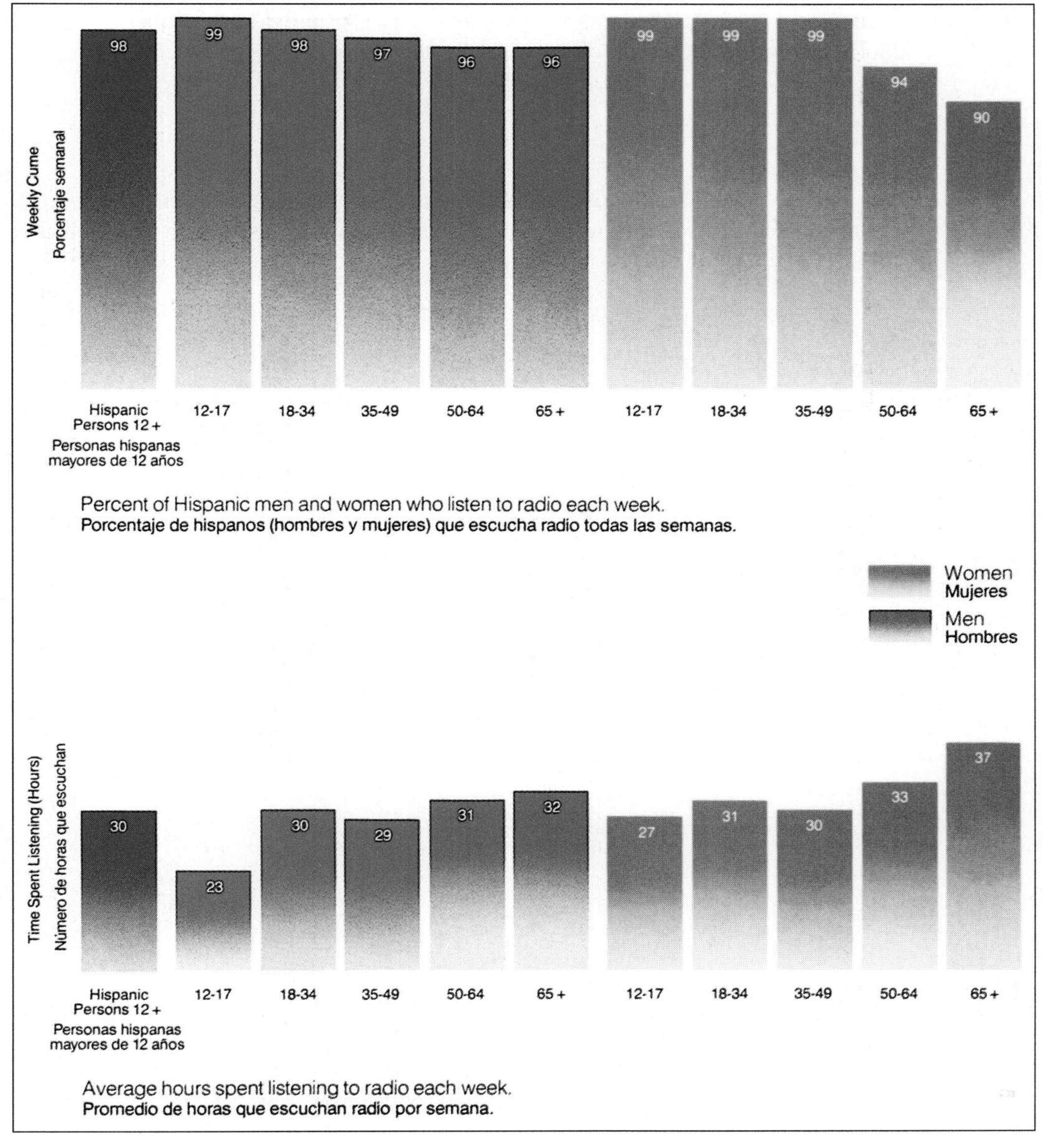

ments are based on information gathered over a 48-week period. Data on radio listening for a one-week period are obtained by daily telephone interviews that use a random dial system to contact respondents.

Respondents are actually contacted up to nine times in a RADAR survey. The first contact is an alert call. The first call for audience information is placed on the first day of the measurement week. In subsequent calls, the respondent is asked about radio listening from the time of the prior call to the present instant. The final call is placed the day after the measurement week ends to complete recording audience information up to midnight of the last day and to ask several demographic questions for classification purposes.

RADAR information is provided in three volumes:

- Volume I, Radio Usage Data. The audience estimates in this report are time period measurements for dayparts or for individual quarter hours (see Exhibit 9.17).
- Volume II, Radio Network Data. This report provides estimates of network audiences for all commercials.
- Volume III, Radio Network Data. This report provides estimates of network audiences for commercials within programs only.

In addition to the standard reports, RADAR can also provide a number of special reports tailored to the needs of specific clients.

RATE CLASSIFICATIONS

Every station establishes its own classifications and publishes them on its rate card. The negotiated cost of time depends on those classifications, which are typically:

EXHIBIT 9.17

(Courtesy: Statistical Research, Inc.)

RADAR 32 - SPRING/FALL 1985

AUDIENCE ESTIMATES FOR ALL AM AND FM RADIO STATIONS
BY DAYPART
NUMBER OF PERSONS IN THOUSANDS

MONDAY THROUGH SUNDAY
LOCAL TIME

	TOTAL PERS 12+	TOTAL ADULTS 18+	MEN TOTAL	MEN 18-49	MEN 25-54	MEN 25+	MEN 35+	WOMEN TOTAL	WOMEN 18-49	WOMEN 25-54	WOMEN 25+	WOMEN 35+	TEENS 12-17
FULL 24 HOUR DAY													
AVERAGE QUARTER HOUR	25075	22680	10551	7936	6354	8353	5242	12129	8166	6806	10012	7313	2395
AVERAGE 1 DAY CUME	153746	135433	65606	47073	38816	53156	35813	69827	46984	38807	57587	40948	18313
7 DAY WEEKLY CUME	184581	163575	78554	54927	45977	64650	44374	85021	55741	46827	71081	50923	21006
6.00 AM TO 12.00 M													
AVERAGE QUARTER HOUR	31055	28095	13025	9743	7845	10356	6508	15070	10176	8512	12463	9081	2960
AVERAGE 1 DAY CUME	151500	133358	64525	46300	38117	52240	35193	68833	46313	38310	56820	40438	18142
7 DAY WEEKLY CUME	184280	163274	78328	54848	45868	64433	44182	84946	55715	46801	71006	50861	21006
6.00 AM TO 10.00 AM													
AVERAGE QUARTER HOUR	38969	36281	16531	11648	10229	13984	9236	19750	12494	11291	17234	12986	2688
AVERAGE 1 DAY CUME	106871	95899	46571	32620	28430	39059	26680	49328	32395	28057	41891	30477	10972
7 DAY WEEKLY CUME	168896	149491	72185	50845	42995	59752	40833	77306	51665	43301	64287	45744	19405
10.00 AM TO 3.00 PM													
AVERAGE QUARTER HOUR	36524	34021	15576	11675	9475	12517	7719	18445	12549	10576	15307	10948	2503
AVERAGE 1 DAY CUME	86804	78265	36543	26822	21408	29062	18728	41722	28737	23382	33961	24050	8539
7 DAY WEEKLY CUME	163471	144987	68420	48907	40161	55460	37297	76567	51534	42772	63189	44731	18484
3.00 PM TO 7.00 PM													
AVERAGE QUARTER HOUR	31966	28433	13486	10455	8330	10551	6533	14947	10562	8627	12059	8585	3533
AVERAGE 1 DAY CUME	87087	76302	37879	29075	23882	30210	19193	38423	27843	22678	30945	21053	10785
7 DAY WEEKLY CUME	160000	140102	67810	49485	40959	55005	36541	72292	50823	41799	59060	40611	19898
7.00 PM TO 12.00 M													
AVERAGE QUARTER HOUR	18527	15350	7302	5717	3921	5140	3099	8048	5641	4134	6124	4485	3177
AVERAGE 1 DAY CUME	61272	50568	24734	19358	14029	17979	11316	25834	18425	13949	19932	13944	10704
7 DAY WEEKLY CUME	133060	113868	55627	42666	33627	43365	27981	58241	42366	33395	46105	31091	19192
12.00 M TO 6.00 AM													
AVERAGE QUARTER HOUR	7133	6433	3126	2512	1878	2341	1441	3307	2137	1687	2661	2009	700
AVERAGE 1 DAY CUME	35348	31807	15649	11931	9466	12241	7894	16158	11069	9123	13139	9744	3541
7 DAY WEEKLY CUME	83458	72696	36416	28531	21541	27521	17648	36280	26303	20056	28006	19589	10762

Drive time. *The early morning and late afternoon periods when most radio stations have their largest audiences and highest ad rates.*

The most *desired* and *costly* time on radio is *drive time,* which also has the highest ratings. As a result, commercial script writers know the reader is preoccupied, but a "captive" audience—so by using the following guidelines, the best radio commercials should emerge: (1) keep it simple; (2) use a dramatic device or provocative statement *early;* (3) speak in the audience's language; (4) repeat product name often; (5) be specific—make every word count; (6) emphasize important, unusual ideas; and (7) give helpful *visual* hints.

- *Drive time:* The most desired and costly time on radio, it varies by community and usually has the highest ratings.
- *Run-of-station (ROS):* The station has a choice of moving the commercial at will, wherever it is most convenient. Preemptible ROS is the least costly time on the rate card.
- *Special features:* Time adjacent to weather signals, news reports, time signals, or traffic or stockmarket reports usually carries a premium charge.

Package Plans

Most spot time is sold in terms of weekly package plans, usually called *total audience plans,* or TAP. A station offers a special flat rate for a number of time slots divided in different proportions over the broadcast day. A typical TAP plan distributes time equally throughout the broadcast day.

An advertiser can buy the total plan or parts of it. In all instances, there is a quantity- or dollar-discount plan, depending upon the total number of spots run during a given period of time (Exhibit 9.18).

Negotiations

In buying spot radio time, as in buying spot TV time, negotiation is the rule rather than the exception. The successful media planner is a hard, but reasonable, bargainer. There is no formula to determine what radio spots should cost; therefore, negotiation is crucial to cost efficiency for the advertiser. Radio advertising time is basically worth whatever the advertiser will pay for it. As we have seen, the number of stations, formats, and purchase plans make buying radio extremely complex. Regardless of whether you enter media negotiations as a buyer or a seller, several points are key to an efficient buy:

1. *Do your homework.* The media buyer should know the demand for various dayparts and the general pricing policies of each station in a market. The salesperson should know the marketing strategy of advertisers, budgets available for radio, and the media mix of the advertisers with whom he or she is dealing.
2. *Be fair.* Advertising sales depend on mutual respect between buyer and seller. The media buyer often looks to the media salesperson as a source of information beyond the buy at hand. The seller who takes advantage of this relationship by offering spots that do not fulfill the advertiser's goals is making short-term gains at the risk of future loss of sales.
3. *Know your counterpart.* The astute negotiator knows not only the rating numbers, but also the personalities of those with whom he or she deals and what techniques work with them.
4. *Don't be greedy.* The best negotiator knows when to close the deal. There is a fine line between tough negotiating and losing a sale by keeping the price unrealistically high or losing a spot by refusing to pay a reasonable rate.

Obviously, negotiation is something that can be learned only by doing. This is why most of the top broadcast salespeople and media buyers started in small markets or as media research assistants in agencies and worked up slowly to larger markets and greater agency buying responsibility.

EXHIBIT 9.18
Total audience plan

*Number of Times**	8	12	20	32	40
1 minute, $	110	100	92	86	79
30 seconds, $	88	80	74	69	63

*Per week (1/4 A.M., 1/4 P.M., 1/4 housewife, 1/4 night).

Buying Radio

The two primary characteristics of radio time are that it is sold on the basis of narrow audience segments and that it is perishable. As we have noted throughout the text, advertisers are increasingly concerned about the quality (i.e., the reach of prime prospects) as well as the quantity of the audience.

Today radio research data and advertising buys give primary consideration to stations and formats that reach some selective audience segment. Exhibit 9.19 shows how radio can reach a particular market such as tape and record purchasers. In radio, being number one may not be as important to the success of a station as its demographic rank in a particular daypart.

In addition, buyers are aware of the perishability of radio time, especially when sales are slow. The competitive bidding for unsold inventory on radio stations has severely depressed the average cost-per-spot in some markets. Dan Flambert of RAB believes this panic selling stems from a failure to appreciate the concept of price integrity.[3] As airtime for an unsold spot approaches, it is very tempting for a station sales department to unload commercial time to salvage some revenues. The larger a station's unsold inventory, the more likely its sales department is to disrupt the price scale within a market.

USING RADIO RATINGS

Unlike television, radio audiences restrict their listening to three–four stations per week—according to the programs they prefer. For executives and professionals—those with incomes over $60,000 or more—The Wall Street Journal Radio Network claims the *most loyal listeners* of all information-related broadcasts.

In Chapter 8, Using Television, we discussed the basic rating and share-of-audience formulas. These formulas are the same in both radio and television, but the lack of distinct programs makes the use of these ratings much different in radio.

From a media-planning perspective, radio is a very different medium from television. Radio *stations* are like television *programs*. Listeners choose specific stations to meet their needs. Most listeners tune in to no more than three or four stations a week, with less than three being the average. Even the largest radio stations typically reach only a portion of their markets, while television stations usually reach over 90 percent of the audience weekly.[4]

There are several definitions we need to understand before we can use radio ratings in media planning. For simplicity, we will use terminology from the Arbitron rating service.

[3]"Attracting New-to-Radio Clients a Key Station Priority," *Television/Radio Age,* September 1, 1986, p. 45.

[4]Robert Galen, "The GRP Trap," *Avoid Radio Planning Errors,"* a publication of the Radio Advertising Bureau, p. 3.

EXHIBIT 9.19

Media buyers are interested in the preferred formats of various consumers. (Courtesy: Radio Advertising Bureau.)

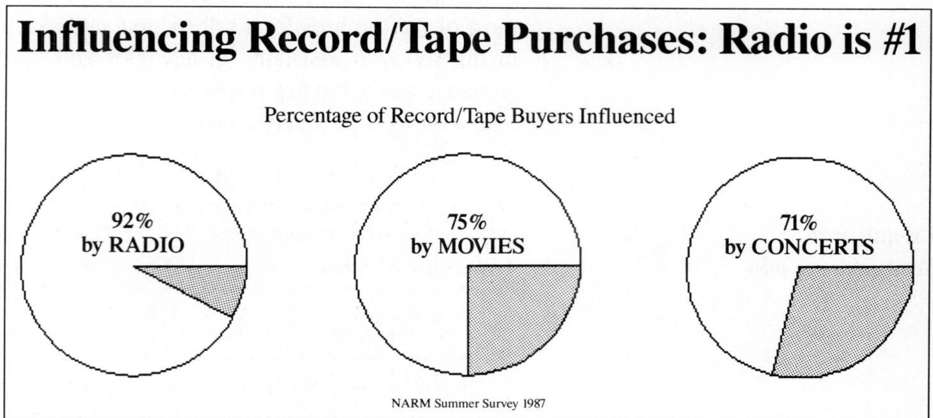

Geographical Patterns of Radio Ratings

Metro Survey Area (MSA). *The central city within a radio station's listenership.*

Radio audience ratings use two geographical boundaries to report audiences: metro survey area (MSA) and total survey area (TSA). Typically, the majority of a station's audience comes from within the MSA.

Metro Survey Area. An MSA always includes a city or cities whose population is specified as that of the central city together with the county (or counties) in which it is located.

Total Survey Area. The TSA is a geographic area that encompasses the MSA and certain counties located outside the MSA that meet specified listening criteria.

Definitions of the Radio Audience

You will recall that the basic audience measures for television are the rating and share of audience for a particular show. In radio, audience estimates are usually given by either average quarter-hour (AQH) audiences or the cumulative or unduplicated audience (Cume) listening to a station over several quarter hours or dayparts.

Average quarter hour estimates. *The period of time during which most radio ratings are calculated. That is, an estimate of the number of people who listen to a station during one or some combination of quarter hours.*

Average Quarter-Hour Estimates (AQHE). Average quarter-hour persons are the estimated number of people listening to a station for at least 5 minutes during a 15-minute period.

The average quarter-hour rating is the AQH persons calculated as a percentage of the population being measured:

AQH persons/population × 100 = AQH rating

The average quarter-hour share is the portion of the average radio audience that is listening to a certain station. It is calculated thus:

AQH persons to a station/AQH persons to all station × 100 = share

Cume Estimates. Cume estimates are used to determine the number or percentage of different people who listen to a station during several quarter hours or dayparts.

Cume persons are the number of *different* people who tuned in to a radio station for at least five minutes.

A Cume rating is the percentage of different people listening to a station during several quarter hours or dayparts:

Cume persons/population × 100 = Cume rating

Now let's look at a typical station's audience and calculate these formulas.

Station XYYY, M-F 10 A.M.–3 P.M., Adults 12+

AQH persons = 20,000
Cume persons = 60,000

Metro survey area population = 500,000
Metro survey area AQH persons = 200,000

For station XYYY:

AQH rating = 4/ (20,000/500,000)[5]

[5]Decimals are not used in reporting rating and share figures.

EXHIBIT 9.20

Media buyers must carefully analyze all data from radio rating sources to measure efficiency. (Courtesy: Radio Advertising Bureau.)

Lower GRPs May Give Equal Or Greater Reach						
Station	**# of Spots**	**AQH Rtg.**	**Cume**	**GRPs**	**Reach**	**Frequency**
Major						
Midwestern Mkt.						
WCCC	12	1.8	130,300	87.0	11.7	7.5
WDDD	12	1.5	159,600	72.8	13.4	5.4
Station "D" delivers 16% less GRPs but delivers 15% more reach than station "C"						

Cume rating = 20 (60,000/300,000)

AQH share = 10 (20,000/200,000)

Using our XYYY example, we can also calculate the following:

Gross impressions. *The total number of audience exposures (as opposed to number of listeners) accumulated during a specific radio advertising schedule.*

Gross impressions (GI) = AQH persons × number of commercials

If we buy 6 commercials on XYYY, we have purchased 120,000 impressions (20,000 AQH persons × 6 spots). Remember, these are *impressions,* not people.

Gross rating points = AQH rating × number of commercials

Again, 6 commercials would deliver 24 GRPs (4 AQH rating × 6 spots).

Listeners per dollar (LPD) = AQH persons/spot cost

If a spot on XYYY costs $500, then the LPD is $40 (20,000 AQH persons/$500).

The media planner must be able to manipulate the various radio data to develop a plan suitable for a particular client. While the computer can do these manipulations quickly, it can't make up for a planner's ignorance of the basic process. The same budget, and even the same number of spots, used in different dayparts and across multiple stations delivers vastly different results. Exhibit 9.20 shows how as few as 12 spots bought on two stations in the same market result in major differences in cume, reach, and frequency.

THE RADIO BUY

To this point, we have examined the stations, formats, and costs of the radio stations in the markets we wish to consider. We have evaluated radio as a medium, and the available stations in light of other media alternatives, our marketing strategy (both quantitative and qualitative factors), and advertising requirements such as compensating for the medium's lack of a visual element. It is now time to actually schedule the radio spots for our campaign.

The first step in radio buying is to rank the stations in each market against the previously defined target market. With the use of lifestyle data, such as PRIZM, the advertisers can identify the stations that *best* meet their criteria. For reaching "intelligent, sophisticated, high-powered people," WBBM, Chicago's All News station says it's the one. . . . and so does 5 agency reps in their ad.

Scheduling for Radio

The first step in buying a radio schedule is to rank the stations in each market against the previously defined target market for your product. In the past, stations would be ranked according to standard demographic data. Let's assume that we are selling luxury cars and we know that our target market is men aged 35 to 64. Using Arbitron ratings, we rank the following stations against this group of prospects:

Market population = 455,900
Monday–Friday, 6–10 A.M.
Men 35–64

Station	*AQH (00)*	*Avg. Rating*	*Market Rank*
WXXX	252	5.5	1
WAAA	211	4.6	2
WYYY	190	4.1	3
WZZZ	129	2.8	4

Remember, the media planner of the 1980s has much more powerful marketing tools than were available in previous decades. As you will recall from Chapter 7, Basic Media Strategy, the use of lifestyle data such as PRIZM allows us to more narrowly identify market segments. Let's assume that our prime prospects for luxury cars are in the Blue Blood and Pools and Patios categories. Our computer model now ranks our stations on the basis of cluster ratings rather than demographic ratings, with the following results:

	Demographics Avg.			*Cluster Ratings*		
Station	**AQH (00)**	**Rating**	**Rate**	**AQH (00)**	**Avg. Rating**	**Rate**
WXXX	252	5.5	1	101	2.2	2
WAAA	211	4.6	2	96	2.1	3
WYYY	190	4.1	3	109	2.4	1
WZZZ	129	2.8	4	88	1.9	4

By using lifestyle measures, we are able to identify those stations that best reach more narrowly targeted markets of upscale men. The next step is the actual scheduling of the spots on each station. Computer technology and statistical estimates make these calculations fairly routine.

Intermedia Scheduling in a Market

Since radio listeners are often light users of other media, radio is an excellent means of extending both reach and frequency of an advertising schedule. As already discussed, radio is most often used as a supplemental medium. The media planner is frequently asked to schedule radio in combination with other media in a manner that yields the best results per dollar.

For several years now, the RAB has studied the role of radio combined with other advertising media. As Exhibit 9.21 shows, radio in combination with newspapers is much more effective than either medium alone.

EXHIBIT 9.21

Newspaper/radio mix comparisons by market size—adults 18+. (Courtesy: Radio Advertising Bureau.)

	Full-Page Ad	*½ Page + Station A*
	Reach × Freq. = GRPs	**Reach × Freq. = GRPs**
Top 10 Markets	18 × 1.0 = 18	29 × 2.3 = 66
Markets 26–50	20 × 1.0 = 20	30 × 2.5 = 75
Markets 101–150	11 × 1.0 = 11	32 × 3.6 = 115
Markets 151–200	20 × 2.0 = 40	31 × 2.2 = 68
Markets 201–250	28 × 1.0 = 28	63 × 3.3 = 208

A single selected market was used for purposes of comparison from each of the above groups. (AM/FM combination shown as one station.)

(Sources: Arbitron, Metro Area, Spring 1984.)

SUMMARY

It is difficult to predict the future of radio. However, some trends can be foreseen for the near future. They represent both opportunities and challenges for this exciting medium.

1. *Continuing audience fragmentation and competition for audiences.* The number of stations continues to grow and the fierce competition of recent years should go on unabated through the 1990s. The problem of price competition will continue to plague the profit side of the industry, while benefiting advertisers. This competition within the medium will prevent the radio industry from devoting as much time and effort as it would like to competing with other media.
2. The radio industry, through Arbitron, Birch, and RADAR, will continue to improve rating techniques and methodology. The competition for advertising dollars will result in even better audience data for agencies and their clients in the future.
3. AM radio will continue to experience problems. With current audience share down to 25 percent, further sharp declines are unlikely. However, AM's inability to reach the younger, more affluent market segments will continue to plague the industry.
4. Radio will go on improving its image with both advertisers and the public. Stereo FM and creative delivery of varied formats for all segments make radio a popular entertainment medium. The ability to deliver fast-breaking news makes it extremely popular as an information medium. The astute marketing techniques of recent years, along with radio's inherent positive characteristics, make the medium extremely popular with both local and national advertisers.

SUGGESTED EXERCISES

- How many radios do you own (including car radios)? How much time do you listen to each one on an average day?
- How many different radio formats are offered by radio stations in your community?
- During a typical hour of radio listening, keep track of the advertisers using the medium. How many of them were local businesses?

QUESTIONS

1. Discuss some of the marketing techniques that have allowed radio to compete with television as an advertising medium.
2. What are the primary advantages and disadvantages of radio as an advertising medium?
3. Briefly discuss the differences between AM and FM radio as advertising media.
4. Discuss the status of network radio and its development during the last few years.
5. Identify and describe the three primary radio ratings services for local and network radio audiences.
6. Define:
   (a) drive time
   (b) package plans
   (c) MSA
   (d) cume
   (e) average quarter-hour rating
7. Discuss some of the primary reasons for the emergence of FM radio.
8. How is radio used by most advertisers in their media planning?

READINGS

''Following the Formats,'' *Broadcasting,* February 27, 1989, p. 40.

MEYER, MARIANNE: ''New Age: The Next Rage in Radio?'' *Marketing & Media Decisions,* February 1988, p. 45.

''More Voices Join Satellite-Delivered Talk Format,'' *Broadcasting,* February 20, 1989, p. 46.

SWISSHELM, GEORGE: ''Newspapers Support Radio Station Viewers Ad Pushes,'' *Television/Radio Age,* February 6, 1989, p. 42.

TEN

Using Newspapers

Newspapers attract more advertising revenue than other medium. Despite a "not so great" year, ad revenue during the first half of 1988 advanced 5.2%. And on the forecast of strong ad dollars, Ingersoll Publications will launch the *St. Louis Sun,* a *new* daily newspaper.

Retailers have relied on *newspapers,* primarily, to get their messages out. In launching their new "Groceries-By-Phone" service, Dominick's Jewel, Big Bear, and Gooding's Supermarkets will advertise heavily in their local newspapers. "When it comes to getting out the facts for changing strongly-held habits, like grocery shopping," Jeno Paulucci, the service's founder, says, "I recommended *large, direct-worded ads*—followed up by coupon books, samples, and an information hot-line."

American Newspaper Publishers Association (ANPA). *Industry-wide newspaper publishers group that provides research and information on the state of the newspaper industry.*

The daily newspaper remains the undisputed leader in attracting advertising dollars. For most of this century, newspapers' leadership in advertising volume was based on their virtual monopoly among local advertisers. A local newspaper had a practically clear field because there were no competing newspapers in most markets; radio was in a transition period and could not mount strong competition for retailers' ad dollars, direct mail had not become a viable local medium, and most television stations did little retail promotion.

The competitive situation has changed dramatically in the last decade. Metropolitan growth has shifted away from the central city, and suburban newspapers and free shoppers have become major competitors for retail advertising dollars. Likewise, preprinted inserts and direct mail have either cut newspapers' profits or allowed large retailers to move out of the medium altogether. Both radio and television have mounted major efforts to encourage retailers to move into the broadcast medium. Cable channels and independent television stations offer extremely competitive spot costs, making it possible for even small retailers to experiment with television.

In addition to competitive pressure from other media, newspapers are also plagued by rising costs as they attempt to stay competitive for advertising dollars. For example, the price of newsprint rose over 400 percent between 1970 and 1990. The cost of labor and printing rose approximately 6 percent a year throughout the 1980s, a time of almost flat circulation. Newspapers ranked second only to network television in CPM increase during that decade.

Despite all these problems, the medium is extremely healthy. One of the major reasons for the industry's optimism is the dearth of internal competition. Daily newspapers can present a united front to advertisers since they are not fighting among themselves to the degree prevalent in other media. According to the American Newspaper Publishers Association, there are approximately 1,640 daily newspapers, a decrease of some 100 papers since 1980. Of these, 530 are morning, 1,110 are evening, and 820 are Sunday newspapers. These figures do not include weekly papers, which we will discuss separately.

In recent years, we have seen the rise of the national newspaper. Long-established specialized publications such as *The Wall Street Journal* and a few nationally distributed newspapers such as *The New York Times* and *The Washington Post* were joined in 1983 by *USA Today* as the first general-readership national newspaper. *USA Today* has a paid circulation of approximately 1.3 million and is available in most markets.

The jury is still out on whether *USA Today*, or any national newspaper, will ever prove profitable. Despite an upscale readership and high visibility and publicity, the paper has lost money every year of its existence. *USA Today's* problem may be finding an advertising niche. As one media planner pointed out, "*USA Today* won't give you great impact across the country. Advertisers use it as an overlay. You would never buy *USA Today* to transplant your more targeted, local media buys."[1]

Although *USA Today* is a newspaper in format, it appeals to national advertisers who traditionally use magazines or television as their primary medium. *USA Today* has already proved that a general national newspaper can sustain high levels of readership. What remains to be seen is whether the paper can attract enough advertising support to make it profitable.

MARKETING THE NEWSPAPER

Newspaper marketing. *Competition for readers and advertising has resulted in newspapers undertaking major marketing and promotional efforts in recent years.*

There is no question that the contemporary daily newspaper is a tremendously popular medium of information, entertainment, and advertising. However, unlike its predecessors, the contemporary newspaper must market itself to readers and advertisers to stay in business. The newspaper industry is well aware of the need to position itself for the twenty-first century and, with that goal in mind, has commissioned a number of studies to see what readers like and dislike about their newspapers. While these studies have come up with various recommendations, all emphasize the need for newspapers to market their product. Consequently, publishers are finally acknowledging that the newspaper is a product and, like all products, must be promoted aggressively if it is to be successful.

NEWSPAPER MARKETING AND MERCHANDISING SERVICES

As we made clear earlier, newspapers are facing growing competition for the advertising dollar. In order to meet this competition, they are marketing the medium more aggressively than ever before. The new emphasis on marketing has taken several forms, the most common of which are:

1. *Retaining and increasing circulation by promoting the newspaper as the best source of information, entertainment, and advertising*. Newspapers use a vast array of promotional devices to gain readership. Some papers give free delivery for a week, others devise contests and sweepstakes for readers, and, of course, heavy advertising in other media is quite common. In addition, individual features such as well-known local and syndicated columnists and special feature sections are promoted to gain readership.
2. *Promoting the newspaper as an advertising medium to local retail accounts*. A strong effort is being made to maintain present business, increase usage among current advertisers, and develop new accounts among recently established businesses or retailers that are currently using other advertising vehicles.
3. *Promoting both the newspaper and the local market as a necessary part of a national advertiser's media schedule*. The approach to national advertisers is usually twofold: First, newspapers show the value of adding the medium to the advertising schedule in conjunction with

Newspapers "promote" themselves to national advertisers by emphasizing their close ties to *local* markets. *The Plain Dealer* of Cleveland, Ohio claims it ranks #2 nationally in city zone penetration of the top 20 newspapers in national circulation. Its daily penetration figure is 58% of the Northeast Ohio market, while that figure jumps to 74% on Sunday!

[1]Patrick Reilly, "*USA Today* Future Colored by Red Ink," *Advertising Age*, July 18, 1988, p. 47.

other media. Second, newspapers located in markets outside the top 10 or 20 heavily promote their markets as important to national advertisers, often by comparing the local market to others that national advertisers might be considering.

Marketing to Readers

The lack of readership, especially among the *young*, is a worrisome trend among newspapers. In trying to reverse that trend, special sections devoted to *entertainment* have been created—which also appeals to companies, trying to sell to that profitable market. When Hartmarx adopted a new strategy to attract *young men* buyers of their clothing, they selected ''upbeat'' weekend inserts to feature their Grethel and Sansabelt lines.

American Society of Newspaper Editors (ASNE). *Newspaper editor organization primarily concerned with matters or editorial content and readership of newspapers.*

Among the major problems newspapers face are retaining present readers and gaining new ones, especially teenagers and young adults. No meeting of newspaper editors or publishers is complete without stories, predictions, and tips on the perplexing problem of readership retention. Exhibit 10.1 shows that the decline in newspaper circulation as compared to population is a 40-year trend. In 1946, there were 1.3 newspapers per household; today that figure is 0.6.

Several studies addressing the problem of declining readership have been conducted, and the consistent finding is that ''a lack of time'' is the primary deterrent to reading a newspaper. Newspapers are dealing with a population much different from that of a few decades ago. Americans of the 1990s are better educated, more affluent, and older than those of past generations. They marry later, are more likely to be childless, and are less tied to either the geography or mores of their parents. Over half of all women work, and the occupational alternatives for women and minorities have never been greater.

The problem of falling newspaper readership must be tackled on several fronts. A study sponsored by the American Society of Newspaper Editors found three areas to be crucial for increasing readership:

1. *Content:*
   - Respect people's time constraints
   - Help readers be efficient ''information retrievers''
   - Make content more compelling
   - Improve local news coverage
   - Pay attention to advertising, TV listings, etc.
2. *Circulation:*
   - Devise programs for grappling with readers' mobility

EXHIBIT 10.1

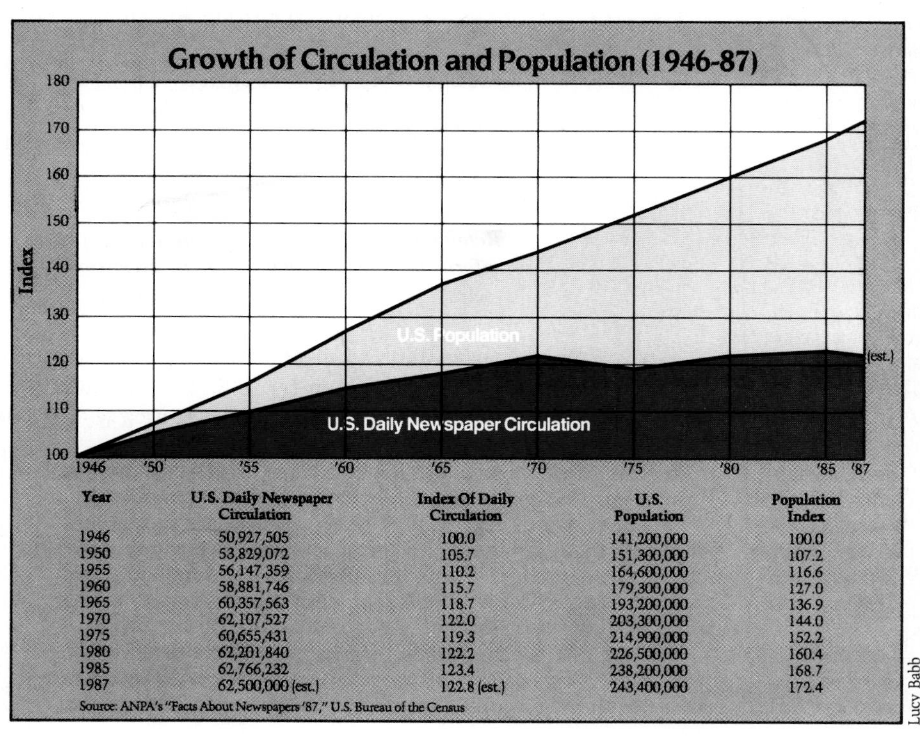

Year	U.S. Daily Newspaper Circulation	Index Of Daily Circulation	U.S. Population	Population Index
1946	50,927,505	100.0	141,200,000	100.0
1950	53,829,072	105.7	151,300,000	107.2
1955	56,147,359	110.2	164,600,000	116.6
1960	58,881,746	115.7	179,300,000	127.0
1965	60,357,563	118.7	193,200,000	136.9
1970	62,107,527	122.0	203,300,000	144.0
1975	60,655,431	119.3	214,900,000	152.2
1980	62,201,840	122.2	226,500,000	160.4
1985	62,766,232	123.4	238,200,000	168.7
1987	62,500,000 (est.)	122.8 (est.)	243,400,000	172.4

Source: ANPA's "Facts About Newspapers '87," U.S. Bureau of the Census

- Accept some churn as a cost of doing business and plan for it
- Periodically verify circulation records with subscribers
- Remember the importance of single-copy sales

3. *Promotion:*
   - Use promotion to create daily brand loyalty
   - Promote newspapers as an excellent way to keep informed
   - Find ways to encourage people to ''voluntarily'' start reading a newspaper
   - Promote more of everything to women; target more toward men's specific interests[2]

More *color, graphics,* and *special sections* give newspapers more advertising appeal. Kraft will use Sunday newspapers to assist in the in-store cookbook promotion it's planning. The promotion will consist of a national, free-standing insert, which is actually a page from the cookbook!

Readership is not a consistent problem with every newspaper, and the solutions that work for one paper may be dismal failures with others. Some publishers have radically redesigned their papers using more color and graphics. Others have begun special-topic sections (entertainment, business, the arts, etc.). A few have even resorted to money-back guarantees to subscribers. It is the rare newspaper that is not engaging in or considering some method of dealing with declining readership.

Marketing to Advertisers

Gaining readership is only part of the marketing task for newspapers. The newspaper industry is well aware of the need to promote the medium to advertisers, who have many alternatives for their advertising dollar. A study sponsored by the Newspaper Advertising Bureau, called *Readers: How to Get Them and Retain Them,* outlines three steps necessary to the future of the newspaper as an advertising medium:

1. Newspapers must reverse the erosion they have suffered in share of advertising in order to preserve their traditional position as the premier communications medium in the United States.
2. The newspaper industry must seize a developing opportunity to strengthen its competitive position, especially vis-à-vis television.
3. Increases in circulation and readership are essential to the industry's efforts to raise its share of advertising dollars.

Newspaper Advertising Bureau (NAB). *Group whose primary mission is to promote newspapers as a major advertising medium. Particularly concerned with increasing national advertising in recent years.*

In order to accomplish these goals, newspaper publishers must learn to take advantage of the opportunities their medium can offer advertisers. Craig Standen, president of the Newspaper Advertising Bureau, has pointed out several of these opportunities:

1. The increasing regionalization of national advertising strategies has opened the way for newspapers to capture additional national business.
2. Nearly one-third of all television commercials are 15 seconds. Newspapers offer advertisers a flexible format with less clutter.
3. Newspapers offer retailers the ability to reach customers quickly, efficiently, and dependably.
4. Newspaper advertising can offer retailers immediate, provable results in terms of day-after sales.[3]

The *flexibility* and *accountability* of newspapers make it the ''perfect'' vehicle for local merchants. Rather than rely on price discounting, Stop 'n' Go convenience stores will be adopting *quarterly promotions*. ''That way,'' admitted Jayal Daily, vice-president, advertising and sales promotion, ''we can change our strategy quickly, if it doesn't generate enough in-store traffic and demand for our advertised goods.''

In addition to these industry-wide efforts, individual newspapers are meeting increased competition by selling local and national advertisers on the vitality of both newspapers and their local markets. It is, after all, the success of each local newspaper that will in the end determine the success of the industry. There are many examples of this newfound emphasis on marketing by local newspapers (see Exhibit 10.2). Throughout this chapter, we will discuss some of the means newspapers have used to market themselves.

---

[2]*Seminar Participants Look for Ways to Retain Readers,* ICMA Update, a publication of the International Circulations Managers Association, Inc., December 1987, p. 2.

[3]''Despite Competitive Challenges, the Outlook for Newspapers Remains 'Tremendous,' Craig Standen Tells Publishers at ANPA Convention,'' *SNPA Bulletin,* May 11, 1988, p. 1.

DATA DARTS

MARKETING FACTS FROM THE ATLANTA JOURNAL AND CONSTITUTION MARKETING DEPARTMENT

The Atlanta Market

Atlanta's Strength

You may not have realized how strong the Atlanta market is or how impressively it stacks up among the top 20 markets in the U.S.

Here's where we stand:

The Atlanta MSA

	12/31/85	**12/31/86**	**% Change**	**Top 20 Rank**
Population	2.5M	2.54M	+3%	10th
Households	902,700	938,700	+4%	9th
Total EBI*	$31.3B	$34.2B	+9%	11th
EBI per HH (Avg. HH EBI)	$34,679	$36,517	+5%	12th
Total Retail Sales	$17.4B	$19.0B	+9%	10th
Retail Sales Per HH	$19,296	$20,295	+5%	5th

*Effective Buying Income

Selected Retail Sales By Category				**Top 20 Per HH Rank**
Furniture, Home Furnishings and Appliance Stores	$817.2M	$945.3M	+16%	9th
Automotive Dealers	$4.3B	$5.0B	+15%	1st
Drugstores	$507.4M	582.1M	+15%	11th
Eating & Drinking Places	$1.8B	$2.0B	+10%	4th
Apparel & Accessories Stores	$762.7M	$861.0M	+13%	14th
Building Materials & Hardware Stores	$1.1B	$1.2B	+15%	2nd

(M=million, B=billion.)

Our strong economic climate provides many opportunities and challenges for retailers--particularly those prepared to capitalize on Atlantans' willingness to spend, and flexible enough to adjust to the market's changing needs. But how do you reach these Atlantans who are your best prospects?

In the Atlanta Journal-Constitution. Last Sunday, 70% of Atlanta adults with household incomes of $35,000-plus read the Journal-Constitution. Reach your best prospects in the advertising medium that combines broad reach and the permanence of print--the Atlanta Journal-Constitution.

Sources: The 1986 Scarborough Atlanta Market Study.
Sales & Marketing Management Survey of Buying Power, 1986 & 1987.

df/24

The Atlanta Journal
THE ATLANTA CONSTITUTION

EXHIBIT 10.2

Zoning and the Total Market Coverage Concept

Two terms have entered newspaper vocabulary with the marketing revolution: *zoning* and *total market coverage*. These services are the industry's recognition of the diverse needs of the various newspaper advertisers.

> ***Zoned editions.*** *Large newspapers often provide weekly inserts directed to specific areas (zones) of a metropolitan area.*

Zoned-editions provide the "ultimate" target market for advertisers who can't afford wasted circulation. *Newsday*, the successful *Long Island* daily, has introduced *New York Newsday*—to cover New York City and its 4 boroughs, *exclusively*. That audience ranks well above the market average in income, with 37% more $50,000+ households—as compared with the entire New York/Long Island market.

Zoned Editions. Zoned editions, also called *mininewspapers,* are usually carried as weekly inserts with news and advertising of interest to a single suburb of a metropolitan area. In most cases, zoned editions or pages are carried in the regular paper, but sometimes they are mailed separately. Zoned editions provide two basic advantages in the marketing strategy of a daily newspaper:

1. They create additional readership by carrying content of interest to a particular area. Often space considerations or a lack of interest outside the particular community would rule out publishing this information in the general daily. News of local business openings, school activities, cultural events, and even personal notices such as hospital admissions make up much of the content of the typical zoned edition.
2. Zoned editions are an excellent means of increasing advertising linage. A small retailer operating one suburban store cannot afford the waste circulation and expense of advertising in a large daily newspaper. The zoned edition, which only reaches customers in a relatively small section of the city, is ideal for this retailer. Large retailers, or even national advertisers, may want to supplement their general media advertising with extra promotion to a specific target segment concentrated in one area of a city.

The most successful zoning efforts appear to be edited to meet specific objectives, whether *offensive* or *defensive*. If, for example, a metro newspaper faces a strong suburban daily, well-edited zoned pages or sections can be focused on retention, defending against potential circulation attrition and loss of the metro's perceived local relevance in those communities. Zoning can also meet potential offensive objectives; leveraging the newspaper's greater resources to provide the breadth and depth of local coverage that prevents the birth (or growth) of competitors.[4]

> ***Total Market Coverage (TMC).*** *Where newspapers augment their circulation with direct mail or shoppers to deliver all households in a market.*

For those retailers desiring *total market coverage* (TMC), such as larger discounters like K-Mart, they advertise in the newspaper's main sections—and supplement that coverage with *inserts* and *direct mail*. To battle the fast-growing Wal-Mart Stores and other retailers, K-Mart will use television, radio, circulars, and *print* to kickoff K-Mart's new $20 million "At Home With Martha Stewart" campaign. "The campaign is targeted at women of America, ages 25–44," revealed Barbara Loren, president of Loren Snyder Marketing, "who need to be *shown how easy and affordable* K-Mart can help redecorate a home in a classy way."

Total Market Coverage. At the opposite end of the marketing spectrum is the total market coverage (TMC) plan. As the name implies, TMCs are designed to give advertisers full market coverage for their messages, including both newspaper subscribers and nonsubscribers. Large retail outlets such as K Mart and Sears demand that all households be reached with their advertising. Since the daily newspaper penetration in major markets falls far short of total coverage (see Exhibit 10.3), retailers obviously cannot achieve this goal by simply advertising in the daily newspaper. Normally they use preprinted advertising supplements, and if a newspaper cannot provide TMC with these, the retailers will go with direct mail.

A newspaper may achieve total market coverage in a number of ways: by making weekly deliveries of a nonsubscriber supplement carrying mostly advertisements, by using direct mail to nonsubscribers, or even by delivering the newspaper free to all households once a week. Whatever the method, it is clear that eventually even smaller newspapers will have to offer total coverage to advertisers.

CATEGORIES OF NEWSPAPER ADVERTISING

As we have seen, the newspaper industry is extremely healthy. With its new emphasis on marketing to readers and advertisers, predictions are for even greater advertising growth in the future.

Newspaper advertising is composed of several categories and subcategories, each

[4]Christine Urban, "Zoning: The Prescription for Lack-of-Local Disease," *AMPE News,* May 1987, p. 5.

MSA Market (Edition)	Total Circ. (000)	% Homes Covered: Home County	MSA	ADI	DMA	Duplication by Outside Papers (% MSA Cov.)
DAYTONA BEACH, FL						
a) Daily Papers						
Daytona Beach News-Journal (M)	78	65.7	65.7	12.5	12.5	Orlando Sentnel (12.1)
De Land Sun News (E)	9	6.1	6.1	—	—	
b) Weekend Papers						
Daytona Beach News-Journal (S)	94	60.3	60.3	11.6	11.6	Orlando Sentinel (15.4)
De Land Sun News (S)	9	6.5	6.5	—	—	
DECATUR, IL						
a) Daily Papers						
Decatur Herald & Review (M)	44	58.7	58.7	12.2	12.3	
b) Weekend Papers						
Decatur Herald & Review (S)	56	66.8	66.8	15.0	15.0	
DENVER, CO						
a) Daily Papers						
The Denver Post (M)	230	26.6	26.8	20.5	20.7	
Rocky Mt. News (M)	332	42.4	39.5	29.8	30.1	
b) Weekend Papers						
The Denver Post (S)	404	40.2	48.4	37.3	37.6	
Rocky Mt. News (S)	373	46.7	44.6	34.3	34.7	
DES MOINES, IA						
a) Daily Papers						
Register (M)	214	57.3	53.0	37.3	38.2	
b) Weekend Papers						
Register (S)	364	70.5	68.2	56.0	56.9	
DETROIT, MI						
a) Daily Papers						
Detroit Free Press (M)	649	32.8	30.5	29.7	29.9	
Detroit News (A)	687	41.6	36.0	34.2	34.4	
b) Weekend Papers						
Detroit Free Press (S)	733	32.7	32.4	31.8	31.9	
Detroit News (S)	838	51.8	46.7	44.3	44.5	
Pontiac Oakland-Press (S)	81	20.7	5.0	—	—	
DOTHAN, AL						
a) Daily Papers						
Dothan Eagle (M/E)	23	43.0	35.3	20.9	20.9	

EXHIBIT 10.3

Newspapers vary significantly in their coverage of a market. Any coverage above 60 percent is considered good. (Courtesy: Bethlehem Publishing Company.)

with its own pattern of users and expenditures. The two major types of newspaper advertising are *display* and *classified*. Within the display category, there are *local* (also called *retail*) and *national* advertisers. The breakout of these categories according to advertising expenditures is as follows:

	$	%
Classified	13.3	36.9
Local	18.4	51.1
National	4.3	12.0

Classified advertising. *In columns so labeled published in sections of a newspaper of magazine set aside for certain classes of goods or services, for example, Help Wanted, Positions Wanted, Houses for Sale, Cars for Sale. The ads are limited in size and illustrations.*

Classified ads are the *major* profit centers for the typical newspaper. "The way to get $2 billion in revenue is to never forget that *every little ad adds up,*" says the Knight-Ridder newspaper ad. They feature letters of appreciation from customers who used their classified ad sections and were very satisfied. Most said they'd continue to use their papers' classified—and tell family, neighbors, and friends to do the same. . . .

Classified Advertising

Those little want ads, often overlooked unless we are in the market for a car, a house, or a used guitar, are major profit centers for the typical newspaper. Classified advertising is concentrated in three categories: employment, real estate, and automotive. These three categories account for approximately 75 percent of all classified expenditures. In fact, classified advertising is considered an excellent barometer of the nation's economic health. Economists watch the employment notices, in particular, to see the ratio of "help wanted" to "positions sought" advertisements.

Newspapers also carry advertisements with illustrations in the classified section. These are known as *classified display* notices, and normally are run in the automotive and real estate sections. All fall under the heading of classified advertising, which is usually a department in itself and has its own rate card. Classified advertising is sold by salespeople who call on accounts just like their counterparts in display advertising. However, a great deal of classified is sold to readers who simply call in to place an ad on a one-time basis. This over-the-transom trade is what makes classified such a profitable part of a newspaper's advertising business.

Local advertising. *Placed and paid for by the local merchant or dealer, in contrast to national, or general, advertising of products sold by many dealers.*

Display advertising includes 2 categories of advertisers: *local* (retail) and *national*. Many local businesses, however, defer to their *centralized offices* for promotion decisions. The local outlet of Ralph Lauren/Polo clothing in Hyde Park/Tampa, Florida joins other merchants in shopping center ads in the local newspapers during heavy shopping seasons. However, most of its promotion is handled by the central office, which concentrates its "image projections" in large metropolitan newspapers—under the assumption that these national ads will "rub off" on local markets.

Display Advertising

All other newspaper advertising is display advertising, which has two classes: local and national.

Local Advertising. For years, local advertising has been the primary revenue source for daily newspapers. *Local advertising* refers to all the advertising placed by local businesses, organizations, and individuals. In recent years, it has become a tremendously competitive arena, with a growing number of media vehicles vying with newspapers for this lucrative market.

The local advertising category includes businesses as diverse as the corner bakery and the largest chain discount or department store. However, because of the significant consolidation of retail companies in recent years, 20 companies account for almost half of all retail advertising carried by newspapers today. This consolidation has changed the way retail advertising is bought. Currently, retail advertising decisions for many chain stores such as J. C. Penney, Target, and Venture are likely to be made at the regional or national level.

This change has had an obvious effect on the way newspaper executives approach retail ad sales. "They're no longer just working on building rapport with the local store manager; they're also taking time to call on regional managers and, two to three times a year, to visit the corporate office."[5] Media planning for many retail chains has become

[5]Rachel Kaplan, "Retail Consolidation Prompts Newspapers to Change Tactics," *Inside Print,* June 1988, p. 17.

similar to that for other large advertisers, and newspapers must deal with this new reality.

Despite the changes in the decision-making process, local advertising continues to be characterized by price competition. Local newspaper advertising tends to be more straight sales oriented than advertising in other media—that is, it emphasizes price, place, and product, with few advertising frills. Most local newspaper advertising attempts to create results that the retailer can see within 24 hours.

National advertising. *Smallest category of newspaper advertising and one newspapers are attempting to increase. Only 12 percent of national ad dollars are placed in newspapers.*

The emphasis in *national* advertising is on *the brand name*—unlike local advertising, which stresses the retail outlet. Benefitting from consumer interest in nutritious foods and a successful new ad campaign, *V-8's* brand name developed new resurgence. The national newspaper ads targeted a *general* audience—anyone who's on a *diet* and over 35. Coincidently, newspaper readership is *heaviest* with the older age groups, where they receive most of their *credible information.*

By *standardizing ad sizes,* local newspapers have interested more national firms in local newspaper advertising. It makes national newspaper space easier to buy—with less variation in the size and type of ads. That's what prompted John Howell, president of Miles' Consumer Healthcare Division, to choose print ads for launching Alka-Seltzer II, the acetaminophen antacid. Howell considers the use of the Alka-Seltzer name "a household word" in most locations, so enlarging the A-S product line via local media is good targeting to reach its primary customers—the over 50 age group.

Standard Advertising Unit (SAU). *Allows national advertisers to purchase newspaper advertising in standard units from one paper to another.*

National Advertising. National advertising, also referred to as *general advertising,* is advertising placed by any marketer who seeks to get readers to ask for a branded product or identified service at any store, showroom, or agency office dealing in such products or services. In recent years, newspapers have become much more aggressive in going after national advertising. There are several reasons for this.

1. As the competition for local advertising dollars has heated up, newspapers see national sales as an important source of new revenue.
2. Regionalization of national advertising accounts has created opportunities for newspapers to compete for national dollars. "Regionalization of advertising buys is not always good news for newspapers—with retail ads, for example, moving the decision making away from the local community is a negative development. But when it occurs with national advertising the net result is positive, according to executives of firms that specialize in representing newspapers to national advertisers."[6]
3. National advertisers are more willing to complement local retailers' promotional efforts, and thus help increase distribution and local retailer support.

National advertising is a huge, and still largely untapped, market for newspapers. At present, national newspaper advertising accounts for only 12 percent of national advertising expenditures. Thus, even a small increase in national advertising dollars would be significant to newspaper profitability. The obvious question, then, is: Why has the leading advertising medium performed so poorly in the national sector? One answer is that until recently newspapers failed to recognize the opportunity and potential profits in national advertising, absorbed as they were in selling to local retailers.

As a result, national advertisers believed that newspapers were indifferent to their needs. Their perception was that newspaper advertising cost too much, was too hard to buy, and was difficult to evaluate. Once newspapers recognized that they had to become more competitive for national advertising dollars, they started to accommodate national advertisers with pricing flexibility and wider acceptance of standardized advertising positions and invoices as well as technical advances in the transmission of ads.[7] Accommodation to the needs of national advertisers has largely centered on three areas:

- Standardization
- Positioning and reproduction quality
- Local versus national rate differentiation

STANDARDIZATION. For many years, publishers and advertisers alike have recognized that standardization of newspaper formats and practices is one of the keys to growth in national advertising. The most important step in the process toward standardization was the 1981 introduction of the Standard Advertising Unit (SAU) system developed by the American Newspaper Publishers Association and the Newspaper Advertising Bureau. The present version of the SAU, was established in 1984, and provides for 56 standard ad sizes. Exhibit 10.4 describes the SAU system.

[6]Margaret G. Carter, "Regional Marketing," *presstime,* January 1988, p. 10.

[7]Amy Alson, "The 1987 Newspaper Brans Leaders," *Marketing & Media Decisions,* June 1988, p. 65.

The Expanded SAU® Standard Advertising Unit System

Depth in Inches	1 COL. 2-1/16"	2 COL. 4-1/4"	3 COL. 6-7/16"	4 COL. 8-5/8"	5 COL. 10-13/16"	6 COL. 13"
FD*	1xFD*	2xFD*	3xFD*	4xFD*	5xFD*	6xFD*
18"	1x18	2x18	3x18	4x18	5x18	6x18
15.75"	1x15.75	2x15.75	3x15.75	4x15.75	5x15.75	
14"	1x14	2x14	3x14	4x14	N 5x14	6x14
13"	1x13	2x13	3x13	4x13	5x13	
10.5"	1x10.5	2x10.5	3x10.5	4x10.5	5x10.5	6x10.5
7"	1x7	2x7	3x7	4x7	5x7	6x7
5.25"	1x5.25	2x5.25	3x5.25	4x5.25		
3.5"	1x3.5	2x3.5				
3"	1x3	2x3				
2"	1x2	2x2				
1.5"	1x1.5					
1"	1x1					

13"

1 Column 2-1/16"
2 Columns 4¼"
3 Columns 6-7/16"
4 Columns 8⅝"
5 Columns 10-13/16"
6 Columns 13"

Double Truck 26¾"
(There are four suggested double truck sizes:)
13xFD* 13x18
13x14 13x10.5

*FD (Full Depth) can be 21" or deeper. Depths for each broadsheet newspaper are indicated in the Standard Rate and Data Service. All broadsheet newspapers can accept 21" ads, and may float them if their depth is greater than 21".

Tabloids: Size 5 x 14 is a full page tabloid for long cut-off papers. Mid cut-off papers can handle this size with minimal reduction. The N size, measuring 9⅜ x 14, represents the full page size for tabloids such as the New York Daily News and Newsday, and other short cut-off newspapers. The five 13 inch deep sizes are for tabloids printed on 55 inch wide presses such as the Philadelphia News. See individual SRDS listings for tabloid sections of broadsheet newspapers.

Printed in U.S.A. 11/83

EXHIBIT 10.4

(*Source: Guide to Quality Newspaper Reproduction,* joint publication of the American Newspaper Publishers Association and Newspaper Advertising Bureau, 1986.)

Suggested SAU® Nomenclature

Depth in inches	1 Column Width (2 1/16″)	2 Columns Width (4 1/4″)	3 Columns Width (6 7/16″)	4 Columns Width (8 5/8″)	5 Columns Width (10 13/16″)	6 Columns Width (13″)	13 Columns** Width (26 3/4″)
1	1×1						
1.5	1×1.5						
2	1×2	2×2					
3	1×3	2×3					
3.5	1×3.5	2×3.5					
5.25	1×5.25	2×5.25	3×5.25	4×5.25			
7	1×7	2×7	3×7	4×7	5×7	6×7	
10.5	1×10.5	2×10.5	3×10.5	4×10.5	5×10.5	6×10.5	13×10.5
13	1×13	2×13	3×13	4×13	5×13		
14	1×14	2×14	3×14	4×14	5×14	6×14	13×14
15.75	1×15.75	2×15.75	3×15.75	4×15.75	5×15.75		
18	1×18	2×18	3×18	4×18	5×18	6×18	13×18
FD*	1×FD*	2×FD*	3×FD*	4×FD*	5×FD*	6×FD*	13×FD*

*FD (Full Depth) can be 21″ or deeper. Depths for each broadsheet newspaper are indicated in the Standard Rate and Data Service. All broadsheet newspapers can accept 21″ ads, and may float them if their depth is greater than 21″.
**Double truck sizes.
The N size, measuring 9 3/8″ by 14″, represents the full page size for short cut-off tabloids such as the New York Daily News and Newsday.

Going, going,

Soon 1984 will be gone. And even sooner all the 1984 model Hondas will be gone. For good. Including this Accord LX 4-Door Sedan.
So if you're thinking of buying a 1984 Honda, you'd better hurry. Get going, going, and go to your Southern California Honda Dealer. Today.

Southern California Honda Dealers.

HONDA

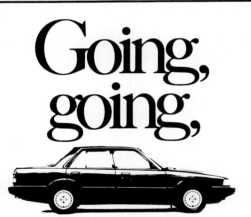

The base ad—to dealer segment—is described in SAU® nomenclature as a 6×14: six columns wide by 14 inches deep; 84 column inches. Local variables such as dealer names can be added to a base ad in 1/4″ ad-wide increments.

Measurement: Column inches replace agate lines

Ads are sized in columns and inches instead of agate lines. All ordering, measuring and billing is done in column inches. An ad 1 column wide by 1 inch deep (the smallest available) is described as a 1×1 (one by one) and is measured and billed as 1 column inch. An ad 2 columns wide by 3 inches deep is described as a 2×3 (two by three), and is measured and billed as 6 column inches. A horizontal half-page is described as a 6×10.5 (six by ten-and-a-half), and measured and billed as 63 column inches. And so on.

Special 1/4-inch increments for variables such as dealer listings

Space for dealer listings, theater names and similar needs may be added to SAU® sizes in 1/4-inch increments for the full width of the ad. Thus, a 3×7 ad with 3/4-inch added at the bottom for theater listings would be described as a 3×7.75 (three by seven and three-quarters) and is measured and billed as 23.25 column inches:

Base ad: 3 × 7.00 = 21.00 column inches
Listings: 3 × .75 = 2.25 column inches
Total ad: 3 × 7.75 = 23.25 column inches

An ad in one of the 56 standard sizes of the Standard Advertising Unit (SAU®) System—shown in reduction on the SAU® Grid at right—will fit virtually every broadsheet newspaper in the United States; 33 will fit tabloids.

EXHIBIT 10.4 (continued)

The importance of the SAU system in gaining more national newspaper advertising cannot be overemphasized. Now national advertisers know that they can purchase space in virtually every major U.S. paper and prepare one ad that will be accepted by all. The SAU system has also opened the way for other types of procedural standardization for national newspaper advertisers.

Other areas of standardizing are now under study, including a standard ad invoice, so that national advertisers can develop a standard accounts payable procedure; standard retail research guidelines, so that information is comparable across markets; and a proposal to extend the SAU system to classified advertising. The ultimate goal of standardization is to make national newspaper space easier to buy and thereby increase the share of national advertising going to newspapers.

Positioning. *Some advertisers prefer certain positions in a newspaper. Positioning may refer to position on a page, position in a certain section of the paper (sports), or position within the paper such as toward the front (far forward).*

Positioning of ads, while an area of disagreement between newspapers and national advertisers, nevertheless may have real merit in increasing awareness and response. The launching of "light whiskey" by Seagram's—with one-third the calories and kick of regular whiskey—needed to be seen by the "right targets," stated company officials. They have requested placement of their Mount Royal ads in the sports and business sections to reach the "active" male.

Those advertisers who choose to use *preprinted ads* do so, in many cases, to get better detailed reproduction. To put a full-court marketing press behind its *Micro Channel-Equipped IBM PS/2 personal computer,* the giant computer company will be distributing their own ads to large metropolitan-area dailies. According to Doug LaGrande, IBM marketing and services director/desktop systems, "IBM is striving to *impress* its business markets by conveying *proprietary technology.*" It's currently up against heavy promotion from Compaq and other rival competitors.

POSITIONING AND COLOR REPRODUCTION QUALITY. National advertisers talk a great deal about the positioning of their advertising, and most of what they have to say is unfavorable to newspapers. Generally, they believe that newspapers are inflexible in the positioning of their advertising and/or relegate them to an inferior position relative to retail advertisements. Actually, the positioning controversy deals with three separate problems:

1. *Position on the page.* While newspapers generally contend that page position makes very little difference in readership, a study by Starch/INRA/Hooper found that right-hand page and placement on the outside of the page gain higher readership than left-hand page or gutter position.
2. *Position within the newspaper.* Advertisers often request that their ads be placed in a "far forward" position, either in the newspaper or in a particular section. Here again, advertisers and newspapers disagree about the importance of positioning.
3. *Availability of special sections.* National advertisers think that retail accounts are given special treatment in sports, travel, financial, and other sections of the paper. However, many advertisers admit that as more newspapers offer new feature sections, national advertisers are gaining an advantage of position for their ads. Many of these feature sections are targeted to relatively narrow segments of consumers, and these target markets are often of more value to a national advertiser than to a local retailer, especially department stores. Consequently, feature sections may be a common ground for newspapers and their national advertisers.

Newspapers claim that many of the disagreements concerning positioning occur because media planners' major experience is with broadcast and magazines. "They [media planners] want to have their spots in the newspaper equivalent of inside the show, not on the outside, when people may be switching channels. . . . Or they want, because it seems to work in the best consumer magazines, their ads right up front in the newspaper—as in *Vogue,* where they sometimes have 50 pages of advertising before they even get to the masthead."[8]

Regardless of what newspaper executives think of media planners' demands for positioning, they will have to accommodate them if newspapers are to significantly increase their national linage. In fairness to newspapers, many have attempted to be more flexible in positioning national advertisements. One recent example is the introduction of the island position. In 1988, the Newspaper Advertising Bureau (NAB), in cooperation with over 250 major newspapers, offered an island position on the financial pages. As the term *island* implies, the advertisements are completely surrounded by editorial matter, often stock quotations, with no competing advertising on the same page.

Color reproduction is a second area of concern to national advertisers. Again, newspapers have tried to ensure consistent quality to national advertisers. One example is the Four-Color Newspaper Network, whose 250 member newspapers guarantee state-of-the-art color reproduction. Moreover, the network allows national advertisers to

[8]Richard Szathmary, "Positions of Influence," *Inside Print,* June 1988, p. 60.

place ads in any or all of its member newspapers with one insertion order and one invoice.

Newspapers are particularly sensitive to the problems of color reproduction since many national advertisers are using preprinted inserts in unprecedented numbers. Today the preprint business accounts for more than 15 percent of daily newspaper display advertising, or over $5 billion. Despite the revenue produced by preprints, they are a headache for publishers for two reasons. First, preprints are much less profitable than ROP advertising. Second, they shrink the space available for editorial matter (the so-called newshole), and this is a serious concern to newspaper publishers.

Nonetheless, newspapers recognize that preprints are a fact of doing business, so much so that the NAB has a division devoted to promoting inserts with a one insertion/one invoice procedure (see Exhibit 10.5). Publishers have come to understand that it is much better to cooperate with preprint advertisers than see them switch to direct mail.

> ***Rate differential.*** *The controversial practice of newspapers charging significantly higher rates to national advertisers as compared to local accounts.*

LOCAL VERSUS NATIONAL NEWSPAPER RATES. A long tradition in newspaper advertising says that national advertisers pay significantly more than local advertisers for the same space. In addition, space discounts, commonly given to local advertisers, are usually denied national advertisers. Obviously, this practice is resented by national advertisers and makes newspapers' efforts to increase national linage very difficult. Publishers defend the rate differential in two ways:

1. Retailers provide consistent support for the newspaper and are guaranteed customers over a long period of time, while the scheduling of many national advertisers is sporadic.
2. Most retail advertising is placed directly with the newspaper, so no agency or rep commissions are paid.

Still, national advertisers are skeptical that the margin of differentiation is justified. Further—and most exasperating for national advertisers—the differential between

EXHIBIT 10.5

Newspaper insertion and purchase order. (Courtesy: Newspaper Advertising Bureau, Inc.)

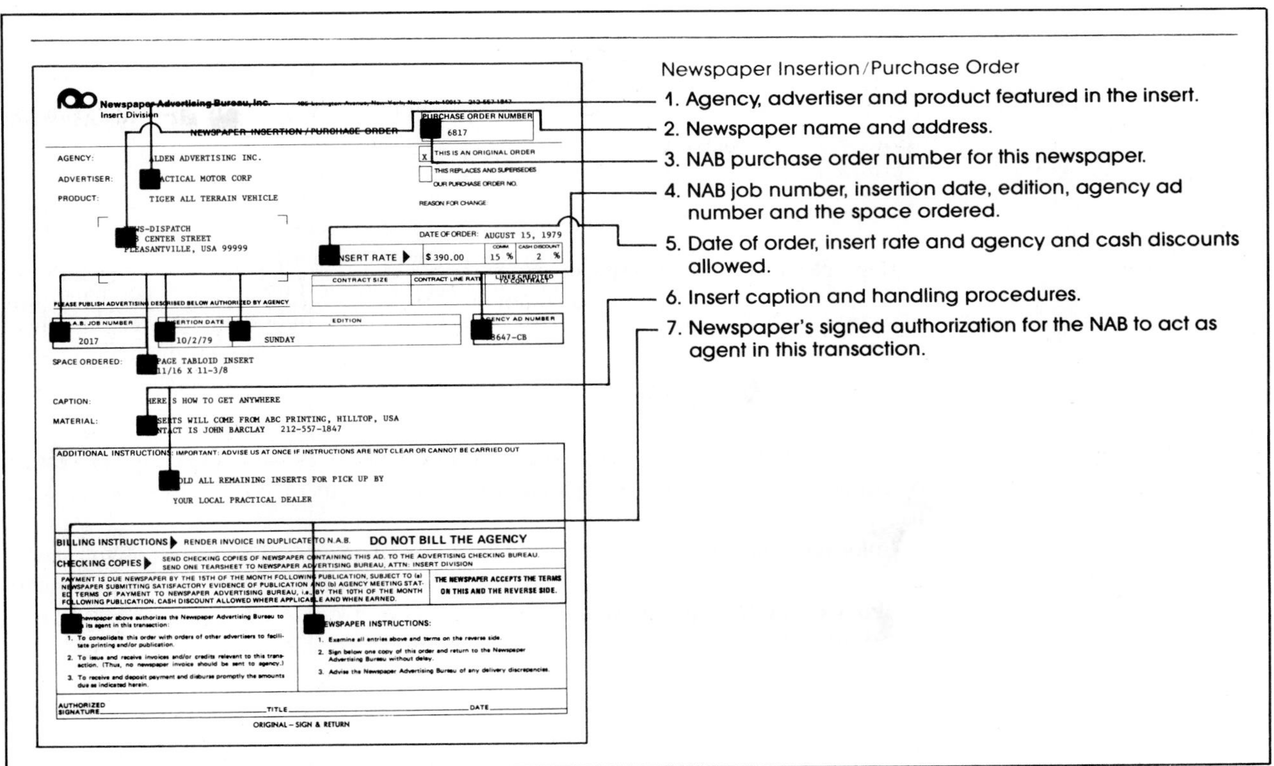

Newspaper Advertising Bureau, Inc.
Insert Division

NEWSPAPER INSERTION / PURCHASE ORDER

PURCHASE ORDER NUMBER: 6817

X THIS IS AN ORIGINAL ORDER
THIS REPLACES AND SUPERSEDES OUR PURCHASE ORDER NO.
REASON FOR CHANGE

AGENCY: ALDEN ADVERTISING INC.
ADVERTISER: PRACTICAL MOTOR CORP
PRODUCT: TIGER ALL TERRAIN VEHICLE

NEWS-DISPATCH
CENTER STREET
PLEASANTVILLE, USA 99999

DATE OF ORDER: AUGUST 15, 1979

INSERT RATE	COMM	CASH DISCOUNT
$ 390.00	15 %	2 %

CONTRACT SIZE	CONTRACT LINE RATE	LINES CREDITED TO CONTRACT

PLEASE PUBLISH ADVERTISING DESCRIBED BELOW AUTHORIZED BY AGENCY

N.A.B. JOB NUMBER	INSERTION DATE	EDITION	AGENCY AD NUMBER
2017	10/2/79	SUNDAY	8647-CB

SPACE ORDERED: PAGE TABLOID INSERT 11/16 X 11-3/8

CAPTION: HERE'S HOW TO GET ANYWHERE
MATERIAL: INSERTS WILL COME FROM ABC PRINTING, HILLTOP, USA
CONTACT IS JOHN BARCLAY 212-557-1847

ADDITIONAL INSTRUCTIONS: IMPORTANT: ADVISE US AT ONCE IF INSTRUCTIONS ARE NOT CLEAR OR CANNOT BE CARRIED OUT
HOLD ALL REMAINING INSERTS FOR PICK UP BY
YOUR LOCAL PRACTICAL DEALER

BILLING INSTRUCTIONS ▶ RENDER INVOICE IN DUPLICATE TO N.A.B. DO NOT BILL THE AGENCY

CHECKING COPIES ▶ SEND CHECKING COPIES OF NEWSPAPER CONTAINING THIS AD. TO THE ADVERTISING CHECKING BUREAU. SEND ONE TEARSHEET TO NEWSPAPER ADVERTISING BUREAU, ATTN: INSERT DIVISION

PAYMENT IS DUE NEWSPAPER BY THE 15TH OF THE MONTH FOLLOWING PUBLICATION, SUBJECT TO (a) NEWSPAPER SUBMITTING SATISFACTORY EVIDENCE OF PUBLICATION AND (b) AGENCY MEETING STATED TERMS OF PAYMENT TO NEWSPAPER ADVERTISING BUREAU, i.e., BY THE 10TH OF THE MONTH FOLLOWING PUBLICATION. CASH DISCOUNT ALLOWED WHERE APPLICABLE AND WHEN EARNED.

THE NEWSPAPER ACCEPTS THE TERMS ON THIS AND THE REVERSE SIDE.

Newspaper above authorizes the Newspaper Advertising Bureau to act as its agent in this transaction:
1. To consolidate this order with orders of other advertisers to facilitate printing and/or publication.
2. To issue and receive invoices and/or credits relevant to this transaction. (Thus, no newspaper invoice should be sent to agency.)
3. To receive and deposit payment and disburse promptly the amounts due as indicated herein.

NEWSPAPER INSTRUCTIONS:
1. Examine all entries above and terms on the reverse side.
2. Sign below one copy of this order and return to the Newspaper Advertising Bureau without delay.
3. Advise the Newspaper Advertising Bureau of any delivery discrepancies.

AUTHORIZED SIGNATURE ______ TITLE ______ DATE ______

ORIGINAL – SIGN & RETURN

The rate differential between national and local advertisers exists to give *local, loyal* businesses "a break." National advertisers often resort to *cooperative advertising,* which is placed by the local retailer at the local rate, but paid for, all or in part, by the national firm. When Levi's "900 Series" hits retail shelves, in addition to their *national* print campaign, cooperative advertising money will be offered to department stores to "beef up" the new appeal to "earthy" women via store ads and in-house catalogs.

local and national rates is presently at an all-time high. Exhibit 10.6 shows the historical pattern of rate differentiation found in a study conducted by the 4A's. Note that the increase in national versus local rates has been particularly significant since 1975. Exhibit 10.7 shows that newspapers with circulations above 250,000 had a rate differential of over 90 percent, up from 88 percent in 1985. This increase is particularly troubling to national advertisers since these are the newspapers they use most often.

Newspapers have made some attempts to deal with the rate differential problem. One such effort is the Packaged Goods Rate Plan (PGRP), introduced in 1986. It offers a discount in some 300 newspapers for packaged-goods manufacturers. While the plan has been used by some major advertisers, it has been criticized for several reasons:

- The plan's minimum frequency of 13 insertions of a quarter-page or more makes it expensive to use on a national basis.
- Some newspapers will not allow coupons in copy placed under the plan.
- The types of discounts are inconsistent among the participating newspapers and are subject to change without notice.
- Non–package-goods advertisers such as airlines resent the discrimination in favor of one product category.

National advertisers recognize *three major difficulties* to increasing their usage of newspapers: (1) red-tape in making multi-newspaper buys; (2) limited creative; and (3) appeal of television. Recognizing advertisers' problems, Maxwell AD/SAT emphasizes that it's a "cost efficient time saver." It can send ads to *any or all* of its 117 network newspapers—"in minutes."

Individual newspapers have modified the PGRP to provide more flexibility for national advertisers. For example, the *Boston Globe* gives a 35 percent discount for 13 insertions. The minimum schedule to qualify is six insertions and a one-sixth page advertisement. The discounted rate is the equivalent of the retail rate marked up to account for the agency commission.[9]

In the view of some national advertisers, the rate discount for national advertising will help, but newspapers still face a number of hurdles in increasing national advertising. Primarily, they need to overcome, "the daunting bureaucratic difficulties involved in making multi-newspaper buys, limited creative in newsprint and advertisers' long-standing loyalty to television."[10]

Cooperative Advertising

One of the outgrowths of the local/national rate differential is a substantial increase in cooperative (co-op) advertising. We will discuss cooperative advertising more fully in Chapter 14, Sales Promotion, but it is such an important part of newspaper advertising that we need to mention it here.

Co-op advertising is placed by a local advertiser, but paid for, altogether or in part, by a national advertiser. The national manufacturer usually provides the ad, allowing space for the retailer's logo. National advertisers vary widely in the amount of compensation they give retailers, but it is in the range of 50 to 100 percent.

In Chapter 14, we will examine a number of the techniques and merchandising strategies associated with co-op advertising. Here it is important to note that since co-op is placed by local dealers, it qualifies for the local rate. In fact, the major reason for the growth of newspaper co-op is to circumvent the national rate charged by most publishers.

The Future of National Newspaper Advertising

Despite the many problems involved in increasing national advertising dollars, newspapers are clearly aware of the need to step up their efforts. In a study conducted by the

[9]Alan Radding, "Rate Differential Issue Still a Cloudy One," *Newspaper Marketing,* March 1988, p. 48.
[10]Rachel Kaplan, "Newspaper Routes," *Inside Print,* May 1988, p. 44.

A History of Rate Differentials Since 1933
(Dailies—General versus Retail)

YEAR (AS OF FIRST OF THE YEAR)	%	YEAR (AS OF FIRST OF THE YEAR)	%	YEAR (AS OF FIRST OF THE YEAR)	%
1933	37.9	1953	54.5	1975	50.3
1934	39.6	1954	55.6	1976	50.5
1935	38.3	1955	55.9	1977	50.6
1936	40.2	1956	56.5	1978	51.1
1937	41.6	1957	57.7	1979	52.9
1938	43.4	1958	59.5	1980	54.5
1939	44.7	1959	59.4	1982+++	59.8
1940	46.3	1960	59.5	1983	++
1941	46.8	1963+	61.7	1984	60.5
1942	47.6	1964	58.1	1985	64.6
1943	48.6	1965	55.7	1986	++
1944	49.8	1966	55.2	1987++++	66.2
1945	++	1967	++		
1946	50.0	1968	49.4		
1947	53.6	1969	50.4		
1948	51.8	1970	50.7		
1949	53.9	1971	50.0		
1950	55.7	1972	48.3		
1951	53.4	1973	48.2		
1952	53.6	1974	49.5		

+ In 1963, method of computing was simplified so that study could be made more current — hence the omission of 1961 and 1962.

++ Study not compiled.

+++ Rates as of January 1; previous years were as of September 1. Hence, there is no report for 1981.

++++Rates as of July 1, 1987.

EXHIBIT 10.6

Despite complaints from national advertisers, the difference between national and retail ad rates has never been greater. (Courtesy: American Association of Advertising Agencies.)

1987 Newspaper Rate Differentials

Total for Newspapers Listed (1,000 inches per year)

All Daily Newspapers

A.B.C. CIRCULATION	PAPERS	RETAIL RATE	GROSS GENERAL RATE	GENERAL VERSUS RETAIL	RETAIL VERSUS GENERAL
Less than 25,000	533	$3,009.588	$4,390.261	+45.88%	-31.45%
25,001—50,000	225	2,190.298	3,331.018	+52.08%	-34.25%
50,001—100,000	122	1,985.845	3,124.134	+57.32%	-36.44%
100,001—250,000	76	2,189.410	3,973.032	+81.47%	-44.89%
Over 250,000	44	2,961.270	5,687.957	+92.08%	-47.94%
TOTAL	1,000	$12,336.411	$20,506.402	+66.23%	-39.84%

Totals in the summary are based on data for 1,000 A.B.C. daily newspapers. Where national advertising is sold on an optional combination basis, totals include rates for the optional combination, and such combinations are counted as one newspaper.

General rates are shown *before* deduction of agency commission and cash discount, if allowed.

EXHIBIT 10.7

The larger a newspaper's circulation, the more likely it will charge national advertisers significantly more than retail clients. (Courtesy: American Association of Advertising Agencies.)

International Newspaper Advertising and Marketing Executives, advertising directors projected the following trends in newspaper advertising:

- The national/local rate differential will be reduced.
- Preprints will continue to increase at the expense of ROP advertising.
- The quality of ROP (run-of-paper) color will improve significantly.
- Newspaper networks will grow to serve the needs of national advertisers.
- Rep firms will take on a bigger role in helping newspapers pursue national advertising, just as they have for many years in broadcast.[11]

Note that all of these trends for the future of newspaper advertising involve national advertising.

NEWSPAPERS AS AN ADVERTISING MEDIUM

Newspapers are a basic local medium, with all the advantages of local media for the national advertiser: (1) freedom to advertise to a widespread audience when and where desired; and (2) the ability to conduct a national campaign, adapting the headline to

[11] Maureen Goldstein, "Forecast: Improved Sales Forces Ahead," *Inside Print,* October 1988, p. 27.

each city market or running test ads in a number of markets. Reading newspapers is a daily ritual in most homes and on commuter trains. Family shoppers carefully read supermarket ads for prices, cents-off coupons, and offerings. They study department store ads, not only for planned purchases, but also to keep abreast of fashion and lifestyle trends. While reading through the world and local news, financial pages, and sports and entertainment sections, newspaper readers often look at ads for cars, household items, sports equipment, family purchases, and clothing. That all of these can be illustrated and described in detail is one of the great advantages of newspapers. They can even carry full-page color reproductions.

A national advertiser can get an ad in a newspaper quickly—overnight, if necessary—an advantage much prized by advertisers, who sometimes are in a hurry to make a special announcement.

Readers consider *newspaper advertising* to be the most believable, most used, and most sought form of advertising. That's why Ralph Ammeriti, founder of Ammeriti-Puris, recommends *The Wall Street Journal* for his most important clients, like BMW. The *Journal* is able to provide upscale clients the "clean" creative point of view.

Most important to advertisers is the attention and value readers place on newspaper ads. Studies conducted during the last several years by a variety of sources have consistently found that newspaper advertising is the most believable, most used, and most sought form of advertising. In addition to providing high readership for a single ad, the newspaper is also an excellent medium for providing both reach and frequency over several insertions. Exhibit 10.8 shows how reach and frequency accumulate over multiple insertions on the basis of the percent of the audience who see an ad.

The Rate Structure

Discounts are offered to national advertisers by newspapers which offer *open* rates—usually based on *frequency* or *bulk purchasing of space*. National Co-op Network offered its best rate to Zenith Data Systems for four ads, to be customized for *240* newspapers! Zenith's order totaled $1 million.

The local advertiser, dealing with one or two newspapers, has a fairly easy job buying newspaper space. The rate structure and discounts for any one newspaper are usually straightforward. However, as we have seen, the national advertiser has a much more difficult time. An advertiser buying space in a number of newspapers confronts an unlimited set of options and price structures, including discounts, premium charges for color, special sections, preferred positions, and zoned editions.

The SAU system has vastly simplified the placing of national advertising. Similarly, Newsplan, a cooperative effort to offer national advertisers discount rates, has accommodated, at least to a small extent, the high-frequency national advertiser. In the following paragraphs, we look at some of the primary options and rate decisions that an advertiser must make.

EXHIBIT 10.8

Estimated net reach and frequency of multiple ad insertions. (Courtesy: Newspaper Advertising Bureau.)

	Number of Ads in Campaign:					
Noted Score	**Two**	**Three**	**Four**	**Five**	**Six**	**Seven**
20% net reach:*	30%	38%	45%	50%	55%	58%
avg. freq:	1.3	1.6	1.8	2.0	2.2	2.4
25% net reach:	37%	46%	53%	59%	63%	66%
avg. freq:	1.4	1.6	1.9	2.1	2.4	2.6
30% net reach:	43%	53%	61%	67%	71%	74%
avg. freq:	1.4	1.7	2.0	2.2	2.5	2.8
35% net reach:	50%	60%	68%	74%	78%	80%
avg. freq:	1.4	1.8	2.1	2.4	2.7	3.1
40% net reach:	55%	65%	73%	79%	83%	85%
avg. freq:	1.5	1.8	2.2	2.5	2.9	3.3
45% net reach:	60%	70%	78%	84%	87%	89%
avg. freq:	1.5	1.9	2.3	2.7	3.1	3.5
50% net reach:	65%	75%	83%	88%	90%	91%
avg. freq:	1.5	2.0	2.4	2.9	3.3	3.8

Explanation: If 30 percent of a population see one ad, we can estimate that 43 percent of the audience will see two ads, 53 percent three ads, and so on. After seven ads, 74 percent of the population will have seen at least one ad. The average exposure will be 2.8 ads.

*Net reach = percent of exposed audience reached one or more times.

Open rate. *In print the highest advertising rate on which all discounts are placed. It is also called Basic rate, Transient rate, or One-time rate.*

Flat rate. *A uniform charge for space in a medium, without regard to the amount of space used or the frequency of insertion. When flat rates do not prevail, time discounts are offered.*

ROP. See *Run-of-paper position.*

Combination rate. *A special space rate for two papers, such as a morning paper, owned by the same publisher.*

Discounts. Newspapers are divided into two categories: those with a uniform *flat rate* that offers no discounts, and those with an *open rate* that provides some discount structure. The open rate also refers to the highest rate against which all discounts are applied. The most common discounts are based on *frequency* or *bulk* purchases of space. A bulk discount means there is a sliding scale so that the advertiser is charged proportionally less as more advertising is purchased. A frequency discount usually requires some unit or pattern of purchase in addition to total amount of space. Examples of each discount are shown in Exhibit 10.9.

ROP and Preferred-Position Rates. The basic rates quoted by a newspaper entitle the ad to a run-of-paper (abbreviated ROP) position anywhere in the paper that the publisher chooses to place it, although the paper will be mindful of the advertiser's request and interest in getting a good position. An advertiser may buy a choice position by paying a higher, preferred-position rate, which is similar to paying for a box seat in a stadium instead of general admission. A cigar advertiser, for example, may elect to pay a preferred-position rate to ensure getting on the sports page. A cosmetic advertiser may buy a preferred position on the women's page. There are also preferred positions on individual pages. An advertiser may pay for the top of a column or the top of a column next to news reading matter (called *full position*).

Each newspaper specifies its preferred-position rates; there is no consistency in this practice. Preferred-position rates are not as common as they once were. Now many papers simply attempt to accommodate advertisers who request a position, such as "Above fold urgently requested."

Combination Rates. A number of combinations are available to advertisers. What they all have in common is the advantage of greatly reduced rates for purchasing several papers as a group. The most frequently seen combination rate occurs when the same publisher issues both a morning and an evening paper. By buying both papers, the advertiser can pay as little as one-third to one-half for the second paper. This type of combination may involve as few as two papers in a single metropolitan market or many papers bought on a national basis. In either case, the advertiser has to deal with only one group and pays a single bill.

EXHIBIT 10.9
Types of discounts.

Frequency Within 52-Week Contract Period Full-Page Contract	
Open Rate	**$2.50/Column Inch**
10 insertions	2.30
15 insertions	2.20
20 insertions	2.10
30 insertions	2.00
40 insertions	1.90
50 insertions	1.80
Bulk Within 52-Week Contract Period	
Open Rate	**$2.50/Column Inch**
500 column inches	2.40
1,500 column inches	2.30
3,000 column inches	2.20
5,000 column inches	2.10
10,000 column inches	2.00
15,000 column inches	1.90

Preferred positions do command higher rates by newspapers—but provide advertisers with *large audiences* they prefer. Since Citizen Watch has decided to launch a new ad campaign for its *upscale, Noblia line,* it selected major market newspapers as one of its vehicles. "The quality-oriented approach," said Carol Shainswit, Citizen's director of advertising, "is aimed at career women, who read the *features* and *fashion* sections, first and foremost."

The Rate Card

A publisher's rate card contains more than rates; on it is all the information that an advertiser needs to place an order (including copy requirements and mechanical requirements), set in a standardized, numbered sequence. Most advertising offices subscribe to the Standard Rate & Data Service (SRDS), which publishes in full all the rate-card information in monthly volumes, kept up-to-date by monthly supplements. Exhibit 10.10 shows this information for *The San Diego Union* and *The Tribune*. Note the designation for both Newsplan and the SAU system.

EXHIBIT 10.10

The SRDS listing shows rates as well as which papers are members of services such as Newsplan and SAU. (Courtesy: Standard Rate & Data Service.)

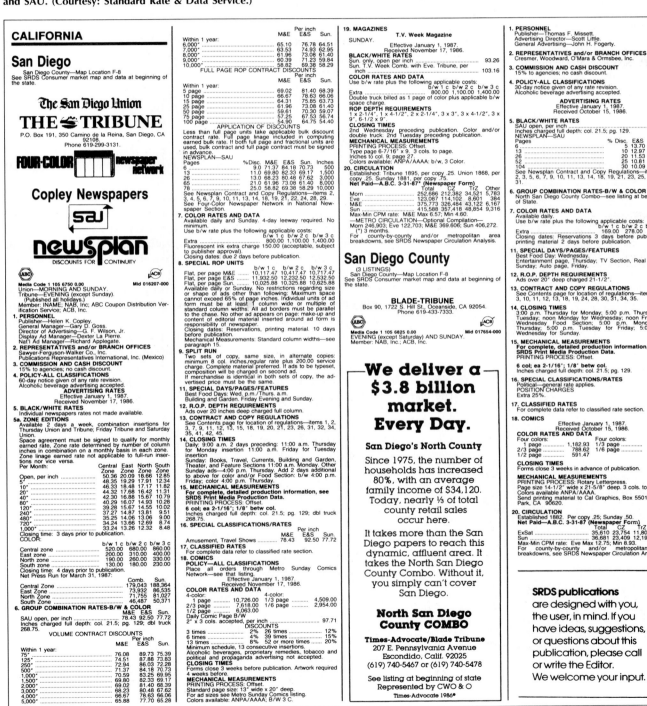

CALIFORNIA

San Diego

San Diego County—Map Location F-8
See SRDS Consumer market map and data at beginning of the state.

The San Diego Union
THE TRIBUNE
P.O. Box 191, 350 Camino de la Reina, San Diego, CA 92108.
Phone 619-299-3131.

FOUR-COLOR newspaper network

Copley Newspapers

sau

newsplan DISCOUNTS FOR CONTINUITY

ABC ACB

Media Code 1 105 6750 0.00 **Mid 016207-000**
Union—MORNING AND SUNDAY.
Tribune—EVENING (except Sunday).
(Published all holidays.)
Member: INAME; NAB, Inc; ABC Coupon Distribution Verification Service; ACB, Inc.

1. PERSONNEL
Publisher—Helen K. Copley.
General Manager—Gary D. Goss.
Director of Advertising—G. F. Wilson, Jr.
Display Ad Manager—Dexter La Pierre.
Nat'l Ad Manager—Richard Applegate.

2. REPRESENTATIVES and/or BRANCH OFFICES
Sawyer-Ferguson-Walker Co., Inc.
Publications Representatives International, Inc. (Mexico)

3. COMMISSION AND CASH DISCOUNT
15% to agencies; no cash discount.

4. POLICY-ALL CLASSIFICATIONS
60-day notice given of any rate revision.
Alcoholic beverage advertising accepted.

ADVERTISING RATES
Effective January 1, 1987.
Received November 17, 1986.

5. BLACK/WHITE RATES
Individual newspapers rates not made available.

5a. ZONE EDITIONS
Available 2 days a week, combination insertions for Thursday Union and Tribune; Friday Tribune and Saturday Union.
Space agreement must be signed to qualify for monthly earned rate, Zone rate determined by number of column inches in combination on a monthly basis in each zone. Zone linage earned rate not applicable to full-run insertions nor vice versa.

Per Month:	Central Zone	East Zone	North Zone	South Zone
Open, per inch	50.36	20.09	18.66	12.85
5"	48.35	19.29	17.91	12.34
10"	46.33	18.48	17.17	11.82
20"	44.32	17.68	16.42	11.31
40"	42.30	16.88	15.67	10.79
80"	40.29	16.07	14.93	10.28
120"	39.28	15.67	14.55	10.02
240"	37.27	14.87	13.81	9.51
480"	35.25	14.06	13.06	9.00
720"	34.24	13.66	12.69	8.74
1,000"	33.24	13.26	12.32	8.48

Closing time: 3 days prior to publication.
COLOR:

	b/w 1 c	b/w 2 c	b/w 3 c
Central zone	520.00	680.00	860.00
East zone	200.00	310.00	400.00
North zone	190.00	260.00	330.00
South zone	130.00	180.00	230.00

Closing time: 4 days prior to publication.
Net Press Run for March 31, 1987:

	Comb.	Sun.
Central Zone	179,043	188,364
East Zone	73,932	86,535
North Zone	71,755	81,027
South Zone	46,487	50,371

6. GROUP COMBINATION RATES-B/W & COLOR

	M&E	E&S	Sun.
SAU open, per inch	78.43	92.50	77.72

Inches charged full depth: col. 21.5; pg. 129; dbl truck 268.75.

VOLUME CONTRACT DISCOUNTS

Within 1 year:	M&E (Per inch)	E&S	Sun.
75"	76.08	89.73	75.39
125"	74.51	87.88	73.83
250"	72.94	86.03	72.28
500"	71.37	84.18	70.73
1,000"	70.59	83.25	69.95
1,500"	69.80	82.33	69.17
2,000"	69.02	81.40	68.39
3,000"	68.23	80.48	67.62
4,000"	66.67	78.63	66.06
5,000"	65.88	77.70	65.28
6,000"	65.10	76.78	64.51
7,000"	63.53	74.93	62.95
8,000"	61.96	73.08	61.40
9,000"	60.39	71.23	59.84
10,000"	58.82	69.38	58.29

FULL PAGE ROP CONTRACT DISCOUNTS

Within 1 year:	M&E (Per inch)	E&S	Sun.
5 page	69.02	81.40	68.39
10 page	66.67	78.63	66.06
15 page	64.31	75.85	63.73
25 page	61.96	73.08	61.40
50 page	59.61	70.30	59.07
75 page	57.25	67.53	56.74
100 page	54.90	64.75	54.40

APPLICATION OF DISCOUNTS
Less than full page units take applicable bulk discount contract rate. Full page linage included in computing earned bulk rate. If both full page and fractional units are used, bulk contract and full page contract must be signed in advance.
NEWSPLAN—SAU

Pages	%Disc.	M&E	E&S	Sun.	Inches
6	9.0	71.37	84.18	70.73	500
13	11.0	69.80	82.33	69.17	1,500
26	13.0	68.23	80.48	67.62	3,000
65	21.0	61.96	73.08	61.40	8,000
78	25.0	58.82	69.38	58.29	10,000

See Newsplan Contract and Copy Regulations—items 2, 3, 4, 5, 6, 7, 9, 10, 11, 13, 14, 18, 19, 21, 22, 24, 28, 29.
See Four-Color Newspaper Network in National Newspaper Section.

7. COLOR RATES AND DATA
Available daily and Sunday. 4-day leeway required. No minimum.
Use b/w rate plus the following applicable costs:

	b/w 1 c	b/w 2 c	b/w 3 c
Extra	800.00	1,100.00	1,400.00

Fluorescent ink extra charge 150.00 (acceptable, subject to publisher approval).
Closing dates: due 2 days before publication.

8. SPECIAL ROP UNITS

	b/w 1 c	b/w 2 c	b/w 3 c
Flat, per page M&E	10,117.47	10,417.47	10,717.47
Flat, per page E&S	11,932.50	12,232.50	12,532.50
Flat, per page Sun.	10,025.88	10,325.88	10,625.88

Available daily or Sunday. No restrictions regarding size or shape of ads other than following: Maximum space cannot exceed 65% of page inches. Individual units of ad form must be at least 1 column wide or multiple of standard column widths. All ad borders must be parallel to the chase. No other ad appears on page: make-up and content of editorial material inserted around ad form is responsibility of newspaper.
Closing dates: Reservations, printing material. 10 days before publication.
Mechanical Measurements: Standard column widths—see paragraph 15.

9. SPLIT RUN
Two sets of copy, same size, in alternate copies: minimum 8 col. inches,regular rate plus 200.00 service charge. Complete material preferred. If ads to be typeset, composition will be charged on second ad.
If merchandise is identical in both sets of copy, the advertised price must be the same.

11. SPECIAL DAYS/PAGES/FEATURES
Best Food Days: Wed. p.m./Thurs. a.m.
Building and Garden. Friday Evening and Sunday.

12. R.O.P. DEPTH REQUIREMENTS
Ads over 20 inches deep charged full column.

13. CONTRACT AND COPY REGULATIONS
See Contents page for location of regulations—items 1, 2, 3, 7, 9, 11, 12, 13, 15, 18, 19, 20, 21, 23, 26, 31, 32, 34, 35, 41, 42, 45.

14. CLOSING TIMES
Daily: 9:00 a.m. 2 days preceding: 11:00 a.m. Thursday for Monday insertion 11:00 a.m. Friday for Tuesday insertion
Sunday: Books, Travel, Currents, Building and Garden, Theater, and Feature Sections 11:00 a.m. Monday. Other Sunday ads—4:00 p.m. Thursday. Add 2 days additional to above for color and/or Food Section: b/w 4:00 p.m. Friday; color 4:00 p.m. Thursday.

15. MECHANICAL MEASUREMENTS
For complete, detailed production information, see SRDS Print Media Production Data.
PRINTING PROCESS: Offset.
6 col; ea 2-1/16"; 1/8" betw col.
Inches charged full depth: col. 21.5; pg. 129; dbl truck 268.75.

16. SPECIAL CLASSIFICATIONS/RATES

	M&E (Per inch)	E&S	Sun.
Amusement, Travel Shows	78.43	92.50	77.72

17. CLASSIFIED RATES
For complete data refer to classified rate section.

18. COMICS
POLICY—ALL CLASSIFICATIONS
Place all orders through Metro Sunday Comics Network—see that listing.
Effective January 1, 1987.
Received November 17, 1986.
COLOR RATES AND DATA

4-color:		4-color:	
1 page	10,726.00	1/3 page	4,509.00
2/3 page	7,618.00	1/6 page	2,954.00
1/2 page	6,063.00		

Daily Comic Page B/W
2" x 3 cols. accepted, per inch ... 97.71
DISCOUNTS

3 times	2%	26 times	12%
6 times	4%	39 times	15%
13 times	8%	52 or more times	20%

Minimum schedule, 13 consecutive insertions.
Alcoholic beverages, proprietary remedies, tobacco and political and propaganda advertising not accepted.
CLOSING TIMES
Forms close 3 weeks before publication. Artwork required 4 weeks before.
MECHANICAL MEASUREMENTS
PRINTING PROCESS: Offset.
Standard page size: 13" wide x 20" deep.
For ad sizes see Metro Sunday Comics listing.
Colors available: ANPA/AAAA; B/W 3 C.

19. MAGAZINES
T.V. Week Magazine
SUNDAY.
Effective January 1, 1987.
Received November 17, 1986.
BLACK/WHITE RATES
Sun. only, open per inch ... 93.26
Sun. T.V. Week Comb. with Eve. Tribune, per inch ... 103.16
COLOR RATES AND DATA
Use b/w rate plus the following applicable costs:

	b/w 1 c	b/w 2 c	b/w 3 c
Extra	800.00	1,100.00	1,400.00

Double truck billed as 1 page of color plus applicable b/w space charge.
ROP DEPTH REQUIREMENTS
1 x 2-1/4", 1 x 4-1/2", 2 x 2-1/4", 3 x 3", 3 x 4-1/2", 3 x 9", 6-1/2 x 9".
CLOSING TIMES
2nd Wednesday preceding publication. Color and/or double truck: 2nd Tuesday preceding publication.
MECHANICAL MEASUREMENTS
PRINTING PROCESS: Offset.
Type page 6-7/16" x 9. 3 cols. to page.
Inches to col. 9; page 27.
Colors available: ANPA/AAAA: b/w, 3 Color.

20. CIRCULATION
Established: Tribune 1895, per copy .25. Union 1868, per copy .25. Sunday 1881, per copy .75.
Net Paid—A.B.C. 3-31-87* (Newspaper Form)

	Total	CZ	TrZ	Other
Morn	252,686	212,382	34,521	5,783
Eve	123,087	114,102	8,601	384
M&E	375,773	326,484	43,122	6,167
Sun	415,588	357,418	48,854	9,316

Max-Min CPM rate: M&E Max 6.57; Min 4.60.
—METRO CIRCULATION—Optional Compilation—
Morn 246,903; Eve 122,703; M&E 369.606; Sun 406,272.
(*) 3 months.
For county-by-county and/or metropolitan area breakdowns, see SRDS Newspaper Circulation Analysis.

San Diego County

(3 LISTINGS)
San Diego County—Map Location F-8
See SRDS Consumer market map and data at beginning of the state.

BLADE-TRIBUNE
Box 90, 1722 S. Hill St., Oceanside, CA 92054.
Phone 619-433-7333.

ABC ACB

Media Code 1 105 6825 0.00 **Mid 017654-000**
EVENING (except Saturday) AND SUNDAY.
Member: NAB, Inc.; ACB, Inc.

We deliver a $3.8 billion market. Every Day.
San Diego's North County
Since 1975, the number of households has increased 80%, with an average family income of $34,120. Today, nearly ⅓ of total county retail sales occur here.
It takes more than the San Diego papers to reach this dynamic, affluent area. It takes the North San Diego County Combo. Without it, you simply can't cover San Diego.
North San Diego County COMBO
Times-Advocate/Blade Tribune
207 E. Pennsylvania Avenue
Escondido, Calif. 92025
(619) 740-5467 or (619) 740-5478
See listing at beginning of state
Represented by CWO & O
Times-Advocate 1986•

1. PERSONNEL
Publisher—Thomas F. Missett.
Advertising Director—Scott Little.
General Advertising—John H. Fogerty.

2. REPRESENTATIVES and/or BRANCH OFFICES
Cresmer, Woodward, O'Mara & Ormsbee, Inc.

3. COMMISSION AND CASH DISCOUNT
15% to agencies; no cash discount.

4. POLICY-ALL CLASSIFICATIONS
30-day notice given of any rate revision.
Alcoholic beverage advertising accepted.

ADVERTISING RATES
Effective January 1, 1987.
Received October 15, 1986.

5. BLACK/WHITE RATES
SAU open, per inch ... 14.41
Inches charged full depth: col. 21.5; pg. 129.
NEWSPLAN—SAU

Pages	% Disc.	E&S	Inches
6	5	13.70	774
13	10	12.97	1,677
26	20	11.53	3,354
52	25	10.81	6,708
104	30	10.09	13,416

See Newsplan Contract and Copy Regulations—items 1, 2, 3, 5, 6, 7, 9, 10, 11, 13, 14, 18, 19, 21, 23, 25, 26, 30, 31.

6. GROUP COMBINATION RATES-B/W & COLOR
North San Diego County Combo—see listing at beginning of State.

7. COLOR RATES AND DATA
Available daily.
Use b/w rate plus the following applicable costs:

	b/w 1 c	b/w 2 c	b/w 3 c
Extra	169.00	278.00	389.00

Closing dates: Reservations 3 days before publication; printing material 2 days before publication.

11. SPECIAL DAYS/PAGES/FEATURES
Best Food Day: Wednesday.
Entertainment page, Thursday; TV Section, Real Estate, Sunday; Auto page, Friday.

12. R.O.P. DEPTH REQUIREMENTS
Ads over 20" deep charged 21-1/2".

13. CONTRACT AND COPY REGULATIONS
See Contents page for location of regulations—items 1, 2, 3, 10, 11, 12, 13, 18, 19, 24, 28, 30, 31, 34, 35.

14. CLOSING TIMES
3:00 p.m. Thursday for Monday; 5:00 p.m. Thursday for Tuesday; noon Monday for Wednesday; noon Friday for Wednesday Food Section; 5:00 p.m. Monday for Thursday; 5:00 p.m. Tuesday for Friday; 5:00 p.m. Wednesday for Sunday.

15. MECHANICAL MEASUREMENTS
For complete, detailed production information, see SRDS Print Media Production Data.
PRINTING PROCESS: Offset.
6 col; ea 2-1/16"; 1/8" betw col.
Inches charged full depth: col. 21.5; pg. 129.

16. SPECIAL CLASSIFICATIONS/RATES
Political—general rate applies.
POSITION CHARGES
Extra 25%.

17. CLASSIFIED RATES
For complete data refer to classified rate section.

18. COMICS
Effective January 1, 1987.
Received October 15, 1986.
COLOR RATES AND DATA

Four colors:		Four colors:	
1 page	1,182.93	1/3 page	394.31
2/3 page	788.62	1/6 page	197.16
1/2 page	591.47		

CLOSING TIMES
Forms close 3 weeks in advance of publication.
MECHANICAL MEASUREMENTS
PRINTING PROCESS: Rotary Letterpress.
Page size 14-1/2" wide x 21-5/8" deep. 3 cols. to page.
Colors available ANPA/AAAA.
Send printing material to Cal Graphics, Box 5501, Buena Park, CA 90620.

20. CIRCULATION
Established 1882. Per copy .25; Sunday .50.
Net Paid—A.B.C. 3-31-87 (Newspaper Form)

	Total	CZ	TrZ	Other
ExSat	35,610	23,754	11,806	1,050
Sun	36,681	23,409	12,191	1,081

Max-Min CPM rate: Eve Max 12.75; Min 8.93.
For county-by-county and/or metropolitan area breakdowns, see SRDS Newspaper Circulation Analysis.

(C-N1)

SRDS publications are designed with you, the user, in mind. If you have ideas, suggestions, or questions about this publication, please call or write the Editor. We welcome your input.

The rates published in SRDS are applicable only to national advertisers. Local advertisers must obtain a separate rate card showing retail rates.

Comparing Newspaper Advertising Costs

Advertisers, signing *space contracts,* estimate the amount of space they'll use during the next 12 months—at an agreed-on rate. The proposed rate is *lower* than if they had contracted for every insertion individually. Sears and Gannett, the country's largest newspaper publisher, have signed a national advertising agreement, covering *all* Sears businesses. The deal, which includes almost *80* newspapers, centralizes placement and lowers billing costs for the huge retail chain.

National advertisers, many of whom consider hundreds of newspapers in a single media plan, want to make cost comparisons among their potential newspapers buys. For many years, the standard measure for comparing the cost of newspaper space was the milline rate.[12] The milline rate has been replaced in recent years by the CPM comparison we discussed earlier.

Using the CPM for newspaper rate comparisons has two advantages:

1. It reflects the move to page and fractional-page space buys. Media planners are much more comfortable using the SAU than line or column-inch space buys.
2. Comparisons among media are more easily calculated using a standard benchmark such as the CPM. While qualitative differences among newspapers and other media must still be considered, the CPM does offer a consistent means of comparison (see Exhibit 10.11).

The Space Contract, The Short Rate

Short rate. *The balance advertisers have to pay if they estimated that they would run more ads in a year than they did and entered a contract to pay at a favorable rate. The short rate is figured at the end of the year or sooner if advertisers fall behind schedule. It is calculated at a higher rate for the fewer insertions.*

If a paper has a flat rate, obviously there is no problem with calculating costs—all space is billed at the same price regardless of how much is used. However, space contracts in open-rate papers must have flexibility to allow advertisers to use more or less space than they originally contracted for. Normally, an advertiser will sign a *space contract* estimating the amount of space to be used during the next 12 months. Such a space contract is not a guarantee of the amount of space an advertiser will run, but rather an agreement on the rate the advertiser will finally pay for any space run during the year in question.

The space contract involves two steps: First, advertisers estimate the amount of space they think they will run and agree with the newspaper on how to handle any rate adjustments needed at the end of the year; they are then billed during the year at the selected rate. Second, at the end of the year, the total linage is added, and if advertisers ran the amount of space they had estimated, no adjustment is necessary; but if they failed to run enough space to earn that rate, they have to pay at the higher rate charged for the number of lines they actually ran. That amount is called the *short rate.*

The Newsplan contract outlines the arrangement as follows:

> Advertiser will be billed monthly at applicable contract rate for entire contract year. At end of contract year advertiser will be refunded if a lower rate is earned or rebilled at a higher applicable rate if contract is not fulfilled.

EXHIBIT 10.11

Newspaper rate comparisons using the CPM.

Newspaper	*Open-Rate Page Cost*	*Circulation*	*CPM*
A	$5,400	165,000	$32.72
B	3,300	116,000	28.45

Example: $\frac{\$5400 \times 1000}{165,000} = \$32.72$

[12]The milline rate is a hypothetical figure that measures what it would cost per agate line to reach a million circulation of a paper, based on the actual line rate and circulation. The formula is:

$$\text{Milline} = \frac{1{,}000{,}000 \times \text{rate per line}}{\text{circulation}}$$

As an example, let's assume that a national advertiser plans to run advertising in a paper whose rates are as follows:

Open rate, $5.00 per column inch
1,000 column inches, $4.50/column inch
5,000 column inches, $4.00/column inch
10,000 column inches, $3.50/column inch

The advertiser expects to run at least 5,000 column inches and signs the contract at the $4.00 (5,000 column-inch) rate (subject to end-of-year adjustment). At the end of 12 months, however, only 4,100 column inches have been run; therefore, the bill at the end of the contract year is as follows:

Earned rate:	4,100 column inches @ $4.50 per column inch =	$18,450
Paid rate:	4,100 column inches @ $4.00 per column inch =	16,400
	Short rate due =	$ 2,050

or

Column inches run × difference in earned and billed rates
= 4,100 column inches × 0.50
= $2,050

Rebate. The amount owed to an advertiser by a medium when circulation falls below some guaranteed level or the advertiser qualifies for a higher space or time discount.

If the space purchased had qualified for the 10,000 column-inch rate ($3.50), the advertiser would have received a *rebate* of $5,000. The calculation then would be:

Paid rate:	10,000 column inches @ $4.00 per column inch =	$40,000
Earned rate:	10,000 column inches @ $3.50 per column inch =	$35,000
	Rebate due =	$ 5,000

Newspapers will credit a rebate against future advertising rather than actually pay the advertiser. Some papers charge the full rate and allow credit for a better rate when earned.

The Audit Bureau of Circulations (ABC) provides advertisers with reliable information about newspaper *circulation and demographic data* for many United States' markets. Penetration figures—as supplied by the *Circulation and Penetration Analysis of Print Media*—can assist the media planner to match areas of *best sales potential* with media circulation. ABC recently rated *The Enquirer's* circulation at 4.3 million. It's additional attractive feature is its *clout* in supermarket checkout lines—where it's the number one "impulse" reading item among a large, diverse market.

CIRCULATION ANALYSIS

The Audit Bureau of Circulations (ABC)

Until the founding of the ABC in 1914, advertisers had little reliable information about newspaper circulation. Since its establishment, the mission of the ABC has been to standardize, verify, and disseminate circulation information for the benefit of its members.[13]

The organization serves advertisers, agencies, and publishers. It is a self-regulating and self-supporting cooperative body. Revenues for the ABC come from annual dues paid by all members and auditing fees paid by publishers.

The verification process involves three reports: two publisher's statements and the ABC audit. The publisher's statements are issued for six-month periods ending March 31 and September 30. The ABC audit is conducted annually for 12-month periods ending either March 31 or September 30. Advertisers can also get summary information in reports called FAS-FAX, which are available more quickly than the full reports. Exhibit 10.12 is a portion of an ABC audit report. It should be noted that the information in ABC reports is constantly changing in response to subscribers' needs.

[13] *Academic Casebook,* a publication of the Audit Bureau of Circulations.

Audit Bureau of Circulations

AUDIT REPORT: Newspaper

THE TRIBUNE (Evening)
Anytown (Red County), Illinois

TOTAL AVERAGE PAID CIRCULATION FOR 12 MONTHS ENDED SEPTEMBER 30, 19--:

	Evening
1A. TOTAL AVERAGE PAID CIRCULATION (BY INDIVIDUALS AND FOR DESIGNATED RECIPIENTS):	41,315

1B. TOTAL AVERAGE PAID CIRCULATION (BY INDIVIDUALS AND FOR DESIGNATED RECIPIENTS) BY ZONES:
(See Par. 1E for description of area)

CITY ZONE

	Population	Occupied Households
1980 Census:	80,109	29,143
#12-31-87 Estimate:	80,500	30,000

Carrier Delivery office collect system, See Pars. 11(b) & (c)	1,875
Carriers not filing lists with publisher	18,649
Single Copy Sales	2,168
Mail Subscriptions	47
School-Single Copy/Subscriptions, See Par. 11(d)	50
Employee Copies, See Par. 11(e)	100
Group (Subscriptions by Businesses for Designated Employees), See Par. 11(f)	50
TOTAL CITY ZONE	22,939

RETAIL TRADING ZONE

	Population	Occupied Households
1980 Census:	268,491	75,140
#12-31-87 Estimate	272,000	79,000

Carriers not filing lists with publisher	15,138
Single Copy Sales	1,549
Mail Subscriptions	908
School-Single Copy/Subscriptions, See Par. 11(d)	25
Employee Copies, See Par. 11(e)	25
Group (Subscriptions by Businesses for Designated Employees), See Par. 11(f)	50
TOTAL RETAIL TRADING ZONE	17,695
TOTAL CITY & RETAIL TRADING ZONES	40,634

	Population	Occupied Households
1980 Census:	348,600	104,283
#12-31-87 Estimate:	352,500	109,000

ALL OTHER

Single Copy Sales & Carriers not filing lists with publisher	256
Mail Subscriptions	375
School-Single Copy/Subscriptions, See Par. 11(d)	20
Employee Copies, See Par. 11(e)	20
Group (Subscriptions by Businesses for Designated Employees), See Par. 11(f)	10
TOTAL ALL OTHER	681
TOTAL PAID CIRCULATION (BY INDIVIDUALS AND FOR DESIGNATED RECIPIENTS)	41,315

1C. THIRD PARTY (BULK) SALES:

Airlines — Available for passengers	1,000
Hotels, Motels — Available for guests	500
Restaurants — Available for patrons	500
Businesses — Available for employees	50
Other	600
TOTAL THIRD PARTY (BULK) SALES	2,650

#S&MM Estimate. See Par. 11(a).

EXHIBIT 10.12

ABC reports provide valuable information concerning the distribution patterns of newspapers and type of purchase. (Courtesy: Audit Bureau of Circulations.)

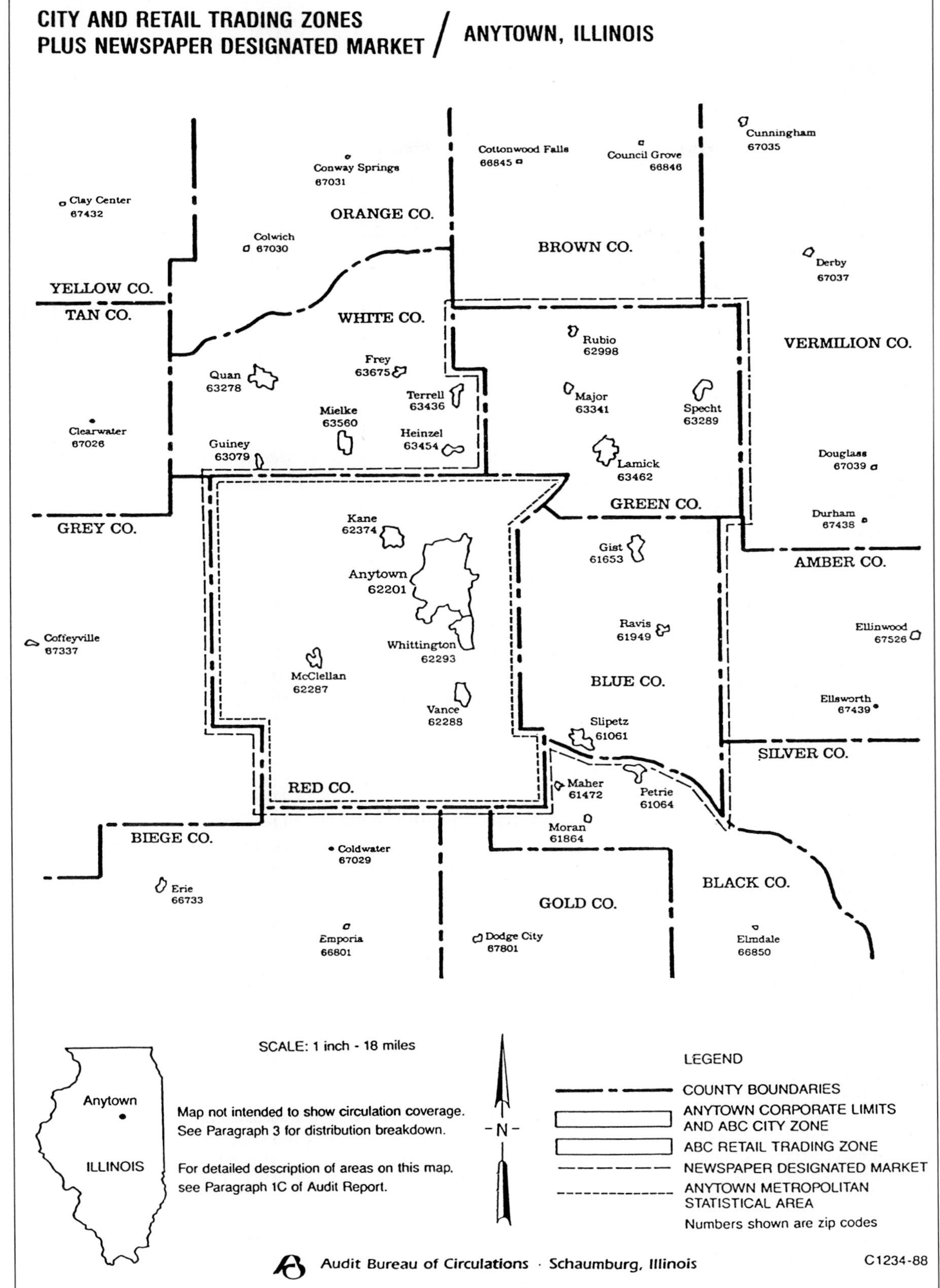

CITY AND RETAIL TRADING ZONES
PLUS NEWSPAPER DESIGNATED MARKET / ANYTOWN, ILLINOIS
Cottonwood Falls
66845
Council Grove
66846
Cunningham
67035
Conway Springs
67031
Clay Center
67432
ORANGE CO.
Colwich
67030
BROWN CO.
Derby
67037
YELLOW CO.
TAN CO.
WHITE CO.
Rubio
62998
VERMILION CO.
Frey
63675
Quan
63278
Terrell
63436
Major
63341
Specht
63289
Mielke
63560
Clearwater
67026
Heinzel
63454
Guiney
63079
Lamick
63462
Douglass
67039
GREEN CO.
Durham
67438
GREY CO.
Kane
62374
Gist
61653
AMBER CO.
Anytown
62201
Ravis
61949
Ellinwood
67526
Coffeyville
67337
Whittington
62293
McClellan
62287
BLUE CO.
Vance
62288
Ellsworth
67439
Slipetz
61061
SILVER CO.
RED CO.
Maher
61472
Petrie
61064
Moran
61864
BIEGE CO.
Coldwater
67029
Erie
66733
BLACK CO.
GOLD CO.
Emporia
66801
Dodge City
67801
Elmdale
66850
SCALE: 1 inch - 18 miles
Anytown
ILLINOIS
Map not intended to show circulation coverage.
See Paragraph 3 for distribution breakdown.
For detailed description of areas on this map.
see Paragraph 1C of Audit Report.
-N-
LEGEND
COUNTY BOUNDARIES
ANYTOWN CORPORATE LIMITS
AND ABC CITY ZONE
ABC RETAIL TRADING ZONE
NEWSPAPER DESIGNATED MARKET
ANYTOWN METROPOLITAN
STATISTICAL AREA
Numbers shown are zip codes
Audit Bureau of Circulations · Schaumburg, Illinois
C1234-88

EXHIBIT 10.12 (continued)

Primary information reported includes:

Audit Bureau of Circulations. *Independent organization that verifies audience data of most major newspapers and magazines.*

1. Total paid circulation.
2. Amount of circulation in the city zone, retail trading zone, and all other areas. (*Note:* The city zone is a market made up of the city of publication and contiguous built-up areas similar in character to the central city. The retail trading zone is a market area outside the city zone whose residents regularly trade with merchants doing business within the city zone.)
3. The number of papers sold at newsstands.

The ABC reports have nothing to do with a newspaper's rates. They deal with circulation statistics only. Publishers have always been glad to supply demographic data on their readers, but the ABC now has its own division for gathering demographic data for many of the markets in the United States. All data are computerized and quickly available.

Circulation and Penetration Analysis of Print Media

The *Circulation and Penetration Analysis of Print Media* is a reference source that offers media planners a method of determining the penetration of various print media throughout the United States. The service includes audience-penetration information for daily and Sunday newspapers, newspaper supplements, and leading national magazines. Penetration figures are given by major geographic division: counties, states, metropolitan areas, and television viewing areas (see Exhibit 10.13).

By using the penetration data, a media planner can match areas of best sales potential with print media circulation. The service also allows the planner to determine those areas that should be given more spot TV or radio advertising because of sparse print coverage. The analysis is invaluable for national advertisers, such as franchise food outlets, that must coordinate national and local advertising weights.

Syndicated Research Services

Scarborough Research Corporation. *One of the major organizations providing research on newspaper readership demographics and consumer behavior.*

Independent, standardized research for newspapers is conducted by Simmons Major Market Research and Scarborough Research Corporation. Typical demographic, psychographic, life-style, and frequency of use data are collected. Citing a recent Scarborough report, *The Los Angeles Times* advertisers that it researches 73% of all Los Angeles and Orange County adults with incomes of $75,000+. Their audience has more than half of the area's new car buyers and boasts *$58 billion* in buying power!

Since newspapers did not show a significant interest in national advertising until fairly recently, national audience surveys conducted for newspapers are a recent practice. It is clear, however, that independent, standardized research is a must to accommodate national advertisers, since virtually all competing media have provided such research for many years. The two major companies in the syndicated newspaper research field are Simmons Major Market Research, Inc., and Scarborough Research Corporation.

> Typically, survey results tell how many people live in an average household, how many newspapers they read a week, their types of employment, whether they own their homes, the kinds of cars they drive, household income, etc. They also cover such things as family ownership of stocks and bonds, ownership of electronic equipment, frequency of air travel, and spending for groceries.
>
> The same questions are asked in every market surveyed, and the same methodology is used. Thus, a national advertiser such as Procter & Gamble has a standard, uniform look at people all over the country who might buy its products. This is what differentiates national syndicated surveys from local surveys that newspapers might conduct themselves.[14]

Exhibit 10.14 shows examples of a Scarborough report giving readership demographics and reader shopping patterns for a major-market newspaper.

---

[14]Gene Goltz, "Syndicated Research," *presstime,* November 1987, p. 16.

TELEVISION VIEWING AREA (ADI/DMA) PRINT ANALYSIS

ORLANDO-DAYTONA BEACH-MELBOURNE ADI/DMA

POPULATION 2,041,000 HOUSEHOLDS 809,700 RETAIL SALES $ 13,927,000,000 AVG HSLD INC $30,451 9 COUNTIES

FLA BREVARD 18.8%,FLAGLER 1.0%,LAKE 7.2%,MARION 8.7%,ORANGE 29.0%,OSCEOLA 4.4%,SEMINOLE 11.8%,SUMTER 1.4%,VOLUSIA 17.6%

	Total Daily within ADI	Total Daily Penetration	A.M. or All Day within ADI	A.M. or All Day Penetration	Evening within ADI	Evening Penetration	20% MAC DAILY* Circulation	20% MAC DAILY* Penetration	20% MAC DAILY* Hslds (000)	Sunday within ADI	Sunday Penetration	20% MAC SUNDAY* Circulation	20% MAC SUNDAY* Penetration	20% MAC SUNDAY* Hslds (000)
★ DAYTONA BEACH NEWS,JOURNAL	79,092	10%	79,092	10%			79,092	52%	151	92,817	11%	92,817	61%	151
★ DE LAND SUN NEWS	8,431	1%			8,431	1%				8,917	1%			
★ FLORIDA TODAY	64,300	8%	64,300	8%			63,843	42%	152	85,511	11%	84,718	56%	152
JACKSONVILLE FLA TIMES-UN,JRNL	873	-%	869	-%	4	-%				1,039	-%			
★ LEESBURG COMMERCIAL	23,571	3%			23,571	3%	23,571	34%	70	25,668	3%	25,668	37%	70
MIAMI HERALD, NEWS	1,372	-%	1,372	-%						2,520	-%			
★ OCALA STAR-BANNER	36,977	5%	36,977	5%			36,701	52%	71	44,854	6%	44,458	63%	71
★ ORLANDO SENTINEL STAR @	242,391	30%	242,391	30%			199,321	47%	425	317,904	39%	266,542	63%	425
ST PETERSBURG TIMES,INDEPENDNT	1,346	-%	1,346	-%						2,007	-%			
★□SANFORD HERALD	8,602	1%			8,602	1%				8,822	1%			
TAMPA TRIBUNE @	5,817	1%	5,817	1%						8,019	1%			
VERO BEACH PRESS-JOURNAL	1,023	-%	1,023	-%						1,119	-%			
TOTAL NEWSPAPERS	474,640	59%								600,206	74%			
FG CENTRAL FLORIDA GLDN MRKTS GR	61,310	8%					61,310	44%	141	71,280	9%	71,280	51%	141
JS JACKSONVILLE/ST AUGUSTINE COM	873	-%								1,039	-%			
TB TAMPA BAY NEWSPAPER NETWORK	5,817	1%								8,019	1%			
TR TREASURE COAST MARKET GROUP	1,023	-%								1,119	-%			

Magazine	Circ.	%	Magazine	Circ.	%	Magazine	Circ.	%	Magazine	Circ.	%	Magazine	Circ.	%	Magazine	Circ.	%
□USAWKD	85,511	10.6%	ANR WN	134,657	16.6%	MOMAT	207,538	25.6%	NEWSWK	21,712	2.7%	R DGST	168,589	20.8%	TV GUI	116,844	14.4%
□PARADE	176,464	21.8%	BET HO	82,593	10.2%	GDHSK	39,702	4.9%	NWYRKR	2,006	.2%	RED BK	33,390	4.1%	USNEWS	24,916	3.1%
SUNDAY	320,675	39.6%	COSMO	28,256	3.5%	LHJ	48,690	6.0%	PENTHS	18,177	2.2%	17	15,711	1.9%	VOGUE	7,480	.9%
□METROC	331,740	41.0%	F CIRC	56,746	7.0%	MCCL	53,837	6.6%	PEOPLE	26,710	3.3%	SPRTIL	19,257	2.4%	WO DAY	60,496	7.5%
□PUCKCW	92,817	11.5%	FARM J	623	.1%	N GEO	75,406	9.3%	PLAY B	39,949	4.9%	TIME	36,231	4.5%			

OTTUMWA-KIRKSVILLE ADI

POPULATION 77,000 HOUSEHOLDS 29,000 RETAIL SALES $ 342,000,000 AVG HSLD INC $25,261 7 COUNTIES

IA DAVIS 11.4%,JEFFERSON 22.4%,VAN BUREN 10.7%

MO ADAIR 31.7%,PUTNAM 7.2%,SCHUYLER 6.9%,SULLIVAN 9.7%

	Total Daily within ADI	Total Daily Penetration	A.M. or All Day within ADI	A.M. or All Day Penetration	Evening within ADI	Evening Penetration	20% MAC DAILY* Circulation	20% MAC DAILY* Penetration	20% MAC DAILY* Hslds (000)	Sunday within ADI	Sunday Penetration	20% MAC SUNDAY* Circulation	20% MAC SUNDAY* Penetration	20% MAC SUNDAY* Hslds (000)
DES MOINES REGISTER,TRIBUNE	1,978	7%	1,978	7%						6,064	21%	4,690	36%	13
★□FAIRFIELD LEDGER	4,578	16%			4,578	16%	4,285	66%	7					
★□KIRKSVILLE EXPRESS & NEWS	6,768	23%			6,768	23%	6,461	46%	14	7,063	24%	6,756	48%	14
OTTUMWA COURIER	2,092	7%	2,092	7%			1,112	34%	3					
TOTAL NEWSPAPERS	16,827	58%								14,757	51%			
CU CENTRAL IOWA UNIT	2,092	7%					1,112	34%	3					

Magazine	Circ.	%	Magazine	Circ.	%	Magazine	Circ.	%	Magazine	Circ.	%	Magazine	Circ.	%	Magazine	Circ.	%
□USAWKD	6,064	20.9%	ANR WN	16,784	57.9%	MOMAT	5,074	17.5%	NEWSWK	831	2.9%	R DGST	5,997	20.7%	TV GUI	3,847	13.3%
□PARADE	422	1.5%	BET HO	2,690	9.3%	GDHSK	1,947	6.7%	NWYRKR	84	.3%	RED BK	1,557	5.4%	USNEWS	739	2.5%
SUNDAY	1,368	4.7%	COSMO	737	2.5%	LHJ	1,617	5.6%	PENTHS	423	1.5%	17	494	1.7%	VOGUE	148	.5%
□METROC	6,514	22.5%	F CIRC	1,967	6.8%	MCCL	1,901	6.6%	PEOPLE	491	1.7%	SPRTIL	580	2.0%	WO DAY	729	2.5%
□PUCKCW	422	1.5%	FARM J	2,402	8.3%	N GEO	2,161	7.5%	PLAY B	1,084	3.7%	TIME	986	3.4%			

OTTUMWA-KIRKSVILLE DMA

POPULATION 115,000 HOUSEHOLDS 44,600 RETAIL SALES $ 551,000,000 AVG HSLD INC $25,778 8 COUNTIES

IA DAVIS 7.4%,JEFFERSON 14.6%,VAN BUREN 7.0%,WAPELLO 35.0%

MO ADAIR 20.6%,PUTNAM 4.7%,SCHUYLER 4.5%,SULLIVAN 6.3%

	Total Daily within ADI	Total Daily Penetration	A.M. or All Day within ADI	A.M. or All Day Penetration	Evening within ADI	Evening Penetration	20% MAC DAILY* Circulation	20% MAC DAILY* Penetration	20% MAC DAILY* Hslds (000)	Sunday within ADI	Sunday Penetration	20% MAC SUNDAY* Circulation	20% MAC SUNDAY* Penetration	20% MAC SUNDAY* Hslds (000)
DES MOINES REGISTER,TRIBUNE	3,819	9%	3,819	9%						11,056	25%	9,682	34%	29
★□FAIRFIELD LEDGER	4,578	10%			4,578	10%	4,285	66%	7					
★□KIRKSVILLE EXPRESS & NEWS	6,768	15%			6,768	15%	6,461	46%	14	7,063	16%	6,756	48%	14
★ OTTUMWA COURIER	12,017	27%	12,017	27%			11,037	58%	19					
TOTAL NEWSPAPERS	28,619	64%								19,810	44%			
CU CENTRAL IOWA UNIT	12,017	27%					11,037	58%	19					

Magazine	Circ.	%	Magazine	Circ.	%	Magazine	Circ.	%	Magazine	Circ.	%	Magazine	Circ.	%	Magazine	Circ.	%
□USAWKD	11,056	24.8%	ANR WN	18,098	40.6%	MOMAT	8,032	18.0%	NEWSWK	1,138	2.6%	R DGST	9,168	20.6%	TV GUI	7,712	17.3%
□PARADE	422	.9%	BET HO	4,143	9.3%	GDHSK	3,078	6.9%	NWYRKR	113	.3%	RED BK	2,342	5.3%	USNEWS	1,077	2.4%
SUNDAY	1,429	3.2%	COSMO	1,087	2.4%	LHJ	2,357	5.3%	PENTHS	633	1.4%	17	792	1.8%	VOGUE	202	.5%
□METROC	11,567	25.9%	F CIRC	3,152	7.1%	MCCL	2,925	6.6%	PEOPLE	777	1.7%	SPRTIL	862	1.9%	WO DAY	1,959	4.4%
□PUCKCW	422	.9%	FARM J	2,815	6.3%	N GEO	3,189	7.2%	PLAY B	1,847	4.1%	TIME	1,394	3.1%			

PADUCA-CAPE GIRARDEAU-HARRISBURG-MAR

POPULATION 868,000 HOUSEHOLDS 330,100 RETAIL SALES $ 4,574,000,000 AVG HSLD INC $25,725 39 COUNTIES

ILL ALEXANDER 1.4%,FRANKLIN 5.4%,GALLATIN 0.9%,HAMILTON 1.2%,HARDIN 0.6%,JACKSON 7.2%,JOHNSON 1.1%,MASSAC 1.9%,POPE 0.6%
PULASKI 1.1%,SALINE 3.7%,UNION 2.3%,WILLIAMSON 7.5%

KY BALLARD 0.9%,CALDWELL 1.5%,CALLOWAY 3.6%,CARLISLE 0.6%,CRITTENDEN 1.0%,FULTON 0.9%,GRAVES 4.0%,HICKMAN 0.6%
LIVINGSTON 1.1%,LYON 0.7%,MC CRACKEN 7.3%,MARSHALL 3.1%

MO BOLLINGER 1.2%,BUTLER 4.5%,CAPE GIRARDEAU 6.9%,CARTER 0.6%,DUNKLIN 4.0%,MISSISSIPPI 1.6%,NEW MADRID 2.3%,REYNOLDS 0.8%
SCOTT 4.5%,STODDARD 3.4%,WAYNE 1.5%

TENN LAKE 0.8%,OBION 3.9%,WEAKLEY 3.7%

	Total Daily within ADI	Total Daily Penetration	A.M. or All Day within ADI	A.M. or All Day Penetration	Evening within ADI	Evening Penetration	20% MAC DAILY* Circulation	20% MAC DAILY* Penetration	20% MAC DAILY* Hslds (000)	Sunday within ADI	Sunday Penetration	20% MAC SUNDAY* Circulation	20% MAC SUNDAY* Penetration	20% MAC SUNDAY* Hslds (000)
★□BENTON NEWS	5,940	2%			5,940	2%	5,940	34%	18					
★ CAPE GIRARDEAU SE MISSOURIAN	15,643	5%			15,643	5%	11,559	51%	23	18,986	6%	17,142	46%	37
★ CARBONDALE SOUTHN ILLINOISAN	23,092	7%	23,092	7%			22,359	29%	78	28,012	8%	26,981	35%	78
CHICAGO TRIBUNE @	1,190	-%	1,190	-%						1,488	-%			
★□DEXTER STATESMAN	4,800	1%			4,800	1%	4,800	43%	11					
★□ELDORADO JOURNAL	2,000	1%			2,000	1%								
EVANSVILLE COURIER,PRESS	2,747	1%	2,729	1%	18	-%	609	20%	3	5,289	2%	889	30%	3
★□FULTON LEADER	2,533	1%			2,533	1%	1,571	51%	3					
★□HARRISBURG REGISTER	7,300	2%			7,300	2%	7,300	60%	12					
★□KENNETT DUNKLIN DEMOCRAT	6,500	2%			6,500	2%	6,500	50%	13					
LOUISVILLE COURIER-JRNL,TIMES	3,122	1%	3,122	1%						4,167	1%			
★□MARION REPUBLICAN	5,300	2%			5,300	2%	5,300	21%	25					
★□MAYFIELD MESSENGER	6,980	2%			6,980	2%	6,980	53%	13					
MEMPHIS COMMERCIAL APPEAL	4,413	1%	4,413	1%						6,634	2%	656	25%	3
★□MURRAY LEDGER & TIMES	7,490	2%			7,490	2%	7,490	63%	12					
★ PADUCAH SUN	31,395	10%			31,395	10%	28,496	42%	67	34,654	10%	31,671	45%	70
★ POPLAR BLUFF AMERICAN REPUBLIC	12,617	4%			12,617	4%	10,618	49%	22	13,010	4%	10,955	51%	22
ST LOUIS POST-DISPATCH	8,807	3%	8,807	3%						11,029	3%			
★ SIKESTON STANDARD	8,750	3%			8,750	3%	8,218	30%	28	8,910	3%	8,373	30%	28
★ TUCSON STAR, CITIZEN	123,169	37%	71,023	22%	52,146	16%	123,169	49%	253	139,285	42%	139,285	55%	253
★□UNION CITY MESSENGER	8,293	3%			8,293	3%	8,293	64%	13					
★□WEST FRANKFORT AMERICAN	4,609	1%			4,609	1%	4,609	26%	18					
TOTAL NEWSPAPERS	299,400	91%								272,330	82%			
CS CAPE GIRARDEAU/SIKESTON/DEXTE	20,443	6%					16,760	49%	34	18,986	6%	17,142	46%	37
MI MISSOURI GROUP	23,917	7%					23,834	52%	46	13,010	4%	10,955	51%	22
SG ST LOUIS ILLINOIS INTERURBIA	23,092	7%					22,359	29%	78	28,012	8%	26,981	35%	78
SI SOUTHERN ILLINOIS NETWORK	16,152	5%					15,849	37%	43					
SY SOUTHERN ILLINOIS PLUS NETWOR	18,152	5%					15,849	37%	43					
WK WESTERN KENTUCKY GROUP	7,490	2%					7,490	63%	12					

Magazine	Circ.	%	Magazine	Circ.	%	Magazine	Circ.	%	Magazine	Circ.	%	Magazine	Circ.	%	Magazine	Circ.	%
□USAWKD	163,247	49.5%	ANR WN	232,260	70.4%	MOMAT	56,293	17.1%	NEWSWK	7,220	2.2%	R DGST	58,522	17.7%	TV GUI	54,728	16.6%
□PARADE	190,306	57.7%	BET HO	27,847	8.4%	GDHSK	16,171	4.9%	NWYRKR	435	.1%	RED BK	15,817	4.8%	USNEWS	6,767	2.0%
SUNDAY	16,684	5.1%	COSMO	7,393	2.2%	LHJ	18,572	5.6%	PENTHS	2,993	.9%	17	7,260	2.2%	VOGUE	2,125	.6%
□METROC	24,127	7.3%	F CIRC	24,299	7.4%	MCCL	23,181	7.0%	PEOPLE	5,368	1.6%	SPRTIL	5,463	1.7%	WO DAY	21,133	6.4%
□PUCKCW	16,375	5.0%	FARM J	8,301	2.5%	N GEO	17,057	5.2%	PLAY B	9,889	3.0%	TIME	8,518	2.6%			

PADUCAH-CAPE GIRARDEAU-HARRISBURG DM

POPULATION 860,000 HOUSEHOLDS 327,100 RETAIL SALES $ 4,559,000,000 AVG HSLD INC $25,734 38 COUNTIES

ILL ALEXANDER 1.4%,FRANKLIN 5.4%,HAMILTON 1.2%,HARDIN 0.6%,JACKSON 7.2%,JOHNSON 1.1%,MASSAC 1.9%,POPE 0.6%,PULASKI 1.1%
SALINE 3.7%,UNION 2.3%,WILLIAMSON 7.6%

KY BALLARD 0.9%,CALDWELL 1.5%,CALLOWAY 3.6%,CARLISLE 0.6%,CRITTENDEN 1.0%,FULTON 0.9%,GRAVES 4.0%,HICKMAN 0.6%
LIVINGSTON 1.1%,LYON 0.7%,MC CRACKEN 7.4%,MARSHALL 3.1%

MO BOLLINGER 1.3%,BUTLER 4.5%,CAPE GIRARDEAU 6.9%,CARTER 0.6%,DUNKLIN 4.0%,MISSISSIPPI 1.7%,NEW MADRID 2.4%,REYNOLDS 0.9%
SCOTT 4.5%,STODDARD 3.4%,WAYNE 1.5%

TENN LAKE 0.8%,OBION 4.0%,WEAKLEY 3.8%

	Total Daily within ADI	Total Daily Penetration	A.M. or All Day within ADI	A.M. or All Day Penetration	Evening within ADI	Evening Penetration	20% MAC DAILY* Circulation	20% MAC DAILY* Penetration	20% MAC DAILY* Hslds (000)	Sunday within ADI	Sunday Penetration	20% MAC SUNDAY* Circulation	20% MAC SUNDAY* Penetration	20% MAC SUNDAY* Hslds (000)
★□BENTON NEWS	5,940	2%			5,940	2%	5,940	34%	18					
★ CAPE GIRARDEAU SE MISSOURIAN	15,643	5%			15,643	5%	11,559	51%	23	18,986	6%	17,142	46%	37
★ CARBONDALE SOUTHN ILLINOISAN	23,092	7%	23,092	7%			22,359	29%	78	28,012	9%	26,981	35%	78
CHICAGO TRIBUNE @	1,190	-%	1,190	-%						1,488	-%			
★□DEXTER STATESMAN	4,800	1%			4,800	1%	4,800	43%	11					
★□ELDORADO JOURNAL	2,000	1%			2,000	1%								
EVANSVILLE COURIER,PRESS	2,138	1%	2,120	1%	18	%				4,400	1%			

EXHIBIT 10.13

National advertisers are often interested in comparing print media circulation patterns with television viewing patterns. (Courtesy: American Newspaper Markets, Inc.)

READERSHIP

COMBINED DAILY READERS

READERSHIP AMONG METRO ATLANTA ADULTS

TOTAL ADULT POPULATION: 1,924,000

		—AVERAGE ISSUE—			—FIVE ISSUES—		
		No. of Readers	% of Readers	% of Demographic Segment	No. of Readers	% of Readers	% of Demographic Segment
TOTAL ADULTS		963,000	100%	50%	1,481,000	100%	77%
SEX	Male	508,000	53%	56%	740,000	50%	81%
	Female	455,000	47	45	741,000	50	73
HOUSEHOLD INCOME	Under $15,000	86,000	9%	33%	163,000	11%	63%
	$15,000-$19,999	55,000	6	47	91,000	6	78
	$20,000-$24,999	59,000	6	47	85,000	6	69
	$25,000-$34,999	203,000	21	50	319,000	22	79
	$35,000-$49,999	260,000	27	53	399,000	27	81
	$50,000-$74,999	179,000	18	52	268,000	18	78
	$75,000 & over	121,000	13	66	156,000	10	85
AGE	18-24	129,000	13%	47%	215,000	14%	78%
	25-34	258,000	27	48	424,000	29	80
	35-44	237,000	25	53	349,000	24	78
	45-54	137,000	14	55	192,000	13	77
	55-64	104,000	11	52	152,000	10	76
	65 & over	98,000	10	44	149,000	10	68
▶ **RACE**	White	704,000	73%	49%	1,074,000	73%	74%
	Nonwhite	259,000	27	54	407,000	27	85
EDUCATION	Part H.S. or less	180,000	19%	36%	302,000	20%	61%
	High School Graduate	318,000	33	48	505,000	34	76
	Part College	208,000	21	55	320,000	22	84
	College Graduate	159,000	17	65	220,000	15	89
	Post Graduate	98,000	10	65	134,000	9	87
OCCUPATION	White-Collar	465,000	48%	55%	688,000	46%	82%
	Blue-Collar	153,000	16	45	245,000	17	73
	Other Employed	94,000	10	51	147,000	10	79
	Homemakers	88,000	9	42	145,000	10	69
	Not Employed	163,000	17	46	256,000	17	73
MARITAL STATUS	Married	587,000	61%	51%	887,000	60%	77%
	Single	217,000	23	54	332,000	22	82
	Other	159,000	16	43	262,000	18	70
HOME OWNERSHIP	Own	669,000	69%	52%	991,000	67%	77%
	Rent	294,000	31	47	490,000	33	78
TYPE OF DWELLING	Single Family Unit	698,000	72%	51%	1,045,000	71%	77%
	Multifamily Unit	265,000	28	47	436,000	29	77

▶ **HOW TO READ THE CHART:**
Over five weekdays, 407,000 nonwhite Atlanta adults, or 85%, have read one or more issues of the Atlanta Journal-Constitution. This category represents 27% of daily readers.

EXHIBIT 10.14

Scarborough reports offer comparative data for major newspaper markets. (Courtesy: *Atlanta Journal and Constitution*.)

FOOD STORES

WINN-DIXIE SHOPPERS

30-DAY PERIOD

Winn-Dixie has 58 stores in metro Atlanta.

		Atlanta Adults	% of Adults	— WINN-DIXIE SHOPPERS — No. of Shoppers	% of Shoppers	% of Demographic Segment
TOTAL ADULTS		1,924,000	100 %	924,000	100 %	48 %
SEX	Male	908,000	47 %	408,000	44 %	45 %
	Female	1,016,000	53	516,000	56	51
HOUSEHOLD INCOME	Under $15,000	260,000	13 %	128,000	14 %	49 %
	$15,000 - $19,999	117,000	6	55,000	6	47
	$20,000 - $24,999	124,000	6	68,000	7	55
	$25,000 - $34,999	403,000	21	173,000	19	43
	$35,000 - $49,999	491,000	26	243,000	26	49
	$50,000 - $74,999	345,000	18	175,000	19	51
	$75,000 & over	184,000	10	82,000	9	45
AGE	18 - 24	275,000	14 %	133,000	14 %	48 %
	25 - 34	533,000	28	246,000	27	46
	35 - 44	446,000	23	204,000	22	46
	45 - 54	249,000	13	128,000	14	51
	55 - 64	201,000	10	104,000	11	52
	65 & over	220,000	12	109,000	12	50
RACE	White	1,446,000	75 %	694,000	75 %	48 %
	Nonwhite	478,000	25	230,000	25	48
EDUCATION	Part H.S. or less	492,000	26 %	227,000	25 %	46 %
	High School Graduate	658,000	34	332,000	36	50
	Part College	376,000	19	182,000	20	48
	College Graduate	246,000	13	124,000	13	50
	Post Graduate	152,000	8	59,000	6	39
▶ **OCCUPATION**	White-Collar	841,000	44 %	405,000	44 %	48 %
	Blue-Collar	337,000	17	151,000	16	45
	Other Employed	185,000	10	89,000	10	48
	Homemakers	209,000	11	110,000	12	53
	Not Employed	352,000	18	169,000	18	48
MARITAL STATUS	Married	1,147,000	60 %	592,000	64 %	52 %
	Single	406,000	21	173,000	19	43
	Other	371,000	19	159,000	17	43
HOME OWNERSHIP	Own	1,294,000	67 %	639,000	69 %	49 %
	Rent	630,000	33	285,000	31	45
TYPE OF DWELLING	Single Family Unit	1,357,000	70 %	682,000	74 %	50 %
	Multifamily Unit	567,000	30	242,000	26	43

▶ **HOW TO READ THE CHART:**
Of Winn-Dixie's 924,000 adult shoppers, 405,000 or 44% are in white-collar professions. This total represents 48% of all white-collar professionals in Atlanta.

EXHIBIT 10.14 (continued)

NEWSPAPER-DISTRIBUTED MAGAZINE SUPPLEMENTS

Sunday Supplements

Supplements offer newspaper advertisers *an upscale target audience,* on par with general circulation and city and regional magazines. They boast high-quality color reproduction, unduplicated newspaper audiences, and lower CPMs. Total spending in 1987 for supplements was $125 million. *Parade,* the most used supplement nationally, claims it reaches "more people per week than *TV Guide, Reader's Digest—and* the two combined—or 65 million readers every Sunday."

The Sunday supplement is a hybrid of the newspaper industry. It is distributed within the newspaper and therefore, potentially at least, reaches the same audience as the rest of the paper. However, in format, content, and, in many cases, advertising, locally published supplements are treated as magazines. In recent years, major newspapers such as the *Washington Post* and the *Los Angeles Times* have joined *The New York Times* in redesigning their magazines, both graphically and editorially, to appeal to an upscale target audience within the general newspaper readership. High-quality Sunday supplements can compete with both general-circulation magazines and city and regional magazines for national advertising. National advertisers see the Sunday supplement as a media vehicle that delivers both broad coverage and a prestige audience. Sunday supplements can offer high-quality color reproduction, an unduplicated newspaper audience, and, with a national buy, lower CPMs than can be achieved in consumer magazines.

Syndicated Supplements. *Parade* and *USA Weekend* offer national coverage. *Parade* is carried by approximately 315 newspapers with a total circulation of 31 million, and *USA Weekend* is carried by over 286 newspapers with a total circulation of 14.5 million. A full-page, four-color advertisement costs approximately $150,000 in *USA Weekend* and $300,000 in *Parade*. As you can tell from the circulation differential, *Parade* is dominant in larger markets. Like most national magazines, both *Parade* and *USA Weekend* permit advertisers to buy a number of regional editions.

Regional and Specialized Supplements. In addition to the nationally syndicated supplements, there are a number of regional and specialized publications. For instance, *Texas Weekly,* published by Harte-Hanks Communications, is carried by approximately 25 Texas papers, including both Harte-Hanks–owned publications and independents. There are smaller supplements such as *Vista,* targeted to the Hispanic community, and the *National Black Monitor*.

Locally Edited Sunday Supplements. A number of newspapers continue to edit their own Sunday supplements. By far the largest of these local supplements in terms of ad revenue is *The New York Times Sunday Magazine*. Other newspapers with well-known Sunday magazines include the *Los Angeles Times* and the *Washington Post*. Several newspapers with their own Sunday supplements also carry regional or syndicated supplements. However, the number of locally edited Sunday magazines has decreased significantly in recent years. Today, of the more than 500 Sunday newspapers, less than 40 publish local magazine supplements.

Sunday Supplement Networks. Advertisers who want the appeal of locally edited supplements and the convenience of syndication can use the Sunday Magazine Network. The Sunday Magazine Network is an organization of locally edited Sunday magazines that may be bought as a single medium. An advertiser is free to buy any number of these magazines. Individual publishers also maintain networks for their regionally distributed publications (such as *Texas Weekly*), but these carry only a small share of the total advertising invested in supplements.

Weekday Supplements

Recently, newspapers have been providing specialized supplements on days other than Sunday. For instance, *Food* and *Taste* are weekly food supplements in the *Boston Globe* and *Minneapolis Star,* respectively, while *Sportsweek* and *Action* are weekly sports "magazines" in the *Chicago Tribute* and *Louisville Times,* respectively. Advertisers find these weekday supplements excellent outlets to reach specific target markets within a newspaper's total readership.

THE BLACK AND ETHNIC PRESS

Specialized newspapers, catering to ethnics and races, are popular in large metropolitan areas. Some are written in foreign languages. They often feature general *and* specially-targeted products—but mostly endorsed by members of the reference group. *El Diario/La Prensa* reaches 38% of the New York City Hispanic market, while its closest competitor, the *Daily News* is 11 percentage points below.

Black-oriented communications are prospering. Syndicated television shows such as "Essence" and "Soul Train" are extremely profitable. Black performers such as Bill Cosby and Oprah Winfrey have great appeal to both black and white audiences. In addition, magazines targeted to black audiences, such as *Jet, Ebony,* and *Black Enterprise,* have shown gains in both readership and advertising revenue. In radio, the National Black Network and Sheridan Broadcasting continue the traditional appeal of that medium to black audiences.

There are approximately 175 black-oriented newspapers in this country. Most are weeklies and few are audited. Circulations are normally under 10,000, although some, such as New York's *Amsterdam News* (circulation 36,000); *The Call* (circulation 16,500) in Kansas City, Missouri; and the *Los Angeles Sentinel* (circulation 23,500), are ABC-audited and prospering members of the black press.

Daily black-oriented newspapers are found only in the larger markets. The *Atlanta Daily World* and the *Chicago Defender* are examples. One problem faced by black-oriented newspapers is that the metropolitan dailies are becoming more sensitive to covering news of the black community. At one time it was very unusual to see a wedding or funeral announcement for a black person in the major dailies, which also largely ignored cultural and civic events in the black community. As that changes, many people are becoming readers of the metropolitan dailies rather than the traditional black-owned newspapers. Advertising in black-oriented newspapers can be bought nationally through the Amalgamated Publishers, Inc., and Black Media, Inc.

In contrast to black newspapers, the Hispanic press is growing rapidly. There are now about 50 weekly Spanish-language newspapers in the United States, several with circulations in excess of 20,000. In addition, several dailies such as Los Angeles's *La Opinions* (circulation 72,000) and Miami's *Diaris Las Americas* (circulation 65,000) are growing so rapidly that they are competing with metro dailies for certain groups of advertisers. For example, Hispanics in New York City number 2.6 million, and their estimated buying power is $18.9 billion, which equals the GNP of Chile. It is not surprising that advertisers are increasingly catering to this market.[15]

While the Spanish-language press is the largest category of foreign-language newspapers, there are also newspapers available in over 20 foreign languages including Albanian, Croatian, and Finnish.

WEEKLY NEWSPAPERS

America was once a country of weekly newspapers, and to this day there are almost five times as many weekly newspapers as dailies. (A "weekly" is sometimes published two or three times a week.) About two-thirds of these 7,500 weeklies are urban oriented, that is, published in communities in the metropolitan areas or in the suburbs or satellites of the suburbs; one-third serve rural communities. Weeklies range from paid-subscription to partially paid or even free-circulation publications. They have high readership because they offer so much local news. They also contain local shopping information; in fact, many are known as "shoppers" because they carry less than

[15]"Hispanic Hot Spot," *American Demographics,* August 1988, p. 49.

25 percent editorial content. Total weekly newspaper circulation is estimated at 51,600,000 by the American Newspaper Publishers Association.

National advertisers may use suburban papers to round out a promotion they are running in the dailies of the nearby city. Weeklies are often offered as part of a group of papers within the same geographic market; dailies and weeklies are frequently included in the same package buy. However, many weeklies are unaudited and therefore a number of major advertisers and agencies will not consider them.

COMICS

For generations, one of the most popular sections of the Sunday newspaper has been the comics. Some newspaper editors have found to their chagrin that editorial columnists or newswriters can come and go with little fanfare, but if they drop a favorite comic strip, public reaction will be loud and swift. Virtually every Sunday edition has a comic section, with current circulation estimates placing readership at 60 million. The comics have increasingly become an advertising vehicle. Some sections are using what has been called a "spadea wrap." Here advertisements printed at the same time as the comic sections are wrapped around the outside of it. The term was derived from an advertiser with the last name of Spadea who in the 1950s first ordered a wraparound of that kind.[16]

The comics offer advertisers a national network for convenient buying. There are also comic syndicators, such as Puck, that sell advertisements to be carried in all or a portion of the newspapers that carry their comics.

SUMMARY

The modern newspaper is an extremely complex medium with many opportunities for both local and national advertisers. It is also a medium in transition; the industry has learned that it must take a more regional and national stance to gain a greater share of advertising dollars. But newspaper publishers must temper this aggressiveness with a realization that their local advertising base is threatened by a tremendous number of competitors in other media.

In order to position the medium for the twenty-first century, the industry is developing a marketing plan that represents an effective overall strategy for newspapers. This plan consists of five major elements:

1. *The market*. The market, the field of play, is like a road map. It must be studied and understood, because before you can figure out where you are going, you have to know where you are.
2. *The newspaper product*. This is the sum of benefits newspapers provide for readers and advertisers—the content, name, service, utility, convenience, and so on. It is important to know whether readers and advertisers think of the newspaper as the newspaper thinks of itself.
3. *Distribution*. This includes how and how many newspapers are delivered. What is the ratio between subscription and newsstand sales? Is the paper sold at convenience stores or racks? Is delivery dependable?
4. *Pricing*. If a newspaper is sold for less than readers think it is worth, it loses potential revenue. If it is sold for more than readers think it is worth, it loses circulation.

[16]Rosalind C. Truitt, "Printing the Comics Is a Serious Business," *presstime,* March 1988, p. 28.

5. *Sales and promotion*. Newspapers are in the business of communicating news and advertising to readers. They must be as adept at promoting their own product as they are at selling others' products.[17]

QUESTIONS

1. Discuss some of the primary reasons for newspapers' leadership in advertising revenue.
2. Marketing has become a key factor in the success of many newspapers. Discuss.
3. Discuss zoning and total marketing coverage. How do these functions present both problems and opportunities to newspapers?
4. Why have newspapers shown a growing aggressiveness in competing for national advertising in recent years? What are some of the steps newspapers have taken to accommodate national advertisers?
5. Why has the CPM calculation replaced the milline rate in comparing newspaper rates?
6. Why has syndicated audience research only recently become an important part of newspaper advertising?
7. From an advertising and marketing perspective, what is the role of the syndicated newspaper-distributed magazine?
8. Briefly discuss the process of audience verification used by the Audit Bureau of Circulations.
9. Under what circumstances would the short rate be used by a newspaper?
10. Discuss newspaper readership trends in recent years and some of the approaches newspapers have taken to increase their penetration.

SUGGESTED EXERCISES

- Using a Wednesday daily newspaper, categorize the advertisements by type of advertiser (excluding classified). How many of the advertisements have coupons?
- Keep a diary of your newspaper reading for a week. What sections and advertisements did you spend the most time on?
- Collect the freestanding inserts in your local daily newspaper for a week. What is the total value of the coupons offered in these inserts?

READINGS

ANDERSON, MARY A.: "Newspaper Marketing," *presstime,* January 1989, p. 26.

BUSTERNA, JOHN C.: "National Advertising Pricing: Chain vs. Independent Newspapers," *Journalism Quarterly,* Summer 1988, p. 307.

GERSH, DEBRA: "Sears Talks Tough," *Editor & Publisher,* February 4, 1989, p. 7.

GOLDMAN, TAMARA: "Big Spenders Develop Newspaper Strategies," *Marketing Communications,* January 1988, p. 24.

MCCOMBS, MAXWELL E., JOHN B. MAURO, AND JINKO SON: "Predicting Newspaper Readership from Content Characteristics: A Replication," *Newspaper Research Journal,* Fall 1988, p. 25.

PASTERNACK, STEVE, AND SANDRA H. UTT: "Newspapers' Policies on Rejection of Ads for Products and Services," *Journalism Quarterly,* Fall 1988, p. 695.

RYKKEN, ROLF: "Readership Decline Brings Newspapers to Crossroads," *presstime,* March 1989, p. 22.

[17] *Readers: How to Gain and Retain Them,* a publication of the Newspaper Advertising Bureau, pp. 13–14.

ELEVEN

Using Magazines

Magazines were the *first national promotion medium*. Because of their *broad reach,* Frito-Lay's new "grain" chip will be given significant exposure in *family magazines*. "Harvest," a multigrain chip with a wheat flavor and a cracker taste, should appeal to *all* age groups, said a company spokesperson.

Television is responsible for the demise of the big-page, general audience magazines. The mass audience advertisers flocked to TV, which could provide *both* audio and video presentations for their products. *Welch's Foods* will use national TV to break its new "dinosaur glass" campaign. It will *supplement* with magazine inserts, offering a coupon and a mail-in order form for a stuffed animal. At one time, it concentrated its promotional efforts in magazines with *national* circulation—but now, it claims "cartoons and jingles" can sell its character items better.

Magazines were the first medium to successfully offer national advertising. The growth of magazines can be traced to the expansion of markets westward and the development of first water, and then railroad, transportation systems to deliver goods to customers in distant markets. Without a medium such as magazines, there would have been no reason to distribute branded goods nationally. Furthermore, the efficiencies of mass production would have been minimized without the corresponding efficiencies of national promotion.

For a 50-year period from the 1870s to the 1920s, magazines were the only national advertising medium. With the advent of radio in the 1920s, they had to share the national advertising dollar. Still, magazines were the only *visual* medium, a characteristic extremely important to package-goods manufacturers. However, when television was introduced nationally in the 1950s, Americans' reading habits became viewing habits, and national magazines had to change to survive.

National advertising in the days before TV meant advertising in *Life, Look,* or the old *Saturday Evening Post,* the traditional, big-page general magazines designed to appeal to everyone. When people began turning to TV by the millions, advertisers followed the crowd. After spending years and fortunes trying to hold their audiences and advertisers, the big giants of the general-magazine world folded, one by one, the victims of TV and rising paper and postage costs, which particularly hurt the large-size, large-circulation magazines. The demise of the weekly *Life* magazine,[1] the last of the old giants, occurred at the end of 1972. No single event could have marked more clearly the turning point in the revolution that had been taking place in the magazine world since the advent of TV.

Many people hold the mistaken idea that the demise of these magazines was caused primarily by a loss of readership. In fact, the old mass magazines—even at the end—had respectable circulations. It was, rather, the loss of advertising revenue that killed them. For advertisers who wanted a mass audience, TV was the obvious answer. To reach a specialized audience, advertisers looked to alternatives to the mass magazine.

[1]Time, Inc., currently publishes a monthly version of *Life* that has a circulation of 1.3 million readers.

Consequently, the mass-circulation magazines were caught in an advertising and financial no-man's-land.

Meanwhile, as radio had done earlier, magazine publishers began to adjust to a changing marketing environment. They introduced new magazines—or updated old ones—to appeal to specific markets. These publications covered a wide range of interests and audiences. *Playboy, Psychology Today, Sports Illustrated, Cosmopolitan,* and many others all have in common an appeal to a group of readers who share some interest, taste, hobby, or point of view.

> ***Specialized circulation magazines.*** *In the last 30 years the most successful magazines have generally been those with a clearly targeted audience as contrasted to general circulation magazines.*

The *new* magazine market appeals to the growth of *special markets and interests*. In popular "yuppie" magazines, ads for personal care products, such as fragrances, are well targeted. Calvin Klein Cosmetics' ads for "Obsession" are *sensual,* appealing to sophisticated men and women.

The magazine industry of the 1990s will be characterized by the introduction of new titles and fierce competition for readers and advertising dollars among existing magazines. With few exceptions, the key to magazine success will be marketing to fairly narrow target segments (see Exhibit 11.1). However, starting a magazine is extremely risky. Magazines are often established in response to a passing interest that quickly fades, along with reader and advertiser interest. In addition, there are so many new magazines that advertisers hesitate to use less-than-established publications. Conse-

EXHIBIT 11.1

The name of the game for magazines is audience selectivity. (Courtesy: Time, Inc.)

60 Minutes. L.A. Law. Cheers. NBC Nightly News. Not one of them reaches as many professional/managerial adults as we do.

Millions watch these TV shows every week, but millions more read TIME. From 25% to 300% more, as you can see from the figures opposite.

For these professional/managerial adults, and for the 29 million readers of TIME worldwide, there's no substitute.

TIME	*6,105,000
Cheers	4,745,000
60 Minutes	3,507,000
L.A. Law	3,355,000
NBC Nightly News	1,411,000

*Professional/Managerial Adult Audience

Source: 1987 SMRB • ©1988 Time Inc.

quently, most new magazines must be prepared to withstand sizable financial losses before becoming profitable.

Creative media plans often include specialty magazines, along with tie-ins to television and other media vehicles. In launching *Purina Select,* "the only dry cat food with real meat as the main ingredient," the company is using women's magazines, supplemented with TV spots, free-standing inserts in newspapers, and direct-mail coupons. By being "aggressive," the company is trying to increase its share of the premium portion of the $1 billion canned cat food market, the fastest growing segment in the industry.

Magazine specialization is not just a function of editorial content. It also involves marketing and distribution. For example, in December 1988, ESPN, the all-sports network, introduced *TV Sports,* a monthly sports magazine that is delivered on the last Sunday of the month in a number of major newspapers. Delivery is made only to neighborhoods that are wired for cable and that have above-average household incomes. *TV Sports* is further evidence of the crossing of media lines by advertisers seeking creative media plans: It is a magazine format, delivered by newspaper, and sponsored by a television network.

Despite the risks, start-ups of consumer publications average four to six a month, with an equal number failing. *Cooking Light, Longevity, PC Computing,* and *Grandparents* are examples of recently introduced consumer publications. Exhibit 11.2 demonstrates the type of magazines that have been successful in recent years.

Sometimes it seems that all you need to do to be a successful magazine publisher is to find a group of people interested in a particular subject and let the magazine write itself. The danger in this approach is confusing a market with an audience. Special-interest magazines are designed to appeal to an image their readers have of themselves. Magazines are not only a means to inform and educate: They are also mirrors—sometimes flattering and wishful mirrors—of the reader. To some people, subscribing to *Travel & Leisure* means that they are world travelers even if they never leave home. So the special-interest magazine must fall somewhere between a practical service and an idealized self-image, between utility and dream.[2]

In our emphasis on special-interest magazines, we should not overlook the remaining giants of the magazine world. Led by *TV Guide* with a circulation of 17 million, there are some 25 to 30 consumer magazines that have readership of over a million. However, even these publications, which include *Modern Maturity* and *Family Circle,* have a narrowly focused editorial format.

Magazine revenue sources. *The financial support of most consumer magazines require readers to pay a larger proportion of the total cost with advertisers paying less.*

Another major change in consumer magazines in recent years is in the economic support of the typical publication. Over the last two decades, readers have been required to pay a much larger share of magazines' cost through significant increases in both subscription and newsstand prices (see Exhibit 11.3). Advertisers generally applaud this change, not only because it has reduced their own share of the cost of producing a magazine, but also because they believe people who are willing to pay a premium for a publication are serious readers of both its editorial and advertising content.

[2]Henry A.Grunwald, "The Magazine Endures," *Folio,* January 1988, p. 172.

EXHIBIT 11.2

In recent years, the most successful magazines have been narrowly directed to specific audiences. (Courtesy: *Advertising Age.*)

Largest % increase in total paid circulaton

	Magazine	%
1.	**Alfred Hitchcock & Ellery Queen Mystery Magazines**	90.6*
2.	**Game & Fish Magazine**	77.1
3.	**European Travel & Life**	70.5
4.	**Teen Beat**	59.9
5.	**Runner's World**	55.8
6.	**Consumer's Digest**	46.2
7.	**Entrepreneur**	45.9
8.	**Golf Illustrated**	45.1
9.	**Vanity Fair**	42.6
10.	**Bicycling**	42.4

*combined circulation

Source: Audit Bureau of Circulations' FAS-FAX for six months ended Dec. 31, 1987

EXHIBIT 11.3
Magazine revenues are increasingly coming from readers rather than advertisers. (Courtesy: *Marketing Media Decisions*.)

Consumer Magazine Sources of Revenue			
	Advertising	**Subscriptions**	**Single Copy**
1970	64.33%	27.91%	7.76%
1980	51.14	32.67	16.19
1981	51.08	33.30	15.62
1982	50.19	33.32	16.49
1983	49.87	33.70	16.43
1984	51.91	32.97	15.12
1985	49.70	33.29	17.01
1986	50.40	33.60	16.00
1987 (est)	50.08	33.60	16.32

Source: James B. Kobak & Co.

Magazines with high newsstand sales promote the fact that their readers are making a constant buying decision and paying a premium for the publication. For example, *Family Circle, Woman's Day, Cosmopolitan,* and *Mademoiselle* all have more than 70 percent of their sales at the newsstand. This is an important fact in selling reader involvement to advertisers.

ADVANTAGES AND DISADVANTAGES OF MAGAZINES

With audience *selectivity* and *extensive* reach, magazines can appeal to target markets much more efficiently and effectively than less selective mass media, such as television. *Fortune* magazine boasts that its ad pages' growth has been "dramatic," specifically in office equipment, insurance, and telecommunications—because of their "superior brand of journalism in being able to attract premier business segments."

Inflexibility and *adverse positioning* in publications cause some advertisers to use *other methods* to reach specialty targets. However, *Adweek* magazine promotes itself as "America's *only* marketing *weekly*—with 10 times more classified ads. . . ." to carve *a timely position* among the communications industry's publications.

***Ad banking.** Practice of some magazines of clustering ads at the front and back of their publications.*

Since magazines are so diversified, it is difficult to offer a list of advantages and disadvantages common to them all. However, despite the range of titles, formats, and editorial matter, we can state advantages of magazines as an advertising medium:

1. *Audience selectivity*. The successful magazines are those that identify and reach an audience segment of interest to advertisers.
2. *Increased reach among selected audience segments*. Selective magazines can be an excellent means of increasing reach among certain groups, for instance, light users of TV.
3. *Long life*. Magazines are the most permanent of all the mass media. Some magazines are kept for months, so advertising messages are seen a number of times.
4. *Availability of demographic and geographical editions*. Most major magazines allow advertisers to buy partial circulation. The advertiser thereby gains the prestige of appearing in a national publication and the selective audience of a smaller magazine.
5. *Credibility*. Most magazines offer advertisers an extremely credible environment for their advertising.

The primary disadvantages of magazines are:

1. *High cost*. The CPM levels for magazines are very high, often running ten times higher than other media in the case of very selective magazines. This high CPM is tempered somewhat by the ability to keep waste circulation to a minimum.
2. *Long closing dates*. Most magazines require that advertising copy be handed in six to eight weeks prior to publication.
3. *Ad banking*. Some publications, such as *National Geographic,* place all ads in clusters (or banks) at the front and back of the publication. This practice creates advertising clutter and greater competition for the individual ad.

WHY ADVERTISERS CHOOSE MAGAZINES

As we indicated earlier, magazines are a relatively expensive medium. Whenever a medium charges a premium for its audience, quality of readership becomes a primary concern. As we will see in this section, the number of people reading a magazine is in many respects less important than the type of reader and the editorial environment to which readers are exposed.

Magazines can deliver audiences with "quality" characteristics and high attention levels—better than other media. When Giorgio, famous for its potent and boldly-packaged signature scent, goes for women who prefer a quieter, more sophisticated fragrance, it'll break ads in *Elle*, *Town & Country*, *Vanity Fair*, and *Lear's*. These magazines *deliver* the "Red" woman—classically beautiful, self-confident, yet soft.

Audience Quality

There is a magazine for virtually every market segment, but heaviest magazine usage is concentrated in the most upscale segments. Exhibit 11.4 shows that magazines are especially well suited to reaching prime prospects in higher education, income, and occupational categories.

The problem faced by magazines is that virtually all media are courting advertisers with the "quality audience" hook. Radio, cable television, direct mail, newspaper special editions, and even television are using the strategy of appealing to narrowly defined markets. To the extent that these media are successful in convincing advertisers of their audience specialization, it can create problems for advertisers.

Audience involvement. *The degree to which readers show interest in editorial and advertising content of a magazine.*

Audience Involvement

While other media can make a case for delivering audience segments similar to those magazines deliver, they have a hard time showing media involvement close to that

EXHIBIT 11.4

Magazine audiences tend to include a high number of well-educated, upper-income persons. (Courtesy: Magazine Publishers of America.)

Index of Media Exposure

Demography	Magazines	TV	Newspapers	Radio
Age:				
18–24	118	94	83	114
25–34	116	85	93	112
35–44	112	87	107	106
45–54	96	103	110	95
55–64	88	112	117	89
65 & Older	65	131	100	72
Education:				
Attended/Graduated College	129	86	123	103
Graduated High School	98	99	100	105
Did Not Graduate High School	67	121	70	88
Household Income:				
$50,000 & Over	133	80	133	101
$40,000–$49,999	116	83	127	107
$30,000–$39,999	110	87	113	104
$20,000–$29,999	100	99	100	102
$10,000–$19,999	88	110	87	99
Under $10,000	75	131	63	88
Occupation:				
Professional/Manager	129	76	130	102
Technical/Clerical/Sales	118	84	110	114
Precision/Craft	90	85	90	117
Other Employed	98	91	90	106
Not Employed	84	125	90	86

100 = U.S. Average

(Sources: Newsletter of Research, *No. 53, November 1986 [Magazine Publishers Association], p. 6 and SMRB, 1986.)*

achieved by magazines. Put together an upscale audience, a medium that requires high levels of attention, and advertising that is compatible with the specific editorial thrust of the publication and you have a unique selling strategy.

Obviously, readers must give more attention to editorial content than viewers to TV or listeners to radio content. But does this involvement carry over to advertising? In a series of studies, the Magazine Publishers of America (MPA) showed that magazine advertising is more favorably received than advertising in other media, especially in its major competitor, television (see Exhibit 11.5).

Editorial Involvement

No magazine—or any other medium, for that matter—will be included in a media schedule if the numbers are not right. Essentially, that means prime prospects must be delivered at a competitive cost. However, media planners judge magazines by qualitative factors in addition to GRPs, CPMs, reach, and frequency figures. Research indicates that media involvement does carry over to advertising in magazines. Furthermore, magazines compare favorably to television in this regard (see Exhibit 11.6).

Ten Factors Important to Advertisers

In a study published by *Folio* magazine, advertising and marketing executives were asked to rate the ''ten most important factors'' in including a magazine in their media

EXHIBIT 11.5

Magazines score well in terms of audience involvement. (Courtesy: Magazine Publishers of America.)

Magazines		*Television*	
	Men		
Favorable		**Favorable**	
1. Keeps me posted on new products	85%	1. Keeps me posted on new products	79%
2. Appealing	84	2. Appealing	68
3. Helpful as a buying guide	79	3. For quality/dependable products	63
4. Informative about product	76	4&5. Informative about product	62
5. Believable	74	4&5. Helpful as a buying guide	62
Unfavorable		**Unfavorable**	
1. Exaggerated/misleading	43%	1. Exaggerated/misleading	63%
2. Boring/monotonous	33	2. Annoying/irritating	62
3. Confusing/unclear	29	3&4. Boring/monotonous	57
4. Unbelievable	27	3&4. Silly/insulting/juvenile	57
5. Silly/insulting/juvenile	26	5. Unbelievable	46
	Women		
Favorable		**Favorable**	
1. Appealing	89%	1. Keeps me posted on new products	80%
2. Keeps me posted on new products	88	2. Appealing	68
3&4. Helpful as a buying guide	79	3. Informative about product	67
3&4. Informative about product	79	4. For quality/dependable products	64
5. For quality/dependable products	78	5. Helpful as a buying guide	60
Unfavorable		**Unfavorable**	
1. Exaggerated/misleading	40%	1. Exaggerated/misleading	63%
2. Boring/monotonous	30	2. Annoying/irritating	61
3&4. Silly/insulting/juvenile	26	3. Silly/insulting/juvenile	59
3&4. Unbelievable	26	4. Boring/monotonous	58
5. Confusing/unclear	23	5. Unbelievable	51

EXHIBIT 11.6

Magazine advertising is generally regarded as unobstrusive. (Courtesy: Magazine Publishers of America.)

Disposition To Seek Out The Advertising . . .		*Advertising Adds to Interest in Medium*				*Advertising Detracts from Interest in Medium*			
		Men		**Women**		**Men**		**Women**	
		Magazines	**TV**	**Magazines**	**TV**	**Magazines**	**TV**	**Magazines**	**TV**
Total U.S.		37%	13%	39%	13%	36%	74%	32%	71%
By Education:	Did Not Graduate H.S.	31%	19%	48%	21%	40%	68%	20%	60%
	Graduated High School	36	20	40	15	38	68	32	70
	Attended College	40	11	40	14	37	78	34	75
	Graduated College	37	7	30	7	32	81	37	76
By Household Income:	Under $15,000	39%	22%	41%	22%	35%	65%	30%	60%
	$15,000–$24,999	35	16	43	13	43	72	31	74
	$25,000–$34,999	41	17	39	13	36	73	36	73
	$35,000 or More	38	6	33	7	31	84	32	80
By Age:	18–24	47%	18%	62%	29%	37%	76%	26%	62%
	25–34	46	16	43	11	30	73	31	76
	35–44	33	9	33	9	42	76	35	77
	45–54	25	12	29	9	44	76	39	76
	55–64	28	6	34	7	36	83	28	71
	65 & Older	33	20	28	14	32	63	33	65
By Occupation:	Prof./Mgr./Owner	39%	10%	37%	6%	33%	79%	35%	80%
	Wh.Col./Sales/Cler.	41	12	41	12	36	68	31	74
	Blue Collar	39	15	47	25	40	76	24	64
	Not Employed	32	18	37	15	35	69	32	68

schedule. It is instructive to see what factors are most often considered in making these decisions.[3]

The reproductive quality of magazine ads make it a prime advantage for advertisers working to display *fine detail*. Japanese magazines are the prime media for *cars* and *technical products for the home*. Frequently, advertisers will use well-known, American celebrities in their "stage dress" to highlight particular features of the products.

1. Advertising Reproductive Quality. For more than 50 years, magazines have had the advantage of being able to show products in realistic color. While this advantage is no longer unique to magazines, it is still a major element in magazine advertising. Research indicated that a full-page four-color ad is approximately 30 percent more likely to be noticed than the same page in black-and-white. However, the advantages of color are lost if reproduction quality is not of the highest standards.

2. Circulation Audited. We will discuss the auditing of magazines later in this chapter. Here we just note that because of the number of magazines, especially new titles, advertisers are demanding independent verification of circulation claims before they will consider buying a publication.

Facing editorial. *Most magazine advertisers prefer their ads to face an editorial page rather than compete for readers with another ad.*

3. Facing Editorial. Many advertisers avoid publications that concentrate their advertising in a few sections within the magazine. Most media buyers prefer to have their advertisements placed next to editorial content and away from other advertising.

4. Syndicated Audience Research. These services offer estimates of total readership (as contrasted to paid circulation) and, more importantly, give media planners information about audience demographics, psychographics, and product usage not found in audits. We will examine the syndicated research services in detail later in this chapter.

5. Recommendations of Ad Agencies. National advertisers, the group most likely to use magazines, look to their agencies as the media experts. Fully 90 percent of a

[3] "Beyond CPMs with Client Execs," *The Folio: AdGuide*, July 1984, p. 42.

Agency recommendations score highly with advertisers because of the in-depth knowledge agency personnel have of the different magazines. *Vista,* the New York Hispanic magazine, advertises to agency personnel—so *they* can advise clients of its ability to reach *3 million English-speaking Hispanics*.

magazine rep's time is spent with agency media buyers and planners. In fact, many company advertising directors rarely see media salespeople. The fact that agencies are so crucial to magazine advertising is an advantage, particularly to new or small-circulation publications. These magazines would find it impossible to meet with individual advertisers, but they can concentrate their efforts on a few agencies.

6. If Publication Is New or Established. Just as with any brand, buyers are apt to feel more comfortable with and purchase a product they know. A publication such as *Gentleman's Quarterly* is so well known in the fashion industry that it need only run reminder notices to advertisers in order to sell the publication (see Exhibit 11.7). A new publication is almost always competing against an established competitor with a similar editorial format. Breaking new ground is very difficult. Often new magazines offer deep discounts and other special deals to major advertisers to get them to use the publication. Ad reps can then sell other advertisers on the basis that General Motors or Procter & Gamble has already advertised in the magazine.

7. Separation from Competitors. Can the magazine make the case that it holds a unique position among its competitors? How will buying *McCall's* benefit my product

EXHIBIT 11.7

***Gentleman's Quarterly* clearly keeps its name before advertisers. (Courtesy: *Gentleman's Quarterly*.)**

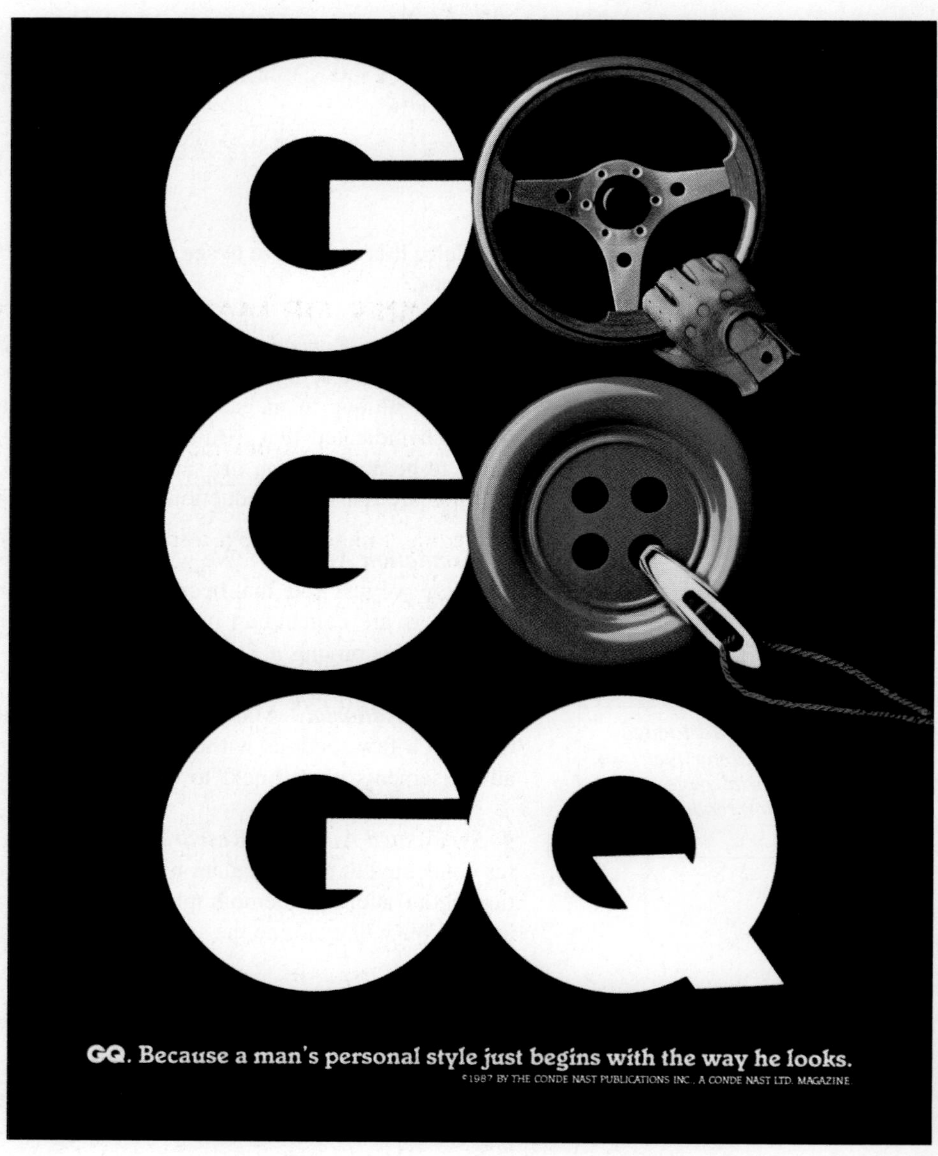
GQ
GQ. Because a man's personal style just begins with the way he looks.
©1987 BY THE CONDE NAST PUBLICATIONS INC., A CONDE NAST LTD. MAGAZINE

in a way that buying *Redbook* or *Family Circle* cannot? One of the most difficult tasks a publisher has is differentiating the publication—but not in a way that drives away potential readers or advertisers. That is, they must find a way that is narrow, but not too narrow.

8. Audience Duplication with Competitors. Because magazine advertising is expensive, audience duplication often results in considerable wasted money. Magazines try to present themselves as reaching a specific market segment that is somehow different from other portions of the market delivered by competing publications. Of course, the largest-circulation magazine in a category stresses that it can provide a single, lower-cost alternative that adequately reaches the entire market. The marketing strategies among magazines are very much like those used by any product in a particular category.

Rate base. *The circulation (or base) on which a magazine determines its advertising rates.*

9. Underdelivery of Rate Base. When advertisers buy space in magazines, they are really buying the delivery of their advertising to a number of people, expressed in terms of circulation. All rates are based on the circulation that a publisher promises to provide, referred to as *guaranteed circulation* or the *rate base*. Later in this chapter, we will discuss in detail the problems that occur when a magazine fails to meet its guarantee.

10. Far Forward. Will the magazine promise an advertiser space toward the front of the publication? Some advertisers think that this favorable placement is an advantage, particularly in reaching casual readers. Many magazines will provide this service at no extra charge to large, continuous users of the publication.

FEATURES OF MAGAZINE ADVERTISING

Fast-Close Advertising

Fast-close. *Some magazines offer short-notice ad deadlines at a premium cost.*

It is a costly process to provide a selected audience, as magazines do. It makes no sense to use this expensive medium if all you want to do is get a short message about a familiar product before the widest possible audience. Magazines are most economical in sending a message about a specialized product to a specialized audience. They are usually least economical in delivering to the general public just the name and a short message about a widely distributed product.

Most magazines, which have closing dates long before publication, are not the best medium for making news announcements, such as a change in an airline schedule. Many magazines close five to seven weeks before publication for black-and-white ads and eight weeks for color ads. The closing date is even further ahead for special editions.

However, several major magazines have introduced fast-close, or short-notice, ads. These permit advertisers to take advantage of timely events that tie in with their products or with changes in marketing or competitive strategy. In most cases, there is no extra charge for this service.

With fast-close service, advertisers are not guaranteed a position or even that the ad will run. To ensure getting space, some advertisers will submit an insertion order but not send the actual ad until the last minute. For instance, a tire company may order space to run an ad the week after the Indianapolis 500. If a car that uses its tires wins the race, an ad making this announcement will run; if not, another, standard ad will be used. As competition has increased for advertising dollars, more and more magazines have begun to offer fast-close services.

Coupon and Direct-Response Advertising

As we will discuss in Chapter 13, expenditures for direct-response advertising are growing at a much faster rate than outlays for general advertising. Magazines are an excellent medium for direct-response ads. They have large pages to accommodate coupons and the ability to reach the selective audiences ideal for many types of direct-response products.

Magazines also, as we noted earlier, have the longest life of any of the mass media. Their long reading life and high pass-along readership contribute to an accumulation of response unequaled by any of the other media. Exhibit 11.8 shows the percentage of direct-response inquiries over time. Six issues after an ad has been placed, inquiries are still being received from readers of both weekly and monthly publications.

EXHIBIT 11.8

Because of their long life, magazines are excellent vehicles for direct-marketing offers. (Courtesy: Magazine Publishers of America.)

With more attention being given to *direct-response,* magazines can provide space for coupons, tear-out post cards, and other promotional tools. Included in promotion industry magazines are "soundsheets" by Eva-Tone. These small 45 RPM records include any message the advertiser wishes—testimonials, sales presentations—and are touted as "standouts" among other types of promotional vehicles. A reply card is attached to the sample recording.

Advertising . . .

7) Accumulation Of Response— Typical Weekly Magazine

After On-Sale Date	Percent of Inquiries The Period	Cumulative
One Week	54	54
Two Weeks	25	79
Three Weeks	7	86
Four Weeks	4	90
Five Weeks	3	93
Six Weeks	2	95
Over Six Weeks	5	100

Source: "An Analysis of 12 Million Inquiries," Daniel Starch.

8) Accumulation Of Response— Typical Monthly Magazine

After On-Sale Date	Percent of Inquiries The Period	Cumulative
One Month	54	54
Two Months	22	76
Three Months	8	84
Four Months	5	89
Five Months	3	92
Six Months	2	94
Over Six Months	6	100

Source: "An Analysis of 12 Million Inquiries," Daniel Starch.

9) Effects On Inquiry Response Rate

Type of Offer in Ad	Index
No Coupon (Free Offer)	100
Coupon (Free Offer)	301
Coupon (Charge Offer)	196

Source: "An Analysis of 12 Million Inquiries," Daniel Starch.

Partial-Run and Regional Magazines

> ***Partial-run editions.** When magazines offer less than their entire circulation to advertisers. Partial runs include: demographic, geographic, and split-run editions.*

Partial-Run Magazines. Say the word "magazines," and most people think of the giants of the industry—*Time, Reader's Digest,* and *Ladies' Home Journal*. These national magazines are really several publications in one. In the 1960s, large-circulation magazines began to offer a portion of their circulation to regional advertisers. Demographic circulation breakouts were added to these geographic editions in the 1970s. The demographic editions usually include those readers residing in high-income ZIP codes.

Today about 13 percent of all magazine advertising revenue comes from either geographic or demographic editions. Together these editions are known as *partial-run* advertising, since the advertiser purchases less than the entire circulation of the magazine. Exhibit 11.9 shows a typical breakout for a magazine sold on a partial-run basis.

EXHIBIT 11.9

Virtually all major magazines offer some type of partial-run opportunities to advertisers. (Courtesy: *Newsweek*.)

Partial-run and *regional editions* afford more direct targeting of specific markets. George Dickel Tennessee Whiskey ads, characterizing the earthy countryside, will be run in the Southeast and Southwest editions of national music, news, and sports magazines. The brand sells in most markets, nationally, but is advertised only in its Southern "heartland," where it gets the bulk of its sales.

Introducing a new business magazine that reaches more business people than Forbes, Fortune or Business Week.

Source: SMRB 1988; Newsweek Composite Factor Method.

When you're trying to reach business people, business publications are a good vehicle. But they're not enough. That's why there's Newsweek Business, our new demographic edition.
With Newsweek Business you will reach nearly 2 million *different* Professionals/Managers than you do in these business magazines. That's 2 million P/Ms you'd miss completely without Newsweek Business. And you reach them more efficiently. Pretty good statistics for a magazine that's not supposed to be a "business book."

Newsweek Business

Major publications such as *Time* and *Newsweek* offer advertisers more than 100 combinations of regional, state, city, and demographic partial-run opportunities. There are several factors to consider when using partial-run advertising.

The partial-run edition allows an advertiser to:

- Relate advertising to territories in which the product is sold
- Support promotions being run in different parts of the country
- Test a campaign in various markets before embarking on a national campaign
- Reach a scattered set of markets with one order
- Encourage local retail support by listing retailers' names as distributors in their home markets

The geographic edition is obviously ideal for local and sectional advertisers. There are, however, some disadvantages to advertising in a geographical edition:

- CPM is higher than in a national edition.
- Forms close much sooner.
- Ads for a given market may not run in every issue.
- Orders must be placed well in advance.
- All local ads may be run back-to-back in an insert—a situation not conductive to high readership. (It is better to place an ad in one of the regional editions with a special localized editorial section for each major split.)

Regional magazine. *A publication that is usually edited for an upscale audience with a particular interest in one geographic area of the country.*

Regional Magazines. Regional publications are a growing segment of the magazine industry. They are in some ways a hybrid between the small-circulation specialty publication and the partial-run edition of national magazines. Regional magazines have an advantage over both in reaching an upscale local audience with editorial and advertising content specifically directed to their interests. Since these publications are usually expensive for advertisers on a CPM basis, they must reach a high-income audience to be an attractive media buy. Successful regional publications fall into one of three categories:

1. *Publications with national appeal.* These are the blue-chippers of the regional field. *Southern Living, Yankee,* and *Sunset* are among the few regional magazines that attract national advertisers and readers outside the region highlighted in the publication.
2. *Utilitarian city magazines.* These magazines offer news of a city. They emphasize utility to the reader with news of cultural and sporting events, restaurant listings, and strong editorial features. They are supported by local advertising.
3. *Atmosphere titles.* Magazines in this category portray a region in a pictorial sense with an emphasis on travel and light editorial. *Washington* magazine and *Arizona Highways* (which accepts no advertising) are examples of this genre.[4]

The problem with most city and many regional magazines is that they appeal to a relatively small group of local advertisers such as specialty store, hotels, and banks (see Exhibit 11.10). When the local economy experiences a downturn, these publications may lose their advertising base very quickly. Exhibit 11.10 shows some of the regional success stories of the 1980s.

Psychographic research. *Research which attempts to go beyond demographic descriptions of an audience to determine how its members think of themselves in terms of lifestyle and purchase behavior.*

Magazine and Psychographic Research

In addition to audience numbers and demographic characteristics, magazines sell a style of living to both readers and advertisers. Advertisers are interested not only in who a magazine's readers are, but also in how these readers think of themselves. The *Playboy* man and the *Cosmopolitan* woman are as much perception as reality. Exhibit

[4]Michael Couzens, "Regional Magazines: Shakeup and Shakeout," *Folio,* May 1988, p. 102.

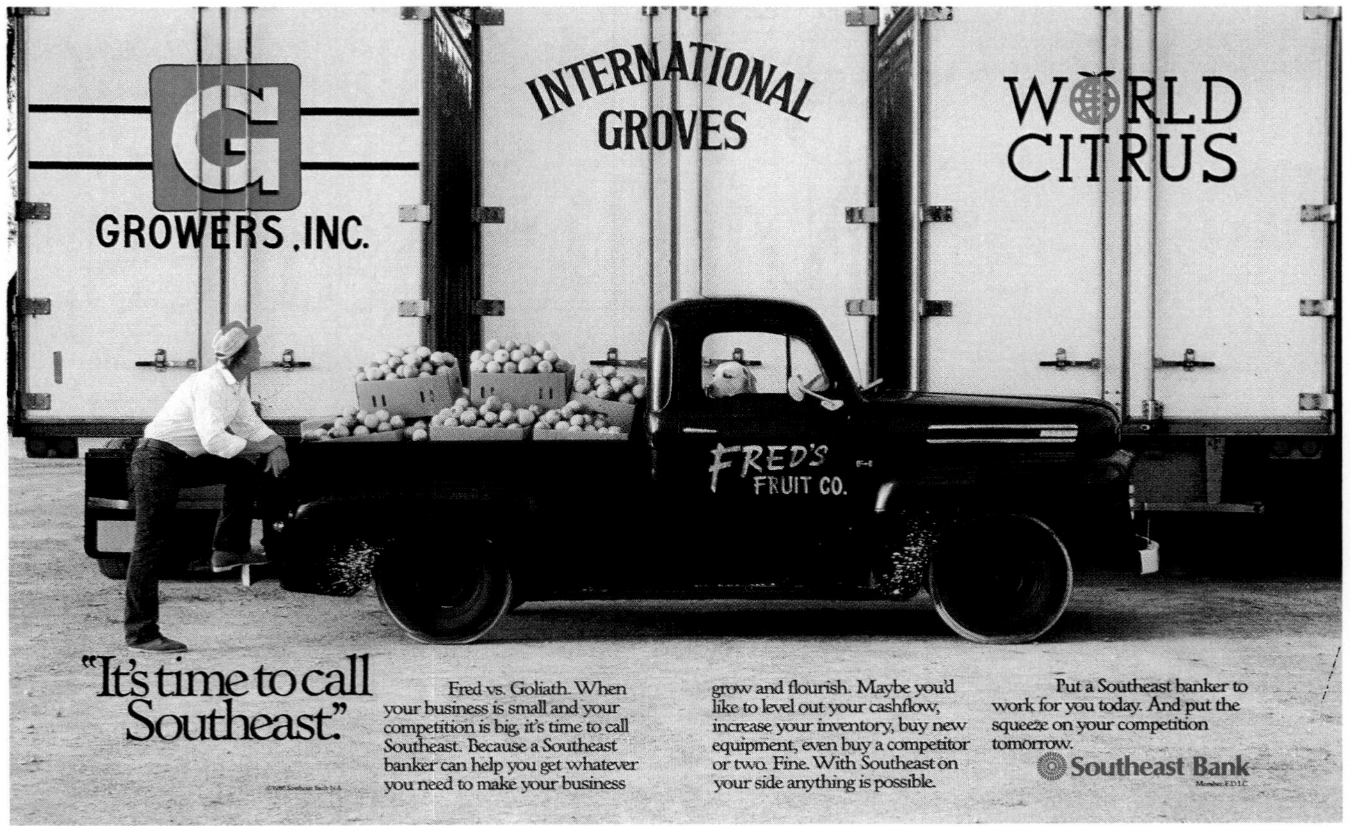

EXHIBIT 11.10
Most city magazines appeal to a relatively small group of advertisers. (Courtesy: Southeast Bank)

11.11 shows how a leading financial publication such as *Barron's* sets its tone and quality image.

Magazines can create a "psychographic" lifestyle. By attaching its seal of approval to home-related items, *Good Housekeeping* magazine is influencing the "new traditionalist." Its editorials feature *trends*, heavily-laden with traditional values—which "spills over" in the ads it attracts.

In Chapter 7, we discussed the PRIZM system of categorizing people by their lifestyle characteristics. Exhibit 11.12 shows how these PRIZM categories can be used to promote the purchase of new cars. (Review Exhibit 7.3 for the explanation of the each of these clusters.)

MAGAZINE ELEMENTS

Sizes

The page size of a magazine is the type area, not the size of the actual page. For convenience, the size of most magazines is characterized as *standard size* (about 8 by 10 inches, like *Time*) or *small size* (about 4⅜ by 6½ inches, like *Reader's Digest*). When you are ready to order plates, you must get the exact sizes from the publisher's latest rate card, because sizes keep changing.

Position and Space-Buying Designations

Cover. *The front of a publication is known as the first cover; the inside of the front cover is the second cover; the inside of the back cover is the third cover; the outside of the back cover is the fourth cover. Extra rates are charged for cover positions.*

The front cover of a magazine is called the *first cover page*. This is seldom, if ever, sold in American consumer magazines (although it is in business magazines). The inside of the front cover is called the *second cover page,* the inside of the back cover is the *third cover page,* and the back cover the *fourth cover page*. For the second, third, and fourth cover positions, you must pay a premium price and may have to get on a waiting list.

Space in magazines is generally sold in terms of full pages and fractions thereof (half

EXHIBIT 11.11

***Barron's* makes clear what readers it is directed toward. (Courtesy: *Barron's*.)**

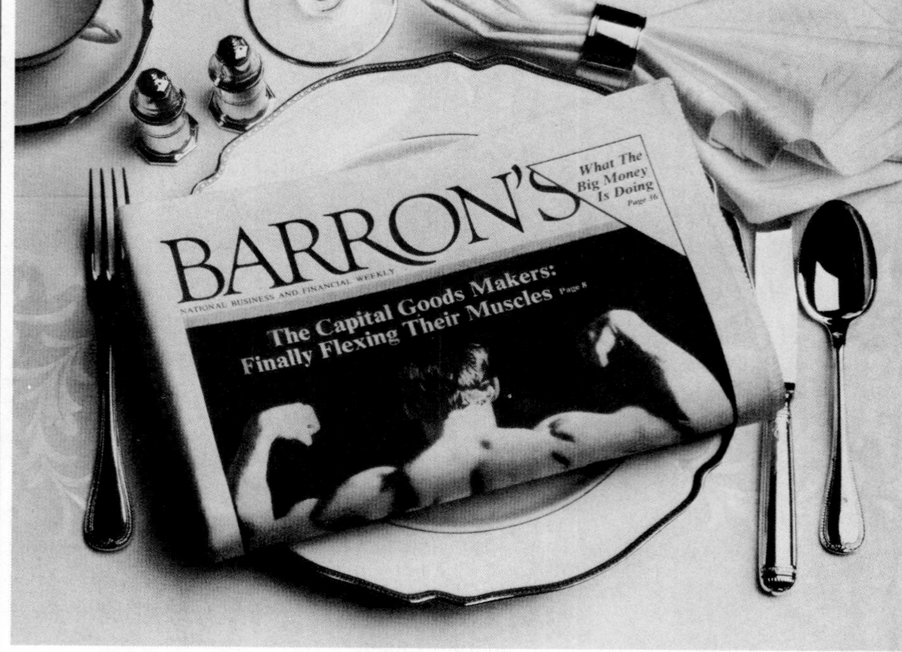

Breakfast Of Millionaires.
BARRON'S
What The Big Money Is Doing
NATIONAL BUSINESS AND FINANCIAL WEEKLY
The Capital Goods Makers: Finally Flexing Their Muscles
You're familiar with what's called the coffee table magazine.
Barron's is something else: a breakfast table magazine.
Every Saturday morning, Barron's reaches the rich and powerful all over America. In fact, an astonishing 37% of all Barron's readers are millionaires.
And unlike magazines that sit on coffee tables and are read with no special urgency (if at all), Barron's is read only hours after it's published.
Eighty-six percent of Barron's readers who go out and buy it on newsstands read it the weekend it appears. For an average of *two* hours an issue.
The importance of all this for advertisers is clear—especially if you've ever suspected that your advertising is languishing somewhere in dens, magazine racks and waiting rooms.
The way to a millionaire's heart may or may not be through his stomach. But the way to his mind is definitely through Barron's.
BARRON'S
HOW THE SMART MONEY GETS THAT WAY.

While special positions in a publication and "bleed" ads will draw more attention, they do add to the final cost. Nevertheless, Delta resorted to the "bleed" approach in luring travellers to the Kentucky Derby. It featured a *blur* of a rider on horseback—almost as if *both were in motion*. Its out-of-focus approach was a noticeable effort to get noticed—regardless of the cost of the time-restricted promotion.

***Bleed.** Printed matter that runs over the edges of an outdoor board or of a page, leaving no margin.*

pages, quarter pages, three columns, two columns, or one column; see Exhibit 11.13.) The small ads in the shopping pages at the back of many magazines are generally sold by the line. Most magazines are flexible about allowing one-page of double-page ads to be broken up into separate units.

Bleed Ads

When an ad runs all the way to the edge of the page, leaving no margin, it is called a *bleed ad* (see Exhibit 11.14). Bleed ads are designed to get extra attention. An ad may bleed on only three sides, or it may bleed on two sides, leaving the white space on the other two sides open for copy.

Although some publications, especially new ones, do not charge for bleeds, usually you must pay an extra 15 to 20 percent whether the ad bleeds on one, two, three, or four sides.

EXHIBIT 11.12

Many magazines sell audience quality and purchase behavior as hard as number of readers. (Courtesy: Magazine Publishers of America.)

23) Personality Profile Index

Self Concept	Media Imperatives Magazine	TV
Affectionate	107	93
Amicable	111	91
Brave	106	95
Broadminded	106	94
Creative	113	86
Dominating	109	88
Efficient	107	95
Egocentric	108	92
Funny	111	91
Impulsive	105	93
Intelligent	116	87
Refined	108	92
Style Conscious	107	91

100=U.S. Average
Source: SMRB, 1987.

24) Target Demographics by VALS Typologies

Typology	% U.S. Adults	Attd./Grad. College %	Attd./Grad. College Index	$40,000+ H.H. Income %	$40,000+ H.H. Income Index	Professional/ Managerial %	Professional/ Managerial Index
Survivors	4.0	0.9	22	*	*	*	*
Sustainers	7.0	2.5	36	0.7	10	*	*
Belongers	38.0	15.4	40	13.3	35	2.7	7
Emulators	10.0	4.9	49	4.9	49	2.9	29
Achievers	21.0	32.6	155	52.0	248	40.3	192
I Am Me	3.0	3.2	106	3.3	109	0.4	13
Experientials	5.0	10.5	210	6.4	127	6.6	132
Societally Conscious	12.0	30.0	250	19.4	162	47.1	393
Total U.S.	100.0	100.0	100	100.0	100	100.0	100

* Less than half of one percent/number too small for reliability.

Source: 1987 SMRB/VALS

25) Media Exposure By VALS Typologies

Typology	Mean Levels Of Exposure: Magazines	Television	Radio	Newspapers
Survivors	56	127	81	61
Sustainers	95	116	101	62
Belongers	84	114	87	93
Emulators	101	89	121	87
Achievers	118	87	108	122
I Am Me	122	90	121	91
Experientials	122	85	108	113
Societally Conscious	120	77	106	125
Total U.S.	100	100	100	100

100=U.S. Average
Source: 1987 SMRB/VALS

26) Market Share By PRIZM Clusters

Magazine Dominant	% U.S. Adults	Percent Unit Sales Of New Car: Under $14,000	$14,000-$15,499	$15,000 & Over
S1	4.2	5.4	6.0	9.9
S2	7.2	8.6	8.6	12.1
S3	10.8	12.6	13.2	14.3
T1	9.4	8.9	10.8	11.2
T2	8.7	10.1	11.0	8.4
U1	7.3	5.3	4.8	5.9
Total	47.6	50.9	54.4	61.8
Television Dominant				
R2	11.7	7.0	6.4	5.4
S4	7.2	12.3	10.5	10.0
U2	8.0	7.1	5.1	4.7
U3	7.7	5.6	4.0	3.5
Total	34.6	32.0	26.0	23.6
Dual/Equal				
R1	7.9	7.6	9.9	6.2
T3	9.9	9.5	9.7	8.4
Total	17.8	17.1	19.6	14.6
Total 12 Clusters	100.0	100.0	100.0	100.0

Source: PRIZM/Propriety Data Base 1987 Model Year

27) Media Exposure By PRIZM Clusters

Magazine Dominant	Media Exposure: Magazine	Television
S1	122	92
S2	108	91
S3	110	93
T1	102	94
T2	103	98
U1	105	100
Total	107	95
Television Dominant		
R2	86	107
S4	92	100
U2	97	106
U3	83	113
Total	89	106
Dual/Equal		
R1	96	97
T3	107	103
Total	102	101
Total 12 Clusters	100	100

100=U.S. Average Reading and Viewing Levels.
Dominance=Advantage of 5% or More.
Source:SMRB 1985-86 SMM/PRIZM.

Inserts and Multiple-Page Units

Multiple-page units. *Multiple-page units are designed to achieve high audience impact, but they often sacrifice CPM efficiency.*

Sometimes advertisers want more impact and dominance than can be achieved with a typical magazine advertisement. Exhibit 11.15 shows how the Aetna Investment Management Network uses a well-designed advertisement to gain attention in an extremely competitive field with a double-page spread. We also have shown how advertisers can use cover foldouts or gatefolds to gain this added attention. In recent years, advertisers have also turned to multiple-page inserts to heighten readership and advertising awareness.

Among the most frequent users of inserts are automobile companies. Car makers are in an extremely competitive market and have a lengthy, technical story to tell about models, engineering features, and special sales promotions. BMW, Nissan, Chrysler, and Ford have all been frequent users of inserts.

EXHIBIT 11.13
Various ways of using magazine space.

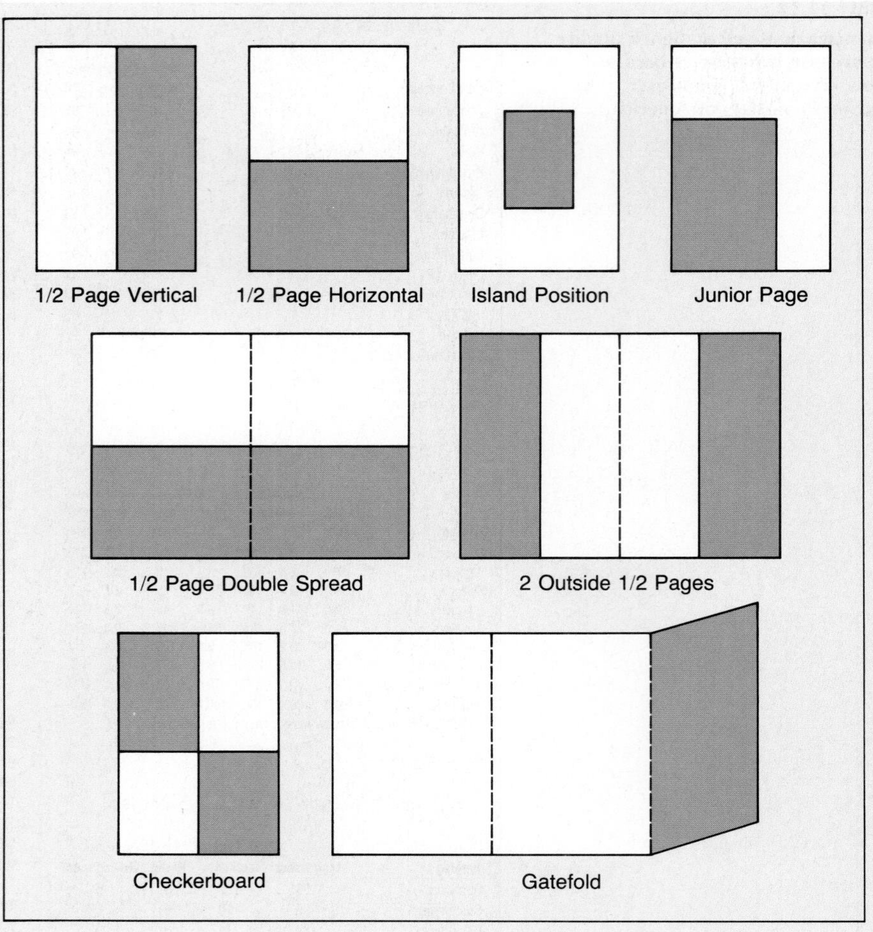

There is no question that inserts gain readership, but they should be used only to fit a specific marketing objective. Among the reasons most often cited by advertisers for using inserts are:

- To gain greater impact when launching a new product
- To develop new marketing strategies
- To change consumers' perceptions of a product
- To showcase a range of products under a single brand name[5]

There are several things an advertiser must consider before planning an insert. First and foremost is cost. The cost of an insert will vary with the publication, but it is common for inserts to cost double the regular four-color rate. In addition, the advertiser is responsible for the cost of design, printing, and paper. If the insert is very large or printed on heavy paper, the magazine may pass on extra postage costs. Rarely will the increase in audience awareness match the added cost of advertising this way. Therefore, the CPM of an insert is significantly higher than for the magazine as a whole.

Another consideration is that the high cost of an insert usually means fewer items in a media schedule. Since the advertiser is putting a disproportionate share of advertising

[5]Abbe Wichman, "Insert Here," *Inside Print,* May 1988, p. 49.

EXHIBIT 11.14

Bleed ads provide opportunities for distinctive creative approaches. (Courtesy: Fireman Fund Insurance Companies.)

"How do you know
what's the right investment strategy?"
"How well do you want to sleep at night?"
At Ætna, we have always maintained an unwavering commitment to the institutional investor: we never forget it's your money, not ours.
That's what makes us take extra care to match your investment performance to your risk tolerance. Even if that means our analysts have to dig deeply to identify the risks involved in alternative investment scenarios. And take the time to communicate these risks clearly and thoroughly to you.
But our digging isn't limited to risk. We also like to uncover the unusual opportunity for our clients. Recently, for example, we re-staged one client's guarantee base, locking in gains already accrued. Even before the contract period was over. In fact, we re-staged it four times.
This level of client dedication may not be every asset manager's cup of tea. But we're willing to bet it's yours. Call us: (203) 275-3635.
Ætna
Ætna Investment Management Network

EXHIBIT 11.15

Multiple-page ads gain high readership but are significantly more expensive on a cost-per-reader basis. (Courtesy: Aetna Investment Management Network.)

money into one or a few vehicles, the likely result is a reduction in reach and frequency compared to a more traditional media plan. Finally, so many advertisers use inserts nowadays that their novelty, as well as their impact on readers, is reduced. The most effective inserts are those with an interesting product, a new story to tell, and a relatively select group of prospects. Computers, financial services, and automobiles will continue to be the largest users of consumer magazine inserts.

HOW SPACE IS SOLD

Magazine Rate Structure

Magazine advertising space is perhaps the most straightforward of all media buys. While regional and other partial-run advertisers may face a number of options, the national, full-run advertising buy is relatively simple. A typical rate card for a weekly publication might look like this:

Living World Bulletin (LWB) Color Rates (4-color)

Space	1 ti	6 ti	12 ti	26 ti
1 page	32,800	29,750	28,150	26,675
⅔ page	24,210	22,950	21,740	20,630
½ page	22,880	18,430	20,615	19,510
¼ page	11,800	11,050	10,550	9,860

An advertiser buying this publication will pay $32,800 for a one-time, four-color, full-page insert. The advertiser who buys at least 26 inserts in the publication will pay only $26,675 per ad for the same space.

Before placing a magazine on its advertising schedule, the advertiser will compute the cost efficiency of that publication against others being considered. Let's assume that *LWB* has an average circulation of 660,132. Using the CPM formula discussed earlier, we can calculate the efficiency of the publication as follows:

$$\text{CPM} = \frac{\text{cost/page}}{\text{circulation (000)}} = \frac{\$32{,}800}{660} = \$49.69$$

Discounts

Frequency discounts. *Discounts based on total time or space bought, usually within a year. Also called bulk discounts.*

Frequency and Volume Discounts. The onetime full-page rate of a publication is referred to as its *basic,* or *open, rate*. In the case of *LWB,* the open rate is $32,800. All discounts are computed from that rate. Most publications present their discounts on a per-page basis in which rates vary according to frequency of insertion during a 12-month period, as we have done here. However, some publications use either *frequency* or *volume discounts* based on the number of pages run. For instance:

Frequency, Pages	Discount, %
13 or more	7
26 or more	12
39 or more	16
52 or more	20

Volume discounts. *Based on total dollars spent for advertising.*

Rates will vary, according to the size of an ad, in units adding up to a full page, and the frequency of insertion. They also are determined by the choice of color or black and white. *Vans' Sneakers* will rebound in the national advertising arena with black and white ads. "While 'trendy,' their lower cost allows us to extend our reach further, since our market is spread among surfers, skateboarders, and BMX bicyclists . . . to name a few. . ." revealed Richard Leeuwenberg, Van's CEO.

In a similar fashion, the volume discount gives a larger percentage discount based on the total dollar volume spent for advertising during a year. The volume discount is convenient for advertisers who are combining a number of insertions of different space units or who are using a number of partial-run insertions. A volume discount might be offered as follows:

Volume, $	Discount, %
83,000 or more	8
125,000 or more	11
180,000 or more	17
260,000 or more	20

Other Discounts. Publishers are always alert to giving special rates to large advertisers and to other advertisers they are eager to attract. Among different magazines, we find various special discounts: mail-order discount, travel discount, trade-book discount. Blanketing all of these is a corporate, or total-dollar, discount. This overall discount (above all the others earned) is based on the total dollars spent by all of the corporation's divisions in a year.

There is obviously no such thing as a standard trade discount or standard use of terms. It pays to ask a lot of questions when buying space.

Remnant space. *Unsold advertising space in geographic or demographic editions. It is offered to advertisers at a significant discount.*

Remnant Space. A number of publishers, especially those with geographic or demographic editions, find themselves with extra space in some editions when they are ready to go to press. Rather than run an empty space, the publisher will often offer this remnant space at a big discount. For direct-response advertisers, whose ads are not part of a continuing campaign but stand on their own, remnant space is an especially good buy. Of course, material for the ad must be ready for instant insertion.

Rate Negotiations

You will recall that broadcast rates are determined by negotiations between advertisers and stations. Some stations don't even print a formal rate card since the cost for spots is determined on an individual basis with each buyer. While rate negotiation has long been the norm in broadcasting, it was considered unusual, even unethical in some quarters, to negotiate rates for print advertising. The practice of negotiating print rates is called *going off the card* and is extremely controversial among advertisers, agencies, and media executives.

Rate negotiation. *Until recently most magazines resisted negotiation of their rates. However, competitive pressure from some publications has caused a number of magazines to engage in rate negotiation.*

Negotiated rates are becoming more common—especially for discounts for *large volume advertisers. Emerge,* a new Black monthly, is anxious to attract advertisers wanting to reach "upwardly mobile Black baby boomers." It promotes its "charter advertiser incentives and guarantees" for those interested in placing multi-insertions.

Nonetheless, all the evidence points to negotiated print rates as the trend of the future. So far, the practice is largely confined to magazines. However, since rate negotiation is largely the result of competitive pressure, many people predict that newspapers may someday follow the lead of magazines in selling space on a negotiated basis.

McCall's magazine took the lead in announcing a willingness to engage in rate negotiation. Few magazines have publicly taken the same position, but several have introduced new discount plans in addition to the traditional volume and frequency discounts. One of the most extensive discount programs is Time, Inc.'s Maximum Advertising Exposure Plan (Max-Plan). This plan offers space credits to any advertisers who increase the percentage of their print advertising budget allocated to any of the eight Time, Inc., publications. Shortly after Time announced the Max-Plan, several other publishers introduced similar programs. Since each package plan is unique to a particular advertiser, negotiation plays a major role in many of these package buys.

Some advertising agencies have begun negotiating units for magazines similar to those established for broadcast buys. While magazine advertising rate negotiation is still not altogether accepted in the industry, it is becoming a fact of life. Yet to be determined is the specific form negotiations and discounts will take.

The Magazine Short Rate

As we have seen, most magazine discounts are based on the amount of space bought within a year. However, the publisher normally requires that payment be made within 30 days of billing. Therefore, an advertiser and a publisher sign a space contract at the beginning of the year and agree to make adjustments at the end of the year if the space usage estimates are incorrect. If the advertiser uses less space than estimated, the publisher adjusts, using a higher rate than contracted for. If more space is used, the publisher adjusts using a lower rate.

Let's look at a typical short rate, using the rate card for *Living World Bulletin*.

> ACME Widgets contracted with *LWB* to run eight pages of advertising during the coming year. At the end of the year, ACME had only run five pages. Therefore, it was short the rate for which it had contracted and an adjustment has to be made, as follows:
>
> Ran 5 times. Paid the 6-time rate of $29,750 per page = (5 × 29,750) $148,750
>
> Earned only the 1-time rate of $32,800 per page = (5 × 32,800) $164,000
>
> Short rate due ($164,000 − 148,750) = $ 15,250

Some publishers charge the top (basic) rate throughout the year but state in the contract, "Rate credit when earned." If the advertiser earns a better rate, the publisher gives a refund. If the publisher sees that an advertiser is not running sufficient pages during the year to earn the low rate on which the contract was based, the publisher sends a bill at the short rate for space already used and bills further ads at the higher rate earned. Failure to keep short rates in mind when you are reducing your original schedule can lead to unwelcome surprises.

PLACING THE ORDER

Insertion order. *Instructions from an advertiser authorizing a publisher to print an ad of specified size on a given date at an agreed rate; accompanied or followed by the copy for the ad.*

A *space contract* will get the advertiser the best rate, such as for the coming 12 months. For contracting for 13 insertions, *Plastics News*, a new magazine aimed at "decision makers in the plastics industry," the advertiser is promised an additional 13 insertions—free!

Placing advertising in a magazine on a 12-month schedule may entail two steps: the space contract and the insertion order. An advertiser who plans to advertise in a particular magazine during the coming 12 months will sign a space contract in order to get the best rate. This is not an order for a specific amount of space but merely an agreement to pay at the current rate schedule for whatever space is used. The advertiser estimates how much space might be run during the year and is billed for the discount rate charged for that amount of space. The contract usually allows the publisher to raise the rate during the contract year, but only with two or three months' notice. The advantage to the advertiser is that during those months no rate increases are permitted.

When the advertiser is ready to run an ad, he or she sends an insertion order to the publisher specifying date of issue, size of ad, and contract rate.

MAGAZINE DATES

There are three sets of dates to be aware of in planning and buying magazine space:

1. *Cover date:* the date appearing on the cover.
2. *On-sale date:* the date on which the magazine is issued (the January issue of a magazine may come out on December 5, which is important to know if you are planning a Christmas ad).
3. *Closing date:* the date when the print or plates needed to print the ad must be in the publisher's hands in order to make a particular issue.

Closing date, closing hour. *The day or hour when all copy and plates or prints must be in the medium's hands if an ad is to appear in a given issue. The closing time is specified by the medium.*

Dates are figured from the cover date and are expressed in terms of "days or weeks preceding," as in the following example:

New Yorker
Published weekly, dated Monday
Issued Wednesday preceding
Closes 25th of 3rd month preceding

MAGAZINE NETWORKS

Magazine networks. *A group of magazines that allows an advertiser to purchase all or several of the titles at a significant discount compared to buying each magazine separately.*

To reach the *same general target market*, advertisers usually purchase space from *several* magazines. Groups of magazines have banded together to form "networks." *Times Mirror Magazines* has 9 special interest magazines—*Home Mechanix, Outdoor Life, Popular Science, Skiing, Yachting, Golf, Ski, Field & Stream,* and *Salt Water Sportsman*—to reach the "active male" market.

It is rare for an advertiser to buy a single magazine. In order to achieve reach and frequency goals, several magazines will normally be included in a national advertising schedule. Usually the magazines bought in such a package will have similar editorial features and appeal to the same general target market. Some years ago, several magazines began to sell themselves as single packages or networks to advertisers. Today there are dozens of these networks, each offering advertisers the efficiency of buying several publications with a single purchase order and one invoice.

There are a number of networks, but all fall into two general types:

1. *Single-publisher networks.* Most networks are offered by publishers who own several magazines of interest to a single audience. For example, the Hearst Corporation offers the "Hearst Man Power" network comprising *Esquire, Sports Afield,* and *Popular Mechanics* (see Exhibit 11.16).
2. *Independent networks.* Independent networks sell competing titles in a single package. The two primary independent networks are ADI Networks and 3M Media Networks. A typical network offered by these companies would be ADI's "Women's Lifestyle Network" comprising *Working Women, McCall's, People,* and *Working Mother*. These services also sell packages on a regional market basis.

EXHIBIT 11.16

Advertisers can realize significant savings by making combination buys of several publications. (Courtesy: The Heart Corporation.)

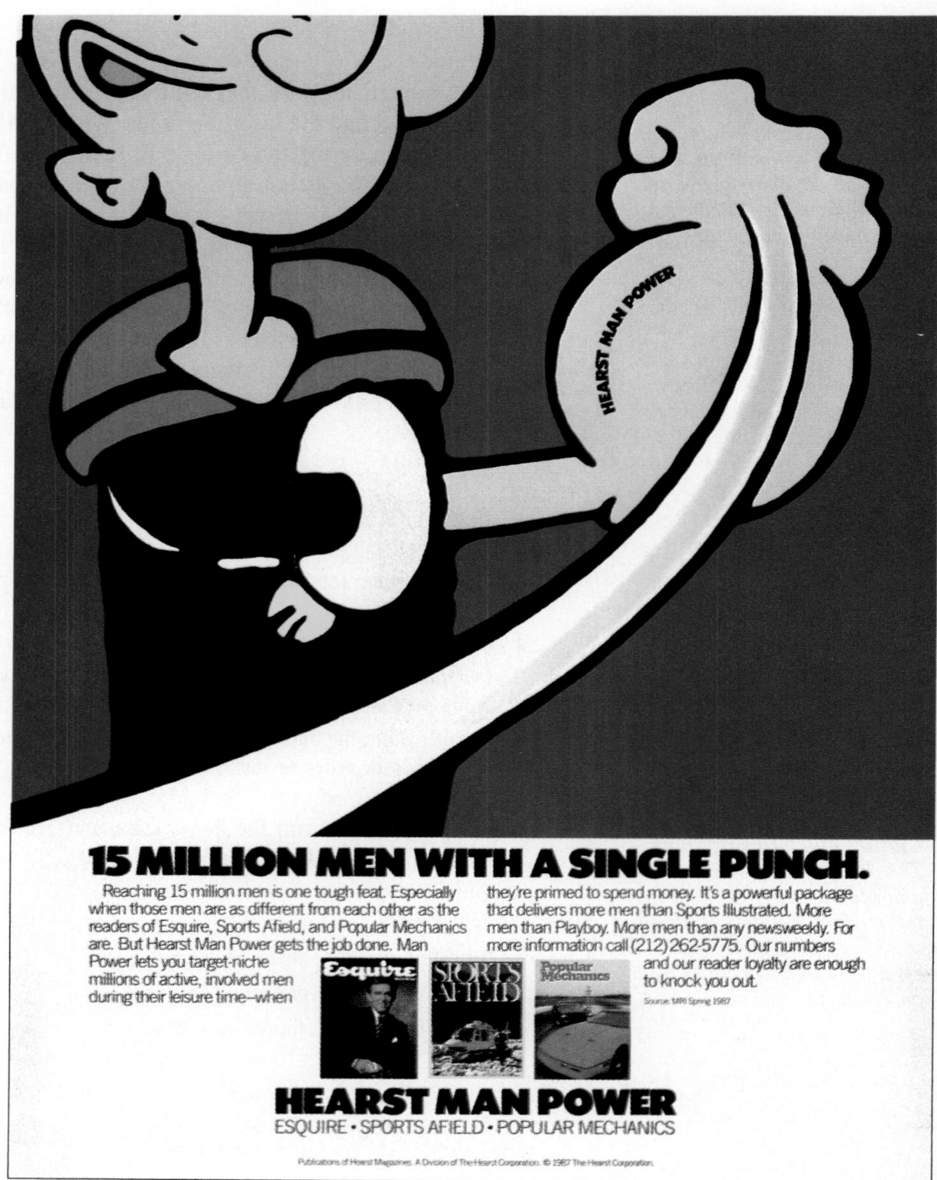

Split-runs afford the advertiser the opportunity to test different ads in the same region or in two or more areas with similar characteristics. When Ore-Ida wanted to reach more military personnel, it resorted to placing ads in *military magazines*. One version of its initial ad was seen in *Exchange and Commissary News,* a male-directed publication. To reach *women,* a different version of the ad was placed in *Family* and *Military Lifestyle*. The coupons in the ads helped determine the more successful approach.

Split-run advertising. *Some publications allow an advertiser to place different ads in the same edition of a publication, that is, to split the press run.*

Split-Run Advertising

Just as Sunday newspaper magazine sections offer split-run advertising, so do many magazines, and for the same purpose: to test different ads against each other. Many magazines also have split-run editions, or more specifically, they divide a geographic edition for testing purposes. In the simplest of such tests, the advertiser supplies two different ads of the same size and shape, each running in the same position in half an edition and each calling for a coupon response. This is called an A/B split. The publisher arranges to distribute both sections equally in the same territory or in two adjacent territories with the same demographics. The advertiser can then readily compare results. The basic principle is that there is to be no difference between places where the ad is run; the only difference is in the two ads.

Those magazines that provide split-run capabilities are listed in a separate section of the *Consumer Magazine Standard Rates and Data*. There are a number of restrictions on using split-runs. For example, ads usually must be full-page insertions and some magazines will accept only four-color ads. Except for the basic A/B split, split-runs normally conform to regional editions—that is, different copy can be provided for different regional editions, but not within a region.

Split-run charges vary from publication to publication. For A/B splits, there is usually an extra flat charge. For multiregional runs, the cost will vary by the number of copy changes and may be expressed as a percentage of the total insertion cost. Premium charges for split-runs are noncommissionable in most magazines.

MAGAZINE CIRCULATION

Media planners don't buy magazines, television spots, or outdoor signs; they buy people. More specifically, they buy certain groups of people who are presently or prospectively customers for their products. As with other media, magazine rates are based on the circulation that a publisher promises to deliver to advertisers, referred to as the *guaranteed circulation*. Since the guaranteed circulation is the number of readers the advertisers pays for, it is also known as the *rate base*. In our discussion, ''readers'' refers to paid circulation rather than pass-along readers.

The failure of a magazine to meet its guaranteed circulation will result in a rebate to the advertiser. However, the damage to a magazine that fails to meet its rate base can be significant far beyond the loss of money. Since there are so many competing magazines, advertisers may well choose other titles if they perceive a magazine's circulation is falling.

Recently, a few magazines have voluntarily reduced their rate base. Usually the reason given is that the magazine wants to consolidate its readership into a more targeted market segment and thereby make itself more attractive and less expensive to advertisers. In fact, advertisers suspect that the magazine lowered its rate base because it knew its circulation was going to decrease.

Regardless of why a particular magazine lowers its rate base, it is clear that publishers are worried about the increasing costs of maintaining circulation. Currently, 27.6 percent of total magazine revenues are allocated to circulation costs. The reduction of a magazine's rate base can save advertising dollars for agencies and circulation dollars for publishers. But can the magazine's image survive such a cut?[6]

Measuring Magazine Audiences

We now turn to the issue of how publishers verify the circulation and readership of their magazines. Advertisers normally will not purchase a magazine unless its publisher can provide independent verification of the magazine's readership.

A magazine's circulation determines its rate base—the larger number of readers, the higher the cost. Audit Bureau of Circulations (ABC), Simmons Market Research Bureau (SMRB), and Mediamark Research, Inc. (MRI) provide circulation and readership data. *Advertising Age*, the *major* trade publication of the advertising industry, boasts 317,382 readers—which has been verified by a new Supplemental Data Report, issued by the Audit Bureau of Circulations. They claim that figure makes it the *leading publication in the ad industry*.

The Audit Bureau of Circulations. The Audit Bureau of Circulations (ABC) is the largest of several auditing organizations that verify magazine circulation. The ABC provides two basic services: the Publisher's Statements, which report six-month periods ending on June 30 and December 31; and the ABC Audit, which annually audits the data provided in the Publisher's Statements. The ABC reports total circulation, as well as circulation figures by state, by county size, and per issue during each six-month period. The ABC reports also state the manner in which circulation was obtained—for example, by subscription, newsstand sales—and any discounts or premiums provided to subscribers. Exhibit 11.17 is a sample of the ABC Publisher's Statement.

The ABC reports are very matter-of-fact documents that deal only with primary readers. They do not offer information about product usage, demographic characteristics of readers, or pass-along readership. These issues are left to another group of companies known as syndicated readership services.

Syndicated Magazine Readership Research. Advertisers are, of course, interested in the primary readers of magazines. But they are also interested in who these readers are

[6]Amy Alson, ''Clip and Save,'' *Marketing & Media Decisions*, February 1988, p. 35.

EXHIBIT 11.17

ABC reports give advertisers insights into the strength and source of magazines' circulation. (Courtesy: The Audit Bureau of Circulations.)

PROTOTYPE MAGAZINE

NEW YORK, NEW YORK 10017

Magazine Publisher's Statement

Average Paid Circulation

For Six Months Ending December 31, (Year)

1,795,598

Publisher's Compilation - Subject to Audit

Audit Bureau of Circulations

123 North Wacker Drive - Chicago, Illinois 60606

and what they buy, as well as in the pass-along readers who are given the publications. Currently there are two primary sources of syndicated readership research: Simmons Market Research Bureau, Inc. (SMRB), and Mediamark Research, Inc. (MRI).

Simmons Market Research Bureau, Inc., (SMRB) and Media-mark Research, Inc., (MRI). *The two major sources of magazine readership and purchase data for consumers magazines.*

SMRB. The older of the two services, SMRB dates to 1963 and is currently owned by the J. Walter Thompson advertising agency. SMRB selects a sample of approximately 25,000 households, which produce 19,000 completed questionnaires. SMRB also measures 110 magazines through personal interviews and leave-behind diaries.

The Simmons interviewer shows the respondent a deck of cards, each with a magazine logo printed on it. The respondent is asked if he or she "did see," "did not see," or "may have seen" that particular magazine. Then the magazines that were not seen are set aside and respondents are asked to look through sample copies of the others and to indicate which specific issues they read. This technique is called *through-the-book*. Finally, respondents fill out an extensive questionnaire indicating purchase behavior, other media usage, demographic characteristics, and psychographic information (see Exhibit 11.18).

MRI. The MRI service is similar in many ways to SMRB. It uses a sample of about 20,000 households and utilizes personal interviews to gather data. MRI uses two waves of 10,000 interviews each to gather information for its two annual reports. As with SMRB, data are gathered concerning a respondent's demographic characteristics, media exposure, and product usage. The primary difference between MRI and SMRB is in how magazine reader exposure is determined. Like SMRB, MRI uses the magazine logo card technique. But instead of asking respondents to actually go through each magazine they indicate they have seen, the interviewer elicits information concerning how recently respondents saw the publication. This is called the *recent-reading* technique. Since this is a faster technique than Simmons's through-the-book method, MRI measures 280 magazines, or more than twice the number Simmons measures.

As is true of most audience research, MRI and SMRB provide only estimates. However, it is rare for a media plan to be presented without some reference to one or both of these services. Advertising agencies and publishers are extremely concerned

0505
P-13

BALL POINT PEN: BOUGHT IN LAST 12 MONTHS AND FOR WHOM
(ADULTS)

0505
P-13

		TOTAL U.S. '000	BOUGHT IN LAST 12 MONTHS A '000	B % DOWN	C % ACROSS	D INDX	FOR SELF A '000	B % DOWN	C % ACROSS	D INDX	FOR SOMEONE ELSE A '000	B % DOWN	C % ACROSS	D INDX	A '000	B % DOWN	C % ACROSS	D INDX
TOTAL		169460	55675	100.0	32.9	100	48346	100.0	28.5	100	17206	100.0	10.2	100				
MAGAZINES	QUINTILE 1	31709	11504	20.7	36.3	110	9811	20.3	30.9	108	3479	20.2	11.0	108				
	QUINTILE 2	36823	13082	23.5	35.5	108	11263	23.3	30.6	107	4132	24.0	11.2	111				
	QUINTILE 3	29136	9323	16.7	32.0	97	8065	16.7	27.7	97	2932	17.0	10.1	99				
	QUINTILE 4	35659	12071	21.7	33.9	103	10759	22.3	30.2	106	3732	21.7	10.5	103				
	QUINTILE 5	36133	9695	17.4	26.8	82	8448	17.5	23.4	82	2932	17.0	8.1	80				
NEWSPAPERS	QUINTILE 1	32367	11022	19.8	34.1	104	9643	19.9	29.8	104	3562	20.7	11.0	108				
	QUINTILE 2	45475	14796	26.6	32.5	99	12767	26.4	28.1	98	4807	27.9	10.6	104				
	QUINTILE 3	24126	7703	13.8	31.9	97	6784	14.0	28.1	99	2293	13.3	9.5	94				
	QUINTILE 4	35013	11747	21.1	33.6	102	10140	21.0	29.0	102	3772	21.9	10.8	106				
	QUINTILE 5	32480	10407	18.7	32.0	98	9012	18.6	27.7	97	2773	16.1	8.5	84				
OUTDOOR	QUINTILE 1	33503	11279	20.3	33.7	102	9971	20.6	29.8	104	3461	20.1	10.3	102				
	QUINTILE 2	33984	11027	19.8	32.4	99	9539	19.7	28.1	98	3353	19.5	9.9	97				
	QUINTILE 3	33294	10745	19.3	32.3	98	9278	19.2	27.9	98	3422	19.9	10.3	101				
	QUINTILE 4	33570	11171	20.1	33.3	101	9585	19.8	28.6	100	3612	21.0	10.8	106				
	QUINTILE 5	35109	11454	20.6	32.6	99	9972	20.6	28.4	100	3359	19.5	9.6	94				
RADIO-DRIVE	QUINTILE 1	33743	11494	20.6	34.1	104	9934	20.5	29.4	103	3831	22.3	11.4	112				
TIME	QUINTILE 2	35287	12026	21.6	34.1	104	10434	21.6	29.6	104	3761	21.9	10.7	105				
	QUINTILE 3	34469	11488	20.6	33.3	101	9969	20.6	28.9	101	3502	20.4	10.2	100				
	QUINTILE 4	31536	10074	18.1	31.9	97	8589	17.8	27.2	95	3289	19.1	10.4	103				
	QUINTILE 5	34425	10594	19.0	30.8	94	9420	19.5	27.4	96	2824	16.4	8.2	81				
RADIO-MID-	TERCILE 1	47608	15761	28.3	33.1	101	13527	28.0	28.4	100	5020	29.2	10.5	104				
DAY	TERCILE 2	47515	15902	28.6	33.5	102	13860	28.7	29.2	102	4946	28.7	10.4	103				
	TERCILE 3	74338	24012	43.1	32.3	98	20958	43.4	28.2	99	7240	42.1	9.7	96				
RADIO-TOTAL	QUINTILE 1	34074	11513	20.7	33.8	103	10029	20.7	29.4	103	3762	21.9	11.0	109				
	QUINTILE 2	34813	12113	21.8	34.8	106	10372	21.5	29.8	104	3807	22.1	10.9	108				
	QUINTILE 3	33542	10811	19.4	32.2	98	9389	19.4	28.0	98	3473	20.2	10.4	102				
	QUINTILE 4	34656	11317	20.3	32.7	99	9732	20.1	28.1	98	3522	20.5	10.2	100				
	QUINTILE 5	32376	9922	17.8	30.6	93	8823	18.2	27.3	96	2642	15.4	8.2	80				
TV-PRIME	QUINTILE 1	34053	10740	19.3	31.5	96	9169	19.0	26.9	94	3388	19.7	9.9	98				
TIME	QUINTILE 2	33672	11138	20.0	33.1	101	9571	19.8	28.4	100	3610	21.0	10.7	106				
	QUINTILE 3	34555	11895	21.4	34.4	105	10210	21.1	29.5	104	3979	23.1	11.5	113				
	QUINTILE 4	33076	11021	19.8	33.3	101	9680	20.0	29.3	103	3202	18.6	9.7	95				
	QUINTILE 5	34104	10882	19.5	31.9	97	9716	20.1	28.5	100	3027	17.6	8.9	87				
TV-DAYTIME	TERCILE 1	48829	15636	28.1	32.0	97	13577	28.1	27.8	97	4811	28.0	9.9	97				
	TERCILE 2	49453	17732	31.8	35.9	109	15552	32.2	31.4	110	5449	31.7	11.0	109				
	TERCILE 3	71178	22307	40.1	31.3	95	19216	39.7	27.0	95	6946	40.4	9.8	96				
TV-TOTAL	QUINTILE 1	33671	10486	18.8	31.1	95	9030	18.7	26.8	94	3129	18.2	9.3	92				
	QUINTILE 2	33378	10984	19.7	32.9	100	9438	19.5	28.3	99	3583	20.8	10.7	106				
	QUINTILE 3	34108	12016	21.6	35.2	107	10484	21.7	30.7	108	3769	21.9	11.1	109				
	QUINTILE 4	34577	11403	20.5	33.0	100	10025	20.7	29.0	102	3537	20.6	10.2	101				
	QUINTILE 5	33727	10786	19.4	32.0	97	9370	19.4	27.8	97	3188	18.5	9.5	93				
MAGAZINES-NEWSPAPERS: DUAL		43365	15507	27.9	35.8	109	13295	27.5	30.7	107	4872	28.3	11.2	111				
MAGAZINE IMPERATIVE		39453	13919	25.0	35.3	107	12014	24.9	30.5	107	4173	24.3	10.6	104				
NEWSPAPER IMPERATIVE		47258	14344	25.8	30.4	92	12666	26.2	26.8	94	4636	26.9	9.8	97				
MAGAZINES-OUTDOOR: DUAL		34635	11494	20.6	33.2	101	9882	20.4	28.5	100	3760	21.9	10.9	107				
MAGAZINE IMPERATIVE		51412	18398	33.0	35.8	109	15768	32.6	30.7	108	5569	32.4	10.8	107				
OUTDOOR IMPERATIVE		52775	16709	30.0	31.7	96	14736	30.5	27.9	98	5052	29.4	9.6	94				
MAGAZINES-RADIO: DUAL		35811	12895	23.2	36.0	110	11070	22.9	30.9	108	4044	23.5	11.3	111				
MAGAZINE IMPERATIVE		49992	16877	30.3	33.8	103	14505	30.0	29.0	102	5156	30.0	10.3	102				
RADIO IMPERATIVE		51616	16237	29.2	31.5	96	14109	29.2	27.3	96	5436	31.6	10.5	104				
MAGAZINES-TELEVISION: DUAL		31205	10364	18.6	33.2	101	8761	18.1	28.1	98	3564	20.7	11.4	112				
MAGAZINE IMPERATIVE		55053	19865	35.7	36.1	110	17256	35.7	31.3	110	5853	34.0	10.6	105				
TELEVISION IMPERATIVE		55985	17635	31.7	31.5	96	15464	32.0	27.6	97	5319	30.9	9.5	94				
NEWSPAPERS-OUTDOOR: DUAL		35670	11896	21.4	33.4	102	10398	21.5	29.2	102	3683	21.4	10.3	102				
NEWSPAPER IMPERATIVE		56671	18671	33.5	32.9	100	16089	33.3	28.4	100	6039	35.1	10.7	105				
OUTDOOR IMPERATIVE		49120	16174	29.1	32.9	100	14027	29.0	28.6	100	4996	29.0	10.2	100				
NEWSPAPERS-RADIO: DUAL		36250	12260	22.0	33.8	103	10461	21.6	28.9	101	4320	25.1	11.9	117				
NEWSPAPER IMPERATIVE		56248	17973	32.3	32.0	97	15765	32.6	28.0	98	5394	31.3	9.6	94				
RADIO IMPERATIVE		49792	17048	30.6	34.2	104	14803	30.6	29.7	104	5148	29.9	10.3	102				
NEWSPAPERS-TELEVISION: DUAL		35932	11703	21.0	32.6	99	10169	21.0	28.3	99	3796	22.1	10.6	104				
NEWSPAPER IMPERATIVE		56808	18962	34.1	33.4	102	16578	34.3	29.2	102	6001	34.9	10.6	104				
TELEVISION IMPERATIVE		49239	16149	29.0	32.8	100	13998	29.0	28.4	100	4642	27.0	9.4	93				
OUTDOOR-RADIO: DUAL		35414	12021	21.6	33.9	103	10475	21.7	29.6	104	3772	21.9	10.7	105				
OUTDOOR IMPERATIVE		52399	16486	29.6	31.5	96	14411	29.8	27.5	96	4902	28.5	9.4	92				
RADIO IMPERATIVE		53418	18172	32.6	34.0	104	15658	32.4	29.3	103	5907	34.3	11.1	109				
OUTDOOR-TELEVISION: DUAL		31694	10398	18.7	32.8	100	9159	18.9	28.9	101	2964	17.2	9.4	92				
OUTDOOR IMPERATIVE		55457	18333	32.9	33.1	101	16048	33.2	28.9	101	5777	33.6	10.4	103				
TELEVISION IMPERATIVE		55404	18066	32.4	32.6	99	15438	31.9	27.9	98	5781	33.6	10.4	103				
RADIO-TELEVISION: DUAL		32024	10716	19.2	33.5	102	9292	19.2	29.0	102	3450	20.1	10.8	106				
RADIO IMPERATIVE		56655	19176	34.4	33.8	103	16571	34.3	29.2	103	6057	35.2	10.7	105				
TELEVISION IMPERATIVE		55753	17682	31.8	31.7	97	15339	31.7	27.5	96	5309	30.9	9.5	94				

SIMMONS MARKET RESEARCH BUREAU, INC. 1985

*A SINGLE ASTERISK IN THE COLUMN OR ROW TOTAL INDICATES THAT THE CORRESPONDING PERCENTAGES DOWN (COLUMN) OR ACROSS (ROW) ARE SUBJECT TO SIGNIFICANT SAMPLING VARIABILITY AND SHOULD BE USED WITH CAUTION
** A DOUBLE ASTERISK IN THE COLUMN OR ROW TOTAL INDICATES THAT THE CORRESPONDING PERCENTAGES DOWN (COLUMN) OR ACROSS (ROW) ARE TOO UNSTABLE FOR RELIABLE USE. THEY ARE SHOWN FOR CONSISTENCY ONLY.

EXHIBIT 11.18

Example of magazine readership data. How to read the SMRB report: Reading from the top, there are 169,460,000 total adults in the United States. Of these, 55,675,000 bought a ball-point pen during the last 12 months, which constitutes 100 percent of the market for pens. It also represents 32.9 percent of total adults. The 32.9 figure then becomes the basic index (100 in column D) for comparisons of other media and market segments. (Courtesy: Simmons Market Research Bureau, Inc.: 1985 Study of Media and Markets.)

about the accuracy of the figures provided by these services, so MRI and SMRB are constantly refining their sampling, methodology, and interviewing techniques to assure the greatest possible accuracy. Exhibit 11.19 offers a summary of both services.

Magazine Merchandising Services

> ***Magazine merchandising.*** *The practice of magazine publishers promoting those companies who advertise in their publications.*

As competition among magazines increases, publishers search for ways to differentiate their publications from others in the same field. The most important way to accomplish this differentiation is through the editorial product. However, since many magazines are very similar in editorial approach, cost, and distribution, publishers are turning more and more to merchandising services to gain a competitive advantage.

Merchandising consists of "benefits given to an advertiser beyond pages in the magazine."[7] Merchandising services can take many forms. Among the most frequently used are:

Magazines "merchandise" themselves—by advertising their other promotion activities to would-be advertisers. *Nation's Business* combines print with television. Their *Ad Plus* plan is aimed at advertisers who buy $100,000 or more in magazine space. They also receive a broadcast schedule equal to half their print investment on ESPN.

1. "As advertised in" point-of-purchase displays and other promotions. These bring the prestige of the magazine to the retail floor and act as an excellent reminder to prospects.
2. Direct-mail campaigns to retailers that alert retailers to future advertising efforts and build retail support for national brands. These mailings can also be used to increase retail co-op advertising.
3. Some magazines provide shopping guides listing the advertisers in each issue. These not only give advertisers additional promotion, but also tell readers where they can write or call for additional product information.
4. Magazines often sponsor shows and in-store promotions to promote themselves and their

[7]"Need More Ad Pages? Try Creative Merchandising," *Folio,* January 1988, p. 57.

EXHIBIT 11.19

MRI and SMRB demonstrate significant differences in their methodologies. (Courtesy: Standard Rates & Data Service.)

HOW SYNDICATED CONSUMER MAGAZINE STUDIES COMPARE

	SMRB	MRI
Who is studied?	Adults 18+	Adults 18+
Areas studied:	Continental U.S.	Continental U.S. & 10 Selected Markets
Method of Data Collection:	Personal Interview & Leave Behind Diary	Personal Interview & Leave Behind Diary
Sampling Method:	Area probability of households with random selection of respondents in each household	Area probability of households with random selection of male or female in each sample household
Who Collects Data:	Interviewers under control of SMAB Field Departments	Chilton Research Services
Number of Interviews Per Year:	19,000 original interviews 16,000 re-interviews 4-6 weeks after original interviews	20,000 national & between 1,500 & 2,000 in each of the 10 selected markets
Incentives Given To Encourage Respondent Cooperation:	N/A	$10.00
Primary Magazine Audience Measurement Technique:	"Through the book" to identify average issue audience	"Recent Reading" to identify the number of people reading any issue of a magazine during its publication period.
Number of Magazines Studied:	110	243
Magazine Measurements Provided:	Average issue audience In-home and total audiences Audience accumulation Net unduplicated audience for various magazine combinations Quintile distribution of magazine readership	Total audience Primary audience Cumulative audience Audience turnover Magazine Page Exposure (MPX)
Qualitative Magazine Measurements available:		Place of reading Reading time Reading days Reader actions Rating of magazine Interest in Advertising Percent of pages opened
Other Media Studied:	Newspapers TV Radio Outdoor Yellow Pages Cable & Pay TV	Newspapers Radio TV Outdoor Cable & Pay TV
Other Measurements:	Demographics Media Imperatives* Product/Brand usage for 800 categories Psychographics	Demographics Lifestyles Product/Brand usage for 450 categories
Report Formats:	Printed volumes On-line access to data base Tape Disk	Printed volumes On-line access to data-base Tape Disk
Contact Info:	SMRB 219 E. 42nd St. NY, NY 10017 (212) 867-1414	Mediamark Research, Inc. 341 Madison Ave. NY, NY 10017 (212) 599-0444

advertisers. For example, *Mademoiselle* and *Seventeen* sponsor fashion events. Other magazines have sponsored cooking, sewing, and similar contests with advertiser tie-ins. One of the most widely recognized consumer merchandising promotions is the *Good Housekeeping* Seal, which carries a limited warranty courtesy of the publisher.

PLANNING A MAGAZINE MEDIA SCHEDULE

Currently more than 50 national corporations are spending at least $20 million in magazine advertising. Magazines occupy an important position in the media plans of some of the nation's most sophisticated advertisers for a number of reasons.

Exhibit 11.20 shows two examples of media plans built around the creative use of

EXHIBIT 11.20

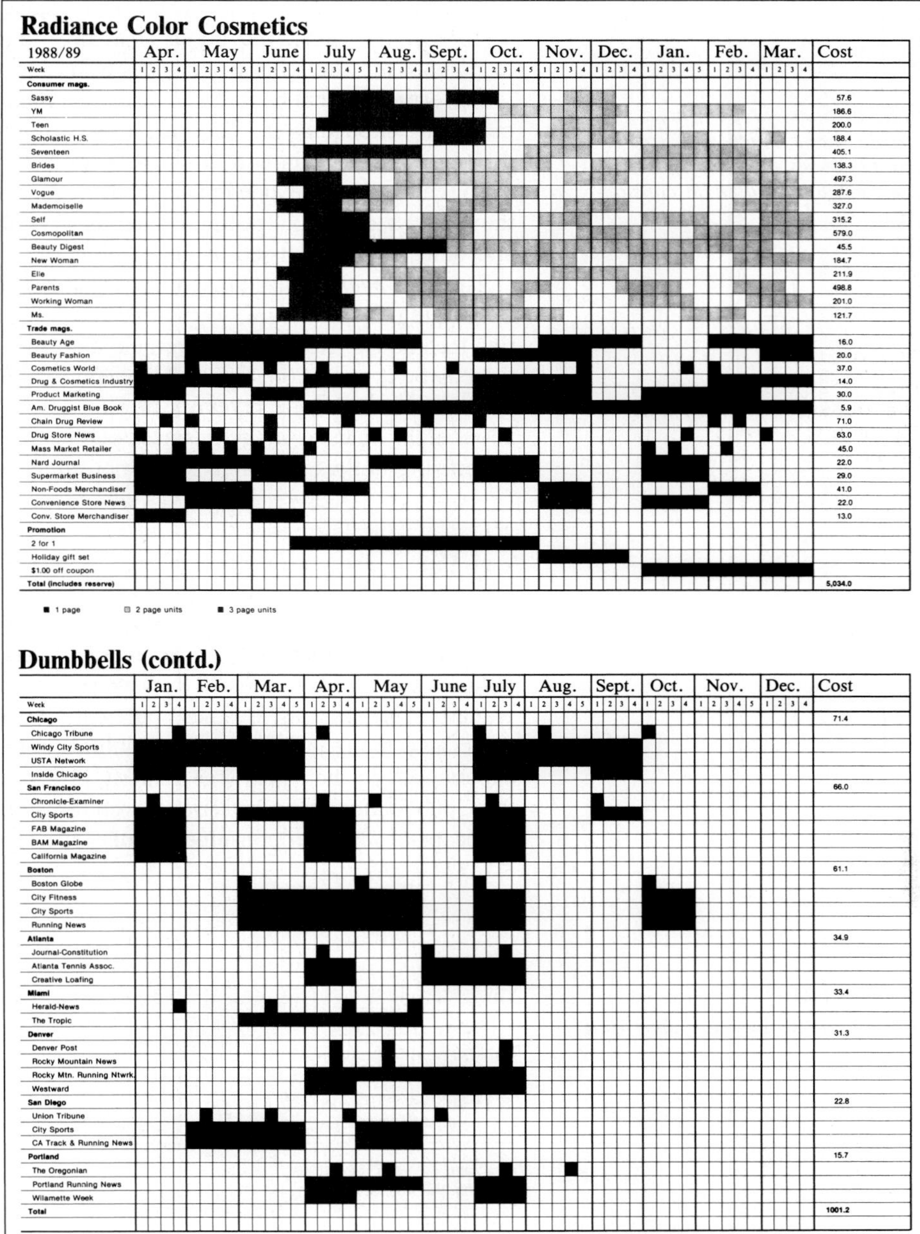

Magazine advertising continues to be popular, with 21% of *national* advertising dollars invested in various periodicals. Only television attracts more national ad revenue. *Gerber Products* uses *both print and television* to capitalize on its image and position as the leading baby food marketer.

magazines. Note the manner in which the media schedules follow logically from the marketing goals.

What did these advertisers have in common that led them to make this type of expenditure in magazines? The common thread is that magazines, either alone or as a supplemental medium, solve specific marketing problems. Advertisers currently invest 21 percent of *national* advertising dollars in magazines, ranking magazines second only to television. Consumer magazines also rank second from the bottom in CPM increases during the last decade. Only radio had a lower rate of increase.

THE BUSINESS PRESS AND BUSINESS-TO-BUSINESS ADVERTISING

A paper company salesperson calls on a grocery chain to sell bags for the checkout counter; a concrete company advertises in a magazine distributed to paving contractors; a resort hotel sponsors a booth at a travel agents' convention. All of these selling techniques are examples of business-to-business marketing, a $100 billion enterprise.

The business press. *Those publications which are directed to audiences in the trade channel, excluding ultimate consumers.*

It is estimated that business advertising accounts for approximately $8 billion of total marketing expenditures. The media mix in the world of business marketing is much different from that in consumer marketing. Exhibit 11.21 gives a breakdown of the major categories of expenditure on business advertising. Note that trade magazines are the largest segment. Expenditures in business advertising also go to publicity, catalogs, and other areas not listed in the exhibit.

The term *media* is used much more broadly in business advertising than in consumer advertising. In the future, we will probably see even greater diversification of promotion techniques. However, the principal characteristic of business advertising will continue to be competition. For example, it is estimated that there are over 9,000 business publications with total revenues of $2.5 billion. To put this in perspective, there are about eight times as many business publications competing for less than one-half the advertising dollars available in the consumer field.

Characteristics of the Business Press

Audiences. The audience of the typical business magazine is much different from its consumer counterpart or the general population. These readers are older, better educated, and have higher incomes than the population as a whole. Exhibit 11.22 compares readers of the average business publication to the general population.

Because the readers of business publications are well trained, highly educated, and experienced in their jobs (see Exhibit 11.23), the advertising and editorial matter in these publications must be serious, well researched, and written at a level that would be unacceptably high in consumer media. (See Exhibit 11.24 for an example.)

EXHIBIT 11.21
Expenditures for business advertising.

Trade magazines	35%
Trade shows and exhibits	12
Direct mail	8
Videocassettes, etc.	4
Telemarketing	1

Source: Neal Weinstock, "Leaner Times Bedevil Business Magazines," Advertising Age, *June 20, 1988, p. S-24.*

EXHIBIT 11.22
Business reader profile.

	Business Reader	*U.S. Population*
Age	42.6 years	30.3 years
Education	17 years	12.5
Family income	$44,000	$33,000

Source: "Profile of the Readers of Specialized Business Magazines," Cahners Advertising Research Report #500.0.

Trade magazines are the largest promotional segment for business. Their stiffest competition is direct mail, which can reach smaller segments of consolidated industries. The Day-Glo Color Corporation is using *both media* to display their brilliant fluorescent colors used in packaging, as well as in fashion and leisure-time products. In addition to the print campaign in *Packaging Digest*, a direct-mail piece featuring fluorescent sunglasses was mailed to select prospects.

Competition. As we saw in Exhibit 11.21, the media mix in the business advertising sector is much different from that in consumer advertising. While business publications get the major share of advertising revenue, they are faced with a growing competitive situation. Since they are designed to reach a targeted audience with a specific message, the CPM level of the typical business publication is extremely high compared to CPMs for consumer magazines and other consumer media.

In this way, business publications resemble direct mail, which is their primary competitor in many market segments. Most experts predict that competition from direct mail will increase as major industries continue to consolidate sales among fewer companies. Fewer customers make techniques such as personal selling and direct mail, perhaps using elaborate videocassettes and other means, more practical options. In many industrial sectors, less than ten companies account for 50 percent or more of total sales. In such a situation, the cost per prospect is an irrelevant figure. At any rate,

EXHIBIT 11.23
On average, the specialized business magazine reader has been in his or her respective industry 13.7 years, and with his or her current company 11.5 years. (Courtesy: Cahners Publishing Company.)

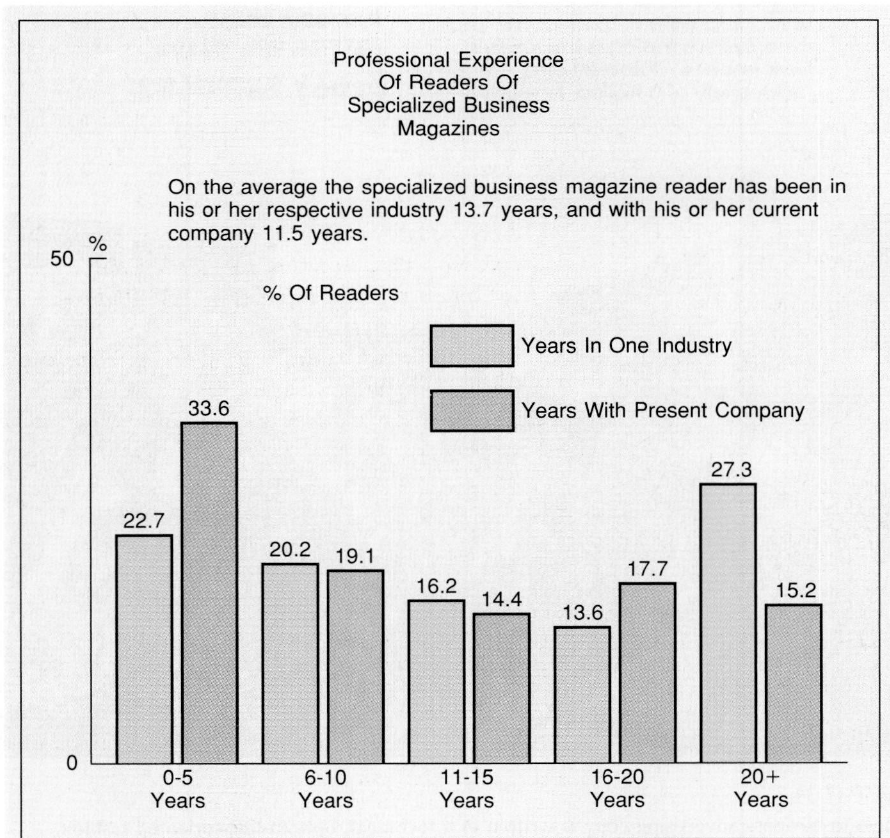

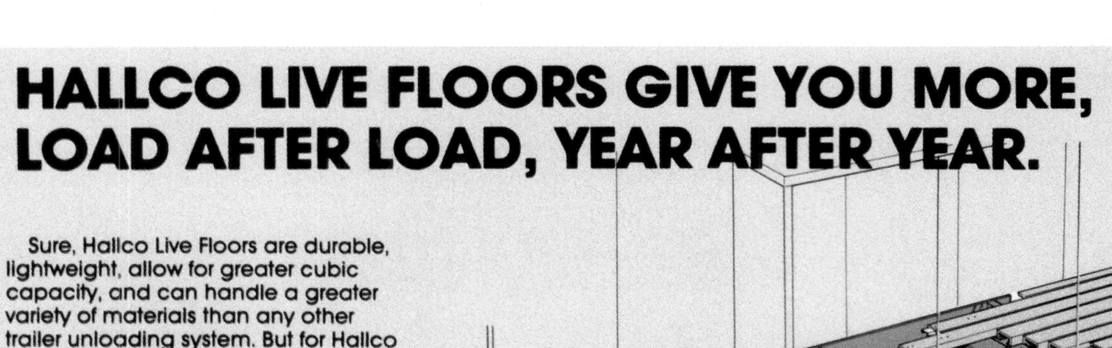

EXHIBIT 11.24

Business-to-business advertising copy is written in a technical, bottom-line–oriented fashion. (Courtesy: Hallco Manufacturing Company.)

EXHIBIT 11.25

Business magazines face stiff competition for ad dollars. (Courtesy: *Advertising Age*.)

Business magazine ad revenues lag in growth

($ in millions)

	Total U.S. ad spending*	% change	Ad revenue for business magazines**	% change**	Business as % of total magazine revenues**	Number of business titles**
1987	$109,800(E)	7.60%	$2,231	3.74%	2.03%	585
1986	102,090	7.90	2,150	1.70	2.11	570
1985	94,750	7.90	2,114	15.75	2.23	600

(E) estimate
Source: *Data provided by McCann-Erickson
**Business magazine revenues provided by MMS-Rome Reports

business magazines have lagged behind growth in general advertising, and their share of total magazine revenues has also declined (see Exhibit 11.25).

Research. The most consistent complaint from business-to business advertisers is the lack of audience research and media performance data. As we will see later in this section, auditing organizations exist to give advertisers basic reader data. However, a majority of publications are not audited, which means there is little independent readership information available in the mode of SMRB or MRI.

One business publication media director described the shortcomings of the field this way: "If the main criteria for measuring the business press is quality of circulation, coverage of buyer/specifiers, editorial quality, readership and response documentation, advertising leadership, etc., then we need better common information than what we now receive.[8]

McGraw-Hill Research has conducted a great deal of research on selling to business. These studies have determined a seven-stage program:

1. Establish contact.
2. Create awareness.
3. Arouse interest.
4. Build preference.
5. Make specific proposals.
6. Close the order.
7. Keep customers sold.[9]

Personal selling. *The business press often complements personal sales approaches which close the deal introduced through business-to-business advertising.*

Indications are that advertising is most efficient in accomplishing steps 1, 2, 3, 4, and 7, but that personal selling is more successful in making specific proposals and closing the order. It is clear from this research that business advertising must complement other sales techniques. Successful business publications realize their role and sell the medium as a *part of,* rather than as the entire, sales function.

Pass-along Readership. The typical consumer magazine has a relatively short life and low pass-along readership. Occasionally a recipe will be clipped or a magazine will be passed on to a neighbor, but consumer magazines are largely read for pleasure and tossed aside. Advertisers in these magazines view pass-along readership as vastly inferior to primary readership.

Business publication advertisers, in contrast, view pass-along readership as quite valuable. For one thing, readers don't normally browse through *Electronic Design* or *Concrete Construction;* they pay close attention to copy. For another, some business publications limit their circulation in a way that forces pass-along readership. Exhibit 11.26 shows that 86 percent of business publication readers pass along or save all or part of these magazines.

---

[8]David Kalish, "Buyer Backtalk," *Marketing & Media Decisions,* May 1988, p. 100.

[9]"Good Advertising: Tracking Performance After Placement," *The SRDS Report,* November 1987, p. 2.

EXHIBIT 11.26

Twenty-four percent of all respondents save their specialized business magazines for future use.

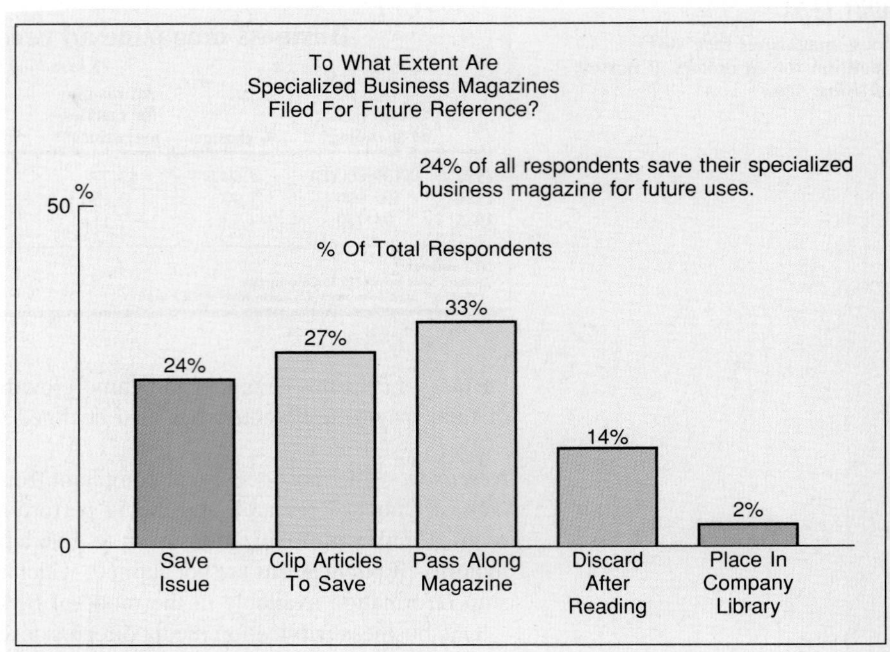

Types of Business-to-Business Publications

Despite the wide array of business publications, they can generally be placed in one of four categories:

- *Trade:* distributive trades
- *Industrial:* manufacturers and builders
- *Management:* top officers of other corporations
- *Professional:* physicians, dentists, architects, and other professional people

Trade papers. *Publications directed primarily to the retail trade.*

Business papers and magazines boast *high editorial and pass-along readership*. That's what The Trump Organization is counting on with its decision to advertise in *Business Week* for its shuttle. *BW* appeals to business executives in a wide variety of markets—but *all* are frequent users of shuttle service. It's also the most frequently distributed magazine in corporate offices, reaching "58% more top managers than *Forbes* and 47% more than *Fortune*."

Trade Papers. Since most nationally advertised products depend upon dealers for their sales, we discuss advertising in trade papers first. Usually, this advertising is prepared by the agency that handles the consumer advertising, and in any new campaign both are prepared at the same time. The term *trade papers* is applied particularly to business publications directed at those who buy products for resale, such as wholesalers jobbers, and retailers. Typical trade papers are *American Druggist, Supermarket News, Chain Store Age, Hardware Retailer, Modern Tire Dealer, Women's Wear Daily,* and *Home Furnishings*.

Almost every business engaged in distributing goods has a trade paper to discuss its problems. Trade papers are the great medium for reporting merchandising news about the products, packaging, prices, deals, and promotions of the manufacturers who cater to the particular industry (see Exhibit 11.27). The chain-store field alone has more than 20 such publications. Druggists have a choice of over 30, and more than 60 different publications are issued for grocers. There are many localized journals, such as *Texas Food Merchant, Michigan Beverage News, Southern Hardware, California Apparel News,* and *Illinois Building News*.

Industrial publications. *Magazines which largely direct their advertising to purchasing agents of major manufacturers.*

Industrial Advertising. As we move into the world where a company in one industry sells its materials, machinery, tools, parts, and equipment to another company for use in making a product or conducting operations, we are in an altogether different ballpark—the industrial-marketing arena.

There are fewer customers in this arena than in the consumer market, and they can be more easily identified. The amount of money involved in a sale may be large—hundreds of thousands of dollars, perhaps even millions—and nothing is bought on

EXHIBIT 11.27

Trade ads are written with the retailer in mind. Note the merchandise display in the insert. (Courtesy: Littelfuse Inc.)

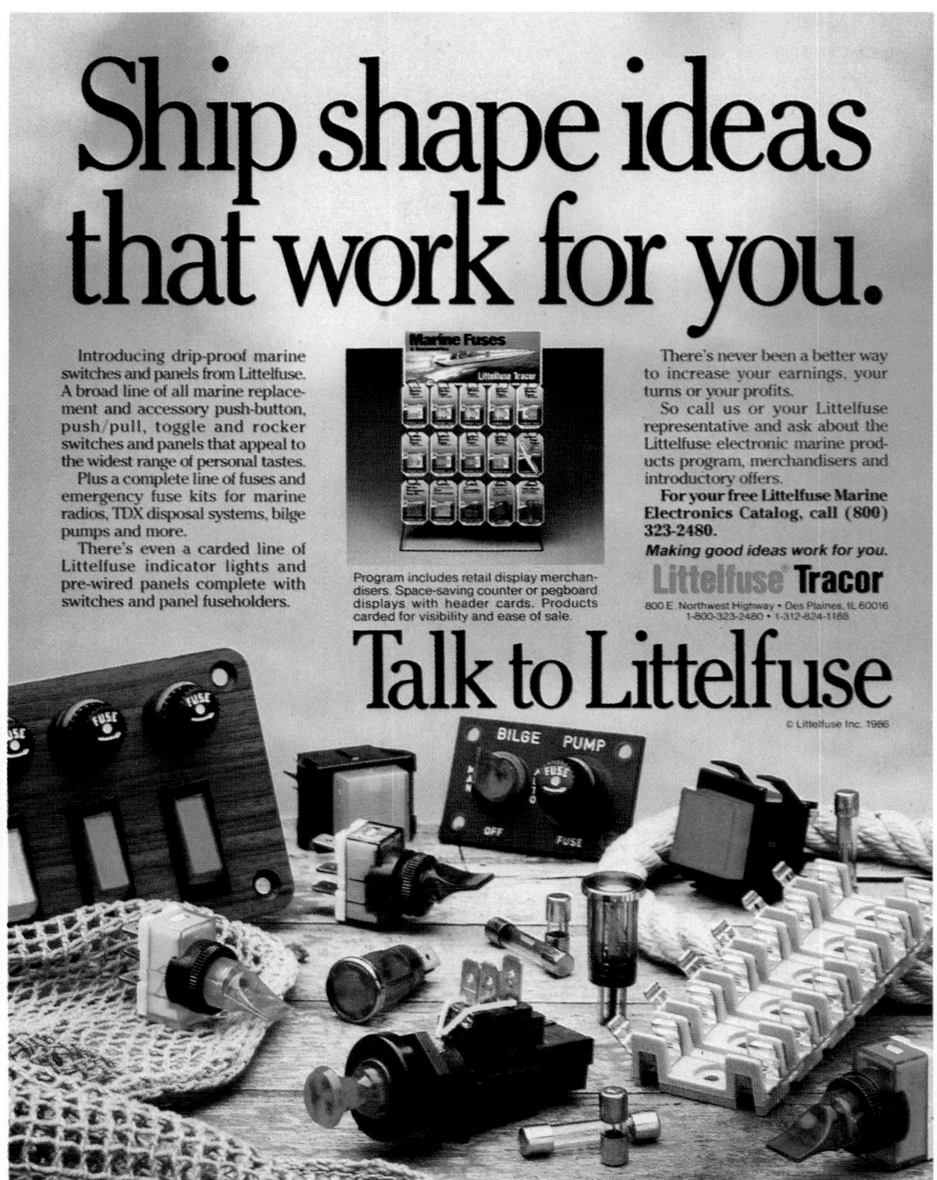

impulse. Many knowledgeable executives with technical skills often share in the buying decision. The sales representative has to have a high degree of professional competence to deal with the industrial market, in which personal selling is the biggest factor in making a sale. Advertising is only a collateral aid used to pave the way for or support the salesperson; hence it receives a smaller share of the marketing budget.

Advertising addressed to people responsible for buying goods needed to make products is called *industrial advertising*. It is designed to reach purchasing agents, plant managers, engineers, comptrollers, and others who have a voice in spending the firm's money (see Exhibit 11.28).

Management Publications. The most difficult group for a publication to reach is managers. After all, even the largest companies have only a relatively few decision makers. When these decision makers are widely dispersed across a number of industries and job descriptions, publications find they must be extremely creative to reach them.

The management category is one that straddles a gray area between consumer and business-to-business publications. Magazines such as *Business Week, Fortune,* and

EXHIBIT 11.28

The typical consumer does not know that many industrial products even exist. (Courtesy: Ashby-Cross Company, Inc.)

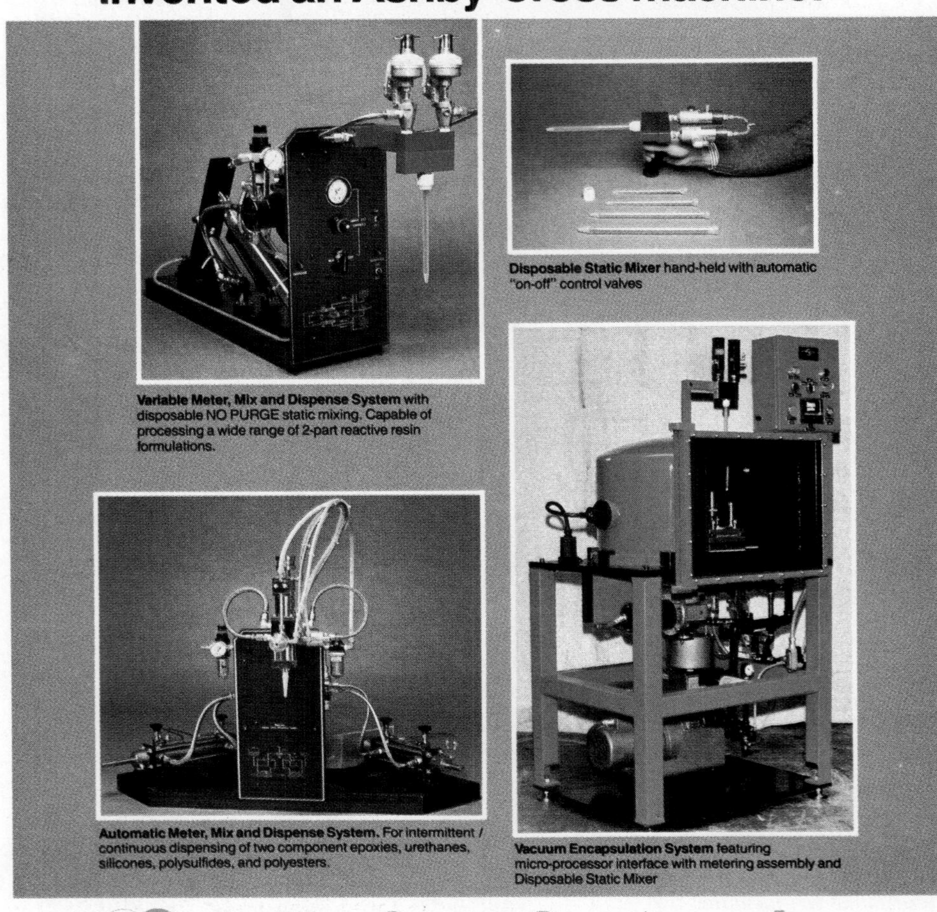

If Leonardo had to cope with Reactive Resins he would have invented an Ashby-Cross machine.
Disposable Static Mixer hand-held with automatic "on-off" control valves
Variable Meter, Mix and Dispense System with disposable NO PURGE static mixing. Capable of processing a wide range of 2-part reactive resin formulations.
Automatic Meter, Mix and Dispense System. For intermittent / continuous dispensing of two component epoxies, urethanes, silicones, polysulfides, and polyesters.
Vacuum Encapsulation System featuring micro-processor interface with metering assembly and Disposable Static Mixer

Ashby-Cross Company, Inc.
P.O. BOX 422, 418 BOSTON STREET, TOPSFIELD, MA 01983 (617) 887-2887

Nation's Business have characteristics that would place them in either the business or the consumer category. Even magazines such as *Time* have at least some of their partial-run editions listed in the *Business Publications SRDS*.

Professional Publications. The Standard Rate and Data Service, in its special business publication edition, includes journals addressed to physicians, surgeons, dentists, lawyers, architects, and other professionals who depend upon these publications to keep abreast of their professions. The editorial content of such journals ranges from reportage about new technical developments to discussions on how to meet client or patient problems better and how to conduct offices more efficiently and profitably. Professional people often recommend or specify the products their patients or clients should order. Therefore, much advertising of a high technical caliber is addressed to them.

Advertising revenue accounts for the major portion of business' magazines financial support. Consumer magazines count more heavily on circulation revenue. *Time,* the number one company with the highest total revenue, $1,752 billion in 1988, had the top revenue magazine, *Time,* in its portfolio. Its ad dollars amounted to $349.7 million, for a 6.4% increase over 1987.

Some Special Features of Business Publication Advertising

Business publications have several practices that are normally not found in consumer magazines. This section briefly discusses the more important ones.

Controlled-circulation business and professional publications. *Sent without cost to people responsible for making buying decisions. To get on, and stay on, such lists, people must state their positions in companies and request annually that they be kept on the list. Also known as qualified-circulation publications.*

Vertical publications. *Business publications dealing with the problems of a specific industry, for example, Chain Store Age, National Petroleum News, Textile World.* See also Horizontal publications.

Horizontal publications. *Business publications addressed to people in the same strata of interest or responsibility, regardless of nature of the company, for example, Purchasing, Maintenance Engineer, Business Week.* See also Vertical publications.

Standard Industrial Classification (SIC). *The division of all industry, by the Bureau of the Budget, into detailed standard classifications identified by code numbers. Useful in making marketing plans.*

Controlled Circulation. In magazine terminology, *free circulation* is called *controlled circulation*. Controlled-circulation publications are delivered to a carefully selected list of people who are influential in making purchase decisions for their industry.

In the early years of business publishing, virtually all subscriptions were paid. During the 1940s, approximately 30 percent of business publishers opted to distribute their publications to readers free of charge. This was the beginning of a growing trend toward controlled-circulation publications.

The trend reached its peak during the 1960s. Since that time, the ratio of controlled to paid circulation has remained constant at about one-third paid to two-thirds controlled.[10] It should be emphasized that a controlled-circulation magazine is not necessarily a secondary publication in the field. Some of the leading business-to-business magazines are distributed this way. Because of the high number of controlled publications, the economics of the business press differs markedly from that of consumer publications. Exhibit 11.29 shows that advertising accounts for approximately 70 percent of business publication revenues, almost 50 percent higher than for consumer magazines.

Vertical and Horizontal Publications. Industrial publications are usually considered either *horizontal* or *vertical*. A vertical publication is one that covers an entire industry. An example is *Baking Industry,* which contains information concerning product quality, marketing, plant efficiency, and packaging.

Horizontal publications are edited for people who are engaged in a single function that cuts across many industries. An example is *Purchasing Magazine,* which is circulated to purchasing managers. It discusses trends and forecasts applicable to all industries.

Standard Industrial Classification System. One thing that greatly facilitates the industrial marketing process is the Standard Industrial Classification (SIC) system, a numbering system established by the United States government. SIC classified more than 4 million manufacturing firms in ten major categories that are subdivided into more specific groups. The code numbering system operates as follows: All major business activities (agriculture, forestry, and fisheries; mining; construction; manufacturing; transportation; communication, and public utilities; wholesale; retail; finance, insurance, and real estate; services, government) are given a two-digit code number. A third and a fourth digit are assigned to identify more specific activities within each major business category. The SIC system works much the same as the Dewey Decimal System. For example:

EXHIBIT 11.29

Unlike consumer magazines, business publications depend overwhelmingly on advertising for financial support. (Courtesy: *Marketing & Media Decisions.*)

Business Magazines' Sources of Revenue

Year	Advertising	Subscriptions
1970	71.1%	28.9%
1977	71.6	28.4
1978	72.6	27.4
1979	71.1	28.9
1980	69.0	31.0
1981	70.0	30.0
1982	70.2	29.8
1983	67.7	32.3
1984	70.0	30.0
1985	71.5	28.5
1986	72.0	28.0
1987	72.2	27.8
1988 (est)	72.6	27.4

Source: James B. Kobak & Co.

[10] "Paid vs. Controlled Circulation . . . Understanding the Numbers Game," *The SRDS Report,* December 1987, p. 1.

- 25 Manufacturers of furniture and fixtures
- 252 Manufacturers of office furniture
- 2521 Manufacturers of wood office furniture
- 2522 Manufacturers of metal office furniture

The great value of the SIC system is that it enables the advertiser to identify and locate specific target markets. Industrial publications usually provide an analysis of circulation by SIC classifications. The advertiser can than pick the publication that reaches the greatest number of people in the appropriate classification, or use the information in buying lists for direct mailings.

Circulation Audits. The leading trade and industrial publications belong to the Business Publications Audit of Circulation, Inc. (BPA), which audits approximately 1,000 business publications (Exhibit 11.30). BPA's audits pay particular attention to the qualifications of people on the controlled list and when they last indicated they wanted the publication.

The Audit Bureau of Circulations performs essentially the same function for over 200 paid-circulation publications, although the ABC's main effort is in the consumer field. Some publications have both ABC and BPA audits, but, as we noted earlier, many, especially the smaller ones, do not offer any circulation-audit report at all.

EXHIBIT 11.30
An example of a BPA circulation audit. (Courtesy: Business Publications Audit of Circulation Report.)

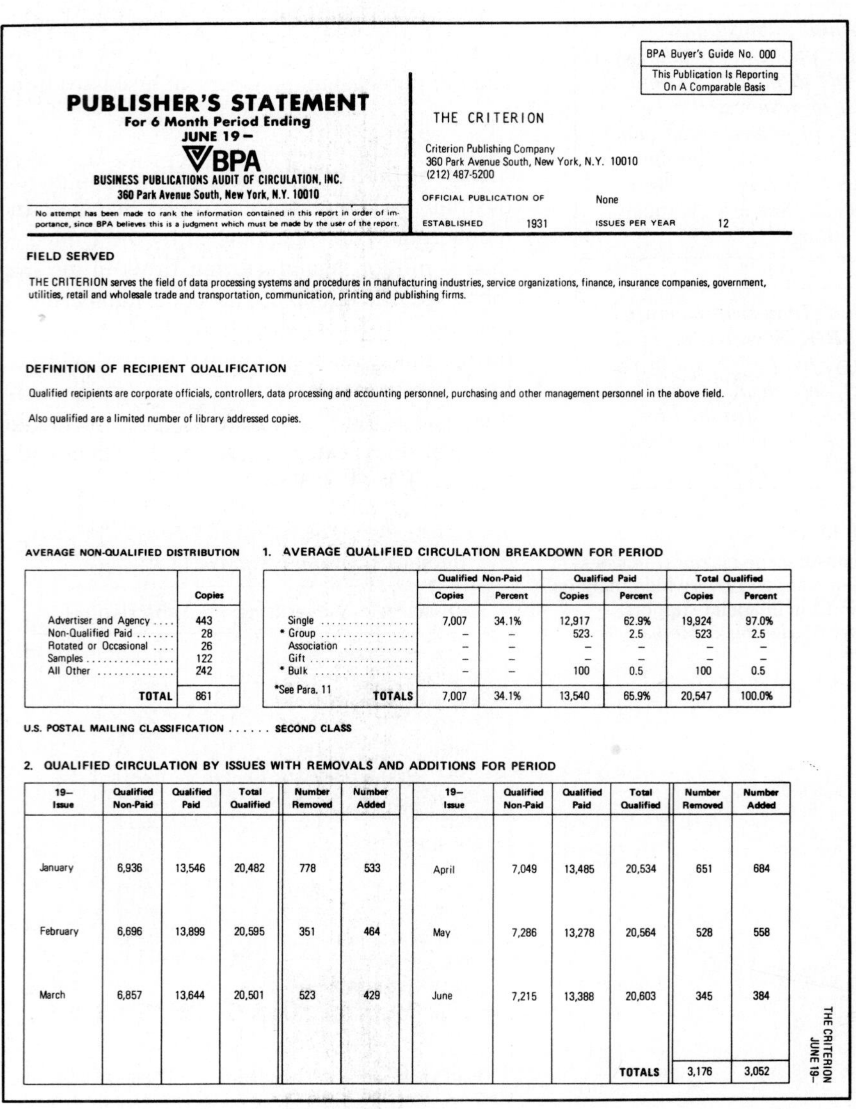

BPA Buyer's Guide No. 000
This Publication Is Reporting On A Comparable Basis

PUBLISHER'S STATEMENT
For 6 Month Period Ending
JUNE 19–
BPA
BUSINESS PUBLICATIONS AUDIT OF CIRCULATION, INC.
360 Park Avenue South, New York, N.Y. 10010

No attempt has been made to rank the information contained in this report in order of importance, since BPA believes this is a judgment which must be made by the user of the report.

THE CRITERION
Criterion Publishing Company
360 Park Avenue South, New York, N.Y. 10010
(212) 487-5200

OFFICIAL PUBLICATION OF None
ESTABLISHED 1931 ISSUES PER YEAR 12

FIELD SERVED

THE CRITERION serves the field of data processing systems and procedures in manufacturing industries, service organizations, finance, insurance companies, government, utilities, retail and wholesale trade and transportation, communication, printing and publishing firms.

DEFINITION OF RECIPIENT QUALIFICATION

Qualified recipients are corporate officials, controllers, data processing and accounting personnel, purchasing and other management personnel in the above field.

Also qualified are a limited number of library addressed copies.

AVERAGE NON-QUALIFIED DISTRIBUTION

	Copies
Advertiser and Agency	443
Non-Qualified Paid	28
Rotated or Occasional	26
Samples	122
All Other	242
TOTAL	861

1. AVERAGE QUALIFIED CIRCULATION BREAKDOWN FOR PERIOD

	Qualified Non-Paid		Qualified Paid		Total Qualified	
	Copies	Percent	Copies	Percent	Copies	Percent
Single	7,007	34.1%	12,917	62.9%	19,924	97.0%
* Group	–	–	523.	2.5	523	2.5
Association	–	–	–	–	–	–
Gift	–	–	–	–	–	–
* Bulk	–	–	100	0.5	100	0.5
*See Para. 11 TOTALS	7,007	34.1%	13,540	65.9%	20,547	100.0%

U.S. POSTAL MAILING CLASSIFICATION ...... SECOND CLASS

2. QUALIFIED CIRCULATION BY ISSUES WITH REMOVALS AND ADDITIONS FOR PERIOD

19– Issue	Qualified Non-Paid	Qualified Paid	Total Qualified	Number Removed	Number Added	19– Issue	Qualified Non-Paid	Qualified Paid	Total Qualified	Number Removed	Number Added
January	6,936	13,546	20,482	778	533	April	7,049	13,485	20,534	651	684
February	6,696	13,899	20,595	351	464	May	7,286	13,278	20,564	528	558
March	6,857	13,644	20,501	523	429	June	7,215	13,388	20,603	345	384
									TOTALS	3,176	3,052

THE CRITERION
JUNE 19–

A third auditing group is the Verified Audit Circulation Company (VAC). Its standards are less strict than those of BPA.

Circulation-audit reports provide the business advertiser with information and statistics to use in selecting the best publications for carrying a product's advertising.

In addition to the auditing companies, there are organizations that track the amount of ad business run in various publications. These services are extremely valuable because they enable a company to follow competitive expenditures and media schedules. One of the major services is the Rome Report (see Exhibit 11.31).

AGRIBUSINESS ADVERTISING

Agribusiness advertising has many similarities to business-to-business advertising. Farm publications are engaged in the same kind of competition business publications face. Although the number of farms and major agribusiness suppliers has decreased in recent years, the number and diversity of media competing for advertising dollars in the sector has grown dramatically. Perhaps the best evidence of the marketing mix in farm advertising is the fact that SRDS has added a section called "Agri-Media" that encompasses Farm Publications, Farm Direct-Response Publications, Agri-Radio, and Agri-Television. In addition to these media, agribusiness firms are increasing their expenditures on sales-promotion campaigns.

There are now approximately 2 million farms, down from 2.37 million in 1983. Annual farm income has remained relatively constant at $50 billion to $60 billion. Exhibit 11.32 shows the growing concentration of farm income among the largest farmers.

In the future, farm magazines will have to compete with other media as a source of in-depth information for farmers. Exhibit 11.33 shows that farm magazines ranked higher than TV and radio in farm news and accuracy of information, which gives them a marketing niche to exploit with both readers and advertisers.

EXHIBIT 11.31

An example of a Rome Report. (Courtesy: Leading National Advertisers.)

TRACKING REPORT FOR WINTERKORN LILLIS - JAN/DEC 1984 — PAGE 14

*** GRAND TOTALS ***

	JAN/DEC 1984			JAN/DEC 1983			CHANGE		
PUBLICATION NAME	PAGES	DOLLARS	%	PAGES	DOLLARS	%	PAGES	DOLLARS	%
AMERICAN LABORATORY	13.75	66,665	9	13.08	56,890	12	0.67	9,775	-4
ANALYTICAL CHEMISTRY	19.00	74,600	10	11.75	43,170	9	7.25	31,430	0
APPLIANCE				0.25	750	0	-.25	-750	0
BIOMEDICAL PRODUCTS	26.75	78,475	10				26.75	78,475	10
BIOTECHNOLOGY				4.00	7,500	2	-4.00	-7,500	-2
CEREAL FOODS WORLD	1.50	2,130	0				1.50	2,130	0
CHAIN ST AGE GEN MER	5.00	29,610	4	4.00	23,460	5	1.00	6,150	-1
CHEMICAL ENGINEERING	1.50	7,890	1				1.50	7,890	1
CHEMICAL EQUIPMENT	1.00	3,500	0				1.00	3,500	0
DISCOUNT STORE NEWS	4.20	21,968	3	3.10	15,201	3	1.10	6,767	0
DRUG & COSMETIC IND	2.25	4,680	1				2.25	4,680	1
ELECTRONIC PRODUCTS	0.25	1,130	0				0.25	1,130	0
ENVIRONMENTAL SCI	6.00	25,170	3	4.00	16,780	4	2.00	8,390	0
FOOD ENGINEERING	1.00	4,240	1	0.75	2,685	1	0.25	1,555	0
GEYERS DEALER TOPICS	2.50	7,950	1	5.00	15,300	3	-2.50	-7,350	-2
GENETIC ENGINEER NEW	13.50	16,790	2	17.50	16,875	4	-4.00	-85	-1
HARDWARE AGE	6.25	29,570	4	4.00	18,060	4	2.25	11,510	0
HARDWARE MERCHANDSR	3.00	12,675	2	3.00	11,655	3	0.00	1,020	-1
HEALTH CARE PROD NEW	1.50	6,840	1	1.50	5,850	1	0.00	990	0
INDUSTRIAL CHEM NEWS	2.00	9,160	1	5.50	20,380	4	-3.50	-11,220	-3
INDUSTRIAL EQPT NEWS	0.50	2,402	0	0.50	3,190	1	0.00	-788	0
INDUSTRIAL RES & DEV				8.50	42,355	9	-8.50	-42,355	-9
JOURNAL WATER POLLU	1.00	1,975	0				1.00	1,975	0
LABORATORY EQUIPMENT	25.46	131,540	17				25.46	131,540	17
LABORATORY MANAGE				1.00	2,575	1	-1.00	-2,575	-1
MATERIAL HAND ENG	1.50	7,050	1				1.50	7,050	1
MEDICAL CARE PROD	3.58	15,950	2				3.58	15,950	2
METLFAX	2.00	2,316	0	2.00	2,184	0	0.00	132	0
MODERN MATERIAL HAND				3.00	14,100	3	-3.00	-14,100	-3
NATIONAL LOCKSMITH	2.00	1,420	0				2.00	1,420	0
NATURE	5.00	12,295	2	3.50	6,830	1	1.50	5,465	0
NEW EQUIPMENT DIGEST	2.75	13,625	2	0.75	3,930	1	2.00	9,695	1
NUCLEAR NEWS	0.25	455	0				0.25	455	0
NUCLEAR PLANT SAFETY	0.25	355	0				0.25	355	0
OFFICE PROD DEALER	5.00	18,250	2	8.00	26,550	6	-3.00	-8,300	-3
OFFICE WORLD NEWS	5.00	16,175	2				5.00	16,175	2
PACKAGING	1.50	6,780	1				1.50	6,780	1
PACKAGING DIGEST	1.00	4,770	1				1.00	4,770	1
PHARMACEUTICAL TECH				7.33	16,576	4	-7.33	-16,576	-4
POWER TRANSMISSION				0.75	2,490	1	-.75	-2,490	-1
RESEARCH & DEVEL	6.25	34,855	5				6.25	34,855	5
SCIENCE	19.25	78,655	10	21.00	77,500	17	-1.75	1,155	-7
TAPPI	0.50	1,788	0	0.25	800	0	0.25	988	0
WATER & WASTES DIG	1.00	2,920	0	1.50	4,005	1	-.50	-1,085	0
WATER TECHNOLOGY				0.50	815	0	-.50	-815	0
****GRAND TOTAL****		756,619			458,456			298,163	65

EXHIBIT 11.32

Farm income is increasingly concentrated in the 1 percent of farms whose income is above $500,000. (Courtesy: Radio Advertising Bureau.)

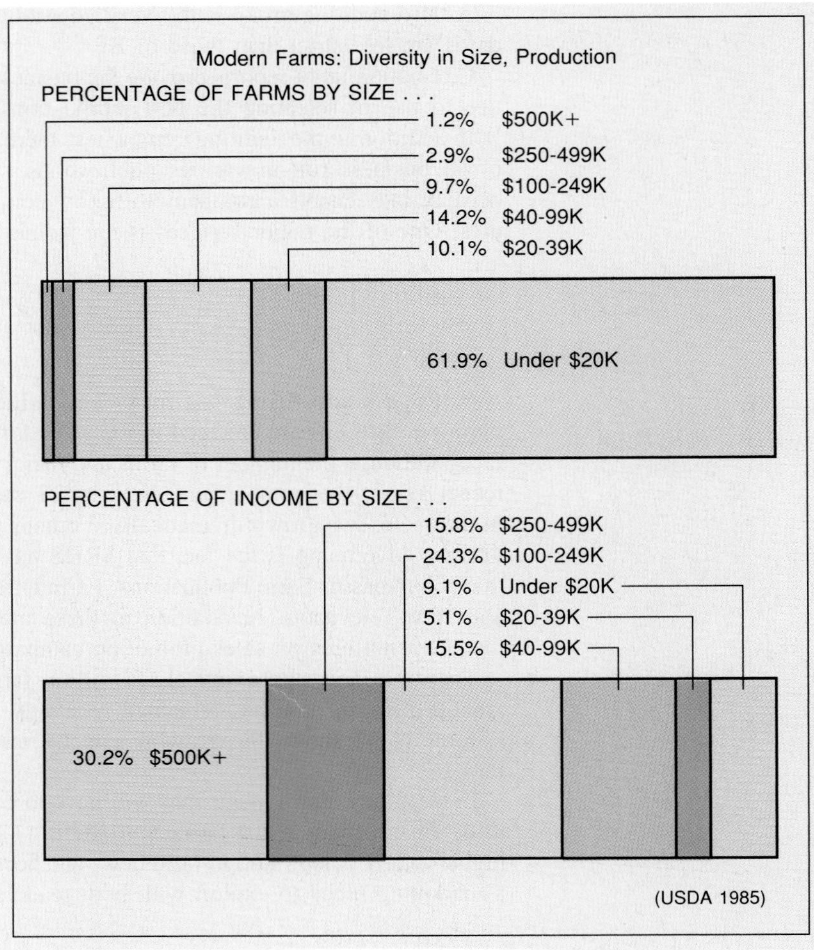

Farm publications are becoming more creative in marketing their publications to advertisers. For many years now, they have been offering advertisers a variety of geographic, demographic, and split-run editions. *Progressive Farmer,* for example, has over 100 combinations of specialized editions. Perhaps no group of businesspersons is more diversified than farmers in terms of product categories, size of operation, and sophistication of individual business.

Farm publications have led the way in reaching specialized markets through a technique called *selective binding.* This involves gathering information on subscribers through questionnaires sent to readers, and then setting up a data base or information bank for each reader. At the printing plant, a computer instructs the machine that binds the magazine to include special sections for subscribers based on their demographic profiles.

To meet the informational needs of *agriculture,* there are three classifications of magazines: (1) general; (2) regional; and (3) vocational. To promote its *horse feed,* Manna Pro of Los Angeles, used *general farm magazines* to get maximum exposure in the market. It mentioned Alysheba, the winningest racehorse ever, as "an opener"—to attract a diversified audience, not just breeders.

The Organization of the Farm Press

Farm magazines may be classified as *general farm magazines, regional farm magazines,* and *vocational farm magazines*. These classifications overlap, however, because a number of the larger magazines have geographical and demographical splits.

General Farm Magazines. The three major publications in this category and their rate bases are: *Farm Journal,* 800,000; *Successful Farming,* 575,000; and *Progressive Farmer,* 525,000. In recent years, each of these publications has lost circulation both because of competition from more specialized media and because of the weak farm economy. The general farm publications are designed to address all aspects of farm

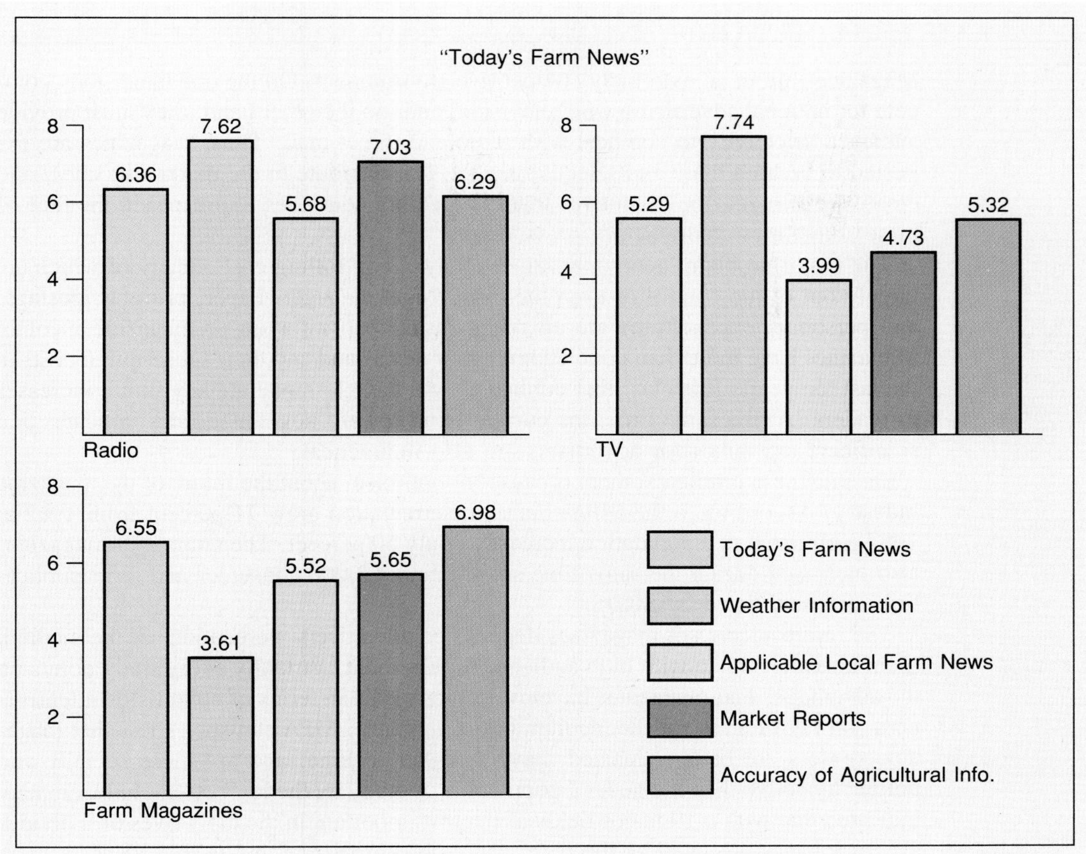

EXHIBIT 11.33
Farm magazines face stiff competition from both radio and TV. (Courtesy: Radio Advertising Bureau.)

life. For instance, the SRDS Publisher's Editorial Profile for *Successful Farming* reads as follows:

> *Successful Farming* editorial is designed as management guidance for business farmers and their families. Articles are written as practical help in making those decisions which directly affect the profitability of the business, and the welfare of the family. Editors seek their information from those in the forefront of farm change, and much editorial is case history reporting of successful innovation. There are also monthly reports on developments in government, finance, equipment, etc. Editorial is 100% business of farming and farm family management.

Regional Farm Magazines. A number of farm publications are directed to farmers in a particular region. These publications tend to be general in nature, but contain little of the family-oriented topics found in the large-circulation farm magazines. They address issues of crops, livestock, and government farm policy unique to a particular region. Among the publications in this category are the *Prairie Farmer,* the majority of whose readers live in Indiana and Illinois; the *Oregon Farmer-Stockman;* and the *Nebraska Farmer.*

Vocational Farm Magazines. The last category of farm publications comprises those devoted to certain types of farming or livestock raising. Typical of these publications are *Soybean Digest, The Dairyman, American Fruit Grower,* and *Tobacco.* Many of the vocational magazines combine elements of both regional and vocational publications; for instance, *The Kansas Stockman* and *Missouri Pork Producer.*

Whatever a farmer's interests may be, a number of publications are edited to cater to them. Many farm homes take several publications.

SUMMARY

Magazines are in an extremely competitive environment. On the one hand, they compete for national advertising with television, and, on the other hand, they must provide audience selectivity to compete with radio and direct mail. Thus, magazines are expected to be both mass and selective media. It is a tribute to the marketing savvy and creativity of magazine executives that the medium continues to prosper in the face of these sometimes contradictory pressures.

The major problem facing magazines today is controlling costs, many of which are largely out of the control of even the most frugal manager. Paper, printing, postage, and personnel expenditures are all rising faster than inflation or magazine income. Magazines have more than doubled both their newsstand and their subscription costs in the last ten years. It is clear that publishers will have to moderate any future increases to readers. At the same time, the current trend toward negotiated rates indicates that significant rate hikes for advertisers are also impractical.

Despite these problems, there is cause for optimism about the future of the magazine industry. According to the MPA, magazine circulation grew 71 percent from 1962 to 1987, compared to a population increase of only 50 percent. The number of magazines also increased during the same time span. Almost 2,000 consumer and farm publications are now listed by SRDS.

The future success of magazines depends on advertisers' perceptions of the medium as an upscale vehicle with high audience involvement. Virtually every study points up the advantages that magazines have over other media in terms of advertising attentiveness and high regard for the medium by its audience. MPA statistics show that magazine readers are better educated, have a higher income, and are more socially and politically active than the general population. A study by the R. Russell Hall Company indicated that within 19 major fields of interest important in the daily lives of individuals, magazines are cited as the main source of knowledge and usable ideas.

QUESTIONS

1. Discuss how magazines began in the 1950s to change their marketing strategy in order to compete with television.
2. How has reader support of magazines changed during recent years? How do advertisers regard this change?
3. Discuss the primary advantages and disadvantages of magazines as a consumer advertising medium.
4. Discuss the qualitative elements of magazines as an advertising medium.
5. Discuss the procedure of the Audit Bureau of Circulations in verifying consumer magazine audiences.
6. Identify the following:
   (a) fast close
   (b) partial-run circulation
   (c) bleed ads
   (d) volume discount
   (e) remnant space
   (f) closing date
   (g) controlled circulation
   (h) industrial publications
7. Why is psychographic research so important to magazines?
8. What are the primary advantages and disadvantages of multipage units and magazine foldouts?
9. What is the role of magazine networks in selling advertising?
10. What is the primary competition for business magazines in gaining advertising dollars?
11. How is pass-along readership viewed by advertisers in consumer and business publications?

12. What is the difference between a vertical and a horizontal industrial publication?
13. Discuss the changing competitive environment for agribusiness publications.

SUGGESTED EXERCISES

- Take a newspaper advertisement for a national product and rewrite it as if it were going to run in *Time* and *Woman's Day*.
- Choose your two favorite magazines and list the primary reasons you read these publications.
- Find three magazine advertisements with (a) a coupon and (b) an 800 telephone number.

READINGS

Angelo, Jean Marie: "One Out of Four Mags Goes Off Rate Card," *Inside Print,* December 1988, p. 21.

Jaben, Jan: "Publishers Join *Soldier of Fortune* in Battling Ad Liability Verdict," *Publishing News,* February 1989, p. 3.

Jaben, Jan: "Sluggish Growth in Magazine Publishing," *Folio,* February 1989, p. 24.

Perry, David: "Performance Advertisers Practice What They Preach," *Business Marketing,* March 1988, p. 86.

Soley, Lawrence C., and R. Krishnan: "Does Advertising Subsidize Consumer Magazine Prices?" *Journal of Advertising,* Vol. 16, No. 2 (1987), pp. 4–9.

"Special Report: Magazine World," *ADWEEK,* February 13, 1989.

TWELVE

Out-of-Home Advertising

In previous chapters, we noted a number of changes in terminology reflecting a transition in usage or marketing strategy of a particular medium. In this chapter, we see yet another example of such a change: The term *out-of-home advertising* is replacing the long-used *outdoor advertising*. This new term reflects the creativity and flexibility that have been introduced in this area of advertising in recent years. These techniques have both augmented traditional outdoor posters with new materials and created new media for the out-of-home market.

Out-of-home advertising. *Inclusive term which includes outdoor poster, transit, shelters, and other forms of similar advertising formats.*

As the Institute of Outdoor Advertising notes, out-of-home is not only the oldest form of advertising, but also the oldest form of mass communication. Wall paintings on tombs and clay tablets set out for public reading date back 5,000 years, to the ancient Egyptians. In more recent times, the tavern signs of fifteenth-century England provided landmarks as well as lodging information for weary and oftentimes illiterate travelers. With the general introduction of the printing press, posters became a popular form of political propaganda and advertising. They were used extensively by the colonists during the Revolutionary War, and Manet and Toulouse-Lautrec created posters for outdoor promotions in nineteenth-century France.

The modern era of advertising can be traced to World War I, when all sides used outdoor advertising as a propaganda device to spur the war effort. After the war, advertisers continued to use it as an efficient means of reaching a mobile, automotive-minded population. During this period, the industry adopted standardized signs; formed the forerunner of its national trade association, the Outdoor Advertising Association of America (OAAA); set up the Traffic Audit Bureau (TAB) to authenticate audience data; and established a national marketing organization, the Institute of Outdoor Advertising (IOA).

Institute of Outdoor Advertising. *The marketing and information arm of the outdoor industry.*

As we will see throughout this chapter, the out-of-home medium comprises a number of advertising vehicles with a common marketing objective. That is, all out-of-home advertising seeks to reach consumers who are in the marketplace, many with a purchase intention. It does so with a colorful, spectacular message that is difficult to ignore. The two primary categories of out-of-home advertising are outdoor and transit.

OUTDOOR ADVERTISING

Out-of-home (outdoor) advertising is the oldest form of advertising. It has always had, as its objective, the goal to reach consumers who are *in the marketplace,* who are likely to purchase goods and services. Tobacco companies know their goods are often bought *on impulse*—after the consumer leaves home and is in the market for other goods. To "beef-up" their no-holes-barred strategy against Philip Morris' Marlboro, R. J. Reynolds is introducing *Vantage Excel 100s.* It's a "breakthrough" cigarette that gives off *less smoke*—"so, it needs as much total exposure as possible to initiate the market," said a company spokesperson. "That's why we're using a heavy outdoor segment."

The most common form of standardized out-of-home advertising is the highway poster or billboard. Approximately $1.5 billion is spent annually on these posters. Only an approximate figure is possible because the diversification of the out-of-home media has made it difficult even to categorize the various options, much less to keep track of their revenues. For instance, a company called American Parking Meter Advertising began selling advertising space on parking meters in Baltimore (see Exhibit 12.1). Is this "medium" outdoor, transit, or a new category? For the sake of simplicity, we will confine our discussion in this section of the chapter to standardized traditional outdoor posters. Then, in later sections dealing with transit advertising, we will deal briefly with some of the newer media.

An Overview of the Outdoor Industry

Outdoor advertising. *The* standardized *posters and painted bulletins comprising the outdoor industry.*

Outdoor advertising—the highway poster or billboard—amasses $1.5 billion per year, but only 1% of total advertising expenditures. However, in 1987, the forecast is for a *7% increase,* as the benefits of localization, contemporary graphics, and creative innovation seek to offset zoning restrictions, the erosion of the alcohol/tobacco base, and the limits of capital. Supermarket chain, Stop 'n' Go, is tying up $500,000 in a sweepstakes campaign, which includes "a heavy chunk" of outdoor promotion to "saturate" its Texas market.

Among the major advertising media, outdoor is the smallest in terms of revenues. In 1990, outdoor revenues will account for about 1 percent of total advertising expenditures. Even though it is not a major medium in terms of revenues, outdoor is an important part of many advertisers' media plans. Outdoor signs are located in over 9,000 communities throughout the United States. As we would expect, most of these signs are found in or near metropolitan areas.

Outdoor advertising is often defined (incorrectly) as any advertisement or identification sign that is located in a public place, such as the signs of varying sizes, shapes, and colors that mark eating places, bowling alleys, motels, movies, and the like. In fact, the outdoor industry is made up only of standardized posters and painted signs.

Outdoor is used primarily as a supplemental medium in an advertising campaign. It is extremely good at extending reach or frequency of other media at an affordable cost (see Exhibit 12.2). Although outdoor has for some time been dominated by national advertisers, in recent years, the medium has been successfully sold to local businesses such as real estate firms, department stores, and insurance companies.

From a marketing standpoint, outdoor tends to be most successful when used by companies that

- are introducing a new product and want immediate brand-name recognition to complement other forms of advertising; or
- are marketing established, well-known, easily recognized brands and want to provide reminder advertising to consumers in the marketplace

The growth of outdoor as an advertising medium was made possible by the automobile. In recent years, mass transit advertising has taken an increasing share of out-of-home expenditures, but the automobile audience remains the foundation of out-of-home media. The lastest figures indicate that private automobile travel accounts for 86 percent of passenger miles compared to 3 percent for local mass transportation. (Most

EXHIBIT 12.1

Out-of-home encompasses a wide array of advertising vehicles. (Courtesy: American Parking Meter Advertising, Inc.)

EXHIBIT 12.2
(Courtesy: Institute of Outdoor Advertising.)

Outdoor is used primarily as a *supplement* in an advertising campaign. Both *national* and *local* advertisers are participants. When Disney launched its newest theme park, *Disney/MGM Studios,* it spent $30 million in marketing and advertising—including television, newspapers, *and billboards.* Another $20 million was invested in promotional tie-ins with Sony and M&M/Mars—all to get a jump on Universal's launching of *its park* next year.

Target Audience: W25–54 Length of Schedule: 8 weeks		
12	**Without Outdoor**	**With Outdoor**
Budget	$108,208	$108,208
% Television	100%	85%
% Outdoor	—	15%
GRP	1000	1594 (+59%)
Cost/Rating Point	$108	$68 (−37%)
% Reach	96.2%	99.1% (+3%)
Average Frequency	10.4X	16.1X (+55%)
Telmar Media Analysis		

of the remaining passenger miles are accounted for by air travel.) As Exhibit 12.3 demonstrates, vehicle ownership is growing faster than either population or households.

Advantages and Disadvantages of Outdoor Advertising

Outdoor advertising has benefited from several factors in recent years. Among the most important are:

Outdoor advertising has benefitted greatly from our increasingly *mobile* population. On the way to East Coast beaches this summer, travellers saw billboards for *Vaseline Intensive Care Sunscreen*—aimed at consumers who are allergic to PABA, a popular sunscreen ingredient. "More suntan products are bought at the beach, than at home, so we're simply informing the beachgoers as they travel . . . ," says a company spokesman.

- An increasingly mobile population and dispersed patterns of shopping and commuting throughout urban and metropolitan centers
- Creation of a modern system of interstate highways
- Legislative and other restrictions banning liquor and cigarettes from the broadcast media

In addition to these societal factors, the outdoor industry, like every other medium, has certain unique characteristics. These advantages and disadvantages ultimately determine whether or not a particular advertiser chooses outdoor.

Among the primary advantages of outdoor are:

1. *Media-mix reinforcement.* Outdoor advertising reaches baby boomers—that elusive, younger, better-educated, and more affluent part of the population who are traditionally light TV viewers and light newspaper readers. It bridges the gap between the in-home message and the out-of-home purchase, while rounding out an existing media mix.
2. *Frequency of exposure.* Outdoor's most notable achievement is its overwhelming superiority

EXHIBIT 12.3
(Courtesy: The Traffic Audit Bureau.)

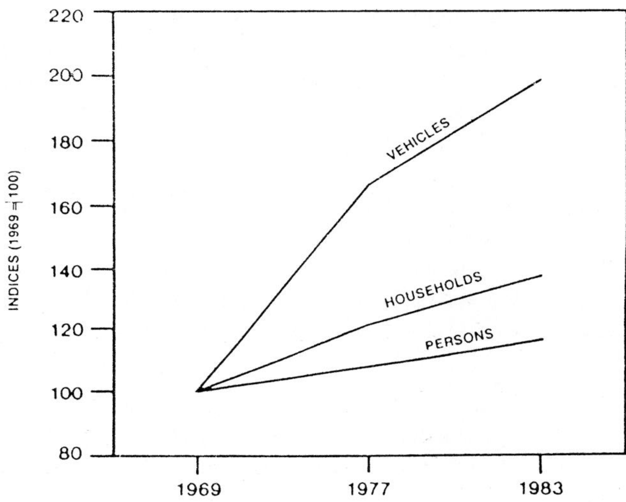

Media mix, outdoor. *Outdoor advertising, as a reminder medium, is normally a supplemental medium within a media plan which includes a number of other vehicles.*

over local competitive media in building frequency of exposure. These superior message repetition values translate into greater advertising awareness and recall.

3. *Strengthened market presence.* Continuous long-term presence is maintained by outdoor advertising exposure—every day, all week, every month.
4. *Target audience capability.* Whether your plan calls for broad marketwide coverage or precise, targeted locations, outdoor advertising offers effective and efficient circulation of your message.
5. *Dominant visual impact.* With a copy area of up to 1,200 square feet, outdoor is the largest major advertising medium available. Bold, colorful, and dramatic displays generate immediate attention to your product or service among consumers.[1]

Some of the disadvantages of outdoor are:

Creative limitations, outdoor. *Most outdoor signs can use no more than 7–10 words effectively.*

In targeting hard-to-reach audiences, such as *single baby boomers* and *teens,* outdoor advertising outweighs other media. Its value is also strengthened by its *frequency of exposure* and *long-term* presence. With *Puma* in an all-out "war" with Nike and Reebok, and with only $8 million to spend on promotion—versus $60 million for Reebok and $40–50 for Nike—it's using *less* spot TV. Instead, it's campaign includes 1,800 transit and outdoor boards with Detroit Piston Isiah Thomas to attract the "active" youth market—especially in the downtown areas of cities.

1. *Creative limitations.* Outdoor advertising can rarely include a complete sales message. Most advertising professionals warn against using more than seven to ten words in an outdoor sign. An advertising message that does not lend itself to a visual interpretation is probably unsuitable for outdoor.
2. *Little audience selectivity.* While certain areas of a market might be pinpointed, outdoor is basically a mass medium. However, it can reach areas of concentrated ethnic populations or upscale markets within a metropolitan center.
3. *The problem of availability.* In some communities, demand for high travel signs is greater than available poster sites. Real estate costs, including high property taxes, are a continuing problem for the industry, and these costs must be passed along to advertisers even though they may be unrelated to higher circulation.

The Image of Outdoor

You will recall that when we discussed magazine advertising we noted that a primary appeal to advertisers was the prestige many magazines hold in the public mind. The association between a medium and the advertising it carries is part of the total perception of the vehicle. That is why most broadcast and print media screen advertising before accepting it and why advertisers consider qualitative factors in media placement.

The image of outdoor has suffered partly because of its association with liquor, beer, and tobacco advertisers. These products are controversial to many people, so some advertisers have shied away from the medium. In recent years, the share of outdoor expenditures devoted to tobacco and alcoholic beverages has declined. "In 1981, tobacco accounted for 42.9 percent of total outdoor dollars and liquor claimed 20.3 percent; today, those figures are 23.5 percent and 9.9 percent respectively."[2]

Though the decline in these categories may result in some shortfall in outdoor revenues during the next few years, some in the industry believe it will prove a healthy long-term trend since it will make outdoor less dependent on a few advertisers. Diversification in outdoor is already evident in the regional strategies increasingly adopted by major advertisers. Some package goods manufacturers view outdoor as a means of selectively targeting high potential markets. The medium also offers advertisers the ability to get a message across with a minimum of clutter. Advertisers such as Colgate-Palmolive, Campbell Soup, Kodak, and Kraft have recently made significant investments in outdoor. Many people believe outdoor executives' ability to market the medium is a major reason for its gains.[3]

Outdoor diversification. *In recent years, outdoor has made significant progress in gaining support from a number of national advertisers and lowered the proportion of space devoted to cigarette and alcoholic beverages.*

Another encouraging trend in outdoor's push for diversification is that retail advertising has replaced alcohol as the second-largest category of advertising. Furthermore, as we can see in Exhibit 12.4, several product categories are spending substantial

[1] *Why Outdoor Advertising?,* a publication of Outdoor Today, a Gannett Company.

[2] David Kalish, "Local Heros," *Marketing & Media Decisions,* August 1988, p. 95.

[3] Alison Fahey, "Outdoor Ads Use Regional Moves as Springboard," *Advertising Age,* October 17, 1988, p. 65.

amounts in outdoor. In every category except tobacco and alcohol, expenditures have risen over the last five years.

Highway Beautification Act of 1965. *Federal law that controls outdoor signs in noncommercial, nonindustrial areas.*

Another reason outdoor suffers from an image problem is that many people regard it as a scenic pollutant. The first organized legislative attempt to control outdoor advertising was the Highway Beautification Act of 1965 (known as the ''Lady Bird bill'' after Mrs. Lyndon Johnson, who actively supported the legislation). The act restricted the placement of outdoor signs along interstate highways and provided stiff penalities for states that failed to control signs within 660 feet of interstate roads. According to the Federal Highway Administration, the number of outdoor posters has decreased by over 50 percent, since 1965 (see Exhibit 12.5). Those that remain are concentrated in commercially zoned areas.

Limitations include brevity, lack of selectivity, and availability of sites. Also detracting some advertisers from using outdoor is its low-scale image in some markets and its former dependency on liquor and tobacco—two industries which are prohibited from television access. But in *foreign markets,* like the Soviet Union, where print and broadcasting time is limited for commercial messages, outdoor advertising is a primary message carrier. Even technical products, like Smith Corona's word processor, the PWP 80, made for the Soviet market, receive their introduction to consumers via well-placed billboards.

Since the passage of national legislation, four states—Alaska, Hawaii, Maine, and Vermont—have totally banned outdoor advertising and major cities such as Denver, St. Louis, and Jacksonville have limited the number and location of outdoor signs. Public interest groups such as the Coalition for Scenic Beauty have launched local campaigns against outdoor throughout the country. Their major effect has been to limit the construction of new billboards. Thus, existing sites have become more valuable and profitable to the outdoor plants that control the space.

Future growth in outdoor will largely come from expansion in the economy and even greater mobility of the population.

> Population increased from 179 million in 1960 to 226 million in 1980. Interstate highway mileage open to traffic increased from 21,185 miles in 1965 to a current 40,936. The Federal-aid primary system has likewise grown. As a result, there has been an increase in the number of commercial and industrial areas in which outdoor advertising may be located.[4]

EXHIBIT 12.4
(Courtesy: *Marketing & Media Decisions.*)

Outdoor's Top Spenders 1987 by Category

	Share of Total Outdoor	Ad Dollars (000)
1. Cigarettes, other tobacco, accessories	23.5%	$164,955
2. Retail	9.9	69,766
3. Liquor, beer and wine	9.9	69,490
4. Automotive	8.2	57,845
5. Business, gov't and consumer services	8.0	56,201
6. Travel, hotels and resorts	7.8	54,882
7. Publishing and media	6.4	44,963
8. Entertainment and amusements	5.8	40,456
9. Insurance and real estate	5.1	36,076
10. Food and food products	2.1	14,978

Source: Leading National Advertisers (actual ad spending may be higher due to under-reporting.)

EXHIBIT 12.5
Outdoor posters, 1966–1986

Total Signs		***Signs per Mile***	
1966	**1986**	**1966**	**1986**
1,100,020	402,062	4.4	0.5

Nonconforming and Illegal Signs to Be Removed		***Signs in Commercial and Industrial Areas***	
1966	**1986**	**1966**	**1986**
839,391	145,523	260,659	256,539

Note: Includes only commercial outdoor advertising signs.

(Source: Outdoor Advertising Myths & Facts, [Outdoor Advertising: Association of America, 1987], p. 1.)

[4] *Outdoor Advertising Myths & Facts,* a publication of the Outdoor Advertising Association of America, Inc., 1985, p. 3.

As we have seen throughout this text, advertisers constantly find ways to deal with new restrictions on marketing their products and services. One such innovation grew out of limitations placed on outdoor advertising along interstate highways. The Interstate Exit Guide (see Exhibit 12.6) gives travelers information about what services and attractions are available at every interstate exit in a particular state. Businesses can

EXHIBIT 12.6

Advertising booklets have replaced outdoor signs on many interstate highways. (Courtesy: Interstate Exit Guide.)

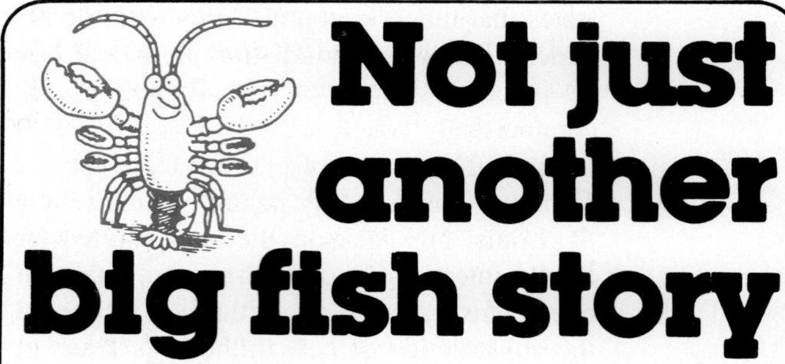
Not just
another
big fish story

When we tell you Red Lobster has the biggest fish story in town. we're not putting you on. What we are putting on is a most spectacular assortment of seafood . . . from sweet scallops to live Maine lobster; from Langostino Nachos to our original Seafood Pastas; from tender shrimp to a wide range of hearty seafood platters. And we've put them all at deliciously reasonable prices that won't take a big bite out of your budget. Great seafood. Great value. Served up in the most relaxed. friendly atmosphere in town. And that's no big fish story.

Red Lobster®

I-4

EXIT	MILE POST		SERVICES
15	26	Gas	Shell*
16	28		None
17	31		None
18	32	Gas	Amoco, Chevron, Exxon,* Gulf, Joy Food Store,* Mobil, Racetrac, Union 76 Truck Stop
		Food	Bill Knapp's Restaurant, Bob Evans, Burger King, Denny's, Jerry's, Kentucky Fried Chicken, Long John Silver's, McDonald's, Sirloin Family Steakhouse, Taco Bell, Waffle House, Wendy's
		Lodging	Days Inn, Foxfire Inn, Howard Johnson, Quality Inn, Red Carpet Inn
		Other	Shopping Centers (2)

advertise in connection with their exit listing, thereby reaching a clearly defined target market.

THE OUTDOOR ADVERTISING PLAN

Planning and executing outdoor demonstrates similarities to and differences from other advertising. The primary difference is that outdoor is usually a secondary medium in a campaign, and therefore its goals and objectives are often determined by other parts of the media plan. It is extremely rare for outdoor to be the primary ''building block'' of a campaign.

This fact should not suggest that the fundamental principles of advertising planning do not apply to outdoor. The Traffic Audit Bureau suggests these five steps in planning for outdoor advertising:[5]

1. *Set clear objectives.* Because of the secondary nature of most outdoor buys, the objectives may be more limited than for other media. Typical objectives are gaining broad awareness, adding seasonal weight, and targeting segments not easily reached by other media.
2. *Choose strategic paths.* Basically, the advertiser must determine how best to use outdoor to complement previously determined objectives. For example: Should outdoor be used regionally or nationally? Can it be used to extend the budget or to accumulate reach quickly?
3. *Define target markets.* You will recall that defining the target market was the first step in media planning. However, since outdoor is a secondary medium, we need to determine the market segments reached by other media before we can determine objectives for outdoor. In this sense, outdoor is said to be ''folded over'' other media; it rarely acts as a primary communication vehicle.
4. *Develop creative executions.* The message is extremely important in outdoor. Though the artwork is usually designed by an advertising agency, most plants have art departments to assist advertisers. Posters require from three to six weeks for printing and should be delivered ten days before the posting date. We will discuss creativity in outdoor later in this chapter.
5. *Arrange production and inspect results.* The basic business unit of the outdoor industry is the local outdoor company, the outdoor *plant*. Its stock in trade is the location it has leased or bought under local zoning regulations permitting the erection of signs. Having acquired a location, the plant builds a structure at its own expense, sells the advertising space on it (technically, it leases the space), posts or paints the advertiser's message, and is responsible for maintaining the board and the ad in good condition during the life of the advertiser's contract. The second part of this step—inspecting the outdoor posters to see that the signs are properly maintained and posted in the agreed-upon locations—is called ''riding the boards.''

Plant operator. *In outdoor advertising, the local person who arranges to lease, erect, and maintain the outdoor sign and to sell the advertising space on it.*

FORMS OF OUTDOOR ADVERTISING

There are two basic forms of outdoor advertising: the poster and the painted bulletin. In both vehicles, the message is designed by the advertising agency. The design is then reproduced on paper and posted on panels. The larger painted bulletins are prepared by outdoor company artists either in a studio or on-site.

Poster Panels

This type of poster is really two posters in one. The 30-sheet and bleed posters, which use the same frame, are the typical highway billboard with which we are all familiar. These posters are available in some 9,000 communities and every state except Maine,

[5]Ken Sammon, *Planning for Out-of-Home Media* (New York: The Traffic Audit Bureau, 1987), p. 15.

> ***Poster panel.*** *A standard surface on which outdoor posters are placed. The posting surface is of sheet metal. An ornamental molding of standard green forms the frame. The standard poster panel is 12 feet high and 25 feet long (outside dimensions).*

> ***Illuminated panels.*** *Most outdoor posters (70–80%) are illuminated so they offer advertising exposures on a 24-hour basis.*

Vermont, Hawaii, and Alaska, where billboards are illegal. Poster buys can be made for anything from a single location to total national coverage.

The standard poster panel measures 12 by 25 feet. The bleed poster either prints to the edge of the frame or uses blanking paper that matches the background of the poster. The term *bleed* is, of course, borrowed from the bleed magazine ad, which has no border. The term *sheet* originated in the days when presses were much smaller and it took many sheets to cover a poster panel. Today presses can print much larger sheets, but the old space designations are still used. Exhibit 12.7 shows a typical configuration of sheets to cover 30-sheet and bleed posters, as well as the painted bulletins discussed later in this chapter.

Poster displays are sold as either *illuminated* or *nonilluminated* panels. Panels in locations with high traffic volume are normally illuminated for maximum 24-hour exposure. A typical poster showing consists of 70–80 percent illuminated posters, and the percentage is increasing slightly each year. When buying an outdoor showing, the advertiser is given the number of displays, the number that are illuminated and nonilluminated, the monthly and per-panel cost, and total circulation or exposure.

The minimum contract period for outdoor posters is normally 30 days, with discounts for consecutive usage up to 12 months. Regardless of the contract period, most posters are changed every 30 days, and the creative execution can be changed then at no additional space charges. Of course, the advertiser will incur higher printing and production costs when messages are changed frequently. Poster positions are often rotated during the period of the contract to give coverage on different thoroughfares.

The Eight-Sheet Poster

In recent years, another form of outdoor advertising, the eight-sheet poster, has gained popularity with advertisers. This size is sometimes called a *junior* poster, but the designation *eight-sheet* is preferred to indicate its proportion to the more popular 30-sheet poster. The eight-sheet poster copy area is 5 feet high and 11 feet wide (see Exhibit 12.8).

> The eight-sheet poster was originally developed to offer affordable outdoor advertising to the small business person. The panels were designed to be placed low and close to the street and thus they command great visibility and impact. Still, they are considerably more reasonable to use than 30-sheet panels both from the standpoint of paper production and average monthly

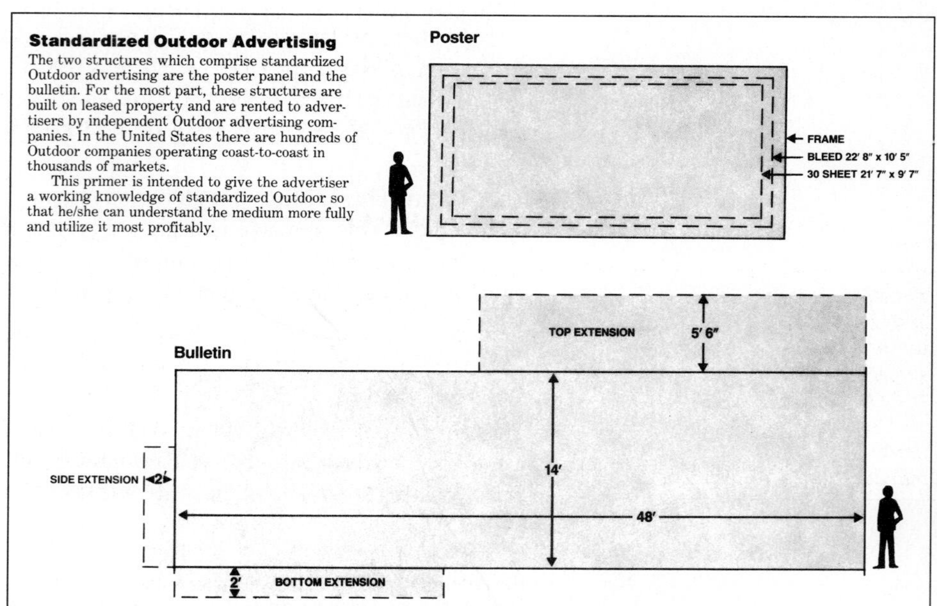

EXHIBIT 12.7
(Courtesy: Institute of Outdoor Advertising.)

EXHIBIT 12.8

Eight-Sheet Outdoor Specifications

The following dimensions and mechanical specifications have been designated as standard by the Eight-Sheet Outdoor Advertising Association, Inc.

DESIGNATION
Eight-Sheet Outdoor is outdoor billboard advertising utilizing poster panels with a live copy area of 5′ x 11′. Although in the past these panels have sometimes been referred to as 6-Sheets, juniors, junior-eights, mini-boards, advertisers and other similar names, the proper designation and the one which should ALWAYS be used to identify this medium is "Eight-Sheet Outdoor."

POSTING SURFACE
The posting surface of an Eight-Sheet poster is 60 inches high and 132 inches wide.

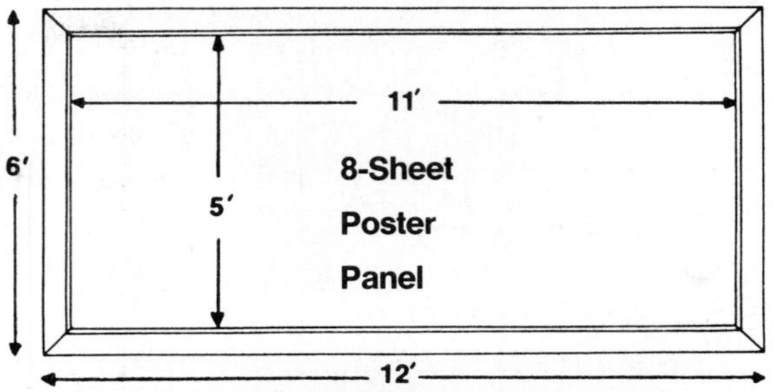

6′
11′
5′
8-Sheet Poster Panel
12′

DESIGN SPECIFICATIONS:
The proportions of an Eight-Sheet poster and a standard 30-sheet poster are the same. Thus the same continuous tone separations may be used for both, thereby reducing litho or four color process printing costs. Designs should restrict live copy to the dimensions indicated under printing specifications. For design purposes, the panels may be considered to be 59 inches by 131 inches. Finished art should be scaled 1″ to 1′.

PRINTING SPECIFICATIONS
Because posting paper has a tendency to stretch when saturated with poster paste, it is necessary to use the following dimensions when printing Eight-Sheet Outdoor poster paper.
Vertical Grain Paper
Poster Size: 129½″ x 60″
Copy Area: 127½″ x 58″
Horizontal Grain Paper
Poster Size: 132″ x 58¾″
Copy Area: 130″ x 56¾″

rental. In many markets, the Out-of-Home Measurement Bureau has conducted audits and certified the circulation of eight-sheet showings. Traffic counts, daily effective circulation and cost per rating point can all be confirmed for the advertising.[6]

In addition, the eight-sheet poster is more likely to meet local outdoor advertising regulations than the standard-size poster. Exhibit 12.9 shows an example of eight-sheet posters.

Since the eight-sheet poster often meets zoning regulations that prohibit traditional posters, it offers advertisers greater geographical flexibility. The eight-sheet poster can be used to reach preselected demographic groups. For example, showings in a financial district or on routes to or from exclusive residential neighborhoods reach high numbers of the more affluent populations; showings near high schools or colleges reach young people.

Eight-sheet posters are available in some 2,500 markets. They are handled by special poster plants and frequently appear concurrently with 30-sheet showings in a market. The Eight-Sheet Outdoor Advertising Association (ESOAA) was founded to promote the interests of the eight-sheet poster medium.

Buying Poster Advertising

***Showing.** Outdoor posters are bought by groups, referred to as showings. The size of a showing is referred to as a 100-GRP showing or a 75- or 50-GRP showing, depending on the gross rating points of the individual boards selected.*

Poster advertising is bought on the basis of *gross rating points* (GRPs) or *showings*. The terms are interchangeable in current practice, with some outdoor companies using one term and some the other. Showings are purchased in units of 100, 75, 50, or 25, and measure the percentage of *duplicated* audience exposed to an advertiser's posters daily. You will recall from our earlier discussions of the broadcast media that a rating point is equal to 1 percent of a population. Therefore, a 50 GRP (showing) will deliver exposure opportunities to an audience equivalent to 50 percent of the market.

Note that the outdoor GRP is a *duplicated* measure, so a 50-GRP buy will not deliver

[6]*Eight-Sheet Outdoor: Cost Efficient Impact*, a publication of the Eight-Sheet Outdoor Advertising Association, Inc.

EXHIBIT 12.9

Eight-sheet posters provide many of the same creative and circulation opportunities as traditional outdoor signs. (Courtesy: Eight-Sheet Outdoor Advertising Association, Inc.)

50 percent of the market (which would be the reach), but rather an audience the size of half the market.

Let's look at a typical calculation for an outdoor showing:

Market: Atlanta

Population: 1,227,000

100 GRPs (showing): 1,227,000 duplicated exposures

50 GRPs: 613,500

$$\text{GRP showing} = \frac{\text{Daily effective circulation (DEC)*}^{7}}{\text{Market population}}$$

[7]The daily effective circulation is the number of people who had an opportunity to see one of the posters in a 24-hour period.

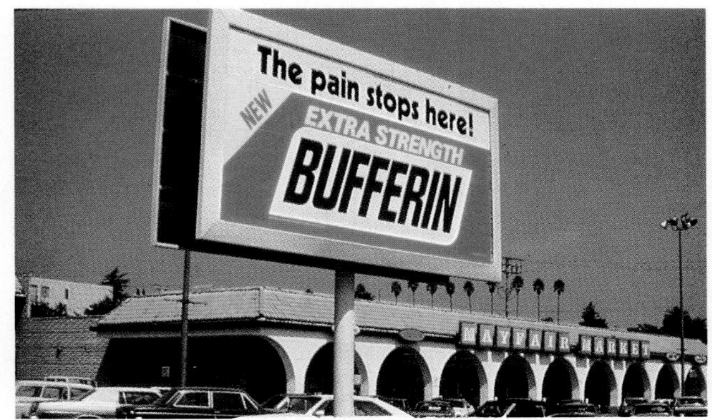

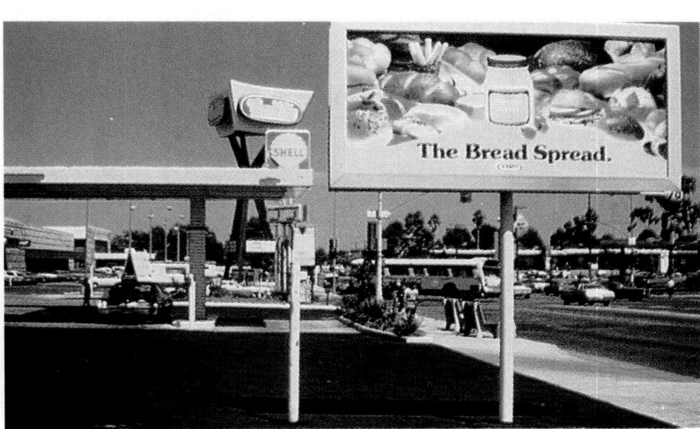

$$50 \text{ GRP showing} = \frac{613{,}500}{1{,}227{,}000}$$

A 100 showing in one city may include fewer posters than the same showing in another, larger city, but it will provide the same intensity of market coverage. Exhibit 12.10 is a rate card showing the number of posters, and their cost, for various GRP levels in the Twin Cities area. Exhibit 12.11 illustrates the placement of outdoor posters for a 50 and 100 showing in the Atlanta market. It should be noted that the standard agency commission in outdoor is 16.67 percent rather than the normal 15 percent.

Outdoor Networks

Since outdoor advertising is primarily a national or large regional medium, advertisers may find themselves dealing with dozens of separate outdoor companies to make a

EXHIBIT 12.10

Most outdoor plants provide a range of posters and showing allocations. (Courtesy: Naegele Outdoor Advertising, Inc.)

Recommended High Impact Coverage
Naegele Outdoor Advertising, Inc.
Twin Cities—1988 Rate and Allotments

Market	Population*	GRPs	Allotment Reg	Allotment Ill.	Total Panels	D.E.C.**	Cost per Month
Minneapolis St. Paul Metro	2,323,300	100	63	147	210	2,777,460	$89,250
		75	47	111	158	2,089,708	67,150
		50	31	74	105	1,388,730	44,625
		25	16	37	53	700,978	22,525
		10	6	15	21	277,746	11,340
Minneapolis Metro	1,410,600	100	38	90	128	1,692,298	$54,400
		75	29	67	96	1,269,696	40,800
		50	19	45	64	846,464	27,200
		25	10	22	32	423,232	13,600
		10	4	9	13	171,938	7,020
St. Paul	912,700	100	25	58	83	1,097,758	$35,275
		75	9	43	62	820,012	26,350
		50	3	29	42	555,492	17,850
		25	6	15	21	277,746	8,925
		10	2	6	8	105,808	4,320

Deluxe Posters: Showing rate per poster—$80 per month; showing rate per backlight poster—$330 per month. Size: 6′ × 12′.
Rotating Painted Bulletin: $2,450 per month (Minimum four consecutive months—rates for less than four months quoted upon request). Size: 14′ × 49′2″ Average D.E.C.: 42,100 Rotation: Every other month.
Deluxe Painted bulletins: $1,675 per month (Minimum four consecutive months—rates for less than four months quoted upon request). Size: 10′6″ × 36′ Average D.E.C.: 28,219 Rotation: Every other month.
Extended Advertising Space: $19 per square foot.

Source: **1987 S&MM Survey of Buying Power.*
***1986 TAB Audited Circulation (Plant average circulation of 13,226 per panel, 70% illuminated and 30% nonilluminated.*

Outdoor network. *Cooperative organizations that allow national advertising to simultaneously make outdoor buys in a number of markets with one insertion order and one invoice.*

Networks exist in outdoor, as in other media, to give advertisers the convenience of *single-source outdoor buys.* When *American Airlines* decided to improve its name in Europe, it enlisted its London ad agency to contract with a European outdoor billboard network to feature its posters in Belgium, France, West Germany, Spain, Sweden, Switzerland, and the United Kingdom. "This is American's first *united* European image campaign," quoted James Simon, managing director of advertising for AA.

single buy. In the past, those who considered using outdoor as a minor part of their schedule may have decided against it simply because they did not want to negotiate with so many individual plants. Knowing this, a number of plant operators combined to offer advertisers the convenience of single-source outdoor buys. These cooperative efforts are similar in marketing intent to the nonwired radio networks and magazine networks.

An example of such a network is Outdoor Network, USA, an organization formed by Gannett Outdoor to serve both Gannett-owned operators and independent plants. Currently the Outdoor Network services 370 cities and provides coverage in approximately 85 of the top 100 markets. As we noted earlier, the competition for advertising dollars has forced all media to offer some form of buying combination for advertisers.

Sources of Outdoor Audience Data

Partly because it is so difficult to accurately measure an audience always "on the go," there are a number of sources of audience data available to the outdoor advertiser. The four primary sources are the Traffic Audit Bureau, the Out-of-Home Measurement Bureau, Simmons Market Research Bureau, and Audience Measurement by Market of Outdoor.

Traffic Audit Bureau (TAB). The TAB is the oldest audience-verification service in outdoor. It was founded in 1933 as a nonprofit organization supported by both industry and advertisers. The TAB audits each market at least once every three years, and provides circulation figures as well as basic information about every local market, including population and coverage within the county.

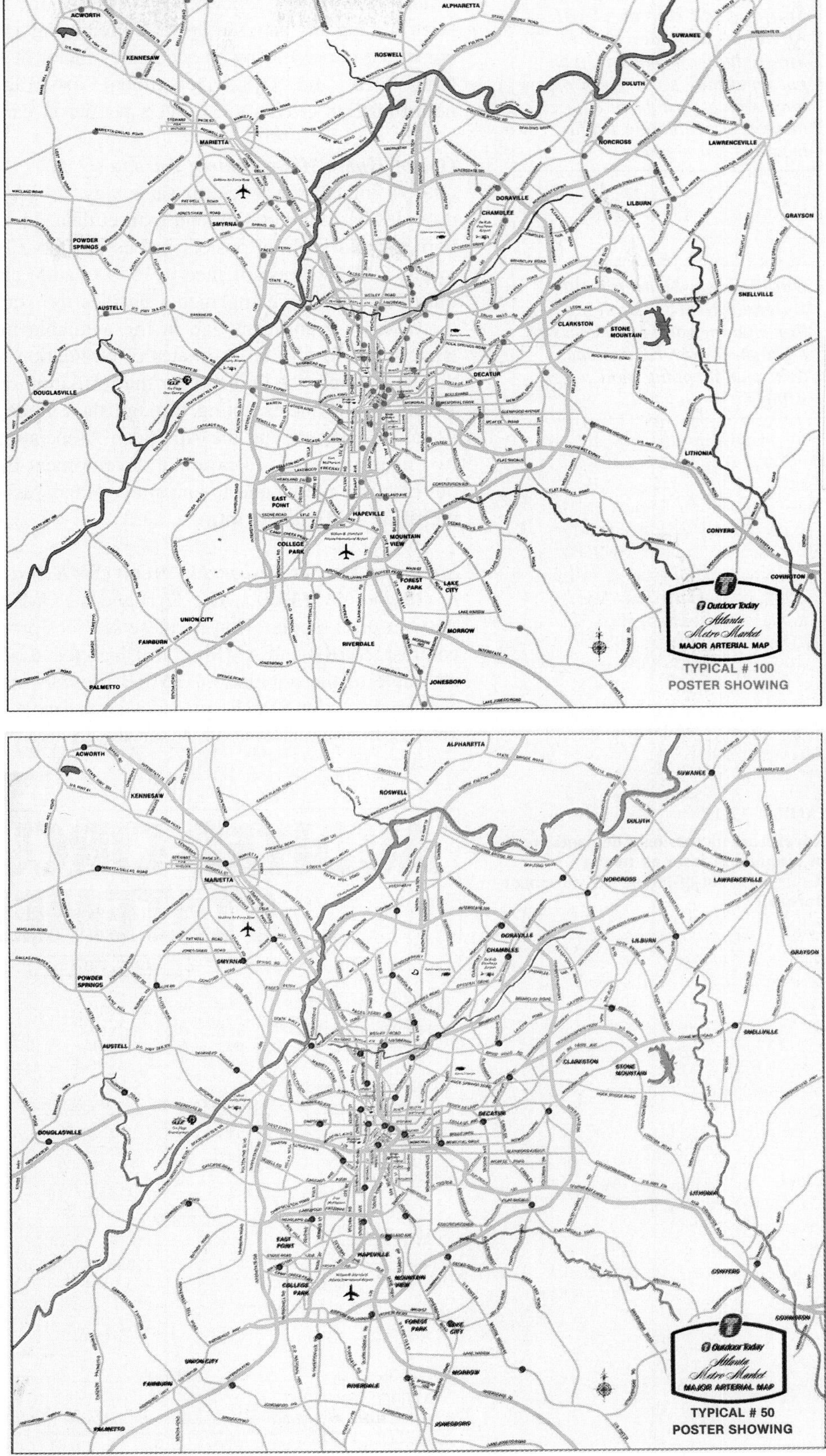

EXHIBIT 12.11

Placement of outdoor posters is extremely important to offer advertisers consistent circulation patterns. (Courtesy: Outdoor Today.)

Traffic Audit Bureau (TAB). *An organization designed to investigate how many people pass and may see a given outdoor sign, to establish a method of evaluating traffic measuring a market.*

Out-of-Home Measurement Bureau (OHMB). *Auditing firm that measures audiences of eight-sheet posters, bus shelters, and shopping mall advertising.*

Four primary sources of outdoor audience data are the Traffic Audit Bureau (TAB), the Out-of-Home Measurement Bureau (OMB), Simmons Market Research Bureau (SMRB), and Audience Measurement by Market of Outdoor (AMMO). Among advertisers ranked 101–200 in terms of total 1987 spending, *Holiday Corporation* (Holiday Inns) had the largest outdoor expenditures—$5 million, out of a total ad budget of $46,000 million.

The TAB audit is obtained by counting the number of pedestrians and/or automobiles passing any advertising structure during a specified time period. Automobiles are converted to persons by an occupancy factor of 1.75 persons per car, a figure based on both TAB and U.S. Department of Transportation national research. Most nonpedestrian circulation reflects people in cars rather than mass transportation.

Out-of-Home Measurement Bureau (OMB). The OMB functions for the eight-sheet outdoor industry in much the same way the TAB does for 30-sheet posters—that is, it provides basic circulation and market data. In addition, the OMB audits other out-of-home media such as posters in bus shelters, shopping malls, and airport terminals.

The OMB was established in 1979 to audit circulation exposure to various forms of out-of-home advertising media besides the standard highway posters. Before 1979, there was a significant gap in the available information about out-of-home media. Buyers had to rely on estimates of circulation for eight-sheet posters and bus shelter displays. Thus, the demand for the formation of the OMB came from advertisers and advertising agencies acting through their trade associations, the Association of National Advertisers and the American Association of Advertising Agencies. OMB has two main purposes: to promote development of credible (audited) information about out-of-home media and to encourage standards of practice. Exhibit 12.12 is an example of an OMB audit form.

Simmons Market Research Bureau (SMRB) and Audience Measurement by Market of Outdoor (AMMO). The TAB and the OMB might be considered analogous to the ABC in print media. That is, these services provide no-frills audience information. In contrast, SMRB and AMMO furnish a great deal of product and media usage data from a sample of the population. SMRB provides national data, and AMMO, working in cooperation with SMRB, provides comparable information for individual major markets. Both companies conduct surveys to determine respondents' actual frequencies of

EXHIBIT 12.12

Advertisers increasingly demand proof of circulation from all media. (Courtesy: Out-of-Home Measurement Bureau.)

AUDITED CIRCULATION STATEMENT

MEDIA TYPE EIGHT SHEETS

1. Market: NEW YORK 2. State: NEW YORK 3. Date of Audit: July-Sept, 1986

4. Plant Name & Address: SALE POINT POSTERS
651 Bergen Street
Brooklyn, NY 11238

5. Market Area Served:

Counties	Pop. (000)	#Panels	Average DEC Per Panel	Average Space Position Value
Bronx	1,120.4	379	12,510	
Kings	2,231.3	626	11,150	
New York	1,485.6	375	16,800	
Queens	1,968.2	359	11,290	
Richmond	395.8	79	12,640	
Totals:	7,201.3	1,818	12,200	

Major Cities	Total City Pop. (000)	Total City #Panels	Black Ethnic Pop. (000)	Black Ethnic #Panels	Hispanic Ethnic Pop. (000)	Hispanic Ethnic #Panels
New York	7,201.3	1,818	1,829.1	983	1,389.9	675

6. Circulation Sources: 100 %Manual ______ %City ______ %State ______ %Other

AUDIT STATEMENT

The traffic counts shown on this statement were prepared according to procedures approved by the Out-of-home Measurement Bureau. The OMB has examined the records of this company and certifies that these data accurately present the circulation and visibility values in this market.

Signed Julian R. Sloan Managing Director

OMB

Out-of-home Measurement Bureau P.O. Box 1201, New Canaan, CT 06840

exposure and to relate exposure to respondents' demographic characteristics and travel behavior.[8]

Painted Bulletins

> ***Painted bulletins.*** *Outdoor signs that are painted rather than papered. More permanent and expensive than posters, they are used only in high-traffic locations.*

There are *two basic forms* of outdoor advertising: the *poster* and the *painted bulletin*. The poster is less expensive, but the painted bulletin is more noticeable at crowded intersections. Both can be rotated to different locations. Proctor & Gamble's latest offering to attract the youth market is a Crest poster—which promotes tartar control Crest. It stresses the "You'd be a lot more popular" theme, using cartoonist Gahon Wilson's big, bold mouth *full* of teeth—which could *hardly be missed*.

Painted bulletins are of two types: *permanent* and *rotary*. The permanent bulletin remains at a fixed location. Since it is fitted to a particular location and never moved, it can vary in size. The permanent bulletin is being phased out by many plants. The more popular rotary bulletin is a standardized sign that is three times larger (14 by 48 feet) than the standard poster. Both types of bulletins are located at choice sites along heavily traveled thoroughfares. They are almost always illuminated.

Bulletins are much more expensive than posters. According to TAB figures, there are approximately 210,000 30-sheet posters in the United States, but only 50,000 painted bulletins. Estimated 1990 revenues for 30-sheet posters are $630 million, and for painted bulletins $753 million. Thus, bulletins are about five times more expensive than posters.

Two factors account for the additional expense of painted bulletins:

1. Production costs are higher since most bulletins are painted and constructed individually.
2. More importantly, bulletins are placed at high-traffic locations. As is the case with any medium, advertisers pay a premium for high circulation.

Special embellishments, such as cutouts, freestanding letters, special lighting effects, fiber optics, and inflatables, may be added to the basic structures. Painted bulletins are usually contracted for a period of one year; however, short-term contracts are available at a higher monthly rate. Costs include painting of a new design three times a year, often with a new message with each painting. Recently, outdoor plants have experimented with one-sheet plastic bulletins that are more durable than paint and seamless to give a better presentation.

The rotary bulletin gives the advertiser the greater impact of the painted bulletin along with more coverage and penetration than a single site could deliver. The rotary bulletin is normally moved every 60 days, so that during a 12-month contract, advertisers will be able to deliver their message throughout the market.

Spectaculars

> ***Spectacular.*** *An outdoor sign built to order, designed to be conspicuous for its location, size, lights, motion, or action. The costliest form of outdoor advertising.*

In an industry known for its jargon, it is refreshing to come upon a phrase that literally means what it says—the outdoor spectacular sign. This is not a standardized sign; it is made by specialists in steel construction. Spectaculars are the most conspicuous and costly outdoor advertisements in terms of cash outlay, although they are low-cost in terms of numbers of people reached. Placed in prime day-and-night locations and designed to attract the attention of a great number of passersby, they are built of steel beams, sheet metal, and plastics. They utilize bright flashing lights and technically ingenious designs. (Everything is subject to local zoning laws and limitations on energy use, of course.) Spectaculars are individually designed; the cost of space and construction is individually negotiated. Changes that entail reconstruction of steelwork and neon lighting are very expensive, so new advertisers often modify their own designs to utilize the construction of existing spectaculars.

Because spectaculars are usually bought on a three- to five-year basis, it takes an experienced and skilled buyer to handle negotiations involving engineering and legal problems as well as the usual advertising considerations. Large outdoor advertisers often use poster displays, painted bulletins, and spectaculars in large cities.

---

[8]Jerome Greene, *How Estimates of Outdoor Audiences Are Reached,* Institute of Outdoor Advertising booklet.

CRITERIA FOR SELECTING OUTDOOR LOCATIONS

Space Position Value (SPV). *The method of evaluating the value of an outdoor site which considers length of approach, speed of travel, angle of the panel, and its relationship to adjacent panels.*

In selecting outdoor sites, *traffic* is a prime consideration—along with obstacles, characteristics of the area, and price. "General Motors will be increasing their promotion budget in 1989 over the $1 billion dollar level of 1988," predicts executive director of advertising, Philip Guarascio. In backing their three new midsize coups, the Buick Regal, Olds Cutlass Supreme, and Pontiac Grand Prix, they'll be seeking highly-trafficked locations, mostly on commuters' routes in upscale suburbs, for additional outdoor boards.

Creativity can be maximized with outdoor advertising—but the agency must emphasize the product, easy-to-read copy, easy-to-see illustrations, simple composition, and bold colors—for the ad to be successful. One of the more creative approaches in billboards is Smith/Greenland's "Dial-a-Date" Johnnie Walker ads. The bathing-suit-clad models face backwards—*with their phone numbers and "JW" in bold print.* "By asking consumers to interact with the billboards," Leo Greenland, chairman of S/G claimed, "you're getting more attention to an otherwise passive product."

Obviously, the most important factor in choosing an outdoor panel site is the volume of traffic. However, traffic volume alone does not make a site inviting for outdoor advertising. The outdoor industry evaluates an outdoor site according to a complex formula that considers four factors: length of approach, speed of travel, angle of the panel, and its relationship to adjacent panels. These factors are combined into a single measure called the *space position value* (SPV).

In picking a location, the following factors should be considered:

- *Length of unobstructed approach:* the distance from which the location first becomes fully visible to people driving.
- *Type of traffic:* the slower the better. Is it all auto, or is it also pedestrian, bus, or a combination of these? Is the traffic toward the location or away from it (e.g., a one-way street)?
- *Characteristics of placement:* angled, parallel to line of traffic, or head-on. Angled is easily seen by cars approaching in one direction; parallel can be viewed by traffic traveling in both directions, but better by people sitting in the car at the near side; head-on is viewed by traffic approaching a location on the outside of a curve or where traffic makes a sharp turn.
- *Immediate surroundings:* Is it close to a shopping center? Is there competition from surrounding signs. Is the sign near a traffic light? Red lights give people more time to read the sign.
- *Size and physical attractiveness of the outdoor sign.*
- *Price:* an area of comparative values and negotiation.

CREATIVITY IN OUTDOOR ADVERTISING

Outdoor is the ultimate visual advertising medium. The outdoor poster utilizes spectacular amounts of space with few words. Most creative directors view outdoor as both a challenge and a great deal of fun. The challenge is in communicating a message with few words. The fun comes from the opportunity to incorporate creative puns and plays on words in addition to the obvious visual elements.

One outdoor advertising creative director summarized his creative strategy for the medium as combining: simplicity; talking *to,* not *at* people; motivation; entertainment; and maximizing the unique characteristics of outdoor.[9] From an art director's viewpoint, maximizing the medium is altogether a matter of design. Since the integration of word and picture is so crucial to the success of an outdoor poster, there is no medium where excellence in design is more important.

In recent years, many advertisers have used a series of outdoor signs for added effect or to give their advertising a "campaign" look (see Exhibits 12.13 and 12.14). Outdoor has also become a popular medium for nonprofit advertisers who wish to reach broad segments of the population as inexpensively as possible (see Exhibit 12.15).

Designing an outdoor poster is such a personal process that it is very difficult to draw up a list of rules for it. Creativity in this area often means breaking the rules—some of the most successful posters have done just that in an unforgettable way. Bearing that in mind, we present seven principles that might prove helpful to individuals designing an outdoor poster:

1. *Product:* Does the advertiser's name or product register quickly?
2. *Short copy:* Is the basic idea expressed to have immediate impact? Use headline copy and keep it brisk, compact, and provocative.
3. *Legible type:* Can the viewer read the copy at a distance while moving? Remember, simple

[9] Pam Janis, "Outdoor's Creative Directors Want Art Added to Medium's Message," *Gannetteer,* May 1988, p. 20.

EXHIBIT 12.13

Effective outdoor advertising is virtually impossible to overlook by the traveling public. (Courtesy: Naegele Outdoor Advertising, Inc.)

EXHIBIT 12.14

(Courtesy: Institute of Outdoor Advertising.)

NIKE SPORTSWEAR

ADVERTISER	NIKE INC. BEAVERTON, OR
ADVERTISING AGENCY	CHIAT/DAY LOS ANGELES, CA OUTDOOR SERVICES, INC. NEW YORK/SAN FRANCISCO

CAMPAIGN DETAILS

NIKE utilized Out-of-Home advertising as the major part of the media mix for national introduction in 1984-85. The focus of the Out-of-Home efforts was to project brand imagery through Painted Bulletins, Painted Walls and Transit Posters.

Successfully achieving this goal, the campaign also gained wide publicity as a kind of new art form. The presentations used the action and drama of athletics in memorable designs made distinctive by extension of the image - an arm, a leg - outside the board limits. Commanding ten-story Painted Walls also captured consumer and news media attention.

So successful was the Out-of-Home effort that it was integrated into award-winning TV commercials that ran during the 1984 Summer Olympics that actually pre-empted official sportswear sponsors.

NIKE established national presence for its line of sportswear by using Out-of-Home to boldly communicate the essence of quality and excitement.

SOURCES: KEVIN BROWN, DIRECTOR OF CORPORATE RELATIONS
NIKE, INC.
GUY DAY
CHIAT/DAY
ROBERT NYLAND
OUTDOOR SERVICES, INC.

EXHIBIT 12.15

With its broad coverage, outdoor is an excellent medium for public-service advertising. (Courtesy: Institute of Outdoor Advertising.)

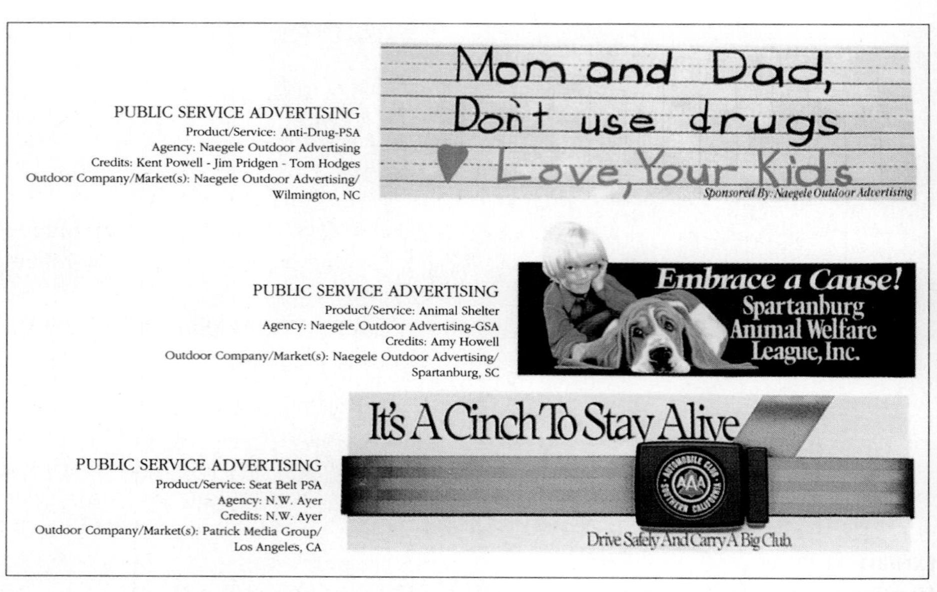
PUBLIC SERVICE ADVERTISING
Product/Service: Anti-Drug-PSA
Agency: Naegele Outdoor Advertising
Credits: Kent Powell - Jim Pridgen - Tom Hodges
Outdoor Company/Market(s): Naegele Outdoor Advertising/
Wilmington, NC
Mom and Dad,
Don't use drugs
Love, Your Kids
Sponsored By: Naegele Outdoor Advertising
PUBLIC SERVICE ADVERTISING
Product/Service: Animal Shelter
Agency: Naegele Outdoor Advertising-GSA
Credits: Amy Howell
Outdoor Company/Market(s): Naegele Outdoor Advertising/
Spartanburg, SC
Embrace a Cause!
Spartanburg
Animal Welfare
League, Inc.
PUBLIC SERVICE ADVERTISING
Product/Service: Seat Belt PSA
Agency: N.W. Ayer
Credits: N.W. Ayer
Outdoor Company/Market(s): Patrick Media Group/
Los Angeles, CA
It's A Cinch To Stay Alive
Drive Safely And Carry A Big Club.

typefaces are more readable from varying distances. Keep capital letters to a minimum and use large type sizes.

4. *Layout:* Do all the elements work together as a single visual unit? Eliminate all nonessential elements—here, less is usually more!
5. *Big illustrations:* Are the pictures large and do they embody elements that identify the product or message? Has the illustration been cropped so the main elements can be magnified greatly?
6. *Simple background:* Does the background promote the basic advertising presentation or interfere with it?
7. *Bold colors:* Are the colors vibrant? Do they project for a fast-moving audience? Do they separate well from the surroundings?[10]

COOPERATIVE ADVERTISING IN OUTDOOR

Outdoor has joined most other media in competing for co-op dollars from major national advertisers. By encouraging manufacturers and retailers to share the cost of space and/or production, co-op increases the dollars available to the medium. Some manufacturers share all costs; some provide (or pay for) paper, but give no space allowances; and some share the cost of space, but stipulate that paper production is the retailer's responsibility. In a typical case, the manufacturer pays for half the space costs and supplies the poster paper, and the retailer pays for the store imprint. Here's how an outdoor co-op buy usually operates:

1. The retailer receives notification of the manufacturer's program, which sets the specifications of the co-op arrangement. The retailer then checks with the manufacturer's representative to see whether he/she has earned enough allowance to be eligible to participate.
2. The retailer and the local outdoor plant agree on showing size, cost, and other details.
3. The retailer orders paper from the manufacturer and has it sent to the outdoor plant, where it is imprinted with the retailer's name and any additional message.
4. The showing is posted and the retailer receives original invoices, proof-of-performance, and a list of all locations. The retailer then arranges for reimbursement from the manufacturer.[11]

---

[10]Ken Sammon, *Planning for Out-of-Home Media* (New York: The Traffic Audit Bureau, Inc.), 1987, pp. 55–56.

[11]From *Co-Op Advertising*, a publication of Naegele Outdoor Advertising, Inc.

TRENDS IN OUTDOOR ADVERTISING

Outdoor advertising is looking to new technology and formats to attract viewers. While promotion companies are consolidating, they are trying to attract *new sponsors,* such as local businesses and *package-goods companies*. Sorrell Ridge, once only found in the condiment section of health food stores, launched an innovative challenge to land in mass outlets. It took on the industry's leader, Smucker's in newspapers, newspaper inserts, and billboards to match their "100% fruit" jams and jellies. Billboards carried a simple 3-line message adjacent to the product—well-positioned near large supermarkets.

Outdoor is in a particularly competitive position because the number of out-of-home competitors is proliferating almost daily at a time when the foundation advertising categories of the industry—tobacco and alcohol—have cut back drastically on their expenditures in outdoor. Attempts to entice other national advertisers to use the medium are succeeding more slowly than anticipated. There are a number of trends of importance to outdoor, but four are paramount:

1. New technology and diversification of formats are changing the out-of-home industry in dramatic ways. Outdoor is beginning to utilize new fabric and plastic materials that offer great illumination and lower maintenance costs. Some observers predict that outdoor advertising of the twenty-first century will consist mainly of spectacular TV screens where messages can be changed immediately by remote control.
2. Consolidation of ownership is as apparent in the outdoor industry as in other media. Multimedia companies such as Gannett and Morris Communications have become major owners of outdoor plants, and they are bringing sophisticated marketing techniques and research to the medium.
3. Outdoor is attempting to diversify the product categories using the medium. Local advertisers have become a major category, but to date, the industry has had less success in selling itself to major package-goods manufacturers. However, even a very small share of the total advertising budget of a company such as Procter & Gamble would have a significant effect on outdoor billings.
4. Plant owners are becoming much more aware of environmental and public policy issues. The number of outdoor signs not in compliance with the Federal Highway Act of 1965 has been reduced dramatically over the last ten years. Throughout the country, new single-pole panels are replacing the older scaffoldlike outdoor panels. In addition, the industry is mounting a communication campaign to tell the public about the positive aspects of outdoor advertising.

TRANSIT ADVERTISING

Transit advertising manages to attract a significant number of metropolitan consumers, who might miss other forms of promotion—the upscale, youth, and working women. AT&T, in trying to reach the college market, chose "wallboards" on kiosks in well-travelled campus locations. Non-resident students were especially respondent—as *frequent* riders of buses and trains and infrequent readers of campus newspapers.

Interior transit signs. *They are carried inside mass transit vehicles, reaching a captive audience which is in the out-of-home marketplace and often intending to make a purchase.*

Exterior transit signs. *These signs expose an advertiser's message to a large segment of the out-of-home market. Major drawback is the difficulty of gaining accurate audience figures.*

After outdoor, the largest segment of the out-of-home advertising industry is transit. In virtually every major market, potential customers are exposed to a wide array of messages on buses, rail cars, subways, taxis, bus shelters, commuter stations, telephone booths, and stations clocks. These diverse forms of transit advertising generally fall into one of three primary categories: interior transit (often called car-cards), exterior transit, and station and shelter advertising. Bus advertising is, by far, the most popular form of transit advertising, using both exterior and interior signs.

The popularity of transit advertising is due to a number of factors:

1. *Broad reach of a mobile population*. Exhibit 12.16 shows the extent of coverage in a typical market. As you can see, every demographic category is well represented.
2. *New transit systems*. During the last decade, a number of mass transit systems have either opened or been renovated. Their appeal to a more upscale audience has brought a number of new advertisers into the medium. The rising number of women in the marketplace, and their usage of mass transit, has also made transit advertising more appealing.
3. *Low cost*. Transit advertising achieves the lowest CPM of any medium—often CPMs of less than 50 cents.
4. *Excellent supplemental and reminder medium*. Transit advertising can supplement more traditional advertising and reach prospects, such as teenagers, who are not heavy users of other media. Exhibit 12.17 shows the manner in which transit accumulates both reach and frequency over a period of time, which makes it an excellent medium for building brand awareness.

The sheer number of exterior and interior signs available (see Exhibit 12.18) gives advertisers great flexibility in using the medium. Interior signs reach a captive audi-

MARK[illegible]MATH, INC.
03/21/[illegible]5

TEAM III -- AUDIENCE OF EXTERIOR BUS ADVERTISING

C.D. WILLIAMS ADVERTISING INC.
TABLE 1

SYRACUSE, NY: #50 SHOWING, 40 BUSES

		SEX		AGE			INCOME			RACE/ETHNIC	
POPULATION 18+	TOTAL 18+	MEN	WOMEN	18-34	35-49	50+	$20K-	$20-35K	$35K+	BLACK	SPANISH
NUMBER (000)	348	163	186	144	80	124	115	102	130	19	NA
PERCENT	100.0%	46.7%	53.3%	41.2%	23.1%	35.6%	33.2%	29.4%	37.4%	5.6%	-
1 MONTH: REACH	90.7%	93.0%	88.7%	94.0%	88.6%	88.2%	90.5%	90.4%	91.1%	94.0%	-
AVERAGE FREQUENCY	13.1X	13.8X	12.4X	13.0X	15.0X	11.8X	13.3X	14.0X	12.1X	14.8X	-
GROSS RATING POINTS	1183	1280	1099	1227	1328	1039	1205	1263	1102	1388	-
NUMBER REACHED	316	151	164	135	71	109	104	93	119	18	-
TOTAL EXPOSURES	4119	2080	2039	1761	1069	1289	1392	1292	1435	270	-
FREQUENCY: 1- 5 TIMES	31.2%	28.6%	32.7%	26.8%	27.6%	33.0%	27.9%	26.6%	29.1%	26.9%	-
6-10	19.5	20.3	19.1	22.7	18.0	19.9	21.0	20.5	22.8	19.8	-
11-20	21.5	23.7	20.3	26.6	21.4	20.6	24.0	24.3	24.8	24.1	-
21-30	9.8	11.0	9.0	11.1	10.6	8.5	10.3	10.9	9.4	11.9	-
31+	8.7	9.4	7.6	6.8	10.9	6.1	7.2	8.1	4.9	11.2	-
2 MONTH: REACH	94.8%	96.4%	93.4%	97.2%	93.0%	93.3%	94.7%	94.5%	95.2%	97.0%	-
AVERAGE FREQUENCY	25.0X	26.5X	23.5X	25.3X	28.6X	22.3X	25.5X	26.7X	23.2X	28.6X	-
GROSS RATING POINTS	2367	2559	2198	2454	2657	2078	2411	2528	2203	2775	-
NUMBER REACHED	330	157	173	139	75	116	109	97	124	19	-
TOTAL EXPOSURES	8238	4160	4078	3522	2139	2577	2783	2585	2871	540	-
FREQUENCY: 1- 5 TIMES	19.2%	16.1%	20.9%	13.0%	17.2%	20.6%	15.0%	14.4%	14.9%	14.9%	-
6-10	14.3	13.9	14.7	14.1	12.7	15.2	14.1	13.4	15.1	13.1	-
11-20	20.4	21.3	20.1	24.0	19.0	21.1	22.4	21.7	24.4	20.7	-
21-30	13.3	14.6	12.7	16.9	13.1	13.2	15.3	15.3	16.2	14.7	-
31+	27.5	30.5	25.0	29.2	31.0	23.1	27.9	29.7	24.6	33.7	-
3 MONTH: REACH	98.3%	97.6%	95.2%	98.2%	94.8%	95.2%	96.3%	96.1%	96.6%	98.0%	-
AVERAGE FREQUENCY	36.8X	39.3X	34.6X	37.5X	42.0X	32.7X	37.6X	39.4X	34.2X	42.5X	-
GROSS RATING POINTS	3550	3839	3297	3681	3985	3117	3616	3788	3305	4163	-
NUMBER REACHED	335	159	177	141	76	118	111	98	126	19	-
TOTAL EXPOSURES	12357	6240	6117	5283	3208	3865	4175	3877	4306	810	-
FREQUENCY: 1- 5 TIMES	14.0%	11.0%	15.6%	8.1%	12.8%	15.1%	10.0%	9.7%	9.5%	10.2%	-
6-10	11.1	10.2	11.6	9.5	9.7	11.9	10.1	9.5	10.5	9.5	-
11-20	17.3	17.3	17.4	18.4	15.6	18.3	18.0	17.1	19.5	16.5	-
21-30	12.8	13.5	12.5	15.5	12.0	13.2	14.4	14.0	15.7	13.2	-
31+	41.2	45.6	38.0	46.6	44.7	36.7	43.8	45.7	41.4	48.7	-

POSTER PLACEMENT	MARKET GEOGRAPHIC DEFINITION
50% LEFT SIDE	ONONDAGA CO., NY
50% RIGHT SIDE	

EXHIBIT 12.16

Transit advertising generates impressive audience figures over relatively short periods. (Courtesy: Transit Advertising Association.)

EXHIBIT 12.17

Typical reach and frequency for exterior transit advertising. *Source:* Market Math, prepared for the Transit Advertising Association.)

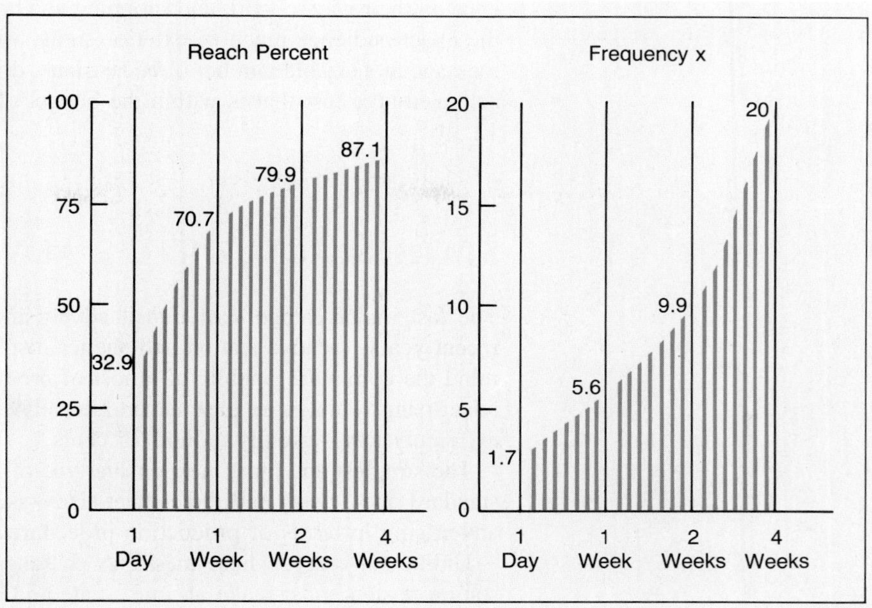
Reach Percent
Frequency x
100
75
50
25
0
32.9
70.7
79.9
87.1
20
15
10
5
0
1.7
5.6
9.9
20
1 Day
1 Week
2 Weeks
4 Weeks
1 Day
1 Week
2 Weeks
4 Weeks

EXHIBIT 12.18

Transit advertising offers advertisers a number of options. (Courtesy: Transit Advertising Association.)

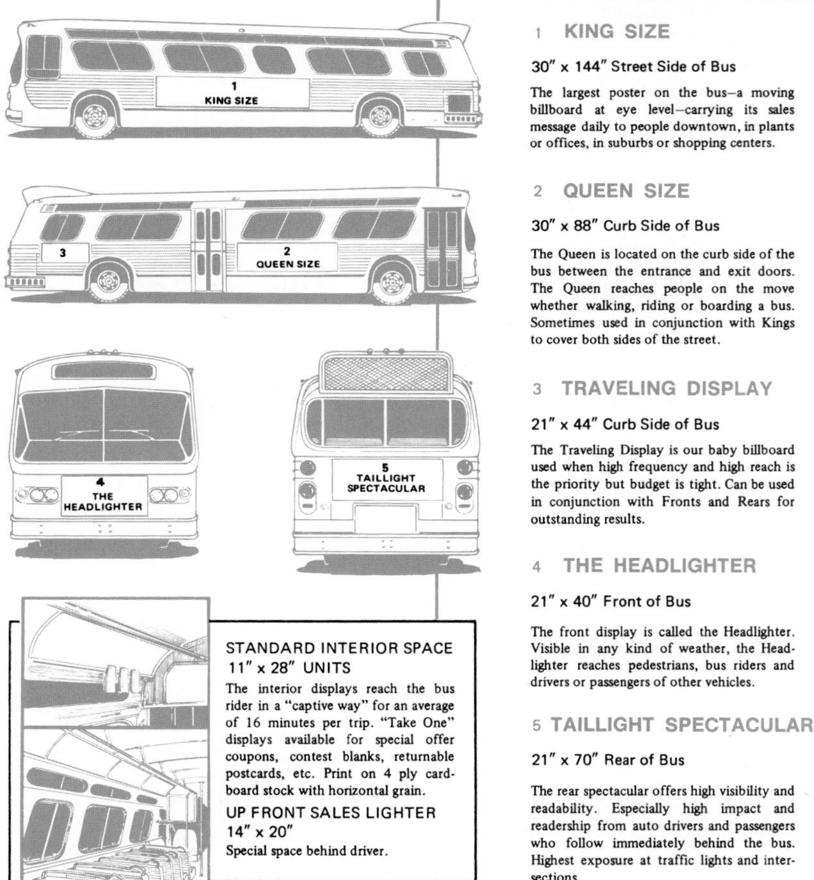
SPECIFICATIONS
Bus Advertising Displays
1 KING SIZE
30" x 144" Street Side of Bus
The largest poster on the bus—a moving billboard at eye level—carrying its sales message daily to people downtown, in plants or offices, in suburbs or shopping centers.
2 QUEEN SIZE
30" x 88" Curb Side of Bus
The Queen is located on the curb side of the bus between the entrance and exit doors. The Queen reaches people on the move whether walking, riding or boarding a bus. Sometimes used in conjunction with Kings to cover both sides of the street.
3 TRAVELING DISPLAY
21" x 44" Curb Side of Bus
The Traveling Display is our baby billboard used when high frequency and high reach is the priority but budget is tight. Can be used in conjunction with Fronts and Rears for outstanding results.
4 THE HEADLIGHTER
21" x 40" Front of Bus
The front display is called the Headlighter. Visible in any kind of weather, the Headlighter reaches pedestrians, bus riders and drivers or passengers of other vehicles.
5 TAILLIGHT SPECTACULAR
21" x 70" Rear of Bus
The rear spectacular offers high visibility and readability. Especially high impact and readership from auto drivers and passengers who follow immediately behind the bus. Highest exposure at traffic lights and intersections.
1 KING SIZE
3
2 QUEEN SIZE
4 THE HEADLIGHTER
5 TAILLIGHT SPECTACULAR
STANDARD INTERIOR SPACE
11" x 28" UNITS
The interior displays reach the bus rider in a "captive way" for an average of 16 minutes per trip. "Take One" displays available for special offer coupons, contest blanks, returnable postcards, etc. Print on 4 ply cardboard stock with horizontal grain.
UP FRONT SALES LIGHTER
14" x 20"
Special space behind driver.
C. Donald Williams Advertising, Inc.
SUITE 200 342 SOUTH SALINA ST. SYRACUSE, NY 13202
CALL COLLECT (315) 422-2213

ence on their way to work and shopping and home again. While it is harder to measure the exact audience reach of exterior signs, we know they do expose an advertiser's message to a sizable number of pedestrians, drivers, and bikers. All of this exposure is achieved at a cost that is within the budget of virtually every advertiser (see Exhibit 12.19).

STATION AND SHELTER ADVERTISING

The last major category of transit advertising is station and shelter advertising. In recent years, creative station and shelter displays have been used to introduce or remind the commuting public of a host of products and services. While many of these advertising vehicles are expensive to install, high pedestrian traffic makes CPM levels extremely low—usually around 25 cents.

The simplest and most inexpensive type of station advertising is the poster. Sold in standard one-, two-, and three-sheet sizes, station posters are very similar to outdoor advertising in terms of production procedures and creative strategy.

Unlike car cards, whose messages passengers have a relatively long time to read, station posters must make an immediate and decisive impact on people hurrying by.

EXHIBIT 12.19

Transit advertising is among the least expensive media, despite its high audience reach. (Courtesy: Transit Advertising Association.)

Rate Sheet

January 1, 1988

Poster	Production	Number of Posters	Poster cost per month for: 1 Month	3 Months	6 Months	12 Months
KING SIZE 30" x 144" Street Side and Curb Side	For frequent copy changes print on 80 lb. paper. Copy which will remain in position for longer periods can be printed on pressure sensitive vinyl or directly on Duron board or Styrene.	80 or more 40 to 79 1 to 39	$ 96.00 98.00 100.00	$94.00 96.00 98.00	$92.00 94.00 96.00	$88.00 90.00 92.00
QUEEN SIZE 30" x 88" Curb Side		80 or more 40 to 79 1 to 39	$70.00 72.00 74.00	$68.00 70.00 72.00	$66.00 68.00 70.00	$62.00 64.00 66.00
TRAVELING DISPLAY 21" x 44" Curb Side and Street Side	For frequent copy changes suggest printing on cardboard. Displays that will remain in position for more than 2 months, printing on styrene is highly recommended for all 3 of these positions.	80 or more 40 to 79 1 to 39	$42.00 44.00 46.00	$40.00 42.00 44.00	$38.00 40.00 42.00	$34.00 36.00 38.00
TAILLIGHT SPECTACULAR 21" x 70" Rear of bus		80 or more 40 to 79 1 to 39	$72.00 74.00 76.00	$70.00 72.00 74.00	$68.00 70.00 72.00	$64.00 66.00 68.00
THE HEADLIGHTER 21" x 40" Front of Bus		80 or more 40 to 79 1 to 39	$50.00 52.00 54.00	$48.00 50.00 52.00	$46.00 48.00 50.00	$42.00 44.00 46.00
INTERIOR SIGNS Backlighted 11" x 28" Both sides of bus	For best results print on a translucent styrene. Opaque cardboard, accepted but not recommended.	Single Poster	$6.00 each	$5.60 each	$5.20 each	$5.00 each
UP-FRONT SALES LIGHTER 14" x 20" Inside back of driver		Single Poster	$12.00 each	$11.20 each	$10.40 each	$10.00 each

COMMISSION 15% to Agencies. No Cash Discount

N

Transit Advertising

Wherever you are... we arE

S

C. Donald Williams Advertising, Inc.

SUITE 200 342 SOUTH SALINA ST. SYRACUSE, NY 13202 (315) 422-2213

One of the fastest growing out-of-home advertising segments is *public transportation shelter ads.* They are inexpensive, provide high frequency, reach targets effectively, and can be illuminated. *Lincoln Savings Bank* hopes to score a "home run" with baseball fans with its new "Subway Series" certificate of deposit. The special 7-month CD offers an interest bonus based on the number of games won by the New York Mets and Yankees baseball teams. The program will receive heavy support with subway and bus shelter billboards—where baseball fans travel to and from the games.

Therefore, the same rules set down for outdoor copy generally apply to transit posters.

Besides posters, station advertising encompasses a number of displays, including showcases, clocks, and floor displays. The more elaborate displays are normally used in the highest traffic areas—they are the transit industry's answer to the outdoor spectacular. It is not uncommon for station advertising to generate a million or more monthly exposures in major markets.

Public transportation shelter advertising is one of the fastest-growing segments of transit advertising. Shelters have a copy area 46 by 67 inches, with virtually no clutter to distract from the message. They provide exposure to car and bus riders as well as to pedestrians. Shelter advertising is one of the least expensive of all media, with average CPM levels in the 50-cent range. (Exhibit 12.20 shows a typical shelter advertising rate card.) Another of its advantages is that it can be targeted to reach specific areas of a market where prime prospects are most likely to live and commute.

Because people's commuting patterns vary little from day to day, shelter advertising generates high frequency as well as reach. Used to complement TV or newspaper advertising, shelter advertising can increase consumer brand recall and awareness at a lower cost than virtually any other promotional or advertising technique. Shelter advertising is used by both national and local advertisers and is available in illuminated signs for night viewing. (See Exhibit 12.21 for some examples of shelter advertising.)

EXHIBIT 12.20

Shelter advertising is becoming an important medium in a number of major markets. (Courtesy: Shelter Advertising Association.)

TRANSTOP

One Appletree Square
Minneapolis, MN 55420
(612) 854-1900

RATES

Effective January 1, 1988 • Cost is per panel per month

Quantity	1 Month	3 Months	6 Months	12 Months
1 - 9	$270	$260	$255	$245
10 - 19	$265	$255	$250	$240
20 - 34	$260	$250	$245	$235
35 +	$255	$245	$240	$230

Agency Commissionable at 15%

TERMS

Bills are rendered monthly and payable on receipt. No cash discounts. Contracts may only be cancelled on ninety (90) days written notice.

ROTATION AND ILLUMINATION

Posters are rotated every 30 days to cover additional audiences every month. All facings are backlit to give the advertiser 24-hour visibility.

AUDITED CIRCULATION DATA*

Average Daily Effective Circulation: **15,420 impressions per panel**

Out-of-Home Media in the Mpls/St. Paul market:

Illuminated bus shelter panel	**15,420**
Illuminated 30-sheet poster	14,720
Unilluminated 30-sheet poster	9,740
Unilluminated 8-sheet poster	7,480

Based on the Average DEC of 15,420, the number of panels per showing are:

Gross Rating Points/ Showings	Number of Illuminated Panels Minneapolis	St. Paul	Twin Cities
100	64	28	92
75	48	21	59
50	32	14	46
25	16	7	23

PRODUCTION

Dimensions:
Overall poster size:
47-½" wide × 68-¾" high
Live copy area: 46" × 67"

Recommended printing stocks are opaline or any paper stock which can be backlit. Cost of production not included in rates. Production estimates and sources for production available on request.

Recommended overage of 10% of panels purchased per month.

Vertical format is proportional to a magazine ad.

SHIPPING

Posters must be received at least 10 days prior to posting date.

Ship to: Transtop, Suite 1026
One Appletree Square
Minneapolis, MN 55420

Number of Shelter Panels
Minneapolis - 400
St. Paul - 200

Posting Date:
Minneapolis - 1st of the Month
St. Paul - 15th of the Month

*Audited by Out-of-Home Measurement Bureau

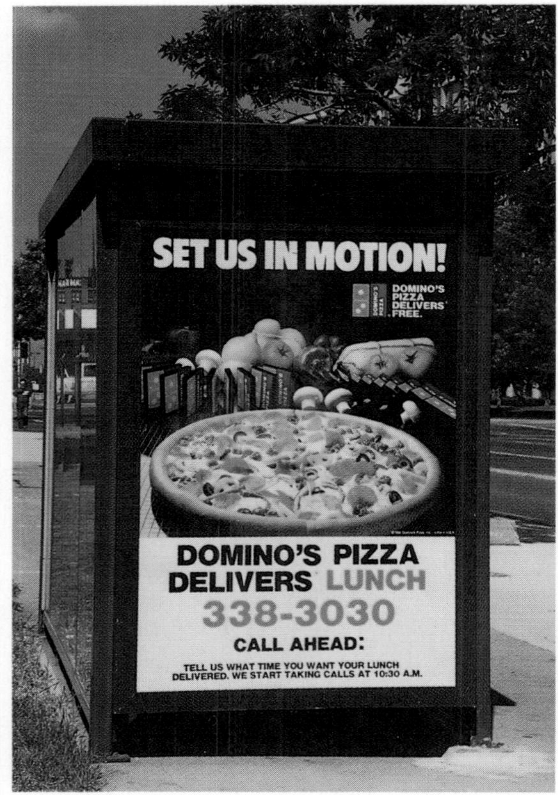

EXHIBIT 12.21

Outdoor shelters provide high visibility for urban audiences. (Courtesy: Shelter Advertising Association.)

Think Of Sushi
As Art You Can Eat.

Rollerblade.
The world's greatest
exercise facility is
right at your feet.

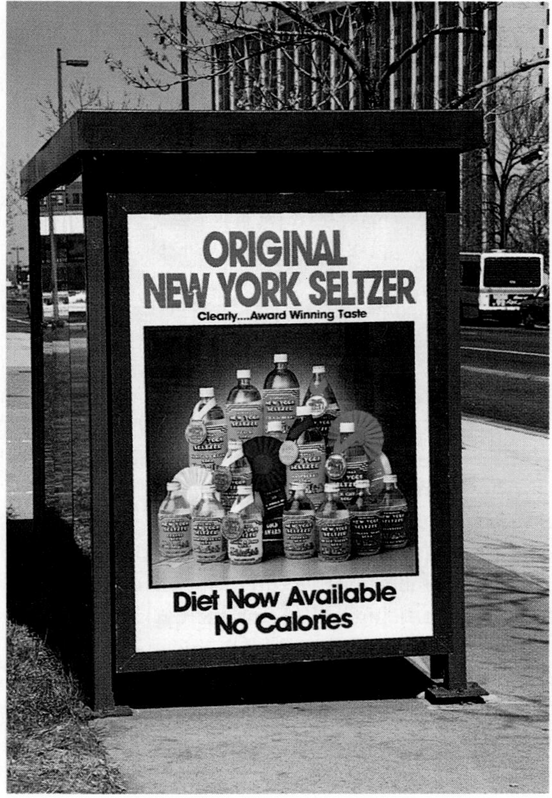
ORIGINAL
NEW YORK SELTZER
Clearly....Award Winning Taste
Diet Now Available
No Calories

WE DELIVER
EXCELLENCE...
FOR LESS.
EXPRESS MAIL
NEXT DAY SERVICE

EXHIBIT 12.22

Services such as ADVAN extend the coverage of traditional transit advertising. (Courtesy: ADVAN.)

A study conducted by Perception Research, Inc., indicated that shelter advertising:

- Attracts attention and generates involvement
- Generates attention in daylight hours and is even more effective when illuminated in evening hours
- Contributes to the overall effort of registering a brand-name with the public and communicating sales messages
- Enhances the effectiveness of the shelter if properly executed
- Evokes favorable comments from shoppers and tends to be viewed as convenient, safe, clean, and easy to see[12]

In addition to the standardized transit advertising found in mass transit systems and stations, trucks and other vehicles are used for advertising purposes. A company called ADVAN contracts with vehicles that circulate in desirable advertising areas such as retail, financial, and commercial centers (see Exhibit 12.22). A sophisticated data-processing program is used to estimate the weekly audience circulation, which is then sold on a GRP basis.

SUMMARY

As advertisers search for affordable alternatives to traditional media, out-of-home is sure to increase in terms of total advertising allocations. Out-of-home media are excellent for introducing, reminding, and increasing brand awareness. And they do so in a largely unobtrusive manner that allows continual exposure of messages to consumers.

If there is a problem with out-of-home, it is that it is a victim of its own success. As more and more companies use this type of advertising, it become increasingly difficult to control quality. Established organizations such as the OAAA and the TAA constantly work with their members and advertisers to ensure that the industry meets high standards, but many nonmember companies don't have the social responsibility of these major out-of-home organizations.

[12]Elliott Young, ''A Researcher's Look at Shelter Advertising,'' speech presented to the Shelter Advertising Association Meeting, New York, September 20, 1983.

QUESTIONS

1. Discuss the two primary types of outdoor advertising.
2. Why has the term *out-of-home* begun to replace *outdoor* in describing the general use of these advertising media?
3. Briefly discuss the major advantages and disadvantages of outdoor advertising.
4. Discuss the image problem of outdoor advertising, noting some ways in which the industry has moved to correct it.
5. Explain the role of the Traffic Audit Bureau and the Out-of-Home Measurement Bureau.
6. Discuss some of the reasons for the growing popularity of the eight-sheet poster.
7. If an advertiser purchases a 50-GRP showing in a market, what audience level is being bought?
8. Discuss some of the major factors in the recent growth of transit advertising.

SUGGESTED EXERCISES

- Note the first ten outdoor signs you see after you read this. Are they promoting local or national advertisers? Are they illuminated? Are they bulletins, 30-sheet, or eight-sheet posters?
- Using the criteria given for selecting outdoor locations in the text, choose an ideal location for an outdoor sign that is not presently being used for that purpose.

READINGS

FLOOD, BOB: ''Surveying the Options,'' *Marketing & Media Decisions,* March 1989, p. 115.

FLOOD, ROBERT: ''Outdoor: Price Right, but Hurdles Remain,'' *Advertising Age,* November 28, 1988, p. S-16.

KALISH, DAVID: ''Outdoor Media All-Star,'' *Marketing & Media Decisions,* December 1988, p. 85.

SAMMON, KEN: *Planning for Out-of-Home Media* (New York: The Traffic Audit Bureau, 1987).

SCOTT, JEFFRY: ''200 mph Billboards Are still Available,'' *ADWEEK,* February 20, 1989, p. 1.

THIRTEEN

Direct-Response and Direct-Mail Advertising

Only a few years ago, direct mail was considered a minor advertising medium. Even though large amounts of money were spent in the medium, its users were primarily those who could not gain access to, or could not afford, traditional media vehicles. The medium was shunned by most major national advertisers. Today the industry has grown and changed in ways that would make it unrecognizable to direct mailers of 20 years ago.

Direct response advertising can target the advertiser's prospects *best* of all leading media in most cases. The lure of a fishing vacation will be directed to residents of the Asheville-Greenville-Spartanburg area of the Carolinas and those of Grand Rapids, Michigan in a 6-week test. "With excellent fishing areas nearby, we're trying to see if we can entice the active 35–54-year-old to investigate the resorts and supply stores we list in our mailer," hopes Tom Conley, president of the American Fishing Tackle Manufacturers Association. Mass advertising was rejected as not reaching fishing's "ideal" target—"the guy who listens to classical, soft rock, or country and western music and prefers to challenge *himself*."

1. *The customer*. Direct response is the prototype medium of the target-marketing era of the 1990s. Advertisers are able to identify and reach prospective consumers to an extent that would have been impossible a few years ago. Basic demographic information has been augmented by purchase-behavior data, media-preference responses, and lifestyle profiles. More importantly, this information is provided on an individual basis rather than in the form of the audience profiles available in most other media.
2. *The media*. Direct response encompasses a number of media vehicles in addition to direct mail. Advertisers are becoming more knowledgeable and sophisticated in adapting media alternatives to different direct-response objectives. Exhibit 13.1 shows the media usage in terms of specific advertising goals for direct response.
3. *The advertisers*. Virtually every major advertiser is making use of some form of direct response. Package-goods manufacturers are sending coupons by mail, financial services are heavily involved in telemarketing, and several business-to-business advertisers are supplementing personal selling with videocassette promotions. This last innovative sales tool has overcome the traditional reluctance to use direct response by Fortune 500 companies.
4. *The products*. Conventional wisdom used to claim that only low-cost items could be sold directly to consumers. Today all sorts of products, from insurance and stocks to jewelry and shoes, are sold successfully through direct response.

Direct-response advertising. *Ads that offer goods and services directly to consumers rather than through a retail outlet.*

Direct marketing is the fastest-growing marketing activity. According to the Direct Marketing Association, expenditures in direct-mail advertising alone more than doubled from $8.9 billion in 1981 to $19 billion in 1987. It is estimated that between $120 billion and $150 billion worth of merchandise is purchased by mail order every year.

Direct response advertising consists of a number of distributive methods, media,

EXHIBIT 13.1

Direct marketing will continue to utilize a number of media outlets as well as direct mail and telemarketing. (Courtesy: *Advertising Age*.)

Media usage
Today's patterns vs. tomorrow's expectations

Media	% For lead generation		% To generate sales		For sales support	
	Today	Tomorrow	Today	Tomorrow	Today	Tomorrow
Direct Mail	61%	52%	66%	56%	24%	22%
Magazines	53%	37%	43%	30%	27%	18%
Catalogs	31%	26%	38%	33%	10%	10%
Telemarketing	30%	32%	42%	42%	15%	17%
Newspapers	30%	21%	26%	17%	19%	11%
Pkg./Stmt. inserts	25%	22%	31%	25%	12%	9%
Free stdg. inserts	22%	18%	24%	18%	11%	8%
Point of sale	19%	13%	18%	14%	11%	8%
UHF/VHF television	15%	17%	15%	14%	15%	13%
Cable TV	11%	20%	13%	19%	8%	11%
Radio	11%	10%	11%	10%	14%	10%

Source: DMA Research Department, Marketing Council, Direct Marketing Practices & Trends Survey, 1986

Direct marketing is the fastest-growing marketing activity. It's forecasted to grow up *9% in 1989*, especially in the areas of *computer targeting* and *enhancing creative and production values*. However, it faces growing concerns about *costs, saturation, and tune-out, plus consumer-perceived abuses*. In a case involving the Home Shopping Network, the sale of "liquidated" dolls for $24.50, versus "the normal retail price" of $49.95, is being challenged by the Council of Better Business Bureaus' National Advertising Division.

***Direct marketing.** Selling goods and services without the aid of wholesaler or retailer. Includes direct-response advertising and advertising for leads for sales people. Also direct door-to-door selling. Uses many media: direct mail, publications, TV, radio.*

Direct marketing allows the advertiser to communicate *directly* with his/her customer, without relying on an intermediate communication vehicle. Optifast, the meal replacement program Oprah Winfrey used to lose 60 pounds, avoids direct consumer advertising because of limits set on consumer advertising of prescription drugs. Instead, it concentrates its promotion on *direct mailings to physicians, hospitals, and clinics*. Sandoz, Optifast's parent, expects sales to increase by 25–30% in 1989, due to increased awareness by the medical community of the health risks of obesity and how successful their product is to treat it.

trade practices, and traditions. We begin our survey of this medium with some definitions.

DEFINITIONS

Direct Marketing

Direct marketing is the general term that encompasses direct-response and direct-mail advertising as well as the research and support activities that make them possible. The term *direct* is used when either the advertiser or the customer deals directly to make a purchase or to promote a product. Direct marketing allows the advertiser greater control over the communication process than traditional forms of media advertising. It is the advertiser who determines the audience, timing, and production techniques, not the medium.

Direct-Response Advertising

The term *direct-response advertising* is supplanting the term *mail-order advertising* because today so much of the business is initiated or shipped by means other than mail. (Later in this chapter, we will look at two of these techniques—telemarketing and broadcast direct sales.)

Still, many people confuse the terms *direct mail* and *direct response,* sometimes even considering them synonomous. In fact, direct-response is any advertising used in selling goods directly to consumers. The message doesn't have to come through the mails (though it often does); it can be an advertisement with a coupon in a newspaper or magazine, or even a telephoned solicitation.

GROWTH OF DIRECT-RESPONSE ADVERTISING

All evidence points to continued growth in direct-response advertising during the next decade. Many factors have contributed to this growth; we discuss some of the major ones here.

"Ideal" targets for direct response advertising are "working" families and senior citizens. *The Insurance Information Institute* is gearing up a $6 million–$8 million campaign to distribute informative material *directly* to subscribers of general household magazines. Also included in the nationwide mailing will be subscribers to *Reader's Digest* and *Modern Maturity*—to reach the older population.

Societal Factors

Our fast-paced lives encourage direct-response advertising. Both the harried executive and the working wife are ideal candidates for catalogs, video shopping services, and mail-order magazine offers because their lifestyles leave them little time to shop. Less obvious prospects are senior citizens. They do not lack the time to shop so much as the transportation and the stamina. In recent years, however, direct-response advertisers have recognized that the over-50 group is an excellent, and largely untapped, market for a host of products and have targeted promotions to them (see Exhibit 13.2).

The Image Problem of Direct Response

We noted at the beginning of the chapter that many major national advertisers long disdained direct marketing. This was largely because direct response had a reputation as a haven for the disreputable.

Despite the industry's efforts to improve both its practices and its image, many customers are still skeptical of direct-response offers, and this skepticism is a major hindrance to further sales increases for the industry. Unfortunately, the problem is not just one of perception. The Better Business Bureau received 70,000 complaints against mail-order firms, and the Federal Trade Commission heard from 11,000 dissatisfied mail-order customers in the first three months of 1988.[1] Clearly, the industry has a formidable public relations task.

[1]Dan Bencivenga, "Polishing Mail Order's Tarnished Image," *Target Marketing*, May 1988, p. 12.

EXHIBIT 13.2

Mature consumers represent excellent prospects for many product categories. (Courtesy: *Marketing & Media Decisions*.)

MATURE PURCHASE PATTERNS

Percentage of those 50-64 who have purchased items via direct-marketing options during the past year.

	Women	Men
Clothing	40%	33%
Books	34%	33%
Seeds, plants	22%	24%
Records, tapes	18%	22%
Hobby, crafts	17%	17%
Vitamins, etc.	16%	17%
Film develop	13%	17%
Shoes	14%	15%
Housewares	16%	14%

Source: Goldring and Co., Chicago

Direct Marketing Association (DMA). *The major trade association which promotes the use of direct marketing.*

An "image problem" exists for direct response—due to disreputable industry participants, who continue to exist. To dispel any doubts among would-be buyers, *quality direct marketers* offer their own "unconditional guaranties," promising to refund the purchase price or replace unsatisfactory merchandise—"at any time, no questions asked." Many of these advertisers belong to the Direct Marketing Association, a trade group which solicits only reputable sellers as members. Credit card companies will also stand behind their *buyers,* if they document legitimate claims against dishonest vendors.

The Direct Marketing Association has taken a leadership role in trying to change consumer perceptions about mail order and in encouraging companies to adhere to strict guidelines in dealing with customers (see Exhibit 13.3). The industry is determined to increase consumer satisfaction and rid mail order of disreputable firms because it knows that the alternative to self-regulation is restrictive legislation. There is already a flood of proposed legislation that would greatly restrict the industry's operations:

> Currently, 31 states have pending or proposed legislation to restrict list access; 33 states have pending legislation to regulate telephone solicitations; 35 states have sales/use taxes pending; and 19 states are seeking to regulate mail order procedures.
>
> This recent spate of restrictive legislation promises to have far-reaching effect within the direct marketing industry. For direct mailers, sales and use taxes can result in greatly increased costs. Reduced list access can dramatically affect targeting. For telemarketing, restrictions on telephone solicitations can adversely impact response and sales.[2]

The Search for Alternative Media by Advertisers

On a CPM/reader or listener basis, direct response is usually very expensive. But on a *CPM/prospect* basis—that is, reaching prime prospects with minimum waste circulation—properly executed direct-response advertising can be a bargain. As advertisers

EXHIBIT 13.3

Self-regulation is extremely important to the image of the direct-marketing industry. (Courtesy: Direct Marketing Association.)

Recommended Practices
For Customer Satisfaction

THE CUSTOMER SHOULD EXPECT:

Order-taking and delivery

- To be given clear, honest and complete information on the exact nature of what is being offered, the price, the terms of payment (including all extra charges) and the commitment the customer is making by placing an order.
- To have included in the promotion or catalog:
  (a) A clear and conspicuous order form or coupon with sufficient space to easily write name and address, item numbers and descriptions, and credit card digits.
  (b) Information on shipping charges, if any, and on any applicable sales/use tax.
  (c) Sizing guidelines to assist in ordering items such as apparel, shoes or jewelry.
  (d) Where practical, instructions regarding ordering, returning and obtaining customer service.
- To have, at or before the time the order is placed or is received by the marketer, information as to when the order will be shipped.
- To find the advertised items in stock, the order promptly processed, and the ordered item or service shipped at the expected time.
- To be advised, as soon as the marketer is aware of the situation, of any delay in shipment of all or any part of the order. To be given, at that time, clear information as to whether the order is being cancelled or will be shipped at a later time, and if so, when.
- To be told, at the time the order is placed, whether there are any additional charges or price changes.

[2] "47 States Propose Restrictive Laws," *Target Marketing,* March 1988, p. 29.

CPM/prospect. *The primary means of measuring efficiency in direct-response advertising. It attempts to reflect the highly selective nature of such advertising.*

The trends are toward more creative messages, aimed at the more discriminating customer, who is more quality sensitive then price sensitive. Chemical Bank is airing a $10 million–$15 million TV, radio, *and direct mail campaign,* its first *image* effort in more than five years. Themed, "The human touch, the financial edge," the campaign aims to strengthen number 2 Chem Bank's position against number 1, Citibank. The direct mail piece is intended to capitalize on the awareness generated by the mass media.

seek methods of pinpointing certain customers, direct response is becoming an even more important part of the total promotional mix—to the point where clutter has become a problem.

A study conducted by the Newspaper Advertising Bureau found that the average American household receives 1.6 pieces of advertising mail each day. In households with incomes above $35,000, the figure is almost two pieces a day. Altogether, third-class mail increased 49 percent from 1982 to 1986, and will probably show a similar increase by the early 1990s.

Given the rising number of competing direct-response messages, it is inevitable that presentations will become more creative, and a greater emphasis on creative values means higher production costs. This is not all bad, however, because the better the communication, the more likely a sale. As one direct marketer commented, "We have a much more discriminating consumer today, one who is not so price sensitive, but very quality sensitive. Most companies are product driven, not customer driven, and I think they've got to change."[3] Thus, the techniques that worked when small, unknown companies sold inexpensive merchandise will not work for national firms selling top-of-the-line products and services to sophisticated buyers.

Target Marketing and Direct Response

In previous chapters, we noted that most media sell themselves to advertisers at least partly on their ability to target certain market segments. The ability to identify individual prospects is the most important feature of direct response. The process of sophisticated audience segmentation began in 1963 when the U.S. Postal Service introduced the ZIP code.

The ZIP code allowed direct-response advertisers to isolate relatively small sections of cities. The next step was to gather as much information as possible about the people living in each ZIP code. The combining of demographic data with ZIP codes greatly enhanced the ability to pinpoint audiences for marketing and advertising purposes.

Next, direct-response advertisers used psychographic information to further identify prospects. As we discussed earlier, psychographics attempts to give advertisers insights into how customers think about themselves and how this self-image is translated into purchase behavior.

Synchrographics. *Market segmentation based on lifestyle changes and the recency of these changes.*

Zip codes, combined with *demographics, psychographics,* and the newer *synchrographics,* can provide the advertiser with the consumer information needed for precise targeting. *May & Speh, Direct Marketing Consultants,* advertise that they'll develop "a complete, confidential data base system that captures customer information from co-op and solo mailings, telemarketing, and mail-in offers." Then, they'll "enrich it" with individual purchasing histories, demographics, and census information. The end result will be *profiles,* identifying the firm's "best customers."

In recent years, a new term has entered the lexicon of target marketing; *synchrographics*. Synchrographics is market segmentation based on lifestyle changes. The theory is that men and women who are changing habits and locations—that is, changing their lifestyles—are excellent customers for certain types of products. For example, new mothers, new retirees, and new homeowners are all excellent prospects for certain products. Synchrographics is the study of *recency* or the *timing* of lifestyle changes.

> Synchrographic thinking urges you to pay more attention to the market—not only consumers' habits and mental images of themselves, but *when* they must buy. The challenge is to steer a market already in motion.
>
> Only lifestyle change marketing promises perpetual markets like these:
>
> - 3.7 million new American babies born each year.
> - 5,500 Americans turn 55 each day
> - 4.2 million new homes purchases annually.[4]

[3] "On the Threshold of Change," *Target Marketing,* July 1988, p. 14.

[4] Robert Perlstein, "The Value of Timeliness," *Target Marketing,* June 1988, p. 25.

Research in Direct Response

Not only does direct response provide immediate sales results, it also allows the advertiser to test a number of variables for future offers. Research in direct mail and direct response dates to the 1920s, when advertisers such as Claude Hopkins studied the effects of direct offers in such works as his classic *Scientific Advertising* (1926). In recent years, virtually every aspect of direct response has been tested and retested to determine the best approach to sales.

Two elements which have given direct marketing the biggest boost are *computers* for targeting and *credit cards* for payment. *Visa* is combining these two features by teaming with MCI Communications. It's using its credit card customers, which also have MCI long-distance service, to test *Visa Phone*, a new service that lets long-distance customers charge calls on their credit cards.

Use of Computers and Credit Cards in Direct Response

In many respects, modern direct marketing was made possible by computer technology. Throughout the remainder of this chapter, we will discuss fundamental techniques of direct response that would be impossible without computers. Computers allow audience segmentation to a degree that would have been impossible only a few years ago. By identifying prime prospects, and thus eliminating the waste circulation that occurs in much mass advertising, the computer justifies the higher cost of direct response. Computers also quickly determine duplication among several lists. Finally, the computer-generated letter has enabled advertisers to personalize direct-response messages.

Another great boon to direct response was the credit card. The widespread use of credit cards has both simplified payment and encouraged purchases of expensive items. Furthermore, recent consumer legislation regarding credit card purchases gives customers greater protection in receiving refunds if the merchandise proves unsatisfactory.

Telemarketing consists of two forms: *inbound*, when consumers respond to phone numbers from another medium, and *outbound*, when the advertiser calls the prospect directly with a sales proposition. *Many service businesses*, such as landscapers, carpet and upholstery cleaners, and home water treatment systems use telemarketing, rather than employ sales personnel or set up showrooms. Their reach is *broad enough* that *blocks* of phone numbers usually net them a sufficient number of prospects to make the "cold calls" economical.

Telemarketing

When the 800 WATS services was introduced in 1961, no one could have imagined the implications it would have for direct marketing. Telemarketing has grown from a supplemental sales technique to the largest source of direct-response sales (although more money is spent on direct-mail advertising). Telemarketing is as close to face-to-face selling as direct response can get. In fact, a recent study indicated that executives spend an average of 14 weeks a year engaged in business calls (see Exhibit 13.4).

EXHIBIT 13.4

The telephone is an indispensable part of doing business. (Courtesy: The Radio Advertising Bureau.)

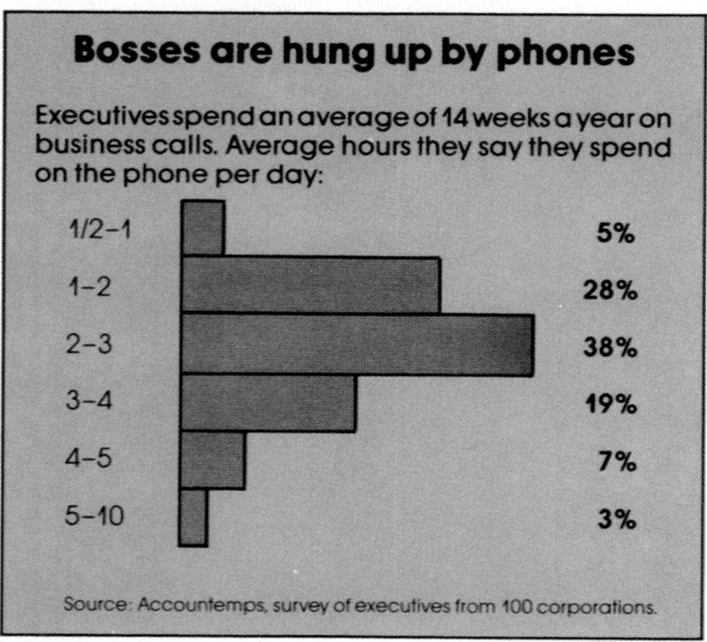
Bosses are hung up by phones
Executives spend an average of 14 weeks a year on business calls. Average hours they say they spend on the phone per day:
1/2–1
5%
1–2
28%
2–3
38%
3–4
19%
4–5
7%
5–10
3%
Source: Accountemps, survey of executives from 100 corporations.

Outbound/inbound telemarketing. *Outbound telemarketing occurs when sellers call prospects to make a sale, in contrast to inbound telemarketing where customers respond to an ad and place an order.*

There are two forms of telemarketing: *outbound* and *inbound*. In outbound telemarketing, the seller calls prospects to make a sale, to determine interest by offering catalogs or other sales material, or to pave the way for a personal sales call at a later date.

Outbound telephone solicitation has several advantages over other techniques. First, it is immediate: The offer and consumer response are practically instantaneous. Second, telephone solicitations are flexible: The sales message can be adapted to the individual buyer as the conversation develops. Finally, telephone offers can be tested quickly and inexpensively.

The second type of telemarketing, inbound, is used in conjunction with some other medium and is normally an order-taking operation. Catalog sales, magazine ads that invite customers to call for addresses of nearby retailers or more information (see Exhibit 13.5), and even product hotlines set up to aid consumers or to process their complaints are all examples of inbound telemarketing.

Perhaps the most familiar type of inbound direct response is the combination of television advertising with an 800 telephone number response capability. The televi-

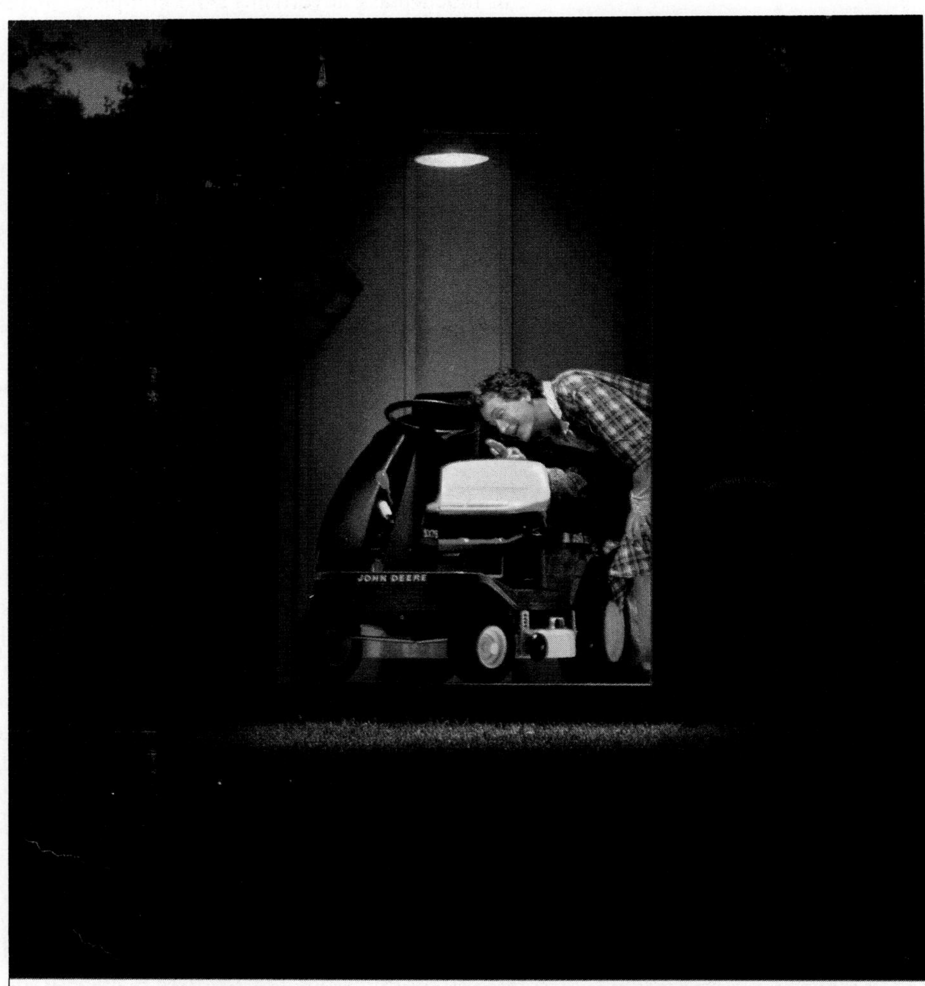

JOHN DEERE
HAVE YOU EVER OWNED THE BEST OF ANYTHING?
We've made a lot of changes in John Deere products over the years, but not in the way we build them. We still use welds where others use bolts. Full-length steel frames instead of half-frames. And heavy-duty engines. You see, we think things should last. And not surprisingly, ours do. For additional details, call 1-800-447-9126. In Illinois, 1-800-322-6796.
JOHN DEERE
NOTHING RUNS LIKE A DEERE®

EXHIBIT 13.5

Telemarketing is often included as a routine part of many ads. (Courtesy: Deere and Company.)

sion ad is a product demonstration, while the 800 number permits an immediate purchase by the consumer. Before initiating any 800 telephone system, the advertiser should be aware that it can be very expensive unless sales volume is high. In the case of television offers, most sales are generated in the few minutes after the commercial runs, but operators must be available throughout the day (often on a 24-hour basis) if customers are to be adequately served.

Successful outbound telemarketing involves several steps:

1. *A targeted list*. As with all direct-response advertising, an up-to-date list is crucial. In addition, there must be some mechanism to make sure the list is continually updated.
2. *Scripts*. The message should be conventional in tone, but not overly familiar. After all, you are a stranger to the prospect.
3. *Testing*. Telemarketing campaigns should be tested before full-scale implementation. One of the advantages of telemarketing is that it lends itself to inexpensive testing of different prospect categories and scripts.
4. *Trained personnel*. The caller must be trained in communication skills, have a thorough knowledge of the product, and be well versed in commonly asked questions. The best telemarketing comes across as a conversation rather than a sales pitch.
5. *Record keeping*. Telemarketing should be used to build and refine your prospect list. Callers should keep records of questions, complaints, and comments about the company or product. Follow-ups are crucial to develop adequate customer service.

Telemarketing is the most controversial of all the direct-response techniques. Legislation to control certain practices of the industry represent a real threat to its future. Several states are considering limiting telemarketing by:

- Requiring telemarketers to register with a state agency
- Prohibiting calls to households where people have notified a special commission that they do not wish to receive such calls
- Limiting calls to some specified hours such as 9 A.M.–5 P.M. on weekdays
- Permitting people to list their phone number with an asterisk beside it to indicate that no calls should be made to that number[5]

Automatic dialing recorded message programs (ADRMP). *Automated, computerized systems that randomly dial prospects and deliver a recorded sales message.*

Recent criticisms of telemarketing are related to random or sequential dialing by recorded message programs and unsolicited sales organizations. Some respondents have complained about 900 numbers' charges and accessibility to underage children. "Under the gun" in Florida are lawyers' promotions on TV, which asks respondents to call 900 numbers for legal advice. The state bar association insists on pre-clearing such solicitations now and is considering making lawyers-advertisers cover the costs involved through special fees.

Many people believe that automatic dialing recorded message programs (ADRMPs) are the major source of telemarketing's recent problems. For less than $1,000, these machines can dial hundreds of numbers a day and deliver a prerecorded sales message. The major complaints concerning ADRMPs come from people with unlisted numbers and others who see indiscriminate random dialing as an invasion of their privacy. One industry critic of random dialing noted, "If you don't know whom you're calling, you shouldn't be calling. There is never a good reason for random or sequential dialing, except maybe to notify people of a nuclear disaster."[6]

While the 800 number revolutionized the direct-response industry, 900 numbers have added a new wrinkle to telemarketing. Whereas the 800 number service is free to the caller, a customer dialing a 900 area code is charged. The 900 number is used for two purposes: to listen to a recorded message or to respond to some sort of opinion poll. During the 1988 presidential election campaign, many radio and television stations used the service to gauge the public's opinion of Bush and Dukakis.

Some 4,000 900 services are in operation today. A company leases a 900 line from AT&T for a onetime rate of $250. Callers to the number generally pay $2 for the first minute and a reduced rate for every minute after that. When 900 numbers are used for polling, the charge is only 50 cents. The per-call revenues are split between the company leasing the line and AT&T.

---

[5]Rebecca Fannin, "Answering the Call for Reform," *Marketing & Media Decisions,* July 1988, p. 24.

[6]David Enscoe, "Automated Junk Calls Threaten Telemarketing," *Target Marketing,* March 1988, p. 16.

The 900 numbers are used for a wide range of services—late sports scores, stock quotations, pornographic monologues, even messages from Jim and Tammy Bakker. Although this service has been generally exempt from the criticisms of outbound telemarketing, there have been complaints about children running up several hundred dollars in charges by calling advertised numbers.

TELEVISION AND DIRECT RESPONSE

Television has been discovered by direct marketing. The creative flexibility of a moving picture combined with precise target marketing is hard for advertisers to resist. There are many uses and formats for televised direct response. We will discuss some of the most popular ones in this section.

The Traditional Straight Sale

Television has been a tremendous stimulus for direct marketing. It starts in motion "the direct response" by referring the prospect to his *phone* to make a purchase or a commitment. The United Way campaign in Richmond, Virginia aired a TV program to recruit volunteers for charity work in the community. People were encouraged to call in and "give" 12 hours of their time for helping the elderly and youth groups. "The response," quoted Roberta Van Der Voort, UW's senior vice-president of marketing, "was so great, we had people calling *the next day,* complaining they couldn't get through!"

Per-inquiry (PI) advertising. *A Medium runs an ad for free and receives a percentage of the sales generated. Mostly used in broadcast.*

Direct-response television advertising consists of several categories. The first is the traditional 30-second-to-2-minute TV commercial offering relatively low-cost merchandise to be ordered through an 800 number. Publications as diverse as *The Wall Street Journal, Playboy,* and *Sports Illustrated* have made television a centerpiece of their marketing strategy. Records and tapes and small appliances make up two other major categories in this segment of TV direct response.

But TV direct response is growing up. While the familiar "greatest hits" offers still show up regularly on late-night TV, the number of companies selling through TV direct response has grown significantly in recent years. Today TV direct response sells products and services ranging from stockbrokers to cruises.

Not only have the products changed, but also the tone of the commercials has become more upscale. Instead of the high-volume hucksterism of former days, TV direct response reflects the corporate image of leading advertisers. By combining TV, telephone, and credit-card selling, advertisers gain immediate response and offer consumers maximum convenience. The purchase of television direct-response advertising is very different from traditional TV advertising. Direct-response advertisers are more likely to buy spots at off-hours, so they can negotiate for low rates. By buying spots at these low prices, they increase the return per dollar.

Other methods of placing direct-response advertising are per-inquiry (PI) and bonus-to-payout. As in magazines, PI means that the station runs the ad as often as it wishes and gets a percentage of the money received or so much for each inquiry. In bonus-to-payout, a fixed schedule of spots is bought, with the station and advertiser agreeing on a certain return. If the advertising fails to generate this level, the station is obligated to run additional spots or provide a rebate to the advertiser. Both PI and bonus-to-payout advertising are usually placed on independent stations or during late fringe time.

Long-Form TV Direct Response

Direct response has borrowed techniques from TV talk shows to create program-length shows featuring topics as diverse as weight loss, hair restoration, and real estate investment. While the stations carrying these programs precede them with a disclaimer saying that the program is a sponsored sales message, the overall impression given is that of a regularly televised interview program. Some of these shows even use personalities such as Robert Vaughn as "interviewers."

Other long-form programs are produced around cooking shows using a particular manufacturer's products, sewing shows using a certain brand of dress pattern, and the like. Whatever the format, most of these shows are aired on UHF independent stations or cable networks. The financial arrangement between the advertiser and the station is similar to that used by major TV evangelists for the last 30 years. Rather than buying commercial time within a program provided by a station, the producer pays the entire fee for time and program production, and is reimbursed out of audience donations (in the case of religious broadcasters) or the proceeds of selling merchandise (in the case of for-profit sponsors).

TV Shopping Networks

If a television spot or a full program works for direct response, why not an entire network? In the last eight years, home shopping television networks have become a major source of direct-marketing revenue. It is estimated that more than $3 billion worth of merchandise is purchased annually through these outlets.

The format and merchandise offered by these networks is very similar, and the tone is that of a fast-paced auction offering jewelry, appliances, and clothing at significant discounts. The TV viewers who are most likely to watch such networks are those in the 55+ age group (see Exhibit 13.6).

Although only about 20 percent of the population are regular viewers of these shows, a high percentage of them have made a purchase. In many respects, home shopping networks are where direct-mail and catalog sales were 20 years ago. These services will almost certainly gain in popularity as they become more established and market their merchandise to a more diversified population. One encouraging factor for these services is that viewer familiarity is consistent across most demographic categories (see Exhibit 13.7).

Home shopping networks have been extremely effective in reaching the ''home-bound'' shopper. J. C. Penney's Telaction interactive cable TV shopping service will prepare for its national rollout in 1990 by expanding its test this year to 39 Chicago suburbs from one. Unlike other TV shopping services that have announcers demonstrating sale items, Telaction resembles a video catalog, offering viewers merchandise ranging from groceries to sweaters and vacations. While grocery areas have proved most popular, especially among working parents, Donald Gordon, Telaction's executive director of consumer marketing, forecasted greater growth in giftware and ''luxury'' items from retirees and elderly shoppers.

Videocassettes

With videocassette recorders in more than 50 million homes and most major businesses, advertisers have naturally come to consider the videocassette as an advertising and sales option. The primary users of videocassettes are business-to-business advertisers, who usually incorporate them as part of a total marketing plan, most often as a follow-up to a personal sales call or as a response to a customer inquiry.

EXHIBIT 13.6

Both awareness and usage of home shopping programs have shown significant increases in recent years. (Courtesy: *Advertising Age*.)

Another stimulus to direct response purchasing is *the videocassette*—or ''a sales pitch on tape.'' It's aimed at *a particular target,* who has been identified as the ''ideal'' viewer of the video *and consumer* of the product by research services. After 12 weeks of release, the ''Moonstruck'' video had been rented 12,472,000 times nationwide, enough to yield the accompanying *Snickers commercial* the equivalent national TV rating of 14.1. Sponsors anticipate an added ''boost'' to video rentals *and* companion products.

Public awareness of TV home shopping programs

	(Base)	Very familiar	Fairly familiar	Only a little familiar	Not at all familiar	Don't know
Total public	(1001)	15%	22	34	28	1
Northeast	(213)	19%	22	31	28	—
North Central	(250)	13%	22	39	25	2
South	(340)	15%	20	33	31	1
West	(198)	13%	26	35	25	—
Non-metro area	(260)	8%	20	37	34	2
Metro area (under 1 million)	(338)	16%	21	32	30	1
Metro area (1 million +)	(403)	19%	25	35	21	—
Less than 35 years old	(366)	17%	24	40	18	1
35–64 years	(498)	15%	24	33	27	1
65 years or more	(130)	8%	12	25	54	1
High school incomplete	(100)	15%	14	26	44	—
High school graduate	(370)	15%	20	32	31	1
College incomplete	(189)	15%	26	34	24	1
College graduate	(330)	15%	25	41	19	—

*Less than ½%

Source: Opinion Research Corporation, April 1987

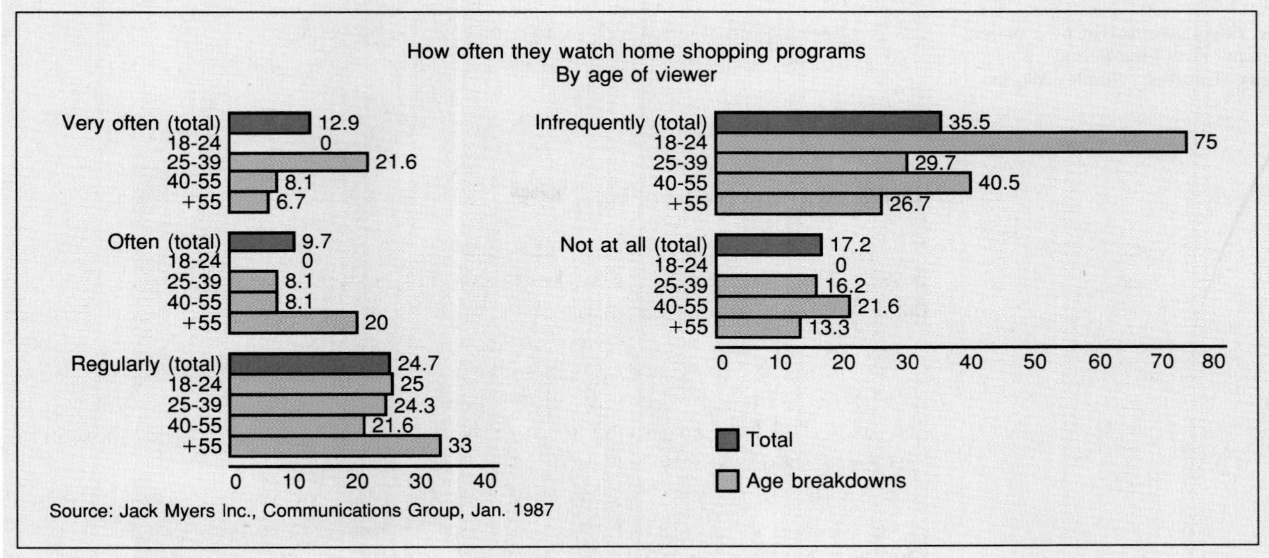

EXHIBIT 13.7

> Industry executives believe the technique is best suited for companies that sell expensive or complicated products, such as financial services and insurance companies, computer system marketers and commercial airlines. Companies eyeing substantial profits per sale from a select list of potential customers will find it easier to justify video marketing's production and distribution costs.[7]

Videologs. *Video cassettes which usually offer specialty products to an upscale audience or business-to-business merchandise, in effect, a video catalog.*

As the costs of cassette production and distribution go down, we will undoubtedly see more consumer distribution. Some advertisers are offering videocassettes as a supplement to print and broadcast advertising (see Exhibit 13.8). In the near future, this use of videocassettes will be a relatively common practice. Already the cost of producing and mailing catalogs is making it more practical to consider *videologs,* or catalogs produced on videocassettes, for specialty, upscale consumer products.

Radio can be effectively used as "back-up" to a direct mail campaign—to remind listeners to "call in" their "purchase." Non-profit groups, such as the Albert Einstein Healthcare Foundation, use radio to stimulate their "targets"—women—to follow up on health care referrals they read about in the AEHF $1 million direct mail campaign. Those receiving foundation brochures were given phone numbers for free medical advice from registered nurses. Radio commercials reiterated the availability of the "Phone-a-Nurse" service.

RADIO AND DIRECT RESPONSE

Because it lacks a visual element, radio is at an obvious disadvantage compared to other direct-response media: The product cannot be shown, no coupons can be provided, and a toll-free number cannot be flashed on a screen. Offsetting these disadvantages is the highly segmented nature of the radio audience. This segmentation is a characteristic made to order for the highly specialized direct-response advertiser.

Radio is often used to supplement other forms of direct response. For example, several publishers use radio to alert people to an upcoming sweepstakes and to encourage their participation.

Radio will never be a major direct-response medium, but it will continue to be valuable as a backup for direct-mail campaigns, as well as for direct use in getting orders by mail and by toll-free telephone. The relatively low cost of radio spots allows a frequency that would be prohibitively expensive in most other media.

[7]Judith Graham, "Selling Through Video Wins Proponents," *Advertising Age,* January 18, 1988, p. S-2.

EXHIBIT 13.8

Soon the videocassette will be a major part of many direct-marketing campaigns. (Courtesy: Stanley Works, Inc.)

MAGAZINES AND DIRECT RESPONSE

Magazines are a major medium for direct response, but the direct-response advertisers' approach to buying space in them is different from that of national advertisers. Many magazines have mail-order sections at the back of each issue; and judging by advertisers' continued use of them, results on the whole must be good. Many a small business has grown into a large one through these advertisements. In direct-response advertising, the question is not what the CPM of the magazine is, but what the cost per order or inquiry will be. Direct-response advertisers can calculate that to the fraction of a cent.

Advantages of Magazines in Direct-Response Advertising

Magazines have several advantages for the direct-response advertiser:

1. *Audience selectivity*. Magazines attract an audience with common interests and characteristics. More importantly, specialized publications offer an editorial environment compatible with the advertising messages they carry, ensuring that the reader will be in the proper "mood" to receive the advertisement.
2. *Distinctive audience*. Magazine readers tend to include light users of other media. Conse-

Mail-order sections in the rear of magazines provide an opportunity for small business to advertise. They can reach *a more selective audience* than other mass media—plus the prestige of the magazine "rubs off." *Adweek*, a popular media magazine, usually contains seven pages of classifieds, containing mostly small ads from specialized firms. The listings are grouped under the *types of services* clients demand in the promotion business—research, production, art/design, copywriting, audio/visual. Boldface and distinct black and white contrast make even the smallest ads noticeable.

quently, magazine direct response can reach an audience that would normally be missed by other media vehicles.

3. *Long life*. Magazines have the longest life of all media. Coupons may be clipped and offers responded to days or weeks after the magazine is received. Pass-along readership expands the potential audience.
4. *Size and color*. The typical magazine advertisement offers enough space to allow for coupons and detailed product information. In addition, excellent reproduction presents products to their best advantage.
5. *Prestige*. Magazines offer many of the advantages of direct mail, but have far more prestige, which transfers to the advertiser.

Some publications will accept a per-inquiry (PI) space, to run at no initial cost. The publisher charges for the advertisement at a certain rate per response received, whether the respondents buy or just make an inquiry.

Most direct-response advertisers expect a full-page magazine advertisement to pull from 0.05 percent to 0.20 percent of circulation—that is, from half of a response per thousand to two responses per thousand—although results can vary enormously from this typical range of figures. According to Frank Vos, an authority on the subject, direct-mail results usually range from 0.7 percent to 5.0 percent of names mailed—that is, from 7 orders per 1,000 to 50 orders per 1,000. You will notice that the ratio of response per thousand between direct mail and magazine space is roughly on the order of 10:1 or 20:1. But since the same ratio applies to the CPM of the two media, many advertisers find that their cost per order for magazine space and direct mail is about the same.

Overall, 40 percent of adults report that they have ordered a product through magazine mail-order advertising (see Exhibit 13.9). Females are only somewhat more likely to order than males, and the region of the country plays no part in determining who will order from magazines. However, as we would expect, the audience for magazine mail order, like that for magazines in general, is skewed toward higher-income and better-educated buyers.

The selectivity of magazine audiences also allows advertisers to be creative in reaching special audiences. For instance, Exhibit 13.10 appeared in *Southern Living* magazine, which is widely read by people interested in homemaking and recipes. Equal artificial sweetner used a direct-response ad to offer booklets to a prime audience for the product.

Discounts

Before placing an ad, ask whether there is a special mail-order rate or a special mail-order section. The mail-order rate can be substantially lower than rates for other classes of advertising. Also ask if the magazine has remnant space (discussed in Chapter 11, Using Magazines). Check all other discounts offered. If your advertising is for a

EXHIBIT 13.9

Magazines offer an excellent, relatively inexpensive means of reaching a selective audience for direct-marketing offers. (Courtesy: *Target Marketing*.)

Distribution of Responses Via Magazine Order Blanks

Ever ordered a product advertised in a magazine **Total 40**

Sex		*Education*		*Annual Household Income*		*Number of Direct Market Purchases in Past 6 Months*	
Male	37	College	44	$10,000–$19,999	42	None	24
Female	43	High school graduate	43	Under $10,000	25	1–2 (Light)	49
Age		Non-High school graduate	28	*Region*		3–5 (Moderate)	59
18–24 years	46			East	40	6 or more (Heavy)	59
25–34 years	47	*Annual Household Income*		Midwest	37		
35–49 years	47	$30,000 or more	47	South	42		
50 and older	30	$20,000–$29,999	44	West	42		

EXHIBIT 13.10

Increasingly, we find magazine ads with either mail or telephone offers. (Courtesy: The NutraSweet Company.)

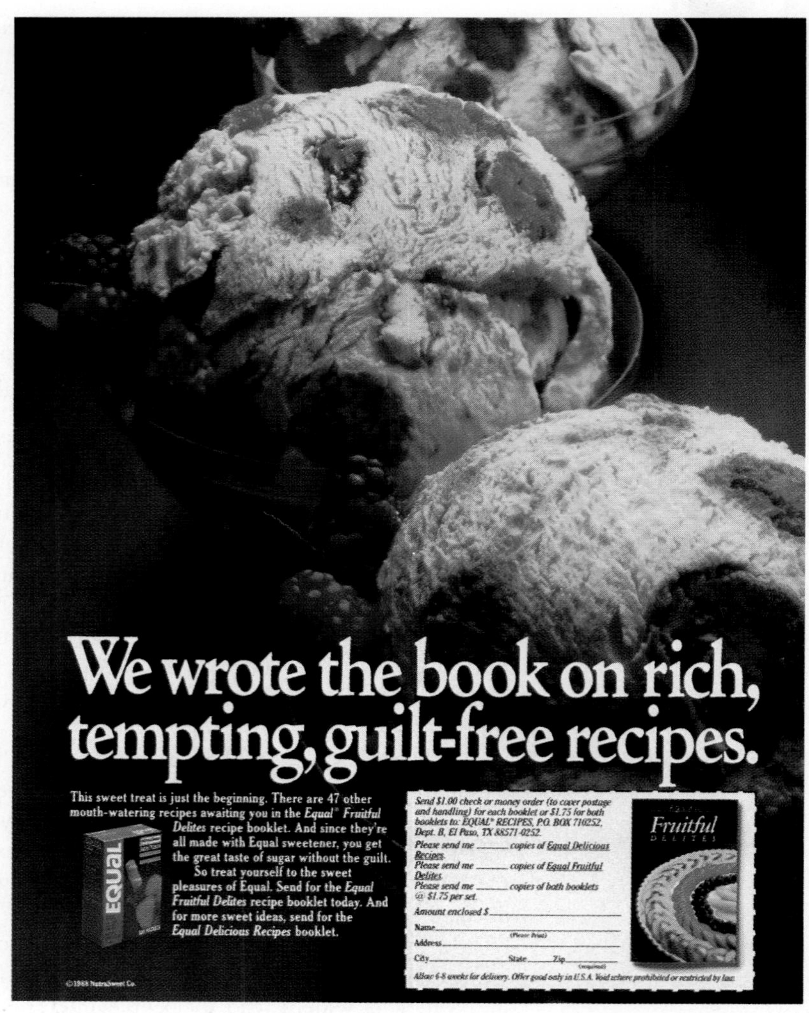

company that is an affiliate of a large advertiser, see whether you can get in under "corporate discounts." Also look into the question of barter space that can be traded for merchandise.

Freestanding inserts frequently promote merchandise which can be ordered by direct mail or phone. In the first test of Rupert Murdock's plan to become *a one-stop shopping service for mass-market advertisers,* the media mogul will put freestanding inserts in his newly acquired *TV Guide*. The move could provide a cornerstone for future multimedia ad buys in his communications empire. Proctor & Gamble, General Foods, and other big-time consumer marketers have been approached.

NEWSPAPERS AND DIRECT RESPONSE

Every week millions of freestanding inserts (FSI) are distributed in local newspapers, many of them promoting some type of direct-response offer. FSI and the use of Sunday supplements to carry direct response make the newspaper a major source of direct-response advertising revenues. FSI is an important medium for direct-response advertisers, and many use devices borrowed from direct mail such as business reply envelopes, die cuts, and punch tokens.

The growth of new techniques for direct response and the increasing use of telemarketing and TV present major competition to newspapers in their quest for direct-response advertising. It is doubtful that newspapers will be able to maintain their present share of the direct-response advertising dollar. Any decrease in newspapers' share of these advertising revenues will reflect more the strength of the competition than a decline in newspapers' ability to produce direct-response sales.

WHAT MAKES A GOOD DIRECT-RESPONSE PRODUCT?

Products lending themselves to direct response marketing are usually *unique, not easily obtained nearby, and be a good value. Florida citrus,* available only during the cooler months, is distributed nationally by mail by many packing houses. Brochures are sent to former customers and to those who inquire from ads placed in large metropolitan newspapers. The oranges and grapefruits, which they receive, are premium grade fruit, not available in most supermarkets, and are priced only slightly above ordinary citrus.

Earlier in the chapter, we noted that until a few years ago, direct response was regarded as a sales tool for relatively inexpensive merchandise. In part, this attitude was due to the risk perceived by customers in purchasing goods by mail from companies with neither local representatives nor established reputations. This situation has changed dramatically. Today major companies routinely engage in direct-response advertising, often directed to a very upscale audience. Because of the high price of merchandise, it is not uncommon for customers to be given the option of paying for products over a three- to six-month period.

While high cost per se is not a detriment to direct-response selling, not every product is suitable for direct-response advertising. Broadly speaking, it should not be the usual product available at a neighborhood store, unless it is being offered at a very special price. It should have some distinguishing quality or render a useful service not generally convenient to buy. It should be small, for mailing, unless it is a costly purchase. It should open the door to repeat business. If it comes with a well-known name backing it, so much the better. Above all, it should be a good value. The advertiser must be geared to handle repeat business, for it is on repeat business that the total marketing business rests.

TYPES OF DIRECT-RESPONSE OFFERS

It should be clear by now that direct-response advertising is an extremely versatile type of promotion. Using virtually all major media, it targets customers to personalize the sale approach for customized products. This section will examine some of the primary means of using direct response. Andi Emerson, president of Emerson Marketing Agency, suggests that direct-response offers should be divided into two categories: direct sales and lead getting.[8]

Category One—Direct Sales

Here the customer is made an offer through one or a series of ads, and responds with a purchase. Direct sales can be a simple, straightforward coupon in a newspaper or a series of elaborate mailing pieces for a cruise or a computer system. Regardless of the simplicity or complexity of the offer, the intent of the promotional effort is to close a sale. Some examples of direct sales offers will be briefly discussed.

Bounce-back circulars. *An enclosure in the package of a product that has been ordered by mail. It offers other products of the same company and is effective in getting more business.*

One-Step Purchase of Specific Product. The simplest examples of this type of direct-response advertising are the small ads one sees in the back of the shopping section of many magazines or in the Sunday newspaper shopping section supplement.

Whoever responds to a mail-order ad will probably receive a package containing the product ordered plus one or more circulars offering other merchandise of related interest. *Bounce-back circulars,* as these are called, can produce as much as 20 to 40 percent additional sales from the same customers and often launch the buyer on the path to becoming a steady customer. The key to the one-step approach is pinpointing the target audience, since you are not depending on follow-ups to complete the sale.

[8] Andi Emerson, "The Magic Seven: Paths to Success in a Direct Response Product Launch," *DM NEWS,* November 1, 1986, p. 31.

The *direct sales method* of reaching consumers can be done with *separate ads* in publications or *with catalogs*. Some companies have *combined* catalog and in-store selling operations. *Saks Fifth Avenue's Folio Division* distributes catalogs of merchandise, which isn't sold in their specialty stores. In addition to these direct sales efforts, the store mails catalogs for merchandise which can be ordered by mail *or* bought in the stores themselves.

Catalogs. The use of catalogs dates at least to the fifteenth century when Aldus Manutius published his book catalog containing 15 titles in 1498. Since its humble beginnings, the catalog has become a keystone of direct marketing. During the late 1800s, both Sears Roebuck & Company and Montgomery Ward brought retail merchandise to every household in the country through their catalogs. Currently, catalog sales account for 4 percent of all retail merchandise sold in the United States.

The early catalogs were primarily directed to low- and middle-income families outside of major cities. Today the catalog business is increasingly directed toward an upscale audience with an interest in specialty merchandise not readily available in retail stores. The typical catalog seller offers a number of books designed to appeal to very specialized audiences. For instance, Spiegel, Inc., publishes more than 20 catalogs, including Eddie Bauer and Honeybee, as well as the more general Spiegel catalog.

Runaway growth is becoming a problem in the catalog industry. During the five-year period starting in 1983, the number of catalogs mailed almost doubled to over 12 *billion*. Total catalog sales are now more than $40 billion a year and are increasing at an annual rate of about 10 percent. The high costs of both mailing and production are making catalog companies vigilant about sending only to prospects. Most companies remove a person from their list if, after three or four catalog mailings, no order has been placed. Other companies will send a catalog only to those who pay for it; when the recipient becomes a customer, the price of the catalog is subtracted from the price of the first purchase.

The catalog business is highly concentrated. The top ten catalogs account for approximately 25 percent of total sales, and the two largest—Sears Roebuck and J. C. Penney—combined have over 10 percent of total catalog sales (see Exhibit 13.11). Yet the number of catalogs distributed continues to increase, making clutter a real problem for the industry.

A leading catalog consultant, John Schmid, has noted several potential pitfalls for new catalog companies:

- Underestimating the amount of capital necessary to start a new business
- Failure to draw up a business plan
- Difficulty getting financing
- Lack of an inventory-control plan
- Failure to find a niche
- Underestimating the time it takes to build a customer list
- Inadequate fulfillment/customer service
- Not building the necessary skills among employees[9]

It is increasingly common for a company to have both catalog sales and retail outlets. Sometimes it was a retail store that started a catalog business; other times it was

EXHIBIT 13.11

Catalog buying has become a popular American pastime. (Courtesy: *Advertising Age*.)

Catalog sales, 1986 ($000,000)*			
1. Sears, Roebuck & Co.	$3,711.4	6. Fingerhut	316.0
2. J.C. Penney Co.	2,332.0	7. Lands' End	265.0
3. Spiegel Inc.	882.2	8. Hanover House	256.0
4. Brylane	475.0	9. Avon Products	216.2
5. L.L. Bean	367.8	10. General Mills	200.0

*Most recent figures available

Source: Blunt, Ellis & Loewi

[9]"8 Pitfalls for New Catalogers," *Target Marketing*, April 1988, p. 32.

CASE HISTORY

The Lord & Taylor "Scents of Beauty" Catalog Case

How does a department store get its fragrance catalog noticed amid the dozens of catalogs its upscale customers receive on a regular basis? Lord & Taylor solved this problem with its "Scents of Beauty" catalog produced by the Petty Company. The catalog provides a scented strip on each page so that customers can sample the fragrances offered by Lord & Taylor.

Who can resist the novelty of a "scented" catalog? (Courtesy: The Petty Company.)

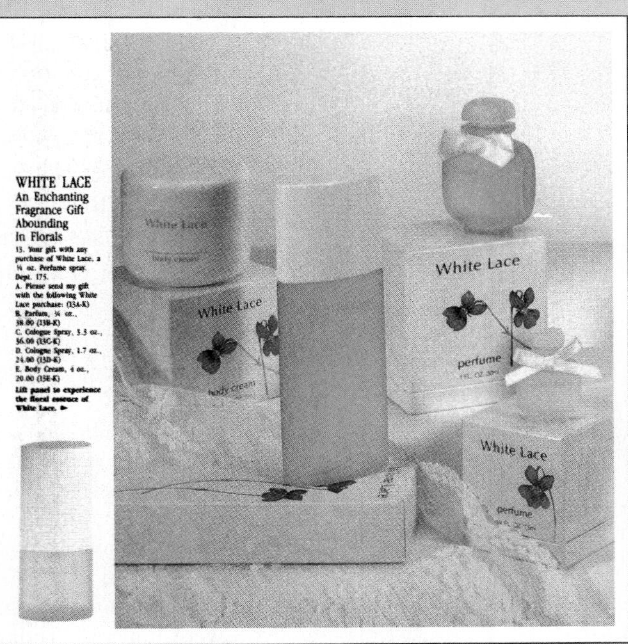

the popularity of a catalog that created the demand for retail outlets. In any case, we will see more of this joint venturing between retail stores and catalogs.

Another common feature of catalogs is advertising. On the one side, catalog companies are seeking additional revenues to offset their rising costs. On the other side, advertisers want to place their messages in vehicles with little waste circulation, be connected to an audience in the mood to purchase, and deliver their messages at a reasonable cost. "Increasingly, catalogers are running ads for merchandise featured in the catalog, melding the moment of impression to the moment of purchase and the medium to the distribution channel."[10]

[10]Ed Fitch, "Catalogs Hit the Target for Advertisers," *Advertising Age*, November 30, 1987, p. S-30.

Magalog. *Catalogs which include some editorial material and even limited advertising.*

Catalog companies are also starting to incorporate some editorial material in their catalogs, recognizing that many specialty catalogs, such as the one for Banana Republic, are read for enjoyment as well as to purchase merchandise. Some people in the industry are predicting the advent of *magalogs,* combining traditional catalog sales with limited advertising and editorial content. Currently catalog advertising accounts for less than $3 million.

Fulfillment firms. *Companies that are responsible for processing direct-response orders and handling customer inquiries and complaints.*

Fulfillment. The product inventory is selected, the colorful and well-written catalog is printed, the mailing list is fine-tuned for prospects only, the timing of the mailing has been tested to the day. All you have to do is wait for the orders and profits to start pouring in. Well, not quite. Who is making sure that the merchandise is sent out properly packed and that any errors are corrected quickly and cordially? This is the job of the fulfillment operation.

The fulfillment function used to be regarded simply as a shipping service that also (sometimes grudgingly) handled complaints. Today fulfillment operations are total customer service departments that include:

- Inquiries
- Order status inquiries
- Liaison with other departments
- Phone-order processing
- Price/availability
- Returns/claims processing
- Mail-order processing
- Field sales support
- Inside rep training
- Sales literature requests

> Despite the obvious rewards of good customer service, it's only recently that some companies have begun viewing it as a marketing strategy. One reason for this is that many marketers see customer service as a complaint department rather than an area to differentiate themselves from competitors. Another is that they (mistakenly) don't believe that better customer service means more sales.[11]

At one time companies like L. L. Bean that put great emphasis on customer service were unusual. Today the competition in direct marketing makes customer service a crucial part of the business. There are simply too many other companies in the field for customers to return to a direct seller with whom they have had an unsatisfactory experience.

> Competition and more demanding consumers may have provided the impetus for faster deliveries, but technological advances have provided the means. Sophisticated computer systems on-line at nearly all big fulfillment houses make order processing faster and more efficient. Today, many services use bar codes to speed up the process even more.[12]

Large firms operate their own fulfillment departments. Others use independent companies that handle responses for a number of firms. Independent fulfillment houses are most commonly used for one-time promotions such as a sweepstakes or premium offer; they are discussed in Chapter 14, Sales Promotion.

Negative Options. Another direct-response technique, often used by record and book clubs, is the negative option. The Book-of-the-Month Club is credited with introducing

[11]"Improve Customer Service . . . Or Else," *Target Marketing,* June 1988, p. 31.
[12]Ibid.

> ***Negative option direct response.*** *Technique used by record and book clubs whereby a customer receives merchandise unless the seller is notified not to send it.*

this method of "one-package-a-month" selling. While book and record clubs are the most common users of negative option selling, other companies have adopted the practice. For example, Franklin Porcelain offers a "subscription" to their porcelain figure collection whereby a different sculpture is sent monthly unless the buyer cancels the order (see Exhibit 13.12). The advantage to the seller is obvious: Once a customer joins the plan, the merchandise is sent automatically unless the customer notifies the company that he or she does not wish to receive it.

Category Two—Lead Getting

Many direct-response offers are designed to pave the way for a sale rather than to close a deal. This is most often true of expensive merchandise, especially in business-to-business sales.

Direct response offers can be used *to generate leads* for salespersons—rather than to close a sale. Business-to-business selling uses this version of direct response frequently to help reduce the cost of unnecessary and costly sales calls. The *Commodore Omega 2000* ad includes an "800" number for inquiries and free brochures. Its "user friendly" ad invites even *unsophisticated computer users* to take advantage of this offer—Commodore's "consumer representatives" will determine which prospects will receive a personal sales call.

The Two-Step Sales Operation. The most frequent lead-getting direct response uses a two-step sales presentation. The first step is to determine potential consumers, and the second is to follow up to close the sale. This second step often consists of a personal or telephone sales call, though some companies choose instead to send more detailed literature or even a product sample. The idea is to generate leads from the company's most profitable customers.

Business-to-Business Direct Marketing. Among the most frequent users of lead-getting direct response are business-to-business sellers, because the target-marketing characteristics of direct response are ideal for this type of marketing. The most important features of business-to-business marketing are:

1. *A relatively small market*. Compared to the typical consumer market, the number of businesses in any industry is quite small. For example, in the industrial sector, it is common for fewer than ten firms to account for 50 percent or more of total sales.
2. *Concentrated buying decisions*. The number of purchasing decision makers on the business side is very small compared to consumer marketing. Therefore, a company can spend a great

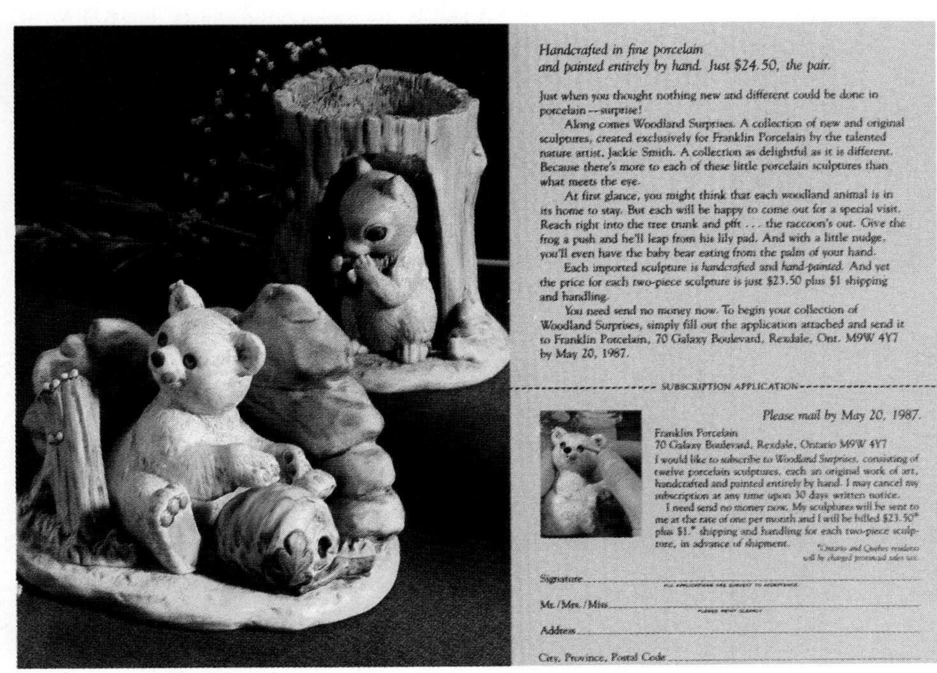

EXHIBIT 13.12

Negative-option offers encompass a number of product categories besides books and records. (Courtesy: The Petty Company.)

deal of money to reach each of these decision makers and still keep its total promotional budget at a reasonable level.

3. *High average per-purchase expenditures*. Business-to-business advertisers are playing for big stakes. Whereas a consumer may buy a $3,000 personal computer, a purchasing agent may buy a multimillion-dollar computer system. Factors such as CPMs that are so important in consumer promotions have little relevance in business marketing.
4. *Flexibility*. Business-to-business direct response can be flexible and adapt to the needs of different industries, or even individuals, in a way that traditional advertising cannot.

Another factor in the growth of the business-to-business advertising segment of direct response is the cost of personal selling. The cost of a typical sales call has risen sharply in recent years and is now over $200 (see Exhibit 13.13). In the future, personal selling will be confined to larger customers, leaving a major role for both direct-response and traditional business-to-business advertising.

DIRECT-RESPONSE COPY

Direct-response advertising is different from general consumer advertising in a number of ways:

1. *It calls for immediate response*. Direct-response advertising wants a sale now. It is not trying to build an image for the advertiser or to subtly put consumers into a positive frame of mind for a future purchase.

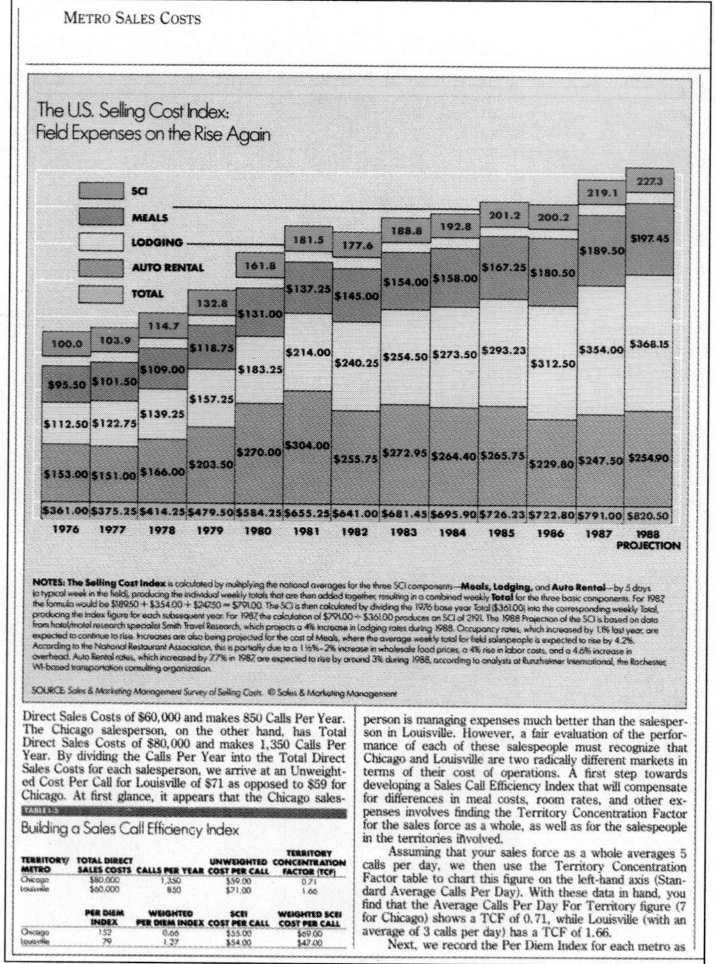

NOTES: The Selling Cost Index is calculated by multiplying the national averages for the three SCI components—**Meals, Lodging,** and **Auto Rental**—by 5 days (a typical week in the field), producing the individual weekly totals that are then added together, resulting in a combined weekly **Total** for the three basic components. For 1987, the formula would be $189.50 + $354.00 + $247.50 = $791.00. The SCI is then calculated by dividing the 1976 base year Total ($361.00) into the corresponding weekly Total, producing the index figure for each subsequent year. For 1987, the calculation of $791.00 ÷ $361.00 produces an SCI of 219.1. The 1988 Projection of the SCI is based on data from hotel/motel research specialist Smith Travel Research, which projects a 4% increase in Lodging rates during 1988. Occupancy rates, which increased by 1.1% last year, are expected to continue to rise. Increases are also being projected for the cost of Meals, where the average weekly total for field salespeople is expected to rise by 4.2%. According to the National Restaurant Association, this is partially due to a 1½%–2% increase in wholesale food prices, a 4% rise in labor costs, and a 4.6% increase in overhead. Auto Rental rates, which increased by 7.7% in 1987, are expected to rise by around 3% during 1988, according to analysts at Runzheimer International, the Rochester, WI-based transportation consulting organization.

SOURCE: *Sales & Marketing Management Survey of Selling Costs.* © Sales & Marketing Management

Direct Sales Costs of $60,000 and makes 850 Calls Per Year. The Chicago salesperson, on the other hand, has Total Direct Sales Costs of $80,000 and makes 1,350 Calls Per Year. By dividing the Calls Per Year into the Total Direct Sales Costs for each salesperson, we arrive at an Unweighted Cost Per Call for Louisville of $71 as opposed to $59 for Chicago. At first glance, it appears that the Chicago salesperson is managing expenses much better than the salesperson in Louisville. However, a fair evaluation of the performance of each of these salespeople must recognize that Chicago and Louisville are two radically different markets in terms of their cost of operations. A first step towards developing a Sales Call Efficiency Index that will compensate for differences in meal costs, room rates, and other expenses involves finding the Territory Concentration Factor for the sales force as a whole, as well as for the salespeople in the territories involved.

Assuming that your sales force as a whole averages 5 calls per day, we then use the Territory Concentration Factor table to chart this figure on the left-hand axis (Standard Average Calls Per Day). With these data in hand, you find that the Average Calls Per Day For Territory figure (7 for Chicago) shows a TCF of 0.71, while Louisville (with an average of 3 calls per day) has a TCF of 1.66.

Next, we record the Per Diem Index for each metro as

TABLE 1-5

Building a Sales Call Efficiency Index

TERRITORY/ METRO	TOTAL DIRECT SALES COSTS	CALLS PER YEAR	UNWEIGHTED COST PER CALL	TERRITORY CONCENTRATION FACTOR (TCF)
Chicago	$80,000	1,350	$59.00	0.71
Louisville	$60,000	850	$71.00	1.66

	PER DIEM INDEX	WEIGHTED PER DIEM INDEX	SCEI COST PER CALL	WEIGHTED SCEI COST PER CALL
Chicago	152	0.66	$35.00	$69.00
Louisville	79	1.27	$54.00	$47.00

EXHIBIT 13.13

As personal selling becomes more expensive, companies increasingly turn to advertising and sales promotion. (Courtesy: *Sales & Marketing Management.*)

PAPA. *A familiar formula for developing an ad or other sales copy. PAPA refers to: promise, amplification, proof, and action.*

Direct response advertising has distinct advantages of being able to present *more informative copy, be more personal in its tone, and receive more immediate response*. College publications often feature their own merchandise in their school publications, which can be ordered directly from the school retail stores. Since they're not buying "space," their merchandise ads tend to be *large*, talk in "familiar language" to students and alumni, and usually limit supplies to seasons or events—which prompts requests. Price is rarely emphasized—authenticity is—for this "familiar" audience.

2. *The copy is longer, more informative, and has a stronger promise-of-benefit headline than general advertising.* Because it is directed to a more selective audience, the copy can go into greater detail about product benefits. The copy writer should marshal all forms of evidence available to give assurance to the reader, specify money-back guarantees, and close with a special bonus for promptness in replying. (This is known as following the PAPA formula: promise, amplification, proof, action.)
3. *Direct response is more personal than general advertising.* The medium is one-to-one, and copy should be written in the same manner as a personal letter or sales call.
4. *Results are immediate in direct response.* Unlike most general advertising (a major exception is retail advertising), direct response provides short-term, accurate, sales-related measures of success. The old adage, "Advertising is salesmanship in print," may well have been referring to direct response.

DIRECT-MAIL ADVERTISING

As noted earlier in the chapter, direct mail is only one of a number of direct-response techniques, yet it is the category most associated with direct-response advertising in terms of both format and execution. It is a rare major advertising campaign that does not at least consider direct mail as a media vehicle. Since it is so clearly related to advertising, we have chosen to discuss direct mail separately from other direct-response media.

Advantages of Direct-Mail Advertising

According to the American Association of Advertising Agencies, direct mail offers five primary advantages to advertisers:

1. *Selectivity.* You can identify exactly the market you want to reach, and cover it the way you want. You can eliminate by region, by state, by market, by individual. You can run lists against each other to eliminate duplication. You can tailor copy to fit known characteristics of a list. Granted, there are errors on most lists. But even so, the medium affords minimum waste and maximum efficiency. You can hit your entire market in a single mailing. Or you can segment your market and mail some prospects six times as often as others.
2. *Ideal for response.* You can include a ready-to-use, postage-paid reply card or envelope to promote maximum immediate response. If you wish, you can employ a window envelope (or die-cut self-mailer) and preaddress your reply element to reduce the amount of effort required to respond to your offer.
3. *Personal impact.* The personal "one-at-a-time" quality of direct mail means your client's prospect or customer is reading your communication without competing, intervening messages. A recipient must do something about a mailing—even if it's only throwing the piece in the wastepaper basket. When you mail by name, you can often credibly adjust your copy appeals and offers to fit things you know about the recipient. The computer letter has made a number of creative possibilities available to copywriters who want to individualize the letters they write. Effectively created mail can achieve high readership and enormous impact.
4. *Flexibility of format and timing.* A mailing requires only minimum standardization of format and timing. You can include additional elements, or adapt pieces to the interests of specific lists. You can utilize special inks that add fragrance; or insert swatches of material, coins, vinyl, records, games—a myriad of attention-getting devices. You can increase or decrease planned mailing quantities to adjust to changing needs. You can delay mailings that are scheduled to go out on specific dates.
5. *Measurability.* Direct mail lends itself to precise calibration of results. You know to whom you mail, and you know who responds. In a lead-getting effort, you can study how prospects are converted into sales. You can analyze response by any variable you wish—each list, each copy approach, each offer.[13]

By using *direct mail*, the advertiser gains the advantage of *personal impact* and *flexibility of format*—utilizing all the elements of *creativity*. Starbucks Coffee, an upscale coffee company, will be expanding its market to Portland and Chicago with mall outlets. Direct mail is planned to those consumers who have charge accounts in the mall's department and specialty shops. Included in personal letters from the president will be packages of coffee beans and ground coffee samples, volunteered Marketing Director Dwight McCabe.

[13]Derry F. Daly and Roger Franklin, "What Every Young Account Representative Should Know About Direct Mail Advertising," a publication of the American Association of Advertising Agencies, 1978, pp. 4–5.

Elements of Successful Direct-Mail Advertising

Direct mail, unlike other forms of advertising, puts the total execution responsibility on the advertiser. Therefore, the successful direct-mail campaign starts with a detailed list of objectives. According to Edith Roman Associates, a leading list broker, direct mail has four primary objectives:

1. *Building sales*. Direct mail can be used to introduce salespeople, promote other forms of advertising, or announce a product introduction. Of course, it can also be used to make the sale.
2. *Cultivating customers*. The sale of a product should not end the relationship with a customer. For example, automobile manufacturers routinely follow up car sales with direct-mail letters congratulating the buyer on making a smart investment and offering help with future service.
3. *Supporting dealers*. Direct mail can alert dealers to future customer promotions, educate them on service problems, and survey them concerning their needs.
4. *Providing internal benefits*. Direct mail can be an important tool for building company morale. Internal newsletters and other employee communications are often used to personalize large corporations.

Direct mail is the only medium where the advertiser must provide the circulation. Modern computer techniques and access to various data bases make it possible to build extremely selective mailing lists. A list will cost between $25 and $125 per 1,000 names, depending on its selectivity. Mailing list costs are similar to those for other circulations: The more upscale and selective the audience, the higher the CPM (see Exhibit 13.14).

EXHIBIT 13.14

Mailing lists are available to reach almost any audience segment at an affordable price. (Courtesy: Alvin B. Zeller, Inc.)

A

QUANTITY		PRICE
679	AAAA Advertising Agencies	$75
3,600	Abattoirs & Slaughterhouses, Meat Packers	$35/M
2,700	Abortion, Birth Control Centers	$40/M
10,100	Abstract & Title Companies	$35/M
9,800	Account Executives, Adv. Agencies	$35/M
206,100	Accountants, Certified Public	$35/M
58,000	Accountants, Partners Accounting Firms	$35/M
40,500	Accountants, Non-Partners Accounting Firms	$35/M
20,400	Accountants Big 8	$35/M
17,700	Accountants, Public	$35/M
55,000	Accountants, Corporate Non-Accounting Firms	$35/M
8,600	Accountants in Government and Education	$35/M
35,300	Accountants, Self Employed	$35/M
25,300	Accountants, Tax Preparation Services	$35/M
24,000	Accountants, Women	$35/M
3,600	Accountants, Auditing Managers	$35/M
23,500	Accounting Firms	$35/M
5,500	Accounting Managers	$35/M
21,000	Acupuncturists	$65/M
4,400	Acoustical Contractors	$35/M
1,770	Actuaries, Pension	$75
6,450	Adding & Calculating Machine Dealers	$35/M
4,000	Addressing & Lettershops	$35/M
5,075	Adjusters, Insurance	$35/M
40,000	Administrators, College (Including Deans)	$50/M
6,772	Administrators, Hospitals	$35/M
1,600	Adoption Agencies	$75
60,000,000	Adults by Age	Inquire
17,500	Advertisers, National	$35/M
1,850,000	Advertisers, Telephone Classifieds	$35/M
24,500	Advertising Agencies	$35/M
4,100	Advertising Agencies (Major)	$35/M
1,700	Advertising Agencies with $1 Million to $10 Million billing	$75
1,350	Advertising Agencies with $10 Million or more billing	$75
679	Advertising Agencies, AAAA	$75
25,300	Advertising Agencies Executives (By Function)	$35/M
5,100	Advertising Managers, Corporate	$35/M
5,625	Advertising Services, Direct Mail	$35/M
8,275	Advertising Novelty Jobbers	$35/M
6,925	Advertising Reps, T.V., Radio, Publishing	$35/M
2,300	Aerial Photographers	$35/M
24,800	Aeronautical, Space Engineers	$35/M
800,000	Affluent & Influential Americans	Inquire
6,800	Agricultural Agents (County)	$35/M
440	Agricultural Laboratories (College)	$75
17,250	Agricultural Machinery & Implement Dealers	$35/M
325	Agricultural Publications	$75
5,025	Air Cargo Services	$35/M
4,150	Air Conditioner Dealers	$35/M
31,500	Air Conditioning Contractors	$35/M
9,400	Air Conditioning Repair	$35/M
2,800	Air & Gas Compressor Dealers	$35/M
10,350	Air Pollution Control Officials	$35/M
4,150	Aircraft Charter Operators	$35/M
9,100	Aircraft Control Tower Operators	$35/M
2,100	Aircraft Dealers	$75
10,300	Aircraft Industry Executives	$35/M
1,200	Aircraft Parts & Supplies Mfrs.	$75
3,850	Aircraft Repair Stations	$35/M
189,800	Aircraft Owners, Including Firms	$35/M
3,600	Aircraft Owners, Jets	$35/M
129,200	Aircraft Owners, Private Individuals	$35/M
24,400	Aircraft Owners, 2 or more Craft	$35/M
6,800	Aircraft Owners, Helicopters	$35/M
28,500	Aircraft Owners, Multi-Engine Craft	$35/M
40,630	Aircraft Flight Engineers, Navigators	$35/M
665,680	Aircraft Pilots	Inquire
148,600	Aircraft Pilots, Commercial	Inquire
33,600	Aircraft Pilots, Helicopter	$35/M
77,300	Aircraft Pilots, Transport (Passenger)	Inquire
128,850	Aircraft Pilots, Students	Inquire
290,960	Aircraft Pilots, Private	Inquire
2,300	Airlines, Passenger & Freight	$35/M
10,500	Airline Executives	$35/M
2,520	Airport Gift Shops	$35/M
11,250	Airports (All)	$35/M
2,590	Airports (Major)	$35/M
9,100	Air Traffic Controllers	$35/M
11,700	Alcoholism Clinics & Centers	$35/M
3,505	Allergists	$35/M
1,400,000	Alumni, College	Inquire
422,000	Amateur Radio (HAM) Operators	$35/M
17,500	Ambulance Services	$35/M
4,100	Ambulance Services (Private)	$35/M
14,800	American Legion Posts	$35/M
90	Ammunition Manufacturers	$75
1,765	Amusement Parks, Centers, Tourist Attractions	$75
13,000	Analysts, Financial (By Speciality)	$35/M
18,300	Anesthesiologists	$35/M
5,200	Animal Hospitals	$35/M
7,100	Animal Kennels	$35/M
7,900	Answering Services (Telephone)	$35/M
26,400	Antiques Dealers	$35/M
62,500	Apartment Buildings	$35/M
35,000,000	Apartment Dwellers	$35/M
4,600	Apparel Chains	$35/M
735	Apparel Mfrs., Children's	$75
3,600	Apparel Mfrs., Men's & Boy's	$35/M
6,100	Apparel Mfrs., Women's	$35/M
12,500	Apparel Retailers, Children's & Infants	$35/M
1,950	Apparel Retailers, Maternity	$35/M
23,000	Apparel Retailers, Men's & Boy's	$35/M
68,250	Apparel Retailers, Women's	$35/M
1,500	Apparel Retailers, Ladies, Couture Shops	$75/M
4,100	Apparel Retailers, Ladies, Large	$40/M
5,300	Apparel Wholesalers, Men's and Boy's	$35/M
10,100	Apparel Wholesalers, Women's & Children's	$35/M
44,000	Appliance Dealers, Retail	$35/M
6,000	Appliance Dealers, Wholesale	$35/M
650	Appliance Manufacturers	$75
16,700	Appliance Repair	$35/M
13,000	Appraisers (Business, Mdse.)	$35/M
1,900	Appraisers, Independent Fee	$75
10,800	Appraisers, Real Estate	$35/M
360	Aquariums & Zoos	$75
3,250	Aquarium Supplies & Tropical Fish Stores	$35/M
578	Arbitrators, Labor	$75
132	Arboreta	$75
30,200	Architects	$35/M
10,800	Architects, Firms (AIA)	$35/M
6,100	Architects, Landscape	$35/M
20,000	Architects Offices	$35/M
3,250	Armature Rewinding — Motor Repair	$35/M
550	Army & Navy Posts	$75
1,100	Army & Navy Stores	$75
2,600	Art Directors	$35/M
12,000	Art Galleries & Picture Dealers	$35/M
452	Art Libraries	$75
790	Art Museums	$75
9,700	Art, Prominent Individuals	$35/M
1,425	Art Schools	$75
3,500	Artificial Flowers & Plant Dealers	$35/M
4,450	Artificial Limbs Dealers	$35/M
13,500	Artists, Commercial	$35/M
7,100	Artists Materials Stores	$35/M
6,600	Artists, Painters & Sculptors	$35/M
17,200	Arts & Crafts Dealers	$35/M
6,500	Assessors, Tax	$35/M
17,900	Associations HQ	$35/M
1,500	Associations, Cultural	$75
1,700	Associations, Health & Medical	$75
1,200	Associations, Scientific & Technical	$75
1,400	Associations, Social Welfare	$75
3,400	Associations, Trade & Business	$35/M
23,600	Athletic Coaches, College	$35/M
3,400	Athletic Directors, College	$35/M
155,500	Athletic Coaches, High School	$35/M
16,800	Athletic Directors, High School	$35/M
150	Athletic Teams (Professional)	$75

Use **HANDY ORDER FORMS** on last page

> *Database marketing.* A process of continually updating information about individual customers. Popular technique with direct-response sellers.

The Mailing List

Data-Based Marketing. The key to successful direct mail is reaching the right persons. The best product, the most creative message, even the lowest price, are all wasted on nonprospects. In the 1990s, the key work in direct mail will be *data-based marketing,* or gaining as much information as possible about prospects and continuing to update it. The process is one of feedback between sellers and their customers to more precisely define the latter's interests and purchase intentions. In its simplest form, data-based marketing is a method of identifying the best prospects for a product from a larger pool of prospects (see Exhibit 13.15).

The concept of data-based marketing can be traced to 1962, when pharmaceutical companies tracked physician preferences for types and volume of prescriptions written. In other words, rather than just making up a list of dermatologists or pediatricians, these companies determined which doctors were most likely to prescribe certain drugs.

Commenting on the development of data-based marketing, one direct mailer noted, ''Back then we had names and addresses but now we have added to that with a tremendous amount of information, like household income, occupation, car ownership and lifestyle characteristics. We probably know seven other products that a customer might be interested in, just from what they have bought in the past.[14]

[14]Eileen Norris, ''Databased Marketing Sets Enticing Bait,'' *Advertising Age,* January 18, 1988, p. S-12.

UNFORTUNATELY,
THE WORLD IS NOT ORGANIZED
THE WAY WE MIGHT LIKE.
WHICH IS WHY NDL DEVELOPED THE LIFESTYLE NETWORK™ DATABASE. IT'S THE BEST WAY TO REACH MORE QUALIFIED PROSPECTS. AT LESS COST.
Target marketing often involves a difficult compromise. To get the market you want, you have to give up saturation. And to get the numbers, you have to give up selectivity.
Until now. The Lifestyle Network offers you the best of both worlds: superb targeting *and* extensive market coverage.
The Lifestyle Network is the new marketing database from NDL, the leader in target marketing with over a decade of experience in building the nation's most detailed consumer databases.
Now you can select your prospective customers from **85 million consumers using a full range of demographic, geographic and lifestyle characteristics.**
You can create custom mailing lists that give you virtual saturation of your prime market, while eliminating those households which don't fit your customer profile.
The Lifestyle Network. Reach. Targeting. And Performance. To learn more, call The Lifestyle Selector Division of NDL, or contact your list broker today.
NDL®
National Demographics & Lifestyles
The Lifestyle Selector® Division
1621 Eighteenth Street, Denver, CO 80202
Phone 303-292-5000 / Toll Free 800-525-3533
NYC: 212-481-9200 / San Diego: 619-488-6070

EXHIBIT 13.15

Data-based marketing is an important aspect of reaching direct buyers. (Courtesy: National Demographics & Lifestyles.)

List broker. *In direct-mail advertising an agent who rents the prospect lists of one advertiser to another advertiser. The broker receives a commission from the seller for this service.*

Renting the List. Most direct mailers use the services of a *list broker*. A list broker obtains lists for clients and also acts as a consultant for the advertiser. Among the responsibilities of a list broker are:

1. Understanding the product so as to know where likely lists of prospects can be obtained.
2. Understanding the total process of putting together the direct-mail marketing plan, not just delivering lists.
3. Negotiating for lists on the advertiser's behalf.
4. Cleaning up lists, especially eliminating duplicate names.
5. Following up after a mailing to determine the performance of various lists.[15]

The *key* to successful direct mail is the *right mailing list;* i.e., *the actual prospects* for the advertiser's product. Lists may be *rented, compiled* from other data sources, or be *derived from responses* to the company's previous solicitations or sales. Many "list houses" send brochures to direct marketers, advertising lists by geographic location, profession, demographic variable, type of business—to name a few categories. One company advertises lists of *14 million businesses,* which they've compiled from yellow pages listings. The advantage of using "ready-made" lists is that they've been pre-screened, usually covering wide areas, and can save the advertiser an enumerable amount of time in solicitations.

List Protection

Mailing lists are extremely valuable commodities and companies go to great lengths to protect them from misuse. The most common list abuse is multimailings beyond the agreed-upon limit. For example, one direct mailer reported that a company rented his list on a onetime basis and used it 13 times.

List owners' traditional protection against such misuse is to include a number of decoy or fictitious names so that the list owner can verify the number of mailings. An even better protection is never to allow renters to take physical possession of the lists. Instead, a third party, such as a letter shop (which we shall discuss later in this chapter), undertakes to address company A's mailing pieces with the names on company B's list. Company A, therefore, sees only the names of people who respond to the mailing.

Types of Mailing Lists

Mailing lists are divided into two categories: *compiled* and *response* (also called *mail-derived*).

List compiler. *Person who sells lists of names to direct mail advertisers.*

Compiled Lists. The list compiler is usually a broker who rents a number of lists from published sources or lists of similar prospects and combines them into a single list. Compiled lists sometimes come from public records such as automobile registrations.

Compiled lists are generally less expensive than response lists. They are also regarded as less valuable by direct mailers because they usually don't offer a previous record of direct-response purchases. Many direct-response advertisers see compiled lists as a supplement to response lists. By combining these two kinds of lists, a mailer can reach both previous customers and a larger pool of prospective customers.

Response list. *List comprised of people who have previously purchased as a result of direct-response offers, either for the same company or another seller.*

Response Lists. Many mailing-list houses sell or rent lists of names of people who have ordered something by mail or who have responded to an ad for further information. The people on response lists are those who are prone to order by mail; therefore, these lists are more productive than compiled lists. A mail-derived list can be your own house list or a response list that you rented from some other advertisers.

HOUSE LISTS. The finest asset that any direct-marketing firm can have is its own list of customers. These customers have shown that they buy by mail, have had dealings with the company, and have confidence in its integrity and merchandise. By the nature of the purchase they have made, they have revealed what type of product interests them. Last but not least, there is no extra cost when a company uses its own house list.

RENTAL LISTS. A major profit center for many firms is the lists of their customers. Magazine publishers are a prime source of such lists since they tend to reach certain

[15]Christine A. Rossell, "Going for Broker," *Target Marketing,* May 1988, p. 75.

demographic groups. Likewise, many record and book clubs and major direct-response firms have formed subsidiaries to sell or rent their lists.

Standard Rate and Data Service publishes a volume devoted to lists available in various categories. Advertisers may buy or rent lists from major magazines such as *U.S. News & World Report* and *Prevention*. They can also buy lists of respondents to all sorts of sweepstakes and premium offerings. For instance, the entrants to the American Family Publishers Sweepstakes are available.

Merge/Purge

Merge/purge (merge & purge). *A system used to eliminate duplication by direct-response advertisers who use different mailing lists for the same mailing. Mailing lists are sent to a central merge/purge office that electronically picks out duplicate names. Saves mailing costs, especially important to firms that send out a million pieces in one mailing. Also avoids damage to the goodwill of the public.*

One of the big problems involved in using a number of lists is that the same name may be on several of them. One person may receive two, three, or even four copies of the same mailing, which results in annoyance to the recipient, extra cost to the advertiser, and perhaps the loss of a prospective customer. For advertisers who send out millions of pieces a year, the losses and expense are considerable.

To deal with this problem, computerized systems have been developed whereby all lists for a mailing are sent directly to a central service equipped to handle what is known as a merge/purge operation. All duplicates are removed from the list so that each recipient gets only one mailing. The merge/purge operation is usually part of a full-service mailing operation rather than a distinct activity.

Other Direct-Mail Techniques

The format and execution of direct-mail campaigns can take many forms. In this section, we will briefly discuss a few of the primary ones.

Package Inserts. For many years, direct marketers have used package inserts to promote additional purchases of the products sent to customers or other items in their product lines. These so-called bounce-back circulars are very inexpensive since they do not involve additional postage costs, but more importantly, they are directed at proven customers who have just made a direct-mail purchase.

Ride-alongs. *Direct-mail pieces that are sent with other mailings such as bills.*

Many direct marketers negotiate with other companies to use inserts in their packages, much as you would buy space in a magazine. These inserts are called *ride-alongs* and can be sent at a fraction of the cost of an independent mailing. Typical ride-along CPMs are in the \$40–\$50 range compared to \$200–\$300 for the simplest direct-mail piece.

There are two basic types of inserts. The first is included in merchandise sent by a company. For instance, L. L. Bean inserts ride-alongs in merchandise it sends to its customers. The second type of insert, and by far the larger category, is included in bills for other companies.

A cable TV system will include an offer to install Showtime or Home Box Office in its statements. Next time you receive a bill from your oil company, it will probably include several ride-along offers. Some retail products purchased at a store carry ride-alongs. For instance, Softcare diapers carry an insert for *Parents Magazine* in each box.

Another advantage of inserts besides their low cost is the implied endorsement they gain for advertisers from the distributing company. Also, the number of ride-along programs available means advertisers get a degree of target marketing that approaches an independent mailing. It is estimated that 20,000 programs are available to advertisers.

Cooperative mailing. *Sent to a select list comprising all the inserts of a group of noncompetitive firms trying to reach the same audience. A way of reducing mailing costs.*

Cooperative (Joint) Mail Advertising. Because of the high cost of postage today, direct mailers often attempt to share expenses through cooperative mailings. A number of firms, such as Donnelley Marketing's Carol Wright program, specialize in joint mailings. These mailings may include as many as 20 different advertising offers in one envelope. Each advertiser provides a coupon or other short message, and the joint mailer handles the mailing and divides the cost among the advertisers.

Cooperative mailings have two major drawbacks. First, they are extremely impersonal since each advertiser's message must be very short. Second, it is difficult for an advertiser to reach specific customers through joint mailings with the precision it would have with its own list. The dilemma of joint mailings is that as the number of participating advertisers increases, the cost per advertiser goes down, but so does the value of the mailing.

Syndicate mailing (direct-response advertising). *The mailing pieces a firm prepares for its products but then turns over to another firm to mail out to the latter's lists. Terms are negotiated individually.*

Syndicate Mailings. Here a marketer prepares a direct-mail piece offering a product or service; but instead of mailing it, he or she makes financial arrangements with other mail-order companies to mail the offer under their letterhead. The marketer supplies material that the mail-order people can use to sell the product under the name of the mail-order house. Thus, Meredith Publishing Company, which publishes the *Better Homes & Garden Family Medical Guide,* might syndicate it to Doubleday Book Clubs, *Encyclopaedia Britannica,* and others that may be able to sell it to their lists of prospective customers. Each of these direct-marketing companies might adapt the syndicator's letter copy to some extent, but most of them will use that circular without change. An important consideration in such arrangements is to keep down the weight of the mailing piece.

Inserts are an economical means to reach desirable prospects for many direct mail vendors. They may be included in *packages, bills, or cooperative (joint) mailings.* New Jersey Governor Tom Kean has launched a statewide $1.2 million campaign to "clean up the image of the state's beaches." In addition to spot TV and posters, inserts in utility bills and bank statements will try to increase state tourism, especially in the spring and summer months. The intent is to reach *all* state residents—"before they commit to an out-of-state vacation."

The Direct-Mail Prospect

A recent Gallup Poll asked respondents if they minded having their names given to other companies for advertising purposes. Over half the respondents said they did not want their names sold to other companies. Not surprisingly, 57 percent of those who had not made a direct-response purchase in the past six months were opposed to the practice of selling names. However, it was somewhat unexpected that 40 percent of the heaviest users of direct marketing (those who had made six or more purchases within six months) also did not want their names sold.[16] Direct mail is simply not considered equal to other forms of advertising—similar polls concerning other media found that readers of both newspapers and magazines regard advertising as an important part of the publications.

Studies such as this Gallup Poll raise another concern of direct mailers. Increasingly, direct mailers ask their customers for permission to sell their names to other companies. If 40 to 50 percent of customers refused to allow this practice, it would be a major blow to direct marketing. In fact, most people, even those who may not like the practice, don't take the time to have their names excluded from lists.

Extensive research has shown that the best prospects for direct marketing are:

The best prospects for direct mail are *previous buyers* or *buyers of similar goods.* Radio Shack, a unit of Tandy Corporation, routinely records the names and addresses of its customers. They, in turn, receive timely brochures of sales, special purchases, and clearances—*before* the general public. *Purchases by former customers* always lead their customer list, says a company official. It's also the *cheapest* form of retail advertising to reach special targets.

- Customers who have recently ordered or who order frequently
- Buyers of similar products
- Volume buyers
- People who have shown interest in a related product; for example, book club members or record and tape buyers
- People who have a demographic interest in a product; for example, parents, who buy encyclopedias; young marrieds, who buy insurance policies
- Those who are known to reply to direct mail (in contrast to those whose response is unknown)

The Direct-Mail Package

All the different pieces that go into one mailing are called its *package.* Each element in a mailing is chosen with care to invite the recipient to open it and then take the desired

[16]"Don't Rent My Name," *Target Marketing,* September 1987, p. 16.

action. Direct mailers test each aspect of the package to find the best combination of pieces to close the sale. Mailers have a number of alternatives to choose from in sending direct-mail advertising.

Envelope. The selling effort begins on the outside of the envelope. Everything depends on rousing curiosity so that the recipient will open it. In fact, 15 percent of the people who receive unsolicited mail in an envelope throw it away unopened because they think they already know what is inside and they are not interested in it. The message on the envelope should not be deceptive; if it is, the reader will feel tricked and toss the whole mailing away after opening it. Most of all, the envelope must break through the barrier of resistance by how it looks and what it says.

In order to *heighten response*, direct mail pieces should be *attractive* and *personalized*. Capitalizing on its success with its *Boys' Life* magazine, National Sales Manager Chuck Carroll advertises its spin-off in sponsoring national festivals and jamborees with the slogan, "I Know What Boys Like." Direct mail solicitations will be mailed to boys on the magazine's mailing list, co-sponsored by organizers such as the Boy Scouts and private camps. Campfires, mountain hiking trails, canoeing in "natural waters" depict typical boys recreation activities.

Letter. The addressee's name may be computerized on it, but usually the letter is personal, establishing contact directly with the reader. It explains the importance of reading the full details given in the handsome brochure enclosed. In fact, the letter's job is to interest the reader in such an enclosure. More recently, the computer has allowed direct-mail letters to be truly personalized by including the name of the recipient in the salutation and even in the body of the letter. This technique heightens interest in the message and increases readership.

Brochure. This is the big selling part of the mailing—a booklet, folder brochure, or broadside, perhaps with color pictures and charts to illustrate everything discussed. This is the workhorse of the team.

Order Form. Requirements for this form are the same as those for the publication advertisement. The direct-mail order form may, however, be considerably larger and may have the addressee's name computerized on it, needing only a signature for ordering.

Act Now. The act-now enclosure may be a different-colored slip offering a special bonus for a prompt reply.

Reply Envelope. An important standard practice, based on experience, is to enclose a return envelope when an order is requested. Convenience encourages the reader to reply.

TESTING DIRECT MAIL

One direct-mail practitioner, when asked to name the three most important factors in his success, said, "Test, test, test!" Direct mailers evaluate the medium on the basis of sales or inquiries. Techniques that contribute to sales are retained, those that don't are excluded from future mailings.

One study found that the majority of respondents in the industry say that direct-mail sales have increased in recent years and will increase even more in the future (see Exhibit 13.16). Since only 20 percent of the population consider themselves regular direct-marketing customers, the other 80 percent constitute a major opportunity for future growth. Research will be the key to tapping this huge potential market for direct mail and other direct-marketing techniques.

In recent years, testing of direct mail has concentrated on three areas: the mailing list, the message, and the timing.

The Mailing List. As we emphasized earlier, an up-to-date mailing list of current or potential prospects is the most important item in the success of a mail campaign. A glance at the direct-mail trade press gives an idea of the number of companies and

EXHIBIT 13.16

More than half of all industry decision makers indicated an increase of purchases by direct mail within the last two years. (Courtesy: Cahners Publishing Company.)

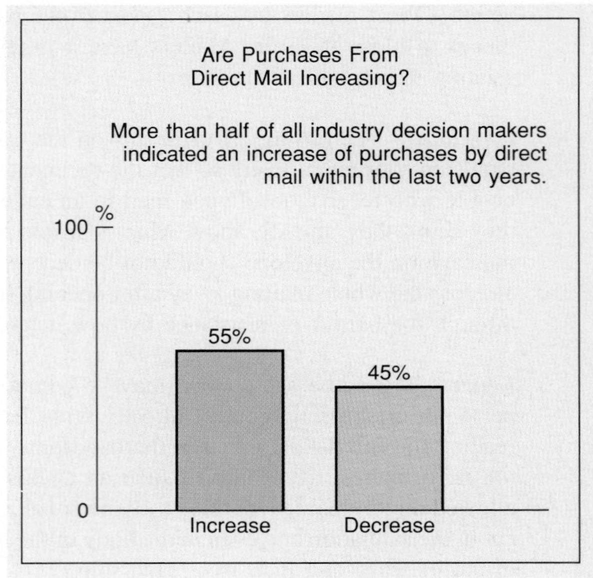

techniques available to enhance a direct marketer's chances of reaching prospects in the most efficient manner (see Exhibit 13.17).

Direct mailers are increasingly interested in determining consumer reading habits. That is, they want to know the odds that a direct-mail message will be considered by a prospect. One study showed that the largest proportion of adults, about one in four (26 percent), said that they throw away unopened less than 10 percent of an average week's mail. When these are added to the 20 percent of respondents who said they never throw their mail away before examining it, it seems direct mailers have a chance to sell their wares to 46 percent of the adult population. The study further divided respondents into age, sex, and geographic categories and noted which were heavy readers of direct mail and which were not. For instance, 25-to-34-year-olds are the most likely group to throw away mail opened.[17]

Testing direct mail's success is concentrated in three areas: the *mailing list*, the *message*, and the *timing*. Advertisers are anxious to know who *keeps*, rather than discards, non-solicited mail, who reads short versus long letters, and which months/seasons elicit the most responses. Most direct mailers depend on research houses, such as *Market Source*, who claim they're "people who reach people you want to reach." They feature sources of *hard-to-reach teens*—"with money to spend"—in addition to college students, military personnel, and young moms and dads "on the move."

The Message. One of the great advantages of direct response is that it allows advertisers to test everything on a small, but meaningful, scale before proceeding on a large scale. Testing is especially simple in direct mail. Say you want to test which of two propositions or two appeals or two different formats is better. You prepare the materials to be tested the way they are to go out. Every other name on a list is sent mailing A; the other half is sent mailing B. All order cards have a code or key number by which replies are identified and tabulated.

To get statistically meaningful differences, you must use a big enough sample of a mailing list. Many list companies will provide a sample of their total list for testing purposes. You must also receive enough responses to show clearly which is the better ad. If mailing piece A produces 14 orders while mailing piece B produces 11, the test result is meaningless. And in order to make the test bed, or mailing, large enough, you have to have some idea of what percentage of response to expect. (This will vary enormously by medium and by offer.) Finally, you must make sure that the names chosen for a direct-mail test are a fair sample of the rest of the list.

These tests of the message look at every aspect of the mailing, from the envelope to the length of the message. For instance, a recent study found that envelopes marked "IMPORTANT," "URGENT," or "OFFICIAL," and resembling government documents are resented by many people. But the degree to which such promotions were

[17]"How Much Mail Is Never Read?" *Target Marketing*, June 1988, p. 40.

EXHIBIT 13.17

The key to successful direct marketing is reaching prospects. (Courtesy: CMG Lists and Doubleday List Marketing.)

regarded as bothersome varied by age. In fact, approximately 67 percent of respondents 18 to 24 years old thought the practice was a satisfactory technique.[18]

Other research has shown that the best length for a direct-mail letter depends on whether you are writing past consumers or new prospects. Generally, long letters get lower overall readership, but the best prospects are most likely to completely read a long letter. On the other hand, letters to current customers should be shorter unless you have a new product or story to tell.

Timing. Consumers are more likely to buy certain products on a seasonal basis. Exhibit 13.18 shows the various timing factors in the purchase of several product categories. For example, during the entire year, 39 percent of respondents indicated they had bought a grooming aid through direct marketing. However, only 19 percent reported buying in March as contrasted to 45 percent in October.

Another timing concern of direct mailers is prompt delivery of mail by the U.S. Postal Service. One study conducted by the Mailing List Users and Suppliers (ML/USA) indicated that approximately 11 percent of third-class mail was not delivered. Four major catalog companies report nondelivery rates of 11–17 percent. Part of the problem is that some postal workers simply dump third-class mail: In one year, 294 USPS employees were fired for doing so.

---

[18] "Official Mail Resented," *Target Marketing,* February 1988, p. 27.

EXHIBIT 13.18

Direct-marketing products demonstrate significant seasonable variations. (Courtesy: *Target Marketing*.)

	Direct Market Product Purchased					
	Personal Grooming	**Household Supplies**	**Leisure/ Hobby**	**Publications**	**Foods**	**Price Paid**
	%	%	%	%	%	
1987	39	21	14	11	3	$73.20
January	32	16	14	13	2	76.40
February	23	14	16	26	6	98.10
March	19	14	10	27	13	75.50
April	41	25	14	9	1	66.40
May	43	22	14	10	0	64.50
June	43	20	11	9	2	82.30
July	43	17	11	13	2	69.30
August	38	29	13	7	2	77.60
September	35	28	15	7	2	92.20
October	45	24	12	6	3	71.10
November	42	20	20	10	3	62.40
December	42	19	16	9	4	70.60

Target Marketing, March 1988, p. 21.

The USPS, while taking some of the blame for nondelivery, cites the direct-mail industry for a large share of the problem. In two studies, one of which was conducted independently of the USPS, between 25 and 33 percent of direct-mail pieces were found to have some form of error in their addresses.[19]

PLANNING AND PRODUCING THE DIRECT-MAIL PIECE

The first step in planning a direct-mail piece is to study the overall marketing and advertising program. Direct marketing is not separate from the firm's other marketing efforts but an integrated part of the system. The first question a direct marketer should ask is: How will my direct marketing efforts complement the total marketing program of my company?

To answer this question, you might ask yourself the following:

Direct mail is usually part of the overall promotion program of the advertiser and should be included *only* if it meshes with the other promotion media. American Express now wants to aim its *Optima revolving credit card* at college students. In addition to direct mail, it has joined with Northwest Airlines to market a new campus magazine. The personalized letter will give *details* of the offer and include a return application form—while the magazine ads will feature travel locations where the card can be used.

- Will the direct-mail effort be supported with media advertising? Before, during, or after the mailing?
- Is the direct-mail message directed at present or potential customers, or both?
- Am I attempting a straight sale or building leads for future follow-up? If the latter, does our sales force know about and understand the purpose of the mailing?

Other questions you ask will, of course, be determined by the specific marketing problem you are trying to solve. However, only after you have approached the direct-mail promotion from the perspective of your marketing goals and objectives are you ready to begin production of your mailing piece.

The creator of direct mail has a wide latitude in format: It may be a single card encompassing a coupon, or it may be a letter with a return card, a small folder, a brochure, or a folded broadside with an order form and return envelope. Each format has a different function and use, depending on the cost of the product being sold, the importance of pictures, and the nature and length of the copy. As a rule, a warm letter, even if not personalized, should accompany any request for the order. This letter

[19]David Enscoe, "Third Class Mail Gets No Respect," *Target Marketing*, July 1988, p. 10.

should stress the product's benefits, describe its key features and their importance, and ask for the order. No matter what kind of material is being sent, it is always possible to present it in an interesting form (within postal limitations).

What a different world direct-mail production is compared to magazine ad production! With magazine ads, the publisher is responsible for the total printing and delivery of the publication. In direct mail, the advertiser undertakes the complete burden of having all the material printed, which involves selecting the paper and the type, establishing prices, and choosing the printer. It also involves selecting a letter shop, whose functions we shall discuss later.

A Mail-Production Program

Perhaps the clearest way to demonstrate what is involved is to work through a schedule and touch on some of the key points.

Checking Weight and Size with Post Office. Everything begins on receipt of a complete dummy of the mailing unit, including copy and artwork from the creative department, along with quantities and mailing dates. The first—and most important—thing to do is to check with the post office on weight and size.

Selecting the Printing Process. In Chapter 18, Print Production, we discuss the three major types of printing: letterpress, offset, and gravure. For the time being, we can say that most direct-mail advertising is printed by the offset method, except very large runs, which may use rotogravure.

Selecting the Paper. Here we have to pause to become familiar with some important things about the choice of paper, as this is not covered elsewhere in the book. The three chief categories of paper ("stocks") used in advertising are writing stocks, book stocks, and cover stocks.

WRITING STOCKS. This class comprises the whole range of paper meant to be written or typed on. Quality varies from ledger stock, used to keep records; to bond stock, for top-level office stationery; to utility office paper, used to keep records; to memorandum paper. If you wanted to include a letter in a mailing, you would find a paper stock in this class.

BOOK STOCKS. Book stocks are the widest classification of papers used in advertising. Chief among the many variations of book stocks are:

- *News stock.* This is the least costly book paper, built for a short life and porous so that it can dry quickly. It takes line plates well. It is used for freestanding inserts in magazines, but is not very good for offset.
- *Antique finish.* A soft paper with a mildly rough finish, antique finish is used for offset. Among the antique classifications are eggshell antique, a very serviceable offset paper; and text, a high-grade antique used for quality offset books, booklets, and brochures (it is often watermarked and deckle-edged).
- *Machine finish.* Most books and publications are printed on machine-finish paper. It is the workhorse of the paper family.
- *English finish.* This paper has a roughened nonglare surface. Widely accepted for direct-mail and sales-promotion printing, it is especially good for offset lithography and gravure.
- *Coated.* This is a paper given a special coat of clay and then ironed. The result is a heavier, smoother paper. Coated paper is not usually used for offset. It can take 150-screen halftones very well for letterpress printing and is therefore frequently used in industrial catalogs, where fine, sharp reproduction is important and where there will be continuous usage over a period of time.

COVER STOCKS. These are strong papers, highly resistant to rough handling. Cover stock is used not only for the covers of booklets, but also sometimes by itself in direct-mail work. Although it has many finishes and textures, it is not adaptable for halftone printing by letterpress but reproduces tones very well in offset.

There are many other types of paper, useful for many purposes, but writing, book, and cover are the chief stocks used in advertising. The printer will submit samples of paper suitable for a given job.

Basic Weights and Sizes. Paper comes off the machine in large rolls. It is then cut into large sheets in a number of different sizes. In that way, many pages can be printed at one time. Paper is sold by 500-sheet reams, and its grade is determined by weight. To meet the problem comparing the weight of paper cut to different sizes, certain sizes have been established for each class as basic for weighing purposes. These are:

- For writing paper: 17 by 22 inches
- For book paper: 25 by 38 inches
- For cover stock: 20 by 26 inches

The advertiser has the responsibility to select the *printing process,* the *paper,* the *printer,* the *mailing house*—and deciding *how* the materials will be *mailed.* Ads by Challenge Graphics in media trade newspapers describe available *catalog papers* and offer a free catalog of their full inventory. Promotional Distribution Services, in the same classified section, specializes in mailing and other distribution tasks. Both companies provide phone numbers and stress *quick service.*

Hence, no matter how large the sheet into which the paper has been cut, its weight is always given in terms of the weight of that paper when cut to its basic size. Thus, one hears a writing paper referred to as a "20-pound writing paper," a book paper referred to as a "70-pound paper," or a cover stock identified as a "100-pound cover."

Paper, which has to be selected in relation to the printing process and the plates to be used, is usually procured by the printer, after a specific choice has been made by the advertiser. In large cities, it may also be bought directly from paper jobbers. Both printers and jobbers will be glad to submit samples. Before you give the final order for paper, you should check once more with the post office for weight, shape, and size of envelope. Check the total package.

In planning direct mail, you must know basic paper sizes and plan all pieces so that they may be cut from a standard sheet size without waste. Before ordering envelopes, check with the post office to learn their latest size restrictions, which are subject to change.

Selecting the Printer. The problem in selecting a printer is, first of all, finding those printers who have the type of presses and the capacity to handle the operation that you have in mind. They may not be located near you. In any case, experience has shown that it is always best to get three estimates. Of course, the reputation of the firm for prompt delivery is important.

Finished mechanicals with type and illustrations or photographic negatives should be made ready to turn over to the printer. Proofs should be checked carefully and returned promptly to the printer.

Letter shop. *A firm that not only addresses the mailing envelope but also is mechanically equipped to insert material, seal and stamp envelopes, and deliver them to the post office according to mailing requirements.*

Selecting the Letter Shop (Mailing House). Once all the material has been printed—including the envelope,which has to be addressed; a letter, possibly calling for a name fill-in; a folder that has to be folded; and a return card, also perhaps with the name imprinted—the whole package goes to a mailing house (in many quarters called a *letter shop*). Many letter shops are mammoth plants in which everything is done by computer. Their computerized letters not only mention the addressee's name, but also include a personal reference. The name is also printed on the return order form. Machines automatically address various units, fold all pieces that need to be folded, collate all material, and insert it in the envelope, which is sealed, arranged geographically for postal requirements, and delivered to the post office. (There is always a question of which is more wonderful: the machines with their swinging arms that do all these things, or the production director who has all the material ready in one place on time.)

Since the letter shop and the printer must work closely together, it is desirable that they be located near each other.

EXHIBIT 13.19

Advertisers use reverse time tables to schedule direct-mail campaigns. (From *The Direct Mail Marketing Manual,* Release 4005, July 1970, Courtesy: Direct Mail/Marketing Association, Inc., New York, N.Y.)

Description of Item or Project: ____________________

REVERSE TIME TABLE

(The purpose of which is to work backwards to make sure enough time is allowed for proper completion.)

Final Date Due in Hands of Recipients ________	This is when you expect the mailing to reach the people who are going to read it and act upon it.
Mailing Date ________	When you must release it to get it there on time. Avoid disappointment by allowing enough time for the P.O.
Assembly Date ________	All material must be in on this date to allow sufficient time for the mailing operations.
Printing Completion Date ________	This could be same as ASSEMBLY DATE except where time is required for shipment to out-of-town point.
Final Artwork Approval Date ________	This is the date the artwork must be ready to turn over to the printer.
Artwork Completion Date ________	Although most details should have been okayed before work actually began, quite often several people must approve the finished artwork. Allow enough time for this approval.
Finished Artwork Assignment ________ Date ________	This is the day the artist or art department gets the job. Allow at least a week. If no type has to be set, the interval can be cut short.
Consideration and Approval Date ________	Allow four or five days for staff members, including legal department if necessary, to see finished copy and layout.
Copy and Layout Assignment Date ________	Allow a week or more to give the copy and layout people time to do their jobs. Give more time when you can; they will more readily come through for you when a rush job is really critical.
Starting Date ________	You need some time to think about the job and draw up a set of instructions.

Production Schedule for Direct Mail

The planning and execution of a direct-mail campaign is not an overnight operation. The advertiser must work backward from the date he or she wishes the customer to receive the mailing piece to determine the necessary lead time. A reverse production timetable can be helpful in planning each step of a project (see Exhibit 13.19).

SUMMARY

By any number of benchmarks, direct marketing is emerging as a major promotional vehicle. Over the last decade, direct marketing's share of promotion and advertising dollars has been surpassed only by cable television. In terms of dollars of sales produced, direct marketing has few peers in either the consumer or the business-to-business sector. All indicators are that the impressive gains of recent years will continue into the future.

Data-based marketing and the capacity of computer technology to identify prospects make direct marketing appealing to even the most sophisticated advertisers. In addition, direct marketing's ability to test and verify results gives it a tremendous advantage over other media. Because of direct marketing's ability to narrowly target prospects, the apparent cost differentials between it and traditional advertising media vehicles have become less of a factor.

Perhaps the biggest challenge facing direct marketers is public distaste for the medium. However, industry-wide efforts sponsored by the Direct Marketing Association and other organizations have improved the industry's image. The fact that most Fortune 500 companies routinely include some form of direct marketing in their promotional plans is testimony to the medium's growing respectability among advertisers and improved credibility among consumers.

QUESTIONS

1. What is meant by the term *direct marketing?*
2. Discuss some of the major societal factors that have led to the significant increase in direct-response advertising in recent years.
3. What steps has the direct-response industry taken to upgrade its image and standing with consumers?
4. What are the primary advantages and disadvantages of the following direct-response vehicles:
   (a) direct mail
   (b) telemarketing
   (c) catalogs
   (d) television
   (e) magazines
5. Briefly discuss the use of inbound telemarketing.
6. Discuss the use of direct-response advertising to build leads as opposed to achieving direct sales.
7. Compare and contrast direct-response advertising with traditional media advertising.
8. Discuss data-based marketing and its application to direct-response advertising.
9. Explain the role of the list broker in building a successful direct-mail advertising program.
10. Identify:
    (a) merge/purge
    (b) ride-alongs
    (c) joint mailings
    (d) the fulfillment function
    (e) 900 telemarketing

SUGGESTED EXERCISES

- Choose a magazine advertisement for a national product and rewrite it as a direct-mail letter.
- Take the same advertisement and write a telemarketing script.

READINGS

AUSTERMAN, DONALD: "Writing Sales Letters That Really Sing," *Sales & Marketing Management,* February 1989, p. 40.

BARTKO, MAXIM C.: "Databases Revisited," *Target Marketing,* January 1989, p. 24.

BENCIN, RICHARD L.: "Electronic Marketing: 1990—A Whole New Selling Approach," *Sales & Marketing Management in Canada,* January 1988, p. 20.

Brown, Herbert E., and Roger W. Brucker: "Just What Is a Direct Response Offer?" *Direct Marketing,* March 1988, p.68.

Herzog, Richard: "Telemarketing Spurs High-Tech Sales," *Direct Marketing,* February 1988, p. 98.

"The Local Database: What's in Store?" *Direct Marketing,* March 1988, p. 46.

Lynton, Linda: "The Fine Art of Writing a Sales Letter," *Sales & Marketing Management,* August 1988, p. 51.

Nuttal, Gwen: "Mail Order: Post Haste," *Marketing,* March 3, 1988, p. 15.

Sovner-Ribbler, Judith: "Which Database Solves Which Marketing Problems?" *Sales & Marketing Management,* July 1988, p. 53.

Schwedelson, Roy: "New Wave Database," *Direct Marketing,* March 1988, p. 35.

"Special Telemarketing Section," *Target Marketing,* September 1988, pp. 47–54.

Stone, Bob: *Successful Direct Marketing Methods,* 4th ed. (Lincolnwood, IL: NTC Business Books, 1988).

FOURTEEN

Sales Promotion

Sales promotion. *(1) Sales activities that supplement both personal selling and marketing, coordinate the two, and help to make them effective, for example, display. (2) More loosely, the combination of personal selling, advertising, and all supplementary selling activities.*

Sales promotion is not advertising. However, it is so closely related to advertising that it would be a serious mistake to ignore it in our discussion.

Sales promotion is much larger than advertising in terms of expenditures and is incredibly diversified. It encompasses many more techniques and formats than advertising. Nonetheless, successful execution of sales-promotion programs requires an understanding of the marketing and advertising objectives of a firm or individual brands. Sales-promotion failures are usually a direct result of poor planning and a lack of integration with the total marketing mix.

PROMOTION AND ADVERTISING

Sales promotion is much *larger* than advertising and is *incredibly diversified*. More techniques and formats are utilized. Hershey Foods budgeted $245 million for promotions in 1988 versus $97 million for advertising, out of a total budget of $342 million. That same approach was seconded by Ralston Purina Chairman, William Stiritz. "There's a great transfer of dollars into promotion at the expense of advertising," he surmised.

Sales promotion is a *temporary* incentive to buy a product or service that is *in addition* to the normal merits of that product or service, its regular price, and its ongoing advertising support.[1] A major problem facing manufacturers is that many consumers are so accustomed to some type of promotion, such as coupons or price reductions, that they have come to expect one with every sale.

> Lots of marketers who turned to sales promotion as a quick fix for a slumping brand or as a way to beat back competitors and then found themselves hooked are searching for ways to break the habit. Promotional experts say marketers have abused incentive programs to the point that brand franchises are being cheapened by too many coupons, sweepstakes, and refunds. Rather than creating long-term brand loyalty, you teach consumers to switch from product to product in search of the best deal. There is also the hazard that brand-loyal consumers will wait for the next promotional offer, then load up the pantry. The marketer would have nabbed those customers anyhow, but now the penalty is a lower profit margin.[2]

---

[1]James H. Naber, "The Sales Promotion Explosion," paper from the James Webb Young Address Series, University of Illinois, October 21, 1986.

[2]Rebecca Fannin, "No Cheap Shots," *Marketing & Media Decisions,* October 1987, p. 104.

Promotion plans are being integrated in the marketing plan for a particular product or service. "It's possible the *food marketing mix* could eventually reach *70% promotion and 30% advertising,*" predicted Bonnie Rivers, A Salomon Brothers analyst. Campbell Soup echoed this forecast for its frozen-food products and Prego spaghetti sauces, where Campbell is locked in a war with Chesebrough-Pond's Ragu.

Manufacturers are attempting to devise complementary programs that can utilize the strengths of both sales promotion and advertising without harming their brands.

The typical national brand is sold through three types of promotion: consumer advertising, consumer promotion (known as *sales promotion* or simply *promotion*), and trade promotion (known as *dealer programs* or *merchandising*). A firm must divide its total promotional dollars among these three functions. Let's take a minute to examine the place of each in the marketing mix and the share of promotional budgets customarily devoted to these promotional categories.

Consumer sales promotion. *Incentives directed to consumers in the form of coupons, sales, etc., to gain immediate sales.*

Trade promotions. *Intended to encourage promotion of a company's products by the trade, especially retailers. Also used as incentives to a company's own sales force.*

1. *Consumer advertising.* Traditional media advertising vehicles promote the basic product attributes, location of dealers, and/or comparisons with other products. Currently, advertising constitutes about 35 percent of promotional expenditures.[3] (*Note:* advertising expenditures are for *measured* media excluding direct mail, which is divided between consumer and trade promotions.)
2. *Consumer sales promotion.* These are sale-promotional incentives directed to the consumer. Cents-off coupons are the most common consumer promotion, but free gifts, rebates, and contests are also used frequently. Some 25 percent of the marketing promotion budget is invested in consumer promotions.
3. *Trade promotion.* Trade incentives are designed to encourage a company's sales force or retail outlets to push its products more aggressively. These are the most expensive types of promotions on a per-person basis. Winning dealers or retailers may get a trip to Hawaii, a new car, or a cash bonus. Trade promotions make up about 40 percent of total promotional expenditures.

Not only is sales promotion growing, but in the largest firms, it is doing so at the expense of traditional advertising (see Exhibit 14.1). In reaction to this trend, many advertising agencies have bought or started promotional firms to handle their clients' requirements. One survey of clients indicated that 77.2 percent of advertising agencies offer them sales-promotion services and these clients consider sales promotion to be one of the most beneficial marketing services they receive.[4]

[3]Share of promotional budget share estimates from Donnelly Marketing Annual Survey.

[4]"Our Readers Tell Us . . . ," *Marketing & Media Decisions,* July 1988, p. 147.

EXHIBIT 14.1

Sales promotion has grown significantly faster than advertising in recent years. (Courtesy: *Marketing & Media Decisions.*)

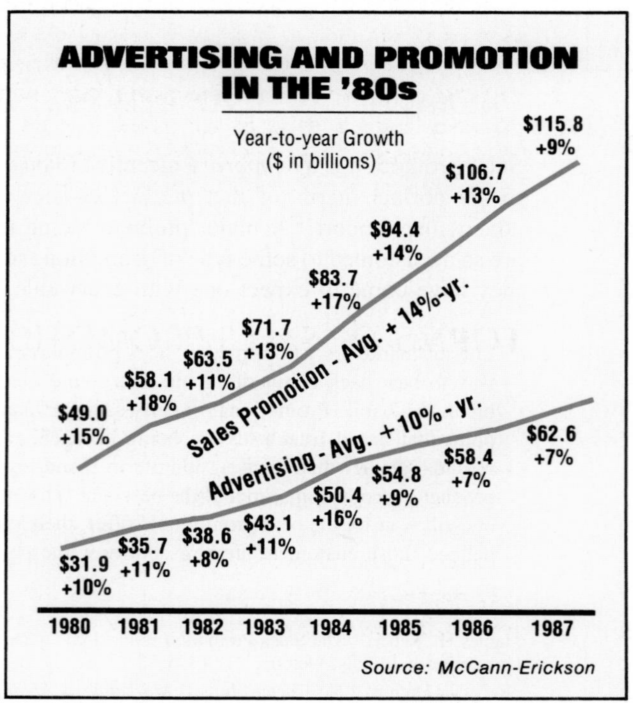

EXHIBIT 14.2

Couponing remains the most popular form of sales promotion. (Courtesy: *Marketing & Media Decisions.*)

CONSUMER-PROMOTION SCORECARD

3-Year comparison of usage levels

Type of Promotion	Percent of respondents who used each option 1987	1986	1985
1. Couponing Consumer Direct	96%	91%	93%
2. Money-back offers/cash refunds	87	85	85
3. Premium offers	74	58	79
4. Sampling new products	71	64	77
5. Cents-off promotions	69	70	78
6. Sweepstakes	66	72	77
7. Sampling established products	65	57	76
8. Couponing in retailers' ads	57	45	56
9. Pre-priced shippers	56	58	70
10. Contests	38	40	55

Source: Donnelley Marketing Annual Surveys of Promotional Practices for 1985, 1986, 1987. Sample = 121 firms

Consumer promotion, such as cents-off coupons, free gifts, rebates, and contests, occupy about 25% of a typical marketing promotion budget. To celebrate the 25th anniversary of its *low-tar Carlton brand,* the American Tobacco Company will offer $1-off coupons on cartons of Carltons and offer smokers a free calculator with proof-of-purchase. The offer, which begins this month, will be supported by point-of-purchase displays.

Incentives given to *dealers,* such as trips, gifts, or cash, are called *trade incentives*—usually costing about 40% of total promotion outlays. Canon, the electronics company, that built its business exporting high-quality, lower-cost products, designed and made in Japan, is in a state of transition. Unlike most other Japanese companies, Canon has relied on overseas markets for 70% of its sales, which hit $7.9 billion in 1987. "To maintain growth, Canon must change from being a product-oriented company to a market-oriented one," admits Eiji Toyosaki, corporate communications manager. Part of their promotion emphasis will now be devoted to *dealer incentives*—since they've recognized that they're the strongest link in the company's distribution channel. Incentives, typically, are "exotic island" trips, personalized gifts, and cash awards—depending on sales!

Promotion expenditures are growing at a *faster rate* than traditional advertising. Their "quick response" encourages advertisers to invest more dollars. Anheuser-Busch has been extremely successful with Bud Light mascot, Spuds MacKenzie's paraphernalia. T-shirts are among the most popular items—*their restricted distribution* has helped to enhance the brand and the product's image as an "adult" beverage, says DDB Needham Worldwide, its agency.

Despite the danger that the clutter of promotional offers might create consumer indifference, the use of promotion continues to grow. As you can see in Exhibit 14.2, a recent survey of a number of companies showed usage levels of promotion techniques ranging from 93 percent for coupons to 55 percent for contests. A comparison of some sales-promotion expenditures with traditional media is also impressive. For instance, the investment in point-of-purchase is greater than advertising expenditures in radio and consumer magazines combined.

There are many reasons for the growth in promotional activities in recent years, among them greater competition in many product categories, reduced consumer spending, and high retail inventories. However, the most appealing feature of sales promotion is its quick payout. In addition to short-term sales, promotions may gain significant free publicity for the sponsor (note the corporate sponsorship of college bowl games such as the Sunkist Fiesta Bowl).

In the future, there will be much more coordination between advertising and promotion. It is tempting to use "cute" ideas in sales promotion, but unless they have an obvious relevance to the product and its prime prospects, the effort (and considerable expense) will be wasted. Successful sales promotion demands the same degree of planning and expertise as the advertising and promotional techniques discussed in earlier chapters. One of the major improvements in sales promotion during recent years is the growing sophistication of these programs and the coordination between them and other area of marketing and advertising.

FORMS OF SALES PROMOTION

In this chapter, we will discuss the primary types of sales promotion. Our emphasis will be on those techniques most associated with advertising, especially at the consumer level. However, we will also look at trade-oriented promotions.

The most frequently used forms (sometimes in combination) of sales promotion are:

- Point-of-purchase advertising
- Premiums
- Specialty advertising
- Coupons
- Sampling

- Deals
- Sweepstakes and contests
- Cooperative advertising
- Booklets and brochures
- Trade shows and exhibits
- Directories and Yellow Pages
- Trade incentives

Sales promotion has become as routine for most product manufacturers as advertising. It is estimated that over 95 percent of firms marketing a consumer product use some form of sales promotion each year.

Point-of-purchase was the fastest-growing promotional category in the 1980s. Revenues increased *100%* between 1982 and 1988. One of the key reasons for P-O-P's successful growth is greater diversity—like *mall* promotions. Joel Benson, president of Shopping Center Network, developer of mall P-O-Ps, comments, "When people walk into a mall, *they want to know*—what's free? what can I do? what can I try? and what can I win? It's an *attitude* that's 'ripe' for clever promotion."

POINT-OF-PURCHASE ADVERTISING

The final battleground for many consumer sales is the aisles and shelves of grocery, drug, and discount stores. These stores represent the last chance for manufacturers to gain a sale from an undecided buyer or to remind an impulse purchaser of items left off a shopping list. The competition for consumers at the retail level is demonstrated by the growth of point-of-purchase advertising. Point-of-purchase was the fastest-growing advertising and promotional category during the 1980s. Revenues grew from less than $6 billion in 1982 to an estimated $14 billion in 1988, an increase of over 100 percent.

Point-of-purchase advertising. *Displays prepared by the manufacturer for use where the product is sold.*

> Point-of-purchase is a subsection of the advertising and promotion element of the marketing mix. Its "four-fold purpose of informing, reminding, persuading, and merchandising" places it squarely across the boundary between advertising and promotion, serving both the purpose of providing information to the consumer and persuading the consumer to purchase.
>
> Marketers have long recognized the ability of point-of-purchase to generate impulse sales, to support consumer price promotions and to reinforce media communications. In recent years, they have come to recognize point-of-purchase's usefulness in many other situations. As consumers make more brand and quantity decisions in the store, as brand loyalty lessens and as the effectiveness of media advertising declines, the value of point-of-purchase as a primary rather than a companion marketing tool has been enhanced.[5]

Point-of-Purchase Advertising Institute (POPAI). *Organization to promote point-of-purchase advertising.*

Point-of-purchase provides a captive audience of consumers in the marketplace, and studies indicate that a large number of them make purchases without prior planning. According to the Point-of-Purchase Advertising Institute (POPAI), two out of every three purchases are decided on while the shopper is in the store (see Exhibit 14.3). The study reported that certain categories are particularly susceptible to impulse buys: candy and gum (85 percent), cosmetics (68 percent), and oral hygiene products (75 percent).

[5]Kristina Cannon Bonventre, *Point-of-Purchase Advertising: A Marketer's In-Store Arsenal,* a publication of the Point-of-Purchase Advertising Institute.

EXHIBIT 14.3

Point-of-purchase takes advantage of the high rate of unplanned retail purchasing. (Courtesy: Point-of-Purchase Advertising Institute.)

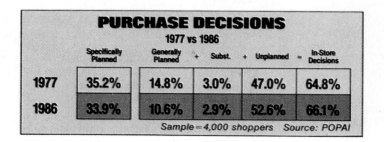

PURCHASE DECISIONS
1977 vs 1986

	Specifically Planned	Generally Planned	+ Subst.	+ Unplanned	= In-Store Decisions
1977	35.2%	14.8%	3.0%	47.0%	64.8%
1986	33.9%	10.6%	2.9%	52.6%	66.1%

Sample = 4,000 shoppers Source: POPAI

With the *decline* of brand loyalty and attention to media advertising, point-of-purchase's role in promotion has increased significantly. Paul Masson Wines offers a refund *on wine and chicken* consumers buy to make Chef Paul Prudhomme's Cajun Chicken Chablis. The bottleneck contains a recipe, and a free spice pack of the famous chef's "Louisiana Cajun Magic" is attached. Last year, the promotion performance made brand history. Displays were up 29% over the previous year; volume was up 11%; and redemption was 31% higher than normal couponing program results.

The popularity of point-of-purchase has resulted in the familiar problem of clutter. With so many advertisers vying for limited space, manufacturers are being forced to invest more money in their displays to enhance the chances of getting them used. Other forms of point-of-purchase are proliferating, such as audio and video material and even messages placed on shopping carts or alongside checkout lanes. Next time you are in a grocery store, look around at the point-of-purchase displays. Notice how many are doubling as product containers (such as magazine racks). Retail floor and shelf space is so scarce in the typical store that a cheap or undistinguished display has little chance of being used.

Uses of Point-of-Purchase Advertising

Point-of-purchase is an extremely flexible form of advertising. According to the Point-of-Purchase Advertising Institute (POPAI), it has four distinct functions in building sales:

1. *Informing*. Signs are the most frequently used informational point-of-purchase tools. Outdoors, they tell customers that a certain brand or category of goods or services is available at that location. Inside a store, signs alert consumers to the actual product and influence them to buy it.
2. *Reminding*. Specific corporate or brand names are usually prominently featured on point-of-purchase signs and displays. Identifying the corporate or brand name just when the customer is ready to buy triggers recall of other selling messages, broadcast commercials, or print advertisements that the consumer has heard or seen. Point-of-purchase reinforces the customer's awareness of a product, helping to influence future purchases.
3. *Persuading*. Selling features of the product, reasons to buy, or details about a promotional offer can be highlighted on point-of-purchase signs and displays. And all can, and do, help persuade consumers to make the ultimate buy decision.
4. *Merchandising*. The final function is the presentation of the product itself. An ingenious display of products naturally attracts attention. It also lets customers carefully inspect the item and evaluate its features for themselves. For many people, "feeling is believing."[6]

Regionalization, sales promotion. *Sales promotion is increasingly adopting a regional strategy to allow promotions to be more specifically adapted to regional interests of various consumer segments.*

A recent change in the strategy of using point-of-purchase and other forms of sales promotion is a more regionalized approach. Until a few years ago, companies would develop a sales-promotion plan and roll it out nationally, much as they would a magazine or network television campaign. However, just as advertisers realized that various target markets must be approached differently, promotion managers also began to adopt a regional strategy. As one sales-promotion executive noted, "The availability of good consumer data also has led manufacturers to become more regional in their marketing, focusing their efforts on specific market areas, or in some cases, specific chains of stores. Marketers are now working with store management to develop specific demographic and psychographic profiles of their customers and then building promotions that specifically target those customers."[7] This regionalization of sales promotion is being made possible by some of the same data-base techniques that we discussed in connection with direct-response advertising.

Point-of-purchase is extremely flexible—from *shopping cart signs* to *regional store displays*—it enhances the *final* presentation of the product. Sears has licensed the McDonald's name for 7 McKids children's apparel stores—with 28 more expected to open by year end. New clothing items will be created—the departments, themselves, will be partitioned from the regular children's departments—and character "guests" will make frequent visits on busy weekends. Videos, music, flashing lights, and plenty of "stuffed reminders" of the McDonald fast-food chain will be for sale.

Forms of Display

Exhibit 14.4 shows some of the variety of point-of-purchase displays. Since manufacturers compete for very scarce floor and shelf space, their point-of-purchase displays must be eye-catching, conserve space, and most of all produce greater profitability for retailers. Note how the prize-winning point-of-purchase displays presented in the exhibit use the product as a focal point.

---

[6]*P/O/P, The Last Word in Advertising,* published by Point-of-Purchase Advertising Institute, Inc., pp. 4–5.
[7]Len Strazewski, "Promotion 'Carnival' Get Serious," *Advertising Age,* May 2, 1988, p. S-2.

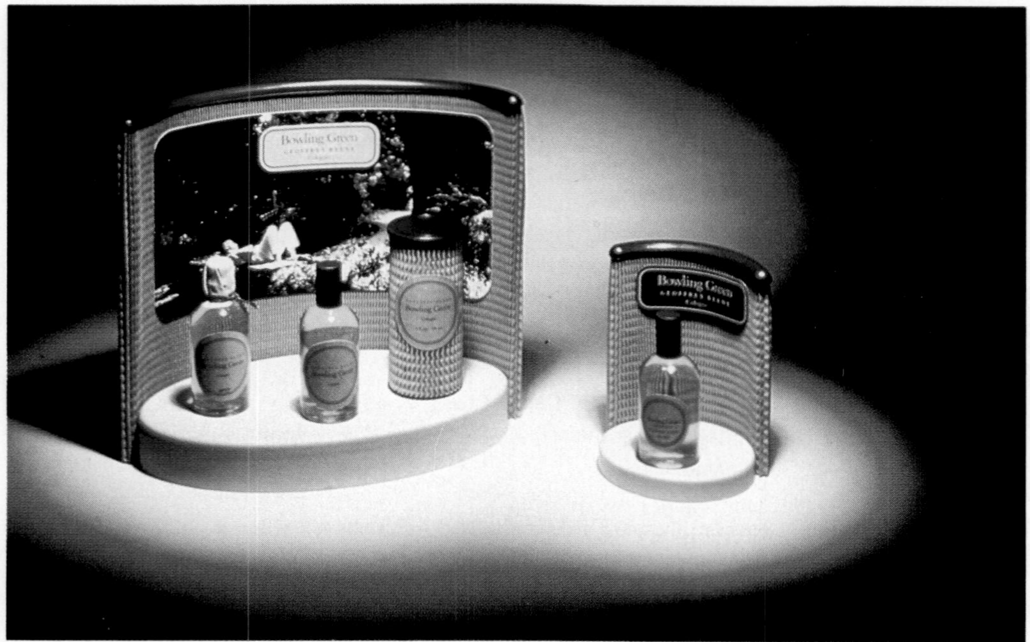

EXHIBIT 14.4A

Bowling Green Introduction Testers: This unit was developed to introduce a new men's prestige fragrance, Bowling Green. Geoffrey Beene's new scent conveys a natural outdoor feeling. Thus the packaging and testers were made of natural materials, i.e., single-face corrugated, bottle covering of natural linen. The color graphics depict a man lying in a field of woods and greenery, conveying the citrus, woody fragrance of Bowling Green. The display uses the same design elements as the primary and secondary containers, enhancing the theme and positioning of the fragrance. The display completely sold out and was reordered.

EXHIBIT 14.4B

Vicks Inhaler Counter Display: This injection-molded gravity-feed display was designed to hold eight dozen inhalers. It is made of translucent blue plastic in order to add visual impact to the unit. To reinforce product identification, vacuum-formed and caps in the shape of the inhaler were used on either side of the unit and labeled to look exactly like the inhaler. Only a few inhalers are exposed at any time, which keeps the product clean. The unit is very compact and easy to refill. The front panel is slid back, a box containing the inhalers is emptied into the unit, and then the panel is closed.

The unit was so successful that the trade placed it right next to cash registers, which is the ideal position for impulse sales. Initial field results indicated sales increases of over 10 percent as compared with the previous gravity-feed unit.

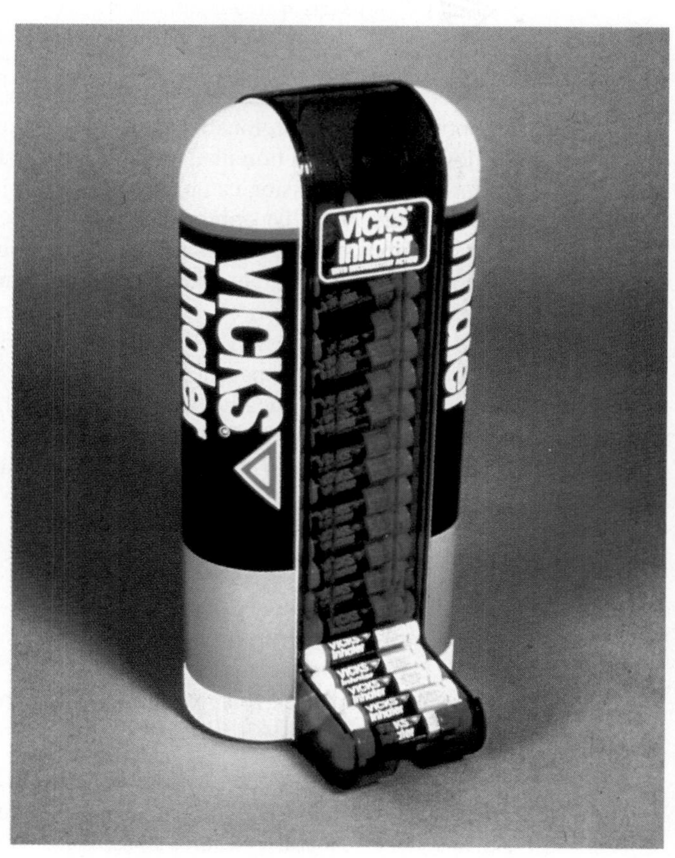

EXHIBIT 14.4C

Kraft Handi-Snack Permanent Floorstand: Kraft wanted to provide a permanent home in grocery stores for its Handi-Snack single packs. In order to have changeable graphics, the unit had to be smaller than the one previously used and movable. Because the unit stacks dump bins vertically, they take up less floor space than the previous model while maintaining the same capacity. Slanting the bins for rear loading assures product rotation. Snap-in glide panels and header provide a medium for changeable graphics and seasonal promotions. Molded-in glides allow the display to be moved around the store easily. The unit's permanence and effective use of floor space persuaded retailers who had not used earlier displays to accept this display.

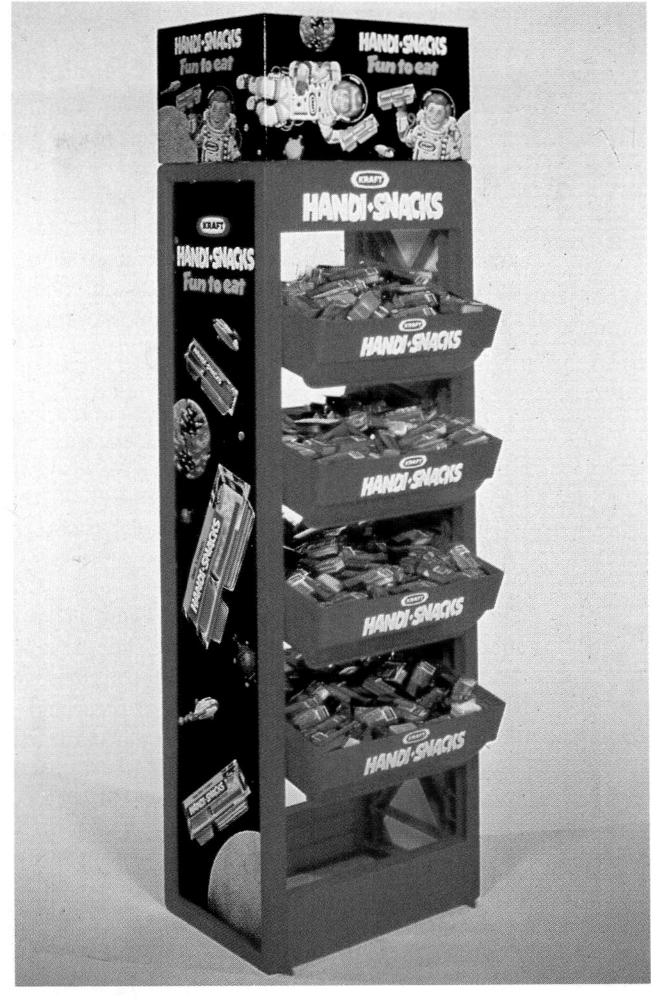

Displays must be eyecatching, conserve space, and enhance profitability for retailers. *Funk & Wagnalls,* one of the 3 major encyclopedia companies, plans to expand sales of its regular sets at the supermarket. Typically, it sets up a *display* in each store about every three and one-half years, depending on the area's birth rates. During the first week, Volume I will be put on display for $.09. With the prices rising each week, shoppers eventually accumulate the full 29-volume set in 18 weeks. The *total cost is $140*—all from self-service displays in nonpersonal settings.

The Display Idea

Like any form of advertising or promotion, successful point-of-purchase must have a unique selling idea that supports general marketing goals. The possibilities are almost unlimited. However, most point-of-purchase plans utilize one of the following ideas:

1. The *product* may be the central theme of a point-of-purchase display. The simplest, yet one of the most effective, displays is a large stack of the product on the floor with a sign stating some of its characteristics. This approach is most used with sale merchandise.
2. *Tie-ins* with other advertising can be extremely effective for point-of-purchase displays. Normally, tie-ins are used in connection with national advertising campaigns, but they can also be used with local promotions or even as part of store-wide promotions such as harvest sales.
3. *Demonstrations* of the product are another approach. Often the display invites the shopper to try out features of the product by pressing a button, looking through an opening, or turning a knob. This is especially good for new types of products.

Audio and Interactive Point-of-Purchase

One of the major changes in point-of-purchase in the last decade is the development of new technology. While the familiar cardboard display is still the most common form of point-of-purchase, new formats are being introduced with some success. In terms of innovative media forms, point-of-purchase is undergoing the same kind of transition as out-of-home advertising. It would be impossible to discuss all these new formats here, but we will look at a few of the more important ones.

Audio Point-of-Purchase. For many years, retailers have provided music for their customers. Often it consisted of no more than piping in a local FM station. Now several companies are providing retailers with the opportunity to turn this "background" music into an aggressive sales tool or *foreground* music. For example, a company called Point-of-Purchase Radio, Inc. (POP Radio) signed a joint operating agreement with Muzak to provide in-store advertising on specialty music programs developed for the audience of a particular store or chain. POP Radio will either produce a commercial or place an agency-produced commercial already running on commercial stations.

> Storecasting offers multiple incentives to retailers—no music licensing fees, controlled programming, the chance of additional revenues from ad sales and/or increased cash register rings. For advertisers, storecast ads offer an alternative to bulky promotional displays and the clutter of intrusive visuals. Furthermore, the customer can respond to in-store radio from anywhere in the store. Finally, smaller brands, which might not have clout in the fight for limited shelf/display space, can use custom-cast ads to get into the point-of-purchase act.[8]

Interactive point-of-purchase. *In-store devices that allow consumers to receive information about a product or product usage, such as recipes.*

Interactive Point-of-Purchase. There are a number of experiments going on with interactive point-of-purchase. One such device is the Cuisine Machine, distributed by Inter-Ad Inc. The machine provides recipes, nutritional information, and cooking instructions for 100 different types of meat and seafood. The consumer can either read the information off a screen or get a printout. In contrast to other store-video point-of-purchase, the consumer determines what information the machine provides. Exhibit 14.5 shows the Cuisine Machine in use.

[8]Marianne Meyer, "Attention Shoppers," *Marketing & Media Decisions*, May 1988, p. 70.

EXHIBIT 14.5

The Cuisine Machine combines features of television, point-of-purchase, and couponing. (Courtesy: Inter-Ad, Inc.)

A new variety of point-of-purchase is "storecasting"—or the broadcasting of commercial messages to shoppers. Other devices use *machines* to provide recipe or nutritional data to customers. *K-Mart Canada* is experiencing better than expected results with its "Amazing Speak 'n' Win" game. Customers choose a flyer, which guarantees a prize. They wave its bar code over a wand—the machine "speaks" to the customers, telling them what they've won. Ted Hains, president of Hains/Roberts, says the voice quality and flexibility of "Speak 'n' Win" make it superior to other similar promotion programs. In the future, the technology can also be wired to display *images* with the winning announcements.

These innovations in point-of-purchase are interesting in themselves. They also point up, once again, how advertising, promotion, and marketing are becoming so interrelated that it is difficult to tell where one stops and the other begins. Managers are more concerned with using whatever works than with categorizing a technique.

The Future of Point-of-Purchase

Point-of-purchase techniques will continue to proliferate. They will also be increasingly designed to reach specific consumers, first at the regional level, and then at the individual store level. Point-of-purchase revenues are growing five times faster than retail floor space and clutter is becoming a major problem. In the future, point-of-purchase will have to find promotional techniques that acknowledge the saturation of both shelf and floor space—for example, packaging (including grocery bags) will be used more frequently as a form of promotion and advertising.

PREMIUMS

Premium. *An item, other than the product itself, given to purchasers of a product as an inducement to buy. Can be free with a purchase (for example, on the package, in the package, or the container itself) or available upon proof of purchase and a payment (self-liquidating premium).*

Premiums are extra incentives to encourage a person at the consumer or trade level to make a purchase. These bonuses make the purchase of a product more inviting and move the buyer to take immediate action. Types of premiums are limited only by the imagination of the companies offering them.

As the term is used in advertising, a *premium* is an item offered in exchange for some customer action. Normally, the consumer must purchase a product to qualify for a premium, but other premiums—known as *traffic-building premiums*—are given merely for visiting a retailer, a real estate development, or an automobile dealer. Annual expenditures for premiums are approximately $6 billion (see Exhibit 14.6).

Like all sales-promotion techniques, premiums should be part of a total marketing and advertising program and should be appropriate and logical for the product with which they are associated. Exhibit 14.7 lists some premium techniques and what marketing goals they are most likely to accomplish. Premiums should be selected with the same care you would use in planning an advertising media buy. Offering a premium without a specific purpose and target market in mind will likely result in an ineffective promotional program and wasted money. To judge the value of a premium, the advertiser should ask: Would this item appeal to my target audience? In other words, is the premium:

- Useful to my customers?
- Unique among competitive promotions?
- Related to my product?
- Easily promoted with the product?
- Of a quality expected by consumers at a price I can afford?

EXHIBIT 14.6

Consumer premiums use a number of formats. (Courtesy: *Advertising Age*.)

	1986 Expenditures	*% Chg.*	*1987 Expenditures*	*% Chg.*	*1987 Expenditures including Retail*
Consumer premiums					
Product promotion:	$3,685,931	1.6	$3,925,162	6.5	$3,925,162
• Mail-in offers	1,864,186	2.0	1,988,071	6.6	1,988,071
• Direct premiums	1,821,745	1.1	1,937,091	6.3	1,937,091
Retail promotion:	$2,411,000	−2.3	$2,512,990	4.2	$1,552,656
• Sweepstakes, games	(Tabulated		185,946		185,946
• Direct, trading stamps	differently		1,366,710		1,366,710
• Trade incentives, gifts	in 1986)		960,334		
Consumer total	$6,096,931	—	$6,438,152	5.6	$5,477,818

EXHIBIT 14.7

Consumer premiums must be carefully planned to promote predetermined objectives. (Courtesy: *Incentive Marketing*.)

CONSUMER PREMIUMS: WHAT THEY CAN DO (% of Users in 1987 Who Consider Each Technique Most Effective for Reaching Each Goal)						
	GET SHELF ATTENTION		SELL-IN TO DEALERS		BOOST REPEAT SALES	
BEST	Direct Premium Factory-Pack	14% 14	Direct Premium Free Mail-In	19% 9	Coupon Plan Direct Premium Free Mail-In	17% 16 16
WORST	Self-Liquidator	2%	Sweepstakes	3%	Self-Liquidator Sweepstakes	2% 2
	SALES TALKING POINT		BUILD USER GOOD WILL		GAIN AD READERSHIP	
BEST	Direct Premium Free Mail-In Coupon Plan	16% 9 9	Direct Premium Self-Liquidator	16% 13	Free Mail-In Coupon Plan	19% 16
WORST	Factory-Pack	2%	Sweepstakes	5%	Factory-Pack	2%
	OBTAIN STORE DISPLAYS		SAMPLE NEW USERS		COST-EFFECTIVENESS	
BEST	Direct Premium Free Mail-In	31% 11	Direct Premium Free Mail-In Coupon Plan	17% 16 16	Direct Premium Self-Liquidator Coupon Plan	16% 11 11
WORST	Self-Liquidator	2%	Sweepstakes	3%	Factory-Pack	6%

"Clutter in the aisles" will force point-of-purchase to seek other methods of projection. *Packaging* innovations are appearing, such as *Henschel-Steinau's freestanding displays*. In addition to being aesthetically attractive, the displays are efficient in building traffic. Products are *housed in displays,* along with descriptive literature and companion items. *By varying sizes and shapes,* these P-O-P display units can fit in corners, at end-of-aisles, near cash registers, or take the place of regular wall units. Clients, such as Philip Morris, Proctor & Gamble, and Max Factor, have redesigned *their* packages—if P-O-P displays will provide greater recognition for their products, says H-S.

Premiums act as extra incentives for browsing or purchasing. To be effective, they should be *appealing* to the target and should have a *specific purpose*. Mooney Aircraft is offering the ultimate premium incentive—free use of a 911 Porsche, if the prospect buys the Porsche-powered plane, the Mooney-Porsche PFM (average flyaway price: $180,000). "We found that almost all of the pilots who bought the PFM at one time had owned a Porsche," admitted Bill Monroe, Mooney's marketing manager. "So we decided to give them one for the hangar and one for the garage."

In recent years, another factor has become a major consideration in selecting premiums—safety. There have been a number of accidents, a few fatal, in which small children have swallowed premiums. In one 1988 case, General Mills recalled 20 million boxes of Cheerios containing a "Powerball" premium after a child choked to death on it. The federal Consumer Product Safety Commission now tests premiums using a cylinder the size of a typical 3-year-old's throat, but several consumer groups have called for stronger controls or the outright banning of such premiums.[9]

Premiums are concentrated among a few major users. By far the largest user of consumer premiums are food-product manufacturers. For some categories, premiums have even become an expected part of the sale. In these high-usage premium categories, it is becoming more and more difficult to differentiate one premium from another.

In the following discussion, we will point out the primary types of premiums and give some examples of each. You will note that some premiums fit into more than one category.

Self-Liquidating Premiums

Self-liquidating premium. *These premiums are offered to consumer in exchange for a full or partial payment to cover their cost.*

Many self-liquidating premiums are sold to consumers at a price that covers the cost of the item as well as handling. Sometimes these premiums actually become a major profit center for a company: Both Marlboro and Budweiser have established subsidiaries to sell their advertising premiums. However, cost is becoming a concern to self-liquidators. A number of companies are starting to pay a larger share of the cost of the premium. Overall, industry figures indicate that approximately 25 percent of the cost of self-liquidating premiums is borne by the advertiser.

The self-liquidating category is one of the largest segments of the premium industry, but recently it has experienced much slower growth compared to some other premium categories. As competition has intensified, companies have turned to free premiums as a greater incentive to purchase.

[9]Judy Biltekoff, "Grocers Field Premium Complaint," *Advertising Age,* January 11, 1988, p. 44S.

Still, a successful self-liquidating program is ideal since it has all the advantages of other premiums without the associated costs. Two examples of self-liquidating premiums are:

1. Sundance natural juice sparkler offered a Sundance/Fuji team cycling jersey for $29.95.
2. Baggies plastic sandwich bags offered a Sony Walkman radio for $9.95.

Manufacturers must be careful about the kind of self-liquidating merchandise they offer because if customers think the merchandise is not worth its price, this will reflect poorly on the product with which the premium is associated. Also, since the self-liquidating premium carries the manufacturer or brand logo, normally only well-known products can successfully market self-liquidators.

2 Direct Premiums

Direct premiums. *Any premium which is given to the consumer at the time of purchase.*

Direct premiums are usually given free to the consumer at the time of purchase. The major advantage of these premiums is the immediate reward they provide for the buyer. In addition, they involve no handling or mailing expenses since the consumer collects the premium at the time of purchase. On the other hand, space limitations restrict the size of the direct premium a manufacturer can offer. There are several types of direct premiums, including on-pack, in-pack, near-pack, and container premiums.

On-Pack Premiums. On-pack premiums are not used as much as other premiums for a number of reasons. Unless the premium is securely attached to the package, pilferage is a problem. A greater concern is the extra shelf space that on-pack premiums sometimes require. Retailers are reluctant to give valuable space to product premiums, especially since they do not provide additional direct profit to the store. Some on-pack premiums, such as the recipes provided with Campbell Soup, overcome these problems.

In-pack premium. *The oldest form of premiums. They are contained in the package.*

Self-liquidating premiums are "sold" to consumers—but face a value appraisal. *Direct premiums,* in contrast, are distributed free. Companies specializing in creating premium merchandise are even broken down by age category—to get the items "right." *The Children's Marketing Experts* advertise that they have the "imagination and expertise" as the nation's largest creator, publisher, printer, and marketer of premiums. As part of a customer's marketing plan, premiums can be created and/or printed for "a unique promotion as *distinctive* as the product or service."

In-Pack Premiums. The oldest type of premium is one that is contained in the package. The in-pack premium can be anything from towels or dishes packed in detergent boxes to the familiar Cracker Jack toy. A common in-pack premium is the sample of washing powder or cleanser shipped with appliances. For example, General Electric dishwashers are delivered with a trial size of Palmolive dishwasher detergent. As we will see later in this chapter, this type of "premium" may also be considered a product sample.

Perhaps the most successful in-pack promotion dates to 1951, when Topps began offering baseball playing cards with its bubble gum. This promotion was so successful that the playing cards became the primary product. Now Topps sells packages of cards rather than one or two in a pack of gum.

A whole industry has developed around this premium turned collectible with privately sponsored trade shows and several publications. If you can get it, the 1952 Mickey Mantle card is estimated to be worth more than $6,500.[10] Not bad for an original investment of a few pennies!

Near-Pack Premiums. Near-pack premiums are items offered by the advertiser that are located in a separate display, usually adjacent to the product. For example, Dearfoam slippers offered a porcelain picture frame with each purchase. Near-pack premiums are the least used of all premiums because they require retailers to provide extra space and sometimes service.

[10]Amy Zipkin, "Premiums from the Past Take on Classic Quality," *Advertising Age,* May 2, 1988, p. S-10.

Container Premiums. Container premiums are reusable containers that serve as the package for the product. This is a good way for the advertiser to increase consumer trials of the product, and the containers act as a constant reminder of the brand. Container premiums are also an extremely efficient form of sales promotion since they cost very little more than a regular product container in most cases.

Free Mail-in Premiums

The free mail-in premium accounts for about 15 percent of all premiums, ranking behind only direct and self-liquidating premiums, and it is growing faster than most other premium categories. It requires that consumers send in a proof-of-purchase in return for a free gift. More than any other sales-promotion technique, free mail-ins tend to be closely tied to some form of advertising or other promotion.

Typically, advertisers promote their mail-in offers through point-of-purchase, direct mail, freestanding inserts, and traditional advertising. Ideally, the customer should know about the offer before the purchase because otherwise it was not an incentive to buy and the money spent on the promotion was wasted. Examples of free mail-in offers are nearly endless. Here are a few made by major companies:

1. Swiss Colony mail-order house offered a free chocolate cake to anyone who ordered a catalog.
2. The purchase of a 16-piece set of Corelle dinnerware qualified the buyer for an eight-inch bud vase.
3. With the purchase of two bottles of Jergen liquid soap, customers could use a mail-in coupon to obtain four bars of Jergen soap.
4. Nutri-Grain cereal offered a set of writing cards with the purchase of a box of cereal.

The free mail-in is the most expensive type of premium offer, which is why you should not consider such a program unless you are sure it will build sales among light users and nonusers of the product. Free mail-ins used only by current customers are a tremendous waste of money.

Tie-in Premiums

More costly premiums are those customers request by mail for proofs of purchase and "tie-in premiums," where additional merchandise of another company is used as a "reward." Stanley Tools tied-in with Coleman in the "Great Outdoors Giveaway." Anyone buying $8 or more worth of Stanley Tools receives a free 2-liter Coleman jug (no postage or handling fees). Research shows that the do-it-yourself market overlaps with those who love the outdoors.

We are seeing an increasing number of tie-in premiums. Formerly, the majority of these programs were used to promote two or more products in the same product line. For example, Nutri-Grain included small in-packs of Raisin Squares, and Aunt Jemima Frozen Waffles were offered free with the purchase of Aunt Jemima Waffles, Pancake Mix, or Syrup.

More recent tie-ins have involved cross-industry promotions. Hasbro toys offered discount coupons when customers bought Kraft products and provided proof-of-purchase. Promise margarine offered 50-cents-off coupons on the purchase of fresh vegetables, Del Monte fruit snacks buyers qualified for $5 rebates on school supplies, and Ragu offered free pasta coupons with the purchase of two jars of its sauces.

The advantage of tie-in premiums is that their cost is shared by two or more companies or brands. A potential disadvantage is that one brand may dominate the promotion and gain most of the benefits. Also, if not handled carefully, joint promotions can damage one of the products. For instance, positioning a product, new or old, as a premium for another brand risks the future image of that product.

Fulfillment

The physical work of opening, organizing, and responding to requests for mail-in premiums is normally handled by fulfillment firms. These firms usually do the work for a fee based on the number of entries. Their operations are critical to the success of any mail-in promotion, so before contracting with a fulfillment firm, you should determine if it is experienced in handling the type of promotion you are planning. Fulfillment is an extension of customer service, and it is your company, not the fulfillment

Fulfillment firm. *Company that handles the couponing process including receiving, verification and payment. It also handles contests and sweepstake responses.*

firm, that will be blamed if something goes wrong. These firms also handle contest and sweepstakes response.

SPECIALTY ADVERTISING

Specialty advertising. *A free gift given to build consumer good will and encourage future purchase of a product.*

In its simplest form, specialty advertising consists of giving gifts to consumers. The idea is to build goodwill that will result in a future purchase. According to the Specialty Advertising Association International (SAAI):

> Specialty advertising is an advertising, sales promotion and motivational communication medium which employs useful articles of merchandise imprinted with an advertiser's name, message or logo. Unlike premiums, with which they are sometimes confused, these articles (called advertising specialties) are always distributed free—recipients don't have to earn the specialty by making a purchase or contribution.[11]

Without making a purchase or commitment to buy, prospects may be offered *free gifts, called advertising specialties*. Items, such as coffee mugs, calendars, bookmarks, paperweights, magnets, etc., build goodwill for consumers *and* distributors. These articles serve as constant reminders of the sponsor. Specialty advertising distributors, such as Gawi-Madison, Madison, New Jersey, has been in business for 35 years, as one of the largest distributors of specialty gifts. Their largest client is the *banking industry*, which distributes small appliances, glassware, and other decorative home items for various investments and new account openings.

Although the specialty industry is geared to major corporations, it is adaptable enough to be a useful marketing tool for even the smallest companies. Annual expenditures for all forms of specialty advertising are now estimated to be over $4 billion.

Specialty items encompass more than 15,000 different articles, from calendars to coffee mugs. Specialties are used to build both consumer and trade support. More expensive trade specialties are called *executive gifts*. They differ from true specialty advertising in that they are often not imprinted with the advertiser's name. Specialty advertising counselors assist their clients with executive gift programs to such an extent (two-thirds of all business gifts are purchased by donors through specialty advertising distributors) that this category is among the leading markets of the industry.

Specialty advertising is an extremely useful marketing tool. Used primarily as a supplement to other promotional and marketing plans, it can accomplish a number of objectives. It fits into even the smallest advertising budget, complements other media advertising, can be directed to selected audiences, and repeats the advertising message, without added cost, each time the advertising vehicle is used. The thousands of advertising specialties available allow flexibility in planning promotional strategies.

Unlike traditional media advertising, specialty advertising provides a continuing reminder of a company to the recipient. Exhibit 14.8 shows the high recall levels and continuing use of three different specialties sent to a sample of businesses and households.

[11] Unless otherwise noted, information in this section is provided by the Specialty Advertising Association International.

EXHIBIT 14.8

Specialty advertising items are used, and company names are recalled, long after the gift is received. (Courtesy: Specialty Advertising Association Internation, Inc.)

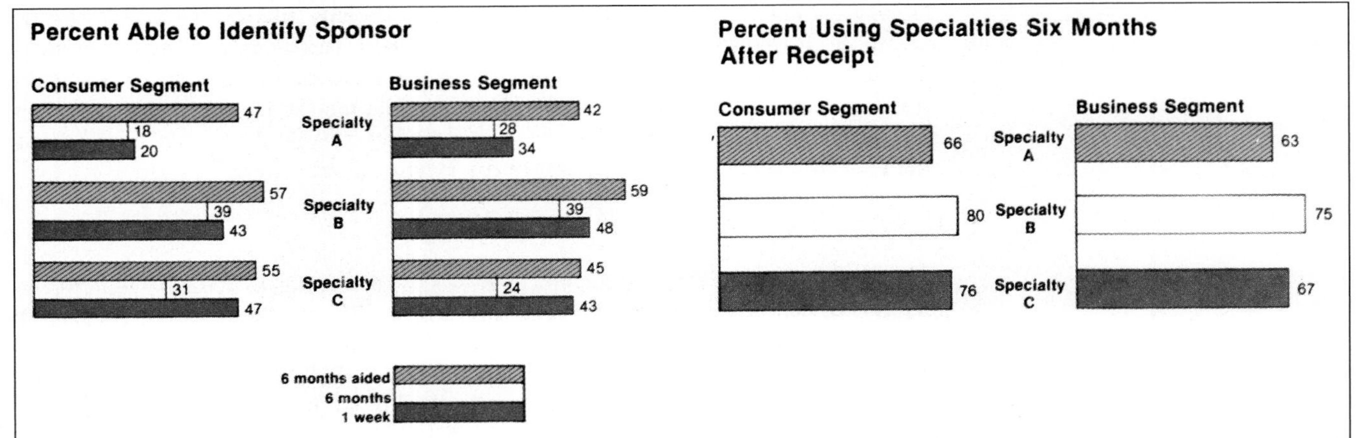

CASE HISTORY
The Typesource

Tampa, Florida
Silver Pyramid
Industrial/Agricultural Promotion—Budget Category L
Objective: To solidify customer loyalty and to secure appointments from prospects.

Strategy and Executions: Since specifying typography from the myriad of available fonts is often like throwing a dart, the advertiser selected a dartboard as a specialty to communicate its services. The shrinkwrapped board illustrated the various popular typefaces. It was accompanied by three darts and a specimen book of the fonts available from The Typesource. The promotional package was shipped via delivery service to the target audience of 250 potential type users—audiovisual studios, printers, graphic designers—in the Tampa Bay area.

Results: The client was said to have been pleased with the results.

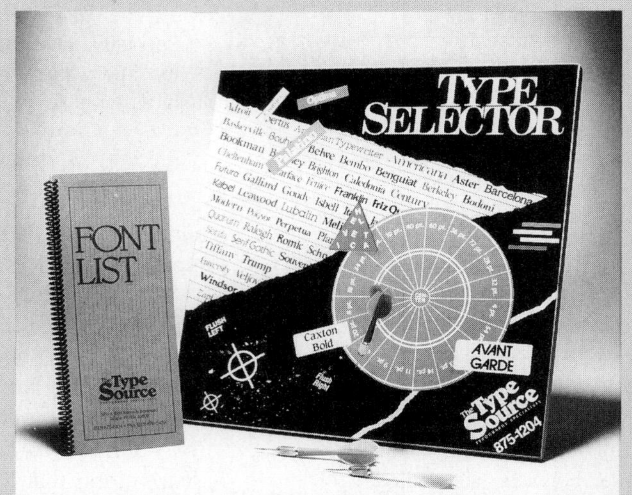

Organization of the Specialty Advertising Industry

Suppliers. The thousands of key chains, balloons, and pens that constitute advertising specialties are manufactured and imprinted by about 1,000 firms.

Distributors. Most specialty merchandise is sold to advertisers by distributors. Distributors contract with one supplier—or, more commonly, a number of suppliers—to provide merchandise to advertisers. There are perhaps 5,000 distributors, ranging from one-person operations to large companies with regional branch offices.

> ***Direct houses.*** *In specialty advertising, firms that combine the functions of supplier and distributor.*

Direct Houses. Among the largest firms in the specialty industry are direct houses. A direct house combines the functions of the supplier and the distributor. It manufactures its own line of merchandise and maintains a sales force to contact advertisers.

The Advertiser. The key to the success of any specialty advertising program is the advertiser. Responsibility for the distribution, timing, and compatibility of the merchandise with the total marketing program largely rests with the advertiser. However, in recent years, distributors have been offering marketing services to advertisers rather than just selling them merchandise.

Calendar Specialties

Calendars are among the most popular specialty items. Writing instruments rank higher in terms of number distributed, but calendars account for the most expenditures of any single specialty and therefore we will discuss them separately. Calendars are an ideal specialty since they are used (and act as a reminder for your company) on a daily basis. One study showed that calendars are used not only as date references, but also for appointments, notes, and even record keeping.

CASE HISTORY
Redding Medical Center

Redding, California
Silver Pyramid
Consumer Promotion—Budget Category H
Objective: To provide a reminder of heart patient's care at the center and to alleviate the discomfort of patients after open heart surgery.

Strategy and Execution: To highlight the personal attention and devotion to heart patients, a special pillow was designed for open heart surgery patients. One side of the pillow depicted a big heart imprinted "To Someone Special . . . from your Redding Medical Center Heart Team." On the other side of the pillow appeared a teddy bear drawn by a member of the cardiac care staff and autographed by the whole team. The pillows, which were given to patients after the surgery, had practical application because they could be held to the chest by the patient to alleviate discomfort while coughing.

Results: The pillows added a "warm, personal touch to a stressful, if not traumatized occasion," reported Redding's public relations director.

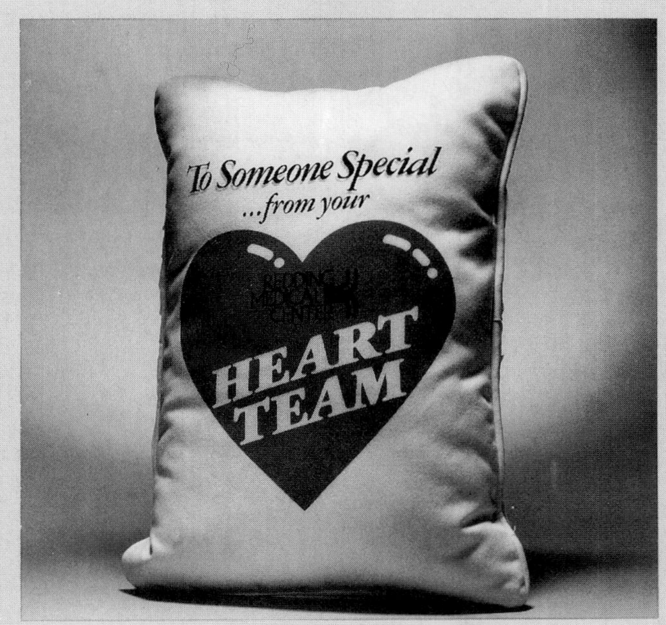

Calendars are among the most widely used specialties—and among the most costly to produce. Nonetheless, it may be the *only* easily recognized, promotional vehicle suitable to reach specialized targets—like the *$270 billion education market. Media Management Services* helps "Fortune 500 companies"—like GTE, Time, Inc., ABC-TV, and McGraw-Hill—"maximize their potential in appealing to educators and students." MMS' introductory direct mail piece for their clients is usually a *calendar*—an item *every* educationally minded target *needs, notices,* and *keeps*. The results, according to President Ed Meell, are "high visibility, early brand loyalty, new sources of business, and a positive corporate image."

The major advantage of specialty calendars is that they are items consumers need. In a survey of recipients of complimentary calendars, most people responded that they would have made an effort to get a calendar if they hadn't received one. How many customers actively seek out other advertising media?

The problem with using calendars as an advertising vehicle is their expense. With the exception of executive gifts, no specialty category has as high an average cost per item. Not only are calendars relatively expensive to produce, but their shipping and handling costs are higher than those for most other items. Ironically, the other drawback to calendars is their popularity. We have mentioned the problem of clutter in connection with several media, and it is no less a problem with calendars. Most businesses, and many households, receive more calendars than they can use. That is why advertisers should avoid cheaply produced calendars: Cheap-looking calendars stand little chance of being used.

Another consideration in using calendars is their format. A study conducted by Richard Manville Research for the SAAI indicated the following preferences for calendars:

Business		***Household***	
Desk	37%	Wall	57%
Wall	36	Desk	13
Book	11	Pocket	11
Pocket	8	Wallet	9
Other	8	Book	4
		Other	6

Executive Gifts

Executive gifts. *A category of specialty advertising intended for a firm's best customers. Often the items are not imprinted.*

Executive gifts are not, strictly speaking, specialty advertising. However, they are included in this section since they are so closely related to the specialty advertising industry and are used for many of the same marketing objectives, as well as because they account for significant revenues for suppliers and jobbers. Executive gifts fall somewhere between specialties and premiums. While recipients are not required to make a purchase to obtain them (which makes them like premiums), they are usually sent to present customers and therefore are rarely "no-strings-attached" gifts (which makes them like specialties).

In a study conducted by Dr. Frank Pierce for the SAAI, 86 percent of businesses surveyed said that they found gifts to be effective to some extent in achieving desired results. The same study indicated that 50 percent of executive gifts are given as Christmas presents. As Exhibit 14.9 shows, when executive gifts are given, they are very much a part of a company's marketing plan.

One respondent to the SAAI survey had this caution about the use of executive gifts: "Always attempt to set an objective when using a gift as a promotion. Try to obtain awareness and response. And try to use gifts in combination with marketing communication elements such as advertising and public relations—to reinforce your marketing program."

A study by *Incentive* magazine estimated that total business gift expenditures were $1.48 billion. The typical gift costs $75, and the median number of gifts given by companies that use this form of promotion is 100. The preferred gift is something for the office, usually the desk, with pen/pencil sets being the most common gift category. (*Note:* You should be aware that most government agencies and some large corporations ban or restrict the type of gift that can be accepted.)

COUPONS

Coupons. *The most used form of sales promotion, offering customers cash rebates against the cost of the product.*

America is flooded with coupons. C. W. Post issued the first coupon in 1885, good for one cent off the price of a box of Grape Nuts Flakes. Since then, coupons have become the most popular form of sales promotion. It is estimated that more than 230 *billion* coupons will be issued in 1990, at a total cost (including redemption and handling) of over $5 billion.

Advertisers have lately been questioning the level and distribution of coupons. Only about 4 percent of coupons are being redeemed, which means that advertisers are paying for almost 200 billion unused coupons. And in some product categories, the redemption rate is significantly less than 3 percent.

An even more pressing problem is coupon clutter. Advertisers are concerned that the number of coupons is reducing the impact that any brand can make through couponing. In some product categories, coupons have been used so frequently that they are hardly

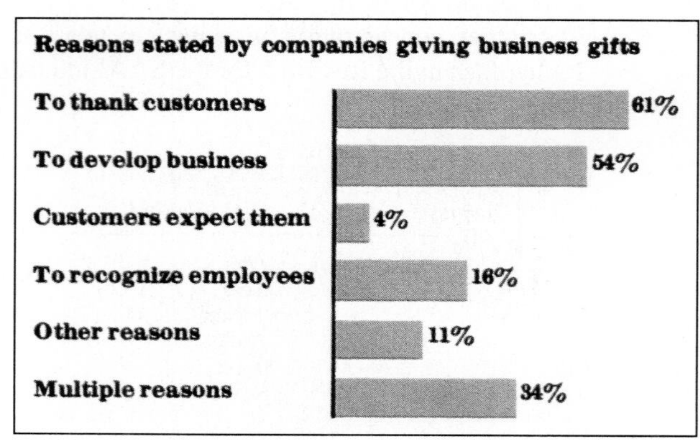

EXHIBIT 14.9
Business gifts, like their consumer counterparts, should be given with specific marketing objectives in mind. (Courtesy: Specialty Advertising Association Internation, Inc.)

While *coupons* are the most recognized sales promotion strategy, their *clutter* and *low redemption rates* keep advertisers striving for more creative strategies to build brand loyalty. By using their new Maxi Flex format, *Select & Save Plus* claims the advertiser will achieve greater reach and increased frequency. "The intelligent Coupon Alternative" provides "maximum consumer response with "personalized" inserts, distributed to "15 million promotionally responsive households." Their increased frequency of distribution—up to 3 programs per year—"guarantees greater success than Carol Wright (direct mail coupons distributor) or FSI's."

noticed by most consumers as a promotional device, while frequent users of coupons regard them as a permanent price discount. Under these conditions, coupons cannot be classified as a sales incentive that builds long-term brand loyalty.

Coupon Distribution

Freestanding Inserts. Coupons are distributed in a number of ways. However, the freestanding insert (FSI), usually provided by national coupon distribution companies in Sunday newspapers, is by far the most popular format (see Exhibit 14.10). FSIs are distributed primarily through three companies: Valassis Inserts, Quad Marketing, and Product Movers. The percent of couponing through FSIs went from less than 20 percent in 1970 to over 70 percent by 1988. The use—some would say overuse—of FSIs has created problems for many advertisers.

First and foremost is the clutter associated with the multitude of coupons vying for consumer attention. FSIs in the same newspaper often carry competing coupons, even though each service guarantees exclusivity within an insert. As we will see, this uncontrolled clutter has caused a number of advertisers to look for alternatives to FSI distribution.

Another problem is the concentration of certain product categories within FSIs. Almost one-third of all FSI coupons are for health and beauty or food products, which makes it extremely difficult for brands within these categories to gain a sales differentiation with coupons. Some advertisers try to gain attention for their coupon efforts by using radio to promote them. Used in conjunction with a mail coupon campaign, radio can provide relatively inexpensive awareness.

Direct-Mail Couponing. Direct-mail coupon distribution is growing more popular. Although direct mail costs significantly more than FSIs, its ability to reach specific target audiences makes it an attractive alternative for some advertisers. Also, redemption rates for direct mail average about 10 percent compared to 3 percent for FSIs.

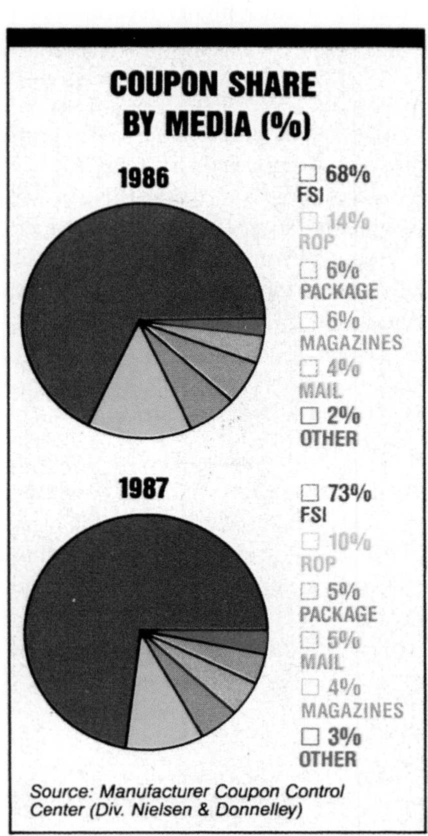

EXHIBIT 14.10

Freestanding inserts are by far the most used method of coupon distribution. (Courtesy: *Marketing & Media Decisions.*)

Among the most popular distribution methods of coupon distribution is the *free standing insert*. Compared to black-and-white newspaper placement, it's *more noticeable and attractive*—and coupons are easier to *remove*. Because women tend to favor disposable razors for "wet shaves," Gilette will concentrate on Daisy Plus. $4 million is being set aside for sales promotion, which includes a free standing insert. Gilette anticipates revenues of $17 million, roughly one-half of the $35 million women's disposable razor market.

Direct-mail coupons have the advantage of *targeted distribution*. Their redemption rates are, also, *higher* than other distribution methods, as they can be directed to "mail-responsive households." *One million* coupons are being distributed by JR Simplot to enhance the sales of their *microwave snacks*. Their target is *families with children,* with "nutritious" snacks, such as sandwiches and pizza.

However, since mail costs are about three times higher than FSI, the CPM/redemption is about the same for both media.

The majority of mail coupons use a co-op program, which we discussed previously in the section on direct mail in Chapter 13. Companies contract with a number of advertisers to conduct a joint mailing. R. R. Donnelley's Carol Wright program is by far the largest co-op mailer, sending out almost 400 million coupons in ten annual mailings. Carol Wright, as well as other programs such as Red Letter Day and Larry Tucker, Inc., offers various demographic mailings.

Larry Tucker, for example, has a full range of demographic mailings targeted to the same kinds of groups magazine demographic and regional editions reach. Its "The Spectrum of American Life" mailings offer segments of 3.5 million new parents, 7 million households with preschool children, 9.5 million homes with school-age children, 5 million households with adults aged 35 to 49, and two segments called "Leisure Years" (mature households with members over 50). Larry Tucker predicts that "within the next few years, targeted mail distribution of coupons will definitely draw business from the shotgun approach of FSIs. Savvy manufacturers want more than relatively low redemption by millions of 'suspects.' They want to concentrate on heavy-user families who buy more product more often. Today's list technology allows us to identify and reach the best prospects—known as mail-responsive households—by current name and address."[12]

In-Store Direct Mail

A number of in-store couponing methods are also used. Act Now provides coupon booklets, hand-delivered in stores, and Shopper's Pay Day distributes copies of their ROP newspaper ads. In addition, many advertisers have moved to in-pack and on-pack (some with immediate redemption) to distribute coupons.

As we mentioned in the point-of-purchase section, a number of experimental computerized coupon dispensers are currently being tested in grocery stores. All of these in-store methods attain a higher redemption rate than most other methods of coupon distribution. However, some in-store methods, rather than being incentives to new purchases, are simply price discounts to people who were already going to purchase the product.

One in-store coupon distribution device brings target marketing to the process. Catalina Marketing Corporation's system is "a supermarket scanner–based technology called the Coupon Solution [that] analyzes a particular customer's purchases and spits out coupons tailored to that buyer. If a shopper buys diapers, for example, the machine may issue a coupon for those diapers or perhaps baby lotion. If a box of cold cereal crosses the scanner, the computer can be programmed to offer a 50-cent coupon to try a competing brand."[13]

Coupon Redemption Fraud

Coupon fraud is big business. The most common type of fraud occurs when unethical retailers send in thousands of dollars' worth of coupons for which no product was purchased. Many manufacturers attempt to curtail the practice by checking product inventory and invoices against coupons submitted. In recent years, the U.S. Postal Service has made a number of arrests for mail fraud in connection with coupon misredemption (the mails are generally used for coupon misredemption).

Postal authorities have had some success in stopping this type of coupon fraud by publishing coupons for nonexistent products: Since no product could have been pur-

[12]Russ Bowman, "Making the Most of the Mail," *Marketing & Media Decisions,* June 1988, p. 153.
[13]Lori Kesler, "Catalina Cuts Couponing Clutter," *Advertising Age,* May 9, 1988, p. S-30.

chased, any coupon redemption request would constitute fraud. This approach has been tried a number of times and has led to the successful prosecution of many retailers—which points up the extent of the misredemption problem.

Coupon Distribution Verification Service. *Service begun by Audit Bureau of Circulations in 1981 to audit newspaper publishers' security and verification of distributed coupons.*

The newspaper industry is particularly concerned about this kind of fraud because newspapers distribute over 70 percent of coupons. Obviously, if manufacturers reduce coupon distribution because of misredemption fears, it would mean a decline in newspaper advertising. In 1981, the Audit Bureau of Circulations established the ABC Coupon Distribution Verification Service, which is basically an audit of publishers' practices concerning security and verification of distributed preprinted coupons. Exhibit 14.11 is an example of an ABC verification form.

Continuing Use of Coupons

Despite some reservations about their misredemption and overuse, coupons continue to be the most popular form of sales promotion. In the future, however, they will probably be used more selectively. Many of the techniques of data-based marketing developed in direct-response advertising will be utilized in couponing. While FSI coupon distribution will continue to dominate, other in-store and direct-mail distribution methods will become more popular. But coupons are here to stay: Consumers have come to expect them, and competitive pressure will force most package-goods manufacturers to continue to provide them.

SAMPLING

Sampling. *One of the oldest (and most expensive) forms of sales promotion. Virtually guarantees initial use of the product.*

Aside from its high cost, *sampling* is a valid strategy to "introduce" a new product to the market. Combined with advertising, it can induce awareness and build customer quality—*better*—than short-term price-cutting. Sample Air, though, has taken targeted sampling of adult men and women to new "heights." It distributes sample consumer goods packets to *airline passengers,* who, the company claims, "are in a receptive mood, ready to break with routine—and ready to try new products." They boast that they're the only national program of its kind, deliver 51% men and 49% women with minimal duplication, and have *proven* "high trial and conversion."

Product sampling is a promotional technique that is growing in popularity. Offering consumers a chance to try the product at no charge guarantees at least an initial trial—which is the objective of most advertising and promotion. Sampling can be extremely effective for a new product with a distinctive benefit, especially one that cannot be conveyed effectively through advertising.

Before undertaking a sampling promotion, you should consider the pros and cons of the technique. "For example, sampling has the following advantages: It reaches new users, helps to introduce the product by building trial, demonstrates product improvement, opens new markets and forces distribution. Its drawbacks? It lacks precision, generating waste and expense."[14]

Successful product sampling must be supported with strong consumer advertising. The advocates of sampling maintain that the combination of sampling and advertising has a much better chance of building a long-term consumer franchise than short-term techniques such as sweepstakes and coupons. In fact, sampling is the ultimate recognition that the success of a product depends on the consumer benefits it provides.

Distribution of Samples

There are several means of distributing samples. Because of the tremendous expense of distribution, manufacturers are constantly looking for ways to hold down costs, but sampling is not a technique that should be considered if cost is a primary concern.

Door-to-Door Delivery. Currently, the only national door-to-door sampling company is Impact Media Associates. IMA contracts with a number of door-to-door distribution companies in various locales and provides its own supervisory personnel to oversee the

[14]Rebecca Fannin, "No Cheap Shots," *Marketing & Media Decisions,* October 1987, p. 104.

I. Security/Storage of Preprinted Coupon Sections:

(a) Publisher's Practices:

It is the publisher's practice to verify the number of free standing coupon inserts at the time of receipt. Records are maintained of differences between the number claimed to have been shipped and the number received. Any differences noted are reported to the printer and advertiser. Run of press coupon sections are printed in advance of issue date and are accounted for by the publisher.

Run of press coupon sections are stored at company owned and independently owned distribution agencies. Free standing coupon inserts are stored at the publisher's mailroom. All storage areas are restricted and accessible only to qualified publishing personnel.

Free standing coupon inserts are inserted into pre-run sections at the publisher's plant. These pre-run sections and run of press coupon sections are inserted into the complete newspaper by carriers and newsdealers at various locations. All leftover preprinted coupon material is baled with other newsprint waste and sold to a local recycling company.

(b) Auditor's Findings:

Publisher's practices were in accord with established guidelines.

II. Unsold Copies Returned to Publisher:

(a) Publisher's Practices:

It is the publisher's policy that all unsold copies of the newspaper are fully returnable from distributors and single copy sales accounts in the City Zone, Balance in Newspaper Designated Market, and Outside Newspaper Designated Market. Whole copy returns and unsold copies from newsdealers in the City Zone are brought back to the publisher's plant, where personnel make spot checks to determine that free standing coupon inserts and/or run of press coupon sections are included. Returned copies are sold to a wastepaper company for recycling.

(b) Auditor's Findings:

Publisher's practices were in accord with established guidelines.

III. Unsold Copies Not Returned to Publisher:

(a) Publisher's Practices:

It is the publisher's policy to require mastheads only for credit from dealers in the Balance in Newspaper Designated Market and Outside Newspaper Designated Market. The publisher requires these dealers to have on file a written statement attesting to the manner in which unsold copies are disposed of to render advertiser coupons unusable.

(b) Auditor's Findings:

Publisher's practices were in accord with established guidelines.

IV. Newspaper Distribution Procedure:

(a) Publisher's Practices:

Distribution of the newspaper is made through employees to single copy sales accounts, independent carriers, independent distributors, and company owned and operated agencies for home delivery and single copy sales. This practice is applicable in the City Zone, Balance in Newspaper Designated Market, and Outside Newspaper Designated Market.

The number of copies to be served to independent carriers, independent newsdealers, and independent distributors is not limited; however, it is the publisher's practice to monitor draw increases.

It is the publisher's practice not to have newsdealers for the Thursday only (coupon) issue. Sunday only newsdealers are permitted.

(b) Auditor's Findings:

Publisher's practices were in accord with established guidelines.

The records maintained by this publication pertaining to data reported for the period covered have been examined in accord with established guidelines. Tests of records and other verification procedures considered necessary were conducted. Based on ABC's examination, the information in this report presents fairly the data verified by Bureau auditors.

(Chicago Tribune, Chicago, Illinois October, 1985 CV#590, 591 AR#140777, 140778
RWM-KSK 01-1110-0)

EXHIBIT 14.11

ABC coupon verification form. (Courtesy: Audit Bureau of Circulations.)

CASE HISTORY

How Kellogg Uses Coupon Distribution Verification Service

In addition to field and internal audits, ABC offers other specialized audits. One of the most requested and one that has an energetic member-following is the Coupon Distribution Verification Service. A newspaper that signs up for CDVS allows an ABC auditor to review the newspaper's records and procedures to verify that its handling, storing, and disposing of coupon inserts meet industry standards. In this way, a newspaper is showing advertisers that it is concerned about coupon security. Advertisers in North America, who lose millions of dollars annually to the theft and fraud of their cents-off coupons, join ABC's CDVS to show their support and to receive reports on coupon security at participating newspapers.

a conversation with Tom Faley

Tom Faley is the manager of coupon services at Kellogg Co.

Faley: We think the Audit Bureau's Newspaper Coupon Distribution Verification Service is a really great program.

Before the advent of the ABC program, few publishers thought of a coupon ad or insert any differently than one without a coupon. ABC has helped to bring about an attitudinal change—one that recognizes that coupons represent our money. As such, coupon sections and preprinted inserts require special handling and must be secured from pilferage.

ABC's program is helping to assure this protection and is alerting us to situations where publishers may not be doing all they can to reasonably provide this protection.

It has brought publishers and manufacturers together to control a part of the costly misredemption problem.

ABC: *Are most of your coupons carried in newspapers?*

Faley: Yes, Historically, we have been heavy in run-of-press—the grocery sections—but recently we have shifted a lot more to free-standing inserts and some direct mail. The switch is mainly tied to the color printing advantages free-standing inserts give us.

ABC: *How large a factor are coupons within your total marketing strategy?*

Faley: Kellogg was into coupons as early as 1908 or 1910. Retailers have gone through trading stamps and all the other phases of coupon development. Our coupon programs have grown and grown—they are a very substantial portion of our budget. I would think that we are one of the nation's biggest couponers.

ABC: *How serious is the misredemption problem for the Kellogg Co.?*

Faley: One of my major responsibilities is to work toward bringing misredemption under control. This is a function that didn't exist two or three years ago. Obviously, the ABC service is just part of our over-all program, but it was one of the early programs that was incorporated into our plans.

ABC: *How do you use the Newspaper Coupon Distribution Verification Reports?*

Faley: We have established a report which lists the areas we feel are a concern to us in controlling newspaper distributed coupons.

We list each of the participating newspapers and, from the ABC reports, note problem areas. Where we feel the problem is sufficiently serious, we contact the newspaper to express our concern.

As we go into the second and third year of this program, we are able to see publishers making changes in their methods of securing and handling coupons. We try to contact the newspaper or its representative to express our appreciation.

Of course, we are able to identify those newspapers that are not participating, or who have dropped out of the ABC service, and call their attention to our interest.

ABC: *Do you feel the ABC service has made publishers more aware of possible areas of misredemption?*

Faley: Oh, yes, most definitely. I think some of the newspapers out there didn't even realize that some handling methods might be encouraging a problem. They see their business as selling newspapers, not controlling coupons.

In fairness, this certainly has not been the situation universally. Some publishers kept these coupons under lock and key long before the ABC program started.

Not only is there a higher level of awareness on the part of the publishers, but with ABC's help the manufacturer is assured that something is being done about problem areas or is alerted to the fact that the newspaper has not taken corrective action.

ABC: *As you go across the list of problem areas on your report, which are your priorities?*

Faley: The most important, as far as preprinted pieces go, is the control of free-standing inserts and supplements. How are they stored and secured?

Falling close behind would be the number of newspapers they allow on best food days—the control of unusual draws by dealers. Do they have limits? Do they check into the reasons why a dealer suddenly ups his draw dramatically? What is happening to those extra copies?

ABC: *How would you react to a situation where you considered a problem existed, but no substantial change had been made from year to year?*

Faley: I would expect to have an explanation from the newspaper as to why it continues to exist. Maybe it is an area where they just can't improve because of union rules, dealer contracts, or something like this. Their hands are tied and I can sympathize with that. Maybe we can work a way around it at some point.

But just their presence of being in the ABC program a second and third year is saying a lot. Conversely, someone who was there the first year and not there the second says a lot, too.

We are not saying the publisher has to get involved with all sorts of costly electronic surveillance equipment. Some of these things are fairly simple to correct.

It's attitude changes. As soon as the publisher realizes that he really has our money sitting around, and understands that his newspaper is somewhat of a bank for us, I think he will begin to appreciate our point of view. Whether the gross redemption value is \$5,000 or \$50,000 shouldn't make any difference.

Certainly, the ABC service has helped us to feel more comfortable.

job. IMA delivers 17 million samples each week in plastic bags hung on doorknobs (see Exhibit 14.12).

Direct Mail. This is becoming a primary means of delivering samples. Often advertisers combine a small trial size of the product with a cents-off coupon for the purchase of the regular size.

Magazines. As we mentioned in Chapter 11, Using Magazines, it is now possible to incorporate certain types of product samples in magazines—for example, preprinted scratch-and-sniff inserts for perfumes. Magazines normally charge a premium for this service. However, it is still inexpensive compared to most other methods of sample distribution.

Coupons. Some manufacturers offer redeemable coupons for full-size or trial-size samples. This method is the least satisfactory for widespread market penetration since many customers will not send in the coupons. Still, it can be effective in reaching a particular segment of customers if the coupons themselves are distributed in a targeted fashion.

In-Store Sampling. In-store sampling is especially effective for prepared food products. Often store sampling is combined with a sale or cents-off coupons. This approach has the advantage of associating the product sample with immediate purchase of the product.

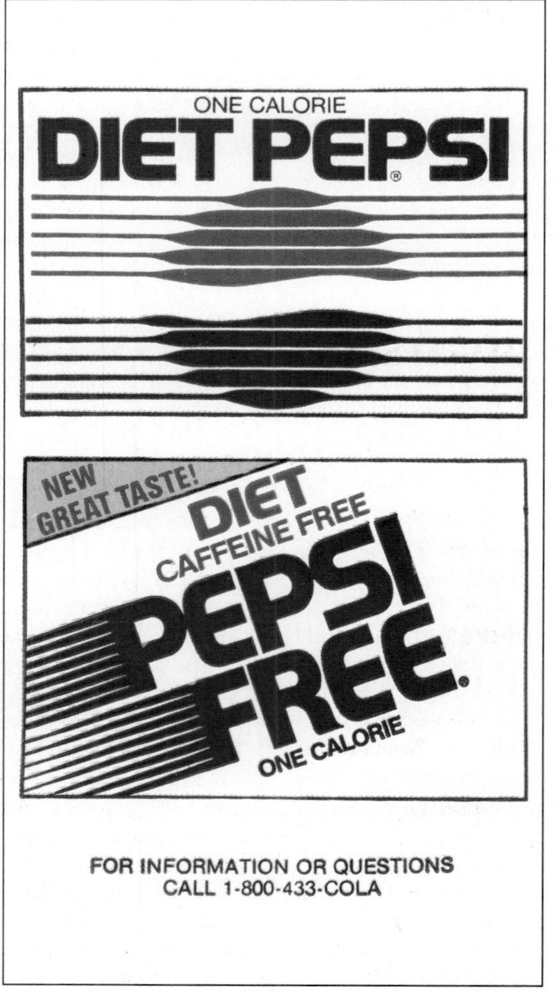

EXHIBIT 14.12

Despite its expense, product sampling can be an effective sales tool for many items. (Courtesy: Impact Media Associates.)

Cooperative Product Sampling. In some cases, manufacturers will arrange for another manufacturer's products to contain a sample. For years, washing machines contained a box of detergent, and Good Seasons Italian salad dressing mix was placed on bottles of Wesson Oil as a promotion.

DEALS

> ***Deals.*** *A consumer deal is a plan whereby the consumer can save money in the purchase of a product. A trade deal is a special discount to the retailer for a limited period of time.*

"Deals," including "2-fers," limited reduced price offerings, rebates, and *tradeins,* are additional promotional inducements. When the Ohio Mattress Company purchased Sealy Mattress Company, it immediately began expanding its product line with *Posturpedic Flotation, its first waterbed*. It looks like an innerspring mattress, can be assembled in 15 minutes with no tools, and holds *60% less water* than other beds. Conventional furniture stores will handle the item—with the added inducement of accepting a mattress and/or a boxspring in trade—compliments of Sealy.

Deals are a catch-all category of promotional techniques designed to save the customer money. The most common deal is a temporary price reduction or "sale." The cents-off coupon is also a consumer deal because it lowers the price during some limited period. Or a deal may be a merchandising deal, in which, for example, three bars of soap are wrapped together and sold at a reduced price. Another possibility is attaching a package of a new member of the product family to a package of an older member. This is an effective way of introducing a new product at little or no extra cost.

Sometimes a deal lets the consumer save money on another product or an additional purchase of the same product. A two-for-one sale offers a free product after the consumer buys the first one. Gatorade offered a free three-pack of drink mix with the purchase of two others. Cash rebates are among the most common deals offered by manufacturers. And, of course, there is hardly a time of the year that some automobile company is not offering a rebate of several hundred dollars or reduced interest rates. One company even offered to pay off the new car purchaser's credit cards up to $3,000.

Automobile deals are a good example of deals that start off as temporary incentives, and then come to be expected by many buyers. The widespread use of rebates in the automobile industry began during the Arab oil embargo of the 1970s, when dealers were stuck with large inventories of new cars. Significant amounts of money were put into moving this stock. The promotions proved so popular they were repeated again and again, until many potential car purchasers learned to wait for the next rebate plan before purchasing a car.

Deals are extremely popular in building sales at the trade level. Trade deals will be discussed later in the chapter as a type of trade incentive.

SWEEPSTAKES AND CONTESTS

Sweepstakes and contests are often lumped together because they both involve consumer participation. However, there are significant differences between these two types of promotion. Sweepstakes, which are based solely on chance, are significantly more popular than contests. Contests involve some element of skill—for example, writing a jingle or completing a puzzle.

Sweepstakes

> ***Sweepstakes.*** *A promotion in which prize winners are determined on the basis of chance alone. Not legal if purchaser must risk money to get it. See Contest.*

Sweepstakes usually depend on some form of random drawing, though many use a continuity format, such as having consumers find bottle caps that spell out a word or phrase. Basically, there are three types of sweepstakes:[15]

1. *Random drawing sweepstakes*. These are the simplest type of sweepstakes to administer and control. The company often requests that a proof-of-purchase accompany the entry, but

[15] Jeffrey P. Feinman, Robert D. Blashek, and Richard J. McCabe, *Sweepstakes Prize Promotions, Games and Contests* (Homewood, IL: Dow Jones–Irwin, 1986), p. 14.

cannot legally require it. Usually a company will ask the consumer to provide a drawing of the product logo if a proof-of-purchase is not included with the entry.

2. *Lucky number sweepstakes*. This type of sweepstakes uses a predetermined winning number. Consumers simply send in their entries and the promoter tells them if they have won. The largest users of this type of promotion are magazines sales organizations such as Publishers Clearing House. Resort developers also use a form of the random drawing sweepstakes. They will guarantee you a prize from a car to a toaster, but you have to bring the entry in person to see what prize you have won.
3. *Games*. Game sweepstakes are popular since they build consumer involvement over a period of time, rather than providing a ''one-shot'' promotional boost. A game is a sweepstakes with the benefits of continuity, involvement, and instant gratification (see Exhibit 14.13).

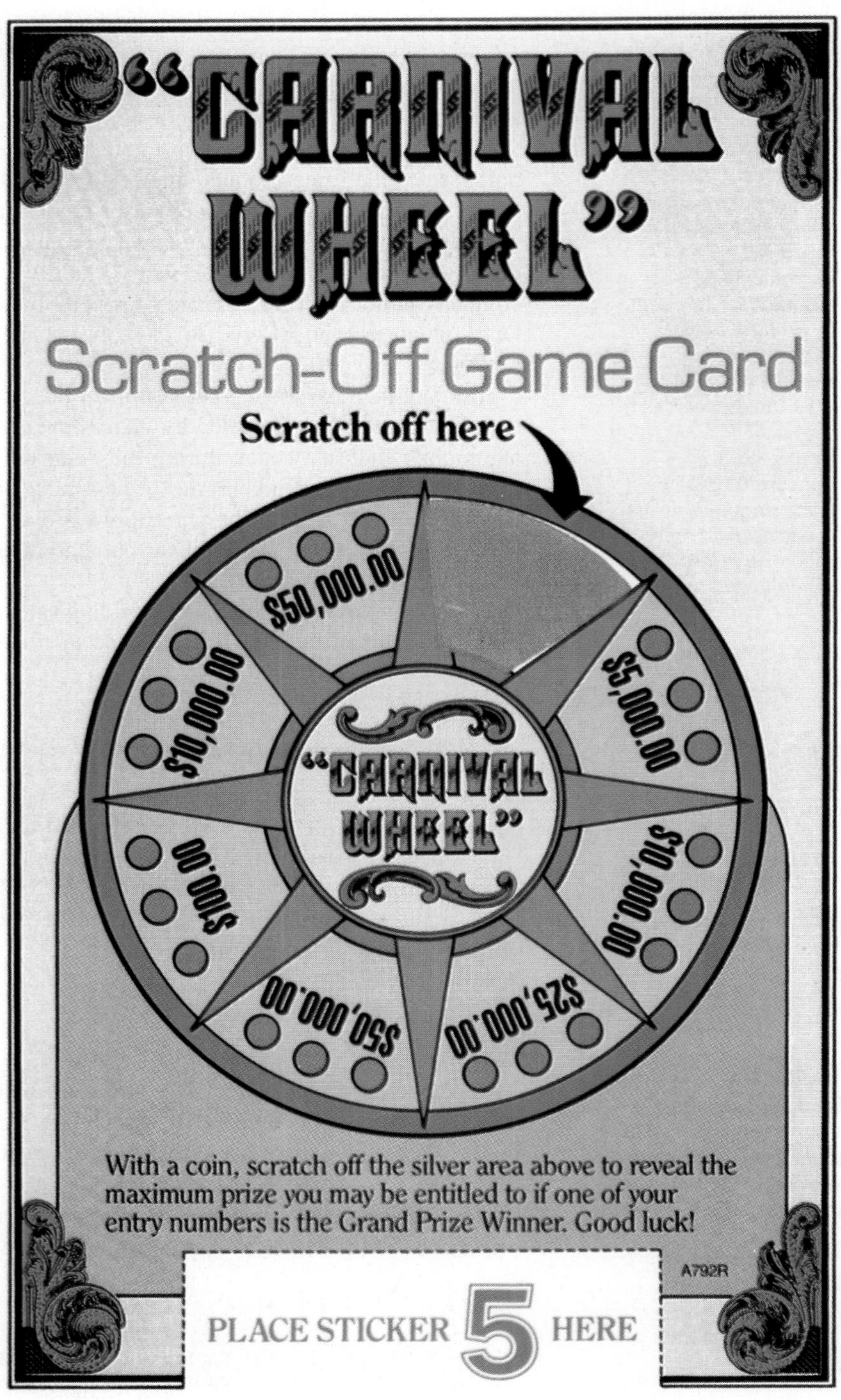

EXHIBIT 14.13
Sweepstakes are used to build consumer interest over a period of time. (Courtesy: The Petty Company.)

Contests

Contest. *A promotion in which consumers compete for prizes and the winners are selected strictly on the basis of skill. See Sweepstakes.*

As mentioned earlier, contests are not nearly as popular as sweepstakes. There are roughly five times as many sweepstakes as contests conducted. Since contests call for some element of skill, there must be a plan for judging and making certain all legal requirements have been met.

The other limitation of contests is the time they require of participants. The majority of consumers are not going to devote the time necessary to complete a contest. Therefore, if the intent of the promotion is to gain maximum interest and participation, a sweepstakes is probably the better choice.

Both sweepstakes and contests are wasted on professional entrants. These are people who have little or no interest in the product and see the promotion as an end in itself rather than as an incentive to purchase a product.

Sweepstakes and *contests* have the advantage of *involving* the prospect in the advertisement. Although they rank *high* in achieving awareness for new products, they also can overshadow the product itself. Nonetheless, in an effort to bring "flash and excitement" to their stores, Sears used a nationwide, newspaper-advertised *sweepstakes*. It was based on charge card customers' account numbers as lottery-type entries. Sears hopes the sweepstakes will drive up sales "dramatically."

National manufacturers often join with their local retailers to advertise jointly. *Co-op advertising* has the advantages of professional composition and partial payment for the local distributor, who can place the ads at local rates, while providing a *regional outlet* for the manufacturers' goods. *Co-op promotions* are just beginning to take hold for some marketers. To put some "spring" back in *Reebok's classic Free Style sneaker*, Very Special Events sponsored a shoe painting contest at 10 malls in major markets. Local outlets provided radio tie-ins, held school poster contests, and informed their markets with advertising. Sales were "up," and awareness increased for the $55 shoe.

Marketing Objectives

Sweepstakes and contests are similar in terms of many of the marketing objectives they seek to fulfill. The goals normally associated with contests and sweepstakes are:

1. *Heightening the involvement of present consumers.* Rather than passively viewing or reading an advertisement, consumers must become actively involved with the promotion in order to participate in a contest or sweepstakes. These promotions are used frequently to increase usage among present consumers.
2. *Differentiating the product from other brands.* A contest or sweepstakes can provide a change of pace from traditional advertising, especially in those product categories where brands are very similar or there is extensive competition. Note how many magazines and cigarettes run contests and sweepstakes.
3. *Introducing a new product.* It is extremely difficult for new brands to gain consumer awareness nowadays. Sweepstakes and contests can generate the type of excitement that gets a brand noticed.
4. *Increasing dealer support.* As we will discuss later, contests and sweepstakes can be very important in gaining trade support for a product.

The key to a successful sweepstakes or contest is a logical tie-in between the promotion and the product. For instance, a Stanback headache powder sweepstakes offered ten years of medical coverage. This prize was of interest to its health-conscious, older target market. A Mars candy sweepstakes appealed to its younger audience by offering a trip to Disney World as the grand prize.

The perennial problem in planning sweepstakes and contests is how to avoid placing the product in a secondary position. Often promoting the prizes seems more important than promoting the product. As one promotion manager noted, "It's difficult enough to announce the sweepstakes without sacrificing the imagery of the product. And, its very difficult to do sweepstakes and instant win without losing the identity of the product. We design for persuasion but never at the expense of the client's communication."[16]

COOPERATIVE ADVERTISING

Cooperative advertising. *(1) Joint promotion of a national advertiser (manufacturer) and local retail outlet on behalf of the manufacturer's product on sale in the retail store. (2) Joint promotion through a trade association for firms in a single industry. (3) Advertising venture jointly conducted by two or more advertisers.*

Cooperative advertising (or *co-op*) is a form of sales promotion whereby national manufacturers reimburse local retailers for placing their advertising in local media. The primary intent of most co-op programs is to exercise control over the type and degree

[16] Amy Zipkin, "1988 Games Perk General Foods Interest," *Advertising Age*, November 16, 1987, p. S-14.

CASE HISTORY

Plymouth/L'Oréal Unbelievable Sundance Sweepstakes

Properly themed and structured, a sweepstakes can dramatically focus attention on a new product or line extension. For a match-and-win sweepstakes, an exciting, on-target concept and design can provide the "hot button" that literally steers consumers to the point of sale. This promotion was created to accomplish these objectives for both companies involved—L'Oréal and Plymouth.

The 1987 Plymouth Sundance, a subcompact mid-priced coupe, has a fun and somewhat fashionable image to appeal to a market heavily skewed to young women. It was introduced into one of the most crowded segments of the auto industry, to compete with approximately 48 domestic and imported nameplates. To create high levels of awareness, generate showroom traffic, and reach female prospects not usually reached via auto advertising, L'Oréal was approached to develop an impactful promotional tie-in with Plymouth Sundance.

The L'Oréal/Plymouth "Unbelievable Sundance Sweepstakes" promotion was a tie-in match-and-win game designed to be used as a vital part of the 1987 Sundance introductory campaign, and simultaneously as L'Oréal's main promotion event for its fall '86 cosmetic color lines of lipsticks and nail enamels.

The main promotion objective for L'Oréal was to deliver store traffic that would generate purchases of featured lipstick and nail enamel products. The main promotion objective for Plymouth was to generate strong levels of traffic among female Sundance prospects to its dealer showrooms, centering on the new Sundance car.

To accomplish these objectives, the promotion maximized product awareness for both companies in an unusual and exciting manner.

To clinch the tie-in, L'Oréal designated a group of top-moving nail enamel and lipstick fall season colors as "Sundance" shades. The exciting promotion motivated salespeople to place special traffic-stopping L'Oréal displays in 16,000 drug and mass merchandise stores, which contained 1.4 million game piece/product units of the L'Oréal Sundance Shade lipstick cases and nail enamel bottles, each with a replica Plymouth ignition key shrink-wrapped on it. Additional awareness was generated via four-color print advertising (with the same graphics as the POP material, featuring L'Oréal model Andie MacDowell). Plymouth ran two-page spread ads with match-and-win key symbols on pop-up bind-in cards. These ads, similar to the one shown, ran in the October 1986 issues of nine women's magazines (*Cosmopolitan, Glamour, Harper's Bazaar, Elle, Mademoiselle, Shape, Ms., Working Woman,* and *Self*) as well as in People magazines), with a total circulation of over 15 million.

Either the replica keys or the game piece inserts could be taken by consumers to any of the 3,700 participating Plymouth dealer showrooms to determine if they were winners. The prize structure appealed to the target audience's interests and tied in with the sweepstakes theme. Not one, but ten Sundance cars were the grand prizes. There were also 15 first prize trips for two to New York for a complete L'Oréal professional make-over (for three days and two nights, including round-trip air fare, hotel, and meals), and 1,000 second prizes consisting of L'Oréal makeup kits. In addition, there was a second-chance sweepstakes to award any unclaimed prizes (with take-one forms at the dealer displays that requested consumer demographic and buying habit data).

This unique tie-in game was extremely well received by all involved, from the L'Oréal sales force and retailers and the Plymouth dealers to the consumers, 170,000 of whom entered the sweepstakes.

L'Oréal Sundance Shade lipstick and nail enamel sales increased more than 10 percent over a comparable sales period. L'Oréal also increased its market share in both lipsticks and nail enamels.

The promotion generated much higher than normal traffic at Plymouth dealers. At least 80,000 sales demonstrations of Sundance were attributed to contest entries.

The promotion was considered by both companies to be a great success, surpassing its predetermined objectives.

of local advertising for national brands and to build trade support. Exhibit 14.14 outlines the major short-term and long-term objectives for co-op advertising to consumers and the trade.

Co-op advertising is big business. It is estimated that over $13 billion will be available for cooperative advertising in 1990, though about half that total will actually be spent. Newspapers are the recipient of perhaps 70 percent of co-op dollars, but both radio and television have been soliciting co-op in recent years.

Co-op dollars are important to manufacturers, retailers, and the media. For the national manufacturer, co-op

(Courtesy: don jagoda associates, inc.)

- Gains local identification for its product
- Creates goodwill among participating retailers
- Saves money by sharing advertising costs with retailers and by allowing the manufacturer to qualify for local rates, especially in newspapers

For the retailer, co-op

- Identifies the local establishment with prominent national brands
- Extends the local advertising budget
- Improves the quality of advertising in cases where ads are supplied by manufacturers to small retailers

EXHIBIT 14.14

Co-Op As A Long-Term And Short-Term Sales Tool

Generally, the objective of a co-op advertising program is to create demand for a company's product as well as generate sales at both the trade and consumer levels. In this case, its value is primarily as a short-term selling tool.

However, as this chart indicates, there are occasions in which co-op advertising is viewed as a tool contributing to long-term strategic goals.

Objectives For Co-Operative Advertising

Intended Audience/ Time Horizon	Consumer	Trade
Short-term	Immediate Purchase	Sell in General influence
	Establish price and location	Competitive parity
Long-term	Brand message reminder and reinforcement	Trade relationships
	Image	Position in merchandise mix

For the media, co-op

- Increases spending by present advertisers in a medium
- Helps attract new advertisers to the media by making additional dollars available to spend on advertising

According to the Radio Advertising Bureau, a typical co-op program comprises the following elements:

1. *Accrual:* the fund a manufacturer sets aside for co-op advertising. It is usually figured according to the amount of purchases by a retailer during the previous year.
2. *Allowance:* the percent of the retailer's advertising that the manufacturer agrees to pay.
3. *Co-op period:* the time period a manufacturer designates for accruing co-op funds.
4. *Cancellation date:* the date that ends the period for a retailer's accrual of co-op funds.
5. *Contact:* the person in the manufacturer's office who administers the co-op program.
6. *General requirements:* the specific requirements that each manufacturer demands of retailers who wish to qualify for co-op. Exhibit 14.15 shows a portion of a co-op listing from the RAB. Similar lists are available from many sources, including SRDS.
7. *Continuity:* commercials or scripts provided by manufacturers. Some manufacturers require that these be used as is, while others will allow modifications.
8. *Billing:* Retailers are expected to pay media bills and are then reimbursed by the manufacturer.[17]

[17]*Radio Co-op Advertising,* a publication of the Radio Advertising Bureau, p. 5.

EXHIBIT 14.15

Companies offer retailers a wide range of co-op advertising opportunities. (Courtesy: Radio Advertising Bureau.)

FOOD, BEVERAGES

4-D HOBE, INC.: 201 So. McKemy, Chandler, AZ 85226. Denise Tabet, (602) 257-1950. 50-50 up to 5% of quarterly net purchases. Expires 3/31, 6/30, 9/30 and 12/31.

AMERICAN HEALTH PRODUCTS, INC.: 70 Hilltop Rd., Ramsey, NJ 07446. Sheila Aigner, (800) 445-7137 or (201) 529-5566. 50-50 up to 5% of previous quarter's sales. Expires 12/31.

ANHEUSER-BUSCH, INC.: D'Arcy & Masius, One Memorial Dr., St. Louis, MO 63118. Rich Meyer, D'Arcy, Masius, (314) 342-8600. 50-50 available to wholesalers. Professional, local and college sports sponsorship only. Expires 12/31.

ARMOUR FOOD CO.: One Central Park Plaza, Omaha, NE 68102. Don Wallen, (402) 449-7385. Varies by geographic region. Expires 5/31.

ARROWHEAD MILLS: P.O. Box 2059, Hereford, TX 79045. Carla Smith, (806) 364-0730. 5% of wholesale purchases during 6 week buy-in period.

BARBICAN BEER NON-ALCOHOLIC: (See Stroh Brewery Co.)

BLACK LABEL: (See G. Heileman Brewing Co., Inc.)

BODY BEAUTIFUL DIET PLAN: (See 4-D Hobe, Inc.)

BOOTH SEAFOOD: 2200 E. Devon, Des Plaines, IL 60018. Michael Yurchesyne, (312) 298-4800. Varies by market.

BRACH STAPLE & SEASONAL PRODS.: (See Jacobs Suchard/Brach, Inc.)

BRACH'S CANDY: (See Jacobs Suchard/Brach, Inc.)

BUDWEISER REGULAR & LIGHT: (See Anheuser-Busch, Inc.)

BUSCH BEER: (See Anheuser-Busch, Inc.)

BUTTER-NUT: (See Coca-Cola Co.)

C.F. SAUER CO.: 2000 W. Broad St., Richmond, VA 23220. Robin Dorsey, (804) 359-5786. 100% up to 5% of current year's purchases. Expires 4/1.

CANADA DRY CORP.: 2600 Century Pkwy., Atlanta, GA 30327. Local Canada Dry Bottler. 40-60 up to specified amount of purchases by bottlers.

CHERRY CRUSH: (See Crush International, Inc.)

CITRUS HILL ORANGE JUICE: (See Procter & Gamble Dist. Co.)

CLAUSSEN: (See Oscar Mayer & Co., Inc.)

COCA-COLA CO. (THE): P.O. Drawer 1734, Atlanta, GA 30301. Marsha Strazynski, (404) 676-2121. Contact local bottler for details.

COLOMBO YOGURT, INC.: Andover Research Pk., 3 Riverside Dr., Andover, MA 01810. Debbie T., (800) 343-8240. 50-50 based on $1 per case during previous 3 months.

COLT 45: (See G. Heileman Brewing Co., Inc.)

CON AGRA POULTRY CO.: P.O. Box 1997, 422 No. Washington, El Dorado, AR 71730. Stewart Bridgeport, (501) 863-1619. 100%, accrual varies by product. Expires 3/31, 6/30, 9/30 and 12/31.

COSMIC NATURAL FOODS: (See Pure & Simple, Inc.)

COUNTRY CLUB: (See Pearl Brewing Co.)

Vendor Programs

Large retailers often use a type of co-op called *vendor programs*. Whereas most co-op programs are initiated by manufacturers, vendor programs are custom programs designed by retailers (often in cooperation with local media). Manufacturers are then approached by retailers to pay all or a share of the program. For example, a department store that is planning a ''Kick Off the Summer'' promotion would request funds from manufacturers of cameras, swimwear, suntan lotions, and sporting goods to support this promotion. Other vendor programs are funded out of unspent manufacturers' co-op money.

Controlling Co-op Dollars

Retailers are paid for advertising when they submit documentation or proof of performance. For newspaper advertisements, they show tear sheets giving the name of the newspaper, the date, and the exact ad copy as it ran. These advertisements are matched with the newspaper invoice stating its cost. For radio and television cooperative ads, proof of performance was a perennial problem until the Association of National Advertisers, the RAB, and the TvB developed an affidavit of performance (see Exhibit 14.16) that documents in detail the content, cost, and timing of commercials. The adoption of stricter controls in broadcast co-op has been a major contributing factor to the growth of co-op dollars for these media.

EXHIBIT 14.16

An affidavit of performance. (Courtesy: Radio Advertising Bureau.)

Use This ANA/RAB "Tear-Sheet To get retailers paid faster

ANA/RAB FORM FOR SCRIPT (IF TAPE IS USED, PREPARE SCRIPT FROM TAPE)

W__ __ __

ANA/RAB RADIO "TEAR-SHEET"

FORM AT BOTTOM OF SCRIPT PERMITS KNOWING HOW MANY TIMES THIS SCRIPT RAN, AT WHAT COST.

Client:	For:

			Begin:	End:	Date:

HERE'S NEWS FOR YOU HANDY HOMEOWNERS. IF YOU'D LIKE TO LEARN HOW TO PUT UP A BEAUTIFUL NEW ARMSTRONG CEILING IN YOUR HOME, COME TO ACE LUMBER THIS SATURDAY AT 10 A.M. ACE LUMBER IS HOLDING A HOME IMPROVEMENT CLINIC. IT WILL TEACH YOU EVERYTHING YOU NEED TO KNOW. YOU'LL LEARN HOW EASY IT IS TO INSTALL ARMSTRONG CEILING TILE IN BASEMENTS, ATTICS, OR ANY ROOM IN YOUR HOME. YOU'LL SEE HOW TO CUT AND FIT BORDER TILES AND HOW TO DO A NEAT JOB AROUND LIGHTING FIXTURES. YOU'LL ACTUALLY INSTALL PRACTICE CEILING TILES YOURSELF. ACE LUMBER IS HEADQUARTERS FOR ALL THE NEW AND EXCLUSIVE ARMSTRONG CEILING DESIGNS, SO IF YOU'RE PLANNING TO REMODEL OR REDECORATE YOUR HOME, IT WILL PAY YOU TO ATTEND THIS CEILING CLINIC. AND THERE'S NO OBLIGATION TO BUY A SINGLE THING. WRITE IT DOWN. THE PLACE IS ACE LUMBER. THE TIME IS THIS SATURDAY AT 10 A.M.

SAMPLE

Hand Billing Form

▼ (STAMP OR PRINT THIS FORM ON THE BOTTOM OF YOUR SCRIPT PAPER)

STATION DOCUMENTATION STATEMENT APPROVED BY THE CO-OPERATIVE ADVERTISING COMMITTEE OF THE ASSOCIATION OF NATIONAL ADVERTISERS

This announcement was broadcast ______ times, as entered in the station's program log. The times this announcement was broadcast were billed to this station's client on our invoice(s) number/dated ____________ at his earned rate of:

$________ each for ______ announcements, for a total of $________
$________ each for ______ announcements, for a total of $________
$________ each for ______ announcements, for a total of $________

Signature of station official

(Notarize above) Typed name and title Station

Computer Billing Form

▼ (STAMP OR PRINT THIS FORM ON THE BOTTOM OF YOUR SCRIPT PAPER)

This announcement was broadcast a total of ______ times at the dates and times coded ______ on our attached invoice(s) numbered/dated ____________, as entered in the station's program log. This announcement was billed to this station's client at a total cost of $ ________.

Sworn to and subscribed before me and in my presence on this ______ day of ______, 19 ____.

Signature of station official

(Notarized above) Typed name and title Station call letters

For details on using this verification document—preferred by hundreds of manufacturers—ask RAB's Co-op Department.

> ***Double billing.*** *Unethical practice of retailer's asking for manufacturer reimbursement at a higher rate than what was paid for advertising time or space.*

Despite these improvements in the process, expenditures of co-op dollars are still allocated improperly out of neglect or inexperience by the retailers and, in a few cases, outright fraud. Most co-op fraud falls into two categories. In the first, retailers bill manufacturers for ads that never ran, using fake invoices and tear sheets. In the second, called *double billing,* the manufacturer is overcharged for the cost of an advertisement; the retailer pays one price to the medium and bills the manufacturer for a higher price by using a phoney (double) bill. Sometimes the medium cooperates in the scheme by billing the retailer at the lower charge and providing a higher bill for the retailer to send to the manufacturer. Only a small minority of retailers and media engage in this unethical practice.

Additional vendor material for outlets include *brochures* and *booklets*, informing customers about installation, upkeep, and companion products. These may be included as part of P-O-P displays. A personal home care agency for the elderly, *VIP Companion Care*, finds it needs a variety of written materials for families, clients, and insurance carriers. In addition to a full description of *services and charges*, Girden Buck, president, says he needs to *differentiate his facility from* those accredited by the National Organization of Private Geriatric Care Managers (NOPGCM). Those organizations typically provide home healthcare—also financial services and counseling. "We're strictly companionship and homemaker services—our *brochures* make that very clear," he declares, "so we have few misunderstandings about our care."

The unique opportunities created by *trade shows and exhibits* are heightened attention by prospects and extensive demonstration capabilities. No longer just considered extensions of the sales process, they function as "live" promotions for a "captive" audience. According to "the experts," many of the 400 new items at the recent *Fancy Food Show* in San Francisco showed plenty of innovative thinking. A lot of attention centered around *Rice Brand Oil*. It's unsaturated, without cholesterol—and contains *bistosteral*, a substance that may actually *reduce* the absorption of cholesterol. Demonstrations "proved" the oil's good taste and "smokeless" cooking.

BOOKLETS AND BROCHURES

Manufacturers of household appliances, cars, motorcycles, and other costly items that give the customer a choice of models or styles usually print colorful booklets or other descriptive pieces free for distribution by the dealer. Because of its clear technical information, this material is especially helpful to distributors who have a high turnover in personnel and a consequent lack of experienced help. Some sales-promotional material is also offered in connection with do-it-yourself equipment sold in hardware stores, where there may be special racks to hold it. In some specialized fields, producers offer booklets—recipe booklets, for example, to liquor stores, or booklets on planting or lawn care where seed and garden equipment are sold. When such booklets have space for the dealer's imprint, they become part of the cooperative advertising plan. Obtaining proper counter space for booklets and making sure they are distributed and used as planned can be a problem.

TRADE SHOWS AND EXHIBITS

Trade shows and exhibits take a growing portion of the promotion budgets of many companies. Events such as car and boat shows have the advantage of reaching both dealers and customers in an environment conducive to current sales and leads to follow up in the future. Trade shows also attract serious prospects with little or no waste circulation. The Trade Show Bureau estimates that more than 31 million prospects attend some 8,000 trade shows annually. Exhibitors spend an estimated $8 billion on these shows and exhibits.

At one time, trade shows were viewed as an extension of a firm's personal selling efforts. However, in recent years, many firms have begun to view them as beneficial for objectives other than making sales, such as enhancing image, gathering competitive information, and improving corporate morale. The broadened perspective on trade shows indicates that they should be considered part of, rather than an appendage to, the firm's total communication program. When other communication tools successfully attract customers, trade shows might emphasize nonselling functions such as customer service and competitor intelligence to round out the communication program. Alternatively, if other communication tools are directed to servicing current customers, trade shows might emphasize opportunities for selling.[18]

A trade show is not just a matter of setting up a booth and waiting for customers. Exhibit 14.17 shows the many elements that go into a successful trade show. Notice that not only do these functions begin as early as a year before the show, but they also run beyond the actual show as manufacturers follow up leads developed during the show.

A trade show should be part of an integrated marketing program that includes promotion of the show, coordination with media advertising, and careful follow-up of leads generated by the show. Exhibit 14.18 illustrates the many variables affecting the successful use of trade shows.

Companies tend to incorporate trade shows into their marketing plans and make more extensive use of trade shows when

- Products are early in the life cycle
- Sales are high
- Customer concentration is low
- The exhibitor has aggressive product plans[19]

[18]Roger A. Kerin and William L. Cron, "Assessing Trade Show Functions and Performance: An Exploratory Study," *Journal of Marketing*, July 1987, p. 88.

[19]Ibid., p. 89.

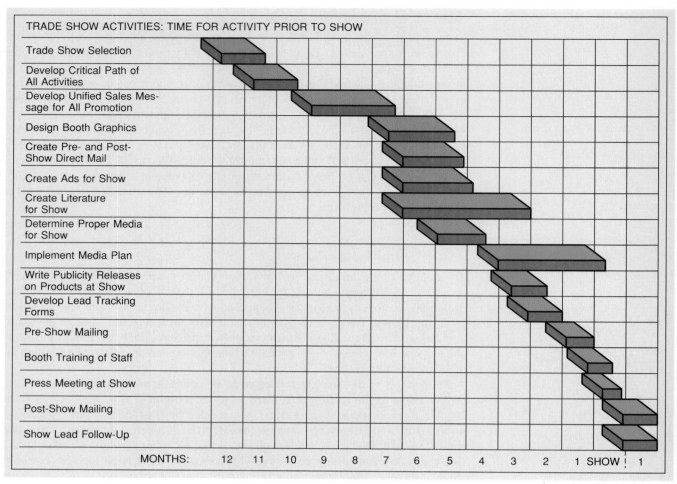

TRADE SHOW ACTIVITIES: TIME FOR ACTIVITY PRIOR TO SHOW

Trade Show Selection
Develop Critical Path of All Activities
Develop Unified Sales Message for All Promotion
Design Booth Graphics
Create Pre- and Post-Show Direct Mail
Create Ads for Show
Create Literature for Show
Determine Proper Media for Show
Implement Media Plan
Write Publicity Releases on Products at Show
Develop Lead Tracking Forms
Pre-Show Mailing
Booth Training of Staff
Press Meeting at Show
Post-Show Mailing
Show Lead Follow-Up

MONTHS: 12 11 10 9 8 7 6 5 4 3 2 1 SHOW 1

EXHIBIT 14.17

The actual show is only one of the many activities that goes into a successful trade show. (Courtesy: *Sales & Marketing Management*.)

EXHIBIT 14.18

The success of a trade show is determined by a number of factors. (Courtesy: *Journal of Marketing*.)

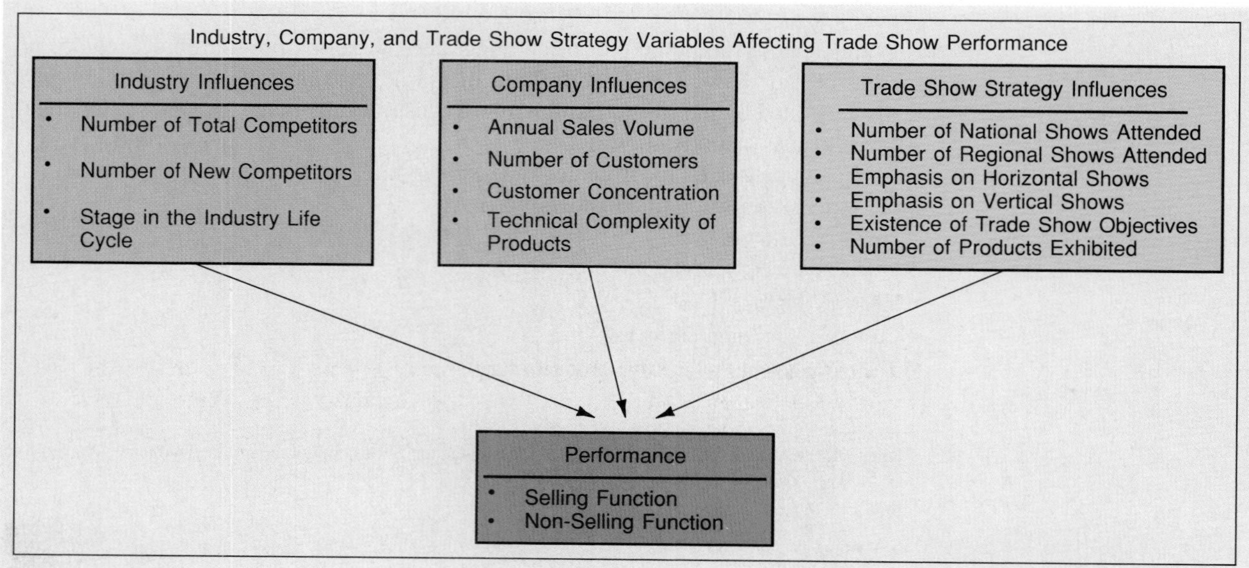

DIRECTORIES AND YELLOW PAGES

A hybrid form of promotion between sales promotion and media advertising is the directory that carries advertising messages. There are over 7,500 directories at both the trade and consumer levels. Directories offer several advantages to advertisers:

1. They reach only prospects. When a person goes to a directory, the need for the product has already been established.
2. Directory advertising is directly associated with product information needed by the customer.
3. Directories are often used by decision makers at the time a purchase is being made.

Consumer Directories

Yellow Pages directories function as regional magazines for local outlets. Their awareness level is the *highest* of any community-based publication. Cross-referencing the Yellow Pages with other media increases *reach* even more effectively. Yellow Pages ad revenues have climbed 10%–12% annually during the past few years, compared with a 7.4% increase in domestic advertising industrywide in 1987 and an 8.4% industrywide increase for 1988. Currently, there are about 6,200 separate directories, issued by more than 200 publishers. But several experts believe *national* advertisers would spend more, if they had usage data "they could trust."

At the consumer level, the most familiar directory is the telephone Yellow Pages. The Yellow Pages have become a major advertising medium. In recent years, they have surpassed both radio and consumer magazines in advertising revenues; expenditures in Yellow Pages for 1989 were over $7 billion. Many agencies treat the Yellow Pages as part of their basic media plan and allocate budgets to these directories as they would to regional and specialty magazines.

The Yellow Pages generate tremendous audience levels at relatively low cost and CPMs to advertisers. A study conducted by Statistical Research, Inc., found:

- 98.5 percent of all adults are familiar with the Yellow Pages.
- The Yellow Pages generate 17.7 *billion* exposures annually.
- 18.4 percent of all U.S. adults use the Yellow Pages daily.[20]

The Yellow Pages are also an extremely efficient means of extending the reach of other media. Exhibit 14.19 shows the level of additional reach achieved when advertising in the Yellow Pages is combined with newspaper, television, and radio advertising.

Many predict that in the near future we will see a new form of directory—the "talking" Yellow Pages. Consumers will be able to call a special number and get information about plumbers, towing services, whatever, and then be connected with the company best suited to take care of their needs. Electronic directories will allow immediate listings of new businesses as well as updated information about business hours, charges, and changes in location.

Trade Directories

Incentives given to the trade *or to a company's own salesforce* can mobilize interest in selling the advertiser's merchandise or services. A recently formed promotion agency, *Fresh Perspectives,* spurred its own executive salesforce to greater heights by having them play their own version of *Super Bowl Sweepstakes*. Successful work and referrals increased the agency 1988 revenues by 280% to $1.9 million—or from 3 staff members to 10! The client list now includes Lever Brothers, Lipton, Hebrew National, and Citibank.

Trade directories must be more sophisticated and detailed than consumer directories. Advertisements in these directories are used to supplement the information given in the listing. However, unlike the common small-space advertisements appearing in the Yellow Pages, trade directory advertising often uses preprinted inserts to gain added space and color, which many directories don't provide.

TRADE INCENTIVES

Marketing strategy dictates that products must be pushed and/or pulled through the distribution channel. Media advertising and consumer sales promotion seek to pull products through the channel by creating demand among ultimate customers. Trade promotion seeks to create product support by pushing the product through the channel.

[20] *Yellow Pages Usage,* a publication of the American Association of Yellow Pages Publishers, 1987, p. 13.

EXHIBIT 14.19

The Yellow Pages, used in combination with other media, increase advertising reach significantly. (Courtesy: American Association of Yellow Pages Publishers.)

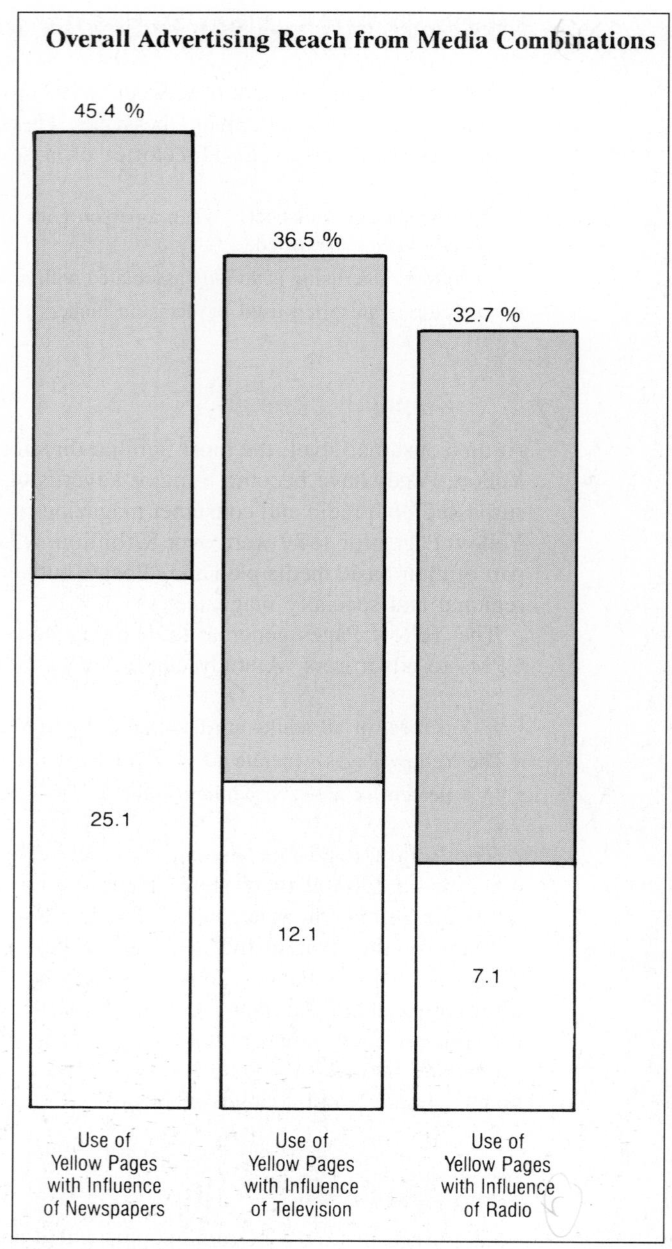

Incentives. *Sales promotion directed to either a company's sales force or dealers.*

Sales promotion to the trade is called *incentives*. There are two types of incentives: *dealer incentives,* which are directed to retailers and wholesalers; and *sales incentives,* which are directed to the company's own salespeople.

The most common incentive given to wholesalers and retailers is price reductions in the form of promotional allowances. In effect, this is comparable to the cents-off promotion at the consumer level. In addition, sweepstakes, contests, and continuity promotions (some with prize catalogs) based on sales volume are all used at the trade level.

An often-used trade incentive is the *trade deal,* which is a special discount to the retailer for a limited period of time. It may involve free goods for a minimum purchase. It may be a sliding scale of discounts, depending on the size of the purchase. The trade deal may be offered in connection with a consumer merchandising deal—for instance, a discount on the purchase of a given number of specific product assortments. Counter displays may be included to help sell the product to the consumer.

CASE HISTORY

Video Magazine Tenth Anniversary Advertising and Subscription Program

PURPOSE

Video magazine sought to establish itself as the preeminent video magazine with both readers and advertisers. On the occasion of its tenth anniversary, the magazine decided to undertake a program to demonstrate to readers and, especially, advertisers that it is the most aggressive and exciting publication in its field.

OBJECTIVES

The first objective was to increase advertising pages among those who had not advertised in the magazine in the past or had done so only infrequently (and, incidentally, among existing advertisers). To achieve this objective, *Video* realized it had to:

- Provide a reason for potential advertisers to advertise in a specific issue of the magazine
- Demonstrate that *Video* magazine is the exciting leader in its field, thereby distinguishing itself from the competition and consequently causing advertisers (and media planners) to think first about *Video* magazine when planning advertising

The second objective was to increase paid subscriptions/circulation among potential readers. This is to be partially achieved by periodically offering readers "something extra" such as sweepstakes.

STRATEGY

The strategy determined upon had two parts. First, it was decided to conduct a reader sweepstakes for the June 1988 issue and offer advertisers the opportunity to participate in the sweepstakes issue. The program was intended to:

- Increase consumer awareness and readership, thereby making *Video* magazine a much more impactful medium than its competition. Thus, the sweepstakes not only acted as a direct incentive for advertisers to advertise in the special issue, but also demonstrated that *Video* was a publication committed to meeting advertisers' needs by doing something extra to get readers more involved with the magazine and, consequently, the advertising.
- Offer readers something extra—an opportunity to win exciting prizes—thereby demonstrating to them that *Video* magazine is the most exciting and rewarding publication in its field.

In essence, this "extra effort" was intended to demonstrate to both

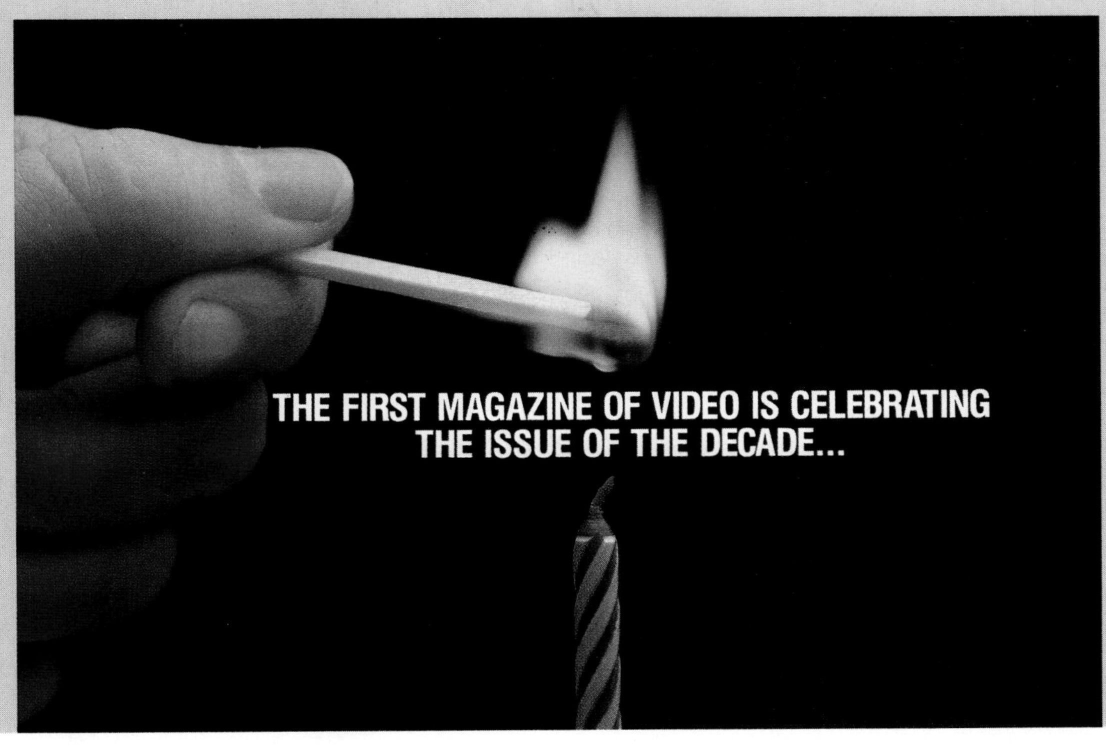

THE FIRST MAGAZINE OF VIDEO IS CELEBRATING
THE ISSUE OF THE DECADE...

current and potential advertisers that *Video* is the leading video magazine, the one they should advertise in.

The second part of the strategy was to use the reader sweepstakes as a focal point for a subscription drive. A properly executed sweepstakes would be the "extra" needed to convince potential new (and former) subscribers to take the magazine. A two-part program was recommended:

1. Subscriptions were promoted by point-of-sale at video retailers. In addition to counter-card displays with "take-one envelopes" for subscriptions, a poster promoting *Video* magazine and the June reader sweepstakes was made available to video retailers. To encourage awareness and promote participation by video retailers in this program, a sweepstakes offering a free trip to the Consumer Electronics Show for video retailers in Las Vegas was conducted.
2. A direct-mail subscription campaign that took advantage of the consumer sweepstakes to renew interest was directed to 100,000 lapsed subscribers.

IMPLEMENTATION

Promotion to Advertisers. The first objective was to get advertisers to participate in the sweepstakes issue. To do that, the following steps were taken:

- *Special bulletin.* A brochure describing the June sweepstakes issue and its advantages was sent to media planners and advertisers in January.
- *Reminder notice.* A postcard-style mailing reminding advertisers of the special June issue was sent out in February.
- *Advertising.* Ads in selected advertising trade journals promoted the sweepstakes issue and made advertisers more cognizant of this special advertising opportunity.

The Sweepstakes. To implement the sweepstakes itself:

- The cover of the June issue boldly announced the sweepstakes to readers. This created interest on newsstands and in video stores, resulting in increased sales of the magazine.
- *Video* magazine sales reps helped participating advertisers provide additional prizes at their expense.
- Promotion Solutions wrote the rules, judged and administered the sweepstakes, and prepared ads and other material for the promotion.

Reader Subscriptions. To encourage *video retailers* to display *Video* magazine promotional/subscription materials, the following was done:

- A promotional brochure, mailed to video retailers, announced/explained *Video* magazine's subscription drive and solicited the video retailer's participation in displaying *Video* magazine materials. It also announced the video retailers' sweepstakes.
- A basic package of retailer display materials, including one counter card (with pocket containing 50 subscription form/envelopes) and one poster, was sent to all video retailers who ordered and agreed to display *Video* magazine subscription materials.

To encourage renewals among lapsed subscribers, the magazine sent them a direct-mail package that included a subscription envelope, a cover memo, and an outgoing envelope.

According to *Incentive* magazine, total trade incentive expenditures now amount to over $8 billion a year. The three primary categories of trade incentives are:

1. Merchandise: $4.4 billion
2. Trade: $1.8 billion
3. Business gifts: $1.3 billion

SUMMARY

It is essential that companies review both the advertising and promotion components of their marketing mix. A company that does not use some combination of trade and retail promotions as well as advertising to carry out its overall marketing objectives is the exception. Successful sales promotion uses the same basic approach as other advertising—that is, it begins with a clearly defined marketing objective, which is then translated into a creative theme appropriate to the intended target audience.

The major difference between sales promotion and other forms of advertising and promotion is that sales promotion is a direct, usually short-term, device to encourage sales. As with advertising, sales promotion should reinforce a positive product image. Because of the higher CPMs of most sales promotion, reducing waste circulation is mandatory.

Advertising and sales promotion must be integrated so that the timing, message components, and overall image that each is creating for the product or service work in synergy. The more these factors are synchronized, the greater is the likelihood that each will cause a positive effect on the other.

The elements of certain promotional activities, particularly those dealing with price-off discounts or some other financial incentive, are very important stimuli in the marketplace. If they are used too frequently, then the consumer will rarely be motivated to purchase the product at full price.[21]

QUESTIONS

1. Compare and contrast sales promotion and advertising.
2. Some advertisers fear that an overuse of sales promotion will damage consumer loyalty created by advertising. Discuss.
3. Point-of-purchase advertising is one of the fastest-growing segments of sales promotion. Why?
4. Compare and contrast premiums and specialties.
5. What is the primary appeal of self-liquidating premiums to advertisers?
6. What is the function of a fulfillment firm?
7. What are the primary advantages and disadvantages of couponing as a sales-promotion technique?
8. Compare and contrast sweepstakes and contests. Why have sweepstakes become more popular in recent years?
9. Discuss the use of cooperative advertising as a sales-promotion device.
10. Discuss, from a marketing standpoint, the advantages and disadvantages of consumer and trade promotions.

[21] Joseph W. Ostrow, "The Advertising/Promotion Mix: A Blend or a Tangle?" *AAAA Newsletter*, August 1988, p. 6.

SUGGESTED EXERCISES

- See how many advertisements you can find that contain some form of sales promotion.
- Take a typical issue of a daily newspaper and look for advertisements run on a co-op basis.
- Find five offers for self-liquidating premiums.

READINGS

DOMMERMUTH, WILLIAM P.: *Promotion Analysis, Creativity, and Strategy* (Boston: PWS-Kent Publishing Company, 1989).

FRANCISCO, ROBERT J.: "Face Up to Winning Exhibit Design," *Business Marketing,* March 1988, p. 80.

FREY, NATHANIEL: "Targeted Couponing: New Wrinkles Cut Waste," *Marketing Communications,* January 1988, p. 40.

FRY, JOHN: "Trade Show Issues: How to Make Them Work," *Folio,* March 1989, p. 139.

HALEY, DOUGLAS F.: "Industry Promotion and Advertising Trends: Why Are They Important?" *Journal of Advertising Research,* December 1987/January 1988, p. RC-6.

WILLIAMSON, HENRY B.: "Yellow Pages: A New Dimension for a Directional Medium," *Marketing & Media Decisions,* April 1988, p. 104.

PART FIVE

Creating the Advertising

We have identified our prime prospects, the marketing, and advertising goals are clear, media planning is beginning—it is time to start the exciting process of creating ads. The advertising process moves from ideas to execution to final production. In Chapters 15 and 16, we discuss the research used to give insights into consumer motivations and behavior and channel messages to these consumer needs.

Chapter 17 discusses the role of the creative team—writer and art director—in developing concepts to use as advertising appeals. This process is one of offering consumers solutions to their problems. It starts by isolating the significant product benefit. The advertiser must make the creative leap from general ideas to specific advertising executions.

In Chapters 18, 19, and 20, we examine the actual production techniques for both print and broadcasts ads. It is extremely important that the creative team understand the opportunities and limitations of production. Poor production planning is one of the major sources of wasted money in advertising.

FIFTEEN

Research in Advertising

Advertisers need to *know* what *motivates* consumers in the marketplace in order to be successful. Once a toy is ''a hit'' in the marketplace, smart toymakers *know* to add items to the product line. Playmates, Los Angeles, is extending its *Teenage Mutant Ninja Turtles line* by adding higher priced accessories and new action figures. Playmates' ad budget for the Turtle toys this year will be about $10 million, more than *double* what it spent in 1988—to coincide with its new ''additions.''

Advertisers need to develop a solid foundation upon which to build their campaigns. They must know the motivations, attitudes, and perceptions behind consumers' choices, because the penalty for not knowing is often failure in the marketplace. If getting consumers to buy a product were easy, the new-product failure rate wouldn't be so high. To enjoy success, all we would have to do is plug in the right marketing and advertising formulas. But predicting consumer behavior is obviously much more complex.

In this chapter, we'll take a look at the various types of research available—product, market, consumer, advertising strategy, and message research—and how they help marketers to better understand the consumer. We'll also examine ways to judge whether a specific ad will communicate effectively to consumers before it is actually run in the media.

Why did you buy any of the products you put in your shopping cart the last time you were at the supermarket? Did you buy peas? Were they Stokely's, Libby's, Green Giant, Del Monte, or the store brand? Why did your hand pick up that specific can? Was it the brand? Price? Quality? You don't know?

You've probably had this sort of discussion with yourself in a department store: ''A lot of these clothes look good, but I can't afford everything I like. Should I buy the Europrep, Genesis, Essentials, the Big Ace, Chaus, or Silk Studio?'' Was your decision based on price? On the kind of fabric? ''I like cotton better than a blend . . . but I really would rather have silk.''

In the drugstore, why did you buy ''your'' deodorant, mouthwash, and toothpaste? Do you really know why you chose any of the products you bought recently? Could you explain the reasons for your preferences to a market researcher?

What kind of advertising motivates you to buy? What was the last ad that made you run out and buy something? As a marketer, how do I reach you?

After marketing research, marketers engage in *advertising research*—to better deliver their message to their chosen targets. Mail order catalogues are following *Banana Republic* and *Lands' End* lead by expanding the use of serious editorial material. It's part of a bid to beat clutter and hold consumers' attention.

WHAT KIND OF RESEARCH IS NEEDED?

Marketing has become far more complex because of the tremendous increase in new products, the high cost of shelf space, the expansion of retailer control over the distribution system, changing media habits, and the bewildering array of communication choices. Market research—*upfront* research—tells us about the product, the market, the consumer, and the competition. Recall from Chapter 3 how the Lintas: Link system's brand equity audit and brand probe set the stage for obtaining this sort of information. After completing market research, we do advertising research—principally pretesting of ads and campaign evaluation—to get the data we need to develop and refine an advertising strategy and message.

The behavioral sciences—anthropology, sociology, and psychology—have had a strong influence on upfront research. We'll review each in turn.

ANTHROPOLOGY AND ADVERTISING

The "emotional connection" consumers have for products can be determined through consumer research. Monticello Cellars, a Napa Valley, California winery, is capitalizing on the nostalgia craze and on the continuing popularity of "tragic" Hollywood stars by affixing prints of Marilyn Monroe to its labels. The new *Marilyn-Merlot 1986* label is designed to heighten attention and stimulate fond remembrances of Marilyn's preoccupation with "pleasure."

Differences in cultures, regions, values, and roles of society is ofttimes appropriately reflected in marketing and advertising strategies. Although *Coca-Cola* has been banned in Saudi Arabia, as in most of the Arab world, for 28 years, because of business ties with Israel, it's been invited back. The reason—Coke is the official sponsor of the Fifth World Youth Soccer Championship. Coke knew that everything the Saudis imported would sell, as the 11–12 million consumers drink 500 million liters of soft drink annually! Equally anxious to promote their non-intrusive entrance was the exclusive distributor, General Trading Company, a division of the Olayon Group.

Cultural anthropologists study the emotional connection between products and consumer values. The creative people in advertising love this kind of research because it shows what people are saying about themselves by choosing a certain type of product. They use consumer research to make what Saatchi & Saatchi executives call "that leap from logic to magic."

Anthropologists have found that certain needs and activities are common to people the whole world over. Bodily adornment, cooking, courtship, food taboos, gift giving, language, marriage, status, sex, and superstition are present in all societies, although each society attaches its own values and traditions to them. Anthropologists see the United States as a pluralistic society made up of an array of subcultures. In each subculture lives a different group of people who share its values, customs, and traditions. Think about the cultural differences among Italians, Poles, blacks, and Hispanics as a starting point.

Some ethnic groups prefer highly spiced foods (Polish or Italian sausage) or distinctively flavored foods (Louisiana chicory-flavored coffee). Indeed, many dishes favored in certain parts of the country identify people in that area with their cultural past: Pennsylvania Dutch cookery, with its fastnachts and shoofly pie, has roots mainly in the valley of the Rhine; in Rhode Island, tourtière (meat pie) reflects the French-Canadian influence; Mexico's influence is revealed in the taco and other Mexican-style foods served in southern California and the Southwest.

There are regional variations in the American language, too. A sandwich made of several ingredients in a small loaf of bread is a "poor boy" in New Orleans, a "submarine" in Boston, a "hoagy" in Philadelphia, and a "grinder" in upstate New York. A soft drink in Syracuse is a "soda," and in Phoenix a "pop." In Virginia, "salad" means kale and spinach. Geomarketing permits advertisers to make use of these cultural differences in food preferences, terminology, and subgroup identities when they advertise their products.

In Chapter 4, we discussed shifting consumer values, the role of working women, and other changes advertisers monitor in order to understand the consumer better. Because it sharpens our understanding of differences in cultural heritage, regional variations, rites of passage, and changing cultural roles, anthropology has significant relevance for marketing and advertising.

SOCIOLOGY AND ADVERTISING

Sociology examines the structure and function of organized behavioral systems. The sociologist studies groups and their influence on, and interaction with, the individual. Advertisers recognize group influences on the adoption of new ideas, media use, and consumer purchase behavior. They use sociological research to predict the probability of product purchase by various consumer groups.

Social Class and Stratification

Just about every society is clustered into classes, determined by such criteria as wealth, income, occupation, education, achievement, and seniority. We sense where we fit into this pattern. We identify with others in our class (''these are my kind of people''), and we generally conform to the standards of our class. Experienced advertisers recognize that people's aspirations usually take on the flavor of the social class immediately above their own.

''Social class'' distinctions often highlight consumer product preferences and are accurate ''barometers'' of brands, retail outlets, and sources of market information. Bowing to is upscale loyal customers, *Timberland,* a marketer of rugged outdoor footwear, will open its second concept store in a ''trendy and pricy'' California location—Sausalito. A midtown Manhattan store opened last spring, after the initial retail outlet ''christening'' in Boston. Print ads in local, upscale magazines and in ''selected'' sections of local newspapers will support the ''price-is-not-the-objective, the boot is'' retailer's openings.

Social-class structure helps explain why demographic categories sometimes fail to provide helpful information about consumers. A professional person and a factory worker may have the same income, but that doesn't mean their interests in products and services will coincide. In today's marketing environment, research has shown that no single variable, such as age, income, or sex, will accurately predict consumer purchases. We have discovered that using several variables gives a more accurate prediction of consumer behavior. Think of the differences between homemakers and working women of the same age, income, and education in food preferences for themselves and their families, usage of convenience goods, child care, and media habits.

CUBE Concept: Consumer Behavior Research

Valentine-Radford's CUBE (Comprehensive Understanding of Buyer Environments) concept is an example of research that goes beyond demographics. CUBE is a means of determining consumer behavior on the basis of habits developed in childhood. It segments the population into eight groups according to three key dimensions of decision making:[1]

1. *How people control their circumstances.* People take control or yield control. *Take-control* people create their own rules. *Yield-control* people follow the existing rules.
2. *How people act. Act-first* people prefer to jump in, make a decision, and worry about the consequences later. *Think-first* people tend to solve problems independently.
3. *How people judge information. Fact-based* people are objective thinkers; they judge information on what they can see, feel, and touch. *Feeling-based* people judge information according to how it makes them feel.

These six variables lead to eight distinct consumer segments with individual profiles:

CUBE analysis of the population yields 8 consumer segments among which are *Aging Hippies. Rolling Stone* magazine, in their ads, capitalizes on the misconception of its *current* readership—it's actually closer to middle America—or so they say—*Their* aging ''hippy'' is quite a modern-day consumer, ''purchasing 80 million items of appeal during the past 12 months''—which should make their current and would-be advertisers very happy. . .

- *Traditionals,* yield-control, act-first, fact-based people, constitute about 14 percent of the population. They are down-to-earth, practical, conventional, and sociable. Somewhat older than some of the other groups, they have lower education and income, attend church often, give or go to dinner parties, and play cards.
- *New Middle Americans,* take-control, act-first, fact-based people, are very sociable, achievement oriented, and concerned with their standard of living. They are somewhat younger and better educated than traditionals, with higher family incomes and fewer children. They make up about 14 percent of the population.
- *Home-and-Community-Centereds* are yield-control, think-first, fact-based people who constitute 13 percent of the population. They are conventional, prim and proper types who are not gregarious. This group is older and better educated than some of the other groups, has a higher income, and contains more males and widowed and divorced people. Home-and-Community-Centereds generally rank low on out-of-home activities.
- *Rising Stars* are take-control, think-first, fact-based types who account for 10 percent of the population. They are intellectually curious but not socially gregarious. Rising Stars are socially conscious and have the highest incomes and education of all the groups, along with the most professionals, entrepreneurs, males, singles, and blacks. They attend museums and con-

[1]Wally Wood, ''Valentine-Radford's CUBE Concept,'' *Marketing & Media Decisions,* April 1988, pp. 140–142.

certs, read books and use the library a lot, and exercise. They are somewhat more apt to watch public television than the other groups.

- *Good Ol' Girls and Boys,* yield-control, act-first, feeling-based people, are about 11 percent of the population. They are practical, down-to-earth, no-nonsense, and sociable, yet cynical. This group contains many women and blue-collar workers who have children in school, but also a lot of retired people. Good Ol' Boys and Girls watch soap operas and game shows, listen to country-and-western music, and like to garden.
- *Young Socials* are take-control, act-first, feeling-based people who account for 13 percent of the population. They are outgoing, warm, intuitive, and have low self-control—''If it feels good, do it.'' They tend to be younger and less educated than some of the other groups; they also have higher incomes. There are more females, health/social workers, and secretaries in this group. They attend the most fitness classes, club meetings, and listen to hard rock.
- *Moralists,* yield-control, think-first, feeling-based, are older than other groups, and have less education and lower income. These people do the most gardening and do-it-yourself work. They also attend church frequently, watch religious programs on TV, and listen to religious music. Moralists are about 13 percent of the population.
- *Aging Hippies,* a take-control, think-first, feeling-based group, are about 12 percent of the population. These people are sensitive, fanciful, unrealistic, and imaginative. They are somewhat younger and better educated than some of the other groups. They exercise and read the most, visit galleries, watch public television, and listen to jazz and folk music.

CUBE can be used by marketers to measure product usage, media preferences, and pinpoint market segments.

Family life cycle analysis can yield significant information about buying behavior. *Both* the State of Connecticut and Pepsi-Cola used such data to enter a ''partnership'' to promote summer tourism activities in the state. Under the agreement, Pepsi drinkers will get free coupons to attend Connecticut tourism attractions when they buy 12-packs of Pepsi in the 400–500 state supermarkets. The ''targets'' are *young families with children,* who account for nearly one-third of the $3.3 billion spent each year on tourist attractions in the state.

Family life cycle. *Concept that demonstrates changing purchasing behavior as a person or family matures.*

Family Life Cycle and Buying Behavior

The basic unit of buying behavior is the family. As Exhibit 15.1 shows, most households pass through an orderly progression of stages, and each stage has special significance for buying behavior. Knowledge about the family life cycle permits you to segment the market and the advertising appeal according to specific consumption patterns and groups.

PSYCHOLOGY AND ADVERTISING

Psychology is the study of human behavior and its causes. Three psychological concepts of importance to consumer behavior are motivation, cognition, and learning. *Motivation* refers to the drives, urges, wishes, or desires that initiate the sequence of events known as ''behavior.'' *Cognition* is the area in which all the mental phenomena (perception, memory, judging, thinking, and the rest) are grouped. *Learning* refers to those changes in behavior relative to external stimulus conditions that occur over time.[2] These three factors, working within the framework of the societal environment, create the psychological basis for consumer behavior. Advertising research is interested in cognitive elements to learn how consumers react to different stimuli, and research finds learning especially important in determining factors such as advertising frequency. However, in recent years, the major application of psychology to advertising has been the attempt to understand the underlying motives that initiate consumer behavior.

VALS 2 segmentation classifies consumers along two key dimensions—*self* and *resources.* ''Lifestyle'' purchases, then, are the result of these two factors. *Izod Lacoste* utilized these two variables for its resurgence in 1985. By capitalizing on its ''famous athlete'' past, it's promoting its sportswear and traditional clothing for ''the educated sportsman.'' And, ''by pricing its standard Izod shirt at $35, we're filling a niche between Polo and private labels,'' stated Walter Kennedy, President, Izod Lacoste Menswear.

Values and Lifestyle 2

A new typology of American consumers, called VALS 2, has been developed by SRI International, the research organization that popularized the lifestyle approach to psychographic segmentation. VALS 2 segments the population into eight clusters of consumers, each with distinct behavioral and decision-making patterns that reflect different self-orientations and available psychological and material resources. The original

[2]James A. Bayton, ''Motivation, Cognition, Learning—Basic Factors in Consumer Behavior,'' *Journal of Marketing,* January 1958, p. 282.

EXHIBIT 15.1

An overview of the life cycle and buying behavior.

Stage in Life Cycle	*Buying Behavioral Pattern*
Bachelor stage: young, single people not living at home	Few financial burdens. Fashion opinion leaders. Recreation-oriented. Buy basic kitchen equipment, basic furniture, cars, vacations.
Newly married couples: young, no children	Better off financially than they will be in near future. Highest purchase rate and highest average purchase of durables. Buys cars, refrigerators, stoves, sensible and durable furniture, vacations.
Full nest I: youngest under 6	Home purchasing at peak. Liquid assets low. Dissatisfied with financial position and amount of money saved. Interested in new products. Buy washers, dryers, TV, baby food, chest rubs and cough medicines, vitamins, dolls, wagons, sleds, skates.
Full nest II: youngest child 6 or over	Financial position better. Some wives work. Less influenced by advertising. Buy larger-sized packages, multiple-unit deals. Buy many foods, cleaning materials, bicycles, music lessons, pianos.
Full nest III: older couples with dependent children	Financial position still better. More wives work. Some children get jobs. Hard to influence with advertising. High average purchase of durables. Buy new, more tasteful furniture, auto travel, nonnecessary appliances, boats, dental services, magazines.
Empty nest I: Older couples, no children living with them, head in labor force	Home ownership at peak. Most satisfied with financial position and money saved. Interested in travel, recreation, self-education. Make gifts and contributions. Not interested in new products. Buy vacations, luxuries, home improvements.
Empty nest II: Older married couples, no children living at home, head retired	Drastic cut in income. Keep home. Buy medical appliances, medical-care products that aid health, sleep and digestion.
Solitary survivor, in labor force	Income still good, but likely to sell home.
Solitary survivor, retired	Same medical and product needs as other retired group. Drastic cut in income.

Source: William D. Wells and George Gubar, "Life Cycle Concept in Marketing Research," *Journal of Marketing Research,* November 1966, pp. 355–63. Reprinted with permission.)

VALS (see Exhibit 15.2) is still a viable typology for uses related to value systems, but VALS 2 is better at predicting consumer behavior, especially purchase decisions. It relies less on political and social issues and more on psychological functions.

VALS 2 classifies consumers along two key dimensions:

1. *Self-orientation:* the fundamental human need to define a social self-image and create a world in which it can thrive.

EXHIBIT 15.2

Values and Lifestyle 1 (VALS 1). (Courtesy: SRI International.)

Need-Driven Consumers: Have to struggle to buy basics.

- Survivors: Aged, poor, depressed, struggling to survive.
- Sustainers: Young, feisty adults on the edge of poverty.

Outer-Directed Consumers: Middle-Americans influenced by what others think.

- Belongers: Want to fit in with the mass.
- Emulators: Ambitious, relatively young, status-conscious.
- Achievers: The establishment.

Inner-Directed Consumers: Along with Achievers, represent the affluent.

- I-Am-Me: Fad starters, the youngest value segment.
- Experimentals: Sensuality and hedonism are major part of their lives.
- Societally Conscious: Live in socially responsible way.

Integrated: Those rare people who have it all together.

I can't wait!

:30 1989 Spring/Summer TV

MUSIC: NERVOUS STACCATO.
Ten reports, nine letters, three memos . . . till my South Carolina vacation . . .

. . . and I CAN'T WAIT!!!

MUSIC: DREAM-LIKE TRANSITION.
SINGERS: I can't wait! I just can't wait— South Carolina!

MUSIC: NERVOUS STACCATO.
Two rush hours and three deadlines to South Carolina . . .

. . . and I CAN'T WAIT!!!

MUSIC: DREAM-LIKE TRANSITION.
SINGERS: I can't wait! I just can't wait— South Carolina!

SINGERS: I . . .

. . . can't . . .

. . . wait . . .

SINGERS: I just can't wait!!

EXHIBIT 15.3

This commercial furnishes a fun solution to everyday problems. (Courtesy: Leslie Advertising, Greenville, SC.)

2. *Resources:* the range of psychological and material resources available to sustain that self-concept.

Values and lifestyle system. *(VALS 1) and (VALS 2) Developed by SRI International to cluster consumers according to several variables in order to predict consumer behavior.*

According to this concept, consumers exhibit three general psychological orientations: principle, status, and action. Consumers with a principle orientation look inside themselves to make choices, rather than to physical experience or social pressure. Those with a status orientation make choices in relation to the anticipated reactions and concerns of others in the groups to which they belong or aspire to belong. Action-oriented consumers base their choices on considerations related to activity. They value feelings only when they result from action.

The second dimension—resources—includes both material and acquired attributes (money, position, education, etc.) and psychological qualities (inventiveness, interpersonal skills, intelligence, energy, etc.).

VALS 2 claims that an individual purchases certain products and services because he or she is a specific type of person. The purchase is related to lifestyle, which in turn is a function of self-orientation and available resources.

VALS 2 is a network of interconnected segments. Neighboring types have similar characteristics and can be combined in varying ways to suit particular marketing purposes. The overall system is highly flexible and predictive of consumer behavior.

Actualizers—or, "take-charge" people—express their "leadership ability" by independence and diversity in their possessions. Rather than advertising "appropriate gift suggestions" to this group, AT&T, Jiffy Lube, major food chains, and New York's Lincoln Center, found greater success with *gift certificates*. In a recent study commissioned by the American Express Company, they found that independent people prefer to give a gift *they'd* like—one which allows freedom of choice of *time* and *date*.

Actualizers. Actualizers are successful, sophisticated, active, "take-charge" people with high self-esteem and abundant resources. They are interested in growth and seek to develop, explore, and express themselves in a variety of ways—sometimes guided by principle, and sometimes by the desire to have an effect, to make a change. Image is important to Actualizers, not as evidence of their status or power, but rather as an expression of their taste, independence, and character. Actualizers are among the established and emerging leaders in business and government, yet they continue to seek challenges. They have a wide range of social and intellectual interests, are concerned with social issues—both in the community and around the world—and are open to social change. Their lives are characterized by richness and diversity. Their possessions and recreation reflect a cultivated taste for the finer things in life.

Principle-minded consumers tend to be conventional people, with established beliefs. Their purchasing pattern is predictable, usually showing preference for *American products and family-oriented items*. *Sears* has been their principal "all purpose" store—and now that their "bread-and-butter" consumer has been "defecting" for the discounters, Sears has launched an "everyday low price" strategy. Appealing to these budget-minded consumers, Sears will rely on TV and FSIs with the slogan, "Your money's worth and a whole lot more."

Fulfilleds and Believers: Principle Oriented. Principle-oriented consumers seek to make their behavior consistent with their views of how the world is or should be.

Fulfilleds are mature, satisfied, comfortable, reflective people who value order, knowledge, and responsibility. Most are well educated, and in, or recently retired from, professional occupations. They are well informed about world and national events and alert to opportunities to broaden their knowledge. Content with their careers, families, and station in life, they tend to center their leisure activities around their homes. Fulfilleds have a moderate respect for the status quo, institutions of authority, and social decorum, but are open-minded about new ideas and social change. Because they are inclined to base their decisions on strongly held principles, they appear calm and self-assured. While their incomes allow them many choices, Fulfilleds are conservative, practical consumers; they care about functionality, value, and durability in the products they buy.

Believers are conservative, conventional people with concrete beliefs based on traditional, established codes: family, church, community, and nation. Many of them have moral codes that are deeply rooted and literally interpreted. They follow established routines, organized in large part around their homes, families, and the social or religious organizations to which they belong. As consumers, Believers are conservative and predictable, favoring American products and established brands. Their education, income, and energy are modest but sufficient to meet their needs.

Achievers and Strivers: Status Oriented. Status-oriented consumers have or seek a secure place in a valued social setting. They make choices to enhance their position or to facilitate their move to another, more desirable group. Strivers look to others to indicate what they should be and do, whereas Achievers, who are more resourceful and

Those who are concerned about status and seek security are *achievers*. They need peer approval of their purchases, so they tend to favor established products. They also tend to rely on "service-minded" establishments, according to a recent survey by Impact Resources, California. While *Sears* in Atlanta rated highly, *Nordstrom* in Salt Lake, Los Angeles, and San Diego is where purchase help is most prevalent among department stores.

active, seek recognition and self-definition through achievements at work and in their personal lives.

Achievers are successful career-oriented people who like to, and generally do, feel in control of their lives. They value structure, predictability, and stability over risk, intimacy, and self-discovery. They are deeply committed to their work and their families. Work gives them a sense of duty, material rewards, and prestige. Their social lives reflect this focus and are structured around family, church, and business. Achievers live conventional lives, are politically conservative, and respect authority and the status quo. Image is important to them. As consumers, they favor established products and services that demonstrate their success to their peers.

Strivers seek motivation, self-definition, and approval from the world around them. They are striving to find a secure place in life. Unsure of themselves and low on economic, social, and psychological resources, Strivers are deeply concerned about the opinions and approval of other people. Money defines success for Strivers, who don't have enough of it, and often feel that life has given them a raw deal. Strivers are easily bored and impulsive. Many of them try to be stylish, in part to mask the lack of sufficient rewards from work, family, or possessions. They emulate those who own more impressive possessions, but what they wish to obtain is generally beyond their reach.

Makers can be approached with *functional* products—by stressing their practicality and individuality. That's the group Seiko and Citizen Watch companies are after. They're "shifting geers" to stress *technology*, instead of fashion in new advertising campaigns. "Technological firsts," such as the first quartz watch powered by a tiny generator that translates the movement of the wearer's wrist into energy, should attract those who are interested in products—not lifestyles," predicted Joe Thompson, editor-in-chief of *Modern Jeweler*.

Experiencers and Makers: Action Oriented. Action-oriented consumers like to affect their environment in tangible ways. Makers do so primarily at home and at work, Experiencers in the wider world. Both types are intensely involved.

Experiencers are young, vital, enthusiastic, impulsive, and rebellious. They seek variety and excitement, savoring the new, the offbeat, the risky. Still in the process of formulating their life values and patterns of behavior, they quickly become enthusiastic about new possibilities, but are equally quick to cool. At this stage in their lives, they are politically uncommitted and uninformed and highly ambivalent about what they believe. Experiencers combine an abstract disdain for conformity and authority with an outsider's awe of others' wealth, prestige, and power. Their energy finds an outlet in exercise, sports, outdoor recreation, and social activities. Experiencers are avid consumers and spend much of their income on clothing, fast food, music, movies, and video.

Makers are practical people who have constructive skills and value self-sufficiency. They live within a traditional context of family, practical work, and physical recreation and have little interest in what lies outside that context. Makers experience the world by working on it—building a house, raising children, fixing a car, or canning vegetables—and have sufficient skill, income, and energy to carry out their projects successfully. They are politically conservative, suspicious of new ideas, respectful of government authority and organized labor, but resentful of government intrusion on individual rights. They are unimpressed by material possessions other than those with a practical or functional purpose (e.g., tools, pickup trucks, fishing equipment).

Strugglers are the most brand loyal—since their knowledge of alternatives is limited and their need for acceptance is great. As a result, they tend to use *coupons* almost twice as often as other households. Since *price* is a factor in their purchasing, strugglers search for *double* redemption stores and multiple purchase "deals."

Strugglers. Strugglers' lives are constricted. Their interests are narrow, their actions and dreams limited by their low level of resources. Chronically poor, ill-educated, low-skilled, without strong social bonds, aging and concerned about their health, they are often despairing and passive. Because they are so limited, they show no evidence of a strong self-orientation, but are focused on meeting the urgent needs of the present moment. Their chief concerns are for security and safety. Strugglers are politically conservative and uninformed, and feel powerless to influence events. They rely on organized religion for moral direction. They are cautious consumers and represent a very modest market for products and services, but they have the strongest brand loyalties of any of the VALS 2 types.

Advertisers can use the VALS 2 typology to segment particular markets, develop marketing strategies, refine product concepts, position products and services, develop advertising and media campaigns, and guide long-range planning.

Nature of Motivation

In the past, most research in consumer behavior was directed toward understanding the underlying reasons for specific consumer demand. In recent years, marketers have taken a broader perspective, viewing marketing science as the behavioral science that seeks to explain exchange relationships. They believe that the marketing system and appropriate advertising appeals must consider behavioral intentions and consequences on the part of buyers, sellers, business institutions, and society as a whole.

RESEARCH TODAY

Research and the Invisible Brand

Ford Motor Company's Mercury line placed last in *brand power*—a research measure tested by Landor Associates among domestic car nameplates in 1988. Mercury didn't have a bad reputation among consumers; rather, it showed little or no presence at all—a problem Mercury has been trying to overcome for some time. Earlier, in the mid-1980s, Mercury executives had been horrified to hear a participant in a focus group say she hadn't seen a Mercury in ten years and was sorry Ford didn't build them anymore. The ad executives' response, as they watched from behind the two-way mirror, was: "Oh, my God, I don't believe this is happening." The result was a "brand campaign" designed to establish the name more firmly in the public eye and mind.

Ford placed a new emphasis on regional marketing, and undertook an aggressive research program to learn why so many people ignore the Mercury brand. As a result of the new marketing, Ford was able to lower the age of the typical Cougar customer from 47 to 42 years, but the average age for all Mercury buyers is still 50.5 years—not a good sign for future sales.

Research showed that the only symbol Mercury customers associate with the car is the cougar, which appeared in 1966 with the first Cougar. It was dropped in national advertising in 1979, although it was retained by dealers in local ads. At dealer request, the cat was revived recently.

The problem the advertising people faced was that the cougar symbol might remind people of the old Mercurys—and scare away younger buyers. They did two things to rejuvenate the cat. First they used a new theme song, "Nothing moves you like a Mercury." Second, since research had shown that the cougar jumping onto its familiar perch atop the Lincoln-Mercury sign tested "old" with today's consumers, they had the cougar in the television ads jump, pivot, and stop quickly to suggest the agility of the brand's newer cars.[3]

Advertisers are primarily concerned with the *images* their products have in the marketplace. Research *clarifies* those images. When Buick wanted to project its Reatta as "a luxury car," consumer recommendations advised that they compare Reatta with other luxury cars on the market, such as BMW and Mercedes-Benz in their ads.

If it weren't for consumer research, a brand might continue to decline without the company having the slightest clue as to why. Consumer research is helping advertisers to create messages that deliver a newer, stronger image to prospects. Once the ads are created, other research measures comprehension, attitudes, and the impact of the message.

The Changing Role of Research

For many advertising agencies, the traditional role of research is changing. During 1989, a number of major agencies restructured or eliminated their research departments. Under the new structures, many researchers have been renamed *account plan-*

[3]Melinda Grenier Guiles, "Ford's Mercury Line Strives to Establish a Firm Identity," *The Wall Street Journal,* April 4, 1989, p. 1B.

EXHIBIT 15.4

Advertising is an innovative way to do consumer research, though the results are not scientific. (Courtesy: United Carolina Bank.)

What Do You Want?

United Carolina Bank wants to get to know you from the inside out. So we want you to tell us what bugs you about most banks. Is it slow loan approvals? Having to show the same teller your I.D. five times in a row? Going through the chain of command just to get an answer?

What do you want above everything else? Special investment expertise? Simple courtesy? To be treated like a person, not a number?

We really want to know. And in the next few weeks, we'll be using your viewpoints to change the face of Carolina banking forever.

You Be The Boss. Tell Us.
UNITED CAROLINA BANK
We appreciate your thoughts and ideas.
Name (Please Print) Phone Address
Mail to: E. Rhone Sasser President and Chief Executive Officer
United Carolina Bank Post Office Box 632 Whiteville N.C. 28472

EXHIBIT 15.5

Advertising the Response to ad illustrated in Exhibit 15.5. The idea is to show consumers that the bank cares about what they think. (Courtesy: Leslie Advertising, Greenville, SC.)

"That's What I Want!"

We're overwhelmed.

It was so simple: to ask you what you want from a bank. And your response went beyond our wildest dreams. Not just from our Customers—but from our friends *outside* United Carolina Bank as well. Thank you all for your ideas and support.

Too bad so many other banks have lost that kind of touch with people.

We asked, and you told us what you want. Keep it up. We want to know more. And in the months ahead, you'll be seeing a lot of *your* ideas put to work at UCB.

That's because our employees know that in everything we do, we have to look at it from your point of view. What do *you* want? How would *you* react? After all, you're why we're here in the first place.

If your bank isn't as interested in what you have to say, maybe it's time you talked to *us*. We're ready to listen.

"That's What I Want!"

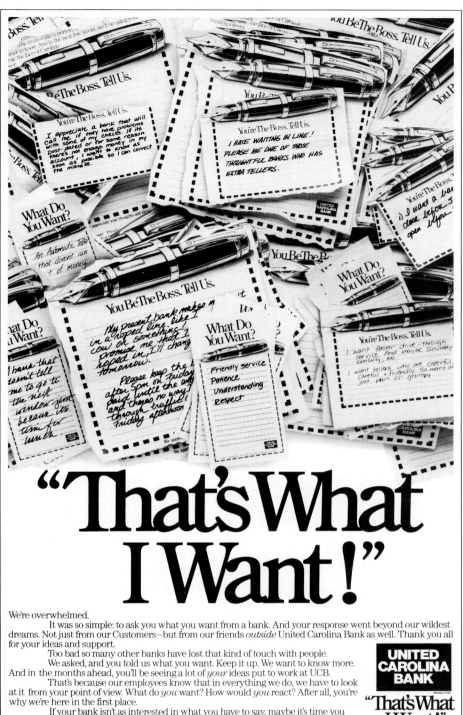

ners or *marketing planners,* and their task now is to discern not just who buys specific brands but why. Chiat/Day was a leader in adopting the British account-planning model, which groups together account, creative, and strategic planning teams for each brand. Most of the changes taking place in agency research departments result from clients' reluctance to pay for traditional agency research because they believe it is outmoded. Many clients are performing more research themselves; others are buying more sophisticated research from independent research companies.

Carnation Company's compensation plan for its ad agencies depends on how the

Research is now being conducted to judge the *effectiveness* of copy. Clients are even targeting compensation to predetermined test scores. Because respondents don't put lemon-lime drinks in the same category as colas, Lowe Marschalk, New York created a *more subtle sales effort* for Sprite. In addition to keeping the 2-year-old theme, "I like the Sprite in you," Ira Gleser, a Coca-Cola USA spokesman (parent company) promised "awareness and excitement" with the new campaign—but no "cola wars." Sprite is the overall lemon-lime leader, with 4.4% of the total $43 billion soft-drink market, and has increased its food-store segment 10% over last year.

An alternative to traditional research is *account planning*—where the agency "builds in" the consumer viewpoint "every step of the way." The objective is to capture "hidden" motivations for purchasing and so base the campaign. . . D'Arcy Masius Benton & Bowles' strategy in buying the Connection Consulting Group was to increase their "resource base" in account planning. DMB&B can now offer advice to clients on product planning sales, public relations, corporate identity, direct marketing, medical specialities, package design, and AV—"based on *benefits* the consumers will accrue," stated George Semko, president of the diversified communications division.

advertising scores in research. The agencies will earn higher pay if their advertising hits preestablished, negotiated target scores in Research Systems Corporation's Advertising Research System tests. The Carnation pay system is based on research rather than sales, profits, or market share because those elements can't always be tied exclusively to advertising.

This system of connecting agency pay to research test scores has stirred great controversy among advertising executives. Robert Schmidt, CEO of Levine, Huntley, Schmidt & Beaver, believes that "Copy testing is one reason advertising is so formulized now." Marvin Sloves, chairman and CEO of Scali, McCabe, Sloves, says: "I believe in research. The more you know, the better you are. But there are some ideas so big, so crazy, so offbeat that no research is going to prove anything. When you do ideas that will research well, you are in danger of not doing great ideas." But Gerald MaGee, executive vice president of Ogilvy & Mather, states: "It's the way of the future. You may not like it, but it is reality. Clients are in the business to get results, not to win Clio Awards."[4]

Account Planners versus Researchers

Account planning is what Chiat/Day does in place of research. The concept was first developed by Stanley Pollitt at BMP agency in London in the 1970s, and Chiat/Day was the first American agency to adopt it. The planning model groups account, creative, and strategic planning teams for a brand. The account person represents the client's point of view, while the strategic planner represents the consumer point of view. Account planning's goal is to define the client's problem, identify the target audience, and provide guidance for the creative department from the very beginning of a project. It attempts to turn advertising from what the client wants to what the client needs.

The Nissan account is an example of how Chiat/Day uses the account-planning system. Account planning identified the target for the Nisson Pathfinder, a Blazer-like half-truck/half-car, as "professionals with a sense of adventure." This insight helped to sell these off-the-road vehicles to yuppies who probably will never in their lives do any off-the-road driving. After finding that this audience's fantasies were far different from their realities, Chiat/Day tapped into the fantasies. The fact that most Pathfinder drivers will never switch the vehicle into four-wheel drive didn't faze the agency, for it recognized that transportation is only one function of a vehicle in the minds of buyers. So the Pathfinder ads feature an Indiana Jones type on a grueling rally up through the muddiest South American countryside.

In the account planning concept, the account planner is a partner in the ad development process at every phase of the process—not just a source of numbers.

Single-Source Data

Single-source data research integrates retail tracking data generated by scanners with household panel data on purchase patterns and ad exposure. The singleness of the source is twofold: The information comes from one supplier and is extracted from a single group of consumers. The major research companies doing true single-source data research are A. C. Nielsen's Learning Labs, Control Data's ScanAmerica, and IRI's Infoscan.

In a presentation to the Advertising Research Foundation, J. Walker Smith, director of marketing research for Dow Consumer Products, predicted that marketers' goals for single-source research would not be realized until the twenty-first century. At present, research firms are far more adept at generating data than most clients are at using the information.[5]

---

[4]Marcy Magiera, "Admen Question Carnation Plan," *Advertising Age,* March 13, 1989, p. 4.

[5]David Kiley, "Making Use of Single-Source Data," *Adweek,* December 5, 1988, p. F.K.36.

THE SERIES OF RESEARCH STEPS IN ADVERTISING

To this point we have examined the relationship of behavioral science research to advertising and looked at some of the implications for target marketing. Before we examine the research process advertisers would use in developing advertising strategy for campaigns (see Exhibit 15.6), let's get a better perspective on gathering research information. Jack Dempsey, former senior vice president of research at Interpublic, Inc., has this to say about information:

> By itself information is of no value. It only acquires value when the strategist takes a point of view about what the information means, a point of view that is relevant to the marketing and advertising issues. You have to get thoroughly involved in all the data at your disposal and, if necessary, fill in some gaps by going out and acquiring more information. But, then you have to step back from it. For the secret of effective strategy formation lies in deciding which data are important and which are not. It's a process of organizing simplicity out of complexity, for the best strategic insights are usually the very simple ones. It is important to take the consumer's point of view. Ask yourself, what is the consumer really buying? Is he or she really buying the product because of its purely functional benefits? How important are the psychological ones? The corporate landscape is littered with examples of companies and industries which failed to appreciate what their consumers were really purchasing, and because of this, they defined their markets inappropriately and often disastrously. Try to see the world with the consumer's eyes.[6]

Research begins with a *situation analysis*—the internal (company) and external (environment) factors which impact on the product. "Con Agra's *Healthy Choice frozen dinners* received their impetus from the growth of the over-50 market," revealed Scott Rahn, president. What also helped launch the low in fat, cholesterol, sodium, and calorie meals was the heart attack the chairman, Mike Harper, suffered four years ago. "Unable to eat oat bran three times a day," Harper encouraged Rahn to contact the American Heart Association for guidelines for a healthful dinner line. Low-calorie frozen dinners and entrees are currently outperforming the rest of the frozen-meal market—according to Business Trends Analysis, a New York-based research company.

Market, Product, Competitive, and Consumer Research

This basic information is gathered and analyzed to determine the marketing strategy for a product or service, projected sales, where the business will come from, pricing and distribution factors, geographical information, and how to develop data to identify the size and nature of the product category. This kind of research includes data on competitors, sales trends, packaging, advertising expenditures, and future trends. The *situation analysis* helps to clearly define the market that the product or service competes in (see Exhibit 15.7).

[6]Jack Dempsey, "Translating Information into Strategy," speech before the Institute of Advanced Advertising Studies/Atlanta, March 1986.

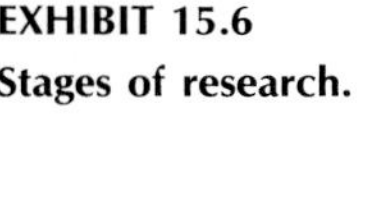

EXHIBIT 15.6
Stages of research.

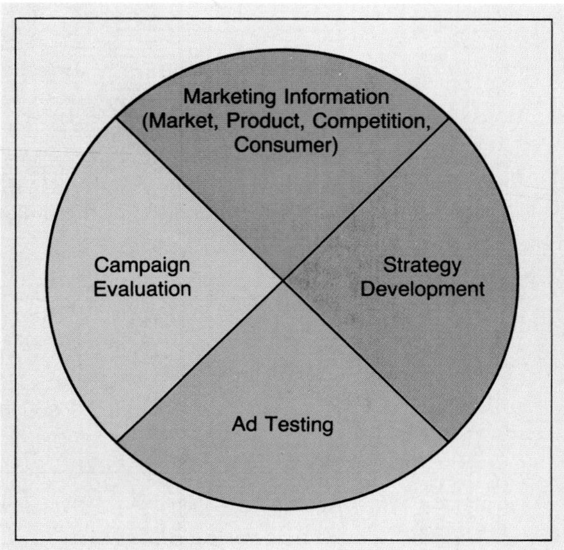

EXHIBIT 15.7

Characteristics that may influence the nature of the consumer decision process.

Market Characteristics	*Product Characteristics*	*Consumer Characteristics*
Relative and projected sales/shares Number of competitors Relative *size* of competitor's marketing efforts Relative *effectiveness* of competitor's marketing efforts The legal environment The economic environment The social/cultural environment The historical environment of the brand/company	Differentiating characteristics Hidden qualities Accompanying service Traditional product classifications Stage in the product life cycle Product's system of distribution Product's tangibility Product's ability to generate involvement Product's image/personality/position	Past experience with the product State of need Basic traits/values Preferred activities, interests, opinions (AIOs) Personal interest in product category Time pressure Demographics

(Source: Spencer Tinkham, "Processes, Procedures, Practicalities: Consumer Research for Advertising Planning," speech before the Institute for Advanced Advertising Studies/Atlanta, March 1986.)

Consumer reaction to the product is the next step. Awareness levels and trial possibilities are particularly important. The National Pork Producers Council noted that since its original ads broke in March, 1987, national pork sales have risen by more than $1 billion to $26.5 billion a year! Council research shows their recent TV spots and magazine ads have increased pork sales—helped with a new, 50% leaner product and a repositioning of the product as "versatile."

Prospect research is crucial to clearly define who is expected to buy the product or service. Studies may identify users, attitudes, lifestyles, and consumption patterns—all of which are needed to identify the prime prospect.

The amounts and kinds of information required will vary according to the product category and marketing situation. Exhibit 15.8 outlines strategy choices indicated by different levels of brand trial and awareness. It is very difficult to talk about strategy until you have information on awareness levels for each brand in the market. "Brand trial" will occur if what consumers know about the brand fits in with their needs and is sufficiently important or motivating. The relationship between a brand's level of awareness and its trial may be expressed as a ratio. A high ratio will suggest one strategy option, a low ratio another. Example: High awareness and low trial (lower left-hand box of Exhibit 15.8) clearly indicates that what people know about the brand is not sufficiently motivating or relevant, and the brand may need repositioning.

Creative Research and Success in Advertising

Research should fuel the creative process. A few years ago, research revealed that the "Weekends Are Made for Michelob" campaign presented a yuppie image that was viewed negatively by some in the target audience. Also negatively viewed was the idea

EXHIBIT 15.8

Brand trial/awareness ratios: strategic options.

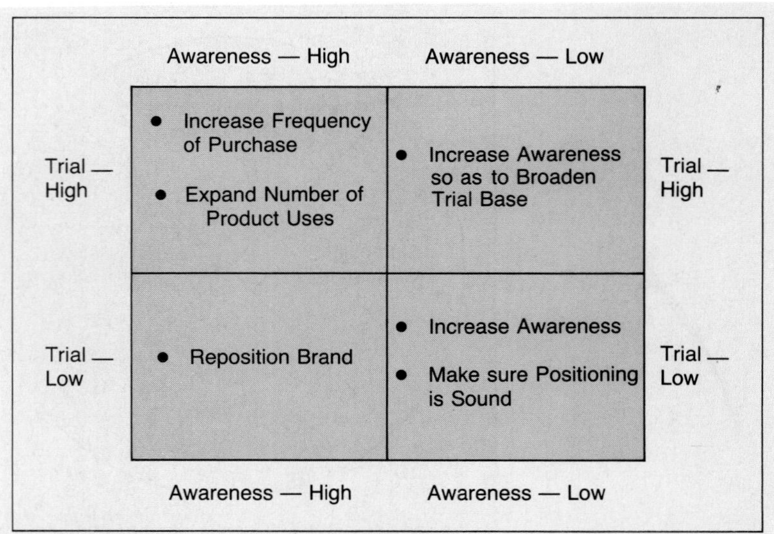

that Michelob was primarily for weekend drinking. The brand personality had always been one of quality, but the target audience of white- and gray-collar men were not clear as to exactly what this meant. They drank super-premium beer (Michelob) on special occasions, but drank premium beer most of the time. For lack of a clear identity, Michelob was losing a good part of its market to imports. The new creative thinking focused on the psychological importance of the night to these consumers, and the result was advertising designed to make the night Michelob's territory. The executions were fast-paced and sexually charged, reinforcing the anticipation of nighttime excitement.

Research doesn't always tell us what we want to hear, which can create problems if we really think an advertising idea is strong. Take the classic ''Avis. We try harder'' campaign. It tested poorly in research. Consumers said the ''We're-number-two'' concept meant Avis was second-rate. Research was against running it, but Bill Bernbach fervently believed in the idea and convinced Avis to take a chance with it. Today the Avis campaign is considered one of the most powerful, memorable ad campaigns in history.

Sometimes a great advertising concept just happens. The campaign that was used to change the name of Budweiser Light to Bud Light featured a customer at the bar asking for a ''light.'' The result was gags played on the customer—dogs jumping through a burning hoop and other kinds of lights being served. The campaign was designed to be an interim campaign of six months. During this time, Spuds Mackenzie, created simply as a college poster for the Southern California college market, became extremely popular. The idea was expanded to a calendar, then to a commercial—and a new campaign was born. Both agency and client agree Spuds never would have survived testing—but the party animal became extremely successful as a campaign.

Advertising Strategy or Message Research

This research is used to identify the most relevant and competitive advertising sales message. It may take many forms: focus groups, brand mapping, usage studies, motivation studies, or benefit segmentation.

To determine the most relevant strategy or message, *focus groups* are frequently called on for ''spontaneous'' reactions to products or ads. *Maybelline's* desire to hone in on the teen cosmetics market began with focus group recommendations to coordinate lip and nail colors. Teenage girls used terms such as ''a perfect match'' and ''made for each other'' to boost the creation of 20 matching lip and nail lines under the Shine Free brand—which also includes face makeup products, mascara, and eye shadow. The resulting TV commercials show off ''an attitude''—not just a product—to appeal to teen-buying tastes.

Focus Group Research. Focus groups, for better or worse, are most marketers' main method of qualitative research—or going beyond the hard numbers to find out why consumers behave as they do. Critics of the emphasis on focus groups point to the fact that good ideas—whether a 30-second commercial or a new product or concept—often get killed prematurely because they didn't find favor with a focus group. Another disadvantage is cost. Moderators, the renting of facilities with two-way mirrors, microphones, and special video setups, and recruiting and paying the respondents can cost anywhere from $2,500 to $4,000 per group. Most clients conduct five or six focus groups around the country. Bruce Meyers, director of research services at BBDO, says: ''Focus groups should never be used as a replacement for quantitative research. But they can work well to determine consumer reaction to certain language in a TV commerical or in the development process for creative.''[7]

Focus groups can elicit spontaneous reactions to products or ads. A trained leader conducts a group of 10 or 12 consumers, usually prime prospects—that is, people who consume relatively large amounts of the product being researched (see Exhibit 15.9). In the food category, for example, respondents would be chosen from the 27 percent of the women who buy 79 percent of prepared cake mixes; in the transportation category, they would be selected from the 20 percent of the men who buy 70 percent of all airline tickets.

[7]Sarah Stiansen, ''How Focus Groups Can Go Astray,'' *Adweek,* December 5, 1988, pp. F.K.4–6.

EXHIBIT 15.9

Copy testing is often conducted *before* the ad is run—either in rough or finished form. Particular attention is focused on the *creative* expression of the ad or commercial. When Bartle Bogle Hegarty, London, wanted to "raise a few eyebrows" for "unspectacular" 501 Levi jeans, it tested a new TV campaign—with an All-American approach. A yuppie couple with car trouble got "help" from a trucker. The stranger took off his "501s" to link the car with his truck—and then he towed the car away! Respondents particularly liked the tag line, "Great for the long haul. . ."

Pretest Research. There are several levels of research aimed at helping advertisers determine how well an ad will perform. Copy testing is done in two stages:

1. Rough copy research is needed to determine if the copy is effectively achieving its goals in terms of both message communication and attitude effects.
2. Finished copy research is done on the final form of the copy to evaluate how well the production process has achieved communication and attitude effects (see Exhibit 15.10).

Remember, copy testing is not a substitute for the other research steps mentioned previously.

Campaign Evaluation Research. Evaluation can be done at various predetermined intervals to measure the effect advertising is having on consumers' awareness, attitudes, and so on. The purpose of this research is to determine if the advertising has achieved its goals (see Exhibit 15.11).

TESTING CREATIVE RESEARCH

Copy testing. *Measuring the effectiveness of ads.*

Creative research takes place within the context of the preceding research stages. This kind of research aids in the development of what to say to the target audience and how to say it. Copy development research attempts to help advertisers decide how to execute approaches and elements. Copy testing is undertaken to aid them in determining whether to run the advertising in the marketplace.

In Chapter 6, PACT (Positioning Advertising Copy Testing) was discussed in the context of the agency-client relationship. Here we need to further examine the role of PACT:

1. A good copy-testing system provides measurements that are relevant to the objectives of the advertising. And, of course, different advertisements have different objectives (e.g., encouraging trial of a product).
2. A primary purpose of copy testing is to help advertisers decide whether to run the advertising in the marketplace. A useful approach is to specify *action standards* before the results are in. Examples of action standards are:
   - Significantly improves perceptions of the brands as measured by ______.
   - Achieves an attention level no lower than ______ percent as measured by ______.
3. A good copy-testing system is based on the following model of human response to communications: the reception of a stimulus, the comprehension of the stimulus, and the response to

EXHIBIT 15.10

These are two in a series of ads with subtle differences to test comprehension and product-benefit recall.

the stimulus. In short, to succeed, an ad must have an effect

- on the eye and the ear—that is, it must be received (*reception*)
- on the mind—that is, it must be understood (*comprehension*)
- on the heart—that is, it must make an impression (*response*)

4. Experience has shown that test results often vary according to the degree of finish of the test.

EXHIBIT 15.11

Effectiveness measures by type of consumer response for copy research.

Response Criterion	*Measurement*
Cognitive (Think)	
• Attention	Eye camera
• Awareness	Day-after recall
Affective (Feel)	
• Attitude	Persuasion
• Feelings	Physiological response
Conative (Do)	
• Purchase intent	Simulated shopping
• Sales	Split cable/scanner

Source: Adapted from John Leckency, "Current Issues in the Measurement of Advertising."

Thus, careful judgment should be exercised when using a less-than-finished version of a test. Sometimes what is lost is inconsequential, at other times it is critical.[8]

Forms of Testing

Each advertiser and agency uses similar but different steps in the testing of creative research. The following are examples of this process.

Concept testing. The target audience evaluation of (alternative) creative strategy. Testing attempts to separate "good" and "bad" ideas and provide insight into factors motivating acceptance or rejection.

Concept Testing. This may be an integral part of creative planning and is undertaken for most clients as a matter of course. Creative concept testing can be defined as the target audience evaluation of (alternative) creative strategy. Specifically, concept testing attempts to separate the "good" ideas from the "bad," to indicate differing degrees of acceptance and to provide insight into factors motivating acceptance or rejection.

There are a number of possible concept tests:

1. *Card concept test.* Creative strategies are presented to respondents in the form of a headline, followed by a paragraph of body copy, on a plain white card. Each concept is on a separate card. Some concepts cannot be tested in card form (e.g., those requiring a high degree of mood, such as concepts based on humor or personalities).
2. *Poster test.* This is similar to a card test except that small posters containing simplified illustrations and short copy are used rather than plain cards without illustrations.
3. *Layout test.* A layout test involves showing a rough copy of a print ad (or artwork of a television commercial with accompanying copy) to respondents. Layout tests are more finished than poster tests, in that they use the total copy and illustration as they will appear in the finished ad. Additionally, whereas a card or poster test measures the appeal of the basic concept, the purpose of the layout test may be to measure more subtle effects such as communication, understanding, and confusion.

Test Commercials. Generally, commercial testing on film or videotape falls into one of four categories:

1. *Animatics.* This is artwork, either cartoons or realistic drawings. Some animatics show limited movement; those that don't are usually called *video storyboards.* Animatics cost from about $1,500 to $4,000 plus artists' fees, although the simplest nonmovement video storyboard may cost as little as $750.
2. *Photomatics.* These are photographs shot in sequence on film. The photos may be stock (from a photo library) or shot on location. Photomatics cost about $10,000 to produce.
3. *Liveamatics.* This involves filming or taping live talent and is very close to the finished commercial. A liveamatic commercial test costs between $10,000 to $20,000 to produce.
4. *Ripamatics.* The commercial is made of footage from other commercials, often taken from ad agency promotion reels. Ripamatics are used many times for experimentation on visual techniques.

Finished Print Tests. This testing procedure can take many forms of measuring the finished ad as it would appear in print. Exhibit 15.12 shows a finished printed ad as consumers would see it.

Finished Commercial Testing. Television testing techniques can generally be classified into two categories:

1. Those that attempt to evaluate a commercial's effectiveness in terms of viewers' recall of a certain aspect of the commercial.
2. Those that attempt to evaluate a commercial's effectiveness in terms of what it motivates a viewer to say or do.

[8]PACT—Positioning Advertising Copy Testing, *The PACT Agencies Report 1982,* pp. 6–25.

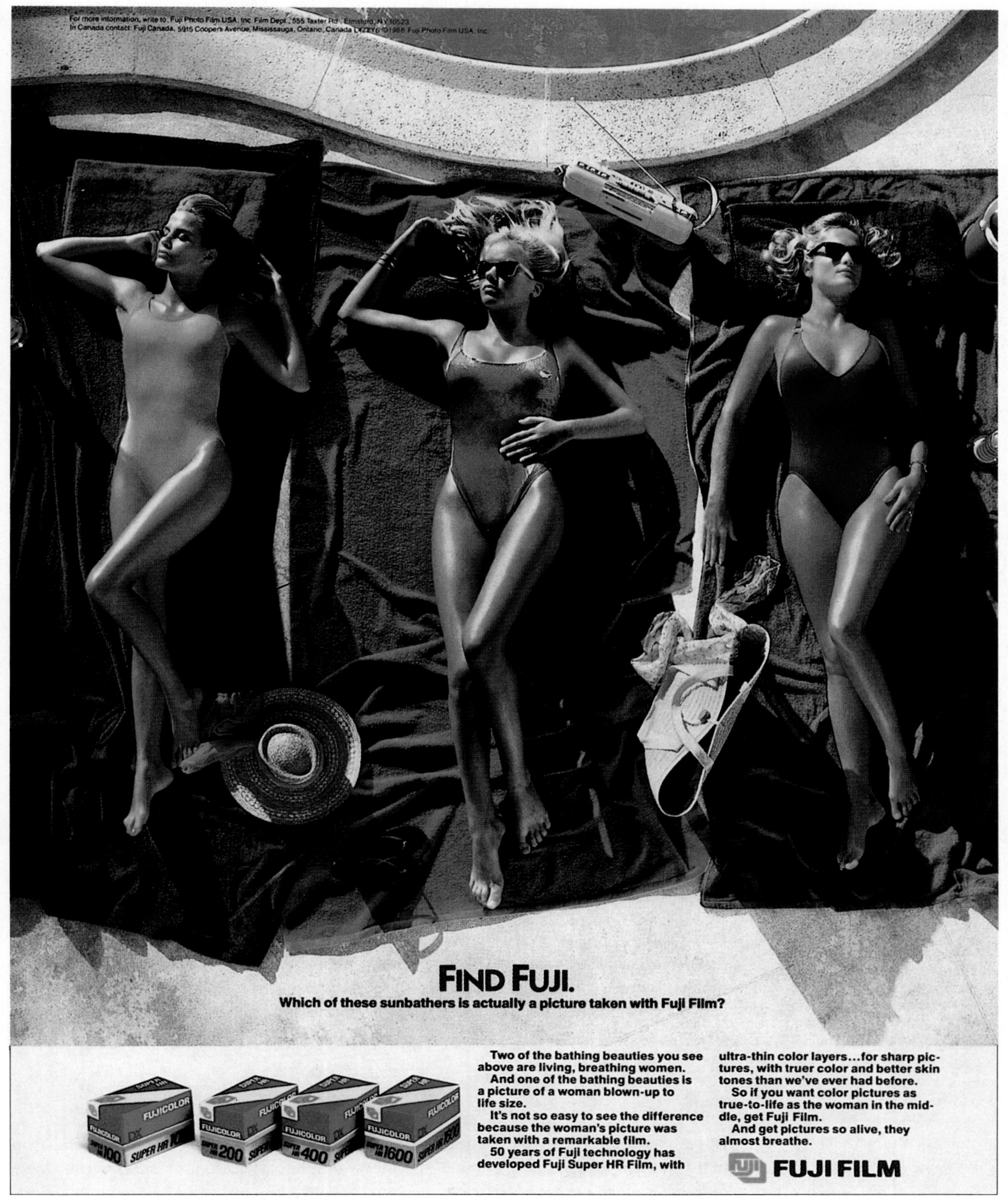

For more information, write to: Fuji Photo Film USA, Inc. Film Dept., 555 Taxter Rd., Elmsford, NY 10523
In Canada contact: Fuji Canada, 5915 Coopers Avenue, Mississauga, Ontario, Canada
©1988 Fuji Photo Film USA, Inc.
FIND FUJI.
Which of these sunbathers is actually a picture taken with Fuji Film?
FUJICOLOR
SUPER HR 100
200
400
1600
Two of the bathing beauties you see above are living, breathing women.
And one of the bathing beauties is a picture of a woman blown-up to life size.
It's not so easy to see the difference because the woman's picture was taken with a remarkable film.
50 years of Fuji technology has developed Fuji Super HR Film, with ultra-thin color layers...for sharp pictures, with truer color and better skin tones than we've ever had before.
So if you want color pictures as true-to-life as the woman in the middle, get Fuji Film.
And get pictures so alive, they almost breathe.
FUJI FILM

EXHIBIT 15.12

Demonstrating the quality of the product.

Recent production technology advances are helping the testing process. The more closely the test spot resembles the finished commercial, the more accurate the test results will be. It is predicted that computer animation will become more economical in the next four or five years, giving rise to more computer-generated artwork in commercial testing.

CASE HISTORY
Prolog Copy Research

Prolog, a division of McCollum/Spielman & Company, has a copy research service that evaluates advertising concepts, storyboards, and rough or finished commercials. Building on what they learned from their child-research division, the Prolog people developed a testing procedure that uses happy faces/sad faces to measure "feelings" about a commercial.

Prolog recruits or intercepts targets at shopping malls. Each respondent sits in front of a television monitor and a special computer keyboard that has five faces down one side hanging from "smile" to a "frown." The procedure goes as follows:

- A respondent first answers a series of demographic questions.
- She or he views eight noncompeting commercials with the test spot always fourth. (If a finished commercial is being tested, all eight commercials will be finished; if an animatic is being tested, all eight will be animatics.)
- The subject sees the eight commercials back to back. The computer then stops the tape, and the screen asks the respondent to write down all the advertisers, brand names, or products she or he can recall.

This measures totally unaided recall. If soft-drink commercials score 87 on average and a test commercial scores 80, it is about average; if the test commercial scores only 20, there is a serious problem.

The procedure used for a new brand is different:

- After viewing the eight commercials and writing down all the brand names she or he can recall, the respondent sees the first four commercials again. The first three are control commercials, the fourth is the test spot.
- The re-viewing instructions tell the respondent to use the face buttons on the keyboard to express feelings about the commercial.
- The first three practice commercials give the respondent a chance to practice with the facial expressions; the fourth measures the respondent's feelings about the test spot.
- Next comes a series of questions. Typically, the first is an open-ended question; then come perception questions; last are the comparative questions.
- After the respondent has answered the diagnostic questions, the computer plays the test commercial once again. This time the commercial stops at five points where the respondent pressed a button. The screen fades out, and the facial expression the respondent chose to express his or her feeling at that point appears, together with the question: "Why were you pressing this face at this point?"

What this test does is collect nonverbal responses at different points in the commercial and ask respondents to interpret their own reactions. Prolog normally tests 100 respondents. Among the things clients get for their $8,000 is a perceptual mapping of a spot's entertainment values, emotional impact, credibility, and product attributes.

POST-TEST RESEARCH

Recall scores are used in *post-test research* for both broadcast and printed media. Each year, Starch measures over 65,000 ads in 700 magazine issues. For an *Advertising Age* special report for the travel category, it identified six 1-page, 4-color ads that performed best in terms of reader "noting"—percentage of readers who remembered having seen the ad in the study magazine. The six winners were *British Airways, Embassy Suites Hotels, Lufthansa German Airlines, Princess Cruises, United Airlines, and the U.S. Virgin Islands.*

Post-test research is used by advertisers as a security check. However, it isn't foolproof. When Life cereal's Mikey campaign was tested, the recall scores of the commercial were weak, although sales of the cereals had increased. The company's decision to continue the campaign despite the low testing scores resulted in one of the country's longest-running commercial characters.

Burke Day-After Recall

Burke has been the premiere company in testing on-the-air television commercials for many years. Burke uses telephone interviews the day after a commercial is run, then gives the advertiser a report on how many people saw and heard the commercial, a summary of all that respondents remembered about the commercial (recall of key advertising messages), and a verbatim transcript of all the ideas they recalled from the commercial (playback).[9]

[9]W. Keith Hafer and Gordon E. White, *Advertising Writing* (St. Paul, MN: West Publishing Co., 1989), p. 256.

Exhibit 15.13 is an example of a television commercial that tested well. This Motorman commercial for Precision Tune achieved a 42 percent recall score against the category norm of 27 percent. Burke Day-After Recall is the kind of measurement that gives advertisers something to compare their advertising to in evaluating its effectiveness.

Starch Reports: Who Reads Magazine Ads?

To find out how effective an ad is, we use research like the Starch Reports. They do personal interviews of readers and, by projecting the results, determine how many people who read the publication noted your ad, associated it with the product, and read most of it.

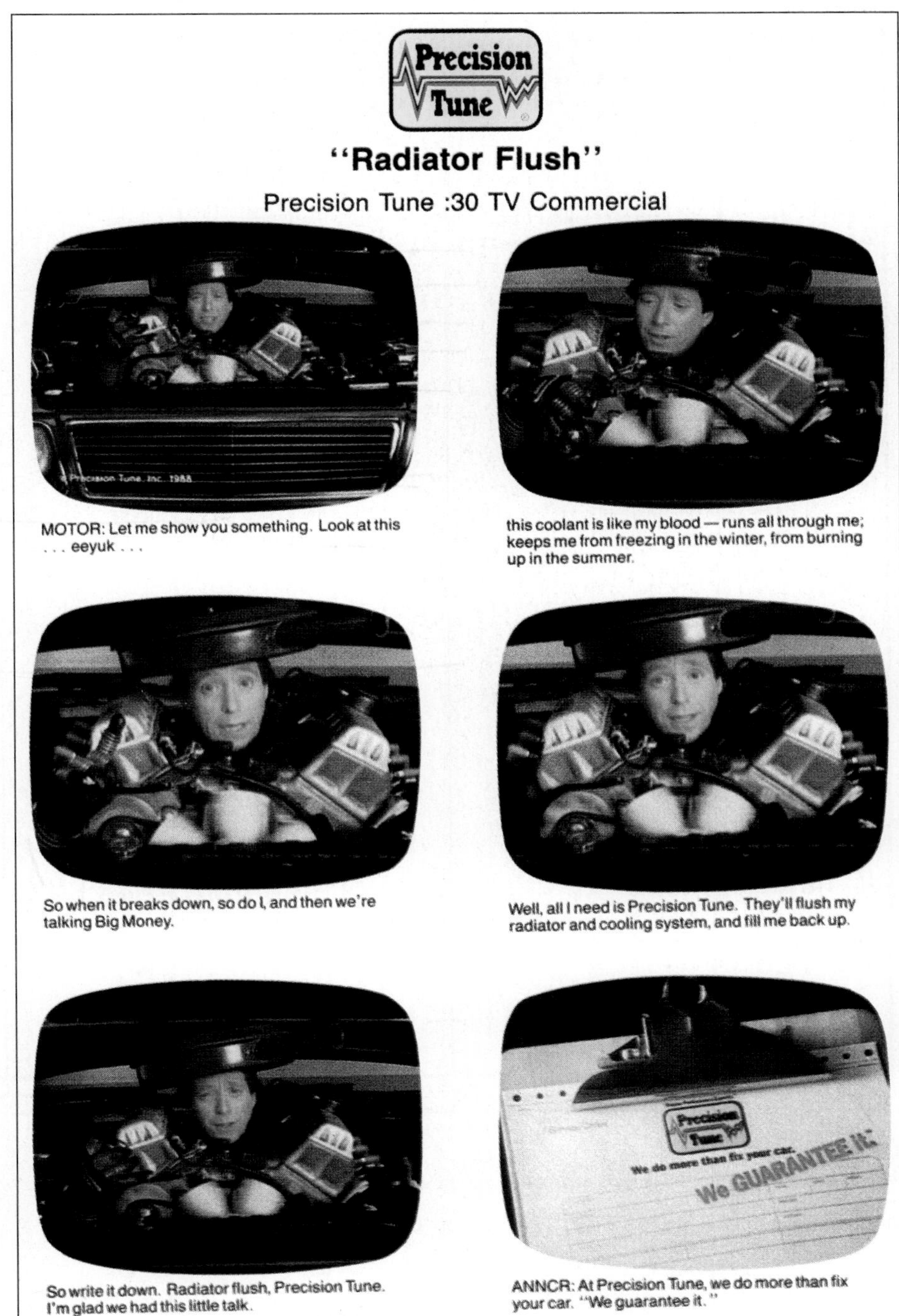

Precision Tune
"Radiator Flush"
Precision Tune :30 TV Commercial
MOTOR: Let me show you something. Look at this . . . eeyuk . . .
this coolant is like my blood — runs all through me; keeps me from freezing in the winter, from burning up in the summer.
So when it breaks down, so do I, and then we're talking Big Money.
Well, all I need is Precision Tune. They'll flush my radiator and cooling system, and fill me back up.
So write it down. Radiator flush, Precision Tune. I'm glad we had this little talk.
We GUARANTEE It.
ANNCR: At Precision Tune, we do more than fix your car. "We guarantee it."

EXHIBIT 15.13

This creative commercial received fantastic recall scores. (Courtesy: PrecisionTune and Leslie Advertising, Inc., Greenville, SC.)

READERSHIP REPORT

For the private use of purchasers only. Reproduction of this report in whole or in part is prohibited. Any reference to this report or any figures in this report in publishers' or advertising agencies' paid advertising or in their printed promotion pieces, must be submitted to the Starch Organization before release. Reference by name to competitive publications or advertisements is expressly prohibited. Use of this report or any figures from this report by non-subscribers is expressly prohibited.

Conclusions drawn from figures shown in this report may not be represented as the opinion of the Starch Organization.

PAGE 3

83 ADS 1/2 PAGE AND OVER
READER'S DIGEST NOVEMBER

MEN READERS

PRODUCT CATEGORIES			COST	RANK IN ISSUE		PERCENTAGES			READERS PER DOLLAR			COST RATIOS		
PAGE	SIZE & COLOR	ADVERTISER	PENNIES PER READER	BY NUMBER OF READERS	BY COST PER READER	NOTED	ASSOCIATED	READ MOST	NOTED	ASSOCIATED	READ MOST	NOTED	ASSOCIATED	READ MOST
(CONT.)		CAMERAS/PHOTOGRAPHIC SUPPLIES												
100	1P4B	KODAK EK4 INSTANT CAMERA	1.0	12	6	56	50	20	112	100	40	187	200	400
213	V1/2P4	EASTMAN KODAK COMPANY G P	.9	33	3	36	31	13	131	112	47	218	224	470
		LUGGAGE/LEATHER GOODS												
238	1P4B	AMERICAN TOURISTER LUGGAGE	1.4	28	22	38	35	12	76	70	24	127	140	240
		PETS/PET FOODS/PET SUPPLIES												
77	1P4B	TABBY CANNED CAT FOOD OFFER	2.6	49	58	30	19	2	60	38	4	100	76	40
		BUSINESS PROPOSALS/RECRUITING												
282	V1/2P	QSP INC BUSINESS PROPOSITION	1.8	64	34	17	13	5	74	57	22	123	114	220
		FLOOR COVERING												
267	1P4B	CONGOLEUM SHINYL VINYL FLOOR	2.0	40	41	34	25	9	68	50	18	113	100	180
		MAJOR APPLIANCES												
8	1P4	SEARS KENMORE COMPACTORS	2.2	45	50	27	23	5	54	46	10	90	92	100
40	X 1S4B	WHITE-WESTINGHOUSE RANGE	4.0	48	71	31	21	4	36	25	5	60	50	50
55	1P4B	K-MART/WHIRLPOOL WASHER & DRYER	1.6	32	27	41	32	1	82	64	2	137	128	20
206	1P	WHIRLPOOL CORPORATION G P	2.4	58	55	19	17	*	46	41	*	77	82	*
248	1P4	KITCHENAID DISHWASHER	3.1	60	65	20	16	2	40	32	4	67	64	40
		SMALL HHLD. APPLIANCES/EQUIP.												
7	1P4	WESTCLOX CLOCKS	1.5	30	25	39	33	2	78	66	4	130	132	40
48	1S4B	K-MART/SMALL APPLIANCES	2.0	17	45	52	46	6	56	49	6	93	98	60
287	1P4B	MR. COFFEE BREWER/FILTERS	1.4	27	20	39	36	8	78	72	16	130	144	160
		RADIOS/TV SETS/PHONOGRAPHS												
20	1P4B	MAGNAVOX TOUCH-TUNE COLOR TV	1.4	28	22	38	35	10	76	70	20	127	140	200
51	1P4B	K-MART/CAPEHART STEREO SYS	1.1	17	10	52	46	11	104	92	22	173	184	220
53	1P4B	K-MART/CAPEHART 1000 STEREO ENSEMBLE	1.0	14	8	54	49	18	108	98	36	180	196	360
57	1P4B	K-MART/PORTABLE RADIO & CASSETTE RECORDER	1.1	19	11	48	45	13	96	90	26	160	180	260
89	1P4B	ZENITH CHROMACOLOR II TV	.9	6	2	60	58	15	120	116	30	200	232	300
229	1P4B	ZENITH ALLEGRO CONSOLE	1.2	22	13	46	43	16	92	86	32	153	172	320
		BUILDING MATERIALS												
17		OWENS-CORNING FIBERGLAS INSULATION/AMERICAN GAS ASSOCIATION SEE COMMUN/PUBLIC UTILITY												
		BLDG. EQUIP./FIXTURES/SYSTEMS												
90	1P4	GE HOME SENTRY SMOKE ALARM	1.0	14	8	51	49	27	102	98	54	170	196	540
		MEDIAN READERS/DOLLAR							60	50	10			

* LESS THAN 1/2 OF ONE PERCENT.

READERS PER DOLLAR ARE BASED ON 12,965,000 MEN READERS AND PUBLISHED ONE-TIME SPACE RATES. READER FIGURES ARE OBTAINED FROM 18,006,799 U.S. A.B.C. CIRC. TIMES MEN PRIMARY READERS PER COPY FROM STARCH ESTIMATES.

EXHIBIT 15.14
A Starch Report showing how well ads get attention and readership.

SUMMARY

Advertising is a people business. Successful advertisers know who their prospects are, and to whatever extent is practical, what their needs and motives are, which results in the purchase of one product and the rejection of another. Consumer behavior is the result of a complex network of influences based on the psychological, sociological, and anthropological makeup of the individual.

Advertising rarely, if ever, changes these influences, but rather channels the needs and wants of consumers toward specific products and brands. Advertising is a mirror of society. The advertiser influences people by offering solutions to their needs and problems, not by creating these needs. The role of the advertiser is to act as a monitor of the changing face of society.

Market research—upfront research—tells us about the product, the market, the consumer, and the competition. After market research, we do advertising research to get the data we need to develop and refine an advertising strategy and message. In research strategy development, information by itself has no value. The data only become useful if they are sifted and reviewed for their relevance to marketing and advertising issues.

A new typology of American consumers, Values and Lifestyle 2 (VALS 2), is better at predicting consumer purchasing decisions than VALS 1. Advertisers can use VALS 2 typology to segment markets, develop marketing strategies, refine product concepts, position their brands, and develop advertising and media campaigns.

The traditional role of research is changing in many of the major agencies. Under new organization structures, many agency researchers have been renamed account planners or marketing planners. The account person represents the client's perspective and the account planner represents the consumer's point of view in the strategic planning process. Today, advertisers are performing more research themselves; others are buying more sophisticated research from independent research companies.

In creative research, there are a number of stages of testing available to the advertiser, ranging from concept testing and commercial testing techniques to finished print and commercial tests. Because of the expense of producing ads, advertisers feel compelled to evaluate concepts and ads prior to buying expensive media schedules to reach consumers.

QUESTIONS

1. What is the role of the social sciences in advertising?
2. How is CUBE (Comprehensive Understanding of Buyer Environments) research used by advertisers?
3. VALS 2 classifies consumers along what two key dimensions?
4. What is single source data?
5. Differentiate between card concept and layout tests.
6. What is the purpose of Burke-Day-After-Recall testing?

SUGGESTED EXERCISES

1. Find three print ads aimed at women that reflect different lifestyles.
2. Find a print ad selling a sports product. Develop three different ad concepts for the same product.
3. Analyze the reasons for your purchasing the deodorant or toothpaste you are currently using. Be specific.
4. Identify and describe your favorite national fast food store. Give specific reasons why this particular company appeals to you.

READINGS

ALWITT, LINDA F., AND ANDREW A. MITCHELL, Eds.: *Psychological Processes and Advertising Effects* (Hillsdale, N.J.: Lawrence Erlbaum, 1985).

DESHPANDE, ROHIT, AND PATRICK F. MCGRAW: "Organizational Culture and Marketing: Defining the Research Agenda," *Journal of Marketing,* Vol. 53, No. 1, 1989, pp. 16–34.

FLETCHER, ALAN D., AND THOMAS A. BOWERS: *Fundamentals of Advertising Research,* 3rd Edition (Belmont, Calif.: Wadsworth Publishing Company, 1988).

KINNER, THOMAS C., AND JAMES R. TAYLOR: *Marketing Research,* 3rd Edition (New York: McGraw-Hill, 1987).

LAZER, WILLIAM: *Handbook of Demographics for Marketing and Advertising* (Lexington, Mass.: Lexington Books, 1987).

PLUMMER, JOSEPH T.: "The Role of Copy Research in Multinational Advertising," *Journal of Advertising Research,* Vol. 26, No. 2, 1986, pp. 11–14.

SCHWARTZ, JOE: "Back to the Source," *American Demographics,* Vol. 11, No. 1, 1989, pp. 22–29.

SUDMAN, SEYMOUR, AND NORBERT SCHWARTZ: "Contributions of Cognitive Psychology to Advertising Research," *Journal of Advertising Research,* Vol. 29, No. 3, 1989, pp. 43–53.

STEWART, DAVID W.: "Measures, Methods, and Models in Advertising Research," *Journal of Advertising Research,* Vol. 29, No. 3, 1989, pp. 54–59.

YALE, LAURA, AND MARY C. GILLY: "Trends in Advertising Research," *Journal of Advertising,* Vol. 17, No. 1, 1988, pp. 12–22.

SIXTEEN

Creating the Copy

Demand for *branded products and memorable advertising* go hand-in-hand. *Nike's* recent resurgence in the athletic shoe field has been attributed to its startling commercials and ads—high on visual images and scarce on "clutter" copy. New ads in *World Tennis* magazine feature a 2-page spread, each with a single "blown-up" sneaker—with captions: "Regular" and "Extra Strength."

The power of advertising is as great today as ever. John Pepper, president of Procter & Gamble, says: "I believe in advertising quite simply because I have seen throughout 25 years that the correlation between profitable business growth on our brands and having *great copy* on our brands isn't 25 percent, it's not 50 percent. It is 100 percent. I have not seen a single P&G brand sustain profitable volume growth for more than a couple of years without having great advertising copy."[1] Yet ask a consumer if he or she is persuaded by ads and the answer is usually a very firm "Absolutely not!" And more times than not, consumers do say no to ads. But they also say yes millions of times a day.

THE NATURE AND USE OF APPEALS

Advertising is written to appeal to consumers' needs for *satisfaction*—which is greater than just the physical product. While business fliers *know* Northwest Airlines will fly them to their destination, they may also feel reassured that the airline is putting new emphasis on comfort and efficiency. From additional first class seats to increased baggage and reservation service, their ads stress the flying "extras" which make "business a pleasure."

Advertising motivates people by appealing to their problems, desires, and goals—and by offering a means of solving their problems, satisfying their desires, and achieving their goals. People purchase products and services because of the benefits they expect from them. As discussed in Chapter 4, to the individual customer, a product is not so much a physical object as a bundle of satisfactions. Automobiles provide transportation, but also status and social and job mobility. Chrysler's TC, built by Maserati, is advertised this way: "When Maserati builds a new convertible, you can expect full-gauge instrumentation in a sea of soft Italian leather and handcrafted European coachwork." The promise includes much more than reliable transporation. Clothing is worn to impress others and to make a statement about oneself, as well as to keep warm. Thus, a Worthington women's clothing ad appeals to working women: "Everyone wonders how you can remain sharp and upbeat when you're juggling two full-time jobs—the second of which begins the moment you arrive home. Worthington Classic

[1] John Pepper, "Great Advertising—It's Purely and Simply a Must," *Viewpoint,* January–February 1989, pp. 12–13.

EXHIBIT 16.1

The ad captures the exuberance a woman experiences wearing hose that make her legs feel good. It also reminds the reader of the high-energy television commercial for the same product. (Courtesy: L'eggs. Photo by George Holz.)

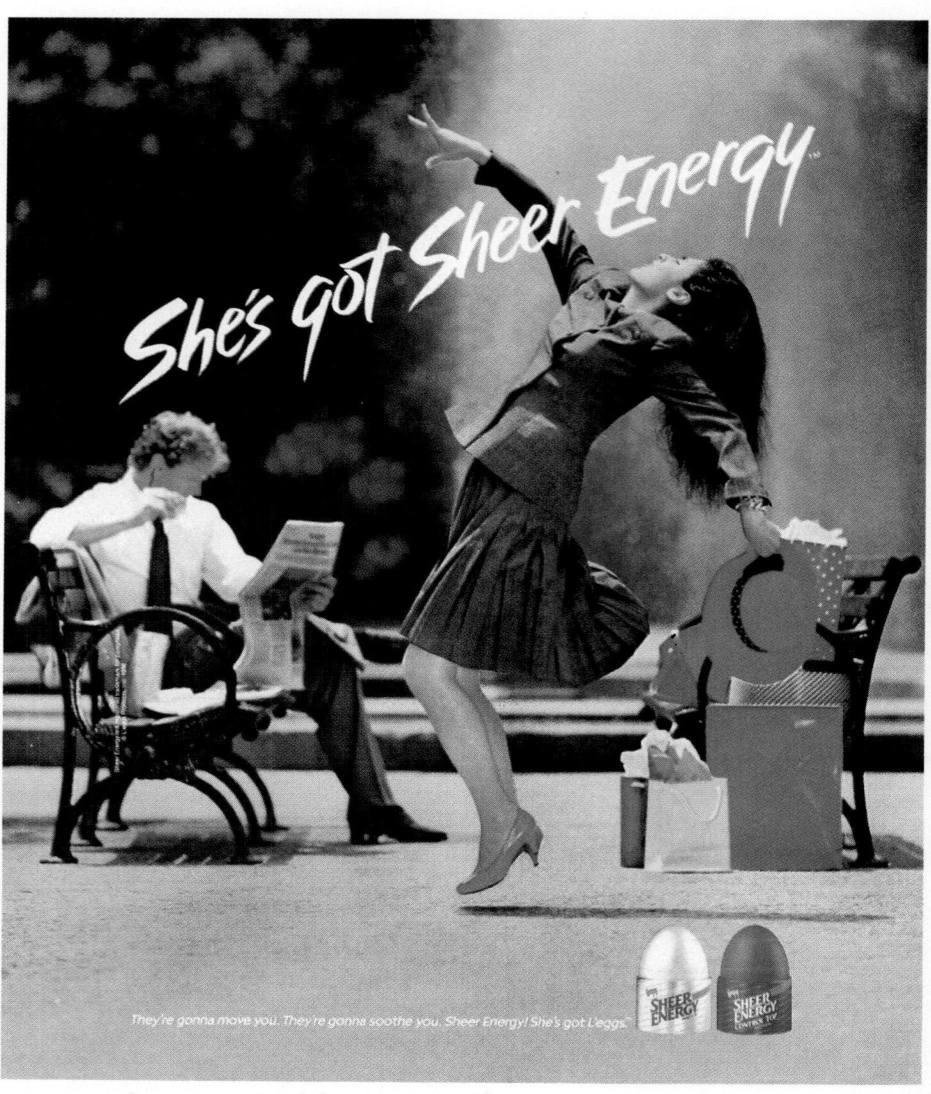

reflections of the woman who wears it.'' The L'eggs ''She's got Sheer Energy'' ad in Exhibit 16.1 appeals to a woman's desire to look fashionable and feel great at the same time.

Selecting the Appeal

Most products have a number of positive appeals that could be successfully promoted. The idea is to choose the one that is most important to the majority of consumers. Since selecting the primary appeal is the key to any advertising campaign, many research techniques have been developed to find which appeal to use. In the last chapter, we discussed some of the aspects of advertising research that help us make strategic and creative decisions. Here we will specifically discuss three techniques to help us decide on appeals: concept testing, focus groups, and motivational research.

Concept Testing. Concept testing is a method to determine the best of a number of possible appeals to use in your advertising. A creative concept is defined as a simple explanation or description of the advertising idea behind the product.

A company planning a promotional campaign for a new line of rental cars listed several appeals that might influence prime prospects to try the product:

In selecting the most important *appeal* to use, the advertiser might present consumers with several *concepts*, from which they choose the one(s) they prefer. When Quaker Oats decided to renew advertising in 1980, consumers "selected" ads which stressed the oatmeal's *nutritional value*. The company, then, decided to treat the age-old brand as "a new product," with actor Wilford Brimley promoting oatmeal as a way for the elderly to avoid cholesterol. Now—*new targets*. . .from kids to grandpops.

1. The lowest-priced full-size car you can rent.
2. Our cars have more extras at no extra cost.
3. Free air-conditioning in each car we rent.
4. No hidden extras when you rent from us. The price we quote is the price you pay.
5. We guarantee the price and the car you reserve.

Using cards with the theme statement and/or sometimes rough layouts, the advertiser tries to obtain:

- A rank of order of consumer appeal of the various concepts
- Diagnostic data explaining why the concepts were ranked as they were

In the case of the car rental company, a test of vacation travelers found that one benefit stood out: The lowest-priced full-size car. The second benefit was: No hidden extras.

One drawback of concept testing is that consumers can react only to the themes presented to them. You may find that they have chosen the best of several bad concepts.

Focus groups offer opportunities for "free" discussion of *a product*—its problems, its attributes, and its benefits for the user. Often, advertisers can use the respondents' words to promote the product's "unique" properties. Focus group research "uncovered" the missing ingredient in 7-Up—*caffeine*. After hearing respondents extolling that unique "virtue" in several meetings across the country, 7-Up executives decided to promote the feature. It prompted other non-colas, like gingerale to do the same—and eventually "forced" the cola makers to come out with non-caffeine versions of their products.

Focus Groups. In the last chapter, we discussed the nature, cost, and typical procedure of focus group research. Here we examine the role of focus groups in selecting the primary appeal. Generally, the interviewer starts by discussing the product category, then proceeds to products within the category, and finally brings up past or current ads for a product or products. And, of course, the focus group can be used to test several new ad concepts of the appeal of print, storyboard, or more finished ad forms. The creative team watching from behind the two-way mirror has the opportunity to hear how participants perceive its products, ads, and ideas.

The leader of the group directs the conversation to determine what problems or "hang-ups" the prime prospects associate with the product. Thus, the answers are not predetermined by the advertiser or the researcher. Rather, they are direct responses to the product and the benefits and problems these prime prospects see in it. Further, because the research is done in a group, people feel less inhibited than they do in one-on-one interviews. The result is usually a good evaluation of the problems, attributes, and particular strengths and weaknesses of the product from the consumer's point of view.

One example of this type research was conducted not long ago by the Atlanta Symphony Orchestra. Its agency interviewed two groups of prime prospects: attendees at regular-season symphony concerts and pop concert goers. The symphony's management wanted to discover prospects' attitudes about programming, length of concerts, and types of soloists. In this case, the results were not surprising. They confirmed management's original perceptions, but provided a more tangible basis for arriving at strategic marketing decisions.

In using motivational research, the researcher seeks the "underlying reasons" for consumer behavior. Researchers discovered that department and specialty store shoppers "refused" J.C. Penney—because of its variety store merchandise, such as gardening supplies and tires. Management decided to upgrade JCP's image by introducing Poyot, an exclusive line of French skincare and makeup products. The company plans an extensive in-store promotional program, including sampling and personal appearances by Mavis Michelle, Poyot's vice president of sales.

Motivational Research. Motivational research has its foundations in the psychoanalytic techniques of Sigmund Freud. Popularized by Ernest Dichter during the 1950s as a marketing tool, this type of research seeks to find the underlying reasons for consumer behavior. Its value rests on the premise that consumers are motivated by emotions they may not be consciously aware of.

Motivational research uses unstructured techniques to elicit open-ended responses that are recorded verbatim. The idea is that among these responses there will be the kernel of an unanticipated consumer motivation that can be translated into a unique advertising appeal. Though motivational research has lost some of its glamour, it still has its advocates in the advertising community.

All research data must be interpreted. In fact, data interpretation may be the most crucial step in effective advertising research. It requires insight and skill. We also must remember that many advertising appeals result from intuition and personal observation. It was an intuition, not research, that prompted Hal Riney & Partners to use the fictitious characters Bartles and Jaymes, not only to name a new wine product from Gallo Wineries, but also to appear as spokesmen for the product in a continuing series of amusing commercials.

Whether created by research or in other ways, the appeal provides the basis of the advertising structure. This appeal can be expressed in many ways. Right now, we will discuss how to make use of words, called *copy,* in presenting the appeal.[2]

STRUCTURE OF AN ADVERTISEMENT

In some instances, the promise is the whole advertisement.

Surf Removes Dirt and Odor

Lipton. The Only Naturally Decaffeinated Tea Bag.

Usually, however, a fuller exposition is required, in which case the promise can act as the headline—the first step in the structure of the advertisement. Most ads are presented in this order:

- Promise of benefit (the headline)
- Spelling out of promise (the subheadline; optional)
- Amplification of story (as needed)
- Proof of claim (as needed)
- Action to take (if not obvious)

The Headline

The *headline,* as the "interest grabber" for the prospect, should *entice* the reader to read on. *Questions* work well as headlines—providing they ask the "right" questions. *Hammermill Papers* ask "What's a desktop publishing system without a desktop paper?"—*to business readers* in *Business Week, Fortune,* and *Forbes.* The copy "quickly" describes the problem of the "wrong" paper—and then remedies the dilemma with "a special family of desktop papers—to make type and graphics come out razor-sharp and clear."

The headline is the most important part of an ad. It is the first thing read, and it should arouse the interest of the consumer so that the person wants to keep on reading and get to know more about the product being sold. If the headline doesn't excite the interest of the particular group of prime prospects the advertiser wants to reach, the rest of the ad will probably go unread.

No formula can be given for writing a good headline. However, there are several factors that should be considered in evaluating an effective headline:

- It should use short, simple words, usually no more than ten.
- They should include an invitation to the prospect, primary product benefits, name of the brand, and an interest-provoking idea to gain readership of the rest of the ad.
- The words should be selective, appealing only to prime prospects.
- They should contain an action verb.
- They should give enough information so that the consumer who reads only the headline learns something about the product and its benefit.

Obviously, many effective headlines violate one or more of these guidelines. However, when you write a headline that excludes any of these points, ask yourself: Would this headline be more effective if it adhered to the guidelines?

---

[2]The term *copy* is a carryover from the days in printing when a compositor, given a manuscript to set in type, was told to copy it. Before long, the manuscript itself became known as copy. In the *creation* of a printed ad, copy refers to all the reading matter in the ad. However, in the *production* of print ads, copy refers to the entire subject being reproduced—words and pictures alike. This is one of those instances in advertising when the same word is used in different senses, a practice that all professions and crafts seem to enjoy because it bewilders the uninitiated.

Most headlines fall into one of four categores:

1. Headlines that present a new benefit.
2. Headlines that directly promise an existing benefit.
3. Curiosity-invoking and provocative headlines.
4. Selective headlines (often combined with one of the others).

Whether promising a new *benefit* or reminding consumers of *existing benefits*, headlines can capture the reasons why consumers use particular products. *Hugo Boss* fashions for men "reminds" its targets that style is "Never Out of Fashion"—against a backdrop of "stylish" males.

Headlines That Present a New Benefit. The moment of peak interest in a product is when it offers a new benefit. That is why, in our innovative society, you often see headlines such as these:

Avis Gives Delta Frequent Flyers a New Lift.
(*Avis*)

Now, feed your entire garden and lawn in minutes.
(*Miracle Gro*)

Finally . . . Equal Treatment for Hands and Nails.
(*Hands & Nail Formula Lotion*)

And now, a word to those who'd like an unscented beauty bar.
(*Unscented Dove*)

Headlines That Directly Promise an Existing Benefit. Products can't be offering new benefits all the time, of course, so headlines often remind consumers of a product's existing features:

The more you travel, the more you appreciate the Clarion difference.
(*Clarion Inns*)

Benchmark performance. Lifetime warranty.
(*Texas Instruments*)

You'll probably spend ten years with your next carpet.
Spend a moment reading why it ought be Du Pont.
(*Du Pont*)

By invoking *curiosity*, the advertiser may get the attention of an otherwise disinterested audience. By using an additional fold inside the front cover of *Time*, Oldsmobile uses this headline alone to invoke curiosity—"To give you more space. . ." The black background of space is the only illustration which appears on the first page. Inside, of course, the new 1990 Cutlass Supreme SL "blasts off."

Curiosity-Invoking and Provocative Headlines. As a change of pace from direct-promise headlines, an advertiser may challenge the curiosity of readers, prompt them to read further, and lead them to the key message:

Fire the Chauffeur.
(*Porsche*)

The Real Poop on Fertilizer.
(*Osmocote Plant Food*)

What it's like to be a gold widow at Grand Cypress Resort.
(*Hyatt Resorts*)

Run Around Naked. Kinda.
(*Nike Air Flow;* see Exhibit 16.2)

Neutral country attacks Germany and Japan.
(*Saab*)

Remember, though, readers do not like to be tricked into reading something that fails to answer their questions or relate the challenge to their self-interest.

Selective Headlines. Readers looking through a magazine or newspaper are more likely to read an ad they think concerns them personally than one that talks to a broad audience. The selective headline aimed at a particular prime prospect who would be most interested in the product is often used.

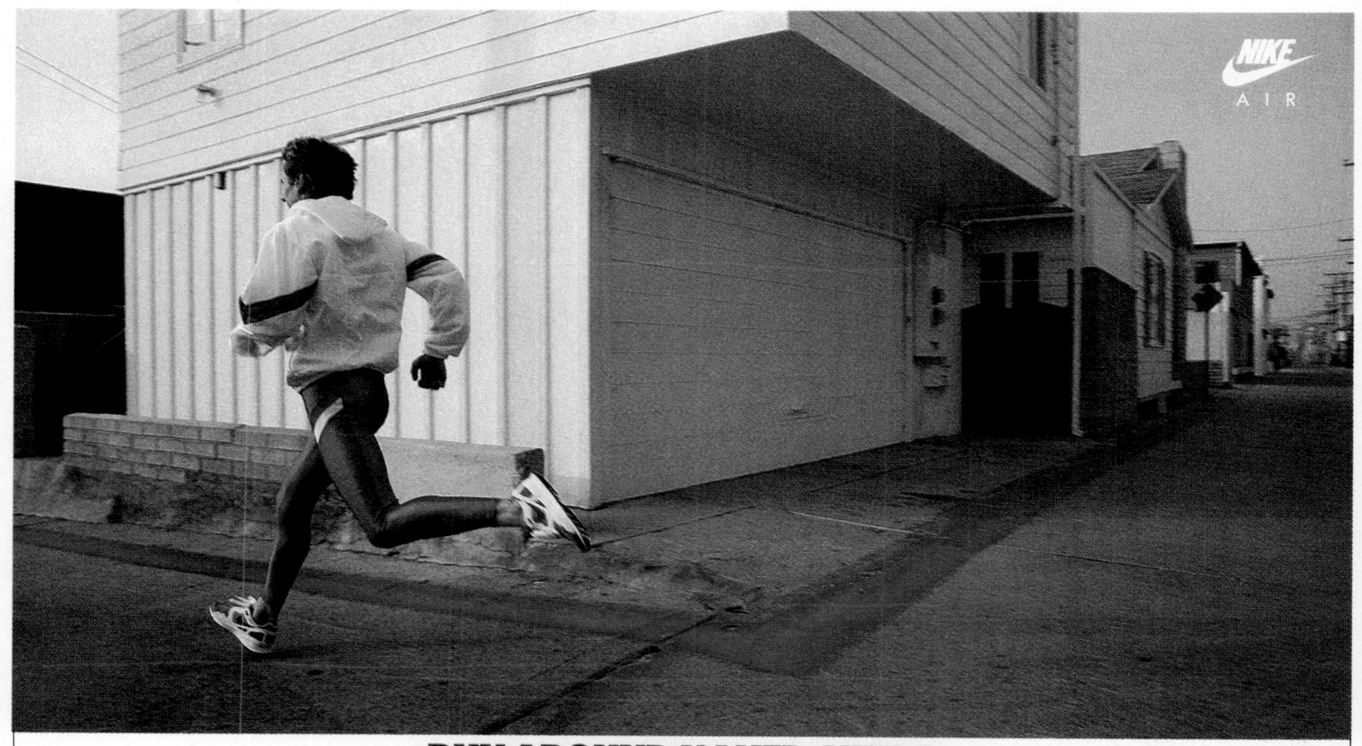

NIKE
AIR
RUN AROUND NAKED. KINDA.
We are talking a *very* light shoe. Try 8.5 ounces in a men's size 9. Oh, it's a training flat, okay. With a Phylon midsole, a 4-way stretch fabric toe, and Nike-Air. It's the Nike Air Flow. Give it a run. Normally, when something feels this good you hope nobody's watching.

EXHIBIT 16.2
The strong illustration and provocative headline attract the reader to this creative ad. (Courtesy: Nike.)

In selecting certain groups out of a general audience to address an appeal, the advertiser may capture the larger segment of product users. *Southpoint* magazine's publishers are targeting the southern region of the country, so their headline reads, "Today's South is ready for a bigger, broader point of view . . . are you?" They're obviously excluding other regions' residents, which is their intention.

Here are four such headlines:

To All Men and Women
To All Young Men and Women
To All College Men and Women
To All College Seniors

The first headline is addressed to the greatest number of readers, but it would be of least interest to any one of them. Each succeeding headline reduces the size of the audience it addresses, and improves the chances of attracting that particular group.

Besides addressing them directly, headlines can appeal to a particular group by mentioning a problem they have in common:

People who have no time for laundry have Speed Queen.

(*Speed Queen*)

Is gentle gentle enough?

(*Clairol Instant Beauty*)

Another vital quality in headlines is specificity. "A sewing machine that's convertible" is better than "A sewing machine with an unusual feature." In fact, specificity is vital to the entire copy of the ad.

The Subheadline

A headline must say something important to the reader. The actual number of words is not the most important factor; long headlines have been known to work as well as short ones. If the message is long, it can be conveyed with a main headline and a subhead-

line. The subheadline can spell out the promise presented in the headline. It can be longer than the headline, it can invite further reading, and it can serve as a transition to the opening paragraph of the copy. For example:
Headline:

Put the whole word in your hand.

Subheadline:

Save $700 on a Radio Shack handheld or $200 on a mobile cellular phone.
(*Radio Shack*)

Subheadlines can be used to "explain" or "defend" the headline. The headline, "Finally an intelligent alternative to the personal computer," leaves the reader "hanging." The subhead "answers" the question—"Smith Corona introduces the world's first laptop word processor."

Headline:

Now, ImageStudio captures the excitement of live video.

Subheadline:

Introducing QuickCapture.
(*Letraset Data Translation*)

Headline:

Introducing Tide with Bleach.

Subheadline:

It'll knock your socks off. And it'll get'em whiter.
(*Tide with Bleach*)

Amplification

To amplify is to explain in body copy what was "hinted at" in the headline and subheadline. In introducing *Desk Mate* to non-technical computer users, Tandy knew it had to include more than pictures and a few headlines. It's headline says DM is "friendly"—the copy provides details of its easy useability, popular programs, and free demonstrations at participating dealers.

The headline is followed by the body copy of the ad. It is here that you present your case for the product and explain how the promise in the headline will be fulfilled. What you say, how deep you go, depends on the amount of information your prime prospect needs at this point in the buying process. A high-cost product, such as a refrigerator or an electric range, probably calls for more explanation than a low-cost product, such as a soup with a new flavor. If a product has many technical advances, such as a new home computer, there probably will not be sufficient room to give a detailed explanation of all its features. In this case, explain just enough to make your prime prospect want to go to a dealer to see a demonstration and be sold in the store.

Amplification should emphasize those product or service features that are of primary importance, but that cannot be included in the headline. A Sun Line ad describes its features in this way (see Exhibit 16.3).

OUR PASSENGERS ARE SPOILED.
NOT OUR DESTINATIONS.

Sun Line sails to islands more likely to be overrun with flowers than with tourists. Because we bypass the crowded tourist centers. . . . Aboard the Stella Oceanis. An intimate cruise ship that carries only 280 passengers. So service is more personal. The friendships closer. . . . Off the ship we offer snorkeling, shopping sprees and a special landing craft to explore secluded beaches that ships can't reach.

The Sun Line ad stops readers with a provocative headline, then immediately explains the kind of islands its ships go to, how Sun Line ships are different from most cruise ships, the activities they offer, where the ships depart from and the lengths of the cruises, savings for early booking, and where to get information.

Our Passengers Are Spoiled. Not Our Destinations.

Sun Line sails to islands more likely to be overrun with flowers than with tourists. Because we bypass the crowded tourist centers. And take your clients, instead, to where the Caribbean is still Caribbean. Like St. Maarten. Soufrieres. Barbados. Bequia. Antigua. Castries. Virgin Gorda. And Tortola. And we take them there in luxury. Aboard the Stella Oceanis. An intimate cruise ship that carries only 280 passengers. So the service is more personal. The friendships closer. On board they'll enjoy classic Continental cuisine and roomy, comfortable cabins. Off the ship we offer snorkeling, shopping sprees and a special landing craft to explore secluded beaches that ships can't reach. We depart from St. Croix for 7- and 14-day cruises through the Caribbean. Book early and you can save your clients up to $300 per person. For reservations or more information, call Sun Line toll-free at: 1-800-872-6400. In New York, 212-397-6400.

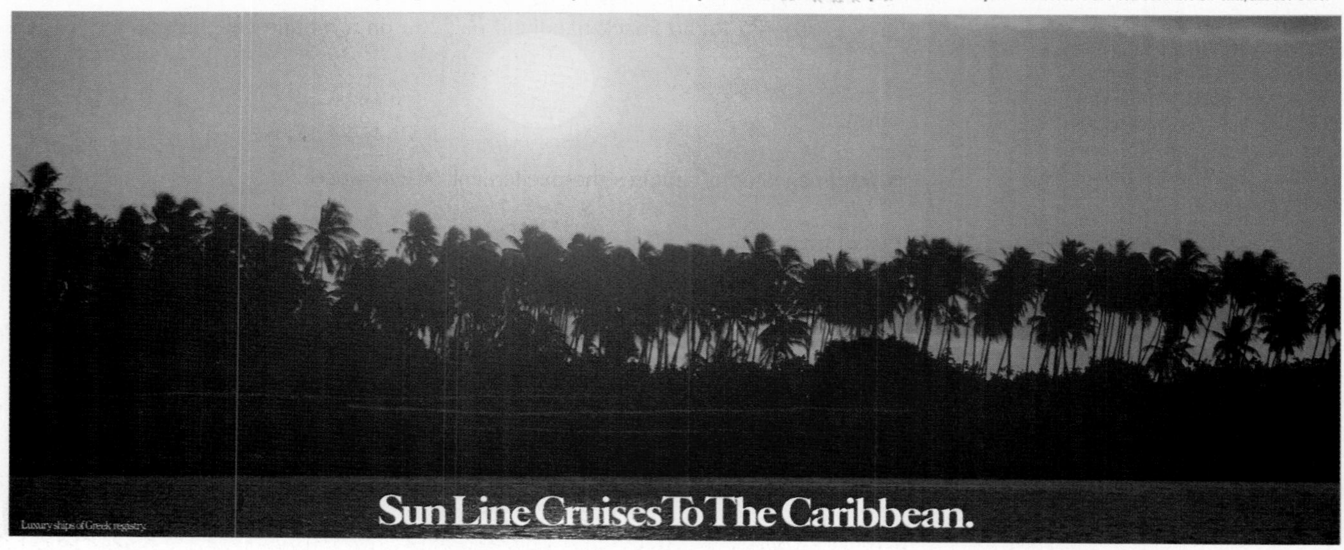

Luxury ships of Greek registry.
Sun Line Cruises To The Caribbean.

EXHIBIT 16.3

The body copy supplies critical information about cruises offered. (Courtesy: Sun Line Cruises/ Cole Henderson Drake, Inc.)

In addition to providing information, the amplification can build confidence in the company's resourcefulness. The Fireman's Fund Insurance Companies' Inland Marine division ad talks about how "At Fireman's Fund, we're keeping pace by taking a different approach to the growing challenges facing us all. . . . We're finding new ways to make unacceptable risks acceptable without lowering our standards" (see Exhibit 16.4).

Proof

Often, consumers look for "proof" in the body copy. Reputation, trials, seals of approval, demonstrations—and celebrity testimonials are frequent strategies to convince targets of claims. Although Carlton cigarettes have been advertising that they're the lowest in tar *and* nicotine, *Now* cigarettes claims that according to "U.S. Government testing method," they're *1 milligram lower in both* categories.

Part of the amplification process is often a reassurance to the consumer that the product will perform as promised. Proof supporting the promises made in an ad is particularly important for high-priced products, health products, and new products with a special feature. The advertiser wants to offer proof of product performance, but does not want to do so in a fashion that will bring up negative features the consumer might not have considered. There are a number of ways in which proof can be offered to prospective consumers.

Emphasizing the Manufacturer's Reputation. "Panasonic alkaline and rechargeable batteries. More than ahead of our time, we are the power behind the name."

Trial Offers. CBS Compact Disc Club offers a ten-day trial period during which discs can be returned and membership canceled.

Seals of Approval. Seals of approval from such accredited sources as *Good Housekeeping, Parent's* magazine, the American Dental Association, the American Medical

EXHIBIT 16.4

The amplification in this copy helps build confidence in the company. (Courtesy: Fireman's Fund Insurance Companies.).

This is no time for ease and comfort.
It is the time to dare and endure.
—Winston Churchill
RESOURCEFULNESS
Inland Marine
The winds of change are gathering strength throughout the insurance industry. At Fireman's Fund, we're keeping pace by taking a different approach to the growing challenges facing us all.
Rather than offer a lesser product at a lower price, our Inland Marine division is working harder to create quality coverages to fit your clients' risks, no matter how tough or unusual. We're finding new ways to make unacceptable risks acceptable without lowering our standards.
Fireman's Fund is committed to the future of Inland Marine. We have full-time Inland Marine underwriters in more cities than any other insurance company. Each of our 48 offices across the country has an experienced Inland Marine specialist with the authority to make local underwriting decisions. So we can take a closer look at how to provide what your clients need.
We'll all be faced with tough decisions in the months ahead. But at Fireman's Fund, we're using our resources to adapt to the changes without compromising our coverages. It's one of the qualities that has kept us in a leadership position for 125 years.
FIREMAN'S FUND
INSURANCE COMPANIES
125 years of tomorrows.

Association, and Underwriters Laboratories allay consumers' fears about product quality.

Demonstrations. Max Factor shows before-and-after unretouched pictures of women who have used Erace Line Filler.

Money-Back Guarantees. Wendy's offered consumers "The best hamburger in the business" with a money-back guarantee.

Warranties. Dodge Dynasty copy says: "And our exclusive 7 year or 70,000 mile protection plan."

Testimonials. Testimonial advertising is popular because it offers proof from a credible source and because it is attention-getting when celebrity endorsers are used. Testimonials should come from persons viewed by consumers as competent to pass judgment on the products they are endorsing. Typar Landscape Fabric used former football great Roger Staubach in its ad: "How a nice guy like Roger Staubach fights nasty weeds" (see Exhibit 16.5).

In the past, most advertisers used only one celebrity endorser for their product. Today, because of the very public problems of so many celebrities (drug use, messy divorces, etc.) many advertisers fear risking their product's credibility on one person.

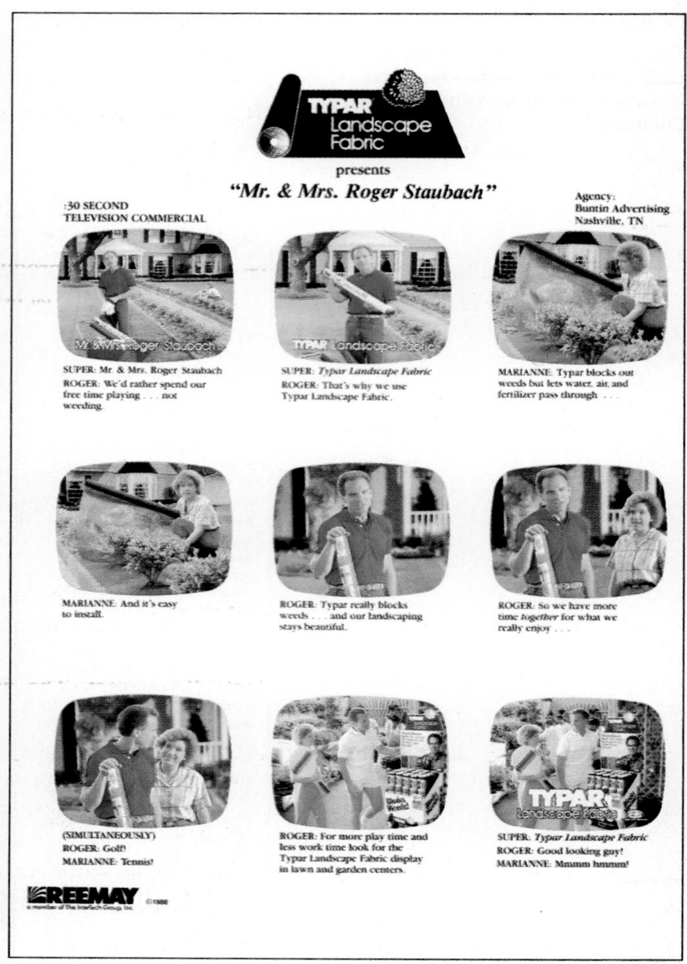

EXHIBIT 16.5

Former football great helps draw attention to product in both print and tv ads. (Courtesy: Reemay, Inc., The Staubach Company, Buntin Advertising, Inc.)

Hence the multiple-celebrity approach to testimonials. Pepsi Cola. Coca-Cola, and Oldsmobile are examples of companies that use several endorsers.

Actor Michael J. Fox and skipper Dennis Connor for Diet Pepsi; musician Michael Jackson for Pepsi; actor Don Johnson and musician George Michael for Diet Coke; models Christie Brinkley and Renee Simonsen for Cover Girl; and, of course, Bill Cosby for Jell-O pudding and frozen deserts, Kodak, and Coca-Cola are among the most popular celebrity endorsers.

COPY STYLE

> ***Copy approach.*** *The method of opening the text of an ad. Chief forms: factual approach, imaginative approach, emotional approach.*

Like people, ads have personalities all their own. Some say what they have to say in a fresh way. They make an impact. Others are boring. Unfortunately, while many of us are polite to a dull person, no one is polite to a dull ad. We simply pass it by.

So far, we have discussed how the building blocks of copy are put together. We will now discuss how the way we say what we have to say can lift copy out of the humdrum. That's style. The creative essence of copywriting is to see a product in a fresh way, to explore its possible effects on the reader, to explain the product's advantages in

"Fresh approaches" attract *and keep* viewers and readers—dull ones "turn off" prospects who, in turn, turn off or by-pass commercials and ads. *Usual* insurance ads feature problems/solutions or "a helpful agent of the month." *Travelers* wanted to demonstrate the intangible benefit of "financial security." Its full page, sun-laden ad shows "promise," and the high, graceful diver portrays "strength"—"to leap beyond the world of worry." While *financial peace of mind* is admittedly difficult to illustrate, the soothing, upbeat colors and the diver's grace—coupled with the popular inside back cover location—will probably attract noteworthy readership.

The *factual approach* in copywriting "talks" of *reality*—the way the product actually is or what it's capable of doing. *Time* magazine advertises to its readers with this headline: "There's no substitute for Good Service." It's a straightforward statement, hardly indisputable, to impress its audience that it will speedily follow through with change-of-address requests, renewals, gift subscriptions, or any other subscription-related requests.

If we use *imagination* in copy, we "highlight" the facts by fantasizing words or scenes—or what the product's attributes can do for its user. *Pro-Kennex* tennis racquets describes its new *Ceramic Destiny* as having a round shaft which "devours vibration, heightens control, and abounds with ideal flex . . . and with a dense string pattern for ultimate control." It concludes the body copy with "a hard punch"—"The Pro-Kennex Ceramic Destiny *is* the natural selection *for victory!*"

Copy can be "emotionally charged"—with words and scenes which provoke love, hate, fear. *Dupont's* Nomex and Kevlar fibers wouldn't ordinarily attract readers for their ads—but when *shown* and *described* as the difference between life and death in a raging 1500 degree Fahrenheit fire, they're sure to make formidable inpressions.

a manner that causes the reader to view the product with new understanding and appreciation.

Most ads end the same way: by asking or suggesting that the reader buy the product. The difference between a lively ad and a dull one lies in the approach to the message at the outset.

The lens through which a writer sees a product may be the magnifying glass of the technician, who perceives every nut and bolt and can explain why each is important; or it may be the rose-colored glasses of the romanticist, who sees how a person's life may be affected by the product. That is why we speak of approaches rather than types of ads. The chief approaches in describing an article are the factual, the imaginative, and the emotional.

Factual Approach

In the factual approach, we deal with reality, that which actually exists. We talk about the product—what it is, how it's made, what it does. Focusing on the facts about the product that are of most importance to the reader, we explain the product's advantages.

An interesting thing about a fact, however, is that it can be interpreted in different ways, each accurate, but each launching different lines of thinking. The most familiar example is that of the eight-ounce glass holding four ounces of water, of which it can be said: "This glass is half full" or "This glass is half empty." Both statements are factually correct. The difference is in the interpretation of reality, as the Asheville tourism ads in Exhibit 16.6 so aptly illustrate. Skill in presenting a fact consists in projecting it in the way that means most to the reader.

An ad for Lean Cuisine low-calorie frozen dinners could have said: "We'll help you lose weight." However, it identified with the plight of every dieter with the headline: "No More Broken Resolutions."

The factual approach can be used to sell more than products. Facts about services, ideas, places—anything an ad can be written for—can be presented with a fresh point of view.

Imaginative Approach

A fact is no less a fact if it is presented imaginatively. The art of creating copy lies in saying a familiar thing in an unexpected way. Speedo swimwear could have said: "You'll look great in our swimwear." Instead, it said: "It's always dangerous to put so much electricity near water," and "Gentlemen, start your engines" (see Exhibit 16.7). The *Boston Globe* could have said: "Get the latest news in the *Globe* every morning." Instead, it said: "The champions of breakfast," and showed not only the *Globe,* but also *The New York Times, The Wall Street Journal,* and several other top newspapers.

Emotional Approach

All good copywriters realize the power of emotion. How someone feels about your product or company can be an important plus or minus. Copy using the psychological appeals of love, hate, or fear has great impact. Usually, you need a strong illustration to support your emotional headline. The copy may continue the emotional appeal, though many times it will take a factual direction and inform the reader about specific features of the product to convince them of its value. Kodak has produced ads so emotional they would bring tears to your eyes. The Kinder-Care ad in Exhibit 16.8 is an example of welding a strong emotional illustration and copy: "We invite you to bring your child to Kinder-Care. And share the joy." This ad would certainly appeal to parents' who want to know their children are learning in a happy environment.

UNCOMMON GROUND.

The moment you and your group arrive, your senses send you a message: This is no ordinary place.

Because off these smoky time-tempered mountains rolls a rare inspiration.

You can hear it in the simple pluck of a shindig fiddler. Or see it in the magnificence of Biltmore Estate. You can breathe it in the earth, the wildflowers, the rock. And touch it in the art of a thousand craftsmen.

Next time you venture out in search of new vistas, come feel our mountain city's fresh and comforting embrace.

And plan on staying a while. Because this land of the sky has an uncommon way of taking hold. And never letting go.

ASHEVILLE
NORTH CAROLINA
It will lift your spirit.

THIS SUMMER, GIVE YOURSELF A WEEK TO GET RICH.

There are many paths to wealth. Here, they just happen to go by unusual names. Like Funnel Top. Butter Gap. Coontree. Dog Loser. And Ferrin Knob.

You can follow trails like these all the way to the golden edge of the sky. And then back down again, into misty coves walled in by million-year-old mountains.

But there are many other ways to uncover the richness of our highlands. Blaze your own trail. To festivals and high country fairs. To a night at the symphony or an afternoon following the Blue Ridge Parkway from one peak performance to the next. And to Biltmore Estate, one of the grandest treasures of them all.

Along every path you'll find hospitality as warm and inviting as a sunrise over Craggy Gardens. And something more, too: when it comes to being rich in this life, you don't always need money. Just time.

ASHEVILLE
NORTH CAROLINA
It will lift your spirit.

EXHIBIT 16.6

These ads use a play on words to get consumers to interpret the reality of Asheville in a new way. (Courtesy: Buncombe County Tourism Authority and Price/McNabb.)

LISTEN TO OUR BLUES.

From these highlands come views you could set to music. Mountains the color of the sky. And clouds that dance through valleys and coves.

Here, too, amidst a million acres of national forests, you will find a city with some very lyrical qualities of its own.

It's a place where you can choose between a night at the symphony or a Shindig on the Green. And where you will find the largest private home in America—Biltmore Estate.

So this summer, take some time to visit our beautiful mountain city. But remember, if you want to see it all, you must listen, too.

ASHEVILLE
NORTH CAROLINA
It will lift your spirit.

For more information, write Asheville Adventures, PO Box 1011P, Asheville, NC 28802 or call toll free 1-800-257-1300 in the East, 1-800-548-1300 in NC, or 1-704-258-3916 from all other areas. © BCTDA 1987

It's always dangerous to put
so much electricity near water.
SPEEDO

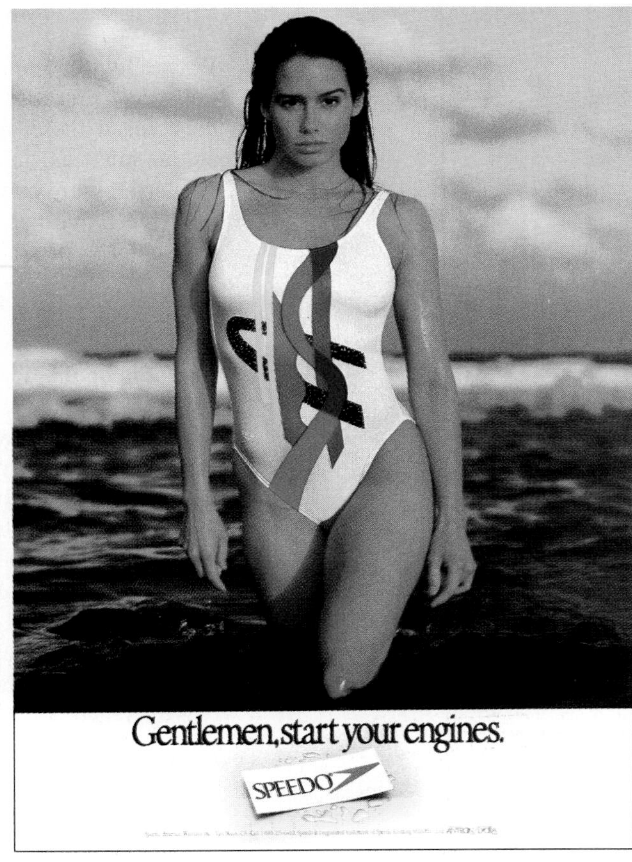

Gentlemen, start your engines.
SPEEDO

EXHIBIT 16.7

This ad uses a familiar saying in an unexpected way. (Courtesy: Speedo America, Warnaco.)

EXHIBIT 16.8

Some ads use strong emotional illustrations and copy. (Courtesy: Kinder-Care and HutchesonShutze.)

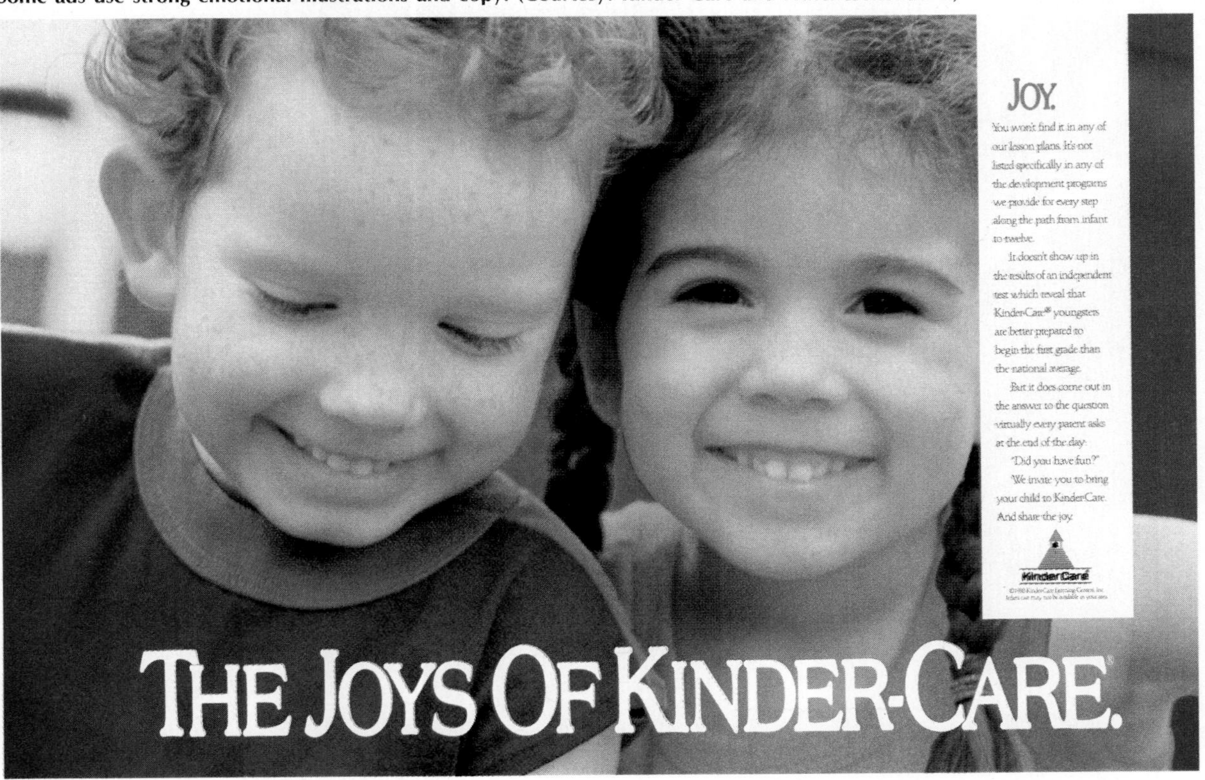

JOY.
You won't find it in any of our lesson plans. It's not listed specifically in any of the development programs we provide for every step along the path from infant to twelve.
It doesn't show up in the results of an independent test which reveal that Kinder-Care® youngsters are better prepared to begin the first grade than the national average.
But it does come out in the answer to the question virtually every parent asks at the end of the day:
"Did you have fun?"
We invite you to bring your child to Kinder-Care. And share the joy.
KinderCare
THE JOYS OF KINDER-CARE.

Copy for Special-Interest Groups

We are living in a diverse world. People are different; they engage in hobbies, vocations, and lifestyles different from those of their friends and neighbors. Advertising must reach these special-interest groups and offer something that appeals to their unique interests. In the future, this trend toward diversity will increase, putting even greater pressure on advertisers to create messages of interest to a fragmented population (see Exhibit 16.9)

COMPARATIVE ADVERTISING

> ***Comparative advertising.*** See *Comparison advertising.*

Another popular approach to creating advertising is to compare your product directly with one or more competitors. Comparative advertising was a little-used technique until 1973, when the Federal Trade Commission encouraged its use by holding that the naming of a competitor's brand would not be considered unfair competition. Until that time, the three major TV networks had banned comparative advertising.

Despite the widespread use of comparative advertising, it is not without problems. Some advertisers hold that it is foolish to spend money to publicize your competition. Others think that it creates an unhealthy atmosphere of name-calling that demeans all advertising. Finally, since statements about competitors have to be fully supportable, an advertiser must exercise caution or be open to legal liability. The legal aspects of comparative advertising are discussed in Chapter 25.

While each comparative ad is unique, there are certain rules of thumb that can be applied to comparative advertising:

1. The leader in a field never starts a comparative campaign.

EXHIBIT 16.9

Clever copy and compeling layout draw attention to Reebok. (Courtesy: Reebok International LTD. Copyright 1988. All Rights Reserved.)

Comparative advertising works best when particular outstanding features of one product can be "isolated" for the target audience—who is led to believe that the competitors can't "measure up." In recent Chrysler ads, they stress their highest customer satisfaction rating, their lowest average safety recall record, and the longest powertrain protection—of all 1988 domestic passenger cars. J.D. Power Associates is listed as the independent research source.

2. The most successful comparison ads are those comparing the product with products identical in every respect except for the specific differential featured in the ad. The stronger the proof that products are otherwise identical, the better.
3. The different features should be of importance to the consumer.

SLOGANS

Derived from the Gaelic *sluagh-ghairm,* meaning "battle cry," the word *slogan* has an appropriate origin. A slogan sums up the theme for a product's benefits to deliver an easily remembered message in a few words. Mr. Goodwrench's slogan says: "No one knows your GM car better. No one" (see Exhibit 16.10)

Used even more often on TV and radio than in print, slogans may be combined with a catchy tune to make a jingle. They are broadly classified as either institutional or hard-sell.

Institutional

Institutional slogans are created to establish a prestigious image for a company. Relying on this image to enhance their products and services, many firms insist that their

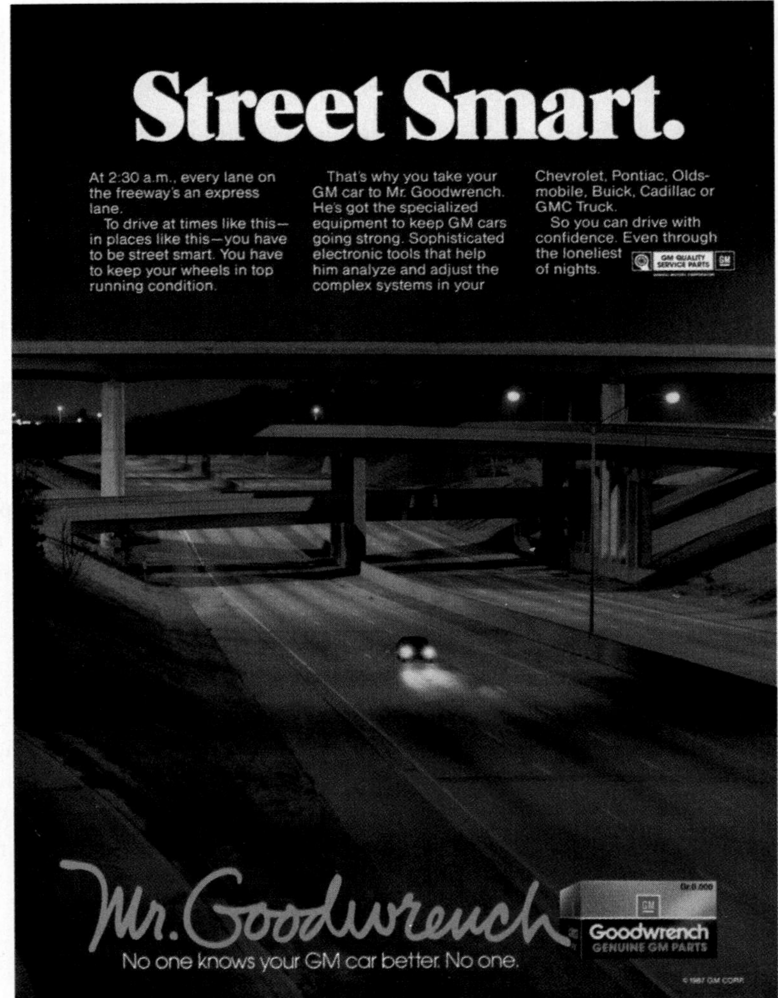

EXHIBIT 16.10

An effective slogan that works to develop brand equity for this GM division. (Courtesy: General Motors Service Parts Operations.)

Slogans, in a few words, can sum up what the company or the product is trying to accomplish. By *repetition* with the name, it becomes "a permanent fixture" with the company or product's identity. *American Express* can "get away" with practically *no copy in its ads—its two slogans* have managed to "speak" for the company—"Membership Has Its Privileges" and "Don't leave home without it."

slogan appear in all of their advertising and on their letterheads. An entire ad may feature the slogan. Some institutional slogans are familiar:

You're in good hands with Allstate.

(*Allstate Insurance*)

In touch with tomorrow.

(*Toshiba*)

The Heartbeat of America.

(*Chevrolet*)

Making it all make sense.

(*Microsoft Software*)

Such policy slogans are changed infrequently, if at all. Stating the platform or virtues of the candidate in a few words, slogans used in political campaigns likewise fall into the institutional-slogan category. Those campaigns expire on election day (as do many of the candidate's promises).

Hard-Sell

To help *sell* a product, a company can employ slogans to advance a particular selling point—in a unique way. *Metropolitan Life* cuts its slogan *short,* given its long company name—"Get Met. It Pays."

These capsules of advertising change with campaigns. They epitomize the special significant features of the product or service being advertised, and their claims are strongly competitive:

The most intelligent cars ever built.

(*Saab*)

The Zero Cholesterol Real Egg Product.

(*Scrambler*)

The most revolutionary advance in copy. Since the copiers.

(*Canon Color Laser Copier*)

The power to be your best.

(*Apple Computers*)

Your foot specialist.

(*Dr. Scholl's*)

Slogans are widely used to advertise groceries, drugs, beauty aids, and liquor. These are products that are bought repeatedly at a comparatively low price. They are sold in direct competition to consumers on the shelves of supermarkets, drug stores, and department stores. If a slogan can remind a shopper in one of those stores of a special feature of the product, it certainly has served its purpose. Slogans can also remind shoppers of the name of a product from a company they respect. Not all advertising needs slogans. One-shot announcements—sale ads for which price is the overriding consideration—usually don't use slogans. Creating a slogan is one of the fine arts of copywriting.

Elements of a Good Slogan

Good slogans are memorable for their *creativity* and *uniqueness*. Hampton Inns, in stressing *comfort and price,* devised this slogan: "Smart style. Smart price. Smart choice."

A slogan differs from most other forms of writing because it is designed to be remembered and repeated word for word to impress a brand and its message on the consumer. Ideally, the slogan should be short, clear, and easy to remember.
Boldness helps:

The smart choice.

(*Tylenol*)

Because you're worth it.

(*L'Oréal*)

Parallelism helps:

Does she, or doesn't she?

(*Clairol*)

Everyday. Everywhere.

(*Lubriderm Lotion*)

The sensitive soap for sensitive people.

(*Neutrogena*)

Aptness helps:

Trusted by more women than any other brand.

(*Massengill*)

More people take our word for it.

(*Webster's Dictionary*)

It is a great advantage to have the name of the product in a slogan:

The American Express Card. Don't leave home without it.

(*American Express Card*)

Slogans are not easy to create. Sometimes they "pop out" of a piece of copy or a TV commercial. Most often, they are the result of hard work and days and months of thinking and discussion by creative and marketing people.

THE CREATIVE WORK PLAN

Before starting an ad, most agencies develop a creative work plan. Recall from Chapter 3 the Lintas: Link creative brief: key observation, communication objective, consumer insight, promise, support, audience, and mandatories. The purpose of the work plan is to provide the proper direction for the creative team prior to ad development. Exhibit 16.11 shows a format different from the Lintas approach. Agencies and clients may have their own format and style for the specific information they think necessary for creative strategy development.

REVIEWING THE COPY

Most good copy positions the brand name clearly in the minds of prospects, as having a strong benefit for the user. "The Big Idea" of *IBM's PS/2's ad* is to present a common business problem—and have PS/2's *Micro Channel* "solve it." The headline/question, "How're you going to do it?" rhymes with the "solution"—"PS/2 it!" IBM, PS/2 and Micro Channel are used frequently in the copy and in the commercial jingle on TV. Additional reinforcement comes from using "PS/2" as the noun ("subject") *and* as a verb ("solution").

After the copy has been written, review it with these questions in mind:

Your copy strategy is *what* you say to *whom* and *why*.

- Does your advertising position the brand clearly?
- Does it tie the brand to a strong benefit?

Does your advertising have a Big Idea?

- Does this idea tie into the strategy and the execution?

How strong is the execution of the Big Idea?

- Does your advertising promote the brand personality?
- Is it bold and unexpected?
- Does it clearly state a promise and reward the prospect?
- Is your advertising single-minded?
- Is the ad visually arresting?

creative work plan

KEY OPPORTUNITY

THE PREMIUM FROZEN ENTREE MARKET IS BECOMING INCREASINGLY CROWDED WITH "ME TOO" PRODUCTS -- MANY SIMILAR PRODUCTS POSITIONED AGAINST SIMILAR TARGETS. THE NEEDS OF THE MALE AUDIENCE, A LARGE PROFITABLE SEGMENT, ARE CURRENTLY BEING IGNORED BY MANUFACTURERS.

TARGET AUDIENCE

PRIMARY: DEMOGRAPHICS

- MALE
- AGE 25-49
- SINGLE OR TWO PERSON HOUSEHOLD
- $25,000+ INCOME
- COLLEGE EDUCATED
- WHITE COLLAR

PSYCHOGRAPHICS

- ACTIVE
- HEALTH CONSCIOUS
- SUCCESS ORIENTED
- DEMANDS QUALITY

TARGET AUDIENCE

SECONDARY: DEMOGRAPHICS

- FEMALE
- MARRIED
- AGE 25-49
- DUAL INCOME HOUSEHOLD
- $25,000+ INCOME
- COLLEGE EDUCATION

PSYCHOGRAPHICS

- ACTIVE
- HEALTH CONSCIOUS
- DEMANDS QUALITY

OBJECTIVES

WHERE DO WE WANT TO BE?

- CREATE AWARENESS AND TRIAL FOR D & R FROZEN ENTREES AMONG TARGET PROSPECTS.
- TO BE RECOGNIZED AS THE PREMIUM FROZEN ENTREE LINE CREATED FOR MALE TASTES AND APPETITE.

STRATEGY

HOW DO WE GET THERE?

- POSITION D & R FROZEN ENTREES AS THE HEARTY AND HEALTHY ALTERNATIVE TO CURRENT FROZEN ENTREE CHOICES, BY COMMUNICATING PRIMARY PRODUCT BENEFITS.

PRIMARY CONSUMER BENEFIT

THAT SATISFIED FEELING YOU GET WHEN YOU HAVE EATEN A DELICIOUS, FILLING, HEALTHY MEAL.

NET IMPRESSION

D & R OFFERS THE BEST FROZEN ENTREE FOR TODAY'S MALE.

SUPPORT

- GREAT TASTING
- LARGER PORTIONS THAN THE COMPETITION
- HEALTHIER: LOW LEVELS OF FAT AND SODIUM
- EASIER PREPARATION -- CONVENIENT PACKAGING, PLUS ALL ENTREES ARE MICROWAVABLE
- MALE ORIENTED MENU

MANDITORIES

- TASTE APPEAL MUST BE STRESSED

CONSUMER RESPONSE STATEMENT

WHAT THE CONSUMER WILL BELIEVE:

"I'M GOING TO TRY D & R FROZEN ENTREES. THEY'RE PERFECT FOR ME. THEY GIVE ME MORE TO EAT, AND THEY HAVE THE FOODS I LIKE."

EXHIBIT 16.11
Creative work plan.

SUMMARY

Advertising motivates people by appealing to their problems, desires, and goals—and offering them a solution to their problems, satisfaction of their desires, and a means to achieve their goals. Selecting the appeal is an important task for the creative team. We sometimes rely on one or more of these techniques to help us decide which appeal is best: concept testing, focus groups, and motivational research.

The structure for most ads is: promise of benefit in the headline (and maybe the spelling out of the promise in a subheadline), amplification of story or facts, proof of claim, and action to take. The headline is the most important copy element. There are numerous methods of approaching headline writing. An effective headline can be long or short, but must contain all the words necessary to communicate your message. The subheadline can help you spell out the promise presented in the headline, and many times serves as a transition between the headline and the first sentence of the body copy. The body copy is where you build your case for the product and support the

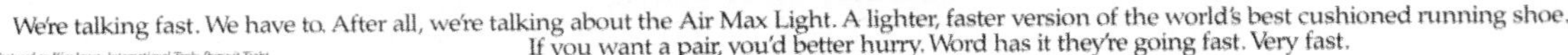

NIKE
AIR
SWOOOOOOOOOOOOSH.
Women's Air Max Light
Men's Air Max Light
We're talking fast. We have to. After all, we're talking about the Air Max Light. A lighter, faster version of the world's best cushioned running shoe.
If you want a pair, you'd better hurry. Word has it they're going fast. Very fast.
Featured on Kim Jones: International Tank: Pursuit Tight.

EXHIBIT 16.12

The creative team can almost make you hear the sound in this imaginative headline and illustration mix. (Courtesy: Wieden & Kennedy, Inc.)

promise in the headline or subheadline. The details about the product or service are presented here, along with support for your claim.

The creative essence of copywriting is to see a product in a different way. The chief approaches used to describe products are the factual, the imaginative, and the emotional. A slogan sums up the theme for a product's benefits. It needs to be a memorable message of few words. Slogans can be developed from several points of view; the institutional and hard-sell viewpoints are the most common.

The place to start planning an ad is the creative work plan or the creative brief. If written properly, the creative work plan will tell you what should be in the ad and what the ad should accomplish. It will keep you from forgetting that every ad must have a specific purpose. However, no work plan will tell you how to execute the copy—that's part of the creative process.

QUESTIONS

1. How do you tell if you have a strong appeal?
2. What does *copy style* mean?
3. Name some factors that should be considered in evaluating strong headlines.

4. Most headlines fall into four categories. Discuss one of them.
5. What makes a good slogan?
6. What do we mean by amplification of the body copy?

SUGGESTED EXERCISES

- Find an example of a testimonial and analyze the copy for credibility.
- Write a testimonial for your favorite movie star. Choose a product you think he or she might use.
- Write a new slogan for either Coke or Pepsi.
- Pick an ad out of a current magazine and, using the same strategy as the ad writer, write ten different headlines that would be effective.

READINGS

BLASKO, VINCENT J., AND MICHAEL P. MOKWA: "Creativity in Advertising: A Janusian Perspective," *Journal of Advertising,* Vol. 15, No. 4 (1986), pp. 43–50.

BURTON, SCOT, AND DONALD R. LICHTENSTEIN: "The Effect of Ad Claims and Text on Attitude Toward the Advertisement," *Journal of Advertising,* Vol. 17, No. 1 (1988), pp. 3–11.

DONATION, SCOT: "Big Gain for Montana in Endorsement Bowl," *Advertising Age,* January 30, 1989, p. 4.

MACHLEIT, KAREN A., AND DALE WILSON: "Emotional Feelings and Attitude Toward the Advertisement: The Roles of Brand Familiarity and Repetition," *Journal of Advertising,* Vol. 17, No. 3 (1988), pp. 22–26.

MORIARTY, SANDRA: *Creative Advertising: Theory and Practice* (Englewood Cliffs, NJ: Prentice Hall, 1986).

SCHULTZ, DON E., AND STANLEY I. TANNENBAUM: *Essentials of Advertising Strategy* (Lincolnwood, Il: NTC Business Books, 1988).

SEVENTEEN

The Total Concept: Words and Visuals

Concept. *The combining of all elements (copy, headline, and illustrations) of an ad into a single idea.*

"A Big Idea" is the total concept behind an ad—one which combines words and visuals. In order to break away from the usual celebrity endorsements, Creative Fragrances of Hollywood, Florida has taken a different approach and created two fragrances based on *theater*. Their first "performance perfume," *Esprit de Phantom,* draws heavily on its connection with the play—print ads show the perfume bottle, a rose, and the phantom's mask, with the headline, "Unmask the Scent." The company's second fragrance, "Gone With the Wind," relies on the famous embrace of Rhett and Scarlett. Lucien Lallouz, president and CEO, said his fragrances will have a better chance of becoming "classics," because they're based on something established!

The dictionary defines a concept as: (1) a general notion or idea; (2) an idea of something formed by mentally combining all its characteristics or particulars. In advertising, the total concept is a fresh way of looking at something. A novel way of talking about a product or service. A dramatic new dimension that gives the observer a new perspective. A concept is an idea. Better yet, a Big Idea. One that is expressed clearly, combining words and visuals. The words describe what the basic idea is, and the visuals say what the words say—even better—or reinforce what the words say, or provide a setting that makes the words more powerful.

This chapter discusses the elements involved in taking an appeal and turning it into a finished ad. In previous chapters, we learned how to identify prospects, evaluate product strengths and weaknesses, and choose the most significant consumer benefits to build brand equity into our product. Here we will learn how to make some ads.

First a word about advertising creatives. The creative team in an advertising agency consists of a writer and an art director (sorry, but we do not know why the artist gets the exalted title of "art director" while the writer is simply a "writer"). Both are concept thinkers. *Both* think in terms of words and pictures. After they are armed with all the information they need and have settled on a creative strategy for the target market, they begin to create. Like any other creative process, the development of an ad is done in a systematic manner, though at times the process can be highly unpredictable and unproductive. Some ideas seem to fall into place, while others are as difficult as giving birth to a rhinoceros. The creative team—artist and writer—worry together, go to lunch together, and talk together. They feed off each other in harmony and conflict until an idea happens. Many times, the artist will supply a good copy line and the writer a strong visual idea. There are no rules (nor should there be) about how you work to develop the Big Idea. The most important thing is that it reflect your creative strategy in solving your prime prospect's problem. The end result of all this collaboration is a Big Idea that says something dramatically in words and pictures.

The idea must come alive—leap off the page of a magazine or grab all your senses while you watch TV. Creative ideas not only grab attention, but do two other important things:

The *creative team*—the artist and the writer—must create "selling" ads and commercials—not merely creative. While seeing a large tiger pounce out of a shipping bag does cause the reader and viewer "to stop in their tracks," it also clearly demonstrates that Federal Express has acquired Flying Tigers. . . and a larger, worldwide shipping company has been formed.

1. Make the prime prospect realize that he or she should consider your product first.
2. Implant your brand name indelibly in the prime prospect's mind and connect it to the positive attributes of the product.

Remember, ideas that are *merely* creative will not help your client. Your creative concept solutions must get across a main selling point and the brand name (see Exhibit 17.1). How often do people who have seen a compelling ad answer: "I don't remember" when someone asks them: "What product, who advertised it?"

VISUALIZING THE IDEA

At this stage of the process, the creative team forms mental pictures of how the basic appeal can be translated into a selling message. You might visualize a sports car as speeding on a mountain road and around hairpin curves. You might see a sedan in front of a country club of understated luxury.

You can describe your mental picture in words or in the crudest sketch. The important thing is to imagine the kind of picture that best expresses your idea. While thinking of the visual form, find the words that work with the visual for the most powerful effect. Make as many versions of the basic idea as you can. Be as imaginative as you want to be, provided the end result delivers the basic message and the brand name.

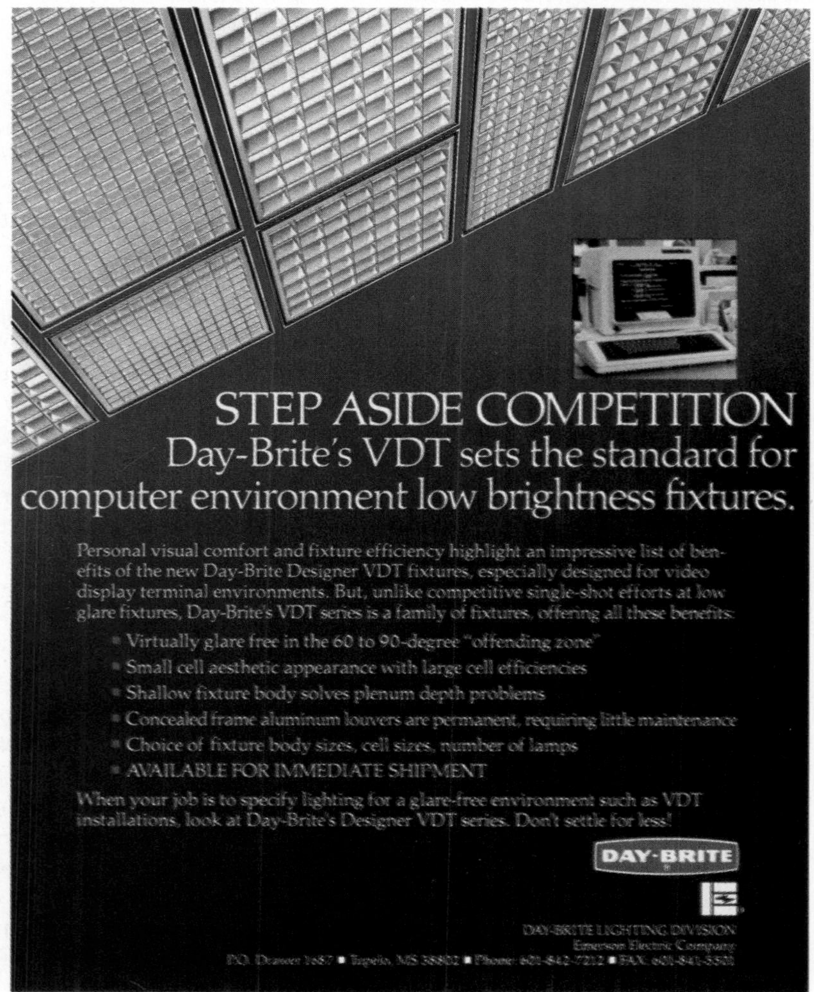

EXHIBIT 17.1

This ad for better computer office environments features unique graphics and head emphasizing product name and benefit. (Courtesy: Emerson Electric Company and Robinson & Associates, Inc.)

Different *visual approaches* to the campaign are considered. Numerous headlines and illustrations are tried, in order to eventually achieve the "creative leap," when the visual and words "mesh." *Spiegel's* usual ads for its catalogs feature well-dressed models, dealing the company's 800 line. Now, Spiegel has directed its attention to the target market it wants to attract the most—*working women*. Knowing their limited calling time at home, its new ads display the office water-cooler—with a bathing suit inside. The headline, "The Blass Swimsuit—Now Available in Offices," should *attract* the office market. . . .

Marketing Approach to Visualization

Each ad is not created for the beauty of its art or prose, but for a specific marketing purpose. Whether or not they appear to be related, all ads for a product should conform to the same set of objectives—and usually use the same slogan or theme. (There is a mistaken notion among some advertisers that media and marketing are closely related, but the linkage is not at all strong with the creative functions of advertising.)

Using all the information you have about the product, write a statement of the one thing you would say about the product if that were all you could say: This is your promise or basic theme.

THE CREATIVE LEAP

Now we are ready to begin to create an ad. During this process of bridging the gap between visualization and concrete words and pictures, the creative team will suggest and reject numerous approaches. The basic appeal will be used to write many headlines. In turn, visual ideas that fit these headlines will be considered. In some cases, headlines will result from an illustration.

This is a period of free association and brainstorming. A crazy idea may spark that elusive "great campaign." Once you get the idea-concept and visual and words that work together as one, you've made the creative leap. Two examples of good ads are shown in Exhibit 17.2.

EXHIBIT 17.2

Very simple concept communicates quickly. (Courtesy: VisiColor.)

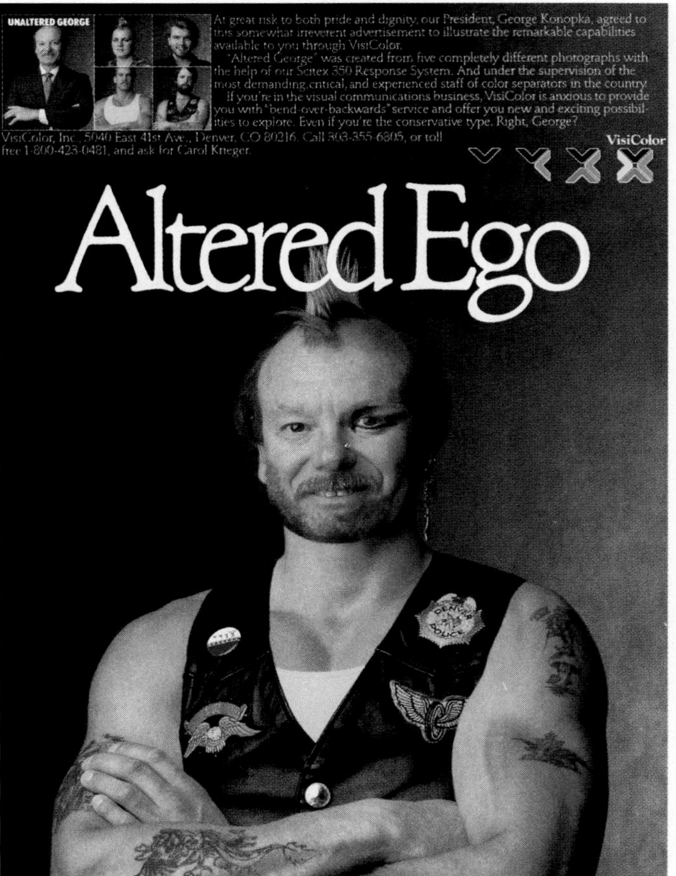

Layout. ***Layout.*** *A working drawing showing how an ad is to look. A printer's layout is a set of instructions accompanying a piece of copy showing how it is to be set up. There are also rough layouts, finished layouts, and mechanical layouts, representing various degrees of finish. The term layout is used, too, for the total design of an ad.*

In designing the *layout* of an ad, all the elements—the headline, the subheadline, the copy, the illustration—*are pulled together*. Radio Shack's ad for Tandy computers features a *dimensional* projection of an office, using spreadsheets. Office personnel, the computer, and a series of spreadsheets are shown at various angles and positions—from close-ups to distant background objects. The copy, however, is listed in the righthand "column" in *one dimension*—leading the reader to the Radio Shack signature and slogan. Although *diverse,* the ad conveys *a singular purpose*—financial computing is efficient.

Illustrations and headlines usually are the key elements for getting ads noticed. In American Marketing Association ads for new members, they created a *distinctive* print style for their bold, black headline: "A New Decade of Growth." They followed it with "a mushroom," composed of the years of the '90s decade—up to the year 2000 in large numerals in the "cap." The concept of *growth* was highly evident, as a result. . . .

THE LAYOUT

The creative leap is only the first step in ad making. The ad itself has a variety of elements: headline, illustration, copy, logotype; maybe a subheadline, several other illustrations of varying importance, a coupon—the number of components varies tremendously from ad to ad. Putting them all together in an orderly form is called making up the layout of the ad. *Layout* is another of those advertising terms that is used in two senses: It means the total appearance of the ad—its overall design, the composition of its elements; it also means the physical rendering of the design of the ad—a blueprint for production purposes. You will hear someone say: "Here's the layout," while handing another person a typed or keyboarded copy and a drawing. Right now, we are talking about the layout as the overall design of the ad.

Layout Person as Editor

Although the person who creates the visual idea may be the same as the one who makes the layout, the two functions are different. The visualizer translates an idea into visual form; a layout person uses that illustration and all the other elements to make an orderly, attractive arrangement.

Before putting pencil to paper, however, the layout person—usually an art director—and the writer review all of the elements. The first task is to decide what is most important. Is it the headline? The picture? The copy? How important is the package? Should the product itself be shown, and if so, should it be shown in some special environment or in use? Is this ad to tell a fast story with a picture and headline, or is it a long-copy ad in which illustration is only an incidental feature? The importance of the element determines its size and placement within the ad.

Working Hard to Get Noticed

Attracting attention. Getting noticed. High visibility. No matter how you say it, this is the primary creative objective of an ad. Today's advertising has to work very hard to get noticed. You can't rely on strategy alone—the positioning, the product appeals, the demographic and psychographic data that tell you what wavelength the consumer is on—to sell the consumer. Obvious as it sounds, you can't sell anyone until you attract their attention. Put another way, people aren't going to read the ad if they don't see it. Remember, your ad is competing with all the advertising clutter and editorial matter in a publication. Unfortunately, most ads in most publications are invisible.

All the creative elements—the visual, the headline, the copy—must be strongly executed if the ad is to succeed (see Exhibit 17.3). Research can't tell us which creative techniques will work best because creative isn't that scientific. Research generally tells us what has been successful, but there are no yardsticks to measure breakthrough advertising ideas. The basic guidelines for writing and designing ads are helpful, but there aren't really any rules. How do you get an ad to stand out? The illustration is usually the key. Either an ad grabs people or it doesn't, and most often it is the illustration that gets them. Of course, many illustrations can't tell the story alone—they require a head to complete the communication. So the headline is extremely important to keep people.

We don't use illustrations solely to attract attention. They must have a strong relationship to the selling concept. A picture is worth a thousand words only if it communicates the selling concept to the reader. Using a shock visual merely to gain attention is generally a mistake. If you're selling a hammer and your dominant visual shows a woman in a bikini, you are using sexist imagery that has no relationship to the product. You are duping people: "Now that we have your attention, buy our hammer." And since most people dislike being duped, they will resent your ad—and often your product as well.

EXHIBIT 17.3
Illustration and headline working together in an interesting way. (Courtesy: Biltmore Estates and Price/ McNabb Advertising.)

There are three basic means of attracting attention:

1. The visual alone
2. The headline alone
3. The combination of the visual and headline

Basic design principles dictate that well-executed ads have *unity and harmony* of design—that they possess a unified design, with elements which work well together. *Dialog Information Services* begins its trade ad with this centered headline in white letters on a black background: "Don't let it happen again." Below, a familiar failure is pictured—*the Edsel grill*. Black copy occupies the lower half of the white space—and the Dialog signature and slogan appear in the predictable lower right corner. The *logic* of its "pieces" make the ad "outstanding."

Don't assume because we put the visual first that the art director is more important than the copywriter. Remember, they are a team working together on both visual and language ideas.

Basic Design Principles

There are some general principles that guide the design of advertising and promotional layouts. Some art directors may use different terminology than that used here, but the basic assumptions are the same.

The following design prinicples, properly employed, will attract the reader and enhance the chances of the message being read.

Unity. All creative advertising has a unified design. The layout must be conceived in its entirety, with all its parts (copy, art, head, logo, etc.) related to one another, to give one, overall unified effect (see Exhibit 17.4).

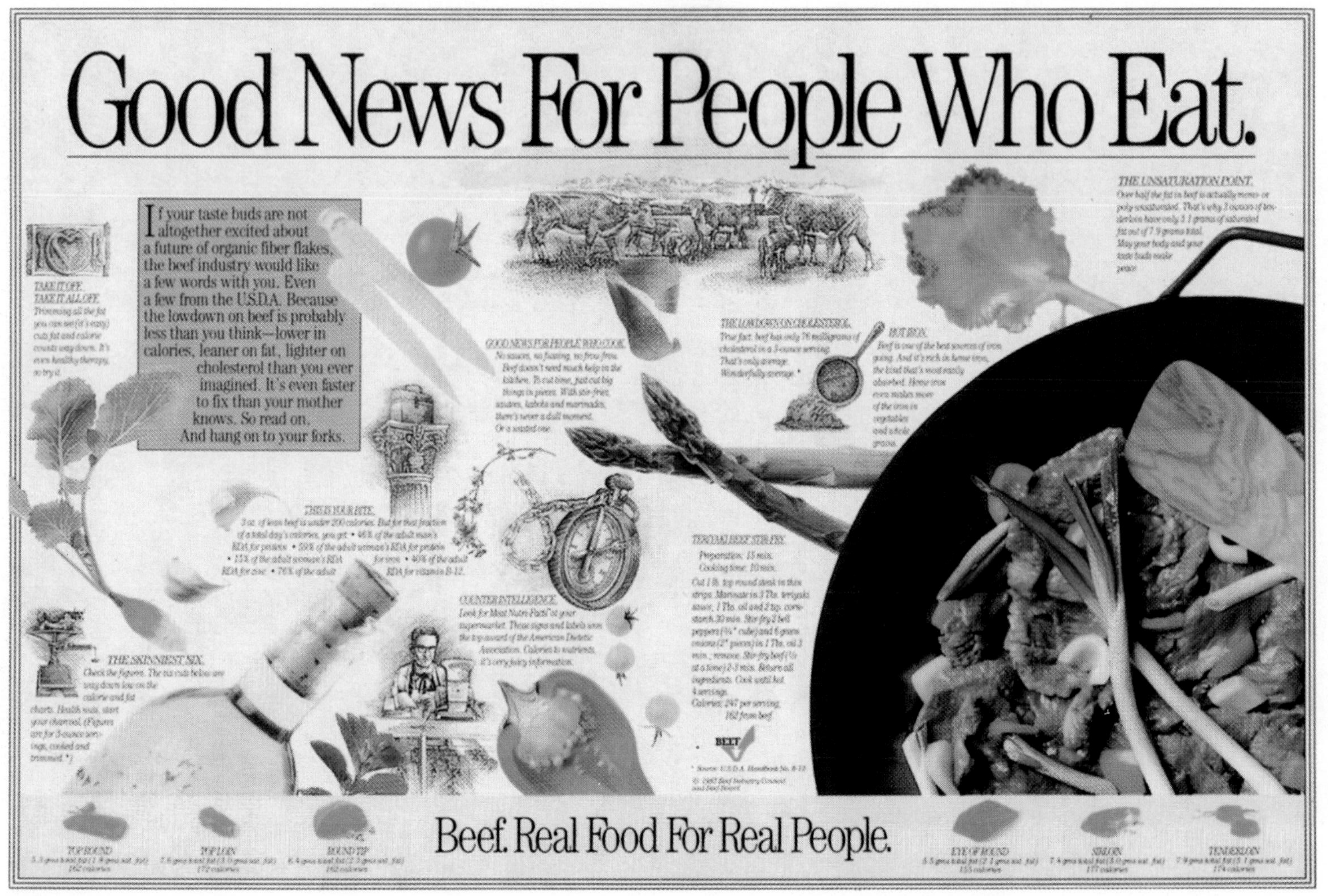

EXHIBIT 17.4
You can't always accomplish your objective with just one illustration. (Courtesy: Beef Industry Council.)

Harmony. All the elements of the layout must work together and not against one another. Shapes, types, tones, and textures must be in harmony so that they are pleasing to the eye.

The logical flow of the ad's elements, with an emphasis on key elements, encourages *readership*. In using a familiar question by a "layman," AT&T "pulls" the reader into its ads for telephone services. By the time the reader gets to the end, he/she has read ¾ of the ad! The reader is encouraged to read the copy—to see if it actually answers the potential customer's question.

Sequence. The ad should be arranged in an orderly manner so it can be read from left to right and top to bottom. The sequence of elements can help direct the eye in a structural or gaze motion. Place the elements so that the eye starts where you want it to start and travels a desired path throughout the ad. "Z" and "S" arrangements are common.

Emphasis. Emphasis is accenting or focusing on an element (or group of elements) to make it stand out. Decide whether you want to stress the illustration, the headline, the logo, or the copy. If you give all of these elements equal emphasis, your ad will end up with no emphasis at all.

Contrast. You need differences in sizes, shapes, and tones to add sparkle so the ad won't be visually dull. Altering type to bold or italic or using extended typefaces brings attention to a word or phrase and creates contrast between type elements. Contrast makes the layout more interesting.

Balance. By balance, we mean controlling the size, tone, weight, and position of the elements in the ad. Balanced elements look secure and natural to the eye. You test for balance by examining the relationship between the right and left halves of the ad. There are basically two forms of balance: formal and informal.

Whether *formal* or *informal* balance is used, the ad should give the impression of *symmetry*. Slaughter/Hanson & Associates, Dothan, Alabama, created *a serious sedate impression* with their ad for Southern Natural Gas. *Formal balance* appears to "suit" a utility, which wants to convey its commitment to long-term service and dependability. Every element in their consumer magazine ad—the headline, the illustration, the copy, the signature, and the slogan is *centered* on the page.

FORMAL BALANCE. A formally balanced ad has elements of equal weights, sizes, and shapes on the left and right sides of an imaginary vertical line drawn down the center of the ad (see Exhibit 17.5). Such symmetrical ads give an impression of stability and conservatism, but at times look unimaginative.

INFORMAL BALANCE. The optical center of a page, measured from top to bottom, is five-eighths of the way up the page; thus, it differs from the mathematical center. (To test this, take a blank piece of paper, close your eyes, then open them, and quickly place a dot at what you think is the center of the page. The chances are that it will be above the mathematical center.) Imagine that a seesaw is balanced on the optical center. We know that a lighter weight on the seesaw can easily balance a heavier one by being farther away from the fulcrum. (The "weight" of an element in an ad may be gauged by its size, its degree of blackness, its color, or its shape.) In informal balance, objects are placed seemingly at random on the page, but in such relation to one another that the page as a whole seems in balance. This type of arrangement requires more thought than the simple bisymmetric formal balance, but the effects can be imaginative and distinctive, as illustrated by Exhibit 17.6.

Other Composing Elements

Color. One of the most versatile elements of an ad is color. It can attract attention and help create a mood. Depending on the product and the advertising appeal, color can be used for a number of reasons:

1. It is an attention-getting device. With few exceptions, people notice a color ad more readily than one in black and white.
2. Certain products can only be presented realistically in color. Household furnishings, food, many clothing and fashion accessories, and cosmetics would lose most of their appeal if advertised in black and white.
3. Color can highlight specific elements within an ad. Occasionally, an advertiser will use spot color for the product in an otherwise black-and-white ad. This not only emphasizes the product as the primary element in the ad, but also saves money compared to four-color processes. (We will discuss the technique of color production in Chapter 18.)

EXHIBIT 17.5

Most formally balanced ads have a few simple elements. This ad is more interesting than the typical ad with formal balance. (Courtesy: South Carolina Tourism and Leslie Advertising, Inc.)

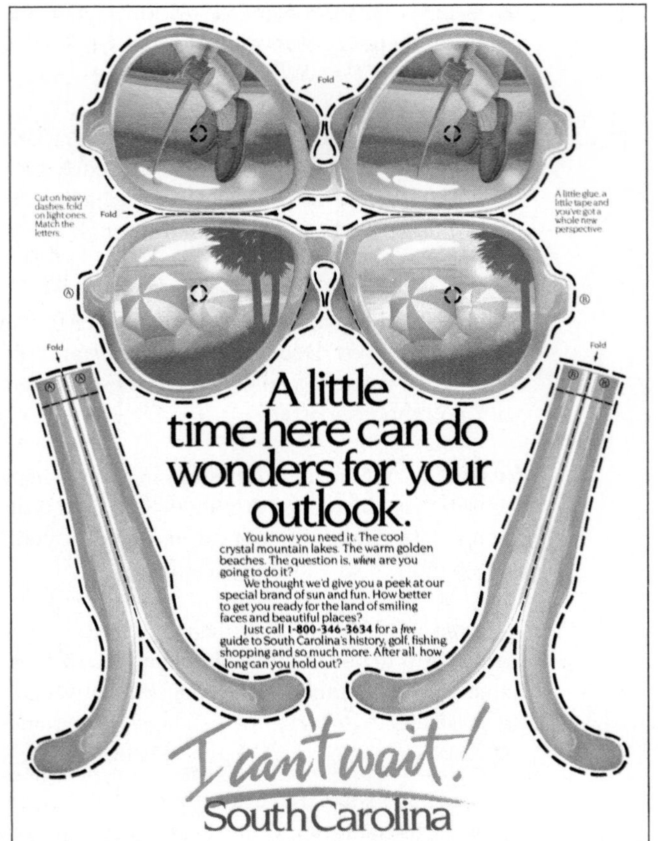

EXHIBIT 17.6

This poster layout format is an example of informal balance. (Courtesy: American Express and Promotion Solutions, Inc.)

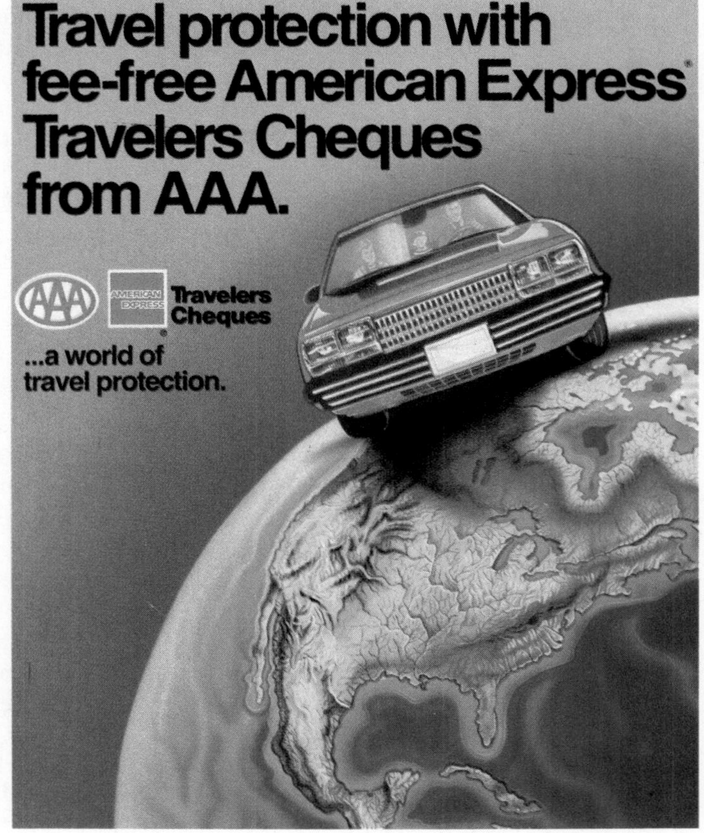

4. Finally, color has a psychological language that sets the mood for the ad. Cool, passive environments are created with blues and pastels, red denotes excitement and warmth, and yellow suggests springtime and youth.

Color can create a recognizable difference in a product. To highlight "a result," SPSS market research software illustrated a manager's success story and picture *in color* in their half-page black-and-white ad. It "drew" the reader to the personal endorsement—and then to the rest of the ad.

Color, a superficial product difference, helped Nuprin analgesic increase its share of the ibuprofen segment of the market. People didn't want to listen to the clinical evidence that Nuprin is better than other pain relievers. Ads saying that research showed two Nuprins give more headache relief than Extra Strength Tylenol failed to advance its share. According to Herb Lieberman, executive vice president of Grey Advertising, New York: "You have to convince consumers that your product is different before they will believe the product is better. The fact that Nuprin is yellow is superficial to the product superiority, yet it opens people's minds that this product is different." The color strategy for Nuprin's print and television campaign was almost an accident. Group creative director Harry Azxorin emptied a whole bunch of pain relievers on his desk, and it hit him—Nuprin was the only yellow tablet there. Color was a way to dramatically and graphically show that Nuprin is different. The first ads showed a black-and-white photo of a hand holding two yellow Nuprin tablets. Television ads in black and white presented testimonials of people explaining that their worst toothaches, back pains, and headaches were relieved with Nuprin. Only the tablets were shown in color. The tagline explained that Nuprin "is for your worst pain."[1]

Color can be extremely important in everything from ad layouts, products, and packaging to the psychological messages consumers perceive.

White Space. One element of design that is often overlooked is white space or blank space. White space can be a strong design tool in helping to unify the ad and emphasize the other elements. The basic rule is to keep it to the outside of the ad. If the designer places too much white space in the middle of the ad, separating other elements, the eye may become confused, as unity breaks down (see Exhibit 17.7).

Search for Distinction

One goal in creating a layout is to make the ad stand out among all the ads in a medium, particularly those for similar products. The first step in this direction is to break away from the layout trend in the same field. There are styles in layouts, and great waves of following the leader sweep over advertisers, with the result that all ads in a field are sometimes in the same mold. Pretend that you are the first person in your field to advertise. Create a layout to fit the mood and nature of your message.

By enlarging the *size* of the illustration, the type, or the ad itself, an advertiser can create distinction. When *Chiquita,* the banana people, wanted to announce that it was now handling *melons* as well, it took out full-page ads in trade magazines. Four different melons were "blown up" to capture the attention of produce buyers—each highlighted against a background of green vines and displaying "an official name tag."

Among the techniques for creating distinction is size. You get more attention if you take a full-page rather than a half-page ad in a newspaper. A double-page spread in a magazine is obviously more attractive than a single page. The problem is cost. Twice as much space does not get you twice as much attention, and large-size ads soon chew up the budget. The only time that use of space may be worth the cost is when you have a special announcement to make.

Another technique is to use an extra-large headline, or the reverse: When everyone else is using large-size type, set the headline around the subject and make it speak softly, yet more powerfully. You can also establish a different style of artwork or create a distinctive art subject.

When Mountain Dew soft drink was introduced, it was promoted with the hillbilly slogan "Ya'hoo, Mountain Dew" and graphics to match. Unfortunately, no known heavy-user segment of soft drinks identified with that appeal. Soon the brand was repositioned to the youthful, fun, carefree image it now promotes. Another way to break away from tradition is to use long narrative copy and catchy headlines.

These are merely a few of the myriad devices for making layouts distinctive. The effort is worth it. When a product becomes known for always having a fresh-looking

[1]Patricia Winters, "Color Nuprin's Success Yellow," *Advertising Age,* October 31, 1988, p. 28.

ADVERTISEMENT

The pyramid of Fantastik bottles seemed to explode as Harold pushed his shopping cart headlong into it. Despite the enormity of the aisle display, Harold ...er saw it until it was too late. Harold's mind was pre- ...ccupied. She ...s tall

blon... Harold had ... lowing her sin... first spied her in th... duce section. He ha... pursued her past "Spice... and Condiments," and up the "Household Items" aisle, cautiously hanging back, glancing toward the shelves whenever she stopp... for fear of being discovered. She was th... most beautifu... creature Harold ha... ever seen, but Harold w... painfully shy, and very se... conscious. And for good reas... Harold had always worn out-of-d... long sleeved paisley shirts, black polyester pants tied off just below his ribcage by a thin black belt and black oversized assembly line shoes. On his nose perched a pair of white-taped black plastic glasses that looked like they belonged with a large rubber nose. He wore his hair combed straight back, slicked down with enough oil to stay in place through a tropical storm. But worst of all, Harold always wore a very strange expression. His entire face stayed squunched up, as if he were constantly staring into the sun.

And now, Harold wore a squunched-up look of embarrassment and disbelief. The blonde had been pushing her cart in the opposite direction when, suddenly, she stopped, turned, and walked directly toward him. Harold had freaked like a scared rabbit, hurtling into the Fantastik. "You clumsy nerd!" an elderly woman ...rked as she pulled herself from ...h the avalanche of white and ...ttles. "You really are a nerd ... you?" a soft voice ...d from behind ... Harold ...ed, and ...ere, ... six ...ches away, ...ood the beautiful blonde.

... g-g-g... so," Harol... replied, staring in a... ment. "But an honest nerd," s...

"I see you use Fantastik, too," the beautiful girl said, nodding toward Harold's basket. They both chuckled a little, as Harold realized that five or six of the bottles had tumbled into his empty cart. "Well, yes, actually I do like Fantastik," Harold answered nervously. "It's great in the kitchen, and I really like to cook!" Harold was excited. They had something in common, even if it was only a preference for the same all-purpose spray cleaner. "I was on my way back to get a bottle of Fantastik when your shopping cart, uh, ran out of control," she said with a smile. Harold squunched his face harder. "You're different," she continued, "different from the other guys I know. Biff, Skippy, Blade... they're so insensitive...but not you. By the way, my name's Susan," she said. Harold took her outstretched hand in his. "Harold," he said with a reluctant sigh. "Ya know, Harold, I like you. You just need a few....alterations." Harold squunched more than ever now. "Some ...thes, shoes, new glasses...and we've got ...do something about that hair...but ...irst Harold..." "Y-y-yes?" Harold ...uttered. "The first thing I'm going to ...o is wipe that silly squunched-up look off your face." At that, she pulled Harold to her, and smothered him with a hot deep kiss that made his knees go weak. "Are you o.k.?" she asked. He nodded. "Harold, it worked. Your face is un-squunched now. You're not bad looking. Not bad at all." Harold blushed. "Harold, would you be so kind as to escort me to the frozen foods?" "Delighted, my dear," Harold answered, surprising himself with the Erroll Flynn-ish tone of his reply. "Yes, you have great potential," Susan ... taking his arm. Harold flashed ... un-squunched smile ...

... away. For a m... that they were sharing one shopping cart, one bottle of Fantastik, one cozy house in the suburbs. 'But hey, slow down' Harold thought, 'just one aisle at a time.'

NEW IMPROVED
FANTASTIK® NOW
OUTCLEANS EVERY
OTHER ALL-PURPOSE
SPRAY CLEANER
on tough greasy dirt in
the kitchen or anywhere else.
MORE POWER FOR
MORE PLACES
fantastik
fantastik
TEXIZE Greenville, SC 29602
Division of Dow Consumer Products Inc. ©1988

EXHIBIT 17.7

This unusual use of white space in a "Z" shape draws the eye to the head and the product. (Courtesy: Dow Consumer Products, Inc.)

ad, each clearly delivering the same story in a different way, you can be sure that the reader will not confuse the brand with others in the field.

Preparing the Layout

Layouts are the actual drawings used in planning the final design of the ad. Different types of layouts represent different stages in the development of the ad. For the first ad of an important new campaign of color magazine ads, an elaborate step-by-step series of layouts may be prepared:

- *Thumbnail sketches:* miniature drawings trying out different arrangements of the layout elements (see Exhibit 17.8A). The best of these will be selected for the next step.
- *Rough layouts:* drawings that are equivalent to the actual size of the ad. All elements are presented more clearly to simulate the way the ad is to look. The best of these will be chosen for the next step (see Exhibits 17.8B and 17.9A).
- *The comprehensive, or mechanical, layout* (often just called the *comp* or the *mechanical*): all the type set and pasted in place exactly as it is to appear in the printed ad. Artwork is drawn one and a half times the actual size it will be in the ad (to be reduced by one-third for sharper reproduction) and is prepared separately; therefore, it is precisely indicated on the comprehensive by blank boxes of the exact final size. This layout will be used not only for client approval but also for making the final print or plate (see Exhibits 17.8D and 17.9B).

Mechanical. *A form of layout. An exact black-and-white copy of the ad as it will appear in printed form. Each element is pasted to an art board in precise position, ready for the camera.*

Exhibit 17.9 illustrates the traditional layout, which uses markers from rough through comp to the finish printed product. In Exhibit 17.8, the rough is more like the comprehensive because a computer was used to give the client a more realistic-looking layout with type in place (not drawn as in 17.9B).

Once the basic ad for a campaign has been approved, layouts for subsequent ads usually consist of just a rough layout and a finished layout.

Computer Design

Comprehensive. *A layout accurate in size, color scheme, and other details to show how final ad will look. For presentation only, never for reproduction.*

In the next chapter, we will talk more about the meshing of computer design functions with production. Here we need to get a brief understanding of the role of the computer in the creative process. For the record, we'll define computer graphics as the ability to draw or display visual information on a video terminal. *Raster Scan Graphics* is the most common computer display. Each spot on the screen, called a *pixel,* represents a location in the computer's memory. The number of individual pixels will determine the resolution of your image: The more pixels, the higher the resolution and the smoother your image. The resolution of a screen controls its clarity and sharpness. Computer software is the prepackaged program that instructs the computer how to operate (see Exhibit 17.10). Such programs allow the artist to manipulate images within defined parameters. Of course, artists may use a digitizing pen and tablet as well as signals from the digitizing camera as sources of images for their designs. The better they understand the program, the greater their flexibility and creativity will be. There are professional systems with a capability of 16 million colors, but these are expensive.[2]

Pixel. *Each spot on computer display screen representing a location in its memory.*

As you can understand, computer design is highly complex, and that has been a problem. Most advertising layout artists simply haven't had the time to become computer experts.

The layout artist of the future, however, will use computer systems as routinely as artists use markers today. The new breed entering the field from design schools have a working knowledge of the power and potential of computers in the graphics process. They can revise a layout merely by manipulating visual elements or changing type size on the screen, which is a real time and cost saver. With a computer system, the

[2]Amy E. Arnston, *Graphic Design Basics* (New York: Holt, Rinehart and Winston, Inc., 1988), pp. 177–188.

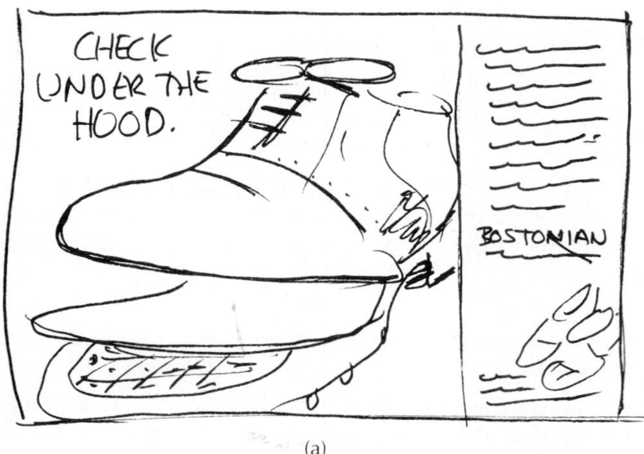

(a)

(b)

(c)

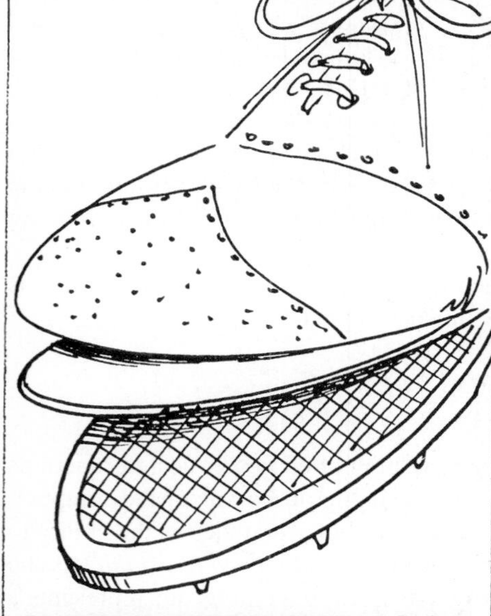

(d)

(e)

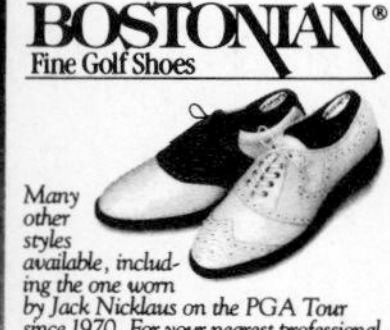

EXHIBIT 17.8

A is an example of a thumbnail sketch. B shows how the computer makes a rough look closer to a comprehensive. C is a computer variation rough changing size. D is the computer comprehensive with all of the copy set in type. E is the finished printed ad as it appeared in magazines.

(a)

(b)

EXHIBIT 17.9

A is a rough layout drawn to actual size, with elements simulated to appear as they will in the ad. B is a comp prepared with color markers, with great detail and every element in its proper place and size. It is shown to the client to get approval for final production. C is the finished color ad as it appeared in publications.

(c)

Today, desktop publishing means more to business than ever before. And Aldus PageMaker® means desktop publishing to more businesses worldwide than any other software program.

Unlike less versatile programs, PageMaker lets you quickly create everything from simple business forms to award-winning brochures. And it makes short work of long documents, too.

Your computer becomes a powerful business communications tool. Which gives you greater control of deadlines and costs while making your document processing more productive.

If you can use a computer, you can create great-looking documents with PageMaker. Professionally designed templates give you a streamlined way to generate hard-hitting reports, manuals, or newsletters. So you don't need a degree in graphic design to make a graphic impression.

Only a program like Aldus PageMaker makes it so easy to incorporate spreadsheets, logos, charts, tables, and other graphics into your documents. Materials that once took days can be produced in hours.

PageMaker works well in your existing business environment, too. It does a beautiful job of integrating with your favorite word-processing and spreadsheet programs. Its files even transfer directly between Macintosh and PC versions. Plus, it works with more business software and printers than any other desktop publishing product available today.

So if you thought desktop publishing was none of your business, think again. And consider how PageMaker can give your business a competitive edge.

See why PageMaker means business.

To see how easily PageMaker can improve your business communications, and your bottom line, visit your authorized Aldus dealer. Or, call 1-800-333-2538, Department 10-B2 for a FREE Aldus PageMaker information packet.*

ALDUS®
The Creative Edge in Business.

AND YOU THOUGHT DESKTOP PUBLISHING WAS NONE OF YOUR BUSINESS.

EXHIBIT 17.10

This computer software ad promotes the use of PageMaker for desktop publishing. (Courtesy: Aldus.)

Computer-designed ads can make creativity and revision relatively simple tasks. *Boston Digital Corporation* became one of the first in its industry to dramatize the machining capabilities of image promotion. The marketing theme, "Master of the Machining Art," was developed for the BostoMatic rollout at the International Machine Tool Show in Chicago in 1988. An ad and general catalogue featured a Venus de Milo replication—one of the finest and most difficult shapes to contour.

Small ads pose a greater challenge to advertisers than large ads—in order to get noticed and convey the intended message. Choosing a well-read part of a page, such as upper-left or right, and using a short, definitive headline make *Namelab* ads stand out. Although less than ¼ of a page, they attract the reader because of their "sharpness."

"roughs" are no longer rough. The comprehensives are better, because the layout and typography are exact. The scanner adds the art and photos, and the system adds color and variations.

By tradition, the creation and production processes in advertising have been separate and distinct. In the future, some experts believe one person will do it all. Others, however, maintain that specialization will continue. In any case, professional mastery of layout increasingly demands a knowledge not only of art, type, and design, but of photography, computers, printers, and electronic imaging as well.[3]

Layouts for Small Advertisements

Small ads are sometimes a greater creative challenge than large ones because they must gain attention in a busy setting. They appear in many magazines, and numerous businesses have been built by them. Successful small ads usually have a strong promise in a selective headline with a functional picture. The eyes take in all of a small ad at one time, so a liberal part of the space must be used merely to get noticed. A good small ad is not a large ad reduced; it is created by abstracting the one or two most essential elements of a large ad (if one has already been created) and emphasizing them.

The Artist's Medium

The tool or material used to render an illustration is called the *artist's medium,* the term *medium* being used in a different sense than it is in the phrase "advertising medium" (as TV or magazines). The most popular artist's medium in advertising is photography. Other popular ones are pen and ink, pencil, crayon, and wash. Perhaps a photograph will be used as the main illustration for an ad, but pen and ink will be used for the smaller, secondary illustration. The choice of the artist's medium depends on the effect desired, the paper on which the ad is to be printed, the printing process to be used, and, most important, the availability of an artist who is effective in the desired medium (see Exhibits 17.8B and 17.9B).

Trade Practice in Buying Commercial Art

Art may be "created" or "bought." Many freelance artists and photographers are concentrated in the largest advertising centers, who will work with various agencies in producing "original" pictures and photographs. For Piggly Wiggly's new "competitive" ads against other supermarkets, it commissioned photographs of women shopping in unlikely settings (warehouses) and with unusual artifacts ("Pinocchio"-style noses). Northwest Productions, Minneapolis, produced the photographs, in conjunction with Sossaman Bateman McCuddy Advertising, Memphis.

Creating an ad usually requires two types of artistic talent: the imaginative person who thinks up the visual idea, with a copywriter or alone, and who makes the master layout; and an artist who does the finished art of the illustrations. Large agencies have staff art directors and layout people to visualize and create original layouts, as well as studios and artists to handle routine work.

In the largest advertising centers—New York, Chicago, Los Angeles, Dallas, San Francisco, and Atlanta—a host of free-lance artists and photographers specializes in certain fields for preparing the final art of such subjects. In fact, agencies in other cities go to one of the major art centers to buy their graphic artwork for special assignments.

There are two important points to observe in buying artwork, especially photographs. First, you must have written permission or a legal release (see Exhibit 17.11) from anyone whose picture you will use, whether you took the picture or got it from a publication or an art file. (In the case of a child's picture, you must obtain a release from the parent or guardian.) Second, you should arrange all terms in advance. A photographer may take a number of pictures, from which you select one. What will be the price if you wish to use more than one shot? What will be the price if you use the picture in several publications?

Free-lance artists' and photographers' charges vary greatly, depending on their reputation, the nature of the work, what medium the work is being used in, and whether the

[3]Frank J. Romano, "Electronic Typesetting and Design," *Art Product News,* January–February 1989, pp. 12–13.

EXHIBIT 17.11

Typical model release used by agencies. (Courtesy: BDA/BBDO, Inc.)

MODEL RELEASE
(MINOR MODEL RELEASE ON OTHER SIDE)

BDA/BBDO
Incorporated
3414 Peachtree Road, N.E., Atlanta, Georgia 30326

DEAR SIRS: DATE ____________

I HEREBY irrevocably consent to the use, for advertising and trade purposes, by BDA/BBDO, Inc., and by advertisers BDA/BBDO, Inc., may authorize or represent, of my name and/or of one or more portraits, pictures and photographs of me and reproductions of the same in any form . . . hereby releasing the above parties from liabilities arising out of what I might deem misrepresentation of me by virtue of distortion, optical illusions or faulty mechanical reproductions. The publicity I receive by virtue of the first such use that may be made thereof shall be full and adequate consideration for this consent. I agree that all such portraits, pictures, photographs, reproductions thereof and plates and negatives connected therewith are and shall remain the property of BDA/BBDO, Inc., or of advertisers represented by BDA/BBDO, Inc. I am over twenty-one years of age. I acknowledge this release constitutes the entire understanding with the above parties, all prior understandings, if any, being merged herein.

Witness my hand and seal below.

WITNESS ____________ SIGNED ____________

EXCLUSIVITY AGREEMENT: In consideration for the payment to be made to me in connection with this modeling for ____________, I hereby warrent that my name and/or likeness has not been used for the past ______ months, nor will be used during the next ______ months, for any competitor's products.

DATE ____________ SIGNED ____________

__Release.__ A legally correct statement by a person photographed, authorizing the advertiser to use that photograph. For minors, the guardian's release is necessary.

ad is to run locally, regionally, or nationally. An art illustration for a magazine may cost $200 if by an unknown artist and up to about $5,000 if by an established artist. A photography session may cost $200 a day for an unknown to about $2,500 for an established photographer. People charge what they think the art or photography is worth or what the client can or is willing to pay. As a result, the better the reputation of the artist or photographer, the more expensive the final product will likely be.

Other Sources of Art and Photography

Clients will not always be able to afford the money or time for original advertising art or photography. There are three basic sources of ready-made images.

"Clipped" or "stock" art and photographs are ready-made designs, which can be adopted for print ads. In the *Sun Bank* ads in *Time* recently, the company wanted to convey "day" *and* "night" to readers. They used two "ordinary" photographs of a quarter moon over water and a rising sun—with the headline: "The Difference Between Our Corporate Financial Services, And All The Rest."

Clip Art. Ready-to-use copyright-free images are available from clip art services. The art is printed in black and white on glossy paper ready for use. All you have to do is cut it out—hence the name "clip art." Almost any kind of image is available from clip art services: families, men and women, children, business scenes, locations (farm, beach), and special events. The negatives to using clip art are that you have to match your idea to the available images and the illustrations are rather average. The advantages are the very reasonable cost and the extensive choice of images. Some clip art services offer a monthly book or books with a wide variety of promotional art; others have specific volumes—restaurant art, supermarket art, hospital art, for example. Once you purchase clip art, it is yours to use as you see fit.

Stock Photos. Over 250 libraries of stock photography are available in this country. Each maintains hundreds or thousands of photographs classified according to subject categories, including children, animals, life-style situations, sports, and models. The cost is based on the nature of the photo and how you are going to use it—in local, regional, or national advertising; in magazines or newspaper; and with what degree of exclusivity. For example, a California stock photo company charges $100 for black-and-white newspaper use, $150 for color newspaper use; the same photo used in magazines costs $150 for black and white and $250 for color; and the same photo used in point-of-sale material costs up to $650.

EXHIBIT 17.12
This photo dominates the layout.
(Courtesy: Speedo America.)

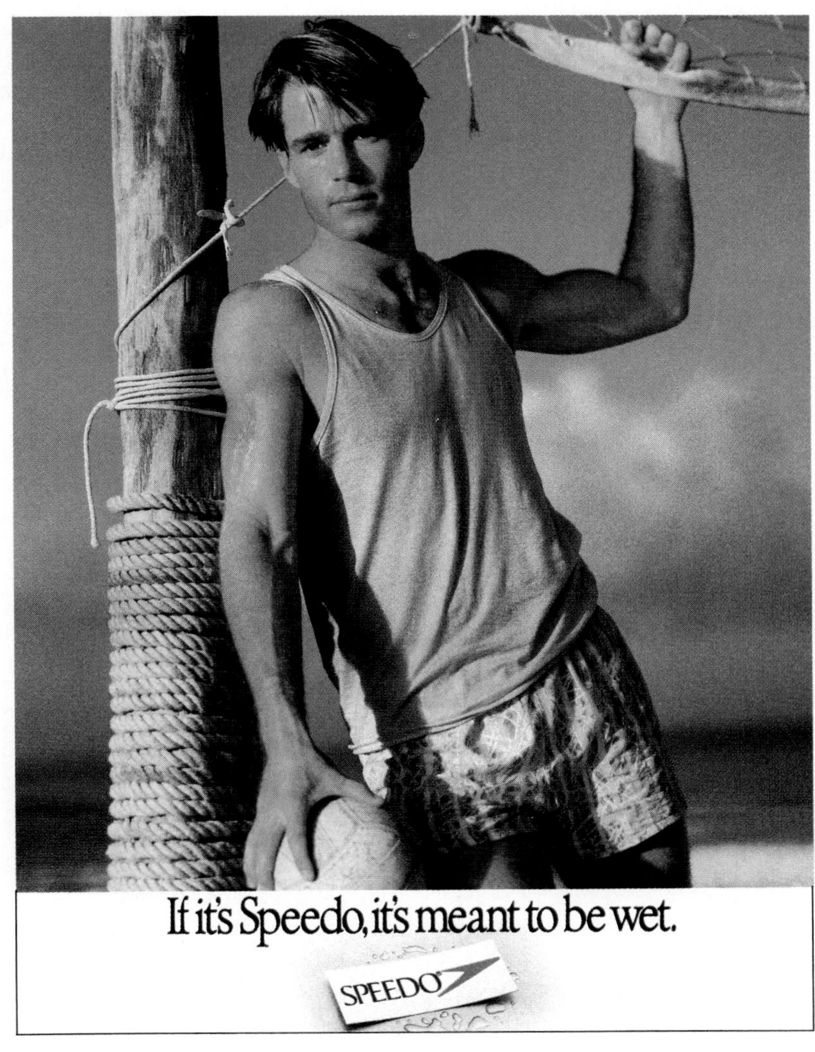

If it's Speedo, it's meant to be wet.
SPEEDO

Computer Clip Art. There are art services that sell software packages of clip art for desktop or other graphic computer uses. Dynamic Graphics's DeskTop Art and DeskTop Graphics provide over 20,000 illustrations to artists. Software companies promote the graphics as a cost and time savings for bulletins, newsletters, flyers, and newspaper ads. The quality of most computer clip art isn't yet good enough for regional and national advertising.

SUMMARY

In this chapter, we made the transition from thinking of ideas to making ads. Ad making begins with finding the primary consumer benefit, the most important thing we can say about our product. The next step is to visualize this basic appeal as a concept that combines words and pictures to express an idea clearly—hopefully, a Big Idea.

The creative team—an art director and a copywriter—next develops the best approach to presenting the concept effectively. Then comes layout preparation (usually done by the art director), in which the various elements of the ad are composed into a unified whole. Because of advertising clutter, getting attention is one of the art director's primary concerns. When arranging the elements of an ad, the layout artist has to consider the principles of design: unity, harmony, sequence, emphasis, contrast, and balance.

Ads usually begin as thumbnail sketches. Subsequent steps are the rough layout, the finished layout, and the comps. The computer simplifies this process: In computer design, the "roughs" are no longer rough and the comprehensives are better, because the layout and typography are exact.

In most cases, art and photography are original executions of the art director's ideas, illustrated or shot according to his or her specifications by free-lance artists or photographers. When time or money is short, clip art or computer art services or stock photography may be used.

QUESTIONS

1. What role does marketing play in visualization?
2. What are the basic design principles?
3. What is informal balance?
4. What is meant by the creative leap?
5. What is the creative team?

SUGGESTED EXERCISES

1. Find two informal and formal balanced ads and discuss their layouts.
2. Find three ads that have distinctive layouts and discuss the design elements of each.

READINGS

BELTRAMINI, RICHARD F., AND VINCENT J. BLASKO: "An Analysis of Award-Winning Headlines," *Journal of Marketing Research,* Vol. 26, No. 2, 1986, pp. 48–52.

HAIGHT, GORDON: "Technology in Advertising," *Desktop,* August 1989, p. 20.

HENCHEY, L. W.: "A New Image," *Inside Print,* June 1988, pp. 40–46.

NELSON, ROY PAUL: *The Design of Advertising,* 6th Edition (Dubuque, Wm. C. Brown Publishers, 1989).

EIGHTEEN

Print Production

So you have developed an idea for an ad, a brochure, or an insert. The copy has been written and the layout and illustrations have been prepared. What's the next step? How do we get a finished product? What do we have to send to the publication people so they can print our ad? What are the preparation and printing procedures for the brochure and insert? How long will all this take?

Advertising and marketing people need to have a working knowledge of production. This conversion process, which is the responsibility of the advertiser or agency, is called *print production*. Production requirements differ from ad to ad. The planning process may involve a great deal of money and many people. The agency production organization varies according to the size of the agency. In small agencies, there may be a single production expert. In large agencies, the production department consists of numerous specialists; buyers who contract with photographers, illustrators, retouchers, and photo labs in cooperation with art directors; typography experts who work with art directors in selecting and developing specifications and purchasing type; producers who work with other agency personnel from traffic to account managers and act as liaison with the publication's production people; and printing buyers who purchase various kinds of printing needed for collateral and newspaper and magazine inserts where the agency and client control the actual printing steps involved. The Komatsu double-page ad in Exhibit 18.1 illustrates many different elements in the production process.

In this chapter, we'll discuss the role of quality in traditional graphics preparation and production and the influence of computer technology.

The computer has enabled one person to create and produce ad layouts. Using a MacIntosh computer, Aldus Persuasion's *Auto Template* software allows the operator to select a design, type in text—and voila! It automatically formats an outline into *a formal layout*. Tables, graphs, charts are included in the program's data sheet—but powerful drawing tools, special effects, and clip art are, also. The operator can easily create flow charts, conceptual diagrams, and logos—and even import art from other graphics programs.

GRAPHICS BY COMPUTER

In Chapter 17, we discussed the computer as a graphics tool for producing layouts and illustrations. This new technology is blurring the creation and preparation aspects of production, as it makes it possible for one person to both create and produce. It is also giving production managers more choices.

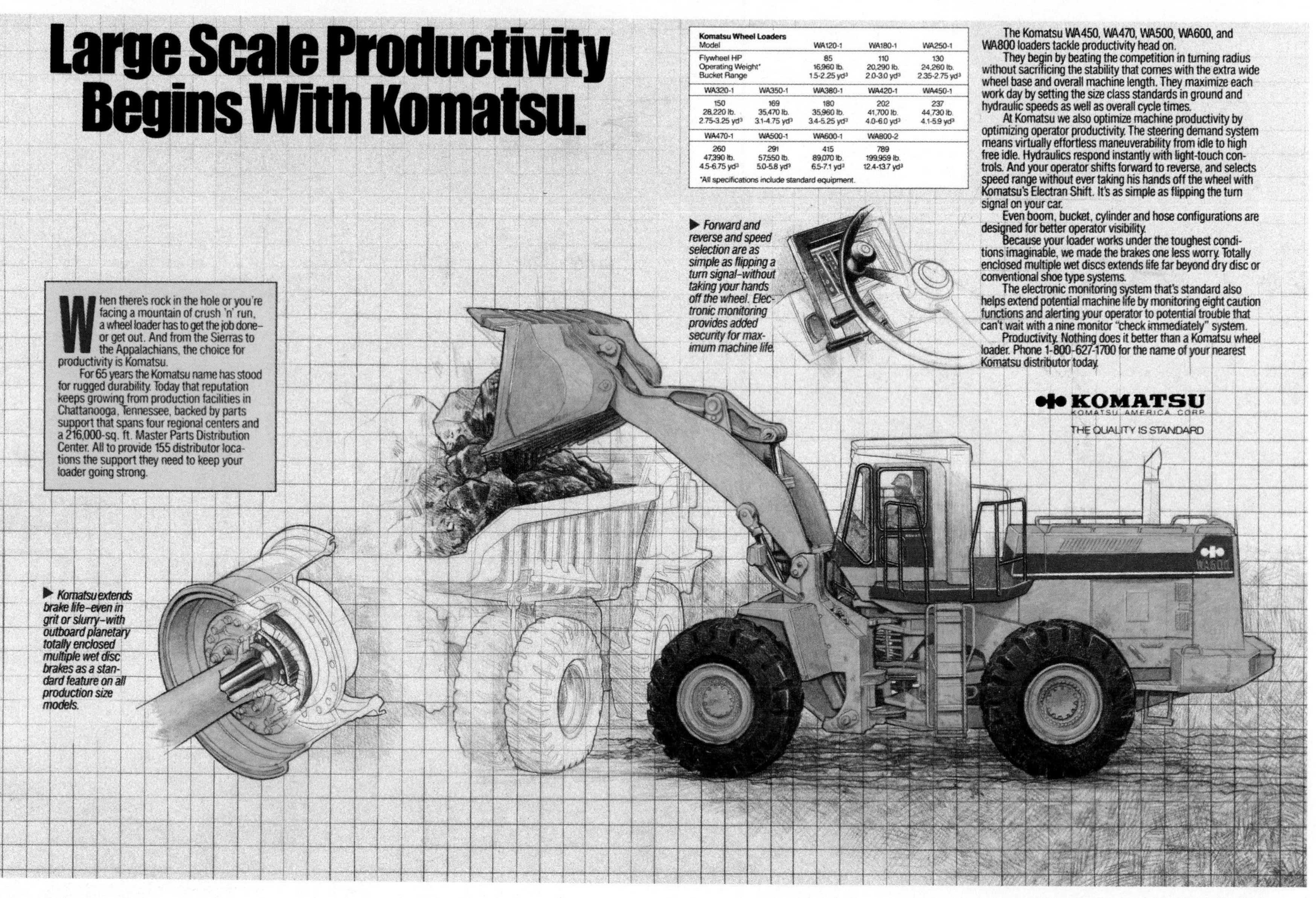

EXHIBIT 18.1

This two-page ad involved many complex production processes. (Courtesy: Komatsu and Sawyer Riley Compton Advertising.)

We visited and conducted a survey of small, medium, and large agencies to get an idea of how much art and production are being created on the computer today. We found that although there is a strong movement toward integrating the computer as a graphic and production tool, only about 10 to 15 percent of the art and production for ads are presently being created on the computer. It appears that the small and medium shops are more prone to use computer graphics than the giants, but Seymour Serle of FCB/Leber Katz predicts that desktop design will become much more common in most agencies within the next two years.

A major hindrance is the time required for the art and production people to learn how to use the software. Art directors who are interested simply lack the time to experiment with computer production. Some agencies have adopted the computer for some kinds of work but not for others. For example, Leslie Advertising, Greenville, South Carolina, has a Macintosh system that it uses primarily for public relations, retail advertising, and promotion typesetting, but it still produces most of the type and layout for ads by traditional methods.

The agencies that do have experience with computer production are highly pleased with the results. Lintas:Campbell-Ewald, a Detroit-based agency, purchased an electronic design and imaging system (Du Pont's Vaster System) three years ago and has used it in developing "The Heartbeat of America" campaign for Chevrolet and Bridgestone tire ads. The computer has actually become a part of the creative team—almost a third person after the writer and the art director. Creating layouts on the computer is much faster than the traditional methods, which might require the art director to send work outside the agency—for color prints, drawings, or illustrations. Instead, using the computer, the artist can do a typical layout in one or two hours, and a simple one in thirty minutes.

Exhibit 18.2A shows an original agency logo as it was scanned into the Macintosh II; 18.2B, C, and D illustrate how the computer can transform the letters' shape, and 18.2E shows how easily you can apply a pattern to the design, then duplicate and manipulate the image. These computer graphics are now ready for the production process.

EXHIBIT 18.2

(a)

(b)

(c)

Advertising

(d)

(e)

1989 Material Due Date Chart

ISSUE		NATIONAL 4c-2c all Nat'l. s/r (7 weeks)	NATIONAL b/w (5 weeks)	REG/STATE/METRO all colors (7 weeks)	SELECT all colors (7 weeks)
JAN:	9	11-21	12-5	11-21	N/A
	16*	11-28	12-12	N/A	11-28
	23	12-5	12-19	12-5	N/A
	30***	12-12	12-26	N/A	12-12
FEB:	6	12-19	1-2	12-19	N/A
	8†	Special Swimsuit Issue—Closes 12-5-88 for all colors & editions			
	13*	12-26	1-9	N/A	12-26
	20	1-2	1-16	1-2	N/A
	27***	1-9	1-23	N/A	1-9
MAR:	6	1-16	1-30	1-16	N/A
	13*	1-23	2-6	N/A	1-23
	20**	1-30	2-13	1-30	N/A
	27***	2-6	2-20	N/A	2-6
APR:	3	2-13	2-27	2-13	N/A
	5†	Special Baseball Preview Issue—Closes 1-30-89 for all colors & editions			
	10*	2-20	3-6	N/A	2-20
	17**	2-27	3-13	2-27	N/A
	24***	3-6	3-20	N/A	3-6
MAY:	1	3-13	3-27	3-13	N/A
	8*	3-20	4-3	N/A	3-20
	15**	3-27	4-10	3-27	N/A
	22***	4-3	4-17	N/A	4-3
	29	4-10	4-24	4-10	N/A
JUNE:	5*	4-17	5-1	N/A	4-17
	12**	4-24	5-8	4-24	N/A
	19***	5-1	5-15	N/A	5-1
	26	5-8	5-22	5-8	N/A
JULY:	3*	5-15	5-29	N/A	5-15
	10	5-22	6-5	5-22	N/A
	17***	5-29	6-12	N/A	5-29
	24	6-5	6-19	6-5	N/A
	31*	6-12	6-26	N/A	6-12
AUG:	7	6-19	7-3	6-19	N/A
	14***	6-26	7-10	N/A	6-26
	21	7-3	7-17	7-3	N/A
	28*	7-10	7-24	N/A	7-10
SEP:	4	7-17	7-31	7-17	N/A
	11***	7-24	8-7	N/A	7-24
	18**	7-31	8-14	7-31	N/A
	25*	8-7	8-21	N/A	8-7
OCT:	2	8-14	8-28	8-14	N/A
	9***	8-21	9-4	N/A	8-21
	16**	8-28	9-11	8-28	N/A
	23*	9-4	9-18	N/A	9-4
	30	9-11	9-25	9-11	N/A
NOV:	6***	9-18	10-2	N/A	9-18
	13**	9-25	10-9	9-25	N/A
	15†	Special Issue—The 80's—Closes 9-11-89 for all colors & editions			
	20*	10-2	10-16	N/A	10-2
	27	10-9	10-23	10-9	N/A
DEC:	4***	10-16	10-30	N/A	10-16
	11	10-23	11-6	10-23	N/A
	18*	10-30	11-13	N/A	10-30
DEC: JAN:	25/ 1	11-6	11-20	11-16	N/A

Mechanical Specifications

All national and less than national editions are printed offset. The SWOP standards for proofing should be followed.

Proofs:

Black and white—10 complete proofs.
Two-color and four-color—10 complete proofs and 10 sets of progressives.

Standard Film Sizes:

Trim-size—8-1/8" x 10-7/8"
Page—7" x 10"
Two pages facing—15" x 10"
Two columns—4-5/8" x 10"
Half-page horizontal—7" x 4-7/8"
One column—2-1/4" x 10"
One column square—4-5/8" x 4-7/8"
Digest size—4-5/8" x 6-15/16"

Bleed Film Sizes:

Page—8-1/4" x 11-1/8"
Two pages facing—16-1/2" x 11-1/8"
Two columns—5-3/8" x 11-1/8"
Half-page horizontal—8-1/4" x 5-5/8"
One column—3-1/8" x 11-1/8"
One column square—5-3/8" x 5-5/8"
Digest size—5-3/8" x 7-11/16"

For bleed pages, columns & halfs keep essential matter 1/2" from top, bottom and sides of all film, and at least 11/16" from front bleed edge on both pages of facing page spread. Live material in facing pages should not be closer than 1/8" to center fold.

Publisher reserves the right to crop up to 3/16" from either side of full page film, 2 column film or one column film to compensate for variation in trim page size.

Engraver's mark must be indicated at the center for spread film as a position guide.

Shipping Instructions:

Send contracts, insertion orders and one proof to:
AD RECORDS DEPARTMENT,
SPORTS ILLUSTRATED,
TIME-LIFE Building
1271 Avenue of the Americas
New York, N.Y. 10020. ATT: JOAN RUSSELL

Send material and copy instructions to:
SPORTS ILLUSTRATED
TIME-LIFE BUILDING
MESSENGER DESK-CONCOURSE LEVEL
1271 AVENUE OF THE AMERICAS
NEW YORK, N.Y. 10020

For additional information or assistance regarding material deadlines, copy changes or the status of material supplied, call New York (212) 522-7607.

SI Regional/State/Metro editions available on alternating weeks with SI Select as listed above.

Any split run, national or regional, regardless of coloration will close seven weeks preceding date of publication.

*SI Prime Issue Dates
**Homeowners Issue Dates
***Circulation identified 50% SI Issue/Dates
†See Special rate card for edition availabilities.

EXHIBIT 18.3
(Courtesy: *Sports Illustrated*.)

PRODUCTION DATA

Each publication determines the due dates and mechanical specifications for an ad. Exhibit 18.3 indicates the due dates based upon the type of *Sports Illustrated* edition desired, the printing process to be used, the kinds of proofs needed, the film size required for specific ad sizes, and other requirements. SRDS (Standard Rate & Data Service) provides mechanical specifications in its print volumes for newspapers, consumer magazines, and so on. However, print production specialists rely heavily on the SRDS *Print Media Production Data* publication, which carries essential production information for the major national and regional publications. Production people must directly contact publications not included in SRDS to obtain their production requirements.

PRODUCTION PLANNING AND SCHEDULING

Scheduling production work varies according to the materials, specifications, *and revisions*. Often, test market results may change an advertiser's mind about a campaign theme. Kentucky Fried Chicken has asked its agency, Young & Rubincam to create a new positioning, since the failure of "Kentucky Fried Chicken is Home." One month is the normal rollout time for new campaigns in competitive markets, so that competitors don't have time to "regroup."

To ensure that the creative and production work moves along with the necessary precision, a time schedule is planned at the outset. The closing date is the date or time when all material must arrive at the publication. Once this is known, the advertiser works backward along the calendar to determine when work must be begun in order to meet the date.

The following can be used as a rule of thumb in determining the length of time needed to make printing materials and revisions: for black-and-white ads, 2–3 working days, depending on the printing process; for process color ads, about 20 working days. You may need another 4 to 5 days to produce progressive proofs and obtain client approvals.

Exhibit 18.4 is a typical time schedule for production of a color ad to be sent to several publications with a closing date of November 1.

Exhibit 18.5 illustrates the job production steps requires.

Now that we better understand the production environment, let's take a look at the key considerations in a number of production steps.

SELECTING THE PRINTING PROCESS

The *printing process*—letterpress, offset, or rotogravure—is determined by what will work best in a particular medium. *Hammermill Papers* uses sheet-fed offset press on their cover stock—to create bright, distinct images with a lustre finish.

In most cases, the printing process used depends on the medium the ad is running in, not on the advertiser or the agency. However, in some areas such as sales promotion, ad inserts, direct mail, and point-of-sale, the advertiser must make the final decision regarding print production. In order to deal effectively with printers, the advertiser

EXHIBIT 18.4
Color ad production schedule.

Work	Date
In order to reach publications by closing date	November 1
Shipping date of duplicate materials	October 29
Start making duplicate materials	October 25
Final photoplatemaker's proof	October 22
Photoplatemaker's first proof available by	October 13
Material to photoplatemaker	September 28
Retouched art and mechanical ready by	September 22
Typesetting order date	September 16
Finished artwork (photograph) delivered by	September 15
Finished artwork (photography) order date	September 7
Creative work (copy and layout) approved by	September 4
Start of creative work	August 23

YOUNG & RUBICAM INTERNATIONAL INC. JOB PRODUCTION ORDER/SCHEDULE – **PRINT** S3 Rev. 6/74

Client

Product

Job #

Subject

Description

Title (Max. 22 characters)

DISTRIBUTION	
Name	Function
	Account Supervisor
	Account Executive
	Assoc. Creative Dir.
	Art Director
	Copywriter
	Art Buyer
	Print Producer

EVENTS/ITEMS	DUE FROM	DATE	NOTES
Briefing Meeting			
Layout & Copy Due			
Layout & Copy Approved by Client			
Estimate Request Prepared			
Estimate Due			
Art Bids Due			
Type Due			
Art Due			
Final Art & Mechanical Due			
Art & Mechanical Approved by Client			
First Proof Due at Y&R			
Final Proof Approved by Client			
All (Duplicate) Materials Ready to Ship			
Materials Due at First Publication			

PUBLICATION	ISSUE	SPACE	SIZE	4/C B/W	N/B BLD.	PUBLICATION	ISSUE	SPACE	SIZE	4/C B/W	N/B BLD.

Job Quote $	Job Billing Requirements	Antic. Mo. 1st Use (Impact)	Antic. Exp. Date

Prepared by: PRODUCTION COORDINATOR Date

Authorized by: ACCOUNT MANAGEMENT AUTHORITY Date

EXHIBIT 18.5

Production schedule indicates the number of steps involved in print production. (Courtesy: Young & Rubicam, Inc.)

must have some knowledge of the basic production techniques and which is the most appropriate for the job at hand.

If the printing process is not predetermined, the first step in the production process is to decide which process is most suitable. There are three major printing processes:

- Letterpress printing (from a raised surface)

Offset's popularity is due to its efficiency—it can print on nearly any surface—and it's economical, compared to letterpress printing. The "World's largest pennant manufacturer," *National Banner Company,* uses offset printing for producing banners, decals, flags, pennants, signs, and tags.

- Offset lithography (from a flat surface)
- Rotogravure (from an etched surface)

Each of these printing processes has certain advantages and disadvantages, but one process may be more efficient for a particular job. Once the printing process has been established, the production process has been dictated, for all production work depends on the process used.

Let's get a basic understanding of these processes.

Letterpress Printing

Letterpress. *Printing from a relief, or raised, surface. The raised surface is inked and comes in direct contact with the paper, like a rubber stamp. See Offset, Gravure printing.*

If you have ever used a rubber ink stamp (with an address or other words), you've applied the principle of letterpress printing—printing from a raised surface. You press the raised stamp against an ink pad. Then, as you press the stamp against paper, the ink is transferred from the stamp to the paper and the message is reproduced.

In letterpress printing, the area to be printed is raised and inked. The inked plate is then pressed against the paper and the result is a printed impression (see Exhibit 18.6).

All types of copy (photographs, type, art) must be converted to a photoengraving (a process of making a raised surface) before printing can occur. The advertiser or agency must supply photoengravings or duplicates of such plates to the newspaper, magazine, or letterpress printer.

Offset Lithography

Offset. *(1) Lithography. (2) The blotting of a wet or freshly printed sheet against an accompanying sheet. Can be prevented by slipsheeting. Antique paper absorbs the ink and prevents offsetting.*

Gravure printing. *A process in which the printing image is etched below the nonprinting area. Instead of plates or forms, gravure printing usually employs a cylinder that is fully inked. The surface is then wiped clean, retaining ink only in the cups (sunken area). Tone variations are mainly achieved by etching cups to different depths. See Rotogravure.*

Offset is a photochemical process based upon the principle that grease and water won't mix. In theory, offset can print anything that can be photographed. In reality, there are some things that won't print very well by offset.

The planographic (flat-surface) process uses a thin, flat aluminum plate that is wrapped around a cylinder on a rotary press. The plate is coated with a continuous flow of liquid solution from dampening rollers that repels ink. The inked plate comes in contact with a rubber blanket on another cylinder. The inked impression goes from the plate to the rubber blanket. The inked blanket then transfers ("offsets") the inked image to the paper, which is on a delivery cylinder. The plate never comes in direct contact with the paper (see Exhibit 18.7).

The photo aspect of the process makes offset very efficient and the most popular printing process in the country. Offset is used to reproduce books (including this text), catalogs, periodicals, direct-mail pieces, outdoor and transit posters, point-of-sale, and over half the newspapers in this country.

This process is capable of printing on almost any surface: paper, plastics, board, cloth.

The advertiser or agency must supply the artwork and mechanicals or films from which offset plates can be made.

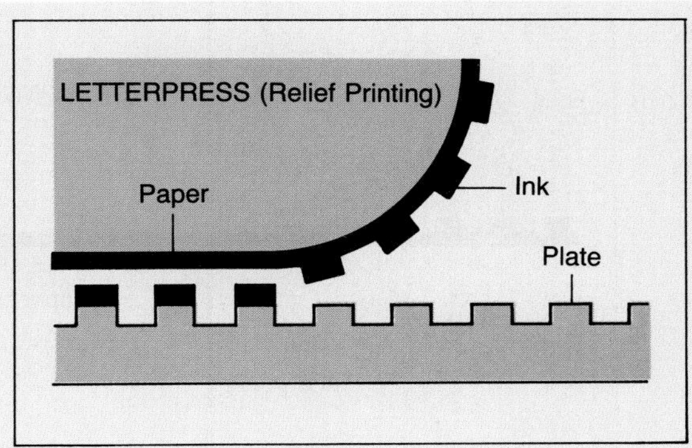

EXHIBIT 18.6

Letterpress printing. Notice the raised surface of the plate.

EXHIBIT 18.7

Offset printing press plate system, showing image coming off plate, onto rubber blanket, and offsetting to paper.

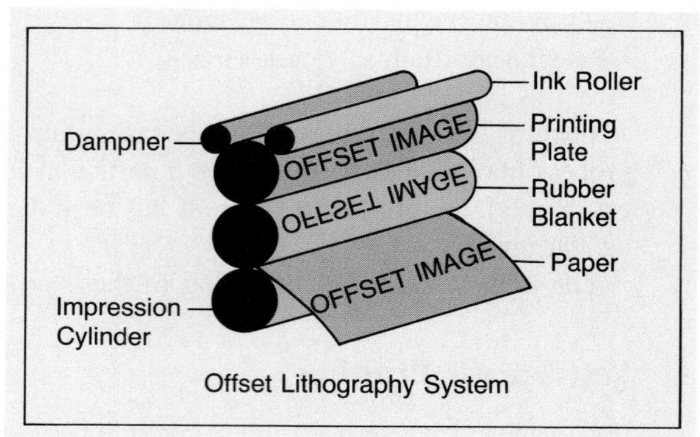

Rotogravure

Sunday supplement magazines, mail-order catalogs, and newspaper inserts are a few examples of rotogravure printing—all requiring long press runs! By adopting gravure printing for its 5 revamped catalogs, *Hanover* hopes to create a fashion image for this once "stodgy" company. Loose assortments of related merchandise are "out;" brand identities and coordination are "in"—for *Halls of Hanover*, *FBS*, and *Domestications*. As a result, Hanover predicts a boost of 30–50% in response rates by 1991, compared with 1988.

Gravure printing is the direct opposite of letterpress printing. The image is etched below the surface of the copper printing plate, creating ink wells (tiny depressed printing areas made by means of a screen). The rotogravure process utilizes a photographic method of transferring the printed image to a large copper cylinder on a rotary printing press. Once the plate is on the press and inked, the surface ink is wiped, so that only the tiny ink wells contain ink. The plate then presses against the paper, causing suction that pulls the ink out of the wells and onto the paper (see Exhibit 18.8).

Gravure is used to print all or parts of many publications, including national and local Sunday newspaper supplements, mail-order catalogs, packaging, and newspaper inserts. The gravure plate is capable of printing millions of copies very efficiently; however, it is not economical for short-run printing. Rotogravure becomes competitive with offset when printing exceeds about 100,000 copies. When printing exceeds a million copies, gravure tends to be more efficient than offset.

Rotogravure prints excellent color quality on relatively inexpensive paper, but the preparatory costs are comparatively high and it is expensive to make major corrections on the press.

Sheet-Fed versus Web-Fed Presses

Letterpress, offset, and gravure printing processes can all utilize sheet-fed or web-fed presses. Sheet-fed presses feed sheets of paper through the press one at a time. The conventional sheet-fed press prints about 6,000 or 7,000 "sheets" per hour. In web printing, paper is fed from a continuous roll and the printing is very rapid—about 1,000 feet per minute. Most major promotional printing utilizes web-fed presses.

EXHIBIT 18.8

Rotogravure. Ink wells fill with ink.

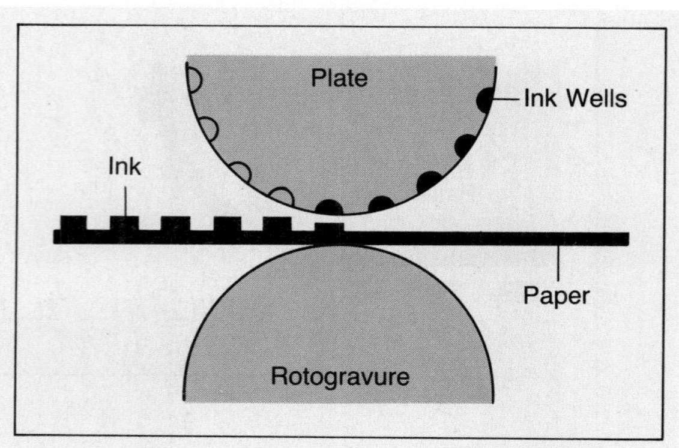

Screen printing is a popular method for printing posters and point-of-sale displays—when broad, flat colors can be applied for relatively short press runs. Bic's pocket-size perfume spritzers will be featured in specially-designed counter displays with large "billboards" proclaiming the theme, "Paris in Your Pocket." Silkscreen printing is responsible for the sharp, distinct impressionistic watercolors.

Screen Printing

Another printing process, screen printing, which is based on a different principle than letterpress, offset, and rotogravure, is especially good for short runs.

This simple process uses a stencil. The stencil of a design (art, type, photograph) can be manually or photographically produced and then placed over a (usually silk) textile or metallic-mesh screen (it actually looks like a window screen). Ink or paint is spread over the stencil and, by means of a squeegee, is pushed through the stencil and screen onto the paper (or other surface), as illustrated in Exhibit 18.9.

Screen printing is economical, especially when you work only in broad, flat colors, as for car cards, posters, and point-of-sale displays.

You can print on almost any surface: wallpaper, bricks, bottles, T-shirts, and so on. Basically, screen printing is a slow short-run process (for one copy to 100 or 1,000 or so copies), although sophisticated presses can print about 6,000 impressions per hour. This expanding printing process is becoming more useful to advertisers.

Screen printing (silk screen). *A printing process in which a stenciled design is applied to a textile or wire-mesh screen and a squeegee forces paint or ink through the mesh of the screen. See Silk screen.*

Flexography

Another printing process that is gaining acceptance in newspaper press rooms is flexography or "flexo"—a process that has long been used by the packaging industry. Newspapers have been successfully testing this system in which the presses are simpler to operate, cheaper to run, and cleaner to use because they print with water-based inks.

Simply defined, flexography is a direct-relief printing process that uses photopolymer plastic plates on web presses. It is the flexibility of the plates, which can be wrapped around a cylinder, that gives the process its name. Flexography involves far fewer components than offset printing. While letterpress is also a direct-relief printing process, flexo's shallow-relief plates and cushioning produce a "light-kiss" impression that yields a sharper image than letterpress. It is predicted that flexo will account for 21 percent of all newspaper printing by 1995. Those newspapers that adopt flexography will use extensive color printing.[1]

DiLitho

A number of newspapers use a process called DiLitho printing. This system combines the use of offset-type planographic plates with direct transfer of the image from the plate to the web.

[1]Rosalind C. Truitt, "Flexo on a Roll at Newspapers," *Presstime,* March 1986, pp. 36–44.

EXHIBIT 18.9
Screen printing.

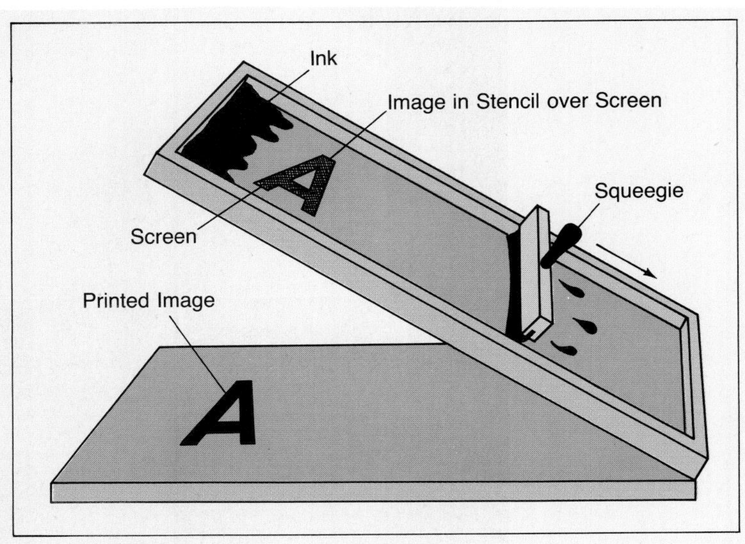

PLANNING THE TYPOGRAPHY

In selecting *type*, advertisers should be aware of the *impression* different faces produce. *Script* conveys upscale feminism, such as that used by Saks Fifth Avenue. The same impression is achieved by the *thin, simple* capital letters *Basile* clothiers of New York uses. ''Signatures'' indicate personal care in producing the product—*Honey* scarfs' ads use that approach. And *Major Damage Jeanswear* resorts to ''warehouse-stamped'' letters to impress readers with their bold, ''take-no-prisoners'' casual wear.

Type does more than just spell out words—it creates a mood, enhances readability, and gives your communication an image. Typography is the art of using type effectively. It entails selecting the style (typeface) and sizes of type, deciding on the amount of space between the letters and words and also between each line, and preparing specifications for the typesetter. Notice the differences in type styles, line length, and spacing in Exhibits 18.10, 18.11 and 18.12.

Changes taking place in typographic technology will continue to have a strong impact on the art director's flexibility in using type. We will discuss some of the basics of type and the changes that are influencing its use.

Typefaces

There are thousands of typeface designs available, each of which can be used to communicate a feeling and complement pictures and words. The selection of the right

EXHIBIT 18.10

This demonstrates reverse copy—white or light type on a dark background—and close letter spacing in the headline. (Courtesy: AGFA Graphics Systems Division.)

EXHIBIT 18.11

Headline and body copy are in sans serif typeface. (Courtesy: Sawyer, Riley, Compton, Inc.)

BUYING POWER

Connecticut's newest indoor shopping mall is the largest in New England. Up to 50,000 people a day shop at the elegant 1.2 million square foot Danbury Mall.

That's a lot of buying power. And the power behind it all travels on wire and cable from Southwire. The one source for both aluminum and copper conductor. Maker of more sizes, colors and types than anyone else in the industry.

The Danbury Mall is just one example of why contractors most often turn to Southwire and Southwire distributors. Who else could have supplied everything from feeders to branch circuits, from 600 MCM color-coded aluminum to 14 AWG copper? Close to a million feet of conductor from one supplier!*

Southwire also has the industry's most fully stocked inventory, a fleet of over 100 trucks that can deliver most orders within 48 hours, responsive service and quality that surpasses the standards. At Southwire we control every step of the process from refining our own metals to delivery and follow-through. You get it all -- what you want, how and when you want it.

From the generator to the switch, power travels on Southwire.

SOUTHWIRE

We Deliver Power.

*Individual stores handled the wiring within their premises and may have used additional sources.

typeface for a particular ad is very important. Exhibit 18.13 illustrates the major classifications of type.

Type Fonts and Families

A type font is a complete assortment of type of one size and face—all the lowercase and capital characters as well as numerals and the usual punctuation marks (see Exhibit 18.14). A font may be roman or italic. A roman (with a lowercase *r*) type refers to the upright letter form, as distinguished from the italic form, which is oblique. Roman (capital *R*) denotes a group of serifed typeface styles.

Type family is the name given to two or more series of types that are variants of one design (Exhibit 18.15). Each one, however, retains the essential characteristics of the basic letter form. The series may be italic, semibold, bold, condensed, expanded, and so forth. A family of type may provide a harmonious variety of typefaces for use within an ad.

EXHIBIT 18.12

Body copy has long line length as it runs around inset photo. The copy is reversed out of photo (white on dark). (Courtesy: Visicolor.)

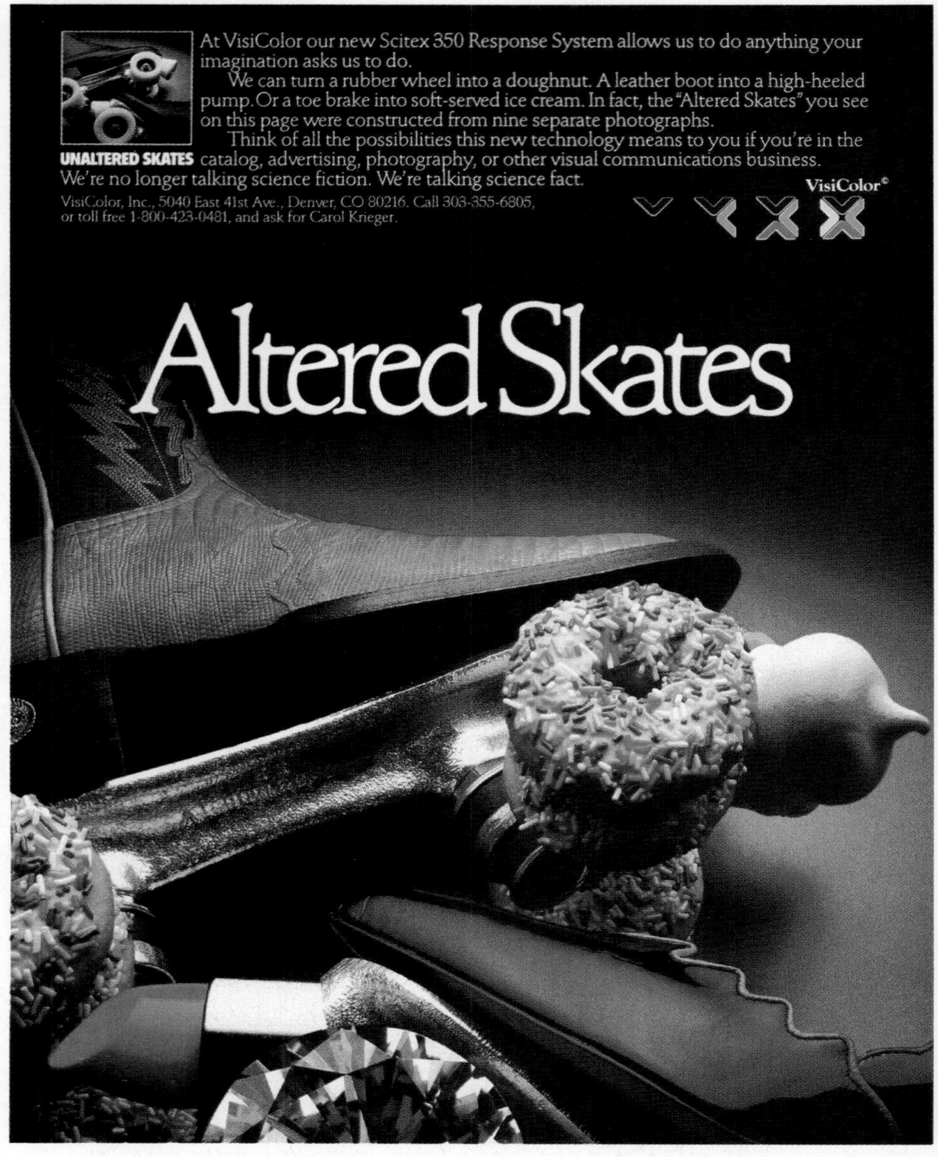

EXHIBIT 18.13

Type classifications.

(a) Times Roman is an example of Text.

(b) Garamond is an example of Old Roman.

(c) **Optima** is an example of Modern Roman.

(d) **Helvetica** is an example of San Serif.

(e) Palatino is an example of Square Serif.

(f) Korinna is an example of Decorative.

Helvetica Medium
abcdefghijklmnopqrstuvwxyz
ABCDEFGHIJKLMNOPQRSTUV
1234567890$(&?!%.',.:;-)* WXYZ

Helvetica Medium Italic
abcdefghijklmnopqrstuvwxyz
ABCDEFGHIJKLMNOPQRSTUVWX
1234567890(&.,:;!?''--•$¢%/£) YZ*

Helvetica Medium Outline
abcdefghijklmnopqrstuvwxyz
ABCDEFGHIJKLMNOPQRSTUV
1234567890(&.,:;?!*—-""""~^«»®+¿¡)
ÆŒØæœøß$¢%/ WXYZ

Helvetica Semi Demi Bold
abcdefghijklmnopqrstuvwxyz
AaBCDEeFGHIJKLMmNnOPQ
RrSTUuVWXYZ-*+®°/ß$¢£
1234567890 &.,:;!?'""( )%,.

EXHIBIT 18.14
Examples of type fonts—Helvetica Medium Outline and Helvetica Semi Demi Bold typefaces.

EXHIBIT 18.15

A family of type retains its basic letterform and style characteristics through all its variations. Some type families consist of only roman, italic, and bold versions. Others, like the popular Helvetica family, have many variations and different stroke thicknesses.

Helvetica Thin
Helvetica Light
Helvetica Light Italic
Helvetica
Helvetica Italic
Helvetica Italic Outline
Helvetica Regular Condensed
Helvetica Regular Extended
Helvetica Medium
Helvetica Medium Italic
Helvetica Medium Outline
Helvetica Bold
Helvetica Bold Compact Italic
Helvetica Bold Outline
Helvetica Bold Condensed
Helvetica Bold Condensed Outline
Helvetica Bold Extended
Helvetica Extrabold Condensed
Helvetica Extrabold Condensed Outline
Helvetica Extrabold Ext.
Helvetica Compressed
Helvetica Extra Compressed
Helvetica Ultra Compressed

Type sizes vary according to placement in an ad. Headlines usually command the largest size type, subheads the next size, and finally copy is the smallest size. However, to appeal to the reader's inquisitiveness, *harve benard clothing company* began its full page ad with copy in the ad's smallest type—albeit beginning the personal anecdote with a very large capital letter. With the "headline" at the *bottom* of the ad, the unusual type placement paid off in "noted" readership.

The amount of space between lines of type can be adjusted by "leading"—creating blank space on the paper. In order to encourage readership about its fabric ingredient, *Lycra,* DuPont has widely-spaced a verticle, right-hand column in a full-page ad. The definition begins at the top with the headline—and "flows" down the side of the page to join the DuPont signature. The spacing has made readership *easy* and *inviting*.

Point (pt). *(1) The unit of measurement of type, about 1/72 inch in depth. Type is specified by its point size, as 8-pt., 12-pt., 24-pt., 48-pt. (2) The unit for measuring thickness of paper, 0.001 inch.*

Measurement of Type

Typographers have unique units of measurement. It is essential to learn the fundamental units of measure if you are going to interact with production people. The *point* and *pica* are two units of measure used in print production in all English-speaking countries. The *point system* is used to measure type sizes and to mark up copy for typesetting: length of line, space between lines, dimensions of type, and so forth. Let's take a closer look at these two units of measure.

Point. A point is used to measure the size of type (heights of letters)—there are 72 points to an inch. You need to know instantly that 36-point type is about ½ inch high and 18-point type is about ¼ inch high. Exhibit 18.16 illustrates the major terms used in discussing the height of type.

Type can be set from about 6 points to 120 points. Body copy is generally in the range of 6 to 14 points; most publications use type of 9, 10, or 11 points. Type sizes above 14 points are referred to as *display* or *headline type*. However, these ranges are simply labels—in many newspaper ads, the body copy is 18 points or so, and there have been ads where the headline was in the body-copy size range. See Exhibit 18.17 for a visual perspective on basic type sizes.

Points are used to measure the height of space between lines, rules, and borders, as well as the height of type.

EXHIBIT 18.16

The size of type is determined by the height of the face (not the height of its letter *x* alone) and includes ascenders, descenders, and shoulders. A point measures almost exactly 1/72 inch. This word is photoset in 72-point Times Roman.

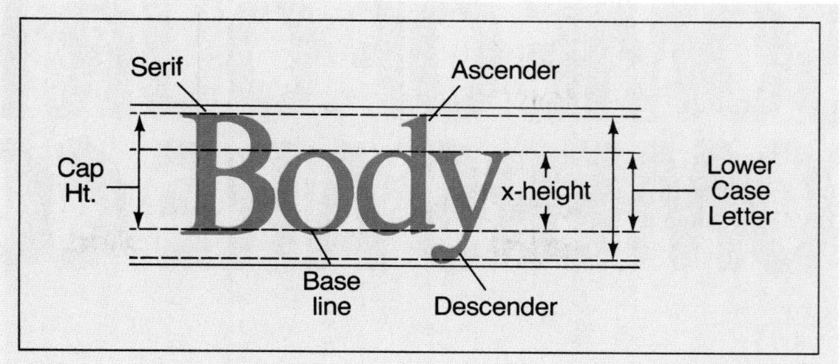

EXHIBIT 18.17

A visual perspective on basic type sizes.

ADVERTISING (6 point)
ADVERTISING (8 point)
ADVERTISING (10 point)
ADVERTISING (12 point)
ADVERTISING (14 point)
ADVERTISING (18 point)
ADVERTISING (24 point)
ADVERTISING (36 point)

> ***Pica, pica em.*** *The unit for measuring width in printing. There are 6 picas to the inch. Derived from* pica, *the old name of 12-point type (1/6 inch high). A page of type 24 picas wide is 4 inches wide (24 ÷ 6 = 4).*

Pica. A pica is a linear unit of measure—12 points of space or 6 picas to an inch. Picas are used to indicate width or depth and length of line.

Em. An em is a square of the type size and is commonly used for indentation of copy blocks and paragraphs.

Agate Line. Most newspapers (and some small magazines) sell advertising space in column inches or by the agate line, a measure of the depth of space. There are 14 agate lines to a column inch, regardless of the width of the column. Newspaper space is referred to by *depth* (agate lines) and *width* (number of columns): For "100 × 2," read "one hundred lines deep by two columns wide."

> ***Leading*** *(pronounced "ledding"). Insertion of metal strips (known as leads) between lines of hot type to create more space between lines. In computer/phototypesetting, referred to as* leading *or* line spacing: *the adding of space between lines, usually in points of space.*

Line Spacing. Also called *leading,* line spacing is the vertical space between lines of type and is measured in points. Lines are said to be set solid when no additional line spacing has been added. Leading is added to make type more readable.

Sawyer Riley Compton, Inc., created two ads (Exhibits 18.18 and 18.19) using similar placements of body copy; however, the line spacing (or leading) between the lines of body copy are significantly different. The rule of thumb is that leading should be no more than 20 percent of the type size. In other words, if you are using 10-point type, the maximum extra space between the lines is 2 points.

Type Specifications

The type of most national advertising is set by an advertising typographer, a firm that specializes in hundreds or thousands of typefaces. Generally, the typographer does not print. Recently, some advertisers and advertising agencies have installed their own

SOME OF OUR BEST CUSTOMERS ARE COLD FISH.

Fish can be pretty tough customers for a lift truck. Especially when they're frozen. Their environment is brutally cold, and they don't tolerate downtime.

At its national distribution center, where the temperature is a constant −20°F, Mrs. Paul's handles almost 3 million pounds of frozen fish a year. *All* of it on Baker lift trucks. Which makes the cold fish at Mrs. Paul's some of our very best customers.

Mrs. Paul's uses a variety of Baker trucks because of their outstanding durability and dependability in a frozen environment. But one of them has almost revolutionized Mrs. Paul's business. The custom-designed Moto-Truc PAL four-way entry pallet truck. Whereas conventional pallet trucks can load only 18 pallets per trailer, the PAL's unique low-profile fork assembly enables it to load 25. That's a whopping 30% increase in loading productivity!

In fact, the PAL four-way entry truck is an efficiency machine. For speed and productivity, it handles standard 40-by-48-inch pallets from all four sides. For superior clearance over dock boards, it has a lowered fork height of two

inches, with six inches of lift. Which means you can use it to load and unload trailers without the help of other types of lift trucks.

And since operator comfort is part of efficiency, the steering handle, attached directly to the drive unit, contains all the controls for travel, lift-lowering and braking. For extra convenience, the travel direction and speed control return to neutral when released. And lifting and lowering are controlled by push button in the control handle.

Add total maintenance and a full parts inventory from the local Baker Dealer–and it's clear why Mrs. Paul's relationship with Baker is no mere fish story.

For the complete story about the PAL four-way entry truck or any other quality Baker lift truck, call us for a free Baker product line brochure and the name of the Baker dealer near you. Baker Material Handling Corporation. At 1-800-627-1700.

Baker
YOU'RE IN GOOD COMPANY.

Mrs. Paul's is a registered trademark of Campbell Soup Company. Used with permission.

EXHIBIT 18.18

The body copy is set without any additional leading between the lines of type. This is called *setting solid.* (Courtesy: Sawyer Riley Compton, Inc.)

EXHIBIT 18.19

Compared to Exhibit 18.18, the body copy here has additional line spacing, opening up the space between the lines. (Courtesy: Sawyer Riley Compton, Inc.)

The most uninhibited vacuum in history.
The power that set it free.
Four and a half years ago, Freedom™ was nothing more than a great idea. Today it's a great product. The world's only full-size vacuum that operates totally cord-free. Only from Eureka. With a little help from Gates Energy Products.
Freedom offers everything you'd ever expect from a Eureka upright–durability, quality and cleaning effectiveness. And, thanks to its revolutionary design, the convenience of cordlessness. Made possible by a rechargeable Gates battery. A 12-volt, 5-amp hour sealed-lead monobloc battery mounted in a portable snap-in battery pack.
Of course, it wasn't easy. And some people said it couldn't be done. How, they asked, could a battery be powerful enough without being too heavy and costly for the market to bear?
But at Gates we believed in Freedom and committed our resources to making it happen. That involved many people and years of close cooperation and hard work. The result was a battery that surpassed all others in run time and shelf life, with the light weight and affordability consumers demand.
Sure, it took time. But that's because we like being a part of your project from the beginning. With a full range of technical and applications engineering support, backed by a broad line of standard and custom-designed rechargeable cells and batteries in both sealed-lead and nickel-cadmium. All intended to help you develop a product that really works.
At Gates we believe that great ideas deserve to become great products. Maybe that's why we're the company the idea people turn to most. So, give us a call at 1-800-627-1700. And experience the power of your great idea.
Gates Energy Products
The power of great ideas.

photographic typesetting equipment and/or some sort of computer typesetting capability, which we will discuss later.

Before the size of type can be chosen, the number of characters in the copy typescript must be determined. Published tables show how many characters of various typefaces and point sizes fit into different widths. In advertising agencies, type specification might be handled by art directors, print production personnel, or specialized type directors.

TYPESETTING METHODS

Radical changes in typesetting technology have recently impacted the typesetting process. In the past, you had a choice between hot and cold composition. Either typographers used line-casting machines to cast each line of hot type (e.g., the linotype machine set a whole line of type in the form of a lead slug) or they used cold composition (strike-on machines similar to typewriters, photocomposition machines converting film strips into letter forms). Most of these processes produced good-quality typeset copy, but the machines required heavy expenditures and by today's standard were slow. Now new technology in reproducing type is running rampant.

Today, if you have a personal computer, you can get varying degrees of sophisticated software to set type directly from your machine; or you can use your disk to input directly into a typographer's sophisticated computer typesetting system where hundreds of type fonts are on-line. Traditionally, most advertisers and agencies have not gone into the typesetting business because of the cost of the hardware and because owning a few typefaces out of thousands of typeface possibilities is too limiting. However, the situation is changing. Some desktop publishing packages offer the advertiser a number of typefaces and reasonable reproduction quality (see Exhibit 18.20).

EXHIBIT 18.20

This ad promotes a software package that allows you to manipulate typography. (Courtesy: Aldus.)

When you combine Aldus PageMaker® with Aldus® FreeHand,™ you have the power to create anything imaginable. And do it faster and easier than ever before.

Today's best-selling desktop publishing and advanced drawing programs give your Macintosh powerful capabilities. And they give you unequaled versatility, control, and productivity for serious desktop publishing.

With Aldus FreeHand, you can produce everything from simple graphics to sophisticated illustrations. Unlike other advanced drawing programs, it lets you see your changes on the monitor while you work. So it's easy to refine a shape or apply PANTONE®* Colors without losing sight of the big picture.

And Aldus FreeHand gives you greater text handling capabilities than any other program. Which gives you total control over typography. Curve text on a path, rotate or stretch type, mix sizes, fonts, and colors. You'll spend less time running back and forth to the typesetter. And less money on type.

After you polish your graphics and display type in Aldus FreeHand, place them into PageMaker. And marvel at how well these powerful design tools work together.

Only PageMaker's unique combination of precision and grace can make page layout such a rewarding experience. For both short and long documents. Ruling, kerning, spot color, text flow, wraps. You name it. It's all there, in a familiar environment as natural as your drawing board.

When you combine Aldus FreeHand and PageMaker, you have more than today's most advanced illustration, design, typography, and page layout capabilities. You have a creative edge in business.

Discover today's powerful design team.

Call 1-800-333-2538, Department J-2, for your FREE copy of the Aldus Design Team information packet.** Or visit your nearest authorized Aldus dealer.

ALDUS®

The Creative Edge in Business.

LOOK WHAT HAPPENS WHEN YOU GIVE PAGEMAKER A FREE HAND.

However, most packages have only limited type choices and mediocre reproduction quality, which may be suitable for some types of newsletters and sales-promotional materials, but not for the production of regional and national ads. Still, the systems and software are getting closer to the reproduction quality of a fine printing process.

Typesetting and Desktop Computers

Desktop publishing is making it possible for advertisers and agencies to "set" type. Using the *G.S./Techtron* electronic design facilities, the operator can instantly size and "crop" a photograph, produce a layout in minutes, or an entire campaign in hours! And, you can transmit images to a client as quickly as they're created. Instructions can be marked up on the screen and seen by the agency and the client *simultaneously*. Once the idea's approved, G.S. Imaging Services can provide high-quality color separations and full pre-press services to bring the job to a finish.

Most agencies still use traditional commercial typesetting methods for ads that are many times more expensive than those designed for the personal computer because of their quality and versatility. Software packages for the microcomputer are usually rather limited, and commercial quality requires expensive output typesetters ranging in cost from about $45,000 to $120,000. Typical desktop laser printers cost from a few thousand dollars (for low resolution) to $7,000 or $8,000 (for high resolution). Obviously, there is a considerable difference in output quality. Each of the Macintosh desktop publishing software packages provides different tools and methods for manipulating type. None of the major packages provides em, en, or thin spacing—all standards in the commercial typesetting world.

Just having good typesetting equipment doesn't guarantee a good final product. Commercial typesetting operators generally have more knowledge of type than desktop system operators, and may spend hours on a single paragraph. The major problem with desktop systems is not the systems themselves, but the lack of a design or typography background on the part of the operators. Still, the computer software is getting better, the printers are becoming better and cheaper, and more people are learning how to effectively use these tools. Moreover, the desktop system offers speed when needed and is a major asset to certain advertisers and agencies. But for now, the typical regional or national ad has its type set by traditional phototypesetting methods.

MECHANICALS AND ARTWORK

After the copy has been set to the proper dimensions (copy fitting) and all corrections have been made, the typographer supplies reproduction-quality proofs. The type is then pasted up on the mechanical in the proper place. At this point, the advertiser reviews the mechanical and artwork. After approval by the advertiser, the mechanical is sent to the photoplatemaker.

Photoplatemaking. *Making plates (and the films preceding the plates) for any printing process by camera, in color or in black and white.*

Typesetting is normally the first step in the production process of an ad. The second step is the preparation of the artwork for printing. This is called *photoplatemaking*—the producing of a printing plate or other image carrier for publication printing. In offset and gravure, films are normally sent to the publication printers, from which they produce their own plates. For letterpress printing, the advertiser produces photoengravings (combining photography and chemical engravings).

The two major forms of letterpress photoengravings are line plates and halftone plates. In offset and gravure photoplatemaking, the basic principles are very similar.

Line Plates

Line drawing. *Made with brush, pen, pencil, or crayon, with shading produced by variations in size and spacing of lines, not by tone.*

Line Art. Artwork drawn in black ink on white paper using lines and solid black areas (only solid color with no tonal value or changes) is called *line art* or *linecuts*. The printer uses a photographic process to get a line negative of the art (the process may vary according to the printing process). Type is an example of line art (if it is in solid form). Most artwork is drawn larger than needed for the mechanical to minimize the art's imperfections when reduced and printed. The negative is used in the appropriate printing-process plate production. (See Exhibit 18.21 for an example.)

Line-Tint. You can give line art some variation in shades by breaking up the solid

EXHIBIT 18.21
Examples of line art. Art is solid black or white with no tonal values or shapes.

color with screen tints or benday screens. Exhibit 18.22 illustrates the adding of a 30 percent screen to line art. The platemaker adds the screens during the film-stripping stage just prior to platemaking.

Line Color Plates. To produce line plates in two, three, or more flat colors, the artwork itself need not be colored. Instead, each extra color is marked on a separate tissue or acetate overlay on the base art as a guide for the platemaker, who then makes a separate plate for each color. Line color plates provide a comparatively inexpensive method of printing in color with effective results.

Halftone Plates

Continuous tone. *An unscreened photographic picture or image, on paper or film, that contains all gradations of tonal values from white to black.*

Photographs and watercolor or oil paintings are not like line art. They have a range of tonal values between pure blacks and pure whites. Such illustrations are called *continuous-tone artwork*. The plates used for them are called *halftone plates*.

To reproduce the range of tones in continuous-tone art, the art must be broken up into dots. Remember that black ink is black ink and not shades of gray, so the production process must create an optical illusion by converting the tonal areas to different-size halftone dots on the printed paper that the eye perceives as gray. However, if you look at the printed halftone gray areas with a magnifying glass, you will see little black

EXHIBIT 18.22

The gray squares are really screened black ink to give the illusion of gray. (Courtesy: First Continental Leasing Corporation and Robinson & Associates, Inc.)

Municipal Lease
Financing:
The Key to Growth

dots and not gray (see Exhibit 18.23 for a magnification). The dots are formed on the negative during the camera exposure when a screen is placed between the film and the photograph (or other kinds of continuous-tone copy). As the film is exposed, light passes through the screen's 50 to 200 hairlines per square inch, and the image reaching the film is in dot form. The size of the dots will vary according to the contrast of tone in the original; this simply means that dark areas in the original photo will give one size dot, medium tones another size dot, and lighter tones still another size dot. The result is a negative with dots of varying sizes, depending on the tonal variations in the original.

After the halftone negative is made, it is placed on a metallic plate just like the line art negative and exposed to the plate. In letterpress printing, the engraving is splashed with acid that eats away the metal, leaving the dots as a raised surface. In offset printing, the dots are transferred to the smooth flat plate photographically.

Halftone screens come in a variety of standard sizes. Each publication has its own requirement for the screen size, dictated somewhat by the printing process and paper

EXHIBIT 18.23

Magnification of a halftone plate, showing light and dark portions of the photographic copy reproduced as dots of different sizes. Lighter dots are freestanding; but at about the 50 percent value (half black, half white), the dots begin to connect. The centers of the dots are equidistant from each other.

EXHIBIT 18.24
(a) 65-line screen; (b) 100-line screen; and (c) 133-line screen of photograph. (Courtesy: Dayton Hudson.)

being used. Most newspaper screens are 55, 65, or 85 lines per inch. Publication screens for magazines and promotional materials generally range from 110 to 133 lines per square inch. In other words, a 133-line screen produces 133 dots to the inch. The more dots per inch, the greater the quality of detail reproduced from the original. However, the higher the screen, the smoother the paper has to be for printing the dots. (See Exhibit 18.24 for examples of different line screens used on the same continuous-tone copy.)

The Halftone Finish. If you want to make a halftone of a photograph, the platemaker can treat the background in a number of ways; that treatment is called its *finish*. Here are a few of the techniques that can be applied to halftones:

- *Square halftone*. A halftone where the background has been retained.
- *Silhouette*. The background in the photograph has been removed by the photoplatemaker (see Exhibit 18.25).

EXHIBIT 18.25
Background has been removed from photo and special technique added. (Courtesy: Day-Brite and Robinson & Associates, Inc.)

- *Surprint*. This is a combination plate made by exposing line and halftone negatives in succession on the same plate, as illustrated in Exhibit 18.26.
- *Mortise*. An area of a halftone is cut out to permit the insertion of type or other matter (see Exhibit 18.27).

Line Conversion. A line conversion transforms a continuous-tone original into a high-contrast image of only black and white tones similar to line art. The conversion transfers the image into a pattern of some kind: mezzotint, wavy line, straight line, or concentric circle.

> ***Duotone.*** *Two halftone plates, each printing in a different color and giving two-color reproductions from an original one-color plate.*

Two-Color Halftone Plates. A two-color reproduction can be made from monochrome artwork in two ways: A screen tint in a second color can be printed over (or under) a black halftone. Or the artwork can be photographed twice, changing the screen angle the second time so that the dots of the second color plate fall between those of the first plate. This is called a *duotone*. It produces contrast in both colors of the one-color original halftone.

> ***Four-color process.*** *The process for reproducing color illustrations by a set of plates, one of which prints all the yellows, another the blues, a third the reds, the fourth the blacks (the sequence is variable). The plates are referred to as process plates.*

Four-Color Process Printing. If you want to reproduce a color photograph in your ad, you use a set of four-color plates: red (magenta), yellow, blue (cyan), and black. Full-color or process requires photographic or electronic scanner separation of the color in the photographs (or other continuous-tone copy) into four negatives, one for each of the process colors. This process of preparing plates of the various colors and black is called *color separation*. Basically, you have a negative that has captured the red light from the photo, another negative that has captured the yellow light, a third negative that has captured the blue light, and a fourth negative that contains the black,

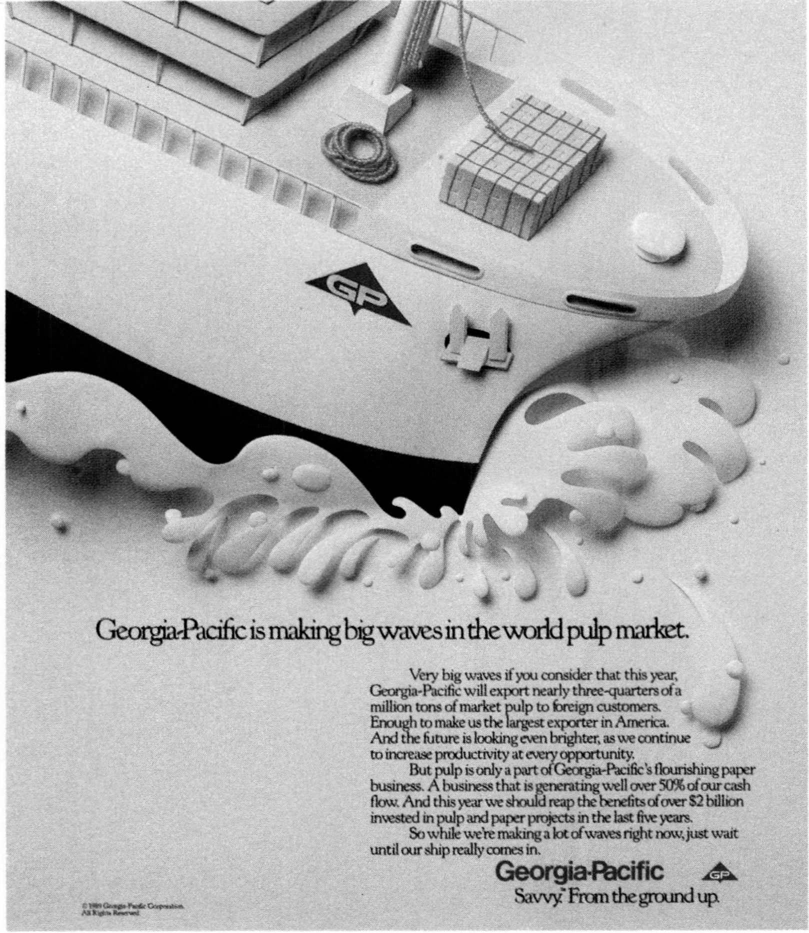

Georgia-Pacific is making big waves in the world pulp market.
Very big waves if you consider that this year, Georgia-Pacific will export nearly three-quarters of a million tons of market pulp to foreign customers. Enough to make us the largest exporter in America. And the future is looking even brighter, as we continue to increase productivity at every opportunity.
But pulp is only a part of Georgia-Pacific's flourishing paper business. A business that is generating well over 50% of our cash flow. And this year we should reap the benefits of over $2 billion invested in pulp and paper projects in the last five years.
So while we're making a lot of waves right now, just wait until our ship really comes in.
Georgia-Pacific
Savvy.™ From the ground up.

EXHIBIT 18.26

This is an example of a surprint or overprint where type is printed over the halftone or art. (Courtesy: Georgia-Pacific and HutchesonShutze.)

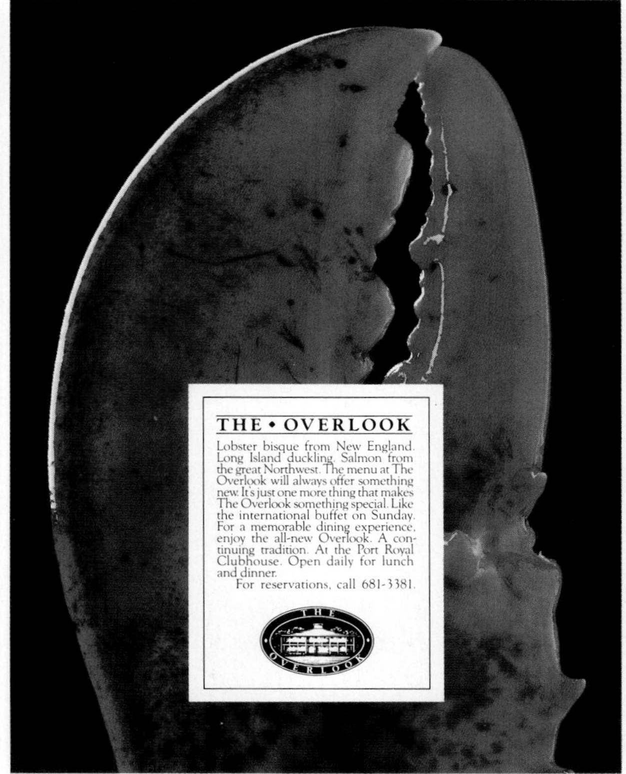

EXHIBIT 18.27
The mortise is a cutout of a portion of the art/photo to permit the insertion of type or another image. (Courtesy: The Overlook.)

which improves the definition and shadow intensity, giving a sharper image. See the process color ad in Exhibit 18.28. If you examine any of the color ads in this text (or any other publication) with a magnifying glass, you will find the halftone dots in four colors.

Desktop Color Separations

One of the outstanding advantages of using *commercial color separating services* is their ability to print "realistic" skintones. Estee Lauder's new "country" ads in *The New York Times Sunday Supplement* features closeups of "The Country Girl," dressed in fall colors. Her predominant orangy skin color and lipstick is highlighted by her matching sweater, "earth" foliage, and complimentary makeup items. By using a professional color service, EL has created a *warm, appealing* ad.

Desktop systems allow agencies and advertisers the opportunity to produce their own color separations at huge savings. However, quality of color separations produced by scanning a photo on a flatbed scanner is inferior to the industry standard. Skin tones can be somewhat off and product colors do not always match. That is why advertisers continue to use commercial color separation services, that can be relied upon to produce top-quality color separations with their complicated, costly equipment and extensively trained operators. It will be some time before the desktop microcomputer can match this high quality.

For the many color jobs that do not require top-quality work, however, the desktop systems offer a fast low-cost alternative. As with type, the software is getting better, and as people improve at using desktop systems, these systems will produce better color separations and be used much more frequently.

Color Proofing

Achieving color reproduction that satisfies demanding ad agencies and advertisers is one of the most crucial roles of the magazine production manager.

Press Proofs. Agencies generally demand to see a proof before the job is printed. For years, press proofs, or progressives, usually made on special proofing presses, were the standard proofs sent to agencies for checking. Today they are still used by many ad

EXHIBIT 18.28 **Yellow plate.**

Progressive steps in four-color process printing. Four plates—yellow, red, blue, and black—combine to produce the desired colors and contrasts. (Courtesy: Canada Dry Corporation.)

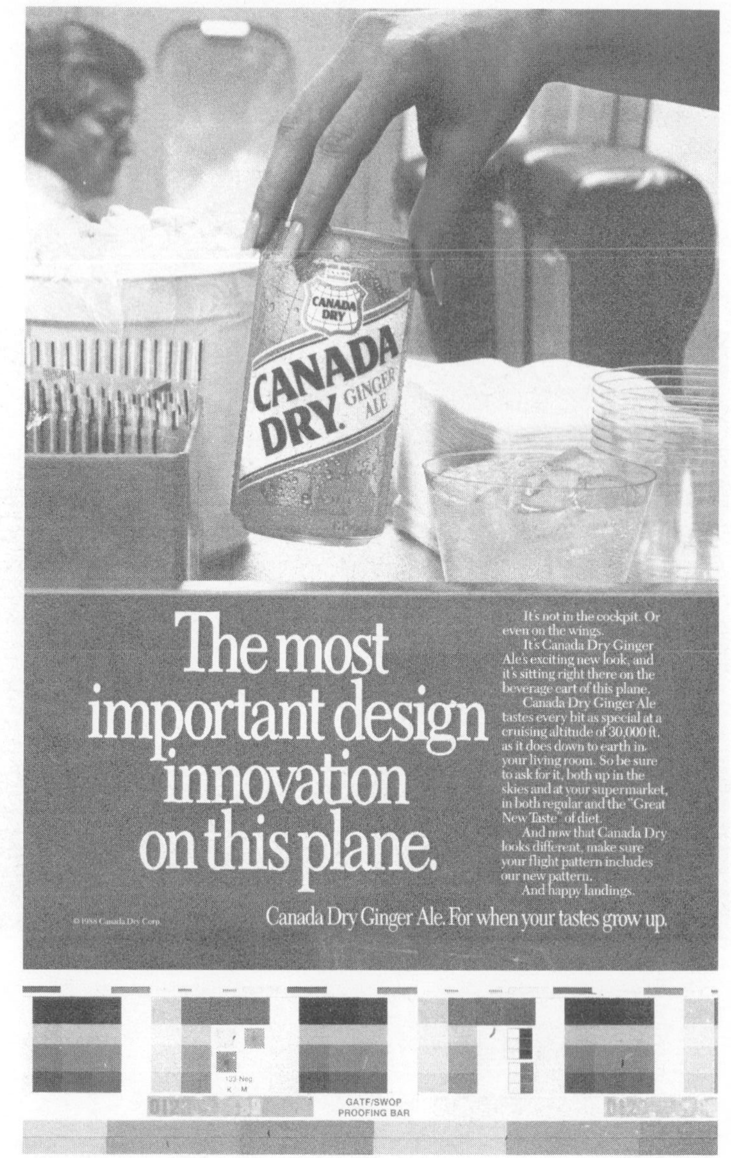

EXHIBIT 18.28 (continued)

Red plate.

EXHIBIT 18.28 (continued)
Yellow and red plates.

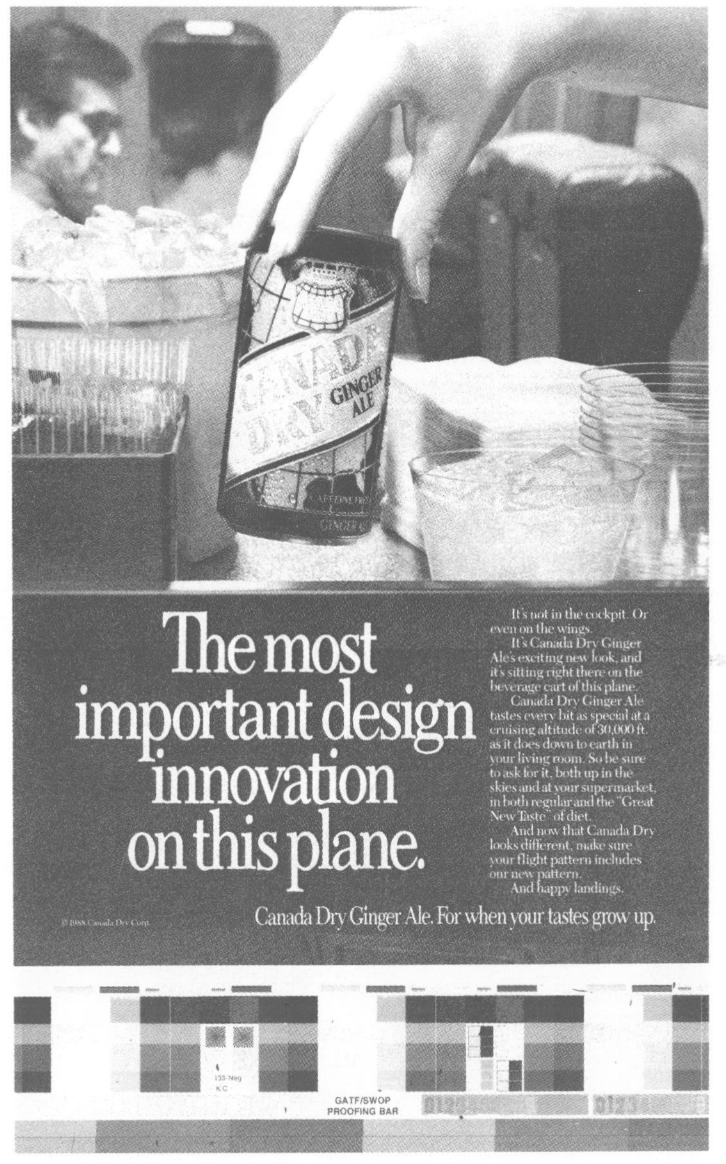

EXHIBIT 18.28 (continued)
Blue plate.

EXHIBIT 18.28 (continued)
Yellow and blue plates.

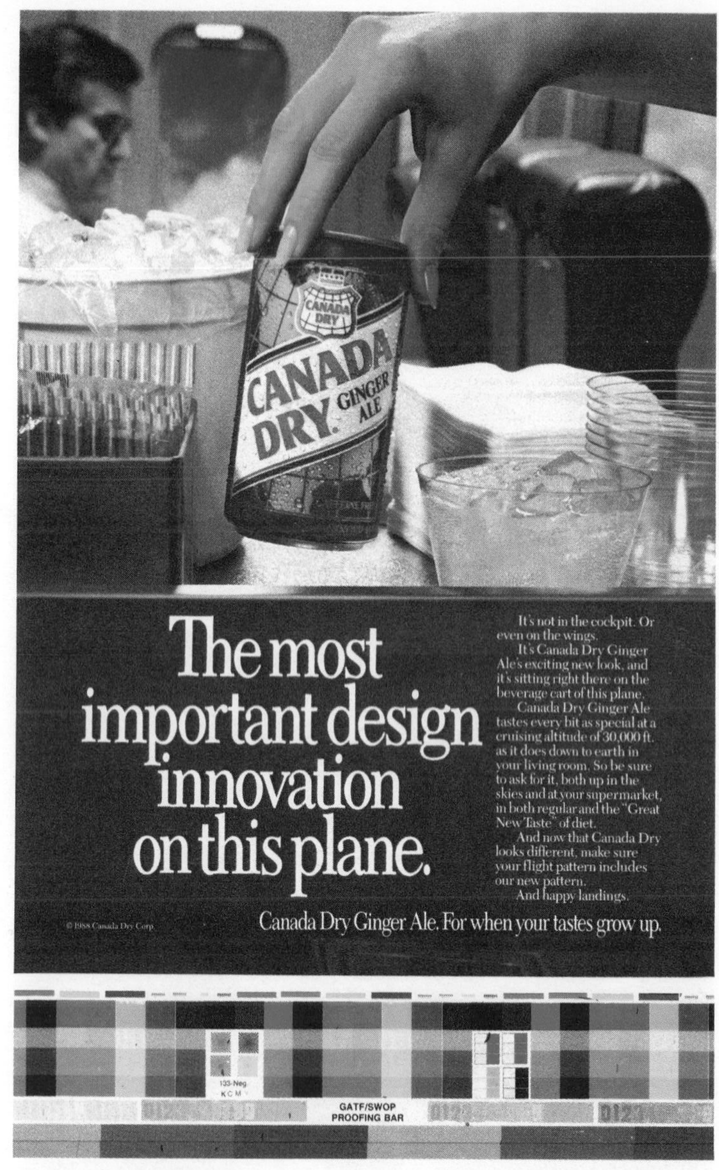

EXHIBIT 18.28 (continued)
Yellow, red, and blue plates.

The most important design innovation on this plane.

It's not in the cockpit. Or even on the wings.
It's Canada Dry Ginger Ale's exciting new look, and it's sitting right there on the beverage cart of this plane.
Canada Dry Ginger Ale tastes every bit as special at a cruising altitude of 30,000 ft. as it does down to earth in your living room. So be sure to ask for it, both up in the skies and at your supermarket, in both regular and the "Great New Taste" of diet.
And now that Canada Dry looks different, make sure your flight pattern includes our new pattern.
And happy landings.

Canada Dry Ginger Ale. For when your tastes grow up.

GATF/SWOP PROOFING BAR

EXHIBIT 18.28 (continued)
Black plate.

EXHIBIT 18.28 (continued)
Finished process color ad showing all colors.

agencies who are willing to pay the steep price for what they believe is the most accurate proof. In theory, press proofs provide a virtually exact representation of the final product.

Progressive proofs (progs) give the advertiser a separate proof for each color (red, yellow, blue, and black), as indicated in Exhibit 18.28, as well as a proof for each color combination (red and yellow, red and blue, blue and yellow)—seven printings in all. After approval by the advertiser and agency, the proofs are sent to the printer to use as a guide in duplicating the densities for each color.

Off-Press Proofs. Less expensive and faster than press proofs, and adequate in most cases, off-press proofs are the usual proof today. No plate or printing is involved. There are numerous types of off-press (prepress) proofing systems. The most popular are overlay and adhesive proofs.

OVERLAY PROOFS. Four sheets of clear polyester are sensitized to a pigment (color), exposed to the color separations, and developed. The four overlays (yellow, red, blue, black) are then stacked to produce a composite image.

ADHESIVE OR TONER TRANSFER PROOF. Du Pont's Cromalin is an example of this technique, which uses dry pigments to produce images on photosensitive adhesive polymers or pretreated carrier sheets. Chromolin is generally considered the superior adhesive process. The proofs are keyed to SWOP (Specifications for Web Offset Publications)/GAA (Gravure Association of America) guidelines, which set standards for inks, density of tones, reverses, and other technical matters.

New digital hard and soft copy systems are more expensive and eliminate film to produce continuous-tone proofs. At this point, their colors are not matched to SWOP. The soft proofing systems allow production and design people to call up a digitized color image and evaluate it before separations are made for an intermediate or position proof. Leo Burnett (Chicago) and Young and Rubicam (New York) are two agencies that use these systems. D'Arcy Masius Benton & Bowles (St. Louis) is the first agency to employ an interactive system, which allows artists to make on-screen adjustments at the agency and instantly relay the changes to the printer to be incorporated into the final proof. The interactive system gives the agency more flexibility about deadlines, and saves time and money for clients.[2]

---

[2]Karlene Lukovitz, "Color Proofing: How Will Digital Change the Market?" *Folio*, June 1988, pp. 111–115.

EXHIBIT 18.29

Strong colors are recreated sharply with good color separations and careful reproduction. The ad bleeds on the left, bottom, and top sides. (Courtesy: Sawyer Riley Compton, Inc.)

OFFSET AND GRAVURE PHOTOPLATEMAKING

In letterpress publication printing, the advertiser or agency furnishes the plate to the publication or printer. Offset and gravure publications only require film from the advertiser, since they make their own plates.

If the agency wishes to retain complete control over the preparatory steps, it usually sends the mechanical and artwork to its own supplier to be prepared for the printer. This can be an offset separation house, a gravure service company, or a company that prepares materials for all printing processes.

The preparatory work for the three major printing processes is very similar. In offset and gravure, the photoplatemaker produces plates merely for proofing purposes. These plates are not sent to the publication—only the final corrected films are sent, along with proof and progs pulled from these plates. As mentioned earlier, in letterpress, actual plates are sent.

MAKING DUPLICATE MATERIAL

Most print ads run in more than one publication. Frequently, advertisers have different publications on their schedules, or they need to issue reprints of their ads or send material to dealers for cooperative advertising. There are various means of producing duplicate material of magazine or newspaper ads.

Letterpress Duplicates

Cronar film and Cronar plates. *A conversion method by which either type of letterpress engraving is transferred directly to film by mechanical means (balls or fingers). This film can then be used to make offset plates, gravure cylinders, or very faithful duplicate letterpress plates.*

There are several kinds of letterpress duplicate plates, because publishers may require a specific type of duplicate plate. Stereotypes are still used to duplicate ads for some newspapers. This process makes a paper or plastic mold or mat, which is sent to the paper. The paper then pours hot molten lead into the mat, converting it into a metal stereotype plate. This process is being replaced by photopolymer plates, which are produced on photosensitive plastic. Electrotype is another duplicate plate produced from a plastic mold using a combination of metals; it is very durable and is capable of printing millions of impressions. Cronapress plates (called *Cronars*) can be made with Du Pont Cronapress film, a pressure-sensitive material capable of duplicating the original impression exactly.

Offset and Gravure Duplicates

Repro proofs (reproduction proofs). *Exceptionally clean and sharp proofs from type for use as copy for reproduction.*

Duplicate material for offset publications can consist of repro proofs (reproduction proofs) or 3M Scotchprints (a plasticized repro proofing material). Usually, photoprints or reproduction proofs are preferred for partial-page newspaper ads; film is often required for full-page newspaper insertions. Duplicate films can also be made from the original artwork or mechanicals. For color gravure magazines or Sunday supplements, duplicate positive films are usually supplied. For black-and-white offset or gravure ads, photographic prints are often substituted for films.

A number of newspapers use satellite transmission systems to send a facsimile of each page of the newspaper to a reception station, where it is recorded on page-size photofilm. The film is then used to make offset plates, which are placed on the presses to reproduce the newspaper in the usual way. This system permits the papers to run different regional editions utilizing the main news items from headquarters, while allowing for variations in advertising content within each regional edition. There are services that can transmit an advertiser's ad by satellite to publications with reception stations in much the same way.

Satellite transmission systems allow newspapers to run different regional editions, utilizing main news items from "headquarters." Dow Jones publishes *12 editions* of *The Wall Street Journal*—to appeal to distinctly different markets, using satellite transmissions. In their case, *speed* and *efficiency* are paramount—yet they must focus on regional news markets for audience appeal.

Color Copiers Come of Age

A variety of color copiers with advanced technology are making their way into ad agency art and production departments. Young & Rubicam has used color copiers for several years, primarily for making comprehensives, TV storyboards, and packaging. Bruno Tomasi, senior vice president, says:

> For print ads we'll use the camera zoom to give several visuals from one piece of art or by changing the focus and retaining the position, we can make up several print ads. We'll do one main drawing and allow a lot of bleed area and then we'll make copies, cropping them so they will fit different layouts. A client needed to imprint their logos on some hats for a company outing. Normally, we would have silk screened, but we didn't have enough time. So we put a special transfer paper with the logo. We matched the color of the logo and were able to transfer the client's logo to the hats. It worked wonderfully.[3]

SUMMARY

Everyone in advertising needs to understand the basics of production. The technical terms, concepts, and processes are not easy to learn, but they are essential to know.

First are the scheduling aspects of production. Planning well in advance of the due date is extremely important.

Then there are the three major processes of printing: *letterpress* (printing from a raised surface), *offset lithography* (printing from a flat surface), and *gravure* (printing from a depressed surface). In addition, there is *silk screen* or screen printing, which has many applications for advertisers. The form of printing affects the type of materials sent to the publication to reproduce your ad.

The computer offers advertisers and agencies more flexibility in typesetting; however, most advertising typography is still set by a printer or typography shop. *Typography* concerns the style (or face) of type and the way in which copy is set. Typefaces come in related designs called *families*. The size is specified in points (72 points per inch). The width of typeset lines is measured in picas (6 picas to the inch). The depth of newspaper space is measured in (agate) lines (14 to the column inch), regardless of the column width. The space between the lines of type is called *leading* or *line spacing;* lines can be set solid (with no extra space) or with extra space up to about 20 percent of the type size.

Typesetting technology is rapidly changing. It is important to check with the typographer so you will know the capabilities of the hardware. Some typographers have very sophisticated systems that can manipulate type in numerous ways; others have typesetting machines with lesser capabilities.

Desktop publishing is suitable for setting some kinds of promotional material. Only the very expensive systems are capable of the crisp quality needed for regional and national ad production.

Graphics and production are complex because what you see isn't always what really is. In halftones, a photoengraving is made of continuous-tone art photographed through a screen and then etched so that the tonal values of the original are reproduced in black dots. The gray tones in a photograph can only be reproduced through the halftone process, which creates an illusion of gray by varying the sizes of the black dots. Line art has no tonal value; it is drawn in black ink on white paper using lines and solid black areas.

---

[3] "A Rainbow of Color and a World of Possibilities," *Art Product News,* July–August 1988, pp. 14–16.

Process color is necessary to reproduce color photographs (halftones) and combinations. Four specific inks are used—red, blue, yellow, and black—and color separations are made of the color continuous-tone copy to isolate each of the four colors of light onto a separate negative. The approval of color proofs is a very important aspect of controlling quality. Proofs for checking color are either progressive (on-press) proofs or nonpress color proofs.

Different publications have different mechanical requirements. These can be learned from SRDS *Print Media Production Data* or from the publications themselves. Both offset and gravure publications accept mechanicals and artwork for ads, although most prefer film.

QUESTIONS

1. Differentiate between letterpress and offset printing.
2. What is continuous-tone copy?
3. When do you need to make a halftone?
4. What are points and picas?
5. What are color separations?
6. What kinds of color proofs do advertisers use?
7. What is line art?
8. What colors are used in process color?
9. Where do you find publication mechanical requirements?

SUGGESTED EXERCISES

- Find examples of halftone and line art in current publication ads.
- Find illustrations with special screens (line conversions) and prepare to discuss how these techniques help the communication process.
- Find type that you think is set solid in an ad. See if you can find an ad that appears to have too much line spacing.

READINGS

ANGELO, JEAN MARIE: "Advertising Inserts: Look for the Danger Signs," *Folio,* June 1989, pp. 110–115.

CROW, WENDELL C.: *Communication Graphics* (Englewood Cliffs, NJ: Prentice Hall, Inc., 1986).

BROWN, ALEX: "How to Avoid Reproduction Problems," *Folio,* April 1988, pp. 100–103.

SAINT JAMES, WATSON: "High-end Software Sharpens Image," *Advertising Age,* November 14, 1988, p. 48.

SHAW, NED: "Forming a Creative Partnership," *Art Product News,* January–February 1989, pp. 16–18.

TOWER, WALTER: "How to Avoid Hazardous Waste," *Adweek,* August 1, 1988.

TRUITT, ROSALIND C.: "Phototypesetters Endure Despite Advent of Laser Printers," *Presstime,* January 1989, pp. 14–16.

NINETEEN

The Television Commercial

Today's television commercial represents *a high order of creativity*—in order to "hold" today's audiences. For Burger King's new campaign theme, "Sometimes you've gotta break the rules," it "broke the rules" and hired *two* agencies. Gary Langstaff, executive VP-marketing, pointed to the new creative as "proof" the decision was a sound one. "This advertising is better and fresher than anything coming out of Oak Brook" (Illinois—headquarters for McDonald's).

Television is the most powerful advertising medium of all because it incorporates sight, sound, and motion. Still, it poses certain problems: commercial clutter that leaves people confused about advertisers, loss of audiences, high production costs and media rates, shrinking commercial lengths, and, of course, zapping.

But adversity breeds innovation. Advertisers have picked up many valuable techniques from MTV for attracting and holding viewers. Rock videos, in fact, have become proving grounds for new techniques. The fear of boring fans forced their producers to experiment, and advertisers have used and refined some of their innovations. Consequently, today's creative team has an array of new techniques and variations on old ones: the serial, the split ad, the documercial, hand-held camerawork, reality advertising. All of these have invigorated the work of writers, art directors, and producers of commercials.

In this chapter, we examine the fundamentals of creating and producing television commercials.

CREATING THE TELEVISION COMMERCIAL

There are two basic segments to developing a TV commercial: the video, the visual part you actually see on the TV screen; and the audio, made up of spoken words, music, and other sounds. Since there are two parts, you usually begin thinking about creating the commercial with pictures and words simultaneously.

Visual Techniques

It isn't sufficient to develop an extremely creative dramatic script with strong sell. That great script idea has to be produced creatively on film or tape. Many good ideas have not come off because the production was not good enough. Let's take a look at some successful visual techniques.

Spokesperson. This technique features a ''presenter'' who stands in front of the camera and delivers the copy directly to the viewer. The spokesperson may display and perhaps demonstrate the product. He or she may be in a set (a living room, kitchen, factory, office, or out of doors) appropriate to your product and product story, or in limbo (plain background with no set). You need to choose as spokesperson someone who is likeable and believable but not so powerful as to overwhelm the product. (see Exhibit 19.1) Remember, the product should be the hero.

Spokespeople ''present'' the products to the viewer. *Testimonials,* on the other hand, are delivered by ''celebrities,'' whose reputation lend credibility to the products. *Holly Farms* chicken products ''jumped to the top of the charts'' with *Dinah Shore* as spokesperson. Since being bought by Tyson Foods, *a fictional farm scientist* has replaced DS, with a new slogan, ''At Holly Farms, we have a natural way with chicken.''

Testimonials. The testimonial by either a known or an unknown individual has been a successful technique for decades. A celebrity personality (e.g., Bo Jackson, Jim Palmer, Joe Montana, Michael Jordan, Christie Brinkley, Bill Cosby) will grab viewers' attention for your commercial. It is important to match the person to the product. You should create your selling strategy first, and then seek the personality for the spot.

You don't need a major celebrity for a testimonial to be effective, especially in an era when even minor stars sometimes demand $250,000 per commercial. Fictional figures often work quite well: Think of Mr. Goodwrench (General Motors), Madge (Bounty), and Motorman (Precision Tune; see Exhibit 19.2). Noncelebrities (''real people'') may add credibility to some spots; for example, a nutritionist or a chef at a

EXHIBIT 19.1

Cates uses a lovable spokesperson to make you believe they produce good-tasting pickles. (Courtesy: Cates Pickle Company.)

EXHIBIT 19.2

Here a personality has been created to talk to the viewer. Who knows your car better than your engine? (Courtesy: Precision Tune and Leslie Advertising, Inc., Greenville, S.C.)

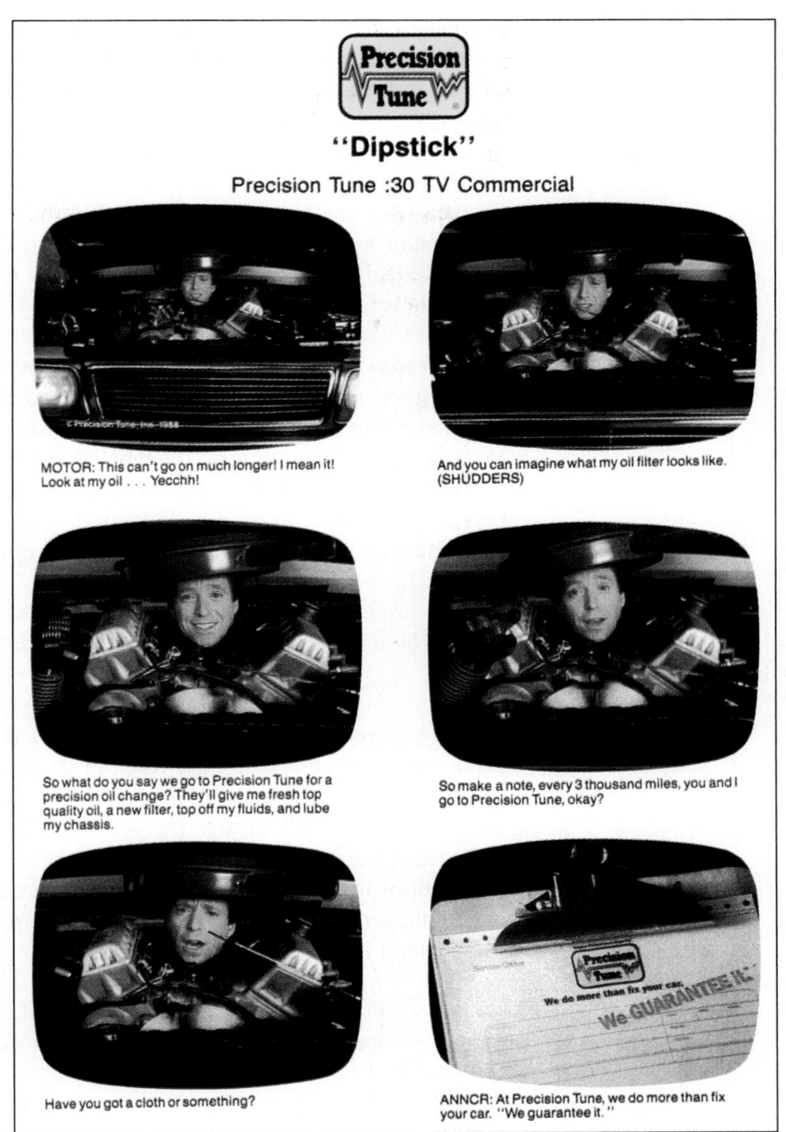

Precision Tune
"Dipstick"
Precision Tune :30 TV Commercial
MOTOR: This can't go on much longer! I mean it! Look at my oil . . . Yecchh!
And you can imagine what my oil filter looks like. (SHUDDERS)
So what do you say we go to Precision Tune for a precision oil change? They'll give me fresh top quality oil, a new filter, top off my fluids, and lube my chassis.
So make a note, every 3 thousand miles, you and I go to Precision Tune, okay?
Have you got a cloth or something?
Precision Tune
We do more than fix your car.
We GUARANTEE IT.
ANNCR: At Precision Tune, we do more than fix your car. "We guarantee it."

famous restaurant might be believable selling a food product. No matter whom you use, celebrity or average housewife, make your commercial sound natural and sincere and be sure that the name of the product comes across loud and clear.

Demonstrations of products are very effective on television. *Most important,* the outcome should be authentic. The British TV spot, titled "Human Condition," depicts the morning woes of a man suffering from a hangover. After a glass of Resolve headache remedy, *he recovers*—and an unknown hand from the medicine chest soothes his brow. He smiles and throws "kisses of thanks. . . ."

Demonstration. This technique is popular for some types of products because TV is the ideal medium for demonstrating to the consumer how the product works: how a bug spray kills, how to apply eye pencils in gorgeous silky colors, or how easy it is to use a microwave to cook a whole meal quickly. When making a demonstration commercial, use close shots so the viewer can see clearly what is happening. You may choose a subjective camera view (which shows a procedure as if the viewer were actually doing whatever the product does), using the camera as the viewer's eyes. Make the demonstration relevant and as involving as possible. Don't try to fool the viewer for two important reasons: (1) Your message must be believable; and (2) legally, the demonstration must correspond to actual usage. For the second reason, most agencies make participants in the commercial production sign affidavits signifying that the events took place as they appeared on the TV screen.

Close-ups. Television is basically a medium of close-ups. The largest TV screen is too small for extraneous details in the scenes of a commercial. A fast-food chain may use close-ups to show hamburgers cooking and the appetizing finished product ready to be consumed. With this technique, the audio is generally delivered offscreen (the voice-over costs less than a presentation by someone on the screen).

Story Line. The story line technique is similar to making a miniature movie (with a definite beginning, middle, and end in 30 seconds), except that the narration is done offscreen. A typical scene may show a family trying to paint their large house with typical paint and brush. The camera shifts to the house next door, where a teenage female is easily spray-painting the house, the garage, and the fence in rapid fashion. During these scenes, the announcer explains the advantages of the spray painter.

Product comparisons today have to demonstrate improved features and unique properties—but may ''anger'' loyal purchasers of the poor-performing product. New TV spots for *Ford Festiva* claim it's *faster* than an Alfa Romeo and has more interior room than a BMW. Another touts the car's *acceleration* as being better than *both* a Pontiac Le Mans or an Alfa Romeo. A third version says the Festiva has more room inside, than either a Toyota Tercel or BMW 635 CSI.

Direct Product Comparison. Do you remember ''brand X,'' the product that was never as good as the advertised brand? The trend now is to use comparative advertising in which both brands are named and compared. You've seen a number of soft-drink ads comparing product qualities. ''Our brand has NutraSweet, their brand doesn't. They are high in sodium. Our brand is sodium-free. Their brand is loaded with caffeine. We never use caffeine.'' Naturally, this kind of commercial answers questions about the two products for the viewer. There are two problems with direct product comparisons, however: In case of a lawsuit by a competitor, you must be prepared to prove in court that your product is significantly superior, as stated; second, you must be credible in the way you make your claim, or the commercial may induce sympathy for the competition.

Still Photographs and Artwork. Using still photographs and/or artwork, including cartoon drawings and lettering, you can structure a well-paced commercial. The required material may already exist, to be supplied at modest cost; or it can be photographed or drawn specifically for your use. Skillful use of the TV camera can give static visual material a surprising amount of movement. Zoom lenses provide an inward or outward motion, and panning the camera across the photographs or artwork can give the commercial motion (*panning* means changing the viewpoint of the camera without moving the dolly it stands on).

Slice-of-life commercials have the advantage of being able to relate to ordinary ''distress'' situations—which the sponsor's product is able to resolve. Four new 30-second TV spots position *regular Dr. Pepper* as ''the product that makes good things happen,'' John Clarke, senior VP-marketing, told Dr. Pepper bottlers at their recent annual meeting. In the spot titled ''Baseball,'' the final batter is an older fellow. Although an unlikely hero, he drinks a Dr. Pepper and hits a homerun to win the game!

By creating fast-paced, exciting scenes, often laced with music and song, motivation is heightened on the part of the audience to want to respond and be part of the ''action.'' That successful technique helped introduce Sunkist Orange Soft Drink. Beach goers frolicking in the sand, surfing amid the waves, and shooting beach balls in the air ''paused'' for refreshing gulps of Sunkist—to the Beach Boy's popular theme, ''Good Vibrations.''

Slice of Life. This approach is based on a dramatic formula: predicament + solution = happiness. The true-to-life or humorous story is dramatized in the hope of involving the viewer to the point of thinking: ''I can see myself in that scene.'' The viewer must see the problem as a real one, and the reward must fit the problem. Since problem solving is a useful format in almost any commercial, slice of life is widely used: Boy meets girl in a close setting. Boy has bad breath. Girl says: ''No.'' Boy is upset. Boy finds the product and uses (mouthwash, toothpaste, gum, breath mints, whatever). Again, boy meets girl in close setting. This time, romance. Problem solved. In this approach, it is important to have a story that the viewer can relate to and at the same time be sure that the product name registers with the viewer.

Customer Interview. Most people who appear in TV commercials are professional actors, but customer interviews involve nonprofessionals. An interviewer or offscreen voice may ask a housewife, who is usually identified by name, to compare the advertised kitchen cleanser with her own brand by removing two identical spots in her sink. She finds that the advertised product does a better job.

Vignettes and Situations. Advertisers of soft drinks, beer, candy, and other widely consumed products find this technique useful in creating excitement and motivation. The commercial usually consists of a series of fast-paced scenes showing people enjoying the product as they enjoy life. The audio over these scenes is often a jingle or song with lyrics based on the situation we see and the satisfaction the product offers.

Humor. Humor has long been a popular technique with both copywriters and consumers because it makes the commercial more interesting. The danger is that the

EXHIBIT 19.3

How about getting an orangutan to sell for a bank? A very creative way to differentiate your advertising and win international ad awards. (Courtesy: South Carolina Federal/HutchinsonSchutz.)

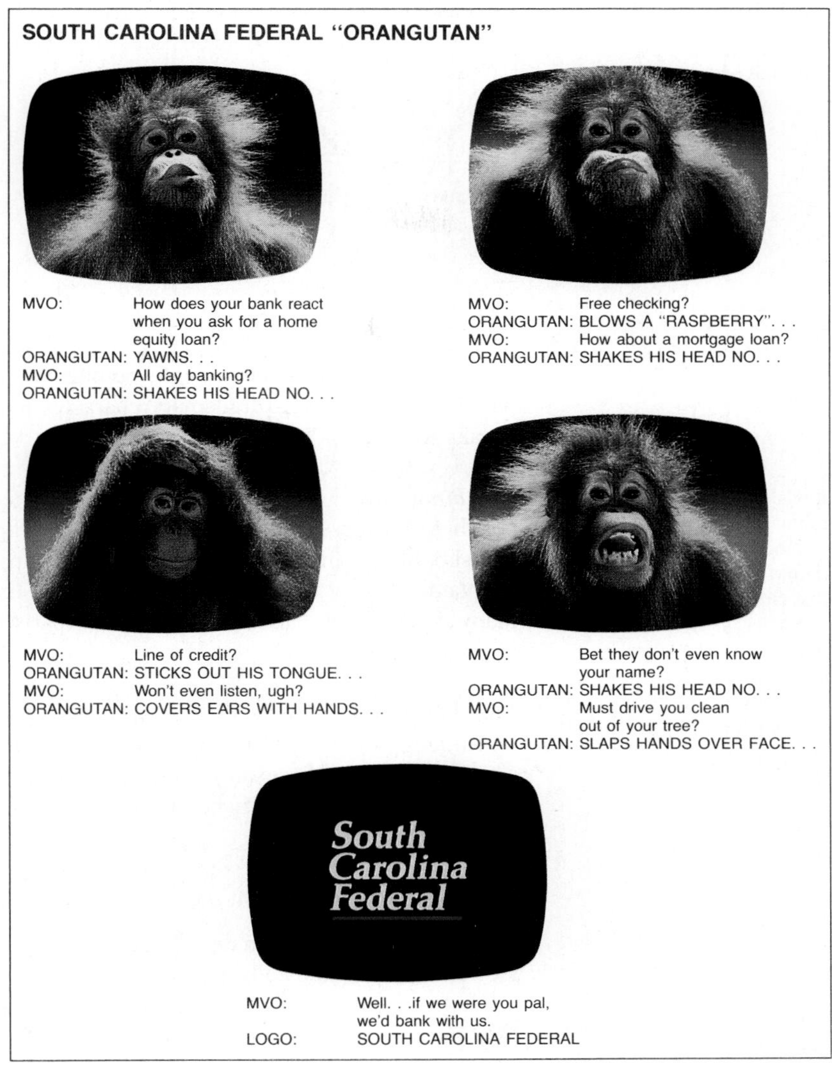

humorous aspects of the commercial will get in the way of the sell and that the viewer will remember the humor rather than the product or the benefit. The challenge is to make the humorous copy relevant to the product or benefit (see Exhibit 19.3).

SOUTH CAROLINA FEDERAL "ORANGUTAN"
MVO: How does your bank react when you ask for a home equity loan?
ORANGUTAN: YAWNS. . .
MVO: All day banking?
ORANGUTAN: SHAKES HIS HEAD NO. . .
MVO: Free checking?
ORANGUTAN: BLOWS A "RASPBERRY". . .
MVO: How about a mortgage loan?
ORANGUTAN: SHAKES HIS HEAD NO. . .
MVO: Line of credit?
ORANGUTAN: STICKS OUT HIS TONGUE. . .
MVO: Won't even listen, ugh?
ORANGUTAN: COVERS EARS WITH HANDS. . .
MVO: Bet they don't even know your name?
ORANGUTAN: SHAKES HIS HEAD NO. . .
MVO: Must drive you clean out of your tree?
ORANGUTAN: SLAPS HANDS OVER FACE. . .
South Carolina Federal
MVO: Well. . .if we were you pal, we'd bank with us.
LOGO: SOUTH CAROLINA FEDERAL

Animation (TV). *Making inanimate objects appear alive and moving by setting them before an animation camera and filming one frame at a time.*

Advertisers use *animation* to attract attention, especially from hard-to-reach audiences (example: young children) and for technical products or applications. The "Pink Panther" is credited with "selling" *more* Owens-Corning Fiberglass than the company's salesforce! He even gets the credit for sales *today*—when the campaign is no longer on the air.

Animation. Animation consists of artists' inanimate drawings, which are photographed on motion-picture film one frame at a time and brought to life with movement as the film is projected. The most common form of animation is the cartoon. A favorite among children but popular with all ages, the cartoon is capable of creating a warm, friendly atmosphere both for the product and for the message. Animation can also be used to simplify technical product demonstrations. In a razor commercial, the actual product may be shown as it shaves a man's face, and an animated sequence may then explain how the blades of the razor remove whisker after whisker. The cost of animation depends on its style: With limited movement, few characters, and few or no backgrounds, the price can be low. (See Exhibit 19.4.)

Stop Motion. When a package or other object is photographed in a series of different positions, movement can be stimulated as the single frames are projected in sequence. Stop motion is similar to artwork photographed in animation. With it, the package can "walk," "dance," and move as if it had come to life.

Rotoscope. In the rotoscope technique, animated and live-action sequences are pro-

EXHIBIT 19.4

Animation commercials use art. (Courtesy: Laura Scudder.)

duced separately and then optically combined. A live boy may be eating breakfast food while a cartoon-animal trademark character jumps up and down on his shoulder and speaks to him.

By combining different techniques, commercials can be made more effective and hold viewers' attention longer. *Bud Light's* use of Spuds MacKenzie, the bull terrier, is a fascinating deployment of vignettes, humor, stop motion, close-ups, and unique story line—all rolled into 1 commercial! Spud's newest venture is *a ninja warrior* episode.

Combination. Most commercials combine techniques. A speaker may begin and conclude the message, but there will be close-ups in between. In fact, every commercial should contain at least one or two close-ups to show package and logo. Humor is adaptable to most techniques. Animation and live action make an effective mixture in many commercials, and side-by-side comparisons may be combined with almost any other technique.

Mood Imagery. This technique is expensive and difficult. It often combines several techniques. The main objective is to set a certain mood and image for the product you are trying to sell. An example of this technique is the GE ''We bring good things to life'' campaign. Or the Michelob Beer campaign—''The night belongs to Michelob.''

The Search for New Techniques

There is a lot of life left in the common techniques we just reviewed, but because of the viewer apathy bred by advertising clutter, creatives continually seek better—or at least different—methods of communicating. Here are a few recent attempts to break out of existing formats.

The newest ''serial''—beginning as a mystery novel would in setting the scene—tells the story of the universe. Each segment shows a familiar scene, invoking memories of remarkable ''works'' of nature: memorable lighting effects, exquisite natural formations, stirring mood settings—all to introduce what promises to be the automobile ''of all time,'' *Infiniti by Nissan*. The idea is to build anticipation *before* the actual introduction of the car.

Serials. Viewers who have watched Frank Bartles and Ed Jaymes sell their wine coolers are familiar with serialization. Another example of a serial is the Nissan ''Road to Rio'' campaign, which portrayed a real-life husband-and-wife team driving a Pathfinder from Chicago to Rio. This campaign had six episodes, each informing consumers about the couple's trip and driving conditions.

The serial can be highly effective in sustaining viewer interest, but it has certain inherent risks. If all the commercials in the series are made in one sweep, and then the first ones don't catch on with consumers, it is very costly to shelve the remaining episodes. Each spot must be able to stand on its own in terms of communicating your objectives. Mary Moore, chief creative officer at Wells, Rich, Green in New York, believes serials are ''a risky strategy. The commercial has a lot of obligations beyond selling. Television viewing is so erratic you can't really expect to sustain interest over a period of weeks or months. It may work better during daytime where you have a dedicated audience watching all the soaps. That works better than stretching it out.''[1] Moore has successfully run serials. Her MCI spots were 15-second commercials resembling a Robert Ludlum suspense novel, each ending with the tagline ''To Be Continued.'' Later a full 60-second spot wrapped up the mystery and introduced a product line. Despite their riskiness, serials offer a great creative opportunity.

---

[1]Ron Gales, ''To Be Continued: Serials Capture Trans-Atlantic Fancy,'' *Adweek,* December 5, 1988, pp. 34–36.

Split and Bookend Spots. A variation on the serial commercial is the split spot: Two related 15-second spots run with a completely unrelated 30-second spot between them. For example, Post Grape-Nuts ran a split spot in which a woman asks a man how long Grape-Nuts stays crunchy in milk. The man doesn't want to find out, but she insists, and viewers are left hanging. Next is an unrelated 30-second commercial for another product. The couple then comes back and she says: "After all this time it's still crunchy."

In the bookend commercial, the first commercial sets up the second, but each works separately. Miller Lite ran two of these commercials 15 minutes apart. In the first segment, former football star Ray Nitschke says all his friends drink Lite. The bar's patrons are all Nitschke look-alikes. In the second spot, former basketball star Bob Lanier says all his friends drink Lite. This bar is also filled with Ray Nitschke look-alikes. Lanier says: "Oops, wrong bar."

In order to "grab" the attention of hard-to-reach (and-hold) audiences, such as business executives, "docummercials" or realistic segments of daily office decision-making are featured. Attention is focused on the discussion of the problem—and then on the "star" decision-maker who chose the "right" product or service. The viewer "sees" and "feels" the decision-making sequence of the communications manager—and "experiences" her satisfaction when the boss commends her decision for choosing MCI. . . .

Roy Rogers, a regional fast food-chain, uses a similar technique to break through TV advertising clutter. In a four-part commercial totaling 30 seconds, Part One, about 6 seconds, features a Roy Rogers menu item—chicken, for example. Part two, 10 seconds long, promotes the sale of that item: A kid who is shown feeding his meal to the family dog. However, when he gets Roy Rogers chicken, he eats it himself, and the dog cries. Part Three, 10 seconds, promotes a sale item—a chicken meal deal. Part Four is a 4-second kicker: The kid says he'll eat the last piece of chicken and the dog cries again.[2]

The theory behind split and bookend commercials is that breaking out of the expected formats will get your product remembered.

Documercials. In the late 1980s, anticommercials—spots that used documentary-style techniques such as hand-held cameras and black-and-white film—pushed TV advertising into the realm of gritty realism. The documercial attempts to make audiences feel as if they're watching real-life events. It can be a powerful tool for exploiting human nature.

Which Technique to Select

With such a variety of techniques to choose from, you might find it difficult to decide which to use. Ask yourself the following questions:

Does your promise of benefit and supporting evidence suggest a particular technique? Do you intend to demonstrate your product? Could it win in a side-by-side comparison with other brands? Is any of your copy based on reports of satisfied users? Is your sales story simple and direct enough to warrant the personal touch that a speaker may provide?

Comparing your technique to competitors' commercials helps to identify *new, creative strategies*. After watching cough/cold market leaders, Nyquil and Alka-Seltzer Plus, "sniffling and sneezing" their way through commercials, Sandoz Pharmaceuticals is introducing *Thera Flu*. Their strategy is to position the product primarily as a *flu and cough remedy*. "The idea is, the flu is *so bad*, it's your worst nightmare," stated Jeffrey Fine, chairman of the Bloom Agency, New York.

What techniques are your competitors using? Although no law prevents you from following their lead, you may want to choose a different direction in order to give your product a distinct TV image.

In previous advertising, has your product or service established a special personality that may suggest continuing a technique?

Do consumer attitudes discovered in research interviews suggest any problems to be met or any special advantages to be stressed for your product?

Does your campaign already exist in print ads? If so, you will probably want your TV effort to bear a visual resemblance. Often the reverse is true: Many print techniques follow the lead set by TV commercials.

How much money is available for production of your commercial? If your budget is modest, you will want to give serious thought to close-ups, artwork, simple sets, or locations with a minimum of personnel.

What production facilities are available? If you plan to produce your commercial in

[2]Stuart Elliott, "Split Ads Vie for Viewers' Full Attention," *USA Today*, May 23, 1988, p. 68.

a large city, you will probably find facilities at hand. Otherwise, the nearest TV station or a free-lance film maker may be your best choice.

What techniques are used in other commercials? Make it your practice to view TV often in order to analyze techniques. This will sharpen your familiarity with the subject, and you may see things that suggest new directions for your product.

PLANNING THE COMMERCIAL

In planning the TV commercial, there are many considerations: cost, medium (videotape or film), casting of talent, use of music, special techniques, time, location, the Big Idea and its relationship to the advertising and marketing objectives and, of course, to the entire campaign.

Let's review some of the basic principles of writing the commercial script or thinking the idea through.

- You are dealing with sight, sound, and motion. Each of these elements has its own requirements and uses. There should be a relationship between them so that the viewer perceives the desired message. Make certain that when you are demonstrating a sales feature, the audio is talking about that same feature.
- Your audio should be relevant to your video, but there is no need to describe what is obvious in the picture. Where possible, you should see that the words interpret the picture and advance the thought.
- Television generally is more effective at showing than telling; therefore, more than half of the success burden rests on the ability of the video to communicate.
- The number of scenes should be planned carefully. You don't want too many scenes (unless you are simply trying to give an overall impression) because this tends to confuse the viewer. Yet you don't want scenes to become static (unless planned so for a reason). Study television commercials and time the scene changes to determine what you personally find effective. As you do this, you will discover the importance of pacing the message—if a scene is too long, you'll find yourself impatiently waiting for the next one.
- It is important to conceive the commercial as a flowing progression so the viewer will be able to follow it easily. You don't have time for a three-act play whose unrelated acts can be tied together at the end. A viewer who can't follow your thought may well tune you out. The proper use of opticals or transitions can add motion and smoothness to scene transitions.
- Television is basically a medium of close-ups. The largest television screen is too small for extraneous detail in the scenes of a commercial. Long shots can be effective in establishing a setting, but not for showing product features.
- The action of the commercial takes more time than a straight announcer's reading of copy. A good rule is to purposely time the commercial a second or two short. Generally, the action will eat up this time, so don't just read your script. Act it out.
- You'll want to consider the use of supers (words on the screen) of the basic theme so that the viewer can see, as well as hear, the important sales feature. Many times, the last scene will feature product identification and the theme line.
- If possible, show the brand name. If it is prominent, give a shot of the package; otherwise, flash its logotype. It is vital to establish brand identification.
- Generally, try to communicate one basic idea; avoid running in fringe benefits. Be certain that your words as well as your pictures emphasize your promise. State it, support it, and, if possible, demonstrate it. Repeat your basic promise near the end of the commercial; that is the story you want viewers to carry away with them.
- Read the audio aloud to catch tongue twisters.
- As in most other advertising writing, the sentences should usually be short and their structure uncomplicated. Use everyday words. It is not necessary to have something said every second. The copy should round out the thought conveyed by the picture.
- In writing your video description, describe the scene and action as completely as possible. ''Open on man and wife in living room'' is not enough. Indicate where each is placed, whether they are standing or sitting, and generally how the room is furnished.

Commercials succeed in holding viewers' attention best when each scene relates a new idea and doesn't become ''static'' on the screen. Viewers still remember Arnold Palmer and O.J. Simpson running through airports—*Hertz* says its executive image has paid off in attracting business travelers. Now, with its new agency, Wells, Rich, Greene, it hopes to turn out a similar, fast-paced campaign to attract ''leisure travelers.''

The *one basic idea* of a commercial should be *stated* first, *supported* next with factual or explanatory evidence, and then *demonstrated*. Howard Johnson Franchise Systems is joining the battle for the frequent business traveler with a campaign that begins—''The *home* of the Road Warriors.'' The voice-over continues—''There's a special breed of people who do battle day after day. . . .'' A Viking, an Indian brave, a *knight, and an Amazon head* down a hotel corridor, only to be ''changed'' into more traditional business attire.

By making use of *sensory appeals*—smell, taste, softness, etc.—viewers can become more easily "involved" with the commercial message. Pontiac has had *an image of excitement* for 8 years, claimed Noel Nauber, senior VP-group creative director. . .so for its new Trans Sport mini-van, it adopted the slogan, "The Pontiac of Minivans." "We wanted to dramatize the *personal* driving characteristics of the vehicle." The TV spot shows a lone driver, weaving through the sandstone landscapes of southern Utah. New, more soulful executions of the 2-year old theme music, "Ride, Pontiac," play in the background.

Sensory Visuals

Television offers you a tremendous opportunity to make consumers use all their senses to feel the product and become involved in the message. In food advertising, you want appetite appeal. You could show a knife gliding like butter through a thick steak. The more sensory your appeal is, the more involved the audience will be. Special effects can aid in appealing to the senses. Remember the slow-motion visual tag that Downy fabric softener used in their commercials to illustrate softness (the container slowly fell into a basket of clothes and gently sank deep into the soft clothes only to bounce back slowly)? Slow motion can illustrate softness, tenderness, and freedom. Motion with meaning can help involve the viewers' kinesthetic sense. The use of mismatched cuts and extended dissolves can give your commercial "feeling."

Script writing necessitates working on the *video* and *audio* portions of the commercial at the same time—to coordinate the words and the action. James Jordan, the creator of "Ring around the collar" for Lever Brothers says he's elated that his 30-year-old son just wrote the campaign's *post script*. The new campaign for Advanced Action Wisk depicts embarrassing food spills—"Tsk, tsk, tsk"—and the detergent's removal—"Wisk, wisk, wisk."

Writing the Script

Writing a TV commercial is very different form writing print advertising. First, you must use simple, easy-to-pronounce, easy-to-remember words. And you must be brief. The 30-second commercial has only 28 seconds of audio. In 28 seconds, you must solve your prime prospect's problem by demonstrating your product's superiority. If the product is too big to show in use, be certain to show the logo or company name at least twice during the commercial. Think of words and pictures simultaneously. You usually divide your script paper into two columns. On the left, you describe the video action, and on the right you write the audio portion, including sound effects and music. Corresponding video and audio elements go right next to each other, panel by panel. Some agencies use specially designed sheets of paper 8½ by 11 inches, with boxes down the center for rough sketches of the video portion (see Exhibit 19.5). For presentations, most agencies use full-size TV storyboards. Write copy in a friendly, conversational style. If you use an off-camera announcer, make certain that his dialogue is keyed to the scenes in your video portion. Though it is not always possible, matching the audio with the video makes a commercial cohesive and more effective. The audio—words, sound effects, or music—in a script is as important as the video portion. They must work together to bring the viewer the message. You need strong copy and sound and strong visuals. All are vital for an effective commercial.

Storyboard. *Series of drawings used to present a proposed commercial. Consists of illustrations of key action (video), accompanied by the audio part. Used for getting advertiser approval and as a guide in production.*

Developing the Storyboard

Once the creative art and copy team has developed a script, the next step is to create a storyboard, which consists of a series of sketches showing key scenes developed in the script. It is a very helpful tool for discussing the concept with other agency or client personnel, who may not know the background or who may not be able to visualize a script accurately. Without a storyboard, each individual may interpret the script's visuals differently.

Storyboards consist of two frames for each scene. The top frame represents the television screen (visual). The bottom frame carries a description of the video (as per script) and the audio for that sequence (some storyboards only carry the audio portion). The number of sets of frames varies from commercial to commercial and is not necessarily dictated by the length of the commercial. There may be 4 to 12 or more sets of frames, depending on the nature of the commercial and the demands of the client for detail.

The ratio of width to depth on the TV screen is 4 by 3 inches. There is no standard-size storyboard frame, although a common size is 4 by 3 inches.

The storyboard is a practical step between the raw script and actual production. It gives the agency, client, and production house personnel a common visual starting point for their discussion. Upon client approval, the storyboard goes into production.

EXHIBIT 19.5

This rough script for an American Express commercial simultaneously shows and tells about the company's reliability. (Courtesy: American Express Company and Ogilvy & Mather.)

After the script, comes *the storyboard,* which shows the script "in action," through sketches. For Sharp's office products, the storyboard begins with "Miss Sharp" "spitting out" the words, "When I say Sharp, I mean business." The second scene focuses on her lips. In the next frame, we see copier results of our heroine, while a voice-over emits the words "copier" and "fax." We then move to the last frame, which displays all of Sharp's office products—and the model—while details of different machine capabilities are revealed.

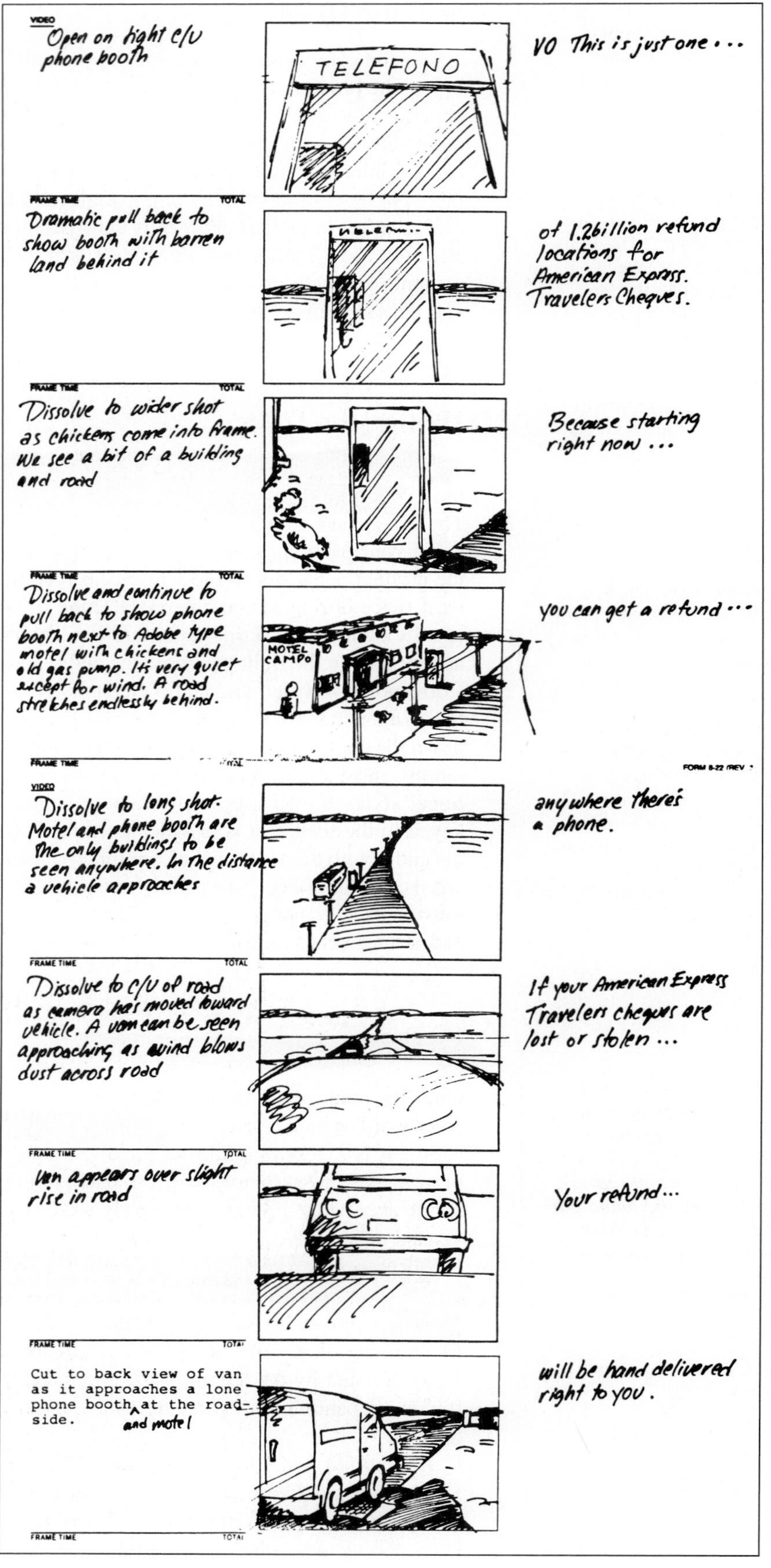

VIDEO
Open on tight c/u phone booth
TELEFONO
VO This is just one...
FRAME TIME
TOTAL
Dramatic pull back to show booth with barren land behind it
of 1.26 billion refund locations for American Express. Travelers Cheques.
Dissolve to wider shot as chickens come into frame. We see a bit of a building and road
Because starting right now...
Dissolve and continue to pull back to show phone booth next to Adobe type motel with chickens and old gas pump. It's very quiet except for wind. A road stretches endlessly behind.
MOTEL CAMPO
you can get a refund...
Dissolve to long shot. Motel and phone booth are the only buildings to be seen anywhere. In the distance a vehicle approaches
anywhere there's a phone.
Dissolve to c/u of road as camera has moved toward vehicle. A van can be seen approaching as wind blows dust across road
If your American Express Travelers cheques are lost or stolen...
Van appears over slight rise in road
Your refund...
Cut to back view of van as it approaches a lone phone booth and motel at the road-side.
will be hand delivered right to you.

PRODUCING THE TELEVISION COMMERCIAL

The job of converting the storyboard into a commercial (see Exhibit 19.6) is done by TV production. In charge of production is the producer, who combines the talents of coordinator, diplomat, watchdog, and businessperson. Some producers are on the staffs of large agencies or advertisers. Many work on a free-lance basis. The work of the producer is so all-embracing that the best way to describe it is to live through the production of an entire commercial. Let's do that first and pick up the details of the producer's job later in the section headed "Role of the Producer."

Elements of Production

Production is a two-part process: shooting and editing. Shooting encompasses the work of filming or videotaping all scenes in the commercial. In fact, several "takes" are made of each scene.

Editing, also known as *completion* or *finishing* or *postproduction,* includes selecting scenes from among those shot, arranging them in their proper order, inserting transitional effects, adding titles, combining sound with picture, and delivering the finished commercial.

Let's begin with the problems of shooting the film, for which a director is appointed by the producer.

EXHIBIT 19.6

The finished commercial as produced from storyboard. (Courtesy: Nike Air and Wieden & Kennedy.)

"WALKING":30
Copy:
I used to like it when she ran.
Copy:
She really didn't go much faster than now when she's walking.
Copy:
But she'd tire out quicker.
Copy:
And then we'd go home and she'd fall asleep in front of the T.V. I used to like that.
Copy:
I'd go sit on the chairs I'm not supposed to and she couldn't do nothing about it.
Copy:
Now, we go 3 miles a day, 10 miles on weekends.
Copy:
You know dogs were meant to sit in the sun and sleep.
Just do it.
Copy:
They ought to engrave that on the president of Nike's forehead.
NIKE
AIR

Director. *The person who casts and rehearses a TV or radio commercial and directs the actual performances.*

The "shooting" of a commercial is "broken" by the need to film indoor, outdoor, and close-up scenes. Each type is shot at the same time and put into proper sequence by the film editor. American Airlines, anticipating growth opportunities in the *leisure travel category,* features shots of exotic locations in its new campaign. Outdoor scenes are interspersed with shots of helpful American travel agents in AA airport terminals, and close-ups of happy passengers, disembarking in sun-drenched Caribbean destinations.

The Director's Function. The key person in the shooting, the director takes part in casting and directing the talent, directs the cameraperson in composing each picture, assumes responsibility for the setting, and puts the whole show together. Before selecting a studio, the agency finds out which director is available. The director may even be the owner of the studio. Because all studios provide basically the same equipment, the director is more important than the studio. A typical director earns $5,000 a day; better-known directors may charge $15,000–$20,000 per day.

Shooting on Film. Most commercials are shot on film, the oldest form of presenting motion pictures. Although the film of finest quality is 35-millimeter (35mm) film, it is expensive. Less costly is 16mm film, used by most local and some national advertisers. Originally, there was a great difference in quality between 35mm and 16mm films, but 16mm film has improved so much that it's now difficult to distinguish between the two.

Unless the action is simple and continuous from beginning to end, the film commercial is generally shot "out of sequence." All indoor scenes are shot as a group, regardless of their order within the final commercial. Close-ups are also generally filmed together, as are outdoor shots. These will all be put in place by the editor (see Exhibit 19.7).

EXHIBIT 19.7A
Production crew on set during shooting. (Courtesy: Leslie Advertising, Inc., Greenville, S.C.)

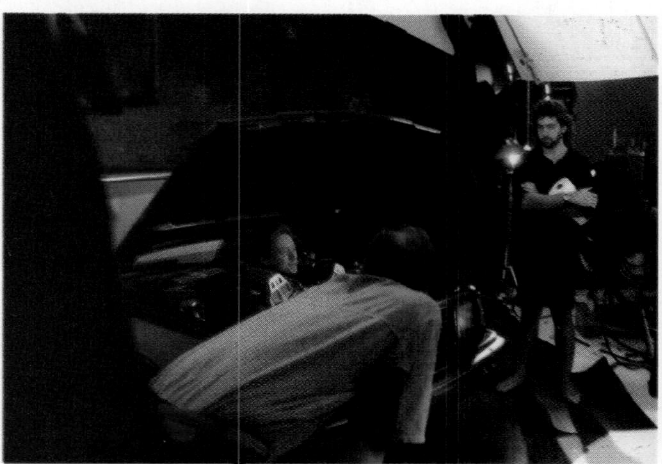

EXHIBIT 19.7B

Finished commercial shot indoors. (Courtesy: Leslie Advertising, Inc., Greenville, S.C.)

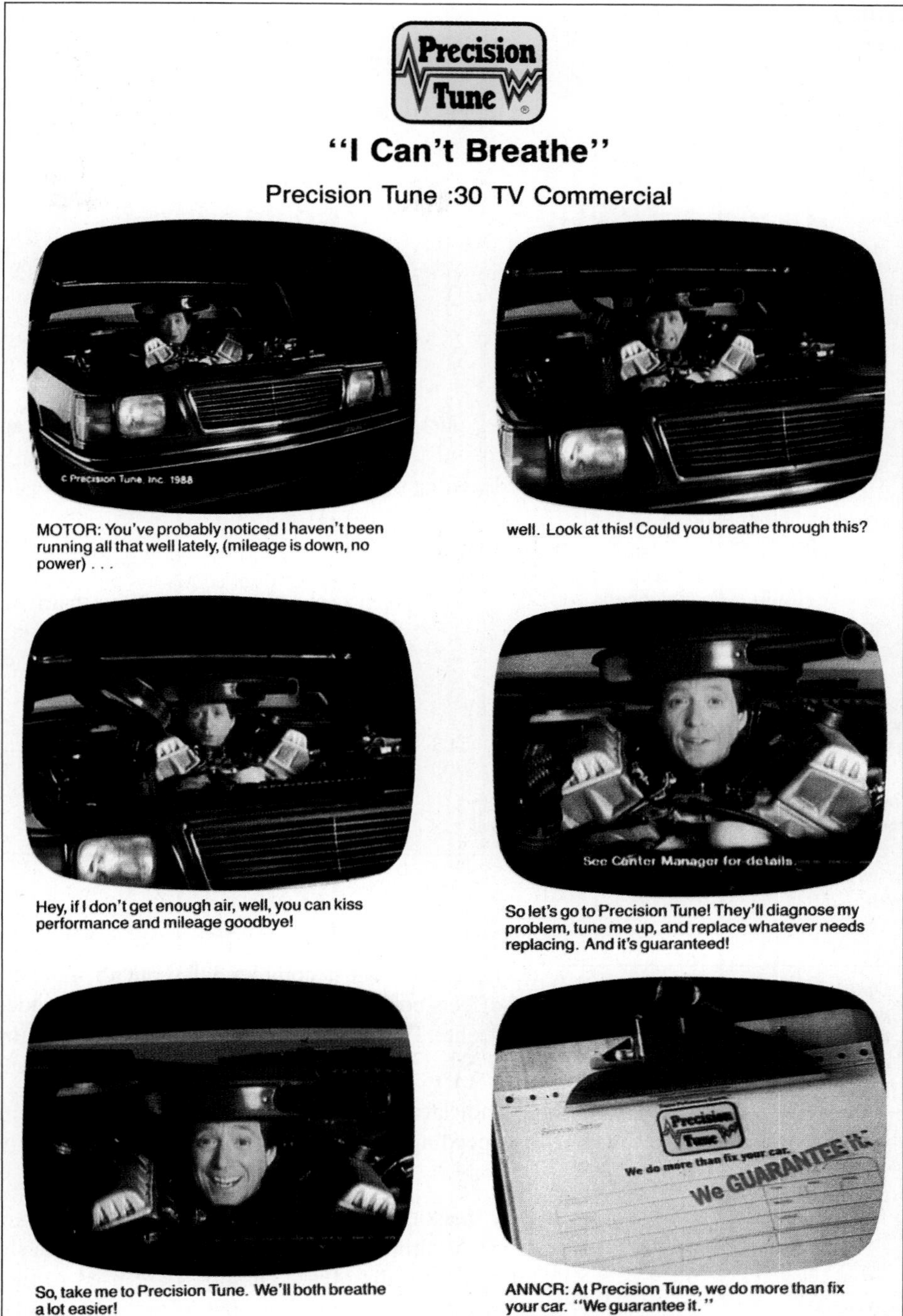

Precision Tune
"I Can't Breathe"
Precision Tune :30 TV Commercial
c Precision Tune Inc 1988
MOTOR: You've probably noticed I haven't been running all that well lately, (mileage is down, no power) . . .
well. Look at this! Could you breathe through this?
Hey, if I don't get enough air, well, you can kiss performance and mileage goodbye!
See Center Manager for details.
So let's go to Precision Tune! They'll diagnose my problem, tune me up, and replace whatever needs replacing. And it's guaranteed!
So, take me to Precision Tune. We'll both breathe a lot easier!
Precision Tune
We do more than fix your car.
We GUARANTEE it.
ANNCR: At Precision Tune, we do more than fix your car. "We guarantee it."

Generally, a scene is shot more than once because the first time or two the performances are unsatisfactory. Even after the director gets an acceptable "take," one more shot may be made for protection. In a normal day's shooting, the camera may expose 4,000 or 5,000 feet of 35mm film (45 feet will be used in the final 30-second commercial) or 1,200 to 2,000 feet of 16mm film (18 feet will be used in the 30-second commercial).

The actual direction of the commercial is the primary function of the director. An experienced director can efficiently tell a story in 30 seconds using a number of different directions (see Exhibit 19.8).

EXHIBIT 19.8
Examples of camera directions.

ECU—An Extreme Close-Up shows, for example, person's lips, nose, eyes.

CU—The Close-Up is a tight shot, but showing face on entire package for emphasis.

MCU—The Medium Close-Up cuts to person about chest, usually showing some background.

MS—The Medium Shot shows the person from the waist up. Commonly used shot. Shows much more detail of setting or background than MCU.

LS—Long Shot. Scene shown from a distance, used to establish location.

In order to move from scene to scene, "cuts," "dissolves," and "fades," are used to make the transition smooth. In the Young & Rubicam TV spot for AT&T's International Long Distance service, two co-workers chat while getting their lunch in the first frame. As the woman mentions that she has just bumped into one of their former colleagues, the scene cuts to a close-up. It cuts again to a close-up of the man—and then fades when he collapses to the floor when he learns the former colleague landed the account he was "pitching." The scene dissolves into a "black" screen; a second later the words, "AT&T—International Long Distance—Don't Wait to Use It," appear in white letters, without audio. . . .

Opticals. *Visual effects that are put on a TV film in a laboratory, in contrast to those that are included as part of the original photography.*

Other Elements of the Commercial

Opticals. Most commercials contain more than a single scene. Optical devices or effects between scenes are necessary to provide smooth visual continuity from scene to scene. They are inserted during the final editing stage. Among the most common are:

CUT. One scene simply cuts into the next. It's the fastest scene change because it indicates no time lapse whatsoever. A cut is used to indicate simultaneous action, to speed up action, and for variety. It keeps one scene from appearing on the screen too long.

DISSOLVE. An overlapping effect in which one scene fades out while the following scene simultaneously fades in. Dissolves are slower than cuts. There are fast dissolves and slow dissolves. Dissolves are used to indicate a short lapse of time in a given scene, or to move from one scene to another where the action is either simultaneous with the action in the first scene or occurring very soon after the preceding action.

FADE-IN. An effect in which the scene actually "fades" into vision from total black (black screen).

FADE-OUT. The opposite of a fade-in. The scene "fades" into total black. If days, months, or years elapse between one sequence of action and the next, indicate "Fade-out . . . fade-in."

MATTE. Part of one scene is placed over another so that the same narrator, for example, is shown in front of different backgrounds. Lettering of slogans or product names can be matted, or superimposed, over another scene.

SUPER. The superimposition of one scene or object over another. The title or product can be "supered" over the scene.

WIPE. The new scene "wipes" off the previous scene from top or bottom or side to side or with a geometric pattern (see Exhibit 19.9). A wipe is faster than a dissolve but not as fast as a cut. A wipe does not usually connote lapse of time as a dissolve or fade-out does. There are several types of wipes: flip (the entire scene turns over like the front and back of a postcard), horizontal (left to right or right to left), vertical (top to bottom or bottom to top), diagonal, closing door (in from both sides), bombshell (a burst into the next scene), iris (a circle that grows bigger is an *iris out*), fan (fans out from center screen), circular (sweeps around the screen—also called *clock wipe*). Wipes are most effective when a rapid succession of short or quick scenes is desired, or to separate impressionistic shots when these are grouped together to produce a montage effect.

ZOOM. A smooth, sometimes rapid move from a long shot to a close-up or from a close-up to a long shot.

Sound Track. The audio portion of the commercial may be recorded either during the film or videotape shooting or at an earlier or later time in a recording studio. When the sound track is recorded during the shooting, the actual voices of the people speaking on camera are used in the commercial. If the sound track is recorded in advance, the film or videotape scenes can be shot to fit the copy points as they occur; or if music is part of the track, visual action can be matched to a specific beat. If shooting and editing

EXHIBIT 19.9
Optical examples.

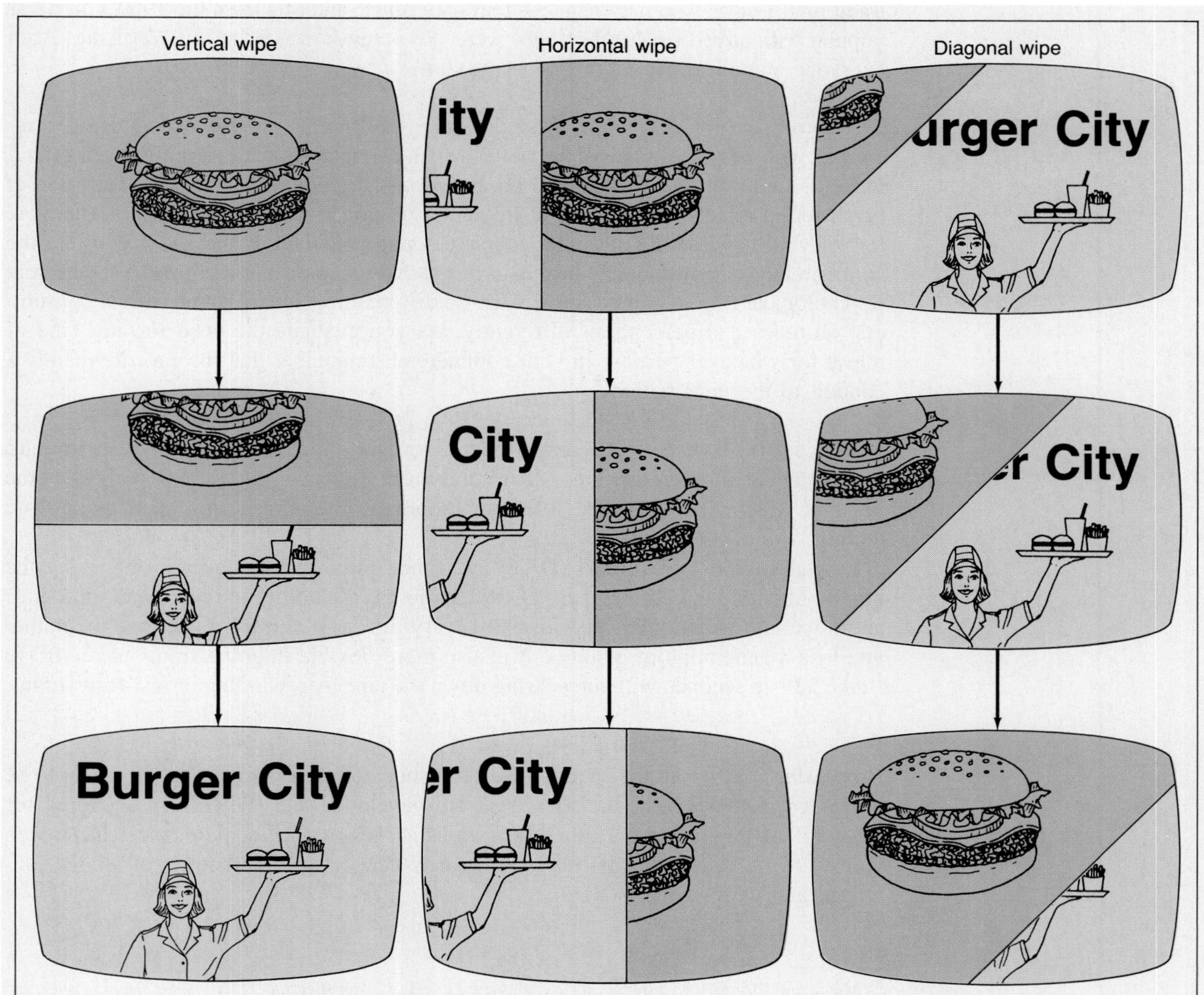

take place before the sound track is recorded, the track can be tailored to synchronize with the various scenes.

Music and song can enhance the creative feature of the commercial, which in turn help *retention* of the advertiser's message. ''The New Generation of Olds'' commercials now feature calypso singer Harry Belafonte's ''grown'' children, singing the Olds tune to HB's hit song. Their resemblance to their father and the island setting ''reinforces'' the Belafonte recollection, while ending on a 90's ''note.''

MUSIC. Music can make or break a TV commercial. It is often used as background to the announcer's copy or as a song or jingle (usually sung off-screen). Effective music can set the mood and tone of the commercial, and can even accent the selling words. Background music is available as stock music, which is usually prerecorded and sold very reasonably by stock music companies; or as original music, which is especially composed and recorded for your very own commercial. Original music is usually done by an independent contractor.

The song or jingle sets the slogan or the lyrics written by the agency or by an outside composer to music. If the melody is original, you must pay a composing fee. If it belongs to a popular or once-popular song, you must get permission from, and usually pay a fee to, the copyright owner. If the music is in the public domain, permission is generally not necessary, but other advertisers may be using it as well as you. Regardless of whether the tune is original or standard, the advertiser must usually pay fees for musical arrangements, to musicians and singers, to a studio for recording the jingle, and for editing to complete the sound track.

As they look for new, more effective ways to attract the viewer's attention and get their message across, agencies, directors, and composers are redefining the kind of music used in commercials, as well as the way those sounds are technically executed. One change is in the jingle: Creatives want music that isn't as ''up ending'' as the traditional jingle. Another change is that rock music and hits from the 1960's aren't as popular with advertisers as they once were. Rock music was a fad in advertising. After everyone started to use it, the effect was lost.

SOUND EDITING. Once the music and various effects have been produced and recorded, you begin to manipulate and shape the sounds to achieve the desired effect. Director Larry Bridges talks about his Lee jeans commercial: ''It's a juxtaposition of harsh sound effects with Mozart's 'Requiem,' dialogue with funeral music. There are lots of very bewildering and imponderable sound associations that draw you into the commercial as an attitude.''[3] Just as in print advertising different colors have different psychological impacts on consumers, so do different music and sounds affect consumers' attitudes and perceptions differently. As you evaluate the need for any kind of music for whatever purpose in your commercial, remember that the ears are merely a conduit to the imagination.

NEW TECHNOLOGY. New sound technology gives the creative team even stronger tools to use in spot production. It isn't unusual for music composers to work at home on their Macintosh, IBM PC, or Commodore Amiga composing, sequencing, and editing.

Digital audiotape recorders (DAT) and other audio technology are improving the quality of sound in commercials. Digital audio has the ability to record and reproduce audio without generation loss (normally every time you dub from one tape to another you lose a generation of quality). It is also more flexible in going from ''take 10'' to ''take 52'' in seconds without wearing down the tape by rewinding or fast-forwarding.

Processing. After all the scenes have been shot, the film is sent to a laboratory to be processed. Often overnight, all scenes are developed and the film is delivered for viewing. At this point, the film is known as *rushes* or *dailies*. After these have been viewed to make certain that no reshooting is necessary, the shoot is officially concluded and editing begins.

---

[3]''Music and Effects for Commercials Reach New Levels of Sophistication,'' *Millimeter,* March 1989, pp. 119–120.

The Film Editor's Function

When the filming of a TV commercial is completed, the work of producing a finished commercial is far from over. The film for a commercial is often a giant jigsaw puzzle. Shots have been taken out of sequence; extra shots have been taken; and some scenes have been reshot several times. The editor must decide how to assemble the shots that will appear in the finished commercial. As we noted earlier, most of what was filmed will be deleted from the final commercial.

Once the editor has assembled the film to be used, the process of coordinating sound and music with the video portion and adding optical effects begins. Since TV commercials have only 15 or 30 seconds to tell a story, this coordination of elements is crucial to success. The editor is responsible for bringing the diverse elements of music, optics, and film together into a meaningful sales message. Exhibit 19.10 shows the stages the commercial passes through up to delivery to stations and networks for airing. Exhibit 19.11 shows the entire production schedule for a 30-second television commercial, from script development to shipping.

Videotape

A commercial can be shot either on film or on videotape. So far, we've discussed filmed commercials, which have to be shot and then developed. Now we're going to talk about a process basically the same as your home video camera, only more sophisti-

EXHIBIT 19.10

The TV commercial production process after shooting.

1. After shooting, the editor and agency screen dailies and select scenes to be used.
2. The agency screens a rough-cut commercial for preliminary approval.
3. Sound and music are recorded on magnetic tracks.
4. All sound tracks are placed on a single magnetic track.
5. Mixed magnetic track and work picture are put together in what is called an *interlock* for client approval.
6. The editor makes changes on interlock.
7. The editor sends the original negative of selected scenes to the lab for a checking copy called an *inter-positive* (IP).
8. The IPs are sent to optics lab to reshoot on negative film, adding title, dissolves, etc.
9. The optical negative is sent to the lab for a silent print called an *answer print optical* (APO). The APO and mixed magnetic track are given final approval.
10. The mixed magnetic track is sent to a lab to make optical track negatives. The optical picture negative is combined with the optical picture negative and color corrections are made.
11. The agency and client view the print for final approval.
12. Release prints are ordered for distribution to stations and networks.
13. Initial airing of commercial.

EXHIBIT 19.11

Production schedule for 30-second 35mm color television commercial.

Script/storyboard development	Tuesday, May 23
Client approves script/storyboard	Friday, June 2
Bids/estimates	Monday–Thursday, June 5–8
Client approves budget	Friday, June 9
Preproduction, casting	Monday–Friday, June 12–23
Shoot	Monday–Tuesday, June 26–27
Edit	Wednesday–Thursday, June 18–29
Client approves rough cut	Friday, June 30
Sound mix, record music	Wednesday–Thursday, July 5–6
Client approves answer print	Friday, July 10
Ship to stations	Friday, July 17

Videotaped commercials provide "instant" playback, the ability to achieve trick effects, and greater definition and clarity than film. "Independents" or "free-lancers" generally advertise their services in trade magazines such as *Adweek*. "Working within a budget," they'll create TV commercials, from concept through to finished production." "Quick turnaround" enables *local merchants* to utilize their "professional services."

cated. With a videotape recording (also called *VTR* or *tape*), we can accomplish everything we can with film, but without any kind of developing. The TV camera electronically carries the impulse through wires to a recorder.

The preference for film or videotape is subjective. It depends on what kind of "look" is desired and what kinds of special effects are needed in the execution of the commercial. Many people feel that film gives a softer, more glamorous image and makes it easier to create some types of special effects. On the other hand, shooting with one-inch state-of-the-art videotape gives you greater definition and clarity.

As technical advances in the shooting and editing process have made videotape much closer to film in quality, videotape has become increasingly popular with both local and national advertisers. Your creative requirements should dictate the choice between the two.

Unique Advantages of Videotape. Editing a film commercial usually takes weeks. Tape can be played back immediately after shooting. With videotape, you can shoot one day and be on the air the next—a boon to many advertisers, particularly retailers who change commercials every few days to feature sale items.

Other Advantages of Videotape. With videotape, you can achieve fascinating trick effects. As one camera focuses on an in-home computer terminal, for example, another camera can focus on the announcer. The two pictures can be combined so that the speaker can appear to walk over the keys of the home computer and be about the size of a doll.

Since no processing is required, shooting ends after the tape has been played back and approved for editing. If the commercial has been conceived as one long take from beginning to end that does not require editing, shooting actually ends after the final version has been approved.

Work print. *An edited form of TV commercial dailies, with no optical effects, titles, or color balance. See Rough cut.*

Videotape Editing. Since the images recorded on the videotape are invisible, the tape editor uses different equipment from that used by the film editor. First, the reel of dailies is screened on a monitor and takes are selected. The various takes are then duplicated and lined up on another monitor in their proper order. This first rough-cut edit, the *work print,* is the early stage in which the rough commercial can be visualized. Once this version is approved, opticals can be added electronically, and titles can be shot separately and matted over any scene in any position.

Today videotape is used to get a final edit of 16mm or 35mm film commercials. The various pieces or clips of the film commercial are edited or conformed on videotape. The videotape is usually 1-inch master tape suitable for broadcast reproduction. Since most clients' and agencies' VCR units are ¾-inch formats, the 1-inch tape is transferred to ¾ tape for final approval by agency and client.

ROLE OF THE PRODUCER

Agency Producer

The producer's role begins before the approval of the storyboard. Conferring with the copywriter and/or art director, the producer becomes thoroughly familiar with every frame of the storyboard.

Producer. *One who originates and/or presents a TV or radio program.*

1. The producer prepares the "specs," or specifications—the physical production requirements of the commercial—in order to provide the production studios with the precise information they require to compute realistic bids. Every agency prepares its own estimate form. The estimate form shown in Exhibit 19.12 gives an excellent idea of the chief elements of such estimates. In addition, many advertisers request a further breakdown of the cost of items such as preproduction, shooting crew labor, studio, location travel and expenses,

EXHIBIT 19.12

An estimate sheet for a commercial. (Courtesy: BBDO.)

BROADCAST PRODUCTION ESTIMATE

Client ______ Code ______ Job Code ______

Product ______ Code ______ Job Name ______

Media ☐ Radio ☐ Television

WORK CODE	WORK CATEGORY	ESTIMATED COST	
A5	Pre-Production		
B2	Production		
B3	Animation		
C4	Artwork		
C6	Color Corr Prod		
D4	Record Studio		
D7	Sound Track		
E2	Talent & P+W		
E5	Tlnt Trvl & Exp		
F3	Music		
F4	Musicians (AFM)		
G2	Editorial		
G5	Vtr/Film Trnsfr		
G7	Cassettes		
G9	Prints & Tapes		
H9	Miscellaneous (Com)		
	COMM SUB-TOTAL		
S2	BBDO Trvl & Exp		
S5	Casting at BBDO		
S8	Contingency		
S9	Weather Contingency		
T3	Handling		
T6	Shipping		
T9	Miscellaneous (Non-com)		
V3	Pyrl Tax & Hndlg		
V5	NY Sales Tax		
V6	NJ Sales Tax		
	N/C SUB-TOTAL		
	COMMISSION		
	GROSS TOTAL		

ESTIMATED BY

APPROVALS

Producer ______ Date

Acct. Exec. ______ Date

Client ______ Date

DATE INPUT

INPUT BY

COMPETITIVE BIDS

1. ______ $ ______
2. ______ $ ______
3. ______ $ ______

RECOMMENDED CONTRACTOR

RECOMMENDED EDITOR

	COMMERCIAL ID. No.	TITLE	LENGTH	COLOR	35mm	16mm	VTR
1.							
2.							
3.							
4.							
5.							
6.							

Further explanation of charges by work category ______

PROD 857 5/80 REV

The producer's role in shooting a commercial is to *finalize all details and execute all procedures* leading to the "final" print. Kathy Mullins, agency producer for Hal Riney & Partners, Chicago, received plaudits recently from *Ad Week's* critic, Barbara Lippert. Her "kinder, gentler" Blue Cross 60-second spots feature "Kids," "Wedding," and "Dawn" themes—with the common reminder tagline, "It's well worth having the piece of mind only this card brings. The one from Blue Cross and Blue Shield. Those who have it feel better than those who don't."

equipment, film, props and wardrobe, payroll taxes, studio makeup, direction, insurance, editing.

2. The producer contacts the studios that have been invited to submit bids based on their specialities, experience, and reputation, meets with them either separately or in one common "bid session," and explains the storyboard and the specs in detail.
3. The production house estimates expenses after studying specs, production timetable, and storyboard. Generally, a 35 percent markup is added to the estimated out-of-pocket expenses to cover overhead and studio profit. Usually, the production company adds a 10 percent contingency fee to the bid for unforeseen problems. The bids are submitted on a standardized production bid form that the producer uses to analyze the bids and recommend the studio to the client.
4. The producer arranges for equipment. The studio may own equipment such as cameras and

lights, but more often it rents all equipment for a job. The crew is also free-lance, hired by the day. Although the studio's primary job is to shoot the commercial, it can also take responsibility for editorial work. For videotape (see Exhibit 19.13), a few studios own their own cameras and production units; others rent these facilities.

5. Working through a talent agency, the producer arranges, or has the production company

EXHIBIT 19.13

A videotape contract showing the details of what is involved in arranging for videotaping. (Courtesy: BBDO.)

Videotape Contract

Agency Production Number TV — This number MUST appear on all invoices and correspondence. If not, invoice payment may be delayed. — Date

AGREEMENT made by and between BATTEN, BARTON, DURSTINE & OSBORN, INC. (hereinafter called "Advertising Agency") on behalf of (hereinafter called "Advertiser") and (hereinafter called "Contractor").

Advertising Agency on behalf of Advertiser hereby agrees to purchase from Contractor and Contractor hereby agrees to produce and sell to Advertising Agency VTR(s) of television commercial(s) in accordance with storyboards and/or scripts furnished by Advertising Agency, subject to the terms and conditions hereinafter set forth.

1. Specifications:

Commercial Identification No.	Title	Length	Color	B&W

2. Disposition of VTR elements:

(a) Number of mixed master(s) to be delivered______

(b) Number of release VTR(s) to be delivered______

(c) Number of release TV film recordings to be delivered______

(d) All elements to be delivered to:

3. Responsibility for requirements:

(a) The Contractor shall supply the following:

(b) The Agency shall supply the following:

4. Production schedule:

(a) Taping to begin on______.

(b) Rough cut VTR(s) to be screened week of______.

(c) Mixed master VTR(s) to be screened on or before______.

(d) Release VTR(s) to be delivered by______.

(e) Release TV film recordings to be delivered by______.

5. Price and payment schedule:

(a) Total cost: $______, including mixed master VTR and one release VTR.

(b) Extra release VTR(s) at $______ each (as an extra charge).

(c) Release TV film recordings at $______ each (as an extra charge).

(d) Price to be paid in following installments:

1. $______ on signing this agreement.
2. $______ on start of taping.
3. $______ on approval of mixed master VTR(s).

6. Miscellaneous:

(a) The authorized representative of the Advertising Agency in the production of this videotape is ______.

(b) The title of Contractor's sample of quality tape is ______.

(c) Final edited original master VTR(s) to be stored by ______, with/without insurance.

(d)

This agreement includes additional paragraphs 7 through 31 set forth on the reverse side hereof.

Batten, Barton, Durstine & Osborn, Inc. by

Agreed and accepted: by

MP 1300 (REV. 2/76)

arrange, auditions. Associates also attend auditions, at which they and the director make their final choices of performers (see Exhibit 19.14). The client may also be asked to pass on the final selection.

6. The producer then participates in the preproduction meeting. At this meeting, the producer, creative associates, account executive, and client, together with studio representatives and director, lay final plans for production. These include what action will take place in each scene, how the sets will be furnished or where the outdoor location will be situated, how the product will be handled, whether the label will be simplified or the color corrected for the camera, what hours of shooting will be scheduled—in fact, all logistics relating to the shooting, which is probably scheduled for only a few days ahead.
7. During the shooting, the producer usually represents both the agency and the client as the communicator with the director. On the set or location, the creative people and client channel any comments and suggestions through the producer to avoid confusion.
8. It is the producer's responsibility to arrange for the recording session. Either before or after shooting and editing, he or she arranges for the sound track, which may call for an an-

EXHIBIT 19.14

Typical commercial production report on talent used for the production of the TV spot. (Courtesy: BBDO.)

Commercial Production Report

Sheet Number | **TV No.**

Client ______ Account Executive ______ Information Received ______
Product ______ BBDO Producer ______ Date Prepared ______
Contractor ______ Shooting Date(s) ______ To Accounting Dept. ______
Recording Studio ______ (Film/Tape, Announcer/Singers) Recording Date(s) ______ (Announcer/Singers) Checks Mailed ______

Commercial Identification Number | **Title** | **Length** | **Film** ☐ | **Tape** ☐ | **SAG** ☐ | **AFTRA** ☐

Basic:
Version:

A **MUSIC AFM** | Contractor ______ Address ______ | Date and place of recording ______ | **Contract No.** | Number of commercials declared

B **SAG/AFTRA** Information (Attach Talent Contracts, Time Cards, and Tax Forms) ★(Ethnic Group indicated as follows: Caucasian (C) Negro (N) Puerto Rican (PR) Mexican (M) Oriental (O)

Paid by BBDO	St'd'o	Compensation Scale/Scale +	Name and Ethnic Group★	★	Camera On	Camera Off	Category	Singers Mult.	Singers Sw't'n'g	Date(s) Worked	Number of Spots	**C** Producer's Remarks Upgrade—Downgrade—Outgrade

Commercial Film/Tape Completion Report:

1. MUSIC ☐ Yes ☐ No

If YES, check and fill in one of the following:
- ☐ Original. You must fill in AFM Information in (A) above.
- ☐ Picked up from: Film/Tape/Ra No. ______ List Contractor's name and AFM contract number in (A) above.
- ☐ Licensed from publisher. Copy of license attached.
- ☐ Stock license. Copy of license attached.

2. SINGERS ☐ Yes ☐ No
- ☐ Original (list singers in (B) above.)
- ☐ Picked up from: Film/Tape/Ra No. ______ (list names in (B) above.)

3. TALENT SAME ☐ Yes ☐ No

If NO, indicate downgrade or outgrade or picked up existing footage from Film/Tape. Indicate commercial Number and name on production report in Section (C) above.

4. EXTRAS ☐ Yes ☐ No

Complete Extras Report and attach to this Completion Report. If Extra upgraded to Principal, list name on Production sheet in Section (B) above. State reason in (C) above.

______ BBDO Producer (Signature) ______ Date

Form No. TV 1399 (August 78)

Talent Control Department

nouncer, actors, singers, and musicians. If music is to be recorded, the producer will have had preliminary meetings with the music contractor.

9. The producer participates in the editing along with the creative team. Editing begins after viewing the dailies and selecting the best takes.
10. The producer arranges screenings for agency associates and clients to view and approve the commercials at various editing stages and after completion of the answer print.
11. Finally, the producer handles the billings and approves studio and other invoices for shooting, editing, and payment to talent.

The "Outside" Producer

This is the person representing a production company whose entire business is film making. He or she is hired by the agency producer to create the television commercial according to agency specifications.

CONTROLLING THE COST OF COMMERCIAL PRODUCTION

The cost of producing a TV commercial is of deep concern to both the agency and the advertiser. The chief reason that money is wasted in commercials is inadequate preplanning. In production, the two major cost items are labor and equipment. Labor—the production crew, director, and performers—is hired by the day, and equipment is rented by the day. If a particular demonstration was improperly rehearsed, if a particular prop was not delivered, or if the location site was not scouted ahead of time, the shooting planned for one day may be forced into expensive overtime or into a second day. These costly mistakes can be avoided by careful planning.

Costs

It is not unusual for national advertisers to pay $100,000–$300,000 for a 30-second commercial. A 2-minute film, which can be replayed over and over to different segments, costs only about $50,000. When the Florida Department of Health & Rehabilitative Services wanted to reach teens throughout the state, it chose 800 movie theaters to air its filmed warning about early sexual activity. "By targeting the heavy movie-going period between Thanksgiving and Christmas, we think the film will reach a lot of teens, on dates, who have serious doubts about whether or not to begin having sexual relationships," quoted Donna Barber, director of the department's Family Planning Division.

Before we cite dollar averages for commercials, we have to note that there are actually two levels of costs: one paid by local advertisers, whose 30-second commercial may cost from $10,000 to $25,000 and more; and the other paid by national advertisers, whose 30-second commercial may cost from around $100,000 to $300,000 or $400,000. The American Association of Advertising Agencies studied over 2,400 spots of different duration, from 15 to 60 seconds, and found the fast-food/beer/soft-drinks/snacks category to be the most expensive for national advertisers at an average of $241,900. The average spot for a national advertiser was $156,000; for regional advertisers, it was $102,000. Only 5 percent of the commercials cost more than the averages, but these expensive spots skewed the sample upward. The average shoot cost per day was $64,000 and the average location cost per day was $75,000. More than 60 percent of the sample contained music, which added, on average, $7,200 to commercial production costs;[4] famous songs added, on average, $19,800.

These cost figures will give you some perspective on television production costs. Actually there isn't any such thing as a true average, for each commercial's cost depends on a number of factors from type and numbers of talent to location. Obviously, small local advertisers need to learn how to produce inexpensive, but effective, television commercials. Spending large sums of money doesn't guarantee an effective commercial.

[4]Gary Levin, "Cost of TV Spot Pegged at $145,600," *Advertising Age,* March 6, 1989.

Union Scale

''Restrictions'' usually mean union restrictions. One of the first facts of life you become aware of in TV production is that it is a highly unionized business. The professional actor usually earns union scale, which is the minimum payment allowed. Personalities are able to demand and negotiate payment above scale. Nonprofessionals, even though they are not members of any union, must be paid union scale if they play a major role in a commercial.

Residual Fees

Residual. *A sum paid to certain talent in a TV or radio commercial every time the commercial is run after 13 weeks, for life of commercial.*

Another major expense is the residual, or reuse fee, paid to performers—announcers, narrators, actors, and singers—in addition to their initial session fees. Under union rules, performers are paid every time the commercial is aired on the networks, the amount of the fee depending upon their scale and the number of cities involved. If a commercial is aired with great frequency, a national advertiser may end up paying more in residuals than for the production of the commercial itself. This problem is less severe for the local advertiser because local rates are cheaper than national rates. The moral is: Cast only the number of performers necessary to the commercial and not one performer more.

PHOTOSCRIPTS

Photoscript (TV). *A series of photographs made at the time of shooting a TV commercial, based on the original script or storyboard. Used for keeping record of commercial, as well as for sales-promotion purposes.*

All advertisers like to be proud of their commercials, and they want to make the best sales-promotion use of them. In addition, they wish to keep a record of the commercials they've made. For this purpose, advertisers often make photoscripts—series of photographic frames taken from key frames of the actual print film, with appropriate copy printed underneath (see Exhibit 19.15).

EXHIBIT 19.15

Photoscript used in sales-promotion efforts. (Courtesy: Precision Tune.)

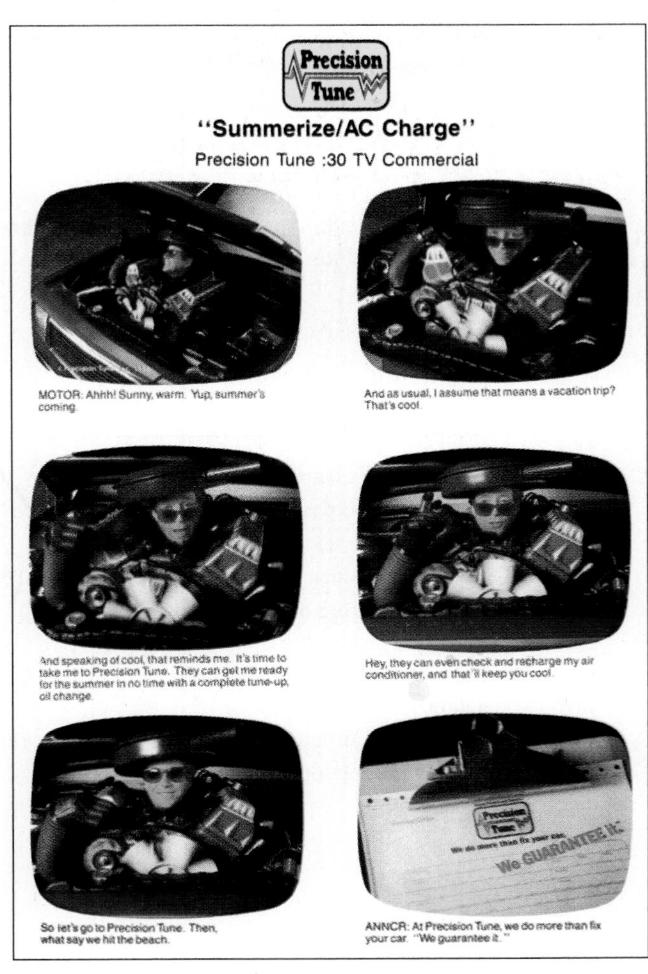

SATELLITE TRANSMISSION OF SPOTS

Cycle Sat sends spot television commercials by satellite transmission to television stations. The company saves agencies money on tape duplication and delivery costs. The ad agency delivers a 1-inch master to a Cycle Sat uplink office (there is one in most major cities), where traffic information is entered onto the computer and the commercial is sent by satellite to only those stations specified on the traffic list. Approximately 380 television stations have satellite decoders for receiving the spots. The equipment at the station records the commercial on the station's 1-inch VTRs and prints hard copy of the traffic instructions for the station.

SUMMARY

Television is the most important advertising medium because of the vast numbers of people it reaches. Creatively, television is powerful because it uses sight, sound, and motion. In developing a television commercial, the creative team has many visual techniques to choose from, among them spokespersons, testimonials, demonstrations, close-ups, humor, and animation. To better hold the viewer's attention, advertisers are constantly trying new techniques like serial commercials and split or bookend commercials, and attempting to build more realism into the ads. Writing and visualizing the commercial in simple easy-to-understand terms is essential to success. Since a good idea can be destroyed by bad production, producing the finished commercial is just as important as conceiving the idea.

Opticals are used as transition devices to get from one scene to the next. The style of music used in commercials has been changing; rock and traditional kinds of jingles have suffered from overuse. Technical advances are allowing much better sound reproduction. Most commercials are shot on film or videotape; each has advantages and disadvantages. The client and agency deal with all types of outside experts in the production of the finished commercial—talent, director, producer, production company crews.

Commercial production can be extremely expensive; it varies with different creative demands and techniques. Today many finished commercials are sent to television stations by satellite transmission.

QUESTIONS

1. What are the elements of a television script?
2. What is the purpose of the television storyboard?
3. Who creates a television script?
4. A commercial that ends with "To be continued" is an example of what technique?
5. How has the role of the jingle changed?
6. What is a residual?
7. Trace what happens to a commercial from after it has been shot until it is delivered to the TV station.
8. What are the differences between shooting on film and shooting on videotape?
9. What is the role of the director?

SUGGESTED EXERCISES

- Find two current commercials using effective opticals and give a brief critique of each.
- Discuss a current commercial that uses the testimonial technique.
- Find an ad in a current magazine that you think is strong and develop a television commercial based upon its concept.
- Create a storyboard for your favorite fast-food product.

READINGS

"Best of '88," *Advertising Age,* May 1, 1989, p. 34.

GILLY, MARY C.: "Sex Roles in Advertising: A Comparison of Television Advertisements in Australia, Mexico, and the United States," *Journal of Marketing,* April 1988, pp. 75–85.

LASKEY, HENRY A., ELLEN DAY, AND MELVIN CRASK: "Typology of Main Message Strategies for Television Commercials," *Journal of Advertising,* Vol. 18, No. 1, 1989.

LIPPERT, BARBARA: "Joe Isuzu Strays from the True Spirit of the Original," *Adweek,* March 13, 1989, p. 21.

KINDEM, GORHAM: *The Moving Image* (Glenview, ILL.: Scott, Foresman and Company, 1987).

"FIFTY TOP PRODUCERS," *Millimeter,* January 1989, pp. 49–82.

WEINBERGER, MARK G., AND HARLAN E. SPOTTS: "A Situational View of Information Content in TV Advertising in the U.S. and U.K.," *Journal of Marketing,* January 1989, pp. 89–94.

TWENTY

The Radio Commercial

Verbal messages need to awaken images in listeners' minds to be successful radio commercials. Hall, Northway & Scofield of Dallas is creating ''inviting'' radio spots for *Steak & Ale* and *Bennigan's*. The restaurants are taking some of their popular sauces and dressings and packaging them for national grocery sale, targeting markets where they have a concentration of restaurants. ''Consumers will 'taste' and 'smell' succulent steak juices and fresh, crisp salads,'' promised Janet Smith, manager of special products, after repeats of ''Just tell them you know the chef at Steak & Ale.'' (or Bennigan's)

Selective programming makes it possible for the radio advertiser to tap many different markets in a unique fashion. For those merchants wanting to reach a predominant Hispanic market, there's *Spanish Radio*. WSUA of Miami serves the specialty Hispanic audience, concentrating on south Florida's growing Nicaraguan, Colombian, and Argentine communities.

In print and television advertising, visuals are an integral part of the communication. Advertisers try to present something interesting, pleasant, bold, or bright to attract and move the reader's/viewer's eyes through a piece of communication. Radio is a different kind of medium, one for the ears alone. It requires a different style of advertising—messages that are developed for the ''theater of the mind.''

Sound messages can be powerful. The classic ''Pepsi-Cola hits the spot'' radio commercial, which ran almost fifty years ago, is proof. Nothing went into the mind via the eye—only through sound, but even today some people need hear only the opening bits of the Pepsi music to be able to recite every word of the jingle. If you use nothing but a verbal message to convince people about a product, people seem to be much more persuaded. The verbal message alone creates in their minds a more positive feeling for the product.

THE NATURE OF THE MEDIUM

As you will recall form Chapter 9, people use radio differently from the way they use other media. They have a tremendous choice of sounds in almost every market: news/talk, New Age, urban contemporary, adult contemporary, country, golden oldies, classical—there is a programming format for almost every taste and lifestyle. Radio is therefore a highly selective medium for the advertiser.

A radio advertiser skilled at tapping the imagination can transport listeners anywhere in the world, treating them to an experience it would take hundreds of thousands of dollars to create on television. The relatively low cost of producing radio spots allows the mass marketer to position a ''sound'' to specific audiences. An advertiser can create different versions of the same basic copy aimed at different radio formats, using voices or music appropriate for each target.

CREATING THE COMMERCIAL

Even though radio requires a different style of advertising, it is very similar to other kinds of advertising in many respects. You've got to know your market, objectives, and positioning and understand what problem you're trying to solve. What are you trying to do? What's in it for the target? How meaningful is your promise? These are the sorts of questions the radio copywriter has to think about when sitting down before the blank page or computer screen.

The writer for radio has the opportunity to develop an entire commercial alone (although in some agencies a creative team may work on a project). That means writing the script, picking the talent, and producing the commercial. In radio, the copywriter enjoys the freedom to create scenes in the theater of the listener's imagination by painting pictures in sound—a car starting or stopping, a phone ringing, water running, ice cubes falling into a glass, crowds roaring, a camera clicking. Remember, sound alone has an extraordinary ability to enter people's minds.

Let's look at three elements the copywriter uses to create mental pictures, memorability, and emotion: words, sounds, and music.

Radio commercials are built on the use of effective *words*. The National Abortion Rights Action League is involved in writing pro-choice radio commercials for New Jersey gubernatorial candidate, Representative Jim Flores, a Democrat. *Abortion* is considered to be the *key issue* in the campaign, and the group's choice of words on this sensitive subject is being guided by Greer, Margolis & Mitchell of Washington.

Words are often reinforced by the use of *sound*—to amplify the mood or make a specific point. While announcing "Lennon: His Last Interview, His Greatest Music," the Beatles music will be heard in the background. An announcement of the sponsors—Sears and Visa—will follow, while the popular theme plays. "The idea of *maintaining* a musical background is to lead the listener from song into the interview sequence—without a "break"—and back," revealed New York on-air personality (WXRK-FM) Jimmy Fink.

Music, in the form of a *jingle,* serves to "announce" and provide "a memorable association" for the product. The Coca-Cola Company's "Coke Is It" jingle is now heard on the radio, as part of a campaign to introduce *Break Mate*—a new, miniature soft drink dispensing unit, designed for small offices. The jingle has been extended to include the tagline, "Coke in the Morning," which should reinforce the beverage company's commitment to replace coffee as the "eye-opener" in the office.

Words

Words are the basic building blocks of effective radio commercials. They are used to describe the product, grab attention, create interest, build desire, and evoke a response from the listener. The warmth of the human voice may be all that is needed to communicate your message.

Sound

Used properly, sound can unlock the listener's imagination and create feelings. Any sound effect used should be necessary and recognizable; you should never have to explain it for the audience.

The sound has to convey a special message or purpose; it has to attract attention and complement the words. Sound can be used to underscore a point; create feelings of suspense, excitement, or anger; and invoke almost any mood you desire.

There are three basic sources of sound effects: manual, recorded, and electronic. *Manual effects* are those that are produced live, either with live subjects or with studio props; opening doors, footsteps, and blowing horns, are examples. *Recorded effects* are available from records, tapes, or professional sound libraries. They offer the copywriter almost every conceivable sound—dogs barking, cats meowing, leaves blowing, thunder crashing, cars racing. *Electronic effects* are sounds that are produced electronically on special studio equipment. The types of electronic effects range from filters (to simulate phone conversations), to oscillators and reverbs. Any sound created by using a device that generates an electrical impulse or other electronic sound is an electrical effect.

Music

Music can be very powerful in catching the listener's attention and evoking feelings. Not for nothing has music been called the "universal language." Different kinds of music appeal to different emotions; a minor is sadder than a major key, an increased tempo creates a sense of anticipation.

Commercials are often set to music especially composed for them or adapted from a familiar song. A few bars of distinctive music played often enough may serve to instantly identify the product. Such a musical logotype usually lasts from four to ten seconds. Jingles are a popular means of making a slogan memorable—think of the music for Coca-Cola, Pepsi, Chevrolet, Oldsmobile, and McDonald's over the years.

DEVELOPING THE RADIO SCRIPT

You will find some differences in the formats used in the script examples in this chapter. This is because most agencies have their own format sheets for copywriters to use. Formats also vary according to how the script will be used: If you are going to be in the studio with the producers and talents, you can verbally explain how the script is to be read or answer any questions that come up. If, however, you are going to mail the script to DJs to be read live, you need to be certain that anyone reading it will understand exactly what you want. The guidelines shown in Exhibit 20.1 illustrate explicit script directions.

STRUCTURING THE COMMERCIAL

Radio must ''grab'' the attention of the listener in the first few seconds of the commercial—and should close each message with a directive to act. To raise funds for Big Brothers/Big Sisters of America, the organization recruited Baseball Hall of Famer Hank Aaron to introduce the campaign. He then instructs listeners to visit Arby's for HA ''Collector's Cups''—with a purchase of Pepsi products. The sign-off includes the limited time period the offer will be available.

There are no hard-and-fast rules about the structure of a radio commercial, but most radio spots contain an introduction or intro (the attention-getter), product benefits, and close. The following thoughts have been selected from the *NAB Guidelines for Radio Copywriting 2*.[1]

It is important to grab the attention of the listener in the first few seconds of the spot. The intro can take the form of a sound effect, a statement, a question, a promise, a benefit, or a number of other methods that will make the audience listen for more. Here are a few techniques to accomplish this:

- Expand on your intro and work it into part of the selling offer. A sound effect can be used to grab attention and then inserted throughout the spot to build interest in the product. A comparison between the quiet purr of a SuperMo lawnmower and an old clickety-clack model, for example, can have great appeal.
- Describe one fundamental aspect of the product: ''A new SuperMo garden mower comes with a free lawn chair to relax in because it takes you half the time to cut your grass.''

[1] Reed Bunzel, *Guidelines for Radio: Copywriting* (National Association of Broadcasters, 1982), p. 18.

EXHIBIT 20.1
Example of radio form directions.

CLIENT: Wild corporation
Length: :60
Job No. 3364

LEFT SECTION OF PAGE IS FOR INFORMATION RELATING TO VOICES, ANNOUNCER, MUSIC, SOUND, USUALLY IN CAPS.	The right section of the script consists of copy and directions. It should be typed double-spaced. Pause is indicated by dots(. . .) or double dash (— —). Underline or use CAPS for emphasis.
MUSIC:	Music is usually indicated by all caps. WILLIAM TELL OVERTURE ESTABLISH AND FADE UNDER. In some cases, music is underlined. Directions may be indicted by parentheses ( ).
VOICE # 1	(LAUGHING LOUDLY) Excuse me sir. . .
OLD MAN	Yes. . .(RAISING VOICE) What do you *want*?
SFX:	SUPERMARKET NOISES, CRASHING NOISES AS SHOPPING CARTS CRASH. Sound effects indicated by SFX: (:08) BUZZER
SINGERS:	He's bright-eyed and bushy-tailed. . .
ANNCR:	This indicates announcer talking.
VO:	Voice Over.

- Emphasize the benefits of owning the product: ''If you get your lawn mowed Saturday morning, you have time to golf all afternoon.''
- Explain the selling points that deliver the desired benefits: ''The SuperMo mower comes with a grass catcher lined with disposable garbage bags to make your job easier.''
- Demonstrate the enjoyment that comes from ownership: ''The SuperMo is so much fun you won't let anyone else use it.''
- Illustrate the disadvantages of not owning the product: ''Everyone on the block owns a SuperMo except the Willetts. And you can't see their house for the grass.''

Every spot should close with an invitation to act, the product theme, the solution to the problem set, or a punch line. The more effective the close, the more effective the spot. Therefore, the close should be set up powerfully, progressing logically from one step to the next. Examples of closings:

- Provide good reasons for buying: ''Tired of paying the kid down the block twenty bucks for cutting your grass? Buy a SuperMo and cut it yourself.''
- Explain how easy it is to buy and select the product: ''Over 50 SuperMo models to choose from at over 1,500 dealers coast-to-coast. Call 1-800-555-MOWER for the nearest dealer.''

WRITING THE COMMERCIAL

Like the television commercial, the radio commercial has as its basic ingredient the promise of a significant and distinctive benefit. Once the promise has been determined, you are ready to use your arsenal of words and sounds to communicate your product message. Here are some ways to vitalize the copy.

A conversational tone, using simple, direct language, will get the *main idea* of the commercial across, in a credible way. That's the hope of Burrell Advertising, the *Metro Atlanta Rapid Transit Authority's* agency. Despite a blitz of radio commercials—along with direct mail, outdoor, print, and TV—Atlanta commuters are still reluctant to pocket their car keys. *Straight forward, common sense advice,* like ''Give your car the day off'' and ''Take the 85¢ Enjoy Ride,'' won Burrell 7 AdWheel creative awards . . . ''So, it's only a matter of time,'' according to Robert Brennan, MARTA assistant general manager, ''that we'll become *part* of the business sector.''

Simplicity. The key to producing a good radio commercial is to build around one central idea. Avoid confusing the listener with too many copy points. Use known words, short phrases, simple sentence structure. Keep in mind that the copy needs to be conversational.

Clarity. Keep the train of thought on one straight track. Avoid side issues.Delete unnecessary words. (Test: Would the commercial be hurt if the words were deleted? If not, take them out.) Write from draft to draft until your script becomes unmistakably clear and concise.

Coherence. Be certain that your message flows in logical sequence from first word to last, using smooth transitional words and phrases for easier listening.

Rapport. Remember, as far as your listeners are concerned, you are speaking only to them. Try to use a warm, personal tone, as if you were talking to one or two people. Make frequent use of the word *you.* Address the listeners in terms they would use themselves.

Pleasantness. It is not necessary to entertain simply for the sake of entertaining, but there is no point in being dull or obnoxious. Strike a happy medium; talk as one friend to another about the product or service.

Believability. Every product has its good points. Tell the truth about them. Avoid overstatements and obvious exaggerations; they are quickly spotted and defeat the whole purpose of the commercial. Be straightforward; you want to convey the impression of being a trusted friend.

Interest Nothing makes listeners indifferent faster than a boring commercial. Products and services are not fascinating in themselves; it is the way you present them that makes them interesting. Try to give your customer some useful information as a reward for listening (see Exhibit 20.2).

Distinctiveness. Sound different from other commercials and set your product apart. Use every possible technique—a fresh approach, a musical phrase, a particular voice quality or sound effect—to give your commercial a distinct character.

Compulsion. Inject your commercial with a feeling of urgency. The first few seconds are crucial ones; this is when you capture or lose the listener's attention. Direct every word toward moving the prospect closer to wanting the product. During the last 10 seconds, repeat your promise of benefit and register the name of your product. And don't forget to urge the listener to act without delay. (It's surprising how many commercials don't do this.)

Getting the listener to act—now—should be the end *result* of the commercial. That's the result the *Tri-State* (New York, New Jersey, and Connecticut) *Acura Dealers* expect from local agencies (billings of $50 million or less). "When you're looking for an up-and-running agency who understands the *volatility* of the marketplace," consultant Herbert Zeltner recommends "small" shops. In the car business, auto associations' spokespeople say, there's no *time* to waste—"Our radio ads are supposed to 'drive' our prospects into the showrooms *today!*"

Some Techniques

Basically a medium of words, radio—more than any other medium—relies heavily on the art of writing strong copy. However, just as print ads and TV commercials include pictures and graphics to add impact to the copy, radio creates mental pictures with other techniques. Radio copywriters can choose among many proven techniques to give more meaning to the copy, to help gain the attention of the busy target audience and hold that attention for the duration of the commercial. Some of these techniques parallel those used in TV.

EXHIBIT 20.2

This commercial combines music and interesting dialogue to attract and hold listeners' attention. (Courtesy: Canon.)

Radio Script **Canon Electronic Typewriters**

Title: THINK AGAIN #1
:60 RECORDED RADIO
:05 DEALER TAG ENDING

1 (GENTLE MUSIC UNDER THROUGHOUT)
2 MAN: Boss, I think our office needs new typewriters.
3 BOSS: I'm with you 100%. What brand of typewriter are you thinking about?
4 MAN: Well, I'm pretty much sold on —
5 FEMALE SINGER: Think Again...
6 BOSS: Yes?
7 FEMALE SINGER: Think Canon.
8 BOSS: You were saying?
9 FEMALE SINGER: Think Again...
10 MAN: Uh, well —
11 FEMALE SINGER: Think Canon.
12 MAN: — We definitely need quiet sturdy machines, with easy-to-use text editing features.
13 BOSS: Agreed.
14 MAN: — And we should get customizeable typewriters that let *us* design the perfect machine for each workstation.
15 BOSS: I like the way you think. So what typewriter company have you decided on?
16 MAN: Well, I think the only choice is —
17 FEMALE SINGER: Think Again..
18 BOSS: Go on.
19 FEMALE SINGER: Think Canon.
20 BOSS: I'm waiting.
21 (MUSIC UNDER)
22 FEMALE ANNCR: Before you make up your mind about office typewriters, Think Again... Think Canon. We make top quality machines that give you everything your office needs.
23 MAN: Canon, sir! I think we should buy Canon typewriters. They make top quality machines that will give us everything our office needs!
24 BOSS: Excellent. You read my mind.
25 SAMPLE LIVE ANNCR: See the complete line of Canon Custom Series typewriters at ABC Office Machines in Boise.
26 FEMALE SINGER: Think Again...
27 ANNCR: For office typewriters —
28 FEMALE SINGER: Think Canon.

Station Manager Please Note: In order for the retailer to receive co-op reimbursement for the cost of broadcasting this commercial, please complete the ANA/RAB documentation statement below.

This announcement and retailer tag was broadcast a total of ________ times at the dates and times coded ____________ on our attached invoice numbered/dated ______________ as entered in the station's program log. This announcement was billed to this station's client at a total cost of $________________.

Sworn to and subscribed before me and in my presence on this ______ day of __________, 19___.

Signature of Station Official

(Notarize above) Typed Name and Title Station Call Letters

Straight Announcer. In this commonly used and most direct of all techniques, an announcer or personality delivers the entire script. Success depends both on the copy and on the warmth and believability of the person performing the commercial.

Two-Announcer. In this format, two announcers alternate sentences or groups of sentences of copy. The commercial moves at a fast pace and generates excitement. This technique gives a news flavor to the commercial.

Announcers often "open" the commercials—but may fade, as *actors, jingles,* or *customers* are interjected to change the pace and add "excitement." Berelson Company, a marketer of imitation shellfish, is rolling out *Mox Lox* imitation salmon in Chicago and New York. A radio campaign features 60-second endorsements by a Joan Rivers impersonator. Rivers is especially well-known in those metro locations. . . .

Announcer-Actor. The listener may identify still more with the situation if the writer includes an actor's or actress's voice reacting to or supplementing the message delivered by the announcer.

Slice of Life. Write dialogue that reenacts a true-to-life scene involving the listener in a problem that the product or service helps solve (see Exhibit 20.3).

Jingle-Announcer. The song or jingle offers two advantages. As a song, it is a pleasant and easily remembered presentation of at least part of the copy. As a musical sound, it is the advertiser's unique property, which sets the commercial apart from every other ad on radio. Generally, an announcer is used in this flexible technique, which may be structured in countless ways. Most common is the jingle at the beginning of the commercial, followed by announcer copy; the commercial is concluded by a reprise of the entire jingle or its closing bars.

Customer Interview. The announcer may talk not with professional talent but with actual consumers, who relate their favorable experience with the product or service or store. As a variation, the satisfied customer may deliver the entire commercial.

Humorous commercials may break the monotony of serious product "pitches"—but should not be remembered for their humor alone. Anne Meara and Jerry Stiller's clandestine meetings over *Blue Nun* wine had listeners anticipating what new adventures they would find themselves embroiled in, while not sacrificing their favorite relaxing beverage. The result was significant added awareness of the *versatility* and *savvy reputation* of *Blue Nun*.

Humor. Tastefully handled, humor may be an ingredient in almost any technique (see Exhibit 20.4). A slice-of-life scene can have humorous overtones, and even straight announcer copy may be written in a humorous vein. Humor is often appropriate for low-priced package products, products people buy for fun, products whose primary appeal is taste, or products or services in need of a change of pace in advertising because of strong competition. Never, however, make fun of the product or the customer or treat too lightly a situation that is not normally funny. The test of a humorous commercial is whether the customer remembers the product, not the commercial. Humor is not called for when your product has distinct advantages that can be advertised with a serious approach. You need a pool of humorous commercials to avoid wearout.

Combination. Radio techniques may be mixed in countless ways, as illustrated in Exhibit 20.5 (combines jingle, dialogue, and announcer). To select the right technique for a particular assignment, follow the guidelines we discussed for selecting TV techniques in Chapter 19.

TIMING OF COMMERCIALS

Time is the major constraint in producing a radio commercial. Most radio stations accept these maximum word lengths for live commercial scripts:

- 10 seconds, 25 words
- 20 seconds, 45 words
- 30 seconds, 65 words
- 60 seconds, 125 words

In prerecorded commercials, of course, you may use any number of words you can

EXHIBIT 20.3

A slice-of-life commercial sells the idea that telephoning makes some things—like asking for a date—easier. (Courtesy: Chuck Blore & Don Richmond, Inc. & AT&T.)

Chuck Blore & Don Richman Incorporated
1606 North Argyle, Hollywood, California 90028 • (213) 462-6944

RADIO SCRIPT

Agency: N W AYER
Client: AT&T
Title: "A Love Story"

Date: 1-22-82
Page 1 of 1
Length: 60" sec.

CATHIANNE: (ON PHONE) Hello.

DANNY: (ON PHONE) Uh, hi. You probably still remember me, Edward introduced us at the seminar...

CATHIANNE: Oh, the guy with the nice beard.

DANNY: I don't know whether it's nice...

CATHIANNE: It's a gorgeous beard.

DANNY: Well, thank you, uh, listen, I'm gonna, uh, be in the city next Tuesday and I was, y'know, wondering if we could sorta, y'know, get together for lunch?

CATHIANNE: How 'bout dinner?

DANNY: Dinner? Dinner! Dinner's a better idea. You could pick your favorite restaurant and...

CATHIANNE: How 'bout my place? I'm my favorite cook.

DANNY: Uh, your place. Right. Sure. That's great to me.

CATHIANNE: Me too. It'll be fun.

DANNY: Yeah...listen, I'll bring the wine.

CATHIANNE: Perfect. I'll drink it.

BOTH: (LAUGH)

DANNY: Well, O.K., then, I guess it's a date. I'll see you Tuesday.

CATHIANNE: Tuesday. Great.

DANNY: Actually, I just, uh, I called to see how you were and y'know, Tuesday sounds fine!

SOUND: PHONE HANGS UP

DANNY: (YELLING) Tuesday...AHHHH...she's gonna see me Tuesday. (FADE)

SUNG: REACH OUT, REACH OUT AND TOUCH SOMEONE

EXHIBIT 20.4

A slice-of-life scene with humorous overtones stresses the trustworthiness of Bell South's car phones. (Courtesy: BellSouth Mobility.)

HutchesonShutze
50 Hurt Plaza, Suite 1500
Atlanta, Georgia 30303 (404) 523-2000

Broadcast Copy

Client: BellSouth Mobility
Product: :60 Radio
Title: "8-Iron"
Code No: **AS PRODUCED**

Date: April 19, 1989
W.O. No: BMI-120L
Radio (Length):
TV (Length): Page 1

Video:

Audio:

```
SFX:    (BIRDS CHIRP, AMBIENT OUTDOOR SFX)
MAN A:  So what do you think, seven-iron?
MAN B:  Are you crazy?  Eight-iron.
MAN A:  From here?
MAN B:  Yes.  Eight-iron.  Trust me.
ANNCR:  What if you had an extra half hour a day.  Or say, a few extra
        hours a week...to do what you want to do?  Well, at BellSouth
        Mobility, we're helping you do the things you have to do.  So you
        can spend more time doing what you want to do.
MAN A:  You're sure.
MAN B:  Absolutely.  Have I ever lied to you?
SFX:    (CLUB BEING TAKEN FROM BAG)
MAN A:  Eight-iron, huh?
MAN B:  Trust me.
MAN A:  Okay.
SFX:    (WHOOSH & WHACK)
ANNCR:  With the resources and advanced technology you'd expect from a
        BellSouth company, we're providing cellular car phones and cellular
        services...with just one purpose in mind.  To help you work
        smarter.
SFX:    (KERPLUNK & SPLASH)
MAN B:  Oh boy....will you look at that?
MAN A:  Well thank you, Mr. Trust Me.
MAN B:  I'm sure it's not very deep.
ANNCR:  At BellSouth Mobility, we figure the sooner you get your work
        done...the sooner you can get busy doing what you'd rather be
doing.
        And isn't that what we're all working for?
MAN A:  You see it in there?
MAN B:  Yeah, just a little to your left.
MAN A:  My left?
MAN B:  Yea.  Right by that big green snake.
MAN A:  Snake!
MAN B:  Trust me.
ANNCR:  BellSouth Mobility.  We're the phone company for your car.  Call
        us.  Because we know what you're working for.
```

EXHIBIT 20.5

This commercial combines dialogue and music to make a point, which the announcer reinforced. (Courtesy: Canon.)

Radio Script — **Canon** Electronic Typewriters

Title: THINK AGAIN #2
:60 RECORDED RADIO
:05 DEALER TAG ENDING

1 (MUSIC UNDER THROUGHOUT)
2 MAN 1: Okay — I've done my homework on different office typewriters.
3 MAN 2: Have you reached a conclusion?
4 MAN 1: I think far and away the best buy on the market is —
5 SINGER: Think Again...
6 MAN 2: You were saying?
7 SINGER: Think Canon.
8 MAN 1: For real typewriter value.
9 SINGER: Think Again...
10 MAN 2: The suspense is killing me.
11 SINGER: Think Canon.
12 MAN 1: Look, we want quiet, state of the art machines that won't break down every 5 minutes, right?
13 MAN 2: Naturally.
14 MAN 1: With loads of features — like easy-to-use text editing, spell checker, the works.
15 MAN 2: Sound reasoning — what typewriter company can give us all that
16 MAN 1: Well, I think the obvious choice is —
17 SINGER: Think Again...
18 MAN 2: Yes?
19 SINGER: Think Canon.
20 MAN 2: Are you collecting your thoughts?
21 ANNCR: If you think there's only one choice for office typewriters, Think Again... Think Canon. Canon typewriters offer you everything you're looking for plus a little bit more.
22 MAN 1: Canon.
23 MAN 2: Canon?
24 MAN 1: Canon typewriters offer us everything we're looking for, plus a little bit more.
25 MAN 2: Good thinking.
26 SAMPLE LIVE ANNCR: See the complete line of Canon Custom Series typewriters at ABC Office Machines, Boise.
27 SINGER: Think Again...
28 ANNCR: For office typewriters.
29 SINGER: Think Canon.

Station Manager Please Note: In order for the retailer to receive co-op reimbursement for the cost of broadcasting this commercial, please complete the ANA/RAB documentation statement below.

This announcement and retailer tag was broadcast a total of________times at the dates and times coded__________on our attached invoice numbered/dated____________as entered in the station's program log. This announcement was billed to this station's client at a total cost of $____________.

Sworn to and subscribed before me and in my presence on
this______day of________, 19___.

Signature of Station Official

(Notarize above) — Typed Name and Title — Station Call Letters

fit within the time limit. However, if you use more than 125 words for a 60-second commercial, the commercial will have to be read so rapidly that it may sound unnatural or even unintelligible. Remember, if you insert sound effects, that will probably cut down on the number of words you can use. If you have footsteps running for 5 seconds, you're going to have to cut 10 to 12 words. You need to time the musical intros and endings or sound effects because each will affect the number of words allowable. It isn't unusual to go into the recording studio with a script that is a couple of seconds short because the extra time allows the talents to sound more natural. Actors need some breathing room to sound sincere.

Music can enhance a commercial message—better than words alone. Advertisers may choose established compositions or may have special songs written for their product. To announce its new *Thunderbird,* Ford will throw an ''American Bandstand''-like party, featuring Dick Clark. The show will air to prime prospects in 30 cities nationwide. After ''live recreations'' of Coasters and Frankie Valli and the 4 Seasons' hits, Ford's commercials will conclude with the long-running song/tag, ''Have you driven a Ford . . . lately?'' Print announcements should ''guarantee'' a ''captive'' audience.

MUSICAL COMMERCIALS

Music can be a powerful tool for getting your product remembered. As musical writer Steve Karmen has said: ''People don't hum the announcer.''[2]

In writing musical commercials, you have to start with an earthquake, then build to something really big. In other words, there's no room for subtlety. The thought process and strategy are different from those in regular songwriting.

There are three main elements to writing commercial music:

- *Intro:* the beginning of the song. The tempo and lyrics may be established here.

[2]Bruce Bendinger, *The Copy Workshop Workbook* (Chicago: Bruce Bendinger Creative Communications, Inc., 1988) p. 214.

- *Verse:* the middle of the song. This is where the message is developed. There may be several verses.
- *Theme or chorus:* may be the conclusion of the song.

Commercial music is very flexible. You may begin with the chorus to establish your theme at the beginning, or you may repeat the theme throughout. The theme is what listeners remember. Some musical forms, such as the blues, can be thought of as both verse and chorus. A theme may serve as a musical logotype for the product, lasting about 4 to 10 seconds. Jingles are also a popular means of making a slogan memorable.

Many commercials are especially composed for the advertiser or product. Others are simply adapted from a familiar song. A melody is in the public domain, available for use by anyone without cost, after its copyright has expired. Many old favorites and classics are in the public domain and have been used as advertising themes. That is one of their detriments: They may have been used by many others.

Popular tunes that are still protected by copyright are available only by (often costly) agreement with the copyright owner. An advertiser can also commission a composer to create an original tune, which becomes the advertiser's property and gives the product its own musical personality.

__Jingle.__ A commercial set to music, usually carrying the slogan or theme line of a campaign. May make a brand name and slogan better remembered.

A mass marketer can position a ''sound'' to a specific audience. This can be done in radio relatively inexpensively compared to TV. Using the same lyrics and tune, BBDO developed four different versions of the same jingle for Delta Air Lines, each aimed at a different radio format: chorus, rock, country and western, and rhythm and blues.

METHODS OF DELIVERY

There are three ways a radio commercial can be delivered: live, by station announcer, and prerecorded.

The Live Commercial

Commercials may be delivered ''live,'' as many local messages are, or may be prerecorded, such as those for national distribution. Chesebrough-Pond's introduction of *Powerstick* antiperspirant/deodorant will be accompanied by *prerecorded radio spots* to air nationally. The strategy is to go head-to-head with Mennen's Speed Stick ''in as many markets as they're in,'' vowed company sources.

A live commercial is delivered in person by the studio announcer, disc jockey, newscaster, or other station personality; or perhaps by a sports reporter from another location. Though generally read from a script prepared by the advertiser, the commercial is sometimes revised to complement the announcer's style. If time allows, the revised script should be approved in advance by the advertiser. Ad-libbing (extemporizing) from a fact sheet should be discouraged since the announcer may inadvertently omit key selling phrases or, in the case of regulated products such as drugs, fail to include certain mandatory phrases.

Some commercials are delivered partly live and partly prerecorded. The prerecorded jingle, for example, can be played over and over with live-announcer copy added. Sometimes the live part (the dealer ''tie-up'') is left open for the tie-in ad of the local distributor.

One advantage of the live commercial is that the announcer may have a popular following and listeners tend to accept advice from someone they like. The other big advantage is cost: Station announcers usually do your commercials free of extra talent costs.

Station Announcer

For a campaign dealing with a retail offer that will change frequently, advertisers often use a station announcer reading copy written by the agency. This is recorded at the station at no charge to the client—sometimes even with the client's musical theme in the background. This type of delivery allows for frequent changes in copy at no cost.

The Prerecorded Commercial

Advertisers undertaking a regional or national campaign will not know local announcer capabilities. In any case, it would be impractical to write a separate script to fit each one's particular style. Commercials for these campaigns are therefore usually prerecorded. Not only does this assure advertisers that the commercial will be identical each time it is aired, but it also allows them to take advantage of myriad techniques that would be impractical in a live commercial. (Actually, in many instances, "live" commercials are recorded by the station so they can run even when the announcer is not on duty.)

PRODUCING THE RADIO COMMERCIAL

Stock music. *Existing recorded music that may be purchased for use in a TV or radio commercial.*

Producing *radio commercials* is less costly and far simpler than those for TV. And, currently, there's a glut of programming at fair prices . . . this spells a big opportunity for advertisers that move into the market *now*. National advertisers who have significantly increased their radio advertising in the last two years are Sears, GM, Campbells Soup, Unilever, and Chrysler.

Although there are certain broad similarities, producing radio commercials is far simpler and less costly than producing TV commercials. First, the agency or advertiser appoints a radio producer, who converts the script into a recording ready to go on the air. After preparing the cost estimate and getting budget approval, the producer selects a recording studio and a casting director, if necessary. If music is called for, the producer calls a music "house" that usually composes, arranges, and takes all steps necessary to get the finished music. If the music is not a big-budget item, the producer may call for "stock" music (prerecorded and used on a rental basis).

After the cast has been selected, it rehearses in a recording studio, which can be hired by the hour. However, since most commercials are made in short "takes" that are later joined in the editing, a formal rehearsal is usually unnecessary. When the producer feels the cast is ready, the commercial is acted out and recorded on tape. Music and sound are taped separately and then mixed with the vocal tape by the sound-recording studio. In fact, by double- and triple-tracking music and singers' voices, modern recording equipment can build small sounds into big ones. However, union rules require that musicians and singers be paid extra fees when their music is mechanically added to their original recording. After the last mix, the master tape of the commercial is prepared. When final approval has been obtained, duplicates are made on quarter-inch tape reels or audiocassettes for release to the list of stations.

Steps in Radio Production

We may summarize the steps in producing a commercial as follows:

1. An agency or advertiser appoints a producer.
2. The producer prepares cost estimates.
3. The producer selects a recording studio.
4. With the aid of the casting director, if one is needed, the producer casts the commercial.
5. If music is to be included, the producer selects a musical director and chooses the music or selects "stock" music.
6. If necessary, a rehearsal is held.
7. The studio tapes music and sound separately.
8. The studio mixes music and sound with voices.
9. The producer sees that the master tape is prepared for distribution on either tape or cassettes and shipped to stations.

You are on the air!

EXHIBIT 20.6

Radio creative services advertise to agencies and corporations. (Courtesy: Chuck Blore & Don Richmond, Incorporated.)

Of Cabbages And Kings

by Bill McDonald

The baby kept us up last night. It gets scary when that happens, especially at night when you're in the dark.

We knew there was something wrong, but we didn't know what — and the baby couldn't tell us. Strange the things that run through your mind at times like those. We conceived this baby, we brought it into our world, nursed it, pampered it and suddenly it's helpless. And so are we.

We try changing it. We lie down with it for awhile. We walk. We wonder. We worry . . . and we wish there were someone we could call. Sometimes, we even get resentful. We wonder why we're here, sitting up half the night with this baby when everyone else is in bed.

Then we look at the baby and we know *exactly* why we're here. We *chose* to be here. Out of love and pride and respect. This will be the best baby ever.

Somewhere between dusk and dawn, instinct took over. It was easy after that. We took our baby back into the studio, fixed what was wrong, then played with it for another hour or so, just to be sure . . . and just for fun.

It's a nice feeling you know. We've been making these babies for twenty years now and we still get that invisible smile inside when we know we've done the best we possibly can, and that our "best" is damn good.

Client called — "This commercial is an award-winner! How do you guys do it?"

Sometimes we do it the hard way, but I'll tell ya, it's worth it. No kid of ours ever leaves home till it feels good.

Chuck Blore & Don Richman
Incorporated

1606 N. Argyle, Hollywood, CA 90028 (213) 462-0944

SUMMARY

Despite its lack of visuals, radio can be an extremely creative medium. It offers great scope to the imagination and the opportunity to play with the listener's mind. Words, sound effects, and music are the tools used in the development of a radio commercial. The biggest constraint is time; you always work against the clock.

Commercial concepts must be kept simple—one main idea. Repetition of the product name and selling premise is generally considered necessary to make an impression on casual listeners. Like television commercials, radio commercials use several techniques and types of format; they differ from TV commercials in that they are simple and economical to produce.

QUESTIONS

1. Describe the characteristics of effective radio advertising.
2. Sound effects can come from what three sources?
3. What kind of sentence structure is used in radio scripts?
4. What do we mean by "theater of the mind"?
5. What is the role of the producer in the process of making a radio commercial?
6. What is the maximum number of words for a 30-second commercial?
7. How can music be effective in reaching different audiences with the same message?

SUGGESTED EXERCISES

- Choose two magazine ads and rewrite each as a radio commercial.
- Select a newspaper department store ad and rewrite it as a 60-second radio commercial. Then rewrite it as a 30-second version of the same commercial.

READINGS

ALTEW, STANLEY R.: *Audio in Media* (Belmont, Cal.: Wadsworth Publishing Company, 1987).

BUNZEL, REED: *Guidelines for Radio: Copywriting* (Washington, D.C.: National Association of Broadcasters, 1982).

EISENSON, JON: *Voice and Diction* (New York: Macmillan Publishing Company, 1985).

O'DONNELL, LEWIS B., CARL HAUSMAN, AND PHILIP BENOIT: *Announcing Broadcast Communicating Today* (Belmont, Cal.: Wadsworth Publishing Company, 1987).

TWENTY-ONE

Trademarks and Packaging

The "power" of a *trademark* and *brand* make it instantly recognizable in the "busy" marketplace. There is no more recognizable trademark around the world than *Coca-Cola*. Not only has Coca-Cola been a century-plus user of the available media to tout its products to the public, but in many instances, it pioneered new avenues of advertising. It was first to use print for soft drinks, first to sponsor national radio and TV broadcasts—and first to employ secondary, promotional media such as P-O-P and coupons.

Think of the power of a strong, effective image—a name, a symbol, a package—in building brand equity. Pepsi, Kodak, Coca-Cola, GE, Du Pont, IBM, and McDonald's have some of the most powerful and memorable brand images in the world. In this chapter, we will examine strategies for creating strong brand names and integrating packaging into the overall marketing program.

When you walk into a supermarket or department store, you frequently encounter products whose packaging and trademarks or logos are familiar to you from advertising, even though you may never have used, or even seen, the actual product. They stand out from lesser-known competitors, inspiring confidence in the companies that make them.

Developing and protecting trademarks, logos, and package designs is an important and expensive task. A company's trademark serves several purposes. It is an important marketing and advertising tool for distinguishing the firm's products from those of competitors. If there were no trademarks, there would be no advertising. Trademarks are an easily identifiable means of promoting a company's products so that they will be instantly recognizable to consumers.

The trademark also serves as a quality control for consumers, assuring them that the individual tube of Crest Toothpaste or can of Dole pineapple will be of the same quality no matter when or where the product is purchased. Without the trademark, a customer could only guess at the quality of most products and manufacturers would have no means of developing customer loyalty.

The brand is one of the most valuable assets of a company, and the trademark is the brand's asset. Consider the financial investment in the name and trademark of Coca-Cola since 1886, when it was first developed. Think of the corporate and financial loss if Coca-Cola lost the exclusive rights to its name and trademark. All companies face this threat, which will be discussed later in the chapter.

There is a strong need to protect the investment in a company name and trademark. In fact, a whole body of law has been developed around this need. Getting legal protection is the province of the attorney; however, it begins with the creation of the trademark itself. Hence, in creating or considering an idea for a trademark, you must understand some of the basic legal ground rules.

TRADEMARKS

What Is a Trademark?

When an advertiser combines a trademark with a "design," he has created a *logo*. *Volkswagen* cars and promotions have always featured an enlarged "V-W," encased in a circle. Even in black-and-white ads, it's been rated one of the most highly recognized logos among domestic and foreign automobile manufacturers.

A trademark is any symbol, sign, word, name, device, or combination of these that tells who makes a product or who sells it, distinguishing that product from those made or sold by others. Its purpose is to protect the public from being deceived and the owner from the unlawful use of his or her property.

There are several types of company and product identifications. The trademark, also called a *brand name,* is the name by which people can speak of the product. Very often a trademark will include some pictorial or design element. If it does, the combination is called a *logotype* (or simply *logo*). The 3M ad in Exhibit 21.1 contains some of the country's best-known corporate names and trademarks.

Logotype design is an extremely important element in the successful marketing of a product. It is very difficult to sell a product until a reasonable level of name recognition is achieved among consumers. In fact, the creation of a logo is so important that a number of firms have been established whose primary function is the design of logos and packages. Most designers attempt to forge a compatible relationship among the package design, logo, and advertising for the product. A strong logo on the package and in product advertising creates an environment of recognition.

Far and away the most successful packages are those that combine an intriguing design scheme with a provocative logotype. A provocative logo is one that if extracted from the package will still project the visual personality of the product. After all, when shoppers pass through the supermarket aisles, the first images to strike their eyes are recognizable brand names.[1]

[1] John DiGianni, "Logotype Impact," *Credits,* Vol. 2, No. 5, p. 23.

EXHIBIT 21.1

This ad shows some of the country's best-known corporation names and trademarks. (Courtesy: 3M Commercial Graphics Division.)

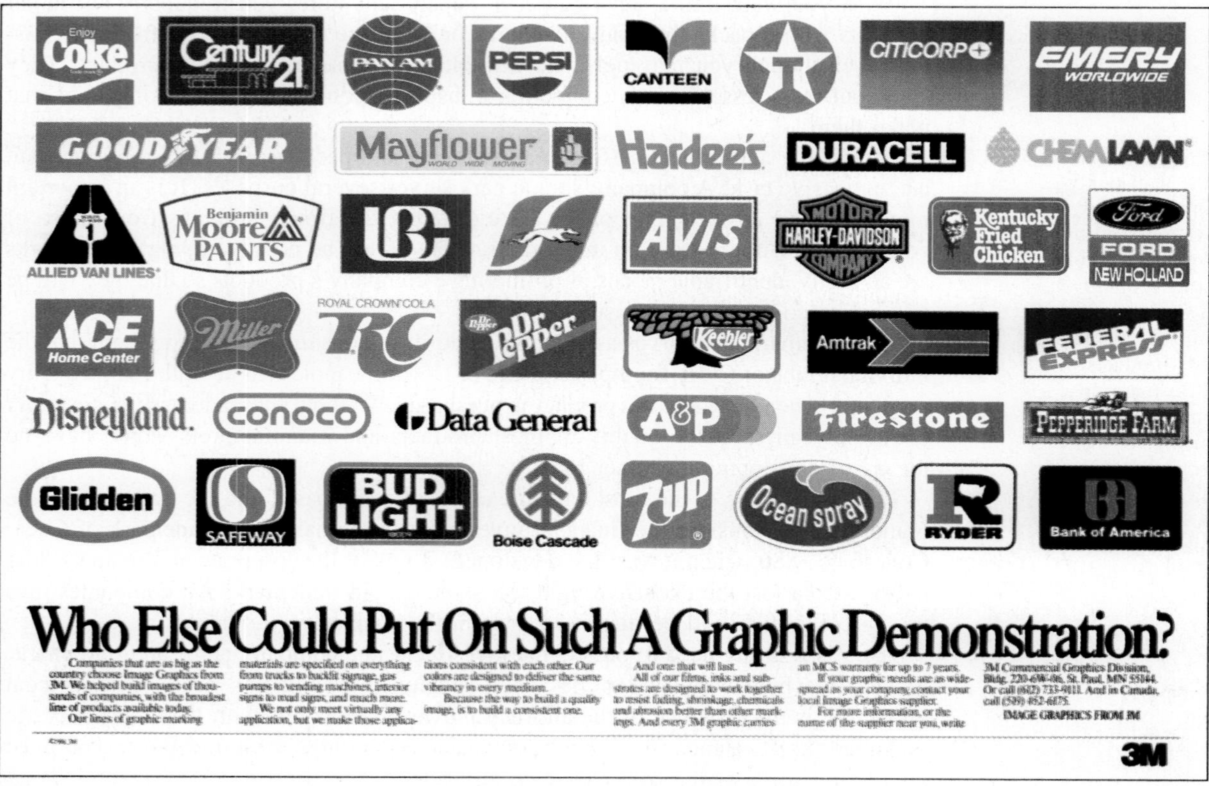

Trade name. *A name that applies to a business as a whole, not to an individual product.*

The trade name is the name under which the company does business. General Motors, for example, is the trade name of a company making automobiles whose trademark (not trade name) is Oldsmobile. The terms *trademark* and *trade name* are often confused. To understand the distinction, think of yourself as a new product. Your surname is your ''trade name'' (Smith). Your sex is the ''product classification'' (Girl Smith). Your given name is the ''brand'' (Judy Smith), as it distinguishes you from other family members.

In order for a firm to qualify for an exclusive trademark, several requirements must be met. If these criteria are not satisfied, the trademark is not legally protected and will be lost to the firm.

Trademarks must have a connection with an actual product, but not be misleading by implying innate qualities which the product lacks. *Eggo* waffles *do* contain eggs; *NutraSweet is* a sweetener for food products; and *Grease Relief does* get rid of grease. Products with family names, by contrast, are considered ''old'' and not often used for today's new introductions—because they don't relate directly to *function*. . . . Hence, it's less likely they'll be remembered.

- The trademark must be used in connection with an actual product. The use of a design in an ad does not make it a trademark, nor does having it on a flag over the factory. It must be applied to the product itself or be on a label or container of that product. If that is not feasible, it must be affixed to the container or dispenser of the product, as on a pump at a service station.
- The trademark must not be confusingly similar to trademarks on similar goods. It should not be likely to cause buyers to be confused, mistaken, or deceived as to whose product they are purchasing. The trademark should be dissimilar in appearance, sound, and significance from others for similar goods. Cycol was held to be in conflict with Tycol (oil), Air-O was held in conflict with Arrow (shirts), and Canned Light was held in conflict with Barreled Sunlight (paint) because of possible confusion. The two products involved need not be identical. The marks will be held in conflict if the products are sold through the same trade channels or if the public might assume that a product made by a second company is a new product line of the first company. Big Boy! powder for soft drinks was held in confusion with Big Boy stick candy.
- A trademark must not be deceptive—that is, it must not indicate a quality the product does not possess. Words that have legally been barred for this reason include Lemon soap that contained no lemon, Half-Spanish for cigars that did not come from Spain; and Nylodon for sleeping bags that contained no nylon.
- A trademark must not be merely descriptive. ''I have often noticed,'' the head of a baking company might say, ''that people ask for fresh bread. We will call our bread Fresh; that's our trademark. How nice that will be for us!'' But when people ask for ''fresh bread,'' they are describing the kind of bread they want, not specifying the bread made by a particular baker. To prevent such misleading usage, the law does not protect trademarks that are merely descriptive and thus applicable to many other products. Aircraft for control instruments and Computing for a weighing scale were disallowed as trademarks because they are merely descriptive. The misspelling or hyphenating of a word, such as Keep Kold or Heldryte, does not make a nondescriptive word out of one that, if spelled correctly, would be descriptive of the product. Although a word must not literally be descriptive, it may suggest certain qualities, and we shall touch upon this matter shortly.

Protecting a Trademark

Because a trademark is so valuable, companies go to great lengths to protect their brand names. In recent years, there have been a number of court cases involving allegations that one company has infringed on the trademark of another.

In deciding where trademark infringement has taken place, several factors are considered by the courts:

1. The distinctiveness of the complainant's mark.
2. The similarity of the marks.
3. The proximity of the parties' products.
4. The likelihood of the complainant bridging the gap between noncompeting products.
5. The similarity of the parties' trade channels and advertising methods.
6. The quality of the alleged infringer's products.
7. The sophistication of the particular customers.

Advertisers sometimes believe that trademark infringement can be avoided by changing a well-known mark or by using it for a dissimilar product. They are wrong, because trademark infringement normally is found when two marks are likely to cause *confusion* as to the source of products or services for which they are used. Complete identity of marks or products is not necessary.

Highly distinctive trademarks, which have well-known reputations—garnered mostly through extensive advertising campaigns—are usually protected by the courts and not often copied. The mere presence of the word, *Tropicana and its Latin female orange bearer,* connote "fresh squeezed" to consumers. Through years of promotion, the company has established its products as "natural" and "wholesome"—thus occupying *a distinct niche* in the crowded, refrigerated juice market.

Recently, a U.S. district court found that the trade name Pegasus Petroleum Corporation infringed Mobil Corporation's registered trademark consisting of the flying horse and the wordmark "Pegasus" for competing petroleum products. Widespread consumer familiarity with Mobil's flying horse design led the court to conclude that the word "Pegasus" as used in the defendant's oil business was the verbal equivalent of Mobil's flying horse symbol. Research presented to the court confirmed the public's association of the word with the design: 74 percent of consumers and 22 percent of oil industry buyers expressed confusion about the corporate connection between the parties. The judge also found a clear intent to trade on Mobil's reputation and name.[2]

The economic value of a trademark is a major consideration in lawsuits. The courts have awarded millions of dollars to companies successfully bringing suit against competitors for trademark infringement. The Goodyear Tire and Rubber Company was required to pay damages of $4.7 million to a company called Big O Tire Dealers. The court ruled that Goodyear had infringed on Big O's trademark for "Big Foot" tires.[3]

There are some common threads running through recent legal decisions. Trademarks that are highly distinctive and well-known and are part of extensive advertising campaigns are considered strong marks that deserve broad protection against unauthorized use. In all these cases, the infringing marks incorporated the dominant element of the registered marks, signaling the infringers' intent to capitalize on the long-standing reputation of the trademark owners. The best evidence in showing confusion has been consumer surveys.

Forms of Trademarks

Trademarks derived from "real," descriptive words are more easily remembered. A new, nutritional magazine has been named, *Cooking Light,* to emphasize its dedication to menus, recipes, articles, and ads, which feature "food for fitness." Introductory ads discuss regular exercise, along with eating the right foods, as being "ingredients" for "a well-balanced lifestyle." Even the cover displays "light" cooking.

Dictionary Words. Many trademarks consist of familiar dictionary words used in an arbitrary, innovative, or fanciful manner. Since advertisers seek a distinctive trademark, they choose a common name as an identifier. Yet many of the most successful products bear dictionary names. Ivory soap, Dial soap, Glad plastic bags, Sunbeam toasters, Shell Oil, and Rise shaving cream are a few examples. This type of trademark must be used in a merely descriptive sense to describe the nature, use, or virtue of the product. The advantages of taking your trademark from the dictionary are that you have so many words from which to choose and the public will recognize them. The task is to get people to associate the word with the product. If you do that, the chances of protection against infringement will be good.

F&P Products Group, Inc., developed a new product for watering plants that has granules that absorb up to 500 times their weight in water. The water is then released as plants need it. To emphasize the product's function, F&P named it Water Grabber (see Exhibit 21.2).

Coined word. *An original and arbitrary combination of syllables forming a word. Extensively used for trademarks, as Acrilan, Gro-Pup, Zerone. (Opposite of a dictionary word.)*

Coined Words. Most trademarks are words made up of a new combination of consonants and vowels. Kodak is the classic forerunner of this school of thinking. We also have Kleenex, Xerox, Norelco, Exxon—the list is long. The advantages of a coined word are that it is new; it can be made phonetically pleasing, pronounceable, and short: and it has a strong chance of being legally protectable. Creating a coined word that is distinctive is the big challenge. One drug company tried using a computer to coin words for its many new products; they were distinctive, all right, but unpronounceable. Still, successful names have been created by computer or mathematical calculations: The name Exxon was created to replace Esso when the federal government ruled that Esso could no longer be used because of a previous right by another company. Exxon

[2] William M. Borchard, "Courts Tend to Favor Trademarks," *Advertising Age,* November 3, 1986, p. 48.

[3] William M. Borchard, "Courts Penalize Trademark Misdeeds," *Advertising Age,* January 6, 1987, p. 34.

EXHIBIT 21.2

This logotype gives a good description of what the product does. (Courtesy: F&P Products Group, Inc., Atlanta.)

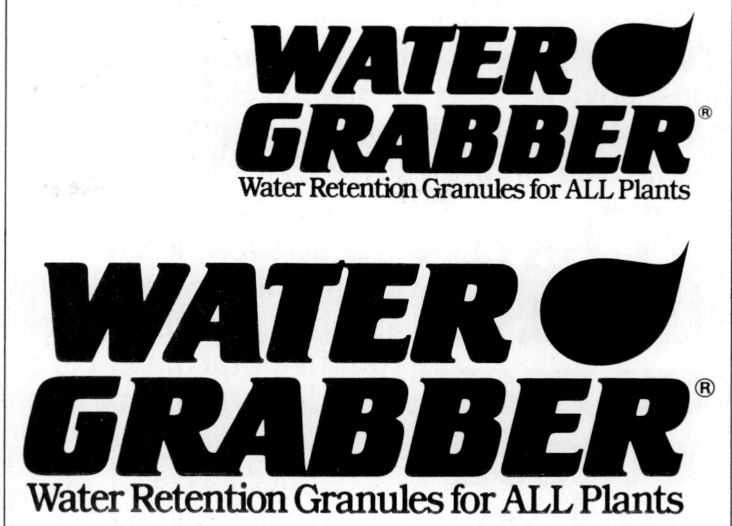

"Coined" or original trademarks excel in distinctiveness—but also must relate to the product and be pronounceable to the general public. *Wet Ones* moist towelettes convey *moisture and single applications. . . .* While napkins and tissues were already on the market for clean-ups, none were "wet" as they were pulled from the package. For *ultimate convenience,* the word "ones" was added—so only the needed sheet would "pop up." Previous to this product's introduction, there wasn't a similar product on the market.

Products using foreign names convey an exotic quality, which may be helpful for promoting *exclusivity*. General Foods is introducing a new Colombian coffee, called "Maxwell House Colombian Supreme." Ann Marks, group product manager indicated that, "Colombian Supreme" will be positioned as "the richest coffee in the world"—the same theme as the National Federation of Coffee Growers' ads featuring Juan Valdez. The "push" for a "Colombian" product is due to the 67% increase in Colombian coffee sales since 1982!

Brand. *Name, term, symbol or design, or some combination of these, that identifies the product or service.*

was one of thousands of names created by a computer printout, and was selected after extensive consumer testing showed it to be recognizable as very similar to the service-station signs and logo already in use for Esso.

When a word is coined from a root word associated with a product, there is a danger that the basic word will be so obvious that others in the field will use it. The result: confusion of similar names. In one issue of the *Standard Advertising Register,* there were 15 trademarks beginning with Flavor or Flava. We also have Lauderdall, Laundromat, and Launderette; and Dictaphone and Dictograph. But if you think of a fresh root concept, you will have the makings of a good trademark.

Personal Names. These may be the names of real people, such as Calvin Klein, Estée Lauder, Sara Lee; fictional characters, such as Betty Crocker; historical characters, such as Lincoln cars; or mythological characters, such as Ajax cleanser. A surname alone is not valuable as a new trademark; others of that name may use it. Names such as Ford automobiles, Lipton teas, Heinz foods, and Campbell's soups have been in use for so long, however, that they have acquired what the law calls a "secondary meaning": That is, through usage the public has recognized them as representing the product of one company only. However, a new trademark has no such secondary meaning.

Foreign names have been successfully used to endow a product with an exotic quality. Arpège perfume, Nina Ricci's L'Air du Temps perfume, and Volkswagen are a few examples of foreign names and words in use. One potential problem is that the name or word may be difficult to pronounce or remember.

Geographical Names. A geographical name is really a place name: Nashua blankets, Utica sheets, Pittsburgh paints. These names are old trademarks and have acquired secondary meaning. Often the word *brand* is offered after the geographical name. The law does not look with favor on giving one person or company the exclusive right to use a geographical name in connection with a new product, excluding others making similar goods in that area. However, if the name was chosen because of a fanciful connotation of a geographical setting, rather than to suggest that it was made there, it may be eligible for protection, as with Bali bras.

Initials and Numbers. Fortunes and years have been spent in establishing trademarks such as IBM, RCA TV, AC spark plugs, J&B whiskey, A-1 sauce. Hence, they are familiar. In general, however, initials and numbers are the hardest form of trademark to remember and the easiest to confuse and to imitate. One issue of the *Standard Advertising Register* listed the following trademarks: No. 1, No. 2, 2 in 1, 3 in 1, 4 in 1, 5 in 1, No. 7, 12/24, No. 14, 77, and 400. (See Exhibit 21.3.)

WD-40's versatility has always been perfect for solving household problems. But now there's one use for WD-40 that could take you right out of your house. And send you on a mystery tour of England.

Find WD-40's® missing use and you may find yourself in London.

Just study the three WD-40 uses pictured in this ad. You'll see that WD-40 silences squeaky hinges. Removes tar from cars. And cleans scuff marks off the floor.

But there's a fourth use that's not shown in this ad. To locate it, look for a hangtag on WD-40 cans at a Missing Use Sweepstakes display.

Discover the missing use on the hangtag, and you'll be eligible to win a trip to the most famous mystery locations in England. Like Baskerville Hall. Sherlock Holmes' address. Plus Scotland Yard. Or you could win a VCR, an exciting mystery video or a murder mystery game.

So tear out this ad now. It'll help you find a WD-40 display at participating retailers. Where you just might turn something that's missing into an incredible find.

?

WD-40'S MISSING USE SWEEPSTAKES.
Discover our missing use and you could land in London.
WD-40

EXHIBIT 21.3
WD-40 uses initials and numbers for their trademark.

Pictorial. To reinforce their brand name, many advertisers use some artistic device, such as distinctive lettering or a design, insignia, or picture. The combination, as we mentioned before, is called a *logotype*.

The Successful Trademark

Whatever the form of a specific trademark, it will only be successful if it is distinctive and complements the manufacturer's product and image. As we mentioned earlier in this chapter, the trademark cannot be considered an isolated creative unit. In most cases, it must be adaptable to a package. It must also be adaptable to many different advertising campaigns, often over a period of many years. The longer a trademark is associated with a brand, the more people recognize it and the greater its value.

Logos to Promote a Distinctive Product or Service

Trademarks have to ''travel'' well—that is, they have to be adaptable to *all media* for effective product identification. The ''Amoco'' logo on the gas pumps appears on the tagline in their print ads and TV commercials. Brightly-colored red, white, and blue ''oval torches'' greet highway travellers on gas station signs and on attendants' uniforms. The same logo appears on credit cards, car maintenance agreements, and bill statements.

When American Express announced its Worldwide Refund Delivery, it used print, television, and collateral advertising. In each case, the logo had to be adapted to the ad and the medium. The continuity of the design was critical in building product recognition. Exhibit 21.4A is an ad announcing this new American Express service to credit unions; Exhibit 21.4B shows the folder that the refunded traveler's cheques are delivered in to the consumer; Exhibit 21.4C shows typical promotion material aimed at informing banks and credit unions about this new service. Note how in each instance American Express marks are clearly visible.

New Trademark Law Aids U.S. in Global Markets

Recent sweeping changes in U.S. trademark law will help American firms compete against foreign companies. Since the 1870s, trademark law has been based on use of the marks in commerce. ''No trade, no trademark'' was the law's basic premise. Since 1946, U.S. trademark owners have been required to submit proof of prior use when they apply to register their marks at the Patent and Trademark Office. The new law permits companies to base trademark applications on an *intent* to use the mark. This brings U.S. policy into harmony with worldwide standards.

The old policy hurt U.S. companies because almost no other nation requires use before registration. Foreign competitors could obtain trademark rights in their own country, which would automatically be valid in the United States, without using their marks anywhere. Thus armed with a U.S.-approved trademark, a foreign company could proceed from product development to the marketplace, confident of its rights to the trademark. In contrast, a U.S. company was unable to register a trademark until it had used it. The company could spend vast sums on packaging, research, and marketing only to find the desired trademark was not available when the product was ready.

The new law permits an applicant with a bona fide intent to use a mark to apply to register it, for example, on January 1, and if the registration is issued eventually—say, on October 31—to trace its rights back to the application date. A registration is issued when the application is approved by the Patent and Trademark Office and confirmed when the applicant submits proof of use within six months of approval. As many as five six-month extensions may be granted, giving the company several years to actually market a product under a particular mark. The registration period has been reduced from 20 to 10 years, but may be renewed indefinitely. This 10-year term is more in keeping with international standards, and allows for clearing the trademark register of ''deadwood.'' The new law also includes prohibiting false statements in advertising about a competitor's product.[4]

[4]Vincent N. Palladino, ''New Trademark Law Aids U.S. in Foreign Markets,'' *Marketing News*, February 13, 1989, p. 7.

EXHIBIT 21.4

A, American Express marks are prominent here. B, Folder for refund of Travelers Cheques. C, Aimed at banks and credit unions. Logo is easily seen. (Courtesy: Promotion Solutions, Inc.)

TELEFONO
This is one of 570,000,000 refund locations
for American Express® Travelers Cheques.
American Express announces Worldwide Refund Delivery, the ultimate in travel protection and convenience.
Now your members can get hand delivered refunds virtually anywhere in the world. If their Travelers Cheques are ever lost or stolen, they can call for a refund toll-free 24 hours a day, seven days a week, 365 days a year. All they have to do is reach for the nearest phone to tap into American Express' worldwide communications network via 12 toll-free numbers. We can make sure that their refunds travel to them, instead of making them travel for a refund.
Worldwide Refund Delivery is the most innovative, convenient, far-reaching refund service ever offered. Only American Express has it! No other travelers cheque even comes close.
This is the kind of quality your members expect from American Express. We'll continue to meet those expectations with the finest in service delivery. We'll meet yours, too—with a new national advertising program especially designed to drive members into your credit union.
For more information about Worldwide Refund Delivery or American Express Travelers Cheques, pick up your phone and call Lou Eiler at 1-800-221-7282.

WORLDWIDE
REFUNDDELIVERY
Travelers
Cheques

(a)

WORLDWIDE
REFUNDDELIVERY
AMERICAN EXPRESS
Travelers
Cheques

(b)

Announcing
Worldwide Refund Delivery
The Ultimate in Travel Security and Convenience
Hand delivered refunds virtually anywhere in the world
Now American Express redefines the level of protection your customers get while traveling away from home. If their Travelers Cheques are ever lost or stolen, they can call for a refund toll-free from any phone 24 hours a day, seven days a week, 365 days a year. Through our worldwide communications network of 12 toll-free numbers and a global courier system, we can make sure that their refunds travel right to them, instead of making them travel for a refund.
What Worldwide Refund Delivery Means to Your Customers
No vacation interruptions: One toll-free phone call is all it takes.
Convenience: Refunds can be hand delivered right to them wherever they travel, virtually anywhere in the world.
Reliability: Backed by our promise of the finest in quality service.
Efficiency: Supported by American Express' worldwide communications network and global courier delivery system.
What Worldwide Refund Delivery Does for You
Worldwide Refund Delivery represents the kind of quality service your customers have come to expect from American Express. It's why they prefer our Travelers Cheque 20:1 over the next selling brand. And why more than 2,495 financial institutions in the past three years have switched to American Express from other brands. By offering American Express Travelers Cheques, you reinforce your relationships with valued customers and offer them the finest travelers cheque product available today.

How Worldwide Refund Delivery Works
Your customer calls our toll-free Refund Hotline with their name, location, and the amount of their loss.
American Express can authorize the refund over the telephone and make delivery arrangements through our exclusive worldwide courier network.
A courier can then hand deliver the refund right to your customer.

TELEFONO

Extensive National Advertising and Marketing
Consumer Advertising: Compelling commercials, featuring Karl Malden, are now promoting Worldwide Refund Delivery on prime time network TV. This ongoing campaign will create consumer awareness, stimulate demand for American Express Travelers Cheques, and generate new business for you.
Merchandising: American Express Travelers Cheques offers colorful new leaflets highlighting Worldwide Refund Delivery. Use them as statement stuffers to generate consumer excitement and sales. They're available now. Order them from your Travelers Cheque representative.
Act Now!
Start promoting this exclusive new American Express Travelers Cheque service today! Worldwide Refund Delivery means greater protection and convenience for your customers, more business, and better customer relationships for you.

WORLDWIDE
REFUNDDELIVERY
Travelers
Cheques

(c)

Trademark Notice

It is extremely important after a trademark has been registered to insert a notice to that effect wherever it appears, such as ® next to the trademark, or “Registered, U.S. Patent Office,” or “Reg. U.S. Pat. Office,” or some similar notice. The exception is when a trademark is repeatedly used in an ad: Some firms require the registration notice on the first use only to reduce the possibility of typographic “bugs.” (See Exhibit 21.5.)

Putting a Lock on Trademarks

To protect a trademark, advertisers must use it with a generic product classification—so the trademark doesn't become the name of the product. Johnson & Johnson always includes the words, “adhesive bandage,” along with the trademark—“Band-Aid” on their products. Should they “forget,” the word, band-aid, may “slip” into the generic category—as did “thermos.” “Jell-O” and “Scotch Tape” are also wary of that predicament and use generic classifications for that reason, also.

We now meet a paradoxical situation, in which the owner of a successful trademark suddenly discovers that anyone can use it—all because certain precautionary steps were not taken. This problem arises when the public begins using a trademark to describe a type of product rather than just a brand of the type of product. Originally, Thermos was the trademark owned by the Aladdin Company, which introduced vacuum bottles. In time, people began to ask: “What brand of thermos bottles do you carry?” The courts held that Thermos had become a descriptive word that any manufacturer of vacuum bottles could use because thermos (with a lowercase *t*) was no longer the exclusive trademark of the originator. Victrola, cellophane, nylon, escalator, aspirin, and linoleum started off as the trademark of one company, but then became generic—words that are public property because their owners failed to take certain simple steps to put a “lock” on their property.

Since large companies often invest millions of dollars establishing their trademarks, most follow very strict rules to protect that investment, with lawyers reviewing every ad and commercial to make certain that all legal “notices” have been included with the trademark.

EXHIBIT 21.5

The registration notice only appears the first time *Pantone* is used in the ad. (Courtesy: Pantone, Inc.)

PANTONE®*
Trademark Notice

PANTONE, PMS, the PANTONE MATCHING SYSTEM and its Color Numbers, Color Names and Color Formulas are protected by registered trademarks and copyrights. They are not generic nor in the public domain and their uses are strictly regulated.

Using our color books to tell your printer which color to print is their prime purpose. However, reproduction rights of PANTONE Color Standards are reserved. If you wish to reproduce a PANTONE Color with its color identification or use any of our trademarks or parts of our copyrighted materials in print, you must first contact us for the rules and regulations governing their use.

Trademark Control Department
Pantone, Inc.
55 Knickerbocker Road, Moonachie, NJ 07074
(201) 935-5500
Telefax: 201-896-0242

*Pantone, Inc.'s check-standard trademark for color reproduction and color reproduction materials. © Pantone, Inc. 1988

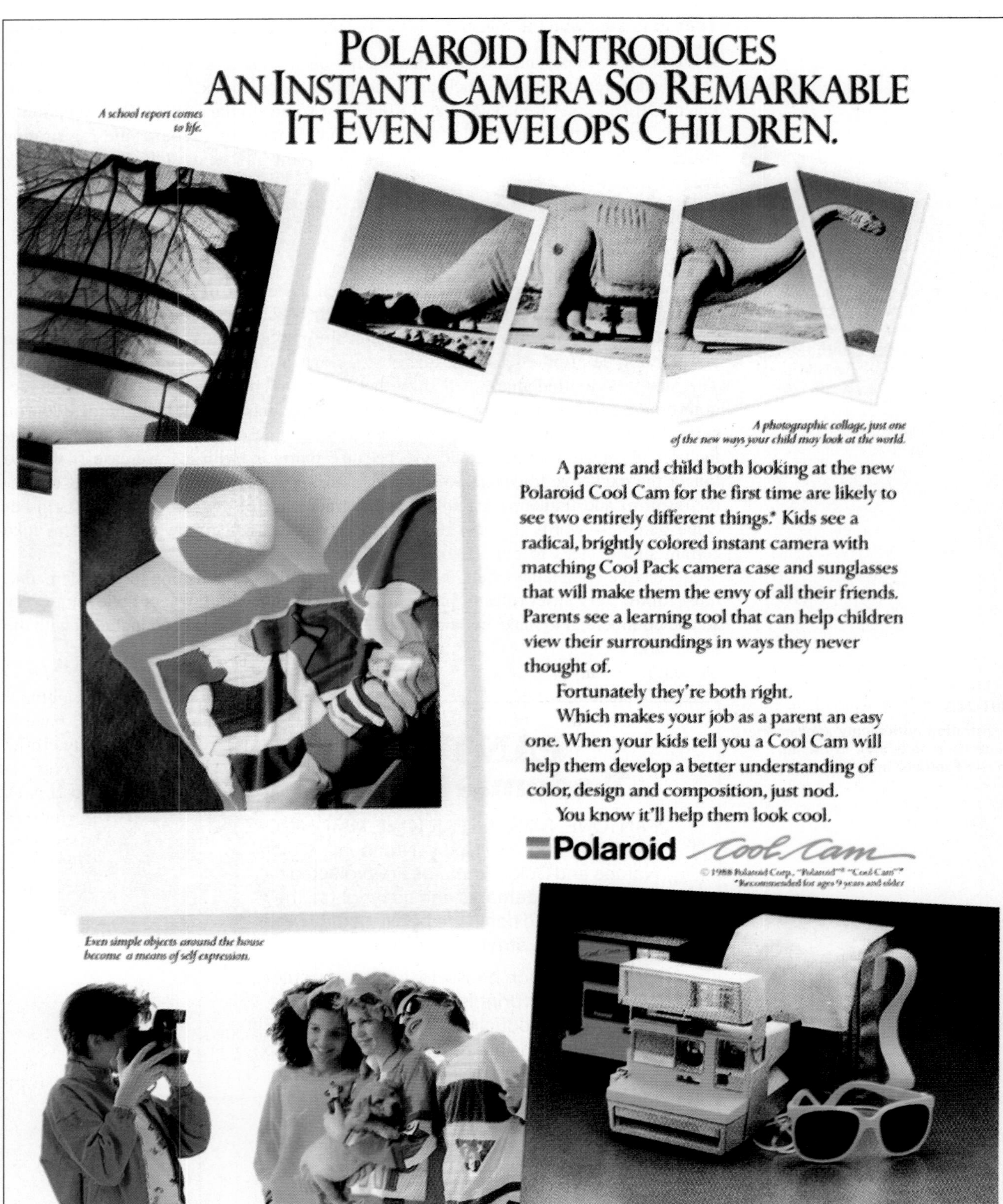

EXHIBIT 21.6

An example of a house mark. (Courtesy: Polaroid.)

Putting a lock on the ownership of a trademark requires taking the following steps:

1. Always make sure the trademark word is capitalized or set off in distinctive type.
2. Always follow the trademark with the generic name of the product: Glad disposable trash bags, Kleenex tissues, Windex glass cleaner.
3. Don't speak of it in the plural, as "three Kleenexes," but rather, "three Kleenex tissues."
4. Don't use it in a possessive form (not "Kleenex's new features," but "the new features of Kleenex tissues") or as a verb (not "Kleenex your eyeglasses," but "Wipe your eyeglasses with Kleenex tissues").

It is the advertising person's responsibility to carry these out legal strictures in the ads.

HOUSE MARKS

House mark. *A primary mark of a business concern, usually used with the trademark of its products.* General Mills *is a house mark;* Betty Crocker *is a trademark.*

As we mentioned earlier in this chapter, trademarks are used to identify specific products. However, many companies sell a number of products under several different trademarks. These companies often identify themselves with a house mark to denote the firm that produces these products. Kraft is a house mark and its brand Miracle Whip is a trademark. In Exhibit 21.6, Polaroid is a house mark and Cool Cam is the trademark.

SERVICE MARKS; CERTIFICATION MARKS

Service mark. *A word or name used in the sale of services, to identify the services of a firm and distinguish them from those of others; for example,* Hertz Drive Yourself Service, Weight Watchers Diet Course. *Comparable to trademarks for products.*

A company that renders services, such as an insurance company, an airline, or even Weight Watchers, can protect its identification mark by registering it in Washington as a service mark (see Exhibit 21.7). It is also possible to register certification marks, whereby a firm certifies that a user of its identifying device is doing so properly. Teflon is a material sold by Du Pont to kitchenware makers for use in lining their pots and pans. Teflon is Du Pont's registered trademark for its nonstick finish; Teflon II is Du Pont's certification mark for Teflon-coated cookware that meets Du Pont's standards. Advertisers of such products may use that mark. The Wool Bureau has a distinctive label design that it permits all manufacturers of pure-wool products to use (see Exhibit 21.8). Certification marks have the same creative requirements as trademarks—most of all, that they be distinctive.

EXHIBIT 21.7
A service mark.

EXHIBIT 21.8
Certification mark.

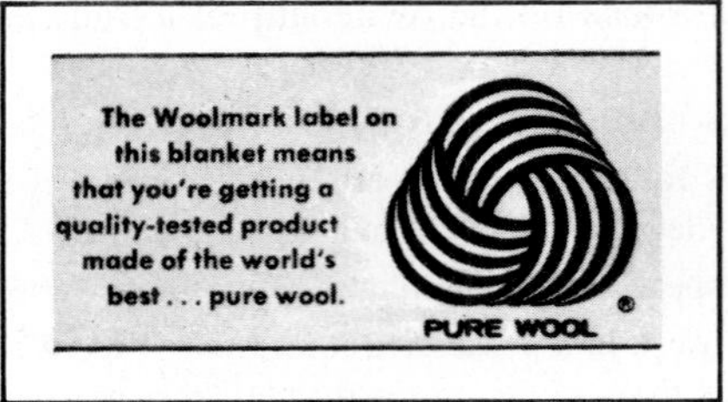

The Woolmark label on this blanket means that you're getting a quality-tested product made of the world's best . . . pure wool.
PURE WOOL

> ***Certification mark.*** *A name or design used upon, or in connection with, the products or services of persons other than the owner of the mark, to certify origin, material, mode of manufacture, quality, accuracy, or other characteristics of such goods or services; for example,* Seal of the Underwriters' Laboratories, Sanforized, Teflon II.

Name changes of companies should be made for the purposes of *simplification* and *clarification*. Often, mergers of professional firms result in names too long to be remembered. Hence, Bozell, Jacobs, Kenyon & Eckhardt have advertised that they'll be known simply as *Bozell*—from this point on. Pencils bearing their once 4-name title were reduced, in their full-page *Advertising Age* ad, to reveal the single designation.

COMPANY AND PRODUCT NAMES

Name Change Craze

There has been a significant increase in the changing of corporate names in recent years. In 1988, a record 1,864 name changes were made; in 1987, there were 1,763 name changes; in 1986, 1,382. Anspach Grossman Portugal's annual survey indicated that 52 percent of the changes made in 1988 were directly related to mergers and acquisitions, and another 23 percent reflected divestitures, spinoffs, sales of assets, and leveraged buyouts. A number of name changes have come about through the increasing foreign ownership of American companies. When Standard Oil was acquired by British Petroleum, it became BP America; First Jersey National Bank became National Westminster Bank NJ; and Firestone Tire and Rubber Company became Firestone Corporation after selling its tire business to Japan's Bridgstone Corporation. Many major Japanese companies simplified their names for U.S. operations: Konishiroko became Konica USA, and Nippon Kogaku became Nikon Corporation. Nearly one-third of all the name changes in recent years have been for financial institutions (for example, First RepublicBank became NCNB Texas National Bank).[5]

Steps for Creating Memorable Names

First, pull together the basic information:

- *Describe What You Are Naming.* Include in your description key features and characteristics, competitive advantages, and anything else that differentiates your company, product, or service from the rest of the field.
- *Summarize What You Want Your Name to Do.* Should it suggest an important product characteristic (e.g., "Blokrot" for treated lumber) or convey a particular image (e.g., "Pandora's Secrets" for an expensive perfume)? Write down the characteristics and images you want your name to convey.
- *Describe Whom You Are Targeting with the Name.* Identify your targets and their demographic/lifestyle characteristics. Would they react more positively to a traditional, conservative name or to a liberal, flashy one? List the name qualities you think would appeal to them (name length, sound, and image).
- *List Names That You Like and Dislike.* Try to come up with a few dozen current names in both categories (include your competitors' names). Note words and roots that might work for your new name and jot them down.
- *Build a List of New Name Ideas.* Start with the list of names that you like and add to it by pulling ideas from a good thesaurus (e.g., *The Synonym Finder* by Jerome Rodale), a book of names (e.g., *The Trademark Register of the United States*), relevant trade journals, a book of root words (e.g., *Dictionary of English Word Roots* by Robert Smith), and other sources.
- *Combine Name Parts and Words.* Take words, syllables, and existing name parts and recombine them to form new names.

[5] "Foreign Ownership Contributes to Name Changes," *Graphic Design:USA,* February 1989, p. 20.

Before selecting a new name for a product, *prospective customers* should be asked their opinions. "Our story is that we're *the ultimate product* for nutrition," stated the Carnation Company in the launch of their new "high-performance" pet food, *Perform*. Focus groups were impressed with the product's *freshness* and its ability to compete, ingredients-wise, with the leaders in nutritional pet foods, such as Hill's Science Diet.

- *Pick Your Favorites*. Select *several* names that meet all your criteria (just in case your top choice is unavailable or tests poorly).

Next verify name availability and test your favorites:

- *Conduct a Trademark Search*. Check to make sure your names are not already in use. Thomson & Thomson in Boston or Compu-Mark in Washington, D.C., can help you check state and U.S. patent and trademark records.
- *Test Your Name Before Using It*. Regardless of how fond you are of the new name, others may have a different opinion. Solicit reactions to your name from prospective customers, stockholders, and industry experts.

Name Assistance

Companies and advertising agencies routinely develop product names independently or together. In addition, there are specialized companies and consultants whose business is helping companies and agencies come up with memorable brand and corporate names (see Exhibit 21.9). The SALINON Corporation sells inexpensive software called NAMER that aids users in creating company, product, and service names.

A *package design* should be *practical*, as well as *marketable*. "Floor wax products must be packaged in easy-to-use containers—or they simply won't sell," revealed Dean Lindsay, a principal of Kornick Lindsay, Inc., the Chicago package-design firm that worked with S. C. Johnson on *Future* floor wax. With new technological changes in plastics manufacturing, Future has been updated with a new spout—with new 90's labeling—"to maintain its 30-year market leadership," said DL.

PACKAGING

In the modern world of self-service marketing, the product package is much more than a container. The package must be designed to take several factors into account. First, it must protect the package contents; every other consideration is secondary to the function of the package as a utilitarian container. Second, the package must meet reasonable cost standards. Since the product package is a major expense for most firms, steps must be taken to hold down costs as much as possible.

Once these two requirements of package protection and cost are satisfactorily met, we move to the marketing issues involved in packaging. These include adopting a package that is conducive to getting shelf space at the retail level. A unique package with strange dimensions or protruding extensions or nonflat surfaces is going to be rejected by many retailers. A package must be easy to handle, store, and stack. It

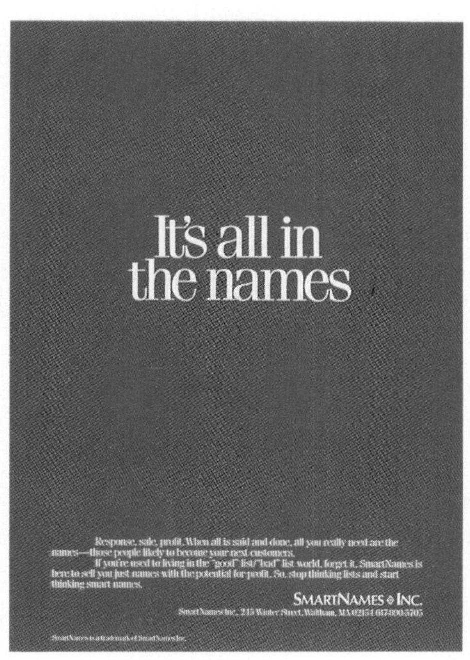

EXHIBIT 21.9
"It's all in the names." (Courtesy: Smart Names, Inc.)

should not take up more shelf room than any other product in that section, as might a pyramid-shaped bottle. Odd shapes are suspect: Will they break easily? Tall packages are suspect: Will they keep falling over? The package should be soil-resistant. Does it have ample and convenient space for marking? The product should come in the full range of sizes and packaging common to the field.

For products bought upon inspection, such as men's shirts, the package needs transparent facing. The package can make the difference in whether a store stocks the item.

Small items are expected to be mounted on cards under plastic domes, called *blister cards,* to provide ease of handling and to prevent pilferage. Often these cards are mounted on a large card that can be hung on a wall, making profitable use of that space. Remember, the buyer working for the store judges how a product display will help the store, not the manufacturer.

Once we have considered the requirements of the retail trade, we can turn our attention to designing a container that is both practical and eye-catching. The package is, after all, the last chance to sell the consumer and the most practical form of point-of-purchasing advertising. Therefore it should be designed to achieve maximum impact on the store shelf. Striving for distinctiveness is particularly crucial in retail establishments such as grocery stores where the consumer is choosing from hundreds of competing brands.

Computers and Package Design

Peterson & Blyth Associates, Inc., a packaging and design firm, researched the impact of computers on marketing and packaging design and found that marketing professionals believe that computers will play an increasingly important role because they make possible quicker design, a more efficient review process, faster approval, and lower design costs.[6]

Changing Package Design and Marketing Strategies

As marketing strategies change, so does packaging designs. *Valvoline Oil Company* recently introduced a new package for its motor oil, after consumer focus groups said the old package looked *dated* and didn't appeal to women or the younger, do-it-yourself market. The type was changed to be comprehensible to "novices"—and more *color* was added to the label.

Design firms redesign packages to suit changing market strategies for existing consumer products and develop new packaging concepts for product introductions. Several trends in package design can be cited. One is the increasing tendency to use packaging to shore up store brands. Another is the use of sophisticated design approaches or unique packaging to establish a high-quality for upscale, private-label brands. There has also been a shift from packaging that suits the convenience of the manufacturer to packaging that is "consumer-friendly" in terms of opening and use, reclosing, and portions. In short, package design is responding to a more sophisticated, discerning consumer.

Today's package design firms do more than provide renderings for clients. They often act as adjunct marketing consultants, providing information on the retail environment and marketing trends, as well as expertise on the roles of positioning, timing, and brand equity in the success or failure of a product.

Canada Dry decided to modernize its package design. In Chapter 18, Exhibit 18 is an ad promoting the company's new can design. Exhibit 21.10 shows the product line's new design.

Packaging and Color Influence

High-quality imagery is changing. Two or three years ago, for instance, black or deep, vibrant colors communicated premium imagery. Today designs for upscale brands use lighter, softer pastel colors. White, once associated with generic brands, is making a

[6] John S. Blyth, "Concern That Computers Will Design a Commodity Is Groundless," *Marketing News,* November 7, 1988, p. 16.

EXHIBIT 21.10

New Canada Dry packaging design. (Courtesy: Canada Dry Corporation.)

Color plays a vital role in package design. It helps determine the perception with which a consumer will view a product. "*Juicy Juice* is a product that kids like," said the business director for the Libby division of Nestle Foods Corporation, "and not just because it tastes good." A lot has to do with the brand's "*lively, primary colors* and pictures of the fruits included." In the year ending last March, JJ's results have shot up *43%*—with the Gerstman & Meyers' children-appealing labels helping to sell $34 million worth of fruit juice!

comeback as an upscale communicator.[7] Exhibit 21.11 shows the Water Grabber package and display package.

Advertisers are very much aware that colors work on people's subconscious and that each color produces a psychological reaction. Reactions to color can be pleasant or unpleasant. Color can inform consumers about the type of product inside the package and influence their perceptions of quality, value, and purity. Thus color in packaging is an important tool in marketing communications.

---

[7]Herbert M. Meyers, "Forecast: Design and Production," *Graphic Design: USA*, January 1989, p. 30.

EXHIBIT 21.11

A, Product and package. B, Package and display package as consumers see it. (Courtesy: F&D Products Group, Inc., Atlanta.)

(a)

(b)

What kind of consumer perceptions would you encounter if you brewed the same coffee in a blue coffeepot, a yellow pot, a brown pot, and a red pot? Would the perceptions of the coffee be the same? Probably not. Studies indicate that coffee from the blue pot would be perceived as having a mild aroma, coffee from the yellow pot would be thought a weaker blend, the brown pot's coffee would be judged too strong, and the red pot's coffee would be perceived as rich and full-bodied.

Packaging and Marketing

Until this century, the role of product packages was generally confined to protecting the product. Only the package label was linked with promotional activities. The Uneeda Biscuit package introduced in 1899 is generally considered to be the first that was utilized for promotion. However, few companies followed Uneeda's lead.

It was during the Depression of the 1930s that the role of packaging as a promotional tool changed dramatically. Most companies had limited advertising funds during this period, so they resorted to using the package as an in-store means of promotion. So successful were their efforts that the role of packaging in the marketing mix became routinely accepted by manufacturers.

Today package design for most products is developed in much the same way as an advertising campaign. While each package is developed, designed, and promoted in a unique fashion, there are some common approaches to the successful use of a package as a marketing tool:

Functional uses of a package—after the product has been used—are often part of the promotional strategy for the brand. *Pepsi-Cola* is rolling out its *Mug root beer*, in an effort to "heat up" to the $1.2 billion RB market, now dominated by A&W Brands. Currently, *Mug* is available in 27% of the country's markets. Spending could reach *$8 million* on this promotion, quoted Lois Pitts Gershon Pon/GGK, New York, PC's agency in this project. TV spots, themed, "I love my Mug," will support.

1. *The type of product and function of the package.* Is the product extremely fragile? Do consumers use the product directly from the package? Are there special storage or shipping problems associated with the product?
2. *The type of marketing channels to be used for the product.* If the product is to be sold in a variety of outlets, will this require some special packaging considerations? Will the package be displayed in some special way at the retail level? Are there special point-of-purchase opportunities for the product?
3. *The prime prospects for the product.* Are adults, children, upper-income families, or young singles most likely to buy the product? What packaging style would be most appealing to the target market?
4. *Promotion and advertising for the product and its package.* Will the package be used to complement other promotional efforts? Are on-pack coupons or premiums being considered? Can standard package-design ideas be adapted to any special promotional efforts being considered?
5. *The relationship to other packages in a product line.* Will the product be sold in different sizes? Is the product part of a product line that is promoted together? Does the product line use the same brand name and packaging style?
6. *The typical consumer use of the product.* Will the package be stored for long periods in the home? Does the product require refrigeration or freezing? Are only portions of the product used from the package?

Obviously, the answers to these and other questions can only be obtained through careful research. The package designer must strive for a balance between creativity and function.

Legal Aspects of Packaging

There are both federal and state laws that regulate packaging and labeling. The Fair Packaging and Labeling Act of 1966 says:

> Informed consumers are essential to the fair and efficient functioning of a free economy. Packages and their labels should enable consumers to obtain accurate information as to the quality of the contents and should facilitate value comparisons. Therefore it is hereby declared to be the policy of the Congress to assist consumers and manufacturers in reaching these goals in the marketing of goods.

EXHIBIT 21.12

Del Monte's logo stands out on all the company's packages. (Courtesy: Del Monte Corporation.)

This is the most far-reaching law affecting packaging and labeling. For example, all food packages must display the ingredients prominently (a loaf of bread lists all of the ingredients in descending order of quantity used); over-the-counter drug products follow the same rule; and drug products must prominently display instructions for use, precautions, and instructions in case of accidental overdose. The Food and Drug Administration is responsible for enforcing the law as it affects foods, drugs, cosmetics, and health devices. The Federal Trade Commission has jurisdiction over ''other consumer commodities.''

Package design can be a *continuation* of the advertising strategy in print ads and broadcast media. When Hamm's brought out their "genuine draft beer," they designed their cans to resemble *beer barrels*—to emphasize the *lengthy, distinctive* brewing technique they were advertising. The design won several awards, including best package design of 1974. Customers were known to ask for the package—"the canned beer in a barrel"—and collect them as show pieces.

Advertising on the Package?

Although featuring key parts of a commercial on the package is rarely done, (a notable exception is Life Cereal, which uses its Mikey commercials on the package), a research report issued by the Ogilvy Center for Research and Development indicates that this idea may be useful. The research consisted of an experiment to find out how showing elements from the advertising on the package affects consumer attitudes toward the brand. It was found that memory cues from the advertising on the package led to higher brand evaluations and purchase intent scores on the part of consumers. The probable explanation, according to O&M, is that commercial cues at the point-of-purchase cause people to retrieve from their memory attitudes they formed toward the brand while viewing its advertising. Evidence suggests this strategy may be particularly useful in more competitive product categories, where people often fail to correctly link a brand name to its advertising.[8]

Design changes in logos, in-store graphics, packaging, and uniforms, etc., often produce *positive* customer reactions. *Just Born,* the Bethlehem, Pennsylvania candy company—found that shoppers skipped over its *Hot Tamales, Jolly Joes,* and *Mike and Ike Treats,* because of their old-fashioned black-and-white packages. So last year, the company introduced a new package featuring a colorful cast of animated grapes and cherries—and sales soared 25%! "Kids say we went from dull and boring to definitely awesome—without a single product change or ad," said a company marketing official.

Corporate Identity: Logo and Whole Package

Hornall Anderson Design Works, a Seattle graphic design firm, has a philosophy of beginning with a corporate mark, signature, or logo that is strong, a quick read, and memorable. A marketing program, however, involves much more than creating an effective, recognizable logo. It incorporates research, corporate definition, and communication.

Tradewell supermarkets, a 50-store chain in Washington State and Oregon, sought revitalization through a new identity. Hornall Anderson built a complete graphics program around Tradewell's new slogan, "Nobody Gives Better Service." The program included store graphics, buttons, aprons, posters, interior and exterior signs, and color schemes. Basic to all these designs would be Tradewell's new logo, which had to convey the company's desired image of the trustworthiness of the "old-time market."

The first step in designing a new logo was research.[9] This included going to local and national supermarkets, collecting logos of chains and trendy designer grocery stores, and working on various treatments from slick san serif to warm and traditional type. The trend in the grocery business is to make stores more human and to concentrate on niche markets by featuring fresh produce, fish, and designer foods. The intention is to create a social experience for customers in addition to the shopping one. For example, aisles are deliberately narrow so that people have to encounter one another. After this basic research, the firm generated many sketches for the client to wade through.

The chosen Tradewell logo (see Exhibit 21.13) has a wood crate appearance, a dated-looking style with a calligraphic flourish intended to evoke tradition, quality, and service. The type used is a modified version of Times Roman. This logo was designed to be used on all Tradewell applications, including signage, in-store graphics, and all print materials from stationery to staff newsletters, direct-mail pieces, flyers, and ads. The new design encompassed specialized store departments, wine and deli packaging, and all aspects of promotion.

[8]"Putting the Advertising on the Package," *Viewpoint,* July–August 1989, pp. 25–27.

[9]Leslee Jaquette, "Corporate Identity Is Order of Business," *Seattle Daily Journal of Commerce,* December 5, 1988, p. 1.

EXHIBIT 21.13

Consumer response to Tradewell's change in corporate identity was a 300–400 percent improvement in activity and sales. The new Tradewell supermarket gives the consumer a warm and cozy shopping experience.

Exhibit 21.14 presents the old Tradewell logo and Hornall Anderson Design Works' quick revision of it. Hornall Anderson developed over 25 variations of logo treatments before deciding on the right one.

Exhibit 21.15 illustrates some of the in-store signage. Wooden plaques placed perpendicularly in the aisles were used for the premium beef market, the chicken segment, the seafood market, and the produce market. These symbols were incorporated into the advertising and promotion. For instance, Tradewell sent out direct-mail pieces using many of these symbols and promoting itself: "We're Proud of Our Produce." Exhibit 21.16 shows the new logo on the shopping bags, wine packages, and deli bags.

Hornall Anderson Design Works uses a very distinctive, but very appropriate, ad for themselves, as shown in Exhibit 21.17.

EXHIBIT 21.14

EXHIBIT 21.15

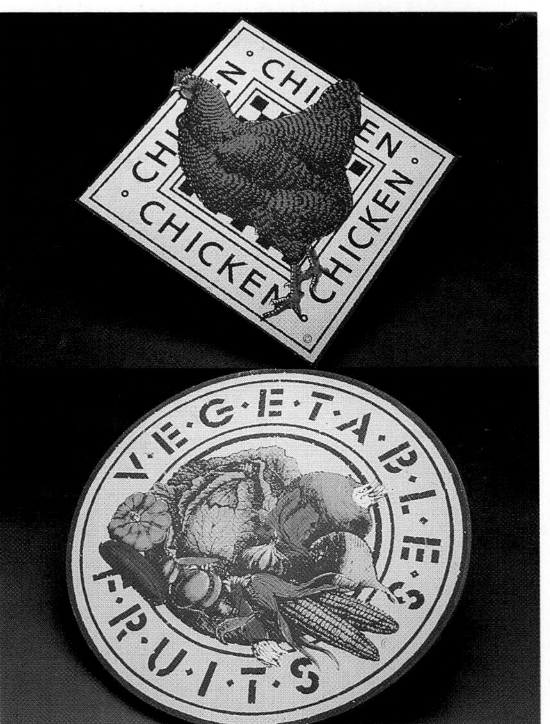

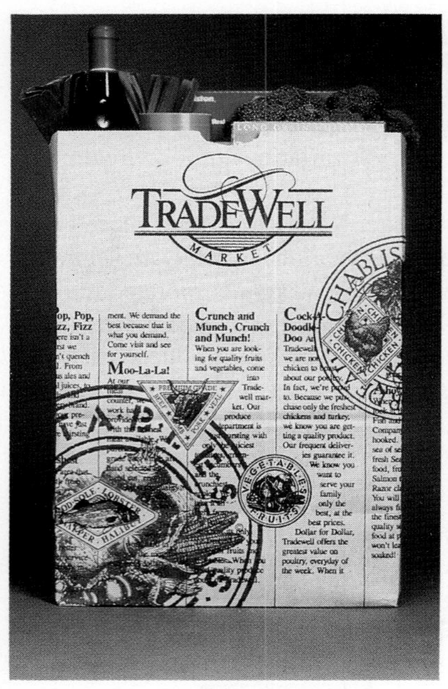
TRADEWELL
MARKET
Pop, Pop, Fizz, Fizz
Crunch and Munch, Crunch and Munch!
Moo-La-La!

TRADEWELL
MARKET
Deli
Wine

TRADEWELL
MARKET

EXHIBIT 21.16

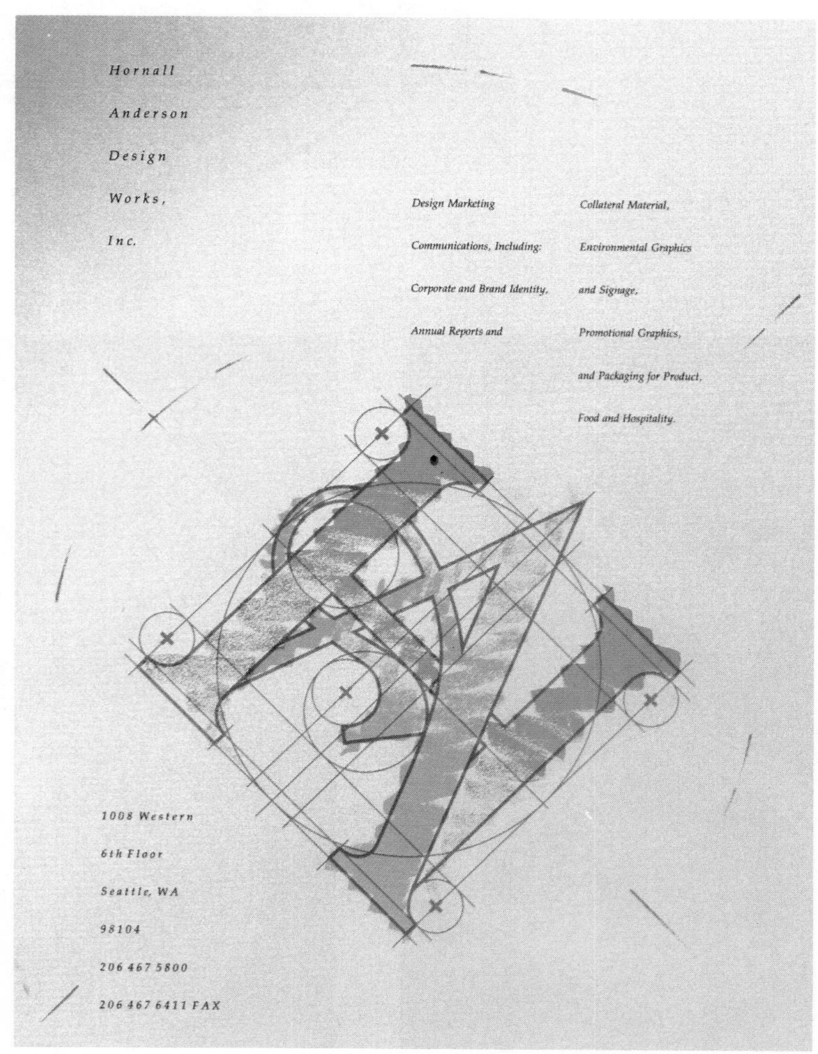
Hornall
Anderson
Design
Works,
Inc.
Design Marketing
Communications, Including:
Corporate and Brand Identity,
Annual Reports and
Collateral Material,
Environmental Graphics
and Signage,
Promotional Graphics,
and Packaging for Product,
Food and Hospitality.
1008 Western
6th Floor
Seattle, WA
98104
206 467 5800
206 467 6411 FAX

EXHIBIT 21.17

SUMMARY

Trademarks serve several purposes: They distinguish your product from the competition and allow easy promotion of a firm's products. They also grow more valuable with familiarity. Trademarks usually, but not always, contain a brand name. A trade name is the company doing business (the Pepsi-Cola Company), not the individual product (Mountain Dew).

Trademark infringement is generally found when one mark is so similar to an earlier, established mark that it is likely to confuse customers.

There are many forms of trademarks. Some use familiar words (like Glad plastic bags), though these words must not be merely descriptive of the product. Other trademarks are coined words (like Kodak); these are advantageous not only because they are legally protectable as original, but also because they are totally new and distinctive. Still other trademarks are personal names (Calvin Klein) or initials or numbers (IBM, WD-40). Most trademarks consist of both words and a symbol; the words are usually lettered in a distinctive style, which is known as a *logotype*.

Recent changes in the U.S. trademark laws brings it closer to international law. A trademark can now be applied for before it is actually used on a product. The company's trademark rights start when the application is made, rather than when the trademark is first used. Companies have six months to actually use the trademark, and can apply for five six-month extensions. The registration period has been reduced from 20 to 10 years, but renewal can be applied for indefinitely. Trademarks must always be capitalized or set off in distinctive type, followed by the generic name of the product (Windex glass cleaner), and never used in the plural or possessive form.

Service marks are used by companies that render a service, such as an airline or insurance company.

The most important steps in creating a product or company name are: pulling together the basic information, verifying name availability, and testing name(s). There are companies that specialize in developing names.

Packaging is an important part of selling. The trend today is toward packaging that is convenient for the consumer rather than for the manufacturer. Recent research has found that placing cues on a package that reinforce media advertising is helpful in highly competitive product categories where consumers easily confuse brand names.

Today's design firms do much more than create logos and/or packaging designs. They are marketing partners who help develop total corporate or brand programs.

QUESTIONS

1. Why does a trademark become more valuable every year?
2. What is a logotype?
3. Briefly discuss the major changes in U.S. trademark laws in recent years.
4. What are the main reasons for so many new corporate names in the last decade?
5. How has high-quality imagery in packaging changed in recent years?

SUGGESTED EXERCISES

- Create a distinctive brand name for a new product that when sprayed on your lawn will prevent the grass from growing.
- Find advertising examples of products using new kinds of packaging.
- Find advertising examples of trademarks and packaging you consider weak. Explain how you would improve each.

READINGS

BLYTH, JOHN S.: "Concern That Computers Will Make Design a Commodity Is Groundless," *Marketing News,* November 7, 1988, p. 16.

BLYTH, JOHN S.: "Other Countries Lead U.S. in Supporting Design Efforts," *Marketing News,* February 13, 1989, p. 16.

ERICKSON, JULIE LIESSE: "The Edge Goes to High Tech," *Advertising Age,* December 12, 1988, p. S-1.

MASTEN, DAVIS L.: "Logo's Power Depends on How Well It Communicates with the Target," *Marketing News,* December 5, 1988, p. 20.

TELZER, RONNIE: "Designer Dares Marketers to Take Risk," *Advertising Age,* December 12, 1988, p. S-4.

TWENTY-TWO

The Complete Campaign

The Link (bond) process of building brand equity described in Chapter 3 focuses on the premise that a brand is a living entity. A brand is created by its communication. It carries its history, which represents its accumulated capital, but it must continue to build new communications by asserting its presence, its sovereignty, and its territory. In so doing, however, it must maintain a consistent identity. The four components (see Exhibit 22.1) of Link are synthesized into an action plan for the development of all communications for the brand, including advertising, promotions, public relations, and direct marketing. The guiding principle is that everything you do should build equity into the brand. The concept of brand equity goes beyond the development of a single ad, commercial, or promotional piece.

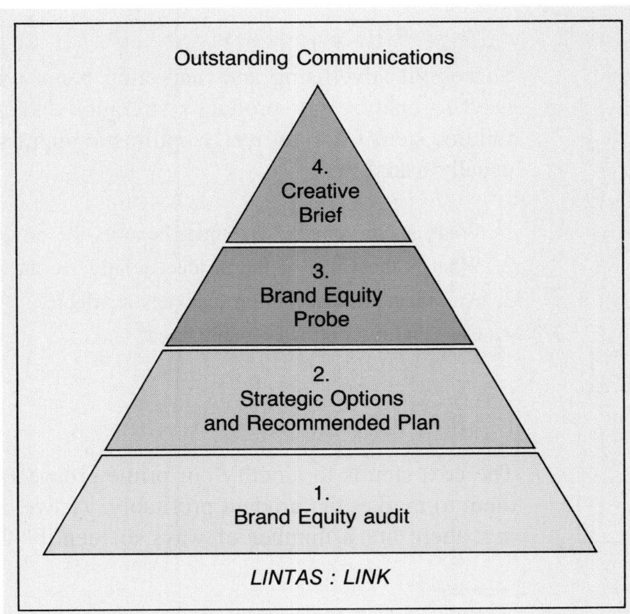

EXHIBIT 22.1

The Link planning process for building strong brand equity in advertising campaigns. (Courtesy: Lintas: New York.)

The campaign—a series of ads and commercials—helps propel *a brand* into prominence before the public. *Evian,* the leading import in still water, credits its growing image to a series of print ads, displaying the drink as a *chic refresher*. ''Evian is growing very fast,'' stated Hellen Berry, associate director of marketing research at *Beverage Marketing*. Sales in 1988 increased 113% over 1987—nonetheless, it's doubling its ad budget and boosting promotions this year to further capitalize on its soaring success.

So far, we've talked mostly about the development of an ad, its placement and testing. Link planning process rejects the practice of thinking in terms of individual ads for companies, products, or services in favor of the type of broader planning called a *campaign*—a series of ads and commercials with an established strategy and goals.

Long-running campaigns are signs that they've continued to be *relevant* and *attention-getting* for the target audience. *Jell-O and Bill Cosby* are virtually synonymous. They'll be together *again* in TV spots, explaining the tie-in between "Duck Tales," a Disney home video release, and the gelatin pudding mix line. The commercials, from Young & Rubicam, are titled, "The fun part of being *a kid*." (à la Cosby!)

The ad campaign doesn't function alone; the advertising is integrated into the sales and marketing program. Generally, campaigns are designed to run over a longer period of time than an individual ad, although there are exceptions. The length of an average campaign, regional or national, is about 17 months, though it is not uncommon for a campaign to go on for three or four years and a few campaigns have lasted much longer. For example, Dewar's scotch whiskey "young achievers" campaign has endured for more than 20 years. It was devised by Leo Burnett Advertising to appeal to up-and-coming young professionals. The campaign has averaged four print ads a year profiling youngish achievers. Burnett put personalities in the foreground of the campaign because people like to read about people. The campaign has evolved over the years, mirroring the changes the country has gone through. "The profiles of social workers and environmentalists that ran in the '60s and '70s have given way to those individuals who clearly represent a more entrepreneurial spirit."[1] One point here is that although Dewar's has used the same campaign for more than 20 years, the *tone* of the 80-plus ads has changed over time. The second point, of course, is that if an ad campaign is working, there is no reason to substitute another because there is no guarantee that the next campaign will be as strong, let alone stronger. So every campaign should be carefully planned.

Campaign. *A specific advertising effort on behalf of a particular product or service. It extends for a specified period of time.*

The campaign must bring together into a unified whole all the advertising elements we have discussed. This calls for an advertising plan. As we have emphasized, good advertising starts with a clear understanding of marketing goals, both short- and long-term. These goals are often expressed as sales or share-of-market objectives to be accomplished for a given budget and over a specified time period.

With our marketing goals in mind, we begin to build the advertising plan with a situational analysis.

SITUATIONAL ANALYSIS

In order to plan and create future advertising, we need to establish a current benchmark or starting point—this is the role of the situational analysis.

The Product

All eyes focus on "the product" at the start of the campaign . . . specifically, *its strengths*. General Foods' Post Division is trying to raise its voice above the oat bran fray by putting a big budget behind its new *Honey Bunches of Oats*. The ad and promotional blitz broke last spring, themed "Good things come in bunches."

Successful advertising and marketing begin with a good product. At this point, we need to analyze our product's strengths and weaknesses objectively. Most product failures stem from an overly optimistic appraisal of a product. Among the questions usually asked are:

1. What are the unique consumer benefits the product will deliver?
2. What is the value of the product relative to the proposed price?
3. Are adequate distribution channels available?
4. Can quality control be maintained?

80/20 rule. *Rule-of-thumb that says a minority of consumers (20 percent) will purchase a large proportion (80 percent) of specific goods and services.*

Prime-Prospect Identification

The next step is to identify our prime prospects and determine if there are enough of them to market the product profitably. As we discussed in Chapter 4, Target Marketing, there are a number of ways to identify the primary consumer of our product.

[1] "Dewar's Campaign Celebrates Its 20th," *Inside Print*, June 1989, p. 15.

Positioning. *Segmenting a market by creating a product to meet the needs of a selective group or by using a distinctive advertising appeal to meet the needs of a specialized group, without making changes in the physical product.*

Advertisers then turn their attention to the "heavy" users of their products—since it's easier convincing them to increase their consumption, than getting non-users to start using a new product. Anheuser-Busch never stops plugging its flagship brand, *Budweiser.* Over the summer, it offered bar owners a softball sales promotion, including a scoreboard, a statistics chalkboard, and a tap marker in the shape of a softball.

Competitors' activities need to be identified to determine their position vis-à-vis the advertised product. American Express, mindful of Visa's ad spending boost for traveler's checks, will focus their new campaign on the ease and convenience with which consumers can get refunds for lost or stolen checks. Most distinctive is the spot's pointed ending, jabbing at banks that *don't* carry Am Ex traveler's checks. . . "So, if your bank doesn't sell them, go to one that does," the voice-over advises.

The *creative theme* of the campaign should be devised with *originality* and *motivation* in mind. . . Ashton-Tate is looking for a fight. The leader in personal computer data-base software began its biggest-ever consumer promotion by tying dBASE IV to the June 12 middleweight championship boxing match between Leonard and Hearns. The campaign goes beyond traditional software marketing efforts—apart from national advertising, the effort uses spot radio, direct mail, P-O-P materials, and a unique instant "electronic" sweepstakes.

1. Who buys our product and what are their significant demographic characteristics? Can we get a mental picture of the average consumer?
2. Who are the heavy users of the product—the prime prospects? Remember the 80/20 rule; we must find those market segments that consume a disproportionate share of our product and determine what distinguishes them from the general population.
3. Finally, we need to examine the prime prospects' problems. Some advertising agencies look for the needs and desires of prime prospects before positioning the product. By discovering what these prospects want in a product, you can adjust your product appeal (and even the product itself) so that the product has a property or difference that will make it more desirable than other products in its category.

Competitive Atmosphere and Marketing Climate

In analyzing the competition, we examine direct and indirect competitors. Which specific brand and products compete with your brand, and in what product categories or subcategories do they belong? Is Mountain Dew's competition 7-Up or Sprite, Mellow-Yellow or Crush, or does it extend to colas, ice tea, and milk? If so, to what extent in each case? The Nissan Sentra competes with the Ford Escort, but not directly with the Buick Park Avenue. Once we determine our specific competition, we need to examine several factors:

1. How do we compare in market position? Is it a market in which a few giant companies claim the major share and remaining sales are divided among a number of firms? How does our geographic distribution compare with that of competitors?
2. What are the specific product features of competing brands? Does our product compare favorably in terms of major consumer benefits?
3. What are competitor's marketing strategies? Pricing, service policies, and distribution are some of the major comparisons we would want to make.

CREATIVE OBJECTIVES AND STRATEGY

At this point, we begin to select those advertising themes and selling appeals that are most likely to move our prime prospects to action. As we discussed in Chapter 16, Creating the Copy, advertising motivates people by appealing to their problems, desires, and goals—it isn't creative if it doesn't sell. Once we establish the overall objectives of the copy, we are ready to implement the copy strategy by outlining how this creative plan will contribute to accomplishing our predetermined marketing goals.

1. Determine the specific claim that will be used in advertising copy. If there is more than one, the claims should be listed in order of priority.
2. Consider various advertising executions. Review the PAPA discussion in Chapter 16 with an eye toward finding the best approach to convince consumers that your product will solve their problem better than any alternative.
3. In the final stage of the creative process, develop the copy and production of advertising.

Creative Criteria for Campaigns

Ken Roman and Jane Maas in *How to Advertise* stress how essential *similarity* between one advertisement and another is in developing successful advertising campaigns. Another term, *continuity,* is used to describe the relationship of one ad to another ad throughout a campaign. This similarity or continuity may be visual, verbal, or sound, attitudinal.[2]

[2]Ken Roman and Jane Maas, *How to Advertise* (New York: St. Martin's Press, 1976), pp. 67–77.

Visual Similarity. All print ads use the same typeface or virtually the same layout format so that consumers will learn to recognize the advertiser just by glancing at the ads. This may entail making illustrations about the same size in ad after ad and/or the headline and body copy very similar in length in each ad. Another device is for all ads in a campaign to use the same spokesperson or a continuing character. Cella Wines used Aldo Cella in ad after ad. Another way to achieve visual continuity is to use the same demonstration in ad after ad. When you look at a Sears or J. C. Penney newspaper ad, you instantly recognize the style and the advertiser. The J. C. Penney layout style is even carried over into the television art direction.

A certain ''sameness'' in characters or words predominating in all the advertisers' ads and commercials establishes *continuity*. Veteran actor, Jesse White was Maytag's perpetually lonely repairman. Although he's been replaced by ''a younger man,'' ''I'll still be out there as Maytag's roving goodwill ambassador,'' claimed Mr. White. He emphasized that while he's been on TV, the company's sales climbed from $186 million in 1967 to $2 billion in 1988!

Verbal Similarity. Oftentimes a campaign will use certain words or phrases in each ad to sum up the product's benefits. Examples are:

We grow great taste.

(Del Monte)

Rugged. Sensitive. Sexy.

(Iron Cologne)

Inside the mind of management.

(Fortune magazine)

It simply works better.

(Compaq computer)

A blending of art and machine.

(Jaguar)

Sometimes the verbal similarity becomes almost a copy format, as in Purina O.N.E. ads:

> When your dog is more than just a pet, you want to feed him more than just a 'dog food.' That's why Purina developed a very special dog food that embodies the kind of nutritional care you want to give your dog. It's Purina O.N.E. brand dog food. . . .

This copy was used as part of every print ad in the series, as well as in a TV ad (see Exhibits 22.2 and 22.3).

EXHIBIT 22.2

These Purina O.N.E. ads have visual and verbal similarities: 90 percent of the copy is identical in each ad. (Courtesy: Ralston Purina.)

EXHIBIT 22.2 (continued)

EXHIBIT 22.2 (continued)

EXHIBIT 22.3

This commercial follows the style of Purina O.N.E.'s print ads featuring the bond between dog owners and their dog—"For that one dog. Yours."

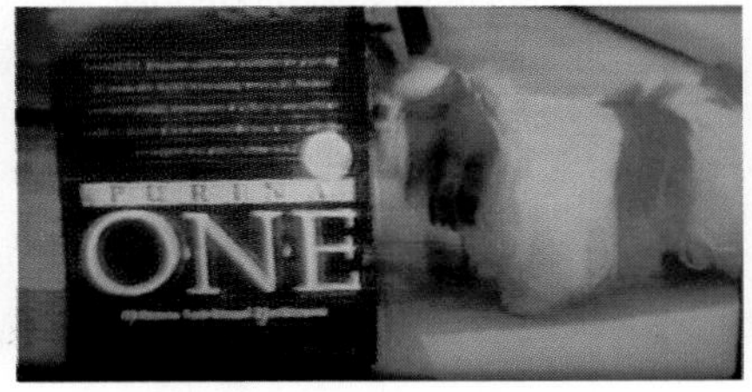

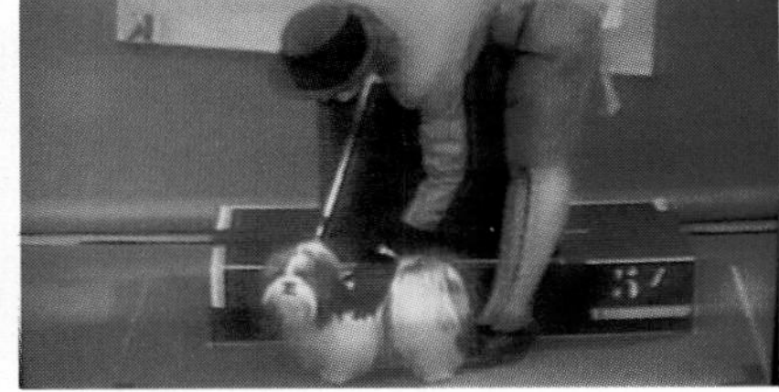

Other examples of verbal continuity are the following themes or slogans:

If you don't look good, we don't look good.

(Vidal Sassoon)

We bring good things to life

(GE)

The technique of verbal similarity may take the form of a tagline used in each television commercial. Some commercials employ identical copy for different slice-of-life commercials.

Repeating the benefits, theme, and key copy points in ad after ad bestows continuity across all media and helps build brand personality.

Sound Similarity. In broadcast, you may use the same music or jingle. Crystal Light used a jingle in their television commercials that instantly identified the ad. Using the same announcer's voice in each ad also helps build continuity. The same sound effect can make the campaign very distinctive. Avon used the sound of a door bell for many years in their ''Avon Calling'' advertising. And Maxwell House used the ''perking'' sound for its Master Blend commercials.

Attitude Similarity. Each ad expresses a consistent attitude toward the product and the people using it. One of the best examples of building a campaign around an attitude is Pepsi Cola's campaign: none of the ads describe what Pepsi taste like. Rather, they all show how the ''Pepsi Generation'' lives. It's an attitude.

These guidelines for building effective advertising campaigns can be used in numerous combinations. Most effective campaigns will use at least one of these techniques to build continuity in ad after ad.

Chosen *media* for the execution of the campaign must ''fit'' the product and the target. In TV and print ads, Orel Hershiser, the highest-paid player in major league baseball, will promote the purchase of a plastic Pizza Hut pitcher, that the restaurant will refill free with Pepsi-Cola. Pizza Hut runs a ''pitcher'' promotion annually—so getting *a star pitcher* to promote their product is ''a natural fit,'' admitted Kirk Wood, OH's agent.

MEDIA OBJECTIVES

While we have chosen to discuss creative strategy before media objectives, both functions are considered simultaneously in an advertising campaign. In fact, creative and media planning have the same foundations—marketing strategy and prospect identification—and cannot be isolated from each other. The media plan involves three primary areas.

Media Strategy

Media strategy. *Planning of ad media buys, including: identification of audience, selection of media vehicles, and determination of timing of a media schedule.*

At the initial stages of media planning, the general approach and role of media in the finished campaign are determined.

1. *Prospect identification.* The prime prospect is of major importance in both the media and the creative strategy. However, the media planner has the additional burden of identifying prospects. The media strategy must match prospects for a product with users of specific media. This requires that prospects be identified in terms that are compatible with traditional media audience breakdowns. You will recall that this need for standardization has resulted in the 4A's standard demographic categories discussed in Chapter 4, Target Marketing.
2. *Timing.* All media, with the possible exception of direct mail, operate on their own schedule, not that of advertisers. The media planner must consider many aspects of timing, including media closing dates, production time required for ads and commercials, campaign length, and the number of exposures desired during the product-purchase cycle.
3. *Creative considerations.* The media and creative teams must accommodate each other. They must compromise between using those media that allow the most creative execution and those that are most efficient in reaching prospects.

Media Tactics

At this point, the media planner decides on media vehicles and the advertising weight each is to receive. The reach-versus-frequency question must be addressed and appropriate budget allocations made.

Media Scheduling

Finally, an actual media schedule and justification are developed, as described in the example in Chapter 7.

THE SALES-PROMOTION PLAN

Along with the *major media* of the campaign—print and broadcast—the agency plans for coordinating *sales promotion*. *Working Woman* magazine joined *Chrysler Corporation* to sponsor a tour of 25 upscale shopping malls nationwide, called "A Preview into the 90's." The tour will feature displays of *Jeep vehicles*.

Usually the earliest planning of a campaign for consumer advertising includes a discussion of the sales promotion plans. These plans may involve dealer displays, premiums, cooperative advertising, and/or couponing offers. Once the theme of the consumer advertising campaign has been established, creative work is begun on the sales-promotion material, which is presented along with the consumer advertising material for final approval. At that time, the production is carefully planned so that all of the sales-promotion material will be ready before the consumer advertising breaks.

GETTING THE CAMPAIGN APPROVED

We now have a complete campaign: the ads, the media schedule, sales-promotion material, and costs for everything spelled out, ready for management's final approval. For that approval, it is wise to present a statement of the company's marketing goals. The objectives may be to launch a new product, to increase sales by x percent, to raise the firm's share of the market by z percent, or to promote a specific service of a firm. Next, the philosophy and strategy of the advertising are described, together with the reasons for believing that the proposed plan will help attain those objectives. Not until then are the ads or the commercials presented, along with the media proposal and the plans for coordinating the entire effort with that of the sales department.

What are the reasons for each recommendation in the program? On what basis were these dollar figures arrived at? On what research were any decisions based? What were the results of preliminary tests, if any? What is the competition doing? What alternatives were considered? What is the total cost? Finally, how may the entire program contribute to the company's return on its investment? Those people who control the corporate purse strings like to have definite answers to such questions before they approve a total advertising program.

RESEARCH—POST-TESTS

Lastly, plans are made for *testing* of the campaign—before and after it's run. The latest addition to McDonald's in Evansville, Indiana, and nearby Owensboro, Kentucky, is a 14-inch pizza, served as an experiment to woo families and couples *for dinner*. "*Local advertising* has been running since July—and tests will soon be conducted to see if the product has been 'noticed'," revealed McD's spokesman, Chuck Rubner.

The final part of the campaign entails testing its success. Post-testing falls into two related stages. In the first, the expected results are defined in specific and measurable terms. What do you expect the advertising campaign to accomplish? Typical goals of a campaign are to increase brand awareness by 10 percent or improve advertising recall by 25 percent.

In the second state, the actual research is conducted to see if these goals were met. Regardless of what research technique is used (for example, test markets, consumer panels), the problem is separating the results of the advertising campaign from consumer behavior that would have occurred in any case. That is, if we find that 20 percent of the population recognizes our brand at the end of a campaign, the question is what would the recognition level have been if no advertising took place. In order to answer this question, a research design is often used as a pretest. The pretest is intended not only to provide a benchmark for the campaign, but also to determine reasonable goals for future advertising.

CASE HISTORY

Avia's "For Athletic Use Only" Ad Campaign

SITUATION

AVIA has been one of the fastest-growing companies in the athletic shoe market. In 1985, their annual sales were $22 million; by 1988, they were $180 million; and current expectations are that they will exceed $200 million by 1990.

In 1989, Avia was the fifth-ranked athletic shoe company, with a 4.2 percent share of the market. Number-one–ranked Reebok had a 27.1 percent market share, and second-place Nike held 22.7 percent. Converse and L.A. Gear were in third and fourth places, respectively.

Avia, which was acquired by Reebok in 1987, planned to increase its 1989 marketing budget 42 percent, to $34 million: $20 million was to be invested in the advertising campaign, and of this, $9 million was reserved for launching the new campaign.

TARGET

Avia primarily targeted fitness fiends between the ages of 25 and 45 who work out at least four times a week. It also believed it could attract many "wannabes," or those who want to be perceived as jocks—in other words, people who dress in workout gear and high-ticket athletic shoes, but don't like to sweat their way through a real workout (see Exhibit A–F).

MEDIA

The "For Athletic Use Only" campaign was introduced to the trade and in collateral material in the fall of 1988. "Believe it or not," read the trade ad, "we're going to spend our millions telling most Americans not to buy our shoes." The consumer campaign

EXHIBIT A

Takeoff on AVIA TV ads as Boz talks tough to consumers, "Don't buy AVIA crosstrainers."

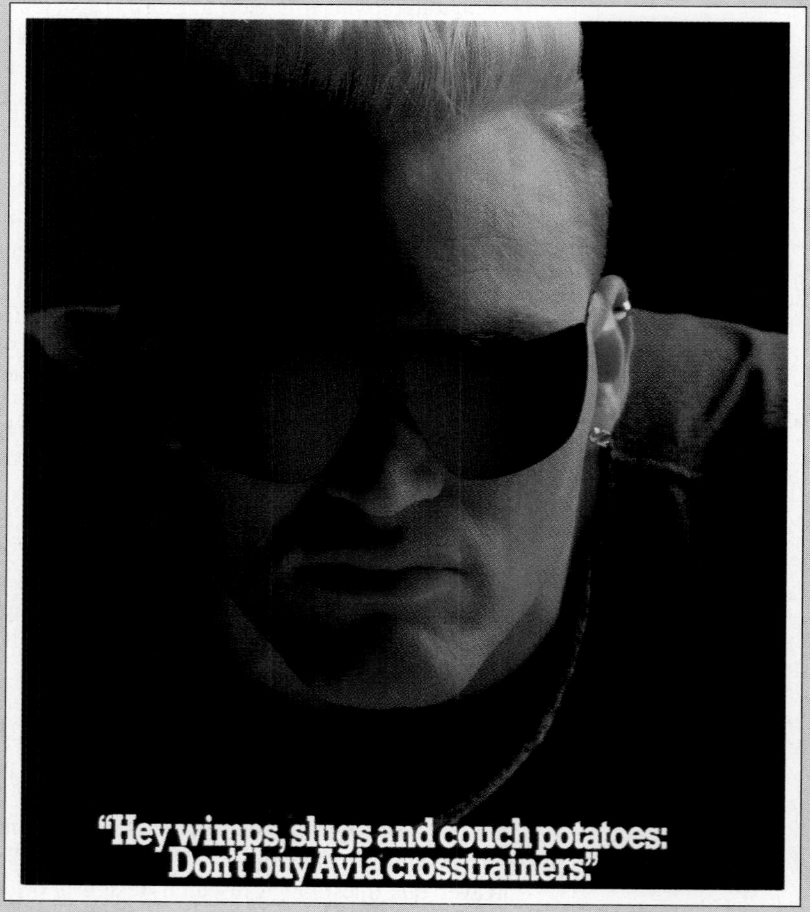

"Hey wimps, slugs and couch potatoes:
Don't buy Avia crosstrainers."

EXHIBIT B
The ad promotes cycling shoes.

If this is an essential component of your bike, don't wear our cycling shoes.

It takes a certain sophistication to appreciate shoes as technical as ours. An aggressive style of riding wouldn't hurt, either. Because Avia® cycling shoes are designed with specific cycling activities in mind. And kicking a stand is not one of them.

To begin with, our multi-density outsole is the first to achieve a stiffness "tuned" to the particular cycling activity. This allows

Clockwise from top left: The AC 80 Technical Racing, AC 70 Triathlon, AC 50 Sportech with recessed cleat and AC 30 Off-Road.

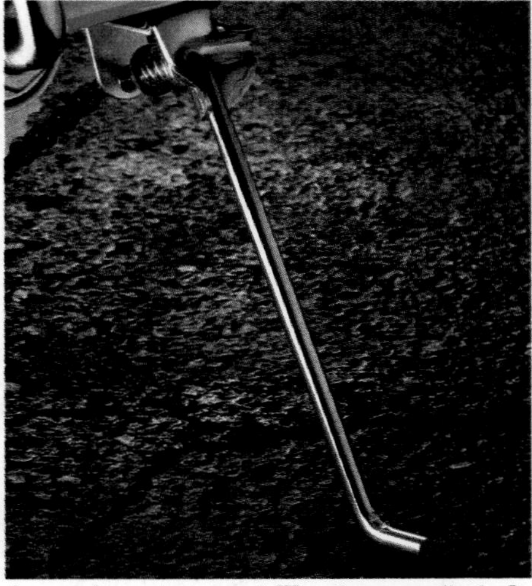

each shoe to deliver maximum efficiency for its intended discipline: be it racing, triathlon, mountain, or fitness cycling. Each shoe also offers unique three- or four-point internal closure systems, to anchor the foot securely between outsole and upper.

And above all, each shoe is built to be pushed.

Wear them accordingly. Or save your money for accessories you can honestly put to use. A bell, for instance.

AVIA
FOR ATHLETIC USE ONLY™

EXHIBIT C
Smokers aren't in AVIA's target.

If this is the only thing that gives your lungs a workout, don't buy our shoes.

Avia® makes authentic, no-nonsense aerobic shoes. Exclusively. They weren't designed to create an image of "fitness" for women who never exercise anything but facial muscles.

We trust you don't fall into that category. We trust you're serious enough about aerobics that you'll need all the cushioning and stability Avia's patented Cantilever® sole can provide.

Please use Avia 455's only for their intended purpose: good, honest workouts.

So if you're in the market for a serious pair of aerobic shoes, we recommend a pair of Avia 455's. If you're not all that serious, we'd rather you wear one of those nice, trendy athletic-*looking* brands available just about anywhere. Because we'd hate to see all our engineering innovations get lost in a puff of smoke.

AVIA
FOR ATHLETIC USE ONLY

EXHIBIT D

Selling AVIA volleyball shoes using strong visual.

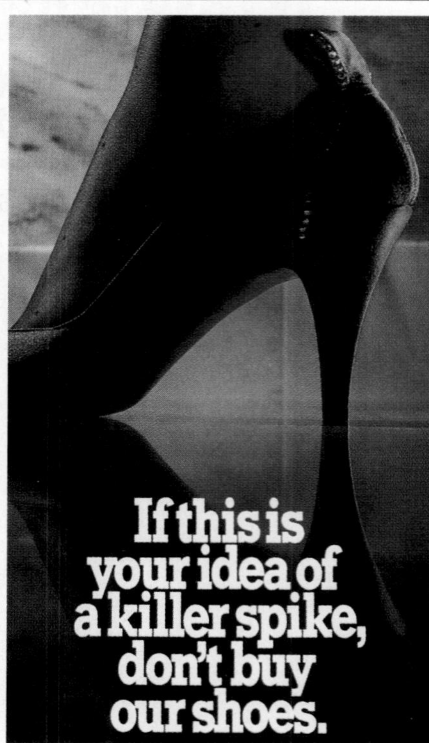

If this is your idea of a killer spike, don't buy our shoes.

Unless you're intimately familiar with lunges, hard landings and rolled ankles, you don't need the Avia® Cantilever® sole, engineered to deflect impact. Or flex joints that work with the foot's natural pivot. Ditto for the traction and lateral stability of gum rubber outsoles and leather forefoot straps.

Avia 285's: use only as directed.

Granted, even you wanna-be volleyball players can appreciate our breathable leather uppers. But then again you have to work up a sweat to do so.

And if that doesn't fit your style, there's no way our shoes ever will.

AVIA®

FOR ATHLETIC USE ONLY™

EXHIBIT E

Four walking shoes are featured in this ad.

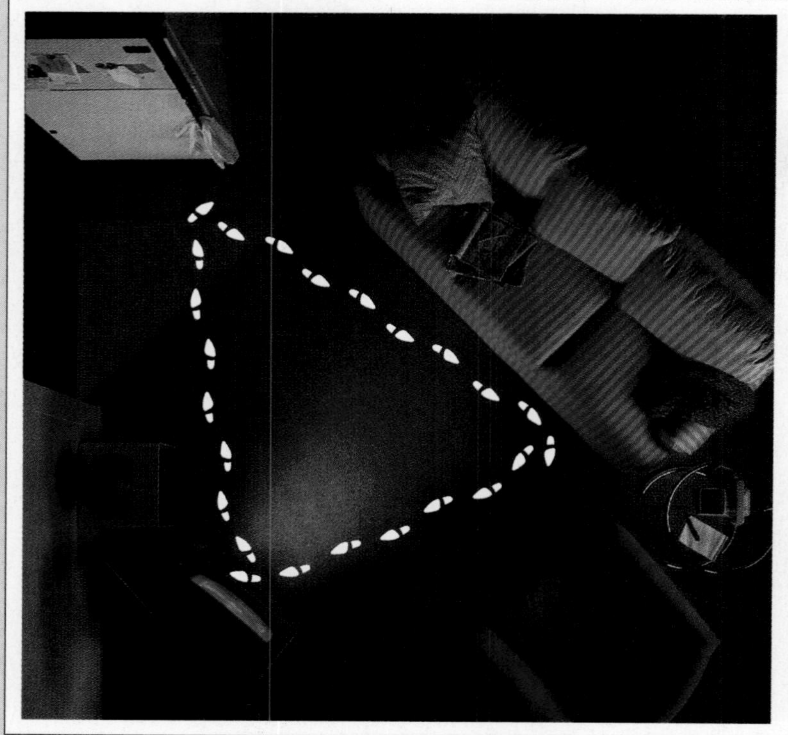

If this resembles your regular walking route, don't buy our shoes.

Mall 310 Street 355 Track 390 Trail 375

Avia® now makes walking shoes for every walking surface. Except carpet. We've purposely excluded people whose idea of a brisk walk is dashing for a bag of pretzels during a commercial break. After all, they'd find little use for the performance features built into Avia shoes.

But if your walking route goes well beyond the front door, we suggest you step outside in a pair of our fitness walking shoes.

As your heel strikes the ground, our unique Cantilever® outsole cushions it. Then, as your foot moves forward, our patented ArchRocker™ takes over and supports your midfoot muscles, while it helps carry your body's momentum forward.

Pick up the pace and you'll find that our track shoes create even more lateral stability from a low profile EVA midsole with lateral support lip. These pace walking shoes are so light you'll only notice them when you slip them on or off.

If you're a more adventurous walker, take a hike. In our rugged walking shoes. As you tread on rocks and roots, a wider ArchRocker stabilizes your foot, and the coiled rubber forefoot pad yields extra cushioning. (This design would be totally wasted on people whose feet never sink into anything tougher than ½" carpet padding.)

Even if you get your exercise in the comfortable confines of shopping malls, we've designed a walking shoe expressly for you—with a nonslip solid rubber outsole and special gum rubber forefoot area.

So no matter where you walk, Avia shoes fit the terrain. Lace up a pair. And then hit the road. Or trail. Or track. Or mall.

But if your idea of a taxing workout is racing to the fridge between soap opera scenes, don't do it in Avia walking shoes.

AVIA

FOR ATHLETIC USE ONLY

Introducing the shoes for people who walk for miles in malls without buying a thing.

Dual-density gum/rubber outsoles were designed for workouts in America's new fitness center—the mall.
It seems some people gain weight everytime they visit the local shopping mall—by loading up with sale items or by over-loading with junk food.
Avia believes that shopping malls are better suited for walking. And walking. And walking. And we've got the shoe to prove it.
The Avia® 310 mall walker's patented Cantilever® outsole cushions your heel on impact. And then two more unique Avia features take-over. The ArchRocker™ supports the midfoot as it helps propel the body's momentum forward. And, as your weight shifts to your forefoot, the gum rubber section of the outsole gives you added traction.
Patented ArchRocker™ supports midfoot muscles and prevents foot fatigue.
Maybe its time you closed the door on bus exhaust fumes, nasty dogs, rain and snow. Lace up the Avia 310 women's or men's mall walking shoes. And hit the mall before the stores open.
AVIA
FOR ATHLETIC USE ONLY

If you'd like to do your walking in malls, check out Avia's Walk 100 Miles program at:
The Athlete's Foot

EXHIBIT F

Targets the mall walker selling benefits of the ArchRocker™.

was previewed to the trade at the Sporting Goods Manufacturers Association's SuperShow/89, held in Atlanta early in February.

The consumer launch began on February 16 with spot television in New York, Atlanta, Boston, Los Angeles, Chicago, Detroit, Philadelphia, and Dallas. The 15- and 30-second spots were also broadcast on national cable networks, including: ESPN, TBS, Lifetime, MTV, USA, and Nickelodeon. Among the consumer magazines used to introduce the campaign were *Rolling Stone, Self, Glamour, The Walking Magazine, Tennis, Triathlete, Runner's World,* and *Bicycling* (see Exhibit G).

STRATEGY

The "For Athletic Use Only" campaign initially included:

- Redesigning shoe boxes to use the "For Athletic Use Only" theme.
- Putting the corporate theme on letterheads.
- Designing point-of-purchase displays to carry the theme.
- Incorporating the theme in Avia's apparel line.
- Using the theme in a trade show display.

CREATIVE

Avia wanted consumers to identify its footwear as the best high-performance shoes available. It determined that telling consumers not to buy its shoes except for athletic use would be the strongest statement it could make to ensure its message came across.

The television and print advertisements contrast an active lifestyle to more sedentary and less healthy behavior. For example, one of the television ads, which opens with a tight shot of two cocktails, says: "If this is what an afternoon of mixed doubles means to you, Avia doesn't want you to wear its tennis shoes" (see Exhibit H for the print version).

If you eat or drink to excess or are, in Seattle Seahawk Brian Bosworth's terms, a wimp, a slug, or a couch potato, Avia doesn't want you to buy their shoes (see Exhibit A). One TV ad has a visual of an overweight man lying on a couch with a TV remote control in his hand and Boz snarling: "If this is the only way you participate in different sports, Avia doesn't want you buyin' their cross-trainers." Boz himself is shown going through a vigorous workout.

The print ads repeat the television theme. One, which pictures a cigarette burning in an ash tray, reads: "If this is the only thing that gives your lungs a workout, don't buy our shoes" (see Exhibits C and I).

EXHIBIT G

Shows specific model shoes and their print ad schedule.

Running	
Models: 2100, 2090 (3 pages)	
Running Times	March, May, July
Runner's World	March, April, July
Models: 2100, 2090 (spread)	
Running Times	April, June, August, September, October, November
Runner's World	May, June, August, September, October, November
Triathlete	April, May, June, September, October, November
Models: 2100, 2090 (1 page regional)	
Competitor Mag. So. Ca.	March, June, December
Florida Running	March/April, May/June, November/December
Florida Sports Review	February/March, August/September, October/November
Houston Health & Fitness	February, April, September
Inside Texas Running	March, October, December
New England Runner	March/April, July/August, September/October
New Jersey Runner	April, July/August, November/December
New York Running News	April/May, June/July, December/January
Northwest Runner	May, June, September
Ohio Runner	May, June, October
Oklahoma Runner	April, May/June, October
Rocky Mountain Sports & Fitness	April, May, October
Running Journal	March, July, October
Southern Runner	March/April, May/June, November/December
Sport Pulse	February, March, September
Washington Running Report	March/April, September/October, November/December
Windy City Sports	March, August, October
Walking	
Models: 390, 375, 355, 310 (3 pages)	
American Health	March
Travel & Leisure	April
Walking	May/June
Working Woman	July
Models: 390, 375, 355, 310 (spread)	
American Health	April
Prevention	March, April, September
The Source Book	Annual
Working Woman	August
Yosemite Magazine	Annual
Model: 310	
New Choices	March, April
Walking	March/April, September/October
Crosstraining	
Model: 1360	
Rolling Stone	February, March, April, May

EXHIBIT G (continued)

Aerobics	
Model: 455	
Glamour	March, April
Self	March, April
Model: 600	
American Fitness	March/April, May/June
IDEA Today	March, April, May, June
Shape	March, April, May
Tennis	
Model: 770 (Spread)	
Tennis	March, April
World Tennis	March
Model: 770 (1 page)	
Inside Tennis Yearbook	January/February
Racquet	February/March, August/September
Tennis	May, July
Tennis Industry	January, February
Tennis Week	March, April, May
World Tennis	April, August
Model: 770 (1 page tab)	
Inside Tennis	March, April, August
Sun Tennis	February, March, April, May
Tennis Northeast	February, March, April, May, July, October
Tennis South	February, March, April, May, July, October
Tennis West	February, March, April, May, July, October
Texas Tennis	February, March, April, May, July, October

Avia's strategy is clear: By positioning the product negatively—that is, by stating emphatically what kind of person the shoes are *not* for—they are identifying the footwear with active lifestyles. The ads are a calculated overstatement so that consumers get the message loud and clear. As Avia's vice president of marketing says: "It's the perfect strategy for our core customers of serious athletes, and, if executed properly, it will be effective with the non-core as well." Avia is banking on the fact that human nature being what it is, a lot of people will desire to buy the shoes just because they have been told not to. Underlying Avia's choice of strategy is the knowledge that the company needs eye-catching advertising to compete against the well-established Reebok and Nike.

RESULTS

The first quarter of the campaign produced a 20–30 percent increase in sales. It also produced complaints from both Philip Morris and Seagram's that Avia was attacking smokers and drinkers. Bill Borders of Avia's agency, Borders, Perrin & Norranger, says: "If we alienate a segment of the zealous nonathletes, we don't care. If they wear our shoes, it's bad advertising for Avia." A gutsy strategy to differentiate a product line against big-spending, highly visible competition.

(Courtesy: AVIA Group International, Inc.)

If this is what an afternoon of mixed doubles means to you, don't buy our shoes.

Avia 770's: use only as directed.

Avia® has taken a curious stance toward part of the tennis shoe market. We don't want it. It's not that we have anything against people whose only regular workout is tossing down cocktails. We'd just prefer that they bought somebody else's tennis shoes. Our shoes are for players at or near the fanatic level.

That's why Avia's patented Cantilever® sole has such a remarkable cushioning effect. It's why we developed lateral/medial forefoot straps, to help control side-to-side movement.

It's why we use Infinity 3000™ compound, to make these shoes last after others have deteriorated into mere sneakers. But those who will use Avia 770's only for marathon drinking sessions should save their money. And to be honest, being seen too often in bars could damage our reputation.

AVIA
FOR ATHLETIC USE ONLY.

EXHIBIT H

Campaign attacks alcohol drinkers.

EXHIBIT I

Running shoes for Athletic Use Only.

If this is the only thing that gets your heart pumping Sunday mornings, don't buy our shoes.

At Avia,® we divide the world into two types of people. Runners and non-runners. If you belong to the latter group, you don't belong in this ad. Kindly turn the page.

That's better. (Having put two years of long days and late nights into developing our new ARC™ running shoes, we don't want people buying them just to look cool standing in brunch lines.) This is radical new technology for running purists only. Anyone else should save their money.

At the heart of it all is our ARC. This ingenious device, made of Dupont's Hytrel®/Rynite® compound, enables our engineers to achieve a level of cushioning never before possible. And, unlike the other cushioning techniques on the market, the ARC retains 100% of its mechanical properties. Meaning it never loses its cushioning ability.

Equally important, the ARC does all this shock absorbing without compromising stability. In truth, it actually enhances stability.

Consider the 2100. Molded into its patented Cantilever® sole is our stability ARC, specifically designed with short, rigid fingers. Working in tandem with the independent lugs of the outsole, this ARC not only helps significantly reduce impact loads, its extended medial fingers help greatly control excessive rearfoot motion. As does the PVC/NBR, lightweight external heel counter.

All of which make the 2100 a godsend for runners with pronation problems.

Our 2090's incorporate a different ARC design with slightly longer, thinner fingers. And considerably different results. These more flexible fingers, coupled with the flared Cantilever sole, result in even greater shock absorption than our 2100 model. For runners less concerned with motion control problems.

While the ARC/Cantilever system is enough to place these two models appreciably ahead of our competitors' shoes, we didn't quit there.

Both also feature our exclusive Dynamic Fit™ lacing system with gore stretch panels that allows the shoe to expand and contract with the foot throughout the gait cycle. (The 2100 even employs a unique symmetrical lacing pattern that distributes lace pressure evenly across the instep.) Each model has a combination EVA/polyurethane midsole for rearfoot and forefoot cushioning. Indy 500® outsole compound for extremely long wear. Scotchlite™ reflective material for 360° nighttime visibility. The list goes on and on.

If you prefer to get your heart pumping by doing at least five or ten miles before a hearty, low sat fat breakfast, we invite you to try on a pair of these very special new shoes.

If, however, you prefer strolling through brunch lines, we invite you to try on a pair of someone else's shoes.

AVIA
FOR ATHLETIC USE ONLY.

CASE HISTORY

Johns Hopkins Health System

BACKGROUND

The Founding of The Johns Hopkins Hospital. More than 100 years ago, The Johns Hopkins Hospital opened its doors to the people of Baltimore, and the world. The hospital was founded by Johns Hopkins, a wealthy Quaker merchant. The following quotations describe his intent:

> To provide for a hospital which shall, in construction and arrangement, compare favorably with any other institution of like character, in this country, or in Europe.
>
> To secure the service of the Hospital, surgeons and physicians of the highest character and greatest skill.
>
> To receive into the Hospital the indigent sick of this city and environs, without charge.
>
> To provide a training school for nurses.
>
> In all arrangements in relation to the Hospital, you will bear constantly in mind that it is my wish and purpose that the institution will ultimately form a part of the medical school.

From Mr. Hopkins' own words, a fivefold mission for the hospital was later developed by its board of trustees:

1. To provide a physical setting that permits physicians to offer the best in medical and surgical care, and that allows for the conduct of biomedical and clinical research.
2. To secure physicians and surgeons of the highest caliber.
3. To provide medical care cost effectively and to assure fiscal viability such that revenues allow the provision of the same medical services without charge to those patients unable to pay.
4. To provide training programs for physicians, nurses, and allied health professionals.
5. To work collaboratively and interdependently with the School of Medicine to assure that the hospital meets the comprehensive medical-care needs of its patients and their families.

The Creation of The Johns Hopkins Health System. By the late 1970s, health-care delivery in this country was changing dramatically. In June 1985, Johns Hopkins trustees and administrators noted the following environmental concerns and market trends:

- The focus of medical practice was shifting from an inpatient setting to ambulatory-care environments.
- The regulatory environment was giving way to competition based on price.
- Patients were being offered more choices by a variety of providers and delivery systems. Greater emphasis was being placed on patient comfort and convenience.
- Hospital occupancies across the country were declining. Physicians were being recruited with incentives that more closely tied them and their patients to specific hospitals.
- A shift to financing practices that use prospective pricing and prepaid health-care systems was taking place.

In response to these concerns, the trustees and administrators decided to create a vertically integrated, multi-institutional system of medical-services delivery in support of the patient care, education, and research missions of The Johns Hopkins Hospital and School of Medicine. Thus in 1986, The Johns Hopkins Health System was born, one of the first nonprofit, academically based health-care systems of its kind in the country.

Purpose of The Johns Hopkins Health System. The new health system had several purposes:

- To make Johns Hopkins quality more accessible.
- To expand patient-care options, including a broad commitment to a health maintenance organization (HMO).
- To protect and extend existing referral sources.
- To reinforce John's Hopkins's dedication to education and research.
- To preserve the hospital's financial position.
- To continue the Hopkins tradition of medical excellence.

Positioning in Preparation for the Introduction of The Johns Hopkins Health System and Its Advertising Program. Considering the significant changes in health care, including complex insurance arrangements, limited reimbursement systems, and shifts in accountability, the board concluded that it was no longer possible for an academic medical center to survive by providing only complex care on a fee-for-service basis. Hence they responded with the creation of JHHS. Before JHHS was created, Johns Hopkins Hospital had never felt the need to advertise. But now they wanted people to know that the newly formed Johns Hopkins Health System (JHHS) includes The Johns Hopkins Hospital, The Francis Scott Key Medical Center, The Wyman Park Medical Center, The North Charles General Hospital, and The Johns Hopkins Health Plan (HMO), and that it provides a wide range of services, financial options, and benefits that are unavailable elsewhere. They decided that an advertising program would be necessary to tell health-care consumers about the options JHHS now offered.

JHHS ADVERTISING PROGRAM FOR FISCAL YEAR 1987

Situation. The Johns Hopkins Health System had just been created. It included:

- The Johns Hopkins Hospital, a world-renowned academic teaching hospital.
- The Francis Scott Key Medical Center, known today as a burn center but also known as the former city hospital.
- The North Charles Hospital, a small, urban community hospital.
- The Wyman Park Medical Center, another urban community hospital, which was formerly a public health service facility (and which continues to serve a large military population).
- The Johns Hopkins Health Plan, a newly created HMO with 16 sites.

Note that only two of the system's five affiliates incorporated Johns Hopkins into their names.

The JHHS was working toward providing quality medicine and patient care across the system, and making it accessible and affordable to all.

Strategy. The plan was to create an advertising campaign that would introduce JHHS and name its affiliates, emphasizing their collective relationship to Johns Hopkins (see Exhibit A–D). Based on the notion of Johns Hopkins's quality, JHHS would be positioned as a consumer's health-care provider of choice no matter how ''routine'' or ''complex'' the level of care needed. All ''customers'' would benefit from Hopkins's experience and research. The affiliates would therefore be positioned as affordable and accessible to all health-care consumers.

The ads, media plan, and collateral materials would be developed in such a way as to advance the system's purpose. A separate campaign would be created to educate consumers about the establishment of a Hopkins HMO and how it is uniquely different from existing HMOs.

Results. Recognition of The Johns Hopkins Health System and awareness of its member affiliates was established by:

- The creation of a JHHS logo, used in all TV and print advertising, print materials, and collaterals.
- The creation of logos for all system affiliates, used in TV and print advertising, print materials, and collaterals as appropriate.
- Print advertising.
- Television and radio advertising.
- Outdoor advertising.
- Collateral materials, including a capabilities brochure and a film.
- Development of a systemwide graphic standards program for printed materials, including, but not limited to, stationery.

EXHIBIT A

Introducing the Johns Hopkins Health System.

HMO membership grew steadily throughout the year and new sites were added.

JHHS ADVERTISING PROGRAM FOR FISCAL YEAR 1988

Situation. The emphasis was to be working toward extending Hopkins quality throughout the system, both internally and externally. Making Hopkins quality medicine affordable and accessible was also to be stressed, particularly through the HMO. Finally, it was decided that the advertising focus in 1988 would be on promoting the HMO.

Strategy. The plan was to create a mixed-media advertising campaign that:

- Emphasized the relationship of The Johns Hopkins Health Plan (JHHP) to JHHS.
- Stressed the affordability and accessibility of Hopkins medicine to all JHHP members.
- Positioned JHHP as the HMO of choice for employers and employees (see Exhibit E).

Collaterals and direct marketing components that would work in concert with the advertising campaign would also be developed.

Results. Membership in JHHP grew significantly. JHHP became an established and respected name in HMOs in the region, and JHHP sites increased to 30 locations. Although a reasonably low advertising profile was maintained throughout the year, JHHS and all hospital affiliates benefited from the comparatively high profile achieved by JHHP advertising and promotional activities.

JHHS ADVERTISING PROGRAM FOR FISCAL YEAR 1989

Situation. As of July 1, The North Charles Hospital and The Wyman Park Medical Center would be known as The Homewood Hospital Center (HHC), south and north campus, respectively.

It was decided that greater emphasis should be placed on the special capabilities of each affiliate, particularly The Francis Scott Key Medical Center (FSK) and both campuses of the newly renamed HHC. It was also decided that given the low profile of hospital affiliates the previous fiscal year and the name changes this year, the affiliates' relationship to the system and to Hopkins medicine needed to be reemphasized.

The centennial celebration of JHH that was to begin at the end of the fiscal year could be used to advantage.

Strategy. The plan for fiscal 1989 was to create an advertising program that:

- Introduced The Homewood Hospital Center, emphasizing its individual campus service strengths and its relationship to the system, using print and direct-mail advertising.

EXHIBIT B

This collateral advertising piece gives more information about service.

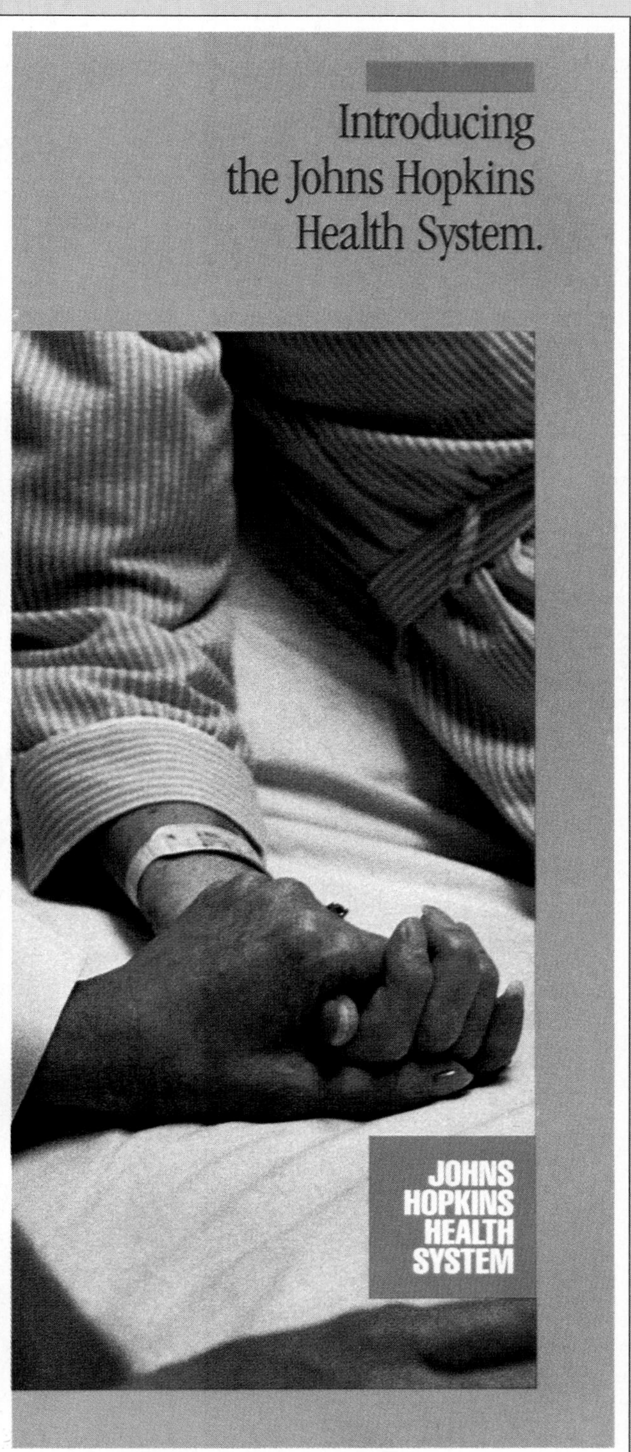

EXHIBIT C

"The biggest name in Health Care just took a giant step in your direction" is in each of the introductory ads.

No job too small.

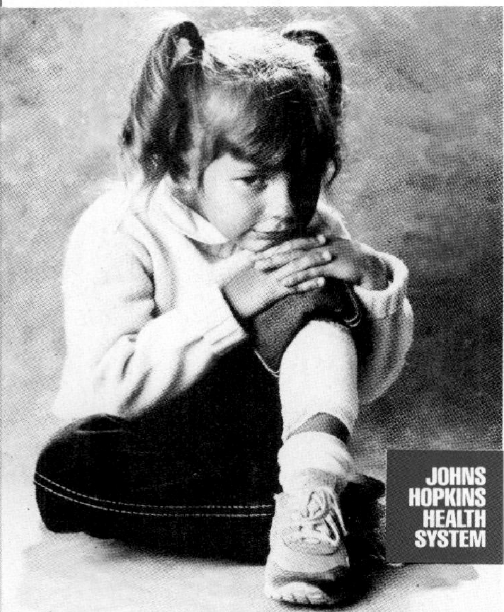

No job too big.

Only Johns Hopkins can offer such a broad spectrum of medical capabilities. From regular checkups to the most highly sophisticated medical procedures in the world, you and your family can access that same Hopkins reputation for medical excellence at 4 hospital sites and 19 Health Plan locations in and around Baltimore.

Now, 100% confidence is 100% convenient!

This is the Johns Hopkins Health System . . . an extensive network of hospitals, physicians and specialists, working to provide Hopkins quality care . . . conveniently and affordably.

Now, you can count on the System to deliver that same level of Hopkins' quality care from the simplest through the most complex medical procedures.

Don't settle for anything less. It's accessible. It's convenient. It's Hopkins.

The biggest name in Health Care just took a giant step in your direction.

The Johns Hopkins Hospital
The Francis Scott Key Medical Center
The North Charles Hospital
The Wyman Park Medical Center
The Johns Hopkins Health Plan

EXHIBIT D

There's no such thing as "routine" surgery.

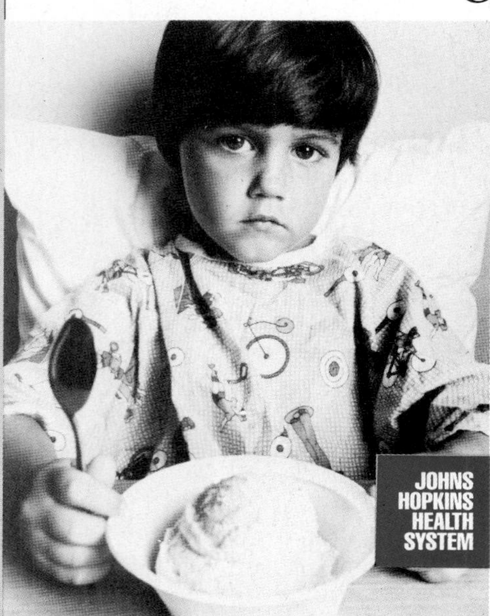

Ask any patient.

Jason's tonsillectomy? Routine? Certainly not to Jason. And certainly not to us. No matter how simple or complex the procedure, your time in the hospital demands nothing less than the very best professional medical care available. Every time.

Now, Johns Hopkins has found a way to *guarantee* that *any* health problem, no matter how big or how small, will be treated with the same level of quality care that Hopkins has been committed to for one hundred years.

Introducing, The Johns Hopkins Health System.

An extensive network of hospitals, physicians and specialists covering every conceivable health service ranging from outpatient services to highly specialized medical procedures. With its four member hospitals and nineteen Health Plan sites, the System works to provide Hopkins quality care . . . conveniently and affordably.

Don't ever settle for anything less. It's accessible. It's convenient. It's Hopkins.

The biggest name in Health Care just took a giant step in your direction.

The Johns Hopkins Hospital
The Francis Scott Key Medical Center
The North Charles Hospital
The Wyman Park Medical Center
The Johns Hopkins Health Plan

THE JOHNS HOPKINS HEALTH PLAN IS NOW OPEN TO STATE EMPLOYEES.
The Hopkins tradition... now, even closer to home.
BALLARD, M.D.
EILHOLZ, M.D.
Hopkins quality health care is just around the corner...
For nearly 100 years, Johns Hopkins has been known throughout the world for outstanding health care. Now you can access that same reputation for medical excellence in your own neighborhood . . . through the Johns Hopkins Health Plan.
Credentialed physicians of the Johns Hopkins Health Plan now have offices conveniently located where you live and work . . . and that puts the resources, specialists and facilities of the entire Hopkins system of health care right at your doorstep.
Hopkins offers total medical coverage for one low fee, backed by an institution that you know and trust. And every health care cost is covered: hospitalization, physician services, emergency care, physicals, X-rays, well baby care, immunizations . . . even routine doctor's office visits.
Get complete health care coverage with complete confidence. The Johns Hopkins Health Plan offers savings and security in protecting your family's precious well being. Trust your health to Hopkins.
Now, we're bringing the Johns Hopkins tradition even closer to home . . . your home, with convenient locations in and around Baltimore.
Enroll through your employer. For more information call 522-9660.
JOHNS HOPKINS HEALTH SYSTEM
The Johns Hopkins Health Plan

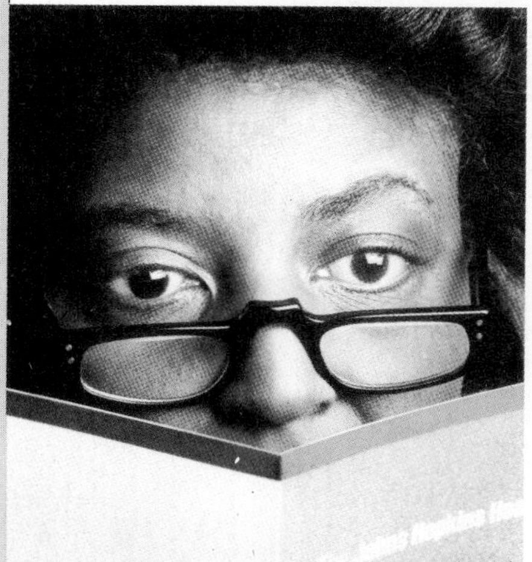

EXHIBIT E

These ads target state employees with a similar format. Each ad's last paragraph is the same, trying to get the reader to call.

- Developed a high-visibility, high-impact television campaign, using testimonials to spotlight the strengths of member institutions.
- Incorporated "brand awareness" and "brand preference" for the system into the television campaign (see Exhibits F and G).
- Supported the JHH Centennial and applied the sense of Hopkins traditions and history to JHHS and all its member affiliates, using print ads (see Exhibit H).

Results. Name recognition of HHC was established and continues to grow. Recognition of JHHS member affiliates and their relationship to the Hopkins name continues to increase, as does the notion of the affordability and accessibility of Hopkins quality systemwide. People's sense of Hopkins traditions and history as they are applied systemwide has been strengthened. JHHP continues to significantly increase membership and has expanded to 40 HMO locations across the state of Maryland.

EXHIBIT F

Johns Hopkins Health Center used a fireman dramatically talking about their Francis Scott Key Burn Center.

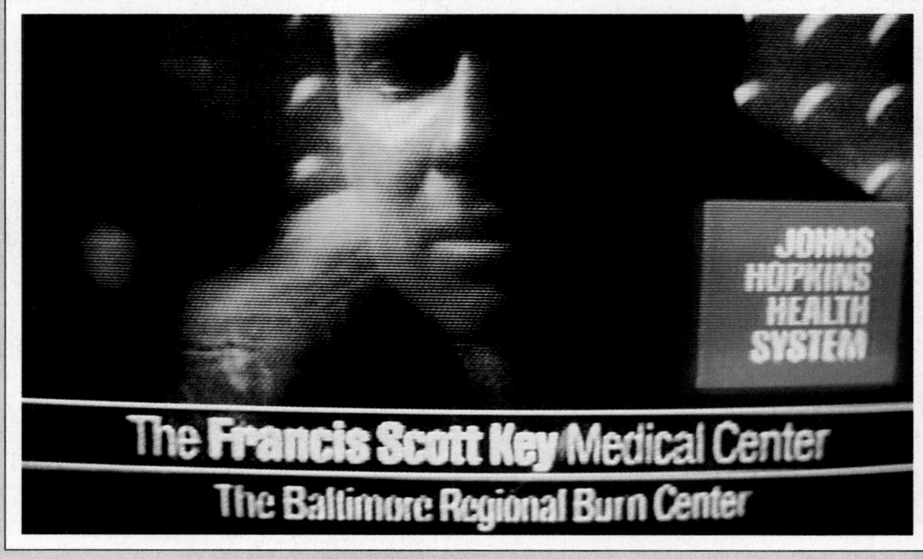

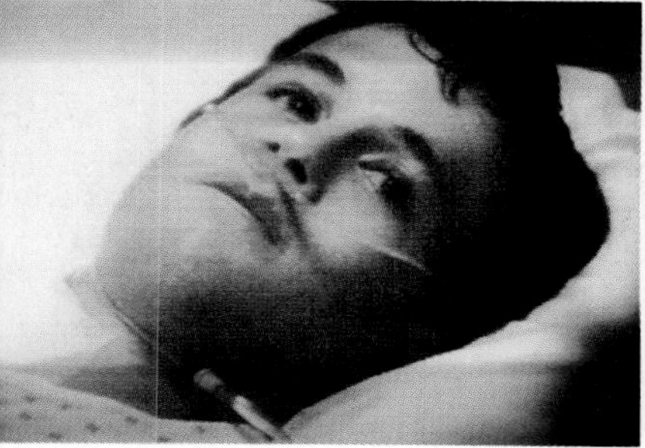

EXHIBIT G

Television commercials were used to promote the Nursing care and dedication of the Johns Hopkins System Hospitals.

EXHIBIT H

This institutional ad promotes the vision and the hospital, Medical Center, Health Plan, and Hospital Center.

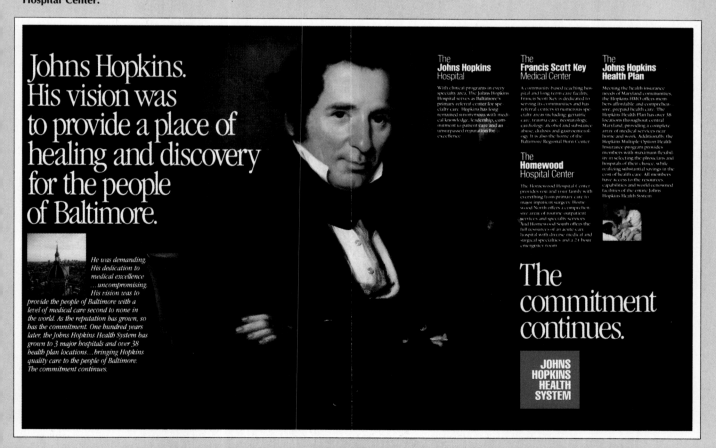

Johns Hopkins. His vision was to provide a place of healing and discovery for the people of Baltimore.

He was demanding. His dedication to medical excellence ...uncompromising. His vision was to provide the people of Baltimore with a level of medical care second to none in the world. As the reputation has grown, so has the commitment. One hundred years later, the Johns Hopkins Health System has grown to 3 major hospitals and over 38 health plan locations... bringing Hopkins quality care to the people of Baltimore. The commitment continues.

The **Johns Hopkins** Hospital

With clinical programs in every specialty area, The Johns Hopkins Hospital serves as Baltimore's primary referral center for specialty care. Hopkins has long remained synonymous with medical knowledge, leadership, commitment to patient care and an unsurpassed reputation for excellence.

The **Francis Scott Key** Medical Center

A community-based teaching hospital and long-term care facility, Francis Scott Key is dedicated to serving its communities and has referral centers in numerous specialty areas including: geriatric care, trauma care, neonatology, cardiology, alcohol and substance abuse, dialysis and gastroenterology. It is also the home of the Baltimore Regional Burn Center.

The **Homewood** Hospital Center

The Homewood Hospital Center provides you and your family with everything from primary care to major inpatient surgery. Homewood North offers a comprehensive array of routine outpatient services and specialty services. And Homewood South offers the full resources of an acute-care hospital with diverse medical and surgical specialties and a 24-hour emergency room.

The **Johns Hopkins Health Plan**

Meeting the health insurance needs of Maryland communities, the Hopkins HMO offers members affordable and comprehensive, prepaid health care. The Hopkins Health Plan has over 38 locations throughout central Maryland, providing a complete array of medical services near home and work. Additionally, the Hopkins Multiple Option Health Insurance program provides members with maximum flexibility in selecting the physicians and hospitals of their choice, while realizing substantial savings in the cost of health care. All members have access to the resources, capabilities and world-renowned facilities of the entire Johns Hopkins Health System.

The commitment continues.

JOHNS HOPKINS HEALTH SYSTEM

SUMMARY

The steps in preparing a national campaign for a consumer product may be enumerated as follows:

1. Situational Analysis
   a. Product analysis.
   b. Prime-prospect identification.
   c. Prime prospects' problem analysis.
   d. Competitive atmosphere and market climate.
2. Creative Objectives and Strategy
   a. Determine specific copy claims.
   b. Consider various advertising executions.
   c. Begin creation of ads and commercials.
3. Media Objectives
   a. Media strategy—includes prospect identification, timing, and creative considerations.
   b. Media tactics.
   c. Media scheduling.
4. The Sales-Promotion Plan
5. Getting the campaign approved.
6. Research—post-tests.

QUESTIONS

1. What is the basic purpose of an ad campaign?
2. What is included in the situational analysis?
3. How does the 80/20 rule relate to prospect identification?
4. What is the advantage of continuity of layout and copy throughout an ad campaign?
5. What is continuity of attitude?
6. Creative and media strategy must be done simultaneously. Discuss briefly.
7. How does a campaign relate to the Link process?

SUGGESTED EXERCISES

- Find three campaign examples of continuity-of-layout format. Be prepared to discuss each campaign.
- Find three campaign examples of verbal continuity.
- Identify the prime prospect for each of the campaigns selected above.

READINGS

HRUBY, F. MICHAEL: "Missing Pieces Analysis Targets the Competitor's Weakness," *Marketing News,* January 2, 1989, pp. 10–11.

LUCK, DAVID J., O.C. FERRELL, AND GEORGE H. LUCAS, JR.: *Marketing Strategy and Plans,* 3rd ed. (Englewood Cliffs, N.J.: Prentice Hall, 1989).

MAGIERA, MARCY: "Avia Gets Nasty," *Advertising Age,* February 13, 1989, p. 4.

SCHULTZ, DON E., DENNIS MARTIN, AND WILLIAM P. BROWN: *Strategic Advertising Campaigns* (Chicago: Crain Books, 1984).

PART SIX

Other Environments of Advertising

To this point in the text our discussion has emphasized national advertising. Those well-known companies and brands that dominate a significant portion of the advertising we see each day have been at the focal point of much of our discussion. However, this last section of the text not only examines some other areas of advertising, but also views the social, legal, and regulatory environment in which it functions.

Chapter 23 covers the fast-paced world of retail advertising where success is measured in tomorrow's sales receipts. Retail marketing is the most competitive segment of product sales. From the major department store and specialized boutique, we turn in Chapter 24 to the multinational advertiser whose concerns are literally worldwide. A few years ago, international marketing meant the export of American products and advertising expertise. Today, Americans drive Japanese cars, wear Italian shoes, and go to work on Swiss time. American companies are as busy protecting their domestic markets from foreign invasion as they are finding profitable overseas markets.

Finally, in Chapter 25 and 26, we conclude the text with a discussion of the regulatory and ethical restraints on advertisers. Its visibility as a business function forces advertising to continually examine itself. In an era of consumer awareness and suspicion of big business, advertising must hold even the appearance of ethical behavior.

TWENTY-THREE

Retail Advertising

When they hear the word *retailers,* most people think in terms of the kinds of stores found in regional shopping malls: the major department stores like Macy's, Lord & Taylor, Rich's, Burdine's, Bloomingdale's, Nordstrom, and Neiman-Marcus; the specialty stores like Victoria's Secret, Toys 'R Us, Herman's, Levitz, The Limited, and Circuit City; the discounters like Wal-Mart, K Mart, and Target; the supermarkets like Kroger's, Winn-Dixie, and A&P; the convenience stores like Circle K and 7-Eleven; and the catalog showrooms like Service Merchandise. The thousands of independent clothing, shoe, grocery, drug, and specialty stores also come to mind. But seldom do people think of warehouse clubs like Sam's and Pace; service retailers such as banks, restaurants, and beauty shops, and mail-order catalog stores such as Sear's, Spiegel, and Lands' End as retailers.

Retailers use more than just newspapers for promotion. . . Lately, radio, TV, cable, catalogs, outdoor, and direct response ads and commercials have been added to their media mix. National clothing and home furnishings chain, *JC Penney* employs, in addition to newspaper ads, radio commercials for "hot sale" promotions, regular and special catalog distributions, colored newspaper inserts, sales promotion activities such as fashion shows and product demonstrations, and attractive billboards near their mall retail stores. Management chalks all this promotion effort to their need for "exposure" in a "crowded" department/specialty store market.

Kotler and Armstrong define retailing as "all activities involved in selling goods or services directly to final customers for their personal, nonbusiness use."[1] Most retailing takes place in retail stores, of course, but in recent years, nonstore retailing—by mail, telephone, door to door, vending machines, and electronically—has grown explosively.

To most people, retail advertising means newspaper ads for the kinds of retailers listed above. Retailers usually carry a variety of brands and/or items. The advertising may focus on many kinds of items, or just a few. The large retailer often uses an extensive media mix—newspapers, radio, television, cable television, catalogs, outdoor, direct response—which necessitates careful planning, identification of the target, and media selection to be successful.

Recently, the scope and diversity of retailing have undergone a dramatic change. The roots of modern retailing can be found in the specialty shops of the 1800s. Typically, these stores carried a single class of merchandise: dry goods, hardware, men's or women's clothing, and so on. Early in this century, retailers began to combine several specialty-store functions under a single roof, initiating the full-service department store

[1]Philip Kotler and Gary Armstrong, *Principles of Marketing* (Englewood Cliffs, NJ: Prentice Hall, 1989), pp. 380–381.

that dominated retail trade for the next 50 years. Retail advertising is the fastest-paced segment of the industry. Large retailers produce ads on a daily basis, and the results of their efforts are measured at the cash register within days. While national advertising expenditures are concentrated among a relatively few advertisers and media, retailers number in the millions and use virtually every advertising and promotion method.

CHANGING RETAIL ENVIRONMENT

Retailing is constantly changing. Let's take a brief look at the evolution over the past several decades.[2]

Retailing in the 1950s and 1960s

This was an era of low prices and cheap goods. Discount department stores adopted self-service to compete against established retailers. Centralized checkout and fewer salespeople brought down labor costs, which can account for as much as 14 percent of sales.

Growth in the 1970s

As hard-goods sales shifted from department stores to discounters, the latter expanded. Their numbers boomed from 1,300 in 1960 to 7,400 by 1977, and the volume of general merchandise sold by discounters eclipsed total department store sales. Not surprisingly, the major retailers decided to enter the discount business. General merchandise sales were fueled in the 1970s by an increase in the number of households, which stimulated one-time purchases to set up housekeeping.

More for Less in the 1980s

With increased consumer sophistication and knowledge of the marketplace, retail promotion has tended to be *better focused*—in *brand names, specific products,* and *competitive prices.* K Mart's Garden Center ads display *a complete array* of seasonal lawn care products—from plant food to marble chips for landscaping. Each item is clearly featured in the sale package, with its brand name prominently displayed. Individual prices are listed in bold, black numerals. . .and the word "sale" appears *only* for applicable items.

Inattention to productivity, fewer price concessions, and customer demand for greater services hiked discounters' expenses. The emphasis in the 1970s was on physical expansion, but little capital was spent on maintaining and implementing support systems. In the 1980s, reduced inflation, new competitive formats, proliferating discount stores, and greater demands on consumers' time caused customers to demand better service, a more attractive ambiance, and more sophisticated merchandise. During this decade, retailing ranged from no-frill warehouses selling brand name general merchandise to customers at lower prices to specialty stores offering a narrow product focus.

Present and Future Trends

Hypermarkets. Hypermarkets, a new concept in retailing, range from 200,000 to 325,000 square feet (that is, three and a half to five football fields). To give an idea of their immensity, the conventional supermarket is only about 30,000 to 35,000 square feet.

Pricing Affects advertising. Some discounters use a pricing strategy of "low everyday prices," that is, the prices of their products seldom change. Others depend on promotional pricing.

---

[2]Martha L. Kimball, "Shake-out Time for Discount Department Stores," *Rab Sound Management,* January 1988, pp. 16–17.

The first category of discounter rarely has sales and does little advertising. These discounters' appeal to consumers is based on the fact that a basket of goods at their outlets will cost less than the same basket of goods at a promotional discounter. Promotional discounters, in contrast, rely on the proposition that "Americans love a good sale." They try to attract customers by offering high savings on certain items, hoping to boost store profits by selling those same customers higher-profit-margin products.

New Formulas for Profit

Retailers are looking to successful competitors for guidance—for example, Nordstrom and Wal-Mart Stores. Although these two retailers are at the opposite ends of the retailing spectrum, both have built their reputations and success on giving consumers service and value. Therefore, other retailers are rushing to copy their formulas, although this may not by the key to success.

Reasons Consumers Patronize a Store

According to a 1989 comprehensive study by Impact Resources, service is not the primary reason shoppers frequent a particular store. Rather, the primary motivations in selecting one store over another are price, selection, and quality, in that order (see Exhibit 23.1).

EXHIBIT 23.1

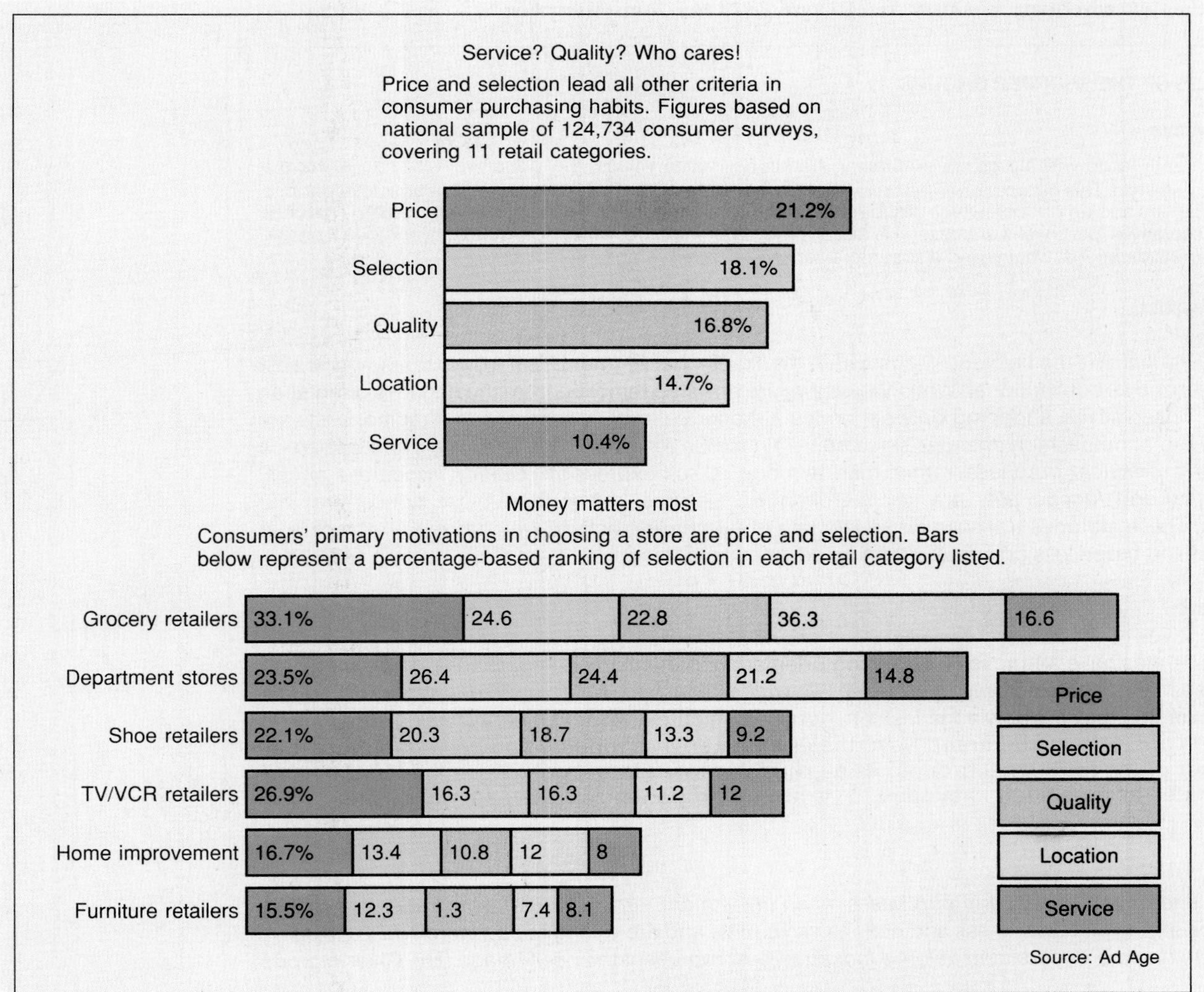

By giving customers "what they want"—*price, service, or quality*—retailers, such as Nordstrom and Wal-Mart have used different appeals in their promotional strategies, but nevertheless, each has been very successful in their respective markets. While Nordstrom is striving for the upscale consumer, Wal-Mart's ads appeal to the bargain-hunter. Nonetheless, consumers rate Wal-Mart *high* in being particularly adept at convincing customers that its prices are *low*, without making people feel that its stores are "too cheap." "The *vests* that Wal-Mart employees wear convey a knowledgeable image—but not too 'snooty' to be interrupted for a question or advice," revealed Chicago-based research firm Leo J. Shapiro & Associates.

Service, however, can function as "tie-breaker" between retailers that already have good prices, selection, and quality. The key reason Nordstrom and Wal-Mart have such excellent reputations is that they have figured out what their customers want and then they give it to them. Nordstrom customers say they place greater importance on the depth and quality of merchandise, whereas Wal-Mart attracts primarily blue-collar, lower income, and less-educated customers who appreciate the chain's biggest attributes: service, price, and location.

A Marketing Emphasis

Retailers are increasingly turning to marketing and marketing research to compete in this new retail environment. The National Retail Merchants Association points out the importance of an organized marketing strategy for retailers:

> Because customers are motivated in their purchases by lifestyle as well as value/price considerations, this has resulted in the segmentation of shoppers according to attitudes, forcing retailers to make clearer distinctions between such segments in their assortments, point-of-sale presentation and advertising.

The NRMA demonstrates the importance of this lifestyle motivation of consumers with its Profiles of the Shopper Groups (see Exhibit 23.2).

EXHIBIT 23.2

The use of detailed consumer profiles is but one more examples of the growing sophistication of retail marketing and advertising. (Courtesy: The National Retail Merchants Association.)

PROFILES OF THE SHOPPER GROUPS

Conservative

Predominantly a downscale group embracing traditional social values, the Conservatives tend to have a sedentary lifestyle. This group is oriented toward **functional, rather than fashion apparel,** due both to economic circumstances and an outlook which discounts apparel as an important means of self-expression. Therefore the Conservatives' purchases are based on **need rather than impulse**, with price, durability and quality being primary considerations. Chains and discounters generate above average interest.

Traditionalist

The Traditionalist is the tie/blend group within the Traditional segment. Its shopping behavior is best characterized as conventional. While their views are one step removed from the negative orientation of the Conservatives, shopping only generates a moderate level of enthusiasm. Traditionalists are reluctant to adopt fashion changes since they *do not wish to appear different.* Therefore, *apparel is seen as a practical purchase* rather than a mode of self-expression. *Quality, moderate prices, wearability and functionality* are key merchandise features, rather than those concerned with fashion. These attitudes translate into a low rate of purchasing activity which is more replacement oriented and based less on impulse than on advanced planning.

Moderate

The Moderates have a functional shopping orientation, particularly in regard to apparel, with such purchases being initiated *only after a trend is well established.* Moderates truly represent Middle America in that they acknowledge fashion, but in their context, *fashion means making sure they do not stand out as being different.* Nevertheless, they *enjoy shopping and browsing* more than any other of the traditional groups. As a group they are budget conscious; hence the name "Moderate" and, as such, they tend to be strong proponents of the national chains.

Classic

Classic shoppers *view apparel purchases as an investment rather than a fashion statement.* They evidence strong self-awareness and definite viewpoints and are willing to *pay more and go to some trouble to find the understated tailored looks*that best represent their self-image. The Classic group tends to be loyal to stores which have *merchandise that embodies their viewpoint* and are the most responsive to *service.* While Classics tend to buy at department stores rather than chains or discount stores, nationally advertised apparel brands are of little interest. Most Classics exercise moderate purchase activity, plan their purchases, and show little interest in sale merchandise.

Transitionalist

The Transitionalist group is the tie group *bridging the gap* between the functionally-oriented Traditional segment and the more fashion-prone Contemporary. These shoppers' attitudes and behavior are in a state of flux as they subscribe equally to both sets of values.

Young Contemporary

The Young Contemporary is distinguished attitudinally from other Contemporary groups by a pattern of *fashion emulation,* rather than leadership. Fashion standards for this group are those associated with high-profile personalities who are accorded recognition by their peers. *Clothes are an important means of self-expression* and of showing others *"I'm with it".* These shoppers are very aware of the latest fashion trends and *wish to be among the first* to be associated with them. Quality is of little importance to a Young Contemporary who becomes bored when apparel is kept too long. They are enthusiastic shoppers, browsers and impulsive buyers. This group has characteristically been an age/size classification.

Update

Updates have an active lifestyle *requiring apparel which expresses their individuality,* but is also functional and appropriate to their variety of activities. While Updates *gravitate toward new fashion trends, they do not seek to be pacesetters* or to buy for the sake of fashion alone. Being self-assured, they display a willingness to experiment with apparel, and do so by *blending classic styles with more advanced forward fashion.* Price and merchandise quality rank lower than fashion appropriateness. While favoring department stores, Updates also frequent small specialty stores and boutiques. Their *high economic value,* based on generally upscale demographics and high rate of purchase activity, makes the Update group a prime target shopper group for upscale department and specialty stores.

Contemporary

The Contemporary shopper group is the tie group within the Contemporary segment, *blending characteristics* of the Young Contemporary, Update and Advanced in a pattern that remains to be defined for this particular market.

Advanced

Representing the most forward position on the fashion attitude spectrum, the Advanced group is composed of the market's *fashion pacesetters.* By anticipating trends, this usually youthful and affluent group has the *confidence and desire to assemble and then introduce new looks.* Advanced shoppers frequent offbeat and small apparel specialty stores. They are impulsive shoppers employing apparel and accessories as a means of expressing their viewpoint, and their prime purchasing consideration is the *ability of merchandise items to make the desired fashion statement.*

Retailers expect the local media vehicles to clearly define their audiences. Newspapers are particularly aware of the need to provide in-depth readership data. They also recognize the importance of relating this readership data to the local retail community. In the future we will definitely see a much greater used of media-generated marketing research in making retail advertising decisions (see Exhibits 23.3 and 23.4).

Perhaps the most used and potentially most beneficial retail research device is the Universal Product Code (UPC). The UPC, developed by IBM and in use since 1974, is on virtually every package-goods product and is expanding into other product categories at a rapid pace. Originally intended to speed up the checking out of customers and to aid in inventory control, it has become an important research tool over the last decade or so. The scanner can determine exactly when and where products are bought.

EXHIBIT 23.3

(Courtesy: Atlanta Constitution and Atlanta Journal.)

DEPARTMENT STORE SHOPPERS

30-DAY PERIOD

Atlanta has a variety of major department stores; several with multiple locations. Over a 30-day period, 1,571,000 Atlanta adults, or 82% shop at one or more of these department stores. The most-shopped is Rich's, with 1,082,000 shoppers.

Atlanta's department store shoppers are among the best readers of the Journal-Constitution. Over four Sundays, 86% have read one or more issues.

And they use Journal-Constitution advertising to make shopping decisions Some 1,160,000 adults, 74% of all department store shoppers, check Journal-Constitution ads before shopping.

Store	No. of Locations	No. of Shoppers	% of Adults
▶ JCPenney	6	668,000	35%
Lord & Taylor	1	97,000	5
Macy's	10	1,045,000	54
Mervyn's	6	349,000	18
Neiman-Marcus	1	137,000	7
Rich's	12	1,082,000	56
Saks Fifth Avenue	1	85,000	4
Sears	7	794,000	41
Uptons	8	289,000	15

▶ HOW TO READ THE CHART:
JCPenney has 668,000 adult shoppers in a 30-day period, or 35% of all Atlanta adults. Note: These totals include only major department store locations.

Retailers rely on local media to have researched their readership and listenership for *target market information*. The *Tampa Bay Business Journal* publishes *The Book of Lists,* which provides the local business community with company names, products made and sold, names of principals, total sales, etc., for business-to-business marketing. Subscribers to the weekly newspaper receive the annual supplement free of charge—which also carries ads, in color and black-and-white.

Sometimes consumer panels are used in conjunction with the scanner so that product purchases can be correlated with consumer demographics and media usage.

DIFFERENCES BETWEEN NATIONAL AND RETAIL ADVERTISING

National advertising. *Advertising by the marketer of a trademarked product or service sold through different outlets, in contrast to* retail advertising.

National advertising is chiefly done by a marketer to get people to buy the marketer's branded goods wherever they are sold. *Retail advertising* is done by local merchants or service organizations to attract customers—in person, by mail, or by telephone—to buy the goods and services they have to offer.

Some firms do both national and retail advertising. The outstanding example is Sears, which produces and advertises goods under its own name and trademark and is one of the largest users of national advertising; but its numerous stores advertise under the Sears name in their communities and thus are local advertisers. Many franchise operations, like the McDonald's fast-food restaurants, use national advertising to get neighborhood business. That both kinds of advertising are sometimes used by a single firm should not obscure the basic differences between the two. In national advertising, the manufacturer says: "Buy this brand product at any store." The retail advertiser says: "Buy this product here. Better come early!"

In order to generate traffic, retailers usually advertise a *variety* of products/services—unlike national advertisers who promote "their own." Drug chains, like Walgreens, use color tabloid inserts to "stand out"—in featuring a large amount of O-T-C drugs, food items, and sundries. While the front page contains name brands, inside sheets carry a high proportion of the company's private label merchandise.

In national advertising, it is difficult to trace the sales effect of a single insertion of an ad. Even tracing the effect of a series of ads takes time and is hard unless the series runs exclusively in one medium. In retail advertising, on the hand, an advertiser can usually tell by noon of the day after an ad appeared how effective it is.

National advertisers speak to a wide and distant audience. Retail advertisers appeal to the local community. They know these people, their lifestyles, their tastes; they know who is likely to be in the market for new home furnishings or whether home computers are likely to be desirable in this area.

Typically, the national advertiser has one product or one line of products to sell at a time. The retailer is faced by a relentless river of new styles and offerings to sell within a week, generating a great sense of urgency in the advertising department. Retail advertising is definitely fast tempo.

In the future, the distinction between national and local advertising at the retail level will become less clear-cut. As more local retail outlets become part of chains and holding companies, we will see a greater coordination of advertising strategy, if not actual preparation of the ads, at the national level.

		Atlanta Adults	% of Adults	RICH'S SHOPPERS No. of Shoppers	RICH'S SHOPPERS % of Shoppers	RICH'S SHOPPERS % of Demographic Segment	LORD & TAYLOR SHOPPERS No. of Shoppers	LORD & TAYLOR SHOPPERS % of Shoppers	LORD & TAYLOR SHOPPERS % of Demographic Segment	MACY'S SHOPPERS No. of Shoppers	MACY'S SHOPPERS % of Shoppers	MACY'S SHOPPERS % of Demographic Segment
TOTAL ADULTS		1,924,000	100 %	1,082,000	100 %	56 %	97,000	100 %	5 %	1,045,000	100 %	54 %
SEX	Male	908,000	47 %	468,000	43 %	52 %	31,000	32 %	3 %	423,000	40 %	46 %
	Female	1,016,000	53	614,000	57	61	66,000	68	6	622,000	60	61
HOUSEHOLD INCOME	Under $15,000	260,000	13 %	97,000	9 %	37 %	10,000	11 %	4 %	63,000	6 %	24 %
	$15,000-$19,999	117,000	6	55,000	5	47	4,000	4	3	49,000	5	42
	$20,000-$24,999	124,000	6	72,000	7	58	4,000	3	3	72,000	7	58
	$25,000-$34,999	403,000	21	206,000	19	51	11,000	12	3	209,000	20	52
	$35,000-$49,999	491,000	26	297,000	27	60	20,000	21	4	296,000	28	60
	$50,000-$74,999	345,000	18	230,000	21	67	18,000	18	5	225,000	21	65
	$75,000 & over	184,000	10	125,000	12	68	30,000	31	16	131,000	13	71
▶ **AGE**	18-24	275,000	14 %	177,000	16 %	64 %	15,000	16 %	6 %	177,000	17 %	64 %
	25-34	533,000	28	298,000	28	56	29,000	29	5	295,000	28	55
	35-44	446,000	23	261,000	24	59	27,000	28	6	266,000	26	60
	45-54	249,000	13	138,000	13	56	11,000	12	5	129,000	12	52
	55-64	201,000	10	104,000	10	52	12,000	12	6	94,000	9	47
	65 & over	220,000	12	104,000	9	47	3,000	3	1	84,000	8	38
RACE	White	1,446,000	75 %	822,000	76 %	57 %	75,000	77 %	5 %	810,000	78 %	56 %
	Nonwhite	478,000	25	260,000	24	54	22,000	23	5	235,000	22	49
EDUCATION	Part H.S. or less	492,000	26 %	189,000	18 %	38 %	9,000	9 %	2 %	188,000	18 %	38 %
	High School Graduate	658,000	34	364,000	33	55	16,000	17	2	329,000	32	50
	Part College	376,000	19	249,000	23	66	25,000	26	7	241,000	23	64
	College Graduate	246,000	13	170,000	16	69	28,000	28	11	170,000	16	69
	Post Graduate	152,000	8	110,000	10	72	19,000	20	12	117,000	11	77
OCCUPATION	White-Collar	841,000	44 %	563,000	52 %	67 %	61,000	63 %	7 %	582,000	56 %	69 %
	Blue-Collar	337,000	17	139,000	13	41	7,000	7	2	116,000	11	34
	Other Employed	185,000	10	81,000	7	44	8,000	8	4	79,000	7	43
	Homemakers	209,000	11	128,000	12	61	10,000	10	5	115,000	11	55
	Not Employed	352,000	18	171,000	16	49	11,000	12	3	153,000	15	44
MARITAL STATUS	Married	1,147,000	60 %	682,000	63 %	60 %	59,000	61 %	5 %	635,000	61 %	55 %
	Single	406,000	21	244,000	23	60	26,000	27	6	248,000	24	61
	Other	371,000	19	156,000	14	42	12,000	12	3	162,000	15	44
HOME OWNERSHIP	Own	1,294,000	67 %	770,000	71 %	60 %	66,000	68 %	5 %	722,000	69 %	56 %
	Rent	630,000	33	312,000	29	49	31,000	32	5	323,000	31	51
TYPE OF DWELLING	Single Family Unit	1,357,000	70 %	796,000	74 %	59 %	68,000	70 %	5 %	743,000	71 %	55 %
	Multifamily Unit	567,000	30	286,000	26	50	29,000	30	5	302,000	29	53

▶ **HOW TO READ THE CHART:**
Of the 1,082,000 adults who shop at Rich's, 298,000 or 28% are 25-34. This total represents 56% of all Atlantans in this age group.

EXHIBIT 23.4

(Courtesy: Atlanta Journal and Atlanta Constitution.)

TYPES OF RETAIL ADVERTISING

Retail advertising is as diverse as the establishments that use it. However, there are certain patterns of retail advertising that reflect the character and goals of various retailers. The Newspaper Advertising Bureau has suggested six categories of retail advertising:[3]

Institutional advertising. *That done by an organization speaking of its work, views, and problems as a whole, to gain public goodwill and support rather than sell a specific product. Sometimes called* public relations advertising.

Highly promotional ads encourage large sales volume and traffic counts—such as those of discounters. *Builders' Square*—in an effort to get a day's jump on Home Depot—distributes its "value booklet" in morning newspapers on Wednesdays. Current sale prices are "guaranteed" for *one week only*—on "100's of items, 1000's of ideas." Every featured item carries a *large* price "tag," and comparison price shopping is encouraged. The impression created? You know what you want *before* you get there—and if you hurry, you'll get *the quantity and the lowest price imaginable!*

1. *Promotional.* Here the emphasis is on sales and high sale volume at a reduced price. Discount stores such as K Mart are the primary users of this type of advertising.
2. *Semipromotional.* In this type of advertising, sale offerings are interspersed with many regular-priced items. Most department stores and supermarkets use this advertising strategy.
3. *Nonpromotional.* Many small shops and specialty stores adopt a no-sale advertising strategy. Their advertising plays down price and emphasizes dignified appeals featuring the quality of the merchandise and the expertise of their sales staffs.
4. *Assortment ads.* The intent of these ads is to show the large variety of products. The ads have an institutional aspect in that they promote the store as a place for one-stop shopping.
5. *Omnibus ads.* Though similar to assortment ads, omnibus ads are usually more clearly sales oriented. These ads may feature related items or a variety of nonrelated items for several departments.
6. *Institutional ads.* Many stores use advertising that emphasizes their unique character. Institutional ads must be careful to tell a story of importance to a store's customers.

Retail Business Cycles

Retailers' selling cycles vary according to the product or service category. Exhibit 23.5 shows that menswear stores' biggest sales month is December; restaurants' best months are July and August; beer sales are strongest in May and July; and more than a third of jewelry store sales occur in November and December. Retailers can use this kind of information in planning their advertising.

Sales and Media Promotions

Everyone is familiar with such retail special promotion times as Christmas, George Washington's birthday, and Father's Day, but there are many, many more opportunities, including National Anti-Boredom Month, Man Watcher's Compliment Week,

EXHIBIT 23.5
Advertiser's Seasonal Business Cycles.

	Jan.	*Feb.*	*Mar.*	*Apr.*	*May*	*Jun.*	*July*	*Aug.*	*Sept.*	*Oct.*	*Nov.*	*Dec.*
All stores & services (%)	7.2	6.9	7.9	8.1	8.6	8.4	8.4	8.7	8.4	8.5	8.5	10.4
Auto dealers, domestic	6.8	7.2	8.3	8.6	9.0	8.9	8.9	9.1	9.6	8.2	7.3	8.1
Auto dealers, import	7.0	6.8	7.6	7.5	8.7	8.6	9.4	9.2	8.8	8.8	8.2	9.4
Beer	7.7	7.4	8.4	9.0	9.6	9.3	9.6	9.0	7.9	8.1	7.0	7.0
Camera stores	7.5	6.8	7.4	7.4	8.0	8.6	8.5	8.3	8.3	8.1	8.0	13.0
Drug stores	7.8	7.4	8.0	8.0	8.3	8.1	8.2	8.3	7.9	8.4	8.3	11.4
Fast food	7.3	6.9	8.1	8.2	8.7	8.7	9.1	9.3	8.3	8.7	8.2	8.5
Jewelry stores	5.6	6.3	6.2	6.3	8.0	6.9	6.4	7.1	6.7	7.4	9.3	23.7
Menswear stores	6.5	5.8	7.1	7.9	8.4	8.1	6.9	7.7	7.3	8.4	9.7	16.3
Movie theaters	7.8	7.5	7.2	8.1	7.4	11.4	12.3	10.0	6.5	6.4	6.8	8.6
Restaurants	7.4	7.1	8.1	8.3	8.8	8.7	9.0	9.2	8.3	8.7	8.1	8.4
Shoe stores	6.6	6.2	8.6	8.8	8.6	8.0	7.2	9.3	8.4	8.3	8.6	11.5
Tire dealers	8.1	6.9	6.6	5.6	6.6	7.5	9.8	9.5	9.8	9.0	8.3	12.1
Women's wear stores	6.4	7.8	7.9	8.2	7.4	8.5	7.5	8.5	8.1	8.7	9.4	13.9

[3] *The I-Wonder-How-to-Set-Up-an-Advertising-Program-and-How-Much-to-Budget Book,* Newspaper Advertising Bureau.

National Library Week, National Singles Week, Pancake Day, Be Late for Something Day, Comedy Celebration Day, and National Pie Day. In the month of May, we normally think of Mother's Day and Memorial Day as retailer promotion periods. Exhibit 23.6 shows a broader range of promotional opportunities for the month of May. Yes, all of these are real special recognition periods for a worthy cause, special interest, or appreciation.

THE RETAIL ADVERTISING MIX

***Target marketing.** Identifying and communicating with groups of prime prospects.*

Like other styles of advertising, retail advertising must (1) determine overall goals and objectives of the marketing and advertising programs, (2) identify target markets, and (3) develop a copy and media strategy to reach these targets. But the way in which retail advertising strategy is carried out differs markedly from that in which national advertising (which we discussed earlier) is carried out.

A retail advertising campaign usually includes media other than newspapers. Radio advertising is used frequently with great success because it is reasonable in cost and easy to produce, and can be changed within hours if necessary. TV is also used more frequently now, although not as often as radio. And many successful campaigns use brochures and catalogs. Frequently, the catalogs are distributed with Sunday newspapers.

Selecting local media is a ''How best to . . . ?'' problem: how best to use newspapers, radio, TV, direct mail—the chief media—alone or in combination to sell merchandise and attract store traffic.

Newspapers in Retailing

While newspapers occupy the greater portion of most retailers' ad budgets, the advertiser is usually *selective* in placing the ads, according to zip code information and sectional opportunities. Most large city newspapers have *regional sections* for neighborhood news—local merchants in Pinellas County/North concentrate their advertising in the section of the *Tampa Tribune,* which exclusively caters to *county news*. Typical advertisers are *restaurants* with purely local ''ties,'' such as *Papa Joe's*.

The days when retail and newspaper advertising were synonomous are over—retailers today use a wide variety of media. Still, newspapers remain the primary local advertising vehicle and newspaper advertising accounts for over 30 percent of all local advertising expenditures. In addition, most research has indicated that both retailers and consumers regard newspapers as the prime medium for local advertising. Newspapers with hold their preeminent position for the foreseeable future, though they face increasing competition from other media, especially broadcast.

To meet the competitive challenge, newspapers are turning to direct mail's strategic selling tool—the ZIP code. Advertisers and agencies can obtain custom newspaper ZIP/postal code circulation reports through the Audit Bureau of Circulations' Data Bank. Retailers employ the newspaper ZIP information not only to target their best customers and make more efficient media buys, but also to locate sites for new outlets

EXHIBIT 23.6

Some promotion events during the month of May.

American Bike Month
Be Kind to Animals Week
Better Sleep Month
Foot Health Month
Better Hearing Month
National Arthritis Month
National Barbecue Month
National High Blood Pressure Month
National Decorating Month
National Physical Fitness and Sports Month
Senior Citizens Month
National Nurses' Day
Astronomy Week
National Health Week
National Hospital Week
National Pet Week
National Wildflower Week
Jewish Heritage Month
Mother's Day
Girls' Club Week
National Historic Preservation Week
National Tourism Week
National Transportation Week
Visit Your Relatives Day
National Shoe Week
International Pickle Week
Memorial Day

and analyze sales performance in existing ones. Most major newspapers offer a number of zones for preprint advertisers to select from in tailoring an advertising program to specific targets.

People normally think of newspaper advertising primarily as ads in certain sections of the paper—sports, editorial, fashion, classified—but there are other advertising opportunities. In many major markets, an advertiser can buy suburban editions that reach select counties or communities. For example, the *Atlanta Journal* and *Constitution* offers *EXTRA* to advertisers—four tabloid-size community newspapers distributed in Cobb and Dekalb counties, North Fulton County, and in-town Atlanta with eight different advertising zones. *EXTRA* is circulated with both the Thursday *Atlanta Constitution* and *Atlanta Journal*. Combined advertising and editorial ''special sections'' are published at intervals throughout the year to promote special interests. In 1989, the first Retail Advertising Conference's survey of its 380 retail members found that the average member spent 55 percent of its advertising budget on newspapers (see Exhibit 23.7).

Radio in Retailing

Radio, because of its *flexibility* and *immediacy*, can assist a successful retail campaign. *Car dealers* often rely on *radio commercials* to supplement their newspaper ads. *Bradenton Volvo's* radio commercial features one of their ''super values''—from a list of immediately available cars in their Sunday, full-page ad. By being able to alternate specific sale items on a *daily* basis, they can keep their radio audience current on what's *still* available.

Local advertising is an extremely important segment of the radio market; of the $7.7 billion spent in radio ad dollars during 1986, $5.9 billion was local. Local radio sales growth was 8 percent from 1987 to 1988.

Radio earns high marks among advertisers for flexibility in spot scheduling. Promotions are another area where radio is strong. It is a good reminder medium, with immediacy as its strong point. Retailers can be very creative with radio. For example, Drive-Up radio provides a retailer with low-power transmitter that broadcasts the advertiser's message and a station tag on a continuous-loop cassette. Signs or billboards alert drivers to hear the message on their car radios. It is sold as part of a radio marketing plan to achieve specific goals. Hardee's installed Drive-Up transmitters at its restaurants in some markets to encourage impulse buying. Drive-Up radio has been particularly successful in real estate promotions.

EXHIBIT 23.7

Retail Advertising Conference Members' Expenditures. (Courtesy: Advertising Age.)

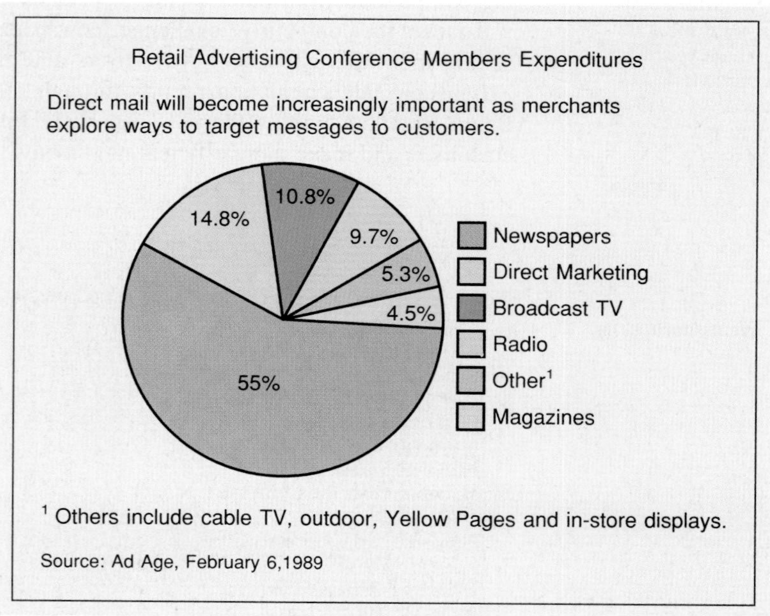

Television in Retailing

Even *small retailers* are finding decided advantages of TV, especially cable networks. *Northwood Chiropractic Center* used to use newspaper inserts as their only advertising vehicle. . . They've found that cable spots during midday and late at night brought in "significant additional clients," stated head doctor, Russel Janssen. "We couldn't demonstrate very well in ads or show off our new, modern offices. . ."

Television made impressive gains in the retail sector during the 1980s. In 1987, local TV advertising passed spot TV in terms of share of total dollars spent in the medium. Currently, local TV advertising is above the $7 billion mark, and predictions are that it will overtake network TV advertising early in the 1990s.

The infusion of retail advertising dollars into local TV has been a result of the growth of independent TV stations and cable outlets. These media offer retailers the creative advantages of TV, a segmented audience targeted to their businesses, and a cost within the reach of even smaller retailers. Spots on both independent stations and local cable are often in the $20–$50 range.

Cable television is the fastest-growing media segment in retail advertising. In 1987, local cable had local sales of $203 million, which increased to $250 million in 1988. This growth has been aided by the spot-buy availabilities on cable networks. The larger cable networks such as ESPN, CNN, and USA offer time to local advertisers, usually at prices significantly lower than those quoted by broadcast stations in the same markets. Even though the CPM figure is generally higher for these cable spots, the actual cost is within the budgets of even small retailers.

Direct Response in Retailing

Direct response advertising, for today's retailers, means using the mail, the telephone, and print and broadcast media—to generate leads or to sell merchandise/services directly to respondents. *Medical care organizations* are discovering that "crisis lines" make responses easier for respondents. Newspaper ads for the *First Hospital Corporation-CompCare Crisis Line* routinely carry "800" or "24-hour" telephone numbers—for "help," consultation, and support groups.

Retailers have long recognized the advantages of direct-mail advertising to promote special sales or reach a specific segment of their customers. Retail direct mail uses various formats, from a postcard to a multipage advertising tabloid.

In addition to traditional direct-mail advertising, retailers are beginning to experiment with new technology in their direct-response promotions. One of the most recent innovations is the video shopping service, in which cable subscribers pay an annual fee for the opportunity to buy discounted merchandise shown on a special shopping-service channel.

Despite the potential of direct response and new technology, direct mail and mail-order catalogs remain the major methods of retail direct response. By the late 1800s, many companies had entered the mail-order field, including Sears & Roebuck and Montgomery Ward. Today a single company such as Horchow will send out multiple catalogs, each aimed at a particular psychographic group. We are also seeing a crossover between mail-order and in-store selling. Retailers are increasingly using catalogs, and direct-mail and catalog sellers such as Eddie Bauer are establishing retail outlets.

Mail-order purchases are covered by the Federal Trade Commission's Mail Order Rule. Under this rule, companies are required to ship the customer's order within the time promised in their advertisement. If no time period is promised, the company must either ship the order within 30 days after it receives it or send an option notice telling the customer there will be a shipping delay and offering the alternative of agreeing to the delay or canceling the order and receiving a prompt refund.

One of the fastest-growing areas of direct marketing is direct-response television advertising. Its purpose is to stimulate product orders or inquiries directly from the viewer. Advertisers know exactly what they are selling in each market, on each station, the next day. Many of these ads use 800 phone numbers, which appeals to consumers who don't like to write out order forms. The first quarter (January–March) is a particularly effective time to use direct-response TV because the large audiences give greater efficiencies. The third quarter (July–September), which has lighter viewership, is often used to test commercials. "Passive" programming, such as movies, dramas, and certain syndicated shows, pull more responses than shows in which viewers are more actively involved, such as sports programs and newscasts.

Associated Financial Services Company developed Moneylink, an easy-to-use service that enables customers to apply for loans by phone. Its key benefit is convenience;

it significantly reduces red tape. The primary objective of the direct-response TV campaign was to generate Moneylink leads by phone (ads used an 800 number). The company had three secondary objectives: to process applications cost effectively over an 800 exchange while simultaneously screening applicants ; to covert a high percentage of leads into real estate loan customers; and to establish new relationships with potential customers. An initial test was conducted with local stations in 10 markets using about 15 commercials a week. Over 5,500 leads were generated, 450 loans were closed, and $2.5 million was borrowed. Associated had set a cost-per-lead goal of $70–$100. Moneylink's direct-response television campaign resulted in a cost per lead of $10–$15.

COOPERATIVE ADVERTISING

Cooperative advertising. *(1) Joint promotion of a national advertiser (manufacturer) and local retail outlet on behalf of the manufacturer's product on sale in the retail store. (2) Joint promotion through a trade association for firms in a single industry. (3) Advertising venture jointly conducted by two or more advertisers.*

Manufacturers wanting local exposure and local advertising rates ofttimes will offer *cooperative advertising* allowance to retailers. "Hot" appliance/hard goods retailer, *Circuit City*, features name brand items, such as *Sony*. Their ads for the internationally known brand are partly paid by the manufacturer—in order to get "featured" and "expert" local exposure with a "premium" retailing outlet.

We have already discussed cooperative advertising allowances from the manufacturer's point of view. Here we will review some of its features from the store's viewpoint. Cooperative advertising is so important in retailing that in some departments it may run as high as 50 percent of total advertising expenditures.

Chief advantages:

- Cooperative advertising helps the buyer stretch his or her advertising capability.
- It may provide good artwork of the product advertised, with good copy—which is especially important to the small store (see Exhibit 23.8).
- It helps the store earn a better volume discount for all its advertising.

Cooperative advertising works best when the line is highly regarded and is either a style or some other kind of leader in its field.

Chief disadvantages:

- Although the store pays only 50 percent of the cost, that sum may be disproportionate for the amount of sales and profit the store realizes.
- Most manufacturers' ads emphasize the brand name at the expense of the store name.

Manufacturers' ads cannot have the community flavor and style of store ads. To localize co-op advertising, some retailers, instead of accepting manufacturer-produced ads, incorporate manufacturer-supplied product information into an ad that conforms to their own advertising style.

Retail stores get far more offers co-op advertising than they can possibly use. Acceptance depends on the importance of the product to the store.

For newspaper advertising, the store sends the vendor a tearsheet of its ad, as evidence that the ad ran, together with its bill for the vendor's share of the cost. Since there are no tearsheets for radio and TV advertising, a special form has been adopted to assure the vendor that the commercials ran as scheduled. Designed by the Association of National Advertisers, the Radio Advertising Bureau, and the Television Bureau of Advertising, it combines in one form the commercial script, the bill, and an affidavit to be signed by the station. A copy of this form is sent to the vendor, who then can be sure that the commercial was broadcast as stated on the form containing the station's affidavit. All stores that do cooperative broadcast advertising use such a form. This dependability in billing has undoubtedly led to the greatly increased volume of TV and radio department store advertising.

There is so much paperwork involved in using cooperative advertising that most stores have a business department inside their advertising department to make sure the store collects all the money due it.

Holland On-The-Double

For a Weekend

Including Airfare & Top Quality Hotels

3 Days/2 Nights in Amsterdam Prices per person based on double occupancy	
Hotel	Golden Tulip Barbizon Palace**
Departure From	
New York	$441*
Chicago	$491*
Atlanta	$491*
Houston	$561*
Los Angeles	$581*
Orlando	$491*
Anchorage	$661*

**Special grand opening rates apply at the 5-Star, deluxe Golden Tulip Barbizon Palace.

Package Includes:
- Round-trip Transatlantic Air Transportation
- The Amsterdam Passport
- Hotel Service Charges and Taxes

Note:
Package not available during holiday blackout period December 11-24, 1988.
*For details and conditions see your travel agent.

Ad Slicks

These easy to understand ad slicks can be used in your agency's newsletter, as a shopping mall hand-out or in direct mail to your client's home or office.

ONE FOURTH PAGE AD SLICK (4″ × 5″)

ONE HALF PAGE AD SLICK (5″ × 8″)

Holland On-The-Double

For a Week

Including Airfare & Top Quality Hotels

7 Days/6 Nights in Amsterdam Prices per person based on double occupancy	
Hotel	Golden Tulip Barbizon Palace**
Departure From	
New York	$575*
Chicago	$625*
Atlanta	$665*
Houston	$695*
Los Angeles	$755*
Orlando	$675*
Anchorage	$805*

**Special grand opening rates apply at the 5-Star, deluxe Golden Tulip Barbizon Palace.

Package Includes:
- Round-trip Transatlantic Air Transportation
- The Amsterdam Passport
- Hotel Service Charges and Taxes

Note:
Package not available during holiday blackout period December 11-24, 1988.
*For details and conditions see your travel agent.

The Reliable Airline KLM Royal Dutch Airlines

EXHIBIT 23.8

Advertiser furnishes these Ad Slicks for use by travel agents—they may or may not be apart of co-op. (Courtesy: KLM/Promotion Solutions, Inc.)

CASE HISTORY

Dayton Hudson's Santabear Promotion

Santabear was first introduced by Dayton Hudson as a purchase incentive during the 1985 Christmas season. For every $50 total purchase, customers could receive Santabear—a $25 value—for only $10. Between November 11 and Thanksgiving, 400,000 Santabears were sold.

In 1986, 1.5 million Santabears were sold, and 200,000 more were given away through the Salvation Army.

By Christmas season of 1987, Dayton Hudson faced two challenges:

1. With other retailers copying the bear promotion, Santabear had to be positioned as the one and only holiday bear.
2. Santabear had to be unique in order to attract new customers and to get current Santabear owners to buy another bear.

Here's how Dayton Hudson met these challenges:

- Santabear was given an exciting new costume, a red flight jacket and helmet, which were designed by a costume designer with the Guthrie Theater and Dayton Hudson's Product Development department.
- Miss Bear, a new plush character, was introduced.
- Customers could receive a "super purchase-with-purchase": Santabear, Miss Bear, and a cardboard airplane container were available for $50 with any $100 purchase. Customers also had the option of buying each separately for $15 with any $50 purchase.
- 160 Santabear-related products ($8.8 million worth) were developed and sold.
- A Santabear press kit featuring a moving airplane propeller was put out. It won an IABC Merit Award.
- Store managers were invited to a Santabear kickoff meeting by way of a wood glider invitation, and the auditorium was transformed into the interior of a jumbo jet.
- Miss Bear was introduced to Twin Cities media at a "Debeartante Tea."
- Santabear and Miss Bear were introduced to Minneapolis society at the second annual Crystal Ball in the Crystal Court of the IDS Center.
- A CBS animated TV special and related book—*Santabear's*

EXHIBIT A

Santabear in new costume with new character, Miss Bear.

EXHIBIT B

Santabear and Miss Bear in their cardboard airplane, "Super Purchase-with-Purchase."

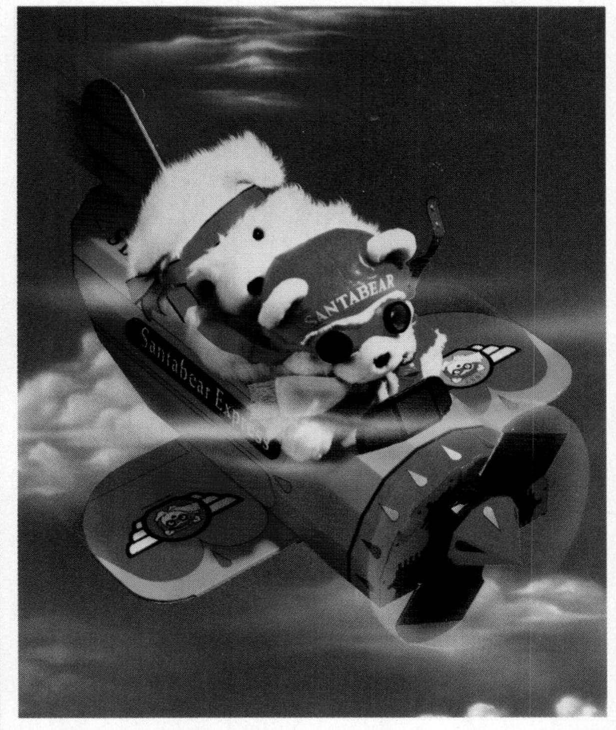

EXHIBIT C

Public Relations effort about the 160 private label Santabear products and quote from Child Psychologist about psycho-sympatico of Santabear.

SANTABEAR PRIVATE LABEL PRODUCTS

The following list is a sampling of the 160 Santabear private label products available at Dayton's and Hudson's department stores.

SANTABEAR'S HIGH-FLYING ADVENTURE ITEMS

- *Miss Bear plush - $30.00
- *Santabear plush - $30.00
- *Cardboard airplane - $20.00
- Santabear's High-Flying Adventure book - $12.99
- Santabear's High-Flying Adventure video - $14.99
- Santabear's High-Flying Adventure book and cassette - $14.99
- Miss Bear's costumes (3) - $9.99 each

GIFTS AND TOYS

- *Santabear waterglobe - $30.00
- *Santabear wreath - $18.00
- *Santabear tree skirt - $45.00
- *Santabear ice scraper - $12.00
- Santabear wall clock - $19.99
- *Santabear Christmas tree ornaments - $2.50 - $9.00

HOME

- Juvenile flannel sheet set, allover Santabear design - $30.00 set
- *Santabear cookie jar - $12.50
- *Santabear glasses - set of 4, $10.00

FOOD

- *Santabear cookies - box of 8 for $6.50

MEN'S

- Allover print brief - $5.00

WOMEN'S

- String bikini, allover Santabear design - $4.00
- Long john sleep shirt (front and back design) - $30.00

INFANTS AND CHILDREN

- Blanket sleeper - $15.00
- Scribble mats - $5.00

SOMETHING FOR EVERYONE

- Santabear front and back fleece sweat shirts for men, women and children - $14.00 - $24.00

* Items shown in accompanying photograph.

PUBLIC RELATIONS • 700 ON THE MALL • MINNEAPOLIS, MN 55402 • 612/375-3015

SANTABEAR IS DEEMED PSYCHO-SYMPATICO BY ESTEEMED CHILDREN'S PSYCHOLOGIST, AUTHOR

HIGH TOUCH SANTABEAR EMBODIES 3 VITAL "C'S" OF GOOD BEARDOM

SANTABEAR - AN EXPERT'S VIEW
BY DR. HELEN BOEHM, DIRECTOR, KIDS CONCEPTS
AUTHOR OF "THE RIGHT TOYS: A GUIDE TO SELECTING THE RIGHT TOYS FOR CHILDREN"

As our society becomes increasingly complex, and sophisticated technology overtakes our lives, it's reassuring to know that cuddly stuffed animals - such as Santabear - are available to calm and comfort. Be it a nursery or a nursing home, the appeal of a soft cozy bear is unparalleled. Santabear communicates warmth and security to children 2 through 92. Snow white and pillow soft, it embodies the three "C's" of bearhood . . . cute, cozy and cuddly.

Research has shown that stuffed animals can aid in psychological development anc social learning. These playthings serve as an emotional anchor, helping ease the transition from an environment which is secure and familiar to experiences which are lesser known. Soft pals provide security for children as they go to sleep or even to school. As an object of affection, a reliever of stress or simply as a cozy, dependable friend, Santabear is the kind of special toy which reminds us that sometimes there are soft answers to hard questions.

\# # #

PUBLIC RELATIONS • 700 ON THE MALL • MINNEAPOLIS, MN 55402 • 612/375-3015

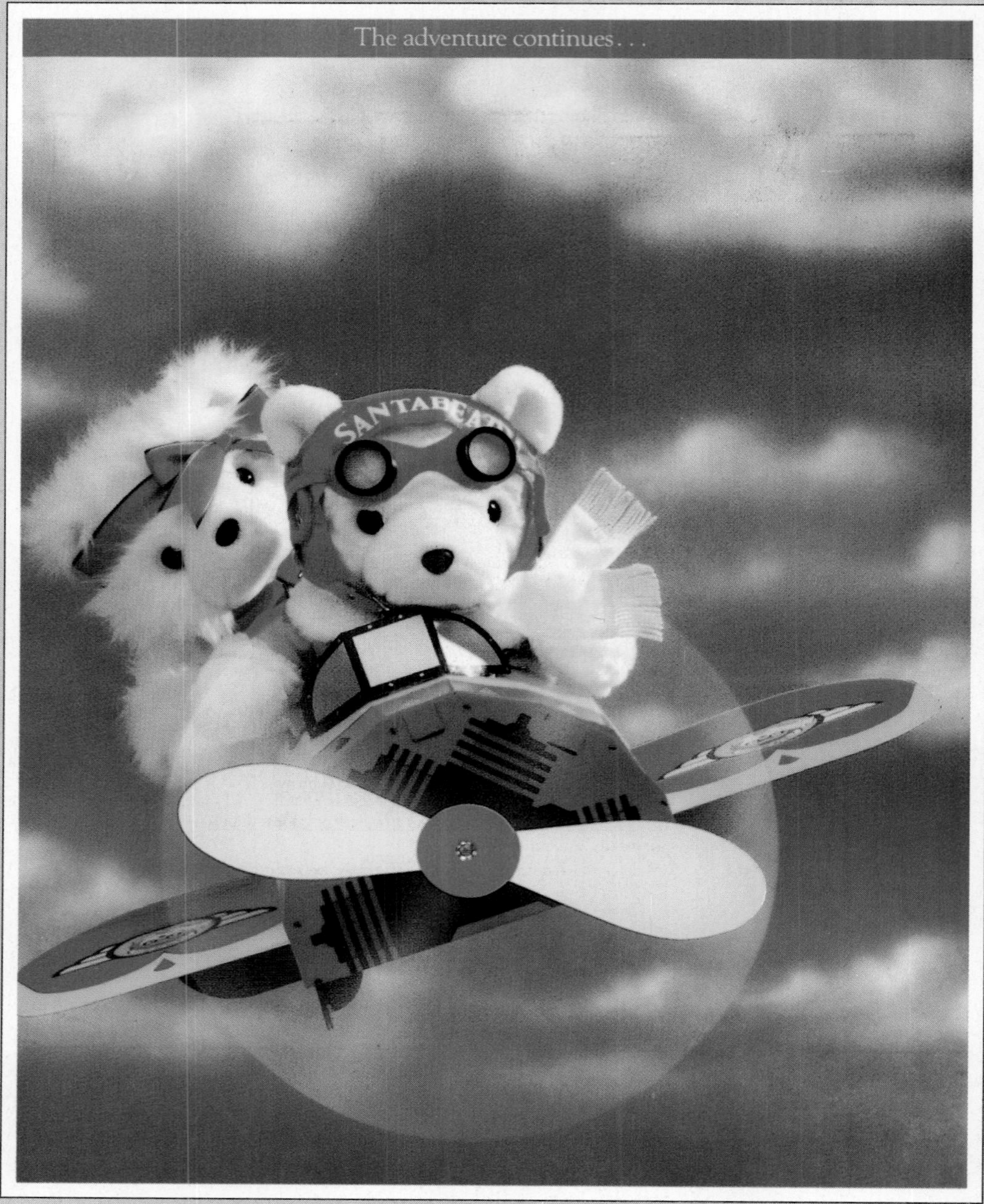
The adventure continues . . .
SANTABEAR

EXHIBIT D
Santabear press kit with moving propeller.

High-Flying Adventure—featured Santabear and his new costume and Miss Bear.

- The Christmas gift catalog featured an ''animated'' Santabear cover.
- A ''Today'' advertising supplement (2.7 million circulation) featured a two-page Santabear kickoff on November 1; six pages of Santabear merchandise in both the November 15 and 22 issues; Santabear's Instant Win contest in the November 29 issue.
- Eight million Santabear Instant Win Sweepstakes game cards were distributed to customers. Top prize was a $25,000 shopping spree. One winner in each of Dayton Hudson's 34 stores received round-trip tickets to anywhere in Europe on American

EXHIBIT E

Christmas gift guide with animated cover.

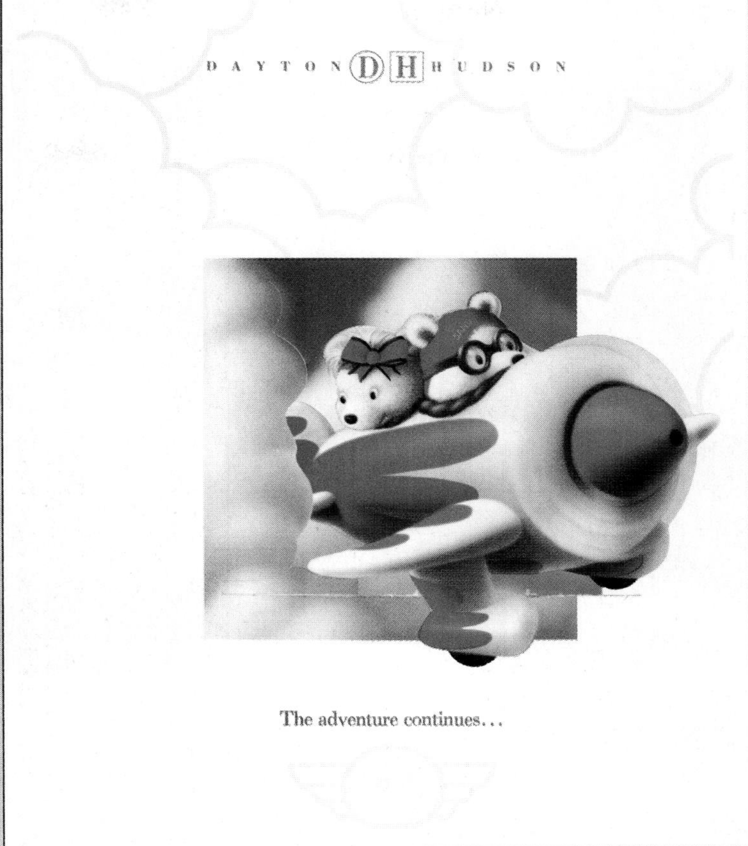

EXHIBIT F

Here are 4 of the 5 different editions of Today Advertising supplement featuring Santabear on covers.

Today Advertising supplements (continued)

EXHIBIT G
Instant Win Sweepstakes game tickets.

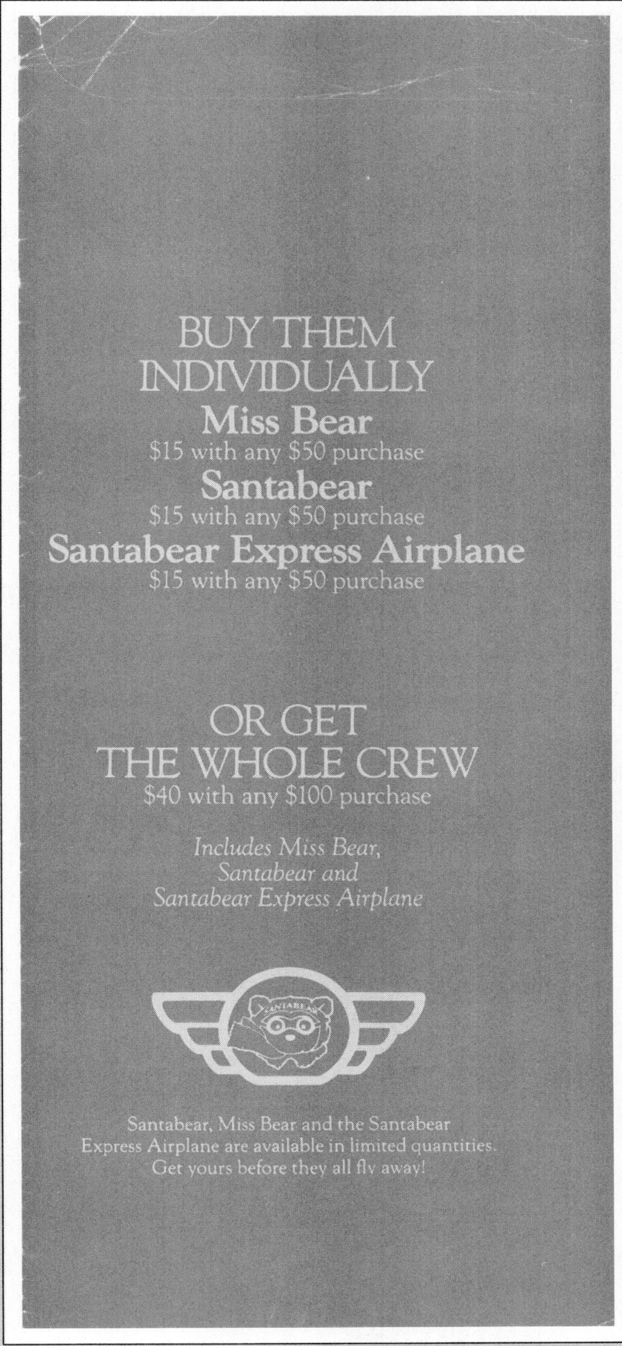

EXHIBIT H

Tie in with American Airlines. "Boarding Pass" envelope distributed in stores to collect receipts.

Airlines. Six customers won trips for two to the Caribbean on a Royal Caribbean cruise ship.

- In-store signs explained the Santabear purchase-with-purchase incentive and the Instant Win contest. Other signs promoted an American Express poster offer, the upcoming Santabear TV special, and the Santabear Christmas auditorium exhibit in the Minneapolis store. (The last was an animated display that attracted over 300,000 visitors.)
- A special Santabear shopping bag was designed.
- A billboard featured a moving propeller.
- A full-page newspaper ad ran on Christmas Eve to promote the Santabear TV special.
- Santabear was used as a prize by General Mills Cinnamon Toast Crunch cereal, and appeared on 5 million cereal boxes distributed nationwide. To support this sweepstakes, General Mills ran a national Sunday supplement ad (circulation 48 million) and television commercials during top time periods for children's programming. In addition, General Mills distributed 17 million coupons for in-store couponing.
- Vroman Frozen Foods added Santabear in an ice-cream/cookie sandwich form to their holiday treat line; 33,000 cases were sold.
- American Express gave away *Santabear's High-Flying Adventure* posters to customers using the American Express Card for purchases at Dayton Hudson stores. American Express also co-sponsored the introductory Santabear ad.
- A special educational supplement with illustrations of Santabear and Miss Bear was printed and distributed to schools in the Twin Cities and Detroit by Knight-Ridder newspapers.
- *St. Paul Pioneer Press Dispatch* and *Detroit Free Press* printed four-color souvenir inserts of Santabear and other characters from *Santabear's High-Flying Adventure*.
- The *Minneapolis Star Tribune* gave copies of *Santabear's High-Flying Adventure* book to elementary school libraries and ran a full-page ad about the gift.
- A children's magazine featured Santabear on the cover and on an inside spread of its November–December issue. A foldout, back-cover ad by Dayton Hudson showcased Santabear and related products.
- Mechanical Santabears appeared in eight stores.
- Costumed Santabears made over 500 appearances from June to December 1987 at community parades, benefits, and orchestra performances.
- Santabear was used as a prop or prize on a number of TV shows.
- The Santabear dance line appeared in Washington, D.C., for the lighting of the Christmas tree at the National Pageant of Peace.
- Santabear was invited to the White House for the Diplomatic Children's Party hosted by First Lady Nancy Reagan.

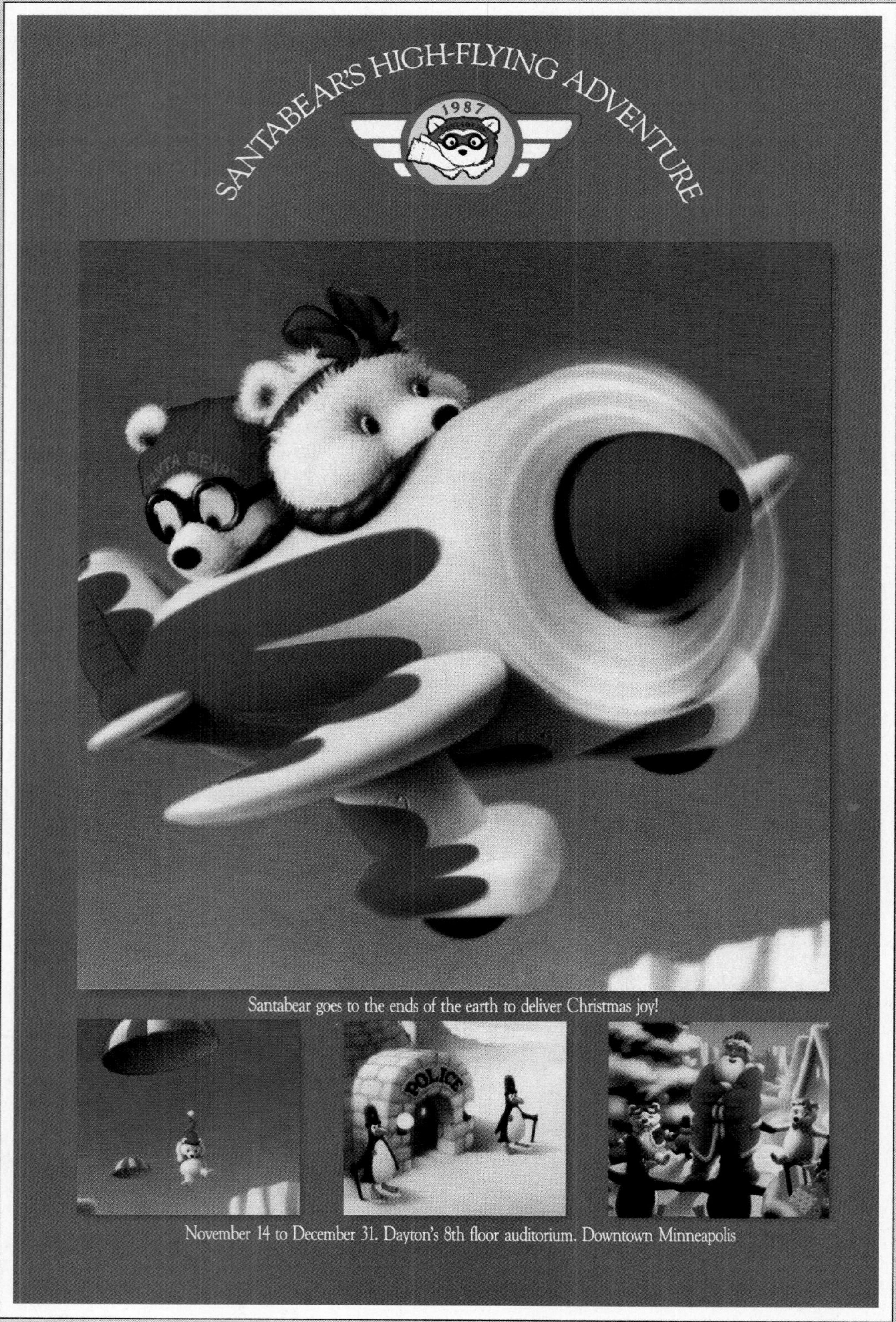
SANTABEAR'S HIGH-FLYING ADVENTURE
1987
Santabear goes to the ends of the earth to deliver Christmas joy!
POLICE
November 14 to December 31. Dayton's 8th floor auditorium. Downtown Minneapolis

EXHIBIT I
This in-store sign promotes the auditorium display.

SHOPPING BAG

A colorful illustration of the Santabear story by artist Leland Klanderman will be appearing on this year's shopping bag.

EXHIBIT J

Santabear christmas shopping bag.

EXHIBIT K

Billboard with moving propeller.

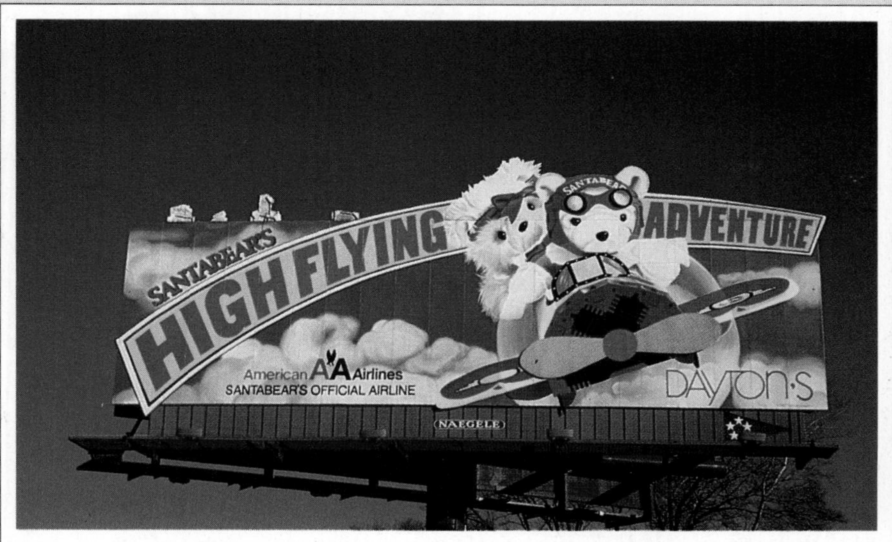

EXHIBIT L

Christmas Eve newspaper ad to advertise the CBS animated Santabear special.

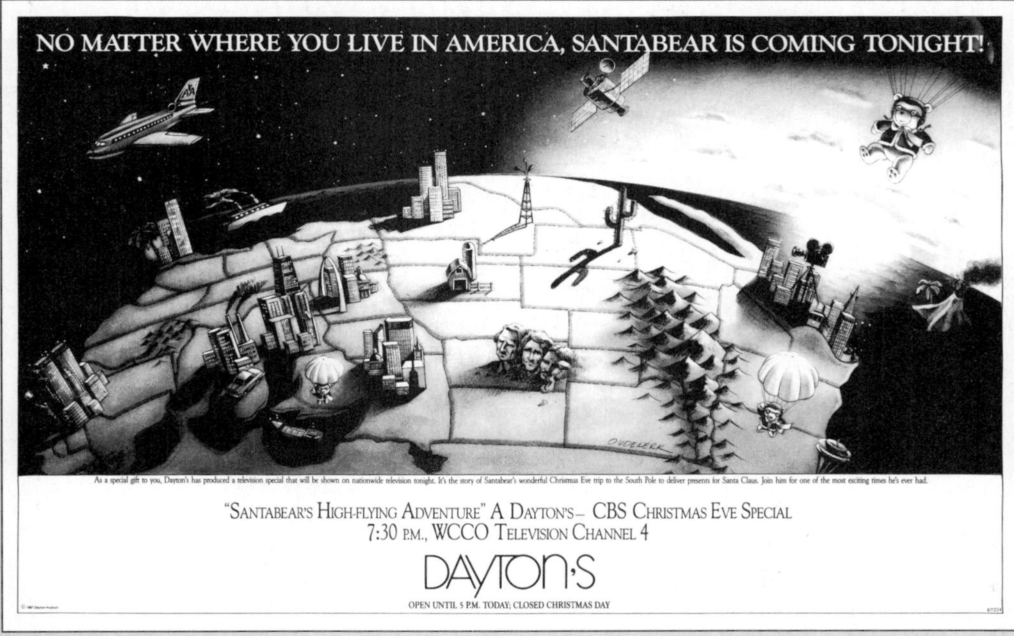

EXHIBIT M

Back of General Mills Cinnamon Toast Crunch cereal box.

EXHIBIT N

Institutional newspaper ads calendar.

Calendar ads (continued)

EXHIBIT O
Child Magazine fold-out back cover ad.

SUMMARY

Retailing consists of all activities involved in selling goods or services directly to final consumers for their personal, nonbusiness use. The 1950s and 1960s were eras of low prices and cheap goods, with discounters gaining strength among consumers. In the 1970s, discounters boomed in terms of numbers of stores and sales. In the 1980s, however, customers began to want more for less: they sought better service and an attractive ambiance. Another 1980s trend was the hypermarket, a super-supermarket selling food and all kinds of goods and services in one gigantic store. Some discounters in that decade used the "low everyday price" concept, meaning they had few sales and did little advertising to attract customers. Other stores used special price promotions to attract customers.

Research indicates that the primary reasons consumers shop at a store are price, selection, quality, location, and service. Retail advertising is done by local merchants or service organizations to attract customers. Some firms do both national and retail advertising. Retail advertisers must determine overall goals and objectives for their marketing and advertising programs, identify target markets, and develop copy and media strategies to reach these targets.

The media mix is getting more complicated with the increase in local media. Advertisers have a number of choices in targeting ads to specific groups. Cooperative advertising can run as high as 50 percent of total advertising expenditure. Despite the many changes in retailing, some elements will remain constant. Retail advertising will be hard sell, with immediate consumer response and immediate results. Retail is the fast-paced, price-and-sale-oriented segment of the advertising industry.

QUESTIONS

1. How does a retailer's pricing policy affect the amount of advertising it does?
2. If price is the main motivator to shop at a store, how does service influence customers?
3. How does retail advertising differ from national advertising?
4. What are the six types of retail advertising?
5. How are newspapers using ZIP/postal codes?
6. What is the fastest-growing medium in retail advertising?

SUGGESTED EXERCISES

- Find an example of co-op advertising.
- List all the advertising opportunities offered by your local newspaper.
- Describe a local radio promotion for retailers.

READINGS

BROWN, PAUL B.: *Marketing Masters Lessons in the Art of Marketing* (New York: Harper & Row, 1988).

FITZGERALD, KATE: "Sears Breaks Biggest Blitz," *Advertising Age,* February 27, 1989, p.2.

GEIGER, BOB: "Hyper in a Hypermarket," *Advertising Age,* May 8, 1989, p. S-11.

GRAHAM, JUDITH: "Retailers Seek to End Era of Price Cuts," *Advertising Age,* February 6, 1989, p.57.

"Walking the Slippery Retail Tightrope," *Advertising Age,* April 24, 1989, p. S-18.

TWENTY-FOUR

International Advertising

Foreign Manufacturers and advertising agencies compete effectively in the United States, *along with domestic companies*, for the same targets. For some foreign agencies, the more prudent approach to domestic markets has been to acquire a United States-based agency. WPP Group of London purchased J. Walter Thompson in 1987 because of its *billings* and its *efficiencies*. The purchase price of $566 million, according to Martin Sorrell, CEO, was considered "an excellent investment"—considering the proximity to the "growth" markets it accomplished.

No segment of the advertising industry has undergone more change in the last decade than the international sector. Not many years ago, international marketing and advertising primarily concerned the export of American products and services to the rest of the world. Today foreign manufacturers have totally taken over some American consumer markets, such as electronic appliances, and have made substantial inroads into others, such as textiles and automobiles. Likewise, foreign advertising agencies not only compete effectively with American agencies, but have taken control of some of the oldest and most prestigious U.S. agencies.

The movement from a situation of total American dominance of international advertising to one of fierce competition is part of a much larger change in the total economic order.

> Dramatic reversal in our nation's international investment position has awakened economists and the American public alike to a new awareness of global capital flows. As recently as 1981, the United States was the world's largest creditor nation; just five years later it had taken on the opposite role, becoming the foremost debtor. Reasons for this extreme shift include the widening of our country's budget and trade deficits as well as foreigners' positive investment response to U.S. tax incentives and growth prospects.[1]
>
> Exhibit 24.1 shows the dramatic change in the U.S. investment posture relative to the rest of the world.

Clearly, American companies must look to international markets for continued growth. Just as clearly, the advertising agencies servicing these multinational companies must have the capability to meet client demands throughout the world. For example, Procter & Gamble spends 21.8 percent of its advertising budget outside the United States. Some other major American corporations and their percentage of non-U.S. advertising spending are: Ford Motor Company, 26.9; Mars, Inc., 39.5; Coca-Cola,

[1]William J. Kahley, "Direct Investment Activity of Foreign Firms," *Economic Review*, Summer 1987, p. 36.

EXHIBIT 24.1

International business no longer means "American dominated." (Courtesy: *Economic Review*.)

U.S. International Investment Position (billions of current dollars)			
Type of Investment	**1980**	**1986**	**Change**
Net position	106.3	−263.6	369.8
U.S. Assets abroad	607.1	1,067.9	460.8
U.S. official reserve assets	26.8	48.5	21.7
U.S. government non-official reserve assets	63.8	89.4	25.6
U.S. private assets	516.6	929.9	413.3
Direct investment abroad	215.4	259.9	44.5
Foreign securities	62.6	131.0	68.4
Other U.S. bank and nonbank claims	238.5	539.0	300.5
Foreign assets in the U.S.	500.8	1,331.4	830.6
Foreign official assets in the U.S.	176.1	240.8	64.7
Other foreign assets in the U.S.	324.8	1,090.6	765.8
Direct investment in the U.S.	83.0	209.3	126.3
U.S. securities	90.2	405.5	315.3
Other U.S. bank and nonbank liabilities	151.5	475.8	324.3

Source: Constructed by the author from data in R.B. Scholl, "The International Investment Position of the United States in 1986" Survey of Current Business, vol. 67, no. 6 (June 1987), p. 40.

Many domestic firms have expanded their *distribution* and *promotion* to reach foreign markets. Proctor & Gamble's total worldwide spending is estimated at *$2.11 billion*, with *$724 million* coming from outside the United States. The *number 1 foreign promoter* is Unilever, however, which invested $731.7 million in 1987. In totaling the top 50 in non-United States spending, *Advertising Age* reports $9.57 billion was recorded for that year, up from $7.3 billion in 1986.

23.1; and Colgate-Palmolive, 40.2.[2] Robert Coen, of McCann Erickson, has estimated worldwide advertising spending for 1989 at $261.6 billion, with the United States contributing $125.6 billion. This is a significant turning point: For the first time, worldwide advertising expenditures exceeded those of the United States. Exhibit 24.2 shows some major advertising countries and the increases in their advertising investment.

GLOBAL MARKETING AND ADVERTISING

Global marketing. *Term that denotes the use of advertising and marketing strategies on an international basis.*

Some companies have adopted a global marketing and advertising strategy—that is, the *same* products are *promoted* similarly around the world—saving tremendous *costs*. Those products which have *general consumer* appeal, such as food, air travel, financial services, communications, automobiles, and tobacco, tend to lend themselves to universal campaigns.

As American companies increasingly seek to sell their products and services abroad, both they and their advertising agencies will need to develop marketing strategies that can be successfully expanded to other markets. The alternative to some commonality of marketing strategy is to develop a unique marketing plan for each country. Not only would this "start-from-scratch" approach involve tremendous expense, but it would deny companies the advantage of using techniques that have already proved successful in a market.

One of the catchphrases of multinational selling is *global marketing*. The term (attributed to Theodore Levitt of Harvard University) suggests that a corporation can develop a master marketing strategy for use wherever it sells its products. At the heart of the concept is the assumption that consumers are basically alike all over the world and will respond to similar appeals regardless of their apparent differences.

Global marketing is extremely appealing to multinational advertisers. First, it allows the development of a single, coordinated marketing strategy. Thus, Coca-Cola, with a presence in more than 150 countries, uses the same basic strategy and advertising themes, adjusted to suit various parts of the world, instead of attempting the nearly impossible task of managing completely unique marketing programs in each country. Second, the international approach dramatically reduces the cost of advertising production. For example, international television commercials require only changes in voice-overs, which is much cheaper than producing completely new commercials for individual countries. Finally, the global strategy, through the introduction of international

[2] "Advertising Age's Top 50 Non-U.S. Marketers," *Advertising Age*, December 14, 1987, p. 58.

EXHIBIT 24.2

With few exceptions, advertising is growing throughout the world. (Courtesy: *Advertising Age*.)

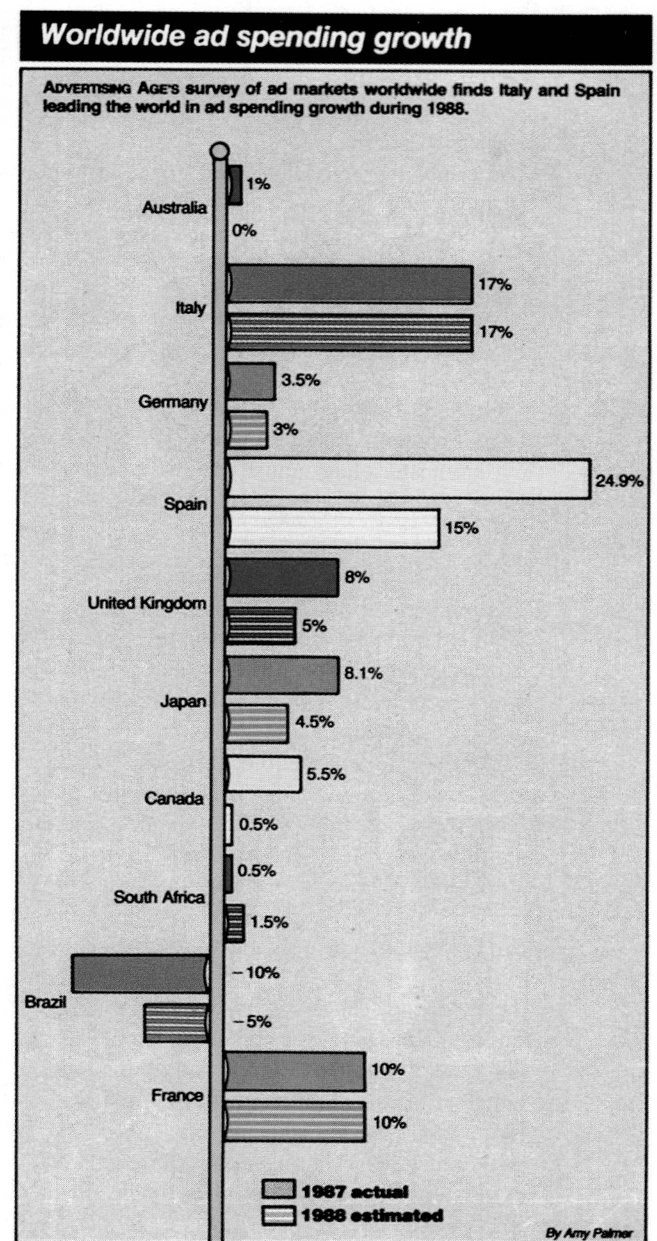

media, saves on media-planning costs and results in lower CPMs through economies of scale.

One of the pitfalls of the strict application of global marketing is it tends to place the corporation's interests above those of the consumer. Howard F. Clark of J. Walter Thompson stresses the importance of taking the consumer perspective when planning multinational advertising:

> They [consumers] search for familiar brands, found in familiar stores, down the aisles where those brands have always been. They develop patterns which they do not seek to alter. They are not in the market for global brands; they are in the market for uncomplicated dependable brands which they can find where they have always found them.

Clark goes on to outline consumer characteristics:

1. Consumers are not themselves "global." The consumer is one person in one place, with a

Some products. . .and some markets have strategic differences, necessitating *unique promotion approaches*. Regardless of the maintenance *or* the removal of physical, fiscal, or technical barriers, cultural differences still remain. Helene Curtis' president-CEO, Ronald Gidwitz, believes his company's future growth lies with its ability to introduce *more products in the United States and overseas*. ''The key to our success is in offering differentiated products. . .on a country-by-country basis,'' says he. The company has launched Finesse shampoo in British Commonwealth counties, and Salon Selectives in Scandinavia.

uniquely personal set of experiences, values, beliefs, and roles. Each consumer chooses and values brands according to that personal set.

2. Consumers do not generally buy ''global'' brands or products. They do not really care where else in the world the same brand is available. Nor do they care much where the brand was manufactured.
3. Since consumers' values are personal and individual, so are the values they place on the brands they buy.
4. Consumers are not sitting around waiting for better brands of anything to be delivered from outside the borders of their country. Foreign origin is not an instant value, but a barrier to overcome. True, in some product categories (French wine, Japanese high tech and cars, and American cola drinks), country of origin has become a value, but in most product categories, manufacturers do not loudly proclaim the factory location as a consumer benefit.[3]

None of this should suggest that the multinational approach to marketing and advertising problems has nothing to offer. The point is that international advertising plans, like domestic plans, must be developed with the consumer uppermost in mind.

1992: The Economic Unification of Europe

Economic unification of the European Community. *In 1992 the 12 nations of the European Community have agreed to virtually eliminate all trade barriers between the countries.*

The practical application of a global marketing strategy will come closer to reality in 1992. In that year, most physical, fiscal, and technical barriers to trade among the 12 nations of the European Economic Community (EEC) will be removed. This economic integration of the various European countries will create a single market of some 300 million customers.

The hope is that people, products, and services will be able to move among EEC nations with the same ease that they now cross U.S. state borders. Health, safety, and other technical requirements will be standardized, making it possible for a product approved for sale in one EEC country to be automatically accepted in all the rest. The 1992 plan envisions uniform standards for TV commercials, which would make it possible for a company to use the same spot across Europe. Though the spots would carry different voice-overs, the savings in production would be huge.[4]

Some people believe that the ''development of pan-European advertising could mean tossing scenes and customs of many European countries into one big cultural vat from which agencies everywhere would extract images.''[5] Actually, the more likely outcome of a unified Europe is that this ''single'' market will exhibit the same type of target segments familiar in the United States. One study has suggested that Spain, Italy, and France make up one group sharing similar lifestyles and Romance languages, while German-speaking Switzerland, Austria and West Germany form another group. A third group would be made up of the United Kingdom and Scandinavia, which have cultural similarities, such as family structures in which young people set up their own homes rather than remain in the extended families common in Italy, Spain, and France.[6]

Global marketing, then, is an ideal rather than a practical blueprint. In those areas of the world where an advertising strategy can be applied across national boundaries, an advertiser would be foolhardy not to use it. However, a blind allegiance to global marketing is no more likely to work than a U.S. marketing strategy that makes no allowances for differences in various consumer segments. Exhibit 24.3 shows that even something as fundamental as attitudes toward advertising show significant differences among several major countries.

[3]Harold F. Clark, ''Consumer and Corporate Values: Yet Another View on Global Marketing,'' *International Journal of Advertising,* Vol. 6, No. 1, 1987, pp. 35–36.

[4]Kevin Cote, ''1992: Europe Becomes One,'' *Advertising Age,* July 11, 1988, p. 46.

[5]Casey Davidson, ''Mass-Marketing, European Style,'' *ADWEEK,* June 6, 1988, p. G. 28.

[6]Janette Martin, ''Beyond 1992: Lifestyle Is Key,'' *Advertising Age,* July 11, 1988, p. 57.

Attitudes Toward Advertising	Hong Kong % Agree	Brazil % Agree	Colombia % Agree	UK % Agree	US % Agree	West Germany % Agree
Consumer Benefits						
Advertising is a good way to learn about new products.	96	90	95	88	91	92
Advertising is a good way to learn about what products and services are available.	95	85	93	83	80	74
Advertising is a good way to find out how products and services work.	87	83	89	71	71	36
Without advertising there would be fewer enjoyable programs on free TV.	86	57	69	63	73	41
Advertising results in better products for the public.	79	72	84	53	57	30
Advertising gives you a good idea about products by showing the kinds of people who use them.	63	66	82	41	40	26
Credibility						
Most ads don't tell facts, but just create a mood.	62	80	75	75	76	80
Most advertising insults the intelligence of the average consumer.	35	64	58	65	72	59
Products don't perform as well as the ads claim.	73	79	87	72	74	82
People really "tune out" ads and don't remember what they've seen or heard soon after.	54	55	58	66	74	68
Most advertising is in poor taste.	25	72	52	35	50	42
Entertainment Value						
A lot of advertising is funny or clever.	79	96	87	83	82	53
A lot of advertising is enjoyable.	66	95	86	66	58	83
Manipulation or Motivation?						
Advertising makes people want things they don't really need.	50	86	86	77	82	85
Most ads try to work on people's emotions.	72	73	92	78	82	91
It is really the manufacturers of products and not the advertising agencies who decide how truthful advertising is and what is said in ads.	73	62	81	59	71	73
In general, advertisements present an honest picture of the products advertised.	31	43	71	40	33	33
Clutter or Intrusiveness						
There are too many commercials in a row on television.	89	83	92	69	91	68
The same ads are constantly shown again and again.	75	82	94	89	89	83

EXHIBIT 24.3

Attitudes toward advertising differ widely from country to country. (Courtesy: *Journal of Advertising*.)

In its pure form, global communications has achieved very little success. For example, in 1988, Rupert Murdoch announced a significant reduction in his Sky Channel as he pulled out of Austria, France, and West Germany.

> After six years of doggedly penetrating cable systems in country after country with his general entertainment, English-language channel, Mr. Murdoch couldn't overcome the trend toward regional broadcasting in viewers' native language.

Aspiring European broadcasters now plan to target single-language groups or are trying to get in on the broadcast revolution locally.[7]

THE MULTINATIONAL ADVERTISING AGENCY

Multinational advertising agencies. *Agencies which are characterized by large clients selling goods in a number of countries. These agencies must have the ability to coordinate client services across a number of countries and branch offices.*

The world of international advertising is dominated by huge agencies and even larger clients. Exhibit 24.4 shows the top 50 advertising agencies. Notice the concentration of income and billings among those at the very top. For instance, the income of the top ten agencies ($5,776.7 million) is greater than that of the next 40 ($4,868.8 million). The advertising agencies of the future will increasingly be split into two groups: large multinational agencies, and small, almost boutique operations that service local and regional accounts. The middle-size agencies of today will either grow and gain an international presence, decrease in size and maintain a client list of small advertisers, or fade away altogether. Regardless of type or size, agencies will be organized and managed according to the needs of their clients.

Building the Multinational Agency

Multinational marketing has accelerated in recent years. This growth has required agencies to expand into a number of countries to serve the farflung interests of their corporate clients. The problems of building an international agency center on two primary areas. The first is how to go about putting together an international agency network.

Agency acquisition. *The primary means of ad agencies expanding into foreign countries is through the acquisition of existing agencies in these countries. Normally, partial ownership is retained by in-country executives of the acquired agency.*

In recent years there has been tremendous growth of the *multinational advertising agency*—to keep pace with the global acceleration of their clients. Saatchi and Saatchi, an agency with a 59% growth rate in profits *each* year for the past 10 years, attributes much of their success to global accounts. They also are considered among the top 5 "best" agencies, handling international accounts such as Burger King, Pfizer, Sunkist soft drinks, Johnson & Johnson—and British Prime Minister Margaret Thatcher's reelection campaign!

In the 1940s and 1950s, when McCann-Erickson and J. Walter Thompson led American agencies into the international arena, they started foreign branches from scratch. Today clients' demands for rapid expansion and the degree of local competition make this method impractical for most agencies. Instead, American agencies generally acquire an in-country agency, or more commonly, a majority interest in one. Acquisition gives the American agency an immediate, experienced presence and provides the minority partner with financial incentives.

We should also mention that acquisition is far from a one-way street. As we noted in our discussion of advertising agencies in Chapter 5, British-based agency holding companies such as Saatchi & Saatchi PLC and WPP Group PLC have already acquired several American agencies, and are on their way to acquiring more.

The second problem in building a multinational agency network is how to keep a sense of corporate identity rather than becoming a number of branch offices linked only by financial interests. "The network should be a brand, and it should be built in a way that you would build a global brand. It should have a sense of identity, it should have a sense of culture and it should have a sense of its own being, and everybody who works within it should share that culture, that sense of belonging."[8]

Since acquisition is the primary means of building an agency network, it is imperative that some degree of corporate compatibility be present in foreign agencies that are bought. It is also imperative to establish a centralized management that can maintain a unified corporate identity among the various agency branches. When one considers differences in language, culture, and national management styles, this assimilation seems a formidable task. Still, there is no escaping it because multinational companies will increasingly demand centrally coordinated ad campaigns from their advertising agencies.

Most multinational advertisers see the following benefits of centrally coordinated campaigns:

[7]Laurel Wentz, "Murdoch's Sky Takes a Fall," *Advertising Age,* October 3, 1988, p. 68.

[8]"Agency Networks: The Why and Wherefore," *Media International,* July 1988, p. 7.

EXHIBIT 24.4

Worldwide advertising is concentrated in a relatively few major agencies. (Courtesy: *Advertising Age*.)

World's top 50 agency groups

Rank '87	Rank '86	Agency	Gross income	Billings
1.	(1)	Dentsu Inc.	$884.5	$6.78 bill.
2.	(2)	Young & Rubicam [1]	735.5	4.91 bill.
3.	(3)	Saatchi & Saatchi Advertising Worldwide [2]	693.6	4.61 bill.
4.	(4)	Backer Spielvogel Bates Worldwide [3]	600.7	4.07 bill.
5.	(7)	BBDO Worldwide [4]	537.0	3.66 bill.
6.	(6)	Ogilvy & Mather Worldwide [5]	528.6	3.66 bill.
7.	(8)	McCann-Erickson Worldwide [6]	512.5	3.42 bill.
8.	(5)	J. Walter Thompson Co. [7]	483.0	3.22 bill.
9.	(15)	Lintas:Worldwide [8]	417.9	2.79 bill.
10.	(12)	Hakuhodo International	383.4	2.90 bill.
11.	(10)	D'Arcy Masius Benton & Bowles [9]	371.3	2.49 bill.
12.	(14)	Leo Burnett Co.	369.2	2.46 bill.
13.	(13)	Grey Advertising	369.2	2.46 bill.
14.	(9)	DDB Needham Worldwide [10]	358.5	2.60 bill.
15.	(11)	Foote, Cone & Belding Communications [11]	344.6	2.30 bill.
16.	(—)	WCRS/Belier [12]	230.2	1.63 bill.
17.	(—)	HDM [13]	204.0	1.38 bill.
18.	(16)	Bozell, Jacobs, Kenyon & Eckhardt	185.2	1.33 bill.
19.	(18)	N W Ayer	166.1	1.22 bill.
20.	(19)	Publicis International	164.3	1.09 bill.
21.	(—)	Lowe Group [14]	137.3	968.3
22.	(26)	Roux, Seguela, Cayzac & Goudard [15]	115.7	830.1
23.	(21)	Wells, Rich, Greene	114.0	765.0
24.	(24)	Tokyu Advertising Agency	113.9	826.8
25.	(22)	Dai-Ichi Kikaku	109.4	836.7
26.	(25)	Daiko Advertising	107.1	879.9
27.	(27)	Scali, McCabe, Sloves [16]	93.1	653.2
28.	(28)	Ketchum Communications	88.1	660.0
29.	(31)	Ogilvy & Mather Direct Response	84.0	560.0
30.	(33)	TBWA	79.0	545.0
31.	(38)	Asatsu Advertising	73.4	489.3
32.	(34)	Ross Roy Inc.	71.3	475.3
33.	(37)	I&S Corp. [17]	65.8	540.4
34.	(41)	Yomiko Advertising	64.7	477.3
35.	(36)	Campbell-Mithun	63.9	425.8
36.	(40)	Wunderman Worldwide	62.1	414.8
37.	(42)	GGK [18]	59.3	415.0
38.	(45)	Asahi Advertising	54.4	340.6
39.	(43)	Chiat/Day	52.5	350.0
40.	(—)	Mojo MDA [19]	52.5	348.0
41.	(—)	Dorland Worldwide	49.6	331.0
42.	(44)	Tracy-Locke	47.3	326.0
43.	(35)	Lowe Marschalk [20]	45.6	304.2
44.	(—)	Doremus & Co.	45.4	304.1
45.	(—)	BDDP Group [21]	44.6	297.6
46.	(—)	George Patterson Pty. [22]	44.3	295.3
47.	(48)	Hill, Holliday, Connors, Cosmopulos	43.4	289.6
48.	(—)	McCaffrey & McCall	42.1	308.9
49.	(47)	Laurence, Charles, Free & Lawson	41.5	302.0
50.	(46)	HBM/Creamer	40.9	272.0

NOTES: Dollars are in millions unless otherwise noted.

Included in agency figures are income and revenues from the following subsidiaries and affiliates:

[1]**Young & Rubicam**: HDM (33%); Wunderman Worldwide; Sudler & Hennessey; Stone & Adler; Creswell, Munsell, Fultz & Zirbel.

[2]**Saatchi & Saatchi Advertising Worldwide**: McCaffrey & McCall; Rumrill-Hoyt; Klemtner Advertising, Cochrane Chase, Livingston & Co. The holding company, Saatchi & Saatchi PLC, London, reported world gross income of $1.68 billion on billings of $11.36 billion.

[3]**Backer Spielvogel Bates Worldwide**: Campbell-Mithun; AC&R/DHB&Bess; Kobs & Draft.

[4]**BBDO Worldwide**:Tracy-Locke; Doremus & Co.; Ingalls, Quinn & Johnson, MARCOA DR Group; Lavey/Wolff/Swift; Frank J. Corbett Inc.; Blair Advertising; Franklin Spier Inc.; Caravetta Allen Kimbrough/BBDO.

[5]**Ogilvy & Mather Worldwide**: Ogilvy & Mather Direct Response; Rolf Werner Rosenthal.

[6]**McCann-Erickson Worldwide**: Part of the Interpublic Group of Cos., New York, which reported world gross income of $992.9 million on billings of $6.62 billion.

[7]**J. Walter Thompson Co.**: Brouillard Communications. JWT Group was acquired in June 1987 by WPP Group PLC, London.

[8]**Lintas:Worldwide**: Part of the Interpublic Group of Cos. In October '87 SSC&B:Lintas and Campbell-Ewald were joined to form Lintas:Worldwide.

[9]**DMB&B**: Medicus Intercon International; Ted Colangelo Associates.

[10]**DDB Needham Worldwide**: Kallir, Philips, Ross; Bernard Hodes Advertising Group; Rapp & Collins USA; Kresser, Craig/D.I.K.

[11]**Foote, Cone & Belding Communications**: Lewis, Gilman & Kynett; Albert Frank-Guenther Law; Vicom/FCB.

[12]**WCRS/Belier**: Della Femina, Travisano & Partners; HBM/Creamer; Creamer Dickson Basford; Heller Breene; Robert A. Becker; Cohn & Wells. In September '87 London-based WCRS acquired 49% of Paris-based Groupe Belier, owned by Eurocom. Earlier in '87 WCRS acquired the Ball Partnership from the Ogilvy Group.

[13]**HDM**: HDM (Havas, Dentsu, Marsteller) is an equal partnership (33 l/3%) between Young & Rubicam, Tokyo-based Dentsu and Havas Conseil.

[14]**Lowe Group**: Lowe International; Allen Brady & Marsh; Laurence, Charles, Free & Lawson.

[15]**Roux, Seguela, Cayzac & Goudard**: includes offices in Austria, Belgium, France (Paris and regional), Germany, Netherlands, Italy, Spain, Sweden, Switzerland, U.K. and O'Rielly O'Brien Clow/RSCG in the U.S. Also, RSCG Export which does business in Africa, the Middle East and French Caribbean and Creative Business International.

[16]**Scali, McCabe, Sloves**: Martin Agency, Fallon McElligott.

[17]**I&S Corp.**: Formerly Dai-Ichi Advertising, Tokyo, which merged in 1986 with SPN Co., a communications and sales promotion company of the Seibu Saison Group.

[18]**GGK Holding**: A Basel, Switzerland-based agency group with offices in Austria, Germany, France, Netherlands, Spain, U.K., Italy and Brazil. Lois Pitts Gershon/GGK, New York, is also part of the group.

[19]**Mojo MDA**: 14 offices in Australia, New Zealand, Hong Kong, Singapore, U.K. and the U.S.

[20]**Lowe Marschalk**: Interpublic Group of Cos. holds 70% of LM; Lowe Howard-Spink & Bell PLC, London, the other 30%.

[21]**BDDP Group**: Boulet, Dru, Dupuy, Petit, Paris, lists nine regional agencies and 10 affiliated companies.

[22]**George Patterson Pty.**: Part of Backer Spielvogel Bates.

Compiled by Ilse Cermak

Within the multinational agency framework, the question becomes one of whether an entire campaign should be *centrally coordinated*—or *developed regionally* according to different cultural tastes. "With continued globalization, I clearly see three or four super global agencies that are truly worldwide," revealed Jagdish Sheth of the University of Southern California, Los Angeles. In these cases, it's predicted that agencies would have about 40% of their revenue coming from *large clients,* who tend to derive benefits from *centralization.* The smaller accounts would be regional and promote only in their local areas.

1. Coordination offers cost savings in terms of client time and manpower and, to some extent, production costs.
2. It facilitates the sharing of experience: Lessons learned in one market can readily be applied in another.
3. It enables the effective control of the overall advertising budget so that funds are spent where and at the level they are needed.
4. The international importance of the account will ensure that it gets the benefit of the agency's top resources locally regardless of the size of the budget for any particular market.
5. Most important, consistency of approach means that a positioning and image for a product can be built over time and across territory, a consideration of growing importance as internationally received media become more commonplace. Instead of being written off as a short-term tactical cost, advertising becomes an investment in an increasingly valuable international asset.

THE ADVERTISING FUNCTION IN INTERNATIONAL ADVERTISING

The basic functions of advertising—research, planning, creative, and media—are the same everywhere. The problem for many American agencies is how to adapt techniques to an unfamiliar marketplace. As in any problem-solving situation, advertising must rely on research to direct planning and execution of the total effort. Research is even more crucial in international advertising, since transcultural assumptions can be both misleading and risky.

Only a few years ago, it was not uncommon for multinational advertisers to treat foreign markets as if they were virtually homogeneous. The same marketer who, at great expense, could segment teens in Seattle from those in New Orleans assumed that every Finn or Columbian was like every other.

Era of homogeneity. *The false assumption that all consumers in a foreign country are similar demographically and in terms of consumer behavior.*

The "era of homogeneity" is behind us. However, even though advertisers now realize the need for demographic, lifestyle, and market research, the available data are too often woefully inadequate. However, research problems, while far from a solution, are showing signs of significant improvement. Certainly in Europe there has been a marked improvement in the quantity and quality of research in just the last decade. Still, many American agencies have been spoiled by their long years of dominance. As one advertiser noted, "U.S. marketing is so computerized. Everybody speaks English; telecommunications connect each state, there's a very robotic approach in the way everything is the same and the way you can measure it. In Asia, you have different cultures, different regulations, a different set of rules."[9]

Advertising research, although *vitally necessary* for domestic agencies involved in foreign markets, is often difficult to execute. *Political restrictions and cultural barriers* proved formidable for *Clayton Research Services,* based in Hong Kong, when clients requested demographic and psychographic information about China. The agency personnel were prevented from "free" travel and were restricted in the content of their questions and to whom they could approach. Obviously, the final reports were less universal and more biased than clients preferred, said an agency spokesperson.

The problems of multinational advertising research are compounded when we attempt to develop common strategies that will cut across national borders. As we noted earlier, advertisers are not confident about the degree of standardization that should be used. One study has indicated that product positioning, campaign themes and objectives, and target markets demonstrate the greatest standardization, while media scheduling, media mix, and creative executions exhibit the lowest.[10]

Creative Considerations

There is hardly an international advertising executive who does not have a favorite (if it happened to someone else!) horror story about the misuse of language.[11] A Moscow periodical gave a misleading twist to its criticism of American life when it translated

[9]Betsy Sharkey, "Getting to Know You," *ADWEEK,* June 6, 1988, p. G. 34.

[10]John K. Ryans, Jr., and David G. Ratz, "Advertising Standardization," *International Journal of Advertising,* Vol. 6, No. 2, 1987, p. 152.

[11]Material in this section is used courtesy of Euramerica, a subsidiary of Ogilvy & Mather, International.

The tendency for *misusing language* can prevent an international campaign from being adopted. "Bloopers" are costly—in time and reputation to the sponsoring firms. When Lone Star beer hits Japan, vice-president for sales, Barry McAlister, knows its current *slogan* will have to be changed. "Although there's a Western craze in Japan and anything wrapped in a Texas approach looks like it will do well, we have to make sure our presentation coincides with Eastern habits," quoted McAlister. "'Lone Star is on the rise again' would just be taken too literally."

our "drugstore" into "narcotics shop." Another Russian blooper transformed a man's career by mistranslating his title on his business card: Instead of reading "Vice President of the International Division," the literal translation militarized the poor man and made him "Vice President of the International *Brigade*"!

An Arabic translation of a truck operator's manual explained that the headlight's blue high-beam indicator would light up at "six o'clock." Not realizing that "six o'clock" meant the lower center position on the lens rather than the time of day, at least one owner returned to the distributor to complain about the broken light that still hadn't lit up at 7:30 P.M. The American automobile named Nova means "bright star" in the United States, but in Latin American idiom, "No va" means "it doesn't go"—not a great name for a vehicle being sold on its dependability. Finally, there was the European ad that turned "body by Fisher" into "corpse by Fisher."

For efficiency's sake, clients demand that creative directors find unified multinational themes. But ideas capable of transcending boundaries often lack the nuances that make advertising so distinctive. Thus, the creative director must constantly balance the forces of efficiency with those of creativity when developing multinational advertising. In the end, however, the communication of a sales message must override all other considerations.

Several factors have made the job of creating international advertising somewhat easier in recent years:

***Global village.** A term popularized by Marshall McLuhan. It refers to the idea that modern technology has created a world of instant communication.*

1. There is a growing cultural understanding and commonality among the nations of the world, especially in the West. Although significant differences still exist in mores and customs, McLuhan's "global village" is much closer to reality than when he announced it more than two decades ago.
2. There is a greater utilization and understanding of the kind of graphic and visual advertising approaches that can overcome cultural differences. An overuse of copy—a verbal approach in general—leads to the comedy of errors we gave examples of at the beginning of this section.
3. Creative directors better understand how to integrate a central theme with local input. For example, DDB Needham ran a campaign for Mobil 1, a lubricating oil for cars, that successfully translated an American commercial for worldwide distribution (see Exhibit 24.5). In producing the international versions, DDB Needham prepared a "generic" European version, a French version, and a Japanese version—each with a different Mobil 1 package. The agency also eliminated the scene in the U.S. version that shows competitive brands of conventional motor oil, since such comparisons are forbidden virtually everywhere in the world except the United States. Also, a Celsius temperature gauge was used in the foreign versions.[12] Otherwise, the commercial ran the same way in every country.

Media Considerations

Almost without exception, international advertisers regard media planning as their biggest headache. The problem is particularly acute in emerging nations such as China. There, "despite the rapid growth in the number of media available, many lack professional services, such as audience and readership profiles, audited circulation and other points of information which media planners expect in developed economies."[13]

Even in the technologically advanced countries of Europe, media buying is more difficult than in the United States. Manufacturers of consumer package goods are especially frustrated by the lack of consistent availability of television advertising. While the number of countries allowing television advertising has increased dramatically in recent years, television remains a tremendously underutilized advertising medium outside of the United States and Japan.

Still, all indications are that television advertising will undergo a period of rapid growth with the 1992 EEC accords:

[12]Letter to author from Mr. Robert Stern, DDB Needham Worldwide Advertising.

[13]"Foreigners Focus on TV Ads for Effect," *Media International*, June 1988, p. 38.

EXHIBIT 24.5

Mobil cleverly created a multinational advertisement. (Courtesy: Mobil Corporation.)

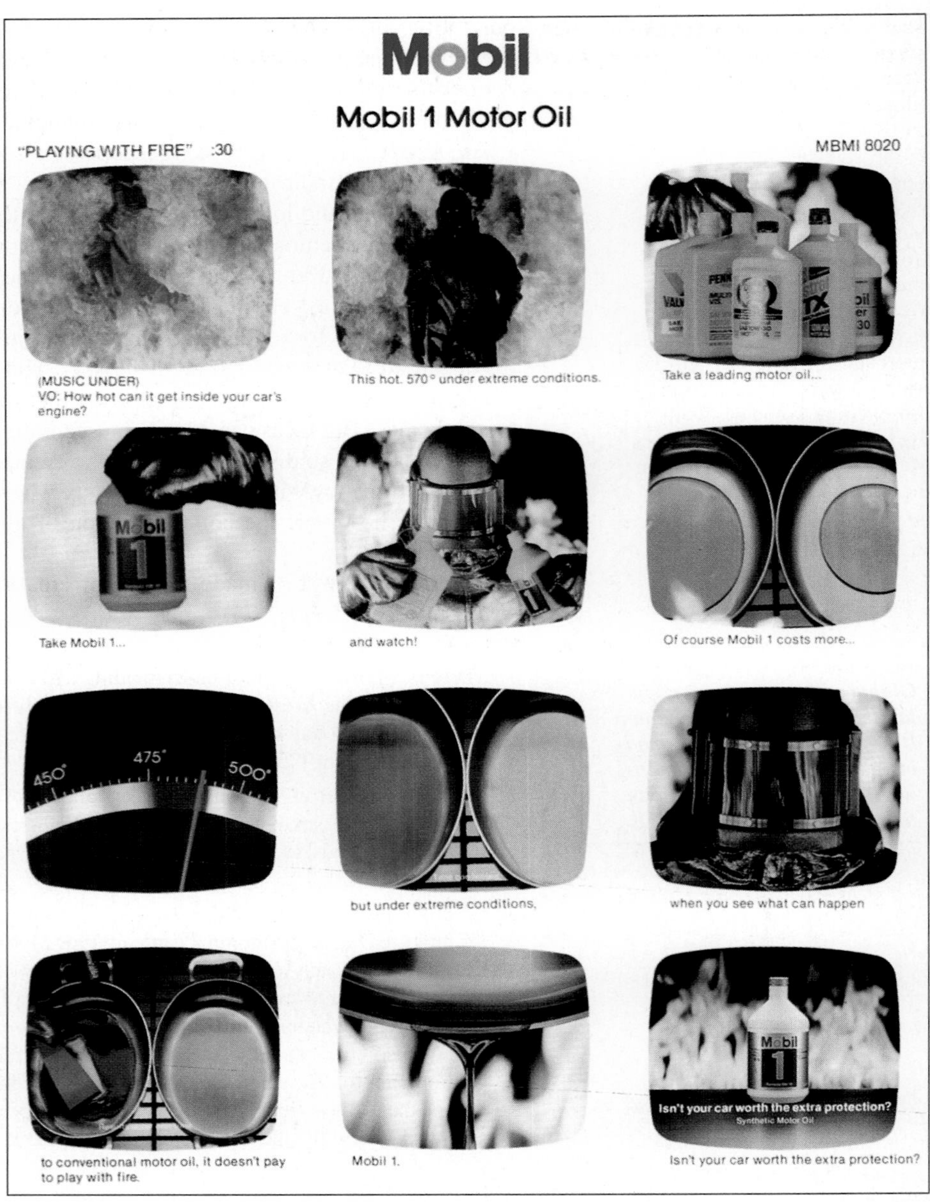

The "business" of *media buying* is complicated by the lack of available vehicles (commercial television) and fragmented systems (*local* or *regional* newspaper syndicates). There's also a *multiplicity of legal ramifications*. Belgium prohibits references to *dieting* in its commercials; in France, premiums can't be worth more than 1% of the product's sale price. Under West German law, comparisons constitute unfair competition.

All over Europe, independently owned broadcast, cable, and satellite stations have sprung to life, challenging the existing state-controlled media and vastly expanding the technological state of the art. According to estimates, by the end of 1990, these new outlets will need an additional 660,000 hours of programming to fulfill the requirements of their 18-hour broadcast days. And if all of these outlets take six minutes of advertising per hour, so the estimates go, then in the next decade European advertisers will have 4 million additional advertising minutes each year.[14]

Large multinational agencies have been exploring the feasibility of cooperating to establish worldwide media operations. These cooperative units would function as global media-buying operations for several agencies. Already multinational agencies such as Ogilvy & Mather have centralized their non-U.S. media buying into a single office. As we move toward the 1992 consolidation of the European Economic Community, such units may become more common.

[14]Sue Woodman, "Looking at the Eurotube," *ADWEEK,* June 6, 1988, p. G. 16.

The appeal of these joint operations stems from several factors:

1. *Growth of non-U.S. billings.* As we discussed earlier, non-U.S. billings have passed domestic advertising expenditures. However, while the dollars invested in global media are growing, the expenditures in many countries remain relatively small, and having separate media departments in each branch office involves substantial overhead.
2. *Coordination of media buys.* Many global media buys cross national boundaries. For instance, television satellite distribution, a few international newspapers, and several magazines distributed worldwide are bought on a continental rather than a national basis. These media buys need to be coordinated among the several countries where they are distributed. (See Exhibit 24.6 for a list of international magazines.)
3. *Buying expertise.* Another factor in considering joint media-buying units is the consolidation of personnel. Only a few people are truly knowledgeable about the complexities of global media. Agencies would gain from having these people buying across a number of agencies.
4. *Availability of media discounts and buying flexibility.* Many non-U.S. media offer volume discounts to agencies regardless of how many clients they are buying for. In other words, the agency is the client. This means that large media-buying combines would have more clout

Pooled media buying. *A proposal that large agencies should create cooperative media buying units to undertake the media function for multinational clients.*

EXHIBIT 24.6

Multinational advertisers have a growing number of media options. (Courtesy: *Advertising Age.*)

Advertising Age's global media lineup

	Title/ publisher/ headquarters	Major printing plants for international editions	Paid North American circulation (% chg '86-'87)	Paid foreign circulation by region (% chg '86-'87)	Worldwide circulation (% chg '86-'87)	Cost of worldwide B&W pg ($/1988)	Global CPM B&W pg ($/1988)	Top worldwide advertisers in 1987
DAILIES	***Financial Times of London*** Financial Times Ltd. London	London Frankfurt Bellmawr, N.J.	16,683[1] (+59.6)	Europe: 258,259[2] (+18.6) Mid. East/Africa: 3,379[2] (−15.2) Asia/Pacific: 3,637[2] (+19.4) Latin America: 182[2] (−4.7) West Indies: 113[2] (−33.9)	311,885[1] (+23.2)	full: 29,568 qtr.: 7,392	94.80	British Airways British Petroleum Hutchison Whampoa Rank Xerox Siemens
	International Herald Tribune New York Times & Washington Post Neuilly, France	10 cities around the world	3,356 (+14.6)	Europe: 128,260[3] (−1.6) Asia Pacific: 27,268[3] (+4.9) Mid. East/Africa: 7,404[3] (−6.0) Sub-Sahara Afr.: 1,274[3] (−27.4) Other: 1,346[3] (+0.9)	168,908[3] (+0.4)	full: 35,616 qtr.: 8,904	210.86	AT&T Republic National Bank Trade Development Bnk Lufthansa Airlines Air France
	USA Today Gannett Co. Arlington, Va.	Singapore Switzerland Hong Kong[4]	1,600,000[1] (+9.7)	Europe: 26,513[1] (+27.0) Asia: 10,130[1] (+29.7)	1,636,643[1] (+10.0)	full: 41,606 qtr.: 15,959	25.42	AT&T Marlboro Stouffers Hotels Visa Volvo
	Wall Street Journal Dow Jones & Co. New York	Hong Kong Singapore Tokyo Heerlen, Neth. Lucerne	2,026,276[5] (+ 2.1)	Asian WSJ: 33,505 (+6.0) WSJ/Europe: 38,631 (+9.2)	2,098,412[6] (+2.2)	full: 109,277 qtr.: 27,319	52.08	Shearson Lehman[8] Merrill Lynch Paine Webber Kidder Peabody Morgan Guaranty
WEEKLIES	***Business Week*** McGraw Hill New York	Philadelphia, Pa.	852,367 (+8.1)	Europe: 52,113 (+7.6) Asia: 25,339 (+11.1) Latin America: 16,248 (−1.9) Other: 1,650 (+3.1)	949,661[9] (+8.3)	full: 38,220	40.57	N.V. Philips[8] AT&T Hitachi Siemens Merrill Lynch
	The Economist The Economist Newspaper London	Virginia London Singapore	125,384 (+11.5)	Europe: 138,060 (+1.5) Asia/Pacific: 31,979 (+30.9) Africa: 7,058 (+5.8) Middle East: 8,285 (+41.7) Ctrl. & Latin Am.: 5,713 (+14.6)	316,479 (+8.9)	full: 7,200[7]	22.75[7]	Singapore Airlines British Aerospace Chemical Bank AT&T Fujitsu
	Guardian Weekly Guardian Newspapers Ltd. Manchester	Montreal Lincoln (U.K.)	25,051 (+2.0)	Europe: 18,320 (−0.3) Asia/Pacific: 13,432 (+2.1) Middle East/Africa: 5,701 (−2.0) Latin America: 1,430 (+4.8) Other: 485 (+6.6)	64,419 (+1.1)	full: 2,745	42.61	Tyndall Managers Amnesty International Nat. West W.T. Fry Standard Chartered Bnk
	Newsweek Newsweek Ltd. New York	Zurich Tokyo Hong Kong Daytona Beach	3,181,187 (+3.0)	Atlantic: 306,189 (−4.2) Latin America: 55,219 (+0.3) Asia: 201,213 (−1.0) So. Pacific: 121,000[10] (N/A) Nihon Ban: 121,297[11] (N/A)	3,986,105 (+1.6)	full: 91,525[7]	22.96[7]	Ruperts International[8] Singapore Airlines Rolex N.V. Philips B.A.T.
	Time Time Inc. Publications New York	Toronto Miami Weert, Neth. Singapore Hong Kong	5,033,558 (−3.3)	Atlantic: 526,897 (−1.6) Asia: 235,485 (−12.6) Latin America: 97,442 (+7.7)	5,893,382 (−5.5)	full: 131,175	22.26	Rothmans Group of Cos. Singapore Airlines Philip Morris IBM Rolex
MONTHLIES	***National Geographic*** Nat'l Geographic Society Washington DC	Corinth, Miss.	9,323,891 (−2.4)	Atlantic: 689,557 (+1.3) Pacific: 357,202 (−4.7) Latin America: 94,333 (+0.1)	10,461,337[9] (−2.1)	full: 127,720	12.42	Canon[8] Iberia Airlines Olympus Lufthansa Airlines Minolta
	Reader's Digest Reader's Digest Assn. Pleasantville, NY	24 cities around the world	18,109,000 (0.0)	Atlantic: 6,863,000 (−1.0) Pacific: 1,658,000 (0.0) Latin America: 1,172,000 (+3.9)	27,802,000 (−0.1)	full: 218,699[7]	7.87[7]	Colgate-Palmolive[8] Franklin Mint Nestle Nissan Motor Co. Toyota
	Scientific American Scientific American Inc. New York	Old Saybrook, Ct.	530,668 (+7.0)	Europe: 57,674 (+4.7) Asia/Pacific: 20,128 (−5.5) Ctrl. & S. Am.: 4,976 (−11.8) Africa: 1,851 (−4.5) Middle East: 1,564 (+2.8)	606,826 (+4.1)	full: 19,450	31.20	McDonnell Douglas Hughes Aircraft General Motors AT&T Hitachi
	South South Publications Ltd. London	London Singapore	6,150 (+0.9)	Africa/Mid East: 32,082 (−6.8) Asia/Pacific: 14,809 (−35.4) Europe: 11,648 (+3.4) Latin America: 12,337 (−2.0)	77,026 (−11.8)	full: 3,067[7]	39.82	British Aerospace Babcock & Wilcox N.V. Philips Hewlett-Packard Isuzu
OTHER	***WorldPaper***[12] World Times Inc. Boston	20 countries around the world	N/A[13]	Latin America: 239,000 (−3.6) Asia: 347,500 (+104.4) Middle East: 69,500 (−18.2)	656,000 (−10.7)	full: 27,522 qtr.: 9,632	42.00	AT&T Hertz American Express IBM
	Fortune Time Inc. Publications New York	Zurich	666,972 (+4.0)	Europe: 61,012 (+10.9) Asia: 36,248 (−5.8) Other: 9,759 (−5.5)	771,988 (+3.6)	full: 31,180	41.30	AT&T IBM General Motors GTE Ford Motor Co.
	Harvard Business Review Harvard Business Review Boston	Glasgow, Ky.	189,638 (−1.5)	Europe: 14,484 (+48.1) Asia/Pacific: 8,652 (+28.1) Ctrl. & S. America: 3,940 (+53.0) Mid. East/Africa: 3,092 (+23.1) Other: 1,208 (+24.2)	220,951 (+2.7)	full: 7,200[7]	32.59	AT&T Morgan Stanley & Co. General Motors Digital Equipment NV Philips

Source: ADVERTISING AGE.

Notes: [1]As of September, 1987. [2]Jan. to June, 1987. [3]Total worldwide circulation Jan.-Dec. 1986. Comparable 1985 figure: 168,189. [4]Plant will start operation April, 1988. [5]As of March 1987. [6]Combines North American figures from March and international figures from June. [7]Page cost is for 1987. [8]All advertisers in category are for non-U.S. editions. [9]Worldwide total exceeds regional total because of different audit dates. [10]April-Dec. 1986 ABC. [11]Japanese language edition of Newsweek. Figure for Jan.-Dec., 1986 Japan Audit Bureau of Circulation. [12]Distributed as a newspaper supplement. [13]Not distributed in North America.

Compiled by Ilse Cermak

with media and be able to obtain deeper discounts for clients. They would also enable agencies to gain flexibility for their clients because they could cancel one client's buy and substitute another.[15]

There are two major drawbacks to pooled buying on a global basis. First is the reluctance of most clients to have a single media-buying organization represent both them and competing brands. As the advertising director of Avon Products noted, "In our executions over the last year, media have become equally as important as the message. We would be concerned that someone buying for our competitor would be aware of important components: timing, media selection and weight. All of these are marketing components you would not want told to competitors."[16]

The second problem is whether media abroad would long be content to deal with these combines as single entities. In the United States, while a very large agency may be somewhat more effective in media negotiations than others, the basic discount structure is determined by the size of the client, not the agency. It is quite possible that global media would adopt the same policy if they found one or two huge media-buying units dictating price or availability on a worldwide basis.

Obviously, global media will continue to change, sometimes in unpredictable ways, during the next decade. However, a number of media trends are already apparent:

The trend is for more United States marketers to look to foreign markets for *expansion*—and with that approach, to search for more efficient means to make wise media buys. Three Proctor & Gamble ad agencies—Leo Burnett, Grey Advertising, and D'Arcy Masius Benton & Bowles—are talking about buying media *together* in Europe to counter rivals' joint media-buying groups there. The positive outcome would be a significant savings in fees—but the downside is a possible conflict of interest between P&G and the agencies' similar accounts.

1. Television in all its diverse forms will grow dramatically on both a household-coverage and a usage basis. The increase will be significant in emerging as well as in developed nations. As more television options come on line, usage of the medium will increase. This should lead to a greater influx of advertising dollars for the available time.
2. Print media will also grow, but at a slower pace. Increased literacy rates in many countries will expand opportunities for print advertising.
3. Advertising expenditures, expressed as a percentage of GNP, will increase around the globe. As many package-goods brands reach maturity in the United States and other developed countries, they will look to worldwide markets for their expansion. This added competition will create higher rates of advertising expenditure in many countries.
4. Major changes in political and economic structures will continue to pave the way for globalization. The most anticipated change is the 1992 consolidation of the EEC market. However, throughout the world, countries such as China are now allowing private marketing to a degree that would have been unthinkable only a decade ago.[17]

SUMMARY

Despite all the problems inherent in international marketing, American companies will continue to expand into these new markets. The profit potential of international markets, especially in Asia, makes it imperative for firms to develop plans to sell their products abroad. Already we see some American products meeting with great success in these countries. For instance, prior to the recent upheaval, the Beijing (China) Kentucky Fried Chicken outlet was number-one among the company's 7,000 worldwide stores in sales of chicken. Likewise, Pepsi Cola has achieved great success in the Soviet Union.[18]

Predicting the future of international advertising is tricky. However, recent trends would lead to the following conclusions:

- Overseas advertising growth will continue to increase at a greater rate than U.S. advertising investment. The rate of non-U.S. advertising investment will probably rise as the largely

[15]Gary Levin, "Wanted: Media Muscle," *Advertising Age,* July 11, 1988, p. 1.

[16]Patricia Winters, "OK with Us, Some Advertisers Say," *Advertising Age,* July 11, 1988, p. 74.

[17]Gordon Link, "Our Global Village," *Marketing & Media Decisions,* May 1988, p. 110.

[18]John Motavalli, "Selling to the Marx Brothers," *ADWEEK,* December 5, 1988, p. F.K. 17.

untapped markets of Latin America and Asia are opened and television becomes more available in Europe.

- Cross-border advertising opportunities will continue to increase. The availability and demand for media are prompting governments to loosen restrictions on commercial media, creating additional advertising opportunities.
- The number of multinational and global brands will continue to expand. As American, European, and few established Asian products seek expanded sales, the whole world will become their marketplace, with resulting fierce competition in countries that until recently did not even have distribution.

Global advertising is interesting to contemplate and certainly holds promise for multinational corporations. However, emerging nations, particularly in Asia, present problems unlike those faced in the United States or Europe. ''It's not a simple thing to have an effective presence in the Pacific. What's done in one country won't fly in another. It's not only complex getting a handle on the many different styles of business cultures and levels of development—it can be hugely expensive.''[19]

As Exhibit 24.7 shows, investment levels in global advertising will exceed those of North American advertising. Given the growth potential and the need for advertising in these markets, an American advertising presence in these countries is essential.

One final note on international advertising: Corporations and their agencies will increasingly have to deal with a multinational/multilingual population in the United States as well as abroad. Net immigration to this country during the 1980s account for one-quarter to one-third of the nation's population growth, according to the Census Bureau, and these figures—are arguably too low because they do not include the American-born children of recent immigrants.[20] Exhibit 24.8 illustrates how culturally diverse our major cities are becoming.

---

[19]Maryanne McNellis, ''Asian Ad Abacus: Marketing by the Numbers,'' *ADWEEK*, October 26, 1987, p. 33.

[20]James P. Allen and Eugene J. Turner, ''The New Immigrants,'' *American Demographics*, September 1988, p. 23.

EXHIBIT 24.7

Worldwide advertising expenditures have shown substantial growth in recent years. (Courtesy: *Advertising Age*.)

	(Current prices)						
	1987 $m	***1988 $m***	***% change***	***1989 $m***	***% change***	***1990 $m***	***% change***
TV, Print, Radio and Outdoor							
North America	$74,484	$80,785	+8.5	$86,248	+6.8	$92,159	+6.9
Europe	42,326	46,914	+10.8	51,521	+9.8	56,334	+9.3
Asia/Pacific	28,957	31,443	+8.6	34,176	+8.7	37,392	+9.4
Latin America	2,980	3,254	+9.2	3,514	+8.0	3,799	+8.1
Africa/Middle East	1,162	1,269	+9.2	1,371	+8.0	1,482	+8.1
Sub-total	$149,909	$163,665	+9.2	$176,830	+8.0	$191,166	+8.1
Below-the-line Activities							
Direct Mail							
North America	20,826	24,074	+15.6	27,608	+14.7	31,665	+14.7
Europe	6,843	8,143	+19.0	9,772	+20.0	11,726	+20.0
Sales Promotion, Point of Sale and Others							
U.S.	21,530	24,329	+13.0	27,005	+11.0	29,976	+11.0
Grand total	$199,108	$220,211	+10.6	$241,215	+9.5	$264,533	+9.7

Source: Saatchi & Saatchi Co.

DESTINATION, U.S.A.

New York is the most popular destination for new immigrants, but 37 other metropolitan areas receive at least 2,000 immigrants a year.

(selected immigrant groups moving to major metropolitan areas, ranked by average annual immigrants received from 1984 to 1986)

metropolitan area	*total**	*Mexico*	*Philippines*	*China***	*S. Korea*	*Vietnam*	*India*	*Dom. Rep.*	*Jamaica*	*Cuba*	*Iran*	*Cambodia*	*Laos*	*Colombia*	*Haiti*	*El Salvador*	*Guyana*
New York, NY	92,345	478	1,761	7,823	2,641	832	3,036	15,554	9,415	647	807	497	39	3,610	5,947	1,162	6,510
Los Angeles-Long Beach, CA	57,912	10,026	6,680	5,081	5,092	3,200	1,139	32	227	1,402	3,883	1,697	122	393	28	2,953	84
Chicago, IL	21,620	4,105	2,178	1,021	1,366	445	2,372	62	323	243	314	185	111	232	207	136	30
Miami-Hialeah, FL	19,609	133	166	114	49	50	95	436	1,153	10,571	66	5	7	1,162	1,067	179	94
San Francisco, CA	16,521	705	3,563	3,793	467	1,200	242	5	22	42	410	341	114	48	17	904	11
Washington, DC-MD-VA	15,636	84	763	972	1,659	1,066	995	188	613	66	901	318	168	201	125	1,066	277
Anaheim-Santa Ana, CA	12,916	1,684	798	924	1,064	3,049	370	4	17	113	696	498	250	90	2	101	4
San Jose, CA	11.665	1,009	1,838	1,495	548	2,305	624	3	14	15	491	413	85	20	3	111	8
Oakland, CA	9,832	727	2,149	1,393	425	645	493	2	24	16	324	143	197	32	3	133	12
San Diego, CA	9,571	2,599	2,314	281	201	934	83	9	9	33	353	343	320	30	2	26	3
Boston, MA	9,325	29	143	905	233	746	374	435	404	56	231	466	114	168	718	90	45
Houston,TX	9,210	2,552	373	504	300	1,030	626	33	95	144	277	160	98	169	10	308	33
Newark, NJ	9,013	15	390	412	265	115	691	263	556	701	63	13	1	579	763	188	360
Nassau-Suffolk, NY	7,621	41	228	424	372	99	566	578	640	63	282	13	16	364	274	574	251
Bergen-Passaic, NJ	7,421	57	332	249	488	34	613	914	460	178	150	6	1	637	28	106	88
Philadelphia, PA	7,117	47	443	458	1,082	437	738	42	429	23	144	380	54	77	69	25	39
Jersey City, NJ	7,093	17	485	110	135	82	656	716	34	1,924	36	—	7	448	64	192	141
Honolulu, HI	6,849	12	3,403	757	888	451	13	1	2	1	7	31	219	2	1	2	2
Dallas, TX	6,378	1,781	205	303	300	494	438	9	33	74	281	245	174	44	4	42	14
Seattle, WA	5,248	84	758	497	553	675	185	1	6	6	150	451	319	25	—	9	2
Detroit, MI	5,116	84	395	217	380	78	508	6	87	14	100	18	42	26	9	11	12
Riverside-San Bernardino, CA	4,282	1,371	414	200	225	330	124	2	17	51	92	66	22	27	1	56	12
El Paso, TX	3,724	3,265	37	16	91	11	15	2	—	6	21	1	—	7	—	7	—
Minneapolis-St Paul, MN-WI	3,697	78	121	154	468	363	164	3	13	11	108	259	607	56	1	8	93
Atlanta, GA	3,409	55	101	195	311	362	172	9	90	86	154	237	89	62	15	15	13
Phoenix, AZ	3,312	1,115	161	209	145	212	96	1	7	9	71	67	15	23	2	23	7
Sacramento, CA	3,181	396	373	343	122	523	92	3	9	5	92	20	255	7	—	28	1
Middlesex-Somerset-Hunterdon, NJ	3,058	22	137	225	168	45	487	425	95	89	34	5	14	85	12	25	59
Denver, CO	3,004	464	104	107	370	428	91	2	6	13	94	115	164	19	1	8	2
Fort Lauderdale-Hollywood-Pompano Beach, FL	2,910	19	57	53	32	33	72	28	637	260	30	—	1	172	227	26	33
Portland, OR	2,832	109	167	200	274	592	75	1	4	16	119	194	217	17	—	8	1
Baltimore, MD	2,785	10	215	177	595	67	252	13	172	3	146	11	4	25	11	16	23
New Orleans, LA	2,702	45	81	83	68	716	88	24	17	175	29	53	34	39	5	49	17
Tampa-St. Petersburg-Clearwater, FL	2,553	107	110	60	90	212	63	26	125	355	52	42	43	66	40	8	16
Fresno, CA	2,542	826	194	83	39	84	171	1	2	1	60	88	610	2	—	10	1
Fort Worth-Arlington, TX	2,513	704	69	138	90	274	135	2	9	16	93	98	117	19	2	10	3
Stockton, CA	2,431	449	398	104	24	340	62	—	1	—	4	404	294	1	—	6	1
McAllen-Edinburg-Mission, TX	2,296	2,189	9	10	7	—	2	2	—	7	3	—	—	4	—	7	—

**Total is the average annual number of immigrants moving to the metropolitan area from 1984 to 1986.*
***Includes immigrants from the Peoples' Republic of China, Taiwan, and Hong Kong.*

Source: U.S. Immigration and Naturalization Service

EXHIBIT 24.8

Even domestic advertisers must be sensitive to a multinational culture, as U.S. population diversity indicates. (Reprinted with permission © *American Demographics,* September 1988, pp. 24–25.

QUESTIONS

1. Why have American advertising agencies become so aggressive in expanding into international markets in recent years?
2. Discuss the concept of global marketing as it relates to advertising.
3. What is the significance of the year 1992 to marketing and advertising in Europe?
4. What are some of the basic strategies used by advertising agencies to expand into international markets?
5. What are the advantages and disadvantages of centralized management by multinational agencies?
6. Discuss the idea of multinational media-buying combines among major advertising agencies.
7. Discuss the ramifications for advertising agencies of the continuing consolidation of worldwide marketing by major corporations.

READINGS

BOLT, JAMES F.: "Global Competition: Some Criteria for Success," *Business Horizons,* January/February 1988, p. 34.

DAWSON, CHARLES: "Television Expands Throughout Europe," *Media International,* January 1989, pp. 12–13.

FRIEDMAN, WAYNE: "Going Behind the Camera in Multi-national Co-ventures," *Cablevision,* February 13, 1989, p. 22.

GILLY, MARY C.: "Sex Roles in Advertising: A Comparison of Television Advertisements in Australia, Mexico, and the United States," *Journal of Marketing,* April 1988, p. 75.

JAIN, SUBHASH C.: "Standardization of International Marketing Strategy: Some Research Hypotheses," *Journal of Marketing,* January 1989, pp. 70–79.

KUPFER, ANDREW: "How to Be a Global Manager," *Fortune,* March 14, 1988, p. 52.

RAO, PRADEEP A.: "Awareness Advertising and International Market Segmentation," *International Journal of Advertising,* No. 4, 1987, p. 313.

RICKS, DAVID A.: "International Business Blunders: An Update," *Business and Economic Review,* January–March 1988, p. 11.

ROSS, BARRY NATHAN, JEAN J. BODDEWYN, AND ERNST LOUIS: "Participation by U.S. Agencies in International Brand Advertising: An Empirical Study," *Journal of Advertising,* Vol. 17, No. 4, 1988.

STEWART, DAVID W., AND KEVIN J. MCAULIFF: "Determinants of International Media Purchasing: A Survey of Media Buyers," *Journal of Advertising,* Vol. 17, No. 3, 1988, p. 22.

WEATHERSBY, WILLIAM, Jr.: "We Are the World," *Public Relations Journal,* September 1988, p. 32.

TWENTY-FIVE

Legal and Other Restraints on Advertising

Advertising is the most regulated of all business enterprises. At the national, state, and local levels, a host of restrictions face the potential advertiser. These cover the range from allowable language in legal and financial advertising to the size and placement of outdoor signs. In addition to complying with legal and regulatory restraints by outside organizations, advertisers must meet the requirements of a number of self-regulatory bodies as well as the media.

Moreover, advertising today operates in a world of heightened consumer knowledge and expectations. The high visibility of most advertising makes consumers more aware of perceived and real abuses than in other areas of marketing. Because of this high visibility and the need for honest and truthful advertising, the legal regulatory environment has become increasingly complex in recent years. Even though advertisers and their agencies have large legal staffs checking all product claims and advertising presentations, companies still run afoul (often innocently) of the legal restraints on advertising.

The consumer *doesn't* have ''perfect'' information about the marketplace—or about the products he/she buys. Consequently, he/she relies on the ''promises'' of marketers, in order to make the best judgements. When an advertiser puts his ''seal of approval,'' such as the *Sunkist stamp,* on citrus, consumers get the impression they are buying a *superior* product. . .even if they have limited knowledge of the category.

There are three primary constraints on advertising:

1. Laws and regulations of legally constituted bodies such as Congress and the Federal Trade Commission.
2. Media control over the kind of advertising acceptable for publication and broadcast.
3. Self-regulation by advertisers through various trade practice recommendations and codes of conduct.

Note that two of these three types of constraints are basically self-imposed. The typical advertiser is as concerned about misleading, false, and inappropriate advertising as any regulatory body. After all, advertising determines, in large measure, how the public perceives the companies, products, and services that advertise. Anything that damages the overall image of advertising hurts the efforts of each advertiser.

Caveat emptor. *Latin for ''Let the buyer beware.'' Represents the notion that there should be no government interference in the marketplace.*

It wasn't always so. In fact, until the twentieth century, the prevailing attitude among advertisers was *caveat emptor,* ''let the buyer beware,'' a libertarian notion rooted in the classical economic perception of a free marketplace of goods and ideas and perfect knowledge on the part of all participants. That is, buyers and sellers had equal information, and it was assumed that both groups, being rational, would make correct economic choices without government interference into business transactions.

In this century, however, the growing complexity of the marketplace led to the rejection of the principle of caveat emptor and its replacement by the idea that consumers cannot hope to have perfect knowledge of the marketplace and must therefore be protected by legal guarantees of the authenticity of advertising claims. Thus, numerous laws have been passed to shield the public from false and misleading advertising. Chief among them is the Federal Trade Commission Act, which we discuss first. We shall then touch on other federal and state laws affecting advertising, and note further steps that have been taken to protect the consumer from misrepresentations.

THE FEDERAL TRADE COMMISSION (FTC)

Federal Trade Commission Act. *Legislation passed in 1914 creating the FTC and making unfair competitive practices illegal.*

Wheeler-Lea Amendments. *Broadened the scope of the FTC to include consumer advertising.*

When the Federal Trade Commission Act was passed in 1914, Congress held that "unfair methods of competition are hereby declared unlawful." Thus, the law was designed to protect one business from another. Commercial actions injurious to consumers, but not to competitors, were not regarded as unfair under the law, and were not thought to come under the FTC's jurisdiction. It was not until 1922, in *FTC v. Winsted Hosiery Company,* that the Supreme Court held that false advertising was an unfair trade practice. In 1938, passage of the Wheeler-Lea amendments broadened this interpretation to include the principle that the FTC could protect consumers from deceptive advertising. This law also gave the FTC specific authority over false advertising in the fields of food, drugs, therapeutic devices, and cosmetics. Today the FTC has wide power over the advertising of all products sold or advertised across state lines.

The FTC possesses authority over false or misleading advertising. In the case of Pat Boone's endorsement of *Acne-Statin,* the FTC discovered that neither he nor his daughters had used the product or would likely use it—nor have they as much investigated the product's claims. Consequently, he was prohibited from *endorsing* the product, and the company from claiming PB's "intimate knowledge" of A-S.

"Bad" publicity from an FTC charge of false advertising can work against a firm's reputation, as to drive it "out" of business. In 1984, when the ads run by Jartran, a consumer "self-move" company, were judged to be "false, misleading, deceptive, and contained incomplete statements of fact"—the company's stock and sales fell drastically—especially when it was announced that it owed U-Haul (its arch competitor) $40 million in damages.

The Role of the FTC

The FTC's view of its role in regulating advertising and the aggressiveness with which it acts tend to vary according to the philosophy of the FTC chairman and the relationship between business and the administration in Washington. However, irrespective of political fluctuations, there are several factors that dictate the FTC's role as an enforcement agency:

1. The FTC cannot satisfy all its constituencies. Public interest consumer groups often charge that the commission is not aggressive enough in its enforcement, while many businesses view it as nitpicking and prone to interfere in trivial areas that are of little consequence to consumers. Daniel Oliver, FTC commissioner under President Ronald Reagan, summarized the overall goal of the commission thus: "Consistent, uniform regulation of interstate commerce is a matter of economic efficiency and common sense, not to mention constitutional law. I have a solution for those concerned about the inconsistent regulation of advertising—cooperation and leadership. The FTC is willing to assume that leadership but will not become a super-regulator. We will regulate only when necessary."[1]
2. The FTC tends to concentrate on major national issues and set the national regulatory agenda for advertising. Advertisers need the "assurance of a fair, consistent and predictable regulatory framework in which to operate. Advertisers simply cannot function efficiently in an environment of crazy-quilt regulations that is constantly changing because of either the political whims of federal legislators and regulators or inconsistent regulations from state to state."[2]
3. The bad publicity generated by an FTC charge of false advertising is often worse than any penalty administered by the commission. One study showed that "when false advertising charges are brought against a company, the market price of that company's stock declines,

[1] Paul Harris, "Will the FTC Finally Wake Up?" *Sales & Marketing Management,* January 1988, p. 60.

[2] *The Role of Advertising in America,* a publication of the Association of National Advertisers, p. 12.

often significantly. This decline is a measure of the market's estimate of the problem the company will have in selling its products as a result of the false advertising charges. [The study found] companies' stock value lost an average of 2.5 percent in the five days following the announcement. The greatest effect was seen in cases in which a company contested the FTC charges in court, but eventually lost.''[3]

Some Basic FTC Rules and Legal Findings

Over the years, ground rules have emerged for applying the FTC law to advertising. Based largely on the regulations of the FTC and on court decisions, these rules include the following important points:

Fairness. The original intent of the FTC Act was to prevent unfairness among businesses. The later charge to the commission to regulate deceptive practices, especially among consumers, has become its major priority. However, the FTC has from time to time moved to prohibit unfairness, especially when it deemed the unfair practice could result in harm to consumers. The FTC may rule an ad unfair even though it is truthful. For instance, the commission stopped ads showing children playing with electrical appliances near water. The ads were not deceptive, but there were legitimate concerns about safety.

Total impression. *The FTC has ruled that advertising deception must consider the overall impression of an ad.*

Total Impression. The courts have held that the overall impression an ad gives is the key to whether it is false or misleading. Thus, in one case, although the term *relief* was used in an ad, the net impression from the entire context was that the product promised a ''cure'' for the ailment. Similarly, words like *stops, ends,* and *defeats* may improperly imply permanent rather than temporary relief. If an ad has even a ''tendency to deceive,'' the FTC may find it illegal.

Clarity. The statement must be so clear that even a person of low intelligence would not be confused by it. The tendency of the law is to protect the credulous and the gullible. If an ad can have two meanings, it is illegal if one of them is false or misleading.

Manufacturers run the risk of legal problems if their claims are so exaggerated that they tend to mislead. The Food and Drug Administration scrutinizes food ads that make *nutritional claims*. In the case of a butter ad that claimed it contained fewer calories than margarine, the company had to provide ''laboratory'' proof to the FDA.

Fact versus Puffery. The courts have held that an advertiser's opinion of a product is tolerated as the legitimate expression of a biased opinion and not a material statement of fact. However, a statement that might be understood by a sophisticated person as trade puffery can be misleading to a person of lower intelligence. Much controversy over misleading advertising hovers around the question: When is a statement trade puffery, and when is it a false claim? All factual claims must be supportable. If you say, ''This is an outstanding leather briefcase,'' and the case is made of vinyl, that is misrepresentation. If you say,''This is an outstanding briefcase,'' that is a matter of opinion and is not illegal.

In addition to the possibility of being cited for exaggerated claims about a product, puffery carries other potential legal consequences. First, puffery may go beyond claims for the product and imply superiority over other brands. Unsubstantiated claims could lead to legal problems with other firms as well as the FTC. Second, an exaggerated claim might be interpreted as as warranty that could lead to liability for the manufacturer. Advertisers must walk a tightrope between creative, attention-getting advertising and claims that can actually mislead a large segment of the public. Beyond the legal ramifications of undue exaggeration, disappointing consumers by creating unreasonable expectations is damaging to the manufacturer's reputation.

Taste. *The FTC generally has held that taste is not a legal issue unless an ad is lewd.*

The Question of Taste. In general, the precedents of advertising law indicate that bad taste (except in advertising that is lewd) is not in itself deceptive or unfair. Hence, bad

[3]''False Advertising Can Cost Firm Dearly, FTC Study Says,'' *The Atlanta Journal,* June 7, 1988, p. 1-C.

taste is not an issue that would involve the FTC (although, of course, it might adversely affect sales).

Demonstrations. Demonstrations of a product or product performance on TV must not mislead viewers. In some cases, product substitutions may be made in a commercial if the intent is not to endow a product with qualities it does not really possess. For instance, the hot lights used in filming commercials do not allow realistic portrayals of some food products. Additives or substitutes may be used if the intent is only to show the product in a normal way or setting and not to upgrade the consumer's perception of the product.

Magnuson-Moss Warranty Act. *Passed in 1977, the act requires specific disclosure of terms of warranties offered to consumers.*

In product demonstrations, the consumer has a right to expect the same performance at home, as was accomplished in the media. *Baking and cooking activities* usually show a before-and-after sequence—but with appropriate time notations—so that consumers will comprehend the *complete* time commitment required to turn out the finished product. *The Pillsbury Doughboy* is used in commercials as a "guide" in the various steps—to help explain the *simplified* process.

Warranties. The major legislation dealing with warranties is the Magnuson-Moss Warranty Act, which became effective in July 1977. This act does not require that products carry a warranty but sets up a framework for disclosure of consumer warranties. It requires that the following information be provided to consumers at the time of purchase: (1) the nature and extent of the guarantee (most guarantees are limited rather than full warranties, and the limitations must be specifically stated); (2) the manner in which the guarantor will perform (what items will be replaced or when refunds will be made and under what conditions); (3) the identity of the guarantor (if the product is defective, should the consumer look to the retailer, distributor, or manufacturer for resolution of a claim?).

"Free." Along with related words, *free* is a popular word in advertising: "Buy one—get one free," "2-for-1 sale," "Gift," "Bonus," and "Without charge." If there are any terms or conditions for getting something free, they must be stated clearly and conspicuously along with the word *free*. If a purchaser must buy something to get something else free, the purchased product must be at its lowest price (same quality, same size) in 30 days. A free offer for a single size may not be advertised for more than 6 months in a market in any 12-month period.

Celebrities often lend their names to products, but they must be typical users of the product. George Plimpton was called on to endorse *Intellivision—versus Atari*—because of his "sports" connections. . . Added to his well-known "field trials" was his in-depth research on various outdoor activities for his many books. . . .

Lotteries. Lotteries are schemes for the distribution of prizes won by chance. If a person has to pay to enter a lottery conducted by an advertiser (except government lotteries), the United States Postal Service calls it illegal and bans the use of the mail for it. If the lottery is advertised in interstate commerce, the FTC also holds it illegal and will proceed to stop it. Prizes in many sweepstakes (which are a form of lottery) are allowable if money need not be paid to enter the sweepstakes. Sponsors of sweepstakes must actually give away all prizes or cash advertised and must disclose the approximate odds of winning. The next time you see a sweepstakes announcement, check whether these conditions are explicitly conformed to.

Testimonials. Testimonial endorsements have become an important method of gaining consumer attention, personalizing a sales message, and adding credibility to product claims. There are several considerations to which a celebrity commercial must conform. If a celebrity or expert endorses a product, he or she should use that product. If comparative claims vis-à-vis other products are made, the endorser should actually have made such comparisons. Claims made by typical endorsers should conform to what average consumers can expect from the product. Furthermore, if an association endorses a product, the endorsement should be based on association members' collective judgment or conform to association standards. The courts have ruled that an endorser who willfully engages in deceptive promotion can be held liable for damages along with the agency and the advertiser.

Consent decrees usually are signed by unlawful advertisers—rather than encounter negative publicity and significant costs in protest. *STP first* signed such a decree, when it was accused by the FTC of deceptive advertising. The company agreed *not* to use "false and misleading advertising" and "to support any claims for the oil additive with competent and reliable scientific tests or other objective data."

Methods of FTC Enforcement

Consent Decrees. When the FTC determines that advertising is deceptive, it notifies the offending advertiser and requests that a consent decree be signed in which the advertiser agrees that the deceptive practice or advertising will be stopped. Signing a

Consent decree. *Issued by the FTC. An advertiser signs the decree, stops the practice under investigation, but admits no guilt.*

consent decree saves the advertiser the cost and bad publicity that would result from a formal FTC complaint. The majority of FTC inquiries are settled by consent decrees without further action. However, any advertiser who fails to abide by the decree is subject to a $10,000-per-day fine.

Cease and desist orders. *If an advertiser refuses to sign a consent decree, the FTC may issue a cease and desist order that can carry a $10,000-per-day fine.*

Cease and Desist Orders. If an advertiser refuses to sign a consent decree, then a formal cease and desist order is issued. Before issuing the cease and desist order, the FTC will make a judgment that the deception is ''substantial'' and that the public interest would be served by formal action against the advertiser. A cease and desist order is a serious matter.

For a cease and desist order to become final, a hearing must be held before an administrative law judge. If the judge upholds the order, the company may appeal the decision to the full commission and then to a federal appeals court. However, this rarely occurs because of the expense and public-relations damage that might be done to the company before the case is finally decided. Still, some companies do appeal, and the case may drag on for years. For example, the FTC finally won a judgment against Geritol 11 years after the original cease and desist order was issued.

Corrective advertising. *To counteract the past residual effect of previous deceptive advertising, the FTC may require the advertiser to devote future space and time to disclosure of previous deception. Began around the late 1960s.*

Corrective Advertising. Although a cease and desist order stops a particular advertising practice, it does not repair any past damage that may have been done by false or misleading advertising. Now a new philosophy has been put into operation: To counteract the residual effects of the deceptive advertising, the FTC may require the advertiser to run advertising at his or her own expense ''to dissipate the effects of that deception.'' The commission appears to require corrective advertising chiefly when major advertising themes are the basis for consumers' choices. In one case of corrective advertising, Listerine was ordered to insert messages in $10 million worth of advertising that Listerine did not cure colds or lessen their severity, which had been a long-running theme of Listerine advertising.

Deception, Standards of Disclosure, and Substantiation

> The basic premise underlying the illegality of deception in advertising is that the receiver of the advertising message will behave in a manner which is different than if the advertisement contained no deception. Therefore, free competition is hindered and firms that deceive are assumed to obtain more business than they otherwise would. Of course, this additional business is assumed to be obtained at the expense of competitors who are engaged in truthful advertising.[4]

Substantiation. *The key to advertising regulation is that advertisers must be able to substantiate the claims made in their advertisements.*

In ruling *against* the legality of an ad, the FTC looks for *deceptive* practices; that is, where the consumer was deceived into believing an ''untruth.'' In a landmark decision ordering corrective advertising, *Profile Bread* had to explain it had fewer calories than other bread—because it was *sliced thinner*. And eating Profile *wouldn't* cause a weight loss, as its lower calories were insignificant, compared to other breads.

One of the crucial elements of effective advertising regulation is substantiation of claims. The public has the right to expect that advertising be factually correct and that any product claims can be substantiated with supportable evidence. Few people disagree that advertising should be truthful, but even among FTC members the definition and implementation of truth and its enforcement are open to many questions and interpretations.

Today substantiation is the key to advertising regulation. Advertisers know that most objective claims concerning safety, performance, or quality are going to be challenged by the FTC, the public, or competitors. Substantiation—or, more correctly, the lack thereof—is the central focus of virtually every advertising disagreement. Basically, an advertising claim that cannot be substantiated runs a great risk of being ruled deceptive—as it should be.

In order to understand the process of advertising deception, let's review some primary considerations of how the law regards deceptive advertising:

1. Intent to deceive is not a factor; deception is unlawful even if entirely unintentional. When

[4]David M. Gardner, ''Deception in Advertising: A Receiver Oriented Approach to Understanding,'' *Journal of Advertising,* Fall 1976, p. 5.

you charge someone with deceptive advertising, you're not saying it was done on purpose—only that it's unlawful and has to stop.

2. It's not *false* advertising that's illegal; but *deceptive* advertising. A recent case involved the true claim for a pain reliever that it "contains no aspirin." Instead, the product contained an ingredient related to aspirin that produces the same side effects as aspirin. The FTC thought the claim "contains no aspirin" would lead consumers to think that the product induced none of aspirin's side effects, and therefore outlawed the claim unless it was properly qualified. In this case, the commission found that true advertising was deceptive because of what it omitted—in other words, it did not tell the whole truth.
3. Perception is a subjective matter, falsity is a matter of fact. When you look for falsity, you compare the advertising claim to the product—you do not examine the consumer. But when you look for deceptiveness, you compare the consumer's perception of the claim to the product.[5]

The problem with judgments about advertising deception is that many advertisements will be deceptive to *someone*. As we have seen, the question of deception involves not only the factual content of an advertising message, but the effect of this message on consumers. This notion of *perceived effect* gave an interesting twist to a case brought by the FTC against Kraft Singles American cheese slices.

The FTC alleged that Kraft "misrepresented the calcium content . . . [and] claimed . . . that a slice of Kraft singles contains the same amount of calcium as 5 ounces of milk, when it does not." In proving that advertisements are deceptive, the FTC must show three things: that there is a misrepresentation or omission that could mislead the consumer; that the misrepresentation or omission is likely to mislead the consumer; and that the misrepresented or omitted information is "material," or important, to consumers.

The first part of Kraft's defense was that its advertising was truthful. The second part of its defense was the ineffectiveness of its advertising—that is, Kraft argued that consumers could not have been misled by advertising that had little or no effect. A study conducted by Kraft indicated "that despite an advertising campaign centered on the milk and calcium content of Singles, only 1.6% of surveyed consumers listed calcium as one of the reasons why they bought Kraft Singles."[6]

The Kraft case raises an interesting question: Does deception occur only when consumers believe an advertisement's claims and alter their consumption as a result? Although Kraft did not acknowledge that its advertising for Singles was factually incorrect, its defense would seem to open the door to using advertising "ineffectiveness" as a defense for deception.

The Robinson-Patman Act and Cooperative Advertising

Robinson-Patman Act. *A federal law, enforced by the FTC. Requires a manufacturer to give proportionate discounts and advertising allowances to all competing dealers in a market. Purpose: to protect smaller merchants from unfair competition of larger buyers.*

The FTC, through its antitrust division, has responsibility for enforcing another law affecting marketing and advertising, the Robinson-Patman Act. This act is part of a three-law "package" that evolved over a period of almost 50 years. These laws and their purposes were:

1. *1890 Federal Sherman Antitrust Act.* The Sherman Act was designed to prevent alliances of firms formed to restrict competition.
2. *1914 Clayton Antitrust Act.* This act amended the Sherman Act. It eliminated preferential price treatment when manufacturers sold merchandise to retailers.
3. *1936 Robinson-Patman Act.* In turn, this law amended the Clayton Act. It tries to prevent manufacturers from providing a "promotional allowance" to one customer unless the allowance is also offered to competitors on a proportionally equal basis.

---

[5]Ivan L. Preston, "Communication Research in the Prosecution of Deceptive Advertising," Working Paper No. 86-2, Department of Advertising, The University of Texas at Austin, May 1986, pp. 3–5.

[6]Julie Liesse Erickson, "Kraft Takes on FTC, Cites 'Ineffective' Ads," *Advertising Age*, July 4, 1988, p. 39.

The background of the Robinson-Patman Act is this: Some manufacturers had found a loophole in the Clayton Act, whereby they could seem to be charging all their customers equitable prices, but actually favor bigger customers by giving them promotional allowances. For example, large retailers might be given co-op advertising allowances that were unavailable to small retailers—which, in effect, lowered the price for the goods paid by these large retailers. Thus, the promotional allowance was an under-the-table rebate.[7]

Since there are fewer independent merchants today, there's *less* of a "push" on enforcing the Robinson-Patman Act in their behalf. In fact, during the 80s, the trend toward government regulation of commerce, in general, spread to the advertising industry. The new philosophy is to let the market adjust on its own to the needs and desires of consumers. If, for example, consumers are annoyed by the advent of a plethora of commercials at each station break, "consumerism" should take over—either by formalized agitation or by individual refusal of commercial messages ("zipping, zapping") and products.

In recent years, the FTC has not given high priority to enforcement of the Robinson-Patman Act. The commission has taken action under Robinson-Patman only when it was clearly in consumers' best interest to do so. One reason for the lack of aggressive enforcement is the changing retail climate since the passage of the act over 50 years ago.

In 1936, Congress was concerned that large chains would drive small independent retailers out of business. Chains were just beginning to play a major role in retailing in the 1930s. They were viewed in many circles as retail predators who would gain a monopolistic advantage once they drove the corner grocer and druggist from the marketplace. Today consumers generally regard chains as a fact of retail life, and a rather economical one at that.

Another factor in the low-keyed enforcement of Robinson-Patman is the generally broader interpretation of what constitutes legitimate business practices today. For instance, quantity discounts to retail customers based on amount of purchases and price-cutting to meet competition are both allowed, so long as there is no collusion in setting prices in violation of antitrust laws. Despite what some observers criticize as a weak enforcement policy, Robinson-Patman remains a strong deterrent to antitrust practices at the retail level.

THE FEDERAL FOOD, DRUG, AND COSMETIC ACT

Food and Drug Administration (FDA). *The federal bureau with authority over the safety and purity of foods, drugs, and cosmetics and over the labeling of such products.*

Ingredients labeling is required by the Federal Food, Drug, and Cosmetic Act. *Mayonnaise* and *ice cream* were among the last two categories of products to resist ingredients labeling—while *Coca-Cola* finally agreed to list its ingredients, *except* those considered "natural flavors."

Alcohol advertising is regulated both by the federal government and by the individual states. While beer and wine ads are permitted on TV, advertisers are prohibited from showing actual consumption by consumers. Only the *products* may be featured.

Closely tied to the Federal Trade Commission Act is the Federal Food, Drug, and Cosmetic Act, passed in 1938, giving the Food and Drug Administration broad power over the labeling and branding—as contrasted with the advertising—of foods, drugs, therapeutic devices, and cosmetics. It is this law that requires food and drug manufacturers to put their ingredients on the labels.

Since the advertising and labeling of a product cannot be contradictory, any rulings by the FDA necessarily affect advertising. For example, the FDA requires that health claims on labels be:

- Truthful and not misleading
- Supported by valid, reliable, publicly available scientific evidence derived from well-designed and well-conducted studies consistent with generally accepted scientific procedures and principles
- Consistent with generally recognized medical and nutritional principles
- Accompanied by the required nutrition information level[8]

In recent years, the FDA has become much more aggressive in examining claims for various cosmetics. In particular, the FDA is concerned with "whether the language used on labels and promotional materials is really a drug claim and not a cosmetic claim. Words like "moisturizing," "smoothing" and "softening" are all viable cosmetic claims, the FDA says. But claims that a product "counteracts," "retards" or

[7]Miles David, *Making Money with Co-op,* a publication of the Radio Advertising Bureau, 1986, pp. 82–83.
[8]"FDA Sets Food Label Guidelines," *The 4A's Washington Newsletter,* December 1987, p. 6.

''controls'' aging or the aging process, and assertions that a product will ''rejuvenate,'' ''repair'' or ''renew'' skin constitute drug claims and are thus unacceptable language for products marketed as cosmetics.''[9] In 1987 alone, the FDA asked 23 cosmetics firms to change such language because it allegedly violated this standard.

OTHER FEDERAL CONTROLS OF ADVERTISING

Alcohol Tax Unit of the United States Treasury Department

The liquor industry has a unique pattern of labeling and advertising under both federal and state laws. For an interesting historical reason, the federal laws are under the jurisdiction of the Treasury Department. The first American excise tax was the one levied under Alexander Hamilton, Secretary of the Treasury, on alcoholic beverages. That department, through its Alcohol Tax Unit, is interested to this day in the labeling, standards of bottle sizes, and advertising of alcoholic beverages.

In addition, each state has its own liquor advertising laws. In some states, you cannot show a drinking scene; in others, you can show a person holding a glass, but not bringing it up to his or her lips; in still others, you can picture only a bottle. In few industries does an advertising person need a lawyer more often than in liquor advertising.

Securities and Exchange Commission

The SEC is the government agency that controls all advertising of public offerings of stocks or bonds. It insists on full disclosure of facts relevant to the company and the stock to be sold so that the prospective investor can form an opinion.

Its insistence on the facts that must be published—including a statement of negative elements affecting the investment—is very firm and thorough. The SEC never recommends or refuses to recommend a security; its concern is with the disclosure of full information.

United States Postal Service

The postal service has the authority to stop the delivery of mail to all firms guilty of using the mails to defraud—which is enough to put any firm out of business. It deals mainly with mail-order frauds.

ADVERTISING AND THE FIRST AMENDMENT

As we noted earlier, advertising is the primary marketing communication tool. It conveys information about new products, competitive promotions, even ideas and opinions. Yet advertising has never been afforded full protection under the First Amendment. Whereas noncommercial speech is offered the widest possible protection, advertising is held to much stricter standards.

In reviewing the First Amendment protection of commercial speech, three things are clear:

1. Commercial speech enjoys *some* protection under the First Amendment.
2. Whether the Founding Fathers intended it or not, a distinction has developed over the past 50

---

[9] ''Watch Your Language,'' *Inside Print,* March 1988, p. 48.

years between the degree and kind of protection to be accorded commercial speech and that given to other forms of speech.

3. Commercial speech is usually viewed as less serious or less important than other forms of speech. In the eyes of many, if not most, Americans, commercial messages are second-class speech.

Many advertisers think that at the heart of the problem is a willingness by the courts to tolerate a degree of restraint that would be totally unacceptable for any other form of speech. There seems to be a belief

> . . . that advertising, employing supple and arcane forms of persuasion, is something a few of us understand and can deal with but that render all those less educated and sophisticated than we submissive and subject to exploitation. The fear underlying the compulsion to censor is groundless. Consumers are protected against untruthful advertising by media and advertising industry self-regulation and, ultimately, by the Federal Trade Commission. Truthful advertising for legal products and services can hurt no one. Indeed, it is inconsistent, if not erratic, to believe that those citizens who can distill the truth about the most complex global issues from the welter of diverse opinion heaved up each day by a free press cannot be trusted to decide, on the basis of commercial messages, which brand of soap or beer or even cigarettes to purchase—or whether to make such a purchase at all.[10]

''Commercial speech'' doesn't enjoy the same protection as free speech. It can be prohibited on the basis of *not* acting in the public's interest. Ads by the National Rifle Association—no matter how *factual*—have been refused by publications for advocating ''injurious'' activity.

In recent decades, commercial speech has been afforded some First Amendment protection. The problem for advertisers, however, is that opinions have been uneven and contradictory. A concrete doctrine of commercial speech has yet to be enunciated by the courts.

In several cases during the 1960s and 1970s, the courts extended some level of free-speech protection to advertising messages. Until 1976, however, the ads at issue did not involve messages dealing with the promotion of a service or product. For instance, in 1975, the Supreme Court overturned a Virginia law making publicizing a New York abortion clinic in a Virginia newspaper a criminal offense. But the Court was careful to note that the ad involved an issue of public interest and did not constitute a purely commercial message. This and similar opinions left open the question of constitutional protection for strictly commercial advertising.

Finally, in 1976, the Court addressed the question of purely commercial speech in the case of *Virginia State Board of Pharmacy v. Virginia Citizens Consumer Council.* The Court ruled that a state law banning the advertising of prescription drug prices was unconstitutional. It said, in effect, that society benefits from a free flow of commercial information just as it benefits from a free exchange of political ideas.

This decision did not result in full constitutional guarantees for commercial speech, for in 1979, in the case of *Friedman v. Rogers,* the Court upheld the right of the state of Texas to prevent an optometrist from using an ''assumed name, corporate name, trade name, or any other than the name under which he is licensed to practice optometry in Texas.'' In its decision, the Court said that First Amendment protection for commercial speech is not absolute and that regulation of commercial speech can be allowed even when the restrictions would be unconstitutional ''in the realm of noncommercial expression.''

Perhaps the best example of this limited protection afforded commercial speech is *Posadas de Puerto Rico Associates v. Tourism Company of Puerto Rico.* This 1986 case involved a Puerto Rican law banning advertising of gambling casinos to residents of Puerto Rico even though casino gambling is legal there. In a 5–4 decision, the Court upheld the Puerto Rico regulation. Clearly, this decision was a setback for the constitutional protection of commercial speech. Even more chilling to advocates of commercial speech protections were statements by Chief Justice William Rehnquist, who wrote the majority opinion on the Puerto Rico case and has long been opposed to

---

[10]John O'Toole, ''Advertising and Democracy: Is Advertising Second-Class Speech?'' *Gannett Center Journal,* Spring 1987, pp. 105–107.

constitutional protections for commercial speech. He wrote that the First Amendment itself is "demeaned" by invoking it to protect advertisements.[11]

The Central Hudson Four-Part Test

Central Hudson four-part test. *Supreme Court test to determine if specific commercial speech is protected under the Constitution.*

To one critic, the Court's almost annual production of commercial-speech decisions shows that it has never quite pinned down its own rationale for the doctrine.[12] If there are any general guidelines as to the type of constitutional protection afforded commercial speech, they are to be found in *Central Hudson Gas & Electric v. Public Service Commission of New York.*

This case concerned a prohibition by the New York Public Service Commission of all promotional advertising by utilities. The rationale was that the ban was compatible with public concerns over energy conservation. In overturning the commission's prohibition, the Court established a four-part test to determine when commercial speech is constitutionally protected and when regulation is permissible:

1. Is the commercial expression eligible for First Amendment protection? That is, is it neither deceptive nor promoting an illegal activity? Obviously, no constitutional protection can be provided for commercial speech that fails this test.
2. Is the governmental interest asserted in regulating the expression substantial? This test requires that the stated reason for regulating the advertisement must be of primary interest to the state rather than of a trivial, arbitrary, or capricious nature.
3. If the first two tests are met, the Court then considers if the regulation of advertising imposed advances the cause of the governmental interest asserted. That is, if we assume that an activity is of legitimate government concern, will the prohibition of commercial speech further the government's goals?
4. If the first three tests are met, the Court must finally decide if the regulation is more extensive than necessary to serve the government's interest.

In the Court's opinion, both the Central Hudson and the Puerto Rico cases met the first three tests. However, the Court ruled that a total prohibition of utility advertising was more extensive than necessary, and overturned the regulation against Central Hudson. In the Puerto Rico case, the ruling was that the prohibition met all four tests, and therefore the Court upheld the ban on casino advertising.

By banning advertising of certain products/services, regulators sidestep the "real" issue of whether the actual product should be banned. That is; if it can't be advertised, why should it be produced? Currently, "hard" liquor is banned from TV, as are smoking products. However, both categories of products can use print and billboards to advertise—and are universally sold throughout the world.

Some observers believe that the current debate over the banning of cigarette advertising represents the most serious challenge to the promotion of legal products since the broadcast advertising ban of cigarette advertising passed by Congress in 1971. Since then, we have seen the elimination of smokeless tobacco products from broadcast media through a law passed in 1986.

The advertising industry is concerned that the Puerto Rico casino gambling case and the earlier bans on broadcast tobacco advertising set a precedent for the selective banning of all sorts of legal product advertising. Howard Bell, president of the American Advertising Federation, summed up the advertising industry's position: "What proponents of ad bans don't realize is that policies which reduce public information only hinder the consumer's ability to make commercial decisions, while they erode the economic structure upon which a free market is based."[13]

In summing up the effects of recent Court cases involving commercial speech, one

[11] Steven W. Colford, "Rehnquist Slams Ads' 1st Amendment Shield," *Advertising Age,* June 30, 1986, p. 12.

[12] P. Cameron DeVore, "Gambling-Ad Decision Weakens Commercial Speech Rights," *presstime,* August 1986, p. 34.

[13] Quote from a speech by Wally Snyder, vice president/government relations, American Advertising Federation, speech to the Better Business Bureau/The Advertising Club of Louisville, November 14, 1986.

media lawyer noted, "What is so troubling about Posadas in the eyes of people who have been dying to ban advertising, [is] it is sort of like a golden key. It's so seductive to ban advertising, as opposed to getting down to the hard question of whether you are going to ban a legal product. It's so simple to say you can't talk about it, instead of attacking an industry or product that is perfectly legal and used by a lot of voters. There's not as big a political price for legislators to pay to enact a ban on words."[14]

ADVERTISING OF PROFESSIONAL SERVICES

One of the most controversial areas of commercial speech involves advertising by professionals, especially attorneys. Two restrictions against legal advertising had long prevailed, one imposed by state laws, the other by bar associations, which had the power to cancel the membership of any attorney who advertised. In the case of *Bates v. State Bar of Arizona,* the Supreme Court ruled that state laws forbidding advertising by attorneys were unconstitutional on First Amendment grounds. The fourth test of the Central Hudson case seems to reinforce the Bates decision. That is, most legal scholars think that the total prohibition of a class of advertising will generally not meet the fourth test since any such total ban will be considered broader than necessary.

In 1988, the Supreme Court extended the right of attorneys to advertise their professional services. A Kentucky lawyer, Richard Shapero, was cited for violating a Kentucky law prohibiting targeted mail solicitation of people who were in need of legal services because of some special circumstance. In this case, Shapero had mailed an advertisement to homeowners facing foreclosure.

The Court ruled that although personal contact by an attorney could be prohibited, a letter posed no threat of undue influence to consumers who are under threat of legal action. The Shapero case had the immediate effect of lifting the ban on targeted letters in the 25 states that prohibited them. In addition, it is predicted that the ruling will remove the stigma attached to such mailings.

The area of *professional advertising* has been explored by the Supreme Court; the current trend is to *permit* such promotion, with professional associations setting appropriate standards. Today, lawyers spend an estimated $60 million a year on TV ad time alone. Joel Hyatt, of Hyatt Legal Services, spends about $5 million a year, advertising his 185 legal clinics in 22 states.

These recent court rulings seem to have made most professional advertising legal. Bar associations and other professional associations still have regulatory powers over the accuracy and scope of their members' advertising, but they can no longer entirely prohibit members from advertising.

Nonetheless, many professionals are still reluctant to support or engage in overt promotion of their services. One study of physicians indicated that over 70 percent opposed unrestricted advertising by doctors because they thought that physician advertising would lower the prestige of the field, not make patients more aware of physician qualifications, and inadequately represent the services provided by individual doctors.[15]

Despite controversy and professionals' misgivings, professional advertising is a growing segment of the advertising business. The Newspaper Advertising Bureau estimates that $1 billion is spent annually on advertising by professionals. The majority of these dollars go into Yellow Pages ads, with newspapers and television advertising trailing far behind. It has been suggested that some professionals prefer to advertise in the Yellow Pages since this form of advertising is not as overt and aggressive as other types. In any event, if the last two years are any indication, professional advertising is bound to increase dramatically in the near future.

---

[14]Margaret G. Carter, "Advertising Curbs," *presstime,* March 1988, p. 11.

[15]Terry Lance Kinney and Karen W. King, "Consumer and Physician Attitudes Toward Advertising by Physicians," *Proceedings of the 1988 Conference of The American Academy of Advertising,* edited by John D. Leckenby, 1988, p. RC-93.

STATE AND LOCAL LAWS RELATING TO ADVERTISING

Printer's Ink *Model Statutes (1911).* *The act directed at fraudulent advertising, prepared and sponsored by* Printer's Ink, *which was the pioneer advertising magazine.*

The first and basic statute in the regulation of advertising, which still represents a landmark in advertising history, is the *Printers' Ink* Model Statute, drawn up in 1911. It attempts to punish "untrue, deceptive, or misleading" advertisers. *Printers Ink* magazine, the pioneer trade paper of advertising, has died; but its model statute, in its original or modified form, lives on in 44 states.

Until recently, the regulation of advertising was rather clearly divided between the federal and state governments. At the national level, the FTC had primary responsibility for regulating advertising in interstate commerce. The individual states were responsible for prosecuting fraud and upholding consumer protection legislation. Most of these state actions dealt with retailers and smaller companies operating within state borders.

National Association of Attorneys General (NAAG). *In recent years, the attorneys general of the various states have taken a more active role in prosecuting illegal advertising. This action has been taken on an individual as well as through the NAAG.*

States are now becoming more involved in setting advertising regulation. All but 4 states have adopted some form of the model statute, introduced by the old *Printer's Ink* magazine in 1911, against deceptive and misleading advertising. However, the cases that are usually brought to trial are the most flagrant and heartless violations—such as robbing "oldsters" of their life savings.

Today state attorneys are bringing more and more suits against national companies for alleged deceptive advertising. The National Association of Attorneys General (NAAG) has been at the forefront of advertising regulation. The organization has formed task forces to review advertising for airline fares and car rental agreements. In addition, major national advertisers such as Nabisco, Procter & Gamble, Sara Lee, and Campbell Soup have been asked to provide information on health claims and other nutritional data appearing in their advertising.

The requests for information and advertising substantiation are nothing new. What is new is the aggressive stance by the states in reviewing national advertising. Advertisers fear that state involvement in national advertising may create 50 different sets of regulations and make national magazine and network television advertising virtually impossible. A spokesman for Campbell Soup summarized the fear this way: "We feel it's more appropriate to be handled on a national scale. Obviously there can be problems with regulations of 50 different states. But this doesn't mean that we reject their right to an inquiry."[16] The FTC also has reservations about the potential fragmentation of advertising regulation among the states. Former FTC Chairman Daniel Oliver has noted that some of the state regulations appear to be stricter than comparable federal standards.

James Mattox, attorney general of Texas, and a strong proponent of the NAAG's efforts in regulating advertising, takes a different position:

> What is new and what has drawn attention to our [NAAG] efforts is that we are now coordinating activities to an unprecedented degree. More and more we see that if one state decides that it is necessary to investigate an advertisement to determine if it is deceptive, that state will get in touch with other states to work together toward our common goal. . . . Our sole goal here is to protect consumers, and we will do so to the fullest extent of our laws.[17]

COMPARISON ADVERTISING

Comparison advertising. *Used interchangeably with the term comparative advertising, it directly contrasts an advertiser's product with other named or identified products.*

Comparison advertising compares a product with a competitive product, usually by name. This kind of advertising is not new; in 1930, J. Sterling Getchell, head of the agency bearing his name, introduced the Chrysler car to the market by inviting customers to "Try all three." For many years afterward, car advertisers compared a feature or the track record of their cars to other named brands. However, the conventional wisdom in the advertising trade was that if you mentioned a competitor's name, you were giving that competitor free advertising.

[16]Jennifer Lawrence, "States Target Campbell Ads," *Advertising Age,* June 27, 1988, p. 107.

[17]James Mattox, "Should States Regulate Ads?" *Advertising Age,* August 8, 1988, p. 18.

The push for comparative advertising came in 1972, when the FTC urged ABC and NBC to allow commercials that named competitors. (Until then, only CBS had permitted such messages; ABC and NBC would allow nothing but ''Brand X''comparisons.) Since 1972, comparative advertising has become a popular, although extremely controversial, advertising technique. The great majority of competitor-initiated complaints about advertising directed to the several regulatory bodies involve comparative advertising.

Types of Comparative Advertising

While *comparison advertising* does provide a tantalizing attraction for viewers, it also invites speculation as to whether the ''superior'' product matches the advantages it claims. To increase credibility, ''actual'' consumer trials of new products are often featured—with the consumer choosing the lesser-known item (example: Blatz Beer over Budweiser). If the audience identifies with the featured ''guinea pig,'' it may increase the probability of success of the new entree's market introduction.

There are basically three types of comparative advertising, each with its own variations.

Head-to-Head Comparisons. It is still common to see ads in which one competitor challenges another by name. However, companies' use of head-to-head comparative advertising as a primary strategy is not as common as it was a few years ago. Visa versus American Express, Now cigarettes versus Carlton, and Duracell versus Kodak batteries somehow don't have the same sting as the original Avis versus Hertz. Still, head-to-head comparisons are fairly popular. They have the advantage of being restrictive in terms of the claims made, so the advertiser must substantiate claims only against a single brand. On the other hand, this type of advertising is not effective unless there is a clear leader in the field against which you can make a comparison.

Your Brand Against the World. Some advertisers have become bolder and made blanket claims against a number of other brands. This type of comparison is more dangerous because it opens you to counterclaims and demands for substantiation from a number of brands. These ads are often based on industry-wide standards.

Brand X Comparisons. The brand X comparison does not mention competing brands by name. In some cases, though, the comparison is to an obvious competitor. For instance, when one advertiser referred to a competing mouthwash as the one that left a ''medicine breath,'' there was little doubt as to the brand being singled out. Other brand X comparisons are the ''your brand against the world'' type: for instance, Kraft Macaroni & Cheese Dinner ''has more cheese than any other brand'' and Advil is better than aspirin. It should be remembered that not naming a competitor will not necessarily protect an advertiser from liability if the claims cannot be substantiated.

Finally, we should mention a quasi-method of comparative advertising that has become popular in recent years. Many products have begun to compare the current version of their product with an earlier model. Headlines promoting the ''best ever,'' ''new and improved,'' and ''now with better taste'' are often promoting improvements of the product rather than making comparisons with other brands. These ads have some of the characteristics of a brand comparison without incurring any of the risks.

In some cases, companies react to comparison advertising by turning the comparisons by other advertisers into a compliment. This technique is used by a brand that regards itself as clearly superior to the competition (see Exhibit 25.1).

In 1974, the American Association of Advertising Agencies issued guidelines for comparative advertising (see Exhibit 25.2). In doing so, the 4A's urged its clients to exercise caution in using comparative ads.

The 4A's word of caution to advertising agencies is important to heed. Penalties for deceptive and damaging comparative advertising under the Lanham Act are extremely harsh:

> Section 43(a) of the Lanham Act, which covers false comparative advertising, prohibits a company from making false or misleading statements about its own goods and services. In recent years, court decisions have greatly expanded the scope and coverage of the Lanham Act, and monetary damages in some cases have been substantial. In *U-Haul International, Inc. v. Jartran, Inc.*, for example, the U.S. Court of Appeals for the Ninth Circuit awarded over $42 million in damages for violations of the Lanham Act. These remedies complement

EXHIBIT 25.1

Effective comparative advertising does not have to "name names." (Courtesy: BMW of North America.)

any action that can be taken by the federal or state governments and serve to further insure that advertisers and their agencies proceed carefully in developing truthful, non-deceptive advertising.[18]

Advertisements and commercials have to "clear" their own organizations' scrutiny, before they can be released. The National Association of Broadcasters (NAB), the Direct Mail Advertising Association (DMMA), and the Outdoor Advertising of America maintain "standards of practice" for their members. While these organizations have no legal clout, they do exert "peer pressure" in encouraging *truthful communication*.

Comparison advertising has lost some of its earlier shrillness in naming competitors. Many advertisers are emphasizing the positive qualities of their own products and making comparative aspects a secondary feature of their advertising (see Exhibit 25.3).

THE ADVERTISING CLEARANCE PROCESS

***Advertising clearance process.** The internal process of clearing ads for publication and broadcast, conducted primarily by ad agencies and clients.*

To this point, our discussion has concentrated on the various legal and regulatory restraints on advertising. It would be a serious mistake to leave the impression that companies must be constrained from producing deceptive advertising by outside orga-

[18] *The Role of Advertising in America,* a publication of the Association of National Advertisers, Inc., p. 10.

EXHIBIT 25.2

Policy statement and guidelines for comparative advertising. (Courtesy: American Association of Advertising Agencies.)

The Board of Directors of the American Association of Advertising Agencies recognizes that when used truthfully and fairly, comparative advertising provides the consumer with needed and useful information.

However, extreme caution should be exercised. The use of comparative advertising, by its very nature, can distort facts and, by implication, convey to the consumer information that misrepresents the truth.

Therefore, the Board believes that comparative advertising should follow certain guidelines:

1. The intent and connotation of the ad should be to inform and never to discredit or unfairly attack competitors, competing products or services.
2. When a competitive product is named, it should be one that exists in the marketplace as significant competition.
3. The competition should be fairly and properly identified but never in a manner or tone of voice that degrades the competitive product or service.
4. The advertising should compare related or similar properties or ingredients of the product, dimension to dimension, feature to feature.
5. The identification should be for honest comparison purposes and not simply to upgrade by association.
6. If a competitive test is conducted it should be done by an objective testing source, preferably an independent one, so that there will be no doubt as to the veracity of the test.
7. In all cases the test should be supportive of all claims made in the advertising that are based on the test.
8. The advertising should never use partial results or stress insignificant differences to cause the consumer to draw an improper conclusion.
9. The property being compared should be significant in terms of value or usefulness of the product to the consumer.
10. Comparatives delivered through the use of testimonials should not imply that the testimonial is more than one individual's thought unless that individual represents a sample of the majority viewpoint.

EXHIBIT 25.3

Low-key comparative ads can be effective sales tools. (Courtesy: Del Monte Corporation.)

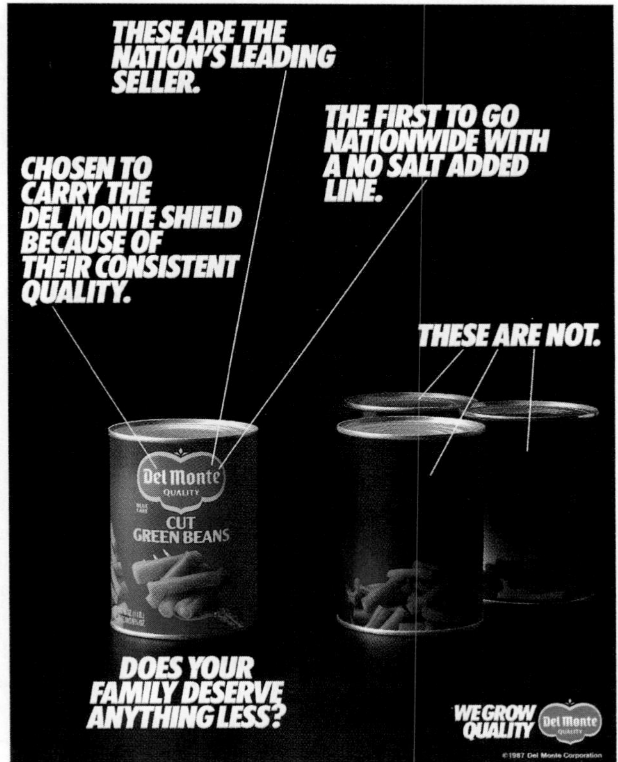

EXHIBIT 25.4

Primary concerns and interests of involved parties. (*Source:* Eric Zanot, "Unseen but Effective Advertising Regulation: The Clearance Process," *Journal of Advertising,* Vol. 14, November 4, 1985, pp. 46–47.)

Agency Creatives	creativity and sales potential primary matters of taste and law secondary
Agency Legal Staff (internal and external)	standards of the media primary matters of law primary pragmatic approach to the process
Advertiser	sales potential primary matters of law primary generally conservative attitude
Media	substantiation of facts primary matters of taste primary matters of law primary creativity and sales potential irrelevant

nizations. In fact, most advertisers, agencies, and media have a sophisticated network for reviewing advertisements.

Starting with the creative team that initiates the ad and ending with the medium that accepts it, an advertisement is reviewed by a number of people. At each step in the process, the ad is looked at from a different perspective (see Exhibit 25.4). The checks and balances of such a process ensure that most national advertising meets all reasonable public standards of ethics and taste as well as legal requirements. Exhibit 25.5 traces this complex process from the creative team to the media, and finally, to the postpublication regulation that might be enforced against a deceptive advertisement.

Virtually every major medium has guidelines for acceptable advertising. Most of the problems appear at the local level. Some local advertisers are simply ignorant of the law. Others are unscrupulous, "fly-by-night" operators who want to rip off customers. In either case, newspapers often form the first line of defense against misleading advertising. They daily deal with issues that rarely come up in national advertising.

The review process of the Orlando *Sentinel* is typical of that of most major newspapers. The *Sentinel* sometimes even goes beyond its own legal staff to make a determination of whether an advertisement should be run. "Questionable copy is scrutinized by the *Sentinel*'s law firm. The Federal Drug Administration is consulted if an advertisement is submitted on an unlicensed drug. If doubts arise about a company's reliability, the Better Business Bureau is contacted."[19] In many cases, a newspaper must simply use its judgment. For example, the *Sentinel* turned down a mail-order advertisement for a machete because it thought it would be too easy for children to order it.

The media, also, have the right to refuse space and time for "questionable" products, which may violate ethical or religious factions. *The New York Times* persuaded Della Femina Travesano & Partners to change the headline, "I enjoy sex" to "I'll do a lot for love" for LifeStyles condoms.

Probably the most formalized systems of media control are found at the three television networks. Their broadcast standards departments tend to deal with questions of taste as opposed to illegality. The large national advertisers that dominate network television rarely submit a commercial that is obviously contrary to federal or FTC regulations. However, in recent years, a number of commercials have been rejected or required to be extensively edited by one or more of the networks. Sometimes a whole class of products, such as condoms, is rejected, but more often it is the execution of a particular commercial that is the problem.

> Although many thousands of storyboards are submitted for approval, relatively few are rejected. Most require some revisions, with the most troublesome involving toys and other children-oriented products; claims made in endorsements, drug and nutrition spots; and a handful of commercials that try to use sex as a selling tool. . . . On top of such clearances, there are between 60 and 85 challenges put forth annually by advertisers who question copy and product claims made in rivals' commercials that had passed muster and got on the air.[20]

---

[19]David Wisor and Ann Patrick, "Ads We Turn Down," *Sentinel Communications Quarterly,* Winter 1986/87, p. 14.

[20]James P. Forkan, "Agencies, Stations Mull Aftermath of Web Censor Cuts," *Television/Radio Age,* October 17, 1988, p. 38.

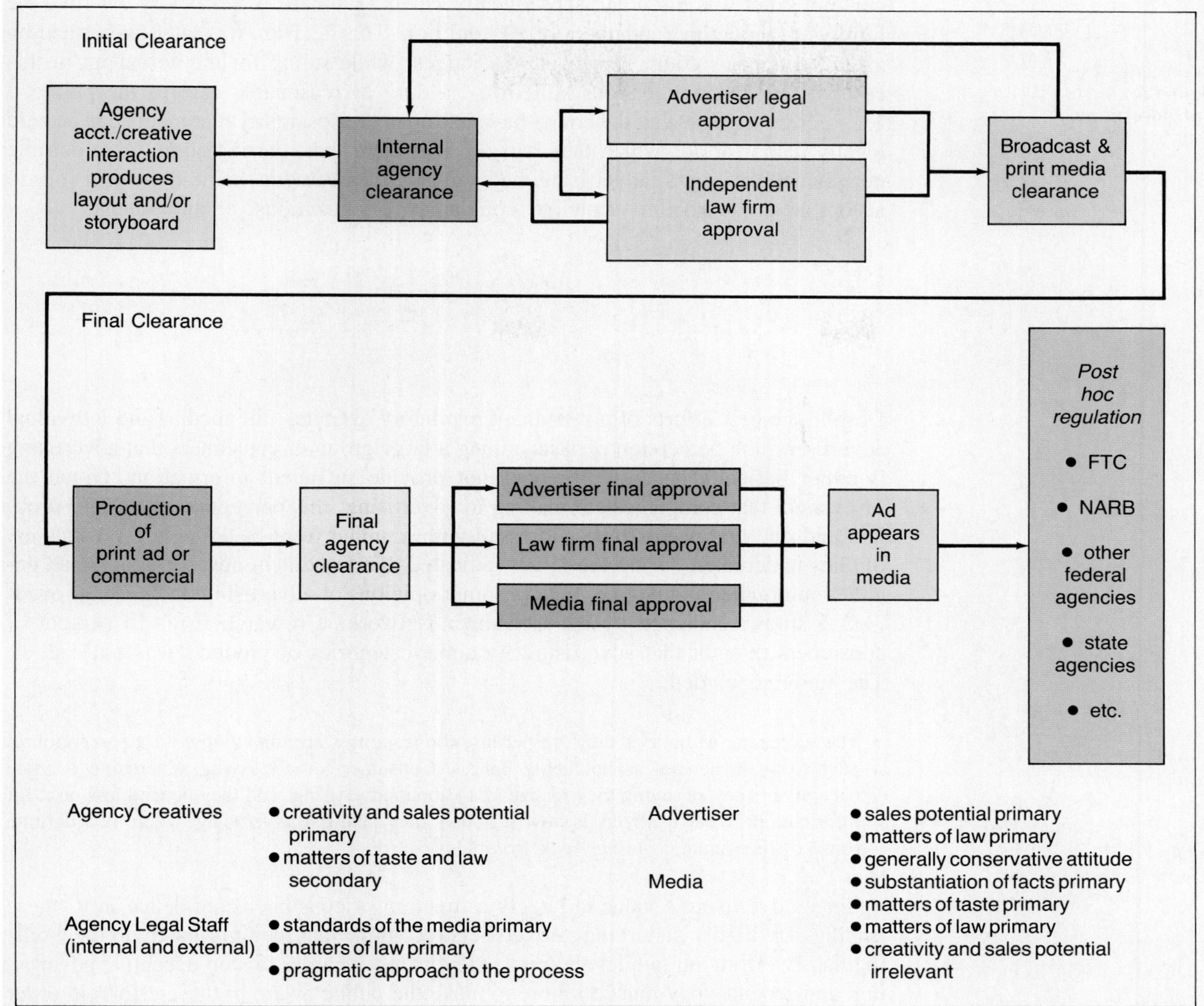

EXHIBIT 25.5

The advertising clearance process. (*Courtesy:* Eric Zanot, "Unseen but Effective Advertising Regulation: The Clearance Process," *Journal of Advertising,* Vol. 14, November 4, 1985, pp. 46–47.)

For the most part, standards are consistent across the networks. Sometimes, however, the networks differ in their standards concerning a particular commercial, which can be really troublesome because it is extremely expensive to produce different versions of a commercial for different networks. Revlon's commercial for Intimate perfume showed a male model stroking the neck of a female model with an ice cube. CBS and ABC accepted an edited version of the commercial, but would run it only after 9 P.M. NBC refused it altogether. By contrast, NBC accepted Sun Country wine cooler spots that were rejected by ABC and CBS until significant editing was done.

Advertising that would be perfectly acceptable in major national magazines or cable television will be questioned by the networks. Advertisers point out that the networks routinely reject commercial scenes that are mild by comparison to their own soap opera story lines.

Besides protecting consumers from offensive or deceptive advertising, the media have another reason for maintaining advertising standards: They might, in extraordinary circumstances, be held liable for advertising they carry. In a well-publicized case, *Soldier of Fortune* magazine ran an advertisement through which it was alleged that a contract killer was hired and subsequently killed a woman. A Texas jury awarded the family of the victim a judgment of $9.4 million. This decision was later overturned by a federal appeals court. However, the judges, while ruling for the defendant in this case, noted that publications still owe "a duty of reasonable care to the public." Therefore, it is clear that the courts have left open the possibility that media can be held legally liable for ads which they carry.[21] It is clear that, barring some more definite decision by the courts, advertising media must use care and restraint in the decisions to accept advertising from suspicious companies, organizations, or individuals.

SELF-REGULATION BY INDUSTRY-WIDE GROUPS

Despite the best efforts of government regulatory agencies, the media, and individual advertisers, the perception persists among a large group of consumers that advertising is either basically deceptive or does not provide sufficient information. Given the investment that companies are making in advertising, this perception is a major problem and one that needs to be addressed with a united front by all honest businesses. Studies undertaken during the 1980s indicated that fraudulent advertisements had declined in number and degree, but consumer opinions of advertising had not improved.

In a study conducted by the Consumer Network, a research firm, 75 percent of consumers thought that advertising for some categories of products was misleading. The study concluded:

Consumers, of late, have been "conditioned" to *not* believing grandiose claims, which extol the virtues of products. Dunlop's ad, claiming their *Maxfli DDH golf ball* is "the longest, most accurate in history" would probably be questioned by most golfers. In fact, their ad breaks with the phrase, "Quite a claim"—as if to indicate to readers, that *doubts are likely*.

> The scores are as poor as they are because the responses are mixed up with a perception of advertising in general as not being honest. Consumers aren't saying advertising is more deceptive. They're saying they realize more about advertising, and they depend less on it for information. What it affects is how seriously they take the advertising. There is a definite sense of [consumers] pulling back from ads.[22]

Since advertising's value is largely a function of consumer confidence in it, these findings are highly disturbing. Advertisers recognize that they must step up their self-regulatory efforts on two levels. First, they must try harder to stop deceptive advertising; and second, they must do more to make the public aware of these efforts in order to maintain and strengthen consumer confidence in advertising.

Better Business Bureaus[23]

***Better Business Bureaus.** An organization, launched by advertisers and now with wide business support, to protect the public against deceptive advertising and fraudulent business methods. Works widely at local levels. Also identified with the National Advertising Review Board.*

One of the best-known, most aggressive and successful organizations in the fight for honest and truthful advertising is the Council of Better Business Bureaus (the national organization) and its affiliated local chapters. The forerunner of the modern Better Business Bureaus dates to 1905, when various local advertising clubs formed a national association that today is known as the American Advertising Federation. In 1911, this association launched a campaign for truth in advertising, establishing various vigilance committees to pressure advertisers. In 1916, these local committees adopted the name Better Business Bureaus, and in 1926, they became autonomous. Today there are almost 200 local bureaus in the United States and Canada.

---

[21] "Common sense on ad liability," *Advertising Age*, August 28, 1989, p. 89.

[22] Janet Neiman, "Misleading Ads Casting Shadow over Entire Industry," *ADWEEK*, September 26, 1988, p. 34.

[23] Information concerning the Better Business Bureaus and the National Advertising Review Council was supplied courtesy of the Council of Better Business Bureaus, Inc.

Although the council and the local bureaus have no legal authority, they exert a major influence on truth and accuracy in advertising. The council uses public opinion and peer pressure to get advertisers to voluntarily comply with industry standards. For example, the council has worked with automobile manufacturers to establish a program for arbitrating consumer complaints. It has also investigated rental car advertising and asked various companies to modify ads the bureaus found to be misleading.

The National Advertising Review Council

National Advertising Review Board (NARB). *The advertising industry's major organization for policing misleading ads.*

In response to the many different consumer groups complaining about deceptive advertising, the chief advertising organizations formed the most comprehensive self-regulating apparatus ever established in advertising. Called the National Advertising Review Council (NARC), its chief purpose is "to develop a structure which would effectively apply the persuasive capacities of peers to seek the voluntary elimination of national advertising which professionals would consider deceptive." Its objective is to sustain high standards of truth and accuracy in national advertising. It consists of the Council of Better Business Bureaus and the three leading advertising groups: the American Advertising Federation, the American Association of Advertising Agencies (the 4A's), and the Association of National Advertisers. The council has two operating arms: the National Advertising Division (NAD) of the Council of Better Business Bureaus and the National Advertising Review Board (NARB).

The NAD is the investigative arm of the NARC. It initiates inquiries as well as taking referrals from other groups such as local Better Business Bureaus.

Sources of NAD Cases, 1987.

NAD monitoring	29
Competitor challenges	39
Local BBB's	13
Consumer complaints	13
Other	4
	98

National Advertising Division (NAD). *The policy-making arm of the National Advertising Review Board.*

Both the *Better Business Bureau* and the *National Advertising Review Council* (NARC) exercise a major influence on discouraging untruthful advertising. They even take out ads themselves to warn consumers about "misleading and deceptive" advertising and to provide an address for reporting such promotion consumers "spot."

After a complaint is received, the NAD determines the issues, collects and evaluates data, and makes an initial decision on whether the advertiser's claims are substantiated. If the NAD finds that substantiation is unsatisfactory, it negotiates with the advertiser to secure modification or permanent discontinuance of the advertising.

In the event of an impasse, the case is referred to the NARB, composed of 50 advertisers, agency personnel, and public members, 5 of whom are assigned to a case—like a court of appeals. If they think the NAD's opinion is justified and the advertiser still refuses to correct the deceptive element, the rules provide that the matter will be referred to the appropriate government agency. The entire process is diagrammed in Exhibit 25.6. In over 15 years of operation, no advertiser who participated in the complete process has declined to abide by the NARB decision. Indeed, only 2 percent of the NAD's decisions have required NARB review.

In discussing the NAD/NARB system, we should understand that it cannot

- Order an advertiser to stop running an ad
- Impose a fine
- Bar anyone from advertising
- Boycott an advertiser or a product

What it can do is bring to bear the judgment of the advertiser's peers that what is being done is harmful to advertising, to the public, and to the offender. This judgment has great moral weight. It is reinforced by the knowledge that if the results of an appeal to the NARB are not accepted, the whole matter will be referred to the appropriate

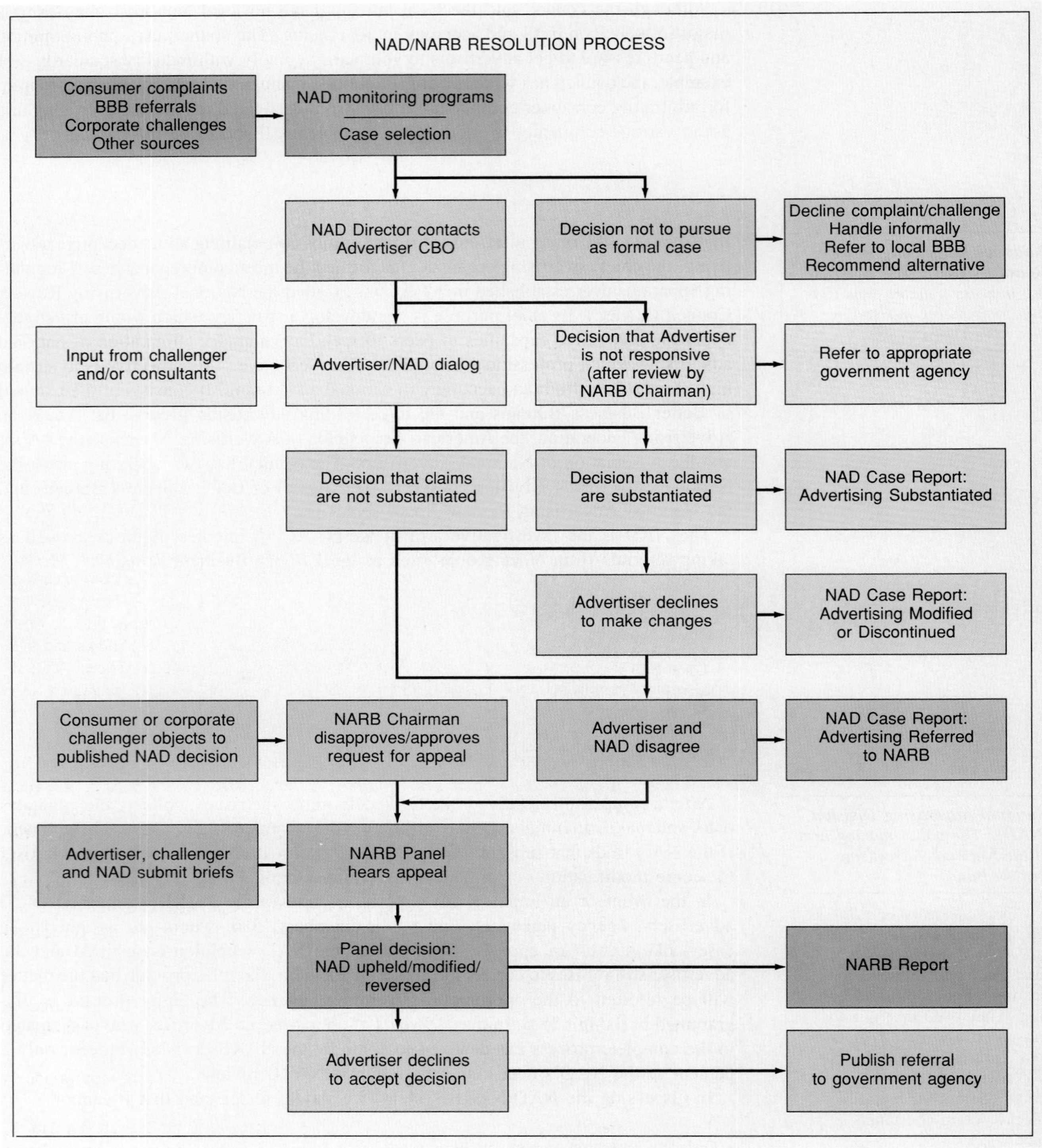

EXHIBIT 25.6
Steps in NAD/NARB process.

government agency and that that fact will be released to the public, together with any statement the advertiser wishes to make. This step, unique in business self-regulation machinery, avoids any problem of violating antitrust laws, presents the entire matter to public view, and still leaves the advertiser subject to an FTC ruling on the advertising. The following case report is typical:

The Children's Advertising Unit of the NAD

Children's Advertising Review Unit (CARU). *The CARU functions much as the NAD to review complaints of advertising to children.*

One of the most controversial areas of advertising is messages directed to children. Obviously, the same standards of deception applied to adult-oriented advertising cannot be applied to advertising intended for children.

> Critics have stated that advertising directed toward children creates materialism, stifles creativity, creates conflict between parent and child, and hinders the development of moral and ethical values. Proponents of advertising to children have attempted to counter the arguments of concerned parents and public interest groups. Advertising, they contend, serves as an information source and teaches children the consumption skills necessary to function in the marketplace.[24]

Of special concern, even to those who generally support children's advertising, are the so-called interactive toy advertisements that have become popular in recent years.

> Today, you invent the toy—then invent the TV show to sell it. According to a count by ACT [Action for Children's Television], no fewer than 72 Saturday morning and afternoon cartoon shows have been toy-based. ABC, NBC, and CBS all have had plenty of shows based on popular toys, from Pound Puppies to Smurfs. But it is on independent stations that the tie-in has been refined as an art, with toy manufacturers themselves creating the shows and syndicating them. With the right distribution windows, the profits can be enormous. Mattel's HeMan—star of stage, screen, tube, and toy itself—is estimated to have generated $350 million in sales.[25]

As Harvard professor Gerald Lesser testified to the House Telecommunications Subcommittee, "To deliberately blur what is program and what is commercial and then leave it to the children to sort it all out for themselves . . . is simply not fair."

Recognizing the special problems of advertising directed to children, in 1974 the advertising industry established the Children's Advertising Review Unit (CARU) of the National Advertising Division of the Council of Better Business Bureaus. Its purpose was to promote truthful, accurate advertising to children that is sensitive to the special nature of its audience. According to the CARU, the most frequently examined areas of children's advertising are:

So-called "children's advertising"—directing promotional messages to *children*—has been criticized for "blurring" the program and commercial messages. A recent Crest TV spot had the hero of the TV program "fighting cavities—just like Crest does." In the last frame, he joins the typical audience of juveniles in praising the "superior" product.

1. *Product presentation.* In toy advertisements, can a child understand what it will be like to actually play with the toy? Do special effects give an unfair depiction of the product and its capabilities?
2. *Adequate disclosure.* Is the product assembled? Are batteries required? Are some products pictured in advertising purchased separately?
3. *Sales pressure.* Do advertisements suggest that children that own a product are superior to others? Are children urged to ask their parents for a product? Are adults who buy a children's product portrayed as being more caring than those who do not?[26]

In the area of children's advertising there are no right answers. Many critics think that no advertising should be directed to children. To these people, no regulation short

---

[24]Robert E. Hite and Randy Eck, "Advertising to Children: Attitudes of Business vs. Consumers," *Journal of Advertising Research,* October/November 1987, p. 40.

[25]Jane Hall, "Aladdin's Lamp Goes Dark," *Gannett Center Journal,* Winter 1988, p. 21.

[26]"An Eye on Children's Advertising," pamphlet published by the Children's Advertising Review Unit.

of a total ban will be satisfactory. However, given the economic support of the media through advertising, it is unlikely that any such ban will ever be permitted. However, it is imperative that all parties involved (media, advertisers, parents, special interest groups) work to insure that children's advertising is appropriate for the audience to which it is intended.

COPYRIGHTING ADVERTISING

Copyrighting has nothing to do with the problems of legal controls over advertising, which we have been discussing in this chapter. However, since copyrighting is a legal procedure related to advertising, it seems appropriate to have this discussion join its legal relatives at this point.

Nature of Copyrights

A copyright is a federal procedure that grants the owner of it the exclusive rights to print, publish, or reproduce an original work of literature, music, or art (which includes advertising) for a specific period of time. January 1, 1978, marked a memorable day in copyright history; for on that day, a new law made the period of time of copyright protection the life of the author plus 50 years (under the old law, established in 1909, copyrights had run for a maximum of 56 years).

A copyright protects an "intellectual work" as a whole from being copied by another; however, it does not prevent others from using the essence of, say, an advertising idea and expressing it in their own way. Copyrighting does not protect a concept or an idea or a theme, but only the expression of it. To be copyrightable, an ad must contain a substantial amount of original text or picture. Slogans and other short phrases and expressions cannot be copyrighted even if they are distinctively arranged or lettered. Neither are familiar symbols and designs copyrightable.

Copyrighting Policy

Some companies make it a policy to copyright all their publication advertising. Most national advertisers, however, deem copyrighting unnecessary in their publication advertising unless it contains a piece of art or copy that they think others will use. Retail newspaper advertising moves too fast for the advertiser to be concerned about having it bodily lifted. But direct-response advertisers often copyright their publication and direct-mail advertising because if an ad is effective, they may want to run it over a long period of time and they don't want to see it used, with minor changes, by someone else.

How to Register a Copyright

Registering a copyright is a simple procedure that can be handled directly by the advertiser, but the steps must be followed precisely.

1. Write to the Register of Copyrights, The Library of Congress, Washington, D.C. 20559, for the proper application form for what you plan to protect.
2. Beginning with the first appearance of the ad, the word *Copyright* or the abbreviation *Copr.* or the symbol © should appear with the name of the advertiser. Add the year if foreign protection is planned. For a booklet or other form of printed advertising besides publication ads, the copyright notice "shall be affixed to the copies in such manner and location as to give reasonable notice of a claim of copyright."
3. As soon as the ad is published, two copies, with the filled-out application form and fee, should be sent to the Register of Copyrights.

SUMMARY

Advertising, more than most businesses, operates within a complicated environment of local, state, and federal statutes and regulations. In addition, the advertising industry itself cooperates with various trade associations, media, and consumer groups, such as Better Business Bureaus, to promote better advertising through self-regulation.

There is no disagreement among responsible parties that truthful and informative advertising is the ideal for which advertisers should strive. For the advertiser, the problem is how to meet the requirements of numerous, sometimes conflicting and constantly changing, advertising regulations. Since the last century, advertising has developed a sense of professionalism and high standards of performance. As in any business, there are unfortunate exceptions to the rule of professionalism. However, the advertiser who uses untruthful or misleading methods will soon be confronted with a number of constraints from both within and without the advertising industry.

QUESTIONS

1. Discuss the three major types of restraints on advertising.
2. Why has the notion of *caveat emptor* been largely rejected by advertising regulators in this century?
3. Discuss the role of the Federal Trade Commission in regulating advertising.
4. Intent is not a relevant factor in determining deceptive advertising. Explain.
5. Discuss the Robinson-Patman Act as it relates to cooperative advertising.
6. Describe the so-called Central Hudson four-part test and discuss its importance.
7. What was the significance of the Shapero case for the advertising of professional services?
8. What are the ramifications to national advertising of recent actions by the National Association of Attorneys General?
9. Why are the television network standards offices of such importance to national advertisers?
10. Briefly outline the steps and procedures used by the National Advertising Review Council.

SUGGESTED EXERCISES

- Find three examples of advertisements or commercials that name competitors.
- How many different examples of professional advertising can you find in your local Sunday newspaper?
- Find good and bad examples of testimonial advertising.

READINGS

BELTRAMINI, RICHARD F.: "Perceived Believability of Warning Label Information Presented in Cigarette Advertising," *Journal of Advertising,* Vol. 17, No. 2, 1988, p. 26.

BLOOMQUIST, RANDALL: "Ad Groups Form Chorus Against Alcohol-Ad Restrictions," *ADWEEK,* February 6, 1989, p. 4.

CAYWOOD, CLAY: "Political Ads in Jeopardy," *Advertising Age,* February 6, 1989, p. 20.

DUHAN, DALE F., AND MARY JANE SHEFFET: "Gray Markets and the Legal Status of Parallel Importation," *Journal of Marketing,* July 1988, p. 75.

NEIMAN, JANET: "Ad Regulation: Everybody Wants to Get into the Act," *ADWEEK,* September 26, 1988, p. 39.

ROTZOLL, KIM: "Advertising and Ethics—Observations on the Dimensions of a Cluttered Battleground," *Advertising Working Papers,* Department of Advertising, University of Illinois, January 1989.

STIPP, HORST H.: "Children as Consumers," *American Demographics,* February 1988, p. 26.

TWENTY-SIX

Economic and Social Effects of Advertising

As a major communication force in society, advertising bears *a social responsibility*. Exxon, the company responsible for the worst inland oil spill in history, donated $4 million for *emergency tourism efforts*. Rod Bradley, president of Bradley Communications, which handles the Alaska Visitors Association account, said the Exxon donation to the association appears to have preserved the 1989 tourism season. "The oil spill couldn't have come at a worse time for us—with virtually all the state's ad money already spent," Mr. Bradley said. State tourism executives reported record numbers of visitors this summer—as a result of the "positive, last minute push. . ."

As we have seen throughout this text, advertising serves many roles and is perceived in a number of different ways by critics and proponents. Advertising's primary purpose is to encourage the consumption of goods and services. However, the power of advertising is not limited to providing the public with persuasive information. Regardless of its overt intent, advertising is a major social force. Some observers claim that it sets the social and cultural agenda for a sizable proportion of the population. Many of our social conventions and much of our behavior are determined by portrayals of situations and people in advertisements. Notice how often the advertising of a product such as cigarettes or condoms becomes more controversial than the actual selling of the product.

Because advertising has an important social component, advertisers have a responsibility to both the businesses they serve and the public they are appealing to. Balancing economic efficiency and social responsibility is not always easy, but most advertising practitioners are sensitive to the need to do so and work at both roles.

This chapter examines these two major roles of advertising. First we discuss advertising's contribution to economic efficiency, exploring the question of whether advertising provides market information in a manner that could not be more efficiently done by other means. Then we discuss advertising's role in the social process, recognizing that advertising has broad, noneconomic effects on society.

THE ECONOMIC ROLE OF ADVERTISING

In examining the economic role of advertising, we must look at several facets of advertising's contribution to economic well-being.

1. Is advertising more efficient than other forms of product-information distribution?

Efficiency can be measured in a number of ways. From a cost standpoint, advertising is clearly the cheapest means of reaching large numbers of consumers. No other personal or promotional sales tool can come close to the cost efficiencies of advertising, where cost per thousand figures typically range from 25 cents to $100.

But remember, simply reaching prospects does not ensure sales. In recent years, companies have been evaluating their advertising in terms of its contribution to sales. Major corporations now make much more stringent demands on their agencies and advertising departments to justify advertising expenditures.

Advertising agencies have responded to these demands by acknowledging the need for greater accountability, but also by pointing out that advertising is only one component of an increasingly complex marketing mix. Nevertheless, there is a clear trend toward tying advertising evaluation directly to sales. For instance, many clients link agency compensation to the increase in product sales and market share.

Advertisers are concerned that this one-to-one relationship between advertising and sales obscures the basic communication foundation of advertising. In addition, this approach places a short-term burden on advertising when a long-term evaluation would normally be more appropriate. Many advertisements reinforce a theme of quality or service built over a number of years (see Exhibit 26.1).

EXHIBIT 26.1

This Yamaha ad depends on the company's long-term reputation for high quality to produce a simple sales message. (Courtesy: Yamaha Music Corporation.)

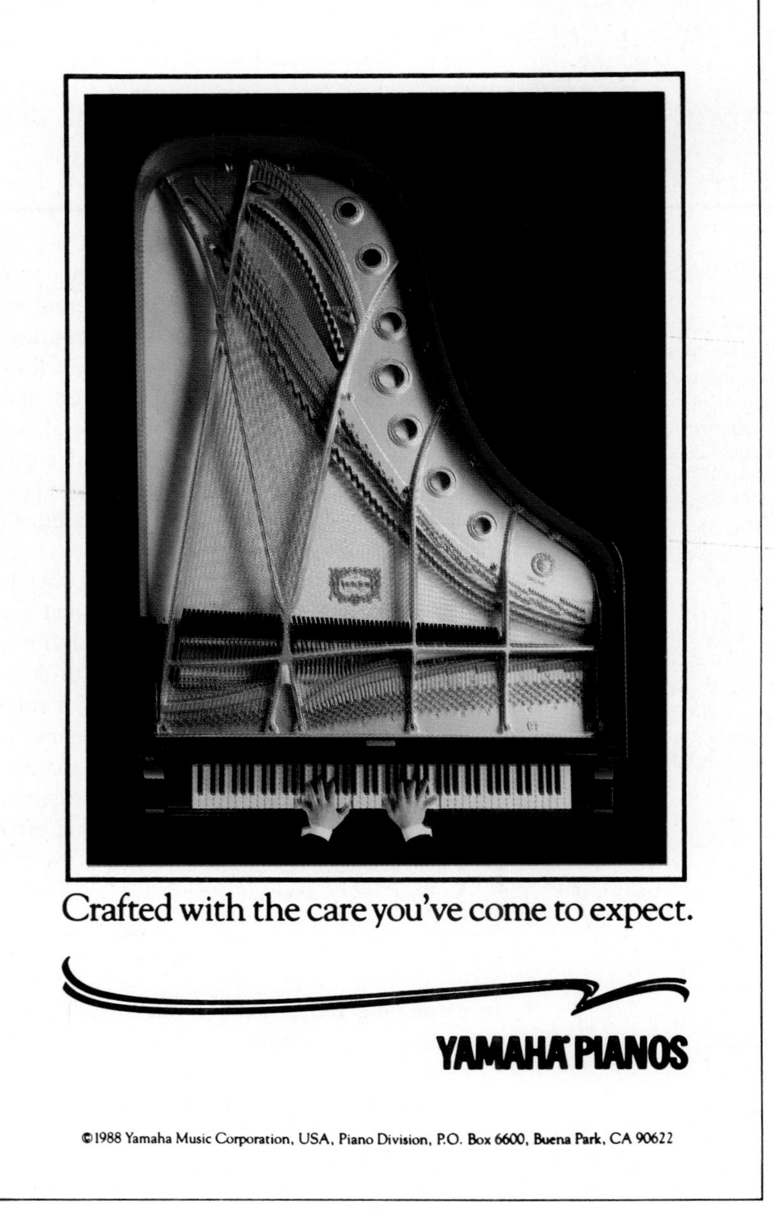

Crafted with the care you've come to expect.
YAMAHA PIANOS
©1988 Yamaha Music Corporation, USA, Piano Division, P.O. Box 6600, Buena Park, CA 90622

Advertising is the *cheapest means* for reaching large numbers of people. That's why off-price retailers, Marshalls and T. J. Maxx, are lining up to spend almost *$50 million* in promotion dollars in the coming year. "We need to tell consumers *who we are,* because there are so many price-oriented messages being thrown at them," explained Karen Claunch, advertising manager at Maxx. "The *off-price marketing challenge* is to 'marry' a price message with a high-quality image message and to differentiate stores from discounters—to claim the leadership in the $3.5 billion-plus business," said she.

Return on investment (ROI). *One measure of the efficiency of a company is the rate of return (profit) achieved by a certain level of investment in the various functions of the business.*

Increased brand/product awareness has been the "traditional goal of advertising." Lately, however, more advertisements have been tied to *sales,* a marketing function. *J. Walter Thompson* agency won over $100 million in *retail* advertising business in the past 12 months—based on sales increases of its "old" retail accounts. . . "We didn't deliberately go out to get them," admitted Bert Metter, chairman of JWT-USA. "But, many retailers have now upgraded their emphases on *brand building*—with a combined effort of increasing sales—that they keep us firmly planted in 'reality'."

When evaluating advertising, the most difficult task is to determine what would have happened to sales and profits if a company had not advertised or had advertised at a reduced level. One approach to this question has been to examine different strategies adopted during periods of business recession.

One study found that companies that advertised aggressively during recessions (see Exhibit 26.2) maintained or increased brand-awareness levels (Exhibit 26.3). The study further indicated that "Increased brand awareness creates an improved potential for market share. Higher market share, in turn, creates a better potential for higher return on investment (ROI). The data demonstrated that most businesses succeeded in realizing these potentials, once the levels of brand awareness were achieved. The start of the process is brand awareness—without it, both market share and ROI are severely jeopardized" (see Exhibit 26.4).[1]

2. Does advertising contribute to corporate profits?

Companies are currently spending some $130 billion a year on advertising. Obviously, they must determine if this gigantic expenditure of resources is contributing to the profitability of their firms. If advertising is not an investment in future profitability, then it cannot be justified. However, the prudent advertiser knows that advertising is only a contributing factor to overall profits. Note how the Norfork Southern advertisement (see Exhibit 26.5) offers basic facts about the company and then invites prospects to call its sales office for additional information. The all-too-often-made mistake is to give advertising too much credit in good times and too much blame in bad times.

[1]"The Role of Advertising in Uncertain Times," Commentary No. 2000.5, Cahners Advertising Research Report, 1980.

EXHIBIT 26.2 & 3

Advertisers can gain a significant competitive advantage by aggressive advertising during periods of business uncertainty. (Courtesy: Cahners Publishing Company.)

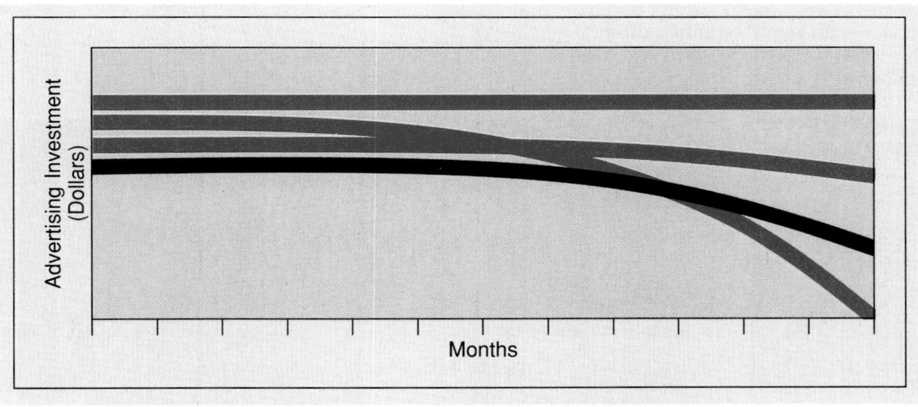

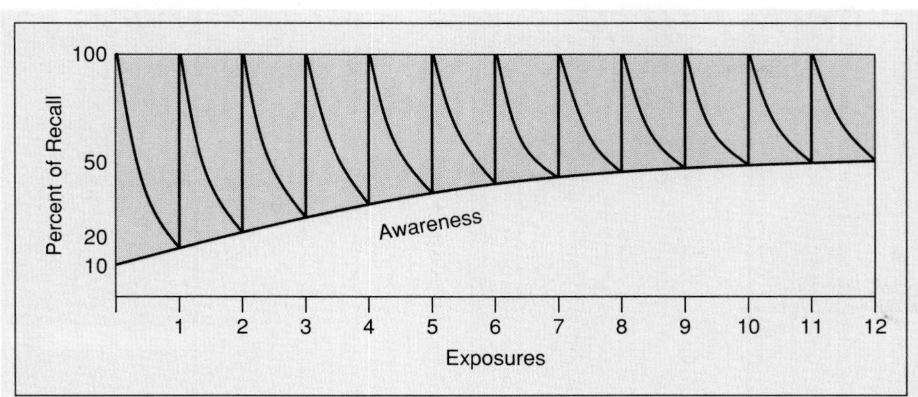

In being able to achieve high levels of awareness and interest in products, advertising has been credited with helping to boost firms' *profitability*. *Philip Morris Companies* became the *first* company to crack the *$2 billion mark* in annual advertising and promotional spending in the US, with an increase of 7.2% to $2.06 billion in 1988. On sales of $20,866,000, they earned almost $4 million or 7.5% over 1987.

EXHIBIT 26.4

A company that has a high market share relative to competitors will usually have higher profits. Effective advertising can enhance brand awareness to create increased market share. (Courtesy: Cahners Publishing Company.)

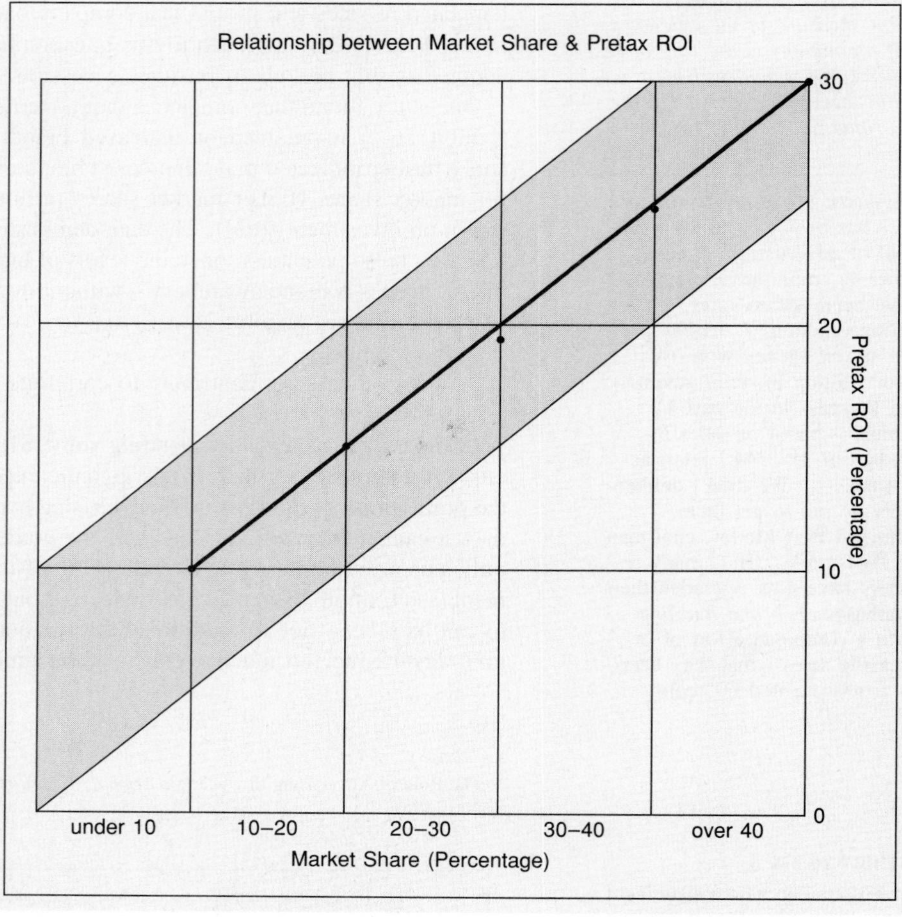

EXHIBIT 26.5

Expensive or complex products and services can rarely be sold entirely through advertising. (Courtesy: Norfork Southern.)

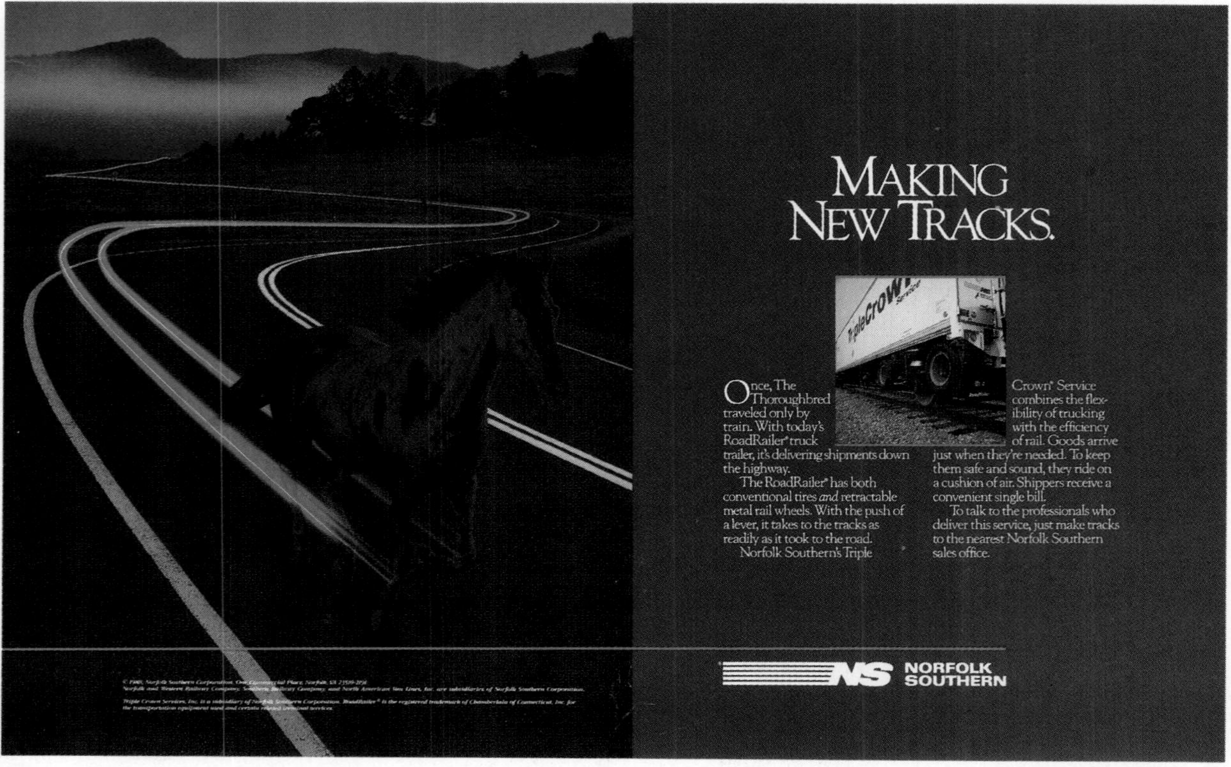

Once we acknowledge the supplementary role of advertising in creating sales, we can make a more reasoned judgment of its value. The key to product success is having a good product, adequate retail distribution, a fair price, and outstanding promotion. Even so, few products can be successfully introduced and marketed without advertising. The requirements of a self-service economy and the economies of scale achieved by mass production demand high levels of product awareness that are made feasible only through advertising.

In addition to advertising-generated profitability achieved directly through product sales, there is a qualitative value created through advertising-created product awareness.

Brand identity. *Strong public awareness of a brand is considered a financial asset for a firm. Advertising is a major component of building such identity.*

> From a financial perspective, what advertising has best been able to help accomplish has never been more important. The marketplace value of major consumer-recognized brands has never been higher—witness the prices of companies with solid brand positions. Strong brand identity is a significant asset, and the cost of acquiring or building one has been escalating. Building and maintaining such brands is a principal task of advertising.
>
> Even for firms which don't sell to household consumers, the salience of company/corporate image has increased. This too is a task for which advertising skills are eminently applicable. One can argue that in a world of more 15-second commercials, image-building will become even more important.[2]

By being *persuasive* (as well as informative), advertising is providing the consumer with "intimate" knowledge of the company and its products. Celebrities, such as baseball great Joe DiMaggio, are used in advertising messages to convey *personal* and *introspective* information about products/services. "As Bowery Savings Bank's spokesman for 18 years, DiMaggio's presence oozes 'credibility'—*better* than the bank can," bragged director Bob Giraldi.

Even the harshest critics of advertising acknowledge its place in modern selling. Increasingly, criticisms of advertising are directed toward its form and execution rather than its existence. One of the most often heard suggestions is that advertising should be informational rather than persuasive—that is, it should be restricted to discussions of price, availability, and basic descriptions of the product or service. John O'Toole, when president of Foote, Cone & Belding, addressed the issue of persuasive advertising in testimony before the Federal Trade Commission:

> Limiting advertising to a discussion of price and function would eliminate, among other things, what I happen to think is an equally essential piece of information these days—what kind of people make and market this product or provide this service. The reputation, the quality standards, the taste and responsibility of the people who put out that product is information that not only is important to the consumer, it's information that's more and more demanded by the consumer.[3]

To suggest that advertising remove the persuasive component is to go against a centuries-old tradition of selling goods. What we must demand is that advertising be completely honest and forthright in the message it communicates. However, this does not mean that advertising should be reduced to the level of a laundry list of product attributes. For example, IBM has an interesting story to tell about one of America's great corporations. It does so in an advertisement that is both informative *and* persuasive (see Exhibit 26.6).

3. Does advertising contribute to the overall welfare of the economy?

Gross National Product (GNP). *The total value of all goods and services produced by a nation in one year.*

Economic productivity must be viewed from the perspective of both the individual firm and the total economy. Clearly, single corporations must advertise to prevent brand-share erosion even in the absence of overall sales increases in a single industry or in the gross national product (GNP). However, most economists are interested in advertising from a macroeconomic perspective. That is, they want to know if advertising contributes to the overall economic system rather than just to the profits of a single firm.

---

[2]Stephen Greyser, "The Importance of Advertising," *Marketing & Media Decisions,* February 1986, p. 150.

[3]J. Robert Moskin, *The Case for Advertising* (New York: American Association of Advertising Agencies, 1973), p. 20.

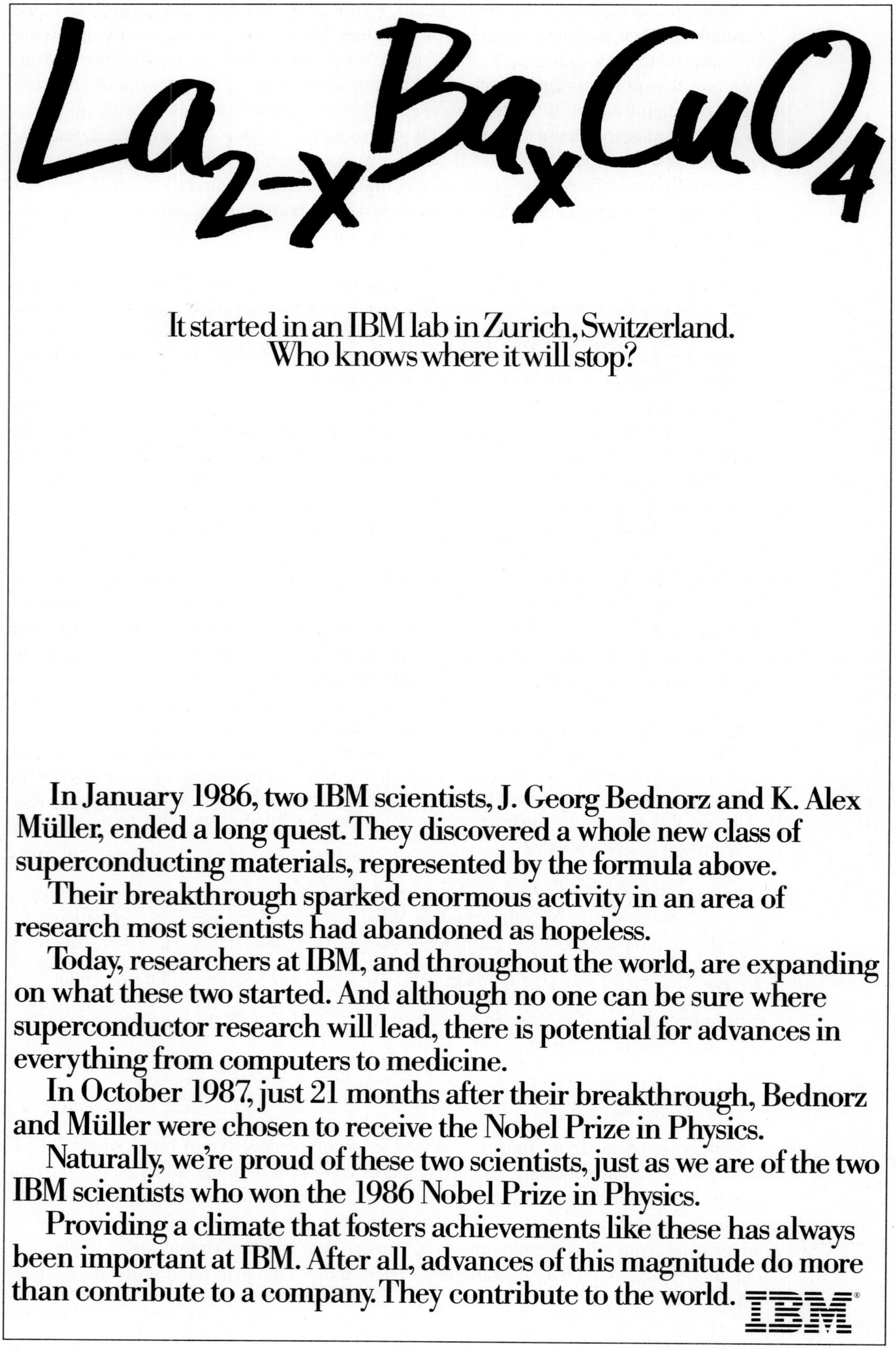

$$La_{2-x}Ba_xCuO_4$$

It started in an IBM lab in Zurich, Switzerland.
Who knows where it will stop?

In January 1986, two IBM scientists, J. Georg Bednorz and K. Alex Müller, ended a long quest. They discovered a whole new class of superconducting materials, represented by the formula above.

Their breakthrough sparked enormous activity in an area of research most scientists had abandoned as hopeless.

Today, researchers at IBM, and throughout the world, are expanding on what these two started. And although no one can be sure where superconductor research will lead, there is potential for advances in everything from computers to medicine.

In October 1987, just 21 months after their breakthrough, Bednorz and Müller were chosen to receive the Nobel Prize in Physics.

Naturally, we're proud of these two scientists, just as we are of the two IBM scientists who won the 1986 Nobel Prize in Physics.

Providing a climate that fosters achievements like these has always been important at IBM. After all, advances of this magnitude do more than contribute to a company. They contribute to the world.

IBM®

EXHIBIT 26.6

This IBM ad is a great selling message without mentioning one of the company's products. (Courtesy: IBM Corporation.)

The ''economic value'' of advertising lies, in part, in its ability to acquaint the market with *new, desired products* and/or *''infant'' companies.* To escape the print/broadcast ''clutter,'' E. G. Smith, a New York-based *specialty sock company,* offers ''thank you'' gift-with-purchase promotions for ''new'' companies wanting to be remembered. This year it's the ''World Home Shopping Bag,'' a footshaped bag and pair of socks offered free for purchasing the company's product. Inside, coordinated response cards invite consumers to share their name, address, birthdate, and personal interests with the distributor. . . What a great way to accumulate a mailing list!

Currently, American advertising accounts for approximately 2½ percent of GNP. While this figure is lower than it was 50 years ago, it still represents a tremendous investment. Economists tend to view advertising's effects on the economy as falling into one of four categories:

1. *Counterproductive:* advertising that raises prices or in some other way creates dissatisfaction with products that still have utility, thereby causing unnecessary consumption of new products.
2. *Unproductive:* advertising that does not increase generic demand, but causes no harm. Advertising designed to create brand switching among present consumers would fall into this category.
3. *Somewhat productive:* advertising that creates an increase in overall demand, but at a level lower than some other technique would achieve, or at an unnecessarily high level of expenditure.
4. *Most productive:* advertising that produces the greatest economic well-being at the lowest possible cost. The implication of this category is that both buyer and seller benefit equally.

It is difficult to deal in generalities when it comes to evaluating the economic value of advertising. The utility of advertising in a market for a relatively new product such as home computers is much different than that for beer or cigarettes, industries that are characterized by flat sales and brand switching among present users.

THE SOCIAL ROLE OF ADVERTISING

Advertising has been accused of ''straying'' from its neutral course in presenting product information. Instead, according to critics, it conveys what advertisers and agencies consider to be ''correct'' behavior. In a novel promotion for *Rascals Candy,* American Chicle has ''created'' a rock band and is distributing its rock video as programming for cable and broadcast TV stations, including MTV Networks' Nickelodeon. Walking a fine line between advertising and programming, the video features the ''Rascalords,'' a group that ''doesn't sing.'' Bob Erlich, category manager at the company, said the aim is to *reach* young people, ages 8 to 14, who regularly watch music video programming.

To this point, we have dealt with advertising's role in the economic system. We have seen that its primary economic role is to provide information on which consumers can base their purchase decisions. Companies view advertising as part of their investment in the marketing mix, which it is hoped will lead to increased sales and profits. In this role, advertising is carrying out its overall function.

Here we will discuss quite another aspect of advertising: its social role. Whatever your view of advertising, you must know that it plays an important role in determining social issues. You have only to review the arguments concerning advertising for controversial products to see its social implications. Few people argue that condoms, feminine hygiene products, and hemorrhoid preparations shouldn't be sold, but many would ban or greatly restrict their advertising. Why?

Those who look at advertising from a social perspective tend to concentrate on its unintended consequences—that is, its effects beyond providing product information. From a social perspective, it has been argued that advertising determines our lifestyle by portraying the ''correct'' products, fads, and even behavior. Others counter that advertising is nothing more than a mirror of society, offering products and services of interest to the majority or a sizable segment of the public. Still another group views advertising as both a shaper and a mirror of society. They see advertising as extending and expanding ideas from one group or area of the country to another.

Regardless of which view you take of the relationship between advertising and society, it is clear that advertising plays a major role in our culture. Obviously, it is more than a neutral source of product information.

Advertising as a Social Force

The more we understand the social aspects of advertising, the more we need to comprehend its role as a cultural communicator. In recent years, there has been a marked shift in the type of criticism and review of advertising. Advertisers are being asked to meet different standards today than in the past.

The public view of advertising standards has altered through three major periods:

1. *The Era of Exaggerated Claims, 1865–1900.* During this period, most people accepted

advertising as "buyer beware" communication in which virtually any claim for a product was allowable. Some advertising claims, especially for patent medicines, were so outlandish that one wonders how anyone could ever have believed them.

2. *The Era of Public Awareness, 1900–1965*. Many responsible advertisers feared for the very existence of the industry as deceptive advertising proliferated during the closing years of the nineteenth century. The Pure Food and Drug Act of 1906 marked the first recognition that the public was demanding truthful portrayals of products and services. The next several decades were characterized by efforts to protect consumers against literal fraud in advertising, a standard most advertisers supported and complied with.
3. *The Era of Social Responsibility, 1965 to the present*. During the last 25 years, advertisers have come to realize that literal truth is not sufficient to meet the demands of many consumers. They know they must meet a standard of social responsibility in addition to providing literally truthful advertising. The consumer movement of the 1960s, concerns with environmental safety, and a heightened awareness of social issues are reflected in modern advertising.

Social responsibility. *During the last 25 years advertising has grown increasingly aware of its responsibility not just to sell goods, but to do so in a manner that fairly reflects the well-being of society.*

"Truthful" advertising has come to mean the *realistic portrayal* of products and services as it's interpreted by the consuming public. In 1986 *Hyundai* scored a hit in the US car market with its *Excel subcompact*. Now the company expects its new mid-sized *Sonata* to do likewise—with the same theme, *economy*. Rather than promise "the moon" and deliver "moon dust," the company's ads say what consumers want to hear about a car—(1) its true price; (2) its extra "values" by category; (3) its warranty; and (4) how to find the nearest dealer (best bet: an "800" number). Right on, Backer Spielvogel Bates!

The public is not content with advertising that communicates truthful product information. Truth in advertising is no more than a minimal standard. Special-interest groups are concerned with how this information is conveyed. They are demanding that advertising fairly reflect the society to which it communicates. Blacks, women, the elderly, ethnic groups, even children's advocates have taken advertisers to task over the way in which these groups are characterized in advertising.

The first step in the process of realistic advertising was to include a diverse population. Until 1970, virtually all advertisements portrayed an all-white society. McDonald's was one of the first major advertisers to hire black and Hispanic advertising agencies to produce advertising directed to specific ethnic groups. Other advertisers quickly followed suit. However, as Elaine Brodey, affirmative action administrator for the Screen Actors Guild commented, "It is not enough to include minority faces and voices in commercials. Those faces and voices must be fairly presented."[4]

Perhaps the ideal we should strive for is advertising that includes minorities without anyone even noticing it. The evidence is that we are slowly reaching that point. Major national advertisers have reacted positively to a changing society. Numerous meetings have been held to open dialogs between advertisers and their customers. The result has been more effective and realistic advertising.

Advertising Restricts Competition and Raises Prices

Brand monopoly. *The concept that large advertisers so overwhelm consumers with their messages that new products have difficulty in gaining entry to the marketplace.*

Advertising is a major means of introducing new products to a general audience. However, critics often claim that advertising contributes to a less-than-free economy by helping to create *brand monopolies* that lessen the opportunity for new products to be introduced. A brand monopoly, in their view, occurs when a brand achieves such predominance in the marketplace that other companies simply do not try to compete. It is charged that advertising is used as a substitute for either price competition or beneficial product improvements. Instead of being of overall economic value to society, advertising, these critics claim, is used as a primary means of creating noncompetitive price structures and persuading customers to switch brands among a few large firms within each product category. There are two implications of this view of advertising: Advertising results in brand switching with no overall economic gain for consumers, and advertising causes higher prices for the buying public.

The advertising industry argues that advertising plays a vital role in our economy and does not produce either less competition or higher prices. Rather than producers dictating product choice, advertisers point out that it is consumers who determine product choice through their purchases. However, consumers generally learn of products through mass advertising and other forms of promotion.

[4]Bill Marvel, "Television Advertisers Reaching Out to Minorities," *TV Week*, November 26, 1988, p. 47.

By emphasizing only well-known, nationally branded products, advertising has been accused of shutting out of the market, lesser-known firms with limited promotional dollars. With a $20 million-plus ad campaign from Ogilvy & Mather, Chicago, *NutraSweet* and its red swirl logo is firmly entrenched in consumers' minds. While Pfizer McNeil Specialty Products, Hoechst Celanese Corporation and United Sweetener, USA aren't exactly "little" companies, "dislodging NutraSweet—with an estimated 65% share of the sugar-substitute market—could be a daunting task," lamented Tom Fucigna, group management supervisor at Pedone & Partners, New York.

In spite of its influence, advertising hasn't been able to "force" consumers to buy *unwanted products/services*. In fact, the opposite is true. While Las Vegas casinos have been very successful in attracting younger players and families, it hasn't worked in Atlantic City. *The Showboat* casino opened in March of '87, *targeting families* with advertising touting *amenities*—such as a bowling center. Didn't work. Industry sources say casinos should target "premium players," instead. Gary Selesman, Trump Plaza director of marketing relies instead on direct mail to reach "high rollers."

Consumer choice as a director of production is a substitute for government-run cartels or even government ownership of the means of producing goods. The very fact that millions of dollars are spent annually on consumer research belies the charge that advertising dictates consumption.

Advertising Promotes Unwanted Purchases

The thesis that advertising fosters unwanted and unneeded purchases assigns to advertising a power it does not have. The idea that persuasive communication (advertising, propaganda, public relations, etc.) can coerce people to take actions they would not otherwise have engaged in presumes a degree of human irrationality that few of us accept. Generally, the assumption among critics has been that *others* are making these advertising-induced purchases. In fact, few, if any, consumers spend their money in such a manner.

Advertising Sells Inferior Products

There is no question that advertising can contribute to the purchase of an inferior product—the first time. However, the function of advertising is usually twofold: to increase the market of a product, and to retain present consumers. How many companies could stay in existence if they sold each potential consumer only one bar of soap or box of cereal? The idea that good advertising is a substitute for bad products is contradictory to the reality of the marketplace.

There are few product categories with so few brands that a consumer would have to purchase an inferior product a second time. An examination of product failures over the last decade shows that product quality is the major determinant of repeat purchases, with product distribution, pricing policies, and service ranking somewhere behind. Advertising can contribute to the success of a superior product, but it can do very little to save a poor one.

Advertising Is an Unnecessary Expense

Some consumers believe that advertising expenditures are unnecessary and that the money should instead be invested in more worthwhile and productive enterprises. Several years ago, a coalition of social activist groups picketed several large advertisers and their agencies, asking that money spent on advertising be diverted to social programs.

There is no question that advertising, like product distribution, salaries, and production costs, is a corporate expense that is passed along to consumers in the price of the products and services they purchase. However, advertising expenditures must be viewed in terms of their contribution to the economic system—both to sellers and to buyers. As we have already said, consumers benefit by having a wider choice of products than they would have without advertising. Advertising also results in lower prices for many products. Sellers benefit in several ways. Advertising allows new products entry into the marketplace. It also allows continuing communication with consumers at a cost per exposure that is far lower than would be possible with available alternatives such as personal selling.

ADVERTISING'S ROLE IN COMMUNICATING SOCIAL ISSUES

Advertising's role in communicating social issues can be characterized in one of three ways:

1. *Direct advocacy of a social-responsibility theme*. Examples of such advertisements are "Don't litter," "Support the government," and "Take safety precautions at work."

2. *Depiction of certain social groups in a favorable light.* Examples are energetic, elderly consumers, informed conservationists, and working women.
3. *Favorable illustration of a social-responsibility goal.* An example is advertising that includes a racially integrated group in an illustration.[5]

Ad Council. *Industry-wide advertising group that enlists advertising professionals to promote social causes.*

The first category, advertising whose primary purpose is social advocacy, is among the fastest-growing type of advertising. We mentioned in Chapter 1 the activities of the Ad Council. It is the oldest and most organized public-service effort in advertising.

The activities of the Ad Council continue because they work. Virtually no American is unfamiliar with Smokey the Bear, and forest fires have been dramatically reduced since this symbol first appeared, even though millions more are using forest recreational areas. In the last decade, the McGruff crime dog campaign has had similar success in inducing people to set up Neighborhood Watch programs and establish McGruff Houses where children can go if they are approached by strangers. Exhibit 26.7 is an example of the Ad Council's continuing campaign on behalf of the Red Cross.

In recent years, the use of advertising to communicate social issues has extended far beyond the Ad Council's efforts. In some cases, advertising campaigns are sponsored by organizations that also provide services, such as food banks and mental health clinics.

Social institutions such as churches have also turned to advertising. While some people have reservations about the role of advertising in promoting certain social institutions and issues, proponents argue that there is no more effective or inexpensive means of getting their messages out.

Finally, we are seeing a number of ads by nonprofit organizations promoting various social issues. This type of advertising will grow as people come to accept the legitimacy of using the mass media as a forum for public issues as well as for communicat-

[5] David J. Lill, Charles W. Gross, and Robin T. Peterson, "The Inclusion of Social-Responsibility Themes by Magazine Advertisers: A Longitudinal Study," *Journal of Advertising*, Spring 1986, p. 37.

EXHIBIT 26.7

The Ad Council proves on a daily basis that advertising can sell ideas and social services. (Courtesy: The Advertising Council.)

ing product information (see Exhibit 26.8). The availability of narrow audience media, such as cable and specialized publications, and their increasing penetration will lead to even more, and perhaps franker, discussions of a host of nonproduct and sometimes controversial topics.

Advocacy advertising. *Term that usually refers to the advertising of social causes, often conducted by nonprofit or public interest organizations.*

While direct advocacy advertising is not a new phenomenon, sensitivity to social problems became much more prevalent among advertisers in the 1980s. Exhibit 26.9 demonstrates several categories of social-responsibility topics and the extent to which magazine advertisers dealt with them over a 17-year period. Advertisers have greatly increased the content of social issues in their advertising in recent years, and there are many causes behind this trend. Primarily, management undertakes socially responsible advertising because it is the right thing to do. Not only is it ethically right, but it allows

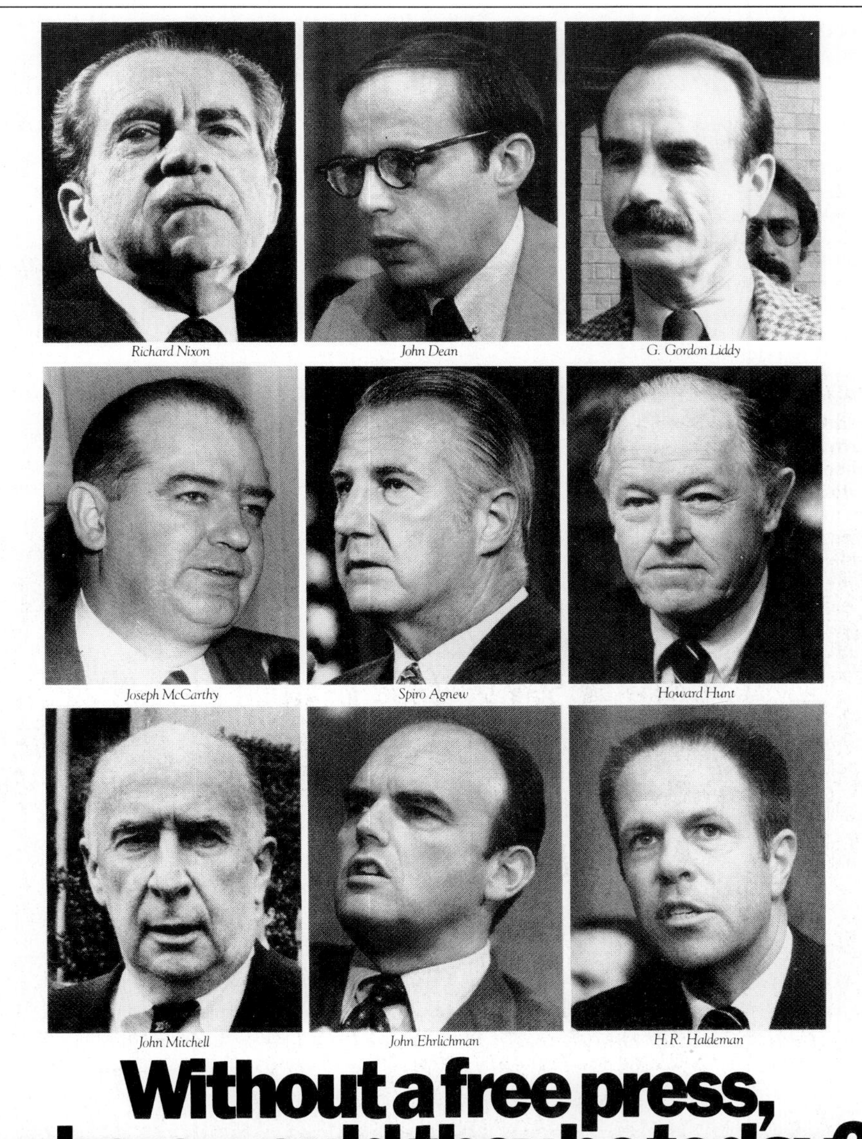

EXHIBIT 26.8

Advertising has become a legitimate vehicle for the communication of public issues. (Courtesy: Freespeech Committee.)

Because of its *pervasive ability* to reach targets and influence their decision-making, advertising has been called on periodically to promote *social issues*. Knowing how influencial *TV* and well-placed *posters* are to young age groups, Yellowhammer Advertising, London created a dramatic pictorial of *multiple needle sharing* for the Central Office of Information. The headline reads, "Sharing your mate's works means sharing with everyone *he's* ever shared with. Shooting up *once* can screw you up. *Forever*." Few could dispute the *impact* of this commercial/ad . . . or think of a more forceful alternative means of conveying the *negative result* of drugs.

EXHIBIT 26.9

Note the increase in social-responsibility themes in advertising, especially those dealing with racial or sexual equality. (Courtesy: *Journal of Advertising*.)

Classification of Advertisements By Social Responsibility Area and Comparison of 1967, 1972, 1975, 1977, and 1984 Frequencies

Classification	1967 No.	1967 %	1972 No.	1972 %	1975 No.	1975 %	19xx No.	19xx %	19xx No.	19xx %
All advertisements examined	9,339	100*	8,113	100*	8,049	100*	14,671	100*		100*
Advertisements containing social-responsibility themes	599	6.4	707	8.7*	813	10.1	1,183	8.06*		15.0*
Advertisements containing direct social-responsibility themes	382	4.1	459	5.6*	547	6.8*	932	6.3*		12.7*
Advertisements containing indirect social-responsibility themes	217	2.3	248	3.1*	266	3.3*	251	1.71		2.3*
Consumerism advertisements with social-responsibility themes**	194	2.1	274	3.4*	323	4.0	106	0.7		3.1*
Ecology & physical environment advertisements with social-responsibility themes**	177	1.9	210	2.6*	314	3.9	329	2.2	448	2.9
Health & safety ads with social-responsibility themes**	91	0.9	211	1.2*	77	0.9	330	2.2	616	4.1*
Public education ads with social-responsibility themes**	56	0.6	32	0.3	35	0.4	144	1.0*	164	1.1
Freedom of the individual ads with social-responsibility themes**	31	0.3	28	0.3	31	0.4	7	0.1	39	0.3*
Employee welfare ads with social-responsibility themes**	36	0.3	27	0.3	17	0.2	35	0.2	68	0.4
Race/civil rights ads with social-responsibility themes**	46	0.4	20	0.2	20	0.2	51	0.4	190	1.2*
Equal opportunity for women ads with social-responsibility themes**	9	0.09	17	0.2	31	0.3	88	0.6	276	1.9
Anti or support of U.S. military with social-responsibility themes**	0	0	6	0.08	0	0	0	0	13	0.1

*Indicates statistically significant changes from previously enumerated to the present year according to t-tests of the difference between two proportions at the .05 level.

**Data in these rows are subsets of data in row 2 (advertisements containing social responsibility themes).

firms to meet legal requirements, foster better relationships with their critics, and enhances their images as good corporate citizens.

For that minority of advertisers who insist on straying from the straight and narrow, there are many public advocacy groups who are quick to make alleged advertising improprieties public. One of the more innovative of these groups is the Center for Science in the Public Interest (CSPI). Each year the CSPI awards a number of Harlan Page Hubbard Lemon Awards for ''the most misleading, unfair, or irresponsible'' ad campaigns of the past year. (Harlan Page Hubbard, in the opinion of the Center, was a pioneer in the use of false and misleading advertising.) The awards, handed out with great fanfare and publicity, are certainly among the most undesirable advertising trophies.

ADVERTISING AND ETHICAL CONSIDERATIONS

As the public, government, and special-interest groups have become more concerned with advertising, the industry has undertaken greater self-examination. As we discussed in Chapters 1 and 25, advertising practitioners have long tried to instill high ethical standards and business practices in their industry. The difference today is that concerns are more openly discussed. Moreover, the industry has conducted formal studies of ethical issues in advertising during the last decade.

These various studies of advertising ethics are interesting on two counts. First, the responses of advertisers demonstrate current thinking about industry ethics. Second, the studies point up the broad range of ethical questions faced by a typical advertiser. Exhibit 26.10 shows the results of a survey on ethics conducted by the Advertising Club of New York. This study is of particular value since it outlines several typical advertising situations and asks whether respondents regard them as ethical or unethical.

EXHIBIT 26.10

How do your ethical responses compare with those of advertising professionals? (Courtesy: *Advertising Age*).

Breaking down ethics responses

1. You are competing with three other agencies for the Magnasonic Consumer Electronics business. Its chief competitor is Rolavision, handled by XYZ Advertising. XYZ's account supervisor on Rolavision has interviewed with you recently for a job. You hire him, specifically to help with the Magnasonic pitch.

	Ethical	Unethical
Agency	75%	25%
Advertiser	74%	26%
Media	78%	22%
Other	64%	36%

2. A good friend of yours calls and says an associate of his is looking for a new advertising agency. His associate knows little about advertising and has asked for his advice. He offers to recommend your company provided he will be paid a finder's fee of $20,000 if you land the business. You agree.

	Ethical	Unethical
Agency	35%	65%
Advertiser	26%	74%
Media	26%	74%
Other	39%	61%

3. Same as Question 2, but your friend is in the business of consulting for clients looking for new advertising agencies, and he is being paid a fee by his client.

	Ethical	Unethical
Agency	44%	56%
Advertiser	22%	78%
Media	35%	65%
Other	52%	48%

4. Your agency is one of four semifinalists asked to participate in a competition for a new-product assignment from a major toy marketer. While the agency has had experience in marketing to children, this assignment would be your agency's first in the toy category—and with a leading manufacturer. During a final briefing your prospective client discloses that the "new product" is a compatible set of war toys complete with pseudo-ammunition, guns, etc. Your agency decides that it will accept the assignment if it is awarded to them.

	Ethical	Unethical
Agency	75%	25%
Advertiser	86%	14%
Media	73%	27%
Other	88%	12%

5. You and two other agencies are in the final stages of a competition. Part of your pitch has to do with recommending and supporting a new marketing strategy. Late one evening, a few days before the scheduled presentation, you are proofing your slides at a slide supply house. By accident, you are handed a fairly complete set of slides put together for one of your competitors. You have enough time to examine and get the gist of it before returning the set to the supplier, who is embarrassed at his mistake. When you return to the office, you make significant changes in the way your agency presents itself so as to attack your competitor's recommended strategy in a direct and forceful manner without, of course, revealing to anyone that you have information on your competitor's actual recommendations.

	Ethical	Unethical
Agency	46%	54%
Advertiser	44%	56%
Media	48%	52%
Other	37%	63%

6. Same as Question 5, except your competitor's slides are in a file folder on the worktable next to you. You have to wait for the supplier to leave the room before you peek at them.

	Ethical	Unethical
Agency	4%	96%
Advertiser	6%	94%
Media	13%	87%
Other	11%	89%

7. You've been invited to compete for the business of a retail chain that has headquarters in the Southeast. The chain is run autocratically by its 75-year-old founder. Every member of his senior management team is white, male and more than 40 years old. In past discussions, you've come away with a clear impression that they are narrow-minded, too. As it happens, a few months ago your agency lost the business of a large New York retail chain. You did excellent work for the chain, and the account supervisor who knows all about the business still works for you but has been without an assignment for more than three months. The problem is, the account supervisor is a 35-year-old woman. You decide not to use her in your presentation.

	Ethical	Unethical
Agency	40%	60%
Advertiser	51%	49%
Media	41%	59%
Other	36%	54%

8. Same as Question 7, except that your account supervisor is male, 45 years old and black. You decide not to include him in the presentation.

	Ethical	Unethical
Agency	38%	62%
Advertiser	49%	51%
Media	45%	55%
Other	31%	69%

9. Your agency is looking to hire a senior account management person. You interview a management supervisor who promises to bring with him one of the accounts he is responsible for at his current agency if you hire him at the salary he is asking. You hire him, and the account comes to you.

	Ethical	Unethical
Agency	84%	16%
Advertiser	63%	37%
Media	87%	13%
Other	73%	27%

10. You and three other agencies are in a competition for a major airline account. As luck would have it, a good friend of yours is sleeping with the secretary for the airline's marketing VP. She's very indiscreet and tells your friend all about the exciting things going back and forth at her company during the review, including the individual views of the members of the airline's agency selection committee. Your friend gives you feedback on all your meetings with the airline.

	Ethical	Unethical
Agency	56%	44%
Advertiser	50%	50%
Media	65%	35%
Other	54%	46%

11. Same as Question 10, except your friend asks for a consulting fee, with a bonus if you get the business.

	Ethical	Unethical
Agency	7%	93%
Advertiser	0%	100%
Media	4%	96%
Other	9%	91%

12. Your agency is being considered by a group of restaurants that offers "good tasting" food at low prices. They ask your company to develop a better "price" story since they will soon be cutting their prices even further. When the agency delves into the reasons why the company can continue to serve the same "good tasting" food at even lower prices, it learns that the group has found a supplier of slightly "off" food. While the food is not yet spoiled, it is close to that stage and requires significant additional seasonings and preservatives. Your agency accepts the assignment.

	Ethical	Unethical
Agency	15%	85%
Advertiser	12%	88%
Media	13%	87%
Other	27%	73%

This questionnaire was created for the Center for Communications, a New York-based group that brings together students and professors with professionals in the communications fields to share practical information rather than theory.

Agencies have expressed reservations about being asked to represent "unethical" products. This is especially true in the case of *alcohol*—in light of the new regulations which require *a stiff wording* on the label for pregnant women and drivers. The NCAA is already talking about banning *beer* advertising during broadcasts—and on July 1, California began treating alcohol as *a carcinogen*, with P-O-P signs on all displays.

Another ethics study was confined to advertising agency executives. The executives were asked, "Will you please briefly describe the aspect of advertising that poses the most difficult ethical or moral problem confronting you in your daily work?" The six most frequently cited ethical problems were:

1. *Treating clients fairly*. This area included billing issues and efforts to balance clients' needs against agency needs.
2. *Creating honest, nonmisleading, socially desirable advertisements*. Clearly, advertising executives are concerned about the effects of the advertising they create.
3. *Advertising unethical products*. Advertisers were troubled by the fact that they sometimes represented clients whose products were not in the public interest. Advertising tobacco and liquor products and political candidates were cited as posing potential ethical problems.
4. *Treating suppliers, vendors, and media fairly*. Agency executives were concerned about the methods used to choose among various suppliers, vendors, and media. They specifically mentioned problems in dealing with gifts, bribes, lunches, kickbacks, and entertainment.
5. *Treating agency employees and managers fairly*. This might be considered a basic ethical issue in all businesses. It includes fairness in hiring and firing employees, counseling incompetent co-workers, handling expense accounts, and a host of similar concerns.
6. *Treating other agencies fairly*. Agency executives were bothered by the practice of pirating work from other agencies and tampering with accounts of other agencies.[6]

SUMMARY

As we conclude our discussion of advertising, it is fitting that we review the broad scope of this powerful communication tool. It is clear that the great majority of advertising expenditures are made to create product awareness and sales. Firms use advertising because it is an important contributor to company profits. It carries out this economic function by providing consumer information, making product comparisons, encouraging customers to take action, and presenting persuasive arguments in favor of specific brands.

However, we have also seen that advertising has other functions of great importance to our society. Advertising supports the mass media and keeps them free from governmental or special-interest control. The independence of the media is assured by the spread-out support of hundreds of advertisers.

Finally, modern advertising provides a platform for the dissemination of divergent ideas of a political or social nature. By buying time or space in the media, a company, a group, or an individual can become editors and discuss ideas that might not be given a hearing in the news and editorials.

No one would argue that advertising is without flaws. However, there is really no more effective or practical means of accomplishing the many tasks presently carried out by advertising. In the future, as society becomes more impersonal and fragmented, advertising may take on even greater importance as a source of information and ideas.

Public scrutiny of advertising, from both an economic and a social-responsibility perspective, will continue and intensify. In what *Advertising Age* has described as a "new assault on advertising," the tax deductibility of advertising as a business expense is now being questioned.[7] Advertisers, and businesses, will have to make a stronger defense of advertising as an efficient method of informing consumers about product improvements, price reductions, and new products and services.

Advertising will also have to come to grips with questions of taste, sexual portrayals, treatment of ethnic groups and women, and other social issues. Certain media,

[6]Shelby D. Hunt and Lawrence B. Chonko, "Ethical Problems of Advertising Agency Executives," *Journal of Advertising*, Winter 1987, p. 19.

[7]"The New Assault on Advertising," *Advertising Age*, June 13, 1988, p. 16.

such as outdoor and telemarketing, will have to defend their very existence to those who would ban or greatly restrict their usage.

The future of advertising will indeed be one of change and adaptation. The public interest will become an increasingly important part of the modern advertiser's agenda.

QUESTIONS

1. Compare and contrast advertising's social and economic roles.
2. What are some of the primary economic roles against which advertising success should be judged?
3. What are the proper sales criteria on which to judge advertising?
4. Is advertising an expense or an investment?
5. Discuss the circumstances in which advertising is most productive in terms of overall economic welfare.
6. Do you think advertising for otherwise legal products should be banned or restricted in some way? Explain.
7. In the text, the present period was characterized as one of social responsibility. How does this period compare to the earlier period of "truth in advertising"?
8. Discuss the concept of a brand monopoly.
9. Discuss truthful advertising and ethical advertising.

SUGGESTED EXERCISES

- Bring in three advertisements whose primary intent is to carry out some social theme as opposed to selling a product.
- In a typical hour of television viewing, keep count of the different characters portrayed in the commercials. Are they treated realistically?

READINGS

HOCH, STEPHEN J.: "Who Do We Know: Predicting the Interests and Opinions of the American Consumer," *Journal of Consumer Research,* December 1988, p. 315.

HOVLAND, ROXANNE, AND GARY WILCOX: *Advertising in Society* (Lincolnwood, IL: NTC Business Books, 1988).

MCAULIFEE, ROBERT E.: *Advertising, Competition, and Public Policy* (Lexington, MA: Lexington Books, 1989).

THORSON, ESTHER: *The Principles of Advertising at Work* (Lincolnwood, IL: NTC Business Books, 1989), pp. 65–75, "Social Critiques and Concerns with Advertising."

P.S.

Getting a Job in Advertising and Succeeding in Your Career

You have decided advertising is the career you want. You have also decided what kind of advertising job appeals to you and fits your talents, aptitudes, and interests.

Advertising is a tough field to break into. The key to finding that first job is preparation: Do your homework before hitting the streets. Develop a marketing plan for yourself. If you can't sell or market yourself, why should anyone hire you to market and sell their products?

Most people think of the advertising agency first—it is, after all, the most conspicuous institution in advertising. But agencies are the source of only a minority of jobs in the field. In fact, they employ less than a quarter of all the people in advertising. Other advertising employers include national, retail, industrial, and direct-response advertisers; TV and radio sales representatives; TV and radio production companies, sales-promotion services; and research companies.

Most advertising functions can be divided into four major areas. The first is creative. Whether writing, production, or art is your primary interest, imagination and an inquisitive mind are prerequisites for working on the creation and production of advertising messages. The ability to see the ordinary in a unique way is needed for success in this area of advertising.

The second primary area of advertising is media. The media function consists either of media planning and buying for a client or of selling time and space for broadcast or print media. In either case, an analytical mind, competency in math, and, in the case of salespersons, persistence are necessary.

The third area is research. There are research divisions in advertising agencies. Researchers also work in the client's marketing department and in separate research companies that service both agency and client on a project-by-project basis.

The last area of advertising jobs is account work. On both the client and the agency side, people who work in these jobs keep the lines of communication open and service the account. This liaison function is crucial to successful advertising. There is no way to estimate the number of accounts that have been lost because of personality conflicts between agency accounts executives and their counterparts on the client side.

Advertisers, agencies, and media use specialized talents and services to implement their communications. There are a lot of opportunities on the "supply side," in advertising specialty companies, art studios, audio/visual specialties, direct-response firms, display companies, film laboratories, film production companies, marketing research firms, typographers, printers, recording studios, and technical writing and illustrating.

Regardless of your area of interest, consider a career in advertising as a career in marketing and advertising, for there is much overlap between these fields. A man or woman who begins as a salesperson in a firm and rises to the position of marketing executive may one day leave the company to become the chief executive of an advertising agency. An assistant account executive may someday become advertising director of a large company with a multimillion-dollar ad budget.

No single type of academic training is recommended for a career in advertising. Most young people entering advertising today were trained in business or journalism schools. However, advertising agencies also hire English, classics, engineering, and psychology majors. Art departments in colleges and art institutes are a major source of art directors.

There is no formula that guarantees success in any of the four categories. Advertising crosses over into other disciplines—marketing, sales, manufacturing, personnel training, engineering, psychology, and many more. The key ingredients for success are an inquisitive, innovative mind, an ability to see through problems quickly, and the capacity to come up with orderly solutions to those problems.

Although, as we have pointed out, the ad agency is the most visible and glamorous part of the advertising business, it is also the most difficult to break into. Very few agencies have training courses; nevertheless, they often accept beginners to work in various departments. The starting pay is low, but after six months to a year—when they have had a chance to reveal their aptitude—beginners' rise in the agency can pick up momentum. After working two years, novices suddenly realize how many opportunities are open for those with "about two years' experience." By the time they are in their early 30s, they may well be making far more money than some of their classmates who went into other fields that offered higher starting salaries but slower potential for moving up. Unlike many other fields, advertising does not deny a person who reveals talent and competence the opportunity of earning good money because he or she is "too young" or because others have more seniority.

The key factors in looking for a job are the letter and resumé and the job interview.

Your letter to a prospective employer should always use the following guidelines:

1. Never address your letter to "Dear Sirs" or "Gentlemen." Write specifically to someone in the company, preferably the head of the department you wish to be employed in.
2. Demonstrate knowledge of the company by talking about its clients or, if it's a media company, its stations or publications.
3. Show how some special interest or training you have can benefit the company. Set yourself apart from the usual letter writer, who talks about *I, me, myself,* by stating clearly what you think you can do for the company.
5. Always close the letter with the statement that you will call for an interview in a few days.

Sidney and Mary Edlund, in their book *Pick Your Job and Land It!,* give good advice on how to turn an interview into a job offer:

- Have a clear picture of what the job calls for.
- Gather all the facts you can about the firm and its products.
- Draw up in advance an outline of the main points you want to cover during the interview.
- Appeal to the employer's self-interest by offering a service or dramatizing your interest in the company.
- Back up all statements of ability and achievement with proof.
- Prepare some questions of your own in advance. Keep etched in mind the two-way character of the interview: It is a mutual exploration.

Start your homework with the *Advertiser* and *Agency Redbook*. Then read everything you can about advertising and job hunting. Here are three titles for starters:

- *How to Get Your First Copywriting Job,* by Dick Wasserman.
- *How to Put Your Book Together and Get a Job in Advertising,* by Maxine Paetro.
- *Getting Hired: Everything You Need to Know About Resumés, Interviews and Job Hunting,* by Ed Rogers.

Sources of Information

PERIODICALS

GENERAL ADVERTISING PUBLICATIONS

Adweek
820 2nd Avenue
New York, New York 10017

Advertising Age
740 North Rush Street
Chicago, Illinois 60611

MARKETING

Marketing & Media Decisions
342 Madison Avenue
New York, New York 10017

DIRECT MARKETING

Direct Marketing
224 7th Street
Garden City, New York 11530

Target Marking
North American Publishing Co.
401 N. Broad Street
Philadelphia, Pennsylvania 19108

TELEVISION AND RADIO

Broadcasting
1735 DeSales Street, N.W.
Washington, D.C. 20036

Television/Radio Age
1270 Avenue of the Americas
New York, New York 10020

PRINT MEDIA

Editor & Publisher
575 Lexington Ave.
New York, New York 10022

Folio
125 Elm Street
New Canaan, Connecticut 06840

Inside Print
Six River Bend
Stamford, Connecticut 06907

PACKAGING

Modern Packaging
205 East 42nd Street
New York, New York 10017

RESEARCH

Journal of Advertising
University of Georgia
Athens, Georgia 30602

Journal of Advertising Research
Advertising Research Foundation, Inc.
3 East 54th Street
New York, New York 10022

Journal of Broadcasting
Broadcast Education Association
1771 N St. N.W.
Washington, D.C. 20036

Journal of Marketing
250 South Wacker Drive
Chicago, Illinois 60606

Journal of Marketing Research
250 S. Wacker Dr.
Chicago, Illinois 60606

Journal of Retailing
P.O. Box 465
Hanover, Pennsylvania 17331

SALES PROMOTION

Incentive Marketing
633 3rd Avenue
New York, New York 10017

INTERNATIONAL ADVERTISING

Advertising World
150 5th Avenue
Suite 610
New York, New York 10011

REFERENCE BOOKS AND INFORMATION SERVICES

Editor and Publisher Market Guide
850 3rd Avenue
New York, New York 10022

Media Market Guide
Conceptual Dynamics
P.O. Box 332
Wakefield, New Hampshire 03598

N.W. Ayer & Sons Directory
of Newspapers and Periodicals
N.W. Ayer & Sons, Inc.
West Washington Square
Philadelphia, Pennsylvania 19106

The Media Book
75 East 55th Street
New York, New York 10022

Newspaper Circulation
Analysis (NCA)
Standard Rate & Data
Service, Inc.
3004 Glenview Rd.
Wilmette, Illinois 60091

Standard Directory of
Advertisers (The Red Book)

Standard Directory
of Advertising Agencies
National Register Publishing Co., Inc.
3004 Glenview Rd.
Wilmette, Illinois 60091

ASSOCIATIONS OF ADVERTISERS AND AGENCIES

The Advertising Council
825 3rd Avenue
New York, New York 10017

American Advertising Federation
(AAF)
1400 K Street N.W.
Washington, D.C. 20005

American Association of
Advertising Agencies (AAAA, 4A's)
666 3rd Avenue
New York, New York 10017

American Marketing Association
(AMA)
250 South Wacker Drive
Chicago, Illinois 60606

Association of National Advertisers
(ANA)
155 East 44th Street
New York, New York 10017

Business & Professional
Advertising Association (BPAA)
205 East 42nd Street
New York, New York 10017

International Advertising
Association (IAA)
475 5th Avenue
New York, New York 10017

International Association
of Business Communicators
870 Market St.
Suite 940
San Francisco, California 94102

National Advertising
Review Board (NARB)
850 3rd Avenue
New York, New York 10022

National Council of Affiliated
Advertising Agencies
6 East 45th Street
New York, New York 10017

SYNDICATED MEDIA-RESEARCH SERVICES

Syndicated media-research services conduct regular surveys to reveal the publications people read, stations they listen to, ads they read, programs they listen to or watch, their reaction to programs and commercials, types of products they use and which brands, and demographic information. Each service focuses on some special phase of the total picture. Since they are continually working to make their output more helpful, no effort is made here to describe the specific services each offers. For latest information communicate directly with them.

The Arbitron Company, Inc.
1350 Avenue of the Americas
New York, New York 10019

Broadcast Advertisers
Report, Inc. (BAR)
500 5th Avenue
New York, New York 10036

The Buyer Guide to
Outdoor Advertising
515 Madison Avenue
New York, New York 10017

Leading National
Advertisers, Inc. (LNA)
515 Madison Avenue
New York, New York 10017

Mediamark Research, Inc.
341 Madison Avenue
New York, New York 10017

A. C. Nielsen Company
Nielsen Plaza
Northbrook, Illinois 60062

Simmons Marketing
Research Bureau, Inc.
219 East 42nd Street
New York, New York 10017

Standard Rate & Data Service, Inc.
3004 Glenview Rd.
Wilmette, Illinois 60091

Glossary

A

Action for Children's Television (ACT). Organization dedicated to the examination and criticism of TV's effects on young viewers.

Ad banking. Practice of some magazines of clustering ads at the front and back of their publications.

Advertising clearance process. The internal process of clearing ads for publication and broadcast, conducted primarily by ad agencies and clients.

Advertising Council. A nonprofit network of agencies, media, and advertisers dedicated to promoting social programs through advertising.

Advertising goals. The communication objectives designed to accomplish certain tasks within the total marketing program.

The Advertising Research Foundation Model for Evaluating Media. A model used to evaluate the methods of measuring a medium's ability to reach prospects versus nonprospects. ''Have you seen this ad before?'' In contrast to *unaided recall:* ''Which ad impressed you most in this magazine?''

Advertorial. Advertising used to promote special views of its sponsors. Name is derived from advertising and editorials.

AIO (activities, interests, and opinions). Widely used in identifying consumers for lifestyle studies.

Air check. A recording of an actual broadcast that serves as a file copy of a broadcast and that a sponsor may use to evaluate talent, program appeal, or production.

A la carte agency. One that offers parts of its services as needed on a negotiated-fee basis; also called *modular service*.

AM. *See* Amplitude modulation.

American Academy of Advertising (AAA). The national association of advertising teachers in colleges and universities and of others interested in the teaching of advertising.

American Advertising Federation (AAF). An association of local advertising clubs and representatives of other advertising associations. The largest association of advertising people. Very much interested in advertising legislation.

American Association of Advertising Agencies (AAAA, 4 A's). The national organization of advertising agencies.

Association of Business Publishers (ABP). An organization of trade, industrial, and professional papers.

American Federation of Television and Radio Artists (AFTRA). A union involved in the setting of wage scales of all performers.

American Newspaper Publishers' Association (ANPA). The major trade association of daily and Sunday newspaper publishers.

Amplitude modulation (AM). The method of transmitting electromagnetic signals by varying the *amplitude* (size) of the electromagnetic wave, in contrast to varying its *frequency* (FM). Quality not as good as FM but can be heard farther, especially at night. *See* Frequency modulation (FM).

ANA. *See* Association of National Advertisers.

Animation (TV). Making inanimate objects appear alive and moving by setting them before an animation camera and filming one frame at a time.

Announcement. Any TV or radio commercial, regardless of time length and within or between programs, that presents an advertiser's message or a public-service message.

ANPA. *See* American Newspaper Publishers Association.

Answer print. A finisher commercial film print that has been corrected for color and density.

Antique-finish paper. Book or cover paper that has a fairly rough, uneven surface, good for offset printing.

Appeal. The motive to which an ad is directed and which is designed to stir a person toward a goal the advertiser has set.

Approach (outdoor). The distance measured along the line of travel from the point where the poster first becomes fully visible to a point where the copy ceases to be readable. (There are *long* approach, *medium* approach, *short* approach, and *flash* approach.)

Arbitrary mark. A dictionary word used as a trademark that *connotes nothing* about the product it is to identify, for example, *Rise* shaving cream, *Dial* soap, *Jubilee* wax.

Arbitron Ratings Company. Syndicated radio and TV ratings company. Dominant in local radio ratings.

Area of dominant influence (ADI). An exclusive geographic area consisting of all counties in which the home-market station receives a preponderance of total viewing hours. Developed by American Research Bureau. Widely used for TV, radio, newspaper, magazine, and outdoor advertising in media scheduling. *See also* Designated Market Area (DMA).

ARF. *See* Advertising Research Foundation.

ASCAP (American Society of Composers, Authors, and Publishers). An organization that protects the copyrights of its members and collects royalties in their behalf.

Ascending letters. Those with a stroke or line going higher than the body of the letter—*b*, *d*, *f*, *h*, *k*, *l*, and *t*—and all capitals. The descending letters are *g*, *j*, *p*, *q*, and *y*.

Association of National Advertisers (ANA). The trade association of the leading national advertisers. Founded 1910.

Association test. A research method of measuring the degree to which people correctly identify brand names, slogans, and themes.

Audience Measurement by Market of Outdoor (AMMO). Audits outdoor audiences in major markets, providing demographic and product-user information.

Audience, primary. In TV and radio, the audience in the territory where the signal is the strongest. In print, the readers in households that buy or subscribe to a publication.

Audience, secondary. In TV and radio, the audience in the territory adjacent to the primary territory, which receives the signal but not so strongly as the latter. In print, the number of people who read a publication but who did not subscribe to or buy it. Also called *pass-along circulation.*

Audience, share of. The number or proportion of all TV households that are tuned to a particular station or program.

Audience composition. The number and kinds of people, classified by their age, sex, income, and the like, in a medium's audience.

Audience fragmentation. The segmenting of mass-media audiences into smaller groups because of diversity of media outlets.

Audimeter. The device for recording when the TV set in a household is on, a part of the research operation of the A. C. Nielsen Company.

Audio (TV). Sound portion of a program or commercial. *See* Video.

Audit Bureau of Circulations (ABC). The organization sponsored by publishers, agencies, and advertisers for securing accurate circulation statements.

Automated Collection of Audience Composition (A-C) meter. A. C. Nielsen device to measure individuals watching TV.

Availability. In broadcasting, a time period available for purchase by an advertiser.

Average quarter-hour estimates (AQHE). Manner in which radio ratings are presented. Estimates include average number of persons listening, rating, and metro share of audience.

B

Background. A broadcasting sound effect, musical or otherwise, used behind the dialogue or other program elements for realistic or emotional effect.

Barter. Acquisition of broadcast time by an advertiser or an agency in exchange for operating capital or merchandise. No cash is involved.

Barter syndication. Station obtains a program at no charge. The program has presold national commercials and time is available for local station spots.

Basic bus. A bus, all of whose interior advertising is sold to one advertiser. When the outside is also sold, it is called a *basic basic bus.*

Basic network. The minimum grouping of stations for which an advertiser must contract in order to use the facilities of a radio or TV network.

Basic rate. *See* Open rate.

Basic stations. TV networks are offered in a list of stations that must be included. These are the basic stations. There is also a supplementary list of optional additions.

Basic weight. The weight a ream of paper if cut to the standard, or basic, size for what class of paper. The basic sizes are: writing papers, 17 by 22 inches; book papers, 25 by 38 inches; cover stocks, 20 by 26 inches.

BBB. *See* Better Business Bureaus.

Better Business Bureaus. An organization, launched by advertisers and now with wide business support, to protect the public against deceptive advertising and fraudulent business methods. Works widely at local levels. Also identified with the National Advertising Review Board.

Billable services. *See* Collateral services.

Billboard. (1) Popular name for an outdoor sign. Term not now generally used in the industry. (2) The TV presentation of the name of a program sponsor plus a slogan, used at the start or close of a program and usually lasting 8 seconds.

Billing. (1) Amount of gross business done by an advertising agency. (2) Name credits of talent in order of importance.

Birch Radio. A local radio ratings service.

Black and white. An ad printed in one color only, usually black, on white paper. Most newspapers are printed in black and white.

Blanking area. The white margin around a poster erected on a standard-size board. It is widest for a 24-sheet poster, for example; narrower for a 30-sheet poster; and disappears on a bleed poster.

Bleed. Printed matter that runs over the edges of an outdoor board or of a page, leaving no margin.

Blister pack. A packaging term. A performed bubble of plastic holding merchandise to a card. Used for small items. Also called *bubble card.*

Block. (1) A set of consecutive time periods on the air or a strip of the same time on several days. (2) Wood or metal base on which the printing plate is mounted. (3) British term for photoengraving or electrotype.

Blowup. Photo enlargement of written, printed, or pictorial materials; for example, enlargement of a publication ad to be used as a poster or transmitted through TV.

BMI. Broadcast Music, Inc. Chief function: to provide music to radio and TV shows with minimum royalty fees, if any.

Boards (outdoor). Poster panels and painted bulletins. Term originated in the period when theatrical and circus posters were displayed on board fences.

Body copy. Main text of ad, in contrast to headlines and name plate.

Body type. Commonly used for reading matter, as distinguished from display type used in the headlines of advertisements. Usually type is 14 points in size or smaller.

Boldface type. A heavy line type; for example, the headings in these definitions.

Bonus-to-payout. Medium agrees to run an ad until some agreed-upon results are achieved.

Book paper. Used in printing books, lightweight leaflets, and folders; distinguished from writing papers and cover stocks. Basic size: 25 by 38 inches.

Bounce back. An enclosure in the package of a product that has been ordered by mail. It offers other products of the same company and is effective in getting more business.

Boutique. A service specializing in creating ads. Often calls in independent artists and writers. This term is usually applied to small groups. Larger groups refer to themselves as *creative services,* and they may develop into full-service agencies.

BPA. *See* Business Publications Audit of Circulation, Inc.

Brand. A name, term, sign, design, or a unifying combination of them, intended to identify and distinguish the product or service from competing products or services.

Brand equity. The value of how consumers, distributors, salespersons, etc., think and feel about a brand relative to the competition over a period of time.

Brands emotional elements. Stem mainly from *HOW* the brand is expressing itself, showing, promising. Part of Brand Equity. *See* Brands Rational Elements.

Brand loyalty. Degree to which a consumer purchases a certain brand without considering alternatives.

Brand manager. See Product manager.

Brand monopoly. The concept that large advertisers so overwhelm consumers with their messages that new products have difficulty in gaining entry to the market place.

Brand name. The spokent part of a trademark, in contrast to the pictorial mark; a trademark word.

Brands rational elements. Stem predominately from *WHAT* the brand is doing, telling, showing. *See* Brands Emotional Elements. Part of Brand Equity.

Bridge. Music or sound-effect cue linking two scenes in a TV or radio show.

Broadcast spectrum. That part of the range of frequencies of electromagnetic waves assigned to broadcasting stations. Separate bands of frequencies are assigned to VHF and UHF TV and AM and FM radio.

Brochure. A fancy booklet or monograph.

Bubble card. *See* Blister pack.

Budget. A plan to organize and allocate future funding of business functions.

Building-block method. The medium with the most effective exposure of prime prospects becomes the foundation of the media schedule. Other media are then added to it.

Bulk discount. *See* Frequency discounts.

Bulk mailing. A quantity of third-class mail that must be delivered to the post office in bundles, assorted by state and city.

Buried offer. An offer for a booklet, sample, or information made by means of a statement within the text of an ad without use of a coupon or typographical emphasis. (Also called *hidden offer.*)

Business Publications Audit of Circulation, Inc. (BPA). An organization that audits business publications. Includes controlled, or "qualified," free circulation.

Buyer's Guide to Outdoor Advertising. Publication of leading national advertisers giving rates for outdoor advertising.

Buying services (media). A professional organization that plans and executes media schedules for agencies and advertisers. Also known as *media services,* operating chiefly in the broadcast field.

Buying space. Buying the right to insert an ad in a given medium, such as a periodical, a newspaper, or an outdoor sign; buying time is the corresponding term for purchase of TV or radio broadcast privilege.

C

Cable networks. Networks available only to cable subscribers. They are transmitted via satellite to local cable operators for redistribution either as part of basic service or at an extra cost charged to subscribers.

Cable television. TV signals that are carried to households by cable. Programs originate with cable operators through high antennas, satellite disks, or operator-initiated programming.

Call letters. The combination of letters assigned by the Federal Communications Commission to a broadcasting station. They serve as its official designation and establish its identity.

Camera light. Pilot light on TV cameras indicating which camera is on the air.

Camera lucids ("lucy"). A device used in making layouts, enabling the artist to copy an illustration larger, smaller, or in the same size.

Campaign. A specific advertising effort on behalf of a particular product or service. It extends for a specified period of time.

Caption. The heading of an ad; the descriptive matter accompanying an illustration.

Casting off. Estimating the amount of space a piece of copy will occupy when set in type of a given size.

Category manager. A relatively new corporate brand position. This manager is responsible for all aspects of the brands in a specific product category for a company including: research, manufacturing, sales, advertising, etc. Each product's advertising manager reports to the category manager. Example: Procter & Gamble's Tide and Cheer detergent brands report to a single Category Manager.

Cathode-ray tube (CRT). Electronic tube used by hight-speed photocomposition machines to transmit the letter image onto film, photopaper, microfilm, or an offset plate.

Caveat emptor. Lating for "Let the buyer beware." Represents the notion that there should be no government interference in the marketplace.

Cease and desist orders. If an advertiser refuses to sign a consent decree, the FTC may issue a cease and desist order that can carry a $10,000-per-day fine.

Center spread. In print the space occupied by an ad or the ad itself on the two facing pages of a publication bound through the center. Otherwise called *double-page spread.* In outdoor two adjacent panels using coordinated copy.

Central Hudson four-part test. Supreme Court test to determine if specific commercial speech is protected under the Constitution.

Certification mark. A name or design used upon, or in connection with, the products or services of persons other than the owner of the mark, to certify origin, material, mode of manufacture, quality, accuracy, or other characteristics of such goods or services, for example, *Seal of the Underwriters' Laboratories, Sanforized, Teflon II*.

Chain. (1) A group of retail outlets with the same ownership, management, and business policy. (2) A regularly established system of TV or radio stations broadcasting through associated stations. (3) A group of media outlets under common ownership.

Chain break. Times during or between network programs when the broadcasting station identifies itself (2 seconds) and gives a commercial announcement (8 seconds). The announcements are referred to as chain breaks or *ID*'s (for identification).

Channel. A band of radio frequencies assigned to a given radio or TV station or to other broadcasting purposes.

Checkerboarding. When a station runs a different syndicated show in the same time slot each day.

Checking copy. A copy of a publication sent to an advertiser or agency to show that the ad appeared as specified.

Children's Advertising Review Unit (CARU). The CARU functions much as the NAD to review complaints of advertising to children.

Circular. An ad printed on a sheet or folder.

Circulation. Refers to the number of people a medium reaches. (1) In publication advertising *prime* circulation is that paid for by the reader, in contrast to *pass-along* circulation. (2) In outdoor and transportation advertising people who have a reasonable opportunity to observe display. (3) In TV usually referred to as *audience*.

Circulation and Penetration Analysis of Print Media. Reference source that gives the penetration of print media by county and ADI.

Circulation waste. Circulation for which an advertiser pays but which does not reach prospects.

Classified advertising. In columns so labeled published in sections of a newspaper or magazine set aside for certain classes of goods or services, for example, Help wanted, Positions Wanted, Houses for Sale, Cars for Sale. The ads are limited in size and illustrations.

Class magazines. Term loosely used to describe publications that reach select high-income readers, in contrast to magazines of larger circulations, generally referred to as *mass magazines*.

Clayton Antitrust Act. Amended the Sherman Antitrust Act to eliminate preferential price treatment when manufacturers sell merchandise to retailers.

Clear. (1) To obtain legal permission from responsible sources to use a photograph or quotation in an ad or to use a certain musical selection in a broadcast. (2) To clear time is to arrange with a TV station to provide time for a commercial program.

Clear-channel station. A radio station that is allowed the maximum power and given a channel on the frequency bank all to itself. Possibly one or two sectional or local stations may be removed from it far enough not to interfere. (*See also* Local-channel station, Regional-channel station).

Clear time. *See* Clear.

Clip. A short piece of film inserted in a program or commercial.

Closed circuit (TV). Live, videotape, or film material transmitted by cable for private viewing on a TV monitor.

Closing date, closing hour. (1) The day or hour when all copy and plates or prints must be in the medium's hands if an ad is to appear in a given issue. The closing time is specified by the medium. (2) The last hour or day that a radio program or announcement may be submitted for approval to a station or network management to be included in the station's schedule.

Cluster sample. A random or probability sample that uses groups of people rather than individuals as a sampling unit.

Clutter. Refers to proliferation of commercials (in a medium) that reduces the impact of any single message.

CMX (TV). Computer editing, in which the videotape of the TV commercial is edited at a console with two side-by-side monitors.

Coarse screen. A compartively low, or coarse, *screen,* usually 60, 65, or 85 lines to the inch, making a *half-tone* suitable for printing on coarse paper.

Coated paper. Coating gives paper a smooth, hard finish, suitable for the reproduction of fine *halftones*.

Coined word. An original and arbitrary combination of syllables forming a word. Extensively used for trademarks, as Acrilan, Gro-Pup, Zerone. (Opposite of a dictionary word.)

Collateral services. An agency term to describe the noncommissionable forms of service that different agencies perform, such as sales promotion, research, merchandising, and new-product studies. Done on a negotiated-fee basis, both for clients and nonclients.

Collective mark. An identification used by the members of a cooperative, an association, collective group, or organization, including marks used to indicate membership in a union, an association, or other organization (for example, Sunkist).

Color bars. A standard method of showing process color inks on a four-color process proof.

Color proof. Combined impressions from separate color plates.

Color transparency. A full-color transparent photographic poitive. A 35mm slide is an example.

Column-inch. A unit of measure in a periodical one inch deep and one column wide, whatever the width of the column.

Combination plate. A *halftone* and *line plate* in one engraving.

Combination rate. A special space rate for two papers, such as a morning paper and an evening paper, owned by the same publisher. Applied also to any other special rate granted in connection with two or more periodicals.

Comic strip. A series of cartoon or caricature drawings.

Commercial. The advertiser's message on TV or radio.

Commercial program. A sponsored program from which broadcasting stations derive revenue on the basis of the time consumed in broadcasting it.

Comparative advertising. *See* Comparison advertising.

Comparison advertising. Used interchangeably with the term *comparative advertising,* it directly contrasts an advertiser's product with other named or identified products.

Competitive stage. The advertising stage a product reaches when its general usefulness is recognized but its superiority over similar brands has to be established in order to gain preference. (*Compare* Pioneering stage; Retentive stage.) *See also* Spiral.

Composite print (TV). A 35mm or 16mm film print of a TV commercial, complete with both sound and picture.

Composition. Assembling and arranging type for printing. (Also called *typography* or *typesetting*.)

Composition (cold). Strike-on, or direct-impression, typesetting by a typewriter.

Comprehensive. A layout accurate in size, color scheme, and other necessary details to show how a final ad will look. For presentation only, never for reproduction.

Computerized composition. The use of a computer in phototypesetting (or, rarely, linecasting) equipment for the purpose of justifying and hyphenating, storing, and typographically manipulating copy after it has been keyboarded but before it is set into type.

Concept. The combining of all elements (copy, headline, and illustrations) of an ad into a single idea.

Concept testing. The target audience evaluation of (alternative) creative strategy. Testing attempts to separate "good" and "bad" ideas and provide insight into factors motivating acceptance or rejection.

Consent decree. Issued by the FTC. An advertiser signs the decree, stops the practice under investigation, but admits no guilt.

Consumer advertising. Directed to people who will personally use the product, in contrast to trade advertising, industrial advertising, or professional advertising.

Contest. A promotion in which consumers compete for prizes and the winners are selected strictly on the basis of skill. *See* Sweepstakes.

Continuity. A TV or radio script. Also refers to the length of time given media schedule runs.

Continuity department (TV). Determines whether or not a commercial is up to the broadcast standards of the station.

Continuity premium. A premium that is part of an ongoing program. The longer a consumer participates, the more valuable the gift becomes. Trading stamps are the most used continuity premiums.

Continuous tone. An unscreened photographic picture or image, on paper or film, that contains all gradations of tonal values from white to black.

Controlled-circulation business and professional publications. Sent without cost to people responsible for making buying decisions. To get on, and stay on, such lists, people must state their positions in companies and request annually that they be kept on the list. Also known as *qualified-circulation publications*.

Cooperative advertising. (1) Joint promotion of a national advertiser (manufacturer) and local retail outlet on behalf of the manufacturer's product on sale in the retail store. (2) Joint promotion through a trade association for firms in a single industry. (3) Advertising venture jointly conducted by two or more advertisers.

Cooperative mailing. Sent to a select list comprising all the inserts of a group of noncompetitive firms trying to reach the same audience. A way of reducing mailing costs.

Copy. (1) The text of an ad. (2) The matter for a compositor to set. (3) Any material to be used in publication. (4) The original photograph, drawing, painting, or transparency used for reproduction.

Copy approach. The method of opening the text of an ad. Chief forms: factual approach, emotional approach.

Copy platform. The statement of the basic idea for an advertising campaign, the designation of the importance of the various selling points to be included in it, and instructions regarding policy in handling any elements of the ad.

Copyright. Legal protection afforded an original intellectual effort. Application blanks for registry are procurable from the Copyright Office, Library of Congress, Washington, D.C. 20559. Copyright notice must appear on ads for this protection.

Copy testing. Measuring the effectiveness of ads.

Copywriter. A person who creates the text of ads and often the idea to be visualized as well.

Corrective advertising. To counteract the past residual effect of previous deceptive advertising, the FTC may require the advertiser to devote future space and time to disclosure of previous deception. Began around the late 1960s.

Cost per order. Method used by direct-response advertisers for comparing results of different ads.

Cost per rating point (CCP). The cost per rating point is used to estimate the cost of TV advertising on several shows.

Cost per thousand (CPM). A method of comparing the cost for media of different circulations. Also weighted or demographic cost per thousand calculates the CPM using only that portion of a medium's audience falling into a prime-prospect category.

Cover. The front of a publication is known as the first cover; the inside of the front cover is the second cover; the inside of the back cover is the third cover; the outside of the back cover is the fourth cover. Extra rates are charged for cover positions.

Coverage. *See* Reach.

Coverage (TV). All households in an area able to receive a station's signal, even though some may not be tuned in. *Grade A* coverage: those households in the city and outlying counties that receive signals with hardly any disturbance. *Grade B:* those on the fringes of the market area receiving signals with some interference.

Cover stock. A paper made of heavy, strong fiber; used for folders and booklet covers. Some cover stocks run into the low weights of paper known as book paper, but most cover stocks are heavier. Basic size, 20 by 26 inches.

Coupon. Most popular type of sales-promotion technique.

Coupon Distribution Verification Service. Service begun by Audit Bureau of Circulations in 1981 to audit newspaper publishers' security and verification of distributed coupons.

CPM. *See* Cost per thousand.

Crash finish. A surface design on paper, simulating the appearance of rough cloth.

Crew (TV). All personnel hired by the production company for shooting a TV commercial.

Cronar film and Cronar plates. A conversion method by which either type of letterpress engraving is transferred directly to film by mechanical means (balls or fingers). This film can then be used to make offset plates, gravure cylinders, or very faithful duplicate letterpress plates.

Cropping. Trimming part of an illustration. Cropping is done either to eliminate nonessential background in an illustration or to change the proportions of the illustration to the desired length and width.

CRT. *See* Cathode-ray tube.

CU. Close-up (in TV). *ECU* is *extra close-up*.

Cue. (1) The closing words of an actor's speech and a signal for another actor to enter. (2) A sound, musical or otherwise, or a manual signal calling for action or proceeding.

Cumes. Cumulative audience. The number of unduplicated people or homes reached by a given schedule over a given time period.

Cut. (1) The deletion of program material to fit a prescribed period of time or for other reasons. (2) A photoengraving, electrotype, or stereotype; derived from the term *woodcut*. In England called a *block*.

D

Dailies (TV). All film shot, developed, and printed, from which scenes are selected for editing into the completed TV commercial. The term may also apply to videotape shooting. Also known as *rushes*.

Database marketing. A process of continually updating information about individual consumers. Popular techniques with direct-response sellers.

Dayparts. Time segments into which a radio or TV day is divided, from first thing in the morning to the last thing at night. The parts are given different names. The cost of time depends upon the size of the audience at the time of each different daypart.

Dealer imprint. Name and address of the dealer, printed or pasted on an ad of a national advertiser. In the planning of direct mail, space is frequently left for dealer imprint.

Dealer tie-in. A national advertiser's promotional program in which the dealer participates (as in contests, sampling plans, cooperative advertising plans).

Deals. A *consumer* deal is a plan whereby the consumer can save money in the purchase of a product. A *trade* deal is a special discount to the retailer for a limited period of time.

Deckle edge. Untrimmed, ragged edge of a sheet of paper. Used for costlier forms of direct mail.

Deck panels (outdoor). Panels built one above the other.

Definition. Clean-cut TV and radio transmission and reception.

Demarketing. A technique of discouraging sales of scarce goods or limiting sales to unproductive market segments.

Demographic characteristics. A broad term covering the various social and economic characteristics of a group of households or a group of individuals. Refers to characteristics such as the number of members of a household, age of head of household, occupation of head household, education of household members, type of employment, ownership of home, and annual household income.

Demographic CPM. *See* Cost per thousand.

Demographic edition. *See* Partial run editions.

Depth interview. A research interview conducted without a structured questionnaire. Respondents are encouraged to speak fully and freely about a particular subject.

Depths of columns. The dimension of a column space measured from top of the page to the bottom, in either agate lines or inches.

Designated market area (DMA). A rigidly defined geographical area in which stations located, generally, in the core of the area attract most of the viewing. A concept developed by the A. C. Nielsen Company. *See also* Area of dominant influence (ADI).

Diary. A written record kept by a sample of persons who record their listening, viewing, reading, or purchases of brands within a specific period of time. Used by syndicated research firms who arrange with a selected sample of people to keep such diaries and to report weekly, for a fee.

Die cut. An odd-shaped paper or cardboard for a direct-mail piece or for display purposes, cut with a special knife-edge die.

Diorama. (1) In point-of-purchase advertising these are elaborate displays of a scenic nature, almost always three-dimensional and illuminated. (2) In TV a miniature set, usually in perspective, used to simulate an impression of a larger location.

Direct Broadcast Satellite Systems (DBS). Transmitting a satellite signal directly to a subscriber via a home receiver dish.

Direct houses. In specialty advertising, firms that combine the functions of supplier and distributor.

Direct-mail advertising. That form of direct-response advertising sent through the mails.

Direct Mail/Marketing Association (DMMA). Organization to promote direct-mail and direct-response advertising.

Direct marketing. Selling goods and services without the aid of wholesaler or retailer. Includes direct-response advertising and advertising for leads for sales people. Also direct door-to-door selling. Uses many media: direct mail, publications, TV, radio.

Direct process. In two-, three-, and four-color process work, color separation and screen negative made simultaneously on the same photographic film.

Direct-response advertising. Any form of advertising done in direct marketing. Uses all types of media: direct mail, TV, magazines, newspapers, radio. Term replaces *mail-order advertising*. *See* Direct marketing.

Director. The person who casts and rehearses a TV or ratio program and directs the actual air performance.

Disk. Circular carrier of negative fonts used in phototypesetting equipment such as Photon or Fototronic.

Disk jockey. The master of ceremonies of a radio program of transcribed music (records).

Display. (1) Attention-attracting quality. (2) Display type is in sizes 18 points or larger. Italics, boldface, and sometimes capitals are used for display; so are hand-drawn letters and script. (3) Display space in newspapers usually is not sold in units of less than fourteen column lines; there is no minimum requirement for undisplay classified ads. (4) Window display, interior display, and counter display are different methods of point-of-purchase advertising. (5) Open display puts the goods where they can be actually handled and examined by the customer; closed display has the goods in cases and under glass.

Display advertising. (1) In a newspaper, ads other than those in classified columns. (2) Advertising on backgrounds designed to stand by themselves (as window displays) or mounted (as tack-on sign).

Dissolve (TV). Simultaneous fading out of one scene and fading in of the next in the TV commercial.

DMA. *See* Designated market area.

Dolly. The movable platform on which a camera is placed for TV productions when different angles or views will be needed.

Double billing. Unethical practice of retailer's asking for manufacturer reimbursement at a higher rate than what was paid for advertising time or space.

Double-leaded. *See* Leading.

Double-page spread. Facing pages used for a single, unbroken ad. Also called *double spread* and *double truck* or *center spread* if at the center of a publication.

Drive time (radio). A term used to designate the time of day when people are going to, or coming from, work. Usually 6 A.M. to 10 A.M. and 3 P.M. to 7 P.M., but this varies from one community to another. The most costly time on the rate card.

Dry run. Rehearsal without cameras.

Dubbing. The combining of several sound tracks for recording on film.

Dubbing in. Addition of one TV film to another, for example, adding the part containing the advertiser's commercial to the part that carries the straight entertainment.

Dubs (TV). Duplicate tapes, made from a master print, sent to different stations for broadcast.

Due bill. (1) In a media barter deal, the amount of time acquired from a station by a film distributor, owner, or producer. (2) An agreement between an advertiser (usually a hotel, restaurant, or resort) and a medium, involving equal exchange of the advertiser's service for time or space.

Dummy. (1) Blank sheets of paper cut and folded to the size of a proposed leaflet, folder, booklet, or book, to indicate weight, shape, size, and general appearance. On the pages of the dummy the layouts can be drawn. Useful in designing direct-mail ads. A dummy may also be made from the proof furnished by the printer. (2) An empty package or carton used for display purposes.

Duplicate plates. Plates made from the same negative as the original engraving, or via DuPont Cronapress conversion, finished in the same manner.

Duograph. A two-color plate made from black-and-white artwork. The second color is a flat color and carries no detail. Less expensive than a *duotone*.

Duotone. Two halftone plates, each printing in a different color and giving two-color reproductions from an original one-color plate.

Dye transfer. A high-fidelity color print made from a color transparency.

E

Early fringe. The time period preceding prime time, usually 4:30 to 7:30 P.M., except in Central Time Zone, where it extends from 3:30 to 6:30 P.M.

Ears (newspaper). Boxes or announcements at the top of the front page, alongside the name of the paper, in the upper right- and left-hand corners. Sold for advertising space by some papers.

Earth station. A TV receiving station designed to capture signals from satellites for relay to broadcasting stations or in time, possibly directly to receiving sets.

ECU (TV). Extra-close-up in shooting a picture.

Editing (TV). Also known as "completion," "finishing," and "postproduction." The second major stage of TV commercial production, following shooting, in which selected scenes are joined together with opticals and titles and sound track into the finished commercial.

Effective frequency. The number of exposures required to achieve a minimal level of communication impact.

Effective reach. The percentage of an audience which is exposed to a certain number of messages or has achieved a specified level of awareness.

Effectiveness. In media planning, those media vehicles best able to communicate a message and reach prospects.

Efficiency. In media planning, the least expensive media that can be included in a media schedule.

Eight-sheet poster. Outdoor poster used in urban areas, about one-fourth the size of the standard 30-sheet poster. Also called *junior poster*.

80/20 rule. Rule-of-thumb that says a minority of consumers (20%) will purchase a large proportion (80%) of specific goods and services.

Electric spectaculars. Outdoor ads in which electric lights are used to form the words and design. Not to be confused with illuminated *posters* or *illuminated painted bulletins*.

Enameled paper (enamel-coated stock). A book or cover paper than can take the highest-screen half-tone. It is covered with a coating of china clay and a binder and then ironed under high-speed rollers. This gives it a hard, smooth finish, too brittle to fold well. Made also in dull and semidull finish.

End-product advertising. Advertising by a firm that makes a constituent part of a finished product bought by the consumer. For example, advertising by DuPont that stresses the importance of Teflon in cooking ware.

Engraving. (1) A photoengraving. (2) A plate in which design is etched for printing purposes.

Equivalent weight of paper. The weight of a paper stock in terms of its basic weight. *See* Basic weight.

Ethical advertising. (1) Standards of equitable, fair, and honest content in advertising. (2) Addressed to physicians only, in contrast to ads of a similar product addressed to the general public.

European Community (EC). The economic integration of Europe is scheduled for 1992. In many respects Europe will become a single market of some 300 million consumers.

Executive gifts. Type of advertising specialty directed to a firm's trade customers. More expensive than consumer specialties and often not imprinted.

Extended covers. A cover that is slightly wider and longer than the pages of a paper-bound booklet or catalog; one that extends or hangs over the inside pages. Also called *overhang* and *overlap. See also* Trimmed flush.

F

Facing text matter. An ad in a periodical opposite reading matter.

Fact sheet. A page of highlights of the selling features of a product, for use by a radio announcer in ad-libbing a live commercial.

Fade. (1) Variation in intensity of a radio or TV signal received over a great distance. (2) *Fading in* is the gradual appearance of the TV screen image, brightening to full visibility. (3) To diminish or increase the volume of sound on a radio broadcast.

Family life cycle. Concept that demonstrates changing purchasing behavior as a person or family matures.

Family of type. *Typefaces* related in design, as Caslon Bold, Caslon Old Style, Caslon Bold italic, Caslon Old Style italic.

Fanfare. A few bars of music (usually trumpets) to herald an entrance or announcement in broadcasting.

Far forward (magazines). Advertisers sometime request a position in the front section of a magazine.

Fast close. Some magazines offer short-notice ad deadlines at a premium cost.

FCC. *See* Federal Communications Commission.

FDA. *See* Food and Drug Administration.

Federal Communications Commission (FCC). The federal authority empowered to license radio and TV stations and to assign wavelengths to stations "in the public interest."

Federal Trade Commission (FTC). The agency of the federal government empowered to prevent unfair competition and to prevent fraudulent, misleading, or deceptive advertising in interstate commerce.

Field-intensity map. A TV or radio broadcast-coverage map showing the quality of reception possible on the basis of its signal strength. Sometimes called a *contour map*.

Fill-in. (1) The salutation and any other data to be inserted in individual form letters after they have been printed. (2) The blurring of an illustration due to the closeness of the lines or dots in the plate or to heavy inking.

Firm order. A definite order for time or space that is not cancellable after a given date known as a *firm-order date*.

Fixed position. A TV or radio spot delivered at a specific time, for example, 8 A.M.

Flag (outdoor). A tear in a poster, causing a piece of poster paper to hang loose. Plant owner is supposed to replace promptly.

Flat color. Second or additional printing colors, using line or tints but not *process*.

Flat rate. A uniform charge for space in a medium, without regard to the amount of space used or the frequency of insertion. When flat rates do not prevail, *time discounts* or *quantity discounts* are offered.

Flexography. A direct-relief printing process that uses polymer plastic plates on web presses, those using a continuous roll of paper. It gets its name from the flexibility of placing plates on press. It gives sharper image than letterpress. More newspapers are adopting this process.

Flight. The length of time a broadcaster's campaign runs. Can be days, weeks, or months but does not refer to a year. A flighting schedule alternates periods of activity with periods of inactivity.

Flush left. Body copy in which there is an uneven or ragged margin on the right and an even margin on the left. When both margins are even, the type is "justified."

Flush right. Body copy in which there is an uneven or ragged margin on the left and an even margin on the right.

FM. *See* Frequency modulation.

Focus group. A qualitative research interviewing method using depth interviews with a group rather than with an individual.

Following, next to reading matter. The specification of a position for an ad to appear in a publication. Also known as *full position*. This preferred position usually costs more than *run-of-paper* position.

Follow style. Instruction to compositor to set copy in accordance with a previous ad or proof.

Font. An assortment of type characters of one style and size, containing the essential twenty-six letters (both capitals and small letters) plus numerals, punctuation marks, and the like. *See* Wrong font.

Food and Drug Administration (FDA). The federal bureau with authority over the safety and purity of foods, drugs, and cosmetics and over the labeling of such products.

Forced combination. A policy of allowing advertising space to be purchased only for a combination of the morning and evening newspapers in the community.

Form. Groups of pages printed on a large single sheet. This book was printed in 32s. (thirty-two pages to one sheet, or *form*).

Format. The size, shape, style, and appearance of a book or publication.

Forms close. The date on which all copy and plates for a periodical ad must be in.

4A's. American Association of Advertising Agencies.

Four-color process. The process for reproducing color illustrations by a set of plates, one of which prints all the yellows, another the blues, a third the reds, the fourth the blacks (sequence variable). The plates are referred to as *process plates*.

Fragmentation. In advertising a term that refers to the increasing selectivity of media vehicles and the segmenting of the audience that results.

Free lance. An independent artist, writer, TV or radio producer, or advertising person who takes individual assignments from different accounts but is not in their employ.

Free-standing inserts. Preprinted inserts distributed to newspapers where they are inserted and delivered within the newspaper.

Frequency. (1) The number of waves per second that a transmitter radiates, measured in kilohertz (kHz) and megahertz (MHz). The FCC assigns to each TV and radio station the frequency on which it may operate, to prevent interference with other stations. (2) Of media exposure the number of times an individual or household is exposed to a medium within a given period of time. (3) In statistics the number of times each element appears in each step of a distribution scale.

Frequency discounts. Discounts based on total time or space bought, usually within a year. Also called *bulk discounts*.

Frequency modulation (FM). A radio transmission wave that transmits by the variation in frequency of its wave, rather than by its size (as in AM modulation). An FM wave is twenty times the width of an AM wave, which is the source of its fine tone. To transmit such a wave, it has to be placed high on the electromagnetic spectrum, far from AM waves with their interference and static. Hence its outstanding tone.

Fringe time. In TV the hours directly before and after prime time. May be further specified as *early fringe* or *late fringe*.

FSI. *See* Freestanding insert.

FTC. *See* Federal Trade Commission.

Fullfillment firm. Company that handles the couponing process including receiving, verification and payment. It also handles contests and sweepstake responses.

Full position. A special preferred position of an ad in a newspaper. The ad either (1) follows a column or columns of the news reading matter and is completely flanked by reading matter or (2) is at the top of the page and alongside reading matter.

Full-service agency. One that handles planning, creation, production, and placing of advertising for advertising clients. May also handle sales promotion and other related services as needed by client.

Full showing. (1) In an outdoor-poster schedule, a 100-intensity showing. (2) In car cards one card in each car of a line or city in which space is bought. The actual number of posters or car cards in a 100-intensity showing varies from market to market.

G

Galley proofs. Sheets, usually 15 to 20 inches long, on which the set type is reproduced for reading before it is made up into pages.

General rate (newspapers). Offered to a nonlocal advertiser. It is also called a *national rate*.

Geographic editions. *See* Partial run edition.

Geostationary (TV). The position of a synchronous satellite, which rotates around the earth at the equator at the same rate as the earth turns. Used for satellite transmission.

Ghost. An unwanted image appearing in a TV picture, for example, as a result of signal reflection.

Ghosted view. An illustration giving an X-ray view of a subject.

Global marketing. Term that denotes the use of advertising and marketing strategies on an international basis.

Grain. In machine-made paper the direction of the fibers, making the paper stronger across the grain and easier to fold with the grain. In direct mail it is important that the paper fold with the grain rather than against it.

Gravure printing. A process in which the printing image is etched below the nonprinting area. Instead of plates or forms, gravure printing usually employs a cylinder that is fully inked. The surface is then wiped clean, retaining ink only in the cups (sunken area). Tone variations are mainly achieved by etching cups to different depths. *See* Rotogravure.

Grid (TV). A system of presenting rates. It assigns various values to each time period. Higher values are assigned to nonpreemptible announcements and to announcements that are telecast during peak periods. Time can be offered and sold in terms of grids.

Gross national product (GNP). The total annual output of the country's final goods and services.

Gross rating points (GRP). Each rating point represents 1 percent of the universe being measured for the market. In TV it is 1 percent of the households having TV sets in that area. In radio it is 1 percent of the total population being measured, as adults, male/female, teenagers. In magazines, it is 1 percent of the total population being measured, as 1 percent of all women or all men of different ages or teenagers, based on census records. In outdoor it is the number of people passing a sign in one day. The percentage is figured on the population of that market. This includes people who pass the sign more than once a day. Gross rating points represent the total of the schedule in that medium in that market per week or per month.

Ground waves. Broadcasting waves (AM) that tend to travel along the surface of the earth and are relatively unaffected by the earth's curvature. *See* Sky waves.

Group discount. A special discount in radio station rates for the simultaneous use of a group of stations.

GRP. *See* Gross Rating Points.

Guaranteed circulation. The circulation that a publication guarantees to advertisers and on which its ad rates are based.

Gutter. The inside margins of printed pages.

H

Halftone. A photoengraving plate whose subject is photographed through a screen (in the camera) that serves to break up the reproduction of the subject into dots and thus makes possible the printing of halftone values, as of photographs. Screens vary from 45 to 300 lines to the inch. The most common are 120- and 133-line screens for use in magazines and 65- and 85-line screens for use in newspapers. *Square half-tone:* The corners are square, and it has an all-over screen. *Silhouette,* or *outline, halftone:* The background is removed. *Vignette halftone;* Background fades away at the edges. *Surprint:* A line-plate negative is surprinted over a halftone negative, or vice versa. *Combination plate:* Line-plate negative is adjacent to (but not upon) halftone negative. *Highlight,* or *dropout, halftone:* Dots are removed from various areas to get greater contrast.

Hand lettering. Lettering that appears drawn by hand, as distinguished from type that is regularly set.

Hand tooling. Handword done on an engraving or plate to improve its reproducing qualities, charged for by the hour. Unless the plate is a highlight halftone, hand tooling is needed to secure pure white in a halftone.

Head. Display caption to summarize contents and get attention. *Center heads* are centered on type matter; *side heads,* at the beginning of a paragraph; *box heads,* enclosed by rules; *cut-in heads,* in an indention of the text.

Head-on position. An outdoor-advertising stand that directly faces direction of traffic on a highway.

Hertz. Frequency per second. *See* Kilohertz.

Hiatus. *See* Flight.

Highway Beautification Act of 1965. Federal law that controls outdoor signs in noncommercial, nonindustrial areas.

Hidden offer. Without calling attention to the offer, something useful or interesting offered free at the end of an ad that is wholly or largely copy. Response to the offer reveals how much attention the ad is drawing.

Holdover audience. The audience inherited from the show immediately preceding.

Horizontal publications. Business publications addressed to people in the same strata of interest or responsibility, regardless of nature of the company, for example, *Purchasing, Maintenance Engineer, Business Week. See also* Vertical publications.

House agency. Owned and operated by an advertiser. May handle accounts of other advertisers, too.

Households using television (HUT). Number of households in a market or nationally watching any TV program.

House lists. Mailing lists that are generated from a company's previous customers.

House mark. A primary mark of a business concern, usually used with the trademark of its products. *General Mills* is a house mark; *Betty Crocker* is a trademark. *DuPont* is a house mark; *Teflon II* is a trademark.

Hypermarket. A hugh retail outlet, typically discount oriented, selling a wide variety of goods.

I

Iconoscope (TV). The special TV camera that picks up the image to be sent.

ID. A TV station break between programs or within a program, used for station identification. Usually 10 seconds, with 8 seconds for commercial.

Inbound telemarketing. Used with offers in other media, buyers call in to place orders.

Incentives. Sales promotion directed to either wholesalers, retailers, or a company's sales force.

Industrial advertising. Addressed to manufacturers who buy machinery, equipment, raw materials, and components needed to produce goods they sell.

Industrial goods. Commodities (raw materials, machines, and so on) destined for use in producing other goods, also called *producer goods* and distinct from *consumer goods.*

In-house agency. An arrangement whereby the advertiser handles the total agency function by buying individually, on a free basis, the needed services (for example, creative, media services, and placement) under the direction of an assigned advertising director.

Interlock film. The capability of running separate TV pictures and track on equipment that enables you to synchronize them.

Interpositive (I.P.). Positive TV print on a fine-grain film stock made from a negative; used for further duplication.

Insert (freestanding). The loose inserts placed between pages or sections of a newspaper or magazine.

Insertion order. Instructions from an advertiser authorizing a publisher to print an ad of specified size on a given date at an agreed rate; accompanied or followed by the copy for the ad.

Inserts (magazine). A card or other printed piece inserted in a magazine opposite the advertiser's full-page ad. Insert is prepared by advertiser at extra cost. Inserts appear in many forms and shapes. Not sold separately.

Institute of Outdoor Advertising (IOA). Organization to promote outdoor advertising and provide information to advertisers concerning the outdoor industry.

Institutional advertising. That done by an organization speaking of its work, views, and problems as a whole, to gain public goodwill and support rather than sell a specific product. Sometimes called *public-relation advertising*.

Intaglio printing. Printing from a depressed surface, such as from the copper plate or steel plate that produces engraved calling cards and announcements; *rotogravure* is a form of intaglio printing. (*Compare* Letterpress and Lithography.)

IOA. *See* Institute of Outdoor Advertising.

IP (TV). Immediately preemptible rate. *See* Preemption.

Island display. A store display placed at the head of an aisle in a store, a choice location.

Island position. (1) In a publication page, an ad surrounded entirely by editorial matter. (2) In TV, a commercial isolated from other advertising by program content.

J

Jingle. A commercial set to music, usually carrying the slogan or theme line of a campaign. May make a brand name and slogan better remembered.

Job ticket. A sheet or an envelope that accompanies a printing job through the various departments, bearing all the instructions and all records showing the progress of work.

Joint venture. Arrangement where an American ad agency will enter a foreign market by purchasing interest in an established agency in that country.

Judgment sampling. *See* Sample.

Junior unit. In print, a page size that permits an advertiser to use the same engraving plates for small- and large-page publications. The ad is prepared as a full-page unit in the smaller publication (such as *Reader's Digest*) and appears in the larger publication (such as *House & Garden*) as a junior unit, with editorial matter on two or more sides.

Justification of type. Arranging type so that it appears in even-length lines, with its letters properly spaced, as on this page.

K

Key plate. Plate in color process with which all other plates must *register*.

Kilohertz. Formerly called *kilocycle*. A way of measuring the frequency per second at which radio waves pass a given point. The words *per second* had long been dropped, and *frequency* alone was not a complete definition. Therefore an international body of scientists decided that a new word was needed for *frequency per second,* and they chose *hertz,* after Heinrich Rudolph Hertz, who produced the first radio waves in a laboratory. 1 kilohertz = 1,000 waves per second; 1 megahertz = 1,000,000 waves per second. Stations are identified by these frequencies.

King-size poster. An outside transit display placed on the sides of vehicles. Size: 30 by 144 inches. *See* Queen-size poster.

Known-probability sampling. *See* Sample.

Kraft. A strong paper used for making tension envelopes, wrappers for mailing magazines, and the like.

L

"Lady Bird bill." *See* Highway Beautification Act of 1965.

Laid paper. Paper showing a regular water-marked pattern, usually of parallel lines.

Lanham Act. The Federal Trademark act of 1946, supplanting the previous federal trademark acts.

Layout. A working drawing showing how an ad is to look. A printer's layout is a set of instructions accompanying a piece of copy showing how it is to be set up. There are also rough layouts, finished layouts, and mechanical layouts, representing various degrees of finish. The term *layout* is used, too, for the total design of an ad.

lc. Lower-case letters.

Leaders. A line of dots or dashes to guide the eye across the page, thus: ....

Lead-in. (1) In relation to *audience flow* the program preceding an advertiser's program on the same station. (2) The first few words of a copy block.

Leading. (pronounced "ledding"). Insertion of metal strips (known as *leads*) between lines of hot type, creating more space between lines. In computer/phototypesetting, referred to as leading or line spacing—the adding of space between lines, usually in points of space.

Leading National Advertisers (LNA). A national service that reports advertising activities of national brands.

Lead-out. In relation to *audience flow* the program following an advertiser's program on the same station.

Left brain. The verbal side of the brain. Controls speech, writing, and thinking. This side thinks in linear terms. *See* Right Brain.

Legend. The title or description under an illustration. Sometimes called *cut line* or *caption*.

Letterpress. Printing from a relief, or raised, surface. The raised surface is inked and comes in direct contact with the paper, like that or a rubber stamp. *See* Offset, Rotogravure.

Letter shop. A firm that not only addresses the mailing envelope but also is mechanically equipped to insert material, seal and stamp envelopes, and deliver them to the post office according to mailing requirements.

Letter spacing. The amount of space between letters.

Lifestyle segmentation. Identifying consumers by combining several demographics and lifestyles.

Limited-time station. A radio station that is assigned a channel for broadcasting for a specified time only, sharing its channel with other stations at different times.

Linage. The total number of lines of space occupied by one ad or a series of ads.

Line. A unit for measuring space: fourteen lines to a column inch.

Line copy. Any copy suitable for reproduction by a *line plate*. Copy composed of lines or dots, distinguished from one composed of tones.

Line drawing. Made with brush, pen, pencil, or crayon, with shading produced by variations in size and spacing of lines, not by tone.

Line plate. A photoengraving made without the use of a screen, from a drawing composed of lines or masses, which can print on any quality stock.

Lintas: Link. Lintas: Worldwide's strategic planning process designed to integrate all communication activities—public relations, sales promotion, advertising, etc.—into a system to build strong brand equity for its clients.

List broker. In direct-mail advertising an agent who rents the prospect lists of one advertiser to another advertiser. The broker receives a commission from the seller for this service.

List compiler. Person who sells lists of names to direct-mail advertisers.

List manager. Promotes client's lists to potential renters and buyers.

Listening area. The geographic area in which a station's transmitting signal can be heard clearly. The area in which transmission is static free and consistent is called the *primary listening area.*

Lithography. A printing process by which originally an image was formed on special stone by a greasy material, the design then being transferred to the printing paper. Today the more frequently used process is *offset* lithography, in which a thin and flexible metal sheet replaces the stone. In this process the design is "offset" from the metal sheet to a rubber blanket, which then transfers the image to the printing paper.

Local advertising. Placed and paid for by the local merchant or dealer, in contrast to national, or general, advertising of products sold by many dealers.

Local-channel station. A radio station that is allowed just enough power to be heard near its point of transmission and is assigned a channel on the air wave set aside for local-channel stations. (*Compare* Regional-channel station, Clear-channel station.)

Local program. A nonnetwork, station-originated program.

Local rate. A reduced rate offered by media to local advertisers. It is usually lower than that offered to national advertisers.

Log. A continuous record by a station, reporting how every minute of its time is used, as required by the FCC for its review when considering renewal of licenses.

Logotype, or logo. A trademark or trade name embodied in the form of a distinctive lettering or design. Famous example: Coca-Cola.

Low Power TV (LPTV). Low powered TV stations. Designed for small towns.

Lower case (lc). The small letters in the alphabet, such as those in which this is printed, as distinguished from UPPER-CASE, or CAPITAL LETTERS. Named from the lower case of the printer's type cabinet, in which this type was formerly kept.

Lucy. *See* Camera lucida.

M

Machine-finish (MF) paper. The cheapest of book papers that take halftones well. A paper that has had its pores filled ("sized") but is not ironed. Thus it possesses a moderately smooth surface. Smoother than *antique,* but not so smooth as *English-finish* or sized and *super-calendered* paper.

Magazine networks. Groups of magazines that can be purchased together using one insertion order and paying a single invoice.

Magazine Publishers of America (MPA). Trade association devoted to promoting magazine advertising.

Magnuson-Moss Warranty Act. Passed in 1977, the act requires specific disclosure of terms of warranties offered to consumers.

Mail-order advertising. See Direct-response advertising (the current term of preference).

Majority fallacy. Mistaken idea that all products should be marketed to majority of consumers, in contrast to market segmentation.

Makegood. (1) In *print* an ad run without charge, in lieu of a prior one that the publisher agrees was poorly run. A print ad run in lieu of a scheduled one that did not appear. (2) In *TV* or *radio* a commercial run by agreement with advertiser, in place of one that did not run or was improperly scheduled. All subject to negotiation between advertiser (or agency) and medium.

Makeready. In letterpress, adjusting the plates for the press to ensure uniform impression. The skill and care in this work serve to make a good printing job.

Makeup of a page. The general appearance of a page; the arrangement in which the editorial matter and advertising material are to appear.

Makeup restrictions. To prevent the use of freak-sized ads which would impair the value of the page for other advertisers, publishers require that ads have a minimum depth in ratio to their width.

Mandatory copy. Copy that is required, by law, to appear on the advertising of certain products, such as liquor, beer, and cigarettes. Also refers to information that, by law, must be on labels of certain products, as foods and drugs.

Market. A group of people who can (1) be identified by some common characteristic, interest, or problem; (2) use a certain product to advantage; (3) afford to buy it; and (4) be reached through some medium.

Market Analysis of Predictable Patterns by Intra-Neighborhood Geo-Demographics. Allows transit advertisers to reach local prime prospects within a market.

Market profile. A demographic and psychographic description of the people or the households of a product's market. It may also include economic and retailing information about a territory.

Market research. Gathering facts needed to make marketing decisions.

Market share. Sales of one brand divided by total product category sales.

Market segmentation. Dividing a total market of consumers into groups whose similarity makes them a market for products serving their special needs.

Marketing concept. A management orientation that views the needs of consumers as primary to the success of a firm.

Marketing environment. The total economic and societal conditions in which advertising operates.

Marketing goals. The overall objectives that a company wishes to accomplish through its marketing program.

Marketing mix. Combination of marketing functions, including advertising, used to sell a product.

Master print (TV). The final approved print of a commercial, from which duplicates are made for distribution to stations.

Masthead. Part of a page devoted to the official heading of the publication and frequently followed by personnel or policy information. In newspapers, it is usually on the editorial page.

Matter. Composed type, often referred to as: (1) *dead matter,* of no further use; (2) *leaded matter,* having extra spacing between lines; (3) *live matter,* to be used again; (4) *solid matter,* lines set close to each other; (5) *standing matter,* held for future use.

Mechanical. A form of layout. An exact black-and-white copy of the ad as it will appear in printed form. Each element is pasted to an art board in precise position, ready for the camera.

Media. The means by which an advertisement is exposed to the public (i.e., magazines, TV, newspapers, etc.)

Media Imperatives. Based on research by Simmons Media Studies, showed the importance of using both TV and magazines for full market coverage.

Media schedule. The detailed plan or calendar showing when ads and commercials will be distributed and in what media vehicles they will appear.

Media strategy. Planning of ad media buys, including: identification of audience, selection of media vehicles, and determination of timing of a media schedule.

Medium. (1) The vehicle that carries the ad, as TV, radio, newspaper, magazine, outdoor sign, car card, direct mail, and so on. (2) The tool and method used by an artist in illustrations, as pen and ink, pencil, wash, or photography.

Merchandising. (1) "The planning involved in marketing the right merchandise or service at the right place, at the right time, in the right quantities, and at the right price" (American Marketing Association). (2) Promoting advertising to an advertiser's sales force, wholesalers, and dealers. (3) Promoting an advertised product to the trade and the consuming public, whether by media, point-of-purchase display, in-store retail promotions, guarantee seals, tags, or other means.

Merge/purge (merge & purge). A system used to eliminate duplication by direct-response advertisers who use different mailing lists for the same mailing. Mailing lists are sent to a central merge/purge office that electronically picks out duplicate names. Saves mailing costs, especially important to firms that send out a million pieces in one mailing. Also avoids damage to the goodwill of the public.

Metro rating area (MRA). Used in broadcast geographic designations. The MRA generally corresponds to the standard metropolitan area.

Milline rate. A unit for measuring the rate of advertising space in relation to circulation; the cost of having one agate line appear before 1 million readers. Calculated thus:

$$\frac{1{,}000{,}000 \times \text{line rate}}{\text{quantity circulation}} = \text{milline}$$

Modern Roman. *See* Old-style Roman.

Motivational research. *See* Research.

Multiple-cable-system operator (MSO). Single firm that owns more than one cable system.

Multi-point Distribution System (MDS). Line-of-sight transmission with a multichannel capacity and a range of approximately 10 miles. Most often used in hotels and apartment houses.

N

NAB. *See* Newspaper Advertising Bureau or National Association of Broadcasters.

NAD. *See* National Advertising Division.

NARB. *See* National Advertising Review Board.

National advertising. Advertising by the marketer of a trademarked product or service sold through different outlets, in contrast to *local advertising.*

National Advertising Division (NAD). The policy-making arm of the National Advertising Review Board.

National Advertising Review Board (NARB). The advertising industry's major organization for policing misleading ads.

National Association of Broadcasters (NAB). Trade association to promote both radio and TV.

National brand. A manufacturer's or producer's brand distributed through many outlets, distinct from a *private brand.*

National plan. Advertising-campaign tactics aimed at getting business nationwide, simultaneously. When properly used, it is the outgrowth of numerous local plans.

Negative-option direct response. Technique used by record and book clubs whereby a customer receives merchandise unless the seller is notified not to send it.

Net audience. Total audience for a schedule in a medium, less duplication.

Network. (1) Interconnecting stations for the simultaneous transmission of TV or radio broadcasts. (2) Any group of media sold as a single unit.

Newshole. The portion of a newspaper available for editorial matter. Largely determined by amount of advertising sold.

Newspaper Advertising Bureau (NAB). Association to promote newspaper advertising, especially co-op and greater use of newspapers by national advertisers.

Newsplan. A system initiated by the Newspaper Advertising Bureau to encourage newspapers to offer national advertising discounts.

Niche marketing. A combination of product and target-market strategy. It is a flanking strategy that focuses on niches or comparatively narrow "windows of opportunity" within a broad product market or industry. Its guiding principle is to pit your strength against their weakness.

Nielsen Station Index (NSI). These reports, issued by the A. C. Nielsen Company, provide audience measurement for individual TV markets.

Nielsen Television Index (NTI). National audience measurements for all network programs.

Nonilluminated (regular). A poster panel without artificial lighting.

Nonstructured interview. An interview conducted without a prepared questionnaire. The respondent is encouraged to talk freely without direction from the interviewer.

Nonwired networks. Groups of radio stations whose advertising is sold simultaneously by station representatives.

NSI. *See* Nielsen Station Index.

NTI. *See* Nielsen Television Index.

O

OAAA. *See* Outdoor Advertising Association of America.

O & O stations. TV or radio stations owned and operated by networks.

Off camera. A TV term for an actor whose voice is heard but who does not appear in a commercial. Less costly than on camera.

Off-screen announcer. An unseen speaker on a TV commercial.

Offset. (1) *See* Lithography. (2) The blotting of a wet or freshly printed sheet against an accompanying sheet. Can be prevented by slipsheeting. Antique paper absorbs the ink and prevents offsetting.

Old English. A style of black-letter or text type, now little used except in logotypes of trade names or names of newspapers.

Old-style Roman (o.s.). Roman type with slight difference in weight between its different strokes, as contrasted with Modern type, which has sharp contrast and accents in its strokes. Its serifs for the most part are oblique; Roman serifs are usually horizontal or vertical.

On camera. A TV term for an actor whose face appears in a commercial. Opposite of *off camera*. Affects the scale of compensation.

One-time rate. The rate paid by an advertiser who uses less space than is necessary to earn a time or rate discount, when such discounts are offered. Same as Transient rate, Basic rate, and Open rate.

Open end. A broadcast in which the commercial spots are added locally.

Open rate. In print the highest advertising rate on which all discounts are placed. It is also called Basic rate, Transient rate, or One-time rate.

Opticals. Visual effects that are put on a TV film in a laboratory, in contrast to those that are included as part of the original photograph.

Optimizing approaches to media planning. Computer solutions that offer a single best media schedule.

Out-of-home media. Outdoor advertising; transportation advertising.

Out-of-Home Media Services (OHMS). Firm that provides agencies with a national buying service for both outdoor and transit advertising.

Out-of-Home Measurement Bureau. Audience auditing for the eight-sheet poster industry. It also audits other outdoor media such as bus shelters.

Outbound telemarketing. A technique that involves a seller calling prospects.

Outdoor Advertising Association of America (OAAA). The trade association of the outdoor-advertising industry. Oldest advertising association.

Overlay. A transparent or translucent covering on artwork where color breakup or other instructions are marked.

Overtime (TV). TV production hours beyond the normal shooting day, when crew costs double, sometimes triple.

P

Package (1) A container. (2) *In radio* or TV, a combination assortment of time units, sold as a single offering at a set price. (3) A special radio or TV program or series of programs, bought by an advertiser (for a lump sum). Includes all components, ready to broadcast, with the addition of the advertiser's commercial. (4) In *direct-response* advertising a complete assembly of everything to be included in the mailing, including the envelope, letter, brochure, and return card.

Package insert. A card, folder or booklet included in a package, often used for recipes, discount coupons, and ads for other members of the product family. When attached to outside of package, called *package outsert*.

Package plan (TV). Some combination of spots devised by a station and offered to advertisers at a special price. Package plans are usually weekly or monthly buys.

Painted bulletins. Outdoor signs that are painted rather than papered. More permanent and expensive than posters, they are used only in high-traffic locations.

Partial run editions. When magazines offer less than their entire circulation to advertisers. Partial runs include: demographic, geographic, and split-run editions.

Pattern plate. (1) An electrotype of extra heavy shell used for molding in large quantities to save wear on the original plate or type. (2) An original to be used for the same purpose.

Pay cable. An additional service offered to cable subscribers at an extra charge. Home Box Office is an example of a pay-cable service.

People meter. Device that measures TV set usage by individuals rather than by households.

Per inquiry (PI). Advertising time or space where medium is paid on a per response received basis.

Personal selling. Face-to-face communication with one or more persons with the intent of making a sale.

Photocomposition (phototypesetting). A method of setting type by a photographic process only. Uses no metal.

Photoengraving. (1) An etched, relief printing plate made by a photomechanical process—as a halftone or line cut. (2) The process of producing the plate.

Photoplatemaking. Making plates (and the films preceding the plates) for any printing process by camera, in color or black and white.

Photoprint. The negative or positive copy of a photograph subject.

Photoscript (TV). A series of photographs made at the time of shooting a TV commercial picture based on the original script or storyboard. Used for keeping record of commercial, also for sales-promotion purposes.

Photostat. One of the most useful aids in making layouts or proposed ads. A rough photographic reproduction of a subject; inexpensive and quickly made (within half an hour if desired).

Phototypesetting. The composition of phototext and display letters onto film or paper for reproduction. Letters are projected from film negative grids and are also stored in a binary form in computer core to be generated through a CRT system. *See also* Photocomposition.

Phototypography. The entire field of composing, makeup, and processing phototypographically assembled letters (photodisplay and phototext, or type converted to film) for the production of image carriers by plate makers or printers.

Pica, pica em. The unit for measuring width in printing. There are 6 picas to the inch. Derived from *pica,* the old name of 12-point type (1/6 inch high). A page of type 24 picas wide is 4 inches wide (24 ÷ 6 = 4).

Picture resolution. The clarity with which the TV image appears on the TV acreen.

Piggyback (TV). The joining of two commercials, usually 15 seconds each, back to back for on-air use.

Pilot file (TV). A sample film to show what a series will be like. Generally, specially filmed episodes of TV shows.

Pioneering stage. The advertising stage of a product in which the need for such product is not recognized and must be established or in which the need has been established but the success of a commodity in filling those requirements has to be established. *See* Competitive stage, Retentive stage, Spiral.

Pixel. The smallest element of a computer image than can be separately addressed. It is an individual picture element.

Plant operator. In outdoor advertising the local person who arranges to lease, erect, and maintain the outdoor sign and to sell the advertising space on it.

Plate. The metal or plastic from which impressions are made by a printing operation.

Plated stock. Paper with a high gloss and a hard, smooth surface, secured by being pressed between polished metal sheets.

Point (pt). (1) The unit of measurement of type, about 1⁄72 inch in depth. Type is specified by its point size, as 8-pt., 12-pt., 24-pt., 48-pt. (2) The unit for measuring thickness of paper, 0.001 inch.

Point-of-purchase advertising. Displays prepared by the manufacturer for use where the product is sold.

Point-of-Purchase Advertising Institute (POPAI). Organization to promote point-of-purchase advertising.

POPAI. *See* Point of Purchase Advertising Institute.

Position (magazine). The place in a magazine where an ad or insert appears. Best position is up front (or as close to it as possible), right-hand side.

Position (newspaper). Where in paper, on what page, and on what part of page the ad appears.

Position (TV and radio). Where in the program your commercial is placed.

Position Advertising Copy Testing (PACT) Report. A report designed to address the question of client versus agency priorities in the evaluation of advertising and marketing objectives.

Positioning. Segmenting a market by creating a product to meet the needs of a selective group or by using a distinctive advertising appeal to meet the needs of a specialized group, without making changes in the physical product.

Poster panel. A standard surface on which outdoor posters are placed. The posting surface is of sheet metal. An ornamental molding of standard green forms the frame. The standard poster panel is 12 feet high and 25 feet long (outside dimensions).

Poster plant. The organization that provides the actual outdoor advertising service.

Poster showing. An assortment of outdoor poster panels in different locations sold as a unit. The number of panels in a showing varies from city to city and is described in terms of a 100 showing, a 50 showing, a 25 showing. This identification has no reference to the actual number of posters in a showing.

Posting date (outdoor). The date on which posting for an advertiser begins. Usually posting dates are every fifth day, starting with the first of the month. However, plant operators will, if possible, arrange other posting dates when specifically requested.

Posting leeway (outdoor). The five working days required by plant operators to assure the complete posting of a showing. This margin is needed to allow for inclement weather, holidays, and other contingencies as well as the time for actual mosting.

Potential Rating Index by ZIP Market (PRIZM). A rank-order description of 40 ZIP-market clusters showing the relative affluence of all ZIP codes in the U.S.

Predate. In larger cities, a newspaper issue that comes out the night before the date it carries, or a section of the Sunday issue published and mailed out during the week preceding the Sunday date.

Preemption, preemptible time. (1) Recapture of a time period by a network or station for important news or special program. (2) By prior agreement the resale of a time unit of one advertiser to another (for a higher rate). Time may be sold as nonpreemptive (NP) at the highest rate, two weeks preemptible (lower rate), or immediately preemptible (IP), the lowest rate.

Preferred position. A special, desired position in a magazine or newspaper, for which the advertiser must pay a premium. Otherwise the ad appears in a *run-of-paper (ROP) position,* that is, wherever the publisher chooses to place it.

Premium. An item, other than the product itself, given to purchasers of a product as an inducement to buy. Can be free with a purchase (for example, on the package, in the package, or the container itself) or available upon proof of purchase and a payment *(self-liquidating premium).*

Primary circulation. *See* Circulation.

Prime prospects. *See* Target audience.

Prime rate. The TV or radio rate for the times when these media reach the largest audience.

Prime time. A continuous period of not less than 3 hours per broadcast day, designated by the station as reaching peak audiences. In TV, usually 8:00 P.M. to 11:00 P.M. E.S.T. (7:00 P.M. to 10:00 P.M. C.S.T.).

Prizm. *See* Potential Rating Index by ZIP market.

Principal register. The main register for recording trademarks, service marks, collective marks, and certification marks under the Lanham Federal Trademark Act.

Printers Ink Model Statutes (1911). The act directed at fraudulent advertising, prepared and sponsored by *Printers' Ink,* which was the pioneer advertising magazine.

Private brand. The trademark of a distributor of products sold only by that distributor, in contrast to manufacturers' brands, sold through many outlets. Also known as *private labels* or *house brands.*

PRIZM (Potential Rating Index by ZIP Market). A method of audience segmentation developed by the Claritas Corporation.

Process plates. Photoengraving plates for printing in color. Can print the full range of the spectrum by using three plates, each bearing a primary color—red, yellow, blue—plus a black plate. Referred to as *four-color plates. See also* Process printing.

Process printing. Letterpress color printing in which color is printed by means of process plates.

Prodigy. A joint venture of IBM and Sears, Roebuck, Co. to provide an in-home shopping/information computer service.

Producer. One who originates and/or presents a TV or radio program.

Product differentiation. Unique product attributes that set off one brand from another.

Product manager. In package goods, the person responsible for the profitability of a product (brand) or product line, including advertising decisions. Also called Brand Manager.

Product protection. Time that a station guarantees between competitive commercials.

Product user segmentation. Identifying consumers by the amount of product usage.

Production. (1) The conversion of an advertising idea into an ad mainly by a printing process. (2) The building, organization, and presentation of a TV or radio program.

Production department. The department responsible for mechanical production of an ad and dealing with printers and engravers or for the preparation of a TV or radio program.

Production director. (1) Person in charge of a TV or radio program. (2) Head of department handling print production.

Professional advertising. Directed at those in professions such as medicine, law, or architecture who are in a position to recommend use of a particular product or service of their clients.

Profile. (1) A detailed study of a medium's audience classified by size, age, sex, viewing habits, income, education, and so on. (2) A study of the characteristics of the users of a product or of a market.

Progressive proofs. A set of photoengraving proofs in color, in which: the yellow plate is printed on one sheet and the red on another; the yellow and red are then combined; next the blue is printed and a yellow-red-blue combination made. Then the black alone is printed, and finally all colors are combined. The sequence varies. In this way the printer matches up inks when printing color plates. (Often called "progs.")

Proof. (1) An inked impression of composed type or of a plate for inspection or for filing. (2) In photocomposition, a proof is made on photographically or chemically sensitized paper. (3) In engraving and etching, an impression taken to show the condition of the illustration at any stage of the work. Taking a proof is "pulling a proof."

Psychographics. A description of a market based on factors such as attitudes, opinions, interests, perceptions, and lifestyles of consumers comprising that market. *See* Demographic characteristics.

Public relations. Communication with various internal and external publics to create an image for a product or corporation.

Public-service advertising. Advertising with a message in the public interest. When run by a corporation, often referred to as *institutional advertising*.

Public-service announcements. Radio and TV announcements made by stations at no charge, in the public interest.

Publisher's statement. Statement of circulation issued by a publisher, usually audited or given as a sworn statement. All publication rates are based on a circulation statement.

Puffery. Advertiser's opinion of a product that is considered a legitimate expression of biased opinion.

Pulsing. *See* Flight.

Q

Qualified circulation. *See* Controlled circulation.

Queen-size poster. An outside transit advertising display placed on the sides of vehicles (usually the curb side). Size: 30 by 88 inches. *See* King-size poster.

R

Radio Advertising Bureau (RAB). Association to promote the use of radio as an advertising medium.

Radio All Dimension Audience Research (RADAR). Service of Statistical Research, Inc., major source of network radio ratings.

Raster graphics. In computer graphics a system in which an electron beam is moved back and forth across the display monitor, activating display units called pixels.

Rate card. A card giving the space rates of a publication, circulation data, and data on mechanical requirements and closing dates.

Rate differential. The controversial practice of newspapers charging significantly higher rates to national advertisers as compared to local accounts.

Rate protection. The length of time an advertiser is guaranteed a specific rate by a medium. May vary from 3 months to 1 year from the date of signing a contract.

Rating points (outdoor). Used in estimating the number of people to whom an outdoor sign is exposed. Each board is rated in terms of 1 percent of the daily passersby in relation to population. In making up a showing of different sizes in market, the total number of rating points of those signs is added and referred to as the *gross rating points* of that showing for that market. The count includes duplication of people who may pass a sign more than once a day.

Rating point (TV). (1) The percentage of TV households in a market a TV station reaches with a program. The percentage varies with the time of day. A station may have a 10 rating between 6:00 and 6:30 P.M., and a 20 rating between 9:00 and 9:30 P.M. (a real hit!) (2) In radio the percentage of people who listen to a station at a certain time. *See* Gross rating points.

Reach. The total audience a medium actually covers.

Reading notices. Ads in newspapers set up in a type similar to that of the editorial matter. Must be followed by "Adv." Charged for at rates higher than those for regular ads. Many publications will not accept them.

Ream. In publishing and advertising, 500 sheets of paper. Thousand-sheet counts now being used as basis of ordering paper.

Rebate. The amount owed to an advertiser by a medium when circulation falls below some guaranteed level or the advertiser qualifies for a higher *space* or *time discount*.

Recognized agency. An advertising agency recognized by the various publishers or broadcast stations and granted a commission for the space it sells to advertisers.

Reduction prints (TV). 16-mm film prints made from 35-mm films.

Register. Perfect correspondence in printing; of facing pages when top lines are even; of color printing when there is correct superimposition of each plate so that the colors mix properly.

Registering trademark. The new trademark law permits an applicant with a bona fide intent to use a mark to apply to register the mark before applicant actually uses mark. Registration is issued when application is approved by the Patent and Trademark Office and proof of use is supplied within six months of approval. Six-months extensions may be granted up to five times to the applicant. The new registration period is 10 years, with indefinite rights to renewal. False statements in advertising about a competitor's product is prohibited. The new trademark law places the United States more in line with international trademark registration procedures and regulations.

Register marks (engraving). Cross lines placed on a copy to appear in the margin of all negatives as a guide to perfect register.

Release. A legally correct statement by a person photographed, authorizing the advertiser to use that photograph. For minors the guardian's release is necessary.

Relief printing. Printing in which the design reproduced is raised slightly above the surrounding, nonprinting areas. Letterpress is a form of relief printing contrasted with intaglio printing and lithography.

Reminder advertising. *See* Retentive stage.

Remnant space. Unsold advertising space in geographic or demographic editions. It is offered to advertisers at a significant discount.

Representative (rep). An individual or organization representing a medium selling time or space outside the city or origin.

Repro proofs (reproduction proofs). Exceptionally clean and sharp proofs from type for use as copy for reproduction.

Research. (1) Structured research: A list of questions is prepared, and subjects are given choices of responses. (2) Unstructured research: Subjects are asked open-ended questions to probe underlying reasons for specific behavior. Also called *motivational*, or *in-depth, research*.

Residual. A sum paid to certain talent on a TV or radio commercial every time the commercial is run after 13 weeks, for life of commercial.

Response list. Direct mail lists compiled of people who have previously ordered by direct mail or other types of direct advertising.

Respondent. One who answers a questionnaire or is interviewed in a research study.

Retail advertising. Advertising by a local merchant who sells directly to the consumer.

Retailer. An individual or organization that sells products to consumers.

Retentive stage. The third advertising stage of a product, reached when its general usefulness is everywhere known, its individual qualities are thoroughly appreciated, and it is satisfied to retain its patronage merely on the strength of its past reputation. *See* Pioneering state, competitive stage, Spiral.

Retouching. The process of correcting or improving artwork, especially photographs.

Reverse time table. Used in direct mail to schedule a job. The schedule starts with the date it is to reach customers and works backward to a starting date.

Reversed plate. (1) A line-plate engraving in which white comes out black, and vice versa. (2) An engraving in which right and left, as they appear in the illustration, are transposed.

Ride-alongs. Direct-mail pieces that are sent with other mailings such as bills.

Riding the boards. Inspecting an outdoor showing after posting.

Right brain. The nonverbal side of the brain. Controls emotions, intuition, psychomotor skills and things that you learn. Thinks in sensory images grasping the whole picture. *See* Left Brain.

Robinson-Patman Act. A federal law, enforced by the FTC. Requires a manufacturer to give proportionate discounts and advertising allowances to all competing dealers in a market. Purpose: to protect smaller merchants from unfair competition of larger buyers.

Roman type. (1) Originally, type of the Italian and Roman school of design, as distinguished from the blackface Old English style. Old style and modern are the two branches of the Roman family. (2) Typefaces that are not italic are called *roman*.

Rome Report. A service of Leading National Advertisers that tracks advertising run in business publications.

Robinson-Patman Act. Required manufacturers to offer promotional allowances to all customers on a proportionally equal basis.

ROP. *See* Run-of-paper position.

ROS. *See* Run of schedule.

Rotary plan (outdoor). Movable painted bulletins are moved from one fixed location to another one in the market, at regular intervals. The locations are viewed and approved in advance by the advertiser.

Rotary press. A printing press having no flat bed, but printing entirely with the movement of cylinders.

Rotation (broadcasting). A technique of moving commercials into different day-parts to expose all categories of viewers and listeners.

Rotogravure. The method of intaglio printing in which the impression is produced by chemically etched cylinders and run on a rotary press; useful in long runs of pictorial effects.

Rotoscope. A technique that combines live and animated characters.

Rough. A crude sketch to show basic idea or arrangement. In making layouts, this is usually the first step.

Rough cut (TV). The first assembly of scenes in proper sequence, minus opticals and titles, in the TV commercial. Also called *work print*.

Routing. The elimination by mechanical means of unwanted printing surfaces of a letterpress engraving or increasing the depth of areas to prevent deposit of ink on paper from nonprinting areas.

Run-of-paper (ROP) position. Any location that the publisher selects in a publication, in contrast to *preferred position*.

Run of schedule (ROS). Commercial announcements that can be scheduled at the station's discretion anytime during the period specified by the seller (for example, ROS, 10 A.M. to 4:30 P.M., Monday through Friday).

Rushes (TV). The first, uncorrected prints of a commercial. Also called *dailies*.

S

SAAI. *See* Specialty Advertising Association International.

Saddle stitching. Binding a booklet by stitching it through the center and passing stitches through the fold in the center pages. Enables the booklet to lie flat. When a booklet is too thick for this method, *side stitching* is used.

SAG. Screen Actors' Guild.

Sales promotion. (1) Sales activities that supplement both personal selling and marketing, coordinate the two, and help to make them effective, for example, displays. (2) More loosely, the combination of personal selling, advertising, and all supplementary selling activities.

Sample; sampling. (1) The method of introducing and promoting merchandise by distributing a miniature or full-size trial package of the product free or at a reduced price. (2) Studying the characteristics of a representative part of an entire market, or universe, in order to apply to the entire market the data secured from the miniature part. A *probability sample* is one in which every member of the universe has a known probability of inclusion. A *random sample* is a probability sample in which, with a fixed mathematical regularity, names are picked from a list. A *stratified quota sample* (also known as a *quota sample*) is one drawn with certain predetermined restrictions on the characteristics of the people to be included. An *area sample* (or *stratified area sample*) is one in which one geographical unit is selected as typical of others in its environment. In a *judgment sample*, an expert's experience and knowledge of the field are employed to choose representative cases suitable for study. A *convenience*, or *batch, sample* is one selected from whatever portion of the universe happens to be handy.

Satellite earth station. A receiving station for domestic satellite transmission, usually to cable-casting systems.

Satellite station. (A term born before we had sky satellites.) A small local TV station that has a feeder line running to a distant larger station (a parent station) so that programs can be relayed from the larger station. Not to be confused with *satellite earth station*.

Saturation. A media pattern of wide coverage and high frequency during a concentrated period of time, designed to achieve maximum impact, coverage, or both.

SC. Single column.

sc. Small caps.

Scanner. Electronic equipment used to make color separations.

Scatter plan (TV). The use of announcements over a variety of network programs and stations, to reach as many people as possible in a market.

Score. To crease cards or thick sheets of paper so that they can be folded.

Scotchprint. A reproduction proof pulled on plastic material from a letterpress plate or form. Normally used in conversion of color plates from letterpress to offset.

Screen (photoengraving). (1) The finely cross-ruled sheet used in photomechanical plate making processes to reproduce the shades of gray present in a continuous-tone photograph. Screens come in various rulings, resulting in more (or fewer) "dots" to the square inch on the plate, to conform with the requirements of different grades and kinds of printing paper. (2) In TV, the surface on which a picture is shown.

Screen printing (silk screen). A printing process in which a stenciled design is applied to a textile or wiremesh screen and a squeegee forces paint or ink through the mesh of the screen. *See* Silk screen.

Script (TV). A description of the video, along with the accompanying audio, used in preparing a storyboard or in lieu of it.

Secondary meaning. When a word from the language has long been used as a trademark for a specific product and has come to be accepted as such, it is said to have acquired a "secondary meaning" and may be eligible for trademark registration.

Secondary service area (radio). The area—beyond the *primary service area*—where a broadcasting station delivers a steady signal; that signal must be of sufficient intensity to be a regular program service of loudspeaker volume, day and night, all seasons.

Segmentation. *See* Market segmentation.

Selective binding. Binding different material directed to various reader segments in a single issue of a magazine.

Self-liquidating premium. A premium offered to consumers for a fee that covers its cost plus handling.

Serial spots. A television commercial technique that is continued in several episodes—each communicating a specific message for the same product.

Serifs. Lines projecting from the top or bottom of a main stroke of a letter, commonly called *roman* letters. Gothic faces lack serifs and are called *sans serif*.

Service mark. A word or name used in the sale of services, to identify the services of a firm and distinguish them from those of others, for example, Hertz Drive Yourself Service, Weight Watchers Diet Course. Comparable to trademarks for products.

Service values. Used in buying interior transit space to determine full, half, quarter coverage of a market.

Sets in use. The number of TV sets and radios turned on at any given time.

Share of audience. The percentage of households using TV tuned to a particular program.

Sheet. The old unit of poster size, 26 by 39 inches. The standard-size posters are 24 sheets (seldom used) and 30 sheets. There are also 3-sheet and 8-sheet posters.

Sherman Antitrust Act. It prevented groups of businesses from forming alliances to restrict competition.

Shooting (TV). The first stage of TV production, which covers the filming or videotaping of all scenes up through delivery of the *dailies*.

Short rate. The balance advertisers have to pay if they estimated that they would run more ads in a year than they did and entered a contract to pay at a favorable rate. The short rate is figured at the end of the year or sooner if advertisers fall behind schedule. It is calculated at a higher rate for the fewer insertions.

Showing. Outdoor posters are bought by groups, referred to as *showings*. The size of a showing is referred to as a 100-GRP showing or a 75- or 50-GRP showing, depending on the gross rating points of the individual boards selected.

Showing transit (exterior). A unit for buying outdoor space on buses. The cards vary according to size, position, and cost per bus.

Showing transit (interior). A unit for buying card space inside buses and subways. A showing usually calls for one card per bus or per car per market.

SIC. *See* Standard Industrial Classification.

Side stitching. The method of stitching from one side of a booklet to the other. Stitching can be seen on front cover and on back. Used in thick-booklet work. Pages do not lie flat. *See* Saddle stitching.

Signal area. The territory in which a radio or TV broadcast is heard. Can be primary, where most clearly heard, or secondary, where there may be more interference.

Signature. (1) The name of an advertiser. (2) The musical number or sound effect that regularly identifies a TV or radio program. (3) A sheet folded and ready for binding in a book, usually in multiples of 32; but 16's and 8's are also possible. A mark, letter, or number is placed at the bottom of the first page of every group of 16 or 32 pages to serve as a guide in folding.

Silhouette halftone. *See* Halftone.

Silk screen. A printing process in which a stenciled design is applied to a screen of silk, organdy, nylon, Dacron, or wire cloth. A squeegee forces paint or ink through the mesh of the screen to the paper directly beneath.

Simmons Market Readership Bureau, Inc. (SMRB). Firm that provides audience data for several media. Best known for magazine research.

Simulation (computer). The process of introducing synthetic information into a computer for testing, an application for solving problems too complicated for analytical solution.

Simulcast. The simultaneous playing of a program over AM/FM radio.

Siquis. Handwritten posters that in sixteenth- and seventeenth-century England were forerunners of modern advertising.

SIU. *See* Sets in use.

Sized and supercalendered paper (s. and s.c.). Machine-finish book paper that has been given extra ironings to ensure a smooth surface. Takes halftones very well.

Sized paper. Paper that has received a chemical bath to make it less porous. Paper sized once and ironed (calendered) is known as *machine finish*. If it is again ironed, it becomes *sized and supercalendered (s. and s.c.)*.

Slotting allowances. Fees demanded of manufacturers by supermarkets for shelf space. Insures advertiser shelf space for 3 to 6 months. Covers supermarket administrative overhead.

Small caps (sc or sm. caps). Letters shaped like upper case (capitals) but about two-thirds their size—nearly the size of lower-case letters. THIS SENTENCE IS SET WITH A REGULAR CAPITAL LETTER AT THE BEGINNING, THE REST IN SMALL CAPS.

Snipe. A copy strip added over a poster ad, for example, a dealer's name, special sale price, or another message. Also referred to as an *overlay*.

Sound effects. Various devices or recordings used in TV or radio to produce life-like imitations of sound, such as footsteps, rain, or ocean waves.

Space buyer. The official of an advertising agency who is responsible for the selection of printed media for the agency's clients.

Space contract. Document that guarantees advertising space costs for some fixed period in newspapers and magazines.

Space discount. Given by a publisher for the linage an advertiser uses. (*Compare* Time discount.)

Space position value. System used in outdoor to judge the value of an outdoor site.

Space schedule. Shows the media in which an ad is to appear, the dates on which it is to appear, its exact size, and the cost.

Specialty Advertising Association International (SAAI). Organization to promote specialty advertising.

Spectacular. An outdoor sign built to order, designed to be conspicuous for its location, size, lights, motion, or action. The costliest form of outdoor advertising.

Spiral (advertising). The graphic representation of the stages through which a product might pass in its acceptance by the public. The stages are *pioneering, competitive,* and *retentive.*

Split run. A facility available in some newspapers and magazines, wherein the advertiser can run different ads in alternate copies of the same issue at the same time. A pretesting method used to compare coupon returns from two different ads published under identical conditions.

Split spots. Two related TV commercials for the same product, run with a completely unrelated spot between them.

Sponsor. The firm or individual paying for talent and broadcasting time for a radio or TV feature; the advertiser on the air.

Spot (TV and radio). (1) *Media use:* purchase of time from a local station, in contrast to purchase from a network. When purchased by a national advertiser, it is, strictly speaking, *national spot* but is referred to as just *spot*. When purchased by a local advertiser, it is, strictly speaking, *local spot* but is referred to as *local TV* or *local radio*. (2) Creative use: the text of a short announcement.

Spread. (1) Two facing pages, a *double-page* ad. (2) Type matter set full measure across a page, not in columns. (3) Stretching any part of a broadcast to fill the full allotted time of the program.

Spread posting dates. Division of outdoor posting dates: One-half the panels of a showing may be posted on one date, the other half later, say, 10 to 15 days.

Staggered schedule. Insertions alternated in two or more periodicals.

The Standard Advertising Unit (SAU). Allows national advertisers to purchase newspaper advertising in standard units from one paper to another.

Standard Industrial Classification (SIC). The division of all industry, by the Bureau of the Budget, into detailed standard classifications identified by code numbers. Useful in making marketing plans.

Standard Rate & Data Service. Company that publishes a series of directories giving media rates and ad production information.

Stand by. *Cue* that a program is about to go on the air.

Stand-by space. Some magazines will accept an order to run an ad whenever and wherever the magazine wishes, at an extra discount. Advertiser forwards plate with order. Helps magazine fill odd pages or spaces.

Station breaks. Periods of time between TV or radio programs or within a program as designated by the program originator.

Station clearance. *See* Clear.

Station satellite. A station, often found in regions of low population density, that is wholly dependent upon another, carrying both its programs and commercials. Purpose is to expand coverage of the independent station and offer service to remote areas. Nothing to do with TV from satellites.

Steel-die embossing. Printing from steel dies engraved by the intaglio process, the sharp, raised outlines being produced by stamping over a counterdie. Used for monograms, crests, stationery, and similar social and business purposes.

Stet. A proofreader's term: "Let it stand as it is; disregard change specified." A dotted line is placed underneath the letter or words to which the instructions apply.

Stock footage (TV). Existing film that may be purchased for inclusion in a TV commercial.

Stock music. Existing recorded music that may be purchased for use in a TV or radio commercial.

Storecasting. The broadcasting of radio programs and commercials in stores, usually supermarkets.

Storyboard. Series of drawings used to present a proposed commercial. Consists of illustrations of key action (video), accompanied by the audio part. Used for getting advertiser approval as a guide in production.

Strip. (1) In *TV or radio* a commercial scheduled at the same time on successive days of the week, as Monday through Friday. (2) In *newspapers* a shallow ad at the bottom of a newspaper, across all columns.

Subcaption (subcap). A subheadline.

Subscription television (STV). A pay-television service that broadcasts a scrambled signal. Homes with a decoder can receive a clear signal for a monthly charge.

Superstations. Local independent TV that is transmitted by satellite to cable systems around the country.

Supplements (newspaper). Loose inserts carried in a newspaper. Printed by advertiser. Must carry "supplement" and newspaper logotype to meet newspaper postal requirements.

Suppliers. Firms that manufacture and imprint specialty items.

Surprint. (1) A photoengraving in which a line-plate effect appears over the face of a halftone, or vice versa. (2) Printing over the face of an ad already printed.

Sustaining program. Entertainment or educational feature performed at the expense of a broadcasting station or network; in contrast to a commercial program, for which an advertiser pays.

Sweepstakes. A promotion in which prize winners are determined on the basis of chance alone. Not legal if purchaser must risk money to get it. *See* Contest.

Sworn statement. When a publisher does not offer a certified audited report of circulation (as many small and new publishers do not), it may offer advertisers a sworn statement of circulation.

Synchrographics. Market segmentation based on lifestyle changes and the recency of these changes.

Syndicate mailings (direct-response advertising). The mailing pieces a film prepares for its products but then turns over to another firm to mail out to the latter's lists. Terms are negotiated individually.

Syndicated research services. Research organizations regularly report on what TV and radio programs are being received, what magazines are read, what products are being used by households, where, and other information. Sold on subscription basis.

Syndicated TV program. A program that is sold or distributed to more than one local station by an independent organization outside the national network structure. Includes reruns of former network entries as well as first run programs produced specifically for the syndication market.

Syndication, trade-out. *See* Trade-out syndication.

T

TAB. *See* Traffic Audit Bureau.

Tag (TV). A local retailer's message at the end of a manufacturer's commercial. Usually 10 seconds of a 60-second commercial.

Take-one. A mailing card or coupon attached to an inside transit ad. The rider is invited to tear off and mail for further information on the service or offering by the advertiser.

Target audience. That group that composes the present and potential prospects for a product or service.

Target marketing. Identifying and communicating with groups of prime prospects.

Tear sheets. Copies of ads from newspapers. Sent to the agency or advertiser as proof of publication.

Telemarketing. Major area of direct marketing.

Telephone coincidental. A broadcast-audience research technique that contacts respondents by telephone during the broadcast being measured.

Teletext. System where "pages" of text are broadcast. Special converters are used to receive the information.

Television Bureau of Advertising (TvB). Association to promote the use of TV as an advertising medium.

TF. (1) Till-forbid. (2) To fill. (3) Copy is to follow.

Theater of listener's imagination. In radio, writer paints pictures in the mind of listener through the use of sound.

Thumbnail sketches. Small layouts used to view various alternatives before finished layouts are drawn.

Till-forbid; run TF. Instructions to publisher meaning: "Continue running this ad until instructions are issued to the contrary." Used in local ads.

Time classifications (TV). Stations assign alphabetical values to specific time periods for easier reference in reading rate cards. The values generally extend from *A* through *D*. In an average market, the classification might work as follows: *AA* and *A* for *prime time; B* for early evening and late news; *C* for daytime (afternoon) and late night; *D* for the periods from 1 A.M. until sign-off and from sign-on until noon.

Time clearance. Making sure that a given time for a specific program or commercial is available.

Time discount. Given for the frequency or regularity with which an advertiser inserts ads. Distinguished from *quantity discount,* for amount of space used.

Tint. A reproduction of a solid color.

To fill (TF). Instructions to printer meaning: "Set this copy in the size necessary to fill the specified space indicated in the layout."

Total audience plan (TAP). In TV and radio, a spot package consisting of a combination that will hit all a station's listeners in a specified time span.

Total impression. The FTC considers the overall impression left by an ad in determining whether or not it is deceptive.

Total market coverage (TMC). Where newspapers augment their circulation with direct mail or shoppers to deliver all households in a market.

Total survey area (TSA). In TV, the geographical area composed of those counties in which at least 98 percent of the net weekly circulation of each home-market station occurs.

Tr. Transpose type as indicated, a proof reader's abbreviation.

Trade advertising. Advertising directed to the wholesale or retail merchants or sales agencies through whom the product is sold.

Trade character. A representation of a person or animal, realistic or fanciful, used in conjunction with a trademark to help identification. May appear on packages as well as in advertising (for example, Green Giant).

Trademark. Any device or word that identifies the origin of a product, telling who made it or who sold it. Not to be confused with *trade name.*

Trade name. A name that applies to a business as a whole, not to an individual product.

Trade-out syndication. A TV program series produced by an advertiser and containing that advertiser's commercials is offered to stations. There are no charges on either side. Stations save the expense of the programs, and advertisers keep other ads away from their own. Stations are free to sell a selected amount of the time at specific points in the program.

Trade paper. A business publication directed to those who buy products for resale (wholesalers, jobbers, retailers).

Traffic Audit Bureau (TAB). An organization designed to investigate how many people pass and may see a given outdoor sign, to establish a method of evaluating traffic measuring a market.

Traffic count. In outdoor advertising, the number of pedestrians and vehicles passing a panel during a specific time period.

Traffic department. In an advertising agency, the department responsible for prompt execution of work in all departments and getting complete material to the forwarding department for shipment on schedule.

Traffic-flow map (outdoor). An outline map of a market's streets scaled to indicate the relative densities of traffic.

Transcription program library. A collection of transcription records from which the radio station may draw. Stations subscribe to various transcription libraries.

Transient rate. Same as One-time rate in buying space.

Transition time. *See* Fringe time.

Transparency. Same as *decalcomania.*

Traveling display. General term for exterior transit advertising.

Trimmed flush. A booklet or book trimmed after the cover is on, the cover thus being cut flush with the leaves. *Compare* Extended covers.

Triple spotting. Three commercials back to back.

TvB. *See* television Bureau of Advertising.

TvQ. A service of Marketing Evaluations that measures the popularity (opinion of audience rather than size of audience) of shows and personalities.

TV week. Sunday to Saturday.

25 × 38–80. (Read "twenty-five, thirty-eight, eighty.") The method of expressing paper weight, meaning that a ream of paper 25 by 38 inches in size weighs 80 pounds. Similarly, 25 × 38–60, 25 × 38–70, 25 × 38–120, 17 × 22–16, 17 × 22–24, 20 × 26–80, 38 × 50–140. Used as a standard for paper sold in any size.

Typeface. The design and style of a type letter.

Type family. A group of type designs that are variations of one basic alphabet style. Usually comprising roman, italic, and boldface, they can also vary in width (condensed or extended) and in weight (light to extrabold). Some families have dozens of versions.

Type page. The area of a page that type can occupy; the total area of a page less the margins.

U

Ultrahigh frequency (UHF). TV channels 14 to 83, operating on frequencies from 470 to 890 MHz.

Unaided recall. A research method for learning whether a person is familiar with a brand, slogan, ad, or commercial without giving a cue as to what it is. "What program did you watch last night?"

Unintended consequences of advertising. The role that advertising plays as a social force, contrasted with its economic role.

Up-front buys. Purchase of network TV time by national advertisers during the first offering by networks. Most expensive network advertising.

V

Verified Audit Circulation Company (VAC). An auditing organization, which believes every publication selling advertising should have an audit available, whatever the circulation method (paid or free).

Value goal. The amount and form of value a company sets out to offer in a product.

Values and lifestyles system (VALS). Developed by SRI International to cluster consumers according to several variables in order to predict consumer behavior.

Velox. A commercial name of photoprint paper. It is broadly applied to any type of line or screened photoprint used for reproduction.

Vendor program. Special form of co-op advertising where a retailer designs the program and approaches advertisers for support.

Vertical publications. Business publications dealing with the problems of a specific industry. for example, *Chain Store Age, National Petroleum News, Textile World. See also* Horizontal publications.

Very-high frequency (VHF). The frequency on the electromagnetic spectrum assigned to TV channels 2 to 13, inclusive. *See* Ultrahigh frequency.

Video (TV). The visual portion of a broadcast. *See* Audio.

Videologs. Catalogs produced on video cassettes, intended for specialized audiences.

Videotape recording. A system that permits instantaneous playback of a simultaneous recording of sound and picture on a continuous strip of tape.

Videotape (TV). An electronic method of recording images and sound on tape. Most TV shows that appear live are done on videotape.

Videotext. Similar to teletext. Instead of a broadcast signal the viewer calls up information from a central computer. It is a flexible, two-way system.

Vignette. A *halftone* in which the edges (or parts of them) are shaded off gradually to very light gray.

Voice-over. The voice of a TV commercial announcer or actor or singer recorded *off camera*. Costs less than if delivered *on camera*.

Volume discounts. Based on total dollars spent for advertising.

W

Wait order. An ad set in type, ready to run in a newspaper, pending a decision on the exact date (frequent in local advertising).

Wash drawing. A brushwork illustration, usually made with diluted India ink or watercolor. In addition to black and white, it has varying shades of gray, like a photograph. *Halftones,* not *line plates,* are made from wash drawings.

Web printing. Also called *roll-fed printing*. In contrast to *sheet-fed printing,* paper is fed into the press from rolls. This method is used in rotogravure, newspapers, magazine presses, packaging presses, and increasingly in offset. Do not confuse with *wet printing* though both may take place simultaneously.

Weighted CPM. *See* Cost per thousand.

Wet printing. Color printing on specially designed high-speed presses with one color following another in immediate succession before the ink from any plate or cylinder has had time to dry.

wf. Wrong font.

Wheeler-Lea Amendments. Broadened the scope of the FTC to include consumer advertising.

Widow. In typography applied to the last line of a paragraph when it has only one or two words.

Wild spot (TV). A commercial broadcast by noninterconnected stations.

Window envelope. A mailing envelope with a transparent panel, permitting the address on the enclosure to serve as a mailing address as well.

Winsted Hosiery Company. The case of *FTC vs. Winsted Hosiery Company* established the precedent that false advertising was an unfair trade practice.

Work-and-turn. Printing all the pages in a signature from one form and then turning the paper and printing on the second side, making two copies or signatures when cut.

Work print. An edited form of TV commercial dailies, no optical effects, titles, or color balance. *See* Rough cut.

Wove paper. Paper having a very faint, clothlike appearance when held to the light.

Wrong font (wf). Letter or letters from one series mixed with those from another series or font. *This sentence is the wrong font.*

Z

Zinc etching. A photoengraving in zinc. Term is usually applied to line plates.

Zoning. Newspaper practice of offering advertisers partial coverage of a market, often accomplished with weekly inserts distributed to certain sections of a market.

Zoom (TV). A camera-lens action or optical effect that permits a rapid move in toward, or pull back away from, the subject being photographed in a commercial.

THE WALL STREET JOURNAL.

MARKETPLACE

MARKETING

Porsche Succeeds in Revving Up U.S. Sales By Throttling Down Prices of Some Cars

By THOMAS F. O'BOYLE
Staff Reporter of THE WALL STREET JOURNAL

STUTTGART, West Germany – When directors of sports-car maker **Porsche** AG decided two months ago to cut the prices of several U.S. models, some may well have feared they were cutting the company's throat.

After all, price reductions are a rarity anywhere in the auto business. But they are particularly dreaded in the luxury-car segment, where image counts as much as engine performance. "There's definitely an unwritten rule that says it makes no sense to lower prices," says Porsche chief executive Heinz Branitzki, "but I felt strongly that this time the rule needed to be broken."

In the end, he persuaded the board to trim the list prices for several U.S. models by 6% to 9%. The result: Porsche has sold as many cars in the two months since the price decrease as it did in the three months prior to it. Although the company's U.S. sales still trail those of a year ago—and will probably never again reach the lofty levels of the mid-1980s—Porsche is showing signs of improvement.

End of a Slide?
Porsche's annual car production for the years ended July 31
(In thousands)

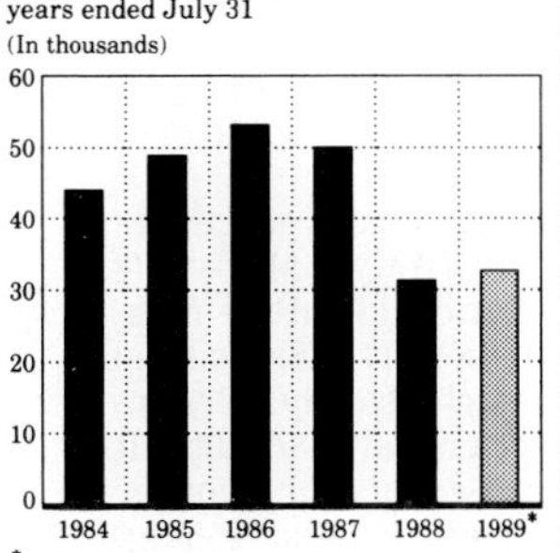

*Company estimate

Strong Balance Sheet

True, the company isn't fully back on track. But its balance sheet, which has no bank debt, remains strong. That—plus the controlling shareholdings held by the Porsche and Piech families—has damped once-persistent speculation that Porsche was about to be gobbled up by a bigger mass-production rival. Mr. Branitzki predicts that earnings for the year ending July 31 will be about 50 million West German marks ($25.5 million), twice what Porsche earned in fiscal 1988.

But whether future earnings will ultimately prove sufficient to guarantee Porsche's independence remains to be seen. The company is increasingly confronted by tough new rivals, including the Japanese, who are pushing sporty luxury cars. Meanwhile, overall sales of luxury cars peaked in 1986 and have been steadily shrinking since. And Porsche's small size allows little room for error. Its average development cost of one billion West German marks for each new model is supported by just three billion marks in annual sales.

For now, however, Mr. Branitzki is being lauded for re-routing a company that only a year and a half ago seemed to be running on empty. "He inherited a very difficult situation, and he has addressed the problems in a very direct and pragmatic manner," says auto analyst Stephen Reitman at UBS Phillips & Drew in London.

Return to Tradition

His turnaround strategy has at its core a return to tradition and the basics that Mr. Branitzki clearly feels were ignored during the go-go years of his flamboyant predecessor, Peter Schutz, who was sacked in December 1987.

An accountant who formerly served as chief financial officer, Mr. Branitzki upon replacing Mr. Schutz immediately set to work lowering costs and reassessing Porsche's model and marketing policy. Since then he has trimmed the white-collar staff by 10% as part of a cost-cutting program that has cut down on frills (including the entertainment at a private casino that Porsche used to offer its customers the night before they picked up their cars). The program is expected to save the company about $100 million this year, savings that, along with the stronger dollar, gave it the latitude to lower U.S. prices.

At the same time, Porsche has discontinued the least expensive of its four model lines and revamped the remaining three in an effort to rebuild its exclusive image. Although the new models are just now coming to the U.S. market, they have been well received in Europe, where customers must wait more than a year for delivery.

That in itself is a change from the excess inventories that crowded dealers' showrooms just a few years ago. Under the direction of Mr. Schutz, Porsche increased its sales goal to 60,000 cars a year mainly by targeting customers in the U.S. for its lower-priced four-cylinder models. Profit zoomed along for a few years. But the company had an earnings blowout when the double shocks of a falling dollar and a crashing stock market jolted U.S. sales.

Now the company aims to sell no more than 40,000 cars a year—about the same as in 1982—and to concentrate on the high end of the market, where it gets most of its earnings. "We're not after volume anymore," says Brian Bowler, the new president of Porsche's U.S. sales unit. "We're going back to our roots, building exclusive, high-priced, high-performance cars."

The building of those cars begins in the Stuttgart suburb of Zuffenhausen, in a factory adjacent to Mr. Branitzki's office. Porsche turns out just 95 cars a day, and the assembly line, when it moves at all, creeps along at a barely discernible pace.

Elsewhere in the factory, workers fashion seat coverings out of the elephant-hide shot by one customer; and they paint a car in the same red shade as the lipstick worn by another customer's wife. "We're a fancy company that sometimes makes crazy things," Mr. Branitzki says.

Too fancy at times for his taste, however. Mr. Schutz, the former chief executive, was an engineer and would often request small modifications that tended to add greatly to costs, company insiders say. One example: At his wife's request, he once asked designers to move the vanity mirror from the passenger's to the driver's side. Although the engineers relented then, they are more cost-conscious now.

"It makes no sense to change a car 100 times a year for small things," says the new chief executive.

The changeover in the executive suite was a U-turn for Porsche. While Mr. Schutz loved publicity and cars, Mr. Branitzki has a personality that reflects his no-frills management style (though he, too, drives a Porsche). He is the first non-engineer to serve as chief executive in the company's 58-year history. And in contrast to the flashy looks of the cars themselves, the 60-year-old executive, who spends his leisure time playing chess, reading history books and hiking in the mountains, has a soft-spoken, unassuming manner.

'A Little Quieter'

"I am a little quieter than my predecessor," he admits, "but our name should be handled discreetly." Instead of boasting, he believes that Porsche should observe noblesse oblige and "not talk too loudly."

Meanwhile, Mr. Branitzki has been trying to steer Porsche back to its engineering roots. Hence, two new models introduced this year, the Speedster and the Carrera 4, are both updated versions of its classic 911 model.

Coming up with new classics will be Porsche's biggest challenge in the future. But the executive appears unfazed. "Can we make it without having a big partner?" Mr. Branitzki asks rhetorically. "Surely we can."

MARKETING & MEDIA

ADVERTISING / By Joanne Lipman

Procter & Gamble Promotions May Be Demoted in Favor of Ads

Procter & Gamble is taking steps to reduce its heavy reliance on promotions and "produce a greater balance toward advertising," said John G. Smale, chairman and chief executive officer.

Mr. Smale's comments come as the trend toward pouring money into promotions—coupons, contests, and discounts to retailers—instead of brand advertising seems finally to be slowing. In recent months, several major consumer companies, including Kraft General Foods, a **Philip Morris** unit, have embarked on aggressive initiatives to strengthen traditional brand advertising. The number of coupons issued has been leveling off. Healthy ad-spending forecasts have been attributed in part to a resurgence in brand advertising by fast-food companies and others.

Mr. Smale was careful to note he isn't "trying to predict that there won't be promotions or allowances in the future." But he did say Procter has taken some cost-cutting steps in the packaging and distribution of its brands, and that promotions will become a smaller part of the marketing mix as a result.

"Our relationship with our customers [retailers] is changing as we develop the capacity to understand costs—their costs as well as ours. We're beginning to work much more cooperatively to reduce those costs. Along with that brings some diminution of the amount of focus brought to promotions, payments and allowances and that sort of thing," he said.

He added: "That will affect the total balance of advertising and promotional support. I think there's an opportunity, not just for Procter alone, for some rebalancing to take place."

Mr. Smale didn't quantify how much the balance would shift away from promotions, and the actual figure is probably relatively small. But any movement at all by Procter, perhaps the company most closely watched by the advertising industry, is significant. No figures are available on promotion spending, but most consumer companies spend more on promotion than they do on advertising.

Procter poured some $1.39 billion into advertising last year, according to Advertising Age, for a stable of brands running the gamut from Crest toothpaste and Ivory soap to Folgers coffee and Citrus Hill orange juice. Although Philip Morris is the country's biggest advertiser following its acquisition of Kraft, Procter still dominates television advertising.

Mr. Smale detailed two Procter efforts to cut promotion spending. First, he said, Procter is "experimenting" with doing away with "price packs"—packages marked with a special price, rebate offer, or other promotion. Not only is the packaging itself expensive to produce, but if Procter makes more product than it can sell to retailers during a given time period, it is left with "remnants" which it must sell at a marked-down price.

If it did away with price packs, Procter would still offer retailers occasional discounts. But by not producing special packaging, it could go back to full pricing after a promotion, instead of unloading specially marked products at a lower price.

Procter is also working on streamlining its distribution of products, in a way that entails cutting back on promotions. Currently, when Procter offers its occasional discounts to retailers, the retailers stock up on the product, then don't buy more for a while. But Procter is working on "continuous supply," in which it would ship the product to retailers on a continuous basis, in a smaller but steady stream.

The new distribution system is less expensive for Procter because it eliminates peaks and valleys of demand; it should save money for retailers, since they won't need to tie up money and warehouse space.

Moreover, the process could reduce promotions in a number of ways. Marketing executives say Procter could cut the number of discount promotions it offers to keep retailers' demand fairly steady. Or, instead of offering occasional discounts, it could offer smaller discounts for a longer period of time to keep demand steady. When it does offer discounts, retailers theoretically would only receive as much as they need, no longer hoarding the product.

Mr. Smale revisited the subject of ad-agency mergers. He was an early and outspoken critic of the huge mergers reshaping the ad business, and Procter pulled business from some agencies following mergers. But the bulk of its business remains at huge agencies, particularly the ultimate symbol of megamergers, Saatchi & Saatchi. Asked if the mergers have affected the quality of the advertising work Procter received in recent years, Mr. Smale said, "It's impossible to say. Would you have gotten more world-class campaigns? I don't know."

ADVERTISING / By Thomas R. King

American Express Ads for Money Transfers Are High on Anxiety

American Express, perhaps the marketing world's prime purveyor of fear and anxiety, knows well the power of well-placed panic. You've seen the ads: Stolen wallets, stranded automobiles and ruined vacations abound. They warn of disaster if Susie is sent off to college without her own charge card.

This month, American Express turns up the heat even more to sell another of its businesses—money transfer—with a set of dramatic television advertisements that portray desperate consumers stuck in bleak situations without cash.

The financial-services giant is trying hard to make a strong impression with the new campaign, and it had better succeed: While American Express is a huge presence in the credit-card and traveler's-checks markets, it's a tiny and relatively new player in the money-transfer business, which is dominated by **Western Union**. The pioneer of money transfers, Western Union, based in Upper Saddle River, N.J., has more than 130 years of experience and boasts a well-established network of more than 13,000 agents.

American Express, meanwhile, is building up its tiny business from scratch. It introduced its money-wiring service, called MoneyGram, in January 1988, but hardly anyone knows yet that it exists. American Express declines to disclose the revenue generated by MoneyGram, but analysts term Western Union's lock on the business a "monopoly." No one else comes close.

Analysts say that American Express, with its strong financial and marketing track record, does have a good chance of making MoneyGram a profitable venture. But the way won't be easy or cheap. Others have failed before. **Citicorp**, for example, introduced Express Money in March 1987, but folded it 14 months later, admitting the road was too difficult. "We couldn't see long-term business propositions," a spokesman says.

Others have failed mostly because start-up costs are prohibitive. Today, only Western Union, American Express and a number of very small competitors are in the business.

But if American Express succeeds with MoneyGram, there is tremendous money to be made. Fees vary based on the amount of money transferred, but American Express charges $11 for every $100 wired, while Western Union charges $14 for each $100. Industry executives say there are currently about 10 million transfers a year totaling some $3 billion; industrywide revenue is estimated at $250 million to $300 million annually.

With stepped-up marketing efforts and cheaper prices, American Express is signaling it plans to become a major player. Since MoneyGram's introduction, the New York-based firm has launched a direct marketing blitz to its cardholders and has been aggressively recruiting its own network of agents, which its says now totals about 6,000. And it claims to have a significant edge in delivering money internationally: Western Union promises money in two to three days; American Express says it'll have it there in less than 10 minutes.

Meanwhile, with a new $7 million ad campaign created by **WPP Group**'s Ogilvy & Mather unit, American Express is playing on everybody's money nightmares—or their guilt. One ad shows a man in his 60s sitting in a modest living room looking somberly at a bill he doesn't have the cash to cover. His wife places a hand on his shoulder. They exchange a saddened, embarrassed look. "Far away, someone you love needs money," the announcer says. "Now you can wire it there in minutes with the American Express MoneyGram."

In another ad, an American teen-ager in Europe is shown stranded on the steps of a church on a cold, stormy night. Lightning flashes as the kid looks nervously up at the sky. "Across the ocean, someone you love needs money," the announcer says.

"We very clearly are taking a serious businesslike tone in these ads," says Rob Ayers, senior vice president at American Express. "We are being careful not to make light of a person's plight."

Western Union, on the other hand, has long been making lighthearted commercials, like the one featuring a doo-wop singing group pulled over by a state trooper. Now, it is girding to take on American Express with a bigger ad budget and a new humorous campaign. Its new commercials, showing mothers whining about their children's spending habits, promotes the company's new toll-free telephone number that can be used to send money by phone.

"We're concerned about the entry of any competitor and what the implications will be to us," says Edward Fuhrman, president of Western Union's consumer services. "But we remain confident that we provide a superior service."

ADVERTISING / By Joanne Lipman

Colgate Tests Putting Its Name On Over-the-Counter Drug Line

Colgate may be a fine name for toothpaste, but do people really want to take Colgate aspirin or Colgate antacid? Would people use Colgate laxative or wash their hair with Colgate dandruff shampoo?

Colgate-Palmolive is about to find out. The massive packaged-goods company has gone to Peoria, Ill., to quietly test market a line of 10 over-the-counter medicines and a shampoo, all using the Colgate name. There's Colgate aspirin-free, to compete with Tylenol, and Colgate ibuprofen, to compete with Advil. There's Colgate cold tablets (like Contac), Colgate nighttime cold medicine (like Nyquil), Colgate calcium antacid tablets (like Rolaids), Colgate natural fiber laxative (like Metamucil), as well as Colgate dandruff shampoo (like Head & Shoulders).

Colgate won't talk about its new line, but Peoria drugstore operators say the company began test-marketing the products last fall. Since then, it has blanketed the town with coupons and ads. A few months ago, it gave away a free tube of toothpaste with any Colgate purchase; it has offered coupons worth virtually the full price of the products and has sent Colgate representatives to local stores to hand out coupons at the door. "They're spending some major money out here," reports Ron Rude, assistant manager of the Super-X drug store on Knoxville Avenue.

If all that weren't enough, the Colgate line is priced well below competing brands, perhaps 20% below, says David Wasson, manager of a local Walgreens. He says sales are strong: "With all the promotion they've done, they should be. They're cheaper, and they've got Colgate's name on them."

Yet even if Colgate's test is a resounding success, marketing consultants say expanding the new line could prove dangerous—and ultimately more expensive than Colgate can imagine. "If you put the Colgate brand name on a bunch of different products, if you do it willy-nilly at the lowest end, you're going to dilute what it stands for—and if you stand for nothing, you're worthless," says Clive Chajet, chairman of Lippincott & Margulies, a corporate identity firm.

Mr. Chajet says that Colgate also might end up alienating customers by slapping its name on so many products. If a consumer "is dissatisfied with one product, they might be dissatisfied with everything across the board. I wouldn't risk it," he says. What would have happened to Johnson & Johnson during the Tylenol poison scare, he asks, if the Tylenol name were plastered across everything from baby shampoo to birth control pills?

Colgate's test is one of the bolder forays into line extensions by consumer products companies. Companies saddled with "mature" brands—brands that can't grow much more—often try to use those brands' solid-gold names to make a new fortune, generally with a related product. Thus, Procter & Gamble's Ivory Soap came up with a shampoo and conditioner. Coca-Cola concocted Diet Coke. Arm & Hammer baking soda expanded into carpet deodorizers.

But unlike those products, Colgate is traveling far afield from its familiar turf. And while its new line is selling well, sales might not stay so strong without the budget prices and barrage of advertising and promotion. "People are looking at it right now as a generic-style product," says Mr. Rude. "People are really price conscious, and as long as the price is cheaper, along with a name that you can trust, people are going to buy that over others."

If Colgate were to raise its prices equal to name-brand prices, "they would have to do more advertising than they're doing," Mr. Rude adds. "They would have to compete more directly with Tylenol" and the other big brands.

Al Ries, chairman of Trout & Ries, a Greenwich, Conn., marketing consultant, questions whether any line extensions make sense—not just for Colgate, but for other strong brand names. He says the reason Colgate has been able to break into the over-the-counter drug market in the first place is because other drugs have expanded and lost their niche; Tylenol and Alka-Seltzer both now make cold medicines, for example, and "that allows an opportunity for the outsiders, the Colgates, to come in and say there's no perception that anybody is any different. The consumer will look for any acceptable brand name."

Mr. Ries says Colgate, and the traditional over-the-counter medicine companies, are basically turning their products into generic drugs instead of brands. They're losing "the power of a narrow focus," he says, adding, "It reflects stupidity on the part of the traditional over-the-counter marketers. . . .if the traditional medicines maintained their narrow focus, they wouldn't leave room for an outsider such as Colgate."

If Colgate is too successful, meanwhile, it also risks cannibalizing its flagship product. Consultants note that almost all successful line extensions, and a lot of not-so-successful ones, hurt the product from which they took their name. They cite Miller High Life, whose share of the beer market has dwindled since the introduction of Miller Lite. "If Colgate made themselves to mean over-the-counter medicine, nobody would want to buy Colgate toothpaste," contends Mr. Ries.

Mr. Chajet agrees. Colgate could "save tens of millions of dollars by not having to introduce a new brand name" for its new products, he says. But in doing so, it might also "kill the goose that laid the golden egg."

ADVERTISING / By Joanne Lipman

Nielsen to Track Hispanic TV Ratings

A.C. Nielsen Co. is close to an agreement to track Hispanic television ratings, a move the nation's two major Hispanic networks hope will help them attract more national advertisers.

The Spanish-language networks, **Telemundo Group** Inc. and **Univision** Inc., said that their boards approved a tentative three-way agreement with Nielsen to set up a Nielsen Hispanic ratings service. John Dimling, executive vice president of Nielsen's media-research unit, said Friday that he wasn't aware that the two boards had already approved the contract, but said that a deal was "very close." He said the agreement should be announced formally within the next few weeks.

For Telemundo and Univision, Nielsen ratings could be the ticket to broader acceptance by the ad community. Henry R. Silverman, Telemundo's president, estimates that the two Hispanic networks combined attract about 5% of the total television audience during prime time—but pull in less than 1% of TV advertising dollars. "We need to be able to prove to the advertisers and their agencies that we really do have 5% of the viewers," he says.

Several research companies follow Hispanic television, but their ratings estimates aren't exactly comparable to Nielsen ratings, which are the industry standard. Nielsen doesn't break out the ratings for the Hispanic networks, but lumps them in its "other" category.

"We want to be able to compete with ABC by showing the same Nielsen results that they do," says Mr. Silverman.

According to the tentative agreement, Nielsen, a unit of **Dun & Bradstreet**, would test-market its Hispanic ratings system in Los Angeles, where it plans to wire 200 Hispanic homes with people meters later this year. After the test is completed next fall, Nielsen would analyze the system and ultimately roll it out nationwide, monitoring 800 Hispanic homes.

If the Nielsen results confirm the Hispanic networks' audience estimates, the networks hope advertisers will give them a second look. Currently Univision, the larger and older of the two, has attracted the nation's 25 largest advertisers, but remains weak in a number of advertiser categories. Insurance companies, corporate accounts, and automobiles are all a hard sell, says Joaquin Blaya, president. Founded 27 years ago, Univision reaches about 85% of the nation's six million Hispanic households.

Telemundo, founded just three years ago, reaches about 75% of the U.S. Hispanic population.

Mr. Silverman estimates that "of the 500 largest advertisers on English-language television, about 100 advertise on Spanish-language television, which means 400 don't. I'd like to get the 80% of advertisers on network TV that don't advertise with us."

Even if Nielsen ratings indicate a large audience, many advertisers may still be put off because the median household income for Hispanic homes is about 80% of that of all U.S. homes. But the Hispanic networks point out that the average Hispanic household is also larger, giving advertisers more viewers per home. And they note that the Hispanic population is growing faster than the general population, making it too important a segment to ignore.

In any case, Telemundo's Mr. Silverman insists most advertisers needn't worry about Hispanics' lower median income. "Perhaps Tiffany won't be a charter advertiser on Telemundo, but 98% of the advertisers on [the big three networks] should be advertising with us," he says. "Consumers are consumers. Their money is green."

Caterpillar Net Fell 2.8% in 2nd Quarter; Higher Costs Cited

By a Wall Street Journal *Staff Reporter*

PEORIA, Ill.—**Caterpillar** Inc. said its second-quarter earnings fell 2.8%, reflecting higher costs resulting from five additional calendar days, material price increases, and wage and benefit increases for all payrolls.

The maker of construction equipment earned $141 million, or $1.39 a share. In the year-earlier quarter, it earned $145 million, or $1.44 a share. Sales rose 17% to $3.04 billion from $2.6 billion.

Caterpillar also cited higher start-up costs, particularly for factory modernization and product introductions.

Most of the sales increase in the quarter reflected higher physical sales volume and stronger demand outside the U.S., Caterpillar said. The company now is reporting financial results based on calendar quarters rather than internally developed cutoff schedules.

The company said that price increases implemented since the first quarter are helping offset inflationary cost increases. Caterpillar said price increases, however, were partially offset by the effects of a stronger dollar.

Caterpillar said sales in the U.S. rose 6%, although dealer machine sales declined as the tight monetary policy of the Federal Reserve Board resulted in reduced construction activity, particularly housing. Sales outside the U.S. continued to post strong gains, rising 28% mostly on physical sales volume.

In the first six months, the company earned $282 million, or $2.78 a share, compared with $263 million, or $2.60 a share, a year earlier. Sales rose 15% to $5.72 billion from $4.98 billion.

ADVERTISING / By JOANNE LIPMAN

From '60s Uniform to '90s Niche: Wrangler Targets the Family Man

Back when you weren't supposed to trust anybody over 30, when boys looked like girls and everybody wore denim, selling blue jeans was as easy as burning a draft card.

Ah, the good old days. Marketers of blue jeans advertised to "the broad market. . . . Jeans were the uniform," says Mary Tetlow, an account supervisor at **Martin Agency** of Richmond, Va. "But times have changed, and people's behavior has changed, and now niche strategies are making more sense."

At least, that's the thinking behind Martin Agency's new campaign for Wrangler jeans. The $10 million effort, breaking today, unabashedly chases a very specific "niche" market: blue-collar family men who wear jeans daily, who are over 30, who love the outdoors, and who, for the most part, live in small towns.

These ads are a very far cry from the ads for trendier blue jeans, like Levi, Lee and Guess, which go after the hip, young, urban crowd. Guess ads revel in ripe young women whose clothes are generally falling off; Levi's 501 jeans ads are shot with a jumpy camera amidst stark, crumbling cityscapes. Few of the actors and models in these ads seem to be over 20, much less listing toward middle age.

The new campaign for Wrangler, a unit of **VF** Corp., by contrast, doesn't even attempt to woo the chic young set. Instead, it embraces the folksy, patriotic America tinged in rose and bathed in warm light that most people see only in commercials, especially in commercials by Hal Riney, the master of Americana whose dulcet voice narrates his own ads for Alamo rental cars, Blue Cross/Blue Shield, and the old Gallo wine campaign.

The Wrangler ads, like the Riney commercials they echo, seek to bring a little tear to the eye with their heartwarming depiction of family men—in this case, beefy family men in blue jeans. In one of the commercials, an unseen wife narrates as her man gets up at the crack of dawn and slips on a pair of "those old jeans" to go fishing. As the camera lovingly pans over the man and his dog sitting in a rowboat by the dawn light, a deep voice intones, "Here's to old dogs, Saturday mornings, and comfortable blue jeans."

In another ad, a father teaches his son to drive an old pickup truck on a dusty country road, and the boy smashes into a mailbox. Instead of getting mad, blue-jeans-clad dad—who bears a passing resemblance to "Roseanne" husband John Goodman—cracks a smile. This one ends with our folksy announcer murmuring, "Here's to fathers and sons, first-time driving lessons, and comfortable blue jeans."

"Our audience lives in blue jeans; they wear them to work, then change into another pair to go out at night," says Mike Hughes, Martin Agency's vice chairman and creative director. "We wanted to talk to people in a different way than Levi's and Lee are talking to people. We want people to know that Wranglers are good-looking jeans, but we also want it to be more real. Our people don't live in the mean streets of New York."

Industry executives say Wrangler's strategy of concentrating on the blue-collar market makes sense. Wrangler is the fourth-largest blue-jeans brand, with about 7% of the market compared with **Levi Strauss**'s 20% of the market. (Lee and Rustler, also units of VF Corp., rank second and third). Slightly cheaper than Levi jeans, with a much smaller ad budget, and distributed through inexpensive mass merchandisers, Wrangler jeans can't exactly compete effectively for the yuppie crowd.

Besides, Levi itself has been making a concerted effort to woo the more upscale thirtysomething man. Its commercials feature images such as a father teaching his young son to fish. Levi's ads are "a little more contemporary, more the yuppie kind of guy" than the Wrangler dad, says Dan Chew, Levi marketing manager.

The Wrangler commercials, and print and radio ads with similar themes, are actually introducing a new Wrangler jean that is cut a bit fuller for—let's be euphemistic now—the "mature" man. But the new jeans' distinguishing features, such as a roomier crotch, aren't alluded to at all in the TV commercials because the ads are supposed to stand "for Wrangler jeans in general," Mr. Hughes says.

Mr. Hughes is convinced that other blue-jeans makers will have to follow in Wrangler's folksy wake. "There's a movement in the country generally for things that are more real," he says. "A lot of the other jeans, especially the ones we think of as hip fashion jeans, are going to be moving towards more real things, too."

Unit of Nestle Settles Dispute On Infant Ads

By ALIX M. FREEDMAN
Staff Reporter of THE WALL STREET JOURNAL

State attorneys general in nine states reached a settlement with **Nestle** S.A.'s Carnation Co. unit over what they claimed was "misleading, deceptive and unfair" marketing and advertising of its Good Start H.A. infant formula.

Under terms of the agreement, Carnation must refrain from using the word "hypoallergenic" to advertise Good Start or any other formula, so consumers won't get the impression that the product can't cause an allergic reaction. Hypoallergenic doesn't mean nonallergenic, but having a reduced potential for allergenic reactions.

Among other stipulations, Carnation is prohibited from asserting that any expert endorses an infant formula without also disclosing whether the individual is affiliated with or has been paid by the company. It also can't falsely represent that its product claims are supported by scientific evidence.

Carnation, which is based in Los Angeles, also agreed to pay $90,000 to cover the costs of the investigation that was launched in March, initially by the states of New York, Texas and California.

"The essence of this settlement is that Carnation simply can't misrepresent that its product is incapable of causing an allergic reaction," said Robert Roth, an assistant attorney general in New York. Mr. Roth added: "This product was being marketed in such a way as to appeal to precisely the parents of those infants who were most at risk."

In a prepared statement, Timm F. Crull, Carnation's chief executive officer, said: "We are convinced the characterizations made by the attorneys general in the settlement agreement are not supported by the facts. However, solely to avoid the time and expense that contesting these characterizations would require, Carnation has entered into this agreement."

State officials acknowleged that the settlement is essentially moot since Carnation—a scant two weeks after the states began to look into its ad claims—hastily made the changes that the states' agreement now stipulates. These included dropping the key claim, hypoallergenic, which appeared in bold type on the front of Good Start cans.

The probe by state officials grew out of Nestle's bid to crack the $1.6 billion U.S. infant formula market in late 1988. Good Start claimed to prevent or reduce sleeplessness, colic, rashes and other ailments in infants because it was hypoallergenic.

But the product quickly came under sharp criticism from some doctors. In February, the Food and Drug Administration began investigating Nestle's aggressive claims for Good Startm as well as six cases of severe reactions in infants for whom the formula wasn't hypoallergenic enough.

For Many, Road to the Right PC Is Paved With Glitches

But Help Is Growing for Entrepreneurs Searching for Computer Systems

By JEFFREY A. TANNENBAUM
Staff Reporter of THE WALL STREET JOURNAL

On his first attempt to computerize his business two years ago, dry cleaner David Berliner wasted $10,000. The Caldwell, N.J., business owner needed all kinds of instantly accessible information, such as the whereabouts of every fur coat entrusted to his shop. But his computer system could do little except write cleaning tickets.

Last year, Mr. Berliner leased an entirely different system. But because of a software glitch, the four terminals couldn't communicate with each other as promised. "I'm still fighting to get my name off the lease," says Mr. Berliner, who had the system yanked out after only two months.

In his third try, Mr. Berliner this year leased yet another system and finally struck pay dirt. Though his business at last is happily computerized, getting there was no fun. "It has been very frustrating and expensive," he says. "If I were starting the process again, I would talk to a lot more people. When I started with this, I wasn't really aware of computers."

He isn't alone. Most small-business owners find buying the right computer system a daunting experience filled with perils. But help is more plentiful than many business owners realize, and it is proliferating.

As computer vendors increasingly subdivide the market into small niches with highly specialized products, more businesses are able to get exactly what they need. But they must know how to find it.

More than 15,000 software packages are being marketed just for International Business Machines Corp. computers and their compatibles, let alone other brands. One package allows video stores to keep track of films. Others help farmers to adjust chicken-feed blends if egg production falters and sausage makers to switch their recipes frequently to capitalize on fluctuations in ingredient costs. Moreover, computers keep getting cheaper and better.

Yet "computer phobia" is still common. "There are business people who know they must have a computer but are terrified by it," says Arlene Borden, owner of **Doc's Computer Center** Inc., Ardmore, Pa. Even calm shoppers face a dizzying proliferation of choices of software, or programming.

Small Businesses Computerize

More than half of U.S. small businesses have at least begun to computerize, usually using personal computers. BIF CAP International, a Norwell, Mass., research and consulting firm, studied the rise in PC ownership over a single year:

NUMBER OF EMPLOYEES	PCT. WITH AT LEAST ONE PC END OF 1987	END OF 1988
Under 5	41.5%	44.2%
5 to 9	48.4	58.5
10 to 19	57.5	67.6
20 to 49	59.7	76.0
50 to 99	67.9	76.0

Business owners say a smart approach can minimize the risks—and give companies a big edge over competitors that shun computer systems or buy them foolishly. From the start, companies must be "absolutely unrelenting" with suppliers, ordering only when the equipment and software fully meet their needs, warns Jim Warnat, financial vice president of **Gordon Aluminum & Vinyl** Inc., Peabody, Mass.

The custom-window maker was awash in paper and losing control of its growing operation when it spent about $40,000 for its first computer system in 1986. "It was a disaster—worse than useless because it made some of our operating personnel a slave to the system," says Mr. Warnat. He adds that the system, paradoxically, was good only at generating more paper.

With a further $60,000 and help from **Grant Thornton**, a New York accounting and consulting firm, Gordon in 1987 got new software and computerized successfully. The computer now speeds order-taking, factory work flow, deliveries, invoicing and accounting; the company has slashed its typical turnaround time on orders to less than two weeks from six. Sales have surged. And customers say they have noticed the better service.

While demanding precisely the right systems, companies must focus on software, the packages of instructions that enable computers to carry out specific tasks, experts say. Software can be costlier than hardware and is crucial in any case. "It's the software that is going to make you or break you," says Amy Wohl, a Bala Cynwyd, Pa., computer consultant.

William M. Zeitler, an IBM marketer in White Plains, N.Y., suggests asking suppliers four fundamental questions related to software: Exactly what applications programs are available? How easy are they to use? What kind of support, such as house calls if trouble arises, does the supplier include in the price? And is the system affordable in the first place?

Though thousands of pre-packaged programs are on the market, they are never in one place. To find what's available, many business owners read trade magazines, visit computer vendors' displays at trade shows and call trade associations. But far more information is handily available than ever before.

In choosing the software, many business owners recommend emphasizing ease of use. For small businesses with many low-skilled workers, this can be crucial. Help teaching the program also counts. Some vendors will enter into long-term service and training contracts.

If computerization poses problems, at least it's getting cheaper. While $15,000 and $25,000 systems are common, very small businesses nowadays can often get by with $3,000 in hardware and less than $200 in software, Ms. Borden says. Even $15,000 systems can be leased for as low as $360 a month over five years, IBM says.

Even companies that have had trouble with computers say the right choice can pay handsomely. In Norwalk, Conn., **Sanitary Cleaners** Inc.'s first computer crashed frequently, plunging the business into chaos for hours at a time. But a new system made the company far more efficient. "I can't believe anyone could run a business without a computer," co-owner Gail Epstein now says. "I don't know how we did it."

During its centennial year, The Wall Street Journal will report events of the past century that stand as milestones of American business history.

CENTENNIAL JOURNAL: 100 Years in Business

Cashing In on Credit Cards, 1950

CREDIT CARDS HAVE BEEN AROUND since 1915, when Western Union and a handful of railroads, hotels and department stores began issuing them to preferred customers, but their real impetus came in 1950 when a New York lawyer found himself short of cash in a Manhattan restaurant. That embarrassing moment prompted Frank X. McNamara to found the Diners Club, which let card-carriers charge their tabs at 27 swank New York eating places. The idea caught on from the start. A year later the club was billing more than $1 million and by 1981, when Citicorp acquired it, it counted more than four million members.

Serious competition came in October 1958, when American Express Co. moved in. In three months that year, American Express signed up 253,000 members. By 1988, it had issued 30 million green, gold and platinum cards, and more than 2.3 million service establishments were accepting them.

Bank cards were another story. After McNamara's cards caught on, more than 100 banks tried them, but their localized programs limited their markets and half soon dropped out. Then, Bank of America, with all of California as its bailiwick, issued its BankAmerica card, which proved so successful the bank was soon franchising it to others. Bank cards exploded when individual institutions worked out interchange arrangements. Four big Chicago banks started MasterCard in 1965; four in California began MasterCharge in 1967.

The BankAmericard eventually evolved into Visa International, a free-standing service company with more than 21,000 financial institutions as members and 187 million cards outstanding. Last year, Visa had world-wide volume of almost $210 billion. MasterCard, its main competitor, claims 29,000 member institutions and 145 million cards.

The "cashless society" was one long step closer.

Pizza Garners a Slice of the Pie, 1949

BY 1949, AMERICA'S VERSION OF ITALIAN PIZZA was starting to become as popular as mom's apple pie.

GIs brought their craving for the cheesy, tomato pies back from Europe after World War II and within five years pizza's soaring sales path was clear. Customers waited in lines outside Pizzeria Uno in Chicago to savor its new deep-dish concoction; Salvatore Marra's in Philadelphia was jammed.

Pizzas had been around since about the year 1000 in the Naples area. They got some zip when Peruvian tomatoes were added in the 1550s and emerged in modern form with mozzarella cheese in 1889 when Raffaele Esposito, a pizzaiolo (pizza cook), made it for Queen Margherita.

Gennaro Lombardi, an Italian immigrant, probably had the first U.S. pizzeria—in New York in 1905. But the round dish stayed mostly in urban Italian neighborhoods until all those ex-GIs' appetites hit the U.S.

Special ovens were built for pizza; Bakers Pride Oven offered a new one in 1946 and Blodgett Co., making bakery ovens since 1848, introduced a special model for the pizza trade early in 1953. Conveyor-belt ovens arrived six years ago.

Pizza parlors swept across the U.S. with such new chains as Pizza Hut, formed in 1958. "By the sixties, pizza was mass-produced, but pizza had arrived," wrote Evelyne Slomon in her "The Pizza Book—Everything There Is To Know About The World's Greatest Pie." She added: "It was one of America's most popular foods—up there with hot dogs."

Pizzerias passed hamburger eateries in 1984 and have kept their lead. In 1988, people in the U.S. chomped a record $20 billion of pizzas, according to the National Association of Pizza Operators.

No Longer a Black-and-White Issue, 1950

COLOR TELEVISION IS THE STORY of how Columbia Broadcasting won all the battles but National Broadcasting won the war.

Peter Goldmark, the legendary head of CBS research, had a color TV system as early as 1940. It was shelved when he went to war to develop radar-jamming devices. It was revived on his return, and CBS was demonstrating baseball games in color by the late 1940s. A major drawback was that the CBS system, which involved a Rube Goldberg arrangement of whirling disks, could not be received on black-and-white receivers—and there were 10 million of these by 1950.

CBS's major rival, Gen. David Sarnoff of RCA and NBC, meanwhile was working on compatible color. This, in effect, sent a color signal over the channel carrying the black-and-white picture. Nonetheless, when the Federal Communications Commission held a showdown session between CBS and NBC, the Goldmark system won the nod. RCA sued all the way to the Supreme Court—and lost. In June 1951, the FCC okayed CBS to start color broadcasts. That November, however, the U.S. banned manufacture of color TV sets because of Korean War shortages, and CBS apparently gave up.

Sarnoff stayed the route, using 100 engineers and $130 million to perfect his compatible system. When the government took another look at color TV in 1953, the National Television Standards Committee gave Sarnoff the victory. RCA and its NBC network would have color TV practically to themselves for 10 years.

Thus Sarnoff had his revenge for the defeat Goldmark had handed him with the long-playing record in 1948, a product RCA eventually had to adopt. But it wasn't a total loss. RCA paid royalties to the CBS engineer for a masking device it used in its sets. And when the Apollo astronauts needed a color-TV system to send back pictures from the moon voyages, they picked Goldmark's.

Index